THE U.S. ARMY IN THE
IRAQ WAR
VOLUME 2

SURGE AND WITHDRAWAL

2007-2011

United States Government

US Army

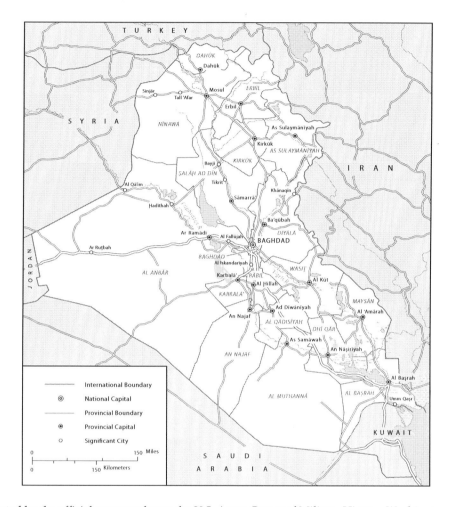

Map created by the official cartographer at the U.S. Army Center of Military History, Washington, DC.

Map 1. Iraq.

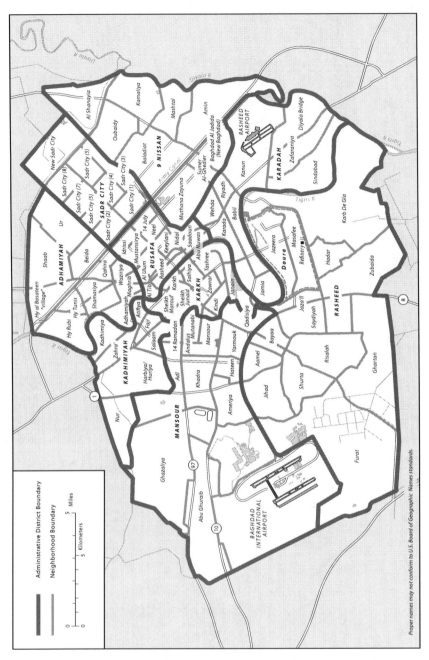

Map created by the official cartographer at the U.S. Army Center of Military History, Washington, DC.

Map 2. Baghdad.

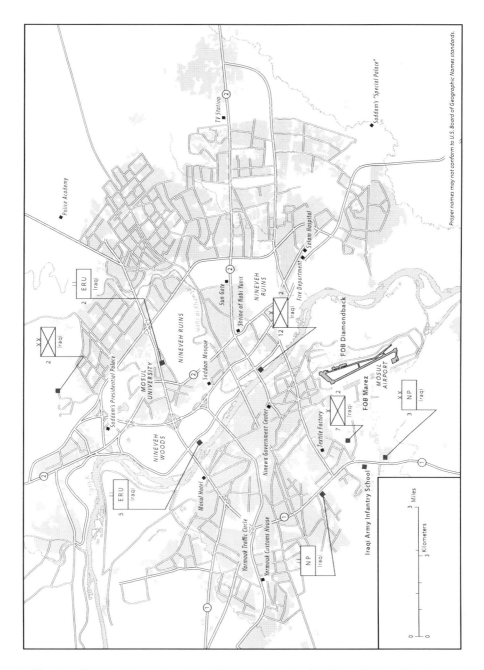

Map created by the official cartographer at the U.S. Army Center of Military History, Washington, DC.

Map 3. Mosul, Iraqi Units, 2006-2008.

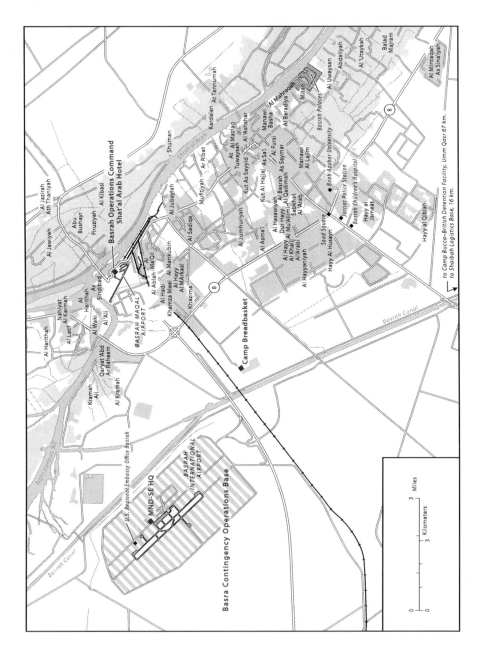

Map created by the official cartographer at the U.S. Army Center of Military History, Washington, DC.

Map 4. Al Basrah, 2007.

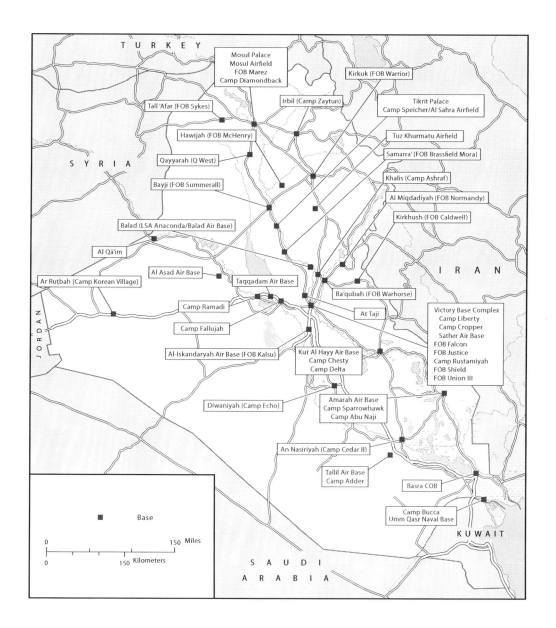

Map created by the official cartographer at the U.S. Army Center of Military History, Washington, DC.

Map 5. Operation IRAQI FREEDOM, Major Camps, 2003–2011.

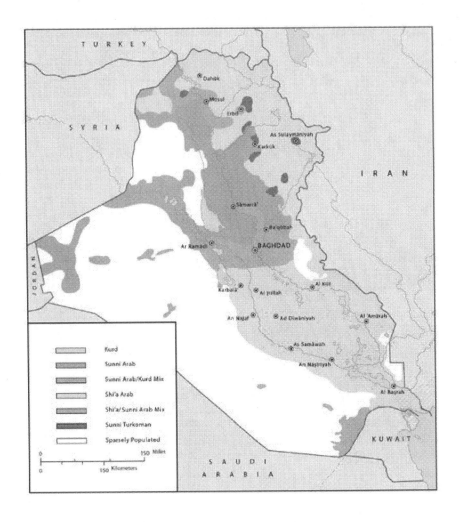

Map created by the official cartographer at the U.S. Army Center of Military History, Washington, DC.

Map 6. Ethno-Religious Groups, Iraq.

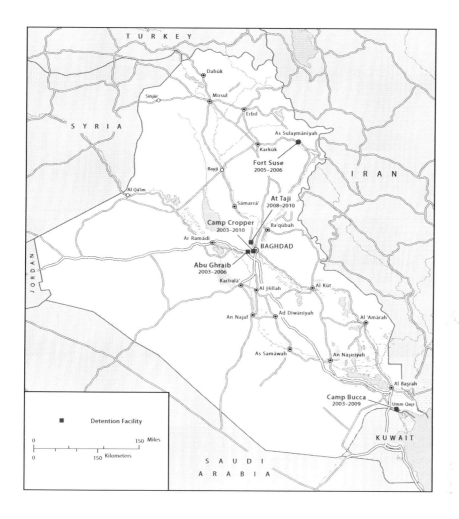

Map created by the official cartographer at the U.S. Army Center of Military History, Washington, DC.

Map 7. Detention Facilities, Theater Level, 2003–2011.

Strategic Studies Institute
and
U.S. Army War College Press

THE U.S. ARMY IN THE IRAQ WAR:
VOLUME 2
SURGE AND WITHDRAWAL
2007-2011

Colonel Joel D. Rayburn

Colonel Frank K. Sobchak

Editors

with

Lieutenant Colonel Jeanne F. Godfroy

Colonel Matthew D. Morton

Colonel James S. Powell

Lieutenant Colonel Matthew M. Zais

January 2019

THE CHIEF OF STAFF OF THE ARMY'S
OPERATION IRAQI FREEDOM STUDY GROUP
2013-2018

Director and General Editor
    2013-2016: Colonel Joel Rayburn
    2017-2018: Colonel Frank Sobchak

Executive Officers/Directors of Research
    Lieutenant Colonel Matthew Hardman
    Lieutenant Colonel Matthew Zais

Senior Fellows
    Lieutenant Colonel Jeanne Godfroy
    Colonel Matthew Morton
    Colonel James Powell
    Colonel Frank Sobchak (2013-2016)

Research Fellows
    Colonel Jason Awadi
    Major Wilson Blythe
    Major Steven Gribschaw

Adjunct Fellows and Contributors
    Michael Bell, Ph.D., College of International Security Affairs, National
      Defense University
    Derek Harvey, University of South Florida
    Major Kelly Howard, U.S. Army Reserve
    Major General (Ret.) Najim Jabouri, Iraqi Ministry of Interior
    Michael Pregent, College of International Security Affairs, National
      Defense University
    Lieutenant Colonel James Sindle, U.S. Army Reserve
    Major General (Ret.) Aziz Swaidy, Iraqi Army

Research Assistants/Interns
    2014: Cadet Andrew Mohr, Jalil Riahi, Lindsey Schmidt, Dillon Shoemaker, and
      Andrew Wickland
    2015: Maura Guyler; Christopher Hartnett; Richard Hulver, Ph.D.; Alexis Knutsen;
      Kelsey Marron; Ashley Rhoades; Alexander Teague; Kate Tietzen; and
      Cameron Zinsou
    2017: Catherine Eatherton, Chasen Glatz

CONTENTS

Foreword by the 39th Chief of Staff, U.S. Army...xxix

Foreword by the 38th Chief of Staff, U.S. Army...xxxi

Preface...xxxiii

Acknowledgments xxxvii

Part I: The Surge, 2007-2008 1

Chapter 1 Strategy in Crisis, October-December 2006 3

    Strategy Options 3

    The Surge Decision 19

    Endnotes - Chapter 1 33

Chapter 2 The Eve of the Surge, December 2006-February 2007 43

    The Hanging of Saddam Hussein.. 43

    The Baghdad Security Plan.. 45

    MNC-I, AQI, and the Baghdad Belts.. 56

    The Shi'a Militants on the Eve of the Surge 65

    The Northern Iraq Conflict Before the Surge 80

    Endnotes - Chapter 2 85

Chapter 3 The New Way Forward, February 2007-April 2007 95

    Petraeus Takes Command 95

    The Iraqi Security Forces in Early 2007 112

    Economies of Force, South and North 117

    Toward a New Joint Campaign Plan 125

    Endnotes - Chapter 3 133

Chapter 4 The Awakening Gathers Momentum 145

    The Expansion of the Anbar Awakening 145

    The Awakening in the Baghdad Belts... 161

    The Awakening Reaches Baghdad 172

    Endnotes - Chapter 4 182

Chapter 5 Summer 2007—The Surge of Operations..195

    Regaining the Initiative: Operation PHANTOM THUNDER 196

    Summer of the Awakening... 215

    The War Against Iran's Militant Proxies 222

MNF-I and the Opposition to the Surge 232

Endnotes - Chapter 5 240

Chapter 6 "The Darkness Has Become Pitch Black" 251

Al-Qaeda in Iraq Loses the Initiative 251

The Awakening, the Maliki Government, and AQI 267

The War Against the Shi'a Militants 273

The Iraqi Surge 278

Planning for Drawdown 286

Iraqi Political Tensions and Progress 288

Endnotes - Chapter 6 295

Chapter 7 Enabling the Surge, 2007-2008 307

Generating Unity of Effort 307

Enabling the Close Fight 311

The Intelligence War 318

Money as a Weapon System 319

Detention and Rule of Law 324

Endnotes - Chapter 7 333

Chapter 8 Crescendo: Maliki Against the Sadrists 341

Operation PHANTOM PHOENIX 341

The Battle for Basrah 350

The Battle for Sadr City 368

Endnotes - Chapter 8 382

Chapter 9 The Surge Culminates, Summer 2008 391

The End of the Surge 391

Operation DEFEAT AL-QAEDA IN THE NORTH 392

Consolidating Victory Against the Shi'a Militant Groups 398

The Unfinished Business of the Surge 404

Maliki's Warning Signs: Diyala, the ISOF, and the SOFA 411

Endnotes - Chapter 9 420

Chapter 10 Conclusion: The Surge, 2007-2008 429

Part II: From Surge to Withdrawal 433

Chapter 11 Zero Attacks, September-December 2008 435

Odierno Takes Command 435

The Northern Iraq Problem 440

The Quest for Stabilization 445

Endnotes - Chapter 11 452

Chapter 12 Out of the Cities, January-June 2009 457

A New Iraq Policy for the United States.. 457

Political Culmination of the Surge: The January 2009 Provincial Elections 458

Drawdown and Change of Operating Posture for MNF-I........................... 459

Iraqi Security Forces Development 461

The Continuing Pursuit of AQI 463

The Challenge of Reconciliation 470

The Iran Problem.. 473

Leaving the Cities... 477

Endnotes - Chapter 12 480

Chapter 13 Toward the Defeat of AQI, August 2009-July 2010 487

The Autumn 2009 Bombings... 487

The "Responsible Drawdown" 491

The Combined Security Mechanism 497

The Evisceration of Al-Qaeda in Iraq, January-May 2010..................... 502

The Iraqi Political Crisis 507

Endnotes - Chapter 13 512

Chapter 14 From NEW DAWN to Zero, August 2010-December 2011 519

The Interregnum 520

Operation NEW DAWN and the "Responsible Drawdown of Forces" 522

Iraq's Political Destabilization.. 532

The Path to Zero 541

Preparing for Exit.. 544

The Retrograde.. 548

Endnotes - Chapter 14 557

Chapter 15 Epilogue: The Office of Security Cooperation and the Return
of the Iraq War, 2012-2014 569

After U.S. Forces-Iraq (USF-I): Crackdowns and Disarray 569

The Unraveling of Iraqi Politics 576

The Spillover of the Syrian Civil War 579

Return of the Sunni Insurgency 582

The Islamic State of Iraq and Syria (ISIS) 585

The Deterioration of the Iraqi Security Forces, 2012-2014............................ 588

The Ascendancy of ISIS.. 592

The Start of Operation INHERENT RESOLVE... 599

Endnotes - Chapter 15 601

Chapter 16 Conclusion: From Surge to Withdrawal.. 609

Part III: Final Conclusions.. 613

Chapter 17 Conclusion: Lessons of the Iraq War 615

Selected Strategic Implications for Future Wars 615

Operational Lessons 622

Tactical and Operational Innovations.. 637

Endnotes - Chapter 17 641

Afterword.. 643

Select Bibliography 645

Interviews... 645

Books... 647

Articles.. 649

Monographs and Reports 653

Unpublished Papers 657

News Outlets and Newspapers 658

Abbreviations 659

Map Symbols 665

About the Contributors 667

CHARTS

Chart 1. U.S. Military Base Closures (December 2010-December 2011). 552

Chart 2. Troop Drawdown and Contractor Drawdown. 553

Chart 3. Transportation Sustainment Spine in Iraq for Operation NEW DAWN...........554

MAPS

Map 1. Iraq i

Map 2. Baghdad ii

Map 3. Mosul, Iraqi Units, 2006-2008 iii

Map 4. Al Basrah, 2007 iv

Map 5. Operation IRAQI FREEDOM, Major Camps, 2003–2011 v

Map 6. Ethno-Religious Groups, Iraq vi

Map 7. Detention Facilities, Theater Level, 2003–2011 vii

Map 8. Before the Surge, Disposition of U.S. Forces Baghdad, January 2007 49

Map 9. Al-Qaeda in Iraq, December 2006 57

Map 10. Disposition of U.S. Forces in Central Iraq, Early 2007 63

Map 11. MND Areas of Operation, June 2007 111

Map 12. Ramadi, February-March 2007 151

Map 13. Operation PHANTOM THUNDER, June-August 2007 196

Map 14. Disposition of U.S. Forces in Central Iraq, June 2007 205

Map 15. Disposition of U.S. Forces in Baghdad, June 2007 209

Map 16. Al-Qaeda in Iraq, 2007 294

Map 17. Operation PHANTOM PHOENIX, January-March 2008 342

Map 18. Basrah Battle, March-April 2008 364

Map 19. Sadr City, March-May 2008 375

Map 20. U.S. Forward Positions, Baghdad, 2007–2008 404

Map 21. MNF-I Unit Disposition, June 2009 459

Map 22. Combined Security Mechanism, 2010-2011 501

Map 23. Disposition of U.S. Forces, USF-I Operation NEW DAWN, September 2010 ... 523

Map 24. ISIS Sanctuary, June 2014 595

ILLUSTRATIONS

Major General Joseph Fil, Jr., Commanding General, MND-B,
With SECDEF Rumsfeld 4

U.S. Ambassador to Iraq Zalmay Khalilzad With General George Casey, Commander,
MNF-I, and Iraqi National Security Adviser Mowaffaq Rubaie 5

President George W. Bush With National Security Adviser Stephen Hadley
and Vice President Richard Cheney 7

President George W. Bush Reaches Out to Iraqi Prime Minister Nuri al-Maliki
in Amman, Jordan 15

President George W. Bush With Vice President Richard Cheney, General Peter Pace,
Admiral Mike Mullen, and Vice Chairman of the Joint Chiefs of Staff Admiral
Edmund P. Giambastiani 25

General Peter Chiarelli Transfers Responsibility of Command of MNC-I to
General Raymond Odierno With General George Casey Officiating 26

BOC Staff General Abud Qanbar, During a Groundbreaking Ceremony in Baghdad ... 46

Major General Joseph Fil, Commanding General of MND-B in the Rusafa Market 48

American and Iraqi Soldiers Wait as U.S. Army UH-60 Black Hawk Helicopters
Approach Their Landing Zone Near Mahmudiyah 52

Colonel Stephen Townsend, Commander of the 3d Stryker BCT, 2d Infantry
Division, With Major General Abdul Ameer al-Lami, Commander of the
Iraqi 6th Division 53

High Rise Apartment Buildings on Haifa Street, the Location of Intense Battles
in Early January 2007 54

The Handwritten Map Depicting AQI's Strategy for Dominating the Baghdad Belts 59

Captain Jason Good During a Patrol in Al Jabor 61

Moqtada Sadr 70

Qais al-Khazali 71

Qassem Soleimani, Commander of the Quds Force of the Islamic
Revolutionary Guard Corps of Iran 72

Soldiers from 1st Squadron, 40th Cavalry Regiment, During Patrols
  in Search of Insurgents in Adwania 74

Hakim Zamili, Iraqi Deputy Minister of Health 79

Major General Benjamin Mixon, Commander MND-N, With Ninawa Provincial
  Governor Duraid Kashmoula.. 81

Colonel Stephen Twitty, Commander, 4th BCT, 1st Cavalry
  Division, With Ninawa Provincial Director of Police
  Major General Wathiq al-Hamdani... 83

General David Petraeus Takes Command of MNF-I From General George Casey......... 98

Colonel Billy Don Farris, Commander of 2d BCT, 82d Airborne Division,
  Meets With Civic Leaders of Sadr City's First Joint Security Station......................... 102

U.S. Army Soldiers Search a House in Zaghiniyat During the
  Early Days of the Surge... 102

Iraqi Police and Paratroopers From 2d BCT, 82d Airborne Division, Patrol
  Adhamiyah in February.. 103

A U.S. Patrol Passes the Ruined Facade of Baghdad's Mutanabi Book Market,
  Destroyed by an AQI Car Bomb in March 2007 104

SECDEF Robert Gates Tours a Joint Security Station With
  Colonel Jeffrey Bannister 105

Colonel J. B. Burton, Commander, 2d BCT, 1st Infantry Division, With
  Major General Abdul Al-Ameer, Commander of the 6th Iraqi Army Division 106

U.S. and Iraqi Soldiers Search for Weapons Caches Near Janabi in March. 106

Colonel Ricky D. Gibbs, Commander, 4th Infantry BCT, 1st Infantry Division,
  With Ambassador Ryan C. Crocker in April 107

Soldiers From 5th Battalion, 20th Infantry Regiment, Fire at Insurgents in Dora.......... 108

Lieutenant General Martin Dempsey, Commanding General, MNSTC-I...................... 113

General Raymond Odierno, With Polish Major General Pawel Lamla,
  MND-CS Commander, and Major General Othman al-Ghanimi, Commander
  of the 8th Iraqi Army Division.. 118

Military Transition Team Members and Iraqi Soldiers During
  Operation BLACK EAGLE 119

SECDEF Robert Gates With British Major General Jonathan Shaw,
Commander of MND-SE, and General Casey 121

Residents of Tel Afar Dig Through Rubble in the Aftermath of the
March 27 AQI VBIED Attack.. 124

SECDEF Robert Gates Meets With Ambassador Ryan Crocker in Baghdad 125

Colonel David W. Sutherland, Commander 3d BCT, 1st Cavalry Division,
Briefs Admiral William Fallon, CENTCOM Commander, and
Major General Benjamin Mixon, Commander of MND-N 130

Lieutenant General Graeme Lamb, Deputy Commander, MNF-I.................................... 146

U.S. Marine Corps Major General Walter Gaskin, Commander MNF-W, and
General Peter Pace, Chairman of the Joint Chiefs of Staff, Tour Ramadi.................. 148

Colonel John Charlton With General David Petraeus... 150

Colonel Michael Kershaw and Colonel William Rapp With Awakening
Members in the Triangle of Death Area 162

The Yusufiyah Power Plant.. 164

Lieutenant Colonel Brian Coppersmith Talks to Abu Maruf, an Awakening
Leader in South Baghdad.. 167

Colonel Michael Kershaw, Commander of the 2d BCT, 10th Mountain Division,
Walks With Colonel Ali Freiji, Commander of the 4th Brigade, 6th Iraqi
Army Division, in the Mahmudiyah Marketplace.. 168

Colonel Michael Garrett, Commander of the 4th BCT (Airborne), 25th Infantry
Division, and Brigadier General Sadiq Jafar Ali, Commander of the
Diwaniya Provincial Iraqi Police 170

Lieutenant Colonel Kurt Pinkerton Meets With Awakening Leader Abu Azzam 175

Staff Brigadier General Nasser Ghanam.. 175

Awakening Leader Abu Abed Meets With Lieutenant Colonel Dale C. Kuehl,
General David Petraeus, and Senior Iraqi Leaders in Ameriyah................................ 178

Colonel David Sutherland With General David Petraeus in Baqubah 199

Soldiers Move Through the Outskirts of Palm Groves in Baqubah
During the Night of March 25.. 200

Soldiers from the 5th Iraqi Army Division and 3d Stryker BCT, 2d Infantry Division, During Operation ARROWHEAD RIPPER 201

U.S. Marines from the 13th Marine Expeditionary Unit During Operations in Karmah 203

Chairman of the Joint Chiefs of Staff Admiral Michael Mullen With Major General Rick Lynch, Commander 3d Infantry Division 206

Sarafiyah Bridge, After Its Destruction by al-Qaeda in Iraq on April 12, 2007 210

Soldiers From 1st Battalion, 26th Infantry Regiment, During a Firefight in Baghdad's Adhamiyah Neighborhood on June 16 212

Bassima Luay Hasun al-Jaidri. 217

Major General John Allen With a Sheikh of the Albu Issa Tribe at Camp Fallujah 221

Fully Constructed EFPs 223

Brothers Qais and Laith Khazali, Commanders of the Militia Group Asa'ib Ahl al Haqq 225

General David Petraeus With Iraqi Police Colonel Naji Rostum Sahra, Also Known as Abu Liqa 228

Rear Admiral James Winnefeld 233

General David Petraeus Testifies Before Congress, September 2007 236

Soldiers From 3d BCT, 2d Infantry Division, During Operations in Muqdadiyah 252

A Soldier From 4th Stryker BCT, 2d Infantry Division, Fires an AT-4 during Operations South of Baqubah 253

Colonel Terry Ferrell, Commander of 2d BCT, 3d Infantry Division, With Sheik Ali Majid, a Concerned Local Citizens (CLC) Leader 254

Ugandan Contractors From a Private Security Company Named SOC, at a Gate at Al Asad Air Base 258

An AQI Foreign Fighter Registration Form Captured in the Sinjar Documents 260

Soldiers From 1st BCT, 10th Mountain Division, Search Remote Terrain in Salahadin Province 265

Colonel Wayne W. Grigsby, Jr., Commander of 3d BCT, 3d Infantry Division, With a Senior Iraqi Officer 266

General Raymond Odierno, Commander of MNC-I, With Local Sheiks. 269

Soldiers From the 101st Airborne Division Conduct Air Assault Operations
    in Ubaydi, December 29, 2007. 271

Lieutenant General James M. Dubik, MNSTC-I Commander,
    Greeting Iraqi Representatives From Anbar Province 279

Jawad Bolani, Iraqi Minister of the Interior (2006-2010) 284

Iraqi Vice President Tariq Hashimi Greets Major General Joseph Fil,
    MND-B, Commander 289

Secretary of Defense Robert M. Gates With U.S. Ambassador to Iraq Ryan Crocker
    and General David Petraeus... 308

An MRAP Vehicle Arrives in Kuwait... 314

Contractors Load Hellfire Missiles onto an MQ-1C Gray Eagle in Iraq 316

U.S. Troops Scan an Iraqi With Handheld Biometric Equipment 317

Soldiers Talk to a Contractor and Local Villagers at a Windmill-Powered
    Ground Water Pump Reconstruction Project 320

Bayji Oil Refinery in June 2007.. 323

Major General John D. Gardner, Commander TF 134....................................... 325

Confiscated Weapons at Camp Bucca Similar to Those Used During
    the April 2007 Riots... 327

Major General Douglas Stone, Commander TF 134 328

General David Petraeus and Colonel James Brown at Camp Bucca 330

Soldiers From the 3d ACR Search for Weapon Caches in Canal Walls of
    "The Breadbasket" 344

Soldiers From 1st BCT, 101st Airborne Division, Fire Artillery During
    Operation PHANTOM PHOENIX 345

Soldiers From the 3d ACR During Combat in Mosul... 346

Sons of Iraq Staff a Checkpoint in Himbus 347

Soldiers Meet With Iraqi National Policemen During a Patrol in Baghdad.................... 348

General David Petraeus Supervising the Change of Command Between
Lieutenant General Raymond Odierno and
Lieutenant General Lloyd J. Austin III..351

Major General Graham Binns, Governor Mohammed Musbeh al-Waeli, National
Security Adviser Mowaffaq Rubaie, and Lieutenant General Mohan al-Freiji
During the Basrah Transfer Ceremony 354

Major General Barney White-Spunner 357

National Security Adviser Mowaffaq Rubaie Informs General David Petraeus
on March 21, 2008, of Prime Minister Maliki's Intention to Initiate
an Offensive in Basrah...358

Marines and Iraqi Forces During Fighting in the Latif District of Basrah on
May 3, 2008..365

A View of the Sadr City Area of Baghdad, March 29, 2008 368

Major General Jeffery Hammond, Commander of MND-B, Greets Baghdad's
Governor Tah'an 370

Soldiers Emplace Concrete Barriers Across Route Gold in Sadr City.............377

A Massive Sandstorm Affected the Battle of Sadr City.......................................378

Kirkuk Governor Abdul-Rahman Mostafa, Major General Mark Hertling,
and Colonel David Paschal...394

Air Force Loadmasters Prepare to Drop Pallets of Humanitarian Aid During
Operation YARBOROUGH 402

Major General Michael Oates, With Major General Othman Ali Farhood al-Ghanimi,
8th Iraqi Army Division Commander..403

Iraqis Celebrate the Removal of Concrete Barriers From a Marketplace in Samarra. ... 405

Tense Discussions on Iraq War Strategy During a Congressional Delegation Visit on
July 21, 2008. 410

Diyala Provincial Police Chief Major General Ghanem al-Qureishi Converses
With a Colleague..413

ISOF Commandos Conduct Night Missions Near Amarah With a CJSOTF Adviser ...415

General Raymond Odierno With Secretary of Defense Robert Gates During
the MNF-I Change of Command Ceremony 435

A U.S. Soldier Plays Foosball With Children in Husseniyah Nahia 437

Prime Minister Nuri al-Maliki at a Ceremony Reopening Baghdad's
    Historic Mutanabi Book Market 437

A Soldier From 3d Armored Cavalry Regiment Conducts a Patrol in Mosul 442

U.S. Soldiers Intercept a Vehicle Whose Occupants Had Been Observed
    Emplacing a Roadside Bomb in Mosul 443

Members of the Gazaliyah Guardians, a West Baghdad Awakening Group,
    Register for Payment From the Iraqi Government 446

An Iraqi Army Officer Pays a Sons of Iraq Member in Ameriyah................................... 446

President George W. Bush and Iraqi Prime Minister Nuri al-Maliki Sign
    the U.S.-Iraq Security Agreement.. 450

U.S. and Romanian Army Soldiers Review Plans During an
    Observation Mission Near Nasiriyah 451

British Major General Andrew Salmon, Commander of MND-SE,
    Hands Responsibility for Southern Iraq to U.S. Major General Michael Oates,
    Commander of MND-C 460

An Explosive Ordnance Technician Prepares to Destroy a Bunker
    During Operations in Diyala Province 464

U.S. Army Soldiers and Iraqi Police Search Houses in West Mosul
    During Operation NEW HOPE.. 465

General Raymond Odierno Meets With MNC-I Commander Lieutenant General
    Charles Jacoby and MND-N Commander Major General Robert Caslen, Jr.,
    in Mosul... 467

RKG-3 Grenades.. 469

Troops of 3d BCT, 82d Airborne Division, Rush to the Scene of Fighting
    Iraqi Security Forces and Adel al-Mashhadani's Sons of Iraq Group 471

Major General Daniel Bolger, Commander of MND-B, Greets General Abud Qanbar
    Hashim al-Maliki, CG, Baghdad Operations Command (BOC) 478

Soldiers Load a C-130 Aircraft at Balad Air Base, Iraq, Bound for Bagram Air Base,
    Afghanistan.. 495

Marines Case the Colors of II Marine Expeditionary Force During a Ceremony
    Marking the End of the Marines' Presence in Anbar Province................................... 495

U.S. Ambassador to Iraq Christopher R. Hill With Iraqi Policemen
in Qadisiyah Province. 496

Ninawa Provincial Governor Atheel Nujaifi Addresses Iraqi Police
Academy Graduates in Mosul 498

An Iraqi Federal Policeman, a U.S. Army Soldier, and a Kurdish Peshmerga Fighter,
Members of the Golden Lions Combined Security Force, on Patrol Near the
Green Line 500

Major General Anthony Cucolo, Commander of MND-N 506

Vice President Joseph R. Biden Meets General Raymond Odierno and
Ambassador James Jeffery in Baghdad...519

General Lloyd Austin During His Assumption of Command of USF-I from
General Raymond Odierno 520

Iraqi and U.S. Soldiers Maneuver During the Battle of the Palm Grove 526

Lieutenant General Robert Cone, USF-I Deputy CG for Operations,
With General Ali Ghaidan, Commander of the Iraqi Ground Forces Command 528

An M1A1 Abrams Tank From the Iraqi 9th Mechanized Division 529

Major General David Quantock With Iraqi Ministry of Justice
Official Dara Nour al-Deen..531

Improvised Rocket-Assisted Munitions. 533

Samir Abd Muhammad al-Khlifawi, Known More Commonly as Hajji Bakr...............537

Major General David G. Perkins, Commander of MND-N, With
Colonel Malcolm Frost, Commander, 2d BCT, 25th Infantry Division,
and Iraqi Officers...540

Soldiers From the Iraqi Army's 12th Division Take Part in Exercise Lion's Leap. 547

Secretary of Defense Leon Panetta Meets With U.S. Troops Following
Negotiations With Iraqi Leaders About an Extension of the U.S.-Iraq Status
of Forces Agreement...549

Airmen of the 407th Air Expeditionary Group Prepare to Depart Iraq in a C-17
Globemaster III Cargo Aircraft 555

General Lloyd Austin Cases the USF-I Colors at Camp Victory on
December 15, 2011..556

The Final USF-I Convoy Reaches the Kuwaiti Border as the Sun Rises
    on December 18, 2011 557

Iraqi Vice President Tariq al-Hashimi With Ninawa Operations
    Commander Lieutenant General Riyadh Jalal Tawfiq in 2008................................... 570

Lieutenant General Robert Caslen With U.S. Division-North (USD-N)
    Commander Major General David G. Perkins. 572

Iraqi Prime Minister Nuri al-Maliki 579

Syrian President Bashar al-Assad... 580

Iraqi Sunni Leader Rafe al-Issawi... 582

A Convoy of ISIS Fighters Moves Through Mosul Shortly After Capturing the City... 594

ISIS Leader Abu Bakr al-Baghdadi.. 597

Prime Minister Haider Abadi.. 598

SECDEF Ashton Carter With U.S. Ambassador to Iraq Stuart Jones and
    ARCENT Commander Lieutenant General James Terry. 600

FOREWORD

BY THE 39TH CHIEF OF STAFF, U.S. ARMY

My predecessor, General (Retired) Ray Odierno, initiated this in-stride study of the U.S. Army's experience in Operation IRAQI FREEDOM (OIF) to share lessons, sharpen thinking, and promote debate.

I applaud and congratulate the team of warrior-scholars that authored this two-volume study, *The U.S. Army in the Iraq War*. These Soldiers devoted countless hours of intellectual energy to help us understand the operational lessons of OIF. They reviewed, analyzed, and synthesized thousands of reports, conducted numerous interviews, and examined the events of a war that defined a generation of Soldiers.

This study is an interim work by design. It is a waypoint on our institution's quest to comprehend the OIF experience. We must continue to evaluate and reevaluate events and the contexts that frame them. Eventually, our Army will have a comprehensive, official "Green Book" history that describes OIF authoritatively, but it will require years of research to get there. There is much left to do, but this analysis starts a long-term historical effort.

We have a professional and moral responsibility to learn the relevant lessons of the recent past. OIF is a sober reminder that technological advantages and standoff weapons alone cannot render a decision; that the promise of short wars is often elusive; that the ends, ways, and means must be in balance; that our Army must understand the type of war we are engaged with in order to adapt as necessary; that decisions in war occur on the ground in the mud and dirt; and that timeless factors such as human agency, chance, and an enemy's conviction, all shape a war's outcome.

Our Army is strong, and getting stronger. We are on azimuth to build a more lethal force that deters adversaries and is capable of a rapid transition to win the ground fight as a member of the joint and coalition forces. Use this work to help you and your team stay ready to defeat any future adversary. Understand that this is likely not the final word, but learn its operational lessons and add them to your kit bag of skills.

Army Strong!

Mark A. Milley
General, United States Army
39th Chief of Staff

FOREWORD

BY THE 38TH CHIEF OF STAFF, U.S. ARMY

In July 2013, 18 months after the last of our operating forces departed Iraq, I directed that the U.S. Army take steps to capture key lessons, insights, and innovations from our more than 8 years of conflict in that country. As the U.S. Army Chief of Staff, I strongly believed that having been at war continuously since the attacks of September 11, 2001 (9/11), it was time to conduct an initial examination of the Army's experiences in the post-9/11 wars, to determine their implications for our future operations, strategy, doctrine, force structure, and institutions. The two-volume study, *The U.S. Army in the Iraq War* by the Chief of Staff of the Army's Operation IRAQI FREEDOM (OIF) Study Group is the first product of that effort.

The story the OIF Study Group has documented of the Army at the operational level is one of units and headquarters working in difficult and complex environments, with leaders at all levels making tough decisions under the pressure of time. As the group's research emerged, I noted a number of their findings whose important implications I saw firsthand as a division, corps, and force commander in Iraq. First and foremost, is the concept that while our technological means may have become more advanced, we cannot ignore operational art, the principles of war, and the importance of terrain. These fundamental concepts were every bit as important to our counterinsurgency and stabilization campaigns in Iraq, as they have been in other, more conventional conflicts. Moreover, it is clear in retrospect, that those who rejected the idea that there is an operational level of war in counterinsurgency were wrong. For our operations to succeed and be sustained, we must have a thorough understanding of the operating environment and the local political and social consequences of our actions, especially when facing an enemy who understands the environment better than we do. When operating among a host nation's population, we must constantly clarify our intentions in order to avoid creating new enemies. In addition, when conditions on the ground change, we must be willing to reexamine the assumptions that underpin our strategy and plans and change course if necessary, no matter how painful it may be.

This account of the Iraq War holds some important strategic and institutional lessons as well. We must seek better ways of operating effectively with our coalition allies, whose constraints are naturally different from ours. We must also employ better ways of generating and partnering with effective and legitimate host nation forces and of accounting for the political pressures that constrain those forces. The Iraq War also teaches us that we should improve the ways in which we develop our strategic leaders. The conduct of war and the nature of decision-making are becoming more decentralized and, as a result, we must develop leaders who are capable of thinking strategically and leading joint, interagency, and multinational teams at an earlier stage in their careers.

We also have seen in the wake of the Iraq War that the United States has entered another historical cycle, like those that followed major American wars in the past, in which our civilian and military leaders debated the utility of landpower for our national objectives. A reading of *The U.S. Army in the Iraq War* indicates that, even at a much higher end strength than they now have, our ground forces were overtaxed by the commitments in Iraq and Afghanistan, and the decision to limit our troop levels in both theaters had severe operational consequences. A review of these volumes also indicates that our adversaries are unlikely to abandon the way of war they adopted in Iraq, and that landpower will remain an important element of strategic deterrence in the future.

For me, as a Soldier of 40 years, the history of the Iraq War is the astonishing story of an Army that reached within itself to learn and adapt in the midst of a war that the United States was well on its way to losing. It was a formative experience for a generation of Soldiers and leaders. In addition, it was a field of sacrifice for many thousands of our fellow countrymen. Above all, these volumes are meant to ensure their sacrifices are never forgotten.

RAYMOND T. ODIERNO
General (Retired), United States Army
38th Chief of Staff

PREFACE

In September 2013, then Army Chief of Staff General Raymond T. Odierno directed the Operation IRAQI FREEDOM Study Group to research and write an operational history of the U.S. Army's experience in the Iraq War from 2003 to 2011. This volume of *The U.S. Army in the Iraq War* is the second of two fulfilling that task. It tells how the surge counteroffensive in 2007-2008 neutralized both the Sunni insurgency and Shi'a militias, bringing Iraq to its most peaceful and stable state since the invasion. It then describes how, with political support for the war waning, consecutive Presidential administrations began to reduce the number of troops in Iraq while Multi-National Force-Iraq (MNF-I) and later United States Forces-Iraq (USF-I) worked hurriedly to prepare the Iraqi military to take responsibility for their nation's security. The speed of the drawdown accelerated significantly after the election of President Barack Obama, culminating in an unexpected complete withdrawal in 2011.

In scope, the study group members consciously modeled this history after the Army's "Green Book" histories of World War II. As the Green Books did, and as General Odierno charged us to do, we focused on the operational level of war. These volumes are narrative histories that tell the story of U.S. forces in Iraq, mainly from the perspective of the theater command in Baghdad and the operational commands immediately subordinate to it. They focus on the decisions and intent of the senior three- and four-star commanders in Baghdad over time.

In writing this history, we strove to evaluate the major decisions those commands faced, to understand what commanders intended to accomplish, and to comprehend how the commands interpreted the situation at the time. We also traced many of those decisions to the tactical level to judge how strategic and operational intent translated into changes on the battlefield. At the same time, we examined the broad trends and tactical developments that affected the operational and strategic levels, including missed opportunities along these lines. Our team also assessed the impact of changes to the institutional army, such as modularization and transformation, on the operational conflict in Iraq. Finally, we explored the assumptions underpinning the U.S. campaign in Iraq at various times and assessed their validity.

We wrote this history with two audiences in mind. For current and future Army leaders, we sought to explain the key operational and strategic lessons from the Iraq War that in our estimation should inform strategy, operations, and the Army as an institution. In addition, we attempted to write this history in an accessible way so that a civilian audience can understand the Army's experience in the war. We believe too few military accounts thus far explain to the American public what the armed forces have gone through in the post-September 11, 2001 (9/11) wars. If unaddressed, this can lead to a gulf between the public and its military.

Although this book is an Army history, we included other military services and international forces in the story, sometimes in great detail. In contemporary warfare, the Army goes to war as part of a joint force and often with coalition partners. It would be impossible to explain what the Army experienced in Iraq without including the story of the U.S. Marines, the British armed forces, and other coalition ground forces.

We also attempted, to the best of our knowledge and ability, to include the enemy perspective, the nature of the operating environment, and the political and social context for the conflict. We have done this to explain why various groups and peoples fought against or alongside coalition forces, what they hoped to achieve, and how their leaders made decisions in response to (or independent of) the coalition's actions.

This volume of *The United States Army in the Iraq War* includes a summary of our major findings concerning the operational and strategic lessons of the war, but readers will see this throughout the themes of our research. The 2007-2008 surge counteroffensive utterly changed the operational situation in Iraq. In late 2006, Iraq was in the throes of a civil war, with its government ministries and security forces barely functioning. Its survival as a unitary state was questionable. By the end of 2008, Iraq's Sunni insurgency had been quashed, with vast groups of insurgents having switched sides and joined the coalition as Sons of Iraq. Similarly, Iranian-backed Shi'a militias had been defeated across southern and central Iraq, and even the militia stronghold of Sadr City had been cleared. Introduction of the surge brigades and Marine forces, combined with the additional manpower from the organic Sunni Awakening, and coupled with operational level guidance to increase the coalition footprint in order to protect the population, had regained the initiative and returned Iraq to a state of near normalcy.

Improvement in Iraq's situation brought paradoxical changes at the strategic level which eventually allowed both Sunni extremist groups and Iranian sponsored militias to recover and again threaten the Iraqi state. As Iraq's security situation improved, its government exerted more influence over its own future. Unfortunately, many of the decisions made by Prime Minister Nuri al-Maliki during this phase proved to be more beneficial to his own political standing and the standing of supportive Shi'a parties than to the long-term viability of the Iraqi state. As a result, the Bush administration was unable to obtain a security agreement to allow U.S. forces to remain in Iraq long enough to ensure the country would not slide off its path toward recovery. Similarly, Iraq's improved situation provided sufficient justification to the Obama administration—elected on a platform of decreasing American involvement in the Middle East—to carry out that very platform. The "Washington and Baghdad clocks" to which General David Petraeus had often alluded had run out. What followed was tragic, but not unexpected. Maliki's sectarianism and authoritarianism only increased as the U.S. presence decreased, and, following the complete withdrawal of forces in December 2011, his actions hollowed out the Iraqi security forces and alienated the Sunni community, leading some of its members to rejoin militant extremists in fighting the central government. Iraq's civil war, which had been smoldering since the departure of U.S. forces, reignited. As Iraq's security forces collapsed in the face of an Islamic State in Iraq and Syria (ISIS) offensive, U.S. forces returned less than 3 years after they had departed.

For the Army, the 5-year period encompassing the surge counteroffensive to the withdrawal of forces from Iraq represents some of the highest and lowest points in its recent history. The surge counteroffensive highlighted how leaders and Soldiers at all levels learned and adapted to a challenging form of warfare. It showed that when the stakes were the highest and the situation most desperate, the Army was able to incorporate new equipment, technology, and tactical innovations. As the Sunni Awakening began to spread, tactical commanders realized its importance and adopted difficult policies that resulted in negotiations with men who had American blood on their hands. Operational and theater-level leaders were similarly able to understand its importance and backed their subordinates as they capitalized on opportunities. By the close of 2008, those adaptations and decisions achieved results far beyond what had been anticipated. But the United States was unable to exploit those gains fully. In the end, those same leaders and Soldiers who had seen free Iraqi elections and the tamping down of the civil war witnessed a Shakespearean-level tragedy as their hard work and sacrifice seemingly came apart when Iraq nearly collapsed in 2014.

In writing this narrative history, we relied to a great degree on military records from U.S. operational headquarters and interviews, most of them not previously accessible to scholars. Mixing oral history interviews with archival documentary research creates, in our opinion, considerable synergy. Some readers, particularly those within the national security community, may be surprised with information revealed in this book. Our study benefited tremendously from U.S. Central Command's (CENTCOM) support in declassifying and/or redacting over 30,000 pages of material selected by our team. We were also aided by the products of an earlier effort led by the researchers of General George Casey's book, *Strategic Reflections*, which had yielded over 10,000 pages of declassified or redacted material. To further ensure we properly safeguarded sensitive national security information, this manuscript underwent security reviews at the Defense Office of Prepublication and Security Review and at the U.S. Army War College. We have also benefited from the fact that much more is known today about the enemy and about the actions of the Iraqi Government than was known during the early years of the war. From our vantage point in 2017, however, we recognize that this is a history of a war that is not yet over. With thousands of U.S. and coalition forces back in Iraq campaigning against an enemy that is a successor to al-Qaeda in Iraq, we understand that there may be many more accounts written before the story truly ends. We do not expect that our work will be definitive. Instead, we hope our contribution helps to open the door to future research by others whose investigations we fully expect will supersede our own.

The scope of this project and the time available prevented us from covering a number of major areas of research that we will have to leave for others to examine. We hope that our work at the operational level will point the way for scholars to research and write the story of U.S. ground forces at the tactical level. Some histories at that level have begun to appear, such as Dale Andrade's *Surging South of Baghdad*, but many more are needed.

Another omission in this history is the role of U.S. special operations forces in Iraq, who were involved in virtually every major development during the war, but whose story we have not been able to adequately tell. The special operations commands are not yet ready to grant researchers complete access to their operational records to chronicle the often amazing tales they contain. In particular, the Combined Joint Special Operations Task Force-Arabian Peninsula (CJSOTF-AP) consistently produced results far above what would normally be expected of a brigade level command, and little has been written about their exploits. The sections of our history that recount the special operations role in Iraq represent a small fraction of what the special operators actually did, and we hope that someday soon that story can be fully told.

We also have not been able to provide a full account of the enemy and Iraqi forces of various kinds that fought during the war, though we have worked hard to assemble as much of that information as we can. Neither the enemy forces nor the Iraqi security forces have yet told their own story, and, until they do, historians' understanding of their perspective is necessarily incomplete.

A few other areas of research were beyond the scope of this history but should be undertaken by researchers, including the shared logistics that supported both Iraq and Afghanistan, air power in Iraq, and the maritime component of the Iraq campaign. The functional areas of information operations and reconstruction efforts deserve their own treatment as well. Even more importantly, the Defense Department needs to produce a history of U.S. Central Command in the post-9/11 wars, so that the operational histories of the Iraq and Afghanistan wars—as well as other smaller operations—can be put into their regional and strategic context. The fight against al-Qaeda in Iraq (AQI) or the Islamic State in Iraq was part of a broader campaign against al-Qaeda and its associated movements. Fighting in Yemen, Somalia, Mali, and other locations was connected through a strategic framework—both ours and our enemies'—with the fighting in Iraq and Afghanistan. This strategic history should be modeled on the U.S. Army in World War II series, *The Supreme Command*, an overarching history of the Allies in the European theater, without which the operational histories of the European theater cannot be fully appreciated.

A history set in Iraq will contain many Arabic personal and place names, many of which have no standard English spelling. In rendering these Arabic names into English, we have followed standard transliteration in many cases, but in others, we have used the spelling most common within the U.S. military, whether that spelling followed transliteration rules or not. We also generally chose to refer to Iraqis using English formalities rather than the more familiar Iraqi style. Therefore, instead of the Iraqi style of referring to General Babakir Zebari as General Babakir, we refer to him as General Zebari. For simplicity's sake, and to reflect U.S. military and Iraqi usage, we have also tended to drop the articles from the spelling of place names in the text. The maps are more formal and retain the article.

Finally, throughout these volumes, we, the authors, retain full responsibility for all matters of interpretation as well as for any errors or omissions of fact.

COLONEL FRANK SOBCHAK
COLONEL JOEL RAYBURN
Washington, DC
May 2017

ACKNOWLEDGMENTS

These volumes could not have been produced without a team effort by a wide range of leaders, experts, and organizations across and outside the Army. Without a doubt, the greatest influence and inspiration came from General (Ret.) Raymond T. Odierno, who conceived this project, provided continuous encouragement, and was generous with his time throughout our work. His support, leadership, and mentorship were invaluable to us. We also want to recognize Brigadier General Bradley T. Gericke, our liaison in the Office of the Chief of Staff of the U.S. Army, who helped us overcome dozens of bureaucratic obstacles while providing the wise counsel of a senior Army historian. Across the Pentagon hallway from General Gericke is Steven J. Redmann, Vice Director of the Army Staff, who was a true champion of our work. He ensured that we had the resources we needed and provided the help of his accomplished team on many occasions. Similarly, Lieutenant General Gary H. Cheek, the Director of the Army Staff, ensured our project remained a high priority after General Mark A. Milley became the Chief of Staff of the Army. Without his stalwart support, it is unclear whether this book would ever have been published. At the National Defense University, Michael S. Bell, Chancellor of the College of International Security Affairs (NDU-CISA), in Washington, DC, provided us a home for more than 2 years and treated us as colleagues, providing resources and people to help us in our work.

We were fortunate to have an external advisory board whose members graciously volunteered their time and advice to help make our work better. Conrad C. Crane and Steven Metz at the U.S. Army War College, Kenneth M. Pollack of the Brookings Institution, and David A. "Scotty" Dawson of U.S. Central Command spent many hours reviewing and rigorously critiquing our draft chapters. Other experts who read all or most of our manuscript and provided valuable input included Seth Center of the U.S. State Department, Peter Bergen of the New America Foundation, and Lieutenant General Herbert Raymond "H. R." McMaster of the U.S. Army Training and Doctrine Command (TRADOC).

As a small team focused on a specific task for a fixed duration, we relied frequently on larger Army and joint organizations that generously contributed their input, time, and resources. Within the Army, we are grateful to the Center of Military History and the Histories Division for providing an array of resources for this project, including historians who helped edit chapters and footnotes, shared ideas, and furnished valuable primary sources. We also would like to thank the Historical Products Branch for its professional editors, cartographers, and visual information specialists who helped turn our manuscript into printed form. Our team is also indebted to the Strategic Studies Institute (SSI) at the U.S. Army War College (USAWC) for further editing and ultimately publishing our work. We owe special thanks to Steve Metz from SSI as well as Conrad Crane and Mike Lynch from the USAWC's Army Heritage and Education Center (USAHEC) for the countless hours they spent scrutinizing our final drafts. Their efforts considerably improved our product.

Several branches of TRADOC provided us with timely assistance and material support. At the USAHEC in Carlisle, PA, Colonel Matthew Q. Dawson and Colonel Robert A. Harney, Jr., offered their assistance and resources, providing workspace for one of our senior fellows and placing their staff at his disposal. USAHEC's Richard Baker,

Ross Webb, Pamela Cheney, Thomas Hendrix, Lieutenant Colonel Christopher Leljedal, and Beth Shaffer freely offered research assistance and advice. At the Combined Arms Center at Fort Leavenworth, KS, Colonel Thomas E. Hanson and Donald P. Wright of the Combat Studies Institute provided us their team's extensive interviews and draft manuscripts of several volumes of the *On Point* series, enabling us to build on their excellent work. Fort Leavenworth's Center for Army Lessons Learned also provided access to its extensive unpublished unit-level studies, particularly to valuable interviews and after action reports from the Office of Security Cooperation-Iraq. At TRADOC Headquarters, Brit McCarley, Karen Lewis, and Lieutenant Colonel (Ret.) Richard Rinaldo opened TRADOC's extensive holdings and offered constructive input during the early stages of this project. We received similar assistance from Robert S. Cameron at the Army's Armor Center at Fort Benning, GA.

The Center for Army Analysis gave us access to its extensive research on the Iraq War and helped us to understand better the vast data the Army collected while in Iraq. The Army's Intelligence and Security Command assisted us with processing our classified and declassified files, without which we could not have fulfilled our mission of establishing a new archive of Iraq War operational records. The Combating Terrorism Center at West Point, NY, assisted us in mining terrorism-related data and also provided numerous declassified reports of interrogations of captured insurgents in Iraq. Finally, we are grateful to the Natick Operations Center at the U.S. Army Natick Soldier Systems Center, MA, especially to Amir Diengdoh and Jacqueline Hope, for providing workspace and many hours of administrative support for one of our senior fellows.

In the joint community and beyond, we owe great thanks to the NDU, which housed the main body of our team for the duration of our project. In addition to our colleagues at NDU-CISA, we received particular support from Colonel (Ret.) John Agoglia, who devoted much time to reviewing our history of the 2003 invasion for accuracy; and from Scott Gower, who, as librarian of NDU's classified collections, generously gave his time to help us mine the classified and unclassified archives that he curates. NDU's Center for Complex Operations gave us access to its extensive archive of documents from the Provincial Reconstruction Teams and other organizations in Iraq.

At the U.S. Central Command History Office, David "Scotty" Dawson and Charles Newell helped us comb through archives and provided their own expert knowledge about the Iraq campaign. Daniel Darling, one of Central Command's finest and most prolific intelligence experts, contributed several monographs that helped unlock some of the mysteries of the Iraqi insurgency. Major General Michael Garrett, U.S. Central Command chief of staff, put his staff at our disposal and accomplished the Army's most extensive document declassification project since World War II in support of these volumes. Their work enabled us to declassify almost 30,000 pages of important operational records.

Many elements from the special operations community provided unique and invaluable support for our project. At U.S. Special Operations Command, the Command History team helped fact-check our data, provided archival research and sources, and helped us gain access to key leaders. We would also like to thank the Center for Counterterrorism Studies and the Command History team at Joint Special Operations Command for enabling us to access their lessons-learned studies and historical archives. Special thanks across these teams go to Shawn Woodford, Colonel (Ret.) Steven Cage, Gaea Lenders, and Colonel (Ret.) James Herson. Likewise, William Knarr of the Joint Special Operations University and the Institute for Defense Analyses provided invaluable primary and secondary sources on Anbar Province across the war, and his interviews of insurgent commanders and Iraqi leaders are unique among the current set of primary sources. We would also like to thank Colonel (Ret.) Mark E. Mitchell, who helped review the special operations sections of our manuscript for accuracy and strength of argument.

Several coalition partners also contributed to our effort. We are thankful for the support we received from senior military officers from the United Kingdom who gave us interviews and helped us to better understand their campaign in southern Iraq. Italian, Danish, and Polish senior leaders were similarly generous with their time and proved indispensable in providing perspective and detail about the efforts of our allies.

We are grateful to Gordon W. Rudd of the Marine Corps University at Quantico, VA, for his insights and providing us with interviews pertaining to the early post-invasion period. Also at the university, the Marine Corps History Division helped us to understand better the Marine Corps' role in Iraq. Fred H. Allison furnished transcribed and digital recordings of key Marine and Army personnel in Multi-National Force-West, Nicholas Schlosser facilitated our access to the unclassified archives at Quantico, and Annette Amerman and Gregory Cina supplied command chronologies and published histories.

At the Institute for Defense Analyses, Kevin M. Woods shared important primary source materials on the Iraqi perspective from the 2003 invasion, as well as materials that yielded insights into Iraqi irregular forces. He also shared the important memoir written by former Iraqi Lieutenant General Raad Hamdani. At the Joint Center for Operational Analysis, Albert Musgrove shared very useful materials from the Joint and Coalition Operational Analysis' Operation IRAQI FREEDOM (OIF) archives. Kyle Orton, a fellow at the London based Henry Jackson Society, provided invaluable assistance with understanding al-Qaeda in Iraq and Islamic State of Iraq and Syria in general and their connections to former Ba'ath officers. Finally, at the Joint History Office of the Office of the Joint Chiefs of Staff, Brigadier General (Ret.) John F. Shortal and his team provided access to a wealth of material pertaining to the 2003 invasion, including documents from the Joint Staff and classified synopses of the Pentagon's planning for OIF.

Outside the Department of Defense, Seth Center of the State Department History Office spent many hours with us discussing his research on the Iraq War and ours, and helping us sharpen our historical arguments. At the RAND Corporation, Colonel (Ret.) David E. Johnson shared his excellent research on the Battle of Sadr City, and Walter L. Perry shared his detailed study on the early phases of the war. At the Central Intelligence Agency (CIA), Clayton D. Laurie and the CIA history staff furnished a manuscript that covered the invasion period of the war. Outside the U.S. Government, Kimberly Kagan and Marisa Cochrane Sullivan of the Institute for the Study of War generously gave us access to their maps, primary source material, and published reports on the Iraq War. We also owe special thanks to Major General (Ret.) Najim Jabouri of Iraq for his many hours of advice and expert input as we developed our manuscript. The ability to draw upon his knowledge enabled us to deepen our understanding and interpretation of many aspects of the war, and to understand why Iraqis were fighting.

Finally, we would like to thank the scores of individuals who granted us interviews or participated in discussions during this project. Their names, except for those who wished to remain anonymous, appear in our bibliographical section. These interviews and meetings enabled us to improve our understanding of the human factor and of command decision-making during the Iraq War. The interviewees, some of whom contributed many hours of their time, helped us clarify topics of concern, provided insight into important decisions, and gave us a more nuanced understanding of previously reported events. We also wish to thank the U.S. Army's General Officer Management Office for helping us connect with many senior leaders from all phases of the war.

PART I:
THE SURGE, 2007-2008

CHAPTER 1

STRATEGY IN CRISIS, OCTOBER–DECEMBER 2006

As 2006 drew to a close, U.S. leaders in Washington and Baghdad grappled with the reality that the transition strategy the U.S.-led coalition had been pursuing for more than 2 years had failed to stabilize Iraq. In the months since the February 2006 bombing of the Shi'a shrine in Samarra, Iraq had descended into a sectarian civil war, with violence worst in the Iraqi capital and its surrounding areas. By mid-October, three successive U.S.-Iraqi operations to tamp down the sectarian attacks in Baghdad had failed, and violence had only increased. The Multi-National Force-Iraq (MNF-I) campaign plan had envisioned a reduction of U.S. forces to about 100,000 by the end of 2006. Instead, MNF-I Commander General George W. Casey, Jr. had been forced to cancel unit redeployments, call forward in-theater reserves from Kuwait, and authorize extensions of U.S. units in response to the dire security situation in Baghdad.

For more than 2 years, Casey, U.S. Central Command (CENTCOM) Commander General John P. Abizaid, and Secretary of Defense (SECDEF) Donald H. Rumsfeld had been the principal architects of U.S. military strategy in Iraq, but their grip on the campaign began to slip in the fall of 2006. In December, the ground would shift under their feet as a variety of high-profile groups offered alternatives to Casey's strategy. In the space of less than 2 months, President George W. Bush would dramatically change the strategy guiding the U.S. campaign in Iraq and would appoint new commanders to implement the revised approach.

STRATEGY OPTIONS

Moving Forward After Operation TOGETHER FORWARD

About 1 week after Abizaid's mid-October message to Casey about the need to change the dynamics in Baghdad (see Volume 1, Chapter 22), Rumsfeld arrived at a similar verdict. The top civilian official in the Pentagon noted the rising violence, abruptly concluded that the Baghdad Security Plan had failed, and invited the MNF-I commander to convince him otherwise.[1]

Casey expected the ensuing video teleconference on November 1, 2006, to be another session in which to communicate his appreciation of the situation. Instead, the general encountered a defense secretary questioning the entire operation. What had been the value of committing 3,000-4,000 more Americans to Baghdad in support of Operation TOGETHER FORWARD, Rumsfeld wondered, if violence had only escalated? "Do you think the Baghdad Security Plan is working?" the secretary pointedly asked.[2] "It is keeping the capital from sliding into anarchy," Casey replied. Sending additional U.S. and Iraqi units to Baghdad had "a dampening effect on sectarian violence," he assessed, but "political action" was needed to shore up security gains.[3]

General Fil, Jr., (left) SECDEF Rumsfeld (right).
Source: DoD photo by Sergeant Nicole Kojetin (Released).

Major General Joseph Fil, Jr., Commanding General, MND-B, With SECDEF Rumsfeld.[4]

Yet making progress on the political front seemed as difficult as it had ever been. This, perhaps, was Rumsfeld's point. To Rumsfeld, the late October 2006 incident (see Volume 1, Chapter 22) in which the Sadrists had forced Prime Minister Nuri al-Maliki to demand the removal of coalition checkpoints from the outskirts of Sadr City demonstrated that Moqtada Sadr exercised more influence over Maliki than the coalition did. The secretary seemed puzzled by Casey's apparent deference to the Iraqi leader and wanted to explore what he saw as a mismatch in leverage. Rumsfeld observed that it looked as if Casey simply bowed to the Prime Minister's will to satisfy Iraqi interests in a case where the coalition had compelling interests of its own. Casey responded to Rumsfeld's prodding with an explanation of his relationship to Maliki. He was in the position of merely providing military advice, and, as Prime Minister, Maliki could take it or leave it. The general had argued that lifting the checkpoints would make recovering the missing American Soldier more difficult and would cast the Iraqi leader as a supporter of Shi'a death squads. Casey related that Maliki understood the risks but had insisted on suspending the checkpoints nonetheless, which had settled the matter in Casey's mind. "I don't see it that way," Rumsfeld pointed out. "You don't work for the PM [Prime Minister]. You report through us—Abizaid and SECDEF—then to POTUS [President of the United States]. We decide. He's not your political leader." Casey acknowledged this fact but noted that he could not ignore Maliki, who was, after all, "my partner." For clarity's sake, the general added that he would never do anything that he felt would disadvantage his Soldiers or jeopardize the mission.[5]

U.S. Ambassador to Iraq Khalilzad (left) General Casey (center).
Source: DoD photo by Captain Amy Bishop (Released).

U.S. Ambassador to Iraq Zalmay Khalilzad With General George Casey, Commander, MNF-I, and Iraqi National Security Adviser Mowaffaq Rubaie.[6]

Rumsfeld persisted. Casey had to make Maliki understand that, in spite of his position as Prime Minister, he did not have carte blanche in matters that involved coalition military operations. Yes, Maliki had the authority to make decisions, but he needed to understand that certain choices came with a price. If the Prime Minister insisted on dismantling the checkpoints along the Army Canal, then Casey should have announced his intention to counter with an action undesirable enough to prompt Maliki's reconsideration. The Iraqi leader was taking advantage of the coalition because he saw no downside to doing so. "I don't want to use the fifty-thousand-mile screwdriver," the secretary ventured, "but I think that if Maliki is responding to Sadr's pressure it's because no pressure is being applied from the other side."[7]

Applying that pressure, as Rumsfeld saw it, was Casey's job. When Chairman of the Joint Chiefs of Staff General Peter Pace and the Under Secretary of Defense for Policy Eric S. Edelman objected, questioning whether it was fair to expect Casey to be a military adviser on one hand while demanding he "push" Maliki with the other, Rumsfeld declared, "I don't know who else it would be!" Adamant to put an end to what he saw as a series of "free lunches" enjoyed by Maliki at American expense, Rumsfeld urged Casey to make the Prime Minister understand that actions taken contrary to expressed U.S. interests had consequences—with troop levels as the most promising lever. "Maybe we should reduce the number of our forces in Baghdad? Maybe you should let him know that you intend to withdraw troops?" suggested Rumsfeld. "Maybe pull a brigade . . . send it after the Iranians and get after EFPs," he added, using the acronym for explosively formed penetrators.[8] Frustrated with Maliki's sluggishness in reducing sectarian violence in Baghdad, Rumsfeld's immediate recommendation was to withdraw American troops from the capital.

Casey and his advisers considered the secretary's suggestions unhelpfully aggressive and confrontational. Pushing Maliki too firmly would make him more reliant on domestic political support and less likely to risk an independent, nonsectarian stand. Furthermore, Casey's determination that MNF-I lacked credible leverage only made his bargaining position worse. "The Iraqis know your hands are tied in Washington," wrote one adviser, offering a bleak assessment of U.S. political will. "They want their view of Iraqi society more than we want our view—and they both know this and know that you know this."[9] With coalition leverage declining, Maliki's demands for sovereignty grew shriller. If Casey and Ambassador Khalilzad responded by taking an even harder line, then the Iraqis might well call their bluff. "Are we irrelevant because of our desire to withdraw?" the general wondered.[10]

After the November 1 video teleconference, Rumsfeld continued to dwell on the prospect of reducing troop levels amid Baghdad's escalating violence. On the eve of congressional midterm elections in the United States, the SECDEF drafted a memorandum that listed an assortment of "new courses of action" for Iraq. "Clearly, what U.S. forces are currently doing . . . is not working well enough or fast enough," he wrote, and proceeded to outline 21 options. Of these, one involved increasing the number of U.S. brigade combat teams (BCTs) in the theater, and he categorized it as a "less attractive option" alongside continuing on the "current path."[11] Further limiting the roles and responsibilities of U.S. forces and reducing their presence through repositioning or drawing down figured much more prominently in the list.[12] There was no question about where Rumsfeld stood when it came to troop levels. The same could be said for the Republican chairman of the Senate Armed Services Committee, Virginia Senator John W. Warner, who sent a memorandum to Casey expressing concern that the MNF-I commander might be considering the prospect of increasing troop strength in Iraq.[13]

The White House Strategy Review

Casey's tense exchange with Rumsfeld on November 1 and the secretary's subsequent input both proved inconsequential. Less than 1 week later, the American people went to the polls to vote in midterm elections and handed the Democrats control of both houses of Congress. Bush used the occasion to replace Rumsfeld, who submitted his resignation a day after the administration's electoral setback, after almost 6 years at the helm of the Pentagon.

Since 2005, National Security Adviser Stephen J. Hadley had peppered Casey with questions related to Iraq operations and strategy. The barrage intensified in summer 2006 as the National Security Council (NSC) staff's slowly developing assessment of the conflict gathered momentum. The general, unaware of this quiet review, saw Hadley's inquiries as a nuisance that bordered on intrusive. Nonetheless, he accepted them (and, at times, dismissed them) as part of the administration's well-intentioned effort to gain an understanding of the complicated and shifting environment in Iraq.[14] Following Hadley's belated trip to Iraq at the end of October, Casey related to Rumsfeld the national security adviser's comment that the situation in Iraq seemed "really complex!"[15] It only later dawned on the general that Hadley was asking the questions in order to develop alternative measures at odds with Casey's strategy.

National Security Adviser Hadley (back, far left).
Source: White House photo by Eric Draper (Released).

President George W. Bush With National Security Adviser Stephen Hadley and Vice President Richard Cheney.[16]

With the election over, the NSC staff ramped up its review of the U.S. Government's Iraq War strategy, considering a broader array of options, to include the deployment of additional brigades—alternatives that Rumsfeld had vehemently opposed.[17] By late 2006, most of the options under consideration were not hasty expediencies, but well-developed proposals. Some were the products of several years of analysis by respected voices both inside and outside of the Bush administration who had long observed that the U.S. campaign in Iraq was in trouble. Among those outside the government, American Enterprise Institute scholar Thomas Donnelly had argued as early as November 2003 that the United States should implement a counterinsurgency approach in Iraq with additional American troops.[18] Brookings Institution scholar Kenneth Pollack had repeatedly argued as early as 2004 that more U.S. troops were needed in Iraq, and he and Georgetown professor Daniel Byman had warned in August 2006 that the strategy of transitioning responsibility to the Iraqis and reducing U.S. troop levels would be insufficient to halt Iraq's civil war, and that it might, in fact, make the war worse.[19] Within the administration, State Department officials Philip Zelikow and James Jeffrey had argued in June 2006 for sending additional U.S. troops to restore order in Baghdad.[20] These critics of the administration's strategy had been consulted by the White House over time, and as Hadley and the NSC staff explored options for a different Iraq strategy, their thinking would be informed by these and other influential scholars and analysts.

On November 8, 2006, the same day as Rumsfeld's resignation, Hadley submitted his observations on the situation in Iraq to Bush, based on Hadley's visit to Baghdad the week before. With its recommendations for "a robust program of embedding coalition forces" and "giving [Maliki] additional control over Iraqi forces" Hadley's memorandum reinforced Casey's idea of speeding up the transfer of security responsibility.[21] Hadley mentioned the possibility of more American forces to help reduce violence and stabilize Baghdad, but he indicated that this idea would be left to the MNF-I commander to approve. Beyond these points, however, Hadley noted that the U.S. strategy in Iraq depended heavily on the Maliki government's success in promoting national reconciliation and reforming the Iraqi security forces, two things the national security adviser doubted that Maliki had either the ability or the will to do.[22]

Hadley was questioning the fundamental assumption that underlay MNF-I's plans, and this skepticism showed in an interagency review of the administration's Iraq policy that Hadley undertook at the President's request. On November 10, deputy national security adviser Jack Dyer "J. D." Crouch launched the review, a step that finally formalized the NSC staff's 5 months of quiet inquiries in search of alternative approaches. The review team included several senior White House officials, including Meghan O'Sullivan and Brett McGurk, who had become frustrated with the MNF-I campaign plan and its inability to halt the violence in Iraq. Crouch and O'Sullivan were concerned that following through on transitioning security responsibility to the Maliki government without first extracting meaningful concessions from the Iraqi leader might be counterproductive. They also believed the United States needed to be more assertive in pushing the Iraqi political factions toward reconciliation. In addition, they consulted U.S.-based defense experts about the idea of a temporary surge of U.S. troops into central Iraq in order to arrest the sectarian violence before handing security responsibility over to the Iraqi Government. Casey had long believed that the United States needed to drawdown its forces in order to foster reconciliation among the Iraqi parties, after which violence would recede. The senior White House officials working on Iraq had come to the opposite conclusion: that U.S. forces needed to remain on the ground in order to tamp down violence and press the Iraqi factions to reconcile.

Casey Doubles Down on the Joint Campaign Plan

From MNF-I's standpoint, the elections and Rumsfeld's resignation brought a sober realization that the country was growing tired and dissatisfied with the war in Iraq.[23] It lent urgency to the command's need to reduce sectarian violence in Baghdad and make progress toward national reconciliation. Casey himself perceived an unsettling change in the President's demeanor. On November 10, during the first video teleconference since the elections, Bush seemed "irritated, distant, and unmistakably cold"—an unpleasant departure from his usual "upbeat, warm and friendly" tone. Casey conveyed his observation to Khalilzad following the meeting and wondered what this stir in the Washington winds portended.[24] He found out soon enough and later recalled that it led "to the most complex period of my command."[25]

As the NSC staff continued to explore ways for the United States to regain control of the security situation in Iraq, Casey's response to the changed dynamics in the aftermath of the November 7 elections was to recommit to the transition strategy. In mid-November, he formulated a new campaign concept in which MNF-I would continue transferring security responsibility to the Iraqis as conditions warranted but would now seek to do so at an accelerated pace. The April 2006 campaign plan that had guided MNF-I's march toward the transfer of security responsibilities had already noted that early opportunities to achieve Provincial Iraqi Control "must be seized and the pace of transition . . . accelerated whenever possible."[26] In fact, MNF-I had dubbed 2006 as the "Year of the Police" in part to highlight the coalition's effort to accelerate the Iraqi police service's development in order to close the gap between its capability and that of the Iraqi Army.[27]

The concept of speeding up the transition also fit naturally with the ongoing effort to link political benchmarks with mutually reinforcing military action to improve the security environment. As early as July 2006, Rumsfeld had called for a set of benchmarks that would ostensibly coax the Iraqi Government toward reconciliation and self-reliance. He had hoped this publicized roadmap would serve as a "new construct for Iraq" and "permit a reduction of coalition forces."[28] When the latest iteration of the Baghdad Security Plan failed to make a satisfactory dent in the levels of sectarian violence, benchmarks reemerged as an idea whose time had come.[29] Casey saw them as political milestones that the Iraqis could achieve by January 2007 with coalition help. The benchmarks included long-standing issues like establishing a date for provincial elections, delineating the powers of provincial governments, de-Ba'athification, hydrocarbon revenue distribution, and several other items related to the rule of law, amnesty, and militias.[30] Successfully tackling this ambitious legislative agenda would set the stage for national reconciliation and the transition of security responsibility during the coming year. Seeking to codify an Iraqi division of power that addressed the competing interests of Kurdish, Shi'a, and Sunni populations, the benchmark legislation formed the basis of an integrated political-military plan.[31] Yet it depended on Iraqi cooperation, and in the fall of 2006, leaders of the competing sects and ethnicities found compromise hard to achieve. Maliki even objected to the term "benchmark" as an affront to his leadership and Iraqi sovereignty.[32]

The crucial question of how long the coalition would be able to exercise its full authority also loomed. MNF-I operated with fairly permissive guidelines under a United Nations (UN) security resolution that could be invalidated by the Iraqi Government at any time. On November 11, 2006, Maliki requested that the coalition's mandate be extended for another year in its current form. However, U.S. officials in Baghdad widely viewed this as the last extension the Prime Minister would grant. Casey fully expected the mandate to expire on December 31, 2007, and, when it did, the coalition would face severe restrictions on the kinds of operations it could conduct.[33] Thus, in the last months of 2006, MNF-I concluded that it had roughly 1 year to set Iraq on a path toward self-reliance—a grim prospect given the self-sustaining cycle of sectarian violence and the government's unwillingness to take meaningful steps toward national reconciliation. This factor also informed Casey's thinking as he pursued an accelerated timeline, even as many officials in Washington were concluding that the time had come to slow down the transition.

The first public debate about Casey's new concept began on November 15 as Abizaid testified before the Senate Armed Services Committee. The CENTCOM commander dismissed an accelerated withdrawal of U.S. troops. He advocated instead a "major change" in U.S. strategy by augmenting the transition teams and reorienting U.S. units from combat operations to training and advising the Iraqi security forces, the very concept that Casey was preparing to implement in Baghdad. When Arizona Senator John S. McCain III suggested that the United States should instead surge 20,000 additional American troops to deal with the security situation directly, Abizaid argued that a surge would be more than U.S. ground forces could handle. He told McCain:

> We can put in 20,000 more Americans tomorrow and achieve a temporary effect. But when you look at the overall American force pool that's available out there, the ability to sustain that commitment is simply not something that we have right now with the size of the Army and the Marine Corps.[34]

Taking a more direct role with more U.S. forces would also discourage the Iraqis from taking responsibility for their own security, Abizaid said. The senator countered, "I regret deeply that you seem to think that the status quo and the rate of progress we're making is acceptable. I think most Americans do not." It was a stark change from their past exchanges, in which McCain had been deferential to Abizaid's expertise on Iraq and the Middle East, and it signaled that those who supported the Iraq War effort were losing patience with the Casey-Abizaid strategy.[35]

The following day, November 16, Casey pitched his new campaign concept to Rumsfeld, now a lame duck serving until the Senate confirmed his nominated successor, Robert M. Gates. The MNF-I commander began with his bottom line: "We are at a position in the campaign where accelerating and completing the transition of security responsibility to capable Iraqi security forces is both strategically appropriate and feasible." When Rumsfeld expressed a mix of surprise and doubt, Casey clarified that the revised plan would not expand the scope of the ongoing transfer, nor would it entail a change to how the transfer would occur. "We are simply saying that there is an opportunity to transfer faster," Casey explained, arguing that the acceleration itself would provide much-needed leverage to coax the Shi'a-dominated government down the road to reconciliation with Sunni Arabs and Kurds. "I thought the administration wants to speed up," Casey added.[36]

Rumsfeld now offered a correction to Casey's interpretation of where the White House desired to steer the U.S. mission in Iraq. "My impression," began the secretary, "is that the president is determined to stay in Iraq for the remainder of his term. . . . He wants success." What the President specifically needed from Casey, Rumsfeld ventured, were options that would not only lead to the accomplishment of the coalition's objectives but also allow the President to defend himself from the critics emboldened by the Republicans' electoral setback. Casey could help the President build political support following the election by telling him what needed to be done to win, particularly an alternative to any stark policy shift the congressionally funded Iraq Study Group might propose. The pace of the transition thus far had been "orderly," Rumsfeld observed, and he was skeptical that a suggestion to speed it up dramatically would be well received. It was true the President wanted new options, Rumsfeld said, but "We don't want to recommend something to the president that is dumb."[37]

Casey went on to propose a five-point plan for an accelerated transition that would ostensibly lead to the implementation of an Iraqi-brokered reconciliation program ending the violence among competing factions. The coalition would push to complete the transfer of security responsibility to the Iraqi Government in 2007. Beginning in 2008, MNF-I would transition to a new mission and establish a new security arrangement with the Iraqis. On its way to this milestone, the force would gradually reduce its presence and visibility—both in terms of troop levels and security-related tasks. Increasing the size of military transition teams would be the primary means of carrying out the acceleration. While these enhanced teams focused on training the Iraqi security forces and coordinating support for their independent combat operations, other coalition forces would concentrate on defeating Sunni and Shi'a terrorists and death squads.[38] As the coalition adjusted its posture to speed up the process of transferring control and improving Iraqi capability, Casey expected Maliki's government to make progress on reconciliation. Specifically, this entailed taking a harder line against Shi'a militia groups and putting a stop to their sectarian cleansing in and around Baghdad. However, the general admitted that it was an open question as to whether the Prime Minister had the political will and courage to do so.[39]

As alternatives, Casey considered maintaining the status quo, raising troop levels, or withdrawing on a fixed schedule. He dismissed outright the last option and opined that additional forces would provide only a "temporary and local solution"—assuming the Iraqis found such a reversal of coalition force levels acceptable in the first place.[40] Not surprisingly, Rumsfeld panned the choice to deploy reinforcements. "More would not be helpful," he declared. It would amount to just "feeding the alligator."[41]

The task of describing how to operationalize the accelerated transition plan fell to Lieutenant General Peter W. Chiarelli. The MNC-I commander explained to Rumsfeld that the new effort, dubbed the transition bridging strategy, would focus on two elements: training the Iraqi security forces and conducting strike operations, both independently against high-value extremist targets and in support of Iraqi-led efforts. Reorienting divisions and BCTs onto these two mission sets would allow them to shed manpower-intensive tasks focused on sustained area security, and thus reorganize their formations along more functional lines. To illustrate the idea, Chiarelli demonstrated how a U.S. brigade would array its forces in a generic province where an Iraqi Army division was assigned. A reinforced battalion would devote one company to help Iraqi units secure the border and to enhance transition teams at the province's ports of entry. Another company would supplement the coalition police transition teams posted in Iraqi police district headquarters and stations. In the most significant change, four companies would support the 14 or so military transition teams embedded with the Iraqi Army brigades and battalions operating in the province. Each transition team of roughly a dozen U.S. troops could be reinforced by one platoon, doubling or tripling the team's size.[42]

In theory, this enhancement provided a number of advantages. It would bolster the inherent combat power of transition teams and allow them to operate farther afield from coalition bases. Additional numbers meant that the team could better supervise the Iraqi unit to which it was assigned down to the company level, an issue that had been debated, but rejected when the teams were first organized in 2005. Chiarelli later described this enhanced capacity as "24/7 coverage" that would deter Iraqi military leaders from implementing sectarian agendas.[43] The BCT would also maintain a "strike battalion"—Chiarelli compared it to a football team's free safety—capable of serving as a quick-reaction force and conducting offensive operations against high-profile targets. Finally, another battalion would assume responsibility for fixed-site security for providing enablers to coalition and Iraqi forces operating in the province.

Two uncertain qualifiers threatened the implementation of the concept at its very outset. First, it depended on the evenhandedness of the Shi'a-dominated Iraqi Government and the willingness of the political elite to make substantive progress toward national reconciliation. Second, it required interagency support. If brigades had to reorganize in order to accelerate the transition, they would have to shed some of the nonmilitary tasks they had been performing due to staffing shortfalls in civilian agencies, Chiarelli said. To illustrate, he mentioned building capacity for the Iraqi Ministry of Health, which, at the moment, had only one adviser while Iraqi security forces personnel occupied over 80 percent of the coalition's military hospital beds.[44]

As he listened to Chiarelli, Rumsfeld pressed the senior military commanders in Iraq to articulate the nonmilitary support they needed in specific terms, such as assistance in tackling corruption and sectarianism within the Iraqi police.[45] On the whole, although Rumsfeld was dubious about Casey's modified strategy, he seemed sold on the transition bridging concept by the end of the session. Granting that the specific numbers for transition-team enhancement still needed to be determined, he labeled the concept as "clear and understandable." The secretary observed that it "seemed inconsistent with 'clear-hold-build' or whatever," and he gave every indication of being comfortable with that fact.[46]

The Council of Colonels

Back at the Pentagon, Chairman of the Joint Chiefs of Staff, Marine Corps General Peter Pace, worked on formulating the Joint Chiefs' input to the White House strategy review. Earlier in the fall, retired General John M. "Jack" Keane had suggested that Pace form a Council of Colonels to conduct an independent assessment of the Global War on Terrorism and generate options regarding the future course of U.S. military policy in Iraq, and Pace had accepted the suggestion.[47] On November 22, the council presented its work to the Joint Chiefs, outlining three broad options for the United States in Iraq: "go big, go long, or go home."[48] Colonel Herbert Raymond "H. R." McMaster, who had commanded the 3d Armored Cavalry Regiment in Tel Afar, Iraq, from 2005 to 2006, championed the "go big" option—formally dubbed the "expanded effort"—in which the United States would "significantly increase economic, political, and military effort to stimulate the economy, strengthen governance, secure the population and regain the strategic initiative." Colonel Peter R. Mansoor, whose 1st Brigade Combat Team, 1st Armored Division, had fought against Jaysh al-Mahdi (JAM) in Karbala in 2004, argued for the "go long" option of deliberately adjusting the provision of resources and support in Iraq and adopting a smaller but "sustainable U.S. military presence" that could help the Iraqis "defeat the insurgency and quell sectarian violence" in a "long-duration effort." Marine Colonel Thomas C. Greenwood, who had served on the NSC staff in 2003 and had commanded the 15th Marine Expeditionary Unit (Special Operations Capable) in Babil Province in 2005, made the case for the "go home," or "strategic disengagement," option, a phased withdrawal from the country by the end of 2007 along with a much less ambitious end state.[49]

Over several weeks of deliberations, a majority of the colonels who comprised the council advocated the "go long" option, and on November 22, they presented to Pace a paper outlining this course of action. "We are losing in Iraq because we are not winning," and as a result the United States should reorient its current effort, they advised.[50] Iraqi governments at the national, provincial, and local levels lacked both legitimacy and effectiveness, as did the indigenous security forces that ostensibly supported them. Caught up in the whirlwind of economic distress, inadequate essential services, lawlessness, destabilizing foreign influences, and sectarian violence, the country was careening toward civil war. "Our modified strategy," the group explained, "is focused on reversing these trends as we transfer responsibility for governance and security to Iraqis."[51] The paper went on to outline a strategic design to "accelerate Iraq in the lead" and pave the way for success by "changing the political and military dynamic on the ground."[52] Given an Iraqi commitment to reconciliation, the U.S. military would "shift its main effort from a U.S.-led counterinsurgency effort to training and partnering efforts."[53] This would entail a gradual, though accelerated, transition of security responsibility. As conditions improved and the Iraqi security forces proved capable of independent operations, U.S. units would adopt a posture of "regional overwatch" and reach a point of sustainable presence in 2008.[54]

Pace provided a copy of the council's paper to Casey, who participated by videoconference with the Joint Chiefs of Staff on the same day. The MNF-I commander was not impressed with the colonels' work. Casey graded their efforts a "C-plus" and dismissed a subsequent version as not very useful. He charged that the colonels had arrived at their recommendations by simply assuming away thorny problems, such as achieving unity of effort among MNF-I, the Embassy, and coalition partners, and obtaining Iraqi Government cooperation on reconciliation and the reduction of sectarian violence.[55] From Casey's perspective, well-intentioned but uninformed officers in Washington had passed over the most difficult tasks facing the coalition in Iraq in order to recommend a strategy that MNF-I was, for the most part, already pursuing. "We're doing most, if not all, of the operational things mentioned, and have been for some time," he wrote in an e-mail to Pace.[56] Casey also believed the chairman's select colonels had failed to appreciate that the struggle in Iraq had everything to do with the struggle for political and economic power. To see the fight as a counterinsurgency spiraling downward into a civil war amounted to a misdiagnosis, he charged. Sectarian violence had emerged as the greatest threat to accomplishing the campaign's objectives, a change that "leads you to the fact that Iraqis have to solve their own problems—including the division of . . . power, and sectarian violence," Casey insisted. "It also leads you to the fact that we have to rely on [the Iraqis] to make the tough choices and expect them to move at a pace that is probably slower than we want."[57] By incorrectly interpreting the basis of the conflict and stretching out the remedy over a long period of time, the Council of Colonels' strategy failed to put sufficient pressure on the Iraqis to force them to change, Casey believed.

Nevertheless, the reorientation of the current effort proposed by the Council of Colonels generally aligned with Casey's concept for accelerated transition. The group found MNF-I's timeline for transferring security responsibilities ambitious and considered the concept for assuming "overwatch" to be too vague, but besides these two issues, the only other major difference revolved around U.S.-Iraqi unit partnership.[58] As a mechanism for facilitating transition, the council recommended partnering a U.S. BCT with each Iraqi division to provide oversight and support. "We're way past that," Casey objected.[59] As more and more Iraqi units assumed the lead, command and control in a partnered arrangement had become too cumbersome, according to Casey. "We want to cut the umbilical cord," he told Pace.[60] Partnership had worked at one time, but now that kind of relationship only hampered progress toward Iraqi self-sufficiency, he argued, even though he and Chiarelli had recommended a similar approach in their session with Rumsfeld a few days before.

Casey had even stronger objections when the discussion with the Joint Chiefs turned to the option of a surge of five U.S. brigades, the same idea that McCain had put to Abizaid 1 week before. Casey acknowledged, as he had earlier in the month, that more troops would have a "temporary, local impact." He doubted, however, that, "the tactical gain was worth possibly unhinging" the ongoing process of transition. Recalling the recent churning of Iraqi politics that stemmed from the coalition's request to commit CENTCOM's MEU reserve to Anbar, the general added that they could not count on unconditional Iraqi Government concurrence. Nonetheless, Casey admitted that, if given extra troops, he would have no trouble finding missions for them in Baghdad or in the rural areas just to the north and south of the capital. Other potential areas where the extra forces would be of use were Diyala, Anbar, and other border provinces. Pace told Casey that the Army Staff and Joint Forces Command had validated the possibility of a surge of 5 BCTs that could bring the force in Iraq up to 20 U.S. brigades from April to October 2007, but Casey reiterated to Pace that existing troop levels were adequate. As he considered the matter from Baghdad, Casey dismissed the chairman's offer as just another staff exercise.[61]

Mixed Messages at Amman

On November 30, 2006, Bush met with Maliki in Amman, Jordan. Seeking Bush's support for his revised Baghdad Security Plan, the Prime Minister risked a politically damaging rift with the Sadrists to attend.[62] Pleased with the plan's Iraqi origin, the President assured Maliki of U.S. assistance. The delegations also discussed the recommendations of the high-level working group on accelerating the transfer of security responsibility.[63] This group, consisting of Casey, Khalilzad, Iraqi national security adviser Mowaffaq Rubaie, and the Iraqi security ministers, had convened the month before and, over the course of November, had identified significant Iraqi military capabilities that could be targeted for acceleration.[64] Bush referred approvingly to this group during a post-meeting press conference and acknowledged the importance of speeding up the training of the Iraqi security forces. The President expressed his confidence in Maliki as a leader and affirmed the Prime Minister's courage and willingness to enforce the law in an evenhanded way. Appearing to see eye to eye on the immediate road ahead, the two leaders also explored the development of a long-term strategic partnership.[65] "The ultimate solution to stabilizing Iraq and reducing violence is true national reconciliation and capable and loyal Iraqi forces dedicated to protecting all the Iraqi people," concluded the two leaders' joint statement.[66]

Source: White House photo by Paul Morse (Released).

President George W. Bush Reaches Out to Iraqi Prime Minister Nuri al-Maliki in Amman, Jordan.[67]

Significantly, however, Bush mentioned his administration's ongoing strategy review and, privately with Maliki, hinted at the prospect of the United States committing tens of thousands more U.S. Soldiers to Iraq. The price of this assistance—assuming the Iraqis wanted it—was the Prime Minister's assurance that he would confront JAM and allow the Americans to do the same.[68] This quid pro quo arrangement must have been confusing to Maliki. Casey had been trying to extract the same concession from him in recent weeks but had linked it to a promise to reduce U.S. presence and involvement. All the same, the Iraqi Prime Minister assured Bush that he would meet this key condition. Casey, for his part, left Amman unaware that Bush considered committing additional forces to be a serious option.[69] In the meeting with the Iraqis—and in public, for that matter—the President's words seemed consistent with the thrust of MNF-I's plan to speed up the pace of transition. Yet Bush recalled in his memoirs that on the way home from Amman, "I thought about the options for a new strategy. Accelerating the handover to the Iraqis was not a viable approach. That sounded a lot like our current strategy, which was failing."[70]

Whatever doubts the President had had in Amman, Casey took the conference as a sign that the President supported his evolving Iraq strategy. In a video teleconference the day after the meeting in Jordan, the general told Bush that his "acceptance, in principle, of acceleration was a very good thing" and that Maliki definitely appreciated the gesture. Sitting alongside Casey in Baghdad, Abizaid agreed, saying that the Prime Minister was pleased with the meeting and was "feeling stronger with respect to the Sadr issue."[71]

Almost immediately though, Bush expressed his doubts. "Does Maliki view with alarm reports that JAM is killing people or that the Sunni are frightened? What will he do?" the President asked. Just over a day after putting Maliki on notice about getting tough on JAM, Bush was growing impatient. "I'm reading reports that JAM is getting ready to kill more people," the President said. "Are we saying to Maliki 'let us take care of this [problem]'?" Bush also expressed hesitation about handing power over to Maliki. What if the Prime Minister decided to use that power for sectarian purposes once it was irretrievably within his grasp? Bush wondered if there was a way to turn over responsibility to the Iraqis without actually giving them control.[72] These were not the ruminations of a President comfortable with Casey's strategy.

The Iraq Study Group

Of the strategic reviews occurring outside the walls of the White House, only the Iraq Study Group's review really mattered to Casey. Chartered by Congress in March 2006, this bipartisan body of elder statesmen, co-chaired by former Secretary of State James A. Baker III and former Congressman Lee H. Hamilton, had engaged in a series of discussions with officials and experts both inside and outside of Iraq. Many U.S. officials expected the long-anticipated Baker-Hamilton report to carry some weight once it appeared, though for his part, the President appeared to worry little about the fallout from the Iraq Study Group's findings and sensed that his advisers fretted a bit too much about it. "Understand that Baker-Hamilton is not setting the orders," Bush reminded video teleconference participants. "I am running this show."[73]

Casey had met with the group during its visit to Iraq in August. Then, he had responded to questions about troop levels by assuring them that the coalition had sufficient forces so long as the Iraqis supplied sufficient numbers of troops and performed adequately. When the Iraqi security forces lagged, U.S. units would support them as needed.[74] In a separate engagement with the group, Chiarelli also rejected the idea of applying more U.S. combat power to the problem. One member recalled him saying, "We're not going to win this thing militarily. We're only going to win it when we provide jobs to people, when we meet their basic needs, when we clean the trash up, when we deliver water, when we deliver electricity. Until we do that, we're fighting a losing war."[75] Later, during a follow-up video teleconference with the group in mid-November, Casey assured the group that "I have the resources I need to succeed," crossing out the word "win" in favor of "succeed" in his talking points. As far as U.S. troops were concerned, the general promised the group that he would continue to ask for whatever he believed he needed, but he judged it a mistake to overemphasize American troops' role in a multifaceted ethno-sectarian struggle over the division of political and economic power. He outlined the danger of ramping up coalition forces: "more [U.S. troops] at this point delays Iraqi movement to self-reliance, gives Iraqi leaders more time to avoid hard decisions, and blame us for their problems, and complicates the ongoing transition."[76]

When it published its findings on December 6, the Baker-Hamilton group proved to be a receptive audience for Casey's message. In its final report, mainly penned by future deputy national security adviser Benjamin J. Rhodes, the Iraq Study Group presented what it called "a new approach" and a "better way forward."[77] However, its findings largely corroborated Casey's viewpoint and endorsed the strategy of drawing down U.S. troops and shifting the coalition's primary mission to one of supporting the Iraqi Army. "The Iraqi government should accelerate assuming responsibility for Iraq security," the report read.[78] That acceleration would be facilitated by the growth of indigenous security forces and a rise in the number of embedded U.S. trainers. The group's philosophical stance echoed the central imperative of Casey's campaign plan, and as Casey and Abizaid had long done, the group assumed that a reduction in the U.S. role would naturally prompt the Iraqi factions to reconcile among themselves. "The most important questions about Iraq's future are now the responsibility of Iraqis," the report concluded. "The United States must adjust its role in Iraq to encourage the Iraqi people to take control of their own destiny."[79] The group also recommended opening negotiations with Iran and Syria to address the destabilizing influence those countries had on Iraq's security.[80]

At Amman a week before the Iraq Study Group report appeared, Maliki and his advisers had pressed Bush for a similar emphasis on handing them security responsibility in an accelerated fashion. However, other Iraqi leaders responded to the report with criticism, Iraqi President Jalal Talabani foremost among them. "As a whole, I reject this report," he told CNN, describing its recommendations for a U.S. troop withdrawal as "very dangerous" and a virtual repeat of the 1991 decision to abandon the Iraqi Kurds and Shi'a as they fought against the Ba'athist regime.[81] In the course of events, Talabani's fear that the United States would adopt the Iraq Study Group's drawdown recommendation proved unfounded. Even as the Baker-Hamilton report reached the public, the Bush administration was already considering options for increasing the U.S. troop presence, not reducing it.

Exploring the Surge Option

Within the Pentagon, U.S. military officials circulated a five-page minority report from the Council of Colonels authored by McMaster, which called for the deployment of additional U.S. brigades.[82] McMaster's paper acknowledged the need for continuing the development of Iraqi security forces and taking steps toward reconciliation, but he argued that a revised military scheme of maneuver could help interrupt the cycle of sectarian violence. With its main effort in Baghdad, MNC-I could ill afford to strip American units from the capital in order to reinforce efforts to disrupt or defeat Sunni and Shi'a extremists elsewhere. Thus, the United States needed more troops. A brigade posted southeast of Baghdad, in Wasit Province, would be able to disrupt the flow of explosively formed penetrators into the country from Iran and serve as a tangible counter to Iran's increasingly malignant influence. One additional brigade would also exploit ongoing success against al-Qaeda in Iraq in Anbar while another could be spread across the belt of towns and rural terrain north of Baghdad to deny the organization sanctuaries and disrupt its campaign to terrorize the capital. Finally, McMaster recommended that a fourth BCT be employed as an offensive force anywhere in Iraq, and that the special operations task force add Shi'a extremists to its target set.[83]

McMaster and other members of the Council of Colonels who dissented from the group's majority endorsement of a gradual U.S. drawdown in Iraq got a chance to present their ideas for a surge to Pace and Vice Chairman of the Joint Chiefs of Staff Admiral Edmund P. Giambastiani. Pace was somewhat sympathetic to McMaster's arguments that the transition strategy was bound to fail because it "underestimated our enemies, and it overestimated the Iraqi government and security forces' will and capability."[84]

McMaster's ideas would not become part of Pace's and the Joint Chiefs' ultimate input to the White House strategy review. Instead, the chairman tasked the group to write a memorandum defending the gradual drawdown that Pace could share with the White House. McMaster, despite being the most vocal critic of the drawdown option, was selected by the group to author the memorandum. Forced to defend an idea he disavowed, McMaster wrote that the only benefit of a drawdown was that it would require no further U.S. troops, but deputy national security adviser Crouch did not include the halfhearted memo in the papers submitted for the NSC principals.[85]

Though the Joint Chiefs of Staff did not adopt McMaster's proposals, the colonel's ideas would soon be closely mirrored by influential work from outside the military, where a consensus began to emerge among defense analysts in Washington that a surge of U.S. troops into Iraq would be needed to secure the country. Along with a handful of other defense analysts, Frederick W. Kagan of the American Enterprise Institute (AEI) had been invited by Stephen Hadley to Camp David in June 2006 during the early stages of the White House strategy review. The former West Point history professor believed the administration had mishandled the occupation of Iraq and took the opportunity to suggest to the President that more U.S. troops would be necessary to salvage the war effort.[86] In the following months, Kagan fleshed out a concept for stabilizing Baghdad that emphasized protecting the population rather than transferring security responsibility to the Iraqis. He saw the development of indigenous forces as essential to progress, but he considered MNF-I's approach inappropriate, given the violence racking the country. Casey's strategy of accelerated transition could not succeed rapidly enough, argued Kagan. Beefing up the number of embedded trainers in the Iraqi security forces would be counterproductive. Shifting the weight of U.S. manpower from combat operations to concentrate mainly on an advisory mission would effectively remove trained and ready forces from the battlefield and likely lead to an escalation in violence far beyond the capabilities of Iraqi units to handle. The effort to develop local security forces had to continue, but hastening the transition without first reducing violence to manageable levels risked pursuing a strategy until it plunged off a cliff.[87]

Kagan also challenged the premise held by Casey and Abizaid that coalition forces were antibodies whose disruptive presence should be mitigated by reducing their involvement. This theory could not be reconciled with the available data. Marked shifts in the levels of violence for a specific area did not correspond with increases or decreases in the number of coalition troops posted there. By late 2006, the violence consisted largely of Iraqi-on-Iraqi incidents, and a drop in attacks on U.S. forces amid sharply rising civilian casualties did not equate to enduring stability. According to Kagan, long-term success required political progress and economic development. However, the equation that yielded this result required rebalancing—and soon.[88]

Retired General Jack Keane had arrived at a similar conclusion. He determined that Casey's Iraq strategy was unraveling under the strain of growing sectarian violence. From his perch on the Defense Policy Board, the former Army vice chief of staff had been making the case for a new strategy to defeat the insurgency since August 2006. The new approach, he believed, needed to start with protecting the population. Doing so required a consistent forward presence in Iraqi neighborhoods and, thus, more troops. He advised

Rumsfeld and Pace that the focus on transition was wrong and pressed them to replace Abizaid and Casey with commanders who would adopt a new approach.[89]

Keane's operational expertise and credibility with senior officials prompted Kagan to invite him to an exercise at the American Enterprise Institute on December 2-3, in which a mix of civilian analysts and retired military officers explored in detail how to implement an alternative concept centered on improving population security. Among the participants were retired Colonel Joel Armstrong, who just a few months before had been McMaster's deputy commander in Tel Afar, and retired Major Daniel Dwyer, who had been McMaster's chief of plans. The two retired officers brought with them an influential testimonial that a surge of U.S. troops executing a counterinsurgency approach could achieve results, as the 3d Armored Cavalry Regiment had done in Tel Afar.[90] AEI's Iraq Planning Group concluded that extending the combat tours of forces already in Iraq and accelerating the deployment for units next to deploy could "produce a surge of two Marine RCTs [regimental combat teams] and five Army BCTs" in March 2007 that could be sustained for a full year.[91] Most of the reinforcements would help secure Baghdad by establishing a continuous presence among the population through small-unit combat outposts and foot patrols. The extra Marines would exploit the burgeoning success in Anbar, where the early signs of a turnaround under Colonel Sean MacFarland and his 1st Brigade Combat Team, 1st Armored Division, could be seen. Kagan originally figured it would take around 10 additional BCTs. Keane had arrived at his own estimate earlier, placing the number between 8 and 10.[92]

Participants in the exercise looked more deliberately into the forces required to deal with the threat groups plaguing each of Baghdad's diverse neighborhoods and then balanced this need with what was possible given the Army's slate of ready and available units. Keane later learned from the Army staff that five brigades were indeed the maximum that could be committed to any "surge."[93] Rather than full regiments, the Marine Corps would send two more battalions. This aside, the exercise confirmed to Keane not only the rationale for dispatching additional troops but also a plan for how they might be applied.[94] As it turned out, the specifics of this blueprint did not directly inform coalition planners in Baghdad.[95] However, the AEI process of deriving it equipped Keane and sympathetic U.S. officials with evidence to argue for a surge of U.S. forces to Iraq.

THE SURGE DECISION

U.S. Leaders Grope for the "New Way Forward"

As the White House continued with its review, the NSC staff began to assemble strategy input from the Pentagon, State Department, CENTCOM, and MNF-I, all of which the NSC principals would consider in a series of meetings beginning December 8. In formulating his input, Casey had to account for some of the competing ideas that had begun to emerge from other quarters in Washington, including the idea of a surge of U.S. troops. In an e-mail sent to Pace and Abizaid on December 6, Casey wrote that if a troop increase was considered, he favored a temporary surge of three Iraqi brigades to Baghdad and remained open to the idea of supplementing this force with coalition units already in Iraq. Alternatively, he could consider moving the 82d Airborne Division's ready brigade to Kuwait from Fort Bragg, NC. Though conceding that the security situation was grim, Casey was not inclined to ask for more troops that first week of December. In spite of the Iraqi security forces' well-known shortcomings, the general gave them the benefit of the doubt. He made a distinction between "poor to fair" police forces and "fair to good" army units and believed that, on balance, they all would continue to improve steadily with coalition support and oversight.[96] In Casey's view, a "fully resourced counterinsurgency strategy" of the kind that the McMaster paper advocated should consist of more U.S. civilian expertise embedded in provincial reconstruction teams, adequate economic investment, and meaningful outreach by the Government of Iraq to assuage the population's grievances.[97] It should not mean sending additional American troops.

On the eve of the NSC principals' meetings, Casey worked to extract political guarantees from Maliki that the Iraqi leader would support the accelerated transition strategy Casey hoped to execute. For some time, Casey and Khalilzad had been urging Maliki to realign his base of political support and allow MNF-I greater latitude in attacking Moqtada Sadr's military organization. However, Maliki's conception of the dominant threat to Iraq differed from the coalition's. In consultations with Casey, the Prime Minister insisted that a Ba'athist resurgence presented the gravest danger to stability. Admitting to a variety of threats, Maliki preferred to approach each in a different way. Terrorists and former regime elements (that is, the Iraqi Government's Sunni enemies) were best dealt with militarily, he asserted, while Shi'a militias were more effectively handled through the political process.[98] The fact that Maliki's political survival relied on an accommodation with the Sadrists explained his reluctance to confront JAM in Baghdad and allow the Americans to conduct raids into the militia's Sadr City sanctuary. MNF-I's apparent fixation on JAM also made the Prime Minister suspicious. On December 6, to allay Maliki's fear that the coalition might ally with the Sunnis in an all-out war against the Shi'a, Casey summoned the coalition's special operations task force commander to Baghdad to brief the Prime Minister on a long-running string of operations against al-Qaeda in Iraq and Ansar al Sunna. The task force's relentless pace (five to seven operations per night, on average), its ability to strike throughout the country, and its focus on Sunni extremists seemed to impress Maliki.[99] The task force commander presented the Prime Minister with a compelling case that the coalition had been pulling no punches in its fight against al-Qaeda in Iraq (AQI).

However, more could be done to undermine the threat posed by Shi'a death squads. When the task force commander explained that JAM's campaign of violence and intimidation tended to drive Sunni citizens into the arms of AQI for protection, Maliki concurred. Admitting that militias were not the all-around positive force that many Iraqis believed, the Prime Minister took the task force commander's point and turned it on its head: Sunnis needed to be persuaded to seek protection only from legitimate government forces.[100] Unsurprisingly, the question of the Prime Minister's willingness to confront JAM would figure prominently in the White House's strategy review.

Back in Washington, Rumsfeld—still serving as SECDEF as Robert Gates prepared to take over—provided his own input to the President on December 8, the same day that the NSC principals began their deliberations. Outlining a strategy for what he called a "new phase," Rumsfeld advised that the United States should "accelerate the transition, refocus the partnership, and stabilize the region," recommendations that drew heavily from the bridging concept briefed by Casey and Chiarelli. "The U.S. military is prepared to do its tasks as recommended in the proposal," Rumsfeld wrote on the cover page. "The test will be whether or not the non-military tasks—the critically needed political objectives—can be achieved and whether we are able to get the necessary cooperation from the Government of Iraq."[101]

From December 8 to 15, the NSC principals met in an intense series of daily discussions, with Abizaid present and Casey participating remotely from Baghdad. Though not all of the participants realized it, by the time these sessions began, Bush had committed to a "new way forward" and intended to announce it in a speech before Christmas. Only the "way" itself was not fully formed. The President wanted to hear options. On the first day of discussions, Crouch, addressing the question of Iraqi security force readiness, laid out two proposals that mainly differed in terms of the level of U.S. military involvement. Neither satisfied the President, who did not want to hand control over to the Iraqis if they were not ready, but also did not want to wait 6 months until the effects of retraining and reform materialized. No one had a problem with transition per se. Bush agreed that the "new way forward" would be about "giving it to the Iraqis," but the question was how fast that transition should take place and under what conditions. He asked Casey what "yardstick" the Prime Minister would use to determine when his military could actually shoulder the burden of independent counterinsurgency operations.[102]

Casey reminded the President about what had been discussed at Amman. The Iraqis would have control over all 10 of their divisions by spring. Baghdad Province was expected to pass to provincial Iraqi control in the summer. In the meantime, U.S. forces would reduce their presence in urban areas and gradually assume an overwatch role. "So 6 more months of the same stuff?" the President asked skeptically. Casey tried to correct what he viewed as an oversimplification of his approach, but Bush's frustration was obvious. Although barely more than a week old, the arrangement struck at Amman seemed stale in the President's eyes. "Does this argue for more U.S. forces as a bridge?" Bush asked the general. "If the Iraqis commit to end sectarian violence and ask us for help, then we should seriously consider adding more forces. But to do this without their commitment or to do it unilaterally? Then that is something we should not do," Casey replied.[103]

When it came to Maliki's commitment to stand up to JAM and mitigate its overtly sectarian agenda, the President voiced similar doubts, finding it ironic that the Iraqi Prime Minister seemed to be the principal "roadblock" to a renewed U.S. effort to stabilize the country. "How do we give [Maliki] responsibility without causing a disaster?" Bush asked. When Casey mentioned that Maliki "lacked political will," the President responded, "One option is to find someone else." In its discussion the following day, the group revisited the possibility of replacing the Prime Minister. Abizaid observed that he had "yet to see Maliki show backbone on anything" and thus saw danger in basing the "new way forward" on the Iraqi leader's political will. Bush reiterated his desire for something "dramatic" or "game-changing." The "new way forward"—whatever form it took—would have to "put us in a position where we can win." He again suggested that it might be "time to choose somebody else," but Khalilzad and the secretary of state convinced him that positioning Maliki for success was the more prudent course.[104]

Reportedly, the Prime Minister had boasted to his close advisers in early December that senior U.S. officials needed him more than he needed them. The Americans, he reasoned, would avoid actions likely to bring about the fall of his government. Nor would they press for a wholesale change in leadership. In the meantime, he could work to consolidate state power.[105] Though a bit overconfident, this stance apparently left some room for give and take. Following their video teleconferences with the President, Casey and Khalilzad made an evening visit to Maliki on December 10 to argue that no illegal armed group, Sunni or Shi'a, should be left with a sanctuary anywhere in Iraq, let alone in the capital. The general began by explaining that coalition and Iraqi staffs were hard at work putting the Prime Minister's revised security plan in place. Transition based on the Amman agreement remained a central element, but a key characteristic of the impending set of operations was the aggressive targeting of all criminal elements. Maliki agreed with Casey in principle and used the acknowledged sectarian behavior of the Iraqi security forces as a lever to press for more specially trained units under his close control. The Prime Minister hoped to dominate the militias not through kinetic operations against their fighters, but by demonstrating the government's unmatched ability to go after Sunni terrorists. Jumping on Maliki's admission that neither terrorists nor militias should be permitted sanctuary, Casey inquired about whether the coalition could carry out raids into Sadr City. The Prime Minister consented to raids led by Iraqi special operations forces with coalition support, to include armor and air assets as required.[106]

When the NSC principals resumed their discussions the following day, Casey reported to the President that Maliki had taken a more positive stance on launching raids into Sadr City. The President accepted this news, but the question still lingered: would the Prime Minister "lose his nerve" when it came time to press the fight against the Shi'a militias? Would he balk when MNF-I ramped up its targeting of Shi'a extremists?[107] In its attempt to persuade Maliki to confront the Shi'a militants, the White House had aimed to place the Prime Minister at the head of a proposed bloc of Shi'a, Sunni, and Kurdish "moderates" (defined by the White House as those who rejected violence and extremism) including Grand Ayatollah Ali Husayni Sistani, Abdul Aziz al-Hakim, and Tariq Hashimi. Hadley and Crouch suggested in the December 11 deliberations that marginalizing extremists on both sides of the sectarian divide would theoretically allow the Prime Minister to act more boldly from a moderate stance.[108] The fact that those viewed as moderates in Iraqi politics had failed thus far to arrive at a basic consensus regarding the future course of Iraq presented an imposing problem, Hadley pointed out.[109] For the President, the pleasantries exchanged at Amman had not satisfied doubts about Maliki's motives and his vision for Iraq. Bush wanted the "new way forward" speech to signify a clearly identifiable departure point, and he wanted Maliki unreservedly along for the ride. The Prime Minister must "stand up" and publicly say that the Iraqi Government will be "going after all outside the law," Bush insisted.[110]

Having upped the ante on what he expected from Maliki, Bush sent Casey and Khalilzad back to the Prime Minister on December 12 for a follow-on discussion in which they obtained new assurances. Maliki would issue a written order directing the Iraqi security forces to pursue and apprehend all lawbreakers regardless of sect and to eliminate their safe havens. Again, the Prime Minister asked about acquiring additional Iraqi forces under his direct control. Casey promised him that he was working on this, as well as the implementation of the revised Baghdad Security Plan. This visit also affirmed the

STRATEGY IN CRISIS, OCTOBER-DECEMBER 2006

understanding between Casey and Maliki that upcoming operations would be set in the
context of an accelerated transition based on the Amman agreement.[111]

The President Decides

Despite Casey and Maliki's discussions, it would soon become clear that the President
of the United States had no intention of proceeding along the lines that Casey and Maliki
believed had been agreed to in Amman. In explaining the violence in Iraq as the result of
a complex communal struggle for power, Casey may have been correct in his diagnosis.
However, Bush had come to disagree with the general's prescription of drawing down
to win. After months of holding his cards close to his chest, the President would finally
make this explicitly clear.

Bush's deepening skepticism of Iraqi political initiatives as the solution to Iraq's chaos
reflected the fact that after almost 2 years of relying on an Iraqi political process as the
key to stability, the President had become convinced that alternative paths to victory in
Iraq were available, in particular the deployment of additional U.S. troops. Soon after
the Amman conference, the White House had asked Casey to address the feasibility of a
surge, to include how more forces might mitigate the risk inherent in an accelerated transition.[112] The President engaged Casey on this question in the NSC principals' discussions
on December 8 and outlined four options for the employment of additional U.S. units in
the deliberations of December 9.[113] Repeatedly, Bush queried Casey and Khalilzad about
the utility of sending more troops, asked if Maliki knew that he could request American assistance in the form of more troops, and emphasized that he—the President—was
willing to deploy more troops.[114] The United States was running out of time in Iraq, but
a surge could buy some back, Bush said, while also demonstrating American commitment.[115] The window was closing on Casey's strategy of accelerated transition as well. On
December 11, amid the NSC principals' deliberations, the President met with Keane and a
coterie of defense intellectuals in the White House. Keane pitched AEI's detailed concept
for how additional brigades might salvage the war effort and enable MNF-I to secure the
population of Baghdad, a task that Bush had already decided to make the centerpiece of
any new strategy.[116] Overall, Keane provided the President an external validation of his
instincts in favor of a troop surge and lent the idea the credibility that could come from a
well-regarded former military leader of Keane's stature.

The following day, December 12, Casey formally provided the President and the other
NSC principals his input to the strategy review, unaware that Keane had met the President the day before to recommend a troop surge. Casey offered a recapitulation of his
plan to accelerate transition in conjunction with the Government of Iraq's commitment to
reconcile, two initiatives that he believed might serve as the "new way forward" the President was looking for. His rationale remained essentially unchanged from what he had
briefed many times before. Iraqis were engaged in a communal struggle for power, with
sectarian violence presenting the gravest threat to stability in the near term. Reconciliation among the competing factions would serve as the basis for the only lasting solution,
and this long-term process was something that—ultimately—only the Iraqis themselves
could undertake. By reducing its presence and passing security responsibility to Iraqi
authorities, the coalition could satisfy a burgeoning Iraqi desire to exercise sovereignty

while buying the additional time needed to bolster indigenous military and governance capacity. In Casey's estimation, the coalition could successfully arrive at its end state in 2009 or 2010. Casey concluded his presentation by commenting on the potential impact of surging additional U.S. forces into Iraq. Of the eight bullet points listed, only two were positive.[117]

Casey did not yet know it, but the President had already decided against his transition strategy. On December 13, the day after Casey's proposal, the President visited the Joint Chiefs of Staff at the Pentagon to discuss the options on the table and sound them out about his preferred option of surging troops. Some of the groundwork had already been laid: on December 11, the same day Keane visited the White House, Pace had visited the White House separately as well and, according to Bush's memoirs, had assured the President that though he would hear some concerns from the Joint Chiefs, they were prepared to support him in a surge decision. Pace also reportedly told Hadley that it would require a surge of 5 brigades, or about 20,000 troops, to make a difference in Iraq.[118]

Even so, once the Pentagon meeting began, Pace presented the Joint Chiefs' collective military advice, which did not recommend a surge option. Before the Council of Colonels had disbanded in mid-December, Pace had asked the group to summarize a draft of the military advice that the Joint Chiefs of Staff could provide the President. The chairman had softened the colonels' hard-hitting assessment of the war to read "we are not losing, but we are not yet winning," but aside from this equivocal rephrasing, the resulting presentation echoed the group's earlier recommendations to "go long" by gradually reducing forces and shifting the main effort to the support of the Iraqi Army.[119] Among the Joint Chiefs themselves, Army Chief of Staff General Peter J. Schoomaker was most vocal in making the case against a U.S. troop surge, telling the President that a five-brigade surge would not reduce the violence and would impose too great a strain on the U.S. ground forces. He also asserted that the impatient U.S. public would not support a surge or allow enough time for a troop increase, to which the President reportedly replied that the Joint Chiefs need not concern themselves with domestic political factors that were the President's to manage.[120] Schoomaker's concern that the nation's twin wars and other military commitments would hollow out and "break" the Army—a concern he shared publicly in congressional testimony on December 14—was shared by many other Army and Marine generals who had served as junior officers in the 1970s and concluded that the Vietnam war had devastated the military. But to the argument that escalating the U.S. commitment in Iraq would break the U.S. ground forces, Bush observed that suffering another humiliating defeat as in Vietnam would be more likely to break the force than a five-brigade troop surge, a point the Joint Chiefs conceded. Some of the service chiefs expressed concern that committing the U.S. strategic reserve to Iraq might be unwise in the event that a conflict flared up elsewhere, such as the Korean Peninsula, but the President replied that he would prefer to win the ongoing war in Iraq rather than hedge against a hypothetical one.[121] "What I want to hear from you is how we're going to win . . . not how we're going to leave," the President reportedly said.[122] After this tense but open discussion—and against their advice—the President informed the Joint Chiefs of his decision to execute the troop surge.[123]

Vice President Cheney (left), General Pace (second from left), Admiral Mullen (second from right), and
Vice Chairman of the Joint Chiefs of Staff Admiral Giambastiani (right).
Source: White House photo by Eric Draper (Released).

President George W. Bush With Vice President Richard Cheney, General Peter Pace, Admiral Mike Mullen, and Vice Chairman of the Joint Chiefs of Staff Admiral Edmund P. Giambastiani.[124]

The Arrival of III Corps

Along with a strategy on the cusp of change, December 2006 brought a shift in one of Casey's major subordinate units. On December 14, the day after Bush's session with the Joint Chiefs of Staff in the Pentagon, Chiarelli relinquished command of MNC-I to General Raymond Odierno in Baghdad. Odierno's arrival introduced another significant factor into the question of whether and how to conduct a U.S. troop surge. For more than a year, his skepticism of the transition strategy had grown. First, as he observed the Iraq campaign from his post as senior military adviser to Secretary of State Condoleeza Rice, and then as he accompanied retired General Gary Luck on a 2005 assessment trip that pronounced Iraqi forces unready to assume responsibility for the country's security. Before deploying to Iraq, the III Corps commander reluctantly had concluded that the campaign would fail if it maintained its projected course. In November, he had had a candid conversation at Fort Hood, TX, with his next-door neighbor, 4th Infantry Division Commander Major General James. D. Thurman, who had arrived home after giving up command of Multi-National Division-Baghdad (MND-B) just days before. Thurman related to Odierno the failures of Operations TOGETHER FORWARD I and II and the destabilizing role played by some of the Iraqi security forces, the same concerns he had voiced to Abizaid in October. Thurman emphasized how limitations in U.S. combat power had hindered him from securing the Iraqi capital. "Just off-ramping is not going to work," he contended. It was a path destined for failure.[125]

General Chiarelli (right) General Odierno (left).
Source: DoD photo by Curt Cashour (Released).

General Peter Chiarelli Transfers Responsibility of Command of MNC-I to General Raymond Odierno With General George Casey Officiating.[126]

Thurman's grim assessment made a deep impression on the future MNC-I commander and validated Odierno's own instinctive skepticism about the transition strategy. As III Corps had prepared for its Iraq rotation in summer and fall 2006, Casey's plan had envisioned the corps inheriting a force of just 13 U.S. BCTs—down from the 15 then deployed throughout Iraq, and Odierno had expected to oversee a continued reduction. As Odierno war-gamed how to employ a shrinking force, he detected a clear mismatch between ends and means. As Thurman had observed, it would be exceedingly difficult to reverse the deteriorating security situation in Baghdad without sufficient coalition troops to confront Iranian meddling, rein in corrupt National Police units, halt an "active Shia plan to control Baghdad," and deal with an Iraqi Government that viewed everything through a "sectarian lens." Meanwhile, in northern Iraq, Odierno also contemplated the worsening Arab-Kurd tensions along the Green Line, a problem he himself had had to confront as commander of Multi-National Division-North Central (MND-NC) in 2003-2004. Iraq's Arab-Kurd conflict would persist even as transition proceeded apace, and there was danger in prolonging the issue as coalition presence and influence dwindled.[127] In Multi-National Division-North (MND-N), Major General Benjamin R. "Randy" Mixon's 25th Infantry Division was having trouble figuring out how to reduce its force from four BCTs to three without losing the operational flexibility needed to deal with the complex northern Iraq conflict. Taken together, these dynamics left Odierno troubled by the prospect of continuing the transition.[128]

What the III Corps commander learned from Chiarelli only deepened his concerns. Shortly after Odierno's arrival in Baghdad on December 5, Chiarelli shared the results of MNC-I's 120-day assessment of the Baghdad Security Plan.[129] Despite "successful tactical efforts," MNC-I concluded, coalition and Iraqi forces had been "unable or not allowed to achieve the stated objectives."[130] The "clear-hold-build approach" seemed sound in concept, but the Iraqis were not up to the task. Anchored to largely ineffective checkpoints, unsupported by key ministries, and infiltrated in many cases by JAM, Iraqi units suffered in terms of both quality and numbers. They proved unable to hold and protect cleared areas, and the reinforcements promised by the ministries had yet to arrive in Baghdad. Furthermore, Prime Minister Maliki had shielded the Shi'a militias from harm by withholding his approval for certain military operations and denying security forces access into sanctuaries like Sadr City. Perhaps most disturbing to Chiarelli, the Prime Minister's government seemed bent on a course leading to Shi'a dominance in Baghdad, a factor that was driving moderate Sunnis into a "marriage of convenience" with al-Qaeda in Iraq.[131] "The self-sustaining cycle of sectarian violence will continue as long as the [Government of Iraq] and certain citizens of Iraq do not see it as a terminal problem for their nation, exercise restraint, and take the appropriate actions to facilitate reconciliation," Chiarelli's assessment somberly concluded.[132]

Though faced with this bleak prognosis for stability in Baghdad, Odierno jumped into a whirlwind of activity in the days leading up to MNC-I's December 14 transfer of authority from V Corps to III Corps. From Casey, the incoming commander received a charge to "change the dynamics in Baghdad" and "break the cycle of sectarian violence."[133] This meant, in effect, adopting an offensive mindset almost immediately, while executing the transition bridging strategy that Chiarelli had been developing. The corps also was falling in on the process of sketching out the revised Baghdad Security Plan with its emphasis on U.S.-Iraqi cooperation and the creation of a unique command-and-control structure. On the evening of December 6, Odierno had wrapped up his first full day in Iraq by joining Casey for a meeting with Maliki's top security advisers in which the MNF-I commander introduced his idea for a "New Year's Offensive" that would demonstrate the Iraqi Government's commitment to imposing law and order. In Casey's mind, the offensive could involve as many as five Iraqi Army divisions operating in the capital and would build much-needed momentum in preparation for the anticipated transfer of responsibilities.[134] Odierno was cheered by his interaction with the heads of Iraq's two key security ministries, but he remained concerned about a rushed transition and saw little prospect for securing Baghdad without significantly more American troops.[135] These views would put him squarely at odds with Casey as the weeks passed.

Confusion Over the Surge Implementation

Although the President had decided in favor of a troop surge on December 13 and all the discussions Bush had held with the NSC principals—Joint Chiefs of Staff and outside surge advocates such as Keane—had revolved around the figure of 5 brigades and at least 20,000 troops, he had yet to direct explicitly that the surge would consist of all 5 of the available brigades. As a result, when it came to the exact size of the surge the President had ordered, an astonishing lack of clarity persisted through Christmas, with Bush, Gates, Casey, and Casey's subordinates all making long-term plans based on different strategies. In the absence of explicit Presidential guidance to deploy all five brigades, many senior military leaders continued to work toward preserving the basic framework of the existing transition strategy by making the troop increase as small as possible.

Casey was foremost among them. In the second week of December, he and Khalilzad published their own progress review of the April 2006 joint campaign plan acknowledging that much had changed for the worse since the spring, but envisioning no major changes to the existing strategy and discounting the benefits of a troop surge. The coalition had failed to achieve its objectives "within the planned timeline" and an increasingly complex threat, the cycle of sectarian violence in Baghdad, and the Iraqi Government's more conspicuous expressions of sovereignty only seemed to promise a harder, slower road ahead.[136] The central tenet of the campaign—that "enduring strategic success will only be achieved by Iraqis"—remained "universally accepted." Casey and Khalizad's review held out a shred of hope that potential surge operations, coupled with political progress, could reduce violence and bring stability in the coming year, but assessed the chances of that as "low-medium," particularly because coalition forces "enmeshed" in an ethno-sectarian struggle might actually be "acting as a catalyst" for violence.[137] Worse still, Casey and Khalilzad's report predicted that the coalition would see many of its powers stripped away or heavily restricted when the United Nations (UN) Security Council resolution expired at the end of 2007, implying that there was little time left for ambitious initiatives like a surge.[138]

MNF-I's lack of enthusiasm for the President's troop surge, coupled with the fact that Bush had yet to specify that all five brigades would be sent to Iraq, ushered in a period of maddening confusion for subordinate units. In his first days as MNC-I commander, Odierno was keen to obtain reinforcements for the Baghdad fight and to exploit the opportunities presented by the Anbar Awakening. First, Odierno wanted to extend the deployment of the 2,200-man 15th Marine Expeditionary Unit (MEU). Casey had requested the MEU, CENTCOM's theater reserve, to reinforce MNF-I's offensive efforts in Ramadi, and the unit had arrived in November.[139] Recognizing that Ramadi would not be secure before the expeditionary unit was scheduled to leave, in mid-December, Odierno raised the question of extending the unit.[140] Doing so would not only strengthen coalition efforts in Anbar, but would also allow Odierno to commit any incoming Army units to Baghdad.[141] Odierno also discussed expanding the size of the Marine contingent in Anbar with I Marine Expeditionary Force (MEF) Commander Lieutenant General James N. Mattis, who noted that there was a possibility that the rotations of two Marine rifle battalions scheduled to leave Anbar in March 2007 could be extended.[142] Given this opening, Odierno pressed the issue. Prolonging the deployments of these two battalions by 60 to 90 days while the units slated to replace them flowed in on schedule would see Multi-National Force-West (MNF-W) through a critical spring and summer.[143] It would also offset the inevitable loss of the 15th MEU, which could not remain in Iraq beyond April.

Casey did not view the situation with the same sense of urgency that Odierno did. He doubted that additional forces in Anbar would be decisive in defeating AQI and looked to Marine Major General Richard C. Zilmer, commander of MNF-W, to back him up. Zilmer did the opposite, siding with Odierno and recommending the addition of one reinforced BCT for employment in Ramadi and Hadithah. While not persuaded, Casey partially relented and on December 17 agreed to extend the 15th MEU.[144]

This debate over additional manpower in Anbar took place as Casey and his subordinate commanders, prompted by the intense policy debate in Washington, DC, considered the larger question of what Bush's new surge strategy would entail. For his part, Odierno judged that the United States would require several more brigades to address the security situation in Baghdad.[145] In his first week in command, Odierno presented a number of surge alternatives to Casey: a "small surge" of three additional brigades in place by early March 2007; a "large surge" of five brigades on the ground by late April; and a "local surge" that would see the deployment of the 82d Airborne Division's ready brigade (the division's 2d Brigade Combat Team) to Baghdad and the extension of one Marine regimental combat team in Anbar. To these three, Odierno added a fourth option: combining the extension of the MEU with the commitment of the 2d Brigade Combat Team, 82d Airborne Division, and the call-up of a heavy BCT already postured in a "prepare to deploy" status.[146] Possible locations for the surge units—in addition to Baghdad and Anbar—included Diyala, southern Salahadin, the Lake Tharthar region just northwest of the capital, the southern belts, and along the Iranian border in Wasit Province.[147]

Casey responded by expressing disappointment that the corps commander had seemed to "put the cart before the horse." It was premature to make a decision on the size of a surge at this point, the MNF-I commander said.[148] The broad span of employment options also left Casey with the impression that MNC-I was attempting to disguise a lack of in-depth analysis. For example, Casey thought it foolish to position a brigade in Wasit, where the unit would likely have no impact on the fight in Baghdad. Finally, dubious about the need for more American troops in the first place, he directed that future plans on the flow of additional forces should include built-in decision points for staunching that flow. There would be no open spigot if the MNF-I commander could avoid it.[149]

The exchange put Odierno in an uncomfortable position. The MNC-I commander believed that virtually all the surge discussions among U.S. leaders in Washington, including the President and the Joint Chiefs, had revolved around a five-brigade surge (with which Odierno strongly agreed), but that Casey intended to shape the implementation of the decision and prevent the full five available brigades from coming to MNC-I. Instructed by the MNF-I commander to continue planning and executing the transition bridging strategy, Odierno sought to buy time until the matter of the surge could be clarified. Under his guidance, MNC-I created a plan under which the implementation of the transition bridging strategy would be drawn out for several months. Rather than start the transition right away, coalition and Iraqi forces would generate momentum with offensive operations through the spring of 2007, leaving the augmenting of advisory teams and the reduction of the coalition presence aside until the conditions were in place for the Iraqi military to become the country's dominant security force.[150] Even this drawn-out timeline was based on far-fetched assumptions that the Iraqi factions would make quick progress on reconciliation and economic development alongside security operations. For Odierno, drawing up the unrealistic plan was a necessary expedient as he waited for an expected change in strategic guidance from Washington.

Meanwhile, Casey continued to operate as though the implementation of the surge would be subject to his control and Maliki's concurrence. On December 20, a week after the President's decision, Casey told Maliki that Bush had promised his full support—including more American troops if the Iraqis wanted them.[151] Major General Joseph F. Fil, Jr., whose 1st Cavalry Division had arrived in November to assume control of MND-B from Thurman's 4th Infantry Division, already had asked Casey and Odierno for two additional BCTs for immediate operations in Baghdad. Despite discussions on increasing the size of U.S. forces in Iraq by two or three brigades, Casey proposed to Maliki an increase of just one. This modest rise was necessary, Casey told the Iraqi leader, in order to have enough coalition battalions to partner with each Iraqi brigade operating in the city. Even so, the MNF-I commander placed more emphasis on the movement of three additional Iraqi Army brigades to the capital than on additional U.S. troops. Making a virtue of the bureaucratic and logistical missteps that had led to prolonged delays in the deployment of these units, Casey described their anticipated arrival on a staggered timeline as a way of maintaining momentum. The periodic infusion of additional Iraqi and American combat power over the course of January and into February would make it easier to sustain progress, the general said. A second U.S. brigade would move into Kuwait as the theater reserve and would be available after mid-February—but only if the situation called for it. Though reluctant about deploying more foreign troops into Baghdad, Maliki approved this scheme.[152]

On the same day that Casey persuaded the Iraqi Prime Minister to accept a small and temporary spike in U.S. force levels, he sought to convince the new U.S. SECDEF not to push for too large an increase. Gates, having replaced Rumsfeld 2 days earlier, landed in Baghdad on December 20 with a team of advisers that included then-Colonel Mark A. Milley. A veteran of four Presidential administrations, Gates had previously visited Baghdad as a member of the Baker-Hamilton Iraq Study Group but had resigned from the group once he had been nominated for the SECDEF position. Joining Pace and Abizaid for consultations with Casey and his generals, Gates discussed the possibility of a more robust surge than the two-brigade option that Casey advocated, however, he left Iraq satisfied that the situation—though tenuous—was on the right track. In spite of the violence, it appeared to Gates that Casey's strategy of preparing the Iraqis to assume the lead for security appeared to have turned a corner. Only a "modest increase of up to two brigades" would be necessary as a bridge to allow the Iraqis to take full control of the capital by summer.[153] The SECDEF sensed a "whiff of disagreement" between Casey and Odierno, but the latter, while notably pessimistic, did not openly challenge his boss' assessment that no more than two brigades were needed.[154] Thus, Gates mistakenly came away with the impression of a consensus on the way ahead among the U.S. commanders in Baghdad. He returned to Washington and presented his recommendation to the President, essentially "parroting" (as Gates himself later ruefully described it) the MNF-I commander's advice.[155] In a separate matter before his departure, Gates offered Casey the Army chief of staff job, and the general, who had served some 30 months in Iraq by that point, accepted.[156] The move was not a surprise; as U.S. leaders in Washington had settled on a new strategy, they had also implicitly agreed that new MNF-I and CENTCOM commanders would be appointed to implement it, and within days speculation would begin on whom those new commanders might be.

Back in Washington, Gates set the Joint Staff to work on plans for a surge of two Army brigade combat teams and two Marine battalions.[157] As the end of the year approached, Casey's intention to hold the line in defense of his strategy, in spite of all the chatter about a surge of considerable size, appeared to be working. Since the beginning of December, Casey had seized on the Iraqi desire to recast the Baghdad Security Plan as an opportunity to further his strategy of accelerated transition. Among the initiatives devised by the Iraqis were standing up a new operations command to coordinate army and police activities in the capital and establishing joint security stations in each administrative district. Casey found this newfound Iraqi energy—along with a tentative willingness on the part of the Prime Minister to target Shi'a militants—encouraging. The MNF-I commander had yielded ground by conceding to MND-B's request for additional brigades and by allowing the division to resurrect unit partnership, but as Casey had related to an uneasy Maliki, though he indeed had requested the temporary deployment of two more BCTs, the circumstances under which he actually would commit the second brigade to Baghdad were quite constrained.[158]

Casey's subordinate commanders in Baghdad saw things differently. At MND-B, Fil had already factored the second surge brigade—initially thought to be a heavy BCT from Fort Stewart, GA—into his scheme of maneuver. In fact, the launching of new operations in Baghdad depended on the brigade's timely arrival. Fil planned to use the new brigade's battalions to reinforce the three BCTs already operating in the capital in order to "assist with partnership." With its subordinate battalions parceled out among MND-B's other units, the newly arrived brigade headquarters would oversee Baghdad's enhanced transition teams as the capital passed to Iraqi control and the division's main effort shifted to the belts.[159]

Odierno concurred with Fil's plan. Troubled by an approach that tied coalition success to Iraqi combat performance, the MNC-I commander worried privately about whether "we have underestimated the number of coalition forces needed and overestimated the capability and motivation of the Iraqi security forces (ISF)." Additional American brigades could serve as a "mitigating factor," he judged.[160] The general believed it was infeasible to launch a combined U.S.-Iraqi offensive while simultaneously parceling out platoon-sized contingents to enhance transition teams. The manpower requirements associated with each concept were in "direct competition," Odierno wrote in his personal notebook on December 28. "We cannot do both at once with the current force structure."[161] In his view, the requirement for significantly more U.S. troops was clear, but this judgment was putting him at sharp odds with Casey. Odierno would later recall that the 2½ months he spent as the corps commander under Casey would be the most difficult period of his 39-year career.[162]

Back in Washington, the U.S. military apparatus had begun work over the Christmas holidays to implement a two-brigade, two-battalion troop surge—much smaller than the five-brigade surge Bush had discussed with the NSC and the Joint Chiefs. The "2+2" option was aligned with the recommendations of Abizaid and Casey but seemed dangerously wrongheaded to Keane, who had just 2 weeks before advised the President that the task in Iraq required at least five additional brigades. Over the previous weeks, Keane had also been in discreet contact with Odierno and knew that the III Corps commander had concluded that a surge of that size would be required to make a serious change in the security situation in Baghdad.[163] Roused by the Pentagon's baffling insistence on committing fewer troops than he believed the commander in chief had authorized, the retired general again reached out to his contacts in the administration and made the case for sending five brigades to reinforce the U.S. forces in Iraq.[164] He gained support from Lieutenant General David H. Petraeus, commander of the Combined Arms Center, who had been brought into the conversation at various points as both a counterinsurgency expert and a potential replacement for Casey. In separate discussions with Keane, Gates, Pace, and White House staffer Meghan O'Sullivan, Petraeus opined that the security situation, as he understood it, called for all the additional BCTs the Army could spare. If it came down to a choice between five and two, then the answer was obvious.[165] Like Keane, Petraeus cautioned that these forces should be approved and committed as a single contingent, not as individual units dispatched based on discrete requests from the theater.[166]

On December 28, Bush finally clarified that he intended to conduct a full five-brigade surge and asked for a video teleconference with Maliki within the week to inform the Iraqi Prime Minister that the surge was coming.[167] Pace conveyed the news to Odierno the following day.[168] Concerned that Maliki's government might undercut the surge of additional American troops by openly condemning it, Bush intended to obtain the Iraqi leader's tacit support for the modified U.S. strategy, as well as his pledge to continue the fight to secure Baghdad until the job was finished. Bush also wanted Maliki's assurance that the Baghdad Security Plan would target all lawbreakers, regardless of sect or political affiliation, and that Maliki would give the coalition a freer hand in operations against Shi'a militias.[169] The President communicated these conditions to Maliki by video teleconference on January 4, and the Prime Minister largely complied in a stirring speech 2 days later.[170]

The President planned to announce the new round of troop deployments publicly in early January, having already postponed plans for a pre-Christmas speech to allow Gates an opportunity to visit Iraq.[171] The deployment of the 15th MEU would be extended, as would those of the two Marine battalions. The 2d Brigade Combat Team, 82d Airborne Division, would arrive in Iraq on January 15, 2007. A heavy BCT would follow, moving into Kuwait in mid-February. Three more brigades would make their way across the Atlantic at a rate of one per month, beginning in March.[172]

***

Home for a short leave following Christmas, Casey learned of Bush's guidance about a five-brigade surge from Pace on December 29. He also learned from a reporter that he would be replaced months earlier than he had anticipated and that White House officials had already informed *The New York Times*. While disappointed that the President had rejected his best military advice, the MNF-I commander was also flabbergasted that administration officials were denigrating his strategy in the press and blaming him for Iraq's descent into violence.[173] "The White House is throwing you under the bus," one contact reportedly informed him.[174]

On January 2, Casey spoke with *The New York Times*, giving what amounted to a critique of the surge decision and a defense of the transition strategy he had formulated 2 years before. Casey said:

The longer we in the U.S. forces continue to bear the main burden of Iraq's security, it lengthens the time that the government of Iraq has to take the hard decisions about reconciliation and dealing with the militias . . . [and] they can continue to blame us for all of Iraq's problems, which are at base their problems.[175]

Responding to criticism that he had declined to ask for more troops when they were needed, the MNF-I commander said, "I have worked very hard to ask for what I need, for what I thought I needed to accomplish the mission. . . . It's always been my view that a heavy and sustained American military presence was not going to solve the problems in Iraq over the long term."[176]

Casey repeated that argument to Pace and Abizaid 2 days later, charging that the impending troop surge would be counterproductive to the long-term campaign. He questioned whether the Iraqis would consent to a U.S. troop increase of the size the President had ordered and saw U.S. military presence in general as "grating on the population, particularly in large urban areas." "We should acknowledge up front that more [coalition] troops won't solve what . . . is inherently a political problem," he insisted.[177] However, the time for protest had passed. On the same day Casey sent his e-mail, January 4, 2007, the 2d Brigade Combat Team, 82d Airborne Division, began its journey to Baghdad. The surge was underway.

ENDNOTES - CHAPTER 1

1. Memo, Donald Rumsfeld, Secretary of Defense, for General Peter Pace, Chairman of the Joint Chiefs of Staff (CJCS), October 23, 2006, sub: Security Plan for Baghdad. All unpublished documents in this chapter, unless otherwise stated, are in the Chief of Staff of the Army (CSA) Operation IRAQI FREEDOM (OIF) Study Group archives, Army Heritage and Education Center (AHEC), Carlisle, PA.

2. Staff Notes, Multi-National Force-Iraq (MNF-I), November 1, 2006. All Staff Notes in this chapter are in the CSA OIF Study Group archives, AHEC, Carlisle, PA.

3. Ibid.

4. DoD photo by Sergeant Nicole Kojetin, "Breakfast in Baghdad [Image 3 of 4]," DVIDS Identifier 33987, December 10, 2006, Released to Public, available from *https://www.dvidshub.net/image/33987/breakfast-baghdad*.

5. Staff Notes, Multi-National Force-Iraq (MNF-I), November 1, 2006. All Staff Notes in this chapter are in the CSA OIF Study Group archives, AHEC, Carlisle, PA.

6. DoD photo by Captain Amy Bishop, "4th Iraqi Army Division assumes security lead [Image 16 of 19]," DVIDS Identifier 27388, August 8, 2006, Released to Public, available from *https://www.dvidshub.net/image/27388/4th-iraqi-army-division-assumes-security-lead*.

7. Staff Notes, Multi-National Force-Iraq (MNF-I), November 1, 2006. All Staff Notes in this chapter are in the CSA OIF Study Group archives, AHEC, Carlisle, PA.

8. Ibid.

9. Ibid.

10. Staff Notes, MNF-I, n.d. [ca. November 2006].

11. Memorandum for Record, Donald Rumsfeld, SECDEF, November 6, 2006, sub: Iraq—Illustrative New Courses of Action.

12. Ibid.

13. Memo, Senator John Warner for General Pace, General John P. Abizaid, and General George W. Casey, Jr., October 25, 2006, sub: Troop Levels in Iraq.

14. Bob Woodward, *The War Within: A Secret White House History, 2006-2008*, New York: Simon & Schuster, 2008, pp. 73-78.

15. Notes from SECDEF Video Teleconference (VTC), November 1, 2006.

16. White House photo by Eric Draper, "President George W. Bush is joined by Stephen Hadley, National Security Advisor, Vice President Dick Cheney and Chief of Staff Josh Bolten Monday, Nov. 13, 2006, during a meeting with the Baker-Hamilton Commission in the Roosevelt Room of the White House. Members of the Commission include: Lee Hamilton, James Baker, Sandra Day O'Connor, William Perry, Vernon Jordan and Lawrence Eagleburger," White House Identifier P111306ED-0104, November 13, 2006, Released to Public, available from *https://georgewbush-whitehouse.archives.gov/news/releases/2006/11/images/20061113-2_d-0104-1-515h.html*.

17. Peter R. Mansoor, *Surge: My Journey with General David Petraeus and the Remaking of the Iraq War*, New Haven, CT: Yale University Press, 2013, pp. 46-47; Woodward, *The War Within*, pp. 196-197, 207-208.

18. Thomas Donnelly and Vance Serchuk, "U.S. Counterinsurgency in Iraq: Lessons from the Philippine War," AEI Online, November 1, 2003, available from *www.aei.org/publication/u-s-counterinsurgency-in-iraq/*.

19. Daniel L. Byman and Kenneth M. Pollack, "What Next?" *The Washington Post*, August 20, 2006, available from *http://www.washingtonpost.com/wp-dyn/content/article/2006/08/18/AR2006081800983_5.html*.

20. Michael R. Gordon, "Troop 'Surge' Took Place Amid Doubt and Debate," *The New York Times*, August 30, 2008, available from *http://www.nytimes.com/2008/08/31/washington/31military.html*.

21. "Text of U.S. Security Adviser's Iraq Memo," *The New York Times*, November 29, 2006, available from *http://www.nytimes.com/2006/11/29/world/middleeast/29mtext.html?pagewanted=all&_r=0*, accessed January 4, 2016.

22. Ibid.

23. George W. Casey, Jr., *Strategic Reflections: Operation IRAQI FREEDOM, July 2004-February 2007*, Washington, DC: National Defense University Press, 2012, p. 126.

24. Woodward, *The War Within*, p. 207.

25. Casey, *Strategic Reflections*, p. 126.

26. MNF-I Joint Campaign Plan, April 28, 2006, p. 23.

27. Ibid., June 9, 2006, p. 11.

28. Paper, Sandy Cochran and Captain Kelly Howard, MNF-I Chronology Reference, November 12, 2008, pp. 306, 329.

29. Memos, Rumsfeld for Pace, October 2, 2006, sub: Time to Work on Benchmarks; Rumsfeld for Stephen Hadley, National Security Adviser, October 5, 2006, sub: My Comments on the Tasking from the September 30 Meeting.

30. PowerPoint Briefing, MNF-I Iraq Update to SECDEF, October 21, 2006, slide 1; PowerPoint Briefing, MNF-I Iraq Update to National Security Council (NSC), October 21, 2006, slide 6.

31. Casey, *Strategic Reflections*, pp. 123-126.

32. Notes from NSC VTC, October 27, 2006.

33. PowerPoint Briefing, MNF-I to SECDEF, VTC, November 16, 2006, slide 3. See also UN Security Council Resolution 1723, November 28, 2006.

34. Thomas E. Ricks and Ann Scott Tyson, "Abizaid Says Withdrawal Would Mean More Unrest," *The Washington Post*, November 16, 2006.

35. Ibid.

36. General George W. Casey, Jr., Notes from SECDEF VTC, November 16, 2006.

37. Ibid.

38. Ibid.; PowerPoint Briefing, MNF-I to SECDEF VTC, November 16, 2006, slide 9.

39. PowerPoint Briefing, MNF-I to SECDEF VTC, November 16, 2006, slide 4.

40. Ibid., slide 8; Casey Notes from SECDEF VTC, November 16, 2006.

41. Casey Notes from SECDEF VTC, November 16, 2006.

42. PowerPoint Briefing, MNF-I to SECDEF VTC, November 16, 2006, slides 10-11.

43. PowerPoint Briefing, Multi-National Corps-Iraq (MNC-I), Transition Bridging Strategy, December 11, 2006, slide 4.

44. Casey Notes from Sec Def VTC, November 16, 2006.

45. Ibid.

46. Ibid.

47. Mansoor, *Surge*, pp. 41-45.

48. Steven Metz, *Decisionmaking in Operation IRAQI FREEDOM: The Strategic Shift of 2007*, Carlisle, PA: Strategic Studies Institute, U.S. Army War College, 2010, p. 33.

49. PowerPoint Briefing, Joint Chiefs of Staff (JCS), "Strategy for the Long War, 2006-2016: Strategic Options Discussion (draft)," November 22, 2006, slide 31.

50. JCS Working Paper (draft, version 8), November 22, 2006, p. 2.

51. Ibid.

52. Ibid., p. 3.

53. Ibid., p. 2.

54. Ibid., p. 3.

55. Casey Notes from JCS VTC, November 22, 2006.

56. JCS Working Paper (draft, version 8), November 22, 2006, p. 2; E-mail, General George W. Casey, Jr., to General Peter Pace, November 26, 2006, sub: Feedback on (v2), November 22 Paper.

57. E-mail, Casey to Pace, November 26, 2006.

58. JCS Group/Office of the SECDEF (OSD)/MNF-I Strategic Option Comparison, n.d. [ca. November 2006].

59. Casey Notes from JCS VTC, November 22, 2006.

60. Ibid.

61. Ibid.

62. "Bush-Maliki meeting likely to go ahead despite Sadr threat," *Iraq News Monitor*, November 25, 2006, available from *http://iraqnewsmonitor.blogspot.com/2006_11_19_archive.html*, accessed May 12, 2016.

63. Casey, *Strategic Reflections*, pp. 138-139.

64. Report from the High-Level Working Group for Acceleration, November 24, 2006, box 115, doc 02634.

65. President George W. Bush, "Joint Statement by the President of the United States and the Prime Minister of Iraq," Washington, DC: The White House, November 30, 2006, available from *http://georgew bush-whitehouse.archives.gov/news/releases/2006/11/20061130-1.html*; Amman Proposed Agenda, n.d. [ca. November 2006].

66. Joint Statement by the President of the United States and the Prime Minister of Iraq, President George W. Bush, Washington, DC: The White House, November 30, 2006, available from *http://georgewbush-whitehouse.archives.gov/news/releases/2006/11/20061130-2.html*.

67. White House photo by Paul Morse, "President George W. Bush reaches out to Iraqi Prime Minister Nouri al-Maliki Thursday, November 30, 2006, following a joint press availability in Amman, Jordan," White House Identifier 20061130-1_p113006pm-0234-515h, November 30, 2006, Released to Public, available from *https://georgewbush-whitehouse.archives.gov/news/releases/2006/11/images/20061130-1_p113006pm-0234-515h.html*.

68. George W. Bush, *Decision Points*, New York: Crown Publishers, 2010, p. 374; Woodward, *The War Within*, p. 256.

69. Woodward, *The War Within*, p. 257. See also Casey, *Strategic Reflections*, p. 139.

70. Bush, *Decision Points*, pp. 374-375.

71. Notes from President of the United States (POTUS) VTC, December 1, 2006, box 116.

72. Ibid.

73. See, for example, Notes from SECDEF VTC, November 1, 2006; Notes from SECDEF VTC, November 25, 2006; Notes from POTUS VTC, December 9, 2006.

74. Notes, Iraq Study Group (ISG) Meeting, August 31, 2006.

75. Quoted in Woodward, *The War Within*, pp. 117-118.

76. MNF-I, Talking Points for ISG, November 13, 2006.

77. James A. Baker III and Lee H. Hamilton, *The Iraq Study Group Report*, New York: Vintage Books, 2006, p. x.

78. Ibid., p. xvi.

79. Ibid., pp. xv-xvi.

80. Ibid., p. xiv.

81. "Iraq President Rejects Baker-Hamilton Report," CNN, December 11, 2006, available from *http://www.cnn.com/2006/WORLD/meast/12/10/iraq.main/index.html?iref=newssearch*.

82. Interview, Colonel Joel Rayburn, Chief of Staff of the Army (CSA) Operation IRAQI FREEDOM (OIF) Study Group, with Lieutenant General H. R. McMaster, May 26, 2016.

83. Ibid., pp. 1-4. By December, MNF-I was already contemplating this rebalancing of the task force mission.

84. Interview, Colonel Rayburn, CSA OIF Study Group, with Lieutenant General McMaster, January 4, 2016.

85. Ibid.

86. Bush, *Decision Points*, p. 364; Mansoor, *Surge*, p. 46.

87. Frederick W. Kagan, *Choosing Victory: A Plan for Success in Iraq, Phase I Report*, Washington, DC: American Enterprise Institute, January 2007, pp. 1-2, 7.

88. Ibid., p. 44.

89. Thomas E. Ricks, *The Gamble: General David Petraeus and the American Military Adventure in Iraq, 2006-2008*, New York: Penguin Press, 2009, pp. 80-81, 84-85, 88-89; Woodward, *The War Within*, pp. 130-135.

90. Interview, Colonel Rayburn, CSA OIF Study Group, with Lieutenant General McMaster, January 4, 2016.

91. Kagan, *Choosing Victory*, p. 37.

92. Interview, Colonel Rayburn, CSA OIF Study Group, with General (Ret.) John M. Keane, May 25, 2016.

93. Ricks, *Gamble*, pp. 94-97.

94. Ibid., p. 98.

95. Interview, CSA OIF Study Group with Lieutenant Colonel Charles Armstrong, MNC-I Plans, March 20, 2014, CSA OIF Study Group archives.

96. E-mail, Casey to Pace and General John P. Abizaid, December 6, 2006, Temp no. 20, Casey Papers electronic finding aid.

97. Ibid.

98. Casey, *Strategic Reflections*, p. 128; Interview, Combat Studies Institute (CSI) Contemporary Operations Study Team with General George W. Casey, Jr., June 16, 2009, pp. 8, 11.

99. Notes from POTUS VTC, December 9, 2006; Task Force Briefing to the Prime Minister on Efforts against al-Qaeda in Iraq, December 6, 2006.

100. Staff Notes, MNF-I, December 6, 2006.

101. Rumsfeld, *Iraq Policy: Proposal for the New Phase* (with attachment), December 8, 2006.

102. Notes from POTUS VTC, December 8, 2006.

103. Ibid.

104. Notes from POTUS VTC, December 9, 2006.

105. Paper, Cochran and Howard, MNF-I Chronology Reference, November 12, 2008, p. 354; Bing West and Max Boot, "Iraq's No. 1 Problem," *Los Angeles Times,* January 28, 2008, available from *http://www. latimes.com/news/la-oe-boot28jan28-story.html.*

106. Staff Notes, MNF-I, December 10, 2006.

107. Notes from POTUS VTC, December 11, 2006.

108. Ibid.

109. Ibid. More fully described in VTC, December 11, 2006.

110. Notes from POTUS VTC, December 11, 2006.

111. Staff Notes, MNF-I, December 12, 2006.

112. Woodward, *The War Within,* pp. 283-284.

113. Notes from POTUS VTC, December 8, 2006; Notes from POTUS VTC, December 9, 2006.

114. Notes from POTUS VTC on December 8, 9, 11, and 15, 2006.

115. Notes from POTUS VTC, December 11, 2006; VTC, meeting summary, December 11, 2006.

116. Peter D. Feaver, "The Right to Be Right: Civil-Military Relations and the Iraq Surge Decision," *International Security,* Vol. 35, No. 4, Spring 2011, p. 106.

117. MNF-I, Iraq—Security Way Ahead, December 12, 2006. See slide 6 in particular.

118. Bush, *Decision Points,* p. 376; Feaver, "The Right to Be Right," p. 109.

119. PowerPoint Briefing, Joint Chiefs of Staff Military Advice (draft, version 1.0), December 13, 2006, slide 2.

120. Feaver, "The Right to Be Right," pp. 107-108.

121. Ibid., p. 108.

122. David E. Sanger, Michael R. Gordon, and John F. Burns, "Chaos Overran Iraq Plan in '06, Bush Team Says," *The New York Times,* January 2, 2007.

123. Mansoor, *Surge,* pp. 52-53; Woodward, *The War Within,* pp. 288-289.

124. White House photo by Eric Draper, "President George W. Bush listens to a reporter's question following his meeting on Iraq with U.S. military leaders at the Pentagon, Wednesday, December 13, 2006, joined by from left, Vice President Dick Cheney; Chairman of the Joint Chiefs of Staff, General Peter Pace, and Vice Chairman of the Joint Chiefs of Staff Admiral Edmund P. Giambastiani, right," White House

Identifier 20061213-5_d-0411-515h, December 13, 2006, Released to Public, available from *http://georgewbush-whitehouse.archives.gov/news/releases/2006/12/images/20061213-5_d-0411-515h.html*.

125. Interview, Colonel Frank Sobchak, CSA OIF Study Group, with James D. Thurman, CG MND-B, Part IV, April 16, 2014.

126. DoD photo by Curt Cashour, "From right: U.S. Army Lieutenant General Peter Chiarelli, commanding general of 5th Corps, looks on as General George W. Casey, Jr., commanding general of Multi-National Force-Iraq, congratulates Lieutenant General Ray Odierno, commanding general of 3rd Corps, during a ceremony marking the transfer of authority over Multi-National Corps-Iraq from 5th Corps to 3rd Corps at Al Faw Palace, Camp Victory, Iraq, December 14, 2006," DoD Identifier 947584-D-RHH62-890, December 14, 2006, Released to Public, available from *http://www.defense.gov/Media/Photo-Gallery?igphoto=2001116310*.

127. Lieutenant General Raymond T. Odierno Iraq Notebook no. 1, entries for October 11 and 16, 2006. Odierno mentions the possibility of drawing down to 10 BCTs in Interview, Colonel Michael Visconnage, MNC-I Command Historian, with Lieutenant General Raymond T. Odierno, June 24, 2007. Attending a briefing in late October 2006, the general also noted that III Corps might be the "last full corps" in Iraq (Odierno, Iraq Notebook no. 1, October 28, 2006, entry).

128. Odierno Iraq Notebook no. 1, entries for October 13, 28, and 31, 2006.

129. Ibid., December 4-5, 2006, entry.

130. PowerPoint Briefing, MNC-I, Baghdad Security Plan: 120-Day Assessment, August 2006-December 2006, December 9, 2006, slide 2.

131. Ibid.

132. Ibid., slide 24.

133. Paper, Cochran and Howard, MNF-I Chronology Reference, November 12, 2008, December 10, 2006, entry, p. 352; Odierno Iraq Notebook no. 1, December 10, 2006, entry; Major James Powell, MNC-I Planner, Notebook no. 2, entries for October 9, 2006, and December 10, 2006; Staff Notes, MNF-I, December 10, 2006.

134. Odierno Iraq Notebook no. 1, December 6, 2006, entry; Staff Notes, MNF-I, December 6, 2006.

135. Odierno Iraq Notebook no. 1, December 6, 2006, entry.

136. MNF-I, Campaign Progress Review, June 2006-December 2006, pp. 2-4.

137. Ibid., pp. 4-5.

138. Ibid., pp. 3, 6-7.

139. Staff Notes, MNF-I, December 6, 2006; Staff Notes, MNF-I, December 16, 2006.

140. Odierno Iraq Notebook no. 1, December 13, 2006, entry.

141. Ibid., December 11, 2006, entry.

142. Powell Iraq Notebook no. 1, December 15, 2006, entry.

143. Ibid., December 14, 2006, entry.

144. Staff Notes, MNF-I, December 17, 2006.

145. Feaver, "The Right to Be Right," p. 102; Odierno Iraq Notebook no. 1, December 9, 2006, entry.

146. PowerPoint Briefing, MNF-I/MNC-I, Surge Options Decision Briefing, version 3, December 14, 2006.

147. Ibid., slides 15-21.

148. Paper, Cochran and Howard, MNF-I Chronology Reference, November 12, 2008, p. 355.

149. Ibid.

150. MNC-I, Fragmentary Order 179, pp. 2-7; Odierno Iraq Notebook no. 2, December 18, 2006, entry.

151. Staff Notes, MNF-I, December 20, 2006.

152. Ibid., December 22, 2006; Paper, Cochran and Howard, MNF-I Chronology Reference, November 12, 2008, December 23, 2006, entry, p. 357.

153. Robert M. Gates, *Duty: Memoirs of a Secretary at War*, New York: Knopf, 2014, p. 42.

154. Ibid., p. 44.

155. Ibid., p. 43.

156. Casey, *Strategic Reflections*, p. 146.

157. Joint Staff, Commander, U.S. Joint Forces Command, *Surge Planning Order*, December 22, 2006, pp. 2-3.

158. Bob Woodward suggests that a skeptical Casey conceded to Fil's request for additional BCTs simply to humor the inexperienced division commander. Woodward, *The War Within*, p. 232.

159. MND-B, *Operation Order (OPORD)* 07-02, December 25, 2006, pp. 11, 14-15; Briefing, MND-B, *Security and Offensive Operations in Baghdad*, December 24, 2006.

160. Odierno Iraq Notebook no. 2, December 23, 2006, entry.

161. Ibid., December 28, 2006, entry.

162. Interview, CSA OIF Study Group with General Raymond T. Odierno, January 24, 2015, Chapel Hill, NC.

163. Ricks, *Gamble*, pp. 91-92.

164. Woodward, *The War Within*, pp. 298-299.

165. Ibid., pp. 294-295, 299-300, 301-302, 305.

166. Ibid., pp. 296-297; Mansoor, *Surge*, p. 54.

167. Bush, *Decision Points*, pp. 377-378.

168. Odierno Iraq Notebook no. 2, December 29, 2006, entry.

169. MNF-I, Agenda for Video-Teleconference, January 4, 2007.

170. Transcript of Prime Minister Maliki's Iraqi Army Day speech, January 6, 2007; MNF-I Commander's notes from NSC VTC, January 8, 2007.

171. Bush, *Decision Points*, p. 377.

172. Odierno Iraq Notebook no. 2, December 29, 2006, entry.

173. Casey, *Strategic Reflections*, pp. 145-46; Woodward, *The War Within*, p. 306; Sanger, Gordon, and Burns, "Chaos Overran Iraq Plan in '06, Bush Team Says."

174. Quoted in Woodward, *The War Within*, p. 306.

175. Sanger, Gordon, and Burns, "Chaos Overran Iraq Plan in '06, Bush Team Says."

176. Ibid.

177. E-mail, Casey to Pace, January 4, 2007.

CHAPTER 2

THE EVE OF THE SURGE, DECEMBER 2006-FEBRUARY 2007

The final days of 2006 were an uncertain time for the U.S.-led coalition in Iraq. President George W. Bush had made the decision to deploy five surge brigades, but almost 2 months remained until a new commander, General David Petraeus, would arrive to implement a new U.S. strategy. In the meantime, General George Casey, Jr., remained in command in Baghdad, overseeing operations under new strategic guidance from the President that Casey had advised Bush not to issue. The 2 months between the surge decision and the arrival of Petraeus would see a widening rift between Casey and his operational commander, Lieutenant General Raymond Odierno, as Odierno began sending his troops forward into Baghdad's neighborhoods and instructing U.S. units to retake lead responsibility for security operations from their Iraqi counterparts. Odierno's approach amounted to a reversal of the course Casey had set for MNF-I more than a year earlier.

One issue on which Casey and Odierno agreed was that the coalition and Iraqi security forces immediately should renew operations to secure Baghdad. As a new Baghdad security plan got underway in early 2007, the warring parties in central Iraq—the coalition, the Iraqi security forces, al-Qaeda in Iraq (AQI), and the Iranian-sponsored Shi'a militant groups—braced themselves for the coming U.S. counteroffensive. In the intensified fighting that resulted as the plan was implemented, the long-deferred war between the coalition and the Iranian regime's militant proxies would reignite.

In the first weeks of 2007, coalition leaders also would shift their attention to the belts that surrounded Baghdad, guided by a new realization that only by controlling the capital's hinterlands could the coalition and its Iraqi partners secure the city itself. Finally, far beyond Baghdad, renewed fighting in northern Iraq would show that even with the coming five-brigade troop surge, there would be important areas of Iraq beyond the coalition's means to pacify, at least in the short term.

THE HANGING OF SADDAM HUSSEIN

The end of 2006 brought with it the end of Saddam Hussein, who had been in U.S. custody since his December 2003 capture. A consummate manipulator, he had cast himself as something of a grandfather to his bemused American guards, dispensing personal advice to those who saw him on a daily basis. In a similar vein, he politely needled the senior officer who visited him every other week at the coalition detention center on Camp Victory, Iraq, where he was held. "You Americans are naïve," he told Major General John D. Gardner, commander of coalition detention operations. "You will be unable to keep the Shi'a, the Sunni, and the Kurds together because you are too kind."[1]

Convicted of "crimes against humanity" for the killing of 148 people in the mainly Shi'a town of Dujail, and sentenced to death by hanging in November 2006, the former dictator learned of the denial of his final appeal on December 26. The Iraqi Government was eager to move forward with the execution but had to satisfy a number of administrative requirements before the United States would transfer custody. The extent of these outstanding legal issues led coalition leaders to assume that the execution was at least 1 to 2 weeks away. When Prime Minister Nuri al-Maliki's representatives notified the U.S. Embassy late on the evening of December 29 that the Iraqi Government intended to hang Saddam the following morning, U.S. Ambassador Zalmay Khalilzad and Casey both were out of the country. Scrambling to try to delay the execution, the Embassy arranged a call between Khalilzad and the Prime Minister and even elevated the matter to Secretary of State Condoleezza Rice. The ambassador and U.S. military officials pressed for a postponement, arguing that the rush was unseemly—particularly given that December 30 was Eid al-Adha, an important religious holiday for both Sunni and Shi'a Muslims. However, Maliki insisted on moving forward, asserting the execution was a matter of Iraqi sovereignty.[2]

Around 3:00 a.m. on December 30, U.S. officials yielded to the Iraqi request and flew Saddam by helicopter from Camp Victory to the Iraqi-run Camp Justice in the Kadhimiyah District of Baghdad. The U.S. military transported Iraqi national security adviser Mowaffaq Rubaie and other Iraqi officials from the Green Zone to the execution site by helicopter as well.[3] Saddam met his fate before sunrise amid a raucous crowd of Ministry of Justice officials and Shi'a militiamen chanting, "Moqtada, Moqtada, Moqtada," a scene captured on cell phone video by Rubaie himself.[4]

For 3 years, the coalition had kept Saddam alive and healthy during his confinement—accommodating his lawyers' demands for access, force-feeding him during his two hunger strikes, and choreographing his safe passage back and forth to the trial—only to accede in the end to the Iraqi Government's haphazard handling and provocative timing of the execution. Maliki's office had brushed aside U.S. concerns over executing Saddam on the day of Eid, stating that it would hang the former dictator well before sunrise. However, citing this technicality as a mitigating factor was merely a smokescreen. The Maliki government fully intended to send a message with the execution. Later that day, Iraqi state television broadcast Rubaie's cell phone video of the former dictator's last moments, and an aide to the Prime Minister labeled Saddam's death as "an Eid gift to the Iraqi people."[5] The message was not lost on Sunni Arabs. In a meeting with Khalilzad in Riyadh, for example, an outraged King Abdullah of Saudi Arabia accused the U.S. Government of complicity in the controversially timed execution.[6] A defiant Maliki answered regional critics 1 week later, "We look strangely at the statements made by some governments who pretend to mourn the dictator for being executed on a sacred day," he intoned, "although these governments know very well that Saddam had desecrated all the sacred things [for] 35 years [while] these governments stood silent."[7]

At coalition headquarters, the incident deepened Odierno's suspicions of the Iraqi Government. The coalition had hoped the execution could be an opportunity for Iraqis to move forward in unity, but news that the government had allowed the event to devolve into a sectarian spectacle dashed these hopes. A disappointed Odierno next found Multi-National Corps-Iraq (MNC-I) embroiled in a dispute over the disposition of the former dictator's remains. The corps transported the Salahadin governor and Saddam's kinsmen to Baghdad for consultations with the Prime Minister's representatives and later flew the body to Tikrit for burial after the issue was decided. Unimpressed with how the central government had handled these negotiations, Odierno was dismayed by the realization that Maliki's aides seemed to be harnessing the powerful emotions associated with the hanging to stoke the sectarian flames. "Rubaie, I believe, has deep ties with Sadr" and "a clear bent toward . . . the protection of Shia extremism," the MNC-I commander wrote after he learned of the national security adviser's involvement, adding that Rubaie "basically turned the execution over to the Sadrists."[8] The distasteful experience left Odierno and other senior U.S. leaders questioning whether the Iraqi Government's partisan stance would derail the impending campaign to secure Baghdad.

THE BAGHDAD SECURITY PLAN

The Maliki Government's New Plan

Saddam's execution took place against a backdrop of intense preparations by Iraqi and U.S. leaders for a renewed Baghdad security plan. Throughout December, as U.S. leaders in Washington hammered out the specifics of a large-scale surge of American troops, Casey and his Iraqi counterparts formulated plans for a surge of Iraqi troops into the capital and additional measures to try to tamp down the sectarian violence there. Casting the operation as a campaign to enforce the law against any militant groups that violated it, Maliki and his officials named the new plan Operation FARDH AL-QANOON, Arabic for "Enforcing the Law." With coalition assistance, the Iraqis developed a unique command-and-control framework for FARDH AL-QANOON that became a mainstay of future operations in the capital.

Representatives from the ministries of defense and interior as well as Maliki's office of the commander in chief would establish a single command—the Baghdad Operations Command (BOC)—to oversee all Iraqi security forces in the capital. Two subordinate commands would divide the city into nine administrative districts: the Rusafa Area Command would oversee the five districts east of the Tigris River, including Sadr City; while the western half's four districts would fall under the jurisdiction of the Karkh Area Command. Police stations in each district would serve as hubs where Iraqi Army units, National Police, and coalition forces would coordinate operations with local police to secure surrounding neighborhoods. Iraqi generals from the army and National Police would lead the Karkh and Rusafa subcommands, respectively, each with a deputy from the other service—an Iraqi-crafted measure instituted to build trust within the security forces and facilitate "joint" operations.[9] The Iraqis' insistence on integrating elements from the ministries of defense and interior into the same headquarters at multiple echelons throughout the capital seemed overly complicated to U.S. officers, but understandable given the pervasiveness of destructive sectarianism. Increasing the linkages among the army, police, and coalition forces meant, in Casey's words, "everyone . . . would be watching each other."[10]

For simplicity's sake, Casey pushed for a combined U.S.-Iraqi command led by Major General Joseph F. Fil, the Multi-National Division-Baghdad (MND-B) commander, and Lieutenant General Ali Ghaidan, the commander of the Iraqi Ground Forces Command (IGFC). Using an existing headquarters building and an experienced staff for the BOC made sense to Casey, who had witnessed MNF-I's own growing pains and also wanted to begin operations quickly.[11] Maliki, however, had other ideas. For weeks, the Prime Minister had pressed the coalition to grant him a responsive military force that reported directly to him. To meld the new command with the IGFC would tie it bureaucratically to the Ministry of Defense rather than directly to the Prime Minister. Creating it as a combined headquarters, meanwhile, would fuse American and Iraqi leaders and staffs together, an idea that Maliki rejected because it seemed to enable the Americans to dodge responsibility for security while providing them with a veto over Iraqi operations. The BOC should be answerable ultimately to the Iraqi Prime Minister alone, Maliki argued. The Prime Minister also had no intention of locating the BOC in the middle of Camp Victory, far from the Green Zone but only a 5-minute walk from MNC-I's headquarters. Preserving his freedom of action mattered more than the strictly military considerations. Instead, the BOC would move into a wing of Adnan Palace near the Green Zone with an ad hoc staff of Iraqi officers from the ministries of defense and interior.[12] Although the coalition would provide a large advisory team, the BOC would be an Iraqi-run organization.

It also did not serve Maliki's political interests to place the IGFC commander, Ghaidan, in charge. Maliki's office instead floated the name of General Mohan al-Freiji as the future Baghdad commander, but MNF-I drew the line at this nomination. At Multi-National Security Transition Command-Iraq (MNSTC-I), Lieutenant General Martin Dempsey judged Freiji "a bad piece of work." Odierno also balked at the proposal, characterizing Freiji as an officer with "extreme Shi'a views," who would be incapable of leading "fair and balanced operations."[13] As a result, the Prime Minister moved on to Lieutenant General Abud Qanbar, a Shi'a officer virtually unknown to the coalition, but a Maliki kinsman who recently had directed the praetorian-like Office of the Commander in Chief. In naming him, Maliki passed over three Iraqi generals Casey had recommended.[14]

Staff General Abud Qanbar (left). Source: DoD photo by Sergeant David Hodge (Released).

BOC Staff General Abud Qanbar, During a Groundbreaking Ceremony in Baghdad.[15]

The coalition headquarters scrambled to assess Baghdad's new commander. Odierno dispatched MNC-I's chief Arabist and political adviser, Colonel Robert Newman, to head the BOC advisory team and report his impressions. Qanbar's postings since 2003 had given him little exposure to the coalition, and he did not yet trust its leaders, tending toward "rudeness" and "a profound lack of respect" in interactions with American and British generals, Newman observed. The American colonel was struck by what he interpreted as the Iraqi commander's baseless self-confidence and dearth of military experience. "[Lieutenant General] Abud believes that he can do anything he wants to do because of his support from the Prime Minister's [PM's] office," Newman reported. "And there is a good chance that most of what he will do will be motivated by sectarian interests."[16] Casey's operations director, Major General David A. Fastabend, met Qanbar soon after his appointment and came away with a similar impression: "Strong hints of Shi'a bias. . . . An officer of average Iraqi competence in the tactical/lower-operational realm. No sign of a grasp of operational/strategic/political complexities. This is not Colin Powell."[17]

However, there was little Casey could do. The security ministers backed Maliki's choice, and the MNF-I commander judged he lacked the influence to contest it. Controversy aside, the BOC was the price the coalition had to pay for a level of Iraqi Government support absent in the Baghdad operations of 2006.

The New Year's Offensive

It would take more than a new commander and headquarters to enforce the law in Baghdad. Early in the process, the Iraqis determined that the revised plan would require a total of 19 brigades from the Iraqi Army and National Police; five more than were actually available.[18] To help correct this shortfall, three additional army brigades were slated to deploy to the capital no later than the end of February.[19] However, the Iraqi plan left many matters unresolved. First, it focused on military details to the exclusion of political and economic issues.[20] Besides a vague reference to raids and patrols, the concept lacked both a scheme of maneuver for units to follow and a prioritization of key terrain in the city. "This is a plan about checkpoints," summarized Fil, the MND-B commander. "There is no mention of the actual offensive."[21] The Iraqi plan went into exhaustive detail about the staffing of static positions, including the Baghdad Barrier, a series of checkpoints ringing the perimeter of the city and an Iraqi fixation that coalition leaders saw as a virtual sinkhole for platoons that could be better employed elsewhere. "We have our doubts on the efficacy of the Baghdad Barrier," commented Fastabend, "but if we unilaterally bring it down it will be the 'Big Excuse' . . . on why things are not going well."[22]

Beyond the matter of the Iraqis' static approach, MND-B recognized that the Iraqi plans did not adequately address the problem of Jaysh al-Mahdi (JAM) and other Shi'a militants—the same shortcoming that had helped to doom the Baghdad security plans of summer and fall 2006. For the past several months or more, JAM elements had been carrying out a systematic campaign of violence and intimidation designed to bring the capital under exclusively Shi'a control. Sunnis had responded by forming "neighborhood watches" to defend their communities and, increasingly, to launch their own extrajudicial killing raids against Shi'a. Al-Qaeda in Iraq (AQI) exploited this growing sectarian rift and co-opted many of these Sunni groups.

Source: U.S. Army photo by Lieutenant Colonel Scott Bleichwehl (Released).

Major General Joseph Fil, Commanding General of MND-B in the Rusafa Market.[23]

MND-B had limited troops at its disposal to address these problems. At the time, three U.S. brigade combat teams (BCTs) operated in the city. The departure of the 172d Stryker BCT from Baghdad without replacement forced MNC-I to relocate Colonel Stephen J. Townsend's 3d Stryker Brigade, 2d Infantry Division, from Mosul to the capital city in December to become MND-B's mobile strike force. Besides these U.S. units, Fil had operational control of seven Iraqi Army brigades and eight National Police brigades in Baghdad. Fil and his division had assumed responsibility for conducting patrols with Iraqi units throughout the city and for holding five "focus areas"—mixed neighborhoods that had witnessed heavy sectarian violence. All these lay in the western half of Baghdad, except for the Sunni enclave of Adhamiyah.[24] MND-B also controlled three U.S. BCTs operating outside the city in the so-called belts—one to the north and two to the south.

To arrest the sectarian violence in Baghdad, Fil and the 1st Cavalry Division argued for collapsing the Baghdad Barrier to free up the Iraqi units that manned it—nearly a brigade of Iraqi combat power—and use them to help clear areas inside the city. They also proposed reinforcing the Army Canal checkpoints on the edge of Sadr City—the same checkpoints Chiarelli unsuccessfully had urged Casey not to remove in late October, just 2 months earlier. The 1st Cavalry Division wished to maintain the checkpoints that limited access to the focus areas, while minimizing other checkpoints to encourage more patrolling and an offensive spirit in Iraqi units.[25] With renewed offensive operations and an extended curfew, MND-B hoped to "surge combat power on focus areas to protect the population."[26]

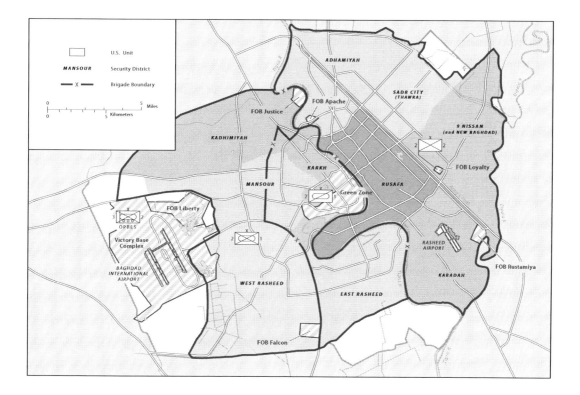

Map created by the official cartographer at the U.S. Army Center of Military History, Washington, DC.

Map 8. Before the Surge, Disposition of U.S. Forces Baghdad, January 2007.

Political pressure accelerated the launch of the new security plan, as Maliki was eager to show progress and Bush was intent on demonstrating the specifics of his "new way forward." On December 22, with Casey and Odierno in attendance, Fil told Iraq's security ministers that a long-term operation would begin within days and last into the summer. During the last week of December, Colonel J. B. Burton's 2d Brigade, 1st Infantry Division, would clear Ghazaliyah, a tough Sunni neighborhood astride a sectarian fault line in west Baghdad. Most MND-B units in the city would spend the first 2 weeks of the new year increasing their presence inside previously cleared areas while conducting raids and patrols to disrupt Sunni and Shi'a militants elsewhere. Meanwhile, Townsend's Stryker brigade would undertake a series of clearing operations across the capital as the division's strike force.[27]

As a strike force, Townsend's brigade would not have a single sector of its own, but instead would lead the effort to remove enemy forces from specific neighborhoods in other BCTs' battle space and to eliminate any support zones or sanctuaries. The unit's additional maneuver battalion and its comparatively large contingent of infantrymen, combined with the Stryker vehicle's mobility, made it well suited for a rapid series of discrete clearing missions. In these operations, coalition and Iraqi troops would move with care through hot-spot neighborhoods, building by building, following up on intelligence or tips from locals to try to find militant operatives, safe houses, weapons, or other aspects of enemy organizations.[28] Clearing operations had been a major part of the coalition's approach in Iraq's urban areas throughout the war, and they often resulted in large-scale captures of enemy operatives and weapons or sparked violent engagements with enemy fighters.

After the New Year, Fil intended for the 3d Stryker Brigade to clear Sha'ab/Ur to the north of Sadr City and prepare the area for the mid-January arrival of the 2d Brigade, 82d Airborne Division, the first of the surge brigades. Townsend's troops would then conduct similar operations over the next several weeks in the troublesome Kadhimiyah, Rashid, and Mansour districts. As the strike force shifted to each follow-on assignment, the American BCT owning the recently cleared battle space would maintain a physical presence there in direct support of Iraqi Army or National Police units. As Sunni and Shi'a militants sought to reassert their influence in these still-contested areas, Iraqi and U.S. formations would remain to protect the population, an element absent from the TOGETHER FORWARD operations in 2006. With a sustained reduction in violence, security forces would turn the cleared areas into "gated communities," as the soldiers liked to call them, surrounded by concrete barriers and with access points controlled by the security forces. As supporting U.S. units reduced their footprint in these areas, the Iraqi Army and National Police would be responsible for ensuring the enemy was not able to reestablish a foothold—though the issue of Iraqi security forces reform would have to be addressed.[29] The traditional counterinsurgency imperative of police primacy informed MND-B's plans. As security improved, control would gradually pass from coalition forces to the Iraqi Army or National Police and finally to local police.[30]

The concept was an advance beyond the flawed approach of Operation TOGETHER FORWARD, but its reliance on the idea of police primacy proved problematic. Putting the Iraqi police on the front lines of the civil war in early 2007 amounted to sponsoring one warring party in a civil war against the other, except in those rare places and units in which the police were thoroughly apolitical and professional. The guiding principle for population security and control within a civil war should have been to prevent all groups from using violence against one another, including the group in control of the government and its security forces. By placing a premium on police primacy while security still hung in the balance, MNF-I had misapplied counterinsurgency doctrine and endangered the operation itself.

Fil's plan also fleshed out the Iraqi concept for joint security stations where American troops, local police, and Iraqi Army and National Police units operating in the same general area would co-locate their headquarters to monitor and synchronize operations. Coalition commanders hoped this move, and its injection of American forces inside Iraqi headquarters, would limit sectarian behavior by Iraqi security force (ISF) members. Starting from a baseline of 9 or 10 "district" joint security stations, MND-B instructed its subordinate BCTs to set up "satellite" stations in the surrounding neighborhoods where company-sized U.S. and Iraqi units would coordinate combined operations, manage routine patrols, process detainees, and engage the local population. Spurred by MNF-I's insistence that the plan complement its transition goals, the division initially proposed that platoons rotate through the company's sector, patrolling in 12-hour shifts before returning to a forward operating base rather than residing in joint security stations. In the view of Casey and MNF-I, the joint security stations were a mechanism for transition as the coalition postured itself for a phased withdrawal from the city.[31]

To ramp up the U.S. and Iraqi security presence on the streets of the capital, MND-B revived the concept of partnership that Casey had eschewed the previous month. The Baghdad Security Plan aligned Iraqi unit sectors and district boundaries, facilitating the pairing of U.S. and Iraqi units that shared battle space. Each of the dozen or so Iraqi Army and National Police brigades posted across the capital's nine security districts would partner with a coalition force battalion. Unlike the 12-man military transition teams advising Iraqi field-grade leaders and their staffs, the newly partnered U.S. units were directed "to increase the capabilities of Iraqi security forces through combined operations and coaching, teaching, and mentoring at all levels."[32] Notably, as additional Iraqi brigades arrived in the capital, more U.S. battalions would be needed to pair with them.

As Fil and his officers saw it, it would take several months of operating within the city before the coalition could transition Baghdad's security to Iraqi control and shift coalition attention to the AQI-dominated areas surrounding Baghdad. Once the threat was sufficiently reduced, local police would take the lead for providing security, allowing the coalition to take the fight into the enemy support zones surrounding the capital while shifting to an "overwatch" posture inside the city itself.[33] Given the forces available, including the two surge BCTs the division hoped to receive from outside the theater, launching a coordinated assault into Baghdad's belts would have to wait until a semblance of stability was restored to the city's core, Fil and his staff judged.[34]

Source: DoD photo by United States Forces Iraq (Released).

American and Iraqi Soldiers Wait as U.S. Army UH-60 Black Hawk Helicopters Approach Their Landing Zone Near Mahmudiyah.[35]

Likewise, a major incursion into Sadr City would not be forthcoming. Washington's interest in the possibility of "taking care of JAM" had prompted a deeper look by Casey in early December. Clearing the densely populated Shi'a slum could be done with the Iraqi and American forces already in and around Baghdad, he concluded. However, if MND-B concentrated its forces on Sadr City, it would leave the west side of Baghdad uncovered, resulting in a high degree of risk.[36] The prospect that engaging JAM in its Sadr City sanctuary could trigger a countrywide backlash gave the MNF-I commander pause as well. "We would expect a tough fight for a week or two," Casey related in an e-mail to Pace and Abizaid, "but we would prevail if the government held tough."[37] Whether the Maliki government would hold remained in question. Maliki had authorized targeted strikes into Sadr City, but he had no appetite for an open confrontation against JAM on its own turf. This suited MND-B just fine. Focused on sectarian fault lines throughout the capital, the division judged that a costly clearing operation into the long-time militia stronghold would likely not end Shi'a death squad activity and argued in favor of a delay. At all levels, U.S. military leaders agreed that it was better in the near term to isolate the stronghold, disrupt JAM through frequent raids against its leadership, and work to weaken the militia's position vis-à-vis the local Iraqi security forces.[38]

To reinforce FARDH AL-QANOON, Odierno ordered MNC-I's units to keep the enemy off-balance with a flurry of simultaneous offensive activity.[39] MND-B had no shortage of hot spots, and Fil quickly began using Townsend's Stryker brigade to address them. The full complement of Townsend's BCT arrived from Mosul in mid-December, ending a 3-week gap during which MND-B operated without a Stryker brigade headquarters or dedicated mobile strike force. The BCT commander's first exposure to Baghdad had come the previous month on a patrol with the unit his brigade was replacing. Townsend had been struck by the absence of American troops in the neighborhoods. "In 5 hours, we saw one other coalition patrol," he recalled.[40] Under the auspices of FARDH AL-QA-NOON, BCTs across Baghdad would now initiate operations to reintroduce U.S. military presence throughout the city.

Source: U.S. Army photo by Sergeant Lance Wail (Released).

Colonel Stephen Townsend, Commander of the 3d Stryker BCT, 2d Infantry Division, With Major General Abdul Ameer al-Lami, Commander of the Iraqi 6th Division.[41]

Battalion-sized strike operations were the raison d'être of Townsend's unit in Baghdad. With his reconnaissance squadron already attached to another BCT, the commander aligned his three remaining maneuver battalions geographically so that they coincided roughly with the sectors of "ground-owning" U.S. brigades, thereby improving responsiveness. Townsend's first large operation occurred in Salman Pak, the mixed-sect town on the southeastern outskirts of the capital where JAM and Sunni militants long had struggled for control and where hundreds of bodies of murdered Baghdadis had washed up from the Tigris in 2005-2006. The second, in New Baghdad, involved three of Townsend's battalions and sought to disrupt Shi'a militant operations while creating the false impression that U.S. forces were gearing up for a major push into Sadr City.[42] During the first week of January, the BCT shifted its combat power to the opposite side of the capital in order to clear the Kadhimiyah District's densely populated Hurriyah neighborhood. Meanwhile, following clearing operations in Ghazaliyah and Ameriyah, Burton's 2d Brigade, 1st Infantry Division, sought to disrupt the Shi'a militants' hold on northern Kadhimiyah and prevent their ongoing forays into Sunni areas just to the south. Two of Townsend's battalions supported this fight. From there, half of the Strykers launched clearing operations in Dora. Remaining in Hurriyah, 1st Stryker Battalion, 23d Infantry Regiment, held the neighborhood, along with an Iraqi Army unit, and waited until reinforcements from the first surge BCT arrived to relieve it.[43]

The Battle of Haifa Street

As FARDH AL-QANOON got underway with these operations in early January 2007, the most difficult fighting emerged around Haifa Street, a busy byway paralleling the west bank of the Tigris River in the Karkh District. Just 2½ miles north of the U.S. Embassy, the neighborhood had become an AQI stronghold and a sectarian battlefield. It lay in the area assigned to Colonel Bryan Roberts's 2d Brigade, 1st Cavalry Division, but had received scant coalition attention for much of 2006—due to the limited forces available and the fact that Dora, in the same BCT sector, was far more violent.

Roberts considered Karkh an economy of force mission. One of his squadrons had responsibility for the area in and around the international zone, with roughly one troop running patrols and monitoring Iraqi checkpoints at any given time.[44] Haifa Street itself ran through a locale inhabited largely by Sunnis, but many Shi'a lived in a neighborhood a few blocks to the west. This sectarian fault-line had become more pronounced in 2006 as Shi'a militants and AQI battled to expand their control.[45] The well-to-do professional class that had once resided in Haifa Street's high-rise apartment buildings had fled as the violence grew intolerable, and those who remained were under the sway of Sunni terrorist groups promising protection in the face of militia intimidation. Just blocks away, in the Shi'a-majority area, a makeshift sign hung on the side of a children's hospital (roughly translated) proclaiming: "Congratulations, President Moqtada al-Sadr, for executing Saddam."[46] As U.S. troops geared up for operations in places like Kadhimiyah, Mansour, and Rashid, Odierno eyed the sectarian tinderbox of Haifa Street as a "big problem."[47]

Source: DoD photo by Staff Sergeant Lorie Jewell (Released).

High Rise Apartment Buildings on Haifa Street, the Location of Intense Battles in Early January 2007.[48]

Matters came to a head during the first week of January 2007. On January 6, a sharp clash in the Haifa Street neighborhood between Sunni gunmen manning a fake checkpoint and Iraqi forces left 30 Sunni fighters dead. Sunni militants retaliated by executing a near-equal number of Shi'a civilians and dumping their bodies in an alleyway, after which emboldened Sunni fighters patrolled the streets practically unchallenged over the next 2 days.[49] When troops of the 1st Brigade, 6th Iraqi Army Division, arrived from nearby Hurriyah to reassert government control, they found themselves overmatched almost immediately. At the request of the commander of an ambushed Iraqi convoy, the 1st Stryker Battalion, 23d Infantry Regiment, dispatched two companies to help.[50] By daylight on January 9, more than 1,000 Iraqi and American troops were engaged in a pitched battle with Sunni insurgents, with the sound of the fighting heard in the U.S. Embassy and MNF-I headquarters a little more than 2 miles away. The enemy appeared well organized and highly trained, maneuvering from position to position, and delivering coordinated mortar fire in support. Defenders occupied several apartment towers some 20 to 30 stories high, making deliberate building-to-building, floor-to-floor, and room-to-room clearing operations infeasible. According to the U.S. commander on the scene, the complexity of the terrain far exceeded the capabilities of available Iraqi-American manpower. When insurgents opted to stay and fight it out rather than melt away after an initial exchange as they typically did, coalition forces employed firepower to bridge the gap. Close air support from rotary- and fixed-wing aircraft targeted snipers. Marking the battle's climax, precision rocket fire from Fallujah some 40 miles away destroyed a heavily defended building with virtually no collateral damage. As darkness fell on January 9, the combined American-Iraqi force consolidated its positions. Over the course of the 11-hour fight, it had suffered six casualties—four American and two Iraqi wounded. About 50 enemy fighters were killed and at least 15 captured, with a handful of Syrians and Egyptians among them.[51] By comparison, the same battalion had netted 16 detainees while reporting no enemy killed the previous week during 5 days of clearing operations in Hurriyah.[52]

Over the next week, the Stryker battalion reduced its forces and left security on Haifa Street in Iraqi hands. The American withdrawal set the stage for the unit's return later in the month. Without U.S. troops present, Haifa Street soon became a scene of sectarian conflict again. JAM, the Badr Corps, and other Shi'a militias renewed their campaign of intimidation in nearby areas and exploited their infiltration of Iraqi forces to target Sunnis. Meanwhile, Sunni extremists also returned to Haifa Street. When their harassing sniper fire paralyzed Iraqi Army units, the Strykers returned to restore stability. On January 24, the battalion attacked with a large force of Iraqis, as well as a troop belonging to 2d Brigade, 1st Cavalry Division. The units undertook more thorough clearing operations than on the previous occasion and over a number of days instituted population-control measures by cordoning off key areas and limiting access to pedestrian traffic. A troop from 4th Squadron, 9th Cavalry Regiment, established a combat outpost alongside troops from the 6th Iraqi Army Division.[53] However, this small presence could not contain the expansion of the Shi'a militias, which imposed a "mafia-like" grip on the neighborhood that persisted for several more months.[54]

The fighting around Haifa Street showcased the shortcomings of the Iraqi security forces in Baghdad relative to the threat. Some of the Iraqi Army troops involved in the early stages of the confrontation appeared to have abandoned their posts. Even the unit sent to Haifa Street to restore order fell victim to an ambush, ran out of ammunition, and was unable to resupply itself.[55] Coalition officials characterized the first day's battle as a success, describing Iraqi forces as maneuvering "aggressively" and enduring "fierce firefights," but in actuality, the Iraqi troops were still no match for the Sunni extremists confronting them.[56] The same units also seemed reluctant to contest the rise of Shi'a militia influence once American forces withdrew from the area.[57] At the same time, the raiding approach of the U.S. units around Haifa Street resembled the failures of Operation TOGETHER FORWARD: U.S. units arrived on the scene reacting to a local security crisis, neutralized the threat, and then pulled out—only to be ordered back when the same problem soon reemerged.

MNC-I, AQI, AND THE BAGHDAD BELTS

During Odierno's fall 2006 preparations to assume command of MNC-I, he noted the lack of corps-level operations in Iraq throughout the previous year. From his perspective, as U.S. units had transitioned battle space and consolidated onto large bases, the U.S. commands had effectively stopped maneuvering and executing at the operational level. Rather than synchronize the multinational divisions toward a common operational goal, MNC-I had tended to structure its campaign as multiple division-sized fights in which subordinate units worked for local economic development, good governance, and trained Iraqi security forces. During summer and fall 2006, this approach had meant that the coalition campaign to secure Baghdad had fallen solely on MND-B and its three U.S. brigades in the city, with the other divisions conducting operations largely disconnected from MND-B's task in the capital.

As the operations of January 2007 got underway, Odierno sought to restore the coalition's operational perspective. From Odierno's vantage point, the coalition's war in Iraq was more properly viewed as countrywide, rather than as a set of discrete province-based campaigns. As MNC-I's main effort, MND-B would establish joint security stations throughout the city, partner with Iraqi units, and adopt a posture that enabled them to maintain a 24/7 presence in their sectors.[58] As Odierno saw it, reversing the cycle of sectarian violence required more than protecting the people of Baghdad and attacking the Sunni and Shi'a militants operating within the city. Any attempt to secure the capital required a concurrent effort to stop violent actors and weapons before they made their way into Baghdad, such as the car bombs that often originated in the belts surrounding the city on their way to targeting Shi'a neighborhoods. Under Odierno's instructions, MNC-I tasked MND-N and MNF-W to support MND-B by interdicting these "accelerants" to violence.[59] By focusing all three U.S. divisions on Baghdad, the corps could create a new, shared responsibility for Baghdad's security and give better shape to the priorities of the outlying divisions. This was particularly true for Major General Benjamin R. Mixon and

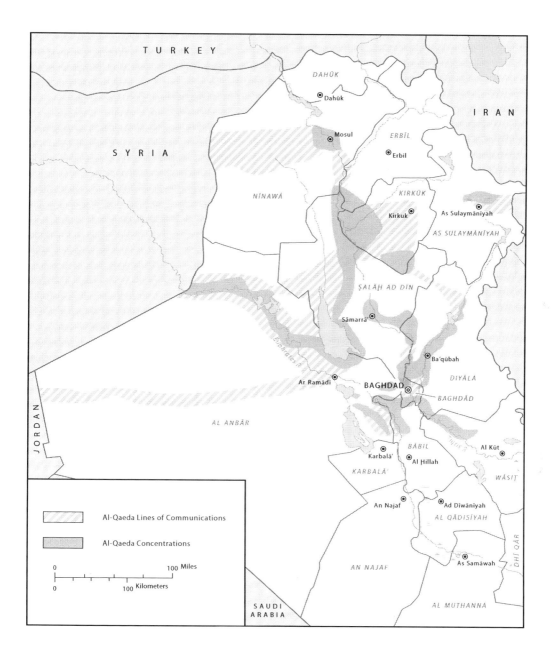

Map created by the official cartographer at the U.S. Army Center of Military History, Washington, DC.

Map 9. Al-Qaeda in Iraq, December 2006.

Multi-National Division-North (MND-N). MNC-I's emphasis on controlling the northern belt running from the Lake Tharthar region into Diyala Province proved more helpful as a guide for managing risk than MNF-I's 2006 framework based on "strategic cities" — four of which lay dispersed across MND-N's vast battle space.[60] Odierno's plan made clear to Mixon that the sectarian battleground between Baghdad and Baqubah should be MND-N's top concern.[61] However, the same principle did not really extend to the non-U.S. divisions. More distant from Baghdad, Multi-National Division-Central South (MND-CS) and Multi-National Division-Southeast (MND-SE) would remain focused on other security problems as the U.S. divisions concentrated on the capital.

Odierno's emphasis on Baghdad's hinterland was new for the coalition, but not for the Iraqis. For quite some time, Iraqis had recognized the areas just beyond Baghdad as crucial to controlling the city, a fact that Defense Minister Ali Allawi had pointed out to Combined Joint Task Force-7 (CJTF-7) in spring 2004. Saddam, too, had viewed controlling the belts as essential and had developed plans to position Republican Guard divisions in defensive zones around the capital.[62] The Iraqi Shi'a leaders saw the problem similarly, with Supreme Council for the Islamic Revolution in Iraq (SCIRI) officials identifying the belts as key terrain in conversations with CJTF-7 officers in 2004. Similarly, in late 2006, Maliki reportedly told his advisers that, after the government successfully excluded the coalition from greater Baghdad, Iraqi forces should move quickly to clear and control an area spanning from Diyala to the southern and western areas of the capital.[63] Within the coalition commands, in 2005 MNC-I commander Lieutenant General John Vines's concern about insurgent support zones in the belts had led him to disagree strongly with Casey's plan to move a division's worth of U.S. combat power from the Baghdad region to the Syrian border zones. To some degree, Casey and MNF-I appreciated the importance of the belts around Baghdad as a support zone for AQI before October 2006, but their focus on transition to Iraqi control, as well as a shortage of U.S. forces, had precluded significant coalition operations in the belts. When Iraqi leaders had insisted on establishing the ring of Baghdad Barrier checkpoints around the city in an attempt to control the routes from the outlying areas into the capital, MNF-I quickly judged it a pointless drain of Iraqi combat power. They missed the key point underlying Iraqi fixation with the ring of checkpoints: securing the city required controlling the outlying rural areas to the north and south. "The role of the support zones in controlling Baghdad is a perceived historical fact to them," Fastabend observed.[64] In their desire to sideline the misguided tactic of staffing stationary checkpoints, coalition leaders before December 2006 had overlooked the significance of this key terrain.

The Taji Documents

One of the most important discoveries of the war validated Odierno's and the Iraqis' instincts about the importance of the Baghdad belts. On December 19, 2006, U.S. Soldiers from 1st Brigade, 1st Cavalry Division, conducting a routine patrol in the Taji market north of the capital, captured a map and other documents that revealed AQI's strategy to control Baghdad. As the U.S. patrol investigated a suspicious vehicle, the men occupying it fled. One wore a suicide vest that detonated when the Americans opened fire. Another claimed to be a hostage. Left in the vehicle was a laptop computer, 450 gigabytes of data, and a hand-drawn map of Baghdad and its environs.[65]

The map and the accompanying Taji documents, as they became known at MNF-I, brought clarity to the coalition's understanding of AQI's battlefield geometry, which was more structured than coalition officials had realized. AQI leaders treated Baghdad as a separate zone, distinguishing between the "metro area" and the surrounding belts, but there was a connection between the two. Securing the key terrain of Rusafa, which AQI leaders seemed to consider a high priority, required the systematic sectarian cleansing of the belts, which would cut off Shi'a lines of communications into east Baghdad and increase the flow of displaced persons to locales known to have poor infrastructure. AQI leaders assumed these developments would tax the already dysfunctional Iraqi Government beyond its capacity and trigger a collapse. "The most important battle, which is happening now," an AQI leader had written in late 2006, "is the Battle of the Baghdad Belt."[66]

The Taji documents showed that AQI leaders believed it was time to intensify this fight. Within Baghdad, they considered the notorious Rusafa car bomb network their principal instrument of violence. Led by an AQI commander called Abu Nur, this network was responsible for the large-scale car bombs that plagued east Baghdad in late 2006 and early 2007. Its sustained success encouraged AQI leaders to accelerate a sectarian conflict with Baghdad's Shi'a they felt confident they could win.[67] From within the Shi'a-majority Rusafa District, Abu Nur's car bombers could easily target the adjacent Sadr City and were also close to a base of support in Adhamiyah, the only Sunni enclave east of the Tigris River. Rumors circulated that some of Abu Nur's operatives were former Shi'a whose Shi'a identities enabled them to move freely in east Baghdad's Shi'a-majority districts, all of which had transitioned to Iraqi police control. Abu Nur's immediate objective was to displace the Shi'a population of central Baghdad into districts like Sadr City and Kadhimiyah, corralling them into besieged pockets for more efficient extermination. At the same time, AQI leaders sought to expand Sunni strongholds in the Ghazaliyah and Ameriyah neighborhoods of west Baghdad, a step toward making the entire northwest quadrant of the capital an "extension of Anbar."[68]

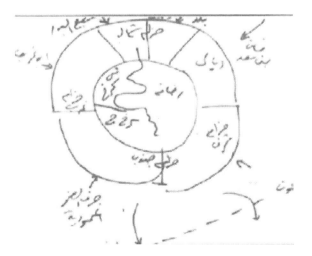

The Handwritten Map Depicting AQI's Strategy for Dominating the Baghdad Belts.[69]

According to the Taji documents, AQI had divided its campaign in the belts into three areas: east, south, and north. The northern belt included Taji, where the documents had been found, and stretched to the lower Diyala Province. Meanwhile, the eastern belt stretched from Salman Pak up through the largely Shi'a Mada'in Qada to the southern reaches of Diyala Province. AQI's emir in the eastern belt, an obscure operative known as Asim, had responsibility for cutting the Kut-Baghdad road and securing a land bridge from the outskirts of the capital up the contested Diyala River Valley to Buhriz and Baqubah. These tasks had been reinforced by AQI in mid-2006.[70] The southern belt stretched west of the Tigris River from Arab Jabour to the border of Anbar Province near Zaidon, an area where a low-grade sectarian civil war pulsed through the key population centers that dotted the heavily irrigated farmland. Arab Jabour remained a Sunni stronghold, as did Yusufiyah at the far end of this portion of the belts. In between, though, JAM and other Shi'a militias were increasing their footholds in the traditionally Sunni towns of Mahmudiyah and Iskandariyah. The stakes were high. Control of Yusufiyah, for example, was vital to AQI, because without it, Baghdad's southern points of entry would be practically inaccessible.[71]

From the coalition's perspective, security in the southern and eastern sections of the belts suffered from a general dearth of friendly forces. At the beginning of 2007, two U.S. BCTs under MND-B had responsibility for the area. With the culturally significant cities of Karbala and Najaf in its sector, Colonel Michael X. Garrett's 4th Brigade, 25th Infantry Division, short one of its maneuver battalions, could project relatively little combat power into the belts adjacent to the capital.[72] The battlegrounds of Arab Jabour and Salman Pak saw little coalition presence, save for forays aimed at disrupting enemy activity. The latest had occurred in December when a battalion from Townsend's 3d Stryker Brigade, 2d Infantry Division, hit high-value targets in Salman Pak.[73] In terms of available troops, 2d Brigade, 10th Mountain Division, was not much better off in the so-called Triangle of Death just southwest of Baghdad, but did have the advantage of a smaller area of operations. Its commander, Colonel Michael M. Kershaw, decided early in his tour to maintain a forward presence among the population through a network of patrol bases, an approach that by early 2007 seemed to be clamping down on AQI's freedom of movement.[74] For example, Abu Dunyah, emir of the southern belt, reported in late 2006 coming under "pressure from the enemy," a development causing infighting among his subordinate leaders.[75]

According to the Taji documents, AQI placed its greatest hope in the operations of Abu Ghazwan, the emir of the northern belt. Imprisoned at Camp Bucca and released from coalition custody in 2005, Ghazwan oversaw the area arcing eastward from Abu Ghraib to the outskirts of Baqubah. He financed himself by extorting money from contractors working for the coalition. He also co-opted local Sunni officials, engaged Sunni tribes in order to cultivate popular support, and steadily pressured Shi'a civilians to relocate at a measured and almost unnoticeable pace of two to three families per day.[77]

AQI's vision of a purely Sunni northern belt underscored the area's operational significance. Critical lines of communications ran through this slice of rural terrain. The

Captain Good (right). Source: U.S. Army photo by Staff Sergeant Sean A. Foley (Released).

Captain Jason Good During a Patrol in Al Jabor.[76]

north-south corridor from Tarmiyah/Taji through Saab al-Bour ran just west of the Tigris into Baghdad's Kadhimiyah District. On the other side of the river, near-parallel roads from Baqubah passed through Hussainiyah and Khan Bani Sa'ad before reaching the fringes of Adhamiyah and New Baghdad, respectively. Large numbers of vehicle-borne improvised explosive devices (VBIEDs) made their way from the Sunni city of Taji into the capital, along with funding for Abu Nur's network. Ghazwan thus managed an indispensable logistical hub for AQI.[78] For its part, JAM enjoyed a safe haven in Hussainiyah, an explosively formed penetrators (EFPs) hot spot that bedeviled the coalition. The Shi'a militia's presence there became problematic for AQI as local JAM intimidation increased and Sunni extremist links to Baqubah grew in importance.[79] As in the south, fighters on both sides of the sectarian divide struggled for control of key crossroads. One distinction of the northern belt, however, was its role as a linchpin in the Sunni terrorist organization's operational infrastructure. The area connected the foreign fighters flowing into Iraq from Syria with the targets they eventually struck in Baghdad. Making their way south along the Tigris River by way of a pre-positioned facilitation network, many foreign fighters paused in Tarmiyah or Taji before making the final leg of their journey to join Abu Nur in the city. Ghazwan's grip on most of the area also enabled AQI to more easily exploit the seam at the convergence of three U.S. division sectors southeast of Lake Tharthar—another safe haven due to the absence of coalition forces.[80]

It was in this area near Taji that Sunni insurgents likely associated with Ghazwan set up deliberate ambush positions, attacking coalition helicopters traversing the busy air routes between Taji and Camp Victory or Balad and Camp Victory, shooting down several helicopters in the early months of 2007. In one engagement on February 2, 2007, insurgents hit the AH-64 Apache helicopter flown by Army Chief Warrant Officer Keith Yoakum, a pilot in the 1st Cavalry Division's aviation brigade. After flying his aircraft safely clear of the ambush zone, Yoakum returned into enemy fire to mount a counter-attack against the insurgent antiaircraft positions. He was able to strike several enemy positions with rockets before his severely damaged helicopter crashed, killing him and his copilot instantly. For his bravery, Yoakum was posthumously awarded the Distinguished Service Cross.

Odierno Changes MNC-I's Operational Concept

MNC-I leaders considered the captured AQI plans from Taji a "serendipitous gold-mine." The documents confirmed that the terrorist organization continued to adhere to Abu Musab al- Zarqawi's strategy of inciting sectarian conflict as a way to overthrow the Iraqi Government and eventually annihilate the Shi'a population. For Odierno, the Taji documents confirmed the importance of the Baghdad belts and the risks of maintaining a too-limited coalition presence in those areas. Odierno would use the refined understanding of the enemy that the documents yielded to help guide the emplacement of the surge brigades as they arrived. Surprisingly, it had become clear that AQI relied on a conventional battlefield architecture. Even terrorist organizations and guerrillas required open lines of communications to conduct resupply, maintain freedom of movement, and shift forces from one geographic area to another. They maintained support zones and rear areas and maneuvered from those places to attack zones. They had command-and-control nodes to orchestrate these movements.

Equipped with this knowledge, Odierno was determined to marshal his available forces to strike the different components of the enemy system simultaneously where he could.[81] With assistance from his staff, the MNC-I commander sketched out three different kinds of areas that U.S. and Iraqi units needed to deny the enemy in order to secure Baghdad. First came the operating zones where the militants attacking Baghdad carried out their attacks, such as Rusafa or Dora. Odierno would seek to deny AQI and its allies access to these and to deny them freedom of movement along the avenues of approach into Baghdad.

Odierno made the next priority the support zones around and beyond the city, the areas such as Adhamiyah, Taji, and the Triangle of Death where AQI and other groups gathered their combat power among local Sunni populations and staged their attacks into the operating zones. In these areas, Odierno intended to employ U.S. and Iraqi units to attack enemy command-and-control hubs, safe houses, and operatives. Finally came the sanctuaries beyond Baghdad usually in quiet, remote areas such as Lake Tharthar, untouched by the coalition or the ISF, where AQI could locate its rear logistics bases, training camps, car bomb factories, and even lodging for its fighters and their camp followers without challenge. In these areas, Odierno intended to disrupt the insurgents, forcing them to abandon their bases and making them more vulnerable to coalition raids while on the move. As the surge units arrived, Odierno and his planning team determined

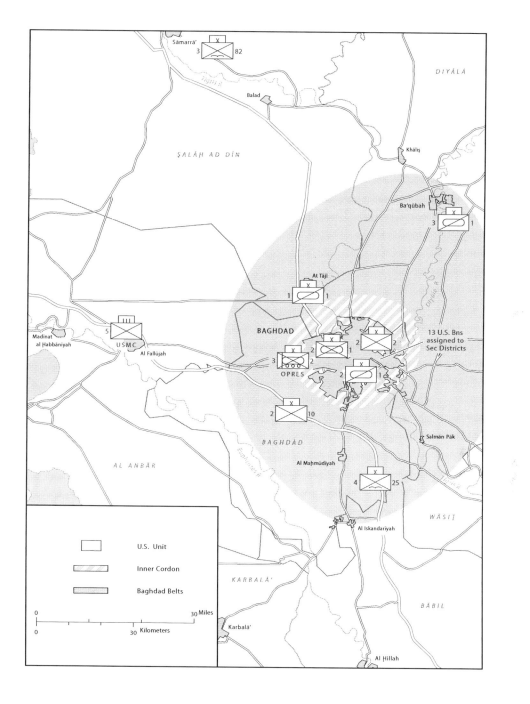

Map created by the official cartographer at the U.S. Army Center of Military History, Washington, DC.

Map 10. Disposition of U.S. Forces in Central Iraq, Early 2007.

where to place them to put simultaneous pressure on all three categories of enemy zones. Of the five surge brigades that Odierno expected to receive, two would flow into Baghdad itself. Exactly where the rest would deploy following their arrival in Kuwait had not been decided, but it was clear to Odierno that a considerable portion of their combat power would need to go into the belts rather than the city.[82] MNC-I's "main security effort" would be "Baghdad and the Baghdad belts, where identified support zones and avenues of approach are used by extremists to accelerate sectarian violence."[83] Over time, MNC-I intended to extend its operating zone, support zone, and sanctuary framework to the fight against Shi'a militants as well.

If the emphasis outside of Baghdad was on disrupting enemy support zones and sanctuaries and interdicting accelerants to violence, then inside the city it was on population control applied in mixed-sect areas in a balanced way. Along with control measures like joint security stations and concrete barriers, Odierno envisioned precision strike operations against extremist operatives and leaders. Units would provide security first, standing ready to follow up with economic development and reconstruction efforts.[84]

Odierno's operational concept signaled a change in the trajectory of the coalition presence and a delay in the coalition's assumption of a mostly supporting role. "There will be no rush to move from [secured] areas to new areas," he decreed. Likewise, "there will be no rush to transition control of security to the ISF, unless the ISF are ready and capable of success."[85] Odierno was determined not to repeat the error of Operation TOGETHER FORWARD II by handing over cleared areas to the Iraqis only to see them slip back into violence. Just as plainly, he did not believe, as Casey had, that "transition" could be used in the near term as leverage over Iraqi factions competing in a violent, high-stakes struggle.

Odierno's difference of opinion with Casey came partly from the MNC-I commander's distrust of the Iraqi Government leadership. Prime Minister Maliki had indicated his support for security operations against lawbreakers on either side of the sectarian divide, but in Odierno's judgment, "It becomes more clear everyday (sic) that [Iraqi leaders] just want us out of the way," as the MNC-I commander noted to himself in his journal. "They see us as an impediment to progress."[86] Odierno's fundamental view of the conflict crystallized during his second month in command. Like Casey, he viewed the war in Iraq as not simply a counterinsurgency, but as a complex communal struggle for power and resources. There were several distinct categories of threat throughout the country, Odierno judged, and each of these "different fights" in "different areas" would require "different approaches." The ubiquitous term "AIF" or "anti-Iraqi forces" was not sufficient to describe threats as diverse as sectarian violence, Sunni and Shi'a militias, AQI's terrorist activities, Kurdish expansionism, Shi'a infighting, malign Iranian influence, and an evolving Sunni insurgency consisting of armed groups open to reconciliation given the right conditions.[87] Putting his own stamp on it, the MNC-I commander visualized the overall problem as a "gap" between Iraqi citizens and the government whose job it was to provide their basic needs. The general's definition of near-term success would be stability, which, if sustained over time, could lead to the "ultimate goal of self-reliance" on the part of the Iraqi Government.[88] Given that the Iraqi Government itself, in Odierno's view, was a threat to stability because of its systemic and often sectarian-based corruption, as well as its lack of capacity and experience, self-reliance was far down the road.

In the meantime the coalition's primary task, as Odierno saw it, was to assist the Iraqi Government in its efforts to "fill the gap," including, whenever necessary, by direct coalition action.[89] It was an approach to addressing the problems in Iraq that would differ markedly from that of MNF-I under Casey.

THE SHI'A MILITANTS ON THE EVE OF THE SURGE

AQI and its Sunni militant allies were not the only group aiming for control of the belts around Baghdad. JAM and other Shi'a militant groups, including the Badr Corps and Asa'ib Ahl al-Haqq, had begun to expand their operations in an effort to seize Sunni towns north and south of Baghdad and control the lines of communications running into the capital. The JAM expansion in fall 2006 to Mahmudiyah, south of Baghdad, served as one of the more dramatic examples. Over the course of 90 days, JAM wrested control of the town through a campaign of targeted killings and the seizure of public services. By October, using Mahmudiyah as a springboard, JAM had begun to conduct similar operations in the nearby town of Yusufiyah.[90] MNC-I's operations to establish control of the belts would have to take the Shi'a militants into account.

During the previous summer, MNF-I had sensed the growing threat that Shi'a militias posed to coalition objectives, though Casey had resisted categorizations that portrayed them as a greater danger than AQI. Militant factions led by one-time Sadr loyalists made the landscape of the Shi'a threat even more complex. Isma'il Hafiz al-Lami, known as Abu Dura, had broken with Sadr in 2004 but still orchestrated death squad and kidnapping operations out of Sadr City, a role that led Western reporters to dub him "the Shia Zarqawi" in 2006.[91] Another former JAM leader who defied Sadr, Abu Gharawi, ran a major EFP network out of Amarah.[92] Some Badr Corps operatives were involved in the shadowy war against the coalition as well. Abu Mustafa al-Sheibani rose to prominence as an intelligence officer and front commander in the Badr Corps before supposedly falling out with the Hakims before the war. In July 2003, he received $40 million from the Iranians to organize a logistics network that would funnel weapons to Shi'a militants.[93] The elusive Sheibani drew upon his prewar experience in clandestine operations, as well as his deep pool of contacts in the Badr Corps to build a potent EFP network. He went on to finance and supply other key networks and remained a key node in the Quds Force's controlled distribution of advanced weaponry.[94]

These and other Shi'a militant networks with shared associations, shifting loyalties, and divergent political aims made for a complex battlefield. Iranian regime support was the common denominator. The major Shi'a militant networks all owed their potency — and even existence — to the Iranian regime's Quds Force and its powerful commander, Qassem Soleimani. The lethal materiel supplied through these networks entered Iraq through ports of entry along the eastern border. Key cities across the southern provinces served as waypoints for the smuggled goods as they traveled hundreds of miles over roads and "ratlines" and passed through multiple tribal areas. Amarah was a major crossroads, from which EFPs were funneled south to Basrah or north through Kut — another critical hub — and Numaniyah, Suwayrah, and eventually Baghdad. Alternatively, facilitators shipped EFPs west from Amarah to Diwaniyah and Najaf and then north through Hillah and Karbala before reaching the outskirts of the capital.[95] A separate "ratline," with the help of Kurdish contacts, began at the border town of Khanaqin and ran south through Diyala Province. Besides providing weapons, training, and periodic sanctuary, Soleimani's Quds Force paid the fighters belonging to JAM Special Groups; supplied their leaders with cars; and offered bonuses for recorded footage of successful rocket, mortar, and IED attacks on coalition forces.[96] In the short term, the Quds Force funneled EFPs to JAM-affiliated or Special Group surrogates using Badr Corps connections. It did so with a view toward the long haul, maintaining financial ties to SCIRI and other players with solid political legitimacy.[97] In short, the Iranian regime was content to fund, train, and supply all parties willing to attack the U.S.-led coalition.

Seeking multiple points to apply leverage in Iraq, the Quds Force also formed a new Shi'a militant group, Kata'ib Hizballah, in early 2007. Its leader, Abu Mahdi al-Muhandis, had the distinction of being a member of the Iraqi Parliament from the SCIRI-Badr bloc, a former Badr Corps commander, and a deputy of Qassem Soleimani. He also had been sentenced to death in absentia by a Kuwaiti court for his role in the 1983 bombings of the American and French embassies in Kuwait City. More so than even Asa'ib Ahl al-Haqq (AAH), Kata'ib Hizballah was designed as a small, disciplined, specially equipped organization of a few hundred highly trained fighters. It remained under the tight control of the Quds Force and would grow in political prominence over time to become one of the most important militant groups in Iraq.[98]

The Quds Force and its Iraqi surrogates were the primary instruments employed by the Iranian regime to wage a proxy war against the United States at minimal cost. Since 2003, the Islamic republic had pursued a regional strategy that sought to promote instability, maximize American casualties, and steadily increase its control over Iraq's Shi'a heartland while maintaining plausible deniability.[99] The politically influential Soleimani reported directly to Iran's supreme leader and oversaw a carefully organized and sustained cross-border operation. His subordinate Ramazan Corps managed the effort in Iraq, with three subcommands responsible for the northern, central, and southern sectors, respectively. Two to three regional offices operated out of each sector.[100] Hundreds of agents were involved, not least Iranian ambassador to Iraq Hassan Kazemi Ghomi, who served as an undercover Quds Force officer. The consulate in Basrah functioned as a similar hub of covert activity for Soleimani.[101]

The level of this network's activity against the coalition in Iraq appeared to have changed over time. In the early months of the war, the Iranian regime seemed to have been careful not to confront the United States, even through proxies, most likely out of fear that the United States might choose to invade Iran next. By 2005 and 2006, the Iranian calculus had apparently changed. As U.S. troops became bogged down in Iraq, the chances of an American invasion of Iran diminished, and it seems likely that Supreme Leader Ali Khamenei and his regime decided to ramp up their anti-U.S. proxy war in Iraq, confident they could so with relative impunity. It is also likely they considered the U.S. outreach to Iraqi Sunni groups in 2005-2006 to be a danger to the Iranian regime's Shi'a and Kurdish client parties. The expanded Iranian role both against U.S. forces and in support of Shi'a sectarian cleansing in central Iraq were probably intended, in part, to counter the American strategy of giving Iraqi Sunnis a greater share of state power. Whatever the motives, by the end of 2006 the Iranian regime's new level of destabilizing activity in Iraq was a threat the coalition could not ignore.

U.S. Special Operations Efforts to Counter Iranian Influence

As the special operations arm of MNC-I, the Combined Joint Special Operations Task Force-Arabian Peninsula (CJSOTF-AP) had seen convincing indicators of nefarious Iranian involvement as early as 2005. However, Casey had been skeptical at the time, concluding that a major shift in MNF-I's campaign was not justified because, in his judgment, the CJSOTF had found no "smoking gun" implicating Iran's Government.[102] MNF-I's intelligence staff had established a cell to focus on Iran in spring 2006, but it had atrophied. In summer 2006, Chiarelli had assembled undeniable evidence that the Iranian regime was responsible for the EFPs causing mounting American casualties and had pressed Casey and MNF-I to take action against the Iranian-sponsored Shi'a militant groups. In late 2006, after months of tracking the increasing strength of the Iranian-sponsored Shi'a militant groups, coalition leaders finally reorganized their forces to counter the growing threat. With EFP attacks on the rise and the quality of ordnance improving, Casey concluded that the Iranian regime had ramped up its campaign in Iraq. On November 7, 2006, he asked his intelligence officers if Iranian support to Shi'a extremists was having a strategic effect and had solicited ideas on how to disrupt Iranian activity. Given the dearth of intelligence on Quds Force agents and infrastructure in Iraq, the coalition had few actionable targets to strike right away. Casey hoped to spin up the effort quickly in the event Iran responded to Western pressure on its nuclear program by retaliating against MNF-I.[103]

Outside U.S. headquarters in Iraq, others took a fresh look at malign Iranian influence as well. Before joining Odierno's headquarters as a senior operations adviser in late 2006, Colonel James Hickey led a project at the Institute for Defense Analyses that had documented in detail the presence and activities in Iraq of the Quds Force and its proxies, including the EFP smuggling networks in the south. At about the same time, the White House gave the go-ahead for the Joint Staff and CENTCOM to develop a plan to counter Iran's destabilizing activities. Secretary of Defense (SECDEF) Donald Rumsfeld also had proposed a more aggressive stance, such as broadening the target set of the special operations task force based in Iraq. A subordinate element of the task force had been boring into Sunni terrorist and insurgent groups with devastating effect. As evidence of Iranian involvement in Iraq mounted, Casey considered applying some of that manhunting capability toward the attrition of their extremist counterparts on the Shi'a side, to include Quds Force agents operating in Iraqi territory. Discoveries inside Iraq of ordnance with 2006 Iranian factory markings reinforced Casey's thoughts on this score, as they convinced the MNF-I commander that the Iranians had become more brazen in their lethal support of Shi'a extremists.[104]

Undertaking the new mission of countering Iranian influence introduced tension between the Green Berets of the CJSOTF and the special operations task force in the country. While the high-end operators had concentrated chiefly on AQI, the U.S. Army Special Forces groups rotating in and out of Iraq during their tours as the CJSOTF had mapped out the Shi'a extremist threat. Special Forces detachments had gone after Shi'a death squads, primarily in partnership with Iraqi special operations forces, but without the far greater quantities of intelligence, surveillance, and reconnaissance assets that the high-end operators controlled. The CJSOTF's broad mission set, which included training indigenous commandos, partnering with Iraqi conventional forces, and providing human intelligence, also meant that it had wider responsibilities than simply killing or capturing militants.[105] Casey wanted MNF-I's campaign against Iranian agents and their surrogates in Iraq to assume a greater level of intensity and focus comparable to other SOF elements' war on AQI—without forsaking the institutional knowledge painstakingly gained through the CJSOTF's years of engagement with tribes and other local networks.

Casey directed the CJSOTF and the special operations task force to cooperate in creating a new subordinate command focused on Shi'a militants that clearly would be separated from the AQI mission set. Since the special operations task force initially would have to rely on the CJSOTF for many targets, as well as the troops to attack them, a cooperative command-and-control relationship was established between the two special operations commands, despite the great disparity in rank between the three-star commander of the special operations task force and CJSOTF commander Colonel Kevin McDonnell. A fusion cell in McDonnell's headquarters at Balad air base in November 2006 was the first embodiment of this focused effort to counter Iranian influence. It would grow in capability in the coming months as both Casey and the commander of the special operations task force sent intelligence specialists to work alongside the CJSOTF.[106] McDonnell thought the new attention on Shi'a extremists also would yield additional unmanned aerial vehicle support for the CJSOTF.[107] However, the special operations task force commander would be the obvious billpayer in this transaction, and he was reluctant to share if it meant reducing his task force's operational tempo against AQI. To better posture itself for countering Iranian influence, the CJSOTF planned to shift four additional U.S. Special Forces detachments to the Shi'a south to join the seven already posted across the southern provinces. Another Special Forces company headquarters also would relocate to the south, bringing the total there to two. The repositioned teams would establish a CJSOTF presence during early 2007 in cities that had long gone without coverage, including the hot spots of Diwaniyah and Amarah.[108]

The original command-and-control arrangement supporting the new Shi'a militant-focused task force did not produce the operational effectiveness that Casey had hoped. Limitations in intelligence, surveillance, and reconnaissance assets hampered the new task force's operations, as did differences in approach.[109] Reliant primarily on human intelligence, McDonnell's CJSOTF tended to conduct operations more deliberately than the special operations task force, which, by contrast, adhered to a rapid, self-sustaining cycle of raids that generated intelligence leading to attacks on subsequent targets.[110] As part of a broader coalition mission to "deny Iranian oppositional influence," MNF-I had instructed the CJSOTF to make direct action against major EFP networks its main effort. McDonnell countered that his main effort should be information operations complemented by well-planned assaults. Working "by, with, and through" indigenous forces and Shi'a tribes was crucial as well, McDonnell argued, and he advocated building popular support so that Iraqis themselves would call for constraining the Iranian regime's destabilizing influence.[111] The special operations task force was impatient with

McDonnell's holistic approach and saw the special operations role in the mission to be primarily "man-hunting."[112] Partnership, tribal engagement, and information operations lay outside its realm of highly refined expertise.

To resolve the competing views about the importance of the Shi'a extremist threat and to address the inherent inefficiencies of the cooperative command-and-control relationship between the CJSOTF and his own command, the special operations task force commander proposed that all special operations forces in Iraq be unified under one command. This change might have mitigated McDonnell's shortfalls in helicopters, surveillance assets, and detention facilities, but it also would have amounted to a hostile takeover of the CJSOTF by another special operations element with a completely different vision, and as a result, McDonnell fought the proposal. Outgunned in a bureaucratic fight with a three-star officer, McDonnell turned to Odierno for support and convinced the MNC-I commander that the corps still required control of the CJSOTF to partner with elite units of the Iraqi security forces and to maintain situational awareness through a countrywide network of contacts.[113] By persuading the MNC-I commander to intervene on the CJSOTF's behalf, McDonnell managed to block the idea of a unified special operations command and maintain his CJSOTF's independence. He also may have ended his own career. Despite his visionary role in confronting the serious but neglected threat posed by the Quds Force and its proxies, the special forces colonel ultimately was passed over for promotion, becoming one of only three wartime CJSOTF-AP commanders—out of 11—not promoted to general officer rank. Despite these disputes over SOF organization and focus, by the end of 2006 the coalition was postured for the first time to apply its potent special operations capabilities to the Shi'a militant networks operating in Iraq. The result in the months to come would be the largest confrontation between the coalition and the Shi'a militants since the battles of August 2004.

The Realignment of the Shi'a Parties and Fracturing of the Sadr Movement

As the coalition was deciding to fight a special operations war against the Shi'a militant groups and, by extension, their Quds Force sponsors, the alignment of the Iraqi Shi'a parties that had given the Sadrist militants political top cover against coalition operations for almost 2 years was changing. In fall 2006, Moqtada al-Sadr and his party continued to pursue the same basic goals they had since 2004: continuing de-Ba'athification, expanding the political and cultural influence of the Sadrist movement, and forcing a withdrawal of coalition forces from Iraq.[114] As the Sadrists and their militant followers largely had been unconstrained by the Baghdad security operations of summer and fall 2006, it had seemed to MNF-I that Sadr's political stock was rising and that the Shi'a cleric had the power to mobilize broad swathes of the Iraqi population against the coalition if he so chose.[115] The fact that Maliki, who owed his election as Prime Minister to the votes of Sadrist Parliamentarians, had intervened repeatedly to block MNF-I from conducting operations against Sadrist militants in Sadr City reinforced this idea.

Yet, when the Sadrist Parliamentary bloc walked out from Parliament on November 30 in protest against Maliki's meeting with Bush at Amman, it became clear that the Sadrists had overreached. Suspending their participation in the central government, politicians affiliated with Sadr had approached other Members of Parliament with a proposal for an alliance that would demand coalition withdrawal, while JAM units had flexed their muscles to intimidate provincial councils and Iraqi security forces across the Shi'a south.[116] These moves were a direct threat to the 6-month-old government of Maliki, and in response, Maliki and his Da'wa

Source: Photo published by Muslim Press.

Moqtada Sadr.[117]

Party allies began to change their political calculus. A few days after the Sadrist walkout from Parliament, Maliki's party struck a new agreement with Abdul Aziz al-Hakim and the Supreme Council for Islamic Revolution in Iraq, cementing a governing coalition that might be powerful enough to hobble the Sadrists' political and military position.[118] At the same time, Maliki and his Da'wa advisers began seeking ways to fracture Sadr's political front and forge alliances with Sadrist leaders disenchanted with Sadr's leadership. The prime target for Maliki's political outreach was the militant organization AAH, headed by Sadr's longtime lieutenant Qais al-Khazali, who since late 2004 had grown into a de facto challenger to Sadr's leadership within the Sadr movement.[119]

Khazali had disagreed with the political overtures that JAM made toward the Iraqi Government after the 2004 Najaf showdown, and along with fellow Sadrist militant Akram al-Kabi he had led a breakaway faction of JAM that allied itself with Iran's Quds Force. For 2 years, Khazali had remained loosely within Sadr's movement, but he had grown more independent over time.[120] As MNF-I puzzled over the array of Shi'a extremists it confronted, analysts differentiated between JAM groups that remained firmly under Sadr's control and "Special Groups" or "secret cells" led by the likes of Khazali.[121] What allowed AAH to operate separately from JAM was the support of Iran's Quds Force. While uncooperative JAM members could be isolated if they failed to "toe the line," Khazali's network maintained its own supply channels and received funding and special training from Iran. JAM had received such support since 2004 or earlier. In 2006, Iran's Quds Force reorganized its effort in Iraq and sought to develop a military organization there similar to the Lebanese Hizballah when Sadr began to appear too powerful for the Iranian regime to control. Still, mainstream JAM continued to derive much support from its vibrant Iranian connections, and Mustafa al-Yaquoubi, Sadr's most trusted adviser, continued to make trips to Iran and Lebanon.[122] As Iranian officials became more concerned about Sadr's future pliability, they sought to strengthen his potential competitors. With combat-experienced leaders, access to the same Sadrist popular base as JAM, and fighters more malleable to Iran's agenda, Khazali's faction fit the bill. By late 2006, Quds Force commander Qassem Soleimani had dispatched senior Lebanese Hizballah operative Ali

Musa Daqduq to serve as an adviser to AAH and to act as a liaison between Khazali and the Quds Force.[123]

In MNF-I's view, AAH, with its connections to the Quds Force and its significant role in the sectarian cleansing of Sunnis from Baghdad, was the most dangerous of the special groups and a prime target for the newly empowered coalition special operations task force. In Maliki's eyes, however, Khazali was an important potential political ally who could be used to reduce Sadr's political power and to co-opt some of the grassroots Sadr movement into the Da'wa Party base, thereby securing Da'wa's long-term leadership of both the Shi'a political bloc and the entire government.[124]

Source: Photo by Meghdad Madadi, Tasnim News Agency.

Qais al-Khazali.[125]

Maliki and MNF-I now approached the Iraqi Shi'a militant problem in nearly opposite ways: MNF-I tended to refer to loyal followers of Sadr as "mainstream JAM" who could be dealt with on a political level, while the special groups were "rogue JAM," irreconcilable extremists who would have to be destroyed through military operations. Maliki, meanwhile, considered Sadr and his loyalists to be political extremists who needed to be constrained, if not destroyed, for the sake of stability, and considered the special groups the more reasonable faction that could be reconciled to the government by political means.

Maliki's newfound hostility to Sadr, in time, would make it easier for the coalition to employ its new anti-JAM task force. However, these sharply different approaches toward the Sadr movement and the special groups created more than a year of tension between Maliki and MNF-I that would give way to an Iraqi Shi'a civil war in 2007 and 2008.

The Raid on SCIRI's Baghdad Compound

Within weeks, the anti-Shi'a militant task force began to have a significant impact. The first high-profile operation came in December 2006, and it swept up ostensible U.S. allies along with Shi'a militant targets. In the aftermath of the 2003 invasion, the United States had worked to build a political alliance with SCIRI and its long-time military wing, the Badr Corps, partly to counter the Sadr movement and partly to sever the two Shi'a parties from the Iranian regime, which had created them during the Iran-Iraq War. The Badr Corps had maintained its close connections to Soleimani's Quds Force after the fall of Saddam's regime and had deliberately integrated into the nascent Iraqi security forces, thus acquiring an institutional foothold that JAM lacked.[126] Because of this development, many of the confrontations between Shi'a extremists and Iraqi Army units were manifestations of an ongoing intra-Shi'a civil war. Stewing for decades, antipathy and distrust between Sadr's forebears and the Hakim family, the exiled founders of SCIRI and the Badr Corps, only exacerbated the tension. In this struggle, the United States had unabashedly taken sides with the Hakims and their allies. Recalling the affiliations of Iraqi Special Weapons and Tactics (SWAT) commanders in key southern cities, one Special Forces officer deadpanned, "We were basically partnering with the Badr Corps."[127]

A large organization, the Badr Corps enrolled many who found it hard to distance themselves from the lucrative business of arms smuggling. Nonetheless, the coalition had given Badr the benefit of the doubt. It was true that some operatives facilitated the flow of EFPs into Iraq, but MNC-I analysts rationalized that they did so against the wishes of Badr Corps commander Hadi al-Amiri and SCIRI chairman Abdul Aziz al-Hakim, both of whom U.S. analysts believed desired a stronger relationship with the United States in the near term.[128] In any case, in terms of the number of casualties it inflicted on coalition soldiers, the Badr Corps was not comparable to JAM.[129] Still, both Badr and its SCIRI affiliates had had a major hand in the bloody sectarian cleansing of 2005 and 2006, but the coalition had penalized neither.

Source: Wikimedia Commons, the free media repository by sayyed shahab-o-din vajedi.

Qassem Soleimani, Commander of the Quds Force of the Islamic Revolutionary Guard Corps of Iran.[130]

Coalition assumptions about SCIRI and Badr were shaken on December 21, 2006, when coalition commandos raided a SCIRI compound on the Karada Peninsula in central Baghdad in pursuit of Iranian military official Mohsen Chizari, head of the Quds Force operations department. Eluding capture earlier in the day, he had absconded to a safe house in a section of the compound belonging to Amiri himself. The special operations task force trailed him there and detained 10 people at the house, including Chizari and three more with connections to the Iranian Embassy. The other six were affiliated with Badr.[131]

Besides living space, the safe house contained a military operations center with maps outlining the Sunni and Shi'a areas of Baghdad and graphics identifying points in the capital apparently where key events had occurred—a visual depiction of the sectarian struggle for Baghdad and its belts that to some degree mirrored the AQI map captured in Taji just 2 days before. When he briefed Maliki on the raid, Casey suggested that the graphics marked the locations of recent (or planned) assassinations and kidnappings. The commandos also recovered computers, videotapes, notebooks, Badr order of battle information, and receipts that logged weapons shipments from Iran. It would take the coalition 14 days to process the volume of material seized.[132] The evidence confirmed the strong links that remained between Quds Force and Badr—not to mention the mutual interests both organizations had in solidifying Shi'a dominance in Iraq. When he had met with U.S. Vice Presidential adviser John Hannah in October, Amiri had denied that his organization was involved in any sectarian activities or that Iranian intelligence agents had infiltrated Badr.[133] Now, 2 months later, MNF-I had captured a high-ranking Quds

Force representative in Amiri's house mulling over Baghdad's sectarian fault lines alongside Amiri's men—some of whom were EFP facilitators.

When U.S. commandos stormed into their compound, it no doubt came as a surprise to Amiri and SCIRI leader Hakim, but it was no less surprising to the White House. Hakim had visited the White House at Bush's invitation earlier in the month, a significant milestone in the Iraqi political party's nascent strategic dialogue with the United States. When told by Abizaid on January 8 that MNF-I "found Iranians in bed with the Iraqis," Bush seemed dumbfounded. "Is SCIRI involved with Iran?" he asked. "Deeply involved," Secretary of State Condoleezza Rice replied. "So they are involved with terrorists?" Bush asked, clearly dismayed. "So I had this guy into the Oval Office who kills our troops?" "No," Rice responded, explaining that SCIRI's military wing did not kill Americans directly, but trained those who might.[134]

Back in Baghdad, the Iranians protested the detentions stridently enough to worry the Maliki administration about potential repercussions. Though not happy with the Quds Force's calculated efforts to destabilize the country, the Prime Minister refrained from taking a hard line, and President Jalal Talabani's pronouncement after the raid that two of the Iranian operatives had come to Iraq at his invitation weakened the coalition's case for holding them. It mattered little that they had crossed the border illegally, under false names. U.S. leaders were not inclined to press publicly for the prolonged detention of Hassan Chizari and his cohorts. The coalition released all four prisoners with ties to the Iranian Embassy by December 25, in time for the visit of Iran's deputy foreign minister. Though bowing to this expected pressure, Casey found satisfaction in the signal the raid sent to Iran and the irrefutable evidence it provided to Maliki regarding Iranian intentions.[135]

The Erbil Five

Three weeks after the December raid on SCIRI's compound, the coalition's anti-Shi'a militant task force crashed another meeting between Iranian agents and their U.S.-allied Iraqi hosts, this time in Kurdistan. The January 11, 2007, raid originally had targeted Brigadier General Mohammad Ali Ja'afari, suspected of guiding Quds Force activities in Iraq, and Hamid Taghavi, the Ramazan Corps operations chief, but somehow the two evaded capture. Ja'afari, incidentally, would take command of Iran's entire Islamic Revolutionary Guards Corps just 8 months after the raid.[136] Illustrating the Quds Force's pervasive hands-on involvement, Ja'afari's comrade, Mansour Taghavi, would be wounded later in 2007 during a gunfight with Iraqi security forces in Diwaniyah and would be killed in December 2014 while advising Iraqi Army units and AAH militiamen as they cleared the Sunni town of Jurf al-Sakhr.

Nonetheless, in January 2007, the special operations task force missed its primary target. U.S. special operators landed by helicopter at Talabani's guesthouse and Erbil airport and hauled away five mid-level Islamic Revolutionary Guard Corps officers. Known as the Erbil Five, they would remain in coalition custody for more than 2 years. In response to this second successful raid against its operations in Iraq, the Iranian regime shut down its Iraqi consulates for a time and instructed Iranian companies doing business in Iraq to remove their computers or to delete all files, lest American commandos capture the information they contained. The Quds Force also scaled down its operations inside the country, recalling many Quds Force officers back to Iran.[137]

The Attack on the Karbala Provincial Joint Coordination Center

Nine days after the raid in Erbil, Soleimani's Iraqi proxies struck back in an apparent attempt to capture American hostages who could be traded for the Erbil Five. Late in the day on January 20, Khazali's AAH militants launched a sophisticated raid against U.S. troops in the government center in the city of Karbala. The small, two-block compound in the middle of a busy neighborhood contained a number of buildings, including the provincial police headquarters and a barracks for the 30 U.S. Soldiers pulling week-long rotational duty there.[138] Toting M4 carbines and wearing American-style combat fatigues, about a dozen AAH fighters arrived at the front gate in a convoy of five-to-seven black sport utility vehicles, and an Iraqi guard waved them through. The vehicles converged on the multi-storied police headquarters, where U.S. advisers, military police, and Soldiers from the 4th Brigade, 25th Infantry Division, in ground-floor offices were wrapping up their daily activities. Outside the headquarters, several AAH attackers moved briskly to the entrance, where they shot and wounded two American guards before bursting into the building and unleashing a hail of grenades and small-arms fire. The operatives surprised and overwhelmed the small U.S. contingent, killing one and wounding three others inside, while seizing four more. Within 30 minutes, the raid was over, and as darkness fell, the militants made their escape with their prisoners, blowing up two High Mobility Multi-Purpose Wheeled Vehicles (HMMWVs) in the process.

Alert Iraqi policemen from nearby Babil Province picked up the trail that evening after the attackers careened through a checkpoint on their flight east toward Hillah.[139] During the pursuit, the attackers either panicked or realized the fruitlessness of evading Iraqi and coalition troops with prisoners in tow. When police found the abandoned vehicles soon after, they found discarded digital camouflage uniforms and the abducted American Soldiers, all of them shot in the chest and head execution style. Two remained handcuffed in the rear of one vehicle while another lay dead on the ground. The fourth—barely alive when the Iraqis recovered him—died of his wounds within the hour.[140]

Source: U.S. Army photo by Staff Sergeant Sean A. Foley (Released).

Soldiers from 1st Squadron, 40th Cavalry Regiment, During Patrols in Search of Insurgents in Adwania.[141]

The brazen raid provoked a vigorous response from the coalition but also sent a chill up and down the chain of command. MND-B had dispatched Apache helicopters to the scene, but they arrived too late to break up the attack and prevent the abduction. The division also mobilized its quick reaction force, sending two companies of Strykers south to help track down the perpetrators once the Iraqi police recovered the remains of the missing Soldiers.[142]

Although it ended quickly, the AAH raid prompted some reflection by U.S. commanders. For a division about to ramp up its forward presence in Baghdad through the construction of dozens of joint security stations and combat outposts, the episode in Karbala provided a sober reminder of the risks involved.[143] Occurring as it did in one of the outlying provinces, the attack also suggested to some coalition officers that MND-B might be overstretched. In the emerging debate over possibly reassigning Baghdad's southern belts to another division headquarters, the assault on the Karbala provincial joint control center underscored the arguments of those who favored reducing MND-B's span of control.[144]

The attack bore the marks of an inside job, carried out with the complicity of the Karbala police. The intruders had detailed information about the compound's security measures, including where and when the unsuspecting Americans likely could be taken. As the gunfire erupted, the Iraqi garrison was absent or inactive, and those officers walking the upstairs halls of the headquarters building or working at their desks showed no interest in organizing a defense. U.S. military policemen racing room to room in search of their comrades swept past Iraqis engaged in hushed conversations. To American troops on rotational duty at the Provincial Joint Coordination Center (PJCC), the incident seemed to cap a period of veiled threats and a nagging feeling of insecurity and distrust of their supposed Iraqi partners.[145] The peculiarities of the day made sense in retrospect: the scarcity of local residents that normally did business in the compound, the early closing of the barbershop and market, and the arrival of a delegation of 15 to 20 "policemen" from Baghdad who had met with local Iraqi commanders ostensibly to plan security for the Ashura celebration. Some had taken pictures of restricted areas. A few had lingered into the evening. A report later concluded they were an advanced team for the attackers.[146]

Within 3 days, six suspects were in custody, and the coalition quickly determined that the perpetrators were AAH members.[147] Not only did the shadowy group's suspected past operations—including the assassination of Lieutenant General Amer Hashimi in October 2006 and the Ministry of Higher Education kidnappings in November—resemble the Karbala attack, but a cell phone belonging to Laith Khazali, the younger brother of AAH's leader, had been active in the local area.[148] The perpetrators made amateurish mistakes during the raid, from grievously wounding their intended captives to leaving behind multiple undetonated explosive devices, suggesting that experienced Quds Force cadre had not participated directly. However, MNF-I saw strong indicators of a Quds Force hand in training AAH and preparing its fighters for the difficult mission.[149] Coalition officers later would discover the existence in Iran of a mock facility, apparently modeled on the Karbala provincial headquarters compound that the Quds Force had likely used to train AAH operatives for the operation.[150]

MNC-I initially explored the theory that the raid stemmed from the Sadrists' desire "to save face" amid mounting pressure and to reassert JAM's dominance in Karbala.

However, given the attack's timing and the tenuous relationship between Khazali and Sadr, the command judged the operation was far more likely an attempt to acquire hostages to trade for the Erbil Five.[151] It was also an escalation in the Iraq-based shadow war between the United States and the Iranian regime.

The Sadrists and the Baghdad Security Plan

The same day that Khazali's operatives were killing U.S. Soldiers at the Karbala PJCC, MNF-I was negotiating with Prime Minister Maliki over the coalition's aggressive new posture against Shi'a militia leaders under the auspices of the Baghdad Security Plan. The day before, January 19, MNF-I had detained the well-known Sadrist cleric and notorious JAM operative Abdul Hadi al-Daraji at his compound just south of Sadr City. Those affiliated with Sadr labeled the detention as a disastrous and foreboding blow.[152]

MNF-I had carried out the Daraji raid with the understanding that, as part of his political battle with the Sadrists, Maliki had loosened restrictions on the coalition's targeting of Shi'a militants in Baghdad. On January 20, the day after the raid, Casey reported to Bush that he noted a marked difference in the Prime Minister's stance. Throughout the fall, Maliki had been "quite agitated" whenever MNF-I conducted operations near Sadr City and often had intervened to secure the release of Sadr allies. Over the intervening months, Casey reported, the situation had eased, allowing MNF-I to target Shi'a militia leaders "without a peep" from the Prime Minister. "We have no present restrictions on Sadr City operations," he declared, adding that this change had diminished senior JAM leaders' boldness and reduced Shi'a death squad activity by 35 percent over the previous 5 weeks.[153] It was perhaps a premature assessment considering that MNF-I already had decided to defer operations against Sadr City and other Shi'a militant strongholds in the capital.

It also was premature where Maliki was concerned. The Prime Minister expressed surprise and irritation over Daraji's detention, thinking the Sadrist cleric had been granted immunity from arrest by the Iraqi interim government in 2004. Despite Maliki's competition with Sadr, his administration was not yet on the same page as the coalition, and his representatives immediately sought to use Daraji's capture by dangling the prospect of the cleric's release in exchange for the Sadrists' return to Maliki's cabinet. Hoping to cut its losses and wrest some guarantees of protection from the New Year's Offensive, Sadr's party announced its intention to return to the government on January 21. Casey protested, however, pointing out that Daraji had links to sectarian violence that more than justified his prolonged detention. The issue escalated into the political realm quickly, and Bush himself directed the MNF-I commander to keep the JAM leader in custody. Mentioning the prisoner to Casey by name, the President viewed his arrest as a test of Maliki's commitment to evenhandedness. In spite of the political discomfort of having to forego his potential deal with the Sadrists, the Prime Minister yielded to the coalition in this case.[154] The exchange showed that just days after the U.S. Government had extracted commitments from Maliki to take action against the Sadrist militants, it would be a challenge to keep the Prime Minister on board.

The Daraji arrest and other coalition operations in January 2007 appeared to put the Sadrists off-balance. Sensing that their top cover had evaporated in the aftermath of the surge announcement, many Shi'a militia commanders hunkered down and adopted a "wait-and-see" approach.[155] Many of those who believed they had made a name for themselves feared capture and fled Baghdad.[156] Confirming this trend, reports reached MNF-I in late January that the Iranian Embassy had issued some 200 special passports to Shi'a militia members. Sadr himself secretly departed for Iran around this time.[157] The flight of the Sadrist leaders within days of the surge announcement illustrated that the psychological effects of the surge would be as important as its physical effects, both in cowing the coalition's enemies and in emboldening its partners. The same effect applied to Abu Mahdi al-Muhandis, who reportedly fled to Iran at the end of January.[158]

Hoping to lower JAM's profile as it braced for more frequent and intense coalition and Iraqi attacks, Sadr called for his militia to stand down following the kickoff of the revised Baghdad Security Plan. Mainstream JAM units generally obeyed. Many leaders that spurned Sadr's instructions did so not for strategic or ideological reasons but to sustain their lucrative criminal enterprises. Groups of loyal fighters formed. The Najaf-based "Golden JAM" and Baghdad's "Noble JAM," as they called themselves, attempted to persuade rogue elements to comply with Sadr's wishes or purged them altogether, showing that the Shi'a militants were fighting one another even as they postured to fight the coalition.[159]

The Battle Against the Soldiers of Heaven

Far from Baghdad, another confrontation took place on the eve of the surge that highlighted the complexity of the Shi'a militant problem. Iraqi and coalition troops found themselves in a strange battle against a Shi'a militia with no ties to the Sadr movement or any other Shi'a extremist faction known to the coalition. Early on the morning of January 28, 2007, 10 miles north of Najaf, Iraqi security forces became embroiled in an unexpected gunfight. The first coalition unit on the scene—a U.S. Special Forces detachment from Najaf—arrived to find dozens of police and troops from the 1st Brigade, 8th Iraqi Army Division, locked in combat with a dug-in, battalion-sized foe reportedly equipped with heavy machine guns, mortars, and rocket-propelled grenades. As the fighting intensified, the enemy's identity and how the battle began remained a mystery to the Americans. Under fire themselves, the Green Berets called for close-air support as reinforcements consisting of Iraqi special operations forces and U.S. advisers from nearby Hillah made their way to the sound of the guns. Multiple strafing and bombing runs from F-16 Falcon jets and A-10 Thunderbolts failed to suppress the enemy position. Rocket fire brought down one AH-64 Apache helicopter that had arrived to help, killing the two pilots when it fell from the sky into no-man's-land between the opposing sides. A U.S. Army transition team returning to the coalition base in Diwaniyah after training with its Iraqi battalion attempted to secure the crash site, but gunfire kept the American Soldiers pinned down. The precarious situation stabilized only when two U.S. Stryker companies arrived at dusk, along with another Iraqi Army company.[160] Taking control of the operation that evening, the Strykers bombarded the enemy position through the night and launched an assault shortly after dawn as the militants began to surrender en masse. The battle ended in a lopsided victory for U.S. and Iraqi troops, with reports of up to 400 militants killed and another 400 people detained.[161]

The coalition soon discovered that the mysterious armed group was a cult-like organization called the Soldiers of Heaven, which had established a commune of sorts on a compound outside Najaf. There, the group's militant members lived with their families, many of whom were detained by the Iraqi troops that overran the compound as the battle ended. Holding a peculiar view of Shi'a Islam, the Soldiers of Heaven believed that the Twelfth or Hidden Imam—who had reputedly disappeared in the 9th century—was on the verge of returning. Their leader, Dhia Abdul Zahra Kadhim, killed in the January 28 fighting, seems to have convinced his followers that he was a reincarnation of the Imam Ali.

No definitive explanation of the origin of the January 28, 2007, battle has ever come to light. Despite its extreme beliefs, the group had displayed no previous violent activity. In the days after the fighting, controversy swirled as details emerged about the group's intentions and the Iraqi Government's motivations surrounding the incident. According to Iraqi Government spokesmen, the Soldiers of Heaven had hoped to hasten the day of the Hidden Imam's return by carrying out a bloody assassination campaign targeting Grand Ayatollah Ali Sistani and other Shi'a leaders in Najaf and occupying the Imam Ali Mosque. While some accounts reported that Iraqi security forces had stumbled into an ambush, others indicated that the troops instigated the conflict but soon found they had kicked over a hornet's nest.[162] Official explanations further clouded the matter. Asad Abu Ghalal, the Islamic Supreme Council of Iraq (ISCI) governor of Najaf, tarred the Soldiers of Heaven as Sunni extremists who had foreign fighters among their ranks. A day later, Major General Qais Hamza al-Mamouri, Babil Province's chief of police, attempted a clarification, describing the group's leader as a Sunni militant masquerading as a co-religionist of his exclusively Shi'a followers. The confusion lingered, with some Iraqi officials speculating about ties to al-Qaeda, while others alleged Iranian connections.[163] One analyst argued that the fighting was a political vendetta against a tribe that locally opposed the Islamic Supreme Council in Iraq and Maliki's Da'wa Party.[164] Related to this was another assertion that Maliki had intended to teach the Sadrists a lesson by confronting a weaker fringe group, thus signaling his readiness to crack down on defiant Shi'a militias, but the operation had met greater resistance than anticipated and had required coalition intervention.

U.S. troops had hastened to answer Iraqi calls for assistance, committing ground, air, and special operations forces with scarcely a thought toward the battle's origins or underlying purpose. Having passed control of security in Najaf province to Iraqi civil authorities in mid-December 2006, MND-B commander Fil naturally highlighted the coalition's military reaction and how it had shored up an unraveling situation. Units had learned about exercising command and control "on the move," Fil observed, as well as valuable lessons on leveraging the operational reach of Stryker formations and marshaling resources for rapid response.[165] Portrayed as a model of how to support contingencies in provinces under Iraqi control, the operation had lacked a logic that connected it to the coalition's broader campaign. Though it was a large battle by Iraq War standards, the government had kept its plans secret until security forces required help. Then, the Americans stepped in and rescued them without knowing who the enemy was, decisively intervening in what may have been an intra-Shi'a political or religious rivalry disguised as a battle against extremists.[166]

Though on Iraq's political and social fringe, the Soldiers of Heaven had maintained offices across the southern provinces. Just as they did not suddenly emerge on the eve of the January 28 battle, neither did they disappear in its wake. Nearly a month later, a joint U.S. and Iraqi force captured over 180 Soldiers of Heaven in a raid in western Qadisiyah Province.[167] Other operations against them would arise in 2008 as well. The sudden appearance of this little-known cultish group showed coalition leaders that stabilizing southern Iraq would likely take more energy and troops than they had expected.

The Zamili Arrest

Barely a week after the battle in Najaf and 3 weeks after the arrest of Daraji, another arrest of a high-profile Sadrist leader suggested there would be some bite to the coalition's bark against the Shi'a militant groups. On February 9, U.S. Special Forces advisers and Iraqi commandos infiltrated the Ministry of Health compound in downtown Baghdad and arrested Hakim Zamili, the Sadrist politician who served as a Deputy Minister of Health. Since 2005, Zamili—a militia commander who purportedly maintained a personal security detail of over 100 men—had masterminded a campaign of terror against Sunni citizens. Under his instructions, government ambulances doubled as troop and weapons carriers for Shi'a death squads, and hospitals became killing grounds for sick or injured Sunni patients. Zamili also was implicated in the November 2006 kidnapping and murder of Ammar Saffar, the other Deputy Minister of Health and Maliki's Dawa Party colleague. Saffar had been compiling a list of the ministry's JAM-sponsored atrocities with the intention of revealing the crimes publicly before gunmen abducted him from his home and eventually murdered him. Seeing Zamili as a mounting liability, Maliki decided to cut ties with the odious health official and authorized MNF-I to detain him so long as it occurred outside of Sadr City. The operation to seize Zamili involved the Iraqi commandos disguising themselves as wounded personnel requiring medical assistance. In this way, they penetrated the outer ring of Zamili's militiamen guarding the compound and captured their quarry without firing a shot.[168]

Source: Photo by Public Relations Department, Ministry of Defence Republic of Serbia.

Hakim Zamili, Iraqi Deputy Minister of Health.[169]

Removing this prominent symbol of corruption and sectarianism from the government sent a powerful signal that the impending surge would involve action against not just Shi'a militant leaders on Baghdad's streets, but potentially against well-connected Shi'a militant politicians. For Casey, evidence pointing to the deep connections between disreputable Iranian actors and their Iraqi partners also suggested something about the difficulties ahead. In one of his last engagements before he departed Iraq in February, the MNF-I commander visited Vice President Adel Abd al-Mehdi and warned him that SCIRI's associations with sectarian thugs threatened the future of his country. Casey had a similar message for Hadi al-Amiri after the Badr Corps chief attended the general's farewell reception: It was time to choose Iraq over Iran and the militias. To Talabani, the MNF-I commander pointedly asked how it was possible for the Iraqi President to thank the United States for the blood and treasure it had expended while maintaining a cordial relationship with Soleimani, whose responsibility for the deaths of American Soldiers now was beyond doubt.[170] By February 2007, the question Casey had put to his staff 4 months before had been answered. The strategic effect of Iranian influence indeed was substantial, if not decisive, with the Quds Force-managed proxy war against MNF-I serving as the clearest indicator.

THE NORTHERN IRAQ CONFLICT BEFORE THE SURGE

With the coalition's focus drawn to Baghdad throughout 2006, the fight in northern Iraq, like that in Basrah and the south, had remained an economy of force operation. Casey's decision to move the Strykers of Colonel Townsend's 3d Brigade, 2d Infantry Division, south from Mosul confirmed the growing centripetal force of the deteriorating state of security in the capital. The Stryker brigade's departure from Mosul in late November left only one U.S. combined-arms battalion from 4th Brigade, 1st Cavalry Division, in a dense, urban area of nearly 2 million people—replicating the situation before the city's collapse in 2004.[171] Mosul itself was a divided city in physical, demographic, and military terms. The Tigris River bisected it, and Sunni Arab and Kurdish enclaves dominated the western and eastern halves, respectively. Mosul similarly was split between the jurisdictions of two Iraqi Army brigades, with a predominantly Sunni Arab unit operating in the west and a former peshmerga unit in the east. The city lay along a fault line where Kurdish expansionism abutted long-time Sunni Arab and Sunni Turkoman interests. Resettling the Mosul area following the collapse of Saddam's regime, the Kurds had secured a strong political position with the help of the Sunni boycott of the 2005 elections and had dominated Ninawa's provincial government ever since. Exacerbating the sense of Sunni disenfranchisement, aggressive peshmerga units routinely crossed the Green Line that marked the western boundary of the Kurdistan Regional Government to establish checkpoints to control the movement of the local population and stake out broader Kurdish territorial claims.[172]

This Arab-Kurd struggle—and a related struggle between Kurds and Sunni Turkomans—provided an opening for AQI and other Sunni insurgents as they moved to solidify their hold on critical terrain. While Baghdad was the prize AQI sought to win, Iraqi Sunni leaders judged that the terrorist group needed Mosul to survive.[173] The city was a crossroads connecting northern Iraq with Syria through the Sinjar-Tel Afar corridor—the same corridor in which Casey had placed the 3d Armored Cavalry Regiment to disrupt foreign-fighter flow in the summer of 2005. Mosul proved relatively hospitable to al-Qaeda in Iraq not only because of its Sunni Arab population's resentment of Kurdish encroachment, but also because it boasted a sizable number of former army officers and Ba'athist officials who opposed the Shi'a-dominated government in Baghdad.[174] Groups like Izzat Ibrahim al-Douri's New Ba'ath Party that sought to expel the coalition and infiltrate Iraq's nascent security apparatus found a relative safe haven in and around Mosul and in the Za'ab Triangle to the south.[175] On the day of Saddam's execution, Douri's militant loyalists in these areas publicly announced the formation of the "Naqshbandi Army," which would function as the militant arm of Douri's wing of the Ba'ath Party. Their heartland was an operationally significant rural area where the only major road between Anbar Province and the upper Tigris River Valley emerged from the southern reaches of the Jazeera Desert to intersect with the Hamrin Ridge running northwest from central Diyala. This combination of factors made it difficult to dislodge AQI, the Naqshbandis, and other militants from Mosul and its environs.

MND-N's Complex Problem Set

Mosul was just one of a host of problems that Mixon's 25th Infantry Division headquarters was responsible for managing. As MND-N commander, Mixon supported the main effort in Baghdad principally by attempting to interdict accelerants of violence emanating from Baqubah and the capital's northern belt.[176] This approach translated into the standard tasks of neutralizing VBIED networks and death squads and denying them safe havens. MND-N's area of responsibility extended from the outskirts of Baghdad north to Turkey and along an east-west axis from the Iranian to the Syrian border, an expansive area whose widely scattered population centers precluded a concentration of ground forces and rapid mutual support between Mixon's units.

General Mixon (right), Governor Duraid Kashmoula (left).
Source: U.S. Army photo by Major Roderick Cunningham (Released).

Major General Benjamin Mixon, Commander MND-N, With Ninawa Provincial Governor Duraid Kashmoula.[177]

In early 2007, Mixon dispersed his four BCTs across the four provinces of Diyala, Salahadin, Kirkuk, and Ninawa, which together formed an area the size of Indiana. Each province held unique problems that added to the dizzying complexity of MND-N's mission. In the far north, the division's complications included the presence of the Kurdistan Workers Party (PKK), an organization that had conducted a 2-decade insurgency against the Turkish Government from bases deep in the mountains of northern Iraqi Kurdistan. The PKK's terrorist attacks inside Turkey sometimes provoked a response from the Turks in the form of limited cross-border operations.[178] Iraq's northern oil fields around Kirkuk and the refinery at Bayji also came within Mixon's purview, saddling him with the unenviable job of assisting the Iraqi Government with improving its oil infrastructure and disrupting smuggling networks that partially bankrolled the insurgency. Given the influx of foreign fighters, the arduous task of border interdiction on the Syrian frontier stretched MND-N's forces even further. Adding to this list of tasks, MNC-I directed the division to neutralize AQI in key cities along the northern Tigris River Valley and to disrupt insurgent activity in the Za'ab Triangle.[179] In the vast territory under Mixon's charge, few areas were unimportant.

MND-N may not have benefited directly from the surge of the first few U.S. brigade combat teams to central Iraq, but the arrival of these forces in Baghdad halted the bone-scraping diversion of coalition combat power from the division's area of operations. Mixon managed the risks posed by a vast, undermanned and trouble-strewn sector in part by leveraging his combat aviation brigade and a recently formed IED-hunting aerial surveillance unit called Task Force ODIN. With these, he organized airmobile platoon and company-sized strike packages targeting insurgent leaders across his area of operations.[180] Given Diyala's connection to the northern belt and the fight in Baghdad, Mixon designated the province and its capital of Baqubah as MND-N's priority effort, and when additional forces began to arrive during spring 2007, Mixon would deploy them there.[181] The BCT stationed in Ninawa thus found itself in the doubly uninviting position of serving as the economy of force element within a division that was itself the corps economy of force.

"Hold Mosul"

Colonel Stephen M. Twitty, the commander of the 4th Brigade, 1st Cavalry Division, understood that MNC-I's primary focus in early 2007 was on reducing the violence in Baghdad, a fact that Odierno made clear in a visit to Mosul. "I know you need more forces," he told Twitty. "But I can't give them to you. . . . Just hold Mosul for us, and don't let it fall. That is your mission."[182] With that guidance, the BCT commander chose to keep his strongest battalion posted at Forward Operating Base Marez on the edge of the city and used these troops to staff combat outposts within the city alongside two Iraqi Army brigades. With his remaining forces, Twitty covered the Syrian border and Tel Afar to the west, and Qayyarah to the south. Twitty's thinly stretched units in Mosul faced the same problems that had emerged during Operation TOGETHER FORWARD in Baghdad. Clearing operations in a specific area temporarily lowered levels of violence, but attacks rose again after the limited surge of U.S. and Iraqi troops moved on to other zones. Twitty could hold Mosul, but the ebb and flow of security developments was such that he could not consolidate his gains with the available forces. The reassignment of three local Iraqi Army battalions to Baghdad as part of the Baghdad Security Plan only lessened his chances of doing so.[183]

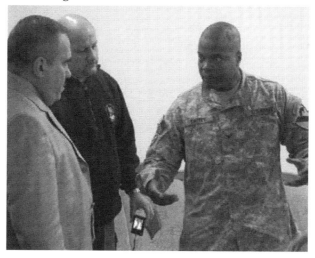

Colonel Twitty (right) with Major General Wathiq al- Hamdani (left).
Source: U.S. Army photo by Major Roderick Cunningham (Released).

Colonel Stephen Twitty, Commander, 4th BCT, 1st Cavalry Division, With Ninawa Provincial Director of Police Major General Wathiq al-Hamdani.[184]

The U.S. commanders in the north judged that the intensifying pressure on the enemy in Baghdad could have a related and undesirable impact elsewhere, as had been the case when the Sunni insurgency responded to the coalition's November 2004 attack in Fallujah with devastating coordinated attacks in Mosul.[185] Local politics did not help. Aggressive peshmerga behavior along with brazen exhibitions of Kurdish nationalism resembled the violent and intimidating activities carried out by some Shi'a-dominated military units in and around Baghdad. Heavily Kurdish outfits lacked legitimacy in the eyes of Mosul's Sunni Arab citizens—often for good reason, and the practice of employing them in Sunni Arab areas constituted a risk to be managed carefully.[186]

Nevertheless, while Casey and Chiarelli's transition bridging strategy had been jettisoned as a corps-wide approach to accelerated transition, Mixon still believed that conditions in MND-N warranted using augmented transition teams to develop the Iraqi security forces in areas where the coalition lacked sufficient combat power to partner with Iraqi units. The continuing improvement of the 2d and 3d Iraqi Army Divisions in Ninawa made the downside of this contentious allocation of manpower more palatable. Both divisions had passed from coalition control to the Iraqi Ground Forces Command by December 2006, just as Twitty's brigade had arrived.[187] In Ninawa, Mixon decided to attach a maneuver squad to the 12-man military transition teams paired with each Iraqi Army battalion and, similarly, one maneuver company covered the brigade of Iraqi border troops posted along the Syrian frontier.[188] For Twitty, this translated into having an entire squadron devoted to training and advising security forces throughout the province.[189]

A crucial part of holding Mosul in early 2007 involved managing the tense relations between local army units and the city's police force. The police in Ninawa's provincial capital were almost exclusively Sunni Arab, making their cooperation with the Kurdish-majority brigade of the 2d Iraqi Army Division difficult. Instances of violence between Iraqi soldiers and police occurred frequently enough for them to be a major concern to Twitty and other U.S. commanders.[190] "That was my biggest worry," Twitty recalled. "If I lost the police and the army, I only had one [U.S.] battalion in Mosul."[191] The dearth of troops meant the coalition was in a precarious situation in a province that would prove to be the most important insurgent stronghold in Iraq. Mosul and the north would pose a thorny problem whether the impending surge operations pacified Baghdad or not.

***

On the eve of the surge counteroffensive in January 2007, U.S. commanders had managed in a matter of weeks to reinitiate a campaign to secure Baghdad. However, the events occurring during the 2 months between Bush's December 2006 decision to deploy the surge troops and the eventual arrival of Petraeus in February deepened senior U.S. leaders' distrust of Prime Minister Maliki and his government. This left them questioning whether an Iraqi Government riven by sectarianism had the will and ability both to attack AQI and rein in Baghdad's Shi'a militant groups.

Yet even before the surge troops began to arrive, the dynamics of the conflict in central Iraq started to change as the warring parties anticipated the additional American troops. Clear signs emerged of what was to come in the remainder of 2007. The coalition's fight against AQI would shift from the streets of Baghdad to the rural areas and suburbs surrounding the city, where AQI had long enjoyed support zones on the edge of the capital. War between the coalition and the Iranian regime's Shi'a militant proxies, relatively quiet since the Sadrist uprising of August 2004, again intensified. War between the Maliki government and the militant arm of the Sadr movement appeared imminent as well, leading to a new alignment of Iraq's Shi'a political parties. Tension grew between MNF-I and the Maliki government over how best to address the Shi'a militant threat, with the two sides appearing to adopt diametrically opposing strategies. There was tension within the coalition command as well, as Odierno began to anticipate the surge and to reverse the transition campaign plan his commander, Casey, had created. Finally, as the coalition commanders gathered U.S. and Iraqi combat power for another Baghdad security plan, the northern Iraq security problem and the Arab-Kurd conflict continued to fester, with neither the coalition nor the Iraqi Government possessing the means to resolve either issue. These were the challenges Petraeus would inherit when he took command of MNF-I in early February 2007.

ENDNOTES - CHAPTER 2

1. Interview, Chief of Staff of the Army (CSA) Operation IRAQI FREEDOM (OIF) Study Group with John D. Gardner, January 14, 2014. All unpublished documents in this chapter, unless otherwise stated, are in the Chief of Staff of the Army (CSA) Operation IRAQI FREEDOM (OIF) Study Group archives, Army Heritage and Education Center (AHEC), Carlisle, PA.

2. John F. Burns, "In Days Before Hanging, a Push for Revenge and a Push Back from the U.S.," *The New York Times*, January 7, 2007.

3. Interview, CSA OIF Study Group with John D. Gardner, January 14, 2014.

4. Anne Penketh, "Guards Taunted Saddam in Final Seconds," *Independent* (United Kingdom [UK]), December 31, 2006.

5. Ibid., pp. 310-311.

6. E-mail, Ambassador Michael Gfoeller to Colonel Joel Rayburn, CSA OIF Study Group, November 12, 2015.

7. Transcript, Republic of Iraq, Premiership Media Office, Iraqi Army Day speech, January 6, 2007.

8. Lieutenant General Raymond T. Odierno, Iraq notebook No. 2, entries for December 30, 2006 and January 2-4, 2007.

9. George W. Casey, Jr., *Strategic Reflections: Operation Iraqi Freedom, July 2004–February 2007*, Washington, DC: National Defense University Press, 2012, pp. 131-132.

10. E-mail, Major General David A. Fastabend to General George W. Casey, Jr., December 20, 2006; quote from Casey, *Strategic Reflections*, p. 132.

11. Staff Notes, MNF-I, December 17-19, 2006. All Staff Notes in this chapter, unless otherwise stated, are in the CSA OIF Study Group archives, AHEC, Carlisle, PA.

12. Staff Notes, MNF-I, December 20, 2006.

13. Odierno Iraq Notebook No. 2, December 29, 2006, entry.

14. In addition to Iraqi Ground Forces Command Commander General Ali Ghaidan, the Iraqi officers whom Casey offered for Prime Minister Nuri al-Maliki's consideration were Lieutenant General Abdul Razaq Yacoob Yousef, director of Joint Headquarters, and Major General Ali Farhood Othman, commander of the 8th Iraqi Army Division. Letter, Casey to Maliki, January 7, 2007.

15. DoD photo by Sergeant David Hodge, "Leaders break new ground in Baghdad [Image 3 of 3]," DVIDS Identifier 100622, July 5, 2008, Released to Public, available from *https://www.dvidshub.net/image/100622/leaders-break-new-ground-baghdad*.

16. E-mail, Robert B. Newman to Casey, January 9, 2007.

17. E-mail, Fastabend to Casey, January 9, 2007.

18. Committee to Plan and Prepare Baghdad Security Plan, Recommendations for Baghdad and surrounding areas Security Plan, n.d., p. 4.

19. Staff Notes, MNF-I, December 22, 2006.

20. E-mail, Fastabend to Casey, December 20, 2006.

21. E-mail, Major General Joseph F. Fil to Frank Hull, December 20, 2006.

22. E-mail, Fastabend to Casey, December 20, 2006.

23. U.S. Army photo by Lieutenant Colonel Scott Bleichwehl, "MND-B commanding general visits Rusafa market [Image 1 of 2]," DVIDS Identifier 37182, March 1, 2007, Released to Public, available from *https://www.dvidshub.net/image/37182/mnd-b-commanding-general-visits-rusafa-market*.

24. PowerPoint Briefing, Multi-National Division-Baghdad (MND-B), Baghdad Security Update and Options, November 24, 2006, slide 9.

25. Ibid., slide 21; PowerPoint Briefing, MND-B, Baghdad Security Update: Information Brief, November 26, 2006, slide 26.

26. PowerPoint Briefing, MND-B, Baghdad Security Update and Options, November 24, 2006, slide 25. For quote, see MND-B, Baghdad Security Update: Information Brief, November 26, 2006, slide 26.

27. Staff Notes, MNF-I, December 22, 2006; Odierno Iraq Notebook No. 2, December 19, 2006, entry; Briefing, MND-B, Security and Offensive Operations in Baghdad—Concept for Clear, Control, and Retain, December 24, 2006.

28. Interviews, Steven Clay, Combat Studies Institute (CSI) Contemporary Operations Study Team, with Colonel Stephen J. Townsend, Part I, January 23, 2008; and Part II, January 24, 2008.

29. MND-B, Security and Offensive Operations in Baghdad, December 24, 2006; MND-B, Operation Order (OPORD) 07-02 (Pegasus Security Forever), December 25, 2006.

30. See the "tiered system" outlined in PowerPoint Briefing, MND-B, Security and Offensive Operations in Baghdad, December 24, 2006, slide 11.

31. An. C, app. 19 (Joint Security Stations), MND-B, OPORD 07-02 (Pegasus Security Forever), December 29, 2006, pp. 1-2.

32. MND-B, OPORD 07-02, December 25, 2006, pp. 10-11.

33. PowerPoint Briefing, MND-B, Baghdad Security Update: Information Brief, November 26, 2006, slides 10-12; MND-B, Security and Offensive Operations in Baghdad, December 24, 2006.

34. MND-B, Breaking the Cycle of Sectarian Violence, December 17, 2006; Odierno Iraq Notebook No. 2, December 26, 2006, entry.

35. DoD photo by United States Forces Iraq, "Dodge the Wash," January 1, 2007, Released to Public, available from *https://www.flickr.com/photos/mnfiraq/4313756175/in/faves-138659840%40N02/*.

36. E-mails, Casey to General Peter Pace and General John P. Abizaid, December 7, 2006, sub: Additional Feedback, Temp no. 25; Fastabend to Casey, December 7, 2006, sub: Commanding General's Questions, Temp no. 76.

37. E-mail, Casey to Pace and Abizaid, December 7, 2006.

38. MND-B, Breaking the Cycle of Sectarian Violence, December 17, 2006; Major James Powell, Iraq Notebook No. 1, December 13, 2006, entry; Staff Notes, MNF-I, December 18, 2006; Staff Notes, MNF-I, December 19, 2006.

39. Briefing, MNC-I, Setting Conditions for Offensive Operations in Baghdad, December 21 Surge Operations, December 17, 2006.

40. Interview, CSI Contemporary Operations Study Team with Colonel Townsend, Part II, January 24, 2008.

41. U.S. Army photo by Sergeant Lance Wail, "Brigades Working together for Baghdad's future [Image 1 of 4]," DVIDS Identifier 40171, March 27, 2007, Released to Public, available from *https://www.dvidshub.net/image/40171/brigades-working-together-baghdads-future*.

42. Interview, CSI Contemporary Operations Study Team with Townsend, Part I, January 23, 2008; and Part II, January 24, 2008.

43. Ibid., Part II, January 24, 2008. See also MNF-I Battle Update Assessments (BUA), December 25, 2006, slide 45; MNF-I BUA, January 1, 2007, slides 44-45; MNF-I BUA, January 8, 2007, slides 46-47; MNF-I BUA, January 9, 2007, slide 44; and MNF-I BUA, January 15, 2007, slides 46-47.

44. Interview, Steven Clay, CSI Contemporary Operations Study Team, with Colonel Bryan T. Roberts, February 22, 2010.

45. Wesley Morgan, "Task Force Warhorse: Classical Counterinsurgency on Haifa Street," *Long War Journal*, August 9, 2007, available from *http://www.longwarjournal.org/archives/2007/08/task_force_warhorse.php*.

46. Michael Hastings, "Iraq: The Battle for Haifa Street," *Newsweek*, January 11, 2007.

47. Odierno Iraq Notebook No. 2, December 16, 2006, entry.

48. DoD photo by Staff Sergeant Lorie Jewell, "Haifa Street in Baghdad," January 2007 est., Released to Public.

49. Kimberly Kagan, *The Surge: A Military History,* New York: Encounter Books, 2009, p. 22.

50. Interview, Steven Clay, CSI Contemporary Operations Study Team, with Colonel Avanulus Smiley, February 25, 2010.

51. Ibid.; Kagan, *The Surge*, p. 23; MNF-I BUA, January 10, 2007.

52. MNF-I BUA, January 8, 2007, p. 47.

53. Interview, Clay, CSI Contemporary Operations Study Team, with Smiley, February 25, 2010; Kagan, *The Surge*, pp. 23-24.

54. Morgan, "Task Force Warhorse."

55. Interview, Clay, CSI Contemporary Operations Study Team, with Smiley, February 25, 2010.

56. MNF-I BUA, January 10, 2007.

57. Hastings, "Iraq: Battle for Haifa Street."

58. MNC-I, Fragmentary Order (FRAGO) 179, pp. 5-6.

59. Ibid., pp. 2, 4, 5, and 7.

60. Interview, CSA OIF Study Group with Ross Coffey, May 8, 2014.

61. Interview, William Epley, U.S. Army Center of Military History, with Major General Benjamin R. Mixon, June 18, 2007.

62. Kagan, *The Surge*, p. 17.

63. Staff Notes, MNF-I, December 2006.

64. E-mail, Fastabend to Casey, December 20, 2006.

65. Briefing, MNC-I, Intelligence Fusion Brief, February 7, 2007.

66. Quote from Briefing, MNC-I, Intelligence Fusion Brief, February 7, 2007.

67. Briefing, MNC-I, Intelligence Fusion Brief, January 31, 2007; Briefing, MNC-I, Intelligence Fusion Brief, February 7, 2007.

68. Briefing, MNC-I, "Intelligence Fusion Brief," February 7, 2007.

69. This map was among the documents captured from AQI operatives in Taji, see the blog by Brian T. Hart, "Battle of the Baghdad Belt, 2006," Minstrel Boy, June 22, 2014, available from *http://minstrelboy. blogspot.com/2014_06_22_archive.html.*

70. Briefing, MNC-I, Intelligence Fusion Brief, February 7, 2007; Briefing, MNC-I, Intelligence Fusion Brief, February 14, 2007.

71. Briefing, MNC-I, Intelligence Fusion Brief, February 7, 2007; Briefing, MNC-I, Intelligence Fusion Brief, February 21, 2007.

72. Interview, Steven Clay, CSI Contemporary Operations Study Team, with General Michael X. Garrett, November 12, 2009.

73. Interview, CSI Contemporary Operations Study Team with Col. Townsend, Part I, January 23, 2008.

74. Michael Kershaw, "Lessons Learned—First 90 Days," November 29, 2006, CSA OIF Study Group Special Collection.

75. Briefing, MNC-I, Intelligence Fusion Brief, February 7, 2007.

76. U.S. Army photo by Staff Sergeant Sean A. Foley, "In the Weeds," December 19, 2006, Released to Public, available from *https://www.flickr.com/photos/mnfiraq/4314478358/in/faves-138659840%40N02/.*

77. Briefing, MNC-I, Intelligence Fusion Brief, February 7, 2007; Briefing, MNC-I, Intelligence Fusion Brief, February 14, 2007.

78. Briefing, MNC-I, Intelligence Fusion Brief, February 7, 2007.

79. Ibid., January 31, 2007.

80. Ibid., February 7, 2007.

81. Interview, Steven Clay, CSI Contemporary Operations Study Team, with Colonel James B. Hickey, Part I, February 23, 2010.

82. Briefing, MNC-I, Operation TOGETHER FORWARD: Brigade Combat Team (BCT) Employment Options, January 29, 2007.

83. MNC-I, Coalition Campaign Operational Concept: Secure and Transition, n.d., p. 15.

84. Ibid., pp. 15-16.

85. Ibid., p. 15.

86. Odierno Iraq Notebook no. 4, February 5, 2007, entry.

87. MNC-I, Coalition Campaign Operational Concept: Secure and Transition, n.d., pp. 2- 6.

88. Emma Sky, *The Unraveling: High Hopes and Missed Opportunities in Iraq*, New York: Public Affairs, 2015, Kindle edition, p. 154; MNC-I, Coalition Campaign Operational Concept: Secure and Transition, n.d., pp. 8-9.

89. MNC-I, Coalition Campaign Operational Concept: Secure and Transition, n.d., pp. 1- 2; Sky, *The Unraveling*, p. 154.

90. MNC-I, *The Perfect Storm*, October 22, 2006, pp. 4-6.

91. MNC-I, Coalition Campaign Operational Concept: Secure and Transition, n.d., p. 16.

92. Briefing, MNC-I, Intelligence Fusion Brief, December 13, 2006.

93. Briefing, MNC-I, Jaysh al-Mahdi (JAM) Special Groups Assessment, Counter-IED Operational Integration Center, July 1, 2007.

94. Paper, C2 Corps Analysis and Control Element (CACE), MNC-I, "Badr Organization: Explosively Formed Penetrators (EFP) Facilitators?" August 8, 2007, p. 1; Marisa Cochrane, "Iraq Report 12: The Fragmentation of the Sadrist Movement," Washington, DC: Institute for the Study of War, January 2009, pp. 20-21.

95. PowerPoint Briefing, Combined Joint Special Operations Task Force-Arabian Peninsula (CJSOTF-AP), overview to Lieutenant General Raymond T. Odierno, January 11, 2007.

96. MNC-I, JAM Special Groups Assessment, July 1, 2007.

97. Paper, C2 Corps Analysis and Control Element (CACE), MNC-I, "Badr Organization: EFP Facilitators?" August 8, 2007, p. 3.

98. Michael Knights, "The Evolution of Iran's Special Groups in Iraq," West Point, NY: Combating Terrorism Center, November 1, 2010, pp. 12-16.

99. Ibid.; Briefing, CJSOTF-AP, overview to Odierno, January 11, 2007.

100. Briefing, MNC-I, JAM Special Groups Assessment, July 1, 2007.

101. Bill Roggio, "General Petraeus: Iran's Ambassador to Iraq 'is a Qods Force Member,'" Small Wars Journal, October 7, 2007; Joel Rayburn, *Iraq After America: Strongmen, Sectarians, Resistance,* Stanford, CA: Hoover Institution Press, 2014, p. 34.

102. Interview, Colonel Frank Sobchak, CSA OIF Study Group, with Colonel Kevin McDonnell, February 10, 2014.

103. Casey, *Strategic Reflections*, pp. 116-117; Staff Notes, MNF-I, January 7, 2007.

104. Staff Notes, MNF-I, November 28, 2006.

105. Interview, Colonel Frank Sobchak, CSA OIF Study Group, with Colonel Mark Mitchell, Special Operations Command CENTCOM (SOCCENT) Joint Planning Group, March 10, 2014.

106. Interview, Colonel Sobchak, CSA OIF Study Group, with Colonel McDonnell, December 1, 2014; Staff Notes, MNF-I, December 19, 2006.

107. Interview, Colonel Sobchak, CSA OIF Study Group, with Colonel Mitchell, March 10, 2014.

108. PowerPoint Briefing, CJSOTF-AP, overview to Odierno, January 11, 2007, slides 22-25.

109. Interview, Colonel Sobchak, CSA OIF Study Group, with Colonel McDonnell, December 1, 2014.

110. Interview, Colonel Sobchak, CSA OIF Study Group, with Colonel Mitchell, March 10, 2014.

111. Quote from CJSOTF-AP, overview for Odierno, January 11, 2007.

112. Interview, Colonel Sobchak, CSA OIF Study Group, with Colonel Mitchell, March 10, 2014.

113. Interview, Colonel Sobchak, CSA OIF Study Group, with Colonel McDonnell, December 1, 2014.

114. Briefing, MNC-I, Intelligence Fusion Brief, January 17, 2007.

115. MNF-I, October Threat Laydown, November 4, 2006.

116. MNF-I BUA, November 30, 2006; MNF-I BUA, December 1, 2006.

117. Photo published by Muslim Press, "Iraqi Shi'ite cleric Moqtada al-Sadr," in "Influential Shi'ite cleric Sadr says Americans should leave Iraq," MuslimPress.com, January 30, 2017, No. 107285, available from *http://www.muslimpress.com/Section-world-news-16/107285-influential-shi-ite-cleric-sadr-says-americans-should-leave-iraq.*

118. Cochrane, "Iraq Report 12: Fragmentation of the Sadrist Movement," p. 22.

119. Briefing, MNC-I, Jaysh al-Mahdi Monthly Update, April 1, 2007.

120. Ibid.; Cochrane, "Iraq Report 12: Fragmentation of the Sadrist Movement," p. 15.

121. Briefing, MNC-I, Intelligence Fusion Brief: K2/JAM Network Update, March 31, 2007; Paper, Coalition Intelligence Operations Center, MNF-I, Summary of Debriefings of Qays Khazali and Associates, Part I, April 8, 2007, p. 1.

122. Briefing, MNC-I, Intelligence Fusion Brief, December 13, 2006.

123. Cochrane, "Iraq Report 12: Fragmentation of the Sadrist Movement," pp. 18-19.

124. Rayburn, *Iraq After America*, pp. 188-189.

125. Photo by Meghdad Madadi, Tasnim News Agency, "Qais Khazali At the Closing of the Worldwide Conference on Lovers of Ahl al-Bayt and the Takfiris issue in Tehran- November 2017," November 23, 2017, modified (cropped), available from *https://newsmedia.tasnimnews.com/Tasnim/Uploaded/Image/1396/09/02/13960902193726558125877784.jpg.*

126. Paper, C2 Corps Analysis and Control Element (CACE), MNC-I, "Badr Organization: EFP Facilitators?" August 8, 2007, p. 2.

127. Interview, Colonel Frank Sobchak, CSA OIF Study Group, with Brigadier General Sean Swindell, Commanding General (CG) Special Operations Task Force-Central, August 27, 2014.

128. Paper, C2 Corps Analysis and Control Element (CACE), MNC-I, "Badr Organization: EFP Facilitators?" August 8, 2007, pp. 2-3.

129. Interview, CSA OIF Study Group with Lieutenant General David H. Petraeus, November 26, 2014.

130. Wikimedia Commons, the free media repository by sayyed shahab-o-din vajedi, "Qasem Soleimani- commander of Quds Force of Army of the Guardians of the Islamic Revolution (IRGC)," n.d., available from *https://commons.wikimedia.org/wiki/File:Sardar_Qasem_Soleimani-01.jpg.*

131. Staff Notes, MNF-I, December 24, 2006.

132. Ibid.; Odierno Iraq Notebook no. 2, December 21, 2006, entry.

133. Paper, Sandy Cochran and Captain Kelly Howard, MNF-I Chronology Reference, November 12, 2008, p. 338.

134. Notes from National Security Council VTC, January 8, 2007.

135. Staff Notes, MNF-I, December 24, 2006.

136. Ja'afari would hold this position for at least 7 years, well into 2015.

137. MNF-I BUA, January 21, 2007.

138. Gordon Cucullu and Chris Fontana, *Warrior Police: Rolling with America's Military Police in the World's Trouble Spots*, New York: St. Martin's Press, 2011, pp. 169-170, 174.

139. Ibid., pp. 183-184.

140. Cucullu and Fontana, *Warrior Police*, p. 185; Paper, C2 Corps Analysis and Control Element (CACE), MNC-I, "Attack on Karbala PJCC," January 21, 2007, p. 3.

141. U.S. Army photo by Staff Sergeant Sean A. Foley, "Roadside Courtesy," January 1, 2007, Released to Public, available from *https://www.flickr.com/photos/mnfiraq/4313755581/in/faves-138659840%40N02/*.

142. Interview, Steven Clay, CSI Contemporary Operations Study Team, with Colonel Townsend, Part II, January 24, 2008.

143. Interview, Major Glenn Garcia, Center for Military History (CMH) with Major General Joseph Fil, Commanding General (CG) MND-B, August 28, 2007.

144. Interview, CSA OIF Study Group with Lieutenant Colonel Charles Armstrong, March 20, 2014.

145. Cucullu and Fontana, *Warrior Police*, pp. 170-173, 175-176.

146. Ibid., pp. 185-386; Paper, C2 Corps Analysis and Control Element (CACE), MNC-I, "Attack on Karbala PJCC," January 21, 2007, p. 3.

147. Staff Notes, MNF-I, January 23, 2007.

148. Ibid.

149. Paper, C2 Corps Analysis and Control Element (CACE), MNC-I, "Attack on Karbala PJCC," January 21, 2007, pp. 2-3.

150. "U.S. General: Iraqi Militants Trained in Iran," CNN, May 25, 2007, available from *http://www.cnn.com/2007/WORLD/meast/05/25/iraq.iran/*.

151. Paper, C2 Corps Analysis and Control Element (CACE), MNC-I, "Attack on Karbala PJCC," January 21, 2007, p. 4.

152. MNF-I BUA, January 21, 2007.

153. Briefing, MNF-I, Maliki Role in ROE, in Meeting with the President, January 20, 2007.

154. Ibid.; MNF-I BUA, January 22, 2007.

155. MNF-I, Deputy Chief of Staff for Intelligence (DCSINT) Monthly Threat Update, January 7, 2007.

156. MNC-I, Weekly JAM Executive Summary, February 9-16, 2007.

157. MNF-I BUA, January 23, 2007; MNF-I BUA, January 29, 2007; MNF-I BUA, February 15, 2007.

158. James Glanz and Marc Santoro, "Iraqi Lawmaker Was Convicted in 1983 Bombings in Kuwait That Killed 5," *The New York Times*, February 7, 2007.

159. Cochrane, "Iraq Report 12: Fragmentation of the Sadrist Movement," pp. 21-26.

160. MNF-I BUA, January 29, 2007, slide 44; Interview, CSI Contemporary Operations Study Team with Garrett, November 12, 2009, p. 12; Dale Andrade, *Surging South of Baghdad: The 3d Infantry Division and Task Force Marne in Iraq, 2007-2008*, Washington, DC: U.S. Army Center of Military History, 2010, p. 68.

161. Interview, Clay, CSI Contemporary Operations Study Team, with Townsend, Part II, January 24, 2008, pp. 22-23; Louise Roug and Saad Fakhrildeen, "Religious Cult Targeted in Fierce Battle near Najaf," *Los Angeles Times*, January 30, 2007.

162. Roug and Fakhrildeen, "Fierce Battle near Najaf."

163. Damien Cave, "Mystery Arises over Identity of Militia Chief in Najaf Fight," *The New York Times*, February 1, 2007.

164. Dahr Jamail and Ali al-Fadhily, "Iran 'Fooling' U.S. Military," Inter Press Service News Agency, February 11, 2007.

165. Interview, Major Garcia, CMH with Major General Fil, August 28, 2007, p. 48.

166. Visser, "When to Confront the Mahdis."

167. MNF-I, Secretary of Defense (SECDEF) Weekly Update, February 24-March 2, 2007.

168. Interview, Sobchak, CSA OIF Study Group, with McDonnell, February 10, 2014; Odierno Iraq Notebook no. 4, February 6, 2007, entry.

169. Photo by Public Relations Department, Ministry of Defence Republic of Serbia, "Minister Gasic talks with President of the Committee for Defence and Security in Iraq," February 24, 2015, modified (cropped), available from *http://www.mod.gov.rs/eng/7871/ministar-gasic-razgovarao-sa-predsednikom-odbora-za-odbranu-i-bezbednost-iraka-7871*.

170. Staff Notes, MNF-I, February 6, 2007.

171. Eric Hamilton, "The Fight for Mosul, March 2003-March 2008," Washington, DC: Institute for the Study of War, n.d., p. 9.

172. Hamilton, "The Fight for Mosul," pp. 3-4; Interview, Steven Clay, CSI Contemporary Operations Study Team, with Brigadier General Stephen M. Twitty, January 8, 2010, pp. 4-6.

173. Interview, Colonel Joel Rayburn, CSA OIF Study Group, with Major General Najim Jabouri, November 12, 2014.

174. Interview, Steven Clay, CSI Contemporary Operations Study Team, with Major General Benjamin R. Mixon, March 9, 2010, p. 7; Hamilton, "The Fight for Mosul," pp. 4-5.

175. MNC-I, Intelligence Fusion Brief, January 10, 2007, slides 7-8.

176. MNC-I, FRAGO 179, p. 17.

177. U.S. Army photo by Major Roderick Cunningham, "Ninewa Province Viewed as Shining Star of Iraq [Image 1 of 2]," DVIDS Identifier 35049, January 11, 2007, Released to Public, available from *https:// www.dvidshub.net/image/35049/ninewa-province-viewed-shining-star-iraq.*

178. MNF-I, SECDEF Weekly Update, April 7-13, 2007; Interview, Contemporary Operations Study Team with Mixon, March 9, 2010, p. 4; Peter R. Mansoor, *Surge: My Journey with General David Petraeus and the Remaking of the Iraq War*, New Haven, CT: Yale University Press, 2013, p. 220.

179. MNC-I, FRAGO 179, p. 17; Interview, Contemporary Operations Study Team with Mixon, pp. 6-7, 10.

180. Report, Task Force Lightening, 25th Infantry Division, September 13, 2006-October 28, 2007, p. 3; Interview, Steven Clay, CSI Contemporary Operations Study Team, with Lieutenant General Mixon, March 9, 2010, pp. 11-12, 19.

181. MNC-I, FRAGO 179, p. 5.

182. Interview, Clay, CSI Contemporary Operations Study Team, with Twitty, p. 5.

183. Ibid., pp. 4-9.

184. U.S. Army photo by Major Roderick Cunningham, "Ninewa Province Viewed as Shining Star of Iraq [Image 2 of 2]," DVIDS Identifier 35048, January 11, 2001, Released to Public, available from *https:// www.dvidshub.net/image/35048/ninewa-province-viewed-shining-star-iraq.*

185. Interview, Clay, CSI Contemporary Operations Study Team, with Townsend, Part II, pp. 2, 4.

186. Ibid., p. 8; Interview, Clay, CSI Contemporary Operations Study Team, with Twitty, pp. 6-7, 13.

187. Report, Task Force LIGHTNING, 25th Infantry Division, September 13, 2006-October 28, 2007, p. 4.

188. MNC-I, Transition Bridging Strategy, December 11, 2006, slide 31; MNF-I, Commander's Conference, February 17, 2007, see slide titled "MND-N Transition Teams."

189. Stephen Twitty, DoD News Briefing, July 27, 2007; Hamilton, "The Fight for Mosul," p. 9.

190. MNF-I, SECDEF Weekly Update, April 21-27, 2007.

191. Interview, Clay, CSI Contemporary Operations Study Team, with Twitty, pp. 6, 13.

CHAPTER 3

THE NEW WAY FORWARD, FEBRUARY 2007-APRIL 2007

In a televised address to the nation on January 10, 2007, President George W. Bush announced his decision to change the U.S. strategy in Iraq. Speaking from the Oval Office, Bush outlined a plan "to help the Iraqis carry out their campaign to put down sectarian violence and bring security to the people of Baghdad." The President explained the plan in unusual detail, to include the new Iraqi command-and-control structure in the capital and the intent behind joint security stations (JSSs). In the past, Iraqi and U.S. force levels proved insufficient to hold "cleared" neighborhoods, he said. This was a primary reason for recent failures, along with unwarranted restrictions on coalition operations against terrorists and insurgents. Explaining how these shortcomings would be addressed, Bush cited Nuri al-Maliki's supportive public comments and revealed his own decision to commit roughly 20,000 additional American troops to Iraq. Besides the 5 brigade combat teams (BCTs) slated to deploy in and around Baghdad, the President mentioned the imminent arrival of another 4,000 Marines in Anbar. While security was the "most urgent priority for success," the plan contained elements covering political, economic, and diplomatic concerns. During his address, the President referred to a "new approach" or a "change" in strategy over a half-dozen times.

A new commander would implement the revised strategy. General David H. Petraeus would take command of Multi-National Forces-Iraq (MNF-I) from General George Casey, Jr., in early February, ending Casey's nearly 3-year tenure in Baghdad. Within days of his arrival in Iraq, Petraeus would reverse the course of the MNF-I campaign plan, sending American troops off their bases and back into Baghdad's neighborhoods to conduct operations against both al-Qaeda in Iraq and the Shi'a militant groups. The days of the transition strategy were over.[1]

PETRAEUS TAKES COMMAND

"Hard is Not Hopeless"

The White House consulted with then-Lieutenant General Petraeus during its fall 2006 Iraq strategy review, and his name had been floated as a potential replacement for Casey in December by Army Chief of Staff General Peter Schoomaker, former Vice Chief General Jack Keane, and Casey himself.[2] Schoomaker had recommended Petraeus to Secretary of Defense (SECDEF) Donald Rumsfeld as a potential successor to Casey as early as fall 2005, when Petraeus had given up command of Multi-National Security Transition Command-Iraq (MNSTC-I) to oversee the Army schools at Fort Leavenworth, KS, with the charter to revise the service's counterinsurgency doctrine in light of the Iraq campaign.[3] Schoomaker also had informed Petraeus at that time that he was the most likely candidate to succeed Casey at MNF-I, a consideration that lent more urgency to Petraeus's work. Other senior officers, including Lieutenant General Peter Chiarelli, had been mentioned as potential new MNF-I commanders, but by the time the President visited the Joint Chiefs of Staff (JCS) in mid-December to issue his guidance to deploy the surge brigades, Petraeus had become the leading candidate. In early January, the President nominated Petraeus for the post. The general enjoyed broad support in Congress and popularity in the media; and the administration looked for him to assume command in Iraq as soon as possible.

Petraeus's two previous tours in Iraq had helped to frame his basic sense of what the coalition's future course should be, and his recent assignment overseeing the development of the Army's new counterinsurgency manual, Field Manual 3-24, provided a doctrinal foundation on which to proceed. The key principle of the new manual—that of population security—was noticeable in Petraeus's January 23 confirmation hearing before the Senate Armed Services Committee, where Petraeus's remarks amounted to a point-by-point repudiation of the transition strategy. "The mission of Multinational Force Iraq will be modified, making security of the population, particularly in Baghdad, and in partnership with Iraqi forces, the focus of the military effort," he told the committee, adding that to secure Baghdad's neighborhoods, "a persistent presence in these neighborhoods will be essential." This change away from a focus on transitioning to Iraqi control was necessary, he explained, because "The escalation of violence in 2006 undermined the coalition strategy and raised the prospect of a failed Iraqi state." Like many of the committee members, Petraeus said he believed the long-term solution to Iraq's problems required more than security, but it was "exceedingly difficult for the Iraqi government to come to grips with the toughest issues it must resolve while survival is the primary concern of so many in Iraq's capital."[4] This fact made a renewed emphasis on "military action to improve security" necessary.

The surge forces would require significant time to flow to Iraq and gain enough understanding of the situation to operate effectively, Petraeus cautioned, taking care to preempt calls to limit explicitly the duration of the surge or to assess its progress too early. "None of this will be rapid," Petraeus said, adding that MNF-I would face "a determined, adaptable, barbaric, enemy . . . [that] will try to wait us out." Perhaps mindful of criticism that Casey had stuck too long with a failing transition strategy, Petraeus assured the senators that "should I determine that the new strategy cannot succeed, I will provide such an assessment." He finished his presentation by cautioning against defeatism, offering, "The way ahead will be very hard . . . But hard is not hopeless."[5]

The President's decision to change commanders in Baghdad prompted a change of commanders at U.S. Central Command (CENTCOM) as well. Like Casey, General John Abizaid recommended against the U.S. troop surge and was skeptical that the addition of five brigades would have a lasting impact on Iraq's security situation. However, Abizaid and other U.S. leaders recognized that a significantly changing strategy would require different commanders in both Baghdad and Tampa, FL. Abizaid had already served at CENTCOM for 3½ years, an unusually long tenure, and was scheduled to retire in April, so moving up his transition was relatively easy. To replace Abizaid and serve as Petraeus's immediate superior, SECDEF Robert M. Gates and JCS Chairman General Peter Pace recommended that Bush select Admiral William J. "Fox" Fallon, then serving as the commander of U.S. Pacific Command (USPACOM).

CENTCOM would be Fallon's fourth post as a four-star admiral, making him the most senior four-star commander in the U.S. military. Petraeus would be the most junior. At 62 years old, Fallon had more than 4 decades of experience in the U.S. Navy and also carried the endorsement of now-retired General Keane, who had worked closely with Fallon in the Pentagon when the two men were vice chiefs of their respective services. Keane believed Fallon's experience as a military diplomat in the Pacific region had equipped him to fill the role of a CENTCOM commander who could engage Middle Eastern leaders across the region to try to mitigate outside intervention in the Iraq conflict.[6] He also believed Fallon would be content to let Petraeus set the U.S. course inside Iraq without interference from CENTCOM, but this was a belief that Fallon soon would dispel.

The Departure of General Casey

Casey tried to put his best foot forward as he entered the home stretch of his prolonged Iraq tour. However, the transition period was far from smooth. Since the summer of 2006, the MNF-I commander had struggled to explain the crux of his approach to the Bush administration—how the United States had to drawdown its forces, transition tasks to the Iraqi security forces (ISF), and get out of Baghdad's neighborhoods in order to win. He had persisted in this line of argument through the exhaustive external strategy review. Surprised and puzzled on occasion as the White House adjusted its Iraq policy, the general believed, in retrospect, that Bush had settled on the surge largely to buy time and build domestic support rather than to achieve success on the ground.[7]

As the administration put its final touches on the "new way forward," Casey found himself again addressing what he considered misperceptions of the approach he had championed for years. In support of the President's January 10 speech, for example, the White House sought to highlight how the revised strategy differed from the preceding one. A list of "key operational shifts" noted that MNF-I's previous security focus had been on transition, while the way ahead would be chiefly characterized by protecting the population.[8] During a meeting with Secretary of State Condoleezza Rice, Gates, Pace, and Stephen J. Hadley, the MNF-I commander protested what he viewed as an incomplete and simplistic depiction of his approach. Casey insisted the coalition had been conducting a counterinsurgency campaign throughout his tenure, adding that he understood the central focus of counterinsurgency as securing the people. He resented the insinuation that MNF-I had neglected it during his watch.[9] The statesman-like Gates cautioned his colleagues against the inclination to set Casey and Abizaid on one side and the "White House, Office of the Secretary of Defense (OSD), and the new people" on the other. "We need to make it seem as if we are all on the same side," Gates advised.[10] This would become increasingly difficult as the MNF-I change of command loomed.

Despite the clear decision in Washington to change course, those at MNF-I watching the President's speech believed they still detected support for the transition bridging strategy. The White House had emphasized protecting the population and identified this as a deviation from the MNF-I campaign plan.[11] However, Bush also mentioned embedding more American advisers and described the training of Iraqi forces as "the essential U.S. security mission in Iraq." The President also announced a doubling of the number of provincial reconstruction teams, a step meant to help "speed the transition to Iraqi self-reliance."[12] The supporting information briefings by the National Security Council (NSC) staff labeled the way ahead as Iraqi-led.[13] Extending these points, Casey claimed at a press conference a few days later that the new plan would "[allow] us to sustain the agreement in Amman . . . to accelerate development of the ISF and the passage of security responsibility." He also described the flow of additional forces as flexible with the ability to "evaluate progress as we went," even though nearly all senior U.S. policymakers by that point had decided that all five surge brigades would deploy.[14]

Back in Baghdad, the process of transition from Casey to Petraeus began uneasily and remained so throughout. Knowing that in his Senate confirmation hearing he would be asked for his opinion on the size of the surge, Petraeus thought it prudent to consult General Raymond Odierno, the operational commander on the ground. Over the phone from Iraq, the Multi-National Corps-Iraq (MNC-I) commander told Petraeus he needed all five brigades, a judgment that matched Petraeus's own.[15] Casey, however, considered the incoming commander's probing as improper meddling and barred Petraeus from communicating directly with MNF-I's subordinate units until after the change of command.[16]

In the brief, one-on-one time the two commanders shared during this rushed transition, Casey observed to his successor, "What we're seeing here is a major shift in strategy from [the Iraqis] doing it to us doing it."[17] Fully aware that Petraeus favored a reversal of his initiative encouraging more Iraqi-led operations, Casey worried about how American troops would adapt to what would effectively be a change of mission. "Whatever you do, whatever you decide, just be clear about it," Casey urged, "because it's a major change."[18] It was indeed, Petraeus agreed, and he was determined to be very clear about it.[19]

The New Commander's Intent

Petraeus took command of MNF-I on February 10 in a ceremony presided over by Abizaid. His introductory letter to the troops issued on that day emphasized security as the foremost task, one that the coalition would achieve in partnership with the Iraqis. Petraeus noted it would require living and fighting alongside those partners. Though the incoming commander echoed the central tenet of his predecessor ("In the end, Iraqis will decide the outcome of this struggle"), not a word was mentioned of transition.[20] The immediate concern was to "gain the time" the Iraqis needed to "save their country."[21]

General Petraeus (second from left), General Casey (right).
Source: U.S. Army photo by Specialist Laura M. Bigenho (Released).

General David Petraeus Takes Command of MNF-I From General George Casey.[22]

Meeting with his subordinate leaders at Al Faw Palace immediately following the change of command ceremony, Petraeus stated that the high level of violence in Iraq had invalidated the current strategy and that a "modification of priorities" was required. Transition remained important, he said, but security had to be recognized as a "prerequisite for the way ahead."[23] Commanders should look for opportunities to put Iraqi security forces in the lead, Petraeus said, "But if we don't get a grip on the violence, then it doesn't matter who is in charge."[24]

As for improving security, Petraeus stressed that how commanders employed the additional surge forces would matter more than sheer numbers. Operationally speaking, the five additional BCTs would be dispatched to help secure Baghdad and interdict accelerants to violence in the surrounding belts, and thus reduce overall violence in the capital. Petraeus considered violence against the population to be the "key metric," and said that tamping it down would be a months-long venture requiring an offensive mindset throughout the process. At the tactical level, adopting a forward presence would be critical, and Petraeus endorsed the construction of JSSs and combat outposts—an effort he would seek to accelerate considerably over time.[25] The first of these had achieved initial operating capability in Ghazaliyah, and there would ultimately be another 76 stood up in Baghdad alone during the surge.[26] However, the new commander branded the JSS concept with his own guidance. Casey originally envisioned JSSs as a mechanism to help Baghdad's police assume control of the city as coalition forces withdrew over time. Each station would serve as a base of operations in a given neighborhood and coordinate patrols. However, Petraeus saw JSSs and combat outposts as a means to ramp up coalition presence on the streets of the capital, and he made clear that he expected each U.S. battalion to locate its command post within the battalion's area of operations, not on distant forward operating bases. The only way to secure the people was to live among them, Petraeus said.[27]

In making clear that coalition commanders had responsibility for bringing violence under control in their areas of operations, Petraeus was not dismissing the importance of cultivating relationships with the Iraqis. He urged leaders to "embrace Iraqi units" and encouraged the rekindling of partnerships with local security forces, a change that would involve BCT commanders more deeply in the daily affairs of Iraqi units with which they shared battle space.[28] Petraeus considered transition teams an important part of this equation, but he intended to attach them formally to the BCTs partnered with the Iraqi formations they advised, thereby making BCT commanders responsible for the development of the security forces in their sectors. Over time, he aimed to work with the Army to deploy the transition teams simultaneously with the BCTs in whose areas of operations they would operate.[29]

Unity of effort extended to relations between the coalition and the Government of Iraq as well. Here, Petraeus, like Casey, signaled his preference to work with the Prime Minister rather than lobby Washington to seek an alternative. "Maliki is our guy," he told his subordinate commanders.[30] Petraeus saw his job—along with Ambassador Zalmay Khalilzad—as facilitating reconciliation and helping the Prime Minister's government improve its capacity. Believing reconciliation to be "key in the long run," the general hoped to draw Maliki to the center by driving a wedge between him and the Sadrists and thus make the government's tribal outreach to Sunnis more credible.[31]

As he sat in the palace luncheon, Odierno jotted down the guidance he heard. The new MNF-I commander, he noted, was not interested in plans for the consolidation of headquarters or schemes related to the so-called BRAC-for-Iraq in which the coalition closed down facilities.[32] After months of disagreements between MNF-I and MNC-I on the way ahead, it appeared the new MNF-I commander and his principal subordinate were at last on the same page.

The Race against Time

As he set about his work in his first weeks in command, Petraeus described MNF-I's mission as "an enormous race against time," and the general intended to do what he could to buy more of it.[33] Petraeus saw the two most concerning security threats as Sunni car-bomb cells and Shi'a death squads. It would be a tough slog against both, and he wanted audiences in Baghdad and Washington to know this. With just one of the five surge BCTs operating in Baghdad and a second on the ground preparing for action, Petraeus emphasized that the coalition counteroffensive would take months to develop. Looking ahead to the arrival of more brigades in March, April, and May, he explained to Gates, "It's much too early to tell how long we'll need to maintain the additional forces."[34] He had an idea, though. The MNF-I commander reassured Odierno of his intent to sustain the surge at 20 BCTs through December 2007.[35]

In the meantime, units in Baghdad continued what they had begun with Operation FARDH AL-QANOON: clearing neighborhoods and establishing a permanent presence in JSSs. This approach, Petraeus believed, "is helping convince Iraqi citizens that we will stick it out with them rather than moving to the next hot-spot."[36] Yet it would take more than forward presence to protect the population in the capital. "We will not be able to reduce substantially the VBIEDs [vehicle borne improvised explosive devices] until we get the final brigades on the ground and can go after the bomb factories that we believe are located in the 'belts' around Baghdad," Petraeus warned.[37]

Well before Petraeus assumed command of MNF-I, he had understood the pressing need to reduce sectarian violence in Baghdad. After falling slightly from December to mid-January, the number of observed incidents of ethno-sectarian violence in the capital leveled off at 150 for over 2 weeks before spiking again to 183 the first week of February. Unsurprisingly, most of the violence had occurred along Sunni-Shi'a fault lines in western Baghdad and across the river in the Sunni enclave of Adhamiyah.[38] Apart from the statistics, the general's impressions after a firsthand look at the bleak conditions in Ghazaliyah and Dora were much worse than he had anticipated. AQI's need for support zones from which to launch attacks inside the city had led to the group's takeover of Sunni areas. The Shi'a militias' campaign of sectarian cleansing further terrorized these besieged Sunni pockets, while pervasive violent crime, like kidnapping, made conditions for families unlivable.

As he traveled around the city in his first days in command, Petraeus was struck at how far conditions had deteriorated since his departure from MNSTC-I 17 months before, though he noted a few bright spots. To Petraeus, Prime Minister Maliki seemed committed to improving security along evenhanded, nonsectarian lines, though he was clearly under heavy Shi'a political pressure. Indeed, Maliki recently had announced to the Iraqi security forces that impending operations in Baghdad would "target anyone and everyone who violates the law" and that "no one can hide behind any political party."[39] After weeks of coordinating with the Iraqis, Multi-National Division-Baghdad (MND-B) had begun to position some of its units in JSSs across the capital. In preparation for the kickoff of the revised security plan, the Baghdad Operations Command (BOC) was establishing itself, albeit slowly. The combination of targeted raids and clearing operations seemed to take their toll on extremist groups, particularly Jaysh al-Mahdi (JAM). Sectarian murders in February decreased by 50 percent from January's total, and population displacement in Baghdad appeared to have stopped. However, Petraeus hastened to put these encouraging signs into their broader, less encouraging context. While some categories of violence had improved slightly from January, late January had been a horrific period of bloodshed, with the Ministry of Interior announcing that more than 1,000 Iraqis had been killed in a single week. February had witnessed the highest number of VBIED attacks in the past year with 77—up slightly from January's 72.[40] There had been 44 VBIEDs in Baghdad alone in February, the most in the capital in any month of the war. The commander expected to see similar levels in the coming weeks as Sunni extremists responded to the new American approach.[41]

"Get Off the FOBs:" Forward Presence Shakes Up East Baghdad

The first surge brigade, 2d Brigade, 82d Airborne Division, was also among the first to implement Petraeus's and Odierno's guidance to move directly into its battle space and operate alongside Iraqi partner units among Baghdad's population. The brigade's arrival in late January had brought the number of U.S. BCTs in the Baghdad security districts to five and marked the start of the surge. Though headquartered in Camp Taji 20 miles to the north, the brigade assumed responsibility for coalition operations in the capital's northeastern security districts of Adhamiyah and Sadr City. With aggressive Sunni and Shi'a elements vying for control, the area seethed with sectarian violence. In the densely populated slums of Sadr City, Sha'ab, and Ur, Shi'a militiamen found safe havens from which to launch raids against Sunni enclaves throughout the city. Adhamiyah, an upscale residential area for military officers and government professionals during the Saddam era, was one such Sunni zone. Nestled along the eastern bank of the Tigris, this neighborhood had served as a support base for al-Qaeda in Iraq's (AQI) Rusafa network, which included the most active and deadly car-bomb ring in the country.[42] In January 2007, amid these two formidable antagonists stood an overmatched U.S. battalion that quartered only one company in the sector. The remainder of the battalion's combat power operated from Camp Taji.[43]

The first surge BCT's deployment to northeast Baghdad effectively increased the number of battalions in the sector from one to three. The first priority for 2d Brigade, 82d Airborne Division, as it formally assumed control of its new section on February 12, was to establish a forward presence with two-thirds of the BCT's combat power. "Get off the FOBs [forward operating bases]," Colonel Billy Don Farris, the brigade commander, told his subordinate leaders.[44] Following several days of targeted raids and cordon and knock/search operations, two battalions from Farris's incoming BCT established combat outposts in their newly assigned sectors in Sha'ab and Ur. The already present 1st Battalion, 26th Infantry, consolidated its position around Old Adhamiyah.[45] The new combat outposts allowed the brigade's three battalions to reduce movement back and forth from the Taji base to their respective sectors, and facilitate interaction with the local population.[46]

Source: U.S. Army photo by Staff Sergeant Michael Pryor (Released).

Colonel Billy Don Farris, Commander of 2d BCT, 82d Airborne Division, Meets With Civic Leaders of Sadr City's First Joint Security Station.[47]

In the coming weeks, Farris's brigade tightened its grip on an area that had seen sparse coalition presence. While combat outposts enabled constant forward presence for U.S. units, JSSs served as command and control nodes for both coalition and Iraqi forces. Farris anticipated that each of his battalions would establish one JSS in existing police stations or government buildings to coordinate local security operations, advise the Iraqis, and encourage their security forces to be an active presence in the community.[48] However, this was problematic, given the lack of Iraqi troops. When Odierno visited Farris on February 24, the BCT commander reported significant shortages in the ranks of the National Police battalion in Sha'ab and Ur—an issue compounded by the Iraqi high command's reluctance to send its army units there.

Source: U.S. Army photo by Staff Sergeant Joann Makinano (Released).

U.S. Army Soldiers Search a House in Zaghiniyat During the Early Days of the Surge.[49]

Initially, Farris was content to isolate Sadr City, given the limited number of maneuver units under his control. He faced practical restrictions when it came to dispatching conventional forces into the dense, inhospitable urban area where JAM dominated. The base of the Iraqi National Police brigade responsible for this security district sat on the northeastern corner of the Shi'a slum, making it difficult for American transition teams to provide oversight. A new JSS planned for the southwestern edge of Sadr City would alleviate this particular problem but introduced another.[50] Committing to a JSS provocatively close to the Sadrist militia's main stronghold would strain the BCT commander's combat power and, in his view, jeopardized clearing operations in Sha'ab and Ur as well as Old Adhamiyah. "These were two very tough nuts to crack," he explained.[51]

Odierno surprised Farris by asking him if he could use another battalion. As Farris mulled this over, the general told him that he and his brigade were doing exactly what Odierno wanted them to do: "Getting into the neighborhoods and integrating the ISF."[52] Petraeus reiterated this guidance in his own visit to Farris's sector 2 days later, telling Farris's Soldiers, "We need to live in the neighborhoods we operate [in]; [we] must break the FOB mentality; [and we] cannot allow ourselves to 'commute' to the fight."[53]

Source: U.S. Army Photo by Staff Sergeant Michael Pryor (Released).

Iraqi Police and Paratroopers From 2d BCT, 82d Airborne Division, Patrol Adhamiyah in February.[54]

Soldiers of 2d Brigade, 82d Airborne Division, established their JSS on the outskirts of Sadr City during the first week of March 2007. U.S. troops cleared the surrounding area using a "soft knock" approach, and Petraeus reported that the population seemed to appreciate it. The National Police battalion proved helpful, its presence apparently setting the people at ease, but the area remained volatile. The Sadr City mayor, after seeking an accommodation with the coalition as it stepped cautiously into the Shi'a militant safe haven, survived an assassination attempt by Shi'a militants on March 15. The following week, the capture of Qais Khazali and other Asa'ib Ahl al-Haqq (AAH) leaders in far-away Basrah stirred fears of another Sadr City uprising. To avoid provoking a large-scale confrontation, Odierno required any raids against high-value targets based in the Sadr

City district come to him for approval. For the time being, the strategic importance of maintaining calm in Sadr City outweighed whatever tactical inroads might be made.[55]

Just south of Farris's area of operations, Colonel Jeffrey Bannister's 2d Brigade, 2d Infantry Division engaged in a similar fight to root out Shi'a extremists while protecting the populace from car-bomb attacks. Before the surge, Bannister's sector had included all of east Baghdad. The BCT had four battalions under its control, but one of these units operated outside the security districts in the sprawling rural Mada'in area. In the neighborhoods for which the brigade was responsible, AQI's Rusafa car-bomb ring had carried out devastating attacks against mostly Shi'a civilians for more than a year. Several market areas in Bannister's sector had been struck by deadly car and truck bombs in late 2006 and early 2007, some of them repeatedly. AQI had bombed the Sadriyah market in December, killing 50 Iraqis, and then struck the market again on February 3 in a massive truck bombing that was one of the war's worst, killing or wounding almost 500 Iraqis. What was likely the same gang followed up on March 5 with a bombing of Baghdad's famed open-air book market on Mutanabi Street, named for Iraq's most famous poet, which killed 26 Iraqis and left the market in ruins.

Source: DoD photo by Staff Sergeant Jason T. Bailey, U.S. Air Force (Released).

A U.S. Patrol Passes the Ruined Facade of Baghdad's Mutanabi Book Market, Destroyed by an AQI Car Bomb in March 2007.[56]

The arrival of Farris's brigade enabled Bannister and his brigade to compress their battle space and focus on securing the frequently bombed districts of New Baghdad, Rusafa, and Karada. As Farris's BCT assumed responsibility for Adhamiyah and Sadr City, Bannister positioned one of his battalions in each of the three remaining security districts for which he now had responsibility.[57] From the two FOBs in his sector—Loyalty and Rustamiyah—his units began to "flood the zone," pushing two-thirds of their combat power forward into a net of combat outposts and converting selected Iraqi police stations into JSSs. Bannister benefited from a small surge of Iraqi security forces as well. The idea to bring Iraqi Army units to Baghdad from less volatile regions of the country had had an unfortunately long gestation, but in January two Iraqi brigades finally arrived. One of them went to Karada, where, according to Bannister, the timely appearance of the additional Iraqi troops helped offset the loss of National Police units pulled offline for much-needed retraining.

SECDEF Gates (center) with Colonel Bannister (right). Source: DoD photo by Cherie Thurlby (Released).

SECDEF Robert Gates Tours a Joint Security Station With Colonel Jeffrey Bannister.[58]

Bannister's BCT eventually reached a total of 6 battalions, enabling it to establish 12 combat outposts and 9 security stations from which his troops and local Iraqi forces would attempt to put an end to the AQI attacks ravaging Rusafa.[59]

The Surge in West Baghdad

In west Baghdad, Colonel J. B. Burton was gratified to hear Petraeus's guidance for coalition forces to increase their presence on the streets of the capital. The commander of 2d Brigade, 1st Infantry Division, had seen the need for that same approach when his headquarters assumed responsibility for the security districts of Kadhimiyah, Mansour, and west Rashid in November 2006. Here, AQI operatives infiltrating Baghdad from the "ratlines" running east from Anbar through Abu Ghraib collided with JAM, AAH, and other Shi'a militants. From support zones in eastern Kadhimiyah, Shi'a militiamen pushed into Sunni neighborhoods in a deliberate effort to expand Shi'a militant control. Like others, Burton understood the problem facing him as more complicated than simple counterinsurgency. His BCT was a third party to an ongoing sectarian war.

Colonel Burton (left) with Major General Abdul Al-Ameer (right).
Source: U.S. Army photo by Staff Sergeant Benny Corbett (Released).

Colonel J. B. Burton, Commander, 2d BCT, 1st Infantry Division, With Major General Abdul Al-Ameer, Commander of the 6th Iraqi Army Division.[60]

The solution, Burton believed, was to insert his forces into the maelstrom. "When I took over, I made it the first order of business to deploy off the FOBs and establish what we called 'combat outposts' along sectarian fault lines," he later said.[61] Combat Outpost Casino, established in the Sunni enclave of Ghazaliyah, was the first of what would become a set of 14 combat outposts and JSSs in Burton's sector.[62] Before the surge announcement, Burton's BCT had been relieved of its responsibility for Abu Ghraib on the outskirts of Baghdad. When 2d Brigade, 82d Airborne Division, arrived in January, one of its battalions was attached to Burton, bringing his total to four. He assigned the incoming paratroopers to the Shi'a militia strongholds in Harbiya and Hurriyah and welcomed them there in the aftermath of a clearing operation conducted by the division strike force.[63]

Source: U.S. Army photo by Sergeant Tierney Nowland (Released).

U.S. and Iraqi Soldiers Search for Weapons Caches Near Janabi in March.[64]

In Petraeus's view, the U.S. battalions in Mansour and Rashid faced the toughest security challenges in Baghdad. For months, these areas had been the scene of the most intense death squad activity, sectarian ISF abuses, and AQI infiltration. The second surge BCT to arrive, Colonel Ricky Gibbs's 4th Brigade, 1st Infantry Division, alleviated some of the pressure in those areas when it hit the ground in mid-February. Its arrival allowed Burton's BCT to concentrate on the northwest quadrant of the capital. In March, 2d Brigade, 1st Infantry Division, combined with Colonel Stephen J. Townsend's Stryker BCT to launch a month-long clearing operation in Mansour. In 35 days of grueling actions, Townsend's units progressively moved through the district, neighborhood by neighborhood, with battalions assigned to Burton establishing cordons in support or patrolling on the flanks. In one of these major clearing operations, U.S. and Iraqi troops discovered components for more than 3,000 IEDs and took 160 suspected insurgents into custody. Forty of these were sent to long-term detention facilities, a number Townsend judged remarkably high for such a short period.[65] Nonetheless, the persistent violence in sectors such as Ameriyah following the departure of the Strykers again showed that clearing operations alone were not enough to solve the problem.[66]

The Rashid District seemed just as troublesome, especially the eastern half of the district centering on the al-Qaeda bastion of Dora. Colonel Bryan Roberts and 2d Brigade, 1st Cavalry Division, had attempted to clear Dora, but the once-flourishing market there remained a battleground when Gibbs and 4th Brigade, 1st Infantry Division, assumed responsibility for the area on March 15. As Gibbs moved into the sprawling district that nearly stretched the length of southern Baghdad from Camp Victory to the Tigris River, Roberts shifted his forces to the center of the capital, turning his brigade's attention to the international zone and the still-smoldering Haifa Street. Roberts took an attached Stryker battalion with him, but he left two infantry battalions to add to Gibbs's cavalry squadron and another infantry battalion—bringing the total number of such units to four where it had been three. Gibbs's BCT also inherited a partnership with elements of three National Police brigades, though they were of dubious utility since National Police units tended to be infiltrated by Shi'a militiamen.[67]

Colonel Gibbs (left) with Ambassador Crocker (front right).
Source: U.S. Army photo by Sergeant 1st Class Robert Timmons (Released).

Colonel Ricky D. Gibbs, Commander, 4th Infantry BCT, 1st Infantry Division, With Ambassador Ryan C. Crocker in April.[68]

Moving into Rashid in mid-March, Gibbs encountered a dichotomous threat like other BCT commanders in the capital. The western half of the district was largely Shi'a, with JAM and the Special Groups posing the greatest danger. In the mostly Sunni neighborhoods east of Route Jackson, AQI ruled, intimidating the local population and using the area as a launching point for violence elsewhere. Instructed on arrival to deploy his subordinate units forward in sector, Gibbs conducted a preliminary operation to establish company-sized combat outposts in hot spots throughout the district.[69] Over the next month, 4th Brigade, 1st Infantry Division built 11 outposts and JSSs—stocking cranes, trucks, and concrete barriers location by location and taking about a week to fortify each position. The move of U.S. units from FOB Falcon back into the Iraqi neighborhoods did not go uncontested. As the new U.S. and Iraqi outposts went into place, they came under frequent attack by Sunni fighters who recognized the danger they posed, such as the March 24 suicide truck bombing against a police station in Dora that killed more than 20 Iraqis, most of them policemen. Militants conducted 711 lethal attacks against Gibbs's troops in March, a monthly figure that would rise to 928 later in the spring.[70] With its forward presence set, the BCT began a long fight in Dora against what would prove to be a fortified AQI headquarters.[71]

Source: U.S. Army photo by Staff Sergeant Sean A. Foley (Released).

Soldiers From 5th Battalion, 20th Infantry Regiment, Fire at Insurgents in Dora.[72]

The Division Fight in Baghdad

At the turn of the New Year, Major General Joseph Fil and the Multi-National Division-Baghdad (MND-B) had had only three U.S. BCTs and a brigade-sized strike force to cover all of Baghdad, but the arrival of both American and Iraqi surge forces in February and March significantly changed the troop density and character of MND-B's operations in the capital. By the end of March, with the arrival of Farris and Gibbs, MND-B had a full five BCTs that owned battle space in the city. More importantly, the territory assigned to each brigade was significantly smaller than it had been in 2005 and 2006, allowing brigade commanders to concentrate more U.S. troops in smaller areas of operations. East of the Tigris, Bannister's 2d Brigade, 2d Infantry Division, saw its area of operations shrink by nearly half while gaining two battalions. Burton's command across the river benefited from the same doubly favorable transaction, employing two more battalions in a sector half the size of what it had been in early January. Finally, Roberts retained control of three battalions, but these massed in Karkh as he shed responsibility for east Rashid. In the coming months, the concentration of American troops in the capital would only grow, and this concentration would factor directly into MND-B's fight against Sunni and Shi'a militants.[73]

The new U.S. troop density also allowed MND-B to partner U.S. forces in Baghdad with Iraqi units at lower echelons as the Iraqi troop density also increased. Senior U.S. commanders had clamored since the previous fall for additional Iraqi battalions to be dispatched to Baghdad. By the first week of March, all had arrived, and by the end of the month, troop strength totaled 61,000 Iraqi security forces in Baghdad, along with 32,000 coalition troops.[74] Another 20,000 Iraqis and 13,000 Americans operated in the belts.[75] In the months ahead, the number of U.S. battalions patrolling the streets of the capital would nearly double from what it had been in late 2006, peaking at 25. Among other things, the additional combat power enabled the rapid creation of more JSSs. After just a month in command, Petraeus noted that 25 already had been established.[76]

This influx of forces gave MND-B far greater means to implement the Baghdad Security Plan than Fil's predecessor, Major General J. D. Thurman, had had for Operations TOGETHER FORWARD I and II. In a broad sense, MND-B's focus remained the same as it had been in late 2006: conduct operations in keeping with the "clear, hold, and build" framework of Operations TOGETHER FORWARD I and II, with an emphasis on neighborhoods located along sectarian fault lines. Yet the marked shift from transition to population security entailed a process whereby areas, once cleared, would be controlled and retained with much more extensive coalition involvement and oversight. This meant instituting more rigorous population control measures—the kind that a persistent forward presence allowed. In one case, a battalion commander in Dora maintained two platoons in Iraqi neighborhoods and began an "ongoing census" that fostered relationships with the locals and helped put a name and a face to friendly and enemy parties.[77] Similarly, in northwest Baghdad, Burton found that the dozen or so JSSs his units created gave Iraqi locals "a constant touch point of security and information inside their neighborhoods."[78]

At the same time, MND-B launched "safe neighborhood" and "safe market" initiatives under which BCTs would erect barriers around vulnerable public areas to frustrate the AQI car and truck bombings that had ravaged Baghdad's markets and open spaces for months. As various kinds of concrete "T-walls" went up throughout Baghdad by the thousands, U.S. troops nicknamed them according to size. The shortest barriers, 3 feet high, were "Jersey barriers." Intermediate-height barriers were either "Virginia barriers" or the slightly taller "Texas barriers." The tallest, over 10 feet high, were "Alaska barriers." In an operation aptly named VIRGINIA CREEPER, Burton's troops lined the route running west out of his sector toward Abu Ghraib with concrete barriers in order to hamper AQI's freedom of movement on this important road.[79] Meanwhile, east of the Tigris River, Farris and 2d Brigade, 82d Airborne Division, built a so-called Great Wall of Adhamiyah to limit unwanted access to the Sunni enclave and adopted a similar tactic to help isolate Sadr City. In all, Farris's units would lay more than 30 miles of concrete barriers during their 15-month deployment.[80] Bannister's 2d Brigade, 2d Infantry Division, hardened nine markets across east Baghdad by enclosing them with concrete T-walls and leaving only a few controlled entrances, converting scenes of former VBIED attacks into pedestrian zones.[81] This barrier sought to deny access to militants on both sides of the sectarian divide, including JAM and other Shi'a militants, and it seemed to have a rapid effect. In one notable case, with the support of local Sunni leaders, Burton's 2d Brigade, 1st Infantry Division, erected concrete walls around northern Ghazaliyah to stymie JAM death squads, after which the neighborhood's murder rate dropped by 50 percent the following week.[82] As these preventive measures appeared around Baghdad, MND-B continued its raids to kill or capture the most dangerous militants, launching the division strike force—3d Stryker Brigade, 2d Infantry Division—on a 2-week clearing operation in March focused specifically on two of Baghdad's major VBIED networks.[83]

For MND-B, more U.S. units in Baghdad also meant more headquarters elements with which to engage Iraqi officials and to partner with ISF units. Fil met regularly with the mayor of Baghdad while his deputy division commanders, Brigadier General John Campbell and Brigadier General Vincent Brooks, engaged with district and neighborhood advisory councils.[84] When General Abud Qanbar and his new Baghdad Operations Command began functioning on March 1, Fil assigned Campbell, MND-B's deputy commanding general for operations, to partner directly with Qanbar, interacting with the Iraqi general and his staff almost daily and encouraging unity of effort between U.S. and Iraqi forces throughout the capital region. MNC-I and Odierno contributed as well, assigning the British deputy corps commander, Major General Gerald Berragan, the task of coaching Qanbar's staff at its Adnan Palace headquarters.[85] These and other related measures mitigated the risk of placing an inexperienced headquarters over Iraqi operations in the capital. Partnerships and transition teams at multiple echelons, including Colonel Robert Newman's newly formed advisory team posted in the BOC itself, were a necessary reinforcement for the Iraqi command as it took control of the 6th and 9th Iraqi Army Divisions and the 1st and 2d National Police Divisions.[86]

Another Division Headquarters: The Creation of MND-Center

To help enable MND-B to secure Baghdad, it was crucial for MNC-I to ensure that the division did not have to focus on matters beyond the city. As some of the arriving surge units began focusing on the belts around Baghdad, Odierno wanted an additional division headquarters to manage those outlying operations. The division's proposed scheme of maneuver involved taking the fight to the belts sequentially—after securing the capital and withdrawing coalition forces to its periphery. However, Odierno intended for operations in these areas to occur simultaneously and strongly believed that separate entities needed to direct them.[87]

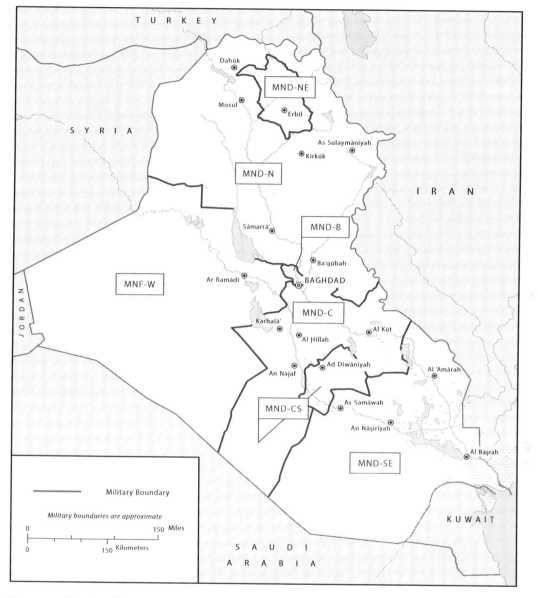

Map created by the official cartographer at the U.S. Army Center of Military History, Washington, DC.

Map 11. MND Areas of Operation, June 2007.

By mid-March, Odierno decided that the third surge BCT arriving later that month would deploy into the portion of the belts south and east of the city, near Salman Pak. The fourth, when it arrived, would cover battle space in the northern belt, near Tarmi-yah—at the nexus of Abu Ghazwan's fiefdom and astride AQI's line of communications from Mosul to Baghdad and, laterally, from Baqubah to Anbar. The fifth BCT, when it appeared, likely would go into the southern belts, but Odierno would finalize that decision at a future date.[88]

According to Army doctrine, commanders positioned units two levels below them in the operational chain. Odierno believed the tactical situation demanded a break with doctrine. Given his limited forces—even with the surge—and the numerous points that required U.S. military presence, Odierno arrayed battalions three levels below him. The break with doctrine displeased some of his division and brigade commanders, but Odierno believed the tactical situation demanded it. While he disliked breaking up organic brigades—as did his brigade commanders—parceling out battalions allowed him to commit a BCT headquarters and one or two of its battalions to the belts while sending the balance into the capital itself, where more manpower but not additional brigade headquarters were still needed. While only 2 of the 5 surge BCTs deployed to the security districts inside the city, more of their maneuver and artillery battalions—12 of 25—took up positions there.[89]

For MND-B, the relief of responsibility for the southern belts meant a loss of responsibilities and resources that Fil and his division preferred to keep for themselves. They were convinced the best use of the additional U.S. forces was to employ them in securing Baghdad itself, leaving the belts for later, and therefore were skeptical about Odierno's approach and the creation of Multi-National Division–Center (MND-C). MND-B's repeated requests for battalions from the later surge BCTs created tension between the corps and division staffs and pestered Odierno to the point of annoyance at least once.[90] MND-B also saw the shifting of battle space as disruptive because it threw unit and municipal boundaries out of alignment, complicating leader engagements with Iraqi civil authorities.[91] This, however, was a small price to pay in Odierno's view: the belts would require their own separate battle, he determined, led by a division dedicated to that task.

THE IRAQI SECURITY FORCES IN EARLY 2007

As the American commander who oversaw the staffing, equipping, and training of Iraqi military and police formations, Lieutenant General Martin Dempsey regarded the surge of U.S. troops with doubt. In the December 2006 deliberations about the surge, Dempsey had advised Casey against asking for more U.S. troops. "If the ultimate goal . . . is to settle the situation to enable better dialogue toward reconciliation," he offered, "then the introduction of additional coalition forces is the wrong answer. [Iraqis] will not reconcile simply because we are separating them."[92] A U.S. troop surge, Dempsey thought, would also give the Iraqis the impression that the U.S. military was inclined to sweep in and take control of every crisis, thus inadvertently holding back the development of their own security forces. The MNSTC-I commander saw more promise in the transition bridging strategy of reinforcing the coalition's advisory effort and the assistance it provided to Iraqi units.[93] Briefing the newly arrived Petraeus on February 17, Dempsey repeated his chief concern that, by putting security responsibility back on the coalition's shoulders, the surge threatened to cause a "loss [of] momentum" for the ongoing transition to the Iraqis. He proposed instead that the surge troops might be used to implement fully the bridging strategy.[94] However, this was an idea Petraeus already had told his subordinate commanders—including Dempsey—a week before that he did not intend to follow.

The Iraqi security forces had grown significantly in the interval since Petraeus had given up command of MNSTC-I in 2005. By early 2007, 10 Iraqi Army divisions operated across the country in sectors established largely along provincial lines. In the far north, the 2d Division—with its mix of Kurdish and Sunni Arab brigades—controlled a sector that included Mosul and half the Kurdish region while, to the west, the Kurdish-majority 3d Division covered most of Ninawa Province. To the south of these two divisions, the brigade sectors of the 4th Division aligned with Salahadin, Kirkuk, and the Kurdish province of Sulaymaniyah. The 5th Division had responsibility for Diyala Province, while the 6th and the 9th Divisions, the latter the Iraqi Army's only mechanized formation, operated in and around Baghdad. In Anbar, the 1st Division sector centered on Fallujah, while the 7th Division spanned much of the Western Euphrates River Valley and extended south across desert terrain to the Jordanian and Saudi borders. Two divisions split the southern provinces, with the 8th Division responsible for Najaf, Karbala, Babil, Qadisiyah, and Wasit and the 10th Division covering Muthanna, Dhi Qar, Maysan, and Basrah.

Source: DoD photo by Staff Sergeant Curt Cashour (Released).

Lieutenant General Martin Dempsey, Commanding General, MNSTC-I.[95]

When first organized, each division had fallen under the operational control of the coalition, but in 2006, MNF-I had begun to pass responsibility for the day-to-day command and control of certain units to the Iraqi Ground Forces Command (IGFC). By the time Petraeus took command, the IGFC controlled five divisions operating in the northern and southern portions of the country. The remaining five, based in Anbar, Baghdad, and Diyala, were slated for transition in the coming weeks and months.[96] At the tactical level, 103 Iraqi Army combat battalions had been fielded. Of these, 93 had the lead for counterinsurgency operations in their areas of responsibility, according to MNF-I.[97] It was a problematic metric that seemed to assess the Iraqi security forces more optimistically than justified. In a late February review conducted at the request of the newly arrived Petraeus, Keane found that virtually all Iraqi units, including those formally in control of territory, still required substantial coalition assistance.[98] The result across Iraq was a collection of Iraqi headquarters that supposedly exercised operational control while their units largely depended on the coalition.

The standing up of the BOC was a promising initiative, and Petraeus reported favorably in March that Qanbar was "leading from the front." While the Iraqi commander was "technically in charge," his headquarters had very limited capacity.[99] Similarly, as clearing operations in Baghdad continued, BCT commanders paid deference to Qanbar's subordinates in Karkh and Rusafa, but they could plainly see that Iraqi units still required a great deal of coaching and material support.[100] Colonel Farris, for example, railed against the Iraqis' cultural inclination to reduce military operations to the practice of staffing checkpoints. He insisted his partnered unit conduct more patrols, pointing out that, even with a "ridiculous amount" of checkpoints in his sector of northeast Baghdad, "we didn't catch one single noteworthy bad guy" at any of them.[101] However, there were bright spots: Roberts partnered with an Iraqi general in Karkh whom he considered "as good as any brigade commander I have ever served with in the United States."[102] Petraeus, in his weekly reports to Gates, noted otherwise unremarkable feats, like staffing fixed positions or establishing outer cordons, as examples of Iraqi competence.[103] Yet, even such ordinary capabilities were absent in many Iraqi units.

Sectarianism and Corruption in the Iraqi Security Forces

In addition to the ISF's uneven capabilities, sectarianism pervaded the force. The transition bridging strategy, with its augmented advisory teams, had been developed by Casey and Chiarelli in part to discourage sectarian behavior in the Iraqi security forces. Though he opted for a different prescription, Petraeus recognized the problem as well and, referencing a list of the 20 worst sectarian actors that he carried in his pocket, often expressed concern to Maliki about its widespread impact.[104] Maliki's own office of the commander in chief was part of the problem, adding an unhelpful layer of bureaucracy to Iraqi military operations and subjecting the Iraqi commands to strong sectarian bias.[105] Among Iraqi tactical units, the sectarian behavior that Thurman and his 4th Infantry Division had observed in Baghdad in fall 2006 was undiminished by spring 2007. In his late February assessment, Keane observed that many Iraqis had come to view the security forces as predators, not protectors.[106] In one high-profile case aired by al-Jazeera, a Sunni woman claimed to have been raped by militia-linked Shi'a police in Baghdad. When Prime Minister Maliki subsequently cleared the policemen of any charges, outraged Sunnis protested, incensed at the tone-deaf nature of the official response.[107]

National Police units in and around Baghdad also remained notorious for their sectarian behavior. MNSTC-I had instituted a "re-bluing" program in the fall of 2006 following the implication of the 8th Brigade, 2d National Police Division, in the kidnapping and execution of Sunni civilians in west Baghdad. The coalition had arrested its officers and pulled the unit off the streets for dedicated vetting and training. In the aftermath of the scandal, the other 8 National Police brigades rotated through a similar, month-long process of re-bluing, so that by March 2007, 5 of the 9 National Police brigade commanders had been replaced, and approximately 2,700 national policemen had been removed from the rolls.[108]

In early April, Petraeus reported that the effort to mold the National Police into an effective and nonsectarian institution was progressing, but its tarnished reputation would be hard to refurbish.[109] At the tactical level, the opinion of the National Police was even less sanguine. The population of east Baghdad still viewed the National Police as an extension of JAM, recalled 2d Brigade, 2d Infantry Division's Bannister.[110] It was not a case of mere perception. Soldiers assigned to Townsend's Stryker brigade discovered that they were especially subject to attack in close proximity to National Police checkpoints.[111] In Rashid, Gibbs found the National Police to be nothing but trouble, recalling later how formations of Shi'a national policemen would storm into the mixed-sect neighborhood of Saidiyah, randomly kill civilians, and force families from their homes.[112] When a Sunni mosque guarded by the National Police in west Rashid blew up, MNF-I concluded that JAM infiltrators had compromised the unit there.[113] When Prime Minister Maliki's initiative to grow the Iraqi security forces included a proviso to establish another National Police brigade to provide security for the Samarra mosque, coalition leaders were understandably wary, especially after Maliki's office produced a roster of recruits for the brigade that was almost 100 percent Shi'a.[114]

Corruption was a related problem. The well-known practice of padding unit rolls with "ghost soldiers" allowed unit commanders to pocket the government salaries of troops who existed only on paper.[115] Systemic corruption stemmed from more than greed, however. Factions competing in a civil war and posturing for an eventual American withdrawal had plenty of incentive to husband resources for themselves, which helped explain missing equipment as well as the general lack of accountability in the security forces.[116] The Iraqi Facilities Protection Service (FPS) typified the problem. This loose affiliation of security details guarded government buildings and officials. Dispersed across 27 ministries and 8 directorates, its 150,000 armed men had a reputation for violence and indiscipline. Attempting to impose order and accountability over the FPS, the Prime Minister had authorized its consolidation under the Ministry of Interior in December 2006, but by late spring 2007, Dempsey reported virtually no progress on this initiative. Unenthusiastic about shedding FPS salaries from their budgets and thus losing leverage over their security guards, the ministries resisted the measure.[117]

General Dempsey and the Gaps in Iraqi Security Forces Development

The ISF suffered not only from state-sanctioned and state-engineered sectarianism and corruption, but from a lack of institutional capacity as well. Their numerical strength in early 2007 stood at 136,000 soldiers, 135,000 police, 24,400 National Police, and 28,400 border troops, for a total force of 323,800 that many outside commentators judged was not nearly enough to meet Iraq's security needs.[118] An army expansion initiative developed by the Prime Minister sought to alleviate this shortfall by fielding two additional division headquarters, six more brigades in central and southern Iraq, and another Special Forces battalion. Implementing this initiative throughout 2007, along with a separate measure to raise the assigned strength of combat battalions, would grow the Iraqi Army by 54,000 men, alongside a more modest increase of roughly 6,000 in Iraq's local and National Police.

Nevertheless, Dempsey concluded in a written "In-Stride Assessment" on the eve of his departure from MNSTC-I that the Iraqi security forces were unprepared to assume full security responsibility, and that the plan for their growth had been far from adequate. The first months of Operation FARDH AL-QANOON had invalidated some of the coalition's key assumptions about the composition and size of units the Iraqis needed, Dempsey judged. The coalition had designed the Iraqi Army with the expectation that it would operate from fixed geographical points in an environment in which the counterinsurgency campaign already had been won. Consequently, when Iraqi units deployed away from their home stations, as several did to support the Baghdad Security Plan, they lacked the logistics and communications capabilities to operate on their own.[119]

The coalition filled this technical gap for the most part, but compensating for a lack of tactical depth proved more difficult. Loath to leave their home bases and battle space unsecure, Iraqi commanders opted to leave, on average, a quarter of their combat power behind when ordered to deploy their units elsewhere for a time.[120] This tendency compounded an already serious personnel shortage. In late 2006, the coalition had decided with the Ministry of Defense to man Iraqi battalions at 110 percent of their authorized strength to compensate for the army-wide practice in which a quarter of a unit's rank and file were away on home leave at any one time. But in the spring of 2007, even this corrective measure appeared insufficient, prompting Petraeus to direct Dempsey to adjust the manning goal to 120 percent, the equivalent of 20,000 extra soldiers, so that the Iraqi divisions could field 80 to 90 percent of their authorized strength even without those on leave.[121]

The additional troops were needed to address another flawed assumption as well. Rather than steadily decreasing over time as coalition planners had predicted, levels of violence had continued to climb. Sunni and Shi'a extremists had shown unexpected resilience and adaptability, and in sustained campaigns against them, the Iraqi security forces had labored under constant troop shortages. According to Dempsey, Iraqi combat units had no "tactical staying power or sufficient capability to surge forces locally"—a critical vulnerability, given the tendency of enemy groups to shift fighters quickly from sector to sector.[122] Furthermore, Iraqi units did not necessarily improve as the months and years passed and as leaders and soldiers accumulated experience. Instead, tactical skills often deteriorated under the combined strains of prolonged combat and unit attrition. This loss of proficiency meant periodic training of Iraqi units was essential, but the Iraqi Army's generous leave policy, potential out-of-sector deployments, demands of routine maintenance, and continuing requirement to secure bases and facilities made it unlikely the Iraqis would develop a sustainable rotation scheme that allowed for collective training and reconstitution. Dempsey concluded that adding more division and brigade headquarters, uniformly raising the number of battalions per brigade from three to four, and bolstering each battalion with more soldiers would go far toward remedying this shortfall.[123]

Turning to issues of quality, Dempsey found that "the Iraqi Security Forces are, for the most part, well-trained, and where military training teams have been present, increasingly well-led," demonstrating both "resolve and capability in battle."[124] Petraeus made a similar report to Gates around this time, noting the Iraqis had been "steadily engaged," suffering an increasing number of combat deaths as Operation FARDH AL-QANOON progressed.[125] Nonetheless, the MNSTC-I commander judged the capabilities of the Iraqi security forces quite harshly relative to the threat they faced. Posing questions as to whether the Iraqis were properly armed, adequately protected, or sufficiently mobile, Dempsey answered "no" on all three counts. They lacked the armor-protected vehicles and weaponry to dominate small-unit engagements and were particularly vulnerable to improvised explosive device (IED) attacks. Maneuvering outside their assigned sectors consistently exceeded their capabilities.[126] "If you pointed them in the right direction, [the ISF] could seize a town, cordon a village, or attack a target," Dempsey recalled later, "but they had nothing—I mean literally nothing—to support that" in the areas of communications, intelligence, logistics, and transportation.[127] He proposed a number of solutions to address these gaps in 2008, including the creation of a corps headquarters for northern Iraq, an engineer regiment for route clearance, an artillery regiment to provide standoff fire support for infantry units that had only 60-mm mortars assigned to them, and the continued enhancement of a logistics architecture that would match the ongoing growth of tactical forces.[128]

As for funding, Dempsey requested that the U.S. Government commit to a budget of $5.5 billion in support of Iraqi security forces development, more than doubling his initial request made less than 1 year before in September 2006.[129] He had worked hard to convince the security ministries to adopt U.S. foreign military sales as the key element of their acquisition process, and believed the more regulated approach had begun to pay off for the Iraqis. "We were able to merge our budgets to advance the issues . . . in a way that we simply could not have [done] if they continued spending money in brown paper bags and flying to Malaysia to buy patrol boats," Dempsey later recalled.[130] In January, Maliki had agreed to Dempsey's recommendation to grant the Ministers of Defense and Interior greater authority to approve foreign military sales contracts, raising the amount the two cabinet ministers could spend independently from $5 million to $50 million.[131] Months later, though, maddening problems hampered the handling of foreign military sales on the American side, where the Washington apparatus treated contracts with Iraq on a routine basis and not with the wartime urgency Dempsey and all other senior U.S. commanders in Baghdad believed they deserved.[132] The U.S. Government had to "squeeze all bureaucratic slack out of the FMS [foreign military sales] process," he argued as his MNSTC-I tour ended. "Time remains the most critical resource," he observed, echoing Petraeus's theme of a "race against time."[133]

After 3 years in which U.S. leaders such as Casey, Rumsfeld, and Abizaid had argued for pulling U.S. troops back from security operations in order to spur the Iraqis to step forward and defend their own country against a complex insurgency and the Shi'a militants, Dempsey's "In-Stride Assessment" showed how deeply flawed that idea had been. The MNSTC-I commander's report documented in great detail the areas in which the Iraqi security forces simply lacked the capacity to take over security responsibility from the coalition, no matter how intensely coalition leaders wished otherwise. As Dempsey made clear, the Iraqis were far from ready for the changeover that Casey and the transition strategy had envisioned for 2007.

ECONOMIES OF FORCE, SOUTH AND NORTH

Trouble in Diwaniya

As the surge brigades began to arrive in the Baghdad region to carry out Petraeus's and Odierno's new guidance for security in the capital and its hinterland, security problems elsewhere in the country continued to simmer, but without sufficient coalition and Iraqi forces to resolve them. Some 80 miles south of the capital, one such problem began to boil over. Across the Shi'a south, the anticipated transition to provincial Iraqi control set the stage for a political battle in which Sadrist foot soldiers and Supreme Council for the Islamic Revolution in Iraq (SCIRI) operatives squared off. Restrained somewhat in the holy city of Najaf, JAM members felt freer to challenge the Badr-infused ranks of the Iraqi security forces in Diwaniya, a Shi'a city of 400,000 and the capital of Qadisiyah Province. Located halfway between Baghdad and Basrah, it sat along the coalition's primary line of communications running south to Kuwait and astride the east-west road connecting

Najaf with the provinces bordering Iran. The governorship of Qadisiyah belonged to SCIRI, and the officer corps of the 8th Iraqi Army Division included a number of former Badr Corps members. However, the Sadrists enjoyed the loyalty of about 1,000 local police, a factor that gave JAM fighters far greater freedom of action in the city than Iraqi or coalition forces could claim.[134]

Diwaniya was therefore a safe destination for many of the Shi'a militia leaders and fighters who decided to flee Baghdad in January 2007 when the new Baghdad Security Plan began to clamp down on JAM and other groups in the capital. By early March, the number of Shi'a militiamen operating in the city had increased from about 600 to over 1,000, and the growing strength of JAM and the Special Groups in Diwaniya became more than the local coalition contingent and the Iraqi Army units posted in Qadisiyah Province could handle.[135] The Polish-led Multi-National Division-Central South (MND-CS) was not staffed or equipped for a forceful campaign against the local Shi'a militias and had long been prevented by national guidance from taking too aggressive an approach in any case, meaning that militia control of Diwaniya spread relatively unhindered in early 2007. The locally based 8th Iraqi Army Division lacked the capability to conduct an aggressive, anti-militia campaign as well, though its commander, Major General Othman Ali Far-hood al-Ghanimi, did as much as he could with his meager troop levels and resources. A Shi'a officer who had served in Saddam Hussein's army as well as a sheikh of the local Ghanam tribe, Othman had been one of Casey's top three Iraqi picks for the Baghdad command and was respected by U.S. leaders for his apolitical stance toward the dominant Shi'a political parties. Proud of the professional reputation he had earned, Othman labeled Badr, JAM, and Iran all as potential enemies of the Iraqi state.[136] As the influence of these three grew across southern Iraq in early 2007, there was only so much that one division commander could do.

General Odierno (center), Major General Pawel Lamla (right) and Major General Othman al-Ghanimi (left). Source: DoD photo by Specialist Jessica Kent (Released).

**General Raymond Odierno, With Polish Major General Pawel Lamla,
MND-CS Commander, and Major General Othman al-Ghanimi, Commander
of the 8th Iraqi Army Division.**[137]

When Petraeus ventured into downtown Diwaniya on patrol with Othman and MND-CS Commander Major General Pawel Lamla in late February, the city had appeared "vibrant, with heavy traffic in the city center."[138] However, this surface impression of a bustling urban area masked growing tensions and violence. The security situation in Diwaniya deteriorated rapidly in early 2007 as the Sadrist militants expanded their presence there and increased weapons smuggling, intimidation tactics, and murderous activities. IED attacks and indirect fire against local coalition and Iraqi troops mounted as well, especially against the MND-CS headquarters at Camp Echo on the outskirts of the city. MND-CS routine business such as conducting security patrols and supervising checkpoints would not be enough to retain control of this key terrain along the coalition's primary supply route. Petraeus, Othman, and Lamla all agreed on the need for a combined operation against JAM in the city.[139]

While Petraeus sought Maliki's endorsement for coalition plans to confront JAM in Diwaniya, MNC-I and the 8th Iraqi Army Division began planning for an operation to be launched following the Muslim holiday of Arba'een. Throughout March, the militia groups expanded their hold on the city, securing support zones and staging areas from which the militiamen maintained a continuous presence in Diwaniya's northern districts. JAM fighters staffed checkpoints in defiance—or with the compliance—of local police and sallied forth to attack Camp Echo with indirect fire. After one such attack wounded eight Polish soldiers, coalition analysts determined that militia groups were bombarding the base from more than a dozen firing points spanning the entire width of the city.[140] The discovery indicated that the ISF in the area were no longer effective. As he reviewed plans for Operation BLACK EAGLE, the impending coalition-Iraqi operation to secure the city, Odierno realized that the Iraqi police in Diwaniya were in a state of collapse and had ceased coordination with the Iraqi Army. To the MNC-I commander's frustration, however, the overly optimistic police transition reports from MND-CS did not reflect this reality or the fact that most of the police were intimidated or under militia influence. This led Odierno to direct that all police transition team reports from Wasit and Qadisiyah Provinces should come directly to him for review.[141]

Source: DoD photo courtesy of Defense Imagery Management Operations Center (Released).

Military Transition Team Members and Iraqi Soldiers During Operation BLACK EAGLE.[142]

Following a week of small-scale strikes by U.S. and Iraqi special operations forces, BLACK EAGLE launched on the evening of April 5. The Iraqi and Polish division commanders hoped that the situation could be remedied with the capture of six local JAM leaders, but as the action unfolded, it became clear the operation would require more than that.[143] Despite the intense battle for Baghdad going on at the time, MNC-I allocated additional forces, intelligence specialists, and aviation assets to the Polish-led headquarters to support raids to kill or capture influential militiamen in Diwaniya.[144] More importantly, Odierno dispatched his operational reserve to the city, sending a battalion-sized Stryker task force from Townsend's brigade in Baghdad that helped the 8th Iraqi Division and MND-CS surprise the local militia enemy. With the Strykers on hand, more than 3,000 coalition and Iraqi troops conducted a series of cordon and search operations that overcame organized resistance and resulted in the capture of 107 JAM fighters over 2 weeks. The population, for its part, appeared to accept the unfamiliar and relatively large-scale presence of U.S. Soldiers in the city. Following this rapid insertion of combat power, Iraqi and coalition troops established two JSSs on the opposite ends of the troublesome northern districts, while the Sadrist militants fell back on rhetoric and propaganda to seek local tribal support.[145] Indirect-fire attacks on Camp Echo—a long-time magnet for rocket and mortar fire—dropped to a historic low.[146] The pause in attacks provided MND-CS and its local Iraqi partners what would be a few weeks' respite from militia pressure as the two sides gathered their strength for the next battle.

A Shift in Focus for Operation SINBAD

South of Diwaniya, Basrah also proved precarious for the coalition. The ongoing Operation SINBAD, begun by Multi-National Division-South East (MND-SE) Commander Major General Richard Shirreff in October 2006, had originated as a plan to subdue JAM and other Shi'a militant groups and restore Basrah to government control, rescuing the British expedition in Iraq from a downward spiral toward humiliation in the process. However, when Shirreff handed command of MND-SE to Major General Jonathan Shaw in January 2007, the new British commander concluded that SINBAD was a case of too little, too late. Though Shirreff slated the operation to continue for several months, Shaw quickly shifted MND-SE from Shirreff's counterinsurgency approach to a scaled-back course inclined toward a political solution.[147]

In doing so, Shaw was following clear guidance he had received on the eve of his departure from Great Britain. In London, the pressure was on to decrease British forces in Iraq in order to increase them in Afghanistan, and it mattered little that the United States had decided that same month to take a divergent path by surging five additional BCTs to the theater. "What the Americans do isn't our concern," Air Chief Marshal Sir Jock Stirrup, Great Britain's Chief of Defence Staff, had told Shaw.

Source: DoD photo by Cherie A. Thurlby (Released).

SECDEF Robert Gates With British Major General Jonathan Shaw, Commander of MND-SE, and General Casey.[148]

"You're to continue to carry on and get out of Iraq."[149] This explicit guidance provided Shaw with a sharp bottom line. Given his command's limited resources and Britain's waning political will, Shaw deemed SINBAD's goals too ambitious, and the approach he inherited from Shirreff a mismatch of ends and means. Beyond the policy and resource constraints, Shaw believed SINBAD's formula of district-by-district clearing operations followed by police training and focused reconstruction projects was the wrong way to stabilize Basrah. To Shaw, Basrah's turbulent local politics resembled "Palermo, not Beirut," meaning that an accommodation among mafia-like groups stood a better chance of stabilizing the city than large-scale clearing operations combined with police development. As Shaw saw it, most of the violence in Basrah took place simply because the British troops were there, so reducing MND-SE's local involvement and force levels would remove the major cause of instability in the city. Instead of using SINBAD to subjugate Basrah's militias and bring them under government control, the general chose to use the operation to facilitate the British drawdown and the transfer of security responsibility to the Iraqis, the same approach Casey had taken in Baghdad the previous summer.[150]

Shaw's change of approach in Basrah promised to widen the gap between MND-SE and its American-led higher headquarters that was about to launch a large-scale counter-offensive. The divergence became clear when Shaw explained his rationale to Petraeus

4 days after the latter arrived in Baghdad in February 2007. Stripping out anti-coalition attacks, the struggle in Basrah boiled down to "power, politics, and gangsterism," Shaw told the new MNF-I commander.[151] The dearth of attacks against local infrastructure suggested to Shaw that intra-Shi'a violence was "self-limiting." Unlike the nihilistic Sunni extremists wreaking havoc in northern and central Iraq, no party vying for power in the Shi'a south was interested in destroying the sources of Basrah's wealth.[152] According to the MND-SE commander, withdrawing coalition forces in Basrah would not only dramatically reduce violence in the city by removing a major source of Iraqi rage, but it also would compel Iraqi leaders to address the intra-Shi'a problem—presumably in a way that the coalition would find in its interests.[153] "The best realistic goal," Shaw argued, would be "a stable linkage" among elements of the Iraqi state, the tribes, and the militias competing for power and resources in the southern provinces. A "pragmatic stability" could only be reached through an accommodation among the key competitors, and any deal had to account for malign Iranian influence and the disruptive activities of death squads.[154] The coalition could not impose a solution in Iraq, Shaw told Petraeus. Rather, one had to emerge out of the natural forces existing in Iraqi society. Outsiders could not "fight the soil," Shaw contended, and because he considered JAM to be one of those natural forces in Basrah, he believed that trying to defeat the militia in the city was futile. "An outright victory for one side is likely to prove a goad to revenge within a culture of 'blood feuds'," the British commander argued. "An accommodation that gives honor to all reconcilable sides is likely to prove more enduring."[155]

As Petraeus politely noted, Shaw's approach was out of sync with the new U.S. strategy and troop surge. It quickly emerged that the British general's concepts were fully in sync with senior British civilian and military leaders in London. On February 21, 2007, 1 day after the 10th Iraqi Army Division passed from coalition control to the control of the Iraqi Ground Forces Command, British Prime Minister Tony Blair announced a gradual drawdown from 7,100 to 5,500 of his country's troops in Iraq.[156] A steady handover of British bases during SINBAD's final weeks followed. By May, British troops had transferred control of three bases to the Iraqis and were operating out of just Basrah Palace and the large air base on the outskirts of the city. A few incidents in the course of the operation had cast greater doubt on the local Iraqi forces to which MND-SE was transferring responsibility. In the worst episode, on March 5, Iraqi special operations forces, U.S. advisors, and British troops had raided the Interior Ministry's intelligence bureau in Basrah—which reported to Engineer Ahmed[157] at the Interior Ministry in Baghdad—and had found 30 prisoners being held there in brutal conditions.[158] Despite these indicators of the ISF's unreliability, Shaw anticipated a shift to Iraqi control of the province as early as November 2007.

Elsewhere, MND-SE transitioned Maysan to Iraqi control in April despite the province's churning intra-sectarian strife and the fact that British troops had no freedom of movement into the provincial capital of Amarah. According to Shaw, this made "readying Maysan for [provincial Iraqi control] . . . hard and very much in the hands of the Iraqis."[159] The British resolve to withdraw gradually, coupled with their view that the "political soil" was impervious to any sort of meaningful retilling, lent a sense of inevitability to MND-SE's slow yielding of control over the Shi'a south.[160] "The accommodation that JAM and Badr . . . made [in Maysan] seemed to look reasonably steady," Shaw recalled later, judging that "it was as good as it was ever going to get."[161] When he recommended transferring the province to Iraqi control, his American military superiors in Baghdad reluctantly agreed to take the risk.

By the time Operation SINBAD ended in May, British and Iraqi forces had killed over 340 militia fighters. The damage inflicted on the Basrah militias was substantial but had come at a cost of 46 British troops killed and 350 wounded, a level of casualties that the British Government and public were unwilling to bear on a sustained basis. While the Iraqi security forces had grown in capability and confidence since the October 2006 beginning of SINBAD, they still lacked the wherewithal to conduct a determined campaign against JAM, as the coming months would show.[162]

Making Much With Little in Mosul

On the opposite end of the country from Basrah, Petraeus viewed the evolving security situation in the north with measured optimism as he took command. As early as March, he expressed the hope of reaching a "sustainable level of violence" in Mosul by summer, despite worrisome incidents like the well-orchestrated insurgent assault on the Badush prison on March 6, which freed about 70 inmates and exposed long-standing corruption in the Iraqi-run facility.[163] As the weeks passed, Iraqi-led operations seemed to be working well enough to keep a lid on the security situation while the coalition's main effort focused on Baghdad. Enabled by tips from local civilians, Iraqi troops captured sizable enemy caches in mid-March, and, in the face of a large, coordinated AQI attack in Mosul in May, Iraqi units maintained their cohesion and fought back as a determined force, something they had failed to do in late 2004.[164] In contrast to the grim assessments of other government agencies at the time — which predicted Mosul's imminent collapse — Petraeus tended to cast the security scene there in hopeful terms, partly due to the crucial role played by the coalition's special operations task force in the city.[165] The task force provided depth to an otherwise thin coalition presence in the north, honing its ability to work with conventional units to amplify the effects of both.[166] The special operations forces (SOF) contingent formed a "fusion cell" of operations and intelligence analysts with the BCT, Combined Joint Special Operations Task Force (CJSOTF) elements, and interagency partners in Mosul to counter the Sunni extremist networks seeking to reestablish a stronger foothold there. Therefore, the SOF contingent was able to keep AQI leaders in northern Iraq off-balance even while Baghdad demanded the preponderance of MNF-I's attention and resources. Reflecting on the close relationship among the task force, conventional units, and other U.S. governmental agencies in Mosul, one BCT commander who had deployed throughout Iraq reported that he never observed a better partnership anywhere else.[167] Despite relegating Mosul to an economy of force effort in 2007, Petraeus thought the provincial capital's security arrangement of "competent Iraqi security forces in the lead, a relatively small U.S. unit in partnership, and a strong special ops capability," might be a model for the future.[168] In the course of events, however, Petraeus would not hold this judgment for long.

AQI's response to combined operations in and around Mosul provided some insight into the terrorist organization's strategy as it sought to reestablish control over this vital area. VBIED attacks in early 2007 increasingly targeted the ISF, indicating a focused attempt to intimidate the army and police and disrupt their activities.[169] Petraeus saw this as a sign that Ninawa's insurgents considered the ISF's growing effectiveness and sense of control a serious threat.[170] Such a pattern may have been related to the enemy's assessment of security force quality, but more likely it suggested that after the departure of Townsend's Stryker brigade for Baghdad in December 2006, the small remainder of U.S. troops in Mosul no longer impinged on AQI's freedom of maneuver to the extent their ISF counterparts did. Sunni extremist targeting of the ISF in the north continued into the spring with multiple VBIED strikes in Mosul and Kirkuk.[171]

High-profile attacks against civilians to stoke ethno-sectarian conflict remained a key part of AQI's strategy in the north as well. Most notably, on March 27, two massive truck bombs struck a market in Tel Afar in one of the largest attacks of the entire war. The bombs collapsed the surrounding buildings, killing 152 Iraqis and wounding almost 350 more, the vast majority of them from Tel Afar's significant Shi'a minority community. Within hours, enraged Shi'a Tel Afari police retaliated by murdering as many as 70 Sunni men and boys elsewhere in the city, with the executions only ceasing once Iraqi Army troops arrived on the scene and arrested the policemen. The incident was a test of the central government's responsiveness and impartiality toward affairs in the distant Sunni-majority province, with MNF-I and the U.S. Embassy trying (but largely failing) to impress on the Maliki government the danger the situation posed to the government's already tenuous legitimacy there. In the end, the Shi'a policemen arrested for the killings of Tel Afari Sunnis were never punished. Meanwhile, the Tel Afar episode illustrated AQI's penchant for stoking ethno-sectarian tension, as well as its desperate need to maintain control over the foreign-fighter pipeline from Syria.[172] Disconcertingly for coalition leaders, the group demonstrated its operational reach with coordinated attacks on two bridges, an Iraqi-run prison, and several police stations in Ninawa's provincial capital on a single day in May.[173] AQI's resilience in Mosul and the far north meant those areas would eventually have to become the coalition's main effort, if and when Baghdad and central Iraq could be pacified.

Source: DoD photo by Sergeant 1st Class Samantha Stryker (Released).

Residents of Tel Afar Dig Through Rubble in the Aftermath of the March 27 AQI VBIED Attack.[174]

TOWARD A NEW JOINT CAMPAIGN PLAN

The Joint Strategic Assessment Team

While MNF-I aimed to regain the initiative through multiple, simultaneous thrusts into long-held al-Qaeda in Iraq sanctuaries, Petraeus and newly arrived U.S. Ambassador Ryan C. Crocker judged that long-term stability in Iraq would require far more than security operations. Together they intended to develop a comprehensive campaign plan to address the diverse array of problems that beset Iraq, from governance and economic development to rule of law and detention. They also hoped to create conditions to foster reconciliation between the Shi'a-dominated Iraqi Government and a Sunni population that had been deeply skeptical of the new government since its inception. While Petraeus judged that the surge operations would visibly improve Iraq's security as the months passed, there were few indicators of progress in Iraqi politics, the area that the U.S. Congress and many critics of the strategy had come to regard as the principal benchmark by which to assess the U.S.-led campaign.

SECDEF Gates (right) with Ambassador Crocker (left).
Source: DoD photo by Cherie Thurlby (Released).

SECDEF Robert Gates Meets With Ambassador Ryan Crocker in Baghdad.[175]

As a new commander implementing a new strategy, Petraeus enjoyed some reprieve from these external stressors. However, pressure was building. In mid-March, Petraeus and Crocker recruited a team of more than a dozen civilian and military experts to review the strategic situation in Iraq and revamp the coalition campaign plan.[176] To lead the team, Petraeus assigned Colonel Herbert Raymond "H. R." McMaster, then on a fellowship in London, while Crocker summoned senior diplomat David D. Pearce from embassy duty in Rome. The two had extensive experience with Iraq and the Middle East. McMaster had led the 3d Armored Cavalry Regiment in Tel Afar in 2005-2006, earning high praise from Bush for the counterinsurgency operations his unit waged there. More recently, he had served on the Council of Colonels organized by Chairman of the JCS General Peter Pace in late 2006 and had accompanied Keane during the latter's assessment trip to Iraq in February. Pearce was a career foreign service officer who had held sensitive posts in Damascus and the Gulf region, in addition to heading the State Department's Iraq desk from 2000 to 2003.

Comprised of distinguished senior officers, diplomats, and scholars, the Joint Strategic Assessment Team (JSAT) represented an unusually comprehensive interagency and multinational effort and was a sharp contrast to normal Army campaign planning efforts. Besides Pearce and McMaster, the team was comprised of regional experts and intellectuals, including Robert S. Ford, an Arabist then serving as ambassador to Algeria, and Molly Phee, a fluent Arabic speaker and Foreign Service officer who had served as the Coalition Provisional Authority's (CPA) governor of Maysan in 2003-2004.[177] Regis W. Matlak, a long-time veteran of the U.S. intelligence community, joined the team, as did Colonel Rick L. Waddell, a Rhodes Scholar and Army reservist with extensive business experience in the oil and gas industry who previously had investigated corruption at the Bayji oil refinery in 2005.[178] Dr. Chris Schnaubelt, a former Air Force colonel who had joined the State Department, served as the U.S. Embassy's lead strategic planner on the team. Former Australian army officer and counterinsurgency specialist David J. Kilcullen served on the team as well, along with civilian scholar Stephen D. Biddle, an Army War College professor and senior fellow for the Council on Foreign Relations who had been among the security experts invited to the White House in December 2006 to discuss Iraq War strategy with Bush.[179] Several British standouts participated, including Toby Dodge, author of two books on Iraq, and Andrew Rathmell, a veteran of the CPA and the chief of an advisory team in Iraq's embattled Ministry of Interior. Emma Sky, Odierno's political adviser, also contributed to the team, as did the British MNF-I planner Colonel James Richardson. The group also included two U.S. Army foreign area officers specializing in the Middle East: Colonel Philip J. "P. J." Dermer, who had served with the CPA and recruited most of the new Iraqi general officer corps; and Colonel Martin Stanton, renowned within the Army for his ill-fated Kuwait City holiday in August 1990. After calling in reports on the Iraqi invasion from his hotel room, then-Major Stanton became a prisoner of war and later an involuntary human shield at Bayji oil refinery.[180]

The JSAT completed its work on April 20, following a 4-week whirlwind of unit visits and senior leader briefings that informed rounds of debate and discussion. The team's final recommendations to the MNF-I commander and U.S. ambassador highlighted the implications of the communal struggle for power in Iraq. Though primarily sectarian in nature, the conflict in Iraq was exacerbated by terrorist activities and external actors, making engagement with reconcilable groups and renewed diplomatic initiatives critical to success. Iraq's communities needed to be pushed toward political accommodation through both bottom-up and top-down efforts, the JSAT recommended, and the coalition should shift to a new strategy that emphasized protecting the population and sought to establish security conditions that would allow for the growth of inclusive governance. It recognized that a transition to Iraqi forces would need to take place, but, by emphasizing population security, it acknowledged the intertwined nature of security and political problems. Population security would lay the groundwork for a political accommodation between Iraq's warring factions that, in turn, would remove support for both AQI and the Shi'a militias.

In addition to a lack of political will among Iraq's warring parties, the JSAT held that a "chronic lack of state capacity" hampered efforts to improve stability. It was thus not enough to press the Iraqis to step up and assume responsibility.[181] Transition to Iraqi responsibility had to be conditions-based, and one of those conditions entailed the removal of "malign actors" from Iraq's Shi'a-dominated government and security forces—a task that required more muscular MNF-I and embassy involvement in the near term. Pointing out that many factions in Iraq were already jockeying for position in a conflict sure to escalate following the coalition's withdrawal, the team hammered home the need to sustain the surge for as long as politically possible.[182] The team's assessment struck Petraeus as "accurate, forthright, and a bit disheartening."[183]

The JSAT paved the way for a new, comprehensive joint campaign plan that sought to achieve "sustainable security" by spring 2008.[184] Describing the plan to Gates, Petraeus posited that two "big ideas" differentiated it from previous coalition efforts: the emphasis on securing the population, and a focus on a political "line of operation."[185] To resolve the conflict, the JSAT concluded the coalition's military objectives should at all times be supportive of and subordinate to political objectives, and the political objectives, in turn, should focus on actions that would enable—or compel—the warring parties to seek their goals through the political process instead of violence.[186] Moreover, Petraeus and Crocker did not assume that Iraqis would reconcile of their own volition over time, and they intended to use the coalition's military operations and political advantage both to bring Sunnis to the negotiating table and to force the Shi'a parties in power to end their sectarian abuses.

The JSAT's leaders believed their most important finding was that Iraq was clearly in the midst of a sectarian civil war and that the Iraqi Government itself had become an accelerant of the conflict. The transition strategy had failed, they judged, because the coalition had worked too uncritically and unconditionally with the government even as the new Iraqi state became captured by sectarian parties who used the machinery of the state to pursue narrow sectarian agendas. The only answer, they argued, was to hold the government leaders accountable for the destabilizing behavior of government-affiliated sectarian killers, and to force the political centrists to purge the extremists—using U.S. military power to compel them if necessary. Too often, McMaster and Pearce concluded, coalition leaders had taken for granted that their job was to empower their government partners, without considering whether those partners might be making the conflict worse with de facto coalition help. The coalition would need to start by forcing the removal of the worst sectarian actors within the Iraqi security forces, especially in the Interior Ministry.[187]

Beyond security, the JSAT's final report laid out detailed analyses and recommended ways forward in more than a dozen areas. To take advantage of the Sunni tribal awakening that had swept Anbar and parts of the Baghdad hinterland, MNF-I should create a strategic engagement cell to coordinate initiatives to split reconcilable militant groups from irreconcilable ones and persuade as many insurgents as possible to switch sides. To reduce the popular discontent with the Iraqi Government that was fueling militant groups on all sides, the coalition should take specific steps to spur economic growth and to get the machinery of the Iraqi state working again, not just in Baghdad but in the provinces as well. There were specific steps the coalition should take to defuse the Arab-Kurd conflict, the JSAT judged, or else the coalition would risk mission failure by the outbreak of a new civil war along the Green Line in the north. This and other aspects of the Iraqi civil war would require the United States to undertake a major diplomatic effort to persuade or coerce Iraq's regional neighbors to cease their destabilizing interventions in the Iraqi conflict—especially Iran, Syria, and Turkey. The coalition would need to take urgent measures to reform its detention operations and its support for rule of law in Iraq, both of which were near the point of collapse.[188]

In addition to its new ideas, the JSAT was an unusual, ad hoc innovation in joint and interagency assessment and planning, an area for which almost no U.S. doctrine existed. With little precedent to guide them, the JSAT's leaders had managed to integrate input from across the multinational coalition and the U.S. and UK (United Kingdom) inter-agencies, producing recommendations that reflected deep expertise no single agency could have mustered by itself. Unlike the MNF-I red teams of the previous 2 years, which had themselves been nondoctrinal innovations, the JSAT had been empowered by senior coalition military and civilian leaders in Baghdad to change the coalition approach to the war. Petraeus, Odierno, and Crocker would use the same JSAT-type model repeatedly to tackle complex problems during their tenures in Iraq and beyond.

Political Violence

The JSAT observed that violence in Iraq was a political phenomenon, a symptom of the war for power and survival among the major Iraqi factions. In the day-to-day bomb-ings and death squad killings, the political motive was sometimes hard to see. Several events during Petraeus's first few weeks in command were examples of political violence that brought the struggle among the Iraqi parties into clear focus. On February 26, as Iraqi Vice President Adel Abdel Mahdi was giving a speech at the Ministry of Public Works, a suicide bomber blew himself up inside the building in what appeared to be an assassination attempt, wounding both the Vice President and the Minister and killing four directors general who had gathered for the occasion.[189] On March 16, assassins shot to death the head of the Adhamiyah district council, a senior Sunni politician, just as they had assassinated his predecessor 3 months earlier. On March 23, less than a month after the attempted assassination of Mahdi, another assassin came close to killing Iraqi Deputy Prime Minister Salam Zobaie in his Baghdad home, setting off a suicide bomb that seriously wounded Zobaie and killed nine others.[190] The Zobaie bombing came just 5 days after Iraqi and coalition troops raided the Green Zone home of Dhafer al-Ani, one of the leaders of the Sunni Parliamentary bloc, and confiscated 65 AK-47s and four cars that bore traces of TNT.[191]

The Ani raid added evidence to the frequent assertion by Shi'a leaders that Sunni politicians were engaged directly in terrorist activities. On April 12 came even stronger evidence. On that day, a suicide bomber entered the Iraqi Parliament building and blew himself up in the building's cafeteria as Members of Parliament were breaking for lunch. The explosion wounded 22 Iraqis and killed a senior Parliamentarian from the Iraqi

National Dialogue party headed by Saleh Mutlaq. Iraqi officials believed the bomber had entered the compound in the entourage of a Sunni Parliamentarian. Over time, Iraqi politicians came to suspect the Speaker of Parliament, Mahmud Mashhadani, with the assistance of Khalaf Ulayan, a Sunni Member of Parliament from Anbar who moonlighted as an insurgent commander in Jaish al-Islami; and Nasser Janabi, another Member of Parliament who secretly commanded the wing of Izzat Ibrahim ad-Douri's Naqshbandi Army based south of Baghdad, orchestrated the bombing.[192] Reacting to the brazen April 12 attack, Maliki government spokesman Ali Dabbagh told reporters, "There are some groups that work in politics during the day and do things other than politics at night."[193]

The Sunni Parliamentarians were not the only senior militants inside the government, however. On February 23, just 2 months after U.S. forces had detained IRGC commander Mohsen Chizari in a SCIRI-Badr compound in Baghdad, U.S. special operators detained SCIRI leader Abdul Aziz al-Hakim's son Ammar after intercepting his convoy crossing from Iran into Iraq. The American troops had discovered a massive collection of weapons and large quantities of money among the vehicles and had concluded that the younger Hakim was up to no good. To minimize the political fallout sure to result from the detention of the SCIRI patriarch's son, Petraeus ordered Ammar al-Hakim's immediate release.[194] In this case, Petraeus saw greater strategic benefit in looking the other way, and Bush agreed. The President told the MNF-I commander the following week to keep SCIRI "in the tent" and to treat Hakim and his party as potential allies, despite their ties to the Iranian regime.[195]

In a few cases, the Iranian regime was involved directly in politically motivated militant events. On March 20 in Basrah, coalition commandos captured AAH leader Qais Khazali and his brother Laith, who had masterminded the January 20, 2007, attack against U.S. Soldiers in Karbala. Along with the Khazali brothers, the coalition troops had captured an unidentified man who pretended initially to be mute but turned out to be senior Lebanese Hizballah commander Ali Mussa Daqduq, the man whom the IRGC Quds Force had assigned to advise AAH in militant operations a few months before. The capture of the Khazalis shocked Prime Minister Maliki, who had hoped AAH could be used as a political counterbalance to Moqtada Sadr and who required explicit evidence of Qais al-Khazali's guilt from Petraeus before he agreed to allow MNF-I to hold Khazali in detention. The capture also robbed Quds Force commander Qassem Soleimani of one of his most effective Iraqi proxy leaders, and the Iranian regime immediately looked for an opportunity to secure Khazali's release. Three days after the capture of the AAH leaders, the IRGC Navy took 15 British sailors hostage in the Persian Gulf, falsely claiming they had strayed into Iranian waters, most likely intending to trade them for the release of the Khazalis and the detained IRGC officials known as the Erbil Five.[196] The February 4 kidnapping of a senior Iranian Embassy official also may have been related to the hostage negotiation. After the unknown gunmen who had abducted the Iranian official released him on April 3, the IRGC released the British sailors the following day.[197] The high profile political posturing of Petraeus's first few weeks in command showed that Iraqi politics remained a turbulent business, with outside powers often closely involved, as the JSAT had found.

"Not in Sync with Us:" Admiral Fallon and the Surge Strategy

Viewing the broader challenge as one of buying time for the Iraqi Government to develop capacity and make progress toward reconciliation, Petraeus hoped to prolong the surge well into 2008. In this aim, he met unexpected pushback from the newly appointed CENTCOM commander. Despite being selected for command as part of Bush's "new way forward," Fallon was deeply skeptical of the U.S. troop surge the President had ordered, and was unsure that Iraq could be stabilized at all. During his January 30, 2007, confirmation hearing before the U.S. Senate, Fallon had admitted plainly enough that "what we've been doing is not working," and that the coalition required a different approach to meet its objectives in Iraq.[198] He had declined to endorse the ideas that Petraeus already had put forward in public. When testifying before the same committee a week earlier, Petraeus had stated his intention to shift the primary mission of U.S. forces from transition to population security, but in his own hearing, Fallon characterized Petraeus's idea as a mere "proposal."[199]

Admiral Fallon (center) and General Mixon (right).
Source: DoD photo by Sergeant Serena Hayden (Released).

Colonel David W. Sutherland, Commander 3d BCT, 1st Cavalry Division, Briefs Admiral William Fallon, CENTCOM Commander, and Major General Benjamin Mixon, Commander of MND-N.[200]

Fallon even had seemed to indicate the surge itself was still in question. Though Bush already had clarified that he intended to send all five available brigades to Iraq, the admiral told senators that he did not yet know how many more troops were needed. "Frankly, I aim to find out and have my own opinions," he avowed.[201] In Fallon's view, the President's statements about the surge were just expressions of policy. It would take a concerted effort to transform the policy into a coherent strategy, and the admiral intended to have a direct role in formulating it. "I'm going to . . . work with General Petraeus and our commanders to figure out how to make an effective strategy," Fallon informed the senate committee.[202] He seemed unaware that Odierno already had begun implementing a new strategy in line with what Petraeus recommended and what the President had envisioned when he approved the surge. There was a similar divergence where the duration of the surge was concerned. Whereas Petraeus and Odierno intended to sustain the troop surge as far into 2008 as possible, Fallon spoke to the senators of being able "to wrap this up and get our troops back," and he cast the campaign in terms of weeks and months, not years as Petraeus did.[203]

Further indicators of future friction emerged the weekend after Fallon took the helm at CENTCOM on March 16, when he held a 2-day commander's conference with representatives from CENTCOM's subordinate commands, including MNF-I. During the proceedings, the admiral reviewed the array of challenges across CENTCOM's area of responsibility and told his new subordinates he believed MNF-I should pursue a much more modest set of objectives, implying that the surge forces either would have no impact or might even make matters worse over time.[204] Fallon's views echoed the accelerated transition strategy that Casey and Abizaid had advocated and that the President had discarded 3 months before—only with more troops, while they lasted. In contrast, Petraeus and Odierno already were gearing up for a surge of U.S.-led offensive operations once all five additional brigades arrived in Iraq in the early summer.[205] When Fallon visited Iraq later that month, Odierno recorded in his journal that the new CENTCOM chief "believes [the] surge will go through October at the latest," and added that Fallon "clearly has a timeline in his mind that is not in sync with us."[206]

Throughout Casey's tenure at MNF-I, he and CENTCOM Commander Abizaid had maintained close alignment in their strategic views, but they were frequently at odds with whomever happened to be MNC-I commander at the time. Now, at the outset of the surge, the tables had turned: under Petraeus and Odierno, MNF-I and MNC-I would act in concert, but at odds with Fallon's CENTCOM. The disconnect between the new CENTCOM commander and his key subordinate commanders in Iraq stemmed partly from the fact that Bush had long since come to consider the MNF-I commander in Baghdad as the main leader of the Iraq campaign, bypassing the CENTCOM commander in Tampa in order to maintain a direct line first to Casey and now to Petraeus. In selecting new commanders in December 2006, Bush had directly tapped Petraeus as MNF-I commander, but he had not been involved in the selection for the CENTCOM post and simply had accepted the Pentagon's recommendation for what he considered merely a supporting command role. As a result, Fallon had taken command at CENTCOM erroneously presuming to operate under a Presidential charter to oversee the Iraq campaign.[207] These misconceptions would cause tension between the different echelons of command in the months to come.

***

By early April 2007, 2 months after he had arrived in Baghdad, Petraeus commanded a force that was postured very differently than it had been in January. Within days of his arrival, Petraeus had given MNF-I a new mission based on population security and had begun work with U.S. Ambassador Crocker on a new campaign plan that would involve much more direct coalition intervention in Iraqi affairs than had been the case in 2006. The coalition also had begun to employ its much-needed surge reinforcements to regain the initiative in Baghdad after a year of worsening sectarian civil war. In the MND-B area of operations, five U.S. brigades held territory where previously there had been only three. Five additional Iraqi Army brigades had arrived as well, bringing the total of U.S. and Iraqi forces inside the city to 93,000—far more than had been on hand for the TOGETHER FORWARD operations of summer and fall 2006. Petraeus and Odierno also had narrowed MND-B's focus, reassigning its vast territory south of Baghdad to the new Multi-National Division-Center (MND-C) that would prosecute a simultaneous campaign in southern belts with more than 30,000 U.S. and Iraqi troops. The additional troops inside and outside the capital city enabled the coalition to intensify its operations on both the east and west sides of Baghdad, and to expand its footprint dramatically in the city after 2 years of steadily shrinking it. By mid-April, Petraeus and Odierno had overseen the creation of more than 20 new U.S.-Iraqi outposts in Baghdad's neighborhoods, a presence that would eventually increase to 77 outposts by the end of the surge. The two U.S. generals had accomplished this significant shift without the support of the new CENTCOM commander, Fallon.

The new approach was not without its serious costs. As U.S. troops fanned out into Baghdad's districts once more, they came head to head with both Sunni and Shi'a militants in the city, and U.S. casualties rose as a result. In February and March, MNF-I suffered 162 U.S. Soldiers killed and another 1,140 wounded, with a worse toll to come in the spring and summer. "We are getting into the fights with both Sunni and Shi'a extremists we knew were coming," Petraeus explained to Gates in early April.[208] MNF-I suffered 35 troops killed in action during the first week of April alone, a number 60 percent higher than the average weekly death toll since December, and Petraeus expected this grim trend to continue as U.S. troops moved farther into enemy-dominated territory.[209]

AQI responded to the new coalition operations with counterattacks of its own, defiantly carrying out some of the war's largest car-bomb attacks against Shi'a civilians both in Baghdad and in the far north and south of the country. Meanwhile, after lying relatively low in January, JAM and other Shi'a militants had responded to the arrival of additional U.S. troops by bombarding the Green Zone periodically, in one case killing two Americans at the U.S. Embassy billeting office a few yards outside Petraeus and Crocker's office windows.[210]

As more U.S. and Iraqi troops moved into Shi'a-militia-dominated neighborhoods, a portion of Baghdad's Shi'a militants had displaced to Diwaniyah, Basrah, and other southern cities and had begun to threaten coalition partners in those territories. While never strong, MND-CS's slipping grip on Diwaniyah and MND-SE's similarly weak hold on Basrah and Amarah in early 2007 were the latest manifestations of a problem that had dogged the U.S.-led occupation since 2003. Operating with coalition partners had been meant to bolster the strategic legitimacy of the U.S.-led campaign, but at the operational level, those same partners often had neither the capability nor the will to achieve the objectives of the U.S.-crafted campaign plan. The deteriorating conditions in the southern cities indicated that MNF-I and MNC-I would eventually have to conduct more extensive operations there after bringing Baghdad under control.

In these areas away from the capital, the coalition could not yet count on Iraqi forces to fill the gap, as Dempsey made clear in his final assessment of the ISF as he prepared to leave command of MNSTC-I; the ISF simply had too many capability gaps to make a transition bridging strategy feasible. Nor could the coalition yet look to Iraqi politics to mitigate security problems in Baghdad or anywhere else. The battles on Iraq's streets were symptoms of the political struggle among Iraq's major parties, not the other way around, reinforcing Carl von Clausewitz's dictum that war was a continuation of politics by other means. The impetus for political reconciliation would have to come from beyond the Green Zone, as the events of spring and summer 2007 were about to demonstrate.

ENDNOTES - CHAPTER 3

1. George W. Bush, "President's Address to the Nation," January 10, 2007, available from *https://georgewbush-whitehouse.archives.gov/news/releases/2007/01/20070110-7.html*, accessed May 19, 2016. All documents in this chapter, unless otherwise stated, are in the Chief of Staff of the Army (CSA) Operation IRAQI FREEDOM (OIF) Study Group archives, Army Heritage and Education Center (AHEC), Carlisle, PA.

2. Interview, Colonel Joel Rayburn and Colonel James Powell, CSA OIF Study Group, with General Peter J. Schoomaker, March 24, 2014; Thomas E. Ricks, *The Gamble: General David Petraeus and the American Military Adventure in Iraq, 2006-2008*, New York: Penguin Press, 2009, pp. 100-101; Bob Woodward, *The War Within: A Secret White House History, 2006-2008*, New York: Simon & Schuster, 2008, p. 295.

3. Ibid.

4. "General Petraeus's Opening Statement," Lieutenant General David Petraeus, Senate Armed Services Committee, *The New York Times*, January 23, 2007, available from *http://www.nytimes.com/2007/01/23/world/middleeast/24petraeustextcnd.html?_r=0*, accessed January 4, 2016.

5. Ibid.

6. Interview, Colonel Joel Rayburn, CSA OIF Study Group, with General (Ret.) John M. Keane, October 8, 2014.

7. Interview, Bob Woodward with General George W. Casey, Jr., Casey Papers, September 30, 2007, pp. 54-55.

8. Briefing, National Security Council (NSC), Highlights of the Iraq Strategy Review, January 10, 2007.

9. MNF-I, Notes from NSC Video Teleconference (VTC), January 8, 2007.

10. Ibid.

11. PowerPoint Briefing, MNF-I, Mission Analysis: President's Speech to the Nation, Casey Papers, January 10, 2006 [sic], slides 2 and 7.

12. George W. Bush, "President's Address to the Nation," January 10, 2007, available from *https://georgewbush-whitehouse.archives.gov/news/releases/2007/01/20070110-7.html*, accessed May 19, 2016.

13. Briefing, NSC, Highlights of the Iraq Strategy Review, January 10, 2007.

14. George Casey, Jr., *Strategic Reflections: Operation IRAQI FREEDOM*, Washington, DC: National Defense University Press, October 2012, p. 148.

15. Woodward, *The War Within*, pp. 300, 309.

16. Ibid., p. 310.

17. Woodward, *The War Within*, p. 328.

18. Ibid.; Interview, Bob Woodward with Casey, Casey papers, September 30, 2007, p. 1.

19. E-mail, General (Ret.) David H. Petraeus to Colonel Joel Rayburn, January 4, 2016.

20. Memo, MNF-I, February 10, 2007, sub: for "the Soldiers, Sailors, Airmen, Marines, and Civilians of MNF-I," Petraeus Papers.

21. Ibid.

22. U.S. Army photo by Specialist Laura M. Bigenho, "Change of command [Image 1 of 3]," DVIDS Identifier 35869, February 10, 2007, Released to Public, available from *https://www.dvidshub.net/image/35869/change-command*.

23. Notes, MNF-I, Commander's Conference (Luncheon), Petraeus Papers, February 10, 2007.

24. Ibid. Incidentally, in spite of all the emphasis on transferring security responsibility, transition to the Iraqis had been gradual under Casey and not far along in terms of its impact "on the ground." The week of the change of command, there were 319 conventional operations of company size or larger. Well over half of these were combined operations, but 125 involved coalition forces only. Just nine were independent Iraqi operations.

25. Notes, MNF-I, Commander's Conference (Luncheon), Petraeus Papers, February 10, 2007.

26. PowerPoint Briefing, MNF-I, Talking Points for POTUS VTC, Casey Papers, February 7, 2007, slide 4; E-mail, Petraeus to Rayburn, January 4, 2016.

27. Notes, MNF-I, Commander's Conference (Luncheon), Petraeus Papers, February 10, 2007.

28. Ibid.

29. E-mail, Petraeus to Rayburn, January 4, 2016.

30. Notes, MNF-I, Commander's Conference (Luncheon), Petraeus Papers, February 10, 2007.

31. Ibid.

32. Lieutenant General Raymond T. Odierno Iraq Notebook No. 4, February 10, 2007, entry.

33. Interview, Michael O'Hanlon with General David H. Petraeus, Petraeus Papers, August 15, 2011.

34. PowerPoint Briefing, MNF-I, Iraq Update, March 2, 2007.

35. Major James Powell Iraq Notebook, March 1, 2007, entry.

36. MNF-I, SECDEF Weekly Update, March 10-16, 2007.

37. MNF-I, SECDEF Weekly Update, March 3-9, 2007.

38. PowerPoint Briefing, MNF-I, Talking Points for POTUS VTC, Casey Papers, February 7, 2007, slide 1.

39. Ibid., slide 2.

40. PowerPoint Briefings, MNF-I, Talking Points for POTUS VTC, February 24-March 2, 2007; MNF-I, Iraq Update, March 2, 2007, slide 3.

41. MNF-I, SECDEF Weekly Update, February 24-March 2, 2007.

42. Memorandum for Record, Historical Command Report, March 15, 2008 (Date mislabeled 2007), sub: 2d Brigade, 82d Airborne Division, pp. 1-2; Briefing, MNC-I, Intelligence Fusion Brief: Hussaniyah, Rusafa, and Sadr City, January 31, 2007.

43. Interview, Dr. Donald Wright and Colonel Timothy Reese, Combat Studies Institute (CSI) Contemporary Operations Study Team, with Colonel Billy Don Farris, Washington, DC, May 6, 2008.

44. 2d Brigade, 82d Airborne Division, Operation Order (OPORD) 07-03 (FALCON STRIKE), January 28, 2007, p. 2.

45. Ibid., pp. 4-5; Interview, Wright and Reese, CSI Contemporary Operations Study Team, with Farris, May 6, 2008.

46. Memorandum for Record, Historical Command Report, March 15, 2008 (Date mislabeled 2007), sub: 2d Brigade, 82d Airborne Division, p. 4.

47. U.S. Army photo by Staff Sergeant Michael Pryor, "New Plan for Greater Security [Image 1 of 2]," DVIDS Identifier 37243, March 1, 2007, available from *https://www.dvidshub.net/image/37243/new-plan-greater-security*.

48. 2d Brigade, 82d Airborne Division, OPORD 07-03 (FALCON STRIKE), January 28, 2007, pp. 2-3, 5-6.

49. U.S. Army photo by Staff Sergeant Joann Makinano, "Clear the Room," April 1, 2007, Released to Public, available from *https://www.flickr.com/photos/mnfiraq/4314528884/in/album-72157623184079079/*.

50. Notes, 2d Brigade, 82d Airborne Division, battlefield circulation with MNC-I Commanding General (CG), February 24, 2007.

51. Interview, Wright and Reese, CSI Contemporary Operations Study Team, with Farris, May 6, 2008.

52. Notes, 2d Brigade, 82d Airborne Division, battlefield circulation with MNC-I CG, February 24, 2007.

53. Ibid., February 26, 2007.

54. U.S. Army Photo by Staff Sergeant Michael Pryor, "Joint Security [Image 1 of 3]," DVIDS Identifier 36592, February 17, 2007, Released to Public, available from *https://www.dvidshub.net/image/36592/joint-security*.

55. MNF-I, SECDEF Weekly Update, March 10-16, 2007; and March 17-23, 2007.

56. DoD photo by Staff Sergeant Jason T. Bailey, U.S. Air Force, "Soldiers assigned to the U.S. Army 3rd Squadron, 89th Cavalry Regiment, Headquarters Troop, 4th Brigade, 10th Mountain Division patrol past the facade of a demolished building in Baghdad, Iraq, on March 27, 2008," DIMOC Identifier 080327-F-SI676-267, March 27, 2008, Released to Public.

57. Bannister had passed control of 1st Battalion, 26th Infantry, to Farris but had accepted one of 2d Brigade, 82d Airborne Division's incoming battalions—the 1st Battalion, 504th Airborne Parachute Infantry Regiment—in exchange.

58. DoD photo by Cherie Thurlby, "Defense Secretary Takes Extensive Tour of Baghdad Operations [Image 24 of 28]," DVIDS Identifier 47690, June 16, 2007, Released to Public, available from *https://www.dvidshub.net/image/47690/defense-secretary-takes-extensive-tour-baghdad-operations*.

59. Interview, Steven Clay, CSI Contemporary Operations Study Team, with Colonel Jeffrey Bannister, January 20, 2010.

60. U.S. Army photo by Staff Sergeant Benny Corbett, "'Torch' lighting the way for Mansour security [Image 1 of 2]," DVIDS Identifier 42724, April 21, 2007, Released to Public, available from *https://www.dvidshub.net/image/42724/torch-lighting-way-mansour-security*.

61. Interview, Jerry England, CSI Contemporary Operations Study Team, with Colonel J. B. Burton, November 29, 2007, pp. 4-5.

62. Ibid.

63. Interview, Steven Clay, CSI Contemporary Operations Study Team, with Colonel Steven J. Townsend, Part II, January 24, 2008.

64. U.S. Army photo by Sergeant Tierney Nowland, "Teamwork," March 1, 2007, Released to Public, available from *https://www.flickr.com/photos/mnfiraq/4314519240/in/datetaken/*.

65. Interview, Clay, CSI Contemporary Operations Study Team, with Townsend, Part II, January 24, 2008.

66. Interview, Steven Clay, CSI Contemporary Operations Study Team, with Colonel Dale Kuehl, January 18, 2010.

67. Interview, Steven Clay, CSI Contemporary Operations Study Team, with Colonel Ricky D. Gibbs, November 30, 2009.

68. U.S. Army photo by Sergeant 1st Class Robert Timmons, "Ambassador visit," DVIDS Identifier 40627, April 5, 2007, Released to Public, available from *https://www.dvidshub.net/image/40627/ambassador-visit*.

69. Interview, Clay, CSI Contemporary Operations Study Team, with Gibbs, November 30, 2009.

70. Ibid.

71. Ibid.

72. U.S. Army photo by Staff Sergeant Sean A. Foley, "Combat Action," March 1, 2007, Released to Public, available from *https://www.flickr.com/photos/mnfiraq/4313783125/*.

73. See, for example, Interview, Clay, CSI Contemporary Operations Study Team, with Bannister, January 20, 2010.

74. MNF-I, SECDEF Weekly Update, March 10-16, 2007; and March 17-23, 2007.

75. Ibid., March 24-30, 2007.

76. Ibid., March 10-16, 2007.

77. Working Paper, Jim Crider, "Inside the Surge: One Commander's Lessons in Counterinsurgency," Washington, DC: Center for a New American Security, June 2009, p. 11.

78. Interview, Kimberly Kagan, Institute for the Study of War (ISW), with Colonel J. B. Burton, Washington, DC, November 14, 2007.

79. Ibid.

80. Interview, CSI Contemporary Operations Study Team, with Farris, May 6, 2008.

81. Interviews, Clay, CSI Contemporary Operations Study Team, with Bannister, January 20, 2010, p. 19; U.S. Army Center of Military History (CMH) with Major General Joseph Fil, Military History Detachment, August 28, 2007.

82. Interview, Kagan with Burton, November 14, 2007.

83. Interview, Clay, CSI Contemporary Operations Study Team, with Townsend, Part II, January 24, 2008.

84. Interview, CMH with Major General Fil, August 28, 2007.

85. Briefing, MNC-I, Training Assistance Strategy, February 21, 2007; Interview, CMH with Major General Fil, August 28, 2007; Interview, CSA OIF Study Group with Colonel Jeffrey Hannon, March 20, 2014.

86. MNF-I, SECDEF Weekly Update, February 24-March 2, 2007; Interview, CMH with Fil, August 28, 2007; Interview, CSI Contemporary Operations Study Team with Brigadier General John Campbell, September 3, 2008; Interview, CSA OIF Study Group with Lieutenant Colonel Charles Armstrong, March 20, 2014.

87. Interview, CSA OIF Study Group with General Raymond T. Odierno, January 25, 2015.

88. MNC-I, Coalition Campaign Operational Concept: Secure and Transition, n.d., pp. 14-15; MNF-I, SECDEF Weekly Update, March 10-16, 2007.

89. Interviews, CSI Contemporary Operations Study Team with Odierno, June 24, 2007, pp. 59-60; Steven Clay, CSI Contemporary Operations Study Team, with Colonel James Hickey, February 23, 2010, p. 15.

90. Powell Iraq Notebook No. 2, February 27, 2007, entry; Interview, CSA OIF Study Group with Armstrong, March 20, 2014.

91. Interviews, CMH with Fil, August 28, 2007; CSA OIF Study Group with Armstrong, March 20, 2014.

92. E-mail, Lieutenant General Martin E. Dempsey to General George W. Casey, Jr., December 7, 2006, sub: Two Questions, Temp No. 77.

93. Notes from Interview, Richard Hooker and Joseph Collins with General Martin E. Dempsey, January 7, 2015, pp. 4-5.

94. Briefing, MNSTC-I, Iraqi Security Forces Update, February 17, 2007.

95. DoD photo by Staff Sergeant Curt Cashour, "Multi-National Security Transition Command—Iraq Changes Command [Image 1 of 4]," DVIDS Identifier 47177, June 10, 2007, Released to Public, modified (cropped), available from *https://www.dvidshub.net/image/47177/multi-national-security-transition-command-iraq-changes-command.*

96. Briefing, MNSTC-I, Iraqi Security Forces Update, February 17, 2007; MNF-I, SECDEF Weekly Update, April 28-May 4, 2007.

97. Report to Congress, *Measuring Stability and Security in Iraq*, Washington, DC: Department of Defense, March 2, 2007, p. 25.

98. Report, H. R. McMaster, Trip Report Based on Visit of General (Ret.) Jack Keane, February 16-24, 2007, and March 4, 2007, CMH files.

99. PowerPoint Briefing, MNF-I, Iraq Update, March 2, 2007.

100. Interviews, Clay, CSI Contemporary Operations Study Team, with Townsend, Part II, January 24, 2008; Interview, Wright and Reese, CSI Contemporary Operations Study Team, with Farris, May 6, 2008, p. 6.

101.Interview, Wright and Reese, CSI Contemporary Operations Study Team, with Farris, May 6, 2008.

102. Interview, Steven Clay, CSI Contemporary Operations Study Team, with Colonel Bryan Roberts, February 22, 2010.

103. MNF-I, SECDEF Weekly Update, March 3-9, 2007; and March 24-30, 2007.

104. Interview, Michael O'Hanlon with Petraeus, Petraeus Papers, August 15, 2011.

105. MNF-I, SECDEF Weekly Update, April 7-13, 2007; and April 29-May 5, 2007.

106. McMaster, Trip Report, CMH files, February 16-24, 2007.

107. MNF-I, SECDEF Weekly Update, February 17-23, 2007; and February 24-March 2, 2007.

108. U.S. Institute of Peace (USIP) Special Report, Robert M. Perito, *The Iraq Federal Police: U.S. Police Building under Fire*, Washington, DC: U.S. Institute of Peace, October 2011, p. 7; Briefing, Brigadier General Dana J. H. Pittard, Iraq Assistance Group, June 25, 2007; Report to Congress, *Measuring Stability and Security in Iraq*, Washington, DC: Department of Defense, March 2, 2007, p. 27.

109. MNF-I, SECDEF Weekly Update, April 7-13, 2007.

110. Interview, Clay, CSI Contemporary Operations Study Team, with Bannister, January 20, 2010.

111. Interview, Clay, CSI Contemporary Operations Study Team, with Townsend, Part II, January 24, 2008.

112. Interview, Clay, CSI Contemporary Operations Study Team, with Gibbs, November 30, 2009.

113. MNF-I, SECDEF Weekly Update, June 3-9, 2007.

114. *Measuring Stability and Security in Iraq*, p. 27.

115. Ibid., p. 28.

116. U.S. House, Armed Services Committee, Subcommittee on Oversight and Investigations, Testimony of Olga Oliker: Iraqi Security Forces: Defining Challenges and Assessing Progress, Washington, DC, 110th Congress, 1st Session, March 2007, pp. 6-7.

117. MNSTC-I, In-Stride Assessment of the Iraqi Security Forces for the FY08 ISFF Budget Review, May 30, 2007, p. 6n.

118. *Measuring Stability and Security in Iraq*, p. 25. For assessments on Iraqi security forces, see McMaster, Trip Report, February 16-24, 2007, pp. 8-9; and Memo, Kagan for MNF-I Commander, May 11, 2007, sub: Kagan Trip Report, p. 6.

119. MNSTC-I, In-Stride Assessment, May 30, 2007, pp. 8, 44.

120. Ibid., p. 11.

121. Ibid., pp. 2-3.

122. Ibid., pp. 8-9. Quote on p. 3.

123. MNSTC-I, In-Stride Assessment, May 30, 2007, pp. 2-3, 10-11, 42-43.

124. Ibid., p. 22.

125. MNF-I, SECDEF Weekly Update, May 27-June 2, 2007. In February 2007, the Iraqi security forces sustained 211 killed in action, compared to 80 American combat deaths that month. In May, the numbers rose to 257 and 124, respectively.

126. MNSTC-I, In-Stride Assessment, May 30, 2007, pp. 10-12.

127. Interview, Lynne Chandler Garcia, CSI Contemporary Operations Study Team, with Lieutenant General Martin Dempsey, June 10, 2008, p. 3.

128. MNSTC-I, In-Stride Assessment, May 30, 2007, pp. 42-44.

129. Ibid., p. 2.

130. Interview, Garcia, CSI Contemporary Operations Study Team, with Dempsey, June 10, 2008.

131. Staff Notes, MNF-I, January 24, 2007.

132. Interviews, Garcia, CSI Contemporary Operations Study Team, with Dempsey, June 10, 2008; Vincent McLean, CSI Contemporary Operations Study Team, with Dempsey, May 6, 2010.

133. MNSTC-I, In-Stride Assessment, May 30, 2007, p. 10.

134. MNC-I, Intelligence Fusion Brief, January 10, 2007, slide 10; MNC-I, Intelligence Fusion Brief, March 3, 2007, slide 8 notes page; MNC-I, Intelligence Fusion Brief, March 10, 2007, slide 4.

135. MNC-I, Intelligence Fusion Brief, March 10, 2007, slide 4.

136. Interview, CSI Contemporary Operations Study Team, with Brigadier General Michael X. Garrett, November 12, 2009, p. 12; Michael R. Gordon, "The Last Battle: The Fight among Iraq's Shiites," *The New York Times Magazine*, August 3, 2008.

137. DoD photo by Specialist Jessica Kent, "security conditions [Image 1 of 2]," DVIDS Identifier 43524, April 25, 2007, Released to Public, available from *https://www.dvidshub.net/image/43524/security-conditions*.

138. In early 2007, Lamla's command included forces from 13 nations, including Armenia, Bosnia-Herzegovina, Denmark, Kazakhstan, Latvia, Lithuania, Mongolia, Romania, El Salvador, Slovakia, and Ukraine, as well as Poland and the United States. It totaled roughly 6,500 troops. Dale Andrade, *Surging South of Baghdad: The 3d Infantry Division and Task Force Marne in Iraq, 2007-2008*, Washington, DC: Center for Military History, November 2010, p. 163.

139. MNF-I, SECDEF Weekly Update, February 17-23, 2007; MNC-I, Intelligence Fusion Brief, March 3, 2007, slide 2.

140. MNC-I, Intelligence Fusion Brief, March 10, 2007, slides 7 and 8; MNF-I, SECDEF Weekly Update, March 17-23, 2007.

141. Odierno Iraq Notebook No. 6, March 27, 2007, entry.

142. DoD photo courtesy of Defense Imagery Management Operations Center, "Operation Black Eagle [Image 17 of 17]," DVIDS Identifier 43679, April 9, 2007, Released to Public, available from *https://www.dvidshub.net/image/43679/operation-black-eagle*.

143. MNF-I, SECDEF Weekly Update, February 17-23, 2007.

144. MNF-I, SECDEF Weekly Update, March 31-April 6, 2007; MNF-I BUA, April 6, 2007, slide 38.

145. MNF-I, SECDEF Weekly Updates, April 7-13, April 14-20, and April 21-27, 2007; MNF-I BUA, April 6, 2007, slide 38; Odierno Iraq Notebook No. 6, April 7, 2007, entry; Patrick Gaughen, "The Fight for Diwaniya: The Sadrist Trend and ISCI Struggle for Supremacy," Institute for the Study of War, Iraq Project, Backgrounder No. 17, Washington, DC, December 2007, p. 3.

146. MNF-I BUA, April 23, 2007, slide 54.

147. Interview, CSA OIF Study Group with Alex Alderson, January 27, 2014.

148. DoD photo by Cherie A. Thurlby, "Secretary of Defense Robert M. Gates shakes hands with British Maj. Gen. J.D. Shaw (right) commander of Multinational Division-South East, as he arrives in Basra, Iraq, on Jan. 19, 2007. U.S. Army Gen. George W. Casey Jr. (left), commander of Multinational Force—Iraq, accompanied Gates," DIMOC Identifier 070119-D-LB417-005, January 19, 2007, Released to Public.

149. Interview, Colonel Joel Rayburn and Lieutenant Colonel Jim Sindle, CSA OIF Study Group, with Major General Jonathan Shaw, January 29, 2014.

150. Justin Maciejewski, "'Best Effort': Operation Sinbad and the Iraq Campaign," in Jonathan Bailey, Richard Iron, and Hew Strachan, eds., *British Generals in Blair's Wars*, Surrey, UK: Ashgate Publishing, 2013, p. 171.

151. E-mail, J. D. Shaw to General Petraeus, Petraeus Papers, February 14, 2007, sub: Background Brief—Multinational Division (Southeast), p. 4.

152. Jonathan Shaw, "Basrah 2007: The Requirements of a Modern Major General," *British Generals in Blair's Wars*, p. 177.

153. For an articulation of this rationale, see Shaw, "Basrah 2007," pp. 177-179; and Maciejewski, "'Best Effort,'" pp. 171-172, both in *British Generals in Blair's Wars*. In retrospect, Air Chief Marshal Sir Jock Stirrup explained that, to end the local violence, MND-SE had to "withdraw our permanently based forces from Basrah city, and to put the Iraqis in the lead there. In our view the Iraqis would then have to deal with the intra- Shia problem." Quote from David H. Ucko, "Lessons from Basrah: The Future of British Counter-Insurgency," *Survival*, Vol. 52, No. 4, August-September 2010, p. 143.

154. E-mail, Shaw to Petraeus, Petraeus Papers, February 14, 2007, sub: Background Brief—Multinational Division (Southeast), pp. 1-3.

155. Ibid., p. 3.

156. "Blair Announces Iraq Troops Cut," BBC News, February 21, 2007; House of Commons Defence Committee, "UK land operations in Iraq 2007," November 20, 2007, pp. 30-31, available from *http://www. publications.parliament.uk/pa/cm200708/cmselect/cmdfence/110/110.pdf.*

157. House of Commons Defence Committee, "UK land operations in Iraq 2007," pp. 30-31. Engineer Ahmed is the nom de guerre for Bashir Nasser al-Wandi, a senior Badr Corps officer and deputy director of the intelligence directorate of the Iraqi Interior Ministry. Ahmed was implicated in multiple events of sectarian malfeasance including the 2005 Jadriyah bunker incident, which involved illegal detention and torture of scores of Sunni civilians.

158. Kirk Semple, "Basra Raid Finds Dozens Detained by Iraq Spy Unit," *The New York Times*, March 5, 2007, available from *http://www.nytimes.com/2007/03/05/world/middleeast/05iraq.html?pagewanted=print&_ r=0*, accessed January 23, 2016.

159. E-mail, Shaw to Petraeus, Petraeus Papers, February 14, 2007, sub: Background Brief—Multinational Division-Southeast, pp. 3 and 3n.

160. Shaw, "Basrah 2007," *British Generals in Blair's Wars*, pp. 176-177.

161. Testimony of Jonathan Shaw, Iraq Inquiry (UK Chilcot Inquiry), January 11, 2010, p. 22, available from *http://www.iraqinquiry.org.uk/media/42237/20100111-shaw-final.pdf*, accessed June 20, 2016.

162. Maciejewski, "'Best Effort'," *British Generals in Blair's Wars*, p. 171.

163. MNF-I, SECDEF Weekly Update, March 17-23, 2007; MNF-I, SECDEF Weekly Update, March 3-9, 2007; MNC-I, Intelligence Fusion Brief, February 7, 2007, slide 4; MNC-I Intelligence Fusion Brief, March 3, 2007, slide 12.

164. MNF-I, Weekly Summaries, March 10-16, 2007, March 17-23, 2007, and May 13-19, 2007.

165. MNF-I, SECDEF Weekly Update, March 17-23, 2007.

166. Ibid., June 10-16, 2007.

167. Interview, Clay, CSI Contemporary Operations Study Team, with Townsend, Part I, January 23, 2008, p. 16.

168. MNF-I, SECDEF Weekly Update, June 17-23, 2007.

169. MNF-I BUA, February 28, 2007, slide 7.

170. MNF-I, SECDEF Weekly Update, April 28-May 4, 2007.

171. Ibid.

172. MNF-I BUA, March 28, 2007, slide 7; MNF-I, SECDEF Weekly Update, March 24-30, 2007; MNF-I, SECDEF Weekly Update, March 31-April 6, 2007.

173. MNF-I, SECDEF Weekly Update, May 13-19, 2007.

174. DoD photo by Sergeant 1st Class Samantha Stryker, "Recovering from a blast in Tal Afar [Image 3 of 7]," DVIDS Identifier 40002, March 29, 2007, Released to Public, modified (cropped), available from *https://www.dvidshub.net/image/40002/recovering-blast-tal-afar.*

175. DoD photo by Cherie Thurlby, "Defense Secretay [sic] Takes Extensives [sic] Tour of Baghdad Operations [Image 17 of 28]," DVIDS Identifier 47702, June 16, 2007, Released to Public, available from *https://www.dvidshub.net/image/47702/defense-secretay-takes-extensives-tour-baghdad-operations.*

176. MNF-I, SECDEF Weekly Update, May 13-19, 2007, February 24-March 2, 2007, and March 17-23, 2007.

177. Ibid., March 24-30, 2007; Press Release, Office of the Press Secretary, Washington, DC: The White House, President Obama Announces More Key Administration Posts, September 17, 2014; Ron Cassie, "Coming Home: Profile on Robert Ford, Former U.S. Ambassador to Syria," *Baltimore Magazine*, November 2014.

178. Interview, CSA OIF Study Group with Rick L. Waddell, June 30, 2014; Regis W. Matlak, *The Nightmare Years to Come?* Washington, DC: National Defense University Press, 2014, p. 51.

179. Peter R. Mansoor, *Surge: My Journey with General David Petraeus and the Remaking of the Iraq War*, New Haven, CT: Yale University Press, 2013, p. 52.

180. Marni McEntee, "Former Army POW Retraces His Captivity," *Stars and Stripes*, June 9, 2003.

181. Briefing, MNF-I, Joint Campaign Plan Development, MNF-I Commander's Conference, Petraeus Papers, June 2, 2007.

182. MNF-I, SECDEF Weekly Update, April 14-20, 2007.

183. Ibid., March 24-30, 2007.

184. Briefing, MNF-I, Joint Campaign Plan Development, June 2, 2007.

185. MNF-I, SECDEF Weekly Update, May 20-26, 2007; Briefing, MNF-I, Joint Campaign Plan Development, June 2, 2007.

186. MNF-I, Joint Campaign Plan Development, MNF-I Commander's Conference, June 2, 2007.

187. Interview, Colonel Joel Rayburn, CSA OIF Study Group, with Major General H. R. McMaster, August 14, 2015.

188. Ibid.

189. "Iraqi V.P. escapes blast in Baghdad; President hospitalized in Amman," *USA Today*, February 27, 2007, available from *http://usatoday30.usatoday.com/news/world/iraq/2007-02-26-car-bomb_x.htm*, accessed January 22, 2016.

190. "Iraq Deputy PM Injured in Blast," BBC News, March 23, 2007, available from *http://news.bbc.co.uk/2/hi/middle_east/6483975.stm*, accessed January 22, 2016.

191. "Iraqi Forces Raid Sunni Lawmaker's Home," CNN, March 18, 2007, available from *http://www.cnn.com/2007/WORLD/meast/03/18/iraq.main/*, accessed January 22, 2007.

192. Joel Rayburn, *Iraq After America: Strongmen, Sectarians, Resistance*, Stanford, CA: Hoover Institution Press, 2014, pp. 113-114.

193. James Palmer, "Security Plan Draws Harsh Critiques after Bombing," *USA Today*, April 13, 2007, p. 6A.

194. Mansoor, *Surge*, pp. 97-98.

195. MNF-I, Commanding General Notes, VTC with POTUS, March 2, 2007.

196. Robin Wright, *Dreams and Shadows: The Future of the Middle East*, New York: Penguin Press, 2008, p. 335.

197. "Kidnapped Diplomat Reveals Details of his Kidnapping in Baghdad," Islamic Republic News Agency, April 7, 2007.

198. Congressional Testimony, William J. Fallon, Before the U.S. Senate Armed Services Committee, January 30, 2007.

199. "General Petraeus's Opening Statement," Lieutenant General David Petraeus, Senate Armed Services Committee, *The New York Times*, January 23, 2007.

200. DoD photo by Sergeant Serena Hayden, "CENTCOM Commander visits Diyala [Image 1 of 4]," DVIDS Identifier 42231, April 21, 2007, Released to Public, available from *https://www.dvidshub.net/image/42231/centcom-commander-visits-diyala*.

201. Congressional Testimony, Fallon, Before the U.S. Senate Armed Services Committee, January 30, 2007.

202. Ibid.

203. Ibid.

204. Interview, CSA OIF Study Group with Colonel (Ret.) Derek Harvey, November 14 and December 11, 2014. Harvey was an MNF-I representative at the CENTCOM commander's conference.

205. Ricks, *Gamble*, p. 232; Mansoor, *Surge*, p. 179.

206. Odierno Iraq Notebook No. 6, March 24, 2007, entry.

207. Interview, CSA OIF Study Group with George W. Bush, April 27, 2015.

208. MNF-I, SECDEF Weekly Update, March 31-April 6, 2007.

209. Ibid.

210. MNF-I, SECDEF Weekly Update, March 24-30, 2007.

CHAPTER 4

THE AWAKENING GATHERS MOMENTUM

During the spring of 2007, the surge of U.S. forces, General David Petraeus's change in strategic guidance, and Lieutenant General Raymond Odierno's shift in operational posture combined to alter the balance of security in the Baghdad region and halt the advance of sectarian forces that had been underway for more than a year. During the same months, coalition commanders compounded these modifications by enabling—or in some cases coercing—the Sunni population of central Iraq to switch sides and take a stand against al-Qaeda in Iraq (AQI) and other Sunni extremist groups. From Multi-National Forces-Iraq (MNF-I) down to the lowest tactical level, coalition commanders worked in concert to expand the Awakening that had begun in Anbar and used it to amplify the effect of the surge. A wave of local cease-fires was about to sweep across western and central Iraq, bringing tens of thousands of Sunni insurgents into a new alliance with the coalition troops they had fought for almost 4 years.

THE EXPANSION OF THE ANBAR AWAKENING

As he prepared to take command of MNF-I, Petraeus had noted with interest the significant changes taking place in Ramadi, where a city once dominated by AQI and its allies had become a stronghold of a new, anti-AQI Sunni movement. During his first weeks, Petraeus encouraged his subordinate commanders to watch for opportunities beyond Ramadi to strike local cease-fires with Sunni fighters to turn one-time enemies into allies—or at least into neutrals. If local Sunnis indicated their willingness to come to an agreement with coalition units, then Petraeus believed coalition commanders should take advantage of the opening. At MNF-I, some of the coalition's senior leaders already had been on the lookout for such overtures. As MNF-I's British deputy commander since September 2006, Lieutenant General Graeme Lamb had begun exploring the possibility of reaching accommodations with select Sunni insurgent leaders along the lines of the Awakening. The former Special Air Service commander believed in negotiation with even staunch enemies. To fellow coalition commanders who might be skeptical about dealing with insurgents responsible for the deaths of American Soldiers, Lamb argued that it would be foolish to bar influential resistance leaders from wading into the political process because they had "blood on their hands."[1] To press his point, the British general often remarked that he himself shared the same condemnable quality, having fought terrorists in Northern Ireland with whom he later negotiated.

Creating a small cell of analysts and military officers on loan from the special operations task force and intelligence agencies, Lamb mapped out the widening rifts in the Sunni insurgency and looked for opportunities to pry loose "reconcilable" factions willing to make a separate peace with the Iraqi Government from the "irreconcilables" not inclined to do so.[2] In keeping with his unorthodox character, the British general occasionally arranged for captured insurgent leaders to be transported individually to his living quarters in the Green Zone to have a discussion over tea and assess whether their release might lead to cease-fires with the groups they led.[3] In December 2006, Lamb arranged for the first "strategic release," setting free the detained Ansar al Sunna cleric Abu Wail without conditions in the hope that his return to the insurgent group would lead to a rift with AQI.[4]

Source: U.S. Air Force photo by Technical Sergeant Dawn M. Price (Released).

Lieutenant General Graeme Lamb, Deputy Commander, MNF-I.[5]

Petraeus encouraged Lamb to continue his efforts and confirmed the coalition's basic approach to reconciliation as "target[ing] the 'irreconcilables' of either sect to reduce their capability and influence, while simultaneously reaching out to those who are reconcilable."[6] Lamb's outreach extended to enemy fighters still at large. Treading lightly to avoid antagonizing Prime Minister Nuri al-Maliki and his advisers, Petraeus and Lamb would keep an eye out for Sunni resistance leaders who recognized the potential for reconciliation at a time when the insurgency seemed increasingly divided. The main effort of MNF-I's Sunni outreach in 2006 had been the U.S. Embassy and Major General Rick Lynch's high-level talks with exiled insurgent (or pro-insurgent) Sunni figures in Jordan and Syria. But under Petraeus, MNF-I's main Sunni outreach effort would shift to a more bottom-up process in which the senior coalition commanders authorized brigade and battalion commanders to follow the openings that presented themselves in their local areas. As those opportunities emerged, the coalition commands in Baghdad would support them with funding or political top cover, and would run interference with the Maliki government as the need arose.

The course of the Awakening in eastern Anbar changed the way Multi-National Corps-Iraq (MNC-I) approached its operations as well. When Odierno had assumed command of MNC-I in late 2006, he had seen reconciliation primarily as a top-down process by the Iraqi Government to gain Sunni allegiance through key legislation and improved essential services.[7] However, as reports of armed Sunni groups seeking agreements with

U.S. units floated up the chain of command, he recognized the Awakening of the tribes in Anbar as significant and explored with Petraeus and Lamb the prospect of reproducing that phenomenon elsewhere.[8] Though MNC-I's collective mindset remained skeptical, and though it would take Odierno a few months to interpret this new development and "decide whether we thought it was real or not," he would soon seize the chance for tactical military leaders to broker local cease-fires and work with former insurgents to defeat AQI.[9]

Visiting Anbar during his first week in command, Petraeus learned of the unexpected progress made in the provincial capital of Ramadi. Days from turning the area over to his successor, Colonel Sean B. MacFarland related how dramatically the security situation had changed since the arrival of his 1st Brigade, 1st Armored Division, in June 2006. Daily attacks on U.S. and Iraqi forces in Ramadi had plummeted. With local tribes dispatching their young men to serve as policemen and hunt down AQI operatives, MacFarland reported that his brigade had "an embarrassment of riches" compared to the meager local Iraqi cooperation it had found when it arrived 6 months earlier. "We have more friendly forces than we almost know what to do with," MacFarland related.[10] He described the Brigade Combat Team's (BCT) tactical approach: quickly establish combat outposts in the city, deliberately expand a forward presence, and cement it with an aggressive information operations campaign.[11] Petraeus approved. Most notably, though, MacFarland's brigade had isolated Ramadi and cut AQI's lines of communications by reaching an accommodation with Sheikh Abdul Sattar Abu Risha and other local leaders whose tribes comprised the Awakening.[12]

However, this new agreement between MacFarland and the Awakening sheikhs led to a disagreement between MacFarland and his superiors at the two-star Marine headquarters on Camp Fallujah. While Major General Richard C. Zilmer of Multi-National Force-West (MNF-W) had tolerated MacFarland's engagement effort in Ramadi, he had been dubious about its long-term effects and mindful of its potential to undermine what the Marine command saw as the more strategically promising track of discussions with the well-connected expatriate sheikhs in Jordan.[13]

Zilmer's successor began his tour intent on emphasizing one approach at the expense of the other. Major General Walter E. Gaskin's II Marine Expeditionary Force (Forward) assumed responsibility for MNF-W on February 9—1 day before Petraeus took the reins at MNF-I. In attendance at MacFarland's meeting with Petraeus, the new Marine commander questioned the relative utility of the BCT's tribal engagement in Ramadi, labeling Sattar a "road thief" and the sheikhs behind the Awakening "small fish."[14] MNF-W's ongoing dialogue with the sheikhs in Jordan had poisoned the well. Alarmed by Sattar's rapid rise to power, many leaders of the more established tribes had denigrated the upstart sheikh as a murderous smuggler to their Marine interlocutors.[15] MacFarland acknowledged Sattar's shady background but suggested to Gaskin that the improved security situation in his sector spoke for itself. When the BCT commander recommended that Petraeus meet with Sattar, Gaskin objected, arguing that such a gesture would lavish the sheikh with undeserved credibility and thus undermine more significant engagements.[16] Nevertheless, persuaded that MacFarland's effort held great promise, Petraeus threw his weight behind it and told Gaskin to put a priority on supporting the Awakening.[17] "This is counterinsurgency," he pressed. "This is how these endeavors end."[18]

Major General Gaskin (right) and General Pace (left).
Source: DoD photo by U.S. Air Force Staff Sergeant D. Myles Cullen (Released).

U.S. Marine Corps Major General Walter Gaskin, Commander MNF-W, and General Peter Pace, Chairman of the Joint Chiefs of Staff, Tour Ramadi.[19]

Gaskin had inherited a dynamic situation. As a supporting effort to Operation FARDH AL-QANOON, he understood his task to be interdicting accelerants to Baghdad's sectarian violence, but he oversaw a province that his superiors considered ripe for exploitation.[20] At the time of Gaskin's arrival in February 2007, the Marine Expeditionary Force (MEF) area of operations included three brigade-sized sectors. Flanking the Army BCT in greater Ramadi were two newly arrived Marine regimental combat teams (RCTs). To the west, Colonel H. Stacy Clardy's RCT 2 had responsibility for the Euphrates River Valley west of the provincial capital to the Syrian border, including the cities of Hit, Haditha, Rawah, and Al Qa'im. Reinforced by the 15th Marine Expeditionary Unit (MEU), its sector extended south of the river over a wide expanse of sparsely populated desert area traversed by a highway and the coalition's main supply route from Jordan. Notably, municipal government had rebounded in al Qa'im as MNF-W's local accommodation with the Albu-Mahal tribe held steady, and Haditha and other population centers had seen drops in violence as well when operations in November caused AQI to disperse. The Marines went on to bulldoze berms around the cities and erect internal barriers to better control access to neighborhoods. Between Ramadi and Baghdad, RCT-6 under Colonel Richard L. Simcock operated in and around Fallujah. Thirty miles from Iraq's capital, Fallujah had offered the most promise in Zilmer's eyes in early 2006, but the situation there seemed tenuous in comparison with Ramadi as Gaskin assumed command 1 year later.[21] Major tribes in the area, like the Jumaili and Zobai, still tended to favor AQI. Extremists held sway in the villages surrounding the city and the long-time sanctuary north toward Lake Tharthar remained.[22]

For the MNF-W commander, the surge meant the extension of the 15th MEU and the imminent arrival of two more formations: 2d Battalion, 5th Marines, which he dispatched to Ramadi in March, and 1st Battalion, 2d Marines, which fell under the command of RCT-2 out west.[23] The surge of U.S. BCTs to Baghdad also reduced the chances that MNC-I would peel away Army units from MNF-W in order to tamp down violence in the capital—a concern not far from the minds of Marine commanders.[24]

Most importantly, following Petraeus's guidance in Ramadi, MNF-W redoubled its support of the Awakening, with Gaskin's deputy, Brigadier General John R. Allen, visiting Sattar at Petraeus's urging. Sattar impressed his guest by assembling more than 100 notables from the surrounding tribes the day of the meeting.[25] The Marine headquarters broadened this promising channel even as it continued talks with the exiled sheikhs biding their time in Jordan. Gaskin sustained tribal engagement along with efforts to build capacity in the Iraqi security forces. He soon discovered there was a direct correlation between the two.[26]

Finishing the Job in Ramadi

On February 18, Colonel John W. Charlton and 1st Brigade, 3d Infantry Division, took over the Ramadi sector from MacFarland's brigade. Though the situation in the city had improved markedly, Charlton saw the fight as far from over. West of the city, tribes loyal to the Awakening dominated, while to the east in Sufiyah cooperation between the coalition and the Albu Soda tribe had disrupted AQI command and control and logistics nodes.[27] Meanwhile, the participation of Albu-Fahad sheikhs in a January reconstruction conference signaled the powerful tribe's new receptivity to the Awakening and thus indicated that the belts surrounding the provincial capital would grow more inhospitable to Sunni militant groups.[28] In Ramadi itself, MacFarland's new combat outposts and security stations manned jointly with the newly formed police force had tamped down violence around the embattled government center.[29]

Yet AQI and its allies had not conceded the struggle. In the northern half of Ramadi, 1st Battalion, 6th Marines, stood poised to advance into the Qatana District in the city's center while Army battalions converged on its southeastern quadrant. MacFarland's brigade had secured a foothold downtown, but the enemy contested it daily with mortar, rocket-propelled grenades (RPGs), and small-arms fire.[30] AQI placed particular emphasis on attacking local police outposts with suicide car bombs—so much so that Odierno expressed concern for Iraqi morale following a string of such attacks, including a February 14 explosion that killed the western Ramadi police chief.[31] Multiple AQI cells clung to safe havens in the central and eastern portions of the city, where they had arrayed improvised explosive device (IED)-laced defenses, manned temporary checkpoints, and enjoyed at least the passive support of the local population. Despite improvements in the overall security situation, six Americans were killed in action during February and another 31 wounded. Fifty-nine IEDs had exploded that month in Ramadi, revealing two major hot spots around the al-Qudar Mosque in the Marine battalion's sector and in the

Mula'ab District on the city's eastern edge.[32] U.S. and Iraqi forces had not established a sustained forward presence in either area.

Colonel Charlton (left) and General Petraeus (right).
Source: DoD photo by Staff Sergeant Lorie Jewell (Released).

Colonel John Charlton With General David Petraeus.[33]

To maintain MacFarland's hard-won momentum, Charlton launched a series of clearing operations that began the day his brigade assumed control of Ramadi.[34] The first focused on Mula'ab, a bad part of town MacFarland had intended to clear late in 2006 before diverting the 1st Battalion, 9th Infantry Regiment, east to rescue the Albu-Soda tribe in its close-run struggle with AQI in Sufiyah and Julaybah.[35] In February 2007, Charlton returned to MacFarland's original plan and dispatched the same combat-experienced battalion into eastern Ramadi after physically isolating the district overnight with the well-choreographed placement of concrete barriers. Two of Charlton's other battalions, accompanied by 1st Brigade, 1st Iraqi Army Division, helped to block fleeing enemy fighters as the U.S. formation cleared Mula'ab. In the first week, the combined force established a fully functional combat outpost, discovered an IED factory, and killed 35 militants.[36] Another clearing operation followed in the sector assigned to 1st Battalion, 6th Marines, repeating the approach of isolating the area and sweeping through it block by block while establishing mutually supporting outposts. The second sweep resulted in about 15 additional insurgents captured, and it enabled more than 200 Iraqi policemen to return to cleared neighborhoods that had been an Ansar al Sunna safe haven.[37]

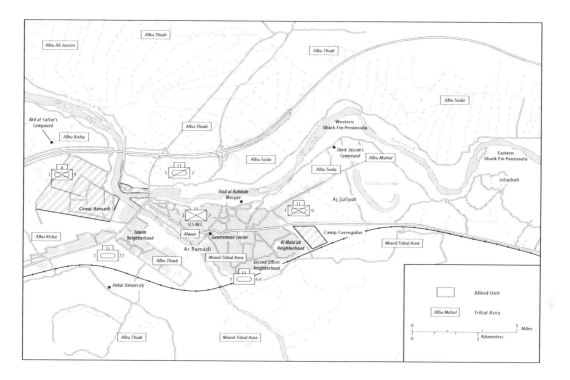

Map created by the official cartographer at the U.S. Army Center of Military History, Washington, DC.

Map 12. Ramadi, February-March 2007.

By mid-March, Petraeus assessed that the coalition had about 70 percent of the provincial capital under control, but entire neighborhoods still were without a credible U.S. presence.[38] On March 17, Charlton launched a third clearing operation, this one in the south-central district of Iskan, where the largest concentration of AQI fighters had sought to regroup.[39] To reinforce the operation, Charlton swapped his smaller but more mobile cavalry squadron for MNF-W's 1,000-man 2d Battalion, 5th Marines, thereby gaining another 500 infantrymen. Charlton committed two infantry battalions—one Army and one Marine—to the final clearing operation.[40] The fighting remained intense, with the Marines calling for a long-range rocket strike to support their offensive.[41]

Charlton's 6-week endeavor to clear Ramadi ended on March 31, a day on which there were no attacks in the provincial capital. The BCT commander remembered that day as "eerily quiet" without the usual cacophony of air strikes, artillery, tank rounds, and machine-gun fire.[42] The Ramadi operations of February 18-March 30 resulted in 36 enemy killed, 8 wounded, and 114 captured. During this period, there had been 515 insurgent attacks in Ramadi, including 82 IED strikes. American troops had suffered 9 killed and 40 wounded.[43] In the aftermath of this tactical victory, U.S. and Iraqi forces consolidated their presence in about 40 positions in the city and began the laborious task of reconstruction. It would take several months and $13 million just to remove rubble from Ramadi's war-ravaged streets.[44]

With violence in the city under control, Charlton set about solidifying his gains. Military operations in Ramadi's tribal belts in April and May coincided with engagement efforts aimed at expanding the Awakening.[45] A breakthrough came when Sattar and Charlton traveled together to the Julaybah area east of the Sufiyah District and met with sheikhs from Albu-Fahad. Though powerful, the tribe had mixed loyalties, and its leader, Khamis Abdul Karim, fled to Jordan in late 2005 following the murder of his brother at the hands of AQI supporters.[46] Once cool to the prospect of aligning with Sattar's movement, tribal elders now treated the Abu Risha sheikh like a "rock star," recalled Charlton, who attributed the warm reception to a growing sense that the tide had turned decisively.[47] When the Albu Fahad joined Sattar, the Awakening's influence spread east into the Habbaniyah area, constricting AQI's freedom of movement along the Ramadi-Fallujah corridor. By early May, MNF-I reported that these developments and Charlton's operations in the belts around Ramadi were forcing AQI's remnants to displace east to Fallujah and Baghdad or north into the remote Lake Tharthar region.[48]

Watching the events in Ramadi, Petraeus quickly latched onto the significance of the connection between local tribal outreach and improved security. He sought to use mounting tribal opposition to AQI by involving the Iraqi Government in a constructive way.[49] He cajoled Maliki into visiting Anbar in early March and hoped the gesture would generate trust among restive Sunnis. Nonetheless, he confided to Gates that considerable challenges remained, pointing out that Sattar took little care to mute his hatred not just of AQI but also of the Iraqi Islamic Party, whose Sunni members dominated the province's elected government. With marked understatement, Petraeus noted, "Reconciliation work, even intra-sect, is obviously difficult."[50]

The momentum generated by the Awakening in Ramadi reverberated across the province. U.S. casualties in Anbar plummeted by 80 percent during the second week of March.[51] Occasional setbacks took place, such as a massive truck bomb that killed 13 policemen in late April.[52] By May, MNF-W witnessed days with fewer than 10 total attacks in all of Anbar Province. During the second half of 2006, attacks in greater Ramadi had averaged 18 per day, with periodic spikes to as many as 40, but from June 2007 to the end of Charlton's tour in March 2008, the daily attack average in Ramadi fell to less than one per day — with some "attacks" nothing more than the discovery of an IED.[53] Petraeus described the overall progress as "stunning," and noted that the security situation in Anbar was "simply unthinkable 6 months ago."[54]

The growth of the police was another indicator of progress. Volunteers came forward in droves after the clearing of Ramadi, gradually adding auxiliaries to the 2,000 policemen Charlton had available and allowing him to hold the city's neighborhoods with few manpower constraints.[55] The Ramadi police force eventually would grow to 9,000 by the end of the surge.[56] The undermanned Iraqi Army brigades operating in Charlton's area of operations also received a boost from the Awakening after the BCT persuaded Sattar to provide local men as army recruits. The sheikh agreed to provide soldiers on the condition that the Sunni men who joined would be posted in Anbar for a minimum of 2 years, thus ruling out deployment to Shi'a provinces where militias might target them, a proviso that coalition leaders readily approved. Five hundred men enlisted at the next recruiting drive for the 7th Iraqi Army Division, exceeding the number of slots the Marines had designated for basic training. Streaming into Sattar's compound to sign up, truckloads of 40 to 50 men rumbled past the gate where the sheikh stood cheering them on.[57]

If security improvements and the continued growth of local security forces firmed up the gains of the Awakening militarily, so too did modest political progress. An enhanced provincial reconstruction team led by a State Department diplomat joined 1st Brigade, 3d Infantry Division, in April, soon after Ramadi had been cleared. Viewing the embedded provincial reconstruction team as a "governance transition team" best employed in partnership with the mayor's office, Charlton built a small compound for it adjacent to the government center.[58] The city council held its first meeting on April 14, and the provincial council returned on May 6, convening after an unproductive year in Baghdad. In a concession to Sattar, the council included for the first time representatives from the Awakening.[59] By July, Petraeus could report that Ramadi was "well into the reconstruction phase," characterizing "the number and breadth of activities" as "very impressive. . . a true example of what right looks like."[60] That same month, during a conference that brought several of Anbar's influential sheikhs, the governor, and the director of police together for the first time, the Sunni leaders "pledged support for Iraq and opposition to al-Qaeda."[61]

A meeting engagement in the desert that same week demonstrated how far AQI's fortunes had fallen since the previous fall when its supporters had marched in armed procession through the streets of Ramadi celebrating the declaration of the Islamic State of Iraq. Acting on a tip, a patrol from Charlton's battalion operating south of the provincial capital made contact with 40 to 50 AQI fighters hiding in a hay-filled flatbed truck. The group had taken months to infiltrate from outside the province, south around Lake Habbaniyah, to an assembly area on the outskirts of Ramadi. The fighters—many wearing suicide vests—engaged the U.S. patrol in the tall grass around a placed dubbed "Donkey Island." Calling in helicopter support, the Americans killed over 30 fighters and recovered a large assortment of weapons at the site, including sniper rifles, grenades, mortar rounds, IED components, and dynamite.[62] The mission of this relatively large AQI force had been to infiltrate into the city and assassinate the leaders of the Awakening, indicating that the terrorist group was now directing much of its resources and men to try to stop their new tribal enemies.

The Awakening in the Western Euphrates River Valley

By summer 2007, the situation looked equally grim for AQI in the population centers to the northwest. Security operations in late 2006 had disrupted the extremist group in the cities between Al Qa'im and Ramadi, but the struggle for the Western Euphrates River Valley remained in question as the New Year began. AQI had cowed and weakened the Jughayfi tribe around highly contested Haditha. To the south in Hit, the Albu-Nimr tribe, unfazed by AQI, tilted strongly toward the coalition but it seemed the coalition had done little to exploit this stance.[63]

Commanding a mechanized infantry battalion attached to RCT-2, Army Lieutenant Colonel Doug Crissman arrived in Hit during February 2007 and surveyed the situation with increasing unease. Home to over 100,000 Iraqis, the district had approximately 650 policemen present for duty, most of them outside the city limits in the Albu-Nimr tribe's traditional strongholds across the river. In Hit itself, Crissman's predecessor had established a single police station under the charge of a charismatic but corrupt Iraqi colonel who showed no reservations about standing up to AQI.[64] All the same, according to Crissman, operations in the city consisted of "going out and hoping you [didn't] get blown up each day, going around, waiting for something to explode, [and] then going after the guys you think might have done it."[65] Finding this pattern unsustainable, the commander, with substantial Iraqi input, compiled a list of some 70 targets and orchestrated a clearing operation led by the police and backed by U.S. transition teams, Combined Joint Special Operations Task Force (CJSOTF) advisers, and conventional patrols. As the combined force swept through Hit in pursuit of insurgents, it established two new police stations and set up checkpoints manned by Iraqis under close American supervision. The battalion facilitated similar operations in towns just to the south.[66]

The expansion of U.S. operations and the tightening of police control in and around Hit coincided with Sheikh Sattar's outreach to the senior Albu Nimr sheikhs. Eager to replicate the gains observed in Ramadi and to strengthen its position vis-à-vis AQI, the tribe joined the Awakening and began boosting the personnel ranks of local security forces with hundreds of recruits.[67] Violence in Hit dropped sharply, enough so that during a visit to the city in early March, a surprised Petraeus reported to Gates that he had not expected to find himself "walking through the market in Hit in a soft cap eating ice cream this soon."[68] In September 2006, the weekly attack average in Hit and Haditha had reached 67 and 58 attacks, respectively. Six months later, these averages had dropped to eight and three.[69] The dramatic change in security conditions came along with changing popular attitudes. Later in March, MNF-I reported that an intense rejection of AQI's extremist ideology had emerged as the predominant theme among the population of western Anbar.[70]

The insurgents still vied for control of the population through a persistent murder and intimidation campaign, but they were now losing ground, as well as allies, because of it. On April 27, a suicide car bomber attacked the residence of the Hit police chief, killing 3 policemen and 10 civilians but leaving the chief himself unscathed.[71] Such efforts failed to stem the spread of local resistance against AQI. By the end of April, the tribal sheikhs of Haditha joined the Awakening and began reporting clan members who continued to support AQI. Sunni resistance fighters of the 1920 Revolutionary Brigades based in Hit also switched sides and aligned themselves with Sattar's movement around this time.[72] By May, cooperation among U.S. and Iraqi forces and local tribes created enough pressure on AQI that the terrorist group's local leaders began to explore the prospects of amnesty.[73] Sunni insurgents maintained a presence throughout villages between Al Qa'im and Rawah, but the struggle for popular allegiance in the Western Euphrates River Valley undoubtedly had shifted against them and in favor of the Awakening.

For tactical commanders like Crissman, this turn of events translated into accelerated recruiting for the Iraqi security forces as the tribes mustered their young men for service in the army, police, or government-sanctioned emergency response units. It also meant making peace with shady characters who had once populated coalition target lists, as well as organizing deliberate, by name detainee releases to demonstrate goodwill and win over local leaders. The effects of such unorthodox actions were not always quantifiable, but Crissman believed one particular metric illustrated the shift: in Hit between

February and September 2007, when his battalion relocated to Rutbah, he lost none of his Soldiers in action.[74]

The Turning of the Fallujah Tribes

The wave of tribal uprisings against AQI that spread across Ramadi and western Anbar in spring 2007 was slower to reach Fallujah, the restive city that twice had been the scene of large-scale fighting in 2004. Fallujah's significantly different tribal and social character proved the main reason for the delay. In Ramadi, the tribes had been able to combine and serve as the foundation for improved security, but those in and around Fallujah were in greater disarray and suspect of the idea of allying with the coalition against Sunni insurgents. The city lay at the convergence of four major tribal areas of influence. Three of these tribes—Mohemdi, Jumayli, and Zobaie—remained sympathetic to AQI in early 2007, while the fourth, the Albu Issa, had split on the issue. With their sheikhs out of the country, all four tribes had lacked senior tribal leadership for some time, making them susceptible to intimidation and internal and external squabbling.[75] A further tribal fault line cut through these tribes' territories, with the Zobaie tribe falling under the Shammar confederation, while the Albu Issa, Mohemdi, and Jumayli belonged to the rival Dulaim confederation.[76]

The Zobaie tribe's area of influence in particular had been fertile ground for insurgent groups since 2003. Dr. Harith al-Dhari, Sunni cleric and chairman of the Association of Muslim Scholars, was a Zobaie tribal leader who also served as a spiritual head of the Sunni insurgency. Dhari's insurgent roots ran deep. His grandfather purportedly had triggered the 1920 revolution in Iraq with the assassination of a British colonel near Fallujah. From his refuge in Jordan, Dhari—a longtime senior member of the Iraqi branch of the Muslim Brotherhood—provided religious endorsement and financial support for insurgent groups such as the 1920 Revolutionary Brigades, a Muslim Brotherhood-associated group in which Dhari's own son was a commander.[77] The Zobaie tribe's strong Salafist culture also proved amenable to the extremist ideology of AQI when it arrived on the scene.[78]

Fallujah's involvement in regional politics was different from Ramadi's as well. The tribes around Ramadi loathed the Iraqi Islamic Party (IIP) and included the removal of IIP Governor Mamoun al-Alwani as a demand in the original draft of the September 2006 proclamation announcing the Awakening.[79] In contrast, the Albu Issa tribe maintained close ties with senior IIP leaders such as Rafi al-Issawi, an Albu Issa member and medical doctor who had treated insurgents in a Fallujah hospital during the November 2004 battle before entering politics. Becoming Maliki's first Minister of State for Foreign Affairs, Issawi would rise to the post of Deputy Prime Minister in 2008. The Zobaie tribe had its high-level connections as well, not only to vehement critics of the Iraqi Government like Harith al-Dhari, but also Salam al-Zobaie, a member of the IIP-led Sunni Parliamentary bloc who had become Iraq's Deputy Prime Minister in May 2006.

Conditions in Fallujah in early 2007 were not ideal for the kind of changes taking place in nearby Ramadi. Two developments in 2006 had worsened Fallujah's security situation. First, between 30,000 and 50,000 internally displaced Sunnis fleeing the sectarian violence in Baghdad had settled in Fallujah, a heavy burden for the city of 400,000.[80] Next, insurgent fighters driven from Ramadi by MacFarland's brigade and the Awakening had migrated to the rural villages surrounding Fallujah, areas that had been a sanctuary for AQI and its allies since they had fled the coalition attack of November 2004.[81] There the insurgents had authority, staffing checkpoints and enforcing curfews in places that saw only intermittent coalition presence. Wedged between the Euphrates River and the Fallujah-Abu Ghraib highway, Zaidon to the southeast stood out as a safe haven that offered access to Baghdad's crucial southern belt, while Karmah to the north served as an AQI logistical hub and transit point. During a mid-February 2007 raid, U.S. and Iraqi troops discovered an elaborate IED factory in Karmah with multiple car bombs in various stages of production, most likely intended for use in Baghdad or its suburbs. Beyond the town of Saqlawiyah to the northwest, AQI enjoyed relative respite in the seam separating the coalition units in Fallujah from those in Ramadi.[82] In these areas within striking distance of Fallujah, AQI and other insurgents gathered their strength and prepared for a confrontation with the coalition and the Iraqi security forces.

The ISF in Fallujah proved unreliable. In keeping with the MNF-I campaign plan, coalition troops had focused on transition mission rather than operating against the insurgents. The Marine regimental combat team in Fallujah shifted responsibility for the city's security to the 1st Iraqi Army Division and afterward maintained only 300 Marines within the city's boundaries.[83] As a result, the security picture was mixed. While recruitment and training woes hampered the Iraqi 1st Division's effectiveness in keeping the city secure, the Fallujah police chief, Colonel Faisal Ismail Hussein, operated against AQI in tandem with the Awakening's militia arm, the Thawar al-Anbar. The two groups had fair results, hauling in 282 suspected AQI fighters in February 2007 alone.[84] Faisal, a former Republican Guard commando and one-time insurgent, formed the "special missions group," which proved especially effective in the hunt for high-value targets, capturing former Ba'athist and prolific AQI financier Brigadier General Ali Dawud Sulayman Nayil al-Khalifawi in March. Khalifawi, prominent in coordinating the insurgency in Fallujah since 2004, continued to support the violence through his ties to the influential Sheikh Abdullah Janabi, whom he visited frequently in Syria.[85] Faisal Hussein also struck ceasefires with Jaysh Muhammad, Jaysh al-Islami, and 1920 Revolutionary Brigades operatives in the city, which likely benefited local police but not U.S. troops.[86]

As for governance, Marine commanders were optimistic for Fallujah's city council, one of the few functioning in Anbar. However, the situation in the city in early 2007 was more fragile than they realized.[87] One week after Colonel Richard Simcock and RCT-6 assumed responsibility for Fallujah in late January 2007, the city council secretary was assassinated—the same fate his predecessor had met 6 months earlier.[88] The targeted killing led the council to adjourn for 1 month and, under the uninspired leadership of a corrupt mayor, the municipal government nearly collapsed.[89]

Tribal outreach in Fallujah had yielded far less than in Ramadi by early 2007. In an attempt to build a "tribal wall" around Fallujah and make the eastern tip of Anbar inhospitable for AQI, deputy MNF-W Commander Major General John R. Allen traveled to Amman, Jordan, every 2 weeks to talk with prominent sheikhs in exile. He managed to extract a few promises to support police recruitment, but he initially failed to persuade many to return and rally their tribes. Sheikh Mishan al-Jumayli, for example, rejected a direct appeal from Allen in the spring, even though Jumayli had driven all night from

Damascus to meet with the Marine general in Amman. Even after assurances that the coalition would fortify his compound and train his personal security detail, the sheikh decided to wait, as did most others like him.[90]

The sheikhs of the Albu Issa proved the exception, and they provided an opening that eventually changed Fallujah dramatically. Courted by Allen's predecessor, Sheikh Aifan Sadoun al-Issawi had a checkered history with the Americans. Mistakenly shot by U.S. troops in 2003, the sheikh later was imprisoned at Abu Ghraib for 9 months. However, as an early outspoken Anbari voice against AQI, he had taken part in the initial CJSOTF efforts to mobilize tribal auxiliaries in 2004-2005, and had been forced to flee with his family to Amman after a failed AQI assassination attempt against him. Following an appeal by Sheikh Sattar, however, he returned and sought to extend the Awakening to Fallujah, a step that put him at odds not just with AQI, but with some members of his own tribe.[91] In early February, the embattled Sheikh Aifan found himself defending his compound outside Fallujah with the help of Marines as he worked to organize an emergency response unit there, a complete turn from his earlier hostility to U.S. troops.[92] Later that month, Iraqi police and Sheikh Aifan's armed Albu Issa fighters, supported by Marine artillery, fought a 2-day battle against 300 Sunni insurgents that resulted in at least 40 insurgents killed. A few weeks later, AQI struck back by launching chlorine-laden suicide car bombs against the Ameriyah Fallujah police station and nearby residence of Sheikh Aifan, just one of many attacks in 2007 in which AQI attempted to use chlorine gas as a chemical weapon.[93] It was also just one of three assassination attempts against Sheikh Aifan that year, all of which he survived, only to be killed by a suicide bomber while serving in the Iraqi Parliament in January 2013.[94] The war against AQI was costly for the Albu Issa, with the tribe losing scores of fighters. In one incident, AQI killed at least 40 Albu Issa tribesmen, dumping them in a mass grave.[95]

Sheikh Aifan's turn against AQI coincided with and benefited from intensified coalition security operations in the Fallujah area in the spring of 2007. With three Marine battalions and two battalion-sized Army units, Simcock had more U.S. forces at his disposal than any of his predecessors in eastern Anbar.[96] Violence inside Fallujah's city limits was a problem, but at an average rate of less than two attacks per day during April, it was not out of control. Thus, the RCT commander focused first on the rural areas south of Fallujah, conducting an operation to secure the route connecting the Ameriyah Fallujah police station to its logistical base near the city.[97] The RCT then shifted its main effort to Zaidon and proceeded counterclockwise around Fallujah's belts, moving north to Karmah and on to Saqlawiyah, where Simcock had the least developed tribal relationships.[98] Adequate U.S. troop levels, along with three Iraqi Army brigades and the establishment of two emergency response police units, enabled the RCT commander to maintain a permanent presence in these outlying areas, even as he turned to clearing Fallujah, where enemy sniper attacks and suicide car bombs were increasing.[99] In late March, for example, insurgents carried out a complex chlorine-augmented IED attack against Fallujah's government center using two suicide truck bombs and two suicide vest bombers, as well as mortar and small-arms fire. Iraqi police disrupted the attack before it caused major damage, but the incident indicated AQI still had a potent presence in the city.[100]

As the Albu Issa tribe was fighting AQI near Ameriyah Fallujah, large portions of the Zobaie tribe joined the battle against AQI as well. As in the Albu Issa area, fighting in the

Zobaie tribal area of Zaidon took the form of an intra-tribal war with the 1920 Revolutionary Brigades fighters loyal to the Dhari house turning against members of al-Faris, a clan closely affiliated with AQI. While the struggle was in part due to Zobaie anger over AQI's indiscriminate targeting of civilians as well as cultural differences like forced marriage, the rival clans' main objective was a grab for power. Observing this Sunni-on-Sunni violence in early March, MNF-W interpreted it simply as insurgents targeting each other.[101]

The conflict began in earnest when squabbling over an inter-clan marriage gone badly and the unrelated murder of a sheikh's son-in-law aggravated an already tense situation. Pressure mounted as related economic factors brought into question which family would control the potentially lucrative transportation corridor running from Fallujah to the outskirts of Baghdad.[102] The internal Zobaie rivalry bled over into Baghdad, with the unsuccessful March 23, 2007, assassination attempt against Deputy Prime Minister Salam Zobaie reportedly carried out by a fellow Zobaie tribe member allied with AQI.[103]

The dispute between the two sides of the Zobaie tribe tipped into open war on March 27, when AQI carried out a suicide attack against the home of Thahir al-Dhari, the most senior sheikh of the Zobaie tribe and the half-brother of Harith al-Dhari. The attack killed Sheikh Thahir's son, a leader of the 1920 Revolutionary Brigades.[104] Angry tribesmen swelled the Revolutionary Brigades' ranks and began fighting AQI in Zaidon. What followed was effectively a switching of sides not only by the 1920 Revolutionary Brigades, but by several other Sunni insurgent groups as well. By mid-May, elements of the 1920 Revolutionary Brigades were negotiating with MNF-W about how best to achieve the common objective of expelling AQI from Anbar.[105] Harith al-Dhari broke publicly with AQI, declaring that it had "gone too far" and that the central leadership in distant Pakistan did not "represent Iraqis."[106]

Joining the 1920 Revolutionary Brigades in its public rupture with AQI was Jaish al-Islami, one of the largest Sunni insurgent groups in Iraq. Just days after the attack on Thahir al-Dhari, Jaish al-Islami announced its decision to "disunite" from AQI.[107] The group's spokesman, Ibrahim al-Shammari, told *al-Jazeera News* that the informal alliance between the two groups had frayed after the death of Abu Musab al-Zarqawi in June 2006 because of AQI's targeting of Jaish al-Islami operatives and its commitment to an expansive Islamic state. Indicators of this rift had come in February 2007, when former Iraqi Parliamentarian Mishan al-Jabouri, who fled the country in late 2005 after his indictment for funneling government money to the insurgency, denounced AQI over the airwaves of the Syrian-based television station he owned. The network typically churned out propaganda for insurgent groups like Jaish al-Islami, but Jabouri used it on this occasion to lambast AQI's campaign of suicide bombings against Shi'a neighborhoods and its cutthroat tactics to intimidate and control rival sheikhs and emirs. The terrorists had done little to make Sunnis in Iraq more secure, Jabouri charged.[108]

In early May, Jaish al-Islami, Jaysh Mujahideen, the 1920 Revolutionary Brigades, and a portion of Ansar al Sunna declared themselves members of a new Jihad and Reform Front united against AQI, a major blow to AQI's support base in Anbar.[109] The turn against AQI in the Fallujah area did not necessarily translate into active partnerships with coalition forces, however. Harith al-Dhari, for example, remained staunchly opposed to the occupation from his perch in Jordan. Nonetheless, local realignments often meant fewer enemies for American troops at the tactical level. Engagement with former insurgents could develop cease-fires into something more, as the Awakening and the fielding of emergency response units had proved. Along these lines, Jaish al-Islami's break from AQI in spring 2007 would pave the way for the eventual expansion of the Awakening beyond Anbar to Abu Ghraib and the southern belts of Baghdad. Within Anbar, tribal rejection of extremist groups like AQI grew quickly in the late spring, taking firmer root in Ameriyah Fallujah and Zaidon and branching out toward Jumayli territory around Karmah to the north.[110]

As Fallujah's hinterland turned increasingly hostile to AQI, RCT-6 and the Fallujah police launched operations in early June to clear the remaining insurgents from the city itself and put an end to large-scale AQI attacks. With the support of a Marine battalion, police units and their coalition advisory teams erected concrete barriers and vehicle checkpoints before sequentially moving through each of the city's 10 precincts, standing up neighborhood watch groups and gathering biometric data in support of ISF recruiting as they went.[111] The cornering of terrorist cells in the city led to some sharp engagements. One U.S.-Iraqi patrol that discovered a car-bomb factory came under attack by AQI operatives wearing suicide vests. After killing seven enemy fighters, the patrol dismantled two trucks carrying thousands of pounds in homemade explosives.[112] Later in June, another combined patrol in the city discovered an insurgent cache containing over 25,000 gallons of nitric acid, enough to produce a large number of IEDs.[113] These deliberate clearing operations by coalition and Iraqi units pushed AQI's remnants out of the city and toward remote areas where they attempted to regroup. With Zaidon and Ameriyah Fallujah no longer hospitable to them, many insurgents headed toward the sparsely populated area north of Karmah, near Lake Tharthar. There they would seek to reestablish themselves, setting up a further round of fighting against coalition and Iraqi troops that would come in the summer.[114]

Cementing Security Gains in Anbar

The rapid improvement of the situation in Anbar created an unexpected decision point for Petraeus and Odierno. Petraeus had been reluctant to shift forces out of Anbar while the situation around Fallujah remained precarious, but the MNF-I commander could not ignore the option, given the province's breathtaking turnaround. With major fighting underway in Diyala and Baghdad, he reported to Gates in late May that Odierno was drafting plans to transfer one Army battalion from Anbar to the southern belts.[115] That adjustment eventually would occur in midsummer when 3d Battalion, 509th Infantry Regiment (Airborne), left eastern Anbar and returned to its parent organization, Colonel Michael Garrett's 4th Brigade, 25th Infantry Division, south of Baghdad. Separately, Odierno entertained the possibility of moving Charlton's BCT to Baghdad, but decided against this significant reallocation of combat units as long as AQI retained enough latent striking power to pose a threat in Anbar.[116]

By early July, Petraeus considered the military fight largely won in Ramadi and Fallujah, judging both cities to be in the "consolidation phase," and with fighting in the urban areas dropping off, the coalition commands moved into a period of cementing the security gains in the province.[117] For MNF-W, the first aspect of this phase was pursuit operations using the additional troops that had come to Anbar as part of the surge.

Between the 13th MEU and 2 more rifle battalions, an additional 4,000 troops arrived in the province by summer 2007, enough manpower to "put us over top" in the words of Allen, MNF-W's deputy commander.[118] Across the province, north and east of Fallujah, south of Haditha, and north and east of Rutbah, the MEF dispatched troops to disrupt long-time AQI safe havens without having to leave the Euphrates River Valley population centers vulnerable. The aim of this widespread pressure was to drive AQI fighters into deserted wadis where unmanned aerial vehicles could find them and indirect fire or airstrikes could target them with little risk of collateral damage, a process that would continue for months.[119]

Back in Anbar's populated areas, MNF-W continued to enroll tribesmen in the security forces and draw formerly hostile or neutral Anbaris into new alliances with U.S. troops. In Allen's judgment, the coalition and the tribal Awakening had been mutually reinforcing. The Awakening had been the idea of the Ramadi tribal leaders, but it "could not have gotten off the ground if it hadn't been supported by coalition forces," he later told historians.[120] Tribal leaders who were skeptical about Anbar's provincial government had resisted MNF-W's entreaties to reconcile, Allen explained, noting that "As long as AQI was a nightmare in their lives every day if they appeared to be aligned with the government . . . then [tribal sheikhs] were on the fence."[121] To encourage reconciliation, MNF-W's strategy had been to empower the sheikhs, connect them to the local government, support them with indigenous security forces, and then provide "security top cover through constant conventional and special operations."[122] By early summer, this multi-pronged approach had paid off, as the tribes had come down on the coalition side of "the fence" and had raised eight emergency response units that changed the security balance in Anbar.[123] The rapid formation of these armed tribal levies had taken AQI by surprise, Allen observed, and the Marine general compared their appearance to the sudden "uncloaking of Klingon warships" in Star Trek.[124]

The resulting numbers were vast. By midsummer 2007, the combined strength of the police and emergency response units in Anbar Province exceeded 20,000. MNF-W aimed to solidify these gains through steps such as the establishment of a large police academy at Habbaniyah that eliminated the logistical and security burden of transporting local recruits to places like Mosul and Jordan.[125] The addition of so many trained policemen in the province enabled the coalition and ISF to hold population centers far more effectively than in previous years, Allen judged. Clearing operations in the past had resembled a boat plying the water, he described, with insurgents returning to an area as the ship's wake settled. However, the growth in police forces had changed this trend. "If you come rolling back into . . . town as al-Qaeda now," Allen observed in late June 2007, "chances are you're going to find yourself in somebody's basement shackled to a pipe until we get around to your case."[126]

As the Awakening grew and security in Anbar improved, MNF-W persisted in its effort to bridge the gap between the tribes and the much-despised provincial government, with mixed results. As they had attempted to do in 2006, MNF-W tried to connect Governor Mamoun and the provincial council in Ramadi with Anbar's outlying municipalities and press provincial officials to be more responsive to local communities' needs. Mamoun labored under a deficit of goodwill due to the provincial government's long-standing ineffectiveness. To help placate indignant municipal leaders, MNF-W requested an infusion of Commanders' Emergency Response Program (CERP) money from MNC-I to enhance the governor's ability to deliver local reconstruction projects, and Odierno responded by approving an additional $50 million.[127] MNF-W also frequently ferried the governor to Baghdad to establish connections with the ministries and favorably facilitate the flow of Iraqi Government money and projects to the province.[128] However, Mamoun and his provincial officials had not played a significant role in Anbar's turnaround between September 2006 and summer 2007. The key Iraqi players instead had been the Anbari sheikhs—particularly local tribal leaders whom the coalition initially had not considered important. In Ramadi, western Anbar, and Fallujah, the turning of the tribes had come because of local dynamics and coalition outreach to local leaders rather than through negotiations with senior Anbari sheikhs in Jordan. The expatriate sheikhs had not led events, but as conditions in eastern Anbar changed, they followed them, joining their more junior tribal leaders who, in some cases, had already expelled AQI from their tribal territories. In early July, as Marine commanders had long wished him to do, Jumayli finally made his way back to Iraq after one of his sons was killed by an IED northwest of Fallujah. The presence of Mishal and others like him provided his tribesmen with the psychological lift for which the Marines had hoped, but not until the security situation had already turned.[129]

In mid-June, the Marines began holding meetings with senior sheikhs who had returned to Anbar after an absence of several years to join forces with Sattar and the Awakening.[130] On June 25, an AQI suicide bomber attacked a number of these sheikhs and Awakening leaders who traveled to the Mansour Hotel in Baghdad for meetings with central government officials. The bomber killed 10 Iraqis, including former Anbar Governor Faisal al-Gaood and Tariq al-Assafi, Sattar's security adviser and a leader of the Awakening in his own right.[131] Though not present, Sattar himself had expected to attend and would have been present in the targeted party had he done so.[132] Reflecting on the near miss, Allen summarized the fragility of the progress in Anbar: "You're only one bomb blast away from the entire calculus changing."[133]

THE AWAKENING IN THE BAGHDAD BELTS

Pacifying the "Triangle of Death"

The Awakening and its associated war within the Sunni tribes did not stop at Anbar's borders. As though channeled by the Euphrates River and the highway system running toward the capital, the tribal movement seeped in early 2007 from MNF-W's area of operations into the sector south of Baghdad dubbed the "Triangle of Death" due to its chronic violence and insurgent influence. AQI and its allies valued this area for its proximity to Baghdad and the access it offered Sunni fighters intent on launching attacks into the capital. The Triangle was an ideal insurgent sanctuary, with many areas difficult for coalition troops to reach. Thousands of small farms dotted a landscape that was crisscrossed by irrigation ditches and 20-foot wide canals, which restricted the movement of U.S. patrols to IED-strewn levee roads. This was the area in which Sunni militants in June 2006 had captured two Soldiers from 2d Brigade, 101st Airborne Division, killing the captive

Americans at an abandoned Russian-built power plant in Yusufiyah that had become an insurgent headquarters for the area.[134]

The western edge of the Triangle of Death was Zobaie tribal land that extended into the areas of Anbar where the Dhari family turned against AQI in spring 2007. Just east of the Zobaie, though, the territories of the Janabi and Karghuli tribes remained particularly hostile to coalition troops and had served as insurgent support bases for several years. In demographic terms, the Triangle was roughly 70 percent Sunni, but with a large Shi'a minority clustered in population centers along Highway 8, the north-south road that fed into southwest Baghdad's troubled Rashid District.[135] These communities were torn by a sectarian struggle for control of the southern belts playing out in Mahmudiyah and Lutu-fiyah, with Shi'a militias successfully shifting the demographics in those traditionally Sunni towns before expanding toward Yusufiyah 8 miles to the west.

Since September 2006, this area had been the responsibility of Colonel Michael M. Kershaw's 2d Brigade, 10th Mountain Division, assigned to Multi-National Division-Baghdad (MND-B) at the time. Kershaw and his troops found themselves facing a violent sector in which the 48th BCT of the Georgia National Guard and the 2d Brigade, 101st Airborne Division, had suffered heavy casualties in the previous year and a half. The brigade's main effort was in the Mahmudiyah area, which in the Saddam Hussein era had been home to the Republican Guard's Medina Division and the location of a major weapons facility—two factors that explained why the area had the ordnance and human capital to sustain a large-scale insurgency.[136]

Colonel Kershaw (right) and Colonel Rapp (left).
Source: DoD photo by Staff Sergeant Lorie Jewell (Released).

Colonel Michael Kershaw and Colonel William Rapp With Awakening Members in the Triangle of Death Area.[137]

To tackle this troublesome insurgent sanctuary, Kershaw had adopted two approaches that were out of step with the MNF-I campaign plan of 2006. First, he had partnered his units with the large 4th Brigade, 6th Iraqi Army Division, embedding his field artillery battalion directly in the brigade rather than simply relying on transition teams. He had worked closely with the Iraqi brigade commander, Brigadier General Ali Freiji, to develop a combined plan for the Triangle of Death. Freiji, a well-regarded nationalist Shi'a officer whom Minister of Defense Abdel Qader described to coalition officers as "the best officer in the Iraqi Army," had a mix of Sunni and Shi'a officers and unusually did not shrink from carrying out operations against Sunni or Shi'a militants alike.[138] Freiji had five battalions of Iraqi troops at his disposal, but few police with whom to partner because the insurgent-dominated area had resisted the establishment of police outposts.

Next, Kershaw had circumvented guidance from MNF-I and MNC-I to close patrol bases in his sector, choosing instead to deploy his companies forward into the area of operations, away from the brigade's base at Camp Striker on the Victory Base complex.[139] "Push units as far forward as possible," the brigade commander advocated in late November 2006, "operate decentralized; gain and maintain contact with the people."[140] By the end of November, 11 of Kershaw's 14 companies were living on forward outposts within the brigade's sector.[141] Establishing the outposts was not easy, and the BCT faced its toughest combat during its initial months as it implemented Kershaw's approach. In its first 90 days in the Triangle of Death, the BCT lost 25 vehicles to roadside bombs, a trend that Kershaw intended to arrest by continuing to place his units forward in the sector and thereby reducing the distance the troops had to travel to operate. The forward presence would also allow for more frequent engagement with the population.[142] The BCT also conducted frequent air assaults to compensate for the difficulty of moving by ground through the segmented terrain of irrigated farmland and canals.[143]

The area most lacking in coalition presence was an inhospitable 20-square-mile patch of ground along a stretch of the Euphrates River near Yusifiyah where Kershaw was determined to expand his brigade's control.[144] In its first operation to enter the area, the brigade encountered a blocking obstacle of 14 IEDs along a section of road 1½ miles in length, indicating that the enemy had prepared a deliberate defense to prevent the penetration of its safe haven.[145] In October, however, the brigade seized the nearby abandoned Yusifiyah power plant and converted the massive concrete structure from an AQI base into a U.S. patrol base. Once gaining access to the enemy safe haven, the brigade captured what amounted to an insurgent arms depot: Kershaw's troops discovered 138 55-gallon drums of ammunition and other materiel buried along previously inaccessible canals within the Shakhariyah Triangle, some of them a mere 500 meters from coalition outposts. The discovery bolstered Kershaw's arguments to his higher headquarters that the area needed more U.S. patrol bases, not fewer. Adding other hubs soon after in a gradually constricting web of positions, the brigade robbed the insurgents of a fortified staging area on the banks of the Euphrates and constricted their ability to maneuver freely.[146]

Source: Photo courtesy of and by Major Adam Scher.

The Yusufiyah Power Plant.[147]

As the surge got underway in early 2007, Kershaw considered the new guidance he received from Petraeus and Odierno to push troops forward into populated areas as validation of a course on which he already had embarked.[148] In April 2007, Kershaw's brigade kept the same battle space but became part of the newly created MND-C area of operations. The arrival of Major General Rick Lynch's 3d Infantry Division as MND-C lent unity of effort to the campaign in the southern belts and to the interdiction of accelerants to Baghdad's sectarian violence, but the principal way that Kershaw pursued his mission — namely by establishing security through forward presence — remained unchanged.[149]

AQI and its allies responded with a wave of attacks against the brigade's new occupied outposts and increased IEDs along the supply routes that linked its hub-and-spoke system of patrol bases.[150] This insurgent counterattack culminated on May 12 with an abduction of U.S. Soldiers by Sunni fighters at almost exactly the location where U.S. Soldiers had been taken the previous year. In a predawn ambush, about a dozen enemy fighters surprised an American patrol watching over a section of road frequently planted with IEDs.[151] The insurgents quickly overwhelmed the crews of the two High Mobility Multi-Purpose Wheeled Vehicles (HMMWVs) there, killing four U.S. Soldiers and an Iraqi soldier during the assault. The attackers snatched three wounded Americans and dragged them east away from the river, disappearing before quick reaction forces from two nearby patrol bases could arrive.[152] It would emerge later that a leader from the local Qarghuli tribe had organized the operation, but AQI claimed responsibility and declared the attack as another retaliation for the rape and murder of a Sunni teenage girl by Soldiers from the 101st Airborne Division in the same area more than a year earlier.[153]

The coalition response to the abduction of Kershaw's three Soldiers was swift and intense. The BCT isolated the area and controlled access to the Euphrates River bridges. Kershaw's battalions began a nonstop series of operations to collect intelligence in support of the search. Within 3 days, the brigade launched 12 air assaults, made possible by the provision of additional UH-60 helicopters. Two Stryker companies from Baghdad also joined the search. These forces ramped up the hunt for insurgent leaders on their target lists, conducting multiple raids each night, and maintaining an exhausting pace for 6 weeks.[154] Colonel Michael X. Garrett, commander of 4th Brigade, 25th Infantry Division, to the south, joined the effort by temporarily pushing troops into the northwestern tip of his sector along an often-neglected tactical seam where he shared a unit boundary with Kershaw on the Euphrates River.[155] Meanwhile, Kershaw's troops descended on Qarghuli village, where a sullen population maintained close ties with AQI. They questioned every military-aged male and acquired biometric data—including fingerprints and other identifying characteristics—on more than 800 people. Similar sweeps occurred elsewhere in the area.[156]

A week after the attack, the BCT had amassed numerous tips from locals, including the tribal elders of Qarghuli village, but neither these nor other intelligence reports could definitively answer questions about the captives' physical condition or location. On May 23, Iraqi police discovered the body of one of the Americans captured on May 12 drifting in the Euphrates River more than 10 miles downstream from the ambush site. The search continued into June as hopes of finding the other two of Kershaw's missing Soldiers alive faded, with a series of brutal battles occurring as a byproduct of the increased operational tempo. While attempting to detain and search an insurgent on June 1, Staff Sergeant Travis W. Atkins from 2d Battalion, 14th Infantry Regiment, became involved in hand-to-hand combat. Noticing the insurgent was about to detonate a suicide vest, Atkins threw himself on his opponent, shielding the other members of his patrol from the blast. For his selfless actions, Atkins was posthumously awarded the Distinguished Service Cross.[157] On June 10, U.S. Soldiers at the scene of a firefight 75 miles away in Samarra recovered personal items belonging to the missing men. Given the expected seriousness of their wounds, it was determined unlikely that the two could have survived a trip that far north.[158] Their remains finally were found more than a year later near Jurf as-Sakhr after a man detained by U.S. special operations forces claimed to have knowledge of the burial place.[159]

Although the search for the missing American Soldiers ended tragically, the operations during the weeks following the Soldiers' May 12 abduction led to dramatic and unexpected changes in the Triangle of Death. The intensity of the coalition's response shocked local Sunni leaders and local insurgent groups, who had witnessed a much milder coalition reaction when insurgents abducted and killed U.S. Soldiers from the same spot a year before.[160] The 6 weeks of pressure against insurgents in the Mahmudiyah District had come just as a violent battle among Sunnis in the area peaked. For nearly a year, tensions between AQI and some local tribal groups had worsened as the terrorist group had murdered and intimidated Sunni opponents and encroached on economic activities that were some tribes' livelihoods. As tribes in eastern Anbar had taken up arms against AQI in early 2007, some tribal groups in the Triangle of Death had begun to do the same.[161] Two of Kershaw's battalions had a front-row seat to this "war within a war," as one commander called it.[162] Down the western slice of the BCT sector, where the Zaidon and Radwaniyah areas straddled the unit boundary with the Marines south of Highway 1, the coalition had little to no military presence. Focused on eliminating the AQI sanctuary in his area of operation (AO) and on helping the Iraqi Army stabilize Mahmudiyah, Kershaw lacked the forces to venture often into Radwaniyah, let alone enough to muster the combat power to stay. Nonetheless, as early as January 2007, U.S. Soldiers observed from their patrol bases the sights and sounds of frequent nighttime skirmishes as AQI and the 1920 Revolutionary Brigades seemed to be fighting.[163]

Throughout the spring, locals began to provide tips to Kershaw's unit and formed neighborhood watch groups in some villages. Kershaw's cavalry squadron commander, who had made inroads with the Khartani tribe on the southern outskirts of Baghdad, conferred with the Marine battalion to his west in Anbar and arranged to meet a leading Zobaie sheikh whose tribal area stretched across division boundaries. The tribe's leadership, he reported to Kershaw afterward, appeared interested in contributing by providing tribal auxiliaries.[164] The brigade commander sensed that this was a positive development but remained circumspect. The Iraqi Army still had to be persuaded.[165]

This approach toward accommodation with formerly hostile or ambivalent tribes accelerated in June. The swarming of U.S. troops in and around the search area after the May 12 abduction, coupled with the spike in raids against insurgent leaders, had an intimidating yet somewhat liberating effect on the population. Special operations forces working closely with Kershaw lent their lethal precision to the fight and, by removing a few key AQI operatives from the battlefield, opened the door to better intelligence-gathering as more civilians came forward with information on the enemy.[166] On June 10, American guards stopped a dump truck laden with 14,000 pounds of explosives as it careened down the market-lined main road of Sadr al-Yusifiyah toward the gate of a patrol base.[167] To local sheikhs caught in the middle but favoring more tight-knit security arrangements with Kershaw's troops, the failed suicide truck bomb attack offered the latest evidence that AQI constituted a threat while the Americans did not.[168]

Sensing that the Americans might be willing to help in their intra-Sunni battle with AQI, local tribal fighters in Kershaw's sector decided to solicit coalition assistance and thus gain some respite in a multi-front war. In mid-June, armed men waving a makeshift flag of truce approached a U.S. patrol in the west of the brigade's sector.[169] This encounter led to a meeting a few days later between two U.S. battalion commanders and one of the group's leaders, a soft-spoken but charismatic man whom U.S. officers described as having a "dastardly" air about him.[170] Intrigued by the man's proposal to join forces against AQI, the U.S. commanders tentatively agreed because they found little to lose from the venture. One gave the insurgent leader a cell phone and a by-name list of the high-value targets his battalion was hunting. In a week's time, the man reported killing two on the list. As proof, the brutal demise of one had been captured on cell-phone video. A third had been brought in alive for the Americans to arrest and interrogate. Told about the outcome of this second meeting, Kershaw instructed his subordinates to exploit what seemed to be a promising development but to proceed cautiously.[171] For the BCT commander, this was uncharted territory, but the killing and capturing of elusive AQI operatives justified the associated risks in his mind.[172] Within 3 weeks, the armed tribesmen delivered an enemy fighter for whom 2d Brigade, 10th Mountain Division, had been searching since September: the infamous Abu Rus, the insurgent who had abducted, tortured, and killed two 101st Airborne Division Soldiers in 2006.[173]

The man behind these meetings was Karim Ismail Hussein, a Zobaie tribesman also known as Abu Maruf who was, almost incredibly, the brother of Colonel Faisal Ismail Hussein, the insurgent-linked Fallujah police chief. Abu Maruf's own shifting allegiances embodied the complexity of the intra-Sunni struggle, as well as the murky origins of the Awakening beyond Anbar. Although he described himself as "an independent," MNF-W in mid-2006 had characterized him as a Zaidon-based AQI leader, and at one time, he had kidnapped two senior members of the 1920 Revolutionary Brigades in order to derail that organization's cease-fire talks with the coalition. By the time Jaish al-Islami and the 1920 Revolutionary Brigades declared themselves against AQI in May 2007, Abu Maruf himself had defected and joined "the 1920," but al-Qaeda retaliated by slitting the throat of his brother Ahmed.[174] As the battle for control in Fallujah swirled into outlying areas like Zaidon, opportunists like Abu Maruf saw a chance to expand the Awakening across the provincial border and gain some relief in their simultaneous struggle against Sunni extremists, the coalition, the Iraqi security forces, and Iranian-backed Shi'a militias.[175]

Source: DoD photo by Sergeant 1st Class Kerensa Hardy (Released).

Lieutenant Colonel Brian Coppersmith Talks to Abu Maruf, an Awakening Leader in South Baghdad.[176]

Kershaw, for his part, welcomed cooperation with Abu Maruf and the tribesmen he led, but this agreement with local insurgents, though the most dramatic in the colonel's sector, was just one of several initiatives there. In Sadr Yusifiyah, a sheikh belonging to the Albu Issa tribe had broached the subject of an armed neighborhood watch group with the U.S. company commander running the nearby patrol base. In another case, the carefully coordinated release of a sheikh's detained son bought enough goodwill to entice local elements of the previously pro-insurgent Khartani tribe into Kershaw's fold.[177] The collective impact of these cooperative security arrangements would be decisive in the Mahmudiyah District, though at the brigade level they appeared disparate and fragmented, slowly gaining traction as battalions built relationships and proceeded through trial and error.[178] Kershaw also noted that reconciliation with erstwhile enemies actually simplified very little. "We are working with a multitude of competing tribes who will consistently seek to gain advantages against the other, and who will lie, cheat, and steal to get a piece of the action that is emerging," he advised subordinates in the summer of 2007. "We are on the cusp of putting these people squarely in our court," Kershaw pressed, "Stay after it."[179]

The final element of Kershaw's approach was to broker peace between the local Sunni fighters and the Iraqi security forces, especially Freiji's Iraqi Army brigade, which had taken heavy casualties against these same insurgents. Once he was satisfied that working with the Sunni locals was a viable approach, Kershaw turned his attention to persuading Freiji and Iraqi 6th Division Commander Major General Abdul Ameer al-Lami of its merits. Freiji was difficult to convince, at one point angrily calling one of Kershaw's battalion commanders, Lieutenant Colonel Mark Suich, a "traitor" for making deals with local insurgents. To involve Freiji closely in the Sunni volunteer initiative, Kershaw assigned his field artillery battalion commander, Lieutenant Colonel Robert Morschauser, to spend most of his time with the Iraqi commander, while Kershaw himself met with Freiji several times a week. As the months passed and Freiji grew more comfortable with the local "volunteers" and with the coalition and ISF oversight of them, he eventually became an advocate for the arrangement in appearances before Iraqi Government committees in Baghdad, with Kershaw accompanying him to those meetings.[180]

Colonel Kershaw (second from left) with Colonel Ali Freiji (center).
Source: DoD photo by 2d Brigade Combat Team, 10th Mountain Division Public Affairs (Released).

Colonel Michael Kershaw, Commander of the 2d BCT, 10th Mountain Division, Walks With Colonel Ali Freiji, Commander of the 4th Brigade, 6th Iraqi Army Division, in the Mahmudiyah Marketplace.[181]

By the time of its departure from Iraq during November 2007, 2d Brigade, 10th Mountain Division, had 8,800 local Iraqi tribesmen incorporated into day-to-day security operations in the brigade's sector, usually paid under security contracts funded by CERP, with Petraeus's and Odierno's blessing.[182] This Sunni tribal cooperation with Kershaw's troops and Freiji's Iraqi Army brigade resulted in a staggering reduction of violence in what had been a solid insurgent stronghold. Kershaw's agreement with tribal irregulars led to the apprehension of 85 insurgents on the brigade's target lists.[183] Where tribal fighters began to cooperate in security operations, IED attacks on Kershaw's troops plunged to nearly zero, while successful raids against AQI operatives skyrocketed. In an area that had seen only a thin security presence in 2006, Kershaw found himself in control of almost 20,000 counterinsurgents, including his 3,300 U.S. troops, Ali Freiji's 5,500-strong Iraqi brigade, 1,500 Iraqi police, and the 8,800 local Awakening members—the equivalent of more than a division's worth of ground troops.[184] After July 2007, the brigade did not suffer another combat death.[185]

The Triangle of Death had experienced a total turnaround. Asked in fall 2007 what percentage of the tribal irregulars in his area had been insurgents, Kershaw paused for a moment and replied, "Probably all of them."[186]

The Awakening in Babil Province

South and east of Kershaw, Garrett's 4th Brigade, 25th Infantry Division, experienced similar summertime breakthroughs with the tribes across the BCT's enormous sector of Karbala, Najaf, and Babil Provinces. The brigade's area, which had long been an economy of force effort for MND-B, was strained by diverse threats at opposite ends of the battle space. In its Shi'a-majority population centers, Shi'a militias such as the Badr Corps and JAM vied for control, occasionally violently. The January battle against the Soldiers of Heaven had occurred in Garrett's sector, as had the AAH raid against U.S. police advisers in Karbala the previous week. These events had pulled the brigade's attention to the south. In the rural areas along the Tigris and Euphrates Rivers, however, Sunni militants held sway, drawing the brigade's attention north.[187] With one of its three maneuver battalions detached to reinforce the Marines northeast of Fallujah, the brigade struggled to control its portion of the southern belts and was forced to focus on the northern half of Babil Province while Iraqi forces assumed responsibility for the rest.[188] Like Kershaw, Garrett maintained a generally favorable view of the Iraqi Army units with which he worked, but could expect little from the police, though Babil police chief Major General Qais Hamaz al-Mamouri proved both popular and dependable. The relative strength of the 8th Iraqi Army Division, under the command of the highly regarded Major General Othman Ali Farhood al-Ghanimi, did not necessarily translate into a lighter burden for Garrett.[189] He still carried the responsibility of supplying and overseeing the military transition teams stationed at the southern reaches of the expansive territory under his purview in Karbala, Hillah, and even Diwaniyah, although Diwaniyah technically lay inside the Polish-led MND-CS area of operations.[190]

Colonel Garrett (left) and Brigadier General Sadiq Jafar Ali (right).
Source: U.S. Army photo by Sergeant 1st Class Steven Childers (Released).

Colonel Michael Garrett, Commander of the 4th BCT (Airborne), 25th Infantry Division, and Brigadier General Sadiq Jafar Ali, Commander of the Diwaniya Provincial Iraqi Police.[191]

In the north, closer to Baghdad, Garrett parceled out his available forces to manage the risk of the vast sector. Jurf as-Sakhr, an insurgent hotbed on the Euphrates and a stronghold of the Janabi tribe, was, according to the BCT commander, a "nasty little place" where "every day was a movement to contact."[192] Without adequate U.S. or Iraqi forces to occupy it, the town remained an enemy safe haven. To the north and east, Lieutenant Colonel Mark Odom's cavalry squadron faced a similar situation in the Arab Jabour region along the Tigris. Headquartered on the southern edge of the capital and somewhat disconnected from Garrett's other battalions, the squadron encountered difficulty expanding its forward presence because of its own limited size and a shortage of capable Iraqi forces.[193] One of Odom's patrol bases astride a prime infiltration route 4 miles outside Baghdad came under attack almost daily. On April 12, AQI struck the company-sized outpost with a truck bomb loaded with 600 pounds of homemade explosives, killing four U.S. Soldiers and wounding nine.[194] Reporting on the attack, Petraeus highlighted the "frontline nature" of such bases, stating that a strategy featuring a "visible, constant presence" was "not without risk."[195] Still, even the right approach required sufficient resources. Without mutually supporting positions and enough U.S. and Iraqi troops to patrol their surroundings, forward bases were exposed and, at times, besieged.

The cavalry squadron abandoned the vulnerable patrol base in mid-June in conjunction with a realignment of battle space as the final surge brigade arrived.[196]

Although Garrett's thinly stretched brigade struggled with its vast battle space, tribal security initiatives accelerated through the spring and began to succeed as Sunni sheikhs who had been fighting a losing battle against both Shi'a enemies and Sunni terrorists approached coalition commanders to offer their cooperation. In early February 2007, Emad Mohammed Talel, a sheikh of the Khartani tribe, met with American leaders at Garrett's headquarters at forward operating base Kalsu in Iskandariyah and proposed raising a force of 5,000 Sunni irregulars to fight AQI and drive JAM from the area. Focused at the time on propping up formal governance and the Iraqi security forces, the brigade discounted his offer as outlandish and risky, not least because Sheikh Emad was reputed to be an AQI leader himself and was known to have carried out attacks on the Iraqi police.[197] However, as other tribal groups continued to approach Garrett's troops to ask for security assistance in exchange for information on insurgent activity, the brigade's judgement changed.[198] Sheikh Emad went on to organize the North Babil Tribal Council, which convened with much fanfare at a May 15 ceremony hosted by Garrett in which council members pledged to support the Iraqi Government, oppose sectarian behavior, and stop intertribal violence.[199] The raising of a tribal security force followed quickly afterward.

Garrett and his brigade threw their weight behind this tribal initiative in part because U.S. leaders had become disillusioned with the abysmal performance of the local Iraqi Government. After several months of frustration, commanders in Garrett's area finally concluded that the official bureaucracy was akin to a sponge, "soaking up assets with no appreciable movement."[200] Finding that such entities "just seemed to swell and ask for more" without benefiting the people, the brigade sought to promote good governance through less formal venues.[201] U.S. Army units elsewhere had arrived at a similar conclusion.[202] So, too, had Petraeus, who had begun to hope that the Sunni movement mobilizing against AQI might lead to the emergence of a more effective alternative to the Iraqi Islamic Party.[203]

The kind of expansion Petraeus envisioned was not far from what the Sunni sheikhs and former insurgent leaders of the Baghdad belts had in mind. As they watched the Zobaie tribe benefit from new security agreements with coalition troops in Anbar and the Triangle of Death, sheikhs from the Dulaimi and Janabi tribes farther down the Euphrates River sought to replicate the Zobaie tribe's accommodation with local coalition forces. Emboldened by Sattar's success in Anbar and sensing their own opportunity, these one-time supporters of the Sunni insurgency turned on AQI rather suddenly. Once the scales tipped—often over the course of tribal infighting—factions choosing not to reconcile with the coalition were betrayed and rooted out quickly.[204] In Jurf as-Sakhr and across the southern swath of Garrett's sector, U.S. forces and tribal leaders soon recruited more than 1,400 irregulars, including Shi'a farmers who signed on to combat the unwelcome militia influence.[205] To the north, in Hawr Rajab on the outskirts of Baghdad, Sheikh Ali Majid al-Dulaimi cut his ties with the insurgency after AQI murdered his father, abducted his cousin, and burned down his house.[206] With coalition support, he would mobilize nearly 200 tribal fighters to secure the town by mid-fall 2007.[207]

Across MND-C's area of operations, agreements like these between sheikhs and former Sunni insurgent leaders on one side and U.S. commanders on the other eventually would generate a massive indigenous force of tens of thousands of Sunni fighters. Most were eventually paid as security contractors, costing the coalition an average of $8 per fighter per day—a price that coalition commanders considered a bargain for the improved security it helped to buy.[208]

THE AWAKENING REACHES BAGHDAD

The Insurgents of Baghdad

The Awakening movement that began in Anbar and spread to the regions south of Baghdad had a profound impact on the various insurgent groups and leaders operating in the Iraqi capital. By early 2007, the Sunni insurgency in the city and its close suburbs had settled into distinct areas where Baghdadis and Iraqi military commanders recognized what groups tended to dominate, and often recognized which insurgent commanders dominated certain neighborhoods. In addition to the presence of AQI in the city and its environs, Iraqi military commanders saw the insurgent enemy organized in seven main geographical areas. East of the Tigris River in Adhamiyah, a contingent of Jaish al-Islami operated under the command of Sheikh Wathiq al-Ubaidi, a Sunni cleric. Also in Adhamiyah, a group of former Iraqi military officers constituted another insurgent network, calling itself the "Free Officers." Iraqi military officials believed the Free Officers were linked to the Iraqi Islamic Party, Iraqi Vice President Tariq Hashimi, and Hashimi's assassinated brother, General Amer Hashimi. Meanwhile, in the farming areas just beyond Adhamiyah, the 1920 Revolutionary Brigades maintained a presence. These three groups were engaged in a violent struggle with the adjacent Shi'a-majority areas of Sadr City, Sha'ab, and Ur. Also east of the Tigris, a group of local Sunni insurgents dominated the Fadhel neighborhood under the command of Adel al-Mashadani, a community strongman whose fighters had purged Fadhel of its minority Shi'a population by early 2007.[209]

West of the Tigris, a contingent of the 1920 Revolutionary Brigades operated in the Hayy al Adel neighborhood under the command of the sons of senior Iraqi Parliamentarian Adnan Dulaimi, himself a former leader of the Iraqi Muslim Brotherhood and one of the leaders of the Sunni Parliamentary bloc. To the south of the Dulaimis' turf, AQI maintained a stronghold in the large Dora neighborhood. To the west, just outside the walls of Camp Victory, a Jaish al-Islami contingent operated in the Ameriyah area under commanders associated with Ameriyah's Firdas Mosque.[210]

On the city's outskirts, major insurgent bases were found in Abu Ghraib and in the Taji area. In Taji and Tarmiyah, in addition to Abu Ghazwan's AQI network, a potent insurgent organization operated under Sunni cleric Sheikh Ahmed al-Dabash. Dabash and his family originally were based in the Shi'a-majority neighborhood of Hurriyah, but when Shi'a militias expelled Sunnis from Hurriyah in the early days of the war, he had relocated to the area near Taji and Tarmiyah and organized his insurgent force under the auspices of both the 1920 Revolutionary Brigades and Jaish al-Islami. Dabash had dispatched fighters and terrorists into west Baghdad to attack the Shi'a population there, especially in his old neighborhood of Hurriyah. Over time, Dabash would pledge his allegiance to al-Qaeda and become a senior AQI commander.[211]

Finally, in Abu Ghraib three major insurgent groups all had a large following. The 1920 Revolutionary Brigades had a sizable organization there under the command of the family of Harith al-Dhari in nearby Zaidon. AQI had a strong presence as well, under the command of a former Iraqi Army officer named Lieutenant Colonel Mohammed, who had been an Iraqi staff college graduate before 2003. Mohammed was captured and held in Camp Cropper in 2006, but his network survived. Finally, Jaish al-Islami had a large contingent under the command of Abu Azzam, who served as Jaish al-Islami's security chief for Anbar Province.[212]

This Iraqi understanding of the geography and leaders of the Sunni insurgency was often more nuanced than the coalition's appreciation of the enemy situation, which tended to focus on the more shadowy, cell-like al-Qaeda in Iraq networks such as the Rusafa car-bomb ring headed by AQI commander Abu Nur. The AQI cells in Baghdad tended to preserve their anonymity, but other insurgent groups were often well known to Baghdadis. It was among these more prominent non-AQI groups that the Awakening would have the greatest impact, as one insurgent commander after another would face a choice between submission to AQI or accommodation with the coalition.

Breakthrough at Abu Ghraib

As the Awakening spread from eastern Anbar into the region south of Baghdad, it also spread to the western outskirts of the capital city. The town of Abu Ghraib, the western gateway into Baghdad, had been a stronghold of the insurgent group Jaish al-Islami for 3 years, but in late 2006, the group's local leader Abu Azzam faced a crisis. He had watched his organization dwindle in relation to AQI, and with Jaish al-Islami's national leadership shifting its emphasis to other parts of Iraq, the cells under Abu Azzam's direction found it difficult to find funding and retain their independence in AQI's shadow. In an insurgency characterized by rapidly shifting alliances and easy individual migration from one group to another, the threat of mass defections to AQI loomed. Meanwhile, Jaish al-Islami ranks thinned as continuous coalition operations took their toll, and the growth of the Awakening took more potential recruits off the board, making combat losses harder to replace. Like other Sunni insurgent groups in the Baghdad belts, the Abu Ghraib insurgents also found themselves increasingly pressured by the Iraqi Government forces and by Shi'a militias, and the idea of a truce with one of their multiple enemies made increasing sense over time.

Unlike Jaysh al-Islami's national leaders, Abu Azzam favored a cease-fire with the coalition in order to improve Jaish al-Islami's position vis-à-vis the Sunni extremists operating in Anbar and, ultimately, as a hedge against Shi'a militias. The insurgent leader met with Iraqi Vice President Hashimi to discuss the terms of a cease-fire several times in late October and shared the idea with other resistance groups, but senior Jaysh al-Islami leader Mahmud Janabi disapproved. Abu Azzam shared his cease-fire idea with other insurgent groups as well, but Ansar al Sunna, for its part, stood opposed to a truce with "unbelievers" on ideological grounds. When AQI began moving against Abu Azzam and his last remaining fighters in December 2006, he turned to Baghdad and the coalition for help.[213] He found a receptive audience at MNF-I, where Abu Azzam appeared to Lamb to be one of those Sunni leaders who "saw the writing on the wall" and realized the Sunni insurgents could not carry on a four-way war against the coalition, the ISF, the Shi'a militias, and AQI all at once.[214]

The local U.S. commander in Abu Ghraib had come to the same conclusion. Arriving in town in November 2006 at the head of 2d Squadron, 5th Cavalry Regiment, Lieutenant Colonel Kurt J. Pinkerton had heard about tentative talks with local insurgents and hoped to use this connection to reduce violence in the restive town.[215] Assigned to Colonel Paul E. Funk's 1st Brigade, 1st Cavalry Division, Pinkerton's squadron shared the two standing tasks of its parent unit: maintaining freedom of movement on the supply routes running out of the city and protecting the flank of MND-B as it secured the population in Baghdad's neighborhoods. Occupying the upper-left quadrant of the belts, Funk's BCT sat astride a major line of communications traversing Tarmiyah and Taji to connect Baqubah with the insurgent stronghold above Fallujah near Lake Tharthar. Its boundaries aligned roughly with the territory of Abu Ghazwan, the al-Qaeda emir whose activity effectively linked Baghdad to foreign fighter facilitation networks in the north.[216] Significant in its own right, Pinkerton's sector on the brigade's southern edge was the gateway to the capital. The squadron's sector included the area where insurgents had destroyed a coalition supply convoy and abducted and killed Army Specialist Keith M. Maupin during the April 2004 uprisings. The local insurgents Pinkerton would engage were likely those who had carried out the attack, and perhaps Abu Azzam among them.

Nonetheless, in the interest of exploring any local engagement that might prevent attacks on his troops, the squadron commander attended a meeting arranged by Lamb's reconciliation cell in late 2006 and began working with Abu Azzam. The Jaish al-Islami security chief told Pinkerton that his fighters could clamp down on AQI operations in and around Abu Ghraib, piquing the colonel's interest but not alleviating his suspicion.[217] Pinkerton approached the relationship cautiously, "building the bridge as he walked across it," as one colleague termed it.[218] In the first months of 2007, Abu Azzam's men helped U.S. troops mainly by providing intelligence tips, but under pressure from AQI and the local Iraqi Army unit, the Jaish al-Islami leader desired to put the agreement with the Americans on a firmer footing. As the Ramadi tribes had done, Abu Azzam eventually hoped to have his men recognized as their area's official security forces and put on the Iraqi Government payroll, an idea Pinkerton endorsed.[219]

This vision put Pinkerton squarely at odds with Brigadier General Nasser Ghanam, commander of the 3d Brigade, 6th Iraqi Army Division, known as the Muthanna Brigade.

Lieutenant Colonel Pinkerton (left) Abu Azzam (right).
Source: DoD photo by Specialist Shea Butler (Released).

Lieutenant Colonel Kurt Pinkerton Meets With Awakening Leader Abu Azzam.[220]

Although Ghanam presented himself as a professional, the general reportedly maintained ties with both Shi'a militia leaders and AQI, periodically releasing prisoners or returning confiscated equipment in exchange for bribes. When Pinkerton approached Ghanam about the budding accommodation with Abu Azzam, the Iraqi commander feigned support — even after receiving instructions from Baghdad to keep his distance. Soon, the Muthanna Brigade began raiding sites where Pinkerton held meetings with former insurgents; however, the U.S. colonel saw through the charade and shifted his meetings to places outside the Muthanna Brigade's sector.[221]

Despite the Iraqi commander's attempts to sabotage the effort, by April 2007, the engagements between U.S. forces and Abu Azzam had reached the point of mobilizing another large emergency response unit of Sunni fighters opposed to AQI and friendly to the coalition. On April 23, Pinkerton drove to a rural schoolhouse to meet again with Abu Azzam, who had pledged to raise a substantial force to assist with security in Abu Ghraib. The view that

Source: U.S. Army photo by United States Forces-Iraq.

Staff Brigadier General Nasser Ghanam.[222]

175

greeted the U.S. commander when he arrived astonished him. As promised, a few thousand Iraqi men—most from the Zobaie tribe—had gathered to enroll in provisional units forming under Abu Azzam. Present at the gathering to help organize the throng of volunteers was Abu Maruf, the 1920 Revolutionary Brigades commander from Zaidon who would soon after strike a cooperative agreement with Kershaw in the Triangle of Death. Abu Maruf's active participation illustrated the interconnected nature of local insurgent groups as they tentatively cast their lot with the coalition in a broader communal struggle for power. It also highlighted the often-neglected agility that tribal ties afforded the insurgency. The fact that Abu Maruf happened to be on Pinkerton's high-value target list suggested something about the complex negotiations that lay ahead as bottom-up reconciliation went mainstream.[223]

At MNC-I, Odierno considered the watershed event of that day and saw it as a chance to shut down AQI in Abu Ghraib and "close the gate to the west." However, Odierno and other coalition leaders were alarmed when it appeared that the fleeing opportunity in Abu Ghraib might soon be lost.[224] In the week after Abu Azzam's recruiting drive, the Muthanna Brigade had gone looking for trouble at the site of the gathering and wound up inciting a mob that threatened to overwhelm an isolated Iraqi Army platoon. Called to the scene, Pinkerton restored order and rescued the platoon by requesting coalition fighter aircraft to buzz the crowd as a show of force. The squadron commander was in the middle of a dispute that would quickly escalate to a major point of contention between U.S. forces and the Maliki government.

Like Odierno, Petraeus was struck by the decline in attacks around Abu Ghraib following the organization of local opposition to AQI and grasped both the potential and urgency of the initiative. On May 12, he reported to Gates that the coalition had "a fairly tight window of opportunity to permanently drive a wedge between Sunnis and AQI."[225] He also noted the challenge of persuading Maliki that the U.S. military's relationship with Abu Azzam supported the fielding of a provisional police force, not the arming of a Sunni militia that would be a threat to the Iraqi Government.[226] For his part, the Prime Minister saw little difference between the two. In his view, Abu Azzam was "tricky as a fox" and "a chameleon who changed his color" to suit the circumstances.[227] Paranoid when it came to anything tinged with the possibility of Ba'athist resurgence, Maliki viewed the developments on Baghdad's doorstep with "considerable angst," as Petraeus put it.[228]

This difference in attitudes between the Iraqi leader and the coalition commanders meant that Maliki was not inclined to rein in Nasser and his troops in Abu Ghraib, where the Muthanna Brigade's aggressiveness toward Abu Azzam's men, and Sunnis in general, jeopardized the fragile accommodation the coalition had forged with insurgent leaders. By mid-May, Abu Azzam and other local Sunni leaders demanded Nasser's reassignment or the removal of his brigade. Elevated to higher echelons, the issue became a matter of priority to MND-B as Odierno's frustration spiked.[229] The engagement, an important test case for the Anbar Awakening's expansion, was "ready to fall apart," Odierno believed.[230] The enmity between Nasser's Muthanna Brigade and Sunni resistance groups at the local level pointed to a more serious obstacle. On June 2, Petraeus offered Gates a rundown of how the Prime Minister and his co-sectarians likely viewed the matter.

If we were to ask the Maliki government if they support Sunni tribal engagement and reconciliation, they would answer "yes." In Sunni provinces like Anbar and Salah ad Din, they would likely mean "yes." Closer to Baghdad, they might say "yes," but would act to slow roll any movement. In places like Diyala, they might say "yes," but would be very unsure of how to proceed. The appetite of the Shi'a leadership for Sunni tribal engagement lessens significantly as the issue gets closer to Shi'a towns and neighborhoods.[231]

In retrospect, it also might have been the case in Abu Ghraib that Maliki was not simply declining to rein in an obstructive Iraqi commander, but was directing the commander's actions. In later years, the coalition would find that Nasser and Maliki had close personal ties that potentially meant Nasser was acting on Maliki's instructions. As the coalition looked to expand the Awakening geographically and to solidify the resulting security gains by integrating Sunni tribesmen into the Iraqi Army and police, the central government's hostility to the idea would prove increasingly problematic.

The Awakening Inside the Capital City

In Baghdad, as in Anbar and Abu Ghraib, the Awakening expanded in the wake of crisis. By 2007, Sunnis in west Baghdad's Mansour District had been pressured for months by the Shi'a militias' expansion across west Baghdad. Living adjacent to the massive coalition base at Camp Victory and at the convergence of two axes of Shi'a militia encroachment, residents in the Sunni enclave of Ameriyah felt especially besieged. Local community leaders with ties to the insurgency initially had regarded AQI as an ally, enough so that in 2004 Abu Musab al-Zarqawi had been able to convene an AQI leadership summit in the neighborhood. However, Ameriyah's residents came to regret this relationship once the terrorist group acquired enough power to dominate the neighborhood.[232] Fighters driven from Haifa Street following U.S.-Iraqi clearing operations in January 2007 gravitated to Ameriyah and reinforced AQI's contingent there.[233] As had been the case in Anbar, the AQI fighters soon alienated Ameriyah's population by carrying out a campaign of murder and intimidation while continuing attacks that shut down the local economy and disrupted basic services. As a result, local leaders began to reconsider the logic that had led them to support the group.[234]

This change in popular attitudes came just as Colonel J. B. Burton and his 2d Brigade, 1st Infantry Division, established a permanent presence among the population through new combat outposts and joint security stations in early 2007. Three additional battalions flowing into Burton's sector between January and May as part of the surge reinforced this effort and allowed Burton to concentrate Lieutenant Colonel Dale C. Kuehl's 1st Battalion, 5th Cavalry Regiment, in Ameriyah as other units focused on curtailing JAM's aggressive sectarian forays elsewhere.[235] As events would soon show, Burton's troops' expanding presence in west Baghdad would enable local Sunnis to challenge AQI.

The first weeks in Ameriyah were difficult, however. Clearing operations in April spearheaded by 3d Stryker Brigade, 2d Infantry Division, seemed to accomplish little, apart from prompting more deadly attacks against coalition forces patrolling the AQI stronghold. Three deep-buried IEDs exploded the first week of May, killing five Soldiers and one interpreter. Kuehl and his battalion responded by ramping up the frequency of patrols and targeted raids while scouting for a suitable site for the battalion's first forward outpost in Ameriyah. When the outpost was emplaced on May 19, another deep-buried IED killed six Americans and one interpreter. The frustrated Kuehl upbraided Sheikh Waleed al-Asawi, an influential cleric at Ameriyah's Firdas Mosque, demanding he do something to assist the coalition's fight against an enemy that threatened both U.S. troops and the local population.[236]

The U.S. battalion commander did not know it at the time, but the backlash against AQI already had begun. Sa'ad Uraibi Ghafari, also known as Abu Abed, a Jaysh al-Islami operative and Saddam-era army officer whose two brothers had been tortured and killed by Shi'a militiamen, had resolved to fight AQI after the group planted an IED near his house despite his objections. With the backing of local clerics, Abu Abed began targeting AQI fighters for assassination.[237] As his military revolt against AQI kicked off, popular dissent against the terrorist group peaked. When AQI operatives tried to kidnap an elderly Christian and, amid the scuffle, humiliated his wife by yanking off her skirt, it struck a nerve among Ameriyah residents. Asawi witnessed the disgraceful scene and, considering the mounting beatings and beheadings AQI had carried out, determined that the time finally had come to take a stand.[238]

Abu Abed (left), Lieutenant Colonel Kuehl (second from left), and General Petraeus (center).
Source: U.S. Army photo by Staff Sergeant Lorie Jewell (Released).

Awakening Leader Abu Abed Meets With Lieutenant Colonel Dale C. Kuehl, General David Petraeus, and Senior Iraqi Leaders in Ameriyah.[239]

On May 29, Sheikh Asawi informed Kuehl that armed volunteers planned to attack AQI at noon the next day. The Americans simply needed to stay out of the way, the religious leader advised. Taken aback by the unexpected development, Kuehl countered by suggesting the U.S. battalion should handle it, but then relented after it became clear that Ameriyah locals intended to carry out the operation with or without his approval.[240] When several mosque loudspeakers broadcast the call to arms, Abu Abed and dozens of fighters attacked the AQI base at the Maluki Mosque, where a chaotic firefight went in the attackers' favor.[241] The euphoric Sheikh Asawi relayed to Kuehl that they had secured two-thirds of the neighborhood by sundown.[242]

However, when AQI launched a furious counterattack the next day, most of Abu Abed's contingent melted away, while a remnant fell back several blocks to the Firdas Mosque and requested American assistance. In a scenario not unlike the late-2006 U.S. rescue of the Albu Soda tribe outside of Ramadi, Kuehl dispatched two Strykers that arrived to find Abu Abed and a half-dozen of his men fighting for their lives against the AQI assault.[243] With the Strykers on site, the AQI attack dissipated. Over the next several days, a combined force of Americans, ISF, and Ameriyah locals reasserted control in the neighborhood, killing 10 enemy fighters and capturing 15 in the process.[244]

During the weeks that followed, Kuehl and Abu Abed forged an informal alliance that Burton sanctioned. The U.S. troops and Iraqis established a joint command and control center in southeast Ameriyah and began to plan operations against AQI. Unknown to Kuehl, Abu Azzam, champion of the April cease-fire in Abu Ghraib, had been summoned to lend his experience to the organization of this latest manifestation of the Awakening. In the meantime, Burton approached the commander of 5th Brigade, 6th Iraqi Army Division, with a request for support. Surprisingly amenable, the Iraqi commander arranged for the delivery of 30,000 rounds of AK-47 ammunition, as well as medical care for Abu Abed's wounded.[245] Formal integration into the security apparatus would take time, but, in principle, the volunteers filled a crucial gap in Ameriyah, where there virtually had been no police and the population distrusted the Iraqi Army.[246] Combined patrols comprised of U.S. Soldiers, Iraqi troops, and Abu Abed's fighters sought to normalize relations between the locals and the ISF, but they also occasionally led to verbal clashes between Iraqi Army commanders and their former insurgent enemies.[247]

Adopting the name "Knights of the Land of Two Rivers," Abu Abed's group grew quickly to 300 fighters in summer 2007, with many of the men serving without pay in the initial months.[248] Clad in tracksuits and toting AK-47s and RPGs, the Ameriyah volunteers looked, to Kuehl's troops, no different from AQI. In a bizarre scene that would become relatively common in 2007, some of the Sunni fighters donned black ski masks as they deployed for security operations atop the American Soldiers' Bradley Fighting Vehicles. The Ameriyah fighters generally impressed American observers with their military bearing and tactical skill. Later, Abu Abed outfitted his men with combat fatigues and gear that gave them the sharp, professional appearance of shade-wearing security contractors but made observers from the Iraqi Government nervous. "Who are these guys really?" one U.S. officer wondered.[249] Indeed, many, like their leader, had prior military experience in addition to their affiliation with Jaysh al-Islami. In an unexpected twist, Kuehl provided this organization of former enemies and once hostile or ambivalent bystanders a dedicated advisory team manned from his own limited ranks.[250] As the U.S.

commander saw it, the Ameriyah Knights provided him with an additional battalion of light infantry, and their impact on security was well worth the investment.[251] After losing 14 Soldiers in May, Kuehl's unit suffered no major attacks from early August until its departure in January 2008. Murders and kidnappings, which had hovered around 30 per month in Ameriyah in the spring, plummeted to an average of 4 during the latter half of the year.[252]

For Petraeus, the events in Kuehl's sector in May and June marked a crucial turning point. By committing their troops to fight alongside erstwhile insurgents and then supplying them with ammunition, Burton and Kuehl both had pushed the limits of acceptable risk. But the spectacle of Baghdad Sunnis decisively cutting their ties to AQI and risking their lives to identify terrorist hideouts, point out IEDs, and locate weapons caches made the MNF-I commander determined to support the initiative in spite of the likelihood of infuriating the Maliki government.[253] In any case, "nothing else worked in Ameriyah," Kuehl observed.[254] A trip to see 1st Battalion, 5th Cavalry Regiment, and observe Abu Abed's men on patrol left Petraeus convinced that what the coalition had witnessed in Anbar could indeed be cultivated elsewhere.[255] "Ameriyah stands as a promising example of the general concept of local people helping secure local neighborhoods," he told Gates on June 9.[256] However, to be sustained, the Awakening's expansion had to be accompanied by a parallel effort to integrate newly allied fighters into the security forces. "The key," Petraeus wrote, "is to formalize the volunteers as quickly as possible by linking them with Iraqi and coalition forces, as we did in Anbar."[257] Each case would be different, he anticipated.[258]

Developments elsewhere in the city showed the MNF-I commander was right. Just north of Ameriyah, another local Sunni security arrangement grew out of stability rather than out of an all-out fight against AQI as Ameriyah had witnessed. In Ghazaliyah, Burton's BCT had established a "safe neighborhood" protected from terrorist attacks by concrete barriers and nearby combat outposts and joint security stations.[259] As they had done so, a former Iraqi Army lieutenant colonel approached locally based U.S. Soldiers to propose a neighborhood watch group that would staff checkpoints and conduct limited patrols. The well-organized Ghazaliyah "Guardians," as they became known, initially performed their duties without weapons, content to leave the hunting of extremists to the Americans and the Iraqi security forces. Even inside a single BCT sector, two sets of volunteers with distinct motivations and characteristics emerged.[260]

East of the Tigris River, by contrast, tensions exacerbated by intra-Sunni violence led to further fracturing in the summer as long-time insurgent Sheikh Wathiq al-Ubaidi openly broke with AQI after extremists murdered two of his nephews in Adhamiya.[261] In nearby Fadhil, Sunni insurgent strongman Adel al-Mashhadani reached an agreement with a battalion commander assigned to 2d Brigade, 82d Airborne Division, after a ferocious gunfight with the Americans and Iraqi troops on April 10, 2007, left about a dozen of his men dead. The arrangement effectively saved the insurgent leader from carrying on an exhausting two-front war, allowing him to focus on the JAM onslaught emanating from Sadr City. Even as U.S. reconstruction money flowed into Fadhil, Adel maintained loose ties to AQI—though he would cut them completely in the fall after a suicide bomber's attempt on his life.[262] Throughout the spring and summer of 2007, a growing number of "awakenings" like these would emerge in the Baghdad region, and coalition commanders would increasingly choose to exploit these opportunities lest they wither on the vine.

***

By the late summer of 2007, the series of local cease-fires between coalition troops and Sunni insurgents accumulated into a broad movement that changed the security conditions and political situation across large regions of western and central Iraq. With more than 20,000 Anbari tribesmen joining security initiatives against AQI, the once-violent Anbar Province was well on its way to becoming the safest region in Iraq less than a year after it had been the location of an al-Qaeda emirate. The region formerly known as the Triangle of Death sat pacified, with almost 9,000 former Sunni insurgents joining the coalition and expelling AQI from one of its former strongholds. The AQI and Jaysh al-Islami bases of Abu Ghraib and Ameriyah had become the headquarters of anti-AQI movements totaling more than 1,500 and 300 Sunni fighters, respectively. Thousands more Sunni fighters mobilized to join similar efforts throughout central Iraq as well.

The effect of these local security arrangements was clear. Though aggregate U.S. casualties and aggregate insurgent attacks in Iraq remained high, in each area where Awakening groups had begun to cooperate with U.S. troops in security operations, attacks dropped to near zero. The value of brokering cease-fires with insurgents and then joining forces with them in the shared fight against AQI went beyond statistics charting the drop in attacks and casualties or the steady rise in caches and IEDs found—as significant as those numbers were. Just as the surge in BCTs extended the operational reach of coalition forces and enabled the clearing of longtime enemy safe havens, so too did the Awakening and the concurrent growth of its members. Throughout central and western Iraq, Sunni fighters allied with the coalition complemented the escalation of U.S. troop levels, limiting AQI's freedom of movement as their presence expanded.[263] After 4 years in which U.S. units had been thinly stretched across violent, vast Iraqi territories, some coalition brigade and division commanders in mid-2007 finally found themselves with enough U.S. troops due to the ongoing surge, enough ISF partners, and enough Sunni auxiliaries to control their areas of operations. In eastern Anbar, the southern belts, and west Baghdad, the counterinsurgent lines had been strengthened enough to force AQI out of its operating and support zones for the first time.

The process of striking these agreements with recent enemies was neither easy nor without risk for many coalition units. After 4 years of warfare against many of these same Sunni fighters, U.S. commanders had to balance caution and trust. Given that many Awakening leaders had been senior insurgents responsible for American deaths, some commanders were reluctant to move too quickly in entering into any agreement with these former enemies. When leaders at the tactical level, such as Kershaw and his subordinates, witnessed the dramatic reduction in violence locally, they measured the gains in terms of the number of American lives saved and found the risks associated with reconciliation worth taking. This was particularly true once it became clear in early 2007 that senior commanders like Petraeus and Odierno stood ready to underwrite those risks— and to make the creation of local cease-fires with Awakening groups a top priority for the coalition for the first time.

For many of the Sunnis who chose to make peace with the coalition and turn against AQI, the impetus to make this fateful change was clear. Fighting a war on multiple fronts against the coalition; AQI and other extremists; the Shi'a-dominant Iraqi security forces; and, in mixed areas, Shi'a militias like JAM, desperate and besieged Sunnis reached out to the foe they deemed least menacing to their way of life. This proved to be the coalition.

However, the participation of the Iraqi Government remained the missing element in the initiative. Prime Minister Maliki and many other senior Iraqi officials looked with alarm on what appeared to them to be a U.S. military campaign to arm and organize Sunnis intent on overthrowing the government. To ease such fears and to solidify the security gains of the Awakening, MNF-I would need to formalize the processes linking local reconciliation efforts with the Iraqi Government, as the Joint Strategic Assessment Team had recommended. Whether the short-term gains in the Awakening areas could be converted into a sustainable long-term arrangement remained to be seen. Tensions between MNF-I and the Iraqi Government over the initiative would take months to settle.

In the meantime, Petraeus and Odierno remained determined to build on the momentum that the surge of U.S. troops and the Awakening had generated. As the final surge brigade arrived in June 2007, they prepared to launch one of the war's largest operations to retake the operational initiative in the Baghdad belts and Diyala, aiming to push AQI out of striking distance from the Iraqi capital for good.

ENDNOTES - CHAPTER 4

1. Interview, Chief of Staff of the Army (CSA) Operation IRAQI FREEDOM (OIF) Study Group with Lieutenant General Graeme Lamb, January 27, 2014; Emma Sky, *The Unraveling: High Hopes and Missed Opportunities in Iraq*, New York: Public Affairs, 2015, p. 179; Peter R. Mansoor, *Surge: My Journey with General David Petraeus and the Remaking of the Iraq War*, New Haven, CT: Yale University Press, 2013, p. 85. All unpublished documents in this chapter, unless otherwise stated, are in the Chief of Staff of the Army (CSA) Operation IRAQI FREEDOM (OIF) Study Group archives, Army Heritage and Education Center (AHEC), Carlisle, PA.

2. Interview, CSA OIF Study Group with Lamb, January 27, 2014, pp. 224-246.

3. Sky, *The Unraveling*, p. 179.

4. Stanley McChrystal, *My Share of the Task: A Memoir*, New York: Penguin Group, 2013, p. 248.

5. U.S. Air Force photo by Technical Sergeant Dawn M. Price, "Polish Army Maj. Gen. Bronislaw Kwiatkowski, left, commander, Multi-National Division - Central South (MND-CS), speaks with British Army Lt. Gen. Graeme Lamb, center, deputy commander, Multi-National Forces-Iraq, at the MND-CS Headquarters building on Camp Echo, Iraq, Oct. 5, 2006, during an office visit to obtain an operations intelligence update and meet with the deputy commanding general of the 8th Division Iraqi Army," DIMOC Identifier 061005-F-XM360-116, October 5, 2006, Released to Public.

6. Multi-National Force-Iraq (MNF-I), Secretary of Defense (SECDEF) Weekly Update, February 17-23, 2007.

7. See, for example, Multi-National Corps-Iraq (MNC-I), Fragmentary Order (FRAGO) 179, January 2, 2007, pp. 2-3.

8. Interview, Colonel Michael Visconage, MNC-I Historian with Lieutenant General Raymond T. Odierno, June 24, 2007.

9. Ibid.

10. Timothy S. McWilliams and Kurtis P. Wheeler, eds., *Al-Anbar Awakening, American Perspectives,* Vol. I, Quantico, VA: Marine Corps University Press, 2009, p. 179.

11. Peter R. Mansoor, *Surge: My Journey with General David Petraeus and the Remaking of the Iraq War,* New Haven, CT: Yale University Press, 2013, p. 133.

12. William Knarr et al., *Al Sahawa — The Awakening,* Vol. IV, "Al Anbar Awakening: AO Topeka, Ramadi Area," Alexandria, VA: Institute for Defense Analyses, 2013, p. A-18.

13. Interview, U.S. Army Center of Military History (CMH) with Brigadier General John R. Allen, April 23, 2009, p. 236.

14. Interview, William Knarr, Lieutenant Colonel Dave Graves, United States Marine Corps (USMC) and Ms. Mary Hawkins with Sterling Jensen, October 20, 2010, p. A-41, in Knarr et al., *Al Sahawa — The Awakening,* Vol. IV.

15. Interview, CMH with Allen, April 23, 2009, p. 236.

16. Interview, Knarr, Graves, and Hawkins with Jensen, October 20, 2010, p. A-41, in Knarr et al., *Al Sahawa — The Awakening,* Vol. IV.

17. Mansoor, *Surge,* p. 134.

18. E-mail, General David H. Petraeus to Colonel Joel Rayburn, February 3, 2016.

19. DoD photo by U.S. Air Force Staff Sergeant D. Myles Cullen, "Pace Visits Troops in Ramadi, Iraq, [Image 6 of 11]," July 17, 2007, Released to Public, available from *http://archive.defense.gov/dodcmsshare/photoessay/2007-07/hires_070717-F-0193C-036a.jpg.*

20. MNC-I, FRAGO 179, p. 7; Interview, Colonel Michael Visconage, MNC-I Historian, with Major General Walter E. Gaskin, June 26, 2007.

21. Interviews, Knarr et al., with Major General Richard C. Zilmer, January 1, 2007, p. 142; Knarr et al., with Robert B. Neller, January 23, 2007, pp. 164, 169-170. Both in William Knarr et al., *Al Sahawa — The Anbar Awakening,* Vol. IIA, "Anbar Province Area of Operations Atlanta — The Insurgency," Alexandria, VA: Institute for Defense Analyses, 2013.

22. William Knarr et al., *Al Sahawa — The Anbar Awakening,* Vol. IIA, pp. 6-1–6-2.

23. MNF-I Battle Update Assessment, BUA, April 8, 2007.

24. Interviews, Knarr et al., with Neller, January 23, 2007, p. 167, in Knarr et al., *Al Sahawa — The Anbar Awakening,* Vol. IIA.

25. Interviews, Knarr, Graves, and Hawkins with Jensen, October 20, 2010, p. A-41, in Knarr et al., *Al Sahawa — The Awakening,* Vol. IV; USMC History Division with Kurt Ebaugh, May 27, 2007, USMC History Division, Quantico, VA.

26. Interview, MNC-I Historian with Major General Gaskin, June 26, 2007.

27. Briefing, MNC-I, Intelligence Fusion Brief, March 14, 2007.

28. Knarr et al., *Al Sahawa — The Awakening,* Vol. IV, pp. 2-24–2-25.

29. Gary W. Montgomery and Timothy S. McWilliams, eds., *From Insurgency to Counterinsurgency in Iraq, 2004-2009: Al-Anbar Awakening*, Vol. II, "Iraqi Perspectives," Quantico, VA: Marine Corps University Press, 2009, pp. 194-195.

30. Interview, Steven Clay, Combat Studies Institute (CSI) Contemporary Operations Study Team, with Colonel John W. Charlton, December 9, 2009.

31. MNF-I, SECDEF Weekly Update, February 17-23, 2007; MNF-I BUA, February 19, 2007; Odierno Iraq Notebook No. 5, February 22, 2007, entry.

32. Briefing, MNC-I, Intelligence Fusion Brief, March 14, 2007.

33. DoD photo by Staff Sergeant Lorie Jewell, "P4 with Colonel Charlton in Ramadi," July 7, 2007, Released to Public.

34. Knarr et al., *Al Sahawa — The Awakening*, Vol. IV, pp. 2-24–2-25.

35. Ibid., p. A-224; Knarr et al., *Al Sahawa — The Awakening*, Vol. IV, pp. A-21–A-22.

36. MNF-I, SECDEF Weekly Update, February 24-March 2, 2007; Interview, CSI with Charlton, December 9, 2009; Interview, CSI with Charlton, December 9, 2009; Interview, CSI with Charlton, October 20, 2010; William Knarr et al., *Al Sahawa — The Awakening*, Vol. IV-A: "Area of Operations Topeka, East Ramadi, and the Shark Fins," Alexandria, VA: Institute for Defense Analyses, 2013, pp. 2-16–2-18.

37. Interviews, CSI Contemporary Operations Study Team with Colonel Charlton, October 20, 2010, pp. A-227–A-228; Briefing, MNC-I, Intelligence Fusion Brief, March 14, 2007.

38. MNF-I, SECDEF Weekly Update, March 10-16, 2007; Interview, CSI Contemporary Operations Study Team with Colonel Charlton, December 9, 2009.

39. Briefing, MNC-I, Intelligence Fusion Brief, March 14, 2007; Interview, CSI with Charlton, October 20, 2010, p. A-228.

40. Interview, CSI Contemporary Operations Study Team with Colonel Charlton, October 20, 2010, p. A-229.

41. Interview, USMC History Division with Craig S. Kozeniesky, June 20, 2007, USMC History Division.

42. Interview, CSI Contemporary Operations Study Team with Colonel Charlton, October 20, 2010, p. A-230.

43. Ibid., p. A-225.

44. Interview, CSI Contemporary Operations Study Team with Colonel Charlton, December 9, 2009, p. 26.

45. Ibid., p. 18; Interview, CSI with Colonel Charlton, October 20, 2010, p. A-250.

46. Knarr et al., *Al Sahawa — The Anbar Awakening*, Vol. IIA, pp. 6-15–6-16.

47. Interview, CSI Contemporary Operations Study Team with Colonel Charlton, October 20, 2010, p. A-240. See also Interview, Knarr, Graves, and Hawkins with Jensen, October 20, 2010, p. A-47, in Knarr et al., *Al Sahawa — The Awakening*, Vol. IV.

48. MNF-I, SECDEF Weekly Update, April 28-May 4, 2007; in Knarr et al., *Al Sahawa — The Anbar Awakening*, Vol. IIA, pp. 6-15–6-16.

49. MNF-I, SECDEF Weekly Update, March 17-23, 2007.

50. Ibid., March 10-16, 2007.

51. Ibid., March 17-23, 2007.

52. Ibid., April 21-27, 2007.

53. Interview, CSI Contemporary Operations Study Team with Colonel Charlton, October 20, 2010, p. A-250.

54. Ibid., MNF-I, SECDEF Weekly Update, May 6-12, 2007; and May 13-19, 2007.

55. Ibid., January 9, 2008, pp. 15-16; December 9, 2009, pp. 16-17; and October 20, 2010, p. A-231.

56. MNF-I, SECDEF Weekly Update, April 7-13, 2007; Interview, CSI Contemporary Operations Study Team with Colonel Charlton, December 9, 2009, p. 14.

57. Interviews, CSI Contemporary Operations Study Team with Colonel Charlton, December 9, 2009, p. 15; and October 20, 2010, pp. A-235–A-236.

58. Ibid., October 20, 2010, p. A-242; Interviews, CSI Contemporary Operations Study Team with Colonel Charlton, January 9, 2008, pp. 20, 23; and December 9, 2009, p. 22.

59. MNF-I, SECDEF Weekly Update, April 14-20, 2007; in Knarr et al., *Al Sahawa – The Anbar Awakening*, Vol. IIA, p. 6-16.

60. MNF-I, SECDEF Weekly Update, July 1-7, 2007.

61. Ibid.

62. Ibid.; Interview, CSI Contemporary Operations Study Team with Colonel Charlton, December 9, 2009, pp. 18-19.

63. Knarr et al., *Al Sahawa – The Anbar Awakening*, Vol. IIA, p. 6-2.

64. Briefing, Multi-National Force-West (MNF-W) update, MNF-I Commander's Conference, February 17, 2007; Interview, Lawrence Lessard, CSI Contemporary Operations Study Team, with Lieutenant Colonel Douglas C. Crissman, December 1, 2009.

65. Interview, CSI Contemporary Operations Study Team with Crissman, December 1, 2009.

66. Ibid.; MNF-I, SECDEF Weekly Update, February 24-March 2, 2007; William Knarr et al., *Al Sahawa – The Awakening*, Vol. IIIB: "Al Anbar Province, Area of Operations Denver, Haditha-Hit Corridor," Alexandria, VA: Institute for Defense Analyses, 2013, pp. 2-22–2-23.

67. Ibid., p. 12; MNF-I BUA, March 5, 2007.

68. MNF-I, SECDEF Weekly Update, March 3-9, 2007.

69. Knarr et al., *Al Sahawa – The Anbar Awakening*, Vol. IIA, p. 6-9. Marines from the 1st Battalion, 2d Marine Regiment, were dispatched to Baghdadi, a town on the Euphrates River roughly halfway between Hadithah and Hit.

70. MNF-I BUA, March 26, 2007.

71. Ibid.; MNF-I, SECDEF Weekly Update, April 21-27, 2007, and April 28-May 4, 2007.

72. MNF-I BUA, April 30, 2007.

73. Ibid., May 28, 2007, and June 11, 2007.

74. Interview, CSI Contemporary Operations Study Team with Crissman, December 9, 2009.

75. Knarr et al., *Al Sahawa – The Anbar Awakening*, Vol. IIA, pp. 6-1–6-2.

76. Interview, Knarr, Colonel Julian "Dale" Alford, USMC, and Major (Ret.) General Thomas Jones, USMC, with Allen, March 16, 2010, pp. A-23–A-24, in William Knarr et al., *Al Sahawa – The Awakening,* Vol. II, "Al Anbar Province, Multi-National Force-West, Area of Operations Atlanta," Alexandria, VA: Institute for Defense Analyses, 2013; Interview, USMC History Division with Kurt Ebaugh, May 27, 2007.

77. Bobby Ghosh, "Al-Qaeda Loses an Iraqi Friend," *Time*, May 14, 2007.

78. Captain Andrew E. Lembke, Commander, Charlie Company, 4th Battalion, 9th Infantry Regiment, "Zaidon Transition Paper," March 2010.

79. Knarr et al., *Al Sahawa – The Awakening*, Vol. IV, p. 2-11.

80. Interview, USMC History Division with Colonel Lawrence D. Nicholson, January 2, 2007, USMC History Division.

81. Bill Roggio, "Securing Eastern Anbar Province," *Long War Journal*, June 15, 2007, available from *http://www.longwarjournal.org/archives/2007/06/securing_eastern_anb.php.*

82. MNF-I, SECDEF Weekly Update, February 17-23, 2007; MNF-I BUA, March 5, 2007, and March 12, 2007; Knarr et al., *Al Sahawa – The Anbar Awakening*, Vol. IIA, pp. 6-3, 6-8.

83. Interview, USMC History Division with Colonel Nicholson, January 2, 2007, USMC History Division.

84. Ibid.; Knarr et al., *Al Sahawa – The Anbar Awakening*, Vol. IIA, pp. 6-7.

85. Knarr et al., *Al Sahawa – The Anbar Awakening*, Vol. IIA, pp. 559-560.

86. MNF-W, Sunni Insurgency Study, June 13, 2007, p. 539.

87. Interview, USMC History Division with Nicholson, January 2, 2007, USMC History Division.

88. Knarr et al., *Al Sahawa – The Anbar Awakening*, Vol. IIA, p. 6-7.

89. MNF-I BUA, February 26, 2007; Interview, CMH with Allen, June 27, 2007.

90. Interview, CMH with Allen, March 16, 2010, pp. A-39–A-41, in Knarr et al., *Al Sahawa – The Awakening*, Vol. IV.

91. Montgomery and McWilliams, eds., *From Insurgency to Counterinsurgency in Iraq, 2004-2009,* pp. 87-88, 91-93; Knarr et al., *Al Sahawa – The Anbar Awakening*, Vol. IIA, p. 6-3.

92. Interview, Montgomery and McWilliams with Sheikh Aifan Sadoun al-Issawi, February 14, 2009, pp. 93-94, in Knarr et al., *Al Sahawa – The Awakening*, Vol. II.

93. Knarr et al., *Al Sahawa – The Anbar Awakening*, Vol. IIA, p. 6-10; Bill Roggio, "The Sunni Civil War," *Long War Journal*, March 27, 2007, available from *http://www.longwarjournal.org/archives/2007/03/the_sunni_ civil_war.php.*

94. Bill Ardolino, "Suicide Bomber Kills Iraqi Lawmaker Who Was Prominent Awakening Leader, and 5 others," *Long War Journal*, January 15, 2013, available from *http://www.longwarjournal.org/archives/2013/01/suicide_bomber_kills_74.php*.

95. MNF-I, SECDEF Weekly Update, June 24-30, 2007.

96. Interview, USMC History Division with Colonel Richard L. Simcock II, June 9, 2007, USMC History Division.

97. Odierno Iraq Notebook No. 7, April 18, 2007, entry.

98. Roggio, "Securing Eastern Anbar Province."

99. Ibid.; Interview, USMC History Division with Simcock, June 9, 2007; MNF-I BUA, May 7, 2007.

100. Knarr et al., *Al Sahawa – The Anbar Awakening*, Vol. IIA, p. 6-10; MNF-I, SECDEF Weekly Update, March 24-30, 2007.

101. MNF-I BUA, March 5, 2007.

102. Lembke, "Zaidon Transition Paper," March 2010.

103. MNF-I, SECDEF Weekly Update, March 17-23, 2007.

104. Ibid., March 24-30, 2007; Knarr et al., *Al Sahawa – The Anbar Awakening*, Vol. IIA, p. 6-13.

105. MNF-I BUA, April 16, 2007, and May 14, 2007.

106. Quoted from Ghosh, "Al-Qaeda Loses an Iraqi Friend."

107. Quoted from Bill Roggio, "Islamic Army of Iraq Splits from al-Qaeda," *Long War Journal*, April 12, 2007, available from *http://www.longwarjournal.org/archives/2007/04/islamic_army_of_iraq.php*.

108. Ibid.

109. Knarr et al., *Al Sahawa – The Anbar Awakening*, Vol. IIA, p. 6-14.

110. MNF-I BUA, May 7, 2007, slide 50. By mid-May, Ansar al Sunna had reaffirmed its allegiance to al-Qaeda. See Knarr et al., *Al Sahawa – The Anbar Awakening*, Vol. IIA, p. 6-17.

111. MNF-I BUA, June 11, 2007; Knarr et al., *Al Sahawa – The Anbar Awakening*, Vol. IIA, p. 6-18.

112. MNF-I BUA, June 4, 2007.

113. MNF-I, SECDEF Weekly Update, June 17-23, 2007.

114. Ibid., June 17-23, 2007; MNF-I BUA, June 18, 2007, and June 25, 2007; Knarr et al., *Al Sahawa – The Anbar Awakening*, Vol. IIA, p. 6-19.

115. MNF-I, SECDEF Weekly Update, May 20-26, 2007.

116. Odierno Iraq Notebook No. 9, May 31, 2007, entry.

117. MNF-I, SECDEF Weekly Update, July 8-14, 2007.

118. Interview, MNC-I Historian with Allen, June 27, 2007, p. 14.

119. Interview, CMH with Allen, March 16, 2010, pp. A-30, A-34–A-35.

120. Ibid., April 23, 2009, pp. 232-333.

121. Ibid., p. 230.

122. Ibid., p. 231.

123. Knarr et al., *Al Sahawa – The Anbar Awakening*, Vol. IIA, p. 6-16.

124. Interview, CMH with Allen, June 27, 2007, p. 71.

125. MNF-I BUA, March 19, 2007, and July 2, 2007; Interview, MNC-I Historian with Gaskin, June 26, 2007.

126. Interview, CMH with Allen, June 27, 2007, pp. 74-75.

127. Ibid., pp. 13, 39.

128. Ibid., pp. 12-13.

129. Ibid., March 16, 2010, pp. A-39–A-41.

130. MNF-I BUA, June 18, 2007.

131. Ibid., June 26, 2007.

132. Interview, CMH with Allen, March 16, 2010, p. A-41.

133. Ibid., June 27, 2007, p. 64.

134. Dale Andrade, *Surging South of Baghdad: The 3d Infantry Division and Task Force Marne in Iraq, 2007-2008*, Washington, DC: U.S. Army Center of Military History, 2010, pp. 55, 58.

135. Press Briefing, Department of Defense, Colonel Michael M. Kershaw, October 5, 2007, available from *http://archive.defense.gov/Transcripts/Transcript.aspx?TranscriptID=4053*, accessed May 20, 2016.

136. Ibid.

137. DoD photo by Staff Sergeant Lorie Jewell, "Colonel Kershaw," October 27, 2007, Released to Public.

138. Interviews, Michael Visconage, MNC-I Historian with Colonel Michael M. Kershaw, September 7, 2007; Steven Clay, CSI Contemporary Operations Study Team, with Colonel Michael M. Kershaw, February 12, 2010.

139. Interview, CSI Contemporary Operations Study Team, with Kershaw, February 12, 2010.

140. Report, Colonel Michael M. Kershaw, Commander, 2d Brigade, 10th Mountain Division, and Major Kenneth Mintz, "Brigade S3, Lessons Learned—First 90 Days," November 29, 2006, CSA OIF Study Group Collection.

141. Ibid.

142. Ibid.

143. Interview, CSI Contemporary Operations Study Team with Kershaw, February 12, 2010.

144. Interview, CMH with Kershaw, September 7, 2007.

145. Interview, CSI Contemporary Operations Study Team with Kershaw, February 12, 2010.

146. Ibid.; Press Briefing, Kershaw, October 5, 2007; Interview, Steven Clay, CSI Contemporary Operations Study Team, with John C. Valledor, Part II, January 22, 2010.

147. Photo courtesy of and by Major Adam Scher, "The Yusufiyah Power Plant," September 2007.

148. Interviews, CSI Contemporary Operations Study Team with Kershaw, February 12, 2010; CMH with Kershaw, September 7, 2007.

149. Interviews, CMH with Kershaw, September 7, 2007; Angela McClain, CSI Contemporary Operations Study Team, with John C. Valledor, Part I, November 24, 2009.

150. Interview, CSI Contemporary Operations Study Team with Kershaw, February 12, 2010.

151. Andrade, *Surging South of Baghdad*, p. 88.

152. Ibid., p. 89.

153. Ibid., pp. 91, 94.

154. Ibid., p. 93; Interviews, CMH with Kershaw, September 7, 2007; CSI Contemporary Operations Study Team with Valledor, Part II, January 22, 2010.

155. Andrade, *Surging South of Baghdad*, p. 108.

156. Ibid., p. 90; Interviews, CMH with Kershaw, September 7, 2007; CSI Contemporary Operations Study Team with Valledor, Part II, January 22, 2010.

157. Military Times Hall of Valor, available from *http://valor.militarytimes.com/recipient.php?recipientid=3667*.

158. Andrade, *Surging South of Baghdad*, pp. 92, 95, 97.

159. Alan Feuer, "With Final Word of Soldiers' Deaths, More Tears, More Sorrow, Some Relief," *The New York Times*, July 12, 2008, available from *http://www.nytimes.com/2008/07/12/us/12soldiers.html?_r=0*.

160. Interviews, CSI Contemporary Operations Study Team with Valledor, Part I, November 24, 2009; Steven Clay with Lieutenant Colonel Mark W. Suich, March 23, 2010.

161. MNF-W, Sunni Insurgency Study, June 13, 2007, p. 328.

162. Interview, CSI Contemporary Operations Study Team with Valledor, Part I, November 24, 2009.

163. Ibid.; Interview, CSI Contemporary Operations Study Team with Suich, March 23, 2010.

164. Interviews, CMH with Kershaw, September 7, 2007; CSI Contemporary Operations Study Team with Suich, March 23, 2010.

165. Interview, CSI Contemporary Operations Study Team with Suich, March 23, 2010.

166. Interview, CMH with Kershaw, September 7, 2007.

167. Andrade, *Surging South of Baghdad*, pp. 110-111.

168. Interview, CMH with Kershaw, September 7, 2007.

169. Interview, CSI with Valledor, Part II, January 22, 2010.

170. Quoted from Ibid.; Interview, CSI Contemporary Operations Study Team with Kershaw, February 12, 2010.

171. Interviews, CSI Contemporary Operations Study Team with Valledor, Part I, November 24, 2009; and Part II, January 22, 2010.

172. Interview, CSI Contemporary Operations Study Team with Kershaw, February 12, 2010, p. 20.

173. Press Briefing, Kershaw, October 5, 2007.

174. Paper, Lembke, "Zaidon Transition Paper," March 2010.

175. Interview, CSI Contemporary Operations Study Team with Valledor, Part I, November 24, 2009.

176. DoD photo by Sergeant 1st Class Kerensa Hardy, "Rakkasan Cavalry Squadron proud of 90-day progress [Image 1 of 2]," DVIDS Identifier 75025, January 29, 2008, Released to Public, available from *https://www.dvidshub.net/image/75025/rakkasan-cavalry-squadron-proud-90-day-progress*.

177. Interview, CMH with Kershaw, September 7, 2007.

178. Interviews, CSI Contemporary Operations Study Team with Kershaw, February 12, 2010; CSA OIF Study Group with Colonel Michael Kershaw, March 14, 2014.

179. Memo, Colonel Michael M. Kershaw for Commanders and Staff, n.d., sub: Thoughts on the Next 90 Days, CSA OIF Study Group Collection. Colonel Kershaw credited his brigade operations officer, Major Kenneth Mintz, as a coauthor of this command guidance.

180. E-mail, Colonel Michael M. Kershaw to Rayburn, February 1, 2016.

181. DoD photo by 2d Brigade Combat Team, 10th Mountain Division Public Affairs, "Commando and Iraqi Troops 'walk the Walk' in Mahmudiyah," DVIDS Identifier 34384, December 21, 2006, Released to Public, available from *https://www.dvidshub.net/image/34384/commando-and-iraqi-troops-walk-walk-mahmudiyah*.

182. Press Briefing, Kershaw, October 5, 2007.

183. Ibid.

184. E-mail, Kershaw to Rayburn, February 1, 2016.

185. Interviews, CMH with Kershaw, September 7, 2007; CSI Contemporary Operations Study Team with Kershaw, February 12, 2010. Of the 2,100 IED "events" observed during the brigade's 15-month tour, all but 100 occurred in first 11 months.

186. Staff Notes, MNF-I, Major Joel Rayburn, September 2007, Chief of Staff of the Army (CSA) Operation IRAQI FREEDOM (OIF) Study Group archives, Army Heritage and Education Center (AHEC), Carlisle, PA.

187. Interview, Steven Clay, CSI Contemporary Operations Study Team, with Brigadier General Michael X. Garrett, November 12, 2009; Unit History, H., 4th Brigade, 25th Infantry Division, 2006-2007 Iraq Deployment, n.d., CSA OIF Study Group Collection.

188. Unit History, 4th Brigade, 25th Infantry Division; Andrade, *Surging South of Baghdad*, p. 63.

189. Interview, CSI Contemporary Operations Study Team with Garrett, November 12, 2009.

190. Unit History, 4th Brigade, 25th Infantry Division.

191. U.S. Army photo by Sergeant 1st Class Steven Childers, "Coordination continues in Diwaniyah [Image 1 of 4]," DVIDS Identifier 41127, April 9, 2007, Released to Public, available from *https://www. dvidshub.net/image/41127/coordination-continues-diwaniyah*.

192. Interview, CSI Contemporary Operations Study Team with Garrett, November 12, 2009.

193. Andrade, *Surging South of Baghdad*, pp. 115-116.

194. Ibid., pp. 73-77; Unit History, 4th Brigade, 25th Infantry Division.

195. MNF-I, SECDEF Weekly Update, April 7-13, 2007.

196. Andrade, *Surging South of Baghdad*, pp. 77-78.

197. Unit History, 4th Brigade, 25th Infantry Division.

198. MNF-I BUA, April 30, 2007.

199. Ibid., May 21, 2007.

200. Unit History, 4th Brigade, 25th Infantry Division.

201. Ibid.

202. For examples, see the aforementioned efforts of 1st Brigade, 1st Armored Division, in Ramadi in late 2006, and the case of 1st Brigade, 1st Cavalry Division, stationed north of Baghdad in Taji throughout 2007. Interview, Steven Clay, CSI Contemporary Operations Study Team, with Colonel Paul E. Funk II and Lieutenant Colonel Patrick R. Michaelis, February 4, 2010.

203. MNF-I, SECDEF Weekly Update, April 28-May 4, 2007.

204. Unit History, 4th Brigade, 25th Infantry Division.

205. Ibid.

206. Michael R. Gordon, "The Former-Insurgent Counterinsurgency," *The New York Times*, September 2, 2007.

207. Unit History, 4th Brigade, 25th Infantry Division.

208. Interview, Steven Clay, CSI Contemporary Operations Study Team, with Major General Rick Lynch, December 4, 2009.

209. Interview, Colonel Joel Rayburn, CSA OIF Study Group, with Major General (Ret.) Aziz Swaidy, February 2, 2016.

210. Ibid.

211. Ibid.

212. Ibid.

213. MNF-W, Sunni Insurgency Study, June 13, 2007, pp. 474-476, 523, and 539-540.

214. Interview, CSA OIF Study Group with Lamb, January 27, 2014, written summary.

215. Interview, CSI Contemporary Operations Study Team with Lieutenant Colonel Kurt J. Pinkerton, July 2, 2010, written responses.

216. Interview, CSI Contemporary Operations Study Team with Funk and Michaelis, February 4, 2010.

217. Interview, CSI Contemporary Operations Study Team with Pinkerton, July 2, 2010, written responses.

218. Interview, CSI Contemporary Operations Study Team with Funk and Michaelis, February 4, 2010.

219. Sky, *The Unraveling*, p. 179; Interview, CSI Contemporary Operations Study Team with Funk and Michaelis, February 4, 2010.

220. DoD photo by Specialist Shea Butler, "Iraqi Citizens Take Part in Their Own Security [Image 1 of 4]," DVIDS Identifier 54131, August 14, 2007, Released to Public, available from *https://www.dvidshub.net/ image/54131/iraqi-citizens-take-part-their-own-security*.

221. Interview, CSI Contemporary Operations Study Team with Pinkerton, July 2, 2010, written responses.

222. U.S. Army photo by United States Forces-Iraq, "File: Staff Brigadier General Nassir al-Hiti & Captain James Văn Thạch.jpg," April 1, 2008, Released to Public, modified (cropped), available from *https://en.wikipedia.org/wiki/File:Staff_Brigadier_General_Nassir_al-Hiti_%26_Captain_James_V%C4%83n_ Th%E1%BA%A1ch.jpg*.

223. Interview, CSI Contemporary Operations Study Team with Pinkerton, July 2, 2010, written responses.

224. Odierno Iraq Notebook No. 8, April 23 and April 30, 2007, entries.

225. MNF-I, SECDEF Weekly Update, May 6-12, 2007.

226. Ibid., May 13-19, 2007.

227. Quoted from Sky, *The Unraveling*, p. 179.

228. MNF-I, SECDEF Weekly Update, May 13-19, 2007. See also Interview, MNC-I Historian with Odierno, June 24, 2007.

229. Briefing, Multi-National Division-Baghdad (MND-B), Reconciliation and the Abu Ghraib Iraqi security forces, May 16, 2007.

230. Odierno Iraq Notebook No. 9, May 17, 2007, entry.

231. MNF-I, SECDEF Weekly Update, May 27-June 2, 2007.

232. Dale Kuehl, "Testing Galula in Ameriyah: The People Are the Key," *Military Review*, March-April 2009, p. 77.

233. Ibid., p. 73.

234. Ibid., p. 77. See also Linda Robinson, *Tell Me How This Ends: General David Petraeus and the Search for a Way Out of Iraq*, New York: Public Affairs, 2008, p. 231; Nir Rosen, *Aftermath: Following the Bloodshed of America's Wars in the Muslim World*, New York: Nation Books, 2010, pp. 323-335.

235. Interview, Kimberly Kagan, Institute for the Study of War, with Colonel J. B. Burton, November 29, 2007.

236. Kuehl, "Testing Galula in Ameriyah," p. 75.

237. Mansoor, *Surge*, pp. 138, 311n; Rod Nordland, "Some Progress Seen in Baghdad," *Newsweek*, November 17, 2007; Ned Parker, "Abu Abed: Ruthless, Shadowy—and a U.S. Ally in Iraq," *Los Angeles Times*, December 22, 2007.

238. Nordland, "Some Progress Seen in Baghdad."

239. U.S. Army photo by Staff Sergeant Lorie Jewell, "Gen. David H. Petraeus and high-level Iraqi officials meet with Abu Abed, a former insurgent commander who now leads Ameriya volunteers fighting against al-Qaeda in Iraq," Image Identifier 20070815-A-4584J-0079, August 15, 2007, Released to Public, modified (cropped).

240. Kuehl, "Testing Galula in Ameriyah," p. 76.

241. Nordland, "Some Progress Seen in Baghdad"; Joshua Partlow, "For U.S. Unit in Baghdad, an Alliance of Last Resort," *The Washington Post*, June 9, 2007.

242. Kuehl, "Testing Galula in Ameriyah," p. 76.

243. Ibid., pp. 76, 78.

244. Partlow, "Alliance of Last Resort."

245. Interview, Institute for the Study of War with Burton, November 29, 2007.

246. Ibid., November 14, 2007.

247. Kuehl, "Testing Galula in Ameriyah," p. 78; Rosen, *Aftermath*, pp. 306-308.

248. Kuehl, "Testing Galula in Ameriyah," p. 78.

249. Partlow, "Alliance of Last Resort." See also Mansoor, *Surge*, p. 139.

250. Kuehl, "Testing Galula in Ameriyah," p. 78.

251. Mansoor, *Surge*, p. 138.

252. Kuehl, "Testing Galula in Ameriyah," p. 80.

253. MNF-I, SECDEF Weekly Update, May 27-June 2, 2007, and June 30, 2007.

254. Partlow, "Alliance of Last Resort."

255. Mansoor, *Surge*, p. 139.

256. MNF-I, SECDEF Weekly Update, June 3-9, 2007.

257. Ibid.

258. Ibid.

259. Interview, Institute for the Study of War with Colonel Burton, November 14, 2007.

260. Ibid., November 29, 2007.

261. Mansoor, *Surge*, p. 140.

262. Geoff Ziezulewicz, "Empowered by the U.S., Imprisoned by the Iraqis," *Stars and Stripes*, September 24, 2009.

263. Interview, Knarr, Alford, and Graves with Colonel (Ret.) Richard Welch, April 25, 2010, p. A-133, in Knarr et al., *Al Sahawa — The Awakening*, Vol. II.

CHAPTER 5

SUMMER 2007—THE SURGE OF OPERATIONS

The surge of additional forces into Baghdad and the gathering momentum of the Awakening movement in Anbar and the belts around the city changed the situation in the Iraqi capital significantly in the first 5 months of 2007. For more than a year, Sunni insurgent groups and Shi'a militias had controlled large swaths of territory inside Baghdad as the Multi-National Force-Iraq (MNF-I) transition strategy played out. By June 2007, the U.S. and Iraqi surges of reinforcements had quieted the Shi'a militias and robbed the Sunni insurgents of most of their territory inside the city, but this progress had come at significant cost. May 2007 had been a harrowing month, with 120 American combat deaths, the worst monthly tally since 2005. "This is a period in which it gets harder before it gets easier," General David H. Petraeus told one journalist at the time.[1] Lieutenant General Raymond T. Odierno had also foreseen this steady increase in violence and was not inclined to abandon his deliberate approach.[2] In a certain sense, the fight had just begun. As the last surge units arrived in May and June 2007, Petraeus and Odierno looked to use their additional forces to extend Multi-National Corps-Iraq's (MNC-I) forward presence deeper into the belts surrounding the city, with the aim of pushing al-Qaeda in Iraq (AQI) and its allies farther away from their former operating zones in Baghdad.

The first step, however, was settling the deployment cycle of the 5 surge brigades and the 15 other brigade-sized U.S. units in Iraq to ensure that the "surge of operations" could extend far enough into 2008 to complete MNF-I and MNC-I's new campaign plan. If these brigades served the usual 12-month rotation period in Iraq, the surge would begin winding down at the end of 2007, little more than 6 months away. To give the campaign plan sufficient time to unfold, the units deployed to Iraq would have to stay longer than the normal year-long combat tour. Petraeus and Odierno recognized this and lobbied Secretary of Defense (SECDEF) Robert M. Gates to extend the length of unit deployments so as to provide, in Petraeus's words, "the flexibility to continue with the new strategy into early 2008 if needed."[3] Convinced, in April Gates announced that he would be extending the deployments of most active-duty Army units stationed in Iraq from 12 to 15 months. Even so, the announcement caught some units off guard. One deploying brigade commander learned of the extension by reading a Department of Defense (DoD) press release on his BlackBerry on his way through Kuwait.[4] The 25th Infantry Division's commander, Major General Benjamin R. Mixon, whose headquarters was responsible for Multi-National Division-North (MND-N), was stunned to see the announcement on an airport television monitor on his way back from mid-tour leave.[5] All the same, the extension seemed the only way to keep force levels in Iraq elevated without shortchanging other Army commitments.[6]

In mid-June, with the future of the surge forces settled, MNC-I would kick off the first of three major operations in 2007-2008 to push AQI out of its support zones and sanctuaries beyond the city and then pursue the group as it displaced in search of new safe havens—a process that Petraeus described as a "surge of operations."[7] After more than 2 years in which MNF-I's insurgent enemies had enjoyed the initiative, the coalition commanders were determined to seize it once again.

REGAINING THE INITIATIVE: OPERATION PHANTOM THUNDER

The first phase of the "surge of operations" was Operation PHANTOM THUNDER, a set of division operations across central Iraq and portions of Anbar and Diyala Provinces in which Odierno and MNC-I intended to stop the "accelerants" that flowed into Baghdad to perpetuate the cycle of sectarian violence. Having created the new Multi- National Division-Center (MND-C) area of operations and redirected MND-N's focus to the lower Diyala River Valley, Odierno intended to send his late-arriving surge units and his operational reserve into those same areas to disrupt or destroy the support zones and sanctuaries from which AQI and its allies had terrorized Baghdad since 2004.[8] To accomplish this objective, Odierno tasked MND-N with conducting a new operation to clear AQI from the lower Diyala Valley, and particularly from the provincial capital of Baqubah. During Operation PHANTOM THUNDER, each of the other U.S. divisions — Multi-National Division-Baghdad (MND-B), MND-C, and Multi-National Force-West (MNF-W) — would mount supporting operations in their own areas of operations at the same time.

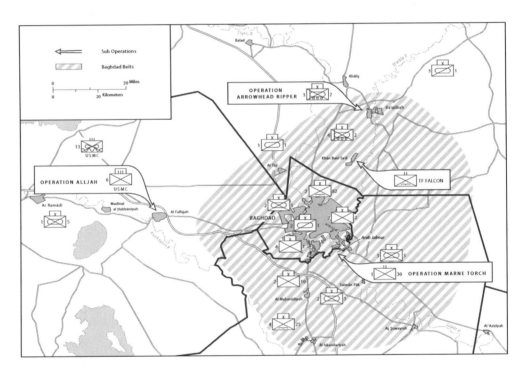

Map created by the official cartographer at the U.S. Army Center of Military History, Washington, DC.

Map 13. Operation PHANTOM THUNDER, June–August 2007.

After 5 months of operating as MNC-I, Odierno and his III Corps staff had zeroed in on the areas they judged to be the most important support zones and sanctuaries for AQI and its allies, and in Operation PHANTOM THUNDER, MNC-I's units would attack into these zones in central Iraq. Within the III Corps staff, Colonel James B. Hickey and his Counter-Improvised Explosive Device (IED) Operations Integration Cell (COIC) had noted particular "no-go" areas that coalition and Iraqi units had come to avoid over time because of the certainty of being attacked there, either by small arms or IEDs. The COIC was especially keen to locate areas where insurgents had had time to emplace belts of blocking obstacles in the form of deep-buried IEDs that could destroy any coalition vehicle, including tanks. As Hickey saw it, those areas were likely the enemy's most important bases, which is why the enemy had set up a deliberate defense of them. Rather than avoid these areas as coalition and Iraqi units had tended to do, Odierno, Hickey, and III Corps intended to attack into them and seize what they believed was key terrain to the enemy.

Hickey and the cell had also drawn from several years of significant activities (SIGACTs) and other data to predict where insurgent groups in each of these zones were likely to displace once they came under pressure. The COIC was able to do so because in almost every case, coalition troops had previously conducted raids into the Sunni insurgency's support zones—sometimes on multiple occasions—and it was possible to examine SIGACT data, intelligence reports, and tribal ties to see where the insurgents had fled on those previous occasions. It had been rare in previous years for the coalition to pursue AQI and other groups into their secondary locations, but in late spring 2007, III Corps aimed to break that pattern and maintain the pressure as the insurgents sought new bases. Using Hickey's analysis, Odierno would plan follow-on operations to disrupt the terrorists before they could establish new support zones elsewhere.

This concept determined where MNC-I deployed the surge units arriving from April onward. Shortly after Gates's announcement of the extended combat tours, the third surge brigade, Colonel Wayne W. Grigsby's 3d Brigade Combat Team, 3d Infantry Division, deployed to MND-C, commanded by Major General Rick Lynch's 3d Infantry Division. Odierno detached Grigsby's tank battalion to MND-B and his artillery battalion to the Camp Bucca guard force, but he sent the remainder of the brigade to a sector where only a handful of Iraqi units guarded the eastern desert approaches to the capital.[9] Though it was difficult to support this remote location in logistical terms, Grigsby's position at a new operating base nearly 32 kilometers east of Baghdad (Forward Operating Base Hammer) placed him astride a troublesome route used by Shi'a weapons smugglers while allowing him to support operations against well-defended Sunni insurgent strongholds south and west of the capital.[10]

When the fourth surge brigade, Colonel Jon S. Lehr's 4th Brigade Combat Team, 2d Infantry Division, arrived in April, Odierno assigned it to Mixon's MND-N and deployed it to Baghdad's northern belt stretching from the Tigris River east toward Diyala Province. By giving Lehr and his brigade responsibility for Tarmiyah, a critical node in AQI and other Sunni insurgents' northern line of communications, Odierno enabled Colonel Paul Funk's MND-B's 1st Brigade Combat Team, 1st Cavalry Division, to shift its focus west toward Sunni insurgent sanctuaries near Lake Tharthar.[11] A few weeks later, the 13th Marine Expeditionary Unit, U.S. Central Command's (CENTCOM) theater reserve, also deployed to the Tharthar region northeast of Fallujah to operate in the "seams" among the MNF-W, MND-B, and MND-N boundaries. Finally, when the last surge brigade,

Colonel Terry R. Ferrell's 2d Brigade Combat Team, 3d Infantry Division, arrived in May, Odierno deployed it into MND-C's area of responsibility to occupy the thin wedge of farmland along the meandering Tigris River south of Baghdad that included the longtime AQI stronghold of Arab Jabour.[12] With the addition of four American brigades' combat power between April and June, III Corps and four American divisions were positioned to apply pressure simultaneously along sectarian fault lines in Baghdad and along the lines of communications essential to controlling the city. It would be the largest operation in the Baghdad region since April 2003.

Clearing Baqubah

Within MND-N, the main task for Operation PHANTOM THUNDER was to retake the city of Baqubah from AQI. Diyala had been the scene of ethno-sectarian violence since the early months of the war. With its volatile mix of Sunni and Shi'a tribes and tensions stemming from Kurdish encroachment, the rural province had often been described as "little Iraq," a microcosm of the broader ethno-sectarian divisions that spanned the country. It was also a key al-Qaeda stronghold. In spring 2006, Abu Musab al-Zarqawi had declared Baqubah the capital of his new "caliphate," and the AQI leader had been killed only a few kilometers west of the city in June 2006.[13] In the first months of 2007, many of the AQI operatives who fled Anbar and Baghdad under the twin pressures of the Awakening and the surge had reestablished themselves in Baqubah, after which the city's security eroded rapidly.[14] By late spring 2007, the city's population was nearly under AQI's control, with the group in control of the city's services, including water and electricity, and the local mosques taken over by AQI imams who began enforcing Sharia law.[15] Coalition analysts estimated there were between 300 and 500 AQI fighters terrorizing the population and preparing a deliberate defense in the city. The situation was exacerbated by the behavior of the Diyala-based 5th Iraqi Army division and the local police, both of whom were led by sectarian commanders who allowed Shi'a death squads to operate in the province.[16]

The extent of AQI's grip on Baqubah stunned Odierno, who described the entire city as a "war zone" after returning from a visit.[17] The sectarian struggle among rival militant groups to control the lines of communication running between Baghdad and Baqubah, along with the Iraqi Government's almost willful neglect of Sunnis in the contested areas of the province, made the dire situation far more than the single U.S. brigade in the province could handle. With responsibility for all of Diyala, Colonel David W. Sutherland's 3d Brigade Combat Team, 1st Cavalry Division, was already stretched thin by its mission to screen the Iranian frontier. Sutherland's remaining units struggled to hold their own both in the city and throughout the highly contested villages along the shifting sectarian fault line near the convergence of the Diyala and Tigris River valleys. As violence in Baqubah rose in early 2007, Mixon and MND-N asked MNC-I for an additional brigade to operate in the lower Diyala River Valley while Sutherland's brigade focused on the upper valley. However, with most of the surge brigades still en route, Odierno had been able to send only an additional battalion from his operational reserve, Colonel Steven Towsend's 3d Brigade Combat Team, 2d Infantry Division, in March. The additional troops, from Lieutenant Colonel Bruce Antonia's 5th Battalion, 20th Infantry, enabled Sutherland's brigade to secure a foothold in eastern Baqubah, but coalition intelligence estimated that AQI had mined the western half of the city with about 175 deep-buried IEDs and had booby-trapped an unknown number of houses to prevent U.S. troops from clearing the area.[18] The group had also dug defensive positions throughout the dense palm groves around the city.

Source: DoD photo by Specialist Benjamin Fox (Released).

Colonel David Sutherland With General David Petraeus in Baqubah.[19]

For U.S. units, the fighting in Diyala in the late spring and summer of 2007 would be some of the most intense of the entire war. Antonia's troops encountered heavy resistance as they attempted to clear the areas surrounding the city, especially in the form of IEDs that destroyed U.S. vehicles on an almost daily basis, sometimes accompanied by insurgent small arms fire. In one instance on April 5, 2007, after an IED destroyed a Bradley fighting vehicle in Baqubah, Specialist Christopher Waiters ignored commands to stay in his nearby Stryker vehicle and braved heavy insurgent fire to pull two wounded Soldiers from the Bradley to safety, returning to remove a third dead Soldier from the vehicle as well. For this act, Waiters received the Distinguished Service Cross. In another incident on April 23, two suicide car bombs rammed a U.S. outpost in the village of Sadah near Baqubah, after which insurgents mounted an unsuccessful ground assault on the troops. The car bombs collapsed a building on the compound, killing 9 Soldiers and wounding 20 more.

Source: DoD photo courtesy 5th Mobile Public Affairs Detachment (Released).

Soldiers Move Through the Outskirts of Palm Groves in Baqubah During the Night of March 25.[20]

As Antonia's battalion fought AQI around Baqubah in April and May, the fourth surge brigade—Lehr's 4th Brigade Combat Team, 2d Infantry Division—flowed into the northern belt, strengthening the coalition position along the western boundary of Diyala and providing another Stryker battalion to operate in the highly violent area between Baqubah and Baghdad. As the Stryker units isolated AQI in Baqubah by clearing the roads and villages surrounding the city, they found that the deep-buried IEDs AQI emplaced on Diyala's roads were often powerful enough to destroy the heaviest American armored vehicles. In early May, deep-buried IEDs destroyed three Stryker vehicles and killed eight U.S. troops in 1 week in the Baqubah area alone. "[W]e're in for some tough challenges in Diyala," Petraeus observed when he reported the incident to Gates.[21] Illustrating his point, later in the month, a deep-buried IED in the city destroyed an M1 tank. The area was dangerous for U.S. aviators as well. In the last week of May, insurgents shot down two U.S. helicopters using truck-mounted heavy machine guns, one of them just northeast of Baqubah.[22]

In the same week, on May 25, U.S. troops attempting to push AQI from the villages south of the city captured a house that AQI had used as an ad hoc prison and liberated 42 Iraqis that AQI fighters had imprisoned and tortured there. The site was just one of multiple "torture houses" that AQI had set up in the area to terrorize the population into submission.[23] The group also took aim at local Iraqi officials for much the same purpose. In a high-profile case, AQI attacked the home of the Baqubah police chief on June 8, killing his wife and 13 others, but missing the police leader himself.[24]

The arrival of the final surge brigades in May and June 2007 finally generated enough combat power for MNC-I to allow Odierno to send an additional brigade to Diyala. In late May, he pulled the rest of the 3d Brigade Combat Team, 2d Infantry Division, from its duties as MND-B's mobile strike force and made them available to MND-N for a decisive operation to retake the whole of the Baqubah area from AQI. It was an operation for which Townsend himself had lobbied for Odierno's support. After dispatching Antonia's 5th Battalion, 20th Infantry Regiment, from his own brigade in March, Townsend had followed the battalion's progress from his headquarters in Baghdad and had seen what he believed was an opportunity to help Sutherland seize most of Diyala from the enemy. Although Major General Joseph F. Fil, Jr., protested the proposed redirection of his strike force, Odierno agreed with Townsend that the coalition now had the opportunity to apply simultaneous pressure on AQI across central Iraq. He also believed that the ongoing surge mitigated the risk of reducing the Strykers in Baghdad, where incoming battalions would offset the departure of Townsend's units. Accordingly, Odierno directed Townsend to take his brigade headquarters and two more Stryker battalions to Diyala to fight alongside Sutherland's 3d Brigade, under MND-N's control.[25]

The Stryker brigade's move to Baqubah marked the beginning of Operation PHANTOM THUNDER for MND-N (and the beginning of Townsend's brigade-level portion called Operation ARROWHEAD RIPPER). On the night of June 18, 2007, one of Townsend's battalions, the 1st Battalion, 23d Infantry Regiment, road marched 90 kilometers from Baghdad to Baqubah while U.S. air strikes pounded AQI positions in the city. The two U.S. battalions already outside the city conducted air assaults into blocking positions to cut off any AQI fighters' escape.

Pausing only briefly outside the city to let the air strikes and air assaults take place, Townsend's troops attacked on June 19 at 1 a.m., assaulting AQI positions in the western side of the city. Within hours, the Strykers and their dismounted infantry squads were moving through the town and pushing back AQI fighters. With the help of tribal irregulars who pointed out about 30 deep-buried IEDs on the main road through the city, Townsend's units lost only 1 Bradley fighting vehicle destroyed on the operation's first day, while killing 36 enemy combatants.[26]

Source: DoD photo by Sergeant Armando Monroig (Released).

Soldiers from the 5th Iraqi Army Division and 3d Stryker BCT, 2d Infantry Division, During Operation ARROWHEAD RIPPER.[27]

MNC-I's operational maneuver appeared to have achieved its aim of surprising the large AQI contingent in Baqubah, which was clearly unprepared for the sudden appearance of a brigade's worth of additional U.S. combat power. Townsend's move to Baqubah doubled the number of coalition forces in the provincial capital and freed up Sutherland's troops to shift their focus northeast toward Muqdadiyah, interdicting enemy fighters as they withdrew north and east up the Diyala River Valley in search of new sanctuaries.[28] Clearing west Baqubah was not easy, even after most AQI fighters had fled. The terrorist group had rigged dozens of houses to explode as U.S. or Iraqi troops entered them, in one case booby-trapping two entire city blocks of houses. Even so, by June 25, Townsend's troops had finished clearing west Baqubah and had enabled local Iraqi security forces, Iraqi officials, and the Diyala provincial reconstruction team to return to the cleared areas. Operations in and around Baqubah continued through July, with elements of the two brigade combat teams (BCTs) implementing tactics similar to those introduced in Baghdad: deliberate house-by-house clearing, followed by the establishment of company-sized combat outposts and the use of concrete barriers to control access to neighborhoods.[29]

In the first month of Operation PHANTOM THUNDER, MND-N's troops in Baqubah killed more than 60 AQI fighters and captured another 215, while eliminating more than 130 IEDs.[30] By July 26, Baqubah was firmly enough in coalition and Iraqi security forces (ISF) control to enable Odierno to take Prime Minister Nuri al-Maliki to the city to meet with local officials and tribal leaders.[31] Iraqi officials responded to urgent coalition appeals to cultivate good will among the populace by arranging for the delivery of food and other supplies in the wake of U.S. clearing operations.[32] Earlier engagement efforts with Sunni tribes in Diyala also bore fruit, maturing more slowly than they had in Anbar, and nascent Awakening groups began to consolidate security gains, while the newly formed Diyala Support Committee worked to improve the fractious political environment.[33]

The province was far from pacified, however. By early July, almost all the surviving AQI fighters and commanders from Baqubah had fled to the Diyala towns of Muqdadiyah, Balad Ruz, Khalis, and Khan Bani Sa'ad and had begun to attack ISF and Shi'a militias in those areas to secure new safe havens.[34] In most of these areas, existing sectarian tensions made the situation ripe for AQI to exploit, as did the corruption and sectarian behavior of the Shi'a-dominated ISF units in the province. By the time Operation PHANTOM THUNDER ended in mid-August, Diyala's provincial capital was back under coalition and Iraqi Government control, but further operations would be needed to roust AQI and its allies from the rest of the province.

Closing the Lake Tharthar Seam

As MND-N battled AQI around Baqubah, other units from MNF-W and MND-N moved to push AQI fighters out of another Sunni insurgent safe haven in the badlands south and east of Lake Tharthar. The sparsely populated area lay at the edge of the division boundaries of MND-N, MND-B, and MNF-W, meaning that no single coalition unit had ever assumed responsibility for securing it. Consequently, the Tharthar area had long served as a base of support for AQI, from which jihadi leaders and fighters could easily transit Anbar, Salahadin, and Diyala without significant coalition interference. The ability to move freely through the Tharthar area enabled Sunni insurgents to attack or control the western and northern belts of Baghdad with relative ease.

As a result of these factors, the AQI fighters driven out of Ramadi, Abu Ghraib, Fallujah, and Baghdad in spring 2007 were able to hold on to support bases in towns such as Karmah, Taji, and Tarmiyah and to mount significant attacks against both the local populace and the thinly stretched coalition units responsible for those areas. In February, for example, Sunni insurgents north of Taji had been able to gather enough combat power to conduct a rare company-sized attack on a U.S. unit in the area. A platoon of Funk's brigade that erected a new combat outpost near Tarmiyah on February 16 found itself attacked 3 days later by a succession of three suicide car bombs that rammed the outpost's entry point and collapsed part of the building where the U.S. element was sleeping. An insurgent infantry assault followed and lasted for several hours before close air support and ground reinforcements helped drive the attackers off. Funk's platoon suffered 2 killed and 17 wounded, rendering it combat ineffective. Meanwhile, Sunni insurgents south of Taji were carrying out attacks against the residents of the Shi'a-majority town of Sab al-Bour, forcing 50,000 of them—90 percent of the population—to flee by March, leaving AQI in charge of the town.

The arrival of Lehr's brigade in April enabled MNC-I to deploy an additional Stryker battalion to the Taji area, but it was not enough to stop insurgents from attacking the lines of communications in the area with large IEDs on an almost daily basis. In one incident on May 22, an IED made of 20 strung-together artillery shells destroyed a Stryker from Lehr's brigade north of Taji, killing or wounding 5 of its 6-man crew. Miraculously unhurt in the blast, the vehicle's driver, Specialist Erik Oropeza, quickly treated a fellow Soldier's mangled leg with a tourniquet and then ran through enemy small arms fire to summon help. For this act, Oropeza would receive the Distinguished Service Cross.[35]

Source: DoD photo by Corporal Neill Sevelius (Released).

U.S. Marines from the 13th Marine Expeditionary Unit During Operations in Karmah.[36]

With these developments and similar attacks in eastern Anbar in mind, Petraeus and Odierno requested that CENTCOM dispatch its theater reserve, the 13th Marine Expeditionary Unit (MEU), to reinforce MNF-W in the Karmah area south of Lake Tharthar. Arriving in June 2007, the Marine unit was on the ground in time to press the fight near Lake Tharthar without requiring Odierno to draw from U.S. units committed elsewhere.[37] Under the leadership of Colonel Carl E. Mundy III, son of a former Marine Corps commandant, the 13th MEU began a large-scale sweep around the crossroads of Karmah on June 24 to disrupt AQI weapons distribution and supply routes. The clearing operation quickly revealed that the area served as a large-scale IED arsenal for AQI and its allies. In their first few days of clearing, the Marines and their partnered Iraqi units discovered car bomb factories, large stocks of nitric acid and explosives, and hundreds of already-built IEDs. One of the caches was large enough that the Marines called in an F-18 Hornet strike to destroy it with a 500-pound bomb.[38] These discoveries reinforced the assessment that the Sunni insurgents who carried out attacks in Baghdad and eastern Anbar had long enjoyed sanctuary in the rural areas northeast of Fallujah. The MEU would remain in the region through the summer to search for and destroy AQI's caches and disrupt the group's ability to produce and employ its weapon of choice.

Interdiction in the Southern Belts

As MND-N cleared AQI from Baqubah, Lynch's MND-C undertook its portion of Operation PHANTOM THUNDER in Baghdad's southern belts by conducting operations to interdict the "accelerants" of sectarian violence that trickled from that area into the capital in the form of car bombs and Sunni insurgents.[39] The division's main effort would come in the areas of Arab Jabour, Mada'in, and Salman Pak, all of which had served as Sunni insurgent support zones and the scenes of sectarian cleansing for several years. The town of Mada'in had been the site of an alleged massacre of dozens of Shi'a townspeople in April 2005 that had sparked a political crisis during the formation of the Ja'afari government. Adjacent to Mada'in, the picturesque river town of Salman Pak, site of an ancient arch marking the one-time Persian imperial capital of Ctesiphon, had been the area where hundreds of corpses dumped into the Tigris in Baghdad had washed ashore in 2005-2006. Between Mada'in and southeast Baghdad, the town of Jisr Diyala had been an Iraqi military housing community and the site of the Iraqi regime's Osirak nuclear reactor destroyed by Israeli planes in 1981. Opposite Jisr Diyala on the west bank of the Tigris, Arab Jabour was home to a Sunni population of 120,000, just 6 kilometers south of Baghdad, close enough to the capital to have served in Saddam Hussein's day as a convenient getaway for prominent Ba'athists, many of whom had built villas there.[40] In short, the area had been a Ba'athist regime stronghold and was fertile ground for the Sunni insurgency.

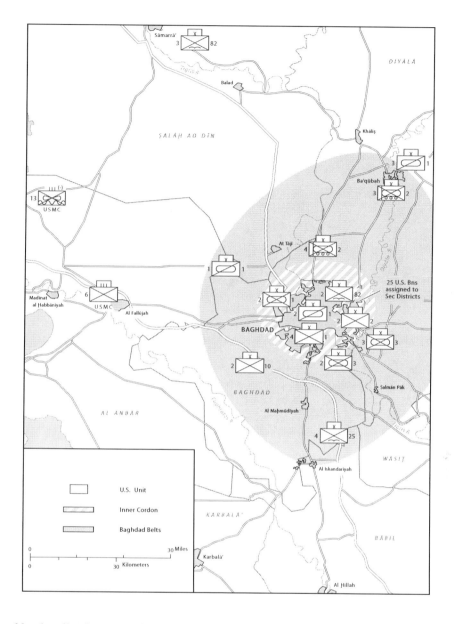

Map created by the official cartographer at the U.S. Army Center of Military History, Washington, DC.

Map 14. Disposition of U.S. Forces in Central Iraq, June 2007.

Source: DoD photo courtesy Defense Imagery Management Operations Center (Released).

Chairman of the Joint Chiefs of Staff Admiral Michael Mullen With Major General Rick Lynch, Commander 3d Infantry Division.[41]

When Colonel Terry Ferrell's 2d Brigade Combat Team, 3d Infantry Division, reached Iraq in May as the fifth and final surge brigade, Odierno and MNC-I gave Ferrell responsibility for the Arab Jabour area just ahead of the start of Operation PHANTOM THUNDER. With two of his battalions already detached to other areas, Ferrell would have two battalions to use for the task. Although coalition special operators had carried out frequent raids in Arab Jabour, the brigade's arrival broke a 3-year streak in which U.S. ground troops had largely steered clear of the stretch of canal-notched farms and palm groves that bordered the Tigris River to the west as it snaked south out of Baghdad. Taking stock of his new area of operations, Ferrell estimated that the safe haven contained about 1,500 AQI operatives, including close to 200 foreigners, with those numbers swelling as the group shifted fighters south from Diyala Province to bolster the Arab Jabour defenses in anticipation of a coalition offensive.[42] The area was a "critical hub for trafficking weapons, bombs, and fighters into Baghdad," Ferrell concluded, with a sophisticated enemy command-and-control structure "on the scale of a conventional military force." In their first month on the ground, the brigade withstood an average of over 40 attacks per week, including the same kind of deep-buried IEDs and explosive-rigged houses that U.S. troops in Diyala were encountering.[43] Like their fellow Soldiers in Diyala and the Tharthar region, Ferrell's troops were dealing with the difficulty of seizing long-uncontested enemy-held territory.

Just across the Tigris near Salman Pak, Grigsby's 3d Brigade, 3d Infantry Division, geared up to move against another AQI transit point that had long fed the violence in Baghdad. Like Arab Jabour, the town of Salman Pak had close historical ties with the Ba'athist regime. Saddam's special intelligence service operated a headquarters there before the coalition invasion, and the dictator had purportedly authorized secretive biological weapons testing at a nearby facility.[44] More recently, Salman Pak had been the scene of a cycle of intimidation, violence, and retribution between Sunnis and a restive Shi'a minority, with the latter backed by National Police units notorious for sectarian abuses. Jaysh al-Mahdi (JAM) had also participated in the fight for control of the critical crossroads—and for good reason.[45] Exploiting Sunni resentment toward the Shi'a-dominated security forces and in an environment characterized by minimal U.S. presence, AQI used the highways running along the Tigris through Salman Pak to attack into eastern Baghdad, particularly Rusafa and Sadr City. The extremist group also funneled men and supplies by boat across the river into Arab Jabour and then north toward staging areas in the Rashid District such as the Dora neighborhood.[46] In June, Grigsby estimated that 20 percent of the attacks occurring in the capital were "facilitated by accelerants moving through AO [area of operation] Hammer," the BCT's sector southeast of Baghdad.[47]

Eager to set the division offensive—labeled Operation MARNE TORCH—in motion, Lynch ordered Ferrell's brigade, along with Iraqis from the 6th Iraqi Army Division, to clear the Arab Jabour region southward from the outskirts of Baghdad and construct combat outposts in the AQI sanctuary. As a supporting effort, Grigsby would advance concurrently along the opposite bank of the Tigris southeast of Salman Pak to block the escape of enemy fighters if they should attempt to cross the river.[48] On June 15, the division carried out ferocious preparatory fires on suspected AQI sites in Arab Jabour, during which 40,000 pounds of ordnance fell in a 10-second span.[49]

Lynch's use of massive demonstrations of firepower in MND-C stood out among the coalition operations in central Iraq in 2007, most of which were characterized by clearing operations, patrolling among the local population, and the kind of restraint that the Army and Marine Corps' new counterinsurgency field manual tended to encourage. "This is all about killing and capturing bad guys," Lynch told his subordinates. "Later, we can do area security. So use anything you can to hit him in the nose. Once he is back on his heels, then we can worry about the population."[50] In this case, the MND-C commander sought to dislocate AQI cells by destroying weapons caches and rendering unusable roads and river crossings that could serve as enemy exfiltration routes. Lynch also acted on the claims by local Iraqis that boats moored along the Tigris or plying its waters belonged exclusively to insurgents or smugglers. Suspicious of the absence of commercial docks along this stretch of the river and the fact that most boats appeared to sail only at night, Lynch concluded that all vessels afloat were likely hostile and ordered them destroyed in support of the operation.[51]

With the American attack driving expectantly into what Ferrell described as a "hornet's nest," progress came slowly.[52] The brigade's calculated advance cleared less than 6 kilometers of Arab Jabour's IED-laden main road over the course of 2 grueling weeks.[53]

Nevertheless, after 1 month, the division operation yielded a number of new patrol bases in rural areas long under AQI's sway. In the process of wresting control of key terrain on either side of the Tigris River, MND-C killed 83 insurgents and captured another 280. Forty of those captured were on coalition high-value target lists. The division also destroyed dozens of boats on the Tigris, many of which when struck produced secondary blasts that suggested they were carrying explosive material, seeming to confirm Lynch's suspicions about their use.[54]

Lynch extended his interdiction efforts to the western half of his sector in July, focusing on enemy lines of communications up the Euphrates River, as well as Highway 8. Spearheaded by Colonel Michael X. Garrett's 4th Brigade Combat Team (Airborne), 25th Infantry Division, and supported by elements of the 6th and 8th Iraqi Army Divisions, operations centered on the mixed-sect Iskandariyah, a small city of 120,000 mostly Shi'a civilians, and on the Sunni town of Jurf al-Sakhr, situated as a gateway on the Euphrates between Anbar and the southern belts.[55] As in Arab Jabour, MND-C began the new operation, called MARNE AVALANCHE, with a striking display of airpower as a single B-1B bomber dropped nearly 10,000 pounds of munitions on selected bridges across the Euphrates to isolate enemy fighters and restrict their maneuver.[56] In a month-long series of platoon- and company-sized attacks and air assaults against militants of both sects, the division killed 16 enemy fighters and captured 110, including local top-level AQI leaders and operatives from JAM mortar-and-rocket teams.

IED attacks in the Euphrates Valley area south of Baghdad fell from 111 in June to 55 the following month, signifying to Lynch that MND-C's approach of highly mobile and firepower-intensive operations was succeeding in disrupting insurgent activity there.[57] Still, by Lynch's own admission, the summertime operations into AQI's sanctuaries had not defeated the terrorist group. As an indication of the enemy's persistent strength in Arab Jabour, for example, four of Ferrell's Soldiers were killed and another four wounded while clearing a booby-trapped house on August 11, and troops elsewhere continued to face roadside IEDs, small-arms fire, and rocket attacks aimed at recently established combat outposts. To be sure, the coalition had seized the initiative and had gained "tactical momentum" in the southern belts, but it had not proceeded as smoothly as Lynch had hoped.[58] The MND-C commander chafed at his division's dearth of engineer support, which meant that he lacked the construction capability required to build patrol bases at a pace aligned with his push into enemy-controlled territory.[59] Regardless of the security gains made, in Lynch's view they could not be confidently sustained without more and better-trained Iraqi forces, which, he believed, needed to triple or quadruple in size for his area of responsibility.[60] Even the notable turnaround in places witnessing a reinvigorated American presence seemed tempered by what some Iraqis viewed as the heavy-handed and unnecessary destruction of local bridges and fording sites upon which so many depended for their livelihood. Once seized, the initiative would still have to be exploited and the security of key terrain solidified by efforts to secure the goodwill of the population through improved governance and economic development.[61]

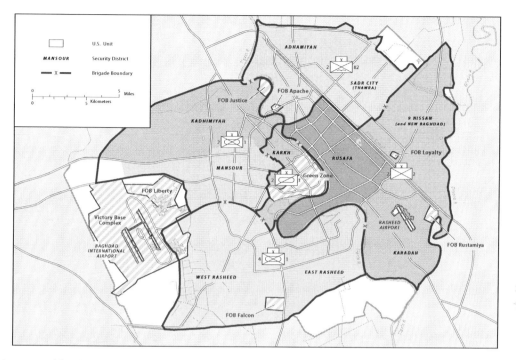

Map created by the official cartographer at the U.S. Army Center of Military History, Washington, DC.

Map 15. Disposition of U.S. Forces in Baghdad, June 2007.

The Continuing Fight for Baghdad

For Fil and MND-B, Operation PHANTOM THUNDER inside Baghdad would be a continuation of Operation FARDH AL-QANOON, the U.S.-Iraqi effort to clear the remaining Sunni insurgent strongholds in the city and to solidify the renewed security presence in the city's neighborhoods. The introduction of the surge units into the city beginning in early 2007 had put AQI and other insurgent groups off-balance, but the first 4 months of the surge in Baghdad had been difficult and violent. The AQI car bomb rings on both sides of the Tigris had continued to do their grisly work, though on a decreasing scale as Fil's troops pressured them and expanded the coalition and ISF footprint. Shi'a death squads had continued to operate as well, though with a greatly reduced freedom of movement. During March through May, Sunni insurgents had attempted to separate the two halves of the city by repeatedly bombing the bridges that spanned the Tigris. One massive truck bombing on April 12 entirely collapsed the spans of the Sarafiyah Bridge between Karkh and Adhamiyah, probably an attempt by Sunni insurgents to stop their Shi'a militant enemies from crossing between the two sides of the city. The following month three successful bridge attacks took place on one day, May 11.[62]

Source: DoD photo by Staff Sergeant Lorie Jewell (Released).

Sarafiyah Bridge, After Its Destruction by al-Qaeda in Iraq on April 12, 2007.[63]

MND-B's share of Operation PHANTOM THUNDER was not just a matter of hunting down AQI and other Sunni insurgent cells, however. As the summer months approached, Colonel J. B. Burton's brigade sector in northwest Baghdad remained one of the most problematic areas in the country because of the activities of both Sunni insurgents and Shi'a militias and death squads. As had been the case in Burton's sector for the better part of a year, U.S. units were bedeviled continually by the sectarian behavior and corruption of the local ISF. The most egregious example was in Baghdad's Kadhimiyah District, where Burton and his subordinates discovered numerous illicit connections between the Sadrists and local security forces and developed Operation SEVENTH VEIL to find guilty Iraqi officials and hold them accountable.[64] Begun as a response to the battery of civilian complaints against units infiltrated by Shi'a militants, this systematic effort eventually led to a violent confrontation at the Kadhimiyah shrine, one of the four holiest sites of Shi'a Islam. Family ties clouded army loyalties and bolstered the Sadrists' position. Sadrist cleric Hazem al-Araji controlled the shrine—a moneymaker during pilgrimage seasons—while his brother Baha al-Araji served in Iraq's Parliament and a cousin, Lieutenant General Faruq al-Araji, directed Maliki's Office of the Commander in Chief, a special action arm that reported directly to Maliki and frequently bypassed the military chain of command in order to pressure Iraqi commanders.[65]

When Burton's troops closed in on the Araji-controlled shrine on April 29, 2007, to detain JAM leaders they knew to be present, they came under rocket-propelled grenade

(RPG) and small-arms fire. The Americans had called on a battalion from the 1st Brigade, 6th Iraqi Army Division, for assistance, but rather than helping them, the Iraqi soldiers came to the aid of JAM militants in the shrine. The ensuing 2-day standoff resulted in the deaths of at least nine Iraqi soldiers who had allied themselves with the militia and ended with a Parliamentary decree barring U.S. troops from a 1-square-kilometer zone around the shrine. In the aftermath of this incident, Petraeus noted that General Abud Qanbar's attitude toward JAM seemed to be hardening—along with that of Maliki's—since the Baghdad commander pressed for fewer restrictions on coalition operations near the militia's strongholds.[66] This, nonetheless, provided little comfort, given the extent of JAM's infiltration of the army in Kadhimiyah. Throughout the summer and the duration of Operation PHANTOM THUNDER, Burton's troops would maintain a tense standoff with both Shi'a militants and pro-militia ISF units in the shrine neighborhood, a factor that complicated the effort to complete the expulsion of Sunni insurgents from other parts of west Baghdad.

Meanwhile, MND-B's main effort was in the AQI-dominated neighborhood of Dora. In the heart of the Rashid District—which Petraeus had labeled as "the most challenging in Baghdad"—the streets bounding the once-vibrant Dora market proved key terrain in a hard-fought sectarian struggle.[67] The neighborhood sat astride an expressway that crossed the nearby Tigris River and fed into Shi'a-dominated eastern Baghdad. Likewise, a well-traveled north-south route provided access to the belt areas of Hawr Rajab and Mahmudiyah. Thus, the Dora neighborhood proved to be an important transit point for insurgents inside the city. Al-Qaeda in Iraq intended to defend the stronghold with a layered network of deep-buried IEDs, sniper positions, and jury-rigged passageways that facilitated maneuver between buildings.[68]

The 4th Brigade Combat Team, 1st Infantry Division, under the command of Colonel Ricky D. Gibbs, had spent the spring closing in on the Sunni extremist fighters ensconced in Dora. After establishing 12 combat outposts and joint security stations across the Rashid District, Gibbs launched a series of clearing operations with support from attached Stryker units and Iraqis from the 2d National Police Division.[69] Perceiving that AQI "wanted to plant their flag and hold" Dora as a launching point to wreak havoc across Baghdad, the colonel marshaled his forces to root out the extremist cells and "send the message to the enemy that we weren't leaving anytime soon."[70] The brigade concentrated on three specific mahallas (neighborhoods) where resistance proved most stubborn and began house-by-house clearing operations on July 1. Gibbs's units netted over 100 suspected AQI fighters and discovered some 200 weapons caches within 2 weeks. Operations in Dora continued through late September when the brigade commander announced the reduction of the Sunni extremist stronghold, along with a general decline in violence. Murders in Rashid, for example, had fallen by 65 percent since the brigade's arrival in mid-March.[71]

The erecting of combat outposts and a sustained presence in neighborhoods, coupled with attacks into erstwhile safe havens, had comparable effects on other Baghdad hotspots. Burton's 2d Brigade Combat Team, 1st Infantry Division, observed a steep drop in violence in Kadhimiyah and Mansour in the 3 months following the kickoff of Operation PHANTOM THUNDER.[72] Burton attributed this improvement to a combination of clearing operations that targeted extremist leaders, the formation of local Awakening groups, and the further development of "safe neighborhoods" and "safe markets," all of which were byproducts of surging additional American troops into his sector.[73] Progress—mixed across Baghdad—had come more quickly in Karkh District, where Colonel Bryan T. Roberts's 2d Brigade Combat Team, 1st Cavalry Division, presided over a dramatic turnaround on Haifa Street. By the summer of 2007, attacks on coalition forces had fallen by 60 percent, with reported civilian murders plummeting at an even faster rate. With violence waning, Roberts focused increasingly on essential services, reviving the local economy, and area beautification.[74] A comprehensive approach that paired security operations with initiatives to improve governance and economic development also bore fruit in eastern Baghdad. There, the 2d Brigade Combat Team, 82d Airborne Division, juggled the AQI threat based in Old Adhamiyah along with the persistent problem of Iranian-supported JAM Special Groups operating out of Sadr City. While attacks against the airborne brigade initially rose with the establishment of forward positions in February, they had declined markedly by August, persuading American leaders to finance local reconstruction projects totaling some $2.5 million—with another bevy of projects costing $8 million scheduled to follow.[75]

Source: U.S. Army photo by Staff Sergeant Michael Pryor (Released).

Soldiers From 1st Battalion, 26th Infantry Regiment, During a Firefight in Baghdad's Adhamiyah Neighborhood on June 16.[76]

Looking at the whole of Iraq's capital as Operation PHANTOM THUNDER wound down in mid-August, Petraeus assessed the results of the operation with a characteristic blend of caution and optimism. "Security has improved in almost every area of Baghdad," he reported to Gates on August 11, adding that, nonetheless, "improvement has been very uneven and remains tenuous" in places.[77]

From Operation PHANTOM THUNDER to Operation PHANTOM STRIKE: Pursuit Operations Against al-Qaeda in Iraq

Operation PHANTOM THUNDER ended on August 15, 2007. In the 60 days of the operation, the coalition divisions had driven AQI out of Dora, Baqubah, and the Fallujah area and had greatly damaged the militant group and its allies in their former safe havens throughout the Baghdad belts. Coalition troops had killed 1,196 enemy fighters, wounded 419, and captured another 6,702, with 382 of the captured considered high-value targets. U.S. and Iraqi troops together had captured more than 1,100 weapons caches, found almost 2,300 IEDs, and disabled 52 car bombs.[78] During the same period, U.S. units lost 150 troops killed by hostile fire, the vast majority of them to IEDs.

The change in the security situation in Baghdad and its environs was significant. In the 5 months before Operation PHANTOM THUNDER, an average of 298 Baghdadi civilians were killed in acts of violence each week. By the end of the operation, the weekly civilian death toll in the capital had fallen to about half of that figure, and from that point to the end of 2007, the weekly average of violent civilian deaths fell to 91, a level not seen in Baghdad since early 2005.

Encouraged by these improved security trends and an overall reduction in violence in and around the Iraqi capital, MNC-I sought to capitalize on those hard-won gains and to continue the pressure against AQI as it attempted to regroup. On August 15, Operation PHANTOM THUNDER gave way to another corps-level operation, Operation PHANTOM STRIKE, designed to serve as a framework for the aggressive pursuit of AQI in the immediate aftermath of operations that had worn down the extremist group's ranks and had rendered longtime sanctuaries increasingly untenable. Like its predecessor, Operation PHANTOM STRIKE consisted of a set of operations oriented on a common purpose but planned and executed by lower echelons of command. Nonetheless, it differed in emphasis, with the clearing of enemy strongholds and the seizure of key terrain that had characterized Operation PHANTOM THUNDER yielding to a focus on solidifying progress. Although U.S. troops maintained a forward presence among the population, they generally refrained from explicit efforts to extend their control into new areas.

This shift did not entail a scaling back in activity, however. Nor was the situation any less dynamic. Sensing that coalition forces had retaken the initiative at the operational level, Petraeus, Odierno, and other coalition commanders looked to keep AQI's leaders off-balance and on the run by orchestrating targeted raids across the country to exploit the enemy's dislocation, drive its center of activity farther from Baghdad, and prevent its consolidation.[79] In MND-B, U.S. troops concentrated on reducing the AQI stronghold in the Hadar neighborhood just south of the Dora expressway running through Rashid. Arriving to replace Townsend's Stryker brigade in late summer, Colonel John S. RisCassi's 2d Stryker Cavalry Regiment became the corps operational reserve and, like its predecessor, served as MND-B's "above-ground" strike force—a role that freed the Stryker unit from responsibility for the security of a particular sector and leveraged the formation's mobility and comparably large infantry troop strength. Supporting Gibbs in Rashid, RisCassi's regiment cleared Hadar while BCTs elsewhere in Baghdad constricted AQI with the help of partnered Iraqi security forces and increasing numbers of Sunni irregulars.[80] The "pursuit" in MNF-W took the form of continued operations northeast of Fallujah, with Marines striking into the hinterlands around Lake Tharthar as the Iraqi police tightened its grip on the city.[81] In Baghdad's southern belts, Lynch faced manpower constraints that discouraged MND-C from expanding its area of control, but, in accordance with Operation PHANTOM STRIKE's intent, the division managed to launch operations designed to keep AQI off-balance. Colonel Daniel L. Ball, commander of the 3d Infantry Division's combat aviation brigade, for example, organized a flurry of raids and air assaults that drew on U.S. conventional and special operations forces to disrupt insurgent staging areas around Mahmudiyah and the Euphrates River Valley.[82] In Arab Jabour, Ferrell's BCT conducted strikes against AQI death squads reportedly formed to assassinate Awakening fighters. Lynch again employed tremendous firepower, and in 1 day alone in September, four B-1B aircraft dropped eight 500-pound and two 2,000-pound laser-guided bombs on enemy targets in Arab Jabour, while the division's artillery fired 45 missions.[83]

For Operation PHANTOM STRIKE, MNC-I intended to pursue AQI fighters who had fled Baqubah farther up the Diyala River Valley to the town of Muqdadiyah and into the remote Hamrin Ridge area, an important insurgent line of communications between Diyala and the Za'ab Triangle south of Mosul. By August, MND-N's task was more difficult than those of the other divisions. As Anbar, the Baghdad belts, and Diyala became dangerous territory for AQI leaders and fighters, they increasingly chose to displace to far northern Iraq, where the coalition and ISF presence was thin. Mixon's main effort, designated Operation LIGHTNING HAMMER, would focus on the upper Diyala Valley beyond Baqubah. Sutherland's 3d Brigade Combat Team, 1st Cavalry Division, would lead the fight for Muqdadiyah and other towns in upper Diyala.

At the same time, however, rising attacks elsewhere in MND-N's area of operations signified that AQI and other insurgents were flowing toward areas where the coalition was weak, as they had done so many times in the past.[84] In Salahadin Province, IEDs and insurgent ground attacks grew in frequency in late summer, with Samarra as particularly contested ground for the 2d Battalion, 505th Parachute Infantry Regiment. In one incident on August 26, more than 40 AQI fighters attacked one of the battalion's observation posts, seeking to abduct the 4 American Soldiers posted there. Two of the American infantrymen were killed in the ensuing firefight, but Specialists Christopher Corriveau and Eric Moser mounted a fierce defense and held off dozens of attackers until a U.S. quick-reaction force arrived. These actions earned the two Soldiers the Distinguished Service Cross.[85]

In another incident in Samarra just 2 weeks later, a team of U.S. special operators and their partnered Iraqi special operations forces conducted a nighttime attack against an AQI hideout that was the suspected location of the city's AQI emir. Blinded by sand kicked up by their own helicopters and cut off from their Iraqi partners, three special operators assaulted the AQI emir's building and found themselves in a close-quarters gunfight with more than a dozen AQI fighters. When his two fellow Green Berets were wounded, Staff Sergeant Jarion Halbisengibbs continued to clear the building by himself in complete darkness, not stopping even when shot in the hand and abdomen. Despite his wounds, he made contact with the Iraqi special operators and reorganized them to continue the attack. During the engagement, Halbisengibbs killed six of the AQI men, including the AQI emir himself. For his actions, the Green Beret sergeant received the Distinguished Service Cross.[86]

The situation was even more dangerous in Ninawa Province, where in late summer and early September Colonel Stephen Twitty's Mosul-based 4th Brigade Combat Team, 1st Cavalry Division, detected a migration of AQI fighters north from Baghdad. The first sign had come when Twitty's troops began capturing enemy fighters who possessed Baghdad area identification cards.[87] As the terrorists arrived, Twitty recorded a corresponding uptick in enemy activity.[88] This migration of AQI fighters to the north led to the Iraq War's most deadly terrorist incident. On August 14, the day before Operation PHANTOM STRIKE began, AQI attacked 2 Yazidi towns near Sinjar with massive truck bombs that killed about 300 civilians and wounded at least 700 more, according to MNF-I's reports.[89] Iraqi reports put the toll even higher, at almost 800 killed and 1,500 wounded. Either way, the attack on the Yazidis resulted in the highest death toll of any single terrorist attack of the entire war, and it indicated AQI's resilience as well as its determination to hold onto Mosul and Ninawa Province despite its loss of almost all of its territory in central Iraq. While the coalition necessarily focused on ending the sectarian civil war in Baghdad, the civil war among ethnic groups and sects in Ninawa had continued, offering a political opening for AQI and other hard-line Sunni insurgent groups. The civil war in the north would flare again as AQI members made their way north and as the group attempted to switch its cross-border infiltration routes from the increasingly difficult Anbar Province to the more AQI-accessible Sinjar-Tel Afar-Mosul corridor.

By intensifying the pressure on Sunni militants and sustaining the surge of operations through Operation PHANTOM STRIKE, Odierno hoped to prevent AQI from carrying out its usual spike in attacks and killings of civilians during the holy month of Ramadan. If the coalition could constrain AQI's normal level of activity once the holy month began on September 12, it would demonstrate the group's waning power and neutralize its psychological effect on Iraqis.[90] For Petraeus, the pursuit of the enemy in August occurred in the context of his impending congressional testimony with Ambassador Ryan Crocker in Washington, where the next month the two men would be expected to report on the first 7 months of the surge. Petraeus would have to assess publicly the interim results of the surge of operations while Operation PHANTOM STRIKE was still underway, a task that would be fraught with political implications. The summer 2007 operations were succeeding in pushing AQI away from Baghdad and the Awakening was turning tens of thousands of local Iraqis against AQI, but it was not yet clear that reconciliation with the Iraqi Government would follow. Ever mindful of the steadily ticking Washington "clock," Petraeus knew that time was running short.

SUMMER OF THE AWAKENING

The Coalition and the Iraqi Government Organize for Reconciliation

In addition to the offensive operations of the four U.S. divisions in central Iraq, the surge of operations of summer 2007 had a significant tribal outreach component. Though senior coalition commanders had been somewhat divided and cautious about the Awakening's potential in early 2007, by late May the unexpected spread of the tribal movement had shown them that they were witnessing a golden opportunity not to be squandered. The MNF-I and MNC-I commanders became determined to continue building the Awakening's momentum and to make the tribal movement a force multiplier in the coalition's major operations, including Operation PHANTOM THUNDER. Petraeus had already told Gates and his coalition subordinates that the tribal movement's continued growth would depend to a great degree on the Iraqi Government's acceptance of it. Accordingly, and as the Joint Strategic Assessment Team had recommended, Petraeus took steps to institutionalize the coalition's oversight of the Awakening and to broker an accommodation between the multiplying Awakening groups and the Maliki government. At MNF-I, the small cell created under British Lieutenant General Graeme Lamb responsible for tribal engagement carried on but expanded in size and scope. In the spring, it received its own co-directors in British Major General Paul R. Newton and Donald A. Blome, a senior aide to the U.S. ambassador. The Force Strategic Engagement Cell, as it came to be called, would have the job of prodding the Iraqi Government as it shuffled down the path toward national reconciliation and attempt to convince Maliki that integrating Sunni tribal irregulars into the security forces lay in his best long-term interests.[91]

One of the cell's initial quandaries was what name should be assigned to the disparate groups that made up the broader Awakening movement. Before creating a standardized name, coalition staff officers referred to the tribal irregulars by a variety of terms including "potential reconcilables," "Sunni groups," "local security forces," and "police support units" before settling on the term "Concerned Local Citizens" in June 2007. Even that term proved unworkable, as coalition leaders soon discovered that "Concerned Local Citizens" was more accurately understood in Arabic as "People who worry a lot." After several more months of searching for an appropriate name, MNF-I staffers settled on the term "Sons of Iraq" in February 2008.[92]

Naming conventions aside, at MNC-I, Odierno, who had been initially cautious regarding outreach to former insurgents, changed course and made the facilitation of bottom-up reconciliation a top-tier priority for his headquarters and subordinate units. By late spring 2007, the MNC-I commander concluded that the short-term security gains realized through bottom-up reconciliation could not be sustained without top-down efforts to integrate armed tribesmen or former insurgents with the Government of Iraq. But he also realized that the Maliki government, for the time being, was at best ambivalent and at worst downright hostile to the Sunni groups with whom MNC-I's units had begun to work. Rather than wait for the Maliki government to move ahead with a formal reconciliation process of its own, Odierno encouraged his subordinate commanders to engage anyone who was willing to talk. In new written guidance to his units in June 2007, Odierno instructed commanders to use dialogue with local groups to stop attacks against the coalition and to broker cease-fires among warring parties. The MNC-I commander's goal was not for his subordinate commanders to pressure extra governmental armed groups to lay down their weapons, but rather that they should convince those groups to turn their weapons against AQI and other irreconcilable terrorists.[93] In writing to MNC-I's units, Odierno conceded that "some may be skeptical" of facilitating bottom-up reconciliation—as he, too, had initially been—but like Petraeus, he believed the initiative to work with Sunnis who had at one time fought against the coalition reflected a new reality.[94] On the streets and in the rural districts of Iraq, insurgent groups and their affiliated tribes were breaking from AQI and seeking local accommodations with the coalition that promised to reduce violence sharply in the near term.

Odierno's June 2007 directives laid out broad guidelines on the use of the tribal irregulars and authorized a wide array of "tools" to reach accommodations, including targeted detainee releases, Commanders' Emergency Response Program (CERP)-funded infrastructure security contracts, and employment in positions that would lead to a more permanent job with the Iraqi police.[95] To help synchronize local engagements throughout the country and implement MNC-I's new guidelines, Odierno created a new reconciliation directorate within MNC-I and encouraged each of his divisions to set up similar "reconciliation cells."[96] Given the rather unconventional directive to facilitate reconciliation, Odierno saw his primary contribution as underwriting the risk subordinate commanders assumed as they engaged with insurgent groups.[97] For the colonels in charge of BCTs and battalions, this top cover afforded by Odierno, as well as Petraeus, allowed for aggressive engagement in an unavoidably decentralized environment in which they often found themselves making "handshake agreements" with recent enemies.[98]

When it came to negotiations with Sunni insurgents, the Maliki administration was less inclined to take such risks. Petraeus found this somewhat understandable, given Iraq's recent history of Ba'athist rule and conspiracy-fueled fears of the party's resurgence, but he believed the time had come to stop the bureaucratic foot-dragging on national reconciliation.[99] Provincial elections would perhaps be the most straightforward way to draw Sunnis into the political process, but in the summer of 2007, prospects for convincing the Iraqi Government to hold new elections were dim. Instead, in June, Prime Minister Maliki formed the Implementation and Follow-Up Committee for National Reconciliation (IFCNR) to manage the Iraqi Government's part in brokering agreements with the many local Sunni groups coming forward.[100] One crucial task for the Iraqi Government, as coalition commanders saw it, involved vetting the names of Awakening members—many of whom were contractors compensated through CERP funds—and then expediting their induction into the Iraqi police and thus onto official government payrolls.

Petraeus considered the IFCNR a good idea in theory but doubted its members would perform their duties in an evenhanded way, especially after Maliki staffed the committee with personnel from the Office of the Commander in Chief (OCINC), the special arm that allowed the Prime Minister to bypass the military chain of command.[101] Moreover, the dominant voice on the IFCNR was Bassima Luay Hasun al-Jaidri, a military technology specialist who had served in Saddam's rocket and missile program before 2003 and since then had become a senior government administrator and a Maliki confidant.[102] In February, Odierno had noted Jaidri's Shi'a sectarian bent and judged that her interference in security

Source: U.S. Army photo by Sergeant 1st Class Kerensa Hardy (Released).

Bassima Luay Hasun al-Jaidri.[103]

affairs was discrediting Baghdad commander General Abud Qanbar.[104] American officers regarded her appointment to be the IFCNR's gatekeeper for the entry of Sunnis into the Iraqi police with disappointment. "The fact that [the IFCNR] is led by Jaidri and other sectarian OCINC personalities makes us a bit cautious as to whether it exists to rapidly assist local accommodation efforts or to protect Shi'a equities while dealing with these tribes or groups," Petraeus wrote to Gates in late June.[105]

The first major task for Jaidri and the IFCNR was dealing with Abu Azzam's large Awakening group in Abu Ghraib. By midsummer 2007, the coalition had registered more than 1,700 of the Abu Ghraib volunteers for potential induction into the Iraqi police and onto government payrolls, a step that coalition commanders believed needed to take place quickly in order to ensure that the volunteers did not become discouraged and drift back into the insurgency.[106] Odierno saw Abu Ghraib as a test case.[107] If the Iraqi Government balked at absorbing Abu Azzam's men into the government security forces, it could undercut the only measurable progress made toward reconciliation and doom the whole venture. To press Jaidri and other IFCNR leaders to see beyond their sectarian perspectives, Odierno dispatched his political adviser Emma Sky to lobby the IFCNR about the benefits of bottom-up reconciliation and specifically to persuade them to issue hiring orders for the Abu Ghraib volunteers. Sky worked to win Jaidri's trust, gradually chipping away at the common perception among the Shi'a ruling class that U.S. cooperation with Sunni groups was part of some American scheme to fuel civil war and hasten Maliki's overthrow. Nonetheless, the Iraqi official still felt strongly that integrating former insurgents into the security forces was equivalent to arming AQI. As Jaidri saw it, American commanders like Odierno seemed obsessed with the Sunni irregulars in nearby Abu Ghraib, and senior American officials' occasional public antagonism toward her only raised her suspicions.[108] Under her leadership, the new IFCNR moved slowly on vetting the Abu Ghraib volunteers, letting the process drag on well into the summer. When coalition commanders learned in late July that the IFCNR was prepared to consider fewer than half the names submitted from Abu Ghraib and, of those, none who had ever been affiliated with Jaysh al-Islami, they braced themselves for a serious confrontation with the Prime Minister. However, at the 11th hour Sky persuaded Jaidri to relent and approve the list in its entirety.[109] The following week, the MNF-I commander conveyed the encouraging news to Gates and hoped the development indicated Maliki's "increased commitment to moving forward on reconciliation—not just in word, but also in deed."[110] However, the action foretold no guarantee of future success.

Control Measures and Tensions Over the Awakening

At the tactical level, the MNF-I and MNC-I commanders' encouragement and guidance about the Awakening came as brigade and battalion commanders were experimenting with ways to work with Sunnis who were mainly former enemies, balancing the need for caution with the need to keep local cease-fires from stalling so that Sunni groups did not drift back into the anti-coalition camp. As U.S. units monitored the activity of Awakening groups in their area, they demanded full transparency of the group's members and required the Sunni fighters to coordinate their operations and movements. Many commanders also devised arrangements that encouraged or even compelled the Sunni groups' cooperation with local Iraqi security forces. In Ameriyah, for example, Lieutenant

Colonel Dale C. Kuehl instituted combined patrols and expected Abu Abed, the local Awakening leader, to post representatives in joint security stations at all times for liaison purposes.[111] To the south around Mahmudiyah, Colonel Michael M. Kershaw's 2d Brigade Combat Team, 10th Mountain Division, "partnered" a U.S. unit with each armed tribal group while ensuring that the local Iraqi Army brigade commander, Brigadier General Ali Freiji, met regularly with Awakening members in his sector.[112] One of Kershaw's battalion commanders even organized his local Sunni irregulars into "platoons" to secure areas that would have stretched the capabilities of available U.S. forces.[113]

To supplement the standard practice of cataloging biometric data and weapon serial numbers, Kershaw required sheikhs to vouch formally for the loyalty of each fighter.[114] He found that this obligation not only yielded insights into the insurgency and its leaders, but it also provided a great deal of leverage over those who had cast their lot with the coalition against AQI.[115] Similarly, in his dealings with Awakening members in northwest Baghdad, Burton employed the contract as a mechanism to apply leverage, investigating alleged violations of the agreed-upon terms and holding offenders accountable.[116] Of course, the fact that the tribal irregulars benefited from stores of U.S. or Iraqi ammunition gave coalition forces considerable leverage.[117] American units also had to deal with the ethically tricky matter of how Awakening groups handled the detainees they captured. Most commanders prohibited unsupervised interrogations by irregular forces and limited the time they were allowed to hold prisoners before transferring them to U.S. or Iraqi units.[118]

Yet in spite of these control measures, enlisting new partners in a multifaceted struggle for stability created its own problems, reminding commanders that accommodations with one-time insurgents stemmed primarily from momentary alignments of interest and thus were delicate in nature and, at times, volatile. Kershaw's involvement with former 1920 Revolutionary Brigades leader Abu Maruf was a prime example. On occasion, Kershaw's brigade employed Abu Maruf and his men in raids, exploiting their general knowledge of enemy tactics as well as their precise intelligence of the locations of extremist leaders. One operation coordinated with Kershaw's troops lasted an entire night as Sunni fighters cleared from Radwaniyah south to the Euphrates River, raiding AQI safe houses and opening an IED-choked road along the brigade's sparsely manned western boundary.[119] Abu Maruf embraced his role as informal ambassador for the Americans among nearby tribes, spurring further local accommodations, but was nonetheless an opportunist at heart.[120] Funk, the 1st Brigade Combat Team, 1st Cavalry Division, commander whose unit was responsible for Taji, also had dealings with Abu Maruf. Since the former insurgent's idea of which Sunnis belonged to AQI seemed contrived and inconsistent, Funk found Maruf capricious.[121] The Awakening leader also magnified the already hostile relations between Sunni volunteers and General Nasser Ghanam's Muthanna Brigade in the Abu Ghraib area. In late summer, Abu Maruf's men launched an independent attack on some of the Muthanna Brigade's checkpoints, having previously warned local U.S. officers that they might do so if tensions with Ghanam's troops continued. When Kershaw learned that the armed tribal group had staged the raid from his sector, the U.S. commander clamped down and directed one of his battalions to act as a buffer between the hostile forces.[122] Though a key figure in rallying the Zobaie tribe in the Radwaniyah-Zaidon area against AQI, Abu Maruf never completely severed his ties with the insurgency and occasionally antagonized even his new American friends by continuing to speak, as he described it, the "language of the resistance."[123]

Like Abu Maruf, Abu Abed also had shown courage in taking on Sunni insurgent cells in Ameriyah in May 2007, as well as a ruthless knack for rooting out their neighborhood sanctuaries. Indeed, U.S.-backed fighters organizing across Baghdad demonstrated this unique expertise—not least because they knew where AQI operatives lived, recognized their faces, and could pinpoint the locations of their weapons caches. The cumulative effect was akin to squeezing the irreconcilable extremists out of Baghdad.[124] Yet, like Abu Maruf, Abu Abed was a controversial partner for U.S. units. A charismatic figure, the self-styled "Robin Hood" made enemies in the Iraqi Islamic Party, whose Sunni power brokers saw his rapid rise in popularity politically threatening, while the Special Weapons and Tactics (SWAT)-like efficiency of his men elicited uneasy scrutiny from the conspiracy-minded Shi'a running the national government. That Abu Abed seemed to embrace the high-profile persona of a temperamental mafia boss did not help. On top of the infighting in his own organization, he occasionally had heated arguments with local Iraqi Army commanders, requiring the Americans to mediate.[125] These factors created challenges in solidifying the security gains in Ameriyah. Recognizing Abu Abed as a leader of influence, the IFCNR engaged him in dialogue but delayed the police enrollment of the Ameriyah "Knights" on the basis of accusations that the armed men carried on like thugs, charges that Kuehl, the U.S. commander of 1st Battalion, 5th Cavalry Regiment, in Ameriyah, investigated but largely dismissed as a disinformation campaign intended to undermine the Awakening.[126]

Despite Petraeus and Odierno's enthusiasm for U.S. units' outreach to local Sunni groups, not all of the higher coalition headquarters' involvement in reconciliation efforts was welcomed at lower unit levels. MNF-I's strategic engagement cell, for example, was established mainly to track and coordinate the dozens of local reconciliation initiatives to prevent divisions from working at cross-purposes, or to identify additional opportunities for reconciliation and pass on the information to subordinate echelons. Lower-level units resented instances when the strategic engagement cell interacted directly with insurgent leaders and appeared to intervene in tactical activities. Marine Brigadier General John R. Allen, deputy commander of MNF-W, considered MNF-I's involvement with tribal engagement disruptive and even harmful, since it potentially undermined the MEF as the coalition's primary interlocutor with the Anbari sheikhs. "We bristle when higher headquarters wants to help us," he told historians in late June 2007, disparaging the strategic engagement cell's efforts to establish a unilateral relationship with the tribes in MNF-W's area of operations.[127] MNF-I's supposed presumption that the delicate nature of reconciliation inside Anbar was best left to "the next group of British officers in the front office" incensed him. "We love them coming down here, and we're happy to brief them . . . and introduce them to people," he offered, but "we don't need their help."[128] Venting just days after a suicide bomber at Baghdad's Mansour Hotel killed several Awakening leaders who had been summoned for talks with the Maliki government, an angry Allen proposed that, rather than try to control negotiations with the sheikhs, higher headquarters should contribute resources instead: "If you want to help me . . . give me $20 million. I'll spend it where I know it'll make some good."[129]

Source: DoD photo by Master Sergeant Paul Bishop (Released).

Major General John Allen With a Sheikh of the Albu Issa Tribe at Camp Fallujah.[130]

In the MND-C area of operations, another serious disagreement over reconciliation matters arose when MND-C commander Lynch developed guidance at odds with ways in which Kershaw's brigade had begun to employ the newly minted Concerned Local Citizens (CLCs). Focused on major combat operations to clear Arab Jabour and Salman Pak as part of Operation PHANTOM THUNDER, Lynch considered MNC-I's guidance to broker cease-fires with local tribes as contradictory with his operations, and a lower priority in any case.[131] When it came to reconciliation, the division would "start small," Lynch determined.[132] Expecting a cool reception from the populace as U.S. forces pressed deeper into AQI sanctuaries, Brigadier General James L. Huggins, one of Lynch's deputies, believed, as late as mid-July, that reconciliation in the area of operations would come primarily "out of the barrel of an M4."[133] By contrast, Kershaw, whose 2d Brigade Combat Team, 10th Mountain Division, had been fighting vigorously in the "Triangle of Death" for 8 months, was pushing ahead of his boss to embrace tribal engagement and incorporate the CLCs into his brigade's security scheme. As the summer progressed, the difference between the two commanders' views grew wider, especially as Lynch, who had ordered 40,000 pounds of munitions dropped in the opening 10 seconds of clearing operations in Arab Jabour, emphasized overwhelming firepower. In the Triangle of Death, Kershaw wanted a more restrained use of firepower and clashed with Lynch on this issue and on the employment of the division's combat aviation brigade. Kershaw frequently used helicopters to enhance his unit's mobility, but he considered the division's AH-64

Apaches too aggressive for a complex battlefield where U.S. and Iraqi troops maneuvered in conjunction with Sunni irregular forces. When MND-C's attack helicopters mistook an armed group of tribesmen in Kershaw's sector for AQI and fired on them, the brigade commander began to rely on OH-58 reconnaissance helicopters for support instead.[134]

Kershaw's decision to employ the CLCs as "shock companies," rather than merely informants or guards at fixed sites, also ran afoul of Lynch's more conservative guidance. Concluding that an auxiliary force of armed tribesmen only would lead to more bloodshed, the MND-C commander initially prohibited the practice. Forbidding his units to issue weapons and ammunition to the CLCs, Lynch also banned the act of fighting alongside them. "They can give us the intel and we will fight al-Qaeda," he directed.[135] Having already gone through months of trial and error with Awakening forces, Kershaw considered Lynch's restriction unnecessary and self-limiting, especially if U.S. units could monitor the armed groups closely and oversee them in operations.[136] Kershaw also disagreed with Lynch's view that the coalition should avoid working with Sunni fighters who had American blood on their hands and dismissed his commander's concern that AQI could infiltrate the armed groups cooperating with the brigade. In a midsummer memorandum to his subordinates, Kershaw emphasized the utility of prudent control measures, but implicitly criticized MND-C's directives by warning against the impracticality of overly prescriptive guidance. "As I look at the daily disposition of the groups, it occurs to me that they exactly mirror the same cells that we were fighting against 2 months ago," Kershaw explained to his units. "We are now working with many of the same people we were fighting against. . . . So, the groups are already 'infiltrated.' Get over it."[137]

THE WAR AGAINST IRAN'S MILITANT PROXIES

EFP Networks and the Iranian Border Problem

As the MNC-I operations against AQI intensified in the Baghdad belts and beyond, the coalition's Shi'a militant problem grew, requiring more attention from U.S. commanders. Taking advantage of MNF-I's renewed focus against Sunni militants elsewhere, Shi'a militants increased their attacks in the first half of 2007, conducting 65 explosively formed penetrator (EFP) attacks against coalition troops in April alone.[138] As in 2006, a well-established network of Iranian-sponsored militants were smuggling EFP devices and other weapons across the Iran-Iraq border in the south and in the Diyala Valley. The most active EFP smugglers were the operatives headed by Abu Mustafa al-Sheibani and his brother Abu Yaser al-Sheibani, who moved the Iranian weapons through Maysan and Wasit Provinces to deliver them to JAM and other militant groups. In addition to the border crossings near Amarah and Kut, coalition analysts suspected the Sheibani brothers and other smugglers were using routes through the vast marshes that spanned the border south of Amara, just as they had done in their shadowy war against Saddam's regime during and after the Iran-Iraq War. Though coalition special operators were able to capture Abu Yaser al-Sheibani on April 20, the incidence of EFP attacks nevertheless increased as the summer approached, eventually rising to 99 attacks during July.[139]

Source: DoD photo by Staff Sergeant Russell Bassett (Released).

Fully Constructed EFPs.[140]

The nature of the EFP smuggling operation and the employment of EFPs left U.S. commanders with no doubt that the weapons were part of an Iranian regime proxy war against the United States and parts of the Iraqi Government, a judgment that Petraeus and Crocker relayed to the visiting Nebraska Senator Charles T. Hagel on April 15.[141] At that time, U.S. analysts believed that 100 percent of EFPs were meant to target coalition troops, though they often killed or wounded Iraqis as collateral damage.[142] The EFPs also never proliferated into the hands of Sunni militants, indicating that the Iranians kept tight control of their distribution.

For coalition commanders, the operational problem was the difficulty of controlling the porous southeastern border—the same problem Lieutenant General Peter W. Chiarelli had reported to Casey almost exactly a year before. Reporting to Gates in mid-May 2007, Petraeus noted that the Iranian regime appeared to be directly involved in the cross-border smuggling, with the coalition detecting at least 10 Iranian helicopter incursions into Iraq in the marsh-covered border area of southeastern Iraq since January. "Most of the observed flight paths followed smuggling routes," Petraeus noted, "which may mean those routes are being reconnoitered to allow smugglers to avoid detection by border patrols and also assess deployed Coalition Forces."[143]

To improve the coalition's monitoring of the troublesome border area, Petraeus and Odierno expected MND-C to deploy coalition combat power to Wasit Province, in addition to its continuing efforts to support the Sunni Awakening and interdict AQI in Baghdad's southern belts. Situated between the Iranian border and Baghdad, Wasit Province contained key routes between Iran and various Shi'a militias and Special Groups, and in the past efforts to disrupt these supply lines suffered from a distinct lack of coalition troops and resources. The closest permanent coalition presence to the main border crossing of Zurbatiyah was a hazardous 80-kilometer drive away from Forward Operating Base Delta, near the city of Kut, and coalition border security teams were able to search only a handful of the approximately 300 trucks that crossed into Iraq daily.[144] The arrival of the 2,000 soldiers of the 3d Infantry Brigade from the Republic of Georgia in July 2007 enabled MNC-I to "thicken" the space between Kut and the border with a coalition troop presence and checkpoints designed to disrupt smuggling of weapons and explosives. In addition to the Georgian checkpoints, coalition commanders made plans to secure the primary border crossings with six new outposts constructed as a secondary screen to the existing Iraqi outposts. These new facilities would be outfitted with X-ray machines that would permit more effective vehicle searches as well as biometric systems to allow guards to identify known terrorists or militants.[145] In September, construction began on Combat Outpost Shocker, which would allow MNC-I to station U.S. troops just 8 kilometers from the Zurbatiyah crossing and allow a permanent coalition contingent on the border.[146] Although smugglers would no doubt still find alternative routes along smaller roads or across the open desert, they would be vulnerable to detection by satellites or aerial surveillance.[147]

South of MND-C's area of operations in Wasit Province, Maysan Province and its unruly capital of Amarah represented another, more complicated problem. In keeping with the transition campaign plan of 2006, the province had been passed to Provincial Iraqi Control in mid-April 2007, making the coalition's ability to operate there unilaterally more difficult.[148] Unlike the border crossing area in Wasit, Maysan's marshy border was largely unwatched by either Iraqi or coalition forces, and coalition commanders suspected Amarah to be a major Shi'a militant logistics hub. The province was riddled with Shi'a militant activity. On June 18, for example, coalition troops conducting a series of raids against the Special Groups (a term referring to highly trained, Iranian-sponsored Shi'a militants such as Asa'ib Ahl al-Haqq) in Amarah and the border town of Majar al Kabir came under heavy small arms and RPG fire. In the ensuing firefight, they killed at least 20 militants before leaving the area with a captured member of an EFP smuggling network.[149] Throughout June and July, coalition troops made similar raids throughout the province to try to stem the flow of EFPs into central Iraq, but with no real coalition presence in Amara or on Maysan's border, U.S. commanders would have difficulty preventing the Sheibani Network or other Shi'a militants from moving lethal materials into Iraq at will.

The Trilateral Talks and Iranian Involvement

In addition to the clear forensic evidence of Iranian-sponsored lethal assistance across the Iran-Iraq border, coalition commanders were learning more about Iranian involvement with Shi'a militant groups from top Shi'a militant leaders themselves. On March 20 in Basrah, coalition troops had captured Qais al-Khazali and his brother Laith al-Khazali based on evidence that the two men and their Asa'ib Ahl al-Haqq group had been behind the January 2007 killing of U.S. military advisers at the police compound in Karbala. They had also captured a third man whose identity was unknown but who had pretended to be mute. On May 1, the third detainee, whom coalition officers referred to as "Hamid the mute," began speaking to his captors in a coalition detention center, revealing himself to be Ali Mussa Daqduq, a senior leader of Lebanese Hizballah's external operations group. Daqduq admitted that he had deployed to Iraq to advise Qais al-Khazali and Asa'ib Ahl al-Haqq in their campaign against the coalition. Once talking, he and Khazali revealed extensive details about their Iranian-sponsored operations. "The evidence is impressive," Petraeus wrote to Gates in late May:

The five-page Qais Khazali sworn statement, made last week and marked with his inked fingerprints, is an unequivocal indictment of Iranian interference. His statement, along with those of his brother and other detainees, provides incontrovertible evidence that Iran is arming, funding, training, equipping, and advising Shi'a extremists operating in Iraq. Iranian interference began shortly after the Coalition began operations, but advanced significantly after the Najaf operation in 2004. The statements of those interrogated are buttressed by dozens of documents taken from the captured laptops. As Qais asserted, without Iranian funding, JAM special groups would not be able to function.[150]

Petraeus had spoken publicly about the implications of this evidence just a few days before, telling an American reporter that Iranian regime activities in Iraq were "absolutely nefarious" and "hugely damaging to Iraq." The Iranian regime had provided millions of dollars to different Shi'a militias since the 2003 invasion, Petraeus noted, and the scale of support was such that it had to denote Iranian regime policy. Asked whether the Iranian Supreme Leader Ali Khamenei might not know about these Quds Force activities, Petraeus was emphatic. "He can't not know," the MNF-I commander said, noting that Quds Force commander Qassem Soleimani reported directly to Khamenei. "It's a massive operation. . . . If he doesn't know about it, it's the most out-of-control operation in the world."[151]

Source: DoD briefing slides (Released).

Brothers Qais and Laith Khazali, Commanders of the Militia Group Asa'ib Ahl al Haqq.[152]

Within 2 weeks, Petraeus began briefing senior Iraqi officials on what MNF-I was learning from Khazali and others. Deputy Prime Minister Barham Saleh and National Security Adviser Mowaffaq Rubaie were "properly taken aback and left for Iran on Sunday determined to take a strong message to Tehran" after they were informed, Petraeus reported to Gates. Interior Minister Jawad Bolani and Foreign Minister Hoshyar Zebari urged Petraeus to broadcast Khazali's and Daqduq's taped confessions on Iraqi television—something Petraeus had to inform them the Geneva Convention would not allow.[153] MNF-I leaders had their own plans to explain to the world the scale of Iranian involvement in any case. On July 2, Petraeus's MNF-I spokesman, Brigadier General Kevin Bergner, held a press conference in Baghdad to lay out the evidence of the Iranian regime's lethal involvement in Iraq, particularly its training and operational direction of the Special Groups. While capturing Qais al-Khazali, the coalition had discovered a 22-page "in-depth planning and lessons learned document" about the January 20 attack

Khazali's operatives had carried out against the Karbala Provincial Joint Coordination Center, Bergner explained, and in the course of their questioning by coalition officials:

> Ali Mussa Daqduq and Qais Khazali state that senior leadership within the Qods Force knew of and supported planning for the eventual Karbala attack that killed five coalition soldiers. Ali Musa Daqduq contends that the Iraqi Special Groups could not have conducted the complex operations without the support and direction of the Qods Forces. Daqduq and Khazali both confirm that Qais Khazali authorized the operation, and Azhar al Dulaimi, who we killed in an operation earlier this year, executed the operation.[154]

Although Petraeus and other coalition officials had previously mentioned their suspicions of Iranian involvement in Iraq, the July 2 press briefing was the most comprehensive public exposure of the evidence of Iran's destabilizing role and Lebanese Hizballah's involvement. As Petraeus described to Gates, the rollout was meant to "put Iran on notice that we know of their activities and that those activities are unacceptable."[155] As if to punctuate MNF-I's point, on the morning of Bergner's press conference Shi'a militants shelled Forward Operating Base Echo in Diwaniya, attacking the Multi-National Division-Central South (MND-CS) base with 80 mortar rounds.

Later the same month, against the backdrop of the public exposition on July 2, Crocker met with Iranian ambassador Hassan Kazemi-Ghomi in the second round of trilateral talks among the United States, Iraq, and Iran, where the American and Iranian representatives agreed on July 24 to form a security subcommittee that would conduct further talks. "On one hand, we'll seek cooperation on an anti-AQI agenda," Petraeus reported to the Pentagon, but "on the other hand, we'll remain firm in showing the Iranians we have extensive knowledge of their activities and will confront them as they support Shi'a militias inside Iraq."[156] With Operation PHANTOM THUNDER pushing AQI away from the capital, MNF-I's statistics showed that Shi'a militias were likely responsible for approximately two-thirds of attacks against U.S. troops in Baghdad, and Petraeus and Crocker intended the coming security talks to be a venue for senior Iraqi and U.S. officials to present a united front against Iranian lethal aid to the militias.[157] On August 6, Bergner and Crocker's political-military counselor, Ambassador Marcie Ries, met with Iranian counterparts again in a meeting hosted by the hard-nosed Iraqi Interior Ministry intelligence chief Hussein Ali Kamal. The "surprisingly good" Kamal "kept [the meeting] focused on AQI and the militias," Petraeus recounted, while the U.S. officials "stressed the need for tangible improvement in reducing EFPs, indirect-fire, and support to special groups." As U.S. officials had noted in the earlier meetings, "the Iranians seemed off-balance in comparison to their Iraqi counterparts' determined leadership of the meeting," Petraeus added in his weekly letter to Gates.[158]

In fact, U.S. officials noted that the Iranian delegates had appeared nervous and unsure of themselves in each of the trilateral meetings, seemingly afraid of being held to account for going beyond a very limited set of talking points. An incident the same week as the August 6 meeting might have explained why. On August 11, Iraqi Minister of State for National Security Affairs Shirwan al-Waeli brought to Petraeus a message from Qassem Soleimani, who told Waeli to relay word that he, Soleimani, was "the sole decision-maker on Iranian activities in Iraq" and that he was willing to decrease the Special Groups activities in exchange for the release of Qais al-Khazali.[159] "I told Waeli to relay back to Soleimani that we believe that Iran has overreached and is on the brink of attracting international isolation," Petraeus reported back to Gates. "I noted that I am not a policy maker," he continued, but:

> as the commander on the ground, I am starting to think that Iran is attacking Iraqi and coalition soldiers through proxies - the JAM they have trained, funded, armed, and in some cases even directed. To provide a bit more jolt, I said that I am considering telling the President that I believe Iran is, in fact, waging war on the US in Iraq, with all of the US public and governmental responses that could come from that revelation. For what it's worth, I do believe that Iran has gone beyond merely striving for influence in Iraq and could be creating proxies to actively fight us, thinking that they can keep us distracted while they try to build WMD and set up JAM to act like Lebanese Hezbollah in Iraq.[160]

Soleimani's message sent two signals. First, it reinforced how important the Special Groups were to the Iranian regime, particularly Qais al-Khazali and Asa'ib Ahl al-Haqq, which Soleimani and the regime clearly considered a vital Iranian instrument inside Iraq. Second, it seemed timed to neutralize the trilateral talks going on in Baghdad and ensure that no other channel might emerge to challenge Soleimani's control of the Iranian regime's operations in Iraq. The Iranian delegates at the trilateral meetings were "on a short string," clearly not empowered to deal substantively with the United States, and "had to take breaks and make frequent calls back" to their superiors for guidance during the talks, one U.S. diplomat recalled.[161] Soleimani, by contrast, demonstrated through his continuing sponsorship of Shi'a militants, and by the toll they took on U.S. troops in summer 2007, that he had a virtually free hand in his Iraq operations.

For American officials in Iraq, expectations for the talks were low at the outset and sank even lower after three rounds of talks that produced nothing. As one senior diplomat put it, "as a practical matter, it was hard to see how you get to a stable arrangement on anything that Iran and its many clients actively opposed, so it was important to make the effort."[162] Crocker and the U.S. Embassy prepared for a planned fourth round of talks in the fall of 2007, bringing some of the State Department's top Iran experts to Baghdad in anticipation of the talks, but as the weeks and then months passed, the Iranians failed to set a return date and let the engagement lapse.[163] In retrospect, the three sessions of the trilateral talks of 2007 may have represented a debate between two camps within the Iranian regime: one that saw some utility in talks with the United States if it would ultimately remove the U.S. military presence in Iraq, and another that believed the talks were, at best, premature. If there was in fact an intra-Iranian policy debate, the latter view apparently prevailed.

The JAM War Against ISCI and the Maliki Government

Despite his assertion that he controlled Iran's Iraq policy and his offer to rein in his Iraqi proxies if the United States was willing to deal with him, in August 2007 Soleimani was in the midst of an intra-Iraqi Shi'a conflict that threatened the viability of his Iraq strategy. Since striking his deal to support the Special Groups and JAM in 2004, Soleimani had sought to maintain a unified Iraqi Shi'a militant front against the U.S.-led coalition, with the aim of forcing the U.S. military out of Iraq. For 3 years, he and his Quds Force generals had been highly active in arming, training, and funding any of the major Shi'a militant factions that were willing to fight against the coalition. By the summer of 2007, it was clear that his militant proxies were fighting each other as much as they were fighting coalition troops, and his continued support to Shi'a militant factions had begun to amount to an arming of Shi'a groups that were in rebellion against a Shi'a government ostensibly aligned with the Iranian regime. In short, by trying to arm all Iraqi Shi'a opponents of the United States, Soleimani and the Quds Force had helped incite a civil war among their top Iraqi clients, and it was unclear whether Soleimani or anyone else was actually in full control of the most active Shi'a militant elements.

A series of high-profile attacks drew attention to the broader intra-Shi'a conflict pulsing ominously throughout the southern provinces. On June 5, the chief Sadrist official in Babil was killed, followed by the murder of a Najafi cleric associated with Sistani. The Shi'a-on-Shi'a violence surged as the summer progressed, with operatives from JAM and Badr engaging in a deadly tit-for-tat as Sadrists and Sistani representatives were killed in rapid succession through July and early August. The tensions between the two sides escalated into larger-scale violence as well. On June 19 and 20, the Nasiriyah Tactical Support Unit, a well-regarded ISF unit headed by Colonel Naji Rostum Sahra (also known as Abu Liqa), came under attack by as many as 200 JAM fighters north of the Euphrates River. Through 2 days of fighting, MNC-I provided close air support and coalition reinforcements as Abu Liqa and his SWAT operators held off their JAM enemies. Prime Minister Maliki and Vice President Adel Abdel Mahdi (himself a Nasiriyah native) gave coalition commanders a green light to attack "any and all JAM elements" in the city, even though the province was already under Iraqi control.[164] At least 20 JAM fighters died in the clashes before calm was restored.[165]

Source: DoD photo by Staff Sergeant Lorie Jewell (Released).

General David Petraeus With Iraqi Police Colonel Naji Rostum Sahra, Also Known as Abu Liqa.[166]

The fighting in Nasiriyah was followed 2 weeks later by another large engagement in still-restive Diwaniya, initiated by a JAM indirect-fire attack against Camp Echo on the same day as Bergner's press conference. Accurate enough to suggest that JAM elements had benefited from "inside help" in their targeting, the barrage of more than 75 rockets and mortars only wounded 1 coalition soldier, but it damaged equipment and came close to igniting critical ammunition stores. F-16 fighters streaked over Diwaniyah in response, destroying three buildings identified as enemy firing points. A raid by U.S. special operations forces against a JAM cell later that week brought a large number of fighters into the streets, where they seemed poised for a march on Camp Echo until an AC-130 strike mowed down scores of fighters, decisively ending the attack.[167] With close air support readily available, the coalition retained ample firepower, but that advantage itself could not prevent JAM from returning to Diwaniya's neighborhoods in strength once again. However, Petraeus noted in his report on the battle that Diwaniya residents—and Prime Minister Maliki as well—had responded favorably to the coalition's actions, while Sadrist leaders had chastised JAM members for firing from inside the city.[168]

The Nasiriyah and Diwaniya clashes were part of an escalating confrontation between JAM and the Special Groups on one side and the Shi'a parties inside the government on the other, with the coalition increasingly active in support of the government and JAM ever more active against the coalition, especially in Baghdad. The same week as the Diwaniyah fighting, coalition troops conducting a raid to arrest a police officer connected to JAM in Sadr City found themselves under heavy fire from other presumably JAM-linked Sadr City policemen as they withdrew from the neighborhood. Four days later, Shi'a militants attacked the International Zone with 35 mortar rounds launched from multiple locations in Sadr City during a 90-second synchronized attack, a sharp change from the Shi'a militants' previous tactics of firing only 1 or 2 rounds at a time. The militia attack on the Green Zone had "a psychological effect" and had even "shaken the Prime Minister a bit," Petraeus reported.[169] The Shi'a militants were shelling the seat of their own government, where the Sadrists still had members in the Parliament.

Meanwhile, the Shi'a militants' assassination campaign in southern Iraq culminated with the killing of two Islamic Supreme Council of Iraq (ISCI) governors in mid-August. On August 11, Qadisiyah Governor Khalil Jalil Hamza and the provincial police chief died amid a hail of small-arms fire and an EFP explosion in Diwaniya. MNF-I quickly concluded that the attack had been carried out by JAM operatives in retaliation for Hamza's support for the ongoing coalition-ISF operations against local JAM groups.[170] Nine days later, Muhammad al-Hassina, a former Badr Corps member who was governor of Muthanna Province, fell victim to a string of EFPs that tore through his convoy. Reeling from these high-profile losses, ISCI politicians blamed the Iranian-backed Special Groups immediately, and by summer's end the new ISCI governor of Qadisiyah was calling for another offensive against the militias in Diwaniya.[171]

Commenting on the two assassinations, Petraeus noted "Tensions between ISCI/Badr and JAM are high now in the southern provinces. This also may heighten tensions with Iran, as there is considerable belief that Iran may have been connected to these events." The events also underscored for Prime Minister Maliki the threat that the Iranian-backed militias posed, Petraeus continued, observing, "Iranian influence appears to be more damaging over time."[172]

It was a judgment that Petraeus had been forming for several months, as the Shi'a militant threat gradually came into greater relief and al-Qaeda in Iraq receded from the Baghdad region. "I tend to agree with the assessment of Ray Odierno and see that JAM is more of a hindrance to long-term security in Iraq than is AQI," he had written to Gates on June 30, adding that, "JAM is a much tougher nut and will require kinetics against the rogue leaders and active engagements to make the mainstream more constructive."[173] In terms of the militias' lethality, Petraeus was right—about two-thirds of U.S. casualties in the following month of July came at the hands of Shi'a militants. The events of the summer also showed a Sadrist militant front that was in disarray as it faced pressure from both the coalition and its rivals in the Iraqi Government. The Sadrists' top problem was that their leader, Moqtada Sadr, appeared not to be in full control of his numerous militant commanders and fighters. In early July, he had suddenly returned to Iran, leaving Sheikh Ahmed al-Sheibani in charge of JAM activities and issuing little guidance to his organization.[174] As Sheibani took command back in Iraq, MNF-I detected that JAM leaders were purging their ranks, and as JAM groups mounted large-scale indirect fire attacks in Baghdad, coalition commanders could not tell how many of the Sadrist militant groups actually followed Sadr's commands.[175] Sheibani left for Iran in mid-July, part of an exodus of JAM commanders who were spending more time in Iran as Maliki consented to more coalition operations against longtime JAM sanctuaries in Baghdad and elsewhere.[176] By mid-August, Petraeus judged that "Sadr is at least a bit marginalized; even the Iranians think he is a weak leader."[177]

The most significant factor working against the Sadrists, however, was that they had worn out their welcome with Nuri al-Maliki, and the Prime Minister was increasingly willing to fight them. After the Sadrists had withdrawn from his cabinet in April, Maliki had spent 3 months working toward fashioning a new governing coalition among Iraq's four major parties that excluded the Sadrists. Petraeus anticipated that Maliki was "setting the stage for a more direct confrontation with the radical elements of JAM."[178] Both Petraeus and the Iraqi Prime Minister detected an erosion of JAM's popular support as well. A late July coalition clash against JAM in Karbala had revealed local disaffection with the militia when JAM fighters commandeered a hospital and demanded that the doctors treat their wounded, instigating a "ruckus" when the doctors refused. "This attitude seems to match that of many Karbala residents, who believe JAM's presence will bring on AQI attacks," Petraeus reported.[179] When an August 8 coalition operation in Sadr City resulted in 32 JAM militiamen killed, Petraeus observed, "while such an operation would have received great opposition only a few months ago, today Iraqis are happy to have these rogue militias cleaned off of their streets."[180]

The Karbala Fiasco and the JAM Freeze

The week following the assassination of Governor Hamza in Diwaniya, Maliki told Petraeus that "many Shi'a communities are getting fed up with JAM," and discussed the Sadrists' prospects among a Shi'a population that was growing resentful of them. Reflecting on the discussions, Petraeus reported to Gates on August 18:

> my take on JAM is that they, like AQI, have overplayed their hand in some areas. . . . JAM continues to demonstrate the destructive nature of their organization, and we are seeing a growing rejection by Iraqi citizens of JAM. JAM protected Shi'a communities when AQI and Sunni insurgents threatened them, but with that threat dissipating in some areas, JAM is being viewed more as criminal gangs and thugs than protectors. Many Iraqi leaders talk about the danger of the Hezbollization of Iraq by

JAM, as well, but both the Prime Minister and I sense that JAM lacks the capability and widespread acceptance among the Shi'a to take on such a role. When the Shi'a communities turn against JAM, as many of the Sunni communities have done against AQI, this effort will turn more to the good.[181]

The turning of the Shi'a population against JAM was not long in coming. The low-level conflict among the Shi'a factions finally boiled over in late August in the shrine city of Karbala. On August 27, Sadrist gunmen attacked Badr-associated government security guards at the Imam Ali shrine, the destination of more than one million pilgrims who had made their way to the city that month to celebrate the birth of the twelfth imam. For weeks, Iraqi security forces and the coalition had made careful plans to guard the pilgrimage against AQI attacks, but had not anticipated that the actual threat would come from the Sadrists. Horrified Iraqis watched footage of the fighting as 52 people were killed and another 279 wounded, many of them pilgrims caught in the crossfire.

The clashes in Karbala quickly set off fighting between JAM and Badr elsewhere, including in Baghdad, where gun battles broke out between the groups for 2 days before finally calming down. The day after the Karbala violence, an enraged Prime Minister Maliki led a 52-vehicle convoy to Karbala to confront JAM fighters and leaders, arrest local officials who had been complicit or incompetent in the JAM attacks, and shut down the pilgrimage, ordering the hundreds of thousands of remaining pilgrims to leave the city for their own safety. The Prime Minister, cheered by crowds along the route from Baghdad, brandished a pistol upon arriving in Karbala and arrested scores of Sadrists implicated in the violence as quick reaction forces from the Interior and Defense ministries deployed to lock down the city, including Major General Othman al-Ghanimi and his 8th Iraqi Army Division.[182]

The Karbala fiasco forced Moqtada Sadr to act quickly to deflect the criticism descending upon his party and repair the embarrassing impression that his movement had become dominated by out-of-control, murderous gangs. The carnage near one of the Shi'a world's holiest sites was a clear sign of the depths to which JAM had sunk: a militant organization formed in 2003 expressly to protect Shi'a pilgrims from violence was now seen on television slaughtering them. Three days after the incident, Sadr's top representatives read out a public statement in which he announced a freeze of all JAM operations for 6 months, during which he encouraged militia members to cooperate with the ISF and refrain from attacking the coalition.[183] Inside the JAM leadership, Sadr went further and ordered his subordinates to overhaul the militia with an educational program for the rank and file, while reportedly clashing with his deputy Ahmed al-Sheibani over Sheibani's handling of the Karbala incident.[184]

The Sadrist fiasco and JAM freeze delivered MNF-I an unexpected respite from the main body of the Sadrist militia organization and also handed Petraeus and coalition leaders a useful tool with which to attack those militias that continued to fight. Coalition leaders could now argue that any Shi'a militants that attacked coalition forces were not a part of Sadr's "honorable" followers, but rather criminal groups who were subject to coalition and ISF targeting. The halt to "mainstream JAM" activities helped coalition commanders identify and target Special Groups, breakaway groups, and rogue militants who distinguished themselves from mainstream JAM by continuing their activities despite Sadr's call for a freeze on activities. Coalition commanders also judged that Sadr, though weakened, had not decided to drop militant resistance against the coalition for good. "They were embarrassed over the Karbala events," Odierno concluded. "I think they called the ceasefire not because they want to stop violent action, but because they want to regroup, reorganize, [and] see if they can get control of their forces so they can continue to influence the future of Iraq."[185]

Some analysts later concluded that the coalition benefited from a strategic windfall as Sadr supposedly unilaterally ordered his militia to stand down from attacks against the coalition. In truth, the JAM freeze was Sadr's desperate attempt to rescue his movement from a severe political backlash inside the Iraqi Shi'a community. The Sadrist stand-down was also, at least in part, a defensive reaction to several months of intensifying pressure on JAM and the Special Groups from both the coalition and the ISF. On a macro scale, it represented the beginning of a reversal of fortunes for Maliki and Sadr. Just as the Karbala incident caused a dramatic change in the Sadrists' near-term political position, it did the same for Maliki. The Prime Minister's decisive action had increased both his stature and his confidence, Petraeus noted a few days later, as well as Maliki's confidence in the ISF units that had responded quickly to secure Karbala.[186] The confrontation with JAM in Karbala marked the beginning of a high-stakes Maliki-Sadrist showdown that would culminate in Basrah and Baghdad the following spring.

MNF-I AND THE OPPOSITION TO THE SURGE

CENTCOM Has Its Doubts, Again

As the operational situation in Iraq began to change in the summer of 2007, the views of the MNF-I and CENTCOM commanders diverged again. Less than 3 months into Admiral William J. Fallon's command, his initial skepticism about the prospects of the surge had developed into virtual opposition to Petraeus's approach. By late May 2007, before the last of the surge units had arrived in Iraq, Fallon concluded that the surge was doomed to strategic failure. He set out to develop an alternative campaign plan for Iraq that would, in his view, allow the United States to regain its strategic flexibility by reducing what he believed was an over-commitment of U.S. military resources to the Middle East. In June, as Petraeus and Crocker's subordinates fleshed out the new joint campaign plan, Fallon dispatched Rear Admiral James "Sandy" Winnefeld to Iraq to assess the situation and formulate a plan to significantly drawdown U.S. troops by year's end, far ahead of the scheduled end of the surge. The Navy men shared the belief that Army leaders had become invested emotionally in Iraq and could no longer clearly judge Iraq's strategic importance and the coalition's chances of success. Journeying to Baghdad to attend the Multi-National Security Transition Command-Iraq (MNSTC-I) change of command in early June, Fallon took it as a bad sign when incoming commander Lieutenant General James M. Dubik delivered his assumption of command speech in phonetic Arabic. Dubik had meant it as a gesture of respect to the assembled crowd of hundreds of Iraqi officers, but Fallon saw it as evidence that Army leaders had become too deeply ensconced in Baghdad.[187] Visiting the vast post exchange at Camp Liberty later, Winnefeld walked through rows of flat-screen televisions for sale to American troops, a sight that seemed to him emblematic of an Army that had settled into a permanent mission in Iraq—though

Petraeus coincidentally had tasked MNF-I Command Sergeant Major Marvin Hill to quietly end such sales.[188] The CENTCOM commander and Winnefeld were determined to help extricate the U.S. military from the Iraq morass. Fallon and Winnefeld's alternative Iraq strategy involved ending the U.S. combat mission in the country and accelerating the transition to Iraqi control, virtually the same concept U.S. forces would adopt during Operation NEW DAWN more than 3 years later.[189]

To assist Fallon in refining this approach, Brigadier General Daniel P. Bolger, having recently served as the commander of the Coalition Military Assistance Training Team, traveled to Tampa to help Winnefeld set down the particulars of how to end combat activities and convert U.S. units into transition teams. As the plan took shape with Bolger's input, Winnefeld shared its details with U.S. commanders in Iraq and the Gulf region. In Kuwait, he met with Army Central commander Lieutenant General R. Steven Whitcomb to discuss ways in which the command could more quickly withdraw the Army from Iraq.[191] In Bahrain, he

Source: U.S. Navy photo by Monica A. King (Released).

Rear Admiral James Winnefeld.[190]

met Marine Corps Central commander Lieutenant General James N. Mattis, but when Winnefeld offered the observation that the surge had failed in its objectives and that U.S. forces should begin to withdraw, an astounded Mattis protested that the Marines in MNF-W were close to winning their war against AQI. Enemy activity had dropped to just a few incidents per week, and the Marines had partnered with the Awakening to mobilize tens of thousands of new Anbari counterinsurgents. However, in his exchange with Winnefeld, it seemed to Mattis that these strategically significant developments in Anbar had somehow escaped CENTCOM's notice. "We've got our boots on their windpipe and you're telling me to lift my foot and let them live," the Marine general declared, incredulously.[192]

In Iraq, Winnefeld met with each of the division commanders and Odierno. The MNC-I commander was not receptive to the CENTCOM commander's withdrawal plans. Odierno believed that Winnefeld's planning was conceptually sound and represented what the United States would eventually have to do in Iraq, but he was alarmed that Winnefeld and Fallon were promoting the idea at such an early stage, when the loss of badly needed combat power would probably ensure the failure of the U.S. campaign.[193] Near the end of the admiral's fact-finding tour, Winnefeld and Petraeus met and calmly debated the competing strategies. In the end, Petraeus noted that he believed the President had given him the task of formulating the mission and campaign plan for U.S. forces in Iraq, and offered, "if someone else is going to present an alternative plan to my boss, then I'm going to have a problem with that."[194]

At a 2-day commanders' conference at CENTCOM's forward headquarters in Qatar the following month, Fallon pressed subtly for a change of mission in Iraq. The admiral told his subordinates that the commands across the CENTCOM area of responsibility were "too operationally and tactically focused" and were failing to be "cognizant of strategic realities that are changing."[195] He also contended that the political dynamics in Washington militated against the continuation of the surge. "We are not going to be able to make any of the domestic political constraints go away," Fallon warned his subordinates. "Dave [Petraeus] is going to have to deal with alternatives . . . that may be pushed on us," the admiral said, and, as a result, MNF-I should, "prepare for a change of mission, the downgrading of population security to secondary concern in favor of transition."[196] Signaling the depth of the divergence in worldviews, as the conference turned to regional security matters beyond Iraq, Petraeus weighed in, offering counterpoints to Fallon's perspectives.[197]

In keeping with his warning, 3 days later Fallon dispatched Winnefeld to Baghdad again to present the conclusions of his campaign assessment to Petraeus. Winnefeld and the CENTCOM commander proposed a gradual troop drawdown to 10 brigades starting in November 2007, with three-quarters of U.S. combat forces departing Iraq by the end of 2009.[198] Just as Casey had recommended in 2006, Winnefeld proposed that U.S. troops should focus on transitioning security responsibility to the Iraqis, while special operations forces continued to hunt AQI and Special Group leaders. Only with this mission change, Winnefeld argued, could the U.S. military restore the strategic flexibility needed to respond to crises in other parts of the world.[199] A puzzled Petraeus replied that, while MNF-I would examine some of Winnefeld's ideas, no one could be expected to come up with a credible Iraq strategy after spending only a few days on the ground as Winnefeld had done.[200] The general pointed out that the last elements of the fifth surge brigade had only arrived in June, and time was needed to gauge the surge's impact. Fallon and Winnefeld's proposal to withdraw troops was also disconnected from major upcoming Iraqi political events, he observed, such as the provincial elections expected in late 2008. What was more, Petraeus argued, their plan was essentially the same one U.S. troops had employed from 2003 to 2006, which had already failed. Petraeus also reiterated that he would protest strongly—even to the point of offering the President his resignation—if someone attempted to present an alternative Iraq strategy to the President or SECDEF.[201]

Comparing notes after the discussion, Fallon and Winnefeld shared the belief that Petraeus was manipulating the President into sticking with a failing surge strategy, and that an intervention by the Joint Chiefs of Staff and the SECDEF was needed.[202] Among the senior Army officers in Baghdad, the Winnefeld-Fallon plan caused confusion and frustration. "[Winnefeld] came here with a conclusion and was looking for evidence," one U.S. commander charged.[203] Instead of attempting to undermine the strategy set by Bush and MNF-I, Petraeus believed that Fallon and CENTCOM should be working to gain support and aid from other Middle Eastern countries and focusing on resolving regional issues, especially by stemming the flow of foreign fighters into Iraq.[204] Senior MNF-I officials also were frustrated at Fallon's seeming obstruction of MNF-I's requests for forces and other resources needed to support the surge. There was a suspicion at the Baghdad headquarters that Fallon's focus on developing an alternative to the surge was distracting him from his other duties.[205] Petraeus followed up his July 17 meeting with Winnefeld by calling Fallon in order to reemphasize his opposition to a what he saw as CENTCOM's "simplistic and strategically unsound proposal." He also registered his disappointment that his immediate boss in the chain of command was undermining—rather than supporting—a surge plan that was only 4 months into execution, with the final surge forces barely established and operating. Commanders in Iraq were beginning to see significant gains from the surge operations, Petraeus said, and further progress appeared likely in the months ahead. He also noted his concern about the amount of time that requests for forces were taking to get through CENTCOM. "I can take 'No' for an answer, admiral," Petraeus said, "but I can't take no answer." Yet if the answer was no, the MNF-I commander said, the admiral should be prepared for Petraeus to raise the issue with the President and SECDEF, given the assurance of support the President had made before Petraeus took command and had reiterated in weekly videoconferences ever since.[206]

Back in Washington, however, an increasing number of U.S. leaders seemed to agree with Fallon's view that the surge was doomed to fail. By midsummer, the odds had grown that the U.S. Congress might pass legislation for an early end to the surge.[207] Eventually, these dynamics influenced Fallon's military advice to his superiors. During a videoconference with Bush on August 30, Fallon questioned whether a continuation of the surge could garner enough congressional support, to which Bush replied that politics and Congress were his concern, not the admiral's. Five days later, the President, accompanied by the other National Security Council (NSC) principals, met with both Fallon and Petraeus at Al Asad air base, where Bush received updates on the situation in Baghdad and also met Sheikh Abdul Sattar Abu Risha, the leader of the Awakening in Ramadi. In the presence of his war cabinet at Al Asad, the President reaffirmed his support for Petraeus's campaign plan, finally and firmly resolving the 5-month-long dispute between the CENTCOM and MNF-I commanders in Petraeus's favor.[208]

The September Congressional Testimony

The President's and NSC principals' visit to Anbar on September 3 took place 1 week before Petraeus and Crocker were scheduled to appear before the U.S. Congress to give their assessment of the surge and its progress. The direction of the Iraq War had become one of the most divisive political issues in the United States since the Vietnam war and the two men's scheduled congressional testimony was a highly anticipated and high-stakes event. Although the summer had passed without a congressional effort to terminate the surge, the idea of a legislative intervention was still a possibility, and much would hinge on whether Petraeus and Crocker could point to an improving situation on the ground. A few late-summer events had greased the rails for the MNF-I commander and U.S. ambassador, most notably a visit to Iraq by influential American think-tank scholars. After touring conflict zones around central Iraq with MNF-I escorts, Kenneth Pollack and Michael O'Hanlon of the Brookings Institution co-wrote a *New York Times* op-ed entitled, "A War We Just Might Win," in which the scholars argued that "we are finally getting somewhere in Iraq," with "sustainable stability" potentially within reach of the U.S.-led coalition due to the significant security gains and the growing competence of the ISF.[209] The article was so effective at slowing the congressional move toward anti-surge legislation that Petraeus referred to it as a new phenomenon, the "strategic op-ed," and thereafter opened Iraq to a series of similar visiting delegations of U.S. scholars and other intellectuals. In addition to these delegations, Petraeus, Crocker, and Odierno had also hosted dozens of members of Congress in Baghdad by the end of the summer, considering the visiting delegations not as a distraction, but rather as opportunities to clarify the situation on the ground to U.S. policymakers.[210]

In his prepared statements to the Foreign Relations and Armed Services committees in both the Senate and House of Representatives on September 10-11, Petraeus gave a data-based assessment of the campaign. "The military objectives of the surge are, in large measure, being met," Petraeus judged, before walking the committee members through a series of detailed statistical reports and charts displayed on easels in the hearing room. Overall, Petraeus noted that security incidents had declined in 8 of the previous 12 weeks, to levels not seen since spring 2006. The decline was mostly because of U.S. and Iraqi troops' success in driving AQI out of its sanctuaries and disrupting the Shi'a militant groups. "The fundamental source of the conflict in Iraq is competition among ethnic and sectarian communities for power and resources," Petraeus testified, and in this regard, it was encouraging that ethno-sectarian deaths had dropped by 55 percent since December 2006 across Iraq, and 80 percent in Baghdad. Iraq as a whole was becoming less volatile, with violent civilian deaths declining by 45 percent since December, and by 70 percent in Baghdad itself.[212]

Source: DoD photo (Released).

General David Petraeus Testifies Before Congress, September 2007.[211]

Petraeus reported that the nascent Awakening among Sunni tribes had had a significant impact on these figures and was spreading quickly from Anbar to other areas, in the process damaging AQI's ability to operate. In 8 months, MNF-I and its Iraqi allies had killed or captured nearly 100 AQI leaders and about 2,500 rank-and-file fighters. They had also robbed AQI of its war-making machinery. "As we have gone on the offensive in former al-Qaeda in Iraq and insurgent sanctuaries, and as locals have increasingly supported our efforts, we have found a substantially increased number of arms, ammunition, and explosives caches," Petraeus noted. U.S. troops had already seized 4,400 caches in 2007, about 1,700 more than MNF-I had discovered in all of 2006. Partly because of this massive loss of materiel, insurgent IED attacks had dropped by one-third during the summer of 2007, and car bombs had declined from a high of 175 in March to about 90 in August. In Anbar, monthly attacks had dropped sharply from 1,350 in October 2006 to just over 200 in August 2007, a decline of more than 80 percent.[213]

At the same time, more than 20,000 Awakening members had come forward to join the Iraqi police and thousands more had hopes of joining the army. The ISF was set to expand from 445,000 to as many as 485,000, and the Iraqi Government was committed to spend $1.6 billion in foreign military sales with the United States. In other words, Petraeus reassured Congress that the Iraqis would soon be paying their own way for their security forces. The general also noted that about 95 of Iraq's 140 combat battalions were now capable of taking the lead, with coalition support.[214]

Alongside these positive signs, Petraeus identified a number of serious obstacles that needed to be dealt with before Iraq could be stabilized. "Foreign and home-grown terrorists, insurgents, militia extremists, and criminals all push the ethno-sectarian competition toward violence. Malign actions by Syria and, especially, by Iran fuel that violence," he reported. He added that "lack of adequate government capacity, lingering sectarian mistrust, and various forms of corruption add to Iraq's challenges." Not all of Iraq's provinces were progressing at the same rate: Ninawa and Salahadin, in particular, remained violent and had not yet experienced the same stabilizing trend that had come to Anbar and Baghdad. The IRGC Quds Force and its Iraqi Shi'a militant proxies were a persistent problem as well. "It is increasingly apparent to both coalition and Iraqi leaders that Iran, through the use of the Quds Force, seeks to turn the Iraqi Special Groups into a Hezbollah-like force to serve its interests and fight a proxy war against the Iraqi state and coalition forces in Iraq," Petraeus noted.[215]

Though MNF-I had increased its targeting of Shi'a militia leaders in the previous 6 months, the Quds Force proxies had still "assassinated and kidnapped Iraqi Governmental leaders, killed and wounded our soldiers with advanced explosive devices provided by Iran, and indiscriminately rocketed civilians in the International Zone and elsewhere."[216] Nevertheless, Petraeus concluded that, based on the prevailing trends, he and Odierno agreed that the surge brigades could be withdrawn from Iraq by summer 2008 without endangering Iraq's security. He added that he would allow the 13th MEU to depart Iraq later in the month without requesting another unit to replace it, followed by the withdrawal of a BCT in December, also without a replacement. Four additional brigades and two Marine battalions would depart without being replaced in the first 7 months of 2008, bringing MNF-I to its pre-surge level of 15 brigade-sized units in mid-July.[217]

From that point, however, Petraeus argued that the drawdown should slow, and that the United States should not yet try to prescribe the troop levels or pace of withdrawal after mid-2008. "In my professional judgment, it would be premature to make recommendations on the pace of such reductions at this time," he offered. "In fact, our experience in Iraq has repeatedly shown that projecting too far into the future is not just difficult, it can be misleading and even hazardous." In this line of argument, Petraeus pushed back directly on Fallon and others who wanted to institute a scheduled drawdown, rather than the conditions-based approach Petraeus favored. Petraeus also argued against Fallon's months-long pressure for a change of mission:

> One may argue that the best way to speed the process in Iraq is to change the MNF-I mission from one that emphasizes population security, counter-terrorism, and transition, to one that is strictly focused on transition and counter-terrorism. Making that change now would, in our view, be premature. We have learned before that there is a real danger in handing over tasks to the Iraqi Security Forces before their capacity and local conditions warrant.[218]

Alongside Petraeus's presentation on Iraq's security, Crocker delivered a sober assessment of the state of Iraqi politics and national reconciliation. Crocker emphasized the enormity of the challenges facing Iraq, a "traumatized society" exiting 35 years of Ba'athist rule. "A new Iraq had to be built almost literally from scratch," he observed, adding that Iraq was "experiencing a revolution, not just regime change." The surge had provided Iraqis with "time and space" to pursue national reconciliation, but "some of the more promising political developments at the national level are neither measured in benchmarks nor visible to those far from Baghdad." The process of stabilizing Iraq "will not be quick, it will be uneven," Crocker judged, meaning that the United States would need to display "strategic patience," especially since, in the ambassador's view, the alternatives—such as withdrawal—would be "far worse" for U.S. vital interests.[219]

Petraeus's testimony that the surge was working and Crocker's judgment that the United States should exercise strategic patience in Iraq prompted endorsements from members of Congress who favored the surge and criticism from those who did not. The two men's hearings before the Senate Committees on Foreign Relations and Armed Services were highly charged, particularly since five Presidential candidates from both parties served on those committees, and the hearing room thus became an extension of the Presidential campaign.[220] Illinois Senator Barack H. Obama was skeptical of Petraeus's reports of progress, arguing "I think that some of the frustration you hear from some of the questioners is that we have now set the bar so low that modest improvement in what was a completely chaotic situation, to the point where now we just have the levels of intolerable violence that existed in June 2006, is considered success. And it's not." Obama judged that the effect of the surge, "has been relatively modest," and added that, "it is not clear to me that the primary success that you've shown in Anbar has anything to do with the surge." Concerning Crocker's plea for strategic patience, Obama offered that the country was already out of patience, and that "the question I think that everybody is asking is: How long will this take, and at what point do we say, 'Enough'?"[221]

For her part, New York Senator Hillary Rodham Clinton expressed deep skepticism of Petraeus and Crocker's reports, telling the MNF-I commander and ambassador that "You have been made the de facto spokesmen for what many of us believe to be a failed policy," and that, despite the two men's efforts, "the reports that you provide to us really require a willing suspension of disbelief." Continuing in Iraq would be counterproductive, she judged, since, "any fair reading of the advantages and disadvantages accruing post-surge, in my view, end up on the downside."[222] Connecticut Senator Christopher J. Dodd, another Presidential candidate, argued, "People are getting tired of hearing that things are better. I don't know anybody who believes that," while Delaware Senator Joseph R. Biden, also a Presidential candidate, told Petraeus, as one reporter put it, that "he had not heard anything that persuaded him that the military was pursuing a new strategy as opposed to new tactics in Iraq."[223]

Despite the vehement response from some senior members of Congress, the Petraeus and Crocker reports offered enough evidence of progress in the surge campaign to begin to relieve some of the pressure to end that campaign early. "Those hearings gained us critical additional time and support, without which it is likely that the mission in Iraq would have failed," Petraeus later wrote.[224] Yet, at the same time the hearings had placed a senior military leader in the awkward role of defending strategy in the political realm.

Two days after Petraeus and Crocker concluded their testimony, Bush gave a televised speech reiterating the evidence the two had given Congress, emphasizing the security gains that had been made in Baghdad, Anbar, and Diyala and highlighting the spread of the Awakening. Now was the time to secure a "return on success," Bush declared, and consequently he had chosen not to replace the 2,200 Marines from the 13th MEU due to redeploy at the end of September and would also consider bringing home an Army BCT before Christmas. These moves would result in a total reduction of 5,700 troops by the end of the year. The President also informed the nation that Petraeus expected to be able to reduce the U.S. presence in Iraq from 20 to 15 brigades by July 2008.[225] The end point of the surge was now a formal U.S. policy.

***

The surge of operations in summer 2007 had enabled the coalition to retake the initiative for arguably the first time since MNF-I's offensive in fall 2004 to clear insurgent sanctuaries before the elections. MNC-I's Operation PHANTOM THUNDER had coordinated the activities of four U.S. divisions to push AQI away from Baghdad and out of support zones and sanctuaries the militant group and its allies had dominated in some cases for more than 3 years. At the same time, MNC-I and MNF-I had taken steps to institutionalize the Awakening by brokering formal agreements between vetted groups of armed Sunnis and the Maliki government, though it was not clear Maliki and his officials could be convinced of the Awakening's merits. Nevertheless, Operation PHANTOM THUNDER had allowed the Awakening to spread even further in the Baghdad belts, Diyala, and southern Salahadin Province and had sent AQI reeling.

By early September, this strategic turn of events and the corresponding drop in violence in Baghdad helped limit the effects of criticism from opponents of the surge in Washington. The Sadrists had inadvertently assisted the coalition, too, by overreaching and creating a backlash among the Iraqi public. Worsening tensions between the Iraqi Government and the Iranian regime's Shi'a militant proxies would occupy more of the coalition's attention as the months passed.

Petraeus and Crocker would return to Baghdad to see the onset of Ramadan amidst the continuing Operation PHANTOM STRIKE. With the main battlefields of the anti-AQI fight shifting to northern Iraq, the coalition commanders were poised to pursue the remaining hardcore Sunni insurgents further from Baghdad than ever and to plan decisive operations to finish them off in early 2008.

However, a single event cast a pall over the September testimony and the security gains the coalition and the Awakening had made. Hours before Bush's nationwide address on September 13, AQI operatives killed Sheikh Abdul Sattar Abu Risha in a car bombing in Ramadi, robbing the Awakening of its most prominent founding leader just 10 days after he had met with Bush at Al Asad and showing that AQI remained a potent threat to the Sunni Iraqi leaders that had begun to turn against it. The war was far from over.

ENDNOTES - CHAPTER 5

1. Quote from Thomas E. Ricks, *The Gamble: General David Petraeus and the American Military Adventure in Iraq, 2006-2008,* New York: Penguin Press, 2009, p. 179. All unpublished documents in this chapter, unless otherwise stated, are in the Chief of Staff of the Army (CSA) Operation IRAQI FREEDOM (OIF) Study Group archives, Army Heritage and Education Center (AHEC), Carlisle, PA.

2. Press Briefing, Lieutenant General Raymond T. Odierno, Department of Defense (DoD), June 22, 2007.

3. MNF-I, Secretary of Defense (SECDEF) Weekly Update, April 7-13, 2007.

4. Interview, Steven E. Clay, Combat Studies Institute (CSI) Contemporary Operations Study Team, with Colonel Jon S. Lehr, December 2, 2009.

5. Interview, Steven E. Clay, CSI Contemporary Operations Study Team, with Lieutenant General Benjamin R. Mixon, March 9, 2010.

6. Dale Andrade, *Surging South of Baghdad: The 3d Infantry Division and Task Force Marne in Iraq, 2007-2008,* Washington, DC: U.S. Army Center of Military History, 2010, p. 42; MNF-I, SECDEF Weekly Update, April 7-13, 2007; Interview, CSI Contemporary Operations Study Team with Mixon, March 9, 2010.

7. MNF-I, SECDEF Weekly Update, June 17-23, 2007; Lieutenant General Raymond T. Odierno, "The Surge in Iraq: One Year Later," Lecture, Heritage Foundation, Washington, DC, March 5, 2008, p. 3; MNF-I, SECDEF Weekly Update, June 3-9, 2007; Kimberly Kagan, *The Surge: A Military History,* New York: Encounter Books, 2009, p. 135.

8. Manuscript (Ms), CSI, *On Point,* Vol. IV, September 25, 2014, Chapter 5.

9. Interview, Major Glenn Garcia, U.S. Army Center of Military History (CMH), with Major General Joseph Fil, August 28, 2007.

10. Andrade, *Surging South of Baghdad,* pp. 22-24.

11. MNF-I, SECDEF Weekly Update, April 29-May 5, 2007; Interview, CMH with Fil, August 28, 2007; Andrade, *Surging South of Baghdad,* pp. 22-23; Interview, CSI Contemporary Operations Study Team with Mixon, March 9, 2010.

12. Interviews, Colonel James Powell, CSA OIF Study Group, with Lieutenant Colonel Kent Strader, MNC-I planner, March 26, 2014; CMH with Fil, August 28, 2007.

13. MNF-I, SECDEF Weekly Update, June 10-16, 2007, p. 2.

14. Interview, CSA OIF Study Group with Lieutenant Colonel Charles Armstrong, March 20, 2014; MNF-I, SECDEF Weekly Update, April 21-27, 2007; Briefing, Multi-National Force-West (MNF-W) update, MNF-I Commander's Conference, February 17, 2007; Interview, CSI Contemporary Operations Study Team with Mixon, March 9, 2010; Interview, Steven Clay, CSI Contemporary Operations Study Team, with Colonel James Hickey, February 23-24, 2010.

15. Ms, *On Point,* Vol. IV, Chapter 5.

16. Ibid.

17. Interview, CSA OIF Study Group with General (Ret.) Raymond T. Odierno, January 25, 2015.

18. Interview, CSI Contemporary Operations Study Team with Colonel Steven Townsend, January 24, 2008; MNF-I, SECDEF Weekly Update, May 6-12, 2007.

19. DoD photo by Specialist Benjamin Fox, "Force commander visits Diyala [Image 2 of 2]," DVIDS Identifier 40977, April 6, 2007, Released to Public, available from *https://www.dvidshub.net/image/40977/force-commander-visits-diyala*.

20. DoD photo courtesy 5th Mobile Public Affairs Detachment, "Night mission in Baqubah [Image 2 of 7]," DVIDS Identifier 39558, March 25, 2007, Released to Public, available from *https://www.dvidshub.net/image/39558/night-mission-baqubah*.

21. MNF-I, SECDEF Weekly Update, May 6-12, 2007, p. 3.

22. Ibid., May 20-26, 2007, p. 1.

23. Ibid.

24. Ibid., June 3-9, 2007, p. 2.

25. Ms, *On Point*, Vol. IV, Chapter 5.

26. Ibid.

27. DoD photo by Sergeant Armando Monroig, "Operation Arrowhead Ripper, Day Four [Image 4 of 6]," DVIDS Identifier 48064, June 22, 2007, Released to Public, available from *https://www.dvidshub.net/image/48064/operation-arrowhead-ripper-day-four*.

28. Kagan, *The Surge*, pp. 121-129; Interview, Clay with Lehr, December 2, 2009.

29. Kagan, *The Surge*, p. 119; Interview, CSA OIF Study Group with Armstrong, March 20, 2014; Interview, CSI Contemporary Operations Study Team with Mixon, March 9, 2010.

30. MNF-I, SECDEF Weekly Update, July 8-14, 2007, p. 1.

31. Ibid., July 1-7, 2007, p. 2.

32. Interview, Dennis VanWey, CSI Contemporary Operations Study Team, with Colonel Walter Piatt, G-3 25th Infantry Division, Multi-National Division-North (MND-N), December 6, 2007.

33. Interviews, CSI Contemporary Operations Study Team with Mixon, March 9, 2010; CSI Contemporary Operations Study Team with Piatt, December 6, 2007; Kim Sanborn, CSI Contemporary Operations Study Team, with Colonel Christopher Gibson, G-3 25th Infantry Division, MND-N, November 4, 2009; Kimberly Kagan, Institute for the Study of War, with Colonel David W. Sutherland, Washington, DC, October 25, 2007; MNF-I, SECDEF Weekly Update, April 21-27, 2007; MNF-I, SECDEF Weekly Update, June 10-16, 2007.

34. MNF-I, SECDEF Weekly Update, July 1-7, 2007, p. 2.

35. Jennifer H. Svan, "Erik Oropeza 'There Was a Sudden White Light'," *Stars and Stripes*, June 14, 2009, available from *https://www.stripes.com/lifestyle/erik-oropeza-there-was-a-sudden-white-light-1.92787*.

36. DoD photo by Corporal Neill Sevelius, "Operation Iraqi Freedom 06-08 Operation Black Diamond [Image 4 of 8]," DVIDS Identifier 51279, June 22, 2007, Released to Public, available from *https://www.dvidshub.net/image/51279/operation-iraqi-freedom-06-08operation-black-diamond*.

37. Press Briefing, Odierno, June 22, 2007.

38. Press Release, 13th Marine Expeditionary Unit, Sergeant Andy Hurt, "3/1 Conducts China Shop," June 25, 2007, available from *http://www.13thmeu.marines.mil/News/NewsArticleDisplay/tabid/1982/Article/532583/31-conducts-china-shop.aspx*, accessed May 18, 2016.

39. Interview, Steven Clay, CSI Contemporary Operations Study Team, with Lieutenant General Rick Lynch, December 4, 2009.

40. Andrade, *Surging South of Baghdad*, p. 117; Kagan, *The Surge*, p. 101.

41. DoD photo courtesy of Defense Imagery Management Operations Center, "Newly appointed Chairman of the Joint Chiefs of Staff [Image 8 of 8]," DVIDS Identifier 61766, October 5, 2007, available from *https://www.dvidshub.net/image/61766/newly-appointed-chairman-joint-chiefs-staff.*

42. Andrade, *Surging South of Baghdad*, pp. 112, 380-381.

43. Press Briefing, Colonel Terry R. Ferrell, DoD, December 3, 2007.

44. Andrade, *Surging South of Baghdad*, p. 39.

45. See, for example, Sabrina Tavernise, "As Iraqi Shiites Police Sunnis, Rough Justice Feeds Bitterness," *The New York Times*, February 6, 2006; and Bing West, *The Strongest Tribe: War, Politics, and the Endgame in Iraq*, New York: Random House, 2009, pp. 127-129, 237-239.

46. Kagan, *The Surge*, pp. 101-102.

47. Quote from Andrade, *Surging South of Baghdad*, p. 152.

48. Ibid., pp. 124-125, 141-142.

49. Interview, CSI Contemporary Operations Study Team with Lynch, December 4, 2009.

50. Quote from Andrade, *Surging South of Baghdad*, pp. 126-127.

51. Ibid.

52. Ibid., p. 131.

53. Ibid., p. 135.

54. Kagan, *The Surge*, p. 151; Ms, *On Point*, Vol. IV, Chapter 5; Kim Gamel, "U.S. Troops Target Bomb Networks," *The Washington Post*, June 26, 2007.

55. Farook Ahmed, "Offensive Operations in MND-C, June 2007-January 2008," Washington, DC: Institute for the Study of War, January 2008, p. 2; Andrade, *Surging South of Baghdad*, pp. 179-181.

56. MND-C Press Release, "Marne Avalanche Starts with a Bang," July 19, 2007.

57. Andrade, *Surging South of Baghdad*, pp. 189-190.

58. Ross Colvin, "5 U.S. Soldiers Killed South of Baghdad," Reuters, August 12, 2007; Tim Kilbride, "Power, Influence Dictate Patterns of Violence in Central Iraq," American Forces Press Service, August 20, 2007.

59. Interview, CSI Contemporary Operations Study Team with Lynch, December 4, 2009.

60. Gamel, "U.S. Troops Target Bomb Networks."

61. Kilbride, "Power, Influence Dictate Patterns of Violence in Central Iraq."

62. MNF-I, SECDEF Weekly Update, May 6-12, 2007.

63. DoD photo by Staff Sergeant Lorie Jewell, "Sarafiyah Bridge, after its destruction by al-Qaeda in Iraq on April 12, 2007," July 7, 2007, Released to Public.

64. Interview, Institute for the Study of War with Colonel J. B. Burton, Washington, DC, November 14, 2007.

65. Joshua Partlow, "Maliki's Office Is Seen behind Purge in Forces," *The Washington Post*, April 30, 2007.

66. MNF-I, SECDEF Weekly Update, May 13-19, 2007.

67. Ibid., May 20-26, 2007.

68. Interview, Steven Clay, CSI Contemporary Operations Study Team, with Colonel Ricky D. Gibbs, November 30, 2009.

69. Ibid.

70. Ibid.

71. "Forces Kill Two Terrorists, Capture 19 in Iraq Today," American Forces Press Service, July 13, 2007; David Mays, "'Dragon' Offensives Destroy al-Qaeda Outposts in Dora with Iraqi Assistance," American Forces Press Service, September 28, 2007.

72. 2d Brigade, 1st Infantry Division, "Dagger BCT Update to the Institute for the Study of War," November 14, 2007, CSA OIF Study Group Collection.

73. Ibid.; Press Briefing, Colonel J. B. Burton, DoD, October 12, 2007.

74. Interview, Steven Clay, CSI Contemporary Operations Study Team, with Colonel Bryan T. Roberts, February 22, 2010; Jim Garamone, "U.S., Iraqi Troops Transform 'Purple Heart Boulevard,'" American Forces Press Service, June 5, 2007.

75. Press Briefing, John Castles, DoD, August 10, 2007.

76. U.S. Army photo by Staff Sergeant Michael Pryor, "Firefight in Adhamiyah: One Insurgent Killed, 3 Captured in Shootout [Image 3 of 4]," DVIDS Identifier 47394, June 16, 2007, Released to Public, available from *https://www.dvidshub.net/image/47394/firefight-adhamiyah-one-insurgent-killed-3-captured-shootout.*

77. MNF-I, SECDEF Weekly Update, August 5-11, 2007.

78. Ms, *On Point,* Vol. IV, Chapter 5; "Operation PHANTOM THUNDER," Washington, DC: Institute for the Study of War, available from *http://www.understandingwar.org/operation/operation-phantom-thunder,* accessed February 10, 2016.

79. MNF-I, SECDEF Weekly Update, August 12-18, 2007; Interview, Colonel Michael D. Visconage, MNC-I historian, with Lieutenant General Raymond Odierno, October 19, 2007; Press Briefing, James E. Simmons, DoD, August 27, 2007, slides 1-2.

80. Press Briefing, Colonel John S. RisCassi, DoD, October 11, 2007, slide 1; Kagan, *The Surge,* p. 157.

81. MNF-I, SECDEF Weekly Update, October 14-20, 2007; Interview, CSI Contemporary Operations Study Team with Colonel Hickey, February 23-24, 2010.

82. Andrade, *Surging South of Baghdad,* pp. 192-196, 198; Kagan, *The Surge,* pp. 153- 154.

83. Andrade, *Surging South of Baghdad,* pp. 243-249, 253-257, and 260-261.

84. Interviews, CSI Contemporary Operations Study Team with Mixon, March 9, 2010; Major Steven W. Richey, CMH, with Christopher P. Gibson, October 24, 2007.

85. Jeff Emanuel, "The Longest Morning," *American Spectator*, November 1, 2007; Jeff Emanuel, "Return from Samarra," *American Spectator*, May 23, 2008.

86. Ann Scott Tyson, "Combat Medal Awarded for Frenzied Iraq Battle," *The Washington Post*, May 15, 2009, available from *http://www.washingtonpost.com/wp-dyn/content/article/2009/05/14/AR2009051404601. html*, accessed February 11, 2016.

87. Ms, *On Point*, Vol. IV, Chapter 5.

88. Interview, Steven Clay, CSI Contemporary Operations Study Team, with Colonel Stephen Twitty, January 8, 2010, pp. 7-8.

89. MNF-I, SECDEF Weekly Update, August 9-25, 2007.

90. Press Briefing, Simmons, August 27, 2007.

91. Peter S. Mansoor, *Surge: My Journey with General David Petraeus and the Remaking of the Iraq War*, New Haven, CT: Yale University Press, 2013, p. 142.

92. E-mails, Colonel James Powell to Colonel Frank Sobchak, "CLC/SOI," March 2, 2017; Mansoor, *Surge*, p. 137.

93. Press Briefing, Odierno, July 19, 2007; Odierno Iraq Notebook No. 10, June 23, 2007, entry.

94. Letter, MNC-I Commander to troops, June 24, 2007, sub: Reconciliation guidance; MNF-I, SECDEF Weekly Update, June 17-23, 2007.

95. MNC-I, Fragmentary Order (FRAGO) 007, June 4, 2007, p. 2.

96. MNC-I, OPORD 07-01, June 1, 2007, p. 14; Interview, William (Bill) Knarr, Colonel Julian "Dale" Alford, United States Marine Corps (USMC), and Lieutenant Colonel David Graves (USMC), with Colonel (Ret.) Richard Welch, April 25, 2010; William Knarr et al., *Al Sahawa—The Awakening*, Vol. II, "Al Anbar Province, Multi-National Force-West, Area of Operations Atlanta," Alexandria, VA: Institute for Defense Analyses, 2013, pp. A-133–A-134; MNC-I, FRAGO 007, June 4, 2007, p. 3.

97. Interviews, CSA OIF Study Group with Odierno, January 25, 2015; Patrecia Slayden Hollis with Odierno, 2008, p. 6, available from *http://sill-www.army.mil/firesbulletin/archives/2008/Mar_Apr_2008/Mar_Apr_2008.pdf*.

98. See, for example, Linda Robinson, *Tell Me How This Ends: General David Petraeus and the Search for a Way Out of Iraq*, New York: Public Affairs, 2008, pp. 238-239. Quote from Press Briefing, Odierno, July 19, 2007.

99. MNF-I, SECDEF Weekly Update, June 10-16, 2007.

100. Ibid., June 17-23, 2007.

101. Partlow, "Maliki's Office Is Seen behind Purge in Forces."

102. Emma Sky, *The Unraveling: High Hopes and Missed Opportunities in Iraq*, New York: Public Affairs, 2015, pp. 187-189.

103. U.S. Army photo by Sergeant 1st Class Kerensa Hardy, "Dr. Bassima Lu'ay Hasun al-Jaidri speaks to representatives from the NP, IA and Coalition Forces Feb. 2 at the Ministry of Defense complex,"

February 2, 2008, Released to Public, in Hardy, "Group to Transition Sons of Iraq," *The Dog Face Daily*, Vol. 1, Iss. 269, February 6, 2008, p. 1, available from *https://www.dvidshub.net/publication/issues/3119*.

104. Odierno Iraq Notebook No. 5, February 22, 2007, entry.

105. MNF-I, SECDEF Weekly Update, June 24-30, 2007.

106. MNC-I, FRAGO 007 (Reconciliation Guidance) to OPORD 07-01, June 4, 2007, p. 1.

107. Interview, CSA OIF Study Group with Odierno, January 25, 2015.

108. Sky, *The Unraveling*, pp. 152-154. See also Interview, CMH with Odierno, October 19, 2007.

109. Sky, *The Unraveling*, pp. 157-158.

110. MNF-I, SECDEF Weekly Update, July 29-August 4, 2007.

111. Interview, Institute for the Study of War with Burton, Washington, DC, November 14, 2007; Dale Kuehl, "Testing Galula in Ameriyah: The People Are the Key," *Military Review*, March-April 2009, p. 78.

112. Interview, CSI Contemporary Operations Study Team with Kershaw, February 12, 2010; Press Briefing, Kershaw, DoD, October 5, 2007, slide 7; Report, Colonel Michael M. Kershaw, Commander, 2d Brigade, 10th Mountain Division, "Thoughts on the Next 90 Days," November 29, 2006, CSA OIF Study Group Collection.

113. Interview, CSI Contemporary Operations Study Team with John C. Valledor, Part I, November 24, 2009.

114. Interview, CSI Contemporary Operations Study Team with Kershaw, February 12, 2010.

115. Kershaw, "Thoughts on the Next 90 Days."

116. Interview, Institute for the Study of War with Burton, Washington, DC, November 14, 2007.

117. Mansoor, *Surge*, p. 142.

118. Interview, Institute for the Study of War with Burton, Washington, DC, November 14, 2007.

119. Interviews, CSA OIF Study Group with Kershaw, March 14, 2014; CSI Contemporary Operations Study Team with Valledor, Part II, January 22, 2010.

120. Interview, CSI Contemporary Operations Study Team with Valledor, Part II, January 22, 2010.

121. Interview, CSI Contemporary Operations Study Team with Colonel Paul E. Funk II and Patrick R. Michaelis, February 4, 2010.

122. Interview, CSI Contemporary Operations Study Team with Kershaw, February 12, 2010.

123. Quote from Ned Parker, "Iraq's Awakening: Two tales illustrate force's birth and slow death," *Los Angeles Times*, April 28, 2009.

124. Interview, Colonel Dale Alford, USMC History Division, and Lieutenant Colonel David Graves, USMC, with Welch, April 25, 2010, USMC History Division, Quantico, VA.

125. Ned Parker, "The Rise and Fall of a Sons of Iraq Warrior," *Los Angeles Times*, June 29, 2008; Nir Rosen, *Aftermath: Following the Bloodshed of America's Wars in the Muslim World*, New York: Nation Books, 2010, pp. 306-308, 311; Robinson, *Tell Me How This Ends*, p. 236.

126. Robinson, *Tell Me How This Ends*, pp. 245-246, 248.

127. Interview, CMH with Brigadier General John R. Allen, June 27, 2007, p. 63.

128. Ibid.

129. Ibid. The June 25, 2007, conference at the Mansour Hotel was an Iraqi initiative that occurred apart from any coaxing by MNF-I's strategic engagement cell. Nonetheless, the deadly attack struck a chord in Allen's mind that roused his anger at what he considered the overbearing involvement of MNF-I.

130. DoD photo by Master Sergeant Paul Bishop, "General presents sheiks with sword [Image 10 of 10]," DVIDS Identifier 75289, January 17, 2008, Released to Public, available from *https://www.dvidshub.net/image/75289/general-presents-sheiks-with-sword*.

131. Andrade, *Surging South of Baghdad*, pp. 218-219.

132. Quote from Andrade, *Surging South of Baghdad*, p. 218.

133. Ibid., p. 220.

134. Interviews, CSI Contemporary Operations Study Team with Lynch, December 4, 2009, p. 7; CSI Contemporary Operations Study Team with Kershaw, February 12, 2010.

135. Quote from Andrade, *Surging South of Baghdad*, p. 220.

136. Interview, CSI Contemporary Operations Study Team with Kershaw, February 12, 2010.

137. Kershaw, "Thoughts on the Next 90 Days."

138. Steven O'Hern, *The Intelligence Wars: Lessons from Baghdad*, New York: Prometheus Books, 2008, p. 100.

139. MNF-I, SECDEF Weekly Update, April 14-20, 2007; Michael O'Hanlon and Jason Campbell, "Iraq Index," Washington, DC: Brookings Institute, March 31, 2008, p. 29.

140. DoD photo by Staff Sergeant Russell Bassett, "CLC Tip Leads Coalition Troops to EFP Factory [Image 5 of 5]," DVIDS Identifier 63719, October 31, 2007, Released to Public, available from *https://www.dvidshub.net/image/63719/clc-tip-leads-coalition-troops-efp-factory*.

141. Notes, Commanding General, meeting at U.S. Embassy with congressional delegation including Senator Charles T. Hagel (NE), April 15, 2007.

142. MNF-I, SECDEF Weekly Update, April 14-20, 2007.

143. Ibid., May 6-12, 2007.

144. Ron Synovitz, "US Building Military Base Near Iraqi-Iranian Border," *Eurasia Insight*, September 29, 2007.

145. Andrade, *Surging South of Baghdad*, pp. 172-173.

146. Synovitz, "US Building Military Base Near Iraqi-Iranian Border."

147. Yochi Dreazen and Greg Jaffe, "U.S. to Target Iranian Arms Entering Iraq," *The Wall Street Journal*, September 10, 2007.

148. MNF-I, SECDEF Weekly Update, April 14-20, 2007.

149. Briefing, MNF-I, Coalition Forces Disrupt Secret Cell Terrorist Network, Combined Press Information Center, Baghdad, Iraq, June 18, 2007.

150. MNF-I, SECDEF Weekly Update, May 27-June 2, 2007.

151. Sean Naylor, "Iran deeply involved in Iraq, Petraeus says," *Military Times*, May 23, 2007.

152. Images taken from Brigadier General Kevin J. Bergner, "Multi-National Force-Iraq Situational Update," briefing slides, July 2, 2007, p. 16, available from *https://www.globalsecurity.org/military/library/ news/2007/07/mil-070702-mnfi-b01.htm.*

153. MNF-I, SECDEF Weekly Update, June 3-9, 2007; MNF-I, SECDEF Weekly Update, June 10-16, 2007.

154. Press Conference, Brigadier General Kevin Bergner, MNF-I, Combined Press Information Center, Baghdad, Iraq, July 2, 2007.

155. MNF-I, SECDEF Weekly Update, July 1-7, 2007.

156. Ibid., July 22-28, 2007.

157. Ibid., July 29-August 4, 2007.

158. Ibid., August 5-11, 2007.

159. Ibid.

160. Ibid.

161. E-mail, Ambassador David Pearce to CSA OIF Study Group, August 30, 2015.

162. Ibid.

163. Ibid.

164. MNF-I, SECDEF Weekly Update, June 17-23, 2007.

165. MNC-I Chronology, June 19-20, 2007.

166. DoD photo by Staff Sergeant Lorie Jewell, "General David Petraeus (left) meets with Iraqi Police Colonel Naji Rostum Sahra (right) also known as Abu Liqa, head of the Nasiriyah Tactical Support Unit, on 21 July 2007," July 21, 2007, Released to Public.

167. MNF-I, SECDEF Weekly Update, July 1-7, 2007; Michael R. Gordon, "The Last Battle: The Fight among Iraq's Shiites," *New York Times Magazine*, August 3, 2008.

168. Patrick Gaughen, "Fight for Diwaniyah: The Sadrist Trend and ISCI Struggle for Supremacy," *Backgrounder 17*, Washington, DC: Institute for the Study of War, January 6, 2008, p. 3, available from *http://www.understandingwar.org/backgrounder/fight-diwaniyah*, accessed May 23, 2016; MNF-I, SECDEF Weekly Update, July 1-7, 2007.

169. MNF-I, SECDEF Weekly Update, July 8-14, 2007.

170. Ibid., August 5-11, 2007.

171. Ibid., August 19-25, 2007; Gaughen, "Fight for Diwaniyah," p. 4.

172. MNF-I, SECDEF Weekly Update, August 19-25, 2007.

173. Ibid., June 24-30, 2007.

174. Ibid., July 1-7, 2007; and July 22-28, 2007.

175. Ibid., July 8-14, 2007.

176. Ibid., July 15-21, 2007.

177. Ibid., August 11-18, 2007.

178. Ibid., July 8-14, 2007; and July 5-21, 2007.

179. Ibid., July 22-28, 2007.

180. Ibid., August 5-11, 2007.

181. Ibid., August 11-18, 2007.

182. Ibid., August 26-September 1, 2007.

183. Ibid.

184. Ibid., September 2-8, 2007.

185. Interview, CMH with Odierno, September 7, 2007.

186. MNF-I, SECDEF Weekly Update, September 2-8, 2007.

187. Interview, Major Wilson Blythe, CSA OIF Study Group, with Colonel Joel Rayburn, March 6, 2015.

188. Interview, Colonel Joel Rayburn, CSA OIF Study Group, with General (Ret.) David H. Petraeus, Febuary 10, 2016.

189. Ricks, *Gamble*, p. 233; Mansoor, *Surge*, p. 179.

190. U.S. Navy photo by Monica A. King, "Admiral James A. 'Sandy' Winnefeld, Jr. Retired 1 Aug 2015," August 3, 2011, Released to Public, available from *http://www.navy.mil/navydata/bios/navybio_ret.asp?bioID=422.*

191. Ibid.; Peter Baker et al., "Among Top Officials, 'Surge' Has Sparked Dissent, Infighting," *The Washington Post*, September 9, 2007.

192. Interview, Colonel Joel Rayburn, CSA OIF Study Group, with Lieutenant General James N. Mattis, April 29, 2015.

193. Interview, CSA OIF Study Group with Odierno, January 25, 2015; Ricks, *Gamble*, p. 233.

194. Interview, Colonel Joel Rayburn and Colonel James Powell, CSA OIF Study Group, with Petraeus, November 26, 2014.

195. Notes, CENTCOM Commander's Conference, July 14, 2007, Petraeus Papers Electronic Finding Aid.

196. Ibid.; Mansoor, *Surge*, p. 179.

197. Interview, CSA OIF Study Group with Brigadier General (Ret.) Michael Meese, Fort McNair, Washington, DC, October 17, 2013.

198. Baker et al., "Among Top Officials."

199. Ibid.

200. Mansoor, *Surge*, p. 179.

201. Interview, CSA OIF Study Group with Petraeus, November 26, 2014.

202. Ricks, *Gamble*, p. 236.

203. Ibid., p. 233.

204. Steve Coll, "The General's Dilemma," *The New Yorker*, September 8, 2008, available from *http://www.newyorker.com/magazine/2008/09/08/the-generals-dilemma*, accessed May 23, 2016.

205. Ricks, *Gamble*, pp. 232, 235.

206. Interview, CSA OIF Study Group with Petraeus, February 10, 2016.

207. Shailagh Murray and Paul Kane, "Key GOP Senator Breaks With Bush," *The Washington Post*, July 6, 2007, available from *http://www.washingtonpost.com/wp-dyn/content/article/2007/07/05/AR2007070501283.html?nav=rss_email/components*; "GOP senator: Iraq plan not working," *USA Today*, June 26, 2007, available from *https://usatoday30.usatoday.com/news/washington/2007-06-25-lugar_N.htm*.

208. Interview, CSA OIF Study Group with Petraeus, February 10, 2016.

209. Michael O'Hanlon and Kenneth Pollack, "A War We Just Might Win," *The New York Times*, July 30, 2007, available from *http://www.nytimes.com/2007/07/30/opinion/30pollack.html?_r=0*, accessed May 23, 2016.

210. Andrade, *Surging South of Baghdad*, p. 209; Interview, CMH with Odierno, September 7, 2007, p. 15.

211. DoD photo, photographer unknown, "PETRAEUS ON IRAQ: U.S. Army Gen. David Petraeus, the top U.S. military commander in Iraq, appears before Congress to testify on assessments of the progress in Iraq, Sept. 11, 2007," VIRIN Identifier 958254-K-RXN96-215.jpg, September 11, 2007, Released to Public, available from *https://www.defense.gov/Photos/Photo-Gallery/igphoto/2001199983/*.

212. General David H. Petraeus, "Report to Congress on the Situation in Iraq," September 10-11, 2007, available from *http://burgess.house.gov/uploadedfiles/petraeus%20testimony.pdf*, accessed February 10, 2016.

213. Ibid.

214. Ibid.

215. Ibid.

216. Ibid.

217. Ibid.

218. Ibid.

219. U.S. Congress, Senate, Joint Hearing Before the Committee on Foreign Affairs and the Committee on Armed Services, Statement of Ambassador Ryan Crocker, 110th Congress, 1st Session, September 10, 2007.

220. Senators Hillary Clinton (D-NY), Joe Biden (D-DE), John McCain (R-AZ), Christopher Dodd (D-CT), and Barack Obama (D-Ill) were all Presidential candidates who served on the Senate committees before whom Petraeus and Crocker appeared.

221. U.S. Congress, Senate, Hearing before the Foreign Relations Committee on Iraq, 110th Congress, 1st Session, September 11, 2007, available from *http://www.gpo.gov/fdsys/pkg/CHRG-110shrg44322/html/CHRG-110shrg44322.htm*.

222. Eli Lake, "Clinton Spars with Petraeus on Credibility," *New York Sun*, September 12, 2007, available from *http://www.nysun.com/national/clinton-spars-with-petraeus-on-credibility/62426/*; John Bresnahan, "Clinton: Believing Petraeus and Crocker Requires 'Willing Suspension of Disbelief,'" Politico Now Blog, September 11, 2007, available from *http://www.politico.com/blogs/politico-now/2007/09/clinton-believing-petraeus-and-crocker-requires-willing-suspension-of-disbelief-003088*.

223. Lake, "Clinton Spars with Petraeus on Credibility."

224. General David H. Petraeus, "How We Won in Iraq," *Foreign Policy*, October 29, 2013.

225. Prepared Text, President George W. Bush's Speech, September 13, 2007, NPR, available from *http://www.npr.org/templates/story/story.php?storyId=14406922*.

CHAPTER 6

"THE DARKNESS HAS BECOME PITCH BLACK"

By early fall 2007, al-Qaeda in Iraq (AQI) had endured more than 3 months of intensifying pressure from coalition operations as well as from Sunni tribes and former insurgents that had turned against the extremist group. For the first time since 2004, AQI lost its support zones inside the capital city and was on the verge of suffering a defeat in the Baghdad belts. At the same time, the Iraqi security forces were growing rapidly, adding to the counterinsurgent forces in the field, although they still suffered from significant shortcomings and sectarian behavior.

These factors alarmed al-Qaeda's senior leaders in Pakistan who had declared the battle for Iraq as central to their global jihadist efforts. As AQI's fighters were forced farther from Baghdad in search of new safe havens, the organization's leaders refocused their forces on slowing the growth of the Awakening, which they had deemed an existential threat to AQI. At the same time, Moqtada Sadr's decision to "freeze" his militia's activities created an opportunity for the coalition to fracture the Shi'a insurgency and hopefully to neutralize the Shi'a groups that had helped plunge the country into civil war. Political reconciliation — the overall goal of the surge — lagged behind the improving security situation because of both tensions among the competing Iraqi political factions and destabilizing interventions by Iraq's neighbors. Coalition leaders would find it difficult to translate the military gains of the surge into political ones.

AL-QAEDA IN IRAQ LOSES THE INITIATIVE

Operation PHANTOM STRIKE Continues

By the time of General David Petraeus's much-anticipated testimony before Congress in early September 2007, coalition operations were "taking out [AQI] networks at a faster rate than they can replicate themselves," Petraeus reported to Secretary of Defense (SECDEF) Robert M. Gates. The coalition had killed or captured more than 2,500 AQI members between February and September, the Multi-National Force-Iraq (MNF-I) commander wrote, including 94 key AQI leaders.[1] One reason for this damage to AQI had been the increasing number of successful intelligence-driven raids by coalition special operators, whose operational tempo in July and August often totaled more than 60 raids per week.[2]

Despite the successes of the special operators, the key to robbing AQI of its vast territory in central Iraq had been the continued, large-scale ground operations led by Multi-National Corps-Iraq (MNC-I). The corps-level Operation PHANTOM STRIKE that jumped off on August 13 was a month old by the time Petraeus and Ambassador Ryan Crocker completed their congressional testimony in Washington. As with the midsummer Operation PHANTOM THUNDER, General Raymond Odierno and MNC-I used Operation PHANTOM STRIKE to synchronize the four U.S. divisions in central and northern Iraq as they conducted division-level operations. These operations caused a visible reversal of

AQI's fortunes in Baghdad, where, by mid-September, insurgent attacks had declined by 70 percent from their peak in 2006 and by 50 percent since the start of Operation FARDH AL-QANOON in January. Car bombs and suicide attacks fell to their lowest levels in a year.[3]

Source: U.S. Army photo by Specialist Shawn M. Cassatt (Released).

Soldiers From 3d BCT, 2d Infantry Division, During Operations in Muqdadiyah.[4]

Also as in Operation PHANTOM THUNDER, MNC-I's main effort in Operation PHANTOM STRIKE was General Benjamin R. Mixon's Multi-National Division-North (MND-N). In June and July, Mixon and MND-N had used Colonel Steven Townsend's 3d Brigade, 2d Infantry Division, to retake Diyala's provincial capital of Baqubah from AQI and reestablish the Iraqi security forces (ISF) and Iraqi Government in the city. In August and September, Mixon followed up by using Colonel David Sutherland's brigade to pursue AQI farther up the Diyala Valley to Muqdadiyah, where many of the surviving insurgent defenders of Baqubah had displaced. In the ensuing MND-N operation, Sutherland's troops forced AQI fighters to withdraw yet again from towns around Muqdadiyah where the extremist group had attempted to regroup, on some occasions fighting pitched battles against company-sized AQI groups. Over the course of 2 weeks, MND-N killed or captured 78 AQI fighters, with the remainder fleeing farther from the Diyala cities to remote areas such as the hills surrounding Hamrin Lake.[5]

Source: U.S. Army photo by 1st Lieutenant Richard Ybarra (Released).

A Soldier From 4th Stryker BCT, 2d Infantry Division, Fires an AT-4 during Operations South of Baqubah.[6]

On September 5, Mixon redirected MND-N's focus to the areas to which the Diyala-based enemy groups were likely to move. In MND-N's Operation LIGHTNING HAMMER II, Mixon shifted the division's main effort from Sutherland to Colonel Stephen M. "Steph" Twitty's 4th Brigade, 1st Cavalry Division, as the latter launched an operation into the long-time insurgent sanctuary in the Za'ab Triangle south of Mosul. Two other brigades supported Twitty's operation to the south, with 3d Brigade, 25th Infantry Division, moving into the Hamrin Mountains between Diyala and Salahadin Provinces and 3d Brigade, 82d Airborne Division, launching operations into enemy strongholds near Bayji and Tikrit. By mid-September, MND-N had killed another 72 enemy fighters and captured more than 600, and Twitty's troops had established several new combat outposts in the Sharqat area and were in a position to control the lines of communications between Mosul and Tikrit.[7] In late September, MND-N shifted its main effort again, this time to Colonel Jon Lehr's 4th Brigade, 2d Infantry Division, in Tarmiyah as the brigade carried out raids against AQI and created new Sunni irregular groups to hold the area that Abu Ghazwan and Ahmed Dabash had controlled with their insurgent armies just months before.[8] This would be the last operation Mixon and his 25th Infantry Division would conduct before being replaced by the 1st Armored Division in October.

Each of the three other U.S. divisions—Multi-National Force-West (MNF-W), Multi-National Division-Baghdad (MND-B), and Multi-National Division-Center (MND-C)—conducted supporting operations in their respective areas as Mixon's brigades operated in August and September. Among these, Major General Rick Lynch's

MND-C conducted the largest-scale supporting operations to continue to push AQI and its allies out of their sanctuaries in the Tigris River towns southeast of Baghdad, forcing the extremist group farther south. MND-C's midsummer operations had disrupted AQI and its allies in Arab Jabour and the Triangle of Death, but it also had stretched Lynch's four maneuver brigades dangerously thin. Only Colonel Peter Baker's field artillery brigade, reassigned from Multi-National Division–Central South (MND-CS) to MND-C in July, remained as a maneuver unit in the Kut sector. With little combat power left to spare for new operations, Lynch used an ad hoc brigade combat team (BCT) under his division aviation brigade commander, Colonel Daniel Ball, to conduct MND-C's portion of Operation PHANTOM STRIKE, called Operation MARNE HUSKY. With one infantry battalion at his disposal, Ball carried out air strikes and raids against suspected AQI hideouts in the Tigris River area between Salman Pak and Suwayrah, the latter of which was the last Sunni-majority town before reaching the overwhelmingly Shi'a area stretching from Kut to the Persian Gulf. As he had done before, Lynch emphasized the use of firepower in Operation MARNE HUSKY and targeted dozens of Tigris River boats. From mid-August to mid-September, the operation yielded 256 enemy fighters killed and captured and pushed AQI to the edges of predominantly Shi'a controlled territory.[9]

To follow up on his operation on the east bank of the Tigris, Lynch shifted his main effort in mid-September to Colonel Terry Ferrell's 2d Brigade, 3d Infantry Division, in Arab Jabour. The midsummer operations had begun to take the riverside town from AQI, but the extremist group had reduced Arab Jabour to one-sixth its normal population and rigged many houses to explode when coalition and Iraqi troops entered. Having established a foothold in Arab Jabour, Ferrell pushed farther west into enemy territory in September and October, creating additional outposts and building new roads to reach them. By mid-October, MND-C had killed or captured another 252 enemy fighters and had planted a large patrol base in the heart of a previously inaccessible canal-crossed agricultural area that had served as an enemy sanctuary.[10]

Source: DoD photo by Sergeant Kevin Stabinsky (Released).

Colonel Terry Ferrell, Commander of 2d BCT, 3d Infantry Division, With Sheik Ali Majid, a Concerned Local Citizens (CLC) Leader.[11]

As Odierno intended, the operations to push AQI farther from Baghdad limited the damage the terrorist group could do during the holy month of Ramadan, which for 4 years had been a period of heightened violence since Abu Musab al-Zarqawi had launched the first "Ramadan Offensive" in 2003. AQI announced its plan to carry out a similar offensive through October 22, 2007, but when the holy month began on September 13, the group and its Sunni allies managed only a 3-day spike in car bombs and suicide attacks against mainly ISF and Awakening targets. Casualties from the worst of these attacks numbered "in the dozens . . . not the hundreds we saw in previous signature [Ramadan] attacks," Petraeus reported to Washington in late September.[12] Odierno observed on September 20 that Iraq was experiencing its lowest levels of violence in the 19 months since the February 2006 Samarra mosque bombing.[13] The overall Iraqi civilian and police death toll for the month-long period was less than half that for the Ramadan period of 2006, and the level of violence for the month was 40 percent lower than in 2006.[14] The reduction in the Sunni insurgents' activities also translated into a reduced level of indirect fire against coalition bases and Iraqi towns, down by nearly 40 percent from the previous month and at its lowest level since 2005.[15]

AQI's decreased ineffectiveness in the capital was partly due to the coalition's continuous clearing of Baghdad's worst neighborhoods. Three days into Ramadan, on September 16, MND-B launched an operation to clear east Rashid, where AQI operatives had long maintained a foothold. After 5 days, MND-B Commander Major General Joseph F. Fil, Jr., reported that the ISF and coalition forces were in control of approximately 56 percent of Baghdad and in the process of clearing another 28 percent. Enemy fighters dominated the remaining 16 percent of the city.[16]

Continued Pressure From the Awakening

The rolls of the Awakening continued to expand through the fall of 2007. Even the AQI assassination of Sheikh Abdul Sattar Abu Risha on September 13, the first day of Ramadan, could not slow the movement's growth. Abu Risha's younger brother Ahmed assumed leadership of the Ramadi Awakening Council the following day, undeterred by AQI's revenge campaign targeting Awakening leaders. Two weeks after Abu Risha's assassination, Petraeus reported that the Awakening's numbers had doubled in a month. In total, more than 52,000 had joined the program throughout Iraq with more than 30,000 being paid wages through Commanders' Emergency Response Program (CERP) contracts.[17]

As the Awakening expanded geographically, it put pressure on AQI in regions where the extremist group had previously faced nominal opposition. In Baqubah, scores of 1920 Revolutionary Brigades members joined the Awakening group dubbed the "Baqubah Guardians" in the wake of Multi-National Division-North's (MND-N) clearing operations in July and August and began assisting Townsend's brigade in attacking AQI cells in the area. The group's emergence prompted AQI to counter with suicide bombings against Baqubah's Awakening leaders, such as the September 24 suicide car bomb at a city mosque that killed 24 attendees of a reconciliation meeting hosted by the Diyala governor. That attack also killed the Baqubah police chief, Ali Dilayan, who had escaped the AQI attack against his home in June. Nevertheless, the Baqubah Guardians continued to grow, reaching more than 1,000 members who patrolled and conducted raids alongside the U.S. troops they formerly had fought.[18]

Similar scenarios emerged elsewhere. After AQI operatives murdered 3 Sunni imams in Mosul on September 27, local volunteers killed 11 AQI members in retaliation the following day.[19] Five days later, a Concerned Local Citizen (CLC) group led Iraqi Army and police units to a foreign fighter base at the abandoned Muthanna chemical complex northwest of Baghdad, where the ISF units and Sunni irregulars jointly attacked militants holding hostages there. The ISF and CLCs rescued 27 hostages while killing 6 militants and capturing 37 more, though 7 ISF members and 1 of the CLC sheikhs were killed in the action.[20]

Meanwhile, in Arab Jabour and adjacent towns, two of Colonel Terry Ferrell's battalion commanders, Lieutenant Colonel Kenneth Adgie and Lieutenant Colonel Mark Odom, were fostering a large Awakening group whose members—many of them admittedly former insurgents—provided detailed intelligence against local AQI members. In Odom's sector, Sheikh Maher Sarhan al-Muini, a Sunni sheikh who had been imprisoned in Camp Bucca earlier in the war, led local fighters who helped hunt down AQI members and pointed out improvised explosive devices (IEDs) to U.S. troops. In Adgie's sector, a former military officer known locally as General Mustafa Jabouri helped establish a group of local scouts that Adgie's men called the "Bird Dogs," whose intelligence tips led to a long string of captures of AQI men. "Where local citizen groups are actively participating in security, violence levels have plummeted," Petraeus noted on October 13.[21] As if to illustrate his point, on October 23, Anbar Province experienced no attacks at all, and 2 days later Baghdad experienced just three attacks, all of which were ineffective.[22] Walking through Arab Jabour on October 26, Petraeus saw the effects of the local Sunni mobilization and Odom's and Adgie's handiwork. "Nearly 700 concerned local citizens have joined with our forces and taken back their villages," he wrote on October 26. "There were no Iraqi police or army forces in the area, and these locals are now under contract to secure their communities."[23]

At the same time, an AQI commander south of Balad made a similar observation that validated Petraeus's assessment. Writing on October 15 in a journal captured by coalition troops a few days later, AQI emir Abu Tariq lamented:

> There were almost 600 fighters in our sector before the tribes changed course 360 [sic] degrees under the influence of the so-called Islamic Army (Deserter of Jihad) and other believer groups. Many of our fighters quit and some of them joined the deserters . . . things started getting worse ever since, and as a result of that the number of [our] fighters dropped down to 20 or less.[24]

On October 28, an embittered Abu Tariq stated that he and his group had been betrayed by the local tribes as they joined the Awakening:

> We were mistreated, cheated, and betrayed by some of our brothers who used to be part of the Jihadi movement . . . [They] were very good faithful Jihadi Fighters, but later on we found out that those people were nothing but hypocrites, liars, and traitors and were waiting for the right moment to switch sides with whoever pays them most and at the end they fought against us and they tried to prevent us from attacking the al-Sahwah [Awakening] groups in [the] area.[25]

It was a stark reversal of fortune for AQI in a district that had been a safe haven for Zarqawi in 2006 and the site of the founding of the Islamic State of Iraq.

The Blackwater-Nisour Square Incident

Despite MNF-I headway against AQI, an incident in an unrelated area showed that the coalition's campaign in Iraq remained in a fragile state. The action also highlighted a troublesome aspect of security operations in a counterinsurgency setting. On September 16, U.S.-Iraqi relations suffered a significant setback when a U.S. Embassy security detail staffed by Blackwater security contractors opened fire on traffic in the busy Nisour Square in west Baghdad, killing 14 civilians and wounding 17 others. Although the Blackwater guards alleged they had taken fire from hostile elements, the incident immediately sparked outrage among Iraqis and a crisis in U.S.-Iraqi Government relations. Prime Minister Nuri al-Maliki charged that Blackwater's actions challenged Iraqi sovereignty, and the Iraqi Government froze the company's operations while government officials moved to ban it from the country.[26]

In the face of the public outcry and "tremendous angst among the Iraqi leadership," as Petraeus put it, the U.S. Government opened several investigations into the incident.[27] Even so, U.S. Embassy leaders had few alternatives to the Blackwater contractors to fulfill the American mission's extensive diplomatic security requirements. Just 5 days before the shootings, Crocker testified to Congress that there was "no way" to provide security in Iraq without contractors. In the wake of the shootings, embassy officials judged that the company's sudden departure would create a security vacuum.[28] As a result, less than a week after the Nisour Square killings, the State Department authorized Blackwater to resume its security escort missions.[29]

The incident highlighted what had been an under-examined aspect of the Iraq campaign: the coalition's heavy dependence on private security contractors (PSC) to perform what in the past had been military missions. These included a broad range of security tasks such as convoy escort, base security, and personal security, as well as intelligence analysis, security training, and operations and movement coordination. As of September 2007, the Department of Defense (DoD) employed an estimated 6,000 PSCs in Iraq, a fraction of the estimated 25,000 to 30,000 contractors employed throughout the country by federal agencies, foreign governments, international organizations, and private firms.[30] On average, only 7 to 10 percent of DoD's security contractors were U.S. citizens, with the remainder coming from more than 30 countries, including Iraq.[31]

The majority of these contractors appeared to perform their duties professionally, but actions by a portion of the foreign security contractors had bred resentment among Iraqis for several years before the Nisour Square incident. Numerous instances occurred of PSCs running Iraqi cars off the road, disabling vehicles by shooting into the engine block, throwing objects at civilians, and in extreme cases, actually shooting civilians—most often in the course of escalation of force incidents. As the 3d Infantry Division's assistant commander in September 2005, Brigadier General Karl R. Horst investigated complaints against security contractors and found that, during a 2-month period, 12 shootings by contractors had resulted in 6 Iraqi civilian deaths in the MND-B area of operations.[32] At the time, Horst—who also discovered the infamous Jadriyah bunker torture chamber in the same period—had said to a reporter that security contractors "run loose in this country and do stupid stuff. There's no authority over them, so you can't come down on them hard when they escalate force. They shoot people, and someone else has to deal with the

Source: DoD photo by Sergeant Marshall Thompson (Released).

**Ugandan Contractors From a Private Security Company Named SOC,
at a Gate at Al Asad Air Base.[33]**

aftermath."[34] In some cases, the contractor shootings had been part of darker incidents than escalations of force. A few months after Horst's comments, security contractors for the United Kingdom-based Aegis Defence Services allegedly assembled a "trophy video" set to Elvis Presley music that showed themselves shooting civilian cars on Iraqi roads. At the same time, contractors working for U.S. security company Triple Canopy alleged their coworkers were firing on Iraqi cars for sport. In December 2006, a Blackwater guard allegedly shot and killed a bodyguard of Iraqi Vice President Adel Abdel Mahdi during an argument in the Green Zone.[35]

The coalition often had difficulty maintaining awareness of the security contractors' activities. A 2007 *Washington Post* investigation found that weapons discharges by PSCs rarely were reported to U.S. or Iraqi authorities, and that the 2007 contractor shooting incidents reported between May 2006 and May 2007 may have represented as little as 15 percent of the actual number.[36] The popular backlash against the contractors after the 2007 Nisour shootings affected the U.S. military campaign, because Iraqis tended not to distinguish between American Soldiers and American-hired security guards. As one Iraqi Interior Ministry official noted, the contractors "are part of the reason for all the hatred that is directed at Americans, because people don't know them as Blackwater, they know them only as Americans."[37] The observation was true even when the contractors were not U.S. employees. In October 2007, MNF-I found itself managing the consequences of an incident in which Australian PSCs killed two Iraqi Christian women. The Iraqi Government "accepted it reasonably well," Petraeus noted, because the Australian company promptly took full responsibility, "acknowledged the event, expressed regret that it happened, made immediate reparations, and pledged full cooperation with the investigation into the incident."[38] Commenting on the episode to Gates, Petraeus judged that "we cannot accomplish our mission in Iraq without Private Security Contractors, but we need to reduce the friction they sometimes cause before the Government of Iraq uses the sovereignty card to try to shut them down completely."[39] When PSCs were involved in 3 escalation of force incidents in a single week a month later, Petraeus decided to gain control of the situation by requiring a meeting between MNF-I's J-3 and 54 leaders of the PSC elements in Iraq to address procedures and the critical nature of their actions.[40]

The shootings in Nisour Square were deeply troubling for a U.S. military force whose commanders had begun to adopt population-centric counterinsurgency tactics throughout the country. One military official opined that the consequences of the Nisour Square shootings "may be worse than Abu Ghraib." From Washington, Gates concluded that security contractors' activities were often "at cross-purposes to our larger mission in Iraq."[41] Petraeus saw the problem as one of fundamentally differing philosophies and roles on the battlefield:

> At the heart of the matter is a subtle, but critical, difference in how [private security contractors] and military elements view their mission. Mission success for [private security contractors] is safe delivery of the "package," and this makes them very risk averse in the battlespace. Our soldiers, focusing on improving security for the population, accept a bit more personal risk and are likely more cognizant of the impact of their actions on civilians.[42]

This difference in missions had the potential to derail even the most carefully conducted military campaign. In the months following the Nisour incident, MNF-I continued to tighten its monitoring of contractor activities, requiring security contractors to clear their operations and locations with coalition units—a policy with which contractors complied unevenly.

The Sinjar Documents

As AQI's situation in central Iraq worsened under the combined pressure of the coalition, the Awakening, and the Iraqi security forces, the terrorist group received another blow in early fall 2007 as its machinery for sending foreign fighters into Iraq came under more intense pressure than ever before. Since 2003, Zarqawi and other insurgents had created networks inside Syria that facilitated the movement of fighters from around the Arab world to be suicide bombers or fighters in Iraq. From the Damascus airport, militant fixers helped foreign fighters move into Iraq's Euphrates River Valley or the Jazeera desert of Ninawa Province. Some of these networks using Ninawa Province had belonged to former Ba'athist regime leaders, such as Mohammed Yunis al-Ahmad. Another significant network belonged to the former Iraqi military officer Suhail Hammo, a Sunni Turkoman from Tel Afar who sent insurgent fighters into Iraq from the Syrian border town of Qamishli and would later be a senior leader in the Islamic State of Iraq and the Levant.[43]

The most prolific network belonged to AQI's top Syria-based facilitator, a young Iraqi named Badran Turki al-Mazidih—also known by the nom de guerre Abu Ghadiyah. From 2003 forward, Abu Ghadiyah split his time between the eastern Syrian cities of Deir ez Zour and Albu Kamal, helping probably thousands of foreign fighters move into Iraq to join AQI's ranks there. Just across the border from the Iraqi city of Al Qa'im in the Western Euphrates River Valley, Albu Kamal was a perfect launching point into Iraq. However, as the anti-AQI Awakening movement took hold in Anbar in fall 2006, AQI's foreign-fighter pipeline through the Euphrates River Valley became increasingly tenuous, and Abu Ghadiyah apparently moved the group's primary facilitation route north to Ninawa. From there, AQI recruits made their way to the town of Sinjar, 30 miles west of Tel Afar, before moving to Mosul or central Iraq.[44]

The flow of foreign fighters through Sinjar was heavy enough that in the fall of 2006 AQI stationed a "border emir" known as Abu Muthanna near the town to receive the fighters Abu Ghadiyah sent into Iraq and send them to their specific assignments.[45] Around the same time, senior AQI leader Abu Usama al-Tunisi assumed overall command of AQI's foreign fighter networks. Considered a likely successor to Abu Ayyub al-Masri, Tunisi had been AQI's military emir in Baghdad's southern belts and had been behind the June 2006 abduction and killing of two American Soldiers from 1st Battalion, 502d Infantry Regiment, near Mahmudiyah, south of Baghdad.[46] His assignment to the management of the foreign fighter influx indicated its importance to AQI's leaders.

According to later coalition estimates, by early 2007 the Abu Ghadiyah-Abu Muthanna northern network was pushing 80 to 110 foreign fighters into Iraq each month. The influx of these foreign fighters coincided with the spring 2007 spike in suicide bombings in Iraq, which peaked at 59 in the month of March 2007.[47] With the onset of summer, the coalition's surge of operations and ramping up of special operations took its toll on the northern facilitation network. As AQI's cells dispersed and its leadership cadre thinned out, coalition leaders determined that the group was suffering a decline in funding, including money from outside donors, and was having difficulty paying its facilitators.[48] By the end of the summer, U.S. officials began to see signs of reticence by outsiders to send their fighters into Iraq, and the flow of foreign fighters dropped to an estimated 60 per month across the country.[49]

In September 2007, the coalition dealt the northern facilitation network two severe blows with raids that killed its most senior leaders. On September 11, coalition special operators located and killed AQI border emir Abu Muthanna near Sinjar.[50] Coalition troops followed that raid a week later with the destruction of 15,000 pounds of explosives in a remote nearby site.[51] The coup de grace for the northern network came a few days later on September 25, when a U.S. air strike killed Tunisi near Musayyib, in Babil Province.[52]

Source: Combating Terrorism Center at West Point (Released).

An AQI Foreign Fighter Registration Form Captured in the Sinjar Documents.[53]

The most significant long-term impact from these operations came not from the killings of the senior AQI men, but from the data yielded from the raid near Sinjar. According to journalists, Abu Muthanna had detonated a suicide vest to evade capture, but the U.S. special operators recovered five terabytes of data and hundreds of personnel files he had maintained onsite, a collection that provided extensive insight into AQI's operations.[54] A subsequent report by the U.S. Military Academy's Combating Terrorism Center, based on access to these "Sinjar Documents" as they became known, painted a detailed picture of AQI's networks of foreign supporters and volunteers. The documents contained personnel files of 606 foreign fighters who entered Iraq between August 2006 and August 2007 by crossing the Syrian border. Many had passed through the important AQI hub of Deir ez Zour in Syria.[55] Among the foreign fighters, 40 percent were from Saudi Arabia, with the largest portion coming from the Saudi capital of Riyadh. Another 8 percent each had come from Yemen and Syria. A surprising 31 percent had come from North Africa, a region that U.S. officials previously had believed provided only a small fraction of foreign fighters.[56] Even more surprising was that about one of every five foreign fighters was Libyan, making that country the highest contributor of foreign fighters per capita. Most of the Libyans came from the cities of Derna and Benghazi and appeared to have a well-established route to Damascus via Egypt. Libyan recruits had surged in spring 2007, apparently coinciding with a new relationship between al-Qaeda and the Libyan Islamic Fighting Group, an organization that would later cooperate with the North Atlantic Treaty Organization (NATO) against the Gadhafi regime in 2011.[57]

As a whole, the foreign fighters depicted in the Sinjar Documents had a median age of 22- to 23-years-old, suggesting that most of them were first-time volunteers. Of those who listed a profession, two-thirds described themselves as students. In Abu Muthanna's files, almost 400 of the foreign recruits had been sorted into specific roles, the most common of which were "suicide bomber" (56 percent) and "fighter" (42 percent).[58] Many of the fighters arrived at Abu Muthanna's processing point on the same day, suggesting they had traveled together in groups. The records listed no fighters entering Iraq in March or April 2007, indicating that the facilitation network may have been disrupted during those months.[59]

As the coalition began to release information about the Sinjar Documents to the media in late 2007, the knowledge that AQI had relied on a large number of foreign suicide bombers and fighters created a public relations problem for the group, which had tried to cultivate the impression within Iraq and the Arab world that it was an Iraqi organization.[60] The disruption of the northern facilitation network also seemed to have had a significant impact on AQI's operations. After the September 2007 raids, MNF-I estimated the number of foreign fighters coming into Iraq each month fell to fewer than 40, and the number of suicide bombings in the country fell to just 16, half the monthly average during the summer.[61] These coincided with a weekly attack average in October that was 64 percent lower than the all-time high of late June 2007, and a U.S. battle death toll of 29, the lowest monthly figure since before the Samarra mosque bombing.[62]

Though he attributed these changes partly to the disruption of AQI's foreign facilitation networks, Petraeus judged that "the trends are the result of many factors," including the rapid coalition-ISF operational tempo against AQI, the emergence of the Awakening, and "the restraint being exercised by some Jaysh al Mahdi elements."[63] He also might have added the fact that the coalition's total strength on the ground had swelled to over 178,000 troops, close to the highest level of the entire war. Even so, the MNF-I commander was guarded in his pronouncements. "We continue to stress the point that success in Iraq will not be like flipping a light switch," he wrote to Gates. "It will emerge slowly and fitfully."[64] It was a prudently optimistic point he already had made to Prime Minister Maliki a few weeks earlier. "The PM [Prime Minister] said he believes he is seeing the beginning of 'victory,' in a psychological sense, given the damage done to AQI and the militias, combined with the people's rejection of them as well," Petraeus reported on September 22. "I cautioned him that we still have much work to do and that achieving political progress is what is needed to move toward that 'victory'."[65]

Osama Bin Laden's Response

On October 21, in response to the situation in Iraq, Osama bin Laden released his third audio recording in 2 months, which aired on al-Jazeera television. Entitled "Message to the People of Iraq," the recording presented a dire assessment of the situation in Iraq, differing greatly from Ayman al-Zawahiri's January 2007 pronouncement that America was "weaker than before" and that the mujahideen in Iraq had already "broke[n] its back."[66] Bin Laden began his October message by extolling his Iraqi audience, declaring that they had been "steadfast in the war against President George W. Bush and his riffraff" while the world had stood "stunned, amazed, delighted and wonder-struck watching America the tyrannical [have] its brigades being wiped out in front of your raids and its battalions being obliterated." He had particular praise for "the champions of the Fedayee [martyr] operations . . . rushing with their car bombs into the midst of the armored vehicles."[67]

The al-Qaeda leader then turned to the grave matter facing him and his followers: the failure of AQI leaders to attract recruits to the Islamic State of Iraq and to prevent the defection of former AQI allies such as the 1920 Revolutionary Brigades, Jaysh Mujahideen, and Jaysh al-Islami, all negotiating truces with the coalition. Addressing "my brothers, the amirs of the Mujahid groups," bin Laden warned that "some of you have been tardy in performing another duty, which is also among the greatest of duties: combining your ranks to make them one rank. . . . the Muslims are waiting for you to gather under one banner." Apparently acknowledging the overbearing AQI behavior and violence that had fractured the Sunni insurgency, he spoke of "the mistakes that take place between the brothers," noting that, "when they happen, differences break out [among] the people." However, he was quick to ascribe some of the Sunni insurgency's infighting to "those in whose hearts there is a disease [who] look for the faults and lapses of the Mujahideen and exaggerate them, and perhaps allege that they are a consequence of the devotion of Jihad, which they label violence and terror."[68]

Turning to the phenomenon of the Awakening that had begun to damage his Iraqi franchise, bin Laden argued that AQI commanders and tribal leaders alike had a duty to resolve the disputes among them. "It is incumbent on the men of knowledge, amirs of the Mujahideen, and Shaykhs of the clans to make every effort to engender reconciliation between every two parties in dispute," he implored. He added an allegation that Saudi Arabia partly was behind the Awakening, asserting that "those in the land of the Two

Sanctuaries [Saudi Arabia] . . . forbid the Mujahideen from fighting the army and police of the traitors—like al-Alawi, al-Jafari and al-Maliki—although they know that they are tools of the American occupation helping it to kill the people of Islam."[69]

Delving into operational matters, bin Laden commented on AQI's diminishing effectiveness on the battlefield, which he partially attributed to a breakdown in operational security. He warned AQI commanders to beware "the hypocrites who infiltrate your ranks to stir up strife among the Mujahid groups," and to:

> protect your secrets and excel in your actions, for among the things which sadden the Muslims and delight the unbelievers is the hindering of some combat operations against the enemy because of negligence in any of the stages of preparation for the operation, whether it be reconnaissance of the target, training, integrity and suitability of weapons and ammunition, quality of the explosive device or other such arrangements. And when you lay a mine, do it right, and don't leave so much as one wounded American soldier or spy.[70]

Bin Laden reserved his most emphatic criticism for Iraqis who had split from AQI's jihad and abandoned the establishment of an Islamic emirate out of sentiment for Iraqi nationalism or tribal affiliation:

> [B]eware of fanatical partiality to men, groups and homelands. . . . The brotherhood of faith is what ties the Muslims together, not belonging to the tribe, homeland or organization. And the interests of the group take priority over the interest of the individual, and the interests of the Muslim state take priority over the interests of the group, and the interest of the Ummah take priority over the interests of the state.[71]

In closing, bin Laden defiantly exhorted "our people in Iraq" to redouble their efforts despite the fact that with the coalition's growing advantage over the insurgency, "the malice has increased, and the darkness has become pitch black."

> The Ummah had reserved you for the darkest of nights, because you are their lions who don't care. . . . You refused to abandon the homeland to the unbelievers, or allow their tanks to roar between the Tigris and Euphrates. . . . You massacred the enemy and applied yourself to fighting them, until they became prisoners of their bases and the Green Zone, fearing danger. So continue to make the soldiers of unbelief drink from the bitter cup of death, and leave not one of them on the soil of Iraq.[72]

For coalition commanders, the al-Qaeda leader's admission of mistakes by his organization's Iraqi branch validated that the Awakening had created major fractures within the insurgency and that surge operations were having a significant impact. Bin Laden's speech also was a windfall for MNF-I's information operations organizations, which acted quickly to turn the al-Qaeda leader's remarks to the coalition's advantage and amplify the message that bin Laden believed his followers were losing in Iraq. "Strategically, we were heartened this past week by Usama bin Laden's admission of mistakes by AQI in their brutal methods and by Al Jazeera's relatively truthful coverage of his admission," Petraeus wrote to Gates 6 days after bin Laden's message. "This crack in Al Qaeda messaging sheds light on the enormous amount of hard work done by our troops and our Iraqi partners over the course of this year."[73]

Operation PHANTOM STRIKE in Salahadin, Nahrwan, and the Euphrates River Valley

The day after bin Laden's message was released, Mixon and the 25th Infantry Division handed command of MND-N to Major General Mark Hertling and the 1st Armored Division. The 1st Armored Division became the first U.S. division headquarters to deploy to Iraq with none of its subordinate brigades, and the division continued MND-N's portion of Operation PHANTOM STRIKE by quickly executing an operation that Mixon already had prepared its brigades to conduct. On November 5, Operation IRON HAMMER shifted MND-N's main effort from the Za'ab Triangle farther south to the Tikrit-Bayji-Hawijah area of Salahadin Province, where Colonel Michael S. McBride and the 1st Brigade, 101st Airborne Division, recently had arrived. Over the next 2 weeks, McBride's Soldiers moved into insurgent-dominated neighborhoods in Bayji and nearby Siniyah, detaining dozens of suspected enemy fighters and raising 230 new recruits for the CLC program. Throughout the division's area of operations, MND-N units captured about 400 suspected insurgents during the same period and established new outposts that encouraged large numbers of locals to join the Awakening. Three weeks after Operation IRON HAMMER began, Colonel David Paschal's 1st Brigade, 10th Mountain Division, coordinated with local tribal leaders in Hawijah to enroll 6,000 security volunteers to work with coalition troops against the militant presence.[74] It was the first major Awakening group to appear in the upper Tigris region and was striking in that it came in Hawijah, a city that was a support base for the Naqshbandi Army, a Ba'athist insurgent group loyal to Izzat Ibrahim al-Douri. The area was also the home territory for the Obaid tribe, some of whose members had been fighting the Kurdish parties since their takeover of Kirkuk in 2003. The Sunni tribal forces would be useful against AQI, but stood to pose a challenge to the Kurds if not watched closely.

The success of coalition operations, coupled with the expansion of the Awakening, drove AQI leaders as well as fighters toward Mosul. Hertling, concerned with the trend, took stock of the broader picture in northern Iraq. Violence in Mosul rose as this relocation took place. From March to September 2007, the city, home to more than 2 million Arabs, Kurds, Turkomans, and other minorities had witnessed about 60 attacks per week, but by late October, the average had risen to 80.[75] At the same time, Tel Afar Mayor Najim Jabouri reported to coalition officers that, although Tel Afar remained in friendly hands, AQI fighters moved freely through Mosul, especially at night, and senior AQI commanders such as Masri had relocated to the area.[76] Coalition officials later noted that Masri traveled through Mosul at least twice during the late fall, validating Jabouri's information.[77] The city felt AQI's impact in neighborhoods west of the Tigris, across the river from the Kurdish-populated areas on which the Kurdish-led local security forces tended to focus. As it had done since late 2004, the terrorist group aimed many of its attacks at the Mosul police, such as the October 17 suicide truck bombing of a west side police station that killed 16 people and wounded another 50, an unusually large attack for the city.[78]

Petraeus echoed Hertling's concern over the worsening situation in Mosul, writing to Gates that the city was "an area of concern that never had an adequate force presence." With all U.S. brigades committed in central Iraq and Diyala, Petraeus and Odierno hoped that the 2d and 3d Iraqi divisions and two U.S. battalions under Twitty's 4th Brigade, 1st Cavalry Division, could keep Ninawa Province under control for the time being.[79] As the

1st Armored Division arrived, Hertling posted one of his assistant division commanders, Brigadier General Raymond A. "Tony" Thomas, in Mosul to keep an eye on the restive city, but the single U.S. battalion stationed there to support the Iraqi 2d Division was insufficient to prevent AQI from ramping up its activity.

There were few Awakening groups in the Mosul area, where rivalry between Kurds and Sunni Arabs and Turkomans meant the local ISF and political leaders discouraged the mobilization of Sunni security volunteers. For Ninawa-based leaders of Massoud Barzani's Kurdish Democratic Party and their local allies, the idea of Ninawa's Sunni Arabs and Sunni Turkomans banding together in armed groups under U.S. sponsorship threatened Kurdish control of the province. MND-N leaders, too, were skeptical of sponsoring Sunni tribal groups that might challenge Ninawa's Kurdish-dominated provincial government, judging that an Awakening there could shatter the fragile political détente and plunge the province into sectarian conflict. The dearth of coalition forces also meant that a critical catalyst for the gestation of such groups was missing.

The security situation in Ninawa reflected this absence of a large-scale local Sunni resistance to AQI. By the end of November, the weekly attack average for the Mosul area rose again to more than 100 incidents, including several major attacks.[80] On November 23, AQI carried out 2 coordinated suicide car bombings against Iraqi police targets, killing 21 Iraqis and wounding 35 more. On the same afternoon, a truck bomb destroyed one span of the Qayyarah Bridge, a major Tigris River crossing about 50 miles south of Mosul, in an apparent attempt to isolate the city.[81]

Source: U.S. Air Force photo by Staff Sergeant Samuel Bendet (Released).

Soldiers From 1st BCT, 10th Mountain Division, Search Remote Terrain in Salahadin Province.[82]

Despite the danger AQI posed to Ninawa, Hertling decided to defend the province by first blocking AQI fighters' escape routes elsewhere. On November 27, he shifted MND-N's main effort farther south again, this time to the area spanning southern Salahadin and western Diyala Provinces where fighters from the Diyala River Valley had been escaping MND-N's operations in the upper Diyala by transiting to the Tigris River Valley. In the towns of Khalis, Hadid, and Hibhib, Lehr's 4th Brigade, 2d Infantry Division, teamed with local units of the 5th Iraqi Army Division to conduct 3 weeks of searches for suspected terrorist safe houses and weapons caches in the area where Zarqawi had located his own hideout and had been killed in June 2006. The operation netted about 60 suspected insurgents and about 80 weapons caches, a reduction in tallies from Diyala operations in previous months, suggesting that most of the remaining AQI cells had probably escaped the trap.[83]

As MND-N conducted its operations in Diyala and Salahadin, Lynch and MND-C continued to seize territory south of Baghdad that militant groups had used as support zones and sanctuaries from which to threaten the capital, including areas dominated by Shi'a militias. As MND-C's main effort from mid-October to mid-November, Colonel Wayne Grigsby and his 3d Brigade, 3d Infantry Division, tightened their control over the Diyala River bridges leading to east Baghdad, making it more difficult for Jaysh al-Mahdi (JAM) and other Shi'a militants to move weapons and fighters into the city. Grigsby also established a new outpost in the town of Nahrwan east of Baghdad, a town of 120,000 that had become a Shi'a militant stronghold. The town's market was adjacent to a large vacant area that local Shi'a and Sunni militants used as a dumping ground for the bodies of their victims. When Grigsby located his new outpost in the middle of the vacant lot, murders in the town nearly ceased overnight and locals began tipping off U.S. troops, who then cracked down on what Grigsby assessed to be a JAM battalion.[84]

Source: DoD photo by Sergeant Natalie Loucks (Released).

Colonel Wayne W. Grigsby, Jr., Commander of 3d BCT, 3d Infantry Division, With a Senior Iraqi Officer.[85]

THE AWAKENING, THE MALIKI GOVERNMENT, AND AQI

One week after Osama bin Laden released his October audio message, AQI already was responding to the increased pressure from the coalition and the Awakening. Signs quickly emerged that AQI's main effort in the weeks following bin Laden's message was to strike back against the CLCs, as well as against the Iraqi police in Sunni areas. The day after Hertling's division took control of the north, a suicide bomber killed 27 policemen in Baqubah by detonating a bomb hidden on a bicycle. In the same week, insurgents killed 11 ISF members in Mosul in 3 separate attacks.[86] The following week, a small war played out between AQI and local Awakening fighters in the area between Baqubah and Samarra. On November 8 in that area, coalition troops killed a senior AQI leader, Mohammed Sulayman Shunaythir al-Zubai. The following day, an AQI suicide bomber killed a coleader of the Diyala Salvation Council, an Awakening umbrella group associated with the Baqubah Guardians, in his home in Khalis. On the same day, November 9, a group of Jaysh al-Islami fighters who had joined the Awakening attacked AQI positions near Samarra and claimed killing 18 AQI members, while losing 15 of their own.[87] In a bigger operation the following day, Awakening fighters and local ISF members attacked an AQI force near Baqubah, reportedly capturing 60 AQI men.[88] On the same day as the Baqubah attack, Petraeus noted to Gates, "while the [Iraqi] Government might underestimate the importance of the CLC movements, AQI certainly does not. AQI's recent targeting of Concerned Local Citizen leaders highlights its awareness that Concerned Local Citizen efforts pose the greatest threat to AQI's freedom of movement and ability to conduct activities."[89]

Events south of Baghdad 2 days later underscored the general's point. On November 12, at least 30 AQI fighters attacked 2 of Odom's and Adgie's partnered CLC detachments in the Arab Jabour area, leading to a long engagement that killed 5 of the CLCs and 18 AQI fighters.[90] Two days later, in the town of Haswa a short distance to the west, a suicide bomber killed Sheikh Emad al-Ghurtani, the Awakening leader who had worked with both Kershaw's and Garrett's brigades to organize 700 Awakening volunteers in the formerly violent area between Haswa and Yusufiyah. Sheikh Ghurtani had met with 3d Infantry Division Commander General Lynch a few days before his death, telling the American general, "Honestly, I'm not going to hide this from you . . . There is some al-Qaeda here in this area. But, God willing, we will get rid of them . . . The citizens are coming out. They're not afraid anymore."[91]

Despite setbacks like the loss of Sheikh Ghurtani, by November 2007 coalition commanders could see their partnership with the Awakening as a potentially decisive change in the war. By mid-November, coalition units had registered 77,000 CLCs, representing an increase of 25,000 in 6 weeks. Of that number, 49,000 CLCs were paid by CERP, and south of Baghdad, MND-C had registered about 20,000 CLCs in only 4 months.[92]

U.S. commanders often described the monetary expense of Sunni irregulars in relative terms, pointing out, as Petraeus did, that "the savings in vehicles not lost because of reduced violence—not to mention the priceless lives saved—have far outweighed the cost of their monthly contracts."[93] Fil, commanding MND-B, noted in late 2007 that the division had spent $17 million to enroll and pay about 67,000 fighters—a sum less than the cost of a single Apache helicopter.[94] In Salahadin Province, Colonel Brian R. Owens

THE U.S. ARMY IN THE IRAQ WAR

and his 3d Brigade, 82d Airborne Division, saw CLCs as a similarly prudent investment. During a visit to Iraq, Senator John S. McCain challenged Owens, "Aren't you just paying them not to emplace IEDs?" Owens responded, "No, I'm giving them an alternative to planting an IED . . . some way to feed their families."[95] Aside from saving CLC soldiers and equipment, the investment pumped money into the local economy, where their enrolled soldiers spent their $300 monthly salary.[96]

Despite the steep decline in violence in large part due to the Awakening, Prime Minister Maliki's and other senior Shi'a leaders' paranoia toward the Awakening increased, further frustrating senior U.S. officials. Concerned that the CLCs would turn their guns toward the Iraqi Government, Maliki pressed his coalition counterparts to slow down the program and announced a freeze on the hiring of CLC members into the Iraqi security forces. This move, if not reversed, would thwart the coalition's plans to transition the CLCs into local police forces in Sunni areas. It validated Petraeus's and Odierno's suspicions that Maliki had created the Implementation and Follow-Up Committee for National Reconciliation under Bassima Luay Hasun al-Jaidari to slow the Awakening rather than to institutionalize it. Petraeus did not hide his concern, "As you would imagine, this has been a frustration for us, as we try to take advantage of what likely is a narrowing window of opportunity to reconcile with Sunni former resistance elements that now oppose AQI," Petraeus reported to Gates on November 17. "Taken together with the halting progress on legislation and the slow movement on provision of services to Sunni communities, the freeze on CLC hiring for the ISF has us concerned that Maliki is not taking the necessary steps to capitalize on a fleeting opportunity to cement fragile gains in the security arena."[97] The Prime Minister, Petraeus observed, was "naturally suspicious and inclined to believe rumors that he hears from his Shi'a advisors, to include the Commander of the Iraqi Ground Forces Command [General Ali Ghaidan]."[98]

At the same time, Maliki repeatedly told his coalition counterparts of his plans to declare an amnesty for those who had been "deceived" into joining the insurgency, a policy that seemed at odds with his suspicions about the CLCs. Maliki described his plan as a general amnesty for those who had been detained for taking up arms against the Iraqi Government—a criterion that seemed to require the freeing of many thousands of detainees being held by the coalition. Alarmed by the prospect of such an arbitrary process, coalition leaders quietly engaged Maliki's national security staff to clarify the policy and apply it only to vetted detainees whose behavior could be guaranteed by local Iraqi leaders.[99]

Maliki's paranoia toward the CLCs manifested itself in the Iraqi capital in November, when General Faruq al-Araji, director of Maliki's Office of the Commander in Chief, came to Maliki with "intelligence" that MNF-I was about to implement a plan under which the CLCs would seize the entry points into Baghdad and then remove Maliki in a coup. The Prime Minister responded to Araji's fantastic rumor by deploying trusted ISF units for a day to checkpoints on the major roads leading into Baghdad, prepared for a supposed U.S.-led coup attempt that did not come. As coalition commanders realized the meaning of the strange ISF movements, astonished coalition officials met with Maliki's Iraqi advisers to assure them that the U.S. military did not intend to lead a coup against him, with the CLCs or with anyone else.[100]

Not all of Maliki's suspicions toward the CLCs were unfounded, however. In mid-November, coalition special operators fought Sunni militants north of Baghdad who had obtained heavy antiaircraft guns. The special operations forces (SOF) operators killed 20 of the militants and destroyed 14 of their machine guns before finding out they were a new CLC group. The incident prompted Petraeus to observe that MNF-I needed "to remain vigilant to the possibilities that some insurgent groups could be using CLC elements as a cover to regroup, rid their areas of al-Qaeda, and retain combat power for the future."[101]

To resolve the CLC impasse with the Iraqi Government, Odierno went before the Iraqi National Security Council on December 2. With the recent history of ISF "ghost soldiers" in mind, Maliki and his advisers had scoffed at reports that the coalition had registered 103,000 CLCs, more than 80,000 of which were Sunnis. The Iraqi leader's skepticism had turned to alarm as Odierno revealed that coalition units had collected individual data, some of it biometric, for each CLC, establishing the accuracy of the figure. Nevertheless, when confronted with the scale of what the coalition already had done, and assured by Odierno that MNC-I would continue to monitor the CLCs' activities to pick out "bad apples," Maliki finally relented. The Iraqi Prime Minister ostensibly accepted the coalition proposal that 20 percent of the CLCs should be absorbed into the ISF and the remainder given public sector jobs with the Iraqi ministries, declaring, "I agree with everything that General Odierno laid out!"[102]

Source: U.S. Army photo by Staff Sergeant Curt Cashour (Released).

General Raymond Odierno, Commander of MNC-I, With Local Sheiks.[103]

The day after Prime Minister Maliki lent his approval to the coalition's partnership with the CLCs—at least for the time being—Abu Umar al-Baghdadi, the leader of the AQI-founded Islamic State of Iraq, called for a campaign of terror attacks against those same Sunni irregulars. "The individual mission of each mujahid," Baghdadi declared, "is to conduct three IED attacks or three attacks with explosives, especially martyrdom attacks, or at least to kill three apostates and traitors" by a deadline of January 29, 2008.[104] Baghdadi also announced the creation of a special "Al Siddiq Corps," that specifically targeted those he considered apostates and heretics—namely Sunnis who had joined the Awakening.[105] AQI kicked off its anti-Awakening campaign with eight attacks during its first five days. Fighting between the Awakening movements and AQI spiked during mid-December as clashes erupted in Baghdad, Anbar, Ninawa, and Diyala Provinces.[106]

At a political level, though, the Awakening showed it had gathered a level of momentum that AQI could not impede. Ten days after AQI's call for terror attacks against the Awakening, Iraqi President Jalal Talabani assembled 750 Sunni and Shi'a tribal leaders in an "Awakening Council" meeting in Baghdad. Attended by Petraeus, who addressed the crowd, and other senior officials, the large gathering showed that in central Iraq at least, the reconciliation movement had begun to gain political traction.[107] The following day, the Sunni insurgency took another blow. Iraq's Government-run Sunni religious endowment evicted Harith al-Dhari's Association of Muslim Scholars from the west Baghdad Umm al-Qura Mosque, the vast complex from which Dhari's colleagues had cheered the attacks against the coalition as well as the Iraqi Government since 2004. The action represented how far in public standing the Sunni insurgency's supporters had fallen.

Despite the Maliki government's lukewarm reception to the Awakening, as well as AQI's vicious hostility toward it, by December 2007, the CLC initiative had grown to an extent that no coalition commander would have thought possible in early 2007. The decision by Petraeus, Odierno, and others to support the mobilization of tens of thousands of former Sunni insurgents had been a serious gamble, and many reasonable coalition officials in spring 2007 had argued against taking the risk—or at least in favor of mitigating the risk by moving more slowly than the MNF-I and MNC-I commanders had decided. The risk had been a political one as well. The coalition commanders had granted their tactical leaders autonomy as well as the latitude to use CERP funds to create a force of more than 100,000 Iraqi security volunteers where none had existed, all with the reluctant agreement of the Maliki government. It would remain to be seen in 2008 whether they could solidify that buy-in to make the Sunnis' rejection of AQI permanent.

The End of Operation PHANTOM STRIKE

The last phase of Operation PHANTOM STRIKE found MND-C as the corps' main effort. The operations south of Baghdad since June had established coalition and ISF control of the Triangle of Death and had forced AQI to move southwest into remote areas across the Euphrates River. In mid-November, MND-C launched an operation to establish a foothold on the south bank of the river using Colonel Dominic Caracillo's newly arrived 3d Brigade, 101st Airborne Division, which had replaced Kershaw and 2d Brigade, 10th Mountain Division. In the final weeks of 2007, Caracillo's troops built a pontoon bridge across the Euphrates at the town of Owesat, the same spot where U.S. troops twice had been abducted and killed by Sunni insurgents in June 2006 and May 2007. On the southern bank, Caracillo's brigade established a new combat outpost and branched out to patrol the local area, raise security volunteers, and drive AQI out of its last large sanctuary in the MND-C area of operations.[108]

Caracillo and his troops inherited a Triangle of Death that bore little resemblance to the violent area that Kershaw's brigade had found on its arrival in fall 2006. Once the heartland of AQI and a major base for the terror attacks that nearly brought the collapse of the Iraqi state in 2006, by late 2007 the area was one of the most peaceful in Iraq. With the manpower raised during the Awakening, Kershaw had created a local army of almost 9,000 former Sunni insurgents, enabling the Awakening to spread beyond Anbar and change the strategic situation in central Iraq in ways that coalition leaders had not thought possible at the beginning of the year. Kershaw himself, however, would reap no professional reward. His clashes with Lynch over the use of firepower and the practice of operating with former insurgents meant that he would finish his career as a colonel. Of the four maneuver brigade commanders in MND-C during summer 2007 who drove AQI from the southern belts, Garrett, Ferrell, and Grigsby later commanded at the division level. Only Kershaw would not be promoted to general officer.

Source: U.S. Army photo by Sergeant Ben Brody (Released).

Soldiers From the 101st Airborne Division Conduct Air Assault Operations in Ubaydi, December 29, 2007.[109]

Across Iraq, Operation PHANTOM STRIKE had maintained the pressure begun by Operation PHANTOM THUNDER and, as the coalition commanders had intended, had disrupted the flow of "accelerants" into the Iraqi capital. The result was a significant drop in violence in central Iraq. Before Operation PHANTOM THUNDER began in June, insurgent attacks had averaged 58 per day, but for the period of July to November, the daily attack average fell to just 27. By the end of 2007, days with no attacks became a common occurrence in Anbar Province. Change also swept Baghdad as well, where surge operations cut violence levels in half. On November 3, Baghdad experienced its first day of no reported violent incidents. On December 7, there were only 13 effective attacks in the country, and overall violence had fallen to levels not seen since 2004.[110] Diyala, Salahadin, Kirkuk, and Babil also experienced steep drops. The surge of operations had resulted in a massive capture of the enemy's munitions as well.[111] By October, U.S. and Iraqi troops in Anbar had found twice as many weapons caches as in 2006.[112] In Baghdad, coalition and Iraqi troops discovered more than 1,000 caches by the end of 2007, compared with 213 in 2006.[113] These captures diminished insurgent means to employ IEDs and other bombs.

Only Ninawa Province did not experience these trends. Violence in Ninawa had risen during the surge of operations to more than 15 attacks per day, making it Iraq's most violent province. "We have seen a general movement of AQI to the north," Petraeus reported during the week following Baghdadi's call for a terror campaign. "Kurdish expansionism and the real/perceived disenfranchisement of the Sunni majority play a role here," the MNF-I commander explained to Gates, "as AQI is able to find some refuge in Sunni communities that feel under pressure."[114] In some cases, AQI also benefited from drought conditions that had devastated the Sunni farmers of Ninawa, with conditions made worse at times in areas where Kurdish parties controlled the water supply, such as the western Ninawa town of Biaj.[115]

The outburst of AQI activity, especially in the far north, made clear that the coalition's hold on Ninawa Province was tenuous and would require reinforcement. The rotation of Colonel Michael A. Bills's 3d Armored Cavalry Regiment and two of its squadrons into Ninawa Province in relief of Twitty's 4th Brigade, 1st Cavalry Division, in early December meant a modest increase in U.S. troop strength in the province, but Odierno and MNC-I doubled the U.S. strength in Mosul by moving the 1st Battalion, 8th Infantry, from Baghdad. With the addition of the battalion, the 3d ACR could split the city between two U.S. battalions, one on each side of the Tigris River. U.S. and Iraqi commanders also recalled two Iraqi battalions that had deployed from the 2d Iraqi Division to Baghdad as part of Operation FARDH AL-QANOON, increasing the number of Iraqi battalions in the city from seven to nine.[116]

To manage the situation in Mosul and the surrounding region better, in December Prime Minister Maliki took a step further and created a Ninawa Operations Command and assigned Lieutenant General Riyadh Jalal Tawfiq, a Sunni officer who had commanded the 9th Division in Baghdad, to head the new command. For Maliki, the new command was a way of balancing "the Kurd dominance of political and military elements in Mosul," a dynamic that he had complained about to Petraeus and Crocker since September. For coalition commanders, the new operations command was a badly needed structure for unifying the effort of the two Iraqi divisions and various police forces spread across Ninawa. Petraeus also noted that the move would "help reassure Arabs in Mosul that Kurds are not running the province," though with the governorship, deputy governorship, provincial council, and police chief posts in the hands of the Kurdish Democratic Party (KDP) and its allies, the Mosul Arabs' perception of Kurdish control was not wrong.[117] As 2007 ended, coalition leaders unanimously judged that with a heavy

AQI presence and a smoldering Arab-Kurd conflict, Ninawa Province would require a full-scale offensive of its own.

THE WAR AGAINST THE SHI'A MILITANTS

Monitoring the Sadrist "Freeze"

As the coalition commanders pressed their operations against AQI, they monitored Shi'a militant activities to gauge the effect that Moqtada Sadr's "freeze" on JAM operations would have on the security situation. Before the late-August Karbala violence and Sadr's damage-controlling response, MNF-I had estimated that Shi'a militant groups were responsible for two-thirds of all attacks on coalition troops in Baghdad, and in the month of July alone, explosively formed penetrator (EFP) attacks had killed 23 coalition troops and wounded another 89.[118] The weeks following the "freeze" declaration seemed to offer hope that political efforts could make Sadr and his organization cease all or most of their attacks. On September 16, senior Sadrist Parliamentarian Baha al-Araji told Petraeus that Sadr was "now open to dialogue with the Coalition."[119] For his part, Prime Minister Maliki told Petraeus that low-level U.S. outreach to Sadrists in Baghdad seemed to be gaining traction and asked that MNF-I "calm down" its raids against targets in Sadr City in order to encourage political reconciliation. Petraeus answered that he would be glad to do so "if there is a reciprocal calming down of EFPs and [indirect fire.]"[120]

The fall 2007 period following Sadr's JAM freeze announcement was marked by the same disconnect between the coalition and the Maliki government that had characterized each side's approach to the Shi'a militant problem since late 2006. While Maliki continued to reach out to Asa'ib Ahl al-Haqq (AAH) and other Special Groups in hopes of using them as a political counterweight against Sadr and "mainstream JAM," whom Maliki considered more threatening than the Special Groups, MNF-I pursued the exact opposite course. Petraeus and other U.S. commanders intended to use Sadr's freeze as a means of splitting the Sadr movement and driving a wedge between those who were "mainstream JAM" followers of Sadr and those in the Special Groups that continued attacks against the coalition and the ISF in defiance of Sadr's instructions. Throughout fall 2007, Petraeus and other coalition spokesmen made frequent public statements clarifying that the coalition did not consider Sadr and his obedient followers to be enemies, while Petraeus continued to order intense targeted operations against the Special Groups that Maliki was trying to entice into politics under the auspices of his Da'wa Party.

As Maliki and his advisers saw it, the Special Groups, especially the imprisoned Qais al- Khazali, were potentially reliable partners for the Maliki government, while the erratic Sadr was immature and troublesome. In mid-October, Maliki's office requested that MNF-I release 40 "reconcilable" Shi'a militants from coalition detention centers. Petraeus responded by authorizing the release of nine that coalition officials deemed safe.[121] Maliki and his advisers also wanted MNF-I to remove a number of prominent Special Groups' leaders from coalition target lists, but reluctant coalition commanders hesitated, given the Special Groups' continued attacks on coalition troops. On October 21, the coalition's operations against the Special Groups collided with Maliki's outreach efforts when U.S. troops conducting a raid against a Special Groups target in Sadr City became engaged in a large-scale firefight. U.S. forces killed an estimated 49 Special Groups fighters in a battle that required air strikes before the raiding party could be extricated. Pro-militia media outlets immediately claimed the coalition troops had killed only 15 people—all civilians, and some of them children. An infuriated Maliki and other Shi'a politicians publicly denounced the raid and MNF-I's "lack of regard for Iraqi sovereignty," showing that the coalition's operations against the Special Groups remained politically sensitive.[122]

Even more politically sensitive were the coalition's activities against the Islamic Revolutionary Guard Corps of Iran (IRGC) Quds Force, which had continued its lethal assistance to the Special Groups and other Shi'a militant proxies. On September 20 in the Kurdish city of Sulaymaniyah, coalition troops captured an undercover Quds Force officer, and the Iranian regime protested by closing several border crossing points with Kurdistan.[123] The following month, more evidence of the Quds Force's activities in Iraq came to light when U.S. troops in Diyala uncovered a cache of 280 fully or partially assembled EFPs and at least 300 pounds of plastic explosives with January 2007 Iranian manufacturing labels, all transported from Iran by a JAM member.[124]

The Quds Force activity presented a problem for the U.S. diplomatic initiative to engage in trilateral security talks with the Iraqis and Iranians in Baghdad. As a result, Petraeus noted to Iraqi leaders, "We believe the caches were established prior to the Iranian leaders pledging that they would stop the arming, training, and funding of Iraqi militia extremists." He added that he and other coalition officials "hope[d] that the Iranian leadership is adhering to the commitment they made to PM Maliki in July and that we welcome the next round of sub-ambassadorial talks with Iranian representatives."[125] On November 9, in a goodwill gesture meant to support the trilateral talks, Petraeus and Crocker released nine Iranian detainees, deemed as no security risk by coalition officials, to Iraqi Government custody so they could be returned to the Iranian Government.[126] Eleven days later, five of the Iranian men were captured attempting to cross back into Iraq, for which they gave the unlikely explanation that Iranian officials had refused to take them back into Iran and had transported them back to the Iraqi border.[127]

Diwaniya, Poland, and the Special Groups

The Special Groups' activities were intensifying as well, partly in response to a new and unexpected assertiveness from the Polish coalition contingent. On September 25, the MND-CS commander, Polish Major General Tadeusz Buk, reversed his command's long-standing caution in Diwaniya and launched Operation OIL DROP to emplace a second joint security station inside the city and extend the Polish and ISF presence there. In this operation, Buk partnered with 8th Iraqi Army Division Commander Major General Othman al-Ghanimi. Both generals were assisted by a small team of U.S. Marines whom Petraeus had assigned to Diwaniya to create a local force of anti-JAM Shi'a tribal auxiliaries, including Captain Seth Moulton, a future U.S. congressman; Captain Ann Gildroy; and Staff Sergeant Alex Lemon. Together, the Polish general, the Iraqi general, and the young Marines put into motion an operation to clear the city of its JAM cells, already under pressure following al-Ghanimi's operations of spring and summer 2007.

In an assault that seemed an apparent response to Operation OIL DROP, on October 2, an Iranian-sponsored Special Groups' cell attacked the Polish ambassador in the

Baghdad neighborhood of Karada, hitting his convoy with several EFPs. The wounded ambassador was evacuated to a U.S. military hospital in Germany. The assassination attempt was clearly meant to intimidate the Poles into ceasing their Diwaniya operations.[128] Two weeks later, Special Groups fighters attacked Buk's troops in Diwaniya, wounding seven American and Polish soldiers and killing four Iraqi civilians in several days of rocket and mortar attacks that JAM-friendly media outlets attempted to attribute to coalition air strikes.[129] During the same week, Special Groups fighters bombarded the U.S. Embassy's regional office in Hillah but caused no casualties.[130]

Back in the Baghdad area, on October 28, a Special Groups cell abducted eight Sunni sheikhs from a nearby area of Diyala, but General Tawfiq—soon to be assigned as the Ninawa operations commander—and troops from his 9th Iraqi Division rescued the sheikhs the following day, though not before one of the hostages was killed.[131] On the same day as the rescue, Brigadier General Jeffrey Dorko, commander of the Gulf Region Division of the Army Corps of Engineers and responsible for most of the coalition's construction projects, was seriously wounded by an IED that hit his convoy as it passed through northern Baghdad. In what was likely a Special Groups EFP attack, Dorko became the highest-ranking U.S. officer wounded in the Iraq War.

Much of the increased Special Groups' activity like this in central and southern Iraq was the handiwork of Akram Kabi and AAH, the militant group commanded by the imprisoned Qais al-Khazali. At the time, MNF-I incorrectly associated the group with a new Special Groups-affiliated political party in Nasiriyah, the Iraqi National Gathering. MNF-I officials did correctly guess that Kabi and AAH were splinter groups that "seem to be rejecting Muqtada al Sadr and reaching out to Hezbollah and Syria along the lines of Arab identity," though they again misjudged that the Iranian-allied AAH were "distancing themselves from overt Iranian connections."[132]

General Buk believed the Special Groups attacks against the Polish ambassador and against his base camp in Diwaniya also were meant to influence the Polish elections to be held in October in much the same way the March 2004 Madrid terrorist attack had influenced the Spanish elections, and had led to the withdrawal of the Spanish military contingent from Iraq. Unfolding events supported Buk's theory. Elections in Poland resulted in a change of government to the anti-Iraq War party of Donald Tusk. On November 14, General Othman launched the ISF-led Operation LIONS' POUNCE to continue pressure against JAM elements in Diwaniya. Two days later, Poland had a new government and a new defense minister who promptly announced on November 17 that Poland would withdraw from its combat mission within months.[133]

Evidence continued to emerge of active Iranian regime sponsorship of AAH and other militant groups. On November 17, coalition troops captured a cell of militants, possibly from AAH, that had returned from Iran in late October after undergoing Quds Force training in explosives, sniper, and other militant activities. Under questioning, the men admitted to crossing the border east of Amarah and being escorted by Quds Force officers to a training camp near Tehran.[134]

The following day, November 18, Special Groups members simultaneously attacked several U.S. bases in the Baghdad area by firing large oxygen cylinders mounted on 107-mm. rocket motors and filled with bulk explosives and ball bearings. It was the first use of an Iranian-designed weapon that coalition troops eventually named the improvised rocket-assisted munition (IRAM) and whose design indicated that it was intended to cause mass casualties. The IRAM's bulkiness meant that it had to be fired from a range of no more than 200 meters, indicating that the Special Groups who fired no fewer than 31 of them on November 18 had been able to come extremely close to the perimeter of U.S. bases. The IRAMs wounded 12 U.S. Soldiers and damaged or destroyed 24 vehicles.[135]

The Special Groups' attacks were not always against coalition troops or political enemies. On November 23, Special Groups' members bombed east Baghdad's Shorja Market, killing eight fellow Shi'a in an attack. The Shi'a militants perversely intended to blame AQI to justify the Special Groups' presence in Shi'a neighborhoods. When four Special Groups' members were arrested shortly after the bombing, they tested positive for handling the type of explosives used in the attack and confessed to having carried out the attack under orders from a Special Groups' leader. "We believe the Special Groups are finding their criminal activities under ever more scrutiny and are trying to justify the need for militia security, and we think they thought they could get away with blaming AQI for the attack," Petraeus explained to Gates on November 25.[136]

Fragmentation of the Shi'a Militants

Despite the continued Special Groups' activity, the Sadrist freeze on JAM activities resulted in fewer than 40 EFP attacks in November, roughly half the number carried out in June.[137] "The Sadrist interlocutors we are engaging [claim] that the decrease in violence toward the Coalition Forces (CF) and ISF reflects good intentions in following Sadr's ceasefire; that the Sadrist trend is a nationalist party with wide support at the grassroots; and that they are committed to fighting Iranian influence over Iraq," Petraeus reported on November 9. It was an opening that the MNF-I commander was eager to exploit. "As I have repeatedly observed, we cannot kill our way out of the JAM problem," he wrote to Gates, "and I don't think we need to, given the increasing sense of extremist rejection."[138] By late November, the Special Groups' disregard for Sadr's freeze order led Petraeus to conclude that:

> JAM no longer exists as a relatively unified entity, and we are working hard to keep it fragmented while peeling away reconcilable elements, similar to what we have done with AQI and the Sunni insurgency. The military arm of the Sadrists is fractured and relatively incoherent, and Sadr himself is being intimidated by his affiliates. . . . Exposing and stopping Iranian influence and destroying the Special Groups without reunifying JAM will require a nuanced approach—reaching out to reconcilables and hammering irreconcilables (quietly), all the while keeping the government of Iraq (GOI) on [our] side and the larger strategic context involving Iran in mind.[139]

In part, the disarray inside the Sadrist militant movement resulted from Sadr's absence and his failure to manage his own organization. He returned to Iraq through the Maysan marshes in early October to try to impose some order over his followers, but by early November, he left for Iran again, claiming he would enter a program of additional religious training, presumably so he could claim ayatollah status at some future point.[140] However, the Sadrist issues also were the culmination of the fissures between Sadr and his senior lieutenants, such as Khazali, in the wake of their defeat in Najaf in 2004. One senior Shi'a militant leader in coalition detention, a former Sadr lieutenant who had been involved in the Karbala Provincial Joint Coordination Center (PJCC) attack, described to coalition officials in late 2007 the reason that so many Special Groups leaders, like Khazali and Kabi, had chosen to break from Sadr:

> [H]e [Moqtada] himself is not stable but he is constantly changing his mind and that reflects on his followers. One day he will tell you that the American forces or CF are an occupying force and he will tell you that we should resist by political means. Then he will draw back from that conclusion and tell you that we must resist by military means. This mind changing creates too much waste, obstacles, and hardships because you do not understand his right clear thinking in order to dialogue or converse with him. We believe that this problem is much greater than if he had a negative assumption or understanding of things. . . . He has demonstrated through time that he is not focused, organized, or competent. He does not take advice from others and often acts unilaterally and makes decisions on his own on matters which he is not knowledgeable on. As a result, two distinct sides have formed within the Sadrist movement. There is [Moqtada] and those who are loyal to him as the leader of the movement and representative of their political interests. Then there is the collection of former associates and supporters of [Moqtada], who still subscribe to the teachings and philosophy of the late Muhammad al-Sadr, but have determined that [Moqtada] is not an appropriate leader or the proper successor to his father.[141]

In a number of ways, Moqtada Sadr had failed to continue his father's practices and ideas, becoming "more dictatorial and controlling in his approach," the detained militant leader said, adding that Sadr was a self-centered leader unconcerned with the welfare of his many followers. He had seen this side of Sadr's character firsthand while hiding Sadr in Baghdad after the August 2004 Battle of Najaf and had "decided to part ways with [Moqtada Sadr] strategically."[142] The militant leader also charged that Sadr had failed to support the Najaf hawza, Shi'a religious colleges, in their competition with the Iranian regime's religious center in Qom, thereby creating a "strategic danger" of deep Iranian influence over Shi'a Iraq.[143]

In December, coalition leaders thought Sadr appeared to be preparing for a violent power struggle with those Sadrist militant leaders who had challenged his leadership. In early December, Interior Minister Jawad Bolani reported to Petraeus that "mainstream JAM members are beginning to bring in information about JAM Special Groups activity."[144] A few days later, Sadrist representatives in Baghdad told journalists that Sadr was "happy with the results of his ceasefire and may even seek to make it permanent, while emphasizing his organization's social role over its armed wing." A JAM commander in southern Iraq added, "we listen to his orders, even if he were to decide to abolish [JAM]. He understands our interests more than ourselves."[145]

As Sadr's militant followers awaited his instructions, the Special Groups struck a serious blow against the ISF in the mid-Euphrates region on December 9 when they assassinated Babil Province police chief Qais al-Mamouri, a nationalist Shi'a officer who had used his highly capable special weapons and tactics (SWAT) battalion against both AQI and Shi'a militant targets for several years. A Special Groups' cell from Sadr City orchestrated the attack, which was carried out with an array of five Iranian-provided EFPs.[146] Within days, coalition special operators struck back by capturing several Special Groups leaders who had received advanced Quds Force training in Iran. By December 23, the coalition had detained 8 of the 16 Special Groups leaders and had begun interrogating them to gain information that could be used in the pending trilateral talks with the Iranians and Iraqi Government.[147] Four days later, coalition special operators carried out another raid near Kut. Eleven Shi'a militants died in the firefight that followed.[148]

Sadr's apparent response to this flurry of Special Groups and special operations activity encouraged coalition leaders. The week after the Kut firefight, Petraeus reported to Gates, "Sadr is upset with the Iranian-supported Special Groups that continue to defy his ceasefire order. . . . He may be on the verge of authorizing their targeting by his own elements."[149] The same week, Sadrist representatives met with Islamic Supreme Council of Iraq (ISCI) leaders in Nasiriyah to solidify an October cease-fire between Sadr and Abdul Aziz al-Hakim's ISCI, after which clerics loyal to Sadr during Friday sermons on January 4 called on his followers to "respect the ceasefire" and make peace with rival factions.[150]

However, on the diplomatic level, the situation was less encouraging. Any hope for the talks faded as it became apparent the Iranians did not intend to continue them. The talks, originally scheduled for August, had been postponed repeatedly, and after setting dates of December 18 and then December 28, the Iranians backed out of the meetings again with no indication they would return.[151]

Some Iraqi leaders believed the December 3 public release of the U.S. national intelligence estimate, which concluded that the Iranian regime had halted its nuclear weapons program, had relieved international pressure on the Iranians, who had consequently seen no reason to return to the negotiations in Baghdad. Iraqi Foreign Minister Hoshyar Zebari also believed the intelligence estimate's publication had emboldened the Iranian regime and would lead to increased assertiveness by both the Iranians and Syrians.[152] The Iranian regime's posture in early 2008 indicated no interest in diplomatic engagement with the United States in Iraq, as Petraeus noted on January 13: "The tri-partite talks between the United States, Iran, and Iraq are again on hold. No date has been negotiated, and the Iranians have spent the week criticizing President Bush's Middle East trip."[153] The expected next round of trilateral talks would never take place.

THE IRAQI SURGE

General Dubik at Multi-National Security Transition Command-Iraq (MNSTC-I)

By fall 2007, the increasing pressure on AQI and other militants came not just from coalition troops and the Awakening, but also from a large-scale expansion of the Iraqi security forces and an improvement in their capabilities. The dramatic expansion coincided with a significant change in the coalition's effort to develop Iraqi forces. Although Lieutenant General James Dubik's MNSTC-I was a peer headquarters to Odierno's MNC-I, Dubik arrived in Iraq in June 2007 with the view that the MNC-I mission should have primacy over that of his own command. Under Lieutenant General Martin Dempsey, MNSTC-I had followed its own campaign plan, setting priorities for resources and areas of Iraq that were not strictly connected to MNC-I's ongoing war against AQI and the Shi'a militant groups. As Dubik saw it, there could be no transition to the ISF unless MNC-I could succeed in improving the overall security situation, and his command should therefore be in a supporting role to MNC-I's campaign plan rather than following a campaign plan of its own.

Source: U.S. Marine Corps photo by Corporal Ira B. Goldfrank (Released).

Lieutenant General James M. Dubik, MNSTC-I Commander, Greeting Iraqi Representatives From Anbar Province.[154]

Beginning in the summer of 2007, Dubik and MNSTC-I let MNC-I's plan for offensive operations drive the creation and replenishment of ISF units. By specifically targeting those ISF units who would play a role in upcoming MNC-I operations, MNSTC-I would work to provide the Iraqi forces required to maintain momentum in areas of Iraq where MNC-I's decisive operations were taking place.[155] MNSTC-I would no longer focus on transitioning to an Iraqi lead in security affairs, but would focus with MNC-I on repairing the security situation itself.

Dubik rejected what he regarded as a "false dilemma" of quality versus quantity. A focus on quantity would result in an ISF composed of "a whole bunch of people that were worthless on the battlefield," he judged, while an overemphasis on quality would result in a campaign timeline "so long that we would not be able to contribute to the counter-offensive and achieve the effects that we knew we needed to achieve on the timeline that General Petraeus had set for us." Instead, Dubik focused on sufficiency: "what is good enough to create the combat power necessary, relative to the enemy? If it was good enough, we fielded it and we augmented 'good enough' with iterative quality improvements."[156] Determining what constituted sufficiency was a subjective matter and Dubik's perspective faced challenges created by Iraqi priorities, the bureaucratic foreign military sales program, and Washington's desire to reduce spending. Dubik also believed the coalition's separate efforts to generate tactical forces and to mentor the security ministries needed to be combined into one effort to build an entire defense and police "enterprise," in which the tactical forces on Iraqi streets reflected a coherent national strategy, with ministries that could plan and sustain a security campaign.[157]

Dubik's tenure led to a dramatic increase in the size of the Iraqi security forces. After taking command, he commissioned several studies to determine the proper size of the ISF for securing the country, and polled his superiors and the Ministers of Defense and Interior on the question. The figure that emerged was an ISF with an end strength between 600,000 and 650,000, very different from the 380,000, evenly split between military and police, which MNF-I and MNSTC-I had previously set as the goal for the ISF.[158]

Dubik's raising of the Iraqi forces' end strength coincided with an "Iraqi surge" that resulted in a net increase of more than 106,000 Iraqi soldiers and police over the course of 2007. "That is a substantial growth for any country, let alone one in the middle of a tough war, lacking mature institutional structures, and hampered by an inefficient, marginally capable government," Petraeus observed on December 23, adding that "quantity has a quality all its own in a COIN fight."[159]

Under MNSTC-I's plans, the rapid increase of 2007 would continue into 2008, when the Iraqi Army would grow by another 41,000 men. The additional troops would enable the Iraqis to staff their 13 existing divisions at close to Petraeus's and Dubik's goal of 120 percent, with some select units at 130 percent. The increase in 2008 would also allow for the creation of 24 new battalions and 5 new brigade headquarters.[160] The vast expansion of Iraqi troops came partly from a significant increase in Iraqi training capacity. In addition to the large combat training center at Besmayah, east of Baghdad, MNSTC-I began creating training centers for each Iraqi division, with a mix of Iraqi and coalition trainers, including a small but important contingent from NATO.[161] Between March and November 2007, 53,000 soldiers were trained at these and other locations, increasing the assigned strength of noncommissioned officers (NCOs) in the Iraqi Army from 33 percent to 43 percent and that of officers from 43 percent to 57 percent. The average daily strength of the Iraqi divisions also rose to 77 percent, a 10 percent increase since June.[162] One important change was that, under Dubik's guidance, MNSTC-I focused not just on generating new Iraqi units, but also on replenishing existing ones that had been much reduced through combat and other attrition. By establishing the "second production line" of replacements for existing units, Dubik aimed to raise the effectiveness and confidence of Iraqi units that in some cases had been worn down by constant combat, losing much of their manpower and their tactical skills as a result. This change also enabled MNSTC-I to accelerate toward its goal of 120 percent staffing of existing Iraqi units even as new formations were being built.[163]

The Awakening helped contribute to the overall ISF expansion as well by providing Sunni recruits, mainly police, in Sunni-majority areas where ISF recruiting had been slow and unpopular before 2007. The integration of Sunnis into the Iraqi Police allowed MNSTC-I to reopen the Habbaniyah police academy and graduate a class of 537 in August 2007, a reversal from 2 years earlier when the academy had been closed for lack of volunteers.[164] The influx of Sunnis spread to Baghdad as well, where they constituted most of the 9,000 new police recruits in the city in January 2008.[165]

The new ISF troops and units were expensive, requiring an outlay of $5.7 billion by the Iraqi Government in 2007, but even this barely kept pace with the ISF expansion. The Ministry of Defense spent a full $1.1 billion through the U.S. foreign military sales (FMS) program to equip its units in 2007, but the Interior Ministry spent nothing through its own FMS accounts for the year, as it had to divert large sums of money to pay salaries for new police officers.[166] MNSTC-I considered the Interior Ministry too inefficient to spend FMS funds for the time being, in any case. "Our priority was the Army initially, then the police," Dubik recalled later. "With the police we had to get the ministry working better and [place] the National Police on a reform agenda. Otherwise any money spent would have been wasted."[167]

This approach collided with differing priorities in the United States. As U.S. leaders in Baghdad planned for the training and equipping of the expanded ISF in 2008, they found themselves in a debate with officials in Washington and at U.S. Central Command (CENTCOM) who favored reducing or postponing the $3 billion the United States had planned to contribute to the Iraqi defense budget in 2008 that would be in addition to the $8 billion the Iraqi Government was able to muster. Gates eventually decided this dispute in MNF-I's favor, but as violence ebbed in Iraq, U.S. agencies were beginning to question U.S. expenditures in the country precisely when Petraeus, Odierno, and Dubik aimed to bolster the ISF to take over territory from departing U.S. units.[168] In the longer term, the Iraqi Government's rising oil revenue and defense expenditures would theoretically make U.S. spending for the ISF unnecessary, but in 2007-2008, there was a funding gap to be bridged, and the U.S. generals in Baghdad believed their Iraqi counterparts were increasingly unwilling to bridge it, regardless of the strategic consequences.

As pressure built to equip the growing Iraqi Army, Iraqi leaders were frustrated by the slowness of the U.S. foreign military sales system to deliver weapon systems, vehicles, and other equipment Iraqi commanders required immediately for the ongoing war against AQI and other insurgent groups. In mid-2007, DoD took an average of 5 months just to approve Iraqi purchase requests, with the actual delivery of equipment taking months longer. "FMS is a peacetime mechanism and not really suited for wartime speed," Crocker noted to a visiting congressional delegation.[169] Through considerable personal attention to the problem inside the Pentagon, Gates and Chairman of the Joint Chiefs of Staff Admiral Mike Mullen were able to cut the FMS request timeline from 5 months to 2½ months, but even so, delays in awarding contracts and in production eroded Iraqi confidence in the system. In one high-profile case, the FMS contract for new Harris radios for the ISF stalled due to DoD's contracting regulations. The radios, which the MNF-I commander deemed critical to ISF capabilities, were scheduled for delivery to Iraq in November 2007, but another vendor protested the award of the contract and initiated a bureaucratic process that delayed delivery for more than 3 months. Over time, MNSTC-I came to rely on FMS for less urgent equipment needs that could be programed over a greater length of time and to use the Iraqi Security Force Fund to direct purchase items that the ISF needed in a more timely manner.[170]

In addition to the bureaucratic demands of the FMS process, there were self-imposed U.S. constraints, such as the U.S. failure to grant Iraq "dependable undertaking status," a category that allowed countries to pay for their equipment purchases in installments. Leaving Iraq out of this category meant that the Iraqi security ministries were forced to pay in full for any equipment before the U.S. Government would deliver it. At MNSTC-I, Dubik warned that the failure to grant the Iraqi Government dependable undertaking status was a "strategic hindrance" that encouraged the Iraqis to purchase arms from other countries that would let them pay over time.[171] In the view of Petraeus and other senior leaders in Baghdad, the U.S. handling of the FMS problem was especially shortsighted because equipment was one of the two main limiting factors in building new Iraqi units, along with the development of Iraqi military leaders.[172] Iraqi Minister of Defense Abdel Qader al-Mufreiji expressed a preference for U.S. military hardware such as the M1 tank, which he believed would raise the prestige of the Iraqi Army and mark a break with Soviet-era equipment. By late 2007, Mufreiji was "shopping for other weapons suppliers due to the time required for FMS deliveries," Petraeus reported. In arms deals with Serbia, Ukraine, and China, the Iraqis ordered 380,000 assault rifles, 110,000 pistols, and over 27,000 machine guns. They sought secondhand helicopters and heavy mortars from Serbia as well. While buying from these countries allowed the Iraqis to get equipment and weapons into their hands more quickly, the result was a mix of different models of hardware that made maintenance and logistics more difficult.[173] Petraeus encouraged Mufreiji and other Iraqi leaders to "[buy] for the long term" and build the Iraqi Army around American-made weapons, vehicles, and aircraft rather than "[get] deflected by apparent bargains from Central Europe."[174]

One idea Dubik, Odierno, and Petraeus formulated to equip the Iraqi Army and police with U.S. hardware was to accelerate greatly the delivery of American up-armored High Mobility Multi-Purpose Wheeled Vehicles (HMMWVs) to the ISF by transferring the vehicles as U.S. units in Iraq began to receive deliveries of mine resistant ambush protected (MRAP) vehicles. Handing the displaced up-armored HMMWVs to Iraqi units would be a welcome change for Iraqi troops that had generally faced the IED threat with soft-skinned vehicles with little protection, and the transfer accordingly promised to increase ISF units' confidence, capability, and operational tempo.

Petraeus hoped to transfer 8,500 of the HMMWVs to the Iraqis in 2008, with the Iraqi Government paying a nominal fee of $1,000 per vehicle. When defense officials in the United States insisted on charging the Iraqis $11,000 per vehicle, however, the Iraqis could only afford to buy about half the 8,500 vehicles in 2008, leaving the rest to be purchased in 2009. In ways that frustrated Petraeus and other U.S. commanders in Baghdad, the policy change slowed the effort to increase the Iraqi troops' mobility and survivability, and further undermined senior Iraqi leaders' confidence in the U.S. Government's commitment to equip the ISF.[175] It also slowed Dubik's plans to use the unwanted U.S. HMMWVs to give the Iraqi Army and police a coherent maintenance program in which drivers, mechanics, and maintenance supervisors throughout the ISF could be trained on the same standard system, with the security ministries using a common vehicle system in their budgeting and staffing.[176]

Aside from the equipping of the ISF, there were problems within the Iraqi security structure. The sectarian power struggle that had manifested itself in incidents such as the assassination of Lieutenant General Amer Hashimi in late 2006 had partially receded by late 2007, but assassinations still occasionally took place. In one high-profile case, the Shi'a deputy commandant of the Iraqi military academy in Baghdad kidnapped and murdered his own commandant, then later kidnapped but did not kill the murdered commandant's successor. When the deputy commandant's role was uncovered, the Ministry of Defense dispatched Iraqi special operations forces to detain him on September 25.[177]

Another problem that bore watching was Prime Minister Maliki's attempt to exert control over the Iraqi Army and police by proliferating regional operations commands. Using the Baghdad Operations Command as his precedent, Maliki created other regional commands in Basrah, Diyala, the mid-Euphrates region, and Ninawa, and others would follow. Initially coalition leaders welcomed the idea of regional commands that could create unity of Iraqi effort, but their enthusiasm faded as Maliki began to use the new headquarters to bypass the formal chain of command. Over time, coalition commanders bristled as Maliki began issuing orders to tactical units through the politically connected General Faruq al-Araji and the Office of the Commander in Chief (OCINC) rather than through the Iraqi Joint Forces Command. Coalition officials noted it was a practice resembling the operating mode of the Saddam Hussein regime and a signal that Maliki might be creating a structure to politicize the Iraqi military as the Ba'ath Party had done. Petraeus shared these concerns but was reluctant to wrestle Maliki over control of the Iraqi military in the midst of a difficult campaign. The MNF-I commander preferred to embed coalition officers as advisers within the OCINC and the regional commands to keep a watchful eye on their behavior instead.[178] MNF-I would then try to undo Maliki's consolidation of control once the crisis of the insurgency had passed.

The Jones Commission and the National Police

During the "Iraqi surge" year, the Interior Ministry remained a problem, with a significant portion of its police forces either ineffective or divided by sectarian behavior. Partly in reaction to coalition reports about the ministry's destructive sectarian role in late 2006, the U.S. Congress in 2007 formed an independent commission of former military officers and senior defense and security officials led by retired Marine General James L. Jones, the former NATO commander and future national security adviser. After months of examination, the Jones Commission released a detailed report on the state of the ISF on September 6, 2007, just 5 days before the Petraeus-Crocker congressional hearings. Among its general findings, the report found that the Iraqi Army was gradually improving, but not ready to operate independently. The commission also noted several major areas in which the Interior Ministry required urgent reforms in order to produce effective police. Its most striking finding stated that the National Police were hopelessly sectarian and should be disbanded:

> The National Police have proven operationally ineffective. Sectarianism in its units undermines its ability to provide security; the force is not viable in its current form. The National Police should be disbanded and reorganized. . . . It should become a much smaller organization under a different name with responsibility for highly specialized police tasks.[179]

The Jones Commission's recommendation to do away with the National Police, which at that time numbered more than 30,000, received a great deal of attention in the United States, but it was an idea with which Petraeus strongly disagreed. Speaking to his senior advisers in Baghdad, the MNF-I commander argued that the United States already should have learned the folly of disbanding large security organizations in Iraq. As bad as the National Police might be, Petraeus judged, it would be better to reform it than to put tens of thousands of armed men out of work as had been done in 2003.[180]

To formulate an alternative to the Jones Commission's recommendations, Petraeus and Dubik pressed Interior Minister Jawad Bolani to present his own plan for reforming his ministry and the National Police, with extensive coalition input. Dubik used the Jones

Commission report as leverage to push Bolani and other Iraqis to accept politically diffi-cult reforms, showing that if the reforms did not come, the U.S. Government in Washing-ton was certain to cut off funding and assistance to the Interior Ministry. This pressure forced Bolani and the Maliki government to institute some of the coalition's recommen-dations, but progress was slow and inconsistent.

Source: DoD photo by Staff Sergeant James Selesnick (Released).

Jawad Bolani, Iraqi Minister of the Interior (2006-2010).[181]

As Dubik pressed Bolani to make these changes, Petraeus tapped Colonel H. R. McMaster to conduct a 2-month countrywide inspection of the Interior Ministry and rec-ommend additional ways to reform it. Going far deeper into the ministry's operations than the Jones Commission had done, McMaster found that corruption and sectarian-ism thrived inside the ministry mainly because of the political pressure that Iraq's major parties placed on it. The ministry and its police forces had become a battlefield among the warring parties, a fact that the coalition's capacity building efforts had naively failed to recognize. The sectarian takeover of the ministry had taken place under the eyes of hundreds of coalition advisers who had done little to stop it, McMaster noted. The worst actors took advantage of the absence of written policies for most of the ministry's activ-ities, creating a gray area in which there were few explicit prohibitions against corrupt, sectarian, and nepotistic behaviors—an underestimated factor in the legalistic Iraqi Gov-ernment system. The ministry's outdated bureaucracy created room for large-scale cor-ruption within its vast budget that could not be easily traced. Against this backdrop, the influence of the Badr Corps was particularly negative, because the Badr Corps officers who had infiltrated senior ministry positions under Bayan Jabr continued to use the min-istry's troops and resources to implement a sectarian agenda.[182]

McMaster also found that there already were a small cadre of reform-minded officials inside the ministry, and if they could be insulated from political pressure, they might have a chance to institute reforms. As Dubik also noted, McMaster discovered that Interior Minister Bolani quietly had begun to purge sectarian officials such as Bashir Nasser al-Wandi, the infamous Engineer Ahmed, shifting some of them to powerless jobs or firing them altogether. In addition, many Interior Ministry officers had served in the Iraqi Army during the Iran-Iraq War and resented the ministry's Badr Corps appointees, most of whom had fought on the Iranian side. These officers were glad to see some of the Badr Corps men sidelined within the ministry and quietly told McMaster so. The McMaster Report concluded that the coalition needed to make dramatic changes, exerting its advantage over the ministry, making its security assistance conditional on appropriate behavior, and strongly supporting the ministry's reformers, if the Iraqi police were to be salvaged.[183]

As McMaster delivered his findings, Dubik saw additional ways the coalition might change its approach and improve the National Police, working closely with National Police commander Lieutenant General Hussein al-Awadi as he did so. In early November, the final National Police unit completed its "rebluing" training and returned to operations in the Baghdad area, where the National Police no longer played as destabilizing a role as they had done in 2006. "Rebluing" was a process where each National Police unit was pulled from security duties and put through a 3- to 4-week program that involved vetting its personnel and retraining in democratic policing and respect for human rights. Many of the units were renamed, and officers were issued new digital camouflage in yet another effort to rebrand the troubled organization. Also in early November, a newly arrived contingent of Italian Carabinieri, operating under Dubik's NATO element at MNSTC-I, began retraining National Police units to operate as a paramilitary gendarme-type force, a process that Dubik and other coalition commanders hoped would help curb the organization's sectarian activities when deployed as reinforcements for local police.[184]

At the same time, General Awadi removed the commander of the notorious "Wolf Brigade," making him the 10th National Police brigade commander to be replaced in 2007, and meaning that all nine of the organization's brigades had seen their commanders replaced—one of them twice.[185] That the diminutive Awadi was bold enough to fire politically well-connected sectarian commanders surprised coalition leaders. At one point in early 2007, coalition commanders misjudged Awadi as a Shi'a sectarian responsible for some of the National Police's destructive behavior—and had even briefly put him on Petraeus's notorious "top 20 sectarian actors" list. Not until working more closely with Awadi to institute reforms in fall 2007 did the general's coalition partners fully realize that he and many other senior Shi'a officers with an Iraqi Army background were nationalists who had been constrained by sectarian political pressure from 2004 onward. Once the coalition helped provide Awadi political top cover, he had been quick to purge many of the sectarian commanders who had caused such trouble in Baghdad in 2006.[186]

PLANNING FOR DRAWDOWN

As the Iraqi security forces continued their expansion in late 2007, coalition commanders already were planning for the reduction of their own troops. The surge was a temporary initiative, and whatever the exact numbers or timeline, MNF-I would need to prepare for its orderly conclusion—though Petraeus and Odierno were loath to signal publicly that the coalition troops who were pressuring AQI and the Shi'a militias would soon begin to leave. The Joint Campaign Plan of June 2007 had assumed that the United States would maintain 20 BCTs in Iraq only through March 2008, though with the Army's extension of unit deployments and individual augmentees from 12 to 15 months, the endpoint of the surge could stretch to June 2008.[187]

As early as June 2007, Odierno judged that conditions likely would allow for a reduction of U.S. troops beginning in December 2007, while Petraeus believed a reduction of approximately 30,000 U.S. troops would be warranted by mid-2008.[188] Together, MNF-I and MNC-I planned for a gradual reduction of U.S. brigades beginning in December 2007, reaching the pre-surge level of 15 in July 2008. Upon reaching 15 brigades, the force level would remain steady for a period of several months as commanders judged whether the security progress of the surge could be sustained with a smaller force. U.S. forces in Iraq at that point would number 137,000, higher than the pre-surge troop total due to the addition of a division headquarters, combat aviation brigade, and a larger number of combat support troops than before the surge.[189] There were also two nonstandard brigade headquarters that controlled almost no subordinate forces but assisted with governance and ISF development in select areas where security had improved.

MNC-I's concept was for U.S. forces to thin out across the country rather than disappear from any particular area in order to maintain situational awareness and to continue the partnering of U.S. units with ISF counterparts at lower echelons. Drawing down by 30,000 troops would be a complex undertaking that depended on a variety of physical factors and policy considerations. Some were straightforward, such as the U.S. Army component of CENTCOM's (U.S. Army Central [ARCENT]) capacity to process only two and half brigades per month through Kuwait. Others were more complicated, such as unanswered questions about which equipment should be turned over to the Iraqi security forces to enhance their capability and interoperability.[190] MNC-I would also have to plan how to administer not just the 15 BCTs but also individual battalions, provincial reconstruction teams, combat support and combat service support units, and ISF formations to cover the country. Instead of closing bases as part of its drawdown scheme, MNC-I would "transition parts of each base by reducing the Coalition 'fence line' within the base simultaneous with conducting a partial handover to the ISF."[191]

In a larger sense, the end of the surge would mean a coalition return to the concept of transition to Iraqi control, the same process that had fallen apart in 2006. As Petraeus described it to British Defence Secretary Desmond Browne, the coalition would move over time from "leading to partnering to over watching" as the Iraqi forces continued to develop.[192] Unlike the premature drawdown of 2006, the coalition hoped that transition to Iraqi control in 2008 would take place "in a deliberate fashion and . . . based on local conditions," according to an MNC-I operations order of December 20, 2007.[193]

The MNC-I order presented two different operational concepts for transitioning security responsibility to the Iraqis and shifting U.S. forces to an overwatch role. In the first approach, military transition teams (MiTTs) in a given area would double or even quadruple in size, as preserving security gains would fall on the shoulders of the ISF, U.S. advisers, and embedded provincial reconstruction teams.[194] A prime example of this approach was in Ramadi where Colonel John Charlton's 1st Brigade, 3d Infantry Division, would not be backfilled after it departed Iraq in April 2008, and MNF-West would lose two additional Marine infantry battalions elsewhere in Anbar the following month.

The second overwatch concept was one of "scalable strike packages," in which Iraqi units would pair with embedded coalition advisers from the Combined Joint Special Operations Task Force (CJSOTF) who would receive priority of fires; intelligence, surveillance, and reconnaissance; and lift assets, while local conventional units would provide a quick reaction force.[195] MNC-I considered Nasiriyah the prime example after Abu Liqaa's specialized police unit and its supporting CJSOTF advisers suppressed a JAM attempt to take over the city in June 2007.[196] In December 2007, MNC-I directed its subordinate units to develop scalable strike packages of their own using Iraqi special operations forces and their CJSOTF advisers.

No matter the approach, it was difficult to mitigate the impending rapid loss of 30,000 U.S. troops. By late 2007, one of Petraeus's biggest challenges was persuading coalition allies to maintain or even expand their troop presence as the United States reduced its own. Like the 2,000-strong Georgian brigade that arrived as MND-C in late summer 2007 making the nation the third-largest contributor of troops to the coalition, Petraeus sought to convince others to increase their participation in the "Coalition of the Willing."[197] In October, MNF-I hosted a conference of 35 partner countries in Bahrain, but it produced no new major troop commitments.

Some countries' commitments to MNF-I were contingent on domestic political developments. In mid-December, Kevin Rudd, Australia's newly elected Labor Prime Minister, informed Petraeus and Crocker that he would withdraw the Australian battle group in August 2008, though Australia would consider providing advisers to build Iraq logistics capacity after that time.[198] Similarly, on November 17, the Polish Defense Minister announced that his country would withdraw its 900-man contingent in MND-CS in 2008, a development Petraeus believed might endanger the gains against JAM in Diwaniya and put Camp Echo outside the city at risk.[199] The Poles also sought an accelerated relief of their responsibilities through the early transfer of Qadisiyah Province to provincial Iraqi control (PIC), but Petraeus replied to the Polish ambassador that Qadisiyah would "PIC when the conditions are right to do so and not when it is politically convenient for the Polish Government."[200] The promise of logistical assistance from MNC-I for the Polish redeployment, coupled with a reminder of the agreement between Bush and the Polish Government, helped convince Polish leaders to maintain responsibility for MND-CS until October 1, 2008.[201] Gains with partner nations proved insufficient, and by the end of 2007, U.S. commanders could see that within months U.S. units would have to expand farther into southern Iraq to cover areas left open by vacating allies. A diminishing number of U.S. troops would be required to hold more territory than ever before.

IRAQI POLITICAL TENSIONS AND PROGRESS

The strategic purpose of the surge had been not just to defeat AQI and other major insurgent groups, but also to create conditions in which the Iraqi political factions would reconcile and use politics rather than violence to pursue their political goals. As the security goals of the surge appeared to come closer to fruition in summer and fall 2007, the political goals remained elusive. Kurdish-Arab tensions simmered, with the governing parties deeply divided over the question of Kirkuk and the future relationship between the Kurdistan Regional Government and the government in Baghdad. The Awakening offered a political opening against the Sunni insurgency, but Maliki and other Shi'a leaders were reluctant to partner with a movement that they considered infiltrated by Ba'athists and sectarian enemies. The Sunni Parliamentary bloc remained outside the government altogether, leaving most of Iraq's Sunni electorate without representatives in the Iraqi cabinet. The large Sadrist bloc remained in opposition to the government as well. As these major political groupings jostled for political power in the Green Zone and in provincial councils, their disputes often fueled violent clashes among their various militias or security forces on the street, and they often seemed more concerned with fighting one another than fighting the worst of the terrorist groups.

A few major political disputes stood out. The fate of Saddam's former senior deputies became a Sunni-Shi'a political divide when Maliki and other Shi'a leaders pressed MNF-I to allow the execution of the men sentenced to death by an Iraqi court for the 1988 chemical weapons attacks against Kurds in Halabjah. The coalition had agreed to the execution of Ali Hassan al-Majid (also known as Chemical Ali) after Jalal Talabani and his Vice Presidents had agreed to sign the execution warrant. A dispute arose, however, when Maliki pressed to execute former Minister of Defense General Sultan Hashem, the Mosul native who had signed the 1991 cease-fire agreement with General Norman Schwarzkopf, and who had surrendered to Petraeus in Mosul in 2003. Many Iraqi Sunnis considered Hashem blameless in the 1988 war crime and looked on him as a potential Sunni political leader. Sunni opposition to his execution was broad; as a result, President Talabani and others had declined to sign his execution order rather than anger the Sunni political parties with what they would consider a sectarian killing. Nevertheless, Maliki pressed MNF-I to release Hashem from coalition detention so that the death sentence could be carried out, something Petraeus and Crocker refused to do without the full approval of Talabani and his Vice Presidents.[202]

The coalition had hoped to encourage the Sunni bloc's return to Maliki's government in fall 2007, but Maliki's ongoing dispute with Vice President Tariq Hashimi and other senior Sunni politicians thwarted this idea. Maliki considered Hashimi a recalcitrant sectarian linked to terrorist groups, and Hashimi had reciprocal feelings about Maliki. Some of Maliki's distrust of the top Sunni Parliamentary leaders seemed warranted when coalition troops raided Sunni leader Adnan Dulaimi's residence in the Green Zone the following month to arrest one of his aides for murder and found Dulaimi's bodyguards with a car bomb at the house. "The incident has created political problems and is likely to heighten sectarian tensions and farther increase the divide between the government of Prime Minister Maliki and the Sunni Tawafuq alliance," Petraeus noted dryly.[203]

Source: DoD photo courtesy of Headquarters, 1st Cavalry Division, Public Affairs (Released).

Iraqi Vice President Tariq Hashimi Greets Major General Joseph Fil, MND-B, Commander.[204]

For its part, the coalition occasionally considered Hashimi difficult to deal with as well, and Petraeus sometimes withheld coalition airlift support for Hashimi in response to his public criticism of the coalition and of Maliki.[205] As Sheikh Ahmed Abu Risha and the Anbar Awakening grew in prominence in fall 2007, both U.S. officials and Maliki considered giving the Awakening the power to name Sunni ministers to fill the cabinet positions Hashimi and the Sunni Parliamentary bloc had abandoned earlier in the year. "We are going to reduce our support for Vice-President (VP) Hashimi and see how Sheik Ahmed performs in a more high profile role for a while," Petraeus reported in early October. "We need to find some Sunni leaders able to bring the Sunni community along the road to reconciliation, and our early impressions are that Sheik Ahmed may fill such a role."[206] Petraeus was reacting partially to a budding intra-Sunni power struggle between the Awakening and Hashimi's Iraqi Islamic Party, the latter of which dominated the Sunni bloc in Parliament. In early 2008, 300 sheikhs in the Awakening met in Ramadi to elect a central committee and announce they would form a political party, called Sahawa al-Iraq. The new political challenge had the potential to create intra-Sunni political violence. "Our message is that both parties have a right to exist, and threats or acts of violence are unacceptable," Petraeus noted.[207]

The intense rivalry among the major parties spilled over into the coalition's detainee releases, as the major political leaders vied to preside over the frequent detainee release ceremonies in order to claim credit for extricating Iraqis from coalition custody. After Vice Presidents Tariq Hashimi and Adel Abdel Mahdi presided over release ceremonies in October, MNF-I held one on November 8 at which Maliki presided. "Hopefully this ceremony (larger than the one at which VP Tariq Hashimi presided) will help compensate the PM's distress over the good will received by the Iraqi vice Presidents when they hosted previous detainee release ceremonies," Petraeus commented.[208] Perhaps carried away by the emotion of the event, Maliki mentioned to Odierno the following day that he was considering declaring a general amnesty for those in detention, an ill-formed idea that alarmed coalition leaders who knew their detention centers still held thousands of hard-core fighters.[209]

The Turkey-Kurdistan Workers' Party (PKK) Crisis

Signs of political discord between Shi'a and Sunni parties in Baghdad were eclipsed by the flaring of ethnic warfare in northern Iraq. The coalition found itself in fall 2007 with yet another conflict on its hands when the decades-long war between Turkey and the Kurdistan Workers' Party (PKK) broke out again. From its bases inside Iraqi Kurdistan, the PKK had launched intermittent attacks against Turkey even before 2003, but the conflict had slackened until several high-profile violent events occurred in 2007. On May 22, a suspected PKK suicide bomber killed eight people in Ankara, after which Turkish leaders threatened to invade Iraqi Kurdistan to root out the PKK, and even to attack Massoud Barzani and the Kurdistan Democratic Party (KDP), whom Turkey blamed for harboring the PKK. Barzani responded by declaring that the peshmerga would resist any Turkish incursion. Turkish troops shelled PKK positions inside Iraq and even briefly crossed into Iraq in "hot pursuit" of PKK fighters.[210]

After an October battle left dozens of Turkish soldiers and PKK fighters dead, the Turkish Parliament authorized its military to use "every kind of measure" against the PKK, including ground operations inside Iraq. Under threat of Turkish attack, Barzani wrote to Petraeus, warning that he would recall Kurdish troops from Iraq to defend the Kurdistan region if necessary.[211] Since Kurdish troops were a key part of Operation FARDH AL-QANOON and the ongoing operations in Ninawa and Salahadin, their withdrawal would put the security of those provinces and Baghdad at risk.

After further bloodshed, Petraeus and Crocker found themselves "in a difficult position with our Iraqi partners and our Turkish NATO allies," as the general put it.[212] Iraqi leaders in Baghdad and Erbil, the capital of Iraqi Kurdistan, protested to U.S. counterparts that Turkey was illegally invading their country, while Turkish leaders in Ankara protested that MNF-I had done nothing to prevent the PKK from using Iraq as a base from which to attack Turkey. The situation worsened when Kurdish peshmerga took several Turkish soldiers who had crossed into Iraq hostage, a crisis that Petraeus defused by taking custody of the Turks and personally returning them to the Turkish Army on November 3.[213]

The Turkish attacks had a significant political impact both in Iraqi Kurdistan and in Baghdad. The Turkish bombing campaign angered the Kurdish public and made it difficult for Kurdish leaders to back down. It also forced Barzani to declare that Turkey's actions violated Iraqi sovereignty, a surprising claim for a Kurdish separatist to make. In Baghdad, the Kurdish parties began to indicate to Maliki and other Iraqi leaders that if the Iraqi Government did not resist future Turkish incursions into Iraq, the Kurdish Alliance would withdraw from the Maliki government, causing its collapse. The crisis thus threatened to leave Iraq without a prime minister and a government—and leave MNF-I without Iraqi Government partners—in the midst of the fragile security gains of the surge.

Petraeus's preferred solution to the crisis was for U.S. leaders to force Turkish representatives to negotiate with the KDP, which had fought a civil war against the PKK in the 1990s and had no fondness for the party.[214] Before diplomacy could be given a chance to work, however, the Turks expanded their operations into a full-scale air campaign against the PKK on December 16. Turkish military leaders, eager to signal that they had American support, announced that the United States had opened Iraqi airspace to Turkish attack aircraft and had provided Turkey with targeting intelligence against the PKK.[215]

In fact, the U.S. European Command and MNF-I had indeed coordinated with the Turkish general staff on the operation in order to restrict its potential damage, but when the bombing actually began, Turkish leaders gave U.S. counterparts a mere 30 minutes notice. The Turkish air strikes also extended far beyond the area MNF-I had agreed could be struck, and angry Kurdish leaders reported to MNF-I that the first air strikes had killed some Iraqi Kurdish civilians.[216] The following day, PKK spokesmen warned, "if colonialist powers in Kurdistan are continued to be supported, it should be known that the Kurdish people have the power to spoil the balances in the Middle East and hurt the interests of Western powers."[217] A letter from the PKK to Petraeus 3 days earlier had been far more conciliatory, asking Petraeus and U.S. leaders to broker a political resolution to the conflict, but lacking policy guidance from Washington, Petraeus did not reply.[218] "It would be most helpful if the Turks would employ some 'constructive ambiguity' and at the least remain quiet about any strikes they conduct," Petraeus wrote to Gates on December 23. He added, "Given the minimal amount of damage we assess they have afflicted on the PKK to date, the better solution is to pressure the Turks to stand down altogether and refocus on a broad, politically-led strategy against the PKK."[219] For the time being, however, the Turks and the PKK remained on a war footing, and the coalition remained braced to deal with the political repercussions.

Political Crisis and Prime Minister Maliki

The crisis in the north came at a time when political tensions between Prime Minister Maliki and the other parties in his government were near the breaking point. A significant factor in the infighting among the major parties was the tendency for Maliki and his personal advisers to make decisions in a secretive, insular fashion without consulting the other parties in the government. The Prime Minister, a deeply distrustful man who had come of age as an exiled Da'wa Party member under constant threat from Saddam's intelligence apparatus, tended to interpret political events as conspiracies and viewed the other parties in his national unity government as potential enemies rather than partners. Before the Turkish campaign against the PKK began, he had begun to take steps in October to curb the KDP's political dominance of Ninawa Province.[220] At the same time, an early October Sadr-Hakim truce that the coalition welcomed as a way of suppressing

291

intra-Shi'a violence seemed to strike Maliki as a potential Sadrist-ISCI alliance against Maliki and Da'wa. By late October, Petraeus noted, "unfortunately, we are beginning to see some suspicion of ISCI and VP Adil Mahdi akin to the suspicion once reserved for VP Hashimi."[221] For their part, the other parties complained to coalition leaders that Maliki had cut them out of the decision-making process and had refused to abide by an agreement among the parties to use a "3+1" arrangement, in which major policy choices would come from consensus among the Prime Minister, President Talabani, and Iraq's two Vice Presidents.[222]

Matters started to come to a head in mid-December as ISCI and the Kurdish parties began to raise the idea that the Iraqi Parliament should vote Maliki out of office. On December 16, the same day that Turkey launched its air campaign against the PKK in Iraqi Kurdistan, Petraeus reported to Gates that Kurdish leaders had "presented a long array of grievances and frustrations with the exclusive and conspiratorial Maliki inner-circle."[223] Three days later, on December 19, several of the same leaders met with visiting Secretary of State Condoleezza Rice in Baghdad and asked for U.S. support for a Parliamentary vote to remove Maliki as Prime Minister. Rice threw cold water on the idea, however, and told the Iraqi leaders that they should look instead to "implementation of the 3+1 concept and true leadership of the [Iraqi Government] to capitalize on the improvements in security that the surge has brought."[224] The matter did not end there. On December 23, Petraeus reported to Washington that almost all of Iraq's major political groups continued to move toward Maliki's ouster. The Kurdish parties were "increasingly frustrated with what its members perceived as Maliki's ineffective leadership and isolated decision-making" and considered withdrawing from the government. Ayatollah Ali Husayni Sistani and other religious leaders in Najaf were "worried about their reputation being tarnished by the GOI's ineffectiveness," while Kurdish leaders and the Iraqi Islamic Party were on the verge of forming an alliance.[225]

The political pressure took its toll on Maliki, who physically collapsed on December 29 and was evacuated to London by the coalition to seek medical treatment for exhaustion and dehydration. "At this point, we don't have any additional evidence that planning for a putsch has progressed," Petraeus noted on December 30, though he reported the following week that Vice President Mahdi was traveling to Tehran seeking Iranian support for Maliki's ouster, while Abdul Aziz al-Hakim visited Ayatollah Sistani in Najaf probably asking for the same.[226]

The UN Security Council Resolution (UNSCR) Rollover

In actuality, coalition leaders had mixed feelings about the prospect of Maliki's replacement. Rice and others were wary of recreating the government vacuum of early 2006, when, for 5 months, Iraq had gone without political leadership and the government machinery ground to a halt. U.S. officials in Baghdad also had seen worrying signs that Maliki and his Da'wa allies were becoming authoritarian and difficult to deal with, especially on issues related to the U.S.-Iraqi security and political relationship.

When the time came in late 2007 to renew the UN Security Council Resolution (UNSCR) that authorized MNF-I's presence in Iraq, U.S. officials in Baghdad found themselves negotiating not with Iraqi ministers, but with Maliki's Da'wa Party advisers, who appeared to discount the U.S. military's role in tamping down the Iraqi insurgency and displayed an ill-informed distrust of common international legal language. Across several weeks of negotiations, the Da'wa men started by "dredging up language from the Amman letter of October 2006" and declaring that they expected the terms under which MNF-I operated to be significantly restricted to reflect "the progress that has been made over the past year."[227] As the talks proceeded, Maliki's advisers insisted that the Iraqi Government be given "all functions and authorities concerning detention, arrest, and imprisonment," which would have prevented coalition units from detaining anyone in Iraq.[228] Only after some dramatic confrontations that Petraeus described as "contentious" did the Maliki government agree to allow the UNSCR to go forward for approval on December 19. The UNSCR "was in question until a few hours before the vote, with Iraqi officials rejecting language in the resolution that suggested their security forces be subjected to international law," Petraeus reported. The general added that the resolution was adopted only after Rice assured Maliki that the resolution's language did not undermine Iraqi control of its security forces. The process left U.S. officials concerned that American plans to negotiate a strategic partnership and bilateral security agreement with the Maliki government in 2008 could run into similar problems.[229] The vast improvement in security during the course of 2007 had not yet made relations among the Iraqi political parties or between the United States and the Iraqi Government much easier.

***

The First Year of the Surge: General Petraeus's Analysis

As 2007 ended, Petraeus took stock of the changed situation in Iraq since the surge had begun almost 11 months earlier. By December 2007, the average number of violent incidents per week in Iraq dropped to less than 40 percent of the peak violence of June 2007 and was on par with the level of violence of early 2005. High-profile bombings had fallen to less than one-third of the June 2007 peak. The number of civilian deaths had fallen to one-sixth the peak total of November 2006, when more than 3,000 civilian deaths had been recorded. In their internal reporting, the coalition commands estimated that over 7,400 enemy fighters had been killed in 2007, compared to about 5,000 in 2006.[230] Conversely, 2007 had been the deadliest year of the war for U.S. troops, with 864 killed, compared to 770 in 2006, but losses had been dropping steadily since the summer. Twenty-two U.S. troops had been lost in December 2007 (seven of them nonbattle deaths), the second-lowest monthly total since the beginning of the war.[231] Among ISF units, 2,452 Iraqi troops and police were killed in 2007, a slight decrease from the 2,590 killed in 2006.[232] "In many ways we spent 2007 creating a new situation—one of reduced violence—that replaced the horrific existence most Iraqis bore for the past 12 to 18 months. Now we obviously need to make the most of the new situation," Petraeus noted as December ended.[233]

On January 6, 2008, the MNF-I commander wrote to Gates to report these figures and to reflect on the dynamics that caused such significant improvements in the security situation. He began by writing, "the past 12 months were made possible by the courageous decision in early December 2006 by General Casey and Ambassador Khalilzad to state that the strategy at the time was not working. This acknowledgement paved the way for the surge—ours and the Iraqis—and for the change in strategy that made securing the population the central tenet."[234] It was a backhanded compliment, considering that Petraeus understood Casey had not agreed that the transition plan needed to be abandoned.

Moving to security arrangements, Petraeus noted that by living in Iraqi communities alongside the ISF, "we not only improved security, we also fostered and supported movements in local communities to reject AQI." As Iraqi tribal leaders had come forward willing to turn against AQI, coalition units had been flexible enough to exploit the opportunity that the Awakening presented. "With experienced leaders like Ray Odierno at the helms of our units, our elements made the most of the situations that developed (validating Seneca's observation that 'Luck is what happens when preparation meets opportunity.')," Petraeus observed. The coalition had also been able to bring local political and economic initiatives to bear along while clearing and holding AQI sanctuaries on a large scale. "[S]uccessful counter-terrorist/counterinsurgency operations on the scale of those in Iraq require conventional forces [and] special forces . . . all working together and augmented by host nation forces and supportive local communities," Petraeus wrote.[235]

A few other factors had contributed to the improvement in security. AQI had exhibited "genuine tone deafness" about the Iraqi population's disapproval of their brutal tactics and ideology, Petraeus noted, making it easier for the coalition and the Iraqi Government to sway public opinion against the terrorist group. The Sadrist cease-fire had been an important development as well, though Petraeus noted that "we remain very wary of the assistance the Quds Force continues to provide" and that MNF-I would not be "handing out any badges for good behavior to Teheran any time soon."[236]

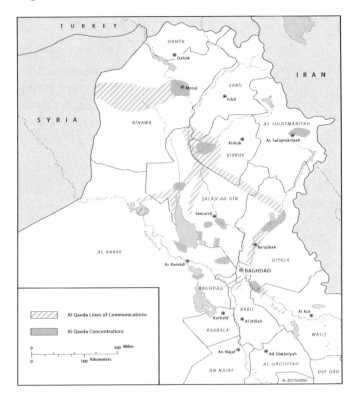

Map created by the official cartographer at the U.S. Army Center of Military History, Washington, DC.

Map 16. Al-Qaeda in Iraq, 2007.

Looking ahead in 2008, Petraeus judged that, although coalition forces had done considerable damage to AQI, more remained to be done because the group was "far from finished" and remained "the most serious near-term threat to Iraq." Where the Shi'a militant groups were concerned, MNF-I would "continue to quietly target members of the JAM Special Groups, to contribute to additional fissures in the Sadr organization, and to cultivate the seeds of a Shi'a Awakening by increasing that community's recognition that Special Group extremists are the long-term threat to security and the rule of law in Iraq." In 2008, Petraeus and MNF-I would seek to replicate the effect of the Sunni Awakening among the Shi'a militant groups' constituencies, based on his judgment that "the same power of the people that made such a profound change in the Sunni communities is present and waiting to be activated, and we have some reason to believe that the basic sensibility of the Iraqi people will lead them to a broader rejection of bad behavior."[237]

Also in 2008, Petraeus reported coalition leaders and units would aim to increase the capacity of the Iraqi Government to try to consolidate the year's security gains. "Given that much of 2007's progress was based on the Iraqi people rejecting extremism, we'll have to work with the GOI [Federal Government of Iraq] and use all of our available means to help the government deliver basic services, job training, and employment to those same people to cement the security gains we've made together," he noted. For that reason, "there will be a need in 2008 for additional aid, advisors, and capacity building efforts in the coming year."[238]

Petraeus's report indicated the growing sense inside the coalition headquarters that the coalition's position was growing stronger week by week. Conversely, for AQI and its allied insurgent groups, the situation bin Laden had described as "pitch black" darkness in October 2007 had become even bleaker by year's end. AQI had lost thousands more fighters killed and captured. The Awakening had become the dominant force in former insurgent strongholds such as the Hawijah and Arab Jabour, and the insurgency's overall prospects looked dim. Across central and northern Iraq, AQI remained strong only in Mosul and its environs, and coalition commanders already were planning a large-scale offensive led by U.S. forces to drive AQI out of Mosul before the departure of the surge brigades. However, as events transpired, it was an offensive that would never take place.

ENDNOTES - CHAPTER 6

1. Multi-National Force-Iraq (MNF-I), Secretary of Defense (SECDEF) Weekly Update, September 2-8, 2007. All unpublished documents in this chapter, unless otherwise stated, are in the Chief of Staff of the Army (CSA) Operation IRAQI FREEDOM (OIF) Study Group archives, Army Heritage and Education Center (AHEC), Carlisle, PA.

2. Ibid., June 3-9, 2007; July 8-14, 2007; July 15-21, 2007; and August 26-September 1, 2007.

3. Ibid., September 16-22, 2007; "U.S.: Violence down across Iraq but not enough," *USA Today*, September 20, 2007.

4. U.S. Army photo by Specialist Shawn M. Cassatt, "Halt!" December 12, 2007, Released to Public, available from *https://www.flickr.com/photos/mnfiraq/4313988397/in/faves-138659840%40N02/*.

5. Manuscript (Ms), *On Point: The United States Army in Operation Iraqi Freedom*, Vol. IV, Chap. 5, Fort Leavenworth, KS: Combat Studies Institute, September 25, 2014.

6. U.S. Army photo by 1st Lieutenant Richard Ybarra, "Fight Fire with Fire," September 8, 2007, Released to Public, available from *https://www.flickr.com/photos/mnfiraq/4314542796/in/photostream/*.

7. Ms, *On Point*, Vol. IV, Chapter 5.

8. Ibid.

9. Ibid.

10. Ibid.

11. DoD photo by Sergeant Kevin Stabinsky, "Seeds of progress spread in Hawr Rajab [Image 2 of 3]," DVIDS Identifier 62194, October 22, 2007, Released to Public, available from *https://www.dvidshub.net/image/62194/seeds-progress-spread-hawr-rajab*.

12. MNF-I, SECDEF Weekly Update, September 23-29, 2007.

13. Press Conference, Lieutenant General Raymond T. Odierno, MNF-I, Combined Press Information Center, Baghdad, Iraq, September 20, 2007, available from *http://www.globalsecurity.org/military/library/news/2007/09/mil-070920-mnfi-b01.htm*, accessed May 25, 2016.

14. Christian Berthelsen, "Attacks during Ramadan fall despite threats," *Los Angeles Times*, October 17, 2007, available from *http://articles.latimes.com/2007/oct/17/world/fg-iraq17*, accessed February 15, 2016.

15. MNC-I Historian's Chronology, 2006-2008, p. 16.

16. Press Briefing, Major General Joseph Fil, DoD, Washington, DC, September 21, 2007.

17. MNF-I, SECDEF Weekly Update, September 23-29, 2007.

18. Peter R. Mansoor, *Surge: My Journey with General David Petraeus and the Remaking of the Iraq War*, New Haven, CT: Yale University Press, 2013, p. 137.

19. MNF-I, SECDEF Weekly Update, September 30-October 6, 2007.

20. Ibid.

21. Ibid., October 7-13, 2007.

22. Ibid., October 21-27, 2007.

23. Ibid.

24. "Al-Qaeda sector leader called Abu Tariq," *Daily Diary*, February 10, 2008, MNF-I translation, available from *http://media.washingtonpost.com/wp-srv/world/pdf/diary_eng_021008.pdf*.

25. Ibid.

26. Alissa Rubin and Andrew Kramer, "Iraqi Premier Says Blackwater Shootings Challenge His Nation's Sovereignty," *The New York Times*, September 24, 2007; Sabrina Tavernise, "U.S. Contractor Banned by Iraq Over Shootings," *The New York Times*, September 18, 2007.

27. MNF-I, SECDEF Weekly Update, September 16-22, 2007. Although an FBI investigation concluded in November 2007 that at least 14 of the shootings at Nisour Square were "unjustified and violated deadly-force rules," the prosecution of the Blackwater guards proved difficult and the case remained mired in various U.S. courts for years. It was not until October 2014 that the case was resolved, with four of the Blackwater employees convicted of various murder, manslaughter, and gun charges. One faces a mandatory life

sentence and the others mandatory minimum sentences of 30 years. Spencer S. Hsu, Victoria St. Martin, and Keith L. Alexander, "Four Blackwater Guards Found Guilty in 2007 Iraq Shootings of 31 Unarmed Civilians," *The Washington Post*, October 22, 2014.

28. David Isenberg, *Shadow Force: Private Security Contractors in Iraq,* London, United Kingdom (UK): Praeger Security International, 2009, pp. 79-80; Rubin and Kramer, "Iraqi Premier Says Blackwater Shootings Challenge His Nation's Sovereignty."

29. Ned Parker, "Blackwater gets OK to resume escorts," *Los Angeles Times*, September 22, 2007.

30. Report for Congress, Moshe Schwartz, "The Department of Defense's Use of Private Security Contractors in Afghanistan and Iraq: Background, Analysis, and Options for Congress," Report No. R40835, Washington, DC: Congressional Research Service, May 13, 2011, p. 22; Policy Paper, P. W. Singer, "Can't Win With 'Em, Can't Go to War Without 'Em: Private Military Contractors and Counterinsurgency," No. 4, Washington, DC: Brookings Institute, September 2007, p. 3.

31. Ibid.

32. Quote from Singer, "Can't Win With 'Em, Can't Go to War Without 'Em," p. 8.

33. DoD photo by Sergeant Marshall Thompson, "Ugandans [Image 2 of 6]," DVIDS Identifier 19607, March 14, 2006, Released to Public, available from *https://www.dvidshub.net/image/19607/ugandans.*

34. Quote from Singer, "Can't Win With 'Em, Can't Go to War Without 'Em," p. 8.

35. Ibid., pp. 7-8.

36. Steve Fainaru, "Guards in Iraq Cite Frequent Shootings," *The Washington Post*, October 3, 2007.

37. Steve Fainaru, "Where Military Rules Don't Apply," *The Washington Post*, September 20, 2007.

38. MNF-I, SECDEF Weekly Update, October 7-13, 2007.

39. "Crocker, Petraeus Testify Before the Senate Armed Services Committee on Iraq," *The Washington Post*, September 11, 2007; MNF-I, SECDEF Weekly Update, October 7-13, 2007.

40. MNF-I, SECDEF Weekly Update, November 11-17, 2007.

41. Thomas Ricks and Sudarsan Raghavan, "Private Security Puts Diplomats, Military at Odds," *The Washington Post*, September 26, 2007; Peter Spiegel, "Gates: U.S., guards are at odds in Iraq," *Los Angeles Times*, October 19, 2007.

42. MNF-I, SECDEF Weekly Update, October 7-13, 2007.

43. Interview, Lieutenant Colonel Joel Rayburn, CSA, OIF Study Group, with Major General (Ret.) Najim Jabouri, Washington, DC, March 12, 2013.

44. Michael Gordon and Wesley Morgan, "The General's Gambit," *Foreign Policy*, October 1, 2012, available from *http://foreignpolicy.com/2012/10/01/the-generals-gambit/*, accessed May 25, 2016.

45. Richard A. Oppel, Jr., "Foreign Fighters in Iraq Are Tied to Allies of U.S.," *The New York Times*, November 22, 2007, available from *http://www.nytimes.com/2007/11/22/world/middleeast/22fighters. html?pagewanted=all.*

46. MNF-I, SECDEF Weekly Update, September 23-29, 2007; Bill Roggio, "Senior al Qaeda in Iraq leader killed in airstrike," *Long War Journal,* September 29, 2007, available from *http://www.longwarjournal. org/archives/2007/09/senior_al_qaeda_in_i.php*, accessed May 25, 2016.

47. Oppel, "Foreign Fighters in Iraq Are Tied to Allies of U.S."

48. MNF-I, SECDEF Weekly Update, July 22-28, 2007.

49. Ibid., August 26-September 1, 2007; Oppel, "Foreign Fighters in Iraq Are Tied to Allies of U.S."

50. Oppel, "Foreign Fighters in Iraq Are Tied to Allies of U.S."

51. MNF-I, SECDEF Weekly Update, September 16-22, 2007, p. 2.

52. Ibid., September 23-29, 2007; Roggio, "Senior al Qaeda in Iraq leader killed in airstrike."

53. Images taken from "PI for 144 Individuals," Reference no. NMEC-2007-657689, West Point, NY: Combating Terrorism Center at West Point, (composite of original PDF p. 2 and English translation completion September 15, 2007, English PDF p. 1), Released to Public, available from *https://ctc.usma.edu/ harmony-program/pi-for-144-individuals-original-language-2/*.

54. Gordon and Morgan, "The General's Gambit."

55. Report, "Al-Qa'ida's Foreign Fighters in Iraq: a first look at the Sinjar Records," West Point, NY: Combating Terrorism Center, December 19, 2007, pp. 6, 21, available from *http://tarpley.net/docs/ CTCForeignFighter.19.Dec07.pdf*, accessed May 25, 2016.

56. Ibid., p. 8.

57. Ibid., pp. 9-10.

58. Ibid., pp. 16-18.

59. Ibid., pp. 22-23.

60. Ibid., p. 3.

61. Oppel, "Foreign Fighters in Iraq Are Tied to Allies of U.S."

62. MNF-I, SECDEF Weekly Update, October 28-November 3, 2007; and November 4-10, 2007.

63. Ibid., October 14-20, 2007.

64. Ibid.

65. Ibid., September 16-22, 2007.

66. Audio Msg, Ayman al-Zawahiri issued by As-Sahab Media to Muslims, The Search for International Terrorist Entities Institute, January 4, 2007, sub: Set Out and Support Your Brothers in Somalia-January 2007.

67. As-Sahab Media Releases Full Bin Ladin Audio Statement October 23, Reston, VA: Open Source Center, October 23, 2007, file no. FEA20071023375906.

68. Ibid.

69. Ibid.

70. Ibid.

71. Ibid.

72. Ibid.

73. MNF-I, SECDEF Weekly Update, October 21-27, 2007.

74. Lauren Frayer, "6,000 Sunnis pact with US in Iraq," Newsmine.org, November 28, 2007, available from *http://newsmine.org/content.php?ol=war-on-terror/iraq/insurgency/2007/07-sep-dec-sadr-ally/6000-sunnis-pace-with-us-in-iraq-November-2007.txt.*

75. Eric Hamilton, "Iraq Report: The Fight for Mosul, March 2003-March 2008," Washington, DC: Institute for the Study of War, March 2008, p. 13.

76. Interview, CSA OIF Study Group with Major General (Ret.) Jabouri, March 12, 2013.

77. Hamilton, "Iraq Report," p. 12.

78. Ibid., p. 13.

79. MNF-I, SECDEF Weekly Update, October 28-November 3, 2007.

80. Hamilton, "Iraq Report," p. 13.

81. MNF-I, SECDEF Weekly Update, November 18-25, 2007.

82. U.S. Air Force photo by Staff Sergeant Samuel Bendet, "Up Hill Battle," November 19, 2007, Released to Public, available from *https://www.flickr.com/photos/mnfiraq/4314589456/in/faves-138659840@N02/.*

83. Ms, *On Point*, Vol. IV, Chapter 5.

84. Ibid.

85. DoD photo by Sergeant Natalie Loucks, "Salman Pak Market Opens [Image 1 of 5]," DVIDS Identifier 80264, March 11, 2008, Released to Public, available from *https://www.dvidshub.net/image/80264/salman-pak-market-opens.*

86. Ms, *On Point*, Vol. IV, Chapter 5.

87. MNF-I, SECDEF Weekly Update, November 4-10, 2007; "Sunni group attacks al-Qaeda base," BBC, November 10, 2007, available from *http://news.bbc.co.uk/2/hi/middle_east/7088013.stm*, accessed May 25, 2016.

88. IntelCenter Terrorism Incident Reference (TIR): Iraq: 2007, Alexandria, VA: Tempest Publishing, 2008, pp. 454-455.

89. MNF-I, SECDEF Weekly Update, November 4-10, 2007.

90. Ibid., November 11-17, 2007.

91. Steven R. Hurst, "Sharp drop seen in U.S. deaths in Iraq," *USA Today*, October 23, 2007, available from *http://usatoday30.usatoday.com/news/world/2007-10-23-104709104_x.htm.*

92. MNF-I, SECDEF Weekly Update, November 11-17, 2007; Hurst, "Sharp drop seen in U.S. deaths in Iraq."

93. Report to Congress, General David H. Petraeus, Situation in Iraq, April 8-9, 2008, p. 3, available from *https://www.longwarjournal.org/multimedia/General%20Petraeus%20Testimony%20to%20Congress%20 8%20April%202008.pdf*, accessed June 4, 2018.

94. Rod Nordland, "Some Progress Seen in Baghdad," *Newsweek*, November 17, 2007.

95. Interview, CSA OIF Study Group with Colonel Brian R. Owens, April 29, 2014.

96. Interview, Combat Studies Institute (CSI) Contemporary Operations Study Team with Colonel Paul E. Funk II and Patrick R. Michaelis, February 4, 2010.

97. MNF-I, SECDEF Weekly Update, November 11-17, 2007.

98. Ibid.

99. Ibid.

100. Emma Sky, *The Unraveling, High Hopes and Missed Opportunities in Iraq*, New York: Public Affairs, 2015, pp. 233-234.

101. MNF-I, SECDEF Weekly Update, November 11-17, 2007.

102. Sky, *The Unraveling,* p. 237; MNF-I, SECDEF Weekly Update, November 26-December 2, 2007.

103. U.S. Army photo by Staff Sergeant Curt Cashour, "Stars & Sheiks," December 18, 2007, Released to Public, available from *https://www.flickr.com/photos/mnfiraq/4314724694/in/faves-138659840%40N02/.*

104. Steve Schippert and Nick Grace, "The Fiction of Abu Omar al-Baghdadi," *Threats Watch*, December 5, 2007.

105. Transcript of December 3, 2007, speech by Abu Omar al-Baghdadi. The Al-Siddiq Corps was a reference to Abu Bakr al-Siddiq, one of Mohammed's earliest supporters and the first Caliph after his death. Siddiq was particularly known for his military prowess and for his service as a protector of Islam.

106. Bill Roggio, "Al Qaeda in Iraq executes bombing offensive," *Long War Journal,* December 8, 2007, available from *http://www.longwarjournal.org/archives/2007/12/al_qaeda_in_iraq_exe.php*, accessed May 25, 2016; Bill Roggio, "The Awakening, al Qaeda clash in Iraq," *Long War Journal*, December 17, 2007, available from *https://www.longwarjournal.org/archives/2007/12/the_awakening_al_qae.php.*

107. Roggio, "Al Qaeda in Iraq executes bombing offensive,"; Roggio, "The Awakening."

108. Ms, *On Point*, Vol. IV, Chapter 5.

109. U.S. Army photo by Sergeant Ben Brody, "Commander's Call," December 29, 2007, Released to Public, available from *https://www.flickr.com/photos/mnfiraq/4314076319/in/photolist-7zdLAc.*

110. MNC-I Historian's Chronology, 2006-2008, p. 22.

111. Michael O'Hanlon and Jason Campbell, "Iraq Index," Washington, DC: Brookings Institution, March 31, 2008, pp. 13, 28.

112. MNF-I, SECDEF Weekly Update, October 14-20, 2007; Interview, Steven E. Clay, CSI Contemporary Operations Study Team, with Colonel James Hickey, February 2010.

113. O'Hanlon and Campbell, "Iraq Index."

114. MNF-I, SECDEF Weekly Update, December 3-9, 2007.

115. Ibid.

116. Hamilton, "Iraq Report," p. 15.

117. MNF-I, SECDEF Weekly Update, December 10-16, 2007.

118. Ibid., July 29-August 4, 2007; Michael R. Gordon, "U.S. Says Iran-Supplied Bomb Kills More Troops," *The New York Times*, August 8, 2007, available from *http://www.nytimes.com/2007/08/08/world/middleeast/08military.html?pagewanted=print&_r=0.*

119. MNF-I, SECDEF Weekly Update, September 16-22, 2007.

120. Ibid.

121. Ibid., September 30-October 6, 2007; October 14-20, 2007; and October 28-November 3, 2007.

122. Ibid., October 14-20, 2007.

123. Ibid., September 16-22, 2007; CSA OIF Study Group Chronology, September 24, 2007.

124. MNF-I, SECDEF Weekly Update, October 21-27, 2007.

125. Ibid., October 26-November 3, 2007.

126. Ibid.; and November 4-10, 2007.

127. Ibid., November 18-25 2007.

128. Ibid., September 30-October 6, 2007.

129. Ibid., October 14-20, 2007.

130. Ibid., October 21-27, 2007.

131. Ibid., October 28-November 3, 2007.

132. Ibid.

133. MNC-I Historian's Chronology, 2006-2008, p. 16.

134. Ibid., November 11-17, 2007.

135. Ibid., November 18-25, 2007.

136. Ibid.

137. Jim Michaels, "Roadside attacks fall in Iraq," *USA Today*, December 11, 2007, available from *http://usatoday30.usatoday.com/news/military/2007-12-10- EFPs_N.htm*, accessed November 4, 2015.

138. MNF-I, SECDEF Weekly Update, November 4-10, 2007.

139. Ibid., November 18-25, 2007.

140. Ibid., September 30-October 6, 2007; and October 28-November 3, 2007.

141. Strategic Debriefing Element Tactical Interrogation Report (SDE TIR) 200243-007, Captive Tag # N1228A-02, 18 1730 June 2007; SDE TIR 200243-041, Captive Tag # N1228A-02, 21 1530 December 2007.

142. SDE TIR 200243-046, Captive Tag # N1228A-02, 06 1930 January 2008.

143. Ibid.

144. MNF-I, SECDEF Weekly Update, November 26-December 2, 2007.

145. Mussab Al-Khairalla, "Powerful Iraq cleric may extend freeze on militia," Reuters, December 20, 2007, available from *http://uk.reuters.com/article/2007/12/20/uk-iraq-sadr- idUKKHA95483820071220.*

146. MNF-I, SECDEF Weekly Update, December 3-9, 2007; and December 10-16, 2007.

147. Ibid., December 17-23, 2007.

148. Ibid., December 24-30, 2007.

149. Ibid., December 31-January 6, 2008.

150. Ibid.

151. Ibid., December 10-16, 2007.

152. Ibid., December 3-9, 2007.

153. Ibid., January 7-13, 2008.

154. U.S. Marine Corps photo by Corporal Ira B. Goldfrank, "U.S. Army Lt. Gen. James M. Dubik, commanding general of Multi-National Security Transition Command, greets various Iraqi representatives from the Al Anbar Province at Al Asad Air Base, Iraq, Nov. 15, 2007," DIMOC Identifier 071115-M-AR449-002, November 15, 2007, Released to Public.

155. Interview, Vincent McLean, CSI Contemporary Operations Study Team, with Lieutenant General James Dubik, Commanding General, Multi-National Security Transition Command-Iraq (MNSTC-I) and Command Sergeant Major Tommy Williams, May 5, 2010.

156. Ibid.

157. Interview, Colonel Joel Rayburn, CSA OIF Study Group, with Lieutenant General (Ret.) Dubik, December 17, 2015.

158. Interview, CSI Contemporary Operations Study Team with Dubik and Williams, May 5, 2010, p. 22; MNF-I, SECDEF Weekly Update, December 10-16, 2007.

159. MNF-I, SECDEF Weekly Update, December 17-23, 2007.

160. Ibid., December 10-16, 2007; December 17-23, 2007; and January 21-27, 2008.

161. Interview, (name redacted) with Brigadier General Robin Swan, MNSTC-I, January 24, 2008; MNF-I, SECDEF Weekly Update, October 28-November 3, 2007; and January 21-27, 2008.

162. Interviews, CSI Contemporary Operations Study Team with Dubik and Williams, May 5, 2010; (name redacted) with Swan, January 24, 2008; MNF-I, SECDEF Weekly Update, November 4-10, 2007.

163. MNF-I, SECDEF Weekly Update, August 12-18, 2007.

164. Ibid., January 14-20, 2008.

165. Ibid., December 10-16, 2007.

166. Interview, CSA OIF Study Group with Lieutenant General (Ret.) Dubik, December 17, 2015.

167. MNF-I, SECDEF Weekly Update, September 16-22, 2007; and September 30-October 6, 2007.

168. Notes, Commanding General, meeting at U.S. Embassy with congressional delegation including Senator Charles T. Hagel (Nebraska), Petraeus Papers, April 15, 2007.

169. MNF-I, SECDEF Weekly Update, November 11-17, 2007; Interview, CSI Contemporary Operations Study Team with Dubik and Williams, May 5, 2010.

170. Interview, CSI Contemporary Operations Study Team with Dubik and Williams, May 5, 2010.

171. Ibid.; MNF-I, SECDEF Weekly Update, August 19-25, 2007; and September 30-October 6, 2007.

172. Interviews, (name redacted) with Swan, January 24, 2008; CSI Contemporary Operations Study Team with Dubik and Williams, May 5, 2010; MNF-I, SECDEF Weekly Update, November 4-10, 2007.

173. MNF-I, SECDEF Weekly Update, December 17-23, 2007.

174. Ibid.; October 14-20, 2007; and December 3-9, 2007.

175. Interview, CSA OIF Study Group with Dubik, December 17, 2015.

176. MNF-I, SECDEF Weekly Update, September 23-29, 2007.

177. Interview, CSA OIF Study Group with General David H. Petraeus, November 24, 2014.

178. Report, "Independent Commission on the Security Forces of Iraq," Washington, DC: Center for Strategic and International Studies, September 6, 2007, available from *https://permanent.access.gpo.gov/lps85852/isf.pdf*, accessed June 4, 2018.

179. E-mail, Lieutenant General H. R. McMaster to Rayburn, Subj: Ministry of Interior 2007, November 14, 2015.

180. Interview, CSA OIF Study Group with Dubik, December 17, 2015.

181. DoD photo by Staff Sergeant James Selesnick, "Paratroopers attend Iraqi police station opening in al-Ameen [Image 1 of 5]," DVIDS Identifier 175388, May 27, 2009, Released to Public, available from *https://www.dvidshub.net/image/175388/paratroopers-attend-iraqi-police-station-opening-al-ameen*.

182. Interview, CSA OIF Study Group with Dubik, December 17, 2015.

183. Ibid.

184. Ibid. MNF-I, SECDEF Weekly Update, November 4-10, 2007.

185. Ibid., November 26-December 2, 2007.

186. Interview, CSA OIF Study Group with Dubik, December 17, 2015.

187. MNF-I, SECDEF Weekly Update, April 7-13, 2007; June 3-9, 2007; and July 22-28, 2007; Notes, CENTCOM Commander's Conference, Petraeus Papers, July 14, 2007.

188. Press Briefing, Lieutenant General Raymond T. Odierno, Commander MNC-I, DoD, June 22, 2007; Discussion notes, Petraeus meeting with Minister of Defense Desmond Browne, Petraeus Papers, September 18, 2007.

189. Interview, Colonel James Powell, CSA OIF Study Group, with Lieutenant Colonel Kent Strader, MNC-I planner, March 26, 2014; MNF-I, SECDEF Weekly Update, November 11-17, 2007; February 25-March 2, 2008; and September 16-22, 2007.

190. Notes, CENTCOM Commander's Conference, Petraeus Papers, July 14, 2007; Interview, CSA OIF Study Group with Strader, March 26, 2014.

191. MNF-I, SECDEF Weekly Update, December 3-9, 2007; and January 7-13, 2008.

192. Discussion notes, Petraeus meeting with Browne, Petraeus Papers, September 18, 2007.

193. MNC-I, Operation Order (OPORD) 08-01, December 20, 2007.

194. MNF-I, SECDEF Weekly Update, July 1-7, 2007; MNC-I, OPORD 08-01, December 20, 2007. The SECDEF Weekly Update of September 23-29, 2007, observed that "of the 133 personnel who were supposed to round out the second tranche of PRTs by 30 September (originally by 31 August), 21 have not arrived and are not projected to arrive until November. Of the 81 civilian surge personnel requested to advise the ministries, 32 have arrived, with no firm date for the remainder."

195. Ibid.; Briefing, MNC-I, Scalable Strike Packages as part of Multi-National Division-Southeast (MND-SE), n.d.

196. MNF-I, SECDEF Weekly Update, July 15-21, 2007; MNC-I, Fragmentary Order 545 (Scaleable Strike Packages) to MNC-I, OPORD 07-01, December 14, 2007.

197. MNF-I, SECDEF Weekly Update, October 7-13, 2007; and December 24-30, 2007.

198. Ibid., September 23-29, 2007; December 24-30, 2007; October 21-27, 2007; and December 17-23, 2007.

199. Ibid., November 11-17, 2007.

200. Ibid., January 14-20, 2008.

201. Ibid.; January 21-27, 2008; and January 28-February 3, 2008.

202. Ibid., October 14-20, 2007; and October 28-November 3, 2007.

203. Ibid., November 26-December 2, 2007.

204. DoD photo courtesy of Headquarters, 1st Cavalry Division, Public Affairs, "Iraqi VP Meets With MND-B CG," DVIDS Identifier 33903, December 06, 2006, Released to Public, available from *https://www.dvidshub.net/image/33903/iraqi-vp-meets-with-mnd-b-cg*.

205. Ibid., November 4-10, 2007.

206. Ibid., October 7-13, 2007; and November 18-25, 2007.

207. Ibid., February 11-17, 2008.

208. Ibid., October 28-November 3, 2007.

209. Ibid., November 4-10, 2007.

210. Peter Symonds, "Turkish military flexes its muscles in northern Iraq," World Socialist Web Site, June 7, 2007, available from *https://www.wsws.org/en/articles/2007/06/turk-j07.html*.

211. MNF-I, SECDEF Weekly Update, October 7-13, 2007.

212. Ibid., October 21-27, 2007.

213. Ibid.; and October 28-November 3, 2007.

214. Ibid.

215. "Turkish jets bomb Kurdish rebel hideouts in northern Iraq," *Jerusalem Post*, January 15, 2008, available from *http://www.jpost.com/Middle-East/Turkish-jets-bomb-Kurdish-rebel-hideouts-in-northern-Iraq,*

accessed May 25, 2016; "Turkey's empty gesture," *The New York Times*, December 18, 2007, available from *http://www.nytimes.com/2007/12/18/opinion/18iht-edturkey.html?_r=0*.

216. MNF-I, SECDEF Weekly Update, December 10-16, 2007.

217. Selcuk Gokoluk, "Turkey says air strikes in Iraq hit their targets," Reuters, December 17, 2007, available from *http://www.reuters.com/article/2007/12/17/idUSL17436786*.

218. MNF-I, SECDEF Weekly Update, December 10-16, 2007.

219. Ibid., December 17-23, 2007.

220. Ibid., October 7-13, 2007.

221. Ibid., October 21-27, 2007.

222. Ibid., November 4-10, 2007.

223. Ibid., December 10-16, 2007.

224. Ibid., December 17-23, 2007.

225. Ibid.

226. Ibid., December 24-30, 2007; and December 31, 2007-January 6, 2008.

227. Ibid., November 18-25, 2007.

228. Ibid., November 26-December 2, 2007; and October 21-27, 2007.

229. Ibid., December 17-23, 2007.

230. Ibid., December 31, 2007-January 6, 2008.

231. Ibid.

232. Ibid.

233. Ibid., December 24-30, 2007.

234. Ibid.

235. Ibid.

236. Ibid.

237. Ibid.

238. Ibid.

CHAPTER 7

ENABLING THE SURGE, 2007-2008

The increase in U.S. forces' operational tempo and effectiveness that General David Petraeus noted in his January 2008 retrospective on the first year of the surge could not have taken place without the addition of thousands of support forces and significant changes in the way the United States prosecuted its campaign in Iraq. The surge in Iraq was substantially more than just the deployment of 21,000 additional combat troops and roughly 8,000 support troops that accompanied them. Several major supporting factors enabled the coalition's combat forces to conduct the security operations of the surge campaign and to pivot into large-scale stabilization activities that helped tamp down Iraq's sectarian civil war. The campaign of 2007-2008 was enabled by an unusual level of U.S. civil-military unity of effort and focus from the strategic to the tactical levels. The fielding and maturation of a series of technological enablers and innovative practices greatly enhanced coalition and Iraqi units' ability to engage in close fights with enemy groups and to survive the improvised explosive devices (IEDs) that had become the most common enemy weapon.

The coalition's intelligence capabilities had matured as well, with thousands of intelligence professionals gaining the experience and knowledge base needed to support counterinsurgency and stabilization operations. Coalition units also enjoyed access to sophisticated intelligence resources at lower echelons than ever before, giving tactical U.S. units an unprecedented advantage in their local operations. The idea of "money as a weapon system" took root at all levels of the coalition's operations, enabling both the spread of the Awakening and the dismantling of important portions of the insurgency's finances. Finally, the coalition was able largely to regain control of its own detention centers, though the results of its rehabilitation programs were mixed. By early 2008, Multi-National Force-Iraq (MNF-I) and its units were operating with new capabilities and new ways of integrating them that gave the operations of the surge campaign a different look and feel than those that had preceded them.

GENERATING UNITY OF EFFORT

The Civil-Military Campaign Plan

Beyond additional troops, implementing the new strategy in 2007-2008 required strategic coherence, active leadership, and an uncommon degree of U.S. civil-military cooperation. President George W. Bush's level of direct involvement in the Iraq campaign had grown over time, as had his direct interaction with senior U.S. officials in Baghdad. By the onset of the surge, the President had instituted regular, typically bi-weekly, meetings of the National Security Council (NSC) Principals Committee on the situation in Iraq that featured the MNF-I commander and the U.S. ambassador reporting via video teleconference from Baghdad, and often included the U.S. Central Command (CENTCOM) commander as well. Throughout the surge, Petraeus and Ambassador Ryan Crocker were able to offer their unfiltered updates on the situation directly to the NSC principals and often received immediate guidance. This arrangement, which had begun when General George Casey, Jr., was in command in Baghdad, was a significant change to the traditional procedure in which the Chairman of the Joint Chiefs of Staff represented the views of field commanders in NSC meetings.

Source: DoD photo by Cherie Thurlby (Released).

Secretary of Defense Robert M. Gates With U.S. Ambassador to Iraq Ryan Crocker and General David Petraeus.[1]

Having the top U.S. military commander and diplomat in Iraq report to the NSC principals as a team also enabled Petraeus and Crocker to keep their respective home agencies' military and diplomatic activities aligned in a way that had been impossible to do in the early years of the war. With the support of Bush and Gates, Petraeus aimed to ensure that MNF-I's security operations supported the larger political goals of the President's New Way Forward. The Joint Strategic Assessment Team (JSAT) launched by Petraeus and Crocker in March 2007 provided the basis for a joint embassy and force campaign plan with a common mission statement and the political line of effort, rather than security, as the main effort.[2]

Petraeus and Crocker oversaw the execution and integration of the joint civil-military campaign plan from offices in Baghdad's Republican Palace that were separated only by a waiting room. The two men met daily to coordinate their activities. About every 6 weeks, they jointly chaired the Campaign Assessment and Synchronization Board, in which senior leaders from the military commands and the U.S. Embassy teamed up to examine each line of effort in the Joint Campaign Plan, with coalition ambassadors and United Nations (UN) representatives usually present. Petraeus and Crocker also met with Prime Minister Nuri al-Maliki together several times a week, usually choreographing what each would say to the Iraqi leader beforehand—sometimes in a "good cop, bad cop" approach.

Within the theater headquarters, Petraeus created or gave new emphasis to several staff elements to execute the surge. Three, in particular, were noteworthy for their contribution to the conduct of a comprehensive counterinsurgency campaign. Headed by a British major general and a senior State Department officer, the Force Strategic Engagement Cell met with Sunni and Shi'a insurgents in an attempt to identify "reconcilables" and bring them into some kind of accommodation with the Iraqi Government. Petraeus had ordered the formation of this cell after he returned to Iraq in 2007, reflecting a tenet in his counterinsurgency guidance: "We must strive to make the reconcilables part of the solution, even as we identify, pursue, and kill, capture, or drive out the irreconcilables."[3] Next, to help sort the reconcilables from irreconcilables, the Strategic Debriefing Element that interrogated high-level detainees took on renewed importance, enabling the command to have extensive conversations with senior detainees and, in the process, "map" enemy networks and better gauge their motivations.

Finally, the MNF-I Information Operations (IO) Task Force provided tailored media products as part of a psychological operations effort to influence attitudes in the Iraqi population and encourage rejection of violent extremists. These sophisticated information operations served as an important force multiplier. Taking guidance from Petraeus, the IO Task Force sought to "turn our enemies' bankrupt messages, extremist ideologies, oppressive practices, and indiscriminate violence against them."[4]

The joint campaign plan also served to align and synchronize all the U.S. military and coalition efforts in theater with the MNF-I strategic approach, as happened when the Multi-National Security Transition Command-Iraq (MNSTC-I) changed its objective in mid-2007 to partnering with and building Iraqi security force (ISF) capacity to better align with MNC-I, the main effort. At the same time, the shift in the theater strategy also served to synchronize the efforts of special operations forces into the overall theater campaign. These organizations all participated in MNF-I's daily Battle Update Assessment, but Petraeus also gathered his senior commanders at weekly meetings in which the commanders of Multi-National Force-West (MNF-W), the U.S. Army Corps of Engineers Gulf Regional Division, the CENTCOM Joint Contracting Command, and Task Force 134 joined as well. These sessions complemented the senior commanders' daily dialogue in the Battle Update Assessment and were typically followed by detailed updates and planning sessions with Petraeus and key subordinate commanders.[5]

The Civilian Surge

Alongside the deployment of additional U.S. troops, 2007 and 2008 witnessed the deployment of a smaller, but significant, contingent of U.S. civilians to help execute the civil-military campaign in Iraq. However, across the U.S. Government, coordination dilemmas, institutional cultures, and a lack of execution oversight or accountability meant that the civilian surge lagged behind the military deployment.

An important component of Bush's New Way Forward strategy was to increase the number of civilians serving with provincial reconstruction teams (PRTs) in Iraq from about

100 civilians in early 2007 to over 450 by the end of the year.[6] In addition to increasing the size of each team, the new PRT program, renamed embedded provincial reconstruction teams (EPRTs), added personnel that specifically focused on facilitating reconciliation initiatives, economic development, and delivery of essential public services at district level and below. By the end of 2008, the State Department had a total of 14 EPRTs in Baghdad, Anbar, north Babil, and southern Diyala.[7]

The civilian staffing for this expansion of the PRT program was a source of friction. The State Department and the U.S. Agency for International Development (USAID) struggled to provide the foreign service officers, administrative personnel, and Arabic language interpreters to fill the new requirements.[8] Diplomats who specialized in the Arab world were already fully committed, and the resulting shortfall had to be filled by the Department of Defense (DoD) or by private-sector experts hired as temporary State Department employees.[9] By the time the second phase of the embedded PRTs came into theater, 99 of the 133 personnel on those teams were DoD military and civilians.[10] Both Gates and Army Chief of Staff General Casey believed the small number of foreign service officers serving on the PRTs represented the State Department's lack of commitment to the Iraq campaign, a sentiment that Secretary of State Condoleezza Rice resented.[11]

The missions of the EPRTs evolved over time. Although the EPRTs were conceived to focus on sustainable, longer-term reconciliation, governance and development projects, their priorities gradually shifted to more immediate stabilization activities that would tamp down attacks against coalition soldiers.[12] Some EPRT leaders were uncomfortable answering directly to military commanders instead of the U.S. Embassy, though Rice recalled that "there was never any question that the PRTs would be run by the battle space owner," and Crocker worked to enforce that arrangement.[13] Additionally, the PRTs and EPRTs both had to rely on U.S. military forces for sustainment and security, particularly those that were co-located with U.S. military units.

In general, shortfalls in the U.S. Government civilian ranks in Iraq in 2007 and 2008 resulted in an increase in contractors providing services ranging from security to engineering and technical support, construction, economic development, and humanitarian assistance.[14] DoD had the lion's share, with 149,000 DoD contract personnel in Iraq and another 30,300 elsewhere in the CENTCOM area of responsibility, though some of the latter supported operations in Afghanistan rather than Iraq. The State Department had approximately 6,700 contractors in Iraq, of which 2,300 were U.S. citizens, and about 40 percent of the department's total provided security. By mid-2007, USAID directly employed another 3,500 contractors, of which about 2,900 were Iraqis, and sponsored programs that employed another 75,000 Iraqis. The Departments of Justice, Homeland Security, Agriculture, Commerce, Transportation, and Treasury employed about 500 additional contractors among them.[15] Throughout the surge, the number of U.S.-employed contractors in Iraq exceeded the strength of U.S. military forces in the country, demonstrating the degree to which MNF-I's operations depended on civilian manpower and support.

ENABLING THE CLOSE FIGHT

Improved Coordination With Special Operations Forces

One of the central components of Petraeus's strategy was to use special operations forces (SOF) to strike at the generators of sectarian violence—namely al-Qaeda in Iraq (AQI) and Shi'a militias—to help buy time and space for the political process to develop. By 2007, a combination of internal developments and improved relationships with conventional forces had enabled special operations forces to fulfill their assigned mission to a degree that had not been possible previously. Better intelligence, surveillance, and reconnaissance assets, as well as revised tactics that sped up the organization's targeting cycle, led the number of monthly raids conducted in Iraq to jump from 18 in August 2004 to 300 in August 2006.[16] The withering series of nightly attacks stunned its sectarian opponents, putting them into a reactive mode that helped tactical commanders regain the initiative on the battlefield as well as operational leaders to advance the political process in Baghdad.

Yet the commandos' crushing pace could not have been implemented without dramatically improved relations with the Army and Marine forces responsible for battle space across Iraq. While some coordination challenges remained, by and large, relations between the two elements had improved considerably from 2005 to 2006—which itself was a period of marked improvement from the beginning of the war. Many leaders on both sides benefitted from trust established across multiple deployments to Iraq or Afghanistan, where the two elements learned how to best partner for synergistic effects. Officers who had been battalion commanders in 2003 and 2004 had returned in 2006 and 2007 as brigade staff officers and commanders, with similar increases in responsibility for more junior officers. Reflecting on that period, one special operations task force commander conceded, "We really didn't mesh completely with the conventional war effort [in Iraq] until 2006 [and] 2007."[17] By 2007, the effects of SOF's pace of intelligence-driven raids against high-value targets and the presence of conventional units often were mutually reinforcing, improving security while accruing additional intelligence to keep the enemy off-balance. A symbiotic relationship had developed in most locations where each element provided its strengths, compensating for the other force's weaknesses. Conventional units provided quick reaction forces, logistics support, evacuation, and an understanding of the local battlefield, while SOF provided intelligence, precision strike capabilities, flexibility, and speed. In particular, when special operations elements shared their in-theater document exploitation capabilities and technical capabilities, conventional forces benefited greatly.

Despite the progress, problems remained. There were still examples in 2007 of poorly coordinated SOF raids that produced collateral damage that set back conventional units' counterinsurgency efforts. In addition, there were problems coordinating priorities between rotating SOF elements that caused a lack of continuity and difficulties synchronizing the SOF effort with MNC-I's priorities. While overall conventional-SOF coordination was indeed getting better, there was still room for improvement.[18]

The Counter-IED Effort and Mine Resistant Ambush Protected (MRAP) Vehicles

From the outset of the surge, Gates placed heavy emphasis on efforts to counter the insurgents' use of IEDs, the weapon that caused a majority of coalition casualties. By late 2006, there were over 1,200 attacks and attempted attacks per week and an average of over 50 IED explosions every day, despite more than 3 years of work by the U.S. military on countermeasures.[19] IEDs had been the insurgents' weapon of choice because of their simple construction, the ready availability of the materials to make them, and their effectiveness against coalition forces' superior military systems and vehicles.[20] In June 2003, Commander of CENTCOM General John Abizaid had declared the IED to be his "No. 1 threat." Almost 3 years later, in March 2006, Bush announced that defeating the IED threat was a top priority.[21] From 2005 until the spring of 2008, IEDs were responsible for well over half of U.S. fatalities in Iraq, and the IED challenge seized media and public attention.

In 2007, counter-IED efforts matured to such a degree, when complemented by the rapid fielding of vehicles with more effective armor protection, that they constituted an essential enabler for the surge of forces. What began as an ad-hoc 12-member Army counter-IED task force in 2003 evolved by 2006 into the Joint Improvised Explosive Device Defeat Organization (JIEDDO), a large DoD sub-agency whose mission was to "defeat the device, attack the network, [and] train the force" by disseminating effective counter-IED tactics, techniques, and procedures to units in the field.[22] By 2007, JIEDDO had a staff of 3,100 and an annual budget of over $4 billion. Under retired Army General Montgomery Meigs, JIEDDO and its predecessor organizations pursued an approach dubbed "left of boom" that, consistent with the U.S. Army's preference for initiative and offensive action, focused on attacking the networks of bomb builders and facilitators in order to find IEDs and prevent them from exploding.[23]

While JIEDDO's early years involved many of the growing pains experienced by newly formed government organizations, by the surge period, the group was having an operational level effect. Between January 2007 and June 2009, from the time the surge was announced to the withdrawal of coalition forces from Iraq's cities, JIEDDO launched 29 different initiatives to counter IEDs, often pushing technical assets down to the brigade level or below in order to enable ground commanders in the tactical fight.[24] Technical advances in IED forensics were some of the most effective initiatives, linking those responsible for the deadly weapons to their progeny with enough confidence to be able to arrest and detain the builders in addition to the triggermen. During the surge, the original IED forensics cell, the Combined Explosives Cell (CEXC), grew into multiple cells that served as crime scene investigation-type teams for the counter-IED fight. CEXC teams consisted of intelligence, law enforcement, and explosives experts, as well as electrical engineers, information technology experts, and intelligence analysts who investigated IED incidents and surveyed post-blast sites for fingerprints, telltale signs of specific bomb makers, and unique aspects of how devices were employed. The counter-IED effort also brought new emphasis on Shi'a militants sponsored by the Iranian regime. JIEDDO funded additional personnel in Iraq from the Defense Intelligence Agency's Joint Intelligence Task Force-Combating Terrorism, to provide advanced analysis and actionable intelligence about Iranian-sponsored militant groups employing IEDs that contained EFPs.

An important part of JIEDDO's operations was the Counter-IED Operations and Integration Center (COIC), which reached full capability in 2007 as a supporting element to General Raymond T. Odierno's III Corps headquarters after the corps assumed duties as MNC-I. The COIC provided essential intelligence for attacking networks of IED makers, trainers, and financiers and maintaining awareness of IED developments worldwide. Under its director, Colonel James B. Hickey, the COIC generated unique analyses of attack trends and helped shed important light on the operational posture and intentions of the coalition's enemies. The COIC played a major role in 2007-2008 by helping Odierno and an adaptive MNC-I make tough choices about how to employ forces and their relationship to key terrain and a thinking enemy. Even so, when XVIII Airborne Corps headquarters assumed the MNC-I mission from III Corps in early 2008, the COIC was dissolved and its functions migrated to other MNC-I staff sections or to JIEDDO.

The integration of U.S. and multinational counter-IED capabilities fell to Combined Joint Task Force (CJTF) TROY. Initially established in 2005, Task Force TROY was staffed by joint service explosive ordinance disposal (EOD) technicians and a diverse group of subject matter experts, including some from the United Kingdom (UK) and Australia, who brought a depth of EOD and electronic warfare expertise to the task. With teams in direct support of multinational divisions and combat brigades, CJTF TROY conducted weapons technical intelligence collection and exploitation to defeat IED networks. It also disseminated actionable intelligence and kept coalition and Iraqi units informed about new counter-IED tactics, techniques, and procedures.[25]

Task Force Observe, Detect, Identify, and Neutralize (ODIN) represented another counter-IED innovation during the surge. In 2006, Vice Chief of Staff of the Army General Richard Cody, who had overseen the creation of the Joint IED Defeat Organization, saw a critical requirement to "win back the roads" from IEDs and help improve the coalition and Iraqi units' freedom of movement.[26] The result was the creation of Task Force (TF) ODIN, an aviation battalion equipped and outfitted to "improve the detection of roadside bombs before they explode[d], and to strike more adversaries safely, from a distance."[27] The TF ODIN battalion consisted of three companies, each with different platforms and equipment to detect and destroy IEDs before coalition troops encountered them. These included C-12 Cessnas refitted for aerial reconnaissance and real-time imagery transmission, the Warrior Alpha and Shadow unmanned aerial vehicles (UAVs), and the Constant Hawk forensic back-tracking system capable of detecting the point of origin for IED attacks.[28] After fielding at Fort Hood, TX, Task Force ODIN deployed to Camp Speicher near Tikrit in July 2007 to support of commanders at the brigade level and below.

The Push for MRAPs

Decreasing the vulnerability of the armored vehicles used by the coalition proved one of the most difficult challenges to the counter-IED effort. Through 2007, the United States and its allies relied heavily upon High Mobility Multi-Purpose Wheeled Vehicles (HMMWVs) for daily operations, but its basic chassis and frame offered limited ability to improve protection against IEDs. As the basic vehicle had been retrofitted as much as possible with armored shields, improved doors, and better floor armor, any further improvements in protection would require the fielding of an entirely new vehicle. Soon after Gates became the Secretary of Defense (SECDEF), he reviewed the programs that aimed to replace the HMMWV and was shocked by what he felt was a lack of progress. After Gates ordered the process accelerated, the search quickly settled on the MRAP vehicle as the best alternative. MRAPs were armored trucks based on South African vehicles used in conflicts in Angola and Rhodesia that had a V-shaped hull designed to channel the blast from land mines or IEDs away from the crew compartment.

Source: DoD photo by Master Sergeant Paul Tuttle (Released).

An MRAP Vehicle Arrives in Kuwait.[29]

Gates believed the program to replace the HMMWV with a more survivable vehicle had languished in the Pentagon from 2004-2006 primarily due to what he called "next war-it is," a focus on preparing for hypothetical future wars rather than winning the current war in Iraq.[30] To a degree, this resistance was a legacy of the 1986 Goldwater-Nichols Defense Reform Act in which the uniformed services focused on organizing, training, and equipping forces for future conflicts while regional combatant commanders had responsibility for conducting contingency operations. That divergence in purpose gave the service headquarters' bureaucracies little incentive to modify their programs for current operations. To complicate matters further, the framers of Goldwater-Nichols had envisioned that future demands on the force would consist of discrete, short-duration contingencies, rather than the extended conflict of Operation IRAQI FREEDOM. Faced with limited budgets, the institutional Army and Marines experienced considerable tension between the demand to field a vehicle such as the MRAP—which might only be useful for the conflict in Iraq—and developing future combat systems that might be needed to fight a peer competitor. The procurement and sustainment costs made funding both priorities impossible, even with the supplemental appropriations received from Congress.

Indeed, the Army's program to field a new reconnaissance helicopter, the Comanche, had already collapsed under the weight of budgetary pressures, and by 2009, the Army's new armored vehicle program would also be canceled. Prior to the surge, this tension between current and future needs had been lessened somewhat by CJTF-7 and MNF-I's campaign plans, which set concrete, even if shifting, dates for troop withdrawals and a transition of security to Iraqi authorities. Bush's decision to surge forces to Iraq and his demand that the war had to be won effectively resolved the tension in favor of developing a new vehicle capable of surviving IEDs and ambushes in Iraq and Afghanistan.

Fielding MRAPs in Iraq quickly became a priority for both Gates and Petraeus because they provided a compounding effect on the battlefield. In addition to being much more effective against the IED threat than other combat vehicles, once fielded in Iraq the MRAPs would free up thousands of HMMWVs that MNF-I could transfer to the Iraqi security forces to replace the ISF's ubiquitous light-skinned commercial pickup trucks.[31] Coalition and Iraqi commanders alike believed the introduction of armored HMMWVs to the ISF would improve Iraqi troops' survivability, freedom of movement, and willingness to patrol.

Once MRAPs began to arrive in Iraq, the advantage of the level of protection they provided became evident quickly. In January 2008, Petraeus notified Gates that "10 MRAPs have been struck by IEDs to date and every soldier has walked away" with only minor injuries.[32] The MRAP was not invincible: on April 12, 2008, the first U.S. Soldier was killed in an MRAP when an EFP pierced his vehicle in Baghdad.[33] Nevertheless, although EFP attacks increased by 40 percent between February and April 2008, deaths from IEDs decreased by 17 percent over the same period. When the first MRAPs arrived in Iraq in 2007, 60 percent of all U.S. casualties were a result of IEDs, but this rate plummeted to 5 percent by the end of 2008, when 10,000 of the vehicles had been fielded.[34] Several U.S. Government studies estimated the impact MRAPs would have had in Iraq had they been fielded when the Defense Department first received an urgent needs request from CENTCOM and MNF-I in February 2005. At the lowest end, these studies estimated that speeding the fielding of MRAPs by 2 years likely would have reduced U.S. casualties by 50 percent. Other estimates ranged as high as an 80 percent reduction in casualties.[35]

The Intelligence, Surveillance, and Reconnaissance (ISR) Surge

In addition to MRAPs, Gates also played a decisive role in deploying additional intelligence, surveillance, and reconnaissance assets to Iraq during the surge. Writing in *Foreign Affairs* in 2009, Gates noted that it had been "necessary to go outside the normal bureaucratic process" to counter-IEDs, build MRAPs, and quickly expand ISR capability.[36] By April 2008, Gates had doubled the ISR capacity in the Iraq theater of operations, but expressed his frustration that "our services are still not moving aggressively in wartime to provide resources needed now on the battlefield." Accordingly, Gates created a new ISR task force to focus on getting additional ISR support to deployed forces and exploring "more innovation and bold new ways" to assist the war fighter.[37] These included small unmanned aerial vehicles (UAVs), blimps and aerostats, Predators, and Task Force ODIN's C-12 aircraft. A program supplied by the National Security Agency (NSA) also helped by speeding up the processing of the information collected by the additional ISR platforms arriving in Iraq.[38]

Source: U.S. Army photo by 1st Lieutenant Jason Sweeney (Released).

Contractors Load Hellfire Missiles onto an MQ-1C Gray Eagle in Iraq.[39]

During 2003-2004, the operational commands in Iraq could count on at most two UAV systems to meet all of their full-motion video (FMV) requirements, and most divisions and brigade combat teams (BCTs) had no capability at all. By 2007-2008, MNC-I had daily support from at least 12 FMV systems and was pushing them to the lowest possible echelon. This increase in ISR capability was most apparent at the BCT level. The BCTs of 2003 had little ISR or analytical capability of their own, but by 2007-2008, BCTs had three times the analytic capability and twice the human intelligence capability of a 2003 brigade combat team. Additionally, each BCT had an organic tactical UAV platoon that could provide 18 hours of full-motion video surveillance coverage a day, and BCTs could often count on additional FMV support from corps' assets allocated to support division operations. The U.S. brigades of 2007-2008 also had much greater bandwidth to handle internal communications needs and to link to higher echelon intelligence organizations.[40] The decentralization of ISR assets and the increased connectivity among brigades, battalions, and companies enhanced commanders' agility while giving corps and higher echelons immediate visibility and support. As Petraeus reported to Gates, by 2007 these factors enabled Army BCTs to execute missions once solely reserved for SOF, including operations against high-value enemy targets. More robust ISR and other intelligence enablers pushed down to lower echelons also provided new support to nontraditional missions such as reconciliation, key leader engagements, border security, ISF development, and detainee release decisions. The units who were carrying out these tasks were among the largest consumers of intelligence information during the surge.[41]

Biometrics and Population Control

Like ISR, the fielding of biometric scanning capability to tactical units proved to be a valuable technological enabler for the coalition. In a campaign in which the enemy hid among the population, coalition units found the Iraqi insurgents' anonymity a constant challenge. The basic task of identifying Iraqis was often a murky proposition. Iraqi personal identification documents were easily forged, while the coalition's sporadic attempts to track the Iraqi population by conducting censuses had sectarian and political implications that made the surveys difficult to perform.[42] Census figures potentially affected the major political parties' claims to particular neighborhoods and could even jeopardize the parties' shares of oil revenues. To identify persons of interest better, MNC-I fielded biometric scanners as the surge began that were portable and simple enough for Soldiers to use on the streets. These biometric tools allowed U.S. forces to scan fingerprints and irises during routine operations and then gradually build a personal identification database.[43] Eventually, the coalition had the means to trace fingerprints found on IEDs and match them to biometric data gathered elsewhere, an effect that was compounded when JIEDDO was able to field remotely operated robots to defuse IEDs and at the same time collect biometric data, rather than having the data disappear upon detonation.[44] By the end of the surge, the coalition had matched over 1,700 sets of fingerprints to those who had placed the IED.[45] The use of biometrics had a palpable effect at the tactical level, where some U.S. officers noted that once enemy fighters lost their anonymity, they were quick to flee for fear of capture.[46]

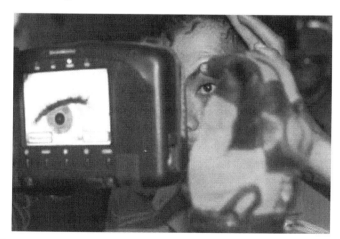

Source: U.S. Army photo by Staff Sergeant Robert DeDeaux (Released).

U.S. Troops Scan an Iraqi With Handheld Biometric Equipment.[47]

Tracking Iraqi identity also extended to the ISF and Awakening. As the coalition began to field M16 rifles to the Iraq military and police in 2007, each weapon was individually tagged to its Iraqi recipient's fingerprint and iris scan.[48] Similarly, the coalition collected biometric data for all concerned local citizens (CLCs), a policy which discouraged those irregular forces from returning to the insurgency. Additionally, as Prime Minister Maliki became concerned toward the end of the surge about the size and potential influence of the CLCs, Petraeus and Odierno tried to mitigate these concerns by showing that rather than constituting a "hidden army" as Maliki feared, the CLCs were identifiable and controllable because their biometric data had been cataloged.[49]

The cataloging of Sunni irregulars was a tool that cut two ways. The gathering of the members' biometric data helped the coalition ensure their good behavior, and knowledge that the database existed helped allay Maliki's concerns about the Awakening in 2007-2008. As U.S. forces began withdrawing from Iraq later in the war, the data would also make it possible for Maliki government officials to track and purge some of the very people who had been most responsible for tamping down the Sunni insurgency.

THE INTELLIGENCE WAR

Innovations among operational and tactical commanders from 2005 to 2007, who learned on the job how to conduct counterinsurgency operations, were equally matched by Army and Marine intelligence personnel who made creative adaptations to doctrine and policies in order to improve their contributions to the war effort. Specifically, organizations and leaders who had spent most of their professional lives training to fight massed armored formations of peer competitors retooled themselves to provide better understanding of the social fissures and political struggles that caused intercommunal violence and fueled Iraq's insurgent groups. By 2007, coalition intelligence leaders and analysts at all levels had begun to accumulate the experience and knowledge needed to understand the motivations and relationships among Iraq's various personalities, groups, and tribes. Four years into the war, the coalition could draw on a large pool of civilians, military service members, and contractors who had served in intelligence roles ranging from the tactical to strategic levels. These professionals were far better equipped than they had been in 2003-2004 to support the full range of missions and tasks demanded by a counterinsurgency and stabilization campaign that varied from combat operations to political-economic issues and security force development.[50]

As coalition intelligence leaders sought to optimize their organizational structure and resources, one approach that proved effective was the assignment of intelligence liaison officers (LNOs) to counterpart organizations. The range of entities that received intelligence LNOs included the Kurdistan Regional Government; Iraqi National Intelligence Service (INIS); Iraqi Operational Centers (National Operations Center, and Baghdad Operations Command); Multi-National Division-South East (MND-SE); Multi-National Division-Central South (MND-CS), and even some military transition teams (MiTTs) operating with ISF. MNSTC-I also assisted in the development of Iraqi intelligence capabilities within the Ministry of Defense and the Ministry of Interior, while helping to coordinate the activities of the INIS and the Iraqi National Security Adviser.[51]

At the tactical level, recommendations made in early 2005 to push intelligence capabilities to division and below bore fruit in 2007. Until that time, the corps and division analysis and control elements were the main hubs of coalition intelligence, in keeping with the Army's traditional doctrinal perspective and reflective of the fact that the signal intelligence, imagery intelligence, and human intelligence capabilities and tools needed for targeting networked insurgent or terrorist organizations simply were not widely available before late 2006. Without those capabilities at division and brigade levels, it was difficult to develop targets and pursue the enemy across different coalition units' areas of operation, particularly because coalition unit boundaries did not match those of enemy networks.[52] But as the coalition commands began to distribute integrated intelligence capabilities more broadly across the force, intelligence cells were able to develop and share good targeting sets across unit boundaries, resulting in more constant pressure on enemy groups.[53] Even before the surge, the Army had recognized the need for dedicated military intelligence personnel at the lowest tactical level to support the coalition campaign's focus on enemy networks and population security. Tactical intelligence leaders often created ad hoc intelligence support teams to bring biometric, analytical, communications, mapping, and document exploitation systems to company and even platoon-level operations. By the time of the surge, these arrangements had become more formal. The BCTs of 2007 and later received national intelligence assets and capabilities to support tactical operations, and often even had national agency personnel such as cryptologists embedded at the brigade level, with connectivity back to their home agencies enabling them to bring intelligence directly to frontline units.[54]

These changes represented a significant shift for the U.S. intelligence community, especially the Defense Intelligence Agency (DIA). The Iraq Study Group (ISG) reported in December 2006 that DIA had fewer than 10 analysts with more than 2 years of experience in studying the Iraqi insurgency and concluded that the U.S. intelligence community should implement "a better personnel system to keep analytic expertise focused on the insurgency. They are not doing enough to map the insurgency, dissect it, and understand it on a national and provincial level."[55] DIA's official response "clarified" that instead of 10 DIA analysts who had studied the Iraq insurgency for more than 2 years, the number was closer to 20. In conjunction with the President's New Way Forward, the ISG report served as a wake-up call that led DIA and other national agencies to change their posture in Iraq.

In early 2007, DIA Director Lieutenant General Michael Maples began committing additional DIA resources and personnel to Iraq, resulting in higher numbers of intelligence operators and analysts forward deployed at lower echelons. Under Maples's direction, DIA established a large forward presence of analytical support in Iraq, while nearly tripling the size of its Pentagon-based Iraq task force to provide enhanced reachback support and to build a cadre of experienced analysts who could rotate into the theater. Other agencies such as National Geospatial Agency, National Ground Intelligence Center, and the NSA followed suit. As an important enabler, DIA coordinated a unified intelligence operation over multiple time zones, managing the flow of personnel, support requirements, and work among Iraq, CENTCOM, and the national level agencies.[56] As these national agencies became integrated into collection and analytical structures in Iraq, they facilitated greatly increased "reach forward" and "reach back" capabilities, integrating the Iraq campaign into the national intelligence structure in a way it had not been before.

MONEY AS A WEAPON SYSTEM

Petraeus's campaign guidance to the force prominently featured the concept of money as an important enabler for commanders on the ground. "Money can be 'ammunition' as the security situation improves," he noted, adding that commanders should "use a targeting board process to ensure the greatest effect for each 'round' expended and to ensure that each engagement using money contributes to the achievement of the unit's overall objectives."[57] MNF-I and its units benefited from a number of important financial initiatives during the surge.

The Commanders' Emergency Response Program

Before the surge, more than 90 percent of U.S. funds intended for Iraq's reconstruction had already been obligated, meaning that commanders had decided on what reconstruction projects to fund, and contracts had been awarded to complete those projects. As a result, the Commanders' Emergency Response Program (CERP) took on greater importance for U.S. military units' local stabilization and reconstruction projects.[58] Initially funded from the seized assets of Saddam Hussein's regime, CERP shifted to congressional funding over time.[59] By summer 2006, over $2.8 billion in U.S. Government funds were spent through CERP on a broad range of items, such as damage compensation, condolence payments for loss of life, medical expenses, infrastructure improvements, and local employment.[60] As U.S. funding to rebuild Iraq dwindled, CERP funds filled the gap, evolving from small-scale disbursement into sometimes massive reconstruction projects. The money dispersed by CERP ranged from $25 to replace a window to $33 million for a hotel, office, and retail complex at Baghdad International Airport.[61] In fiscal year 2007, U.S. units spent $915 million in CERP. "Every one of my commanders will tell you of the incredible vale that funding provided in their battlespace," Petraeus reported to Gates in January 2008.[62] CERP was also the vehicle that allowed the coalition to pay monthly stipends for the CLCs while coalition leaders tried, ultimately unsuccessfully, to persuade the Maliki government to absorb them into the Iraqi security forces or other government jobs.[63] The U.S. Government spent approximately $300 million funding the CLCs through 2008, an amount that Petraeus believed paid for itself in fewer American troops killed or wounded, fewer lost or damaged vehicles, and more secure communities.[64]

Source: DoD photo by Sergeant Natalie Loucks (Released).

Soldiers Talk to a Contractor and Local Villagers at a Windmill-Powered Ground Water Pump Reconstruction Project.[65]

Even so, CERP received sharp criticism from some important quarters. U.S. Government development experts pointed out that, in some cases, short-term CERP projects undermined longer-term economic goals or skewed local economies. In addition, critics noted as CERP-funded projects became more costly and lengthy, problems with corruption and accountability also increased.[66] Some military leaders believed CERP exacerbated intercommunal strife by creating a new source of competition and corruption. In some cases, projects were funded but never completed, leaving only shells of buildings or utilities infrastructure. Reports occasionally surfaced of U.S. military members misusing CERP funds, or of CERP funds making their way to Iraqi insurgents. These were difficult developments for the U.S. Congress to overlook as the Iraqi Government's own revenues grew to surpass $60 billion.[67]

Yet, while CERP had many long-term challenges, there was little doubt that in the short term it helped tamp down violence, as unemployed Iraqis queued up to work on projects as simple as picking up garbage, which helped remove hiding places for IEDs, or laying gravel to make newly established combat outposts more livable. As congressional reluctance to continue funding CERP in the 2008 National Defense Authorization Act began to develop, Petraeus expressed concern that its absence could hinder the projected U.S. military drawdown.[68] Worried that CERP would dry up while it was still relied on heavily in the field, Petraeus advised Gates that "we have often talked about the value of CERP in cementing the gains won through hard kinetic fighting. One of our battalion commanders said recently that 'if money is ammunition, then we are 'black' on ammunition'."[69] Congress eventually made provisions to keep CERP funds going through July 2008, but in light of the U.S. Government's waning interest in spending money in Iraq, Petraeus encouraged the Iraqi Government to supplement CERP and to establish a matching Iraqi-funded "I-CERP" using the same U.S. procurement and disbursement policies already in existence.[70]

The Task Force for Business and Stability Operations

Along similar lines, DoD established the Task Force for Business and Stability Operations (TFBSO) under Deputy Undersecretary of Defense Paul Brinkley in 2006. Brinkley was a former Silicon Valley executive and proponent of establishing a free market system in Iraq. Much like CERP, DoD envisioned TFBSO as a tool for economic growth that could improve Iraq's harsh economic conditions and create jobs for young Iraqis who might otherwise turn to militancy.[71] In the post-World War II era, most of the U.S. Government's major economic reconstruction programs in foreign countries were not orchestrated by DoD, but Brinkley argued that DoD's involvement in the Iraqi economy was necessary because economic improvements went hand-in-hand with improved security.[72] In Brinkley's view, DoD was best suited to handle the economic side of Iraqi reconstruction because the lives of American Soldiers were at risk if security did not improve, and because DoD was the largest industrial enterprise in the world.[73]

Brinkley encouraged private investment in Iraq by inviting American and other foreign industrialists to tour Iraq with U.S. military escorts and survey economic opportunities in the country.[74] Brinkley focused on revitalizing Iraq's state-owned enterprises that had employed an estimated 200,000 Iraqis before 2003.[75] Rather than attempt a "shock therapy" model of quickly privatizing former state-owned businesses—an approach the Coalition Provisional Authority (CPA) had advocated in 2003—Brinkley implemented a gradual privatization process so that the effects of reopening Iraqi companies might improve security in the long term.[76] TFBSO received approximately $103 million dollars to revitalize state-owned enterprises in Iraq between 2007 and 2008 and finalized its first private investment deal in January 2008, working with the Iraqi Ministry of Defense to privatize three state-owned Iraqi cement factories valued at $3 billion and capable of creating 5,000 jobs.[77] Although most investors in the cement plants were foreigners, TFBSO required all state-owned enterprise investments to include at least one Iraqi so that a business leadership base could be developed within Iraq.[78] By late 2009, TFBSO reportedly had helped restart more than 60 Iraqi factories, creating approximately 250,000 jobs.[79]

The Energy Fusion Cell and Task Force Hydra

Iraq's energy sector was problematic for the Iraqi Government and the coalition campaign in two major ways. The Iraqi Government relied on oil production for more than 90 percent of its revenues, but the country's oil production infrastructure suffered from chronic mismanagement and security threats. At the same time, the Iraqi population relied on free state-provided electricity, but the supply constantly suffered from infrastructure and security problems. To help alleviate these problems, MNF-I established an Energy Fusion Cell to "synchronize efforts of different ministries to provide energy to the people of Iraq and facilitate the export of oil."[80] Under the direction of British Brigadier Carew Wilks, the Energy Fusion Cell brought together representatives from the United States and pertinent ministries of the Iraqi Government to overcome departmental infighting and offer solutions to energy problems, such as increasing Iraq's oil exports to generate higher revenues needed to stabilize the state. It was also Wilks's job to help coordinate the various ministries of the Iraqi Government as they quarreled over energy priorities. On one hand, the priority of Prime Minister Maliki and Minister of Oil Hussein al-Shahristani was to generate government revenues by exporting as much oil as possible, not holding it back for domestic use.[81] On the other hand, popular demand for electricity was mounting while oil-fired generator plants throughout Iraq sat idle and produced only one-third of the country's peak demand.[82] Much of the oil used to fuel the generators was imported from Kuwait, while more than 10 percent of Iraq's electricity was imported from Iran.[83]

In addition, there was significant disparity in access to the limited electricity the Iraqi Government grid produced. In 2008, the Energy Fusion Cell had to respond to the problem of outlying provinces (some of which had been starved of resources by Saddam) shutting down transmission lines to Baghdad in order to keep the electricity supply in their own areas rather than sharing it with the capital. Some provinces received an average of 23 hours of government-supplied electricity a day, while Baghdad often received fewer than 12 hours.[84] During the surge campaign, Iraqi public demand for electricity only increased, constantly outstripping supply as Iraqis who felt more secure began purchasing additional electrical appliances.[85] The constant gap between demand and government supply bred resentment among a population accustomed to state-subsidized electricity.

A different coalition organization dealt with the other major problem plaguing Iraq's energy sector: corruption. Corruption was widespread in Iraqi society, with many Iraqis considering a certain amount of bribery and kickbacks simply as the cost of doing business. When international sanctions cut off much of the country's oil revenues, corruption became even worse. In the aftermath of the 2003 invasion, corruption not only threatened to undermine economic recovery and development goals but also, in some cases, funded the insurgency, leading Maliki to declare corruption Iraq's "second insurgency."[86] Corruption in Iraq's oil sector, based on the scale of the money involved, was the major cause of concern.

Before 2006, coalition officials had had trouble defining the problem and accepting the cultural differences associated with it. Often, MNC-I categorized the issue as one of supply and demand of fuel. In the months after the end of major combat operations and the fall of Baghdad in 2003, fuel demand surged, and by late 2005 much of the refined fuel used in Iraq, approximately 40 percent, was being imported from Turkey. After Iraq's State Oil Ministry Office took control of domestic oil refinery operations in late 2004, the coalition lost control of the process, leading to a lack of oversight and rampant corruption. By early 2006, MND-N concluded that corruption at the sprawling Bayji Oil Refinery, itself responsible for a third of Iraq's output, had been financing insurgent activities since the start of the war. To combat this, in late 2007, MNF-I formed a small interagency group named Task Force Hydra, with representatives from the Department of State, Department of Treasury, and CENTCOM focused on AQI's involvement in the flow of black market oil revenues from the refinery. Ultimately, Task Force Hydra uncovered a vast network of smuggling and extortion, about half of whose profits apparently went to AQI.[87]

Source: DoD photo by Staff Sergeant Lorie Jewell (Released).

Bayji Oil Refinery in June 2007.[88]

Task Force Hydra pieced together a 5-year history of illicit activity at the Bayji refinery. The technocrats at the refinery, who had run the facility during Saddam's rule, had few local ties and continued operations regardless of the warfare that raged across the countryside. They made little protest as insurgents skimmed oil, refined product, and cash from the refinery's activities. Local tribes were also involved in the rampant corruption, with three tribes controlling much of the distribution and sale of refined gasoline and other by-products such as kerosene. Not to be left out, the Kurds to the north had a strong financial interest in the continued flow of Kurdish crude oil to the refinery, especially from the nearby Kirkuk oil fields. While any of these actors could have shut down Bayji by pulling out of the illicit arrangement, it was in the best interest of all parties to maintain the status quo.[89] As Task Force Hydra unraveled the intricacies of corruption at Bayji, it concluded that nearly 70 percent of its $2 billion in fuel production in 2007 and at least a third of profits in 2008 were transferred to the black market. Estimates deemed that between $50 and $100,000 a day were being funneled from the refinery to AQI.[90] Uncovering these illicit links helped Task Force Hydra solve the mystery of the timing of recurring attacks on the crude oil lines running from Kirkuk to Bayji: insurgents apparently worked in concert with tribal sheiks to systematically attack certain portions of the 8-inch product line to control the output at Bayji. Task Force Hydra determined that the timing of these attacks was linked to a price fixing scheme rather than to outright insurgent activity.[91]

Revelations like these enabled coalition and Iraqi forces to plan sophisticated operations to take out critical nodes in the illicit northern oil enterprise from 2008 onward, seriously damaging one of AQI's important funding streams. As the task force was successful at diagnosing corruption at the Bayji refinery, the unit was not intended to redress the overall corruption problem in Iraq and its link to the insurgency. Therefore, in spring 2008, MNF-I and the U.S. Embassy established the Iraq Threat Finance Cell (ITFC), a joint venture of the Department of Treasury, law enforcement agencies, and CENTCOM to conduct financial intelligence analysis of insurgent and terrorist elements in Iraq. The ITFC's analysis of insurgent and terrorist finances, both inside and outside Iraq, became an important generator of targets against AQI and other groups as the kinetic aspect of the surge campaign began to wind down in 2008.

DETENTION AND RULE OF LAW

Overcrowding and Other Detention Facilities Problems

By spring 2007, the surge of U.S. BCTs and reinvigorated security operations in the Baghdad region led to a sharp rise in the number of captured insurgents, intensifying already overcrowded conditions in MNF-I's detention facilities. Overwhelmed by the increasing number of prisoners, MNF-I's TF 134 for detention operations lost control of its detention facilities, resulting in a near repeat of the riots and escape attempts of early 2005. This crisis delayed Petraeus's plan to have detention operations serve as an additional enabler for his larger campaign.

The overcrowding challenge had been a problem long in the making. As early as January 2006, Major General John Gardner, who had replaced Major General William Brandenburg as commander of TF 134, warned MNF-I of the danger developing in the camps:

> Gains to the detainee population have outpaced releases almost 2 to 1 since Oct[ober] 2004. The new expansion compounds we are starting to build at [Camp] Bucca will help mitigate the overcrowding, but continued growth at this rate is not sustainable without an increased level of releases or a subsequent major expansion of Bucca and corresponding increase in U.S. personnel. . . . We are approaching an excessive level of crowding throughout the system.[92]

At the same time, continuing pressure from SECDEF Donald Rumsfeld to transfer responsibility for detention to the Iraqis as soon as possible detracted from efforts to regain control of the rapidly expanding detainee population and to institute counterinsurgency measures in the detention facilities.[93] Gardner later recalled that he had been told before deploying to Iraq that he would be the last TF 134 commander and was warned, "If you cannot get the U.S. out of detention, they will replace you with someone else that can."[94] Throughout 2006, Rumsfeld stymied the task forces' operations by reducing its overall funding, and also blocked the task force's new construction plans in order to compel TF 134 to transition its activities to the Iraqi Government. As a result, Gardner was forced to rely on internal initiatives to reduce the mounting detainee population pressure.[96] First, aiming to trim the popula-

Source: U.S. Army photo (Released).

Major General John D. Gardner, Commander TF 134.[95]

tion through increased releases, Gardner doubled the number of Combined Review and Release Boards held each week and created an expedited release program that freed low-threat detainees within the first 30 days of their detention. These changes increased the number of average monthly releases from 650 to 1,100 by mid-2006.[97]

Gardner also aimed to reduce pressure by instituting a "counterinsurgency in the compounds" program that sought to defuse detainee anger and hopelessness that stemmed from an inconsistent and confusing detention process as well as to attack the threat of jihadist radicalization and recruitment inside the camps.[98] The core of this effort came from counterinsurgency teams that paired intelligence personnel with the guard force of each facility, a bold move considering the integration of intelligence personnel with detention guards was believed to have contributed to the detainee abuse scandal at Abu Ghraib in 2004.[99] Brigadier General David Quantock, who would serve as TF 134 commander in 2009, later recalled:

> Abu Ghraib was still fresh in everyone's mind and no one wanted intelligence specialists inside the wire working with the security forces. But General Gardner and his team were able to assemble counterinsurgency (COIN) teams that ran informants in the compounds to really sort out the population. Without the COIN teams figuring out the extremists from the moderates, none of the [later] rehabilitation efforts would have worked.[100]

As the teams slowly worked their way through each camp, they segregated detainees according to the relative danger they posed and placed them in one of five categories: AQI, takfiris, moderate Sunnis, JAM, and moderate Shi'a.[101] Takfiris were considered higher-threat Sunni militants not affiliated with AQI, while moderates were assessed to be less ideologically committed prisoners who might have joined the insurgency for money. Among the moderates, Gardner later opined that perhaps 1 in 10 probably should not have been detained in the first place.[102]

The counterinsurgency programs also included efforts to help reintegrate detainees into Iraqi society upon release: inmates could attend classes taught by fellow detainees who were teachers, outside agencies provided skills training to help newly released Iraqis find jobs, and moderate religious voices provided an alternative to the preaching of more extremist religious figures.[103] With no doctrine to guide their effort, TF 134 applied lessons from the U.S. prison system and experimented with different tactics, techniques, and procedures of its own.

By February 2007, however, it was clear that the change in coalition strategy would dramatically increase the number of the coalition's detainees, with TF 134 officials estimating that the surge could create an additional influx of 2,000 prisoners per month.[104] With a total capacity of 18,000 across all coalition theater detention facilities and a detainee population standing at 15,840, little slack remained in the system to absorb such increases.[105] The same month, TF 134 officials noted that the detainee population could double in 6 months' time, prophetically warning that they were gravely concerned with "maintaining the required guard-detainee ratio to maintain order" as well as the "likelihood of increased violence, escape attempts, and use of lethal force."[106] Gardner's internal measures would not be able to compensate for the expected flood of detainees.

Informed by Gardner of the worsening situation, Petraeus initially hoped transferring detainees to Iraqi-run facilities could relieve some of the pressure. However, after discussing the issue with Maliki in April 2007, the MNF-I commander realized that the Iraqi corrections services would provide no relief to the coalition detention problem in the near term. The Iraqis themselves still struggled with prison capacity, arresting criminals and suspected insurgents in increasing numbers but committing few resources toward building new facilities in which to hold them. Pointing out the equally glaring problem that the Iraqi Government had no reliable judicial system to try prisoners, Petraeus noted that Maliki's unsatisfactory plan for addressing the overcrowding problem was to "cut a political deal, declare amnesty, and release 90 percent of the detainees."[107]

With no help from the Iraqi Government, Gardner moved to address the expected overcrowding by increasing the size of his guard force and by growing the capacity of his facilities. To counter Gardner's insufficient guard-to-detainee ratio, MNF-I requested nine additional U.S. Army military police companies, nearly a brigade's worth of one of the Army's least-populated specialties. When these predominantly reserve component forces proved unable to deploy quickly, MNC-I diverted an artillery battalion from the surge brigades to augment TF 134's guard force.[108] To resolve the mismatch in the detainee population and capacity, Gardner ordered the construction of temporary facilities to meet immediate needs and requested military construction projects for enduring structures through the budgetary process, aiming for a total capacity of 30,000 prisoners.[109] The majority of the new facilities were hastily built by Navy Seabees and consisted of groups of large plywood shacks or air-conditioned tents able to sleep 20 men. Although the new facilities were separated from each other by chain-link fences reinforced with earth-filled HESCO barriers, detainees within subdivided areas could roam freely under the observation of the guard force. By April, only one-third of the new temporary compounds were complete.[110] The longer-term solution, which included additional permanent buildings, a supermax-style facility for hard-core terrorists, and a brick factory where prisoners could work, received funding from Congress in March, but construction did not begin until October 2007.[111]

These changes proved insufficient. As Gardner had predicted, the coalition's detainee population climbed steadily, from 18,000 the week of April 14 to more than 20,000 just 2 weeks later.[112] True capacity never caught up with the tidal wave of new detainees, and many of the crises that had shaken TF 134 in 2005 developed again. In spite of efforts to categorize inmates by sect and threat level, segregation in the relatively open compounds could not curtail intimidation and recruitment by dedicated jihadists.[113] Hardened radicals intimidated and recruited other inmates, with an estimated 1,350 dedicated members of AQI conscripting new members in Camp Bucca daily. Under the weight of overcrowding, many of Gardner's promising "counterinsurgency inside the compounds" programs collapsed, and the coalition again lost control of its major detention facilities.[114]

"COIN Inside the Wire"

As Gardner and his replacement, Marine Corps Major General Douglas Stone, conducted their transition in April 2007, the simmering problem of detention facility overcrowding finally exploded. A riot that included nearly 10,000 detainees broke out at Camp Bucca, where mobs of inmates set fire to their tents and slung "chai balls"—hardened projectiles molded from tea, sand, and milk—at the guard force as it attempted to restore order.[115] As the riot dragged on and worsened, Stone became convinced that decisive action had to be taken to change the way the coalition conducted detention operations.[116] A second riot of several thousand detainees again roiled Camp Bucca in May, and in June guards discovered a completed 80-foot long escape tunnel with an exit outside the wire.[117] When the rioters came close to breaching the perimeter fence during the May riots, Stone called Petraeus in Baghdad to discuss whether to use deadly force to regain control. Such a measure had not been employed at Bucca since 2005, but the prospect of inmates seizing American hostages troubled the new Task Force 134 commander. Not ready to pull the trigger, Petraeus arranged for Multi-National Division- Southeast to mobilize a mechanized quick-reaction force from nearby Basrah for shock effect if needed. In the end, Stone's troops put down the riot with tear gas and nonlethal munitions and corralled extremist ringleaders into the more isolated and recently completed compounds.[118] As the riots overwhelmed TF 134's day-to-day operations, the detainee population reached 22,400, and staff officers predicted the coalition could be holding as many as 53,940 detainees by September 2008.[119]

Source: DoD photo by Staff Sergeant Lorie Jewell (Released).

Confiscated Weapons at Camp Bucca Similar to Those Used During the April 2007 Riots.[120]

Armed with this dire assessment, and having seen firsthand the impact of overcrowding, Stone set about building upon Gardner's efforts to transform detention operations into a crucial arm of the coalition's efforts, viewing the handling of the coalition's detainees as an opportunity to enhance reconciliation within Iraqi society. Stone believed the detainees could be rehabilitated through reeducation and vocational training programs and changed from security threats into assets in the counterinsurgency campaign.[121] As Stone saw it, TF 134's mandate was an integral part of the surge, which aimed to:

> . . . establish an alliance and empower the moderate Iraqis to effectively marginalize the violent extremists. That's what victory means to me [. . .] I'm going to replace that destructive ideology and then, when [a detainee is] assessed to no longer be a threat, I'm going to release the detainee less likely to be a recidivist . . . they're not going out of here unless I can feel comfortable about that.[122]

Stone outlined his plan for "COIN inside the wire" to MNF-I and MNC-I leaders in June 2007. He intended to transform the detention facilities, which he described as "jihadi universities"—where AQI not only recruited new members but intentionally sent experienced cadres to recoup, network, and plan during their temporary incarceration—into facilities that would facilitate ethnic and political reconciliation.[123] Stone's first step was to increase the capacity of the camps to facilitate the segregation of detainees and then, through a program of vetted and targeted releases and job training programs, to reeducate and reintegrate detainees with their local communities, tribes, and families.[124] Toward this end, Stone benefitted from the support of Petraeus, who also saw detention operations as a crucial component of counterinsurgency. Concerned that detention operations were not properly resourced, the MNF-I commander reported to Gates in May that "we have a lot of work to do to provide higher-security detention facilities, more detainee capacity, a carefully developed release program, and a way ahead in coordination with our Iraqi partners."[125] Petraeus conceded that the problem of overcrowding had created a situation in which, "We essentially had maximum security detainees in minimum security facilities."[126]

Source: DoD photo by Cherie Cullen (Released).

Major General Douglas Stone, Commander TF 134.[127]

With support from MNF-I, Stone intended to distribute the detainee population more evenly across Iraq, putting more funding into regional facilities in order to take pressure off of Camp Bucca and better reintegrate detainees into local communities.[128] Stone also proposed that MNF-I establish theater internment facility reconciliation centers at Taji and Ramadi to provide recently released detainees and unemployed adult Iraqi males with vocational and civil training, pay them a small stipend, and maintain a relationship with former prisoners to gain a better understanding of the insurgency.[129]

To reduce the pressure of overcrowding further, Stone proposed expanding the release program, estimating that up to 25 percent of inmates could be released with no issues, 30 percent could not be released under any circumstances based on the gravity of their offenses, and the remainder could go either way.[130] Petraeus approved the proposal, cautioning Stone to avoid any perception of "catch and release" while reducing the overall detainee population to 15,000 or fewer by the end of 2008.[131] TF 134 would accomplish these releases by converting the review board process used by Gardner into a new Multi-National Force Review Committee Process. The revised system added non-U.S. multinational personnel and ensured that the material in a detainee's file could be shared with the detainee, thus demonstrating that a review process was ongoing, reassuring the often-bewildered detainees that their cases were being properly adjudicated.[132] Three coalition military officials reviewed the detainees' files and assessed each prisoner's progress in detention. After hearing the detainees speak in their own defense, they made a recommendation for release or continued detention.[133]

Unfortunately, the new process suffered many of the same problems from the previous process. Neither the multinational members of the committee nor the detainees could review the classified information that might have led to their detention. TF 134 lacked the capacity to convert all of the authorized materials into Arabic for the detainees to read. Another problem pertained to the veracity of information provided by Iraqi informants, many of whom may have had motives for providing false information about the accused.[134]

Yet the revised release system proved effective at controlling the unrestrained growth of the detainee population, which peaked at 25,600 in October. It also drove down the average rates of detention to 333 days, with only 5 percent of the population having been interned over 3 years.[135] At the same time, the changes proved to be controversial, reigniting many of the disputes that existed between the detention command and tactical commanders in 2005.

Detainees nominated for release first went through a screening process at TF 134, which then sent the multinational divisions a list of those nominated for release. In theory, detainees were released only when there was no longer any reason to believe they posed a security threat and only after pledging before an Iraqi judge not to participate in insurgent or criminal activity. Released detainees also required a guarantor who could be held responsible if the released detainee returned to violence.[136] In practice, the process did not always run smoothly, as pressure to reduce the number of detainees was intense. MNF-W deputy commander Brigadier General John R. Allen recalled that, upon receiving a proposed list of detainee releases, MNF-W would circulate the names among local sheikhs and tactical commanders to ensure they were not "introducing cancerous cells back into the living organism of Anbar Province." MNF-W's refusal to take some of the detainees back into Anbar because of suspected insurgent ties created tension with

TF 134, particularly after some of the detainees that MNF-W wanted to remain in TF 134 custody were released anyway. "We know who ought to come back and who shouldn't," Allen told an MNC-I counterpart in January 2008, adding:

> Sometimes they get released anyway and that's where the rub is. It's causing hate and discontent for the Iraqis . . . we want to not create a situation where the Iraqis have become convinced that our rule of law has failed them and they're going to have to take their own measures to protect themselves from detainees being cancerous cells being injected back into their neighborhoods and lives. We want a say in who comes back, and we want that say to be a veto, not a request.[137]

Like Allen, many tactical commanders believed that the release program not only allowed the enemy to reconstitute, but it also psychologically emboldened them as it communicated a lack of will and determination on the part of the coalition. This psychological impact also affected the coalition's soldiers and Iraqi allies — especially informants — who could be put at risk if hardened fighters were released mistakenly.

Large-scale political releases also continued, to the chagrin of some unit leaders who believed MNF-I pushed to release too many detainees too soon. In September 2007, MNF-I approved the release of 50 to 80 prisoners per day during the month-long Ramadan holiday to show goodwill and deter high-profile mass casualty attacks that could derail political support for the surge. MNF-I released 847 detainees in the first 3 weeks of Ramadan alone.[138] By the end of 2007, MNF-I had released a total of 7,510 detainees for that calendar year.[139] In October 2007, TF 134 reported only 70 recaptures of 4,865 former prisoners, a 1.4 percent recidivism rate that was significantly lower than the 6 to 8 percent recidivism rates reported in January 2007 by Gardner.[140] Gardner's estimation itself was far lower than the rate approximated by tactical commanders across the MNDs, and the issue of recidivism became a highly controversial topic that created a wedge of disagreement between tactical and operational commanders. Yet despite the controversy, Petraeus judged the reduction in reported recidivism rates allowed MNF-I to "take more risk in exchange for the payoff of putting Iraqi citizens back in their neighborhoods rather than holding them in detention."[141]

General Petraeus (left). Source: DoD photo by Staff Sergeant Lorie Jewell (Released).

General David Petraeus and Colonel James Brown at Camp Bucca.[142]

The overall impact of TF 134's "COIN inside the wire" initiatives on the insurgency was mixed. When coupled with increases in detainee capacity, they helped end the chaos that had prevailed in the detention centers before summer 2007. By the beginning of August 2007, theater detention facilities reported zero incidents among the 23,000 detainees in coalition custody, a marked improvement from the period leading up to the Bucca riots several months earlier.[143] Stone also reported an incident in October 2007, in which detainees in one of the Camp Bucca compounds presented the guards with a letter declaring an internal Bucca "Awakening" during which a compound of reformed moderates overtook takfiri extremists. "It's never happened before," Stone noted. "Found them [extremists], identified them, threw them up against the fence, and shaved the frickin' beards off of them."[144] Yet MNC-I was skeptical about TF 134's reported rates of recidivism for released detainees, which, Odierno and other senior officers judged, might simply be a recapture rate. In Odierno's view, Stone also seemed to underestimate the possibility that radicalism was still going on inside the wire, however calm TF 134's compounds appeared.[145]

Rule of Law "Green Zones"

In April 2004, the CPA finalized Order 13 that established the Central Criminal Court of Iraq in an effort to create an independent Iraqi judiciary system. In the absence of a secure and stable environment, however, several years passed before the Central Court and the subsidiary provincial courts could operate effectively across the country. Standing up the judicial system in a post-dictatorial state was a significant task further complicated by the murder and intimidation of judges, investigators, and witnesses. By 2007, the court system struggled to make a dent in the growing detention population and was a long way from administering routine civil and criminal case law. To try to reduce the vulnerability of judges and investigators, MNF-I established a secure Rule of Law "Green Zone" in the Rusafa District of east Baghdad that would contain a court, detention facility, and training academy as well as house judges and investigators along with their families.[146]

The Rule of Law Green Zone began to operate on April 2, 2007, after Prime Minister Maliki agreed to support its $50 million annual operating expenses.[147] Petraeus informed Gates, "the investments we've made in it should help improve the institutional legitimacy and effectiveness of the Iraqi judiciary branch," and that "provincial rule of law complexes are being built in Salah ad Din, Mosul, and Ramadi" in the hopes that the judicial system could operate effectively beyond Baghdad as well. By mid-July, the Court had received over 1,900 cases, and its anticipated demand increased as the Federal Bureau of Investigation continued to train more Iraqi investigators.[148] Between April and November, the number of judges across Iraq increased from 570 to 1,160 as well. The infusion of attention and funds from the Iraqi Government along with the protection provided within the system seemed to be having a positive effect.

The Iraqi judicial system's first real test came in February 2008 with the prosecution of former Deputy Minister of Health Hakim Zamili and former Ministry of Health Facilities Protection Service Chief Hamid al-Shammari, two senior Sadrists accused of masterminding sectarian killings across Baghdad in 2006-2007.[149] During the men's tenure at the Health Ministry, officials and security guards had used their identification credentials and medical vehicles, including ambulances, to move freely across Baghdad and operate as death squads against Sunnis.[150] They had also allegedly ordered the killing of Sunni patients in government hospitals in Baghdad.[151] Finally, when their activities had been uncovered by Deputy Health Minister Ammar Saffar, a Da'wa Party official, they had abducted and murdered Saffar as well.

As Zamili and Shammari's trial neared, the coalition took precautions to shield witnesses and judges from intimidation to include having some witnesses temporarily moved out of the country. For some Iraqis, the trial was more important than Saddam's, because it would signal whether or not Iraqi Government officials were above the law, and whether Shi'a militants could behave with impunity. As the trial approached, Petraeus related to Gates:

> This is the first trial in which high-ranking Iraqi officials of a post-Saddam government will be tried for offenses against the Iraqi people, and it promises to set an extremely important precedent. Unfortunately, the FBI has picked up intelligence that there may have been such severe intimidation (despite our detentions of some of the intimidators) that an acquittal may be the outcome. Ryan [Crocker] will meet with the Chief Judge [Medhat al-Mahmoud] to convey concerns that this might be the case. Nothing is easy.[152]

The following week, officials uncovered even more evidence that the trial appeared to be "fixed to assure acquittal" for Zamili and Shammari. Although Iraqi Chief Judge Medhat al-Mahmood initiated an investigation and replaced the judge, on March 3, 2008, both Zamili and Shammari were acquitted of all charges.[153] Prime Minister Maliki, who had asked MNF-I to arrest Zamili in the first place the previous year, "expressed his personal conviction that witnesses had refused to testify or changed their testimony due to intimidation and death threats" and "lamented that the trial meant the entire Iraqi judicial system was in danger."[154] The Rule of Law Green Zones had succeeded in securing Iraq's judicial system and judges from the physical threat of terrorism, but they could not shield the Iraqi courts from political intimidation, casting doubt on Iraq's long-term ability to administer the rule of law.

***

The operations of the surge campaign benefited from a number of enabling activities and capabilities that had matured or evolved since the beginning of the war. Many of these, such as the counter-IED effort, reflected advances made by trial and error as the U.S. military adapted to the character of the Iraq conflict over time. Others reflected the decisions by senior U.S. officials in Washington to commit their organizations more fully to supporting the coalition campaign, such as the forward deployment of the U.S. intelligence community or the expansion of the provincial reconstruction team program. Still others were initiatives that arose in response to requirements that were unusual for a military campaign, such as the Energy Fusion Cell or the TFBSO. A few of these enabling activities had a clear, significantly positive impact on operations. The dramatic increase in ISR available for tactical units, the fielding of MRAPs, and the integration of special and conventional operations stand out in this respect. For some other initiatives, the picture was mixed. For example, it is difficult to judge in retrospect whether the TFBSO contributed to economic stabilization or whether TF 134's deradicalization programs had any effect on Sunni militancy. What can be said for certain is that the military commands in the Iraq campaign had to adapt to address problems that few U.S. leaders, including those who formulated the surge strategy, had foreseen. As they adapted, the military commands developed new capabilities, organizations, and ways of operating not anticipated in U.S. doctrine before their employment or, in most cases, captured in U.S. doctrine after. By early 2008, these adaptations made coalition units and headquarters look and behave very differently than they had in 2005-2006. They would need every new capability at their disposal in order to get through the bloody spring of 2008, when the coalition unexpectedly would have to fight its largest battles since 2004.

ENDNOTES - CHAPTER 7

1. DoD photo by Cherie Thurlby, "Defense Secretay [sic] Takes Extensives [sic] Tour of Baghdad Operations [Image 18 of 28]," DVIDS Identifier 47703, June 16, 2007, Released to Public, available from *https://www.dvidshub.net/image/47703/defense-secretay-takes-extensives-tour-baghdad-operations*.

2. General David H. Petraeus, "Ambassador Ryan Crocker: Diplomat Extraordinaire," *Army*, Vol. 61, No. 4, April 2011, p. 16.

3. General David H. Petraeus, Multi-National Force-Iraq (MNF-I) Commander's Counterinsurgency Guidance, July 15, 2008.

4. Ibid.

5. E-mail, Colonel (Ret.) Michael Bell to Colonel Joel Rayburn, May 20, 2016.

6. Interviews, Chief of Staff of the Army (CSA) Operation IRAQI FREEDOM (OIF) Study Group with George W. Bush, April 27, 2015; CSA OIF Study Group with Robert M. Gates, July 21, 2014; CSA OIF Study Group with Condoleezza Rice, July 12, 2014. All unpublished documents in this chapter, unless otherwise stated, are in the Chief of Staff of the Army (CSA) Operation IRAQI FREEDOM (OIF) Study Group archives, Army Heritage and Education Center (AHEC), Carlisle, PA.

7. John K. Naland, "Lessons from Embedded Provincial Reconstruction Teams in Iraq," Washington, DC: U.S. Institute of Peace (USIP) Special Report No. 290, October 2011, pp. 2, 6, available from *https://www.usip.org/sites/default/files/SR290.pdf*, accessed June 22, 2016.

8. Ibid., p. 2.

9. Interview, CSA OIF Study Group with Rice, July 12, 2014.

10. Naland, "Lessons from Embedded Provincial Reconstruction Teams in Iraq," pp. 2-3; MNF-I, Secretary of Defense (SECDEF) Weekly Update, September 23-29, 2007; and December 10-16, 2007.

11. Interviews, CSA OIF Study Group with Gates, July 21, 2014; CSA OIF Study Group with Rice, July 12, 2014.

12. Naland, "Lessons from Embedded Provincial Reconstruction Teams in Iraq."

13. Interviews, CSA OIF Study Group with Rice, July 12, 2014; CSA OIF Study Group with Bush, April 27, 2015.

14. Congressional Budget Office, *Contractor's Support of U.S. Operations in Iraq*, Washington, DC: U.S. Congress, August 2008, pp. 5, 8-9.

15. Ibid., p. 9.

16. Ibid.

17. Gideon Rose, "Generation Kill: A Conversation with Stanley McChrystal," *Foreign Affairs*, March/April 2013, available from *https://www.foreignaffairs.com/interviews/2013-02-11/generation-kill*.

18. Conrad C. Crane, *Cassandra in Oz: Counterinsurgency and Future War*, Annapolis, MD: Naval Institute Press, 2016, pp. 176-177.

19. MNF-I Commander's Assessment slides contained in Bill Roggio, "Iraq by the Numbers: Graphing the Decrease in Violence," *Long War Journal*, December 17, 2007, available from *http://www.longwarjournal.org/archives/2007/12/iraq_by_the_numbers.php*, accessed June 22, 2016.

20. R. B. Polin, *The Counter-IED Fight in Iraq, P- 4949*, Alexandria, VA: Institute for Defense Analyses, February 2013, pp. 2-1–2-2.

21. Christopher J. Lamb, Matthew J. Schmidt, and Berit G. Fitzsimmons, *MRAPs, Irregular Warfare, and Pentagon Reform*, Institute for National Strategic Studies Occasional Paper 6, Washington, DC: National Defense University, June 2009, pp. 1, 6.

22. Manuscript (Ms), *On Point*, Vol. II, Fort Leavenworth, KS: Combat Studies Institute (CSI), September 25, 2014, p. 577.

23. Rick Atkinson, "'The single most effective weapon against our deployed forces,'" *The Washington Post*, September 30, 2007, available from *http://www.washingtonpost.com/wp-dyn/content/article/2007/09/29/AR2007092900750.html?sid=ST2007092900754*, accessed June 22, 2006.

24. Polin, *The Counter-IED Fight in Iraq*, pp. 5-8.

25. Briefing, Multi-National Corps-Iraq (MNC-I) to the United States Naval Academy Alumni Association, Task Force TROY Counter IED Update, December 4, 2009.

26. Colonel A. T. Ball and Lieutenant Colonel Berrien T. McCutchen, Jr., "Task Force ODIN Using Innovative Technology to Support Ground Forces," Defense Video & Imagery Distribution System, September 20, 2007, available from *https://www.dvidshub.net/news/12463/task-force-odin-using-innovative-technology-support-ground-forces#.VUPAkTaJjIU*, accessed June 22, 2016.

27. Thom Shanker, "At Odds With Air Force, Army Adds Its Own Aviation Unit," *The New York Times*, June 22, 2008, available from *www.nytimes.com/2008/06/22/washington/22military.html?pagewanted=1&r=0&partner=rssnyt&emc=rss*, accessed June 22, 2016.

28. Ball and McCutchen, "Task Force ODIN Using Innovative Technology to Support Ground Forces."

29. DoD photo by Master Sergeant Paul Tuttle, "MRAPs Arrive in Kuwait [Image 8 of 9]," DVIDS Identifier 67332, November 25, 2007, Released to Public, available from *https://www.dvidshub.net/image/67332/mraps-arrive-kuwait*.

30. "Military must focus on current wars, Gates says," Associated Press, May 13, 2008, available from *http://www.nbcnews.com/id/24600218/ns/us_news-military/t/military-must-focus-current-wars-gates-says/#.Vz5ZN5ErKUk*.

31. Christopher J. Lamb, Matthew J. Schmidt, and Berit G. Fitzsimmons, *MRAPs, Irregular Warfare, and Pentagon Reform*, Institute for National Strategic Studies Occasional Paper 6, Washington, DC: National Defense University, June 2009, pp. 1, 6.

32. MNF-I, SECDEF Weekly Update, January 7-13, 2008.

33. Ibid., April 7-13, 2008.

34. Lamb, Schmidt, and Fitzsimmons, *MRAPs, Irregular Warfare, and Pentagon Reform*, pp. 16-17.

35. Ibid.

36. Robert M. Gates, "A Balanced Strategy: Reprogramming the Pentagon for a New Age," *Foreign Affairs*, January-February 2009, available from *www.foreignaffairs.com/articles/63717/robert-m-gates/a-balanced-strategy*, accessed March 6, 2015.

37. Donna Miles, "Gates Forms Task Force to Promote Intelligence, Surveillance for Warfighters," *DoD News*, April 21, 2008, available from *http://archive.defense.gov/news/newsarticle.aspx?id=49639*.

38. Spencer Ackerman, "Killer Drones, Stealth Jets, Spy Planes: Bob Gates' Legacy in Military Tech," *Wired*, June 30, 2011, available from *http://www.wired.com/2011/06/killer-drones-stealth-jets-spy-planes-bob-gates-legacy-in-military-tech/*.

39. U.S. Army photo by 1st Lieutenant Jason Sweeney, "MQ-1C," February 27, 2011, Released to Public, available from *https://www.flickr.com/photos/mnfiraq/5618715985/in/faves-138659840@N02/*.

40. Interview, Major Jeanne Godfroy, CSA OIF Study Group, with Colonel (Ret.) Derek Harvey, October 7, 2014; Raymond T. Odierno, Nichoel E. Brooks, and Francesco P. Mastracchio, "ISR Evolution in the Iraqi Theater," *Joint Force Quarterly*, 3d Quarter, 2008, pp. 51-55.

41. Ibid.

42. Peter Mansoor, *Surge: My Journey with General David Petraeus and the Remaking of the Iraq War*, New Haven, CT: Yale University Press, 2013, p. 74.

43. Ibid., p. 75.

44. Appropriations Committee, Subcommittee on Defense, Testimony of Lieutenant General Tom Metz: The Joint Improvised Explosive Device Defeat Organization Mission, Washington, DC: U.S. House, 110th Congress, 2d Session, February 14, 2008.

45. Mansoor, *Surge*, p. 76.

46. Interview, Kim Sanborn, Combat Studies Institute (CSI) Contemporary Operations Study Team, with Colonel Christopher Gibson, G-3 25th Infantry Division, Multi-National Division-North, November 4, 2009, p. 10.

47. U.S. Army photo by Staff Sergeant Robert DeDeaux, "Eye for an eye," May 3, 2011, Released to Public, available from *https://www.flickr.com/photos/mnfiraq/5716009306/in/faves-138659840%40N02*.

48. Interview, Colonel James Powell, CSA OIF Study Group, with Colonel Jeff Hannon, March 20, 2014.

49. Mansoor, *Surge*, p. 215.

50. Interview, CSA OIF Study Group with Harvey, October 7, 2014.

51. Ibid.

52. Derek Harvey, "Intelligence during the Surge," unpublished manuscript, CSA OIF Study Group archive, May 11, 2015.

53. Ibid.

54. Interview, CSA OIF Study Group with Harvey, October 7, 2014. Tactical U.S. units during the surge period also benefited from other technological initiatives such as Stingray, 3D imaging, unattended ground sensors, Aerostats, Persistent Threat Detection System, or cameras on sticks.

55. James A. Baker III and Lee H. Hamilton, "The Iraq Study Group Report," December 6, 2006, p. 94.

56. Interview, CSA OIF Study Group with Harvey, October 7, 2014.

57. Petraeus, MNF-I, Commander's Counterinsurgency Guidance, July 2008.

58. General David H. Petraeus, "Learning Counterinsurgency: Observations from Soldiering in Iraq," *Military Review*, January-February 2006, p. 5; *CALL Handbook 09-27, Commander's Guide to Money as a Weapons System: Tactics, Techniques, and Procedures,* Fort Leavenworth, KS: Center for Army Lessons Learned, 2009.

59. Master Sergeant Keith Taylor, "CERP Misappropriation," Fort Bliss, TX: U.S. Army Sergeant Majors Academy, April 28, 2011, p. 4.

60. Ibid.

61. Dana Hedgpeth and Sarah Cohen, "Money as a Weapon," *The Washington Post*, August 11, 2008, available from *http://www.washingtonpost.com/wp-dyn/content/article/2008/08/10/AR2008081002512_pf.html*. See also Major Jason Condrey, *The Commander's Emergency Response Program: A Model for Future Implementation,* Fort Leavenworth, KS: School of Advanced Military Studies, July 4, 2010, p. 11.

62. MNF-I, SECDEF Weekly Update, Petraeus reporting to Gates, December 31, 2007, January 6, 2008.

63. CRS Report for Congress, Kenneth Katzman, "Iraq: Post-Saddam Governance and Security," Washington, DC: CRS, July 2008, pp. 24-25; Unit History, 3d Infantry Division, *2007-2008 Surge in Iraq, Operation Iraqi Freedom (March 2007-June 2008) Overarching Overview,* n.d., pp. 9, 54, CSA OIF Study Group archive.

64. Hedgpeth and Cohen, "Money as a Weapon."

65. DoD photo by Sergeant Natalie Loucks, "CERP funded windmills to bring clean water to villages [Image 1 of 5]," DVIDS Identifier 79087, March 1, 2008, Released to Public, available from *https://www.dvidshub.net/image/79087/cerp-funded-windmills-bring-clean-water-villages*.

66. Government Accountability Office, *Military Operations: Actions Needed to Better Guide Project Selection for Commander's Emergency Response Program and Improve Oversight in Iraq,* Washington, DC: U.S. Congress, 2008; and Taylor, "CERP Misappropriation."

67. Taylor, "CERP Misappropriation," pp. 5-6; and Hedgpeth and Cohen, "Money as a Weapon."

68. MNF-I, SECDEF Weekly Update, Petraeus reporting to Gates, December 31, 2007-January 6, 2008.

69. Ibid., January 21-27, 2008.

70. Ibid., December 31, 2007-January 6, 2008; January 21-27, 2008, and March 17-23, 2008.

71. *Final Report on Lessons Learned: Department of Defense Task Force for Business and Stability Operations,* Washington, DC: Center for Strategic and International Studies, June 2010, p. 29.

72. John Dowdy, "Stabilizing Iraq's economy: An interview with the DOD's Paul Brinkley," *McKinsey Quarterly*, March 2010, available from *http://www.mckinsey.com/insights/public_sector/ stabilizing_iraqs_economy_an_interview_with_the_dods_paul_brinkley#*.

73. Ibid.

74. *Final Report on Lessons Learned: Department of Defense Task Force for Business and Stability Operations*, p. 31.

75. *Full Impact of Department of Defense Program to Restart State-Owned Enterprises Difficult to Estimate*, Washington, DC: Office of the Special Inspector General for Iraq Reconstruction, 2009, p. i.

76. Dowdy, "Stabilizing Iraq's economy."

77. MNF-I, SECDEF Weekly Update, Petraeus reporting to Gates, January 7-13, 2008.

78. Ibid.

79. Dowdy, "Stabilizing Iraq's economy."

80. Interview, U.S. Army Center of Military History (CMH) with Major General Peter Devlin, Deputy Commanding General [Canadian] MNC-I, June 18, 2007, p. 19. See also U.S. Congress, *Rebuilding Iraq: Integrated Strategic Plan Needed to Help Restore Iraq's Oil and Electricity Sectors*, Washington, DC: Government Accountability Office, May 2007, p. 45.

81. Glenn Zorpette, "Keeping Iraq in the Dark," *The New York Times*, March 11, 2008, available from *http://mobile.nytimes.com/2008/03/11/opinion/11zorpette.html?pagewanted=print&referrer=&_r=1*, accessed June 22, 2016; Interview, Lieutenant Colonel William Shane Story, MNF-I Historian, with Lieutenant Colonel Scott Kimmell, Chief of Staff, Energy Fusion Cell, January 2, 2008, p. 2. This is not a full transcription, but a summation by the interviewer.

82. Zorpette, "Keeping Iraq in the Dark."

83. Ibid.

84. Interview, Story with Kimmell, January 2, 2008, p. 1.

85. Ibid.

86. Stuart W. Bowen, Jr., *Learning from Iraq: A Final Report from the Special Inspector General for Iraq Reconstruction*, Washington, DC: Government Printing Office, 2013, p. 103.

87. Interview, CSA OIF Study Group with Major General Rick L. Waddell, June 30, 2014. This is a follow-up interview.

88. DoD photo by Staff Sergeant Lorie Jewell, "Bayji Oil Refinery," June 9, 2007, Released to Public.

89. Interview, CSA OIF Study Group with Rick L. Waddell, June 30, 2014. This is a follow-up interview.

90. Ibid.

91. Michael Freeman, *Financing Terrorism: Case Studies*, Burlington, VT: Ashgate, 2012, p. 38.

92. E-mail, Gardner to Casey, January 1, 2006, sub: Initial Assessment.

93. Snowflake, SECDEF Donald Rumsfeld, February 28, 2006, sub: Turning responsibility of detainees over to Iraqis.

94. Notes and Observations, Lieutenant General (Ret.) Jack Gardner, CG, TF 134, Fall 2008; Quote from Interview, Colonel Matt Morton, CSA OIF Study Group, with Lieutenant General (Ret.) Jack Gardner, January 14, 2014.

95. U.S. Army photo, photographer unknown, "Major General Jack D. Gardner—Commanding General," circa 2004, Released to Public, available from *https://web.archive.org/web/20041015012634/http://www.usarso.army.mil/cg/cg.aspx*.

96. Snowflake, Rumsfeld, February 28, 2006, sub: Turning responsibility of detainees over to Iraqis; Cheryl Bernard et al., *The Battle Behind the Wire: U.S. Prisoner and Detainee Operations from World War II to Iraq,* Santa Monica, CA: RAND Corp., 2011, p. 66.

97. Briefing, TF 134, Detention Operations Update, April 27, 2006.

98. Ibid.

99. Notes and Observations, Gardner, 2008.

100. Interview, Robert Rush, CMH, with Brigadier General David Quantock, May 29, 2009.

101. TF 134, Detention Operations, February 10, 2007.

102. Interview, CSA OIF Study Group with Lieutenant General (Ret.) Gardner, February 26, 2015.

103. Bernard et al., *The Battle Behind the Wire*, pp. 59-69; Interview, CSA OIF Study Group with Gardner, January 14, 2014.

104. Briefing, TF 134 to General David H. Petraeus, Detention Operations Review, February 10, 2007.

105. Ibid.

106. Briefing, MNF-I to CG, Camp Bucca, Overview, February 15, 2007.

107. MNF-I, SECDEF Weekly Update, April 14-20, 2007.

108. MNF-I, SECDEF Weekly Update, March 31-April 6, 2007; E-mail, Lieutenant General (Ret.) Jack (John) Gardner to Colonel Frank Sobchak, May 13, 2015, sub: Comments.

109. Briefing, TF 134 to Petraeus, Detention Operations: Strategic Offensive in COIN, on the Way Ahead for Detention Operations, April 12, 2007.

110. Notes and Observations, Gardner, 2008, p. 7; Interview, CSA OIF Study Group with Lieutenant General (Ret.) Gardner, February 26, 2015.

111. Briefing, TF 134 to Petraeus, Detention Operations Review, February 10, 2007; Joseph Jiordono, "Prison Camp in Iraq Once Listed to Close Now Sees Major Upgrades," *Stars and Stripes*, October 31, 2007; Walter Pincus, "U.S. Plans to Expand Detention Centers," *The Washington Post*, March 15, 2007.

112. MNF-I, SECDEF Weekly Update, April 14-20, 2007; MNF-I, SECDEF Weekly Update, April 28-May 4, 2007.

113. Interviews, CSA OIF Study Group with Gardner, January 14, 2014; and February 26, 2015; Michael Weiss and Hassan Hassan, *ISIS: Inside the Army of Terror,* New York: Regan Arts, 2015, p. 86.

114. Elizabeth Detwiler, "Iraq: Positive Change in the Detention System," Washington, DC: U.S. Institute of Peace, July 1, 2008, available from *http://www.usip.org/publications/iraq-positive-change-in-the-detention-system*, accessed May 19, 2016; Interview, CSA OIF Study Group with Gardner, January 14, 2014.

115. Interview, CMH with Major General Douglas M. Stone, U.S. Marine Corps, Deputy Commanding General for Detainee Ops, CG of TF 134, November 13, 2007; Mansoor, *Surge*, p. 151; Thomas E. Ricks, *The Gamble: General Petraeus and the American Military Adventure in Iraq*, New York: Penguin, 2009, p. 194.

116. Interview, CMH with Stone, November 13, 2007.

117. Elaine M. Grossman, "Rehabilitating Iraqi Insurgents," *National Journal*, Vol. 39, No. 33, 2007, pp. 49-51, on EBSCOhost Online Research Database; Alissa Rubin, "U.S. Remakes Jails in Iraq, but Gains Are at Risk," *The New York Times*, June 2, 2008.

118. MNF-I, SECDEF Weekly Update, May 13-19, 2007; Interview, CMH with Stone, November 13, 2007; Mansoor, *Surge*, p. 152.

119. Briefing, TF 134 to Petraeus, Detention Operations, June 1, 2007.

120. DoD photo by Staff Sergeant Lorie Jewell, "Camp Bucca confiscated weapons," November 27, 2007, Released to Public.

121. Colonel James Brown, Lieutenant Colonel Erik Goepher, and Captain James Clark, "Detention Operations, Behavior Modification, and Counterinsurgency," *Military Review*, Vol. 43, May-June 2009, pp. 40-47; Mansoor, *Surge*, p. 154.

122. Major General Douglas Stone, Blogger's roundtable, *The Washington Post*, September 18, 2007.

123. Weiss and Hassan, *ISIS*, pp. 83-86.

124. MNF-I, SECDEF Weekly Update, July 8-14, 2007; Briefing, MNF-I, Detention Operations: Strategic Offensive in COIN, June 1, 2007.

125. MNF-I, SECDEF Weekly Update, May 6-12, 2007.

126. SDW, May 13-19, 2007.

127. DoD photo by Cherie Cullen, "U.S. Marine Corps Maj. Gen. Douglas M. Stone, Commander of Task Force 134, conducts a press conference about his recently completed 14-month tour as Deputy Commanding General for Detainee Operations with the Multinational Force-Iraq at the Pentagon," DIMOC Identifier 080609-D-JB366-002, June 9, 2008, Released to Public.

128. MNF-I, SECDEF Weekly Update, July 8-14, 2007.

129. Bernard et al., *The Battle Behind the Wire*, p. 73; Briefing, MNF-I, Detention Operations: Strategic Offensive in COIN, June 1, 2007.

130. Stone, Blogger's roundtable.

131. MNF-I, SECDEF Weekly Update, April 29-May 5, 2007; and May 6-12, 2007; Briefing, MNF-I, Detention Operations: Strategic Offensive in COIN, June 1, 2007, slide 5; MNF-I, SECDEF Weekly Update, January 28-February 3, 2008.

132. Brown, Goepher, and Clark, "Detention Operations, Behavior Modification, and Counterinsurgency," p. 42.

133. MNF-I, SECDEF Weekly Update, November 26-December 2, 2007.

134. Brian J. Bill, "Detention Operations in Iraq: A View from the Ground," *International Law Studies*, Vol. 86, 2010, pp. 421-426, 455.

135. Alissa Rubin, "U.S. Military Reforms Its Prisons in Iraq," *The New York Times*, June 1, 2008.

136. Briefing, MNF-I Commander's Conference, MNF-I Detainee Operations, October 13, 2007.

137. Interview, Colonel Michael Visconage, CMH with Major General John R. Allen, January 10, 2008, Camp Fallujah, Iraq.

138. MNF-I, SECDEF Weekly Update, September 9-15, 2007; and September 30-October 6, 2007.

139. Ibid., December 10-16, 2007.

140. Briefing, MNF-I Commander's Conference, Detainee Operations, October 13, 2007.

141. MNF-I, SECDEF Weekly Update, November 26-December 2, 2007.

142. DoD photo by Staff Sergeant Lorie Jewell, "P4 briefed by Colonel Brown overlooking Camp Bucca," November 27, 2007, Released to Public.

143. MNF-I, SECDEF Weekly Update, July 29-August 4, 2007.

144. Brown, Goepher, and Clark, "Detention Operations, Behavior Modification, and Counterinsurgency," p. 42; Stone, Blogger's roundtable.

145. CSA OIF Study Group, off-site meeting, January 25, 2015.

146. MNF-I, SECDEF Weekly Update, July 1-7, 2007.

147. Ibid., March 17-23, 2007; March 24-30, 2007; and July 1-7, 2007.

148. Ibid., July 15-21, 2007.

149. Ibid., February 11-17, 2008.

150. Ibid.; Mansoor, *Surge*, pp. 210-211.

151. Interview, Colonel Frank Sobchak, CSA OIF Study Group, with Colonel Kevin Leahy, Commander, AOB, October 31, 2014; and November 7, 2014.

152. MNF-I, SECDEF Weekly Update, February 11-17, 2008.

153. Ibid., March 3-9, 2008.

154. Ibid.

CHAPTER 8

CRESCENDO: MALIKI AGAINST THE SADRISTS

On January 11, 2008, 3 days after the launch of Operation PHANTOM PHOENIX, snow fell on Baghdad for the first time in a century. Iraqis took it as a felicitous omen after the war's most violent 2 years. The following day, President George W. Bush traveled to Kuwait for meetings with General David H. Petraeus and Ambassador Ryan Crocker. While there, the President announced publicly that he had decided to end the surge by midsummer, by which time 20,000 U.S. troops would have returned home without replacement. After a year of intensified operations mainly against al-Qaeda in Iraq (AQI) and other Sunni insurgent groups, the surge was on its downward slope.

Yet, some of the most intense fighting of the Iraq War was in the offing. After 2 months of clearing operations in northern Iraq designed to push AQI ever farther from Baghdad and other Iraqi population centers, the coalition in spring 2008 would find its campaign plan against the Sunni insurgency thrown off course by a high-stakes war between the Nuri al-Maliki government and Iraq's Shi'a militias. The long-simmering confrontation between the Iraqi state and the Iranian regime's Iraqi militant proxies was about to explode into a Shi'a civil war.

OPERATION PHANTOM PHOENIX

On January 8, 4 days before Bush's announcement, Lieutenant General Raymond T. Odierno and Multi-National Corps-Iraq (MNC-I) launched Operation PHANTOM PHOENIX, the final corps-level operation employing all of the surge brigades before the first of them departed Iraq in February. In Operations PHANTOM THUNDER and PHANTOM STRIKE, MNC-I's units had pushed AQI and other Sunni insurgent groups out of Baghdad and much of the surrounding belts. Odierno's specific intent for PHANTOM PHOENIX was to push AQI even farther from Baghdad and to pursue them up the Diyala and Tigris River Valleys, clearing the insurgent support zones in eastern Diyala, Mosul, and the area south of Baghdad known as Arab Jabour. He then intended that MNC-I's units should hold those formerly insurgent-held areas by establishing new combat outposts and joint security stations "to ensure that AQI does not return . . . thereby further denying AQI from reestablishing staging areas throughout the Baghdad Belts."[1] As with the preceding PHANTOM operations, PHANTOM PHOENIX involved all four U.S. division-level commands. Multi-National Division-North (MND-N) led the main effort, conducting large-scale clearing operations in the upper Diyala River Valley and the Mosul area. Multi-National Division-Center (MND-C) conducted a supporting operation to clear AQI from the troublesome Tigris River areas of Arab Jabour and Salman Pak south of Baghdad. Multi-National Force-West (MNF-W) focused on clearing the Jazeera desert and the vicinity of Lake Tharthar, the area that had for several years been a seam among MNF-W, MND-N, and Multi-National Division-Baghdad (MND-B), where those units' boundaries met. In the Baghdad area, MND-B continued operations to root out car-bomb networks.[2] Finally, the coalition launched a supporting effort, Operation HYDRA, in which a joint interagency task force made up of intelligence analysts, law enforcement experts, and even oil sector economists tracked down AQI's financing networks at the

Bayji oil refinery in order to starve the group of the cash it normally generated from black market oil and gasoline.[3]

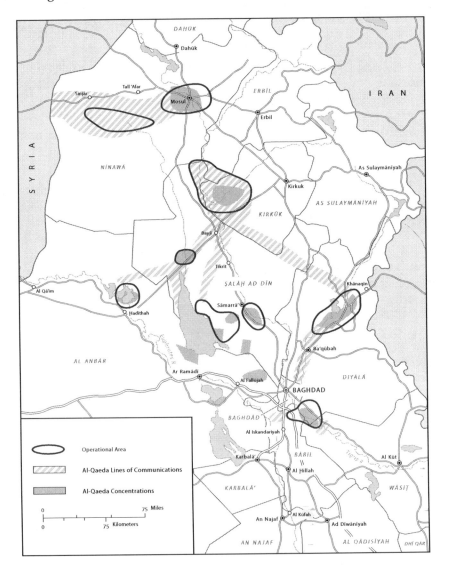

Map created by the official cartographer at the U.S. Army Center of Military History, Washington, DC.

Map 17. Operation PHANTOM PHOENIX, January–March 2008.

Many of the U.S. units that conducted PHANTOM PHOENIX were newly arrived in Iraq, as some of the brigades that had shouldered the burden of the hard fighting of 2007 rotated home. Colonel Michael X. Garrett's 4th Brigade, 25th Infantry Division, handed responsibility for Hillah, Najaf, and Karbala to Colonel Thomas James's 4th Brigade, 3d Infantry Division, in early December. In Baghdad, Colonel Jeffrey Bannister's 2d Brigade,

2d Infantry Division, handed control of the restive southeast Baghdad districts to Colonel Mark Dewhurst's 4th Brigade, 10th Mountain Division, in late December. In January, the first surge brigade, Colonel Billy Don Farris's 2d Brigade, 82d Airborne Division, handed control of Adhamiyah to Colonel John H. Hort's 3d Brigade, 4th Infantry Division, while Colonel Paul Funk's 1st Brigade, 1st Cavalry Division, transferred control of Taji and the northern Baghdad belt to Colonel Todd McCaffrey's 2d Brigade, 25th Infantry Division.[4]

To support MNC-I's main effort, Odierno deployed his operational reserve, a Stryker squadron of the 2d Cavalry Regiment, to eastern Diyala to take part in the clearing operations there.[5] Iraqi reinforcements moved to MND-N as well, with the 3d Brigade, 1st Iraqi Army Division, deploying from Anbar to eastern Diyala with less than a week's notice to take part in the operation.[6] For his part, MND-N commander Major General Mark P. Hertling was not satisfied with the provision of corps-level reinforcements for what he anticipated would be difficult fights in both Diyala and Mosul and asked MNC-I for another U.S. battalion for Mosul. Eventually, a squadron of the 3d Armored Cavalry Regiment (ACR) joined MND-N in the middle of the operation as 3d ACR units began to arrive.

For MND-N's portion of Operation PHANTOM PHOENIX, Hertling had decided that his division would focus on Diyala rather than Ninawa, although Ninawa stood out as the most violent province in the country once the violence in central Iraq waned in late 2007. Hertling believed another major operation would be required in Diyala to flush AQI and its allies out of the province's agricultural areas before MND-N could turn its full attention to Mosul. He also believed that AQI would try to reestablish itself in the Za'ab Triangle rather than Mosul, and that the Za'ab area was where the final battle against AQI would take place.[7]

The focus of the clearing operations in Diyala was a 285-square-kilometer area north of Muqdadiyah that U.S. Soldiers nicknamed "the Breadbasket" for its agricultural terrain. For several years, the towns in the Breadbasket had seen almost no coalition presence, and AQI fighters had used them as staging areas for attacks against Muqdadiyah and Baqubah with impunity. On January 8, troops from Colonel Jon S. Lehr's 4th Brigade, 2d Infantry Division, and troops of the Diyala-based 5th Iraqi Army Division entered the area to hunt for an estimated 200 AQI fighters.[8] The fight was difficult for Lehr's Stryker units. Crisscrossed with irrigation canals, the Breadbasket was an ideal insurgent sanctuary, hard for armored vehicles to access, and covered by dense palm groves and marshes in which enemy fighters could easily hide. The insurgents also had had time to prepare their defenses. On the second day of the operation, January 9, six of Lehr's men were killed and nine wounded when a local Iraqi led them into a house that AQI fighters had rigged to explode. This house-borne improvised explosive device (IED) slowed clearing operations by forcing U.S. units to enter every structure more cautiously and to be more careful about acting on tips from locals. "There is obviously a tradeoff between working with the local population to garner information and being set up by the enemy," Petraeus noted a few days later.[9] In other places, U.S. troops found that inventive insurgents had even rigged date palm treetops with explosives to target U.S. patrols as they passed underneath. By January 20, U.S. and Iraqi troops were uncovering AQI bunkers, tunnel complexes, and weapons caches hidden among "eight-foot-high reeds" and date palms, Petraeus reported.[10]

Source: DoD photo by Private 1st Class Kirby Rider (Released).

Soldiers From the 3d ACR Search for Weapon Caches in Canal Walls of "The Breadbasket."[11]

However, MND-N's clearing operations in the Breadbasket had meager results: only 4 AQI fighters killed and another 30 detained or wounded, although coalition troops did manage an important raid that killed the Syrian AQI leader Abu Layla al-Suri on January 16 near Muqdadiyah.[12] The small number of enemy fighters killed or captured indicated, contrary to MND-N's expectations, that AQI groups already had relocated from the Breadbasket to other areas farther north, such as the Hamrin mountains and Mosul.[13] MND-N's main effort appeared to have gone into an area that AQI's commanders and fighters had already abandoned.

While the MND-N troops cleared the Breadbasket, MND-C troops focused on Arab Jabour a few kilometers south of Baghdad. Despite a nascent Awakening group in the area, Arab Jabour had long been an insurgent support zone used by AQI and other militants to infiltrate fighters and car bombs into Baghdad. Colonel Terry R. Ferrell's 2d Brigade, 3d Infantry Division, oversaw the operations there, reinforced by the 5th Battalion, 7th Cavalry sent from Anbar to give Ferrell three U.S. battalions for the task.[14] Among the Iraqi forces present, Brigadier General Ali Freiji's brigade of the 6th Iraqi Army Division received an additional Iraqi infantry battalion for the operation as well.[15] Under the plans drawn up by MND-C commander Major General Rick Lynch, the clearing of Arab Jabour relied on intense firepower. On January 10, MND-C called in air strikes that dropped 20 tons of munitions on suspected AQI targets in just 10 minutes in an effort to destroy AQI weapons caches and to reduce a defensive belt of IEDs that blocked important roads.[16]

A local Awakening leader estimated that the air strikes killed 20 AQI fighters, including a senior AQI commander.[17] As the MND-C troops progressed deeper into AQI's Arab Jabour sanctuary, they carried out similarly intense air strikes on January 16 and 20.[18] On January 19, however, Ferrell's brigade suffered the first battle death in an MRAP when a 3,000-pound IED flipped over one of the mine-resistant vehicles and killed the gunner.[19]

Farther to the northwest, the Marine and Army troops that had massed to clear the area that MNC-I called area of operation (AO) Bedrock found extensive insurgent outposts in the remote areas east of Lake Tharthar. West of Samarra, the U.S. troops discovered 10 car bombs at a large explosive production facility. On January 17, they also discovered a foreign fighter base camp that had a 300-meter tunnel system with multiple entrances and fighting positions hidden by reeds, all of which the U.S. troops destroyed with incendiary munitions.[20]

Source: U.S. Army photo by 1st Lieutenant Jonathan J. Springer (Released).

Soldiers From 1st BCT, 101st Airborne Division, Fire Artillery During Operation PHANTOM PHOENIX.[21]

Mosul was even more challenging. As clearing operations began with the arrival of 1st Battalion, 8th Infantry, from Baghdad, the AQI fighters who had begun to gather in the Mosul area in fall 2007 repeatedly attacked the tightening ring of Iraqi-manned checkpoints and obstacles that locals dubbed the "Riyadh Line" after the new Ninawa Operations Commander, Lieutenant General Riyadh Jalal Tawfiq. The Ninawa Operations Command began operating on January 15, bringing a much-needed layer of command and control to the city's army and police forces. Still, even with a better command structure, the city of two million was difficult to clear, especially its older west-side neighborhoods with their narrow medieval streets that could not accommodate vehicles. On January 23, Iraqi troops investigating a tip in an apartment building in northwest Mosul found an insurgent cache of at least 20,000 pounds of explosives that detonated when an Iraqi soldier improperly probed the charge. The explosion leveled the entire building, killing 34 Iraqis and wounding 138 more, and leaving an enormous crater. The following morning, when the newly appointed Ninawa police chief, Brigadier General Saleh Jabouri, arrived to investigate the site, he was killed by an AQI suicide bomber dressed as a policeman who wrestled him into a nearby vehicle before detonating a suicide vest.[22]

Source: U.S. Army photo by Specialist Kieran Cuddihy (Released).

Soldiers From the 3d ACR During Combat in Mosul.[23]

The assassination was a serious setback for the new joint Iraqi Army and police campaign to secure the city and, in Petraeus's words, showed that "AQI still has the ability to strike."[24] It also caused a shift in priorities for both the coalition and the Iraqis. Angered by the attack, Prime Minister Maliki dispatched an Iraqi battalion from Baghdad to reinforce the 2d Iraqi Army Division in Mosul, while Hertling responded by changing his division's main effort from Diyala to Mosul and employing the 3d Squadron, 3d ACR, in the city. The arrival of the additional troops was timely. On February 11, the Badush prison outside Mosul, whose inmate population included an AQI command and control node, erupted into a riot that required the quick intervention of the 3d Squadron and 2d Iraqi Army Division to suppress the violent prisoners and prevent a jailbreak.[25]

Farther south of Mosul, MND-N made better progress. In the long-time insurgent stronghold of Hawijah, Sunni insurgents felt increasing pressure from Operation PHANTOM PHOENIX and from the newly formed 6,000-man Awakening group in the area. As a result, insurgent fighters began to come forward seeking amnesty from local Iraqi officials and Colonel David Paschal's 1st Brigade, 10th Mountain Division. Throughout February and subsequent months, Paschal's units publicized a program called "Restore Peace" in which insurgents who turned themselves in could register with the brigade and go through a 6-month reintegration process. A few insurgents turned themselves in during the first weeks of February, but on February 24, more than 100 insurgents walked into Forward Operating Base McHenry in Hawijah to seek amnesty. "I'm tired of being a target and running," one insurgent explained to U.S. troops, while another testified, "I have not slept in my house for a year."[26]

Back in Diyala, sectarian political tensions complicated the operation. On February 8, thousands of Sunni Awakening members, now renamed Sons of Iraq by MNF-I planners, abandoned their checkpoints to join in demonstrations against Diyala police chief Ghanem al-Qureishi, who they accused of sponsoring Shi'a death squads that targeted Awakening members. For several weeks, U.S. commanders in Diyala were forced to scramble to mediate between the Awakening and the Shi'a-dominated Diyala police forces, showing that the province's difficult sectarian politics meant that it was far from stabilized, even if AQI had lost its grip on most of its former territory there.[27]

Source: DoD photo by Staff Sergeant Russell Bassett (Released).

Sons of Iraq Staff a Checkpoint in Himbus.[28]

Diyala was not the only PHANTOM PHOENIX operational area in which the Awakening groups felt themselves under pressure. In January, MNF-I had recorded at least 100 attacks against Awakening groups, almost four times as many as were recorded in December. In Baghdad on February 11, two car bombs had unsuccessfully targeted Sheikh Ali Hatem Suleiman, one of the Awakening leaders from Ramadi. Elsewhere, in separate incidents in Jurf al-Sukhr south of Baghdad and in the Za'ab Triangle in northern Iraqi, U.S. troops mistakenly raided Awakening members, although it was possible the targeted men had in fact been insurgents using the Awakening as a cover.[29]

The stabilization phases of Operation PHANTOM PHOENIX continued until July, but large-scale clearing operations began to wind down in February with coalition and Iraqi troops in possession of large swathes of formerly AQI-held territory. For the whole of the operation, the coalition lost 60 troops killed and the Iraqi security forces more than 500 killed. Meanwhile, the Sunni insurgent groups lost an estimated 900 killed and approximately 2,500 captured.[30] By the end of PHANTOM PHOENIX's clearing operations, most of AQI's networks had been pushed beyond striking distance of Baghdad, although they could still carry out large attacks in the cities of Diyala and maintain a formidable clandestine presence in Mosul, where attack levels remained high. By February 15, MND-C had completed the clearing of Arab Jabour and shifted focus to the clearing of Salman Pak on the opposite side of the Tigris, farther south.[31] After 5 weeks of PHANTOM PHOENIX's clearing and holding operations, insurgent activity had diminished significantly, especially in Baghdad, where AQI no longer had freedom of movement in its traditional support zones around the city. By February, Baghdad had an average of just 11 attacks per day, down from 46 per day in June 2007. On February 17, MNF-I announced that insurgent attacks across Iraq had fallen sharply to an average of 82 per day, down from a daily average of 205 exactly 1 year before.[32]

Source: U.S. Army photo by Specialist Nicholas A. Hernandez (Released).

Soldiers Meet With Iraqi National Policemen During a Patrol in Baghdad.[33]

Political Progress and the Departure of III Corps

The theory behind the surge was that improvements in the security situation and the tamping down of Iraq's ethno-sectarian civil war would give the Iraqi political factions breathing space in which to make progress toward political reconciliation. After a politically turbulent December, the Iraqi Parliament took steps that seemed to lend some credence to the theory. In January and February 2008, the Iraqi political parties began serious negotiations concerning a series of difficult political and security issues. In early February, Maliki began to include his main Sunni rival, Vice President Tariq Hashimi, in cabinet consultations on how to counter AQI's resurgence in Mosul and to give Hashimi the floor in discussions with the Ninawa operations commander and the Ninawa provincial governor.[34] Meanwhile, the Parliament began negotiating the passage of several laws that the coalition considered essential for political reconciliation. These included a law defining the powers of the Iraqi provinces and the central government; a law establishing an amnesty process for those who had decided to abandon resistance against the government; and a 2008 budget that divided oil revenues between the Iraqi Government and the Kurdistan Regional Government (KRG). On February 13, the Parliament passed all three laws at once. Petraeus received the news of the laws' passage while walking through a west Baghdad neighborhood where attacks had fallen to almost zero after 2 years of sectarian violence. "[Parliament speaker Mahmud] Mashadani had threatened the Council of Representatives with dissolution," Petraeus reported, "and then he came right back on Wednesday with a savvy bundling of the three laws that gave everyone something they were looking for—that's politics!"[35]

The legislative breakthrough also came the day before Odierno and the III Corps headquarters handed over the reins of MNC-I to Lieutenant General Lloyd Austin and his XVIII Airborne Corps headquarters, which had returned to Iraq for its second tour as the coalition's operational headquarters. The timing was fitting. In his departing remarks the following day, Odierno noted that the Iraqis' legislative successes were "the best gift [I] could have received."[36]

The change in security conditions from the time of III Corps' arrival in December 2006 was stunning. Odierno and III Corps had taken up their responsibilities at a time when Iraqi civilian deaths averaged 3,500 per month, enemy attacks averaged 1,200 per week, and U.S. military deaths averaged more than 100 per month. By February 2008, those numbers had dropped to fewer than 600 Iraqi civilian deaths per month and fewer than 600 attacks per week, and only 29 U.S. troops had been killed in January 2008. The ethno-sectarian war had lost much of its energy as well: Iraq had witnessed about 2,000 ethno-sectarian killings in December 2006, but that number dropped to just 100 in February 2008.[37]

The dramatic changes were due in large part to III Corps' intense operations against AQI, which by the time of Odierno's departure in February 2008 was a mere shadow of what it had been in late 2006. By attacking AQI's support zones and safe havens around Baghdad, and by synchronizing the operations of the divisions in central and northern Iraq, Odierno and his command had enabled the coalition to retake the initiative for the first time since 2004. Odierno's operations had succeeded in depleting AQI's ranks, decimating the group's leadership, and pushing its fighters into far northern Iraq or into remote areas of the Diyala River Valley far from Iraq's population centers. What remained was to finish the Sunni insurgency in Mosul.

Denouement of the Turkey-Kurdistan Workers' Party War

As Odierno departed Iraq, however, the campaign for Mosul competed with other problems for the coalition's attention. The situation between Turkey and the insurgents of the Kurdistan Workers Party (PKK) remained critical in early 2008. As the Turks continued their air strikes against PKK bases inside Iraq without a decisive result, the PKK continued to hit back inside Turkey, including a bombing attack against a Turkish patrol in Diyarbakir that killed 5 Turks and wounded 110. In early January, the Turkish general staff began to plan a ground incursion into Iraq to wipe out the PKK and requested U.S. intelligence support for their operations. U.S. military leaders outside Iraq were willing to provide this support, but Petraeus advised U.S. leaders "a kinetic-only approach to dealing with the PKK . . . especially with US ISR [intelligence, surveillance, and reconnaissance] support to their operations, will only make matters more difficult in Iraq. Our forces don't need another enemy and we certainly do not want to get into a situation where Iraq raises [United Nations] protection from Turkish action."[38] Petraeus also had doubts about the Turkish operational plan, which Turkish military officers briefed to U.S. counterparts in advance. "The snow depth, the altitude, the vertical feet up [and] down, the distance planned for travel, and the very difficult terrain" all indicated that "no one who planned that operation had been under a rucksack in recent years," Petraeus later recalled.[39]

On February 21, 2008, the Turks launched a ground operation into Iraq with about 800 troops, though the Turkish media outraged the Kurdish public by claiming 10,000 troops had crossed the border. As Petraeus had warned, the Turkish maneuvers immediately bogged down, indicating the Turkish commanders had not prepared well for the harsh winter conditions and the tough resistance from PKK fighters. After a week, the inconclusive operation ended as Turkish units withdrew into Turkey leaving the PKK intact, though the Turks claimed to have killed more than 200 PKK fighters.[40]

In the postmortem analysis of the operation, Petraeus wrote to Secretary of Defense (SECDEF) Robert M. Gates, "We hope that all parties can now move toward political solutions and that we can avoid another large-scale Turkish military intervention that would further endanger the nascent political progress in Iraq."[41] The entire episode, however, demonstrated that there were regional problems affecting the Iraq campaign that only U.S. policymakers in Washington, not U.S. commanders on the ground, had the means to address. If Washington could not formulate a policy to stave off spoiler events such as the Turkish incursion, U.S. units in Iraq would pay the price.

THE BATTLE FOR BASRAH

The Arrival of Lieutenant General Lloyd Austin and XVIII Airborne Corps

Austin's first challenge after he assumed command of MNC-I from Odierno on February 14, 2008, was to continue to keep pressure on AQI and other militant groups as all five of the surge brigades began redeploying. To overcome a looming deficit of combat forces, the 15 remaining brigades needed to expand their areas of operations once again. As Austin took command, he still had seven division-level headquarters with which to work. Major General Jeffery W. Hammond commanded MND-B, the 4th Infantry Division; Lynch headed MND-C and the 3d Infantry Division; and Hertling led MND-N and the 1st Armored Division. Major General Graham Binns, General Officer Commanding the 1st (United Kingdom [UK]) Armoured Division, remained in control of Multi-National Division-Southeast (MND-SE) in Basrah, while Multi-National Force-West (MNF-W) continued in its final year under the U.S. Marines, and a South Korean brigade remained in control of Multi-National Division-Northeast (MND-NE) in Kurdistan. Multi-National Division-Central South (MND-CS), led by a Polish brigade at their headquarters in Diwaniyah, also contained a Georgian brigade and several smaller coalition contingents.

Source: U.S. Army photo by Sergeant Laura M. Bigenho (Released).

General David Petraeus Supervising the Change of Command Between Lieutenant General Raymond Odierno and Lieutenant General Lloyd J. Austin III.[42]

When Austin assumed command of MNC-I, he saw his immediate objectives as holding the line in Baghdad and Anbar, completing the defeat of AQI in Mosul and the Diyala River Valley, and, when he could gather the capacity, gaining greater control of the south, where he believed the coalition had limited situational awareness.[43] Austin believed that to accomplish these objectives, he needed to reapportion his forces significantly across the country. Although the security situation in Baghdad had improved dramatically since early 2007, MND-B in February 2008 remained at peak strength, still in control of 6 brigade combat teams and 44 U.S. combat battalions, far more than either MND-N or MND-C.[44] Austin and XVIII Airborne Corps knew that the security situation in Basrah was deteriorating—although the province recently had been transferred to Iraqi control—and the new MNC-I leaders were determined to turn south to secure the city once AQI had been finished off in the north. This was the coalition's planned campaign sequence as Austin arrived. The new corps commander had little warning that his priorities in the coming months were about to be turned upside down by a massive, unexpected clash between the government of Nuri al-Maliki and the Sadrist militias in Basrah and Baghdad that would bring some of the most intense fighting of the war.

The Rush to Provincial Iraqi Control in Basrah

The spring 2008 war between the Maliki government and the Sadr movement had been coming for a long while. The situation in Basrah had slipped out of control of both the coalition and the government in 2007. When Binns took command of MND-SE in August 2007, he came with strict orders from his British superiors at the UK Permanent Joint Headquarters to follow through on the transition plans begun by Major General Jonathan Shaw, his predecessor. Binns was to complete the withdrawal of British troops from bases inside the city to the Basrah Air Station outside the town, while handing the security portfolios for all of Basrah Province to the Iraqis so British forces could then withdraw from the country. "The UK had indicated that it had no long-term intention to remain in Iraq, and, therefore, exit was inevitable," Binns recalled, "but the strategy, as I was delivering it, was one of transition increasingly to Iraqi security forces, and as a result, we would [drawdown] our presence. . . . I had been told to deliver a transition, and that's what I was doing."[45]

The British Government had been eager to transfer Basrah Province to the Iraqis for some time. Shaw had suggested moving the province to Provincial Iraqi Control (PIC) in April 2007, because British planners were counting on shifting troops from Iraq to Afghanistan even as the U.S. surge into Iraq was getting underway.[46] Like Shaw, Binns also sought an early handover of security responsibility, preferably immediately after UK forces moved out of Basrah city in September to their main base at the Basrah Air Station. The move out of the city would result in provincial control in all but name. After all, British forces were no longer patrolling the streets of Basrah due to the summer 2007 truce with Jaysh al-Mahdi (JAM) leader Ahmed al-Fartusi, and the UK's position was that the Iraqis would never take charge of their own affairs unless the British left.[47] Therefore, Binns pushed to "reduce the gap between leaving the palace and going to PIC."[48]

Earlier proposals to speed up Basrah's transfer to PIC had met with skepticism at coalition headquarters in Baghdad. MNC-I had determined that the Iraqi security forces in the province were not ready, a position generally shared by the central Iraqi Government. In January 2007, Odierno had written to General George Casey, Jr., "the MND-SE [commander] now projects Basra to meet conditions for transfer of security to PIC in April 2007 (previously March 2007). I assess that more time is needed."[49] Petraeus, too, had urged the British Government on at least one occasion not to withdraw its troops too precipitously, and American officers in Baghdad raised doubts that conditions in the province merited a handover of security.[50] It was doubtful that any of the four criteria for transferring to PIC—the level of the threat, the capability of the Iraqi security forces, the capability of the national and provincial governments, and the ability of coalition forces to re-intervene—had been met by the latter half of 2007. However, the temporary reduction in attacks on MND-SE after the truce with JAM may have created that impression.[51]

The summer 2007 truce also had led to a drastic reduction in British operations against Sadrist militias, as the MND-SE headquarters developed highly restrictive rules of engagement to prevent their forces from upsetting the tenuous agreement. American forces in the sector, made up almost exclusively of elements of the Combined Joint Special Operations Task Force (CJSOTF), were expected to follow the same rules — a situation that led to some frustrating episodes from the American perspective. On one occasion in 2008, CJSOTF commander Colonel Christopher Conner requested permission for an air strike against militiamen setting up a rail system frequently used to launch rockets, but MND-SE denied the strike because, as Conner recounted, there was nothing loaded on the rails. When the militiamen began loading a rocket onto the rail, the CJSOTF asked for permission again, but were denied because the rocketeers had not demonstrated hostile intent. As the special operators watched, the militiamen launched the rocket and began breaking down the launch system, but when the CJSOTF Soldiers made one final entreaty, their British counterparts denied the strike with the explanation that since the militiamen had no rockets left, they were not demonstrating hostile intent.[52]

On the streets of Basrah, however, it was clear that militias terrorized the city with impunity, while the city's police were either infiltrated by militiamen or cowed by militia threats. Coalition commanders had deemed the 10th Iraqi Army Division so widely infiltrated by militants that the entire division was transferred north to Maysan and Dhi Qar Provinces. The fledgling 14th Iraqi Army Division that had been created to replace the 10th in Basrah was still being formed and trained. Neither the police nor the army were trustworthy or capable of enforcing the rule of law. On a political level, the provincial council was riven by warring factions incapable of providing public services. Prime Minister Maliki was openly hostile to the Fadhila Party Governor Mohammed Musbeh al-Waeli, who seemed mainly occupied by a scheme to turn the province into a federal region under his rule and keep its massive oil revenues for his party rather than for the government in Baghdad. It was doubtful that MND-SE, with only 4,500 British troops available and an operating posture constrained by JAM accommodation, would be able to re-intervene to help resolve these conflicts.[53]

Despite these dynamics, Binns and MND-SE continued to press for PIC for Basrah Province, pointing to the trend of fewer militia attacks against the British base. In fall 2007, Odierno and Petraeus finally acceded to a policy they believed originated in Whitehall and that they had no hope of altering. On December 16, MND-SE transferred control of the province to Iraqi authorities at a ceremony on Basrah Air Station attended by senior Iraqi officials and UK Foreign Secretary David W. Miliband. The speeches were upbeat about Basrah's future, but hinted that the security environment was dangerous. Miliband admitted that Basrah was not "a land of milk and honey," and Iraqi National Security Adviser Mowaffaq Rubaie stressed that "the rule of law needed to be upheld, only the government should have weapons, and that political parties needed to unite and 'crack down on militias and religious extremists'."[54] Meanwhile, coalition officers judged downtown Basrah too dangerous for Miliband to visit.

Source: U.S. Army photo by Sergeant Nicole Dykstra (Released).

Major General Graham Binns, Governor Mohammed Musbeh al-Waeli, National Security Adviser Mowaffaq Rubaie, and Lieutenant General Mohan al-Freiji During the Basrah Transfer Ceremony.[55]

Because of Maliki's ongoing dispute with Governor Waeli, the Prime Minister was loath to give Waeli control of the province's security affairs, which complicated the terms of the PIC agreement. Waeli assumed responsibility for civil affairs, but he was forced to sign a letter of understanding that security matters were to be handled by the chief of the Basrah Operations Center, Lieutenant General Mohan al-Freiji. U.S. commanders had blocked Freiji from becoming the Baghdad operations commander just months before because he was both sectarian and tyrannical.[56] UK forces formally agreed to continue to provide training to Iraqi security forces, assist Freiji at the Basrah Operations Command, and re-intervene only in extremis and only with Maliki's approval. The latter condition was unlike other PIC agreements, which allowed American troops to re-intervene based on a local Iraqi commander's request.

British forces also assured MNC-I that they would continue to patrol the Iranian border and secure key supply routes.[57] Nonetheless, with provincial Iraqi control came a shift for the British from "tactical overwatch" to "operational overwatch," which Whitehall intended to trigger the long-planned drawdown of troops from 4,500 at the end of 2007 to 2,500 by the spring of 2008.[58]

Iraqi Security Forces in Basrah

Part of the UK leaders' eagerness to leave Basrah was that, throughout 2007, British officials increasingly came to believe that the primary cause of violence in Basrah was the presence of UK forces. "Ninety percent of the violence was directed against us," Binns argued. "If we didn't present the target, then the figures would reduce, and coming out of the city had a dramatic effect on the metrics that we used to measure the violence. I'm not pretending that the security situation significantly improved for Basrawis; it wouldn't, and I knew it wouldn't until the Iraqi security forces got back in there."[59] By this logic, a reduced British presence ostensibly would force the Iraqi security forces to take responsibility for security. Echoing SECDEF Donald Rumsfeld's ideas about the Iraqis' military capacity, Binns also believed the Iraqi security forces "wouldn't get better until they were given responsibility, and it was a bit like . . . taking the stabilisers off a child's bike. They were going to wobble for a while and I was there to make sure they didn't fall over."[60]

In the new post-PIC arrangement, MND-SE would rely heavily on the strength, capabilities, and loyalty of the Iraqi security forces in Basrah, which had been judged thoroughly infiltrated by militias. By September, when the British moved out of Basrah Palace, the new 14th Iraqi Army Division, created to compensate for the corruption of the 10th Iraqi Army Division, was only at half strength and suffering serious equipment shortfalls. Beyond the Iraqi Army, nearly every law enforcement unit in Basrah was under the influence of some political party's militia. JAM had overwhelmingly infiltrated the Iraqi police, the port authority, and the Facilities Protection Service. The Islamic Supreme Council of Iraq (ISCI) and Badr Corps also had infiltrated some of the police units and controlled the National Intelligence Service bureau in the city. Fadhila had firm control over the Oil Protection Force, and Iraqi Hizballah controlled the Customs Police Force.[61] While provincial police Chief Major General Mohammed Jalil Khalaf Shuwayl was regarded favorably by coalition officials in Basrah, his force was heavily infiltrated and corrupt.[62] Jalil's predecessor had said in 2005 that he trusted only a quarter of his officers, a figure Jalil frequently repeated to coalition counterparts.[63] Given the circumstances, Basrah's "good cops" felt outnumbered and intimidated into submission, with much of the militia-infiltrated police effectively a part of a power struggle among militant groups rather than protectors of the population. The day after PIC, Jalil criticized the departing British, declaring to a reporter: "They left me militia, they left me gangsters, and they left me all the troubles in the world."[64]

Basrah's Descent into Chaos

Despite Shaw's and Binns's theory about the proximate cause of Basrah's unrest, violence and crime skyrocketed within the city shortly after the British pullout. With the Iraqi forces too weak and unwilling to confront the militias alone, Basrah's militias had free rein to compete violently for political control, to access economic resources and oil, and to control the security forces especially in neighborhoods such as Qibla and Hayaniyah, Sadr City-like slums developed to accommodate rural migration to the city in the 1970s and 1980s.[65] Kidnapping, murder, extortion, rape, torture, and intimidation became commonplace in a city once a popular vacation destination on the Persian Gulf. On February 11, 2008, CBS reporter Richard Butler was kidnapped from his hotel by JAM members wearing police uniforms.[66] The same month the director of the Basrah Electricity Department was kidnapped. Violence became so prevalent that Basrawis held a protest on March 8 to criticize the security forces for failing to protect the city, while local politicians began calling contacts in the central government for help.[67]

Basrah's intellectuals, doctors, security officials, and former Ba'athists increasingly were targeted as Shi'a militias implemented a strict interpretation of Islamic law, purged secular thinking, and sought revenge against the Ba'ath. Barbers were also singled out for their willingness to commit the heretical crime of shaving beards. Attacks against women, usually carried out by militiamen bent on punishing "prostitutes" (women who were simply not dressed conservatively enough in public), became a focal point for the violence, making international headlines. According to the provincial council, 133 Basrawi women were murdered in 2007, though unofficial numbers were much higher.[68] In late November 2007, police chief Jalil handed coalition officials folders with photographs detailing the murders of 45 women, the majority of them executed in the preceding 3 months for purportedly violating the militia's strict interpretation of Sharia law. Most of the women were shot in the face, two were beheaded, and some tortured to death. Another 35 women reportedly were murdered in the first quarter of 2008.[69]

One of the unintended consequences of repositioning British forces outside the city was the loss of MND-SE's situational awareness inside Basrah. Binns noted that, "coming out of the city did have an impact on my situational awareness. I found it difficult to keep track of what was going on in the city," a factor that made it hard for MND-SE to gauge the downward spiral of the security environment inside the city, 6 kilometers away.[70]

Even the British truce with JAM leader Ahmen al-Fartusi began to break down by January 2008. Once MND-SE released Fartusi in December 2007 and the last remaining JAM prisoner in January 2008, the British no longer had any leverage over the militia. While indirect-fire attacks onto the MND-SE bases had dropped significantly after the accommodation with JAM, they continued nonetheless, with 5 in September, 9 in October, 11 in November, and 12 in December. In January and February 2008, rocket attacks on Basrah Air Station reached levels similar to the previous summer, before the truce with Fartusi.[71] When pressed by MND-SE, Fartusi claimed that rogue or non-JAM affiliated groups were responsible for the renewed attacks.[72] While Fartusi was likely duplicitous, there were doubtless some JAM Special Groups commanders ignoring him, and other militias, like Thar Allah and Sayyed al-Shahadda, who were not beholden to the Fartusi deal or to the mainstream JAM groups.

Eventually word began to reach Baghdad that Basrah was in crisis. Although MND-SE lacked adequate information to report to MNC-I on the security situation inside the city, Iraqi authorities and politicians in Basrah reported independently to Maliki and the Iraqi cabinet on the dire state of affairs. Alarmed by these reports, Maliki dispatched Iraqi vice Chief of Defense General Nasier Abadi from Baghdad in early January to investigate conditions in Basrah, and Abadi returned with a grim report of a city in chaos, with beleaguered Iraqi security forces (ISF) units outgunned and outnumbered by militants. In February 2008, Binns's newly arrived replacement, Major General Barney White-Spunner, General Officer Commanding the 3d (UK) Mechanized Division, quickly reached a similar conclusion. "[I]t was absolutely clear that we needed an operation to clear the Shi'a militias out of the city," White-Spunner later recalled, though for such an operation to be effective, he believed it "really had to be Iraqi-led with us in support."[73] U.S. officials stationed with MND-SE in Basrah also frequently reported on the downward trend in the city in early 2008. "At some point in the very near future coalition forces will need to go kinetic in Basrah—the situation has gotten that bad," one U.S. official told the visiting Odierno in early 2008.[74] Odierno was highly sympathetic to the arguments, but stressed the difficult balance between pushing the British to be more forward leaning and the political imperative to keep them in the coalition. Once MNC-I had dealt with Mosul, it could then turn its attention to Basrah, Odierno said.

Source: DoD photo by Petty Officer 3d Class Jannine Hartmann (Released).

Major General Barney White-Spunner.[75]

General Freiji's Plan to Regain Government Control over Basrah

As the security situation in Basrah worsened, Lieutenant General Mohan al-Freiji formed a plan to regain control of the city, loosely based on the security framework for Belfast in the 1970s and 1980s, as well as on recent U.S. successes in other parts of Iraq.[76] British forces continued to train Iraqi security forces, which would later establish checkpoints and outposts across the city. Over several months, more Iraqi troops became available as they completed their training, and the Iraqi security forces would build new outposts before finally confronting the militias. The plan also called for increased patrols along the border to prevent Iranian assistance to the Shi'a militias. Beginning in the summer of 2008, Freiji envisioned that Iraqi troops would commence a 6-week weapons amnesty and buy-back program, followed by house-to-house clearing operations.[77] Unlike Operation SINBAD, Freiji's plan would put Iraqi troops in the operational lead for the first time, and add sufficient numbers of troops to clear and hold territory.

On March 4 and 5, Freiji briefed his plan to Iraqi and coalition leaders in Baghdad, including Maliki, Petraeus, Austin, White-Spunner, and the Iraqi security ministers.[78] The U.S. officers were not impressed with Freiji's concept or his presentation of it. "Mohan's plan is not fully resourced, and his timeline is overly optimistic," Petraeus reported to Gates.[79] With the total number of U.S. brigades dropping to pre-surge levels by the summer, MNC-I would only be able to tackle one problem at a time and was necessarily

357

focused on finishing the campaign against AQI in Mosul. U.S. commanders also saw some inherent problems with the plan, particularly Freiji's desire to fall back on the Saddam Hussein-era tactics of cordoning and bombarding populated areas, not accounting for the use of special operations, and not having a reconstruction plan. Petraeus directed the Multi-National Security Transition Command-Iraq (MNSTC-I) commander, Lieutenant General James M. Dubik, to help improve Freiji's plan and suggested reconvening on March 21, with coalition plans for the northern offensive against AQI proceeding in the meantime.[80]

As the coalition looked toward Mosul, however, Maliki became more focused on Basrah. The Prime Minister raised the subject during the March 16 Ministerial Committee on National Security, arguing that the lawlessness in the southern city presented a greater problem than Mosul. Maliki and several of his ministers seemed genuinely concerned about Basrah's security. As the U.S.-led surge had begun to quell the Sunni insurgency in late 2007, Maliki could afford to start looking at other areas that posed a threat to his government, and Basrah clearly stood out. Furthermore, Maliki increasingly saw Moqtada Sadr and JAM as his primary political competition. In April 2007, the Sadrists had pulled their six ministers from Maliki's cabinet over their demand for a timeline forcing the departure of U.S. troops, and in September, the Sadrists quit Maliki's United Iraqi Alliance bloc in the Council of Representatives, leaving him to govern with a narrow majority.[81] Maliki also was upset that Basrah's economically vital port of Umm Qasr was entirely under Sadrist control.[82] For Maliki, Sadr was no longer a Shi'a ally of convenience, but a political rival to be eliminated. By breaking the Sadrist grip on Basrah, restoring order, and delivering on economic growth, Maliki likely believed he could set up his Da'wa Party to win the south in the provincial elections scheduled for late 2008.

Source: DoD photo by Staff Sergeant Lorie Jewell (Released).

National Security Adviser Mowaffaq Rubaie Informs General David Petraeus on March 21, 2008, of Prime Minister Maliki's Intention to Initiate an Offensive in Basrah.[83]

At the scheduled March 21 meeting to review Freiji's plan, Rubaie pulled Petraeus aside and informed him that Maliki had decided to accelerate plans for a security operation in Basrah and wanted to meet Petraeus the following day to discuss the matter. When Petraeus met Maliki, the Prime Minister blamed the British for Basrah's faltering security, announced he was deploying additional Iraqi security forces to the city, and revealed that he would travel to Basrah the following day with his own AK47 to deal with the situation. Stunned by Maliki's plans, Petraeus argued vehemently that the government's forces were not ready to execute the operation. If Maliki insisted on an operation in Basrah, Petraeus advised, the Iraqi leader should wait for more deliberate preparations to be made. When Maliki made it clear that he intended to go south immediately, a chagrined Petraeus advised him to "take lots of money to Basra to help with inevitable logistical difficulties." Petraeus offered to provide "movement support, intelligence support, aviation-related maintenance and logistics support, and liaison teams to work with Iraqi special operations forces and to assist with close air support and attack helicopters, should they prove necessary."[84]

The Prime Minister's decision took MND-SE by surprise as well. Having seen at the early March plan briefings in Baghdad that Lieutenant General Freiji's operation was not imminent, White-Spunner had departed on leave to Germany, where he planned to brief the soon-to-arrive British 7th Brigade on the additional resources needed to support Freiji's plan, though the British commander quickly returned on learning of Maliki's new intentions.[85] Sitting in for White-Spunner at a conference with Austin and the coalition division commanders in Baghdad on March 21, the same day Petraeus learned of Maliki's Basrah plans, Brigadier Julian Free, Commander, 4th (UK) Infantry Brigade, had listened to Austin describe the impending MNC-I operation against AQI in the north. "All I need from you, Julian," Austin said, "is to avoid opening a second front for us."[86] The Iraqi Prime Minister's surprise move, however, caused Free to return immediately to Basrah, where the British brigadier found himself reporting to Austin that a second front was indeed opening, less than 24 hours after the MNC-I commander's injunction.[87]

"Maliki Has Bit Off More Than He Can Chew"

Despite their determination to restore Basrah to government control, Maliki and several of his advisers clearly misunderstood the scale of the problem. During the March meetings in Baghdad, Rubaie had charged that Freiji was exaggerating the extent of the problem and characterized it, as former MND-SE commanders Shaw and Binns had done, as a criminal problem rather than an insurgent one.[88] Even Maliki said the problem was caused by "criminals and gang leaders" in his March 22 meeting with Petraeus. Failing to understand how deeply the militias had become entrenched as they vied to take control of Basrah, the Iraqi leaders underestimated how fierce the militia resistance would be.[89] This misperception was likely compounded by Maliki's quick success in leading Iraqi forces to stop the intra-Shi'a violence in Karbala in August 2007. On March 24, Maliki, Minister of Defense Abdel Qader al-Obeidi, Minister of National Security Affairs Shirwan al-Waeli, and military advisers from MNF-I and the CJSOTF arrived at Basrah Palace, where they planned to direct Iraqi operations to retake the city.[90] Interior Minister Jawad Bolani, who feared flying, drove down separately in an armored convoy. Angry with the British for having made an accommodation with Fartusi to cede the city to militia control, Maliki did not consult with MND-SE about the impending operation and even ejected British officers from meetings that day. Despite Maliki's hostility, Brigadier Free took the precautionary step of sending the commander of the Royal Dragoon Guards to help advise Freiji at the Basrah Operations Command in the Shatt al-Arab Hotel.[91]

Confident of an easy victory, Maliki ordered Freiji to execute Operation CHARGE OF THE KNIGHTS (or SAWLAT AL-FORSAN) the next morning, despite the fact that Iraqi reinforcing units, including the 1st Brigade, 1st Iraqi Army Division, with its U.S. Marine military transition teams (MiTTs) were still en route. At dawn on March 25, nearly 10,000 Iraqi police and soldiers of the newly formed 14th Iraqi Army Division convoyed into militia-controlled districts to cordon them off and search suspected militia locations.

They were driving into a trap. Because of militia infiltration in the police and army, JAM commanders had plenty of time to mobilize their estimated 6,000 fighters and pre-pare complex small arms and IED ambushes for the government convoys. Once the Iraqi columns entered militia neighborhoods and met stiff resistance, their advance immedi-ately halted and their units fell into disarray. Without U.S. or British advisers embed-ded in the Iraqi brigades, coalition aircraft could not engage militia targets or evacuate wounded Iraqi soldiers, leaving U.S. F-16s on station merely to fly extremely low in a show of force.

At the Basrah Operations Command, General Freiji seemed to have lost control of the operation. Lacking communications equipment, Freiji relied on several mobile phones and a map to issue orders.[92] The bifurcation of command between Freiji at the operations center and Maliki at Basrah Palace further complicated coordination. Freiji had failed to impress coalition counterparts in his planning, and he did the same when the fighting began. At one point, Freiji asked his British counterparts for air or artillery strikes to take out militia positions. When asked to point out specific locations, he shouted, "Here!" as he waved his arm across the entire map of the city.[93] More importantly, Freiji, under pressure from Maliki, scrapped the methodical plan he had developed with coalition assistance to retake Basrah district by district, and instead began to conduct hasty attacks with little thought for logistics or troop strength.

As Maliki's and Freiji's plans began to break down, JAM indirect-fire teams launched repeated rocket and mortar salvos at Basrah Palace, killing the head of Maliki's security detail and forcing the Prime Minister to seek cover for hours. Frustrated with the ISFs' poor performance and eager to deflect blame, Maliki announced that he was relieving Freiji of command in favor of Major General Abdel Aziz al-Ubaydi, although to every-one's confusion, Freiji remained in his headquarters and continued to issue orders after this edict.[94] Conditions were not any better for Freiji at his operations center in the Shatt al-Arab Hotel, which also was targeted by heavy mortar, rocket-propelled grenades, and sniper fire throughout the day.

By the end of the first day of Operation CHARGE OF THE KNIGHTS, it was clear the militias were winning. JAM ambushes had killed about 50 Iraqi soldiers, wounded another 120, and destroyed dozens of vehicles, while the militia groups had lost approx-imately 40 fighters.[95] Not only did the militiamen prevent the Iraqi Army from achieving any of its objectives, but they also seized some provincial government buildings over-night. The 14th Iraqi Army Division's 52d Brigade, full of new recruits, had fallen into disarray on the first day, with some of its soldiers beginning to desert as the fighting turned to their enemies' advantage.

Similarly, nearly two-thirds of the Iraqi police either deserted or discarded their uniforms to fight alongside the militiamen.[96] Only after Iraqi troops began to stream back into Shaibah Logistics Base west of the city did the 1st Battalion, The Royal Regiment of Scotland (The Royal Scots Borderers), and MND-SE learn how poorly the attack had gone.[97]

U.S. leaders in Baghdad soon realized that Maliki had precipitated a crisis that could derail the entire coalition campaign in Iraq. Conferring among themselves, Petraeus and Crocker concluded that they could not allow the Prime Minister to fail and give the Sadrists a major military and political victory. Even as Maliki's troops reeled from the first day's fighting, Petraeus and Austin quickly shifted resources and key personnel to Basrah, making the Prime Minister's operation the MNC-I main effort. At Tallil Airfield in Dhi Qar Province, four AH-64 Apaches and two UH-60 Black Hawk helicopters were dispatched to provide attack and medevac support. Elements of the Iraqi special operations forces (ISOF) Brigade with their CJSOTF advisers were flown from Baghdad on multiple lifts of MC-130 aircraft, joining the regional ISOF Battalion already stationed in Basrah. The Baghdad Emergency Response Unit and Hillah Special Weapons and Tactics (SWAT), two elite Interior Ministry units similarly advised by CJSOTF operational detachment alpha (ODA) units, also rushed to Basrah.[98] At MND-SE, Brigadier Free also issued a "be-prepared" order for the 1st Battalion, Scots Guards, to reenter Basrah if necessary with 14 Challenger II tanks and 40 Warrior infantry fighting vehicles, a maneuver that Whitehall had expressly forbidden before the battle.[99] On the same night of March 25, special operators from CJSOTF that MND-SE previously had prohibited from entering the city due to the Fartusi truce were able to make their way to Freiji's headquarters, while Rear Admiral Edward G. Winters III, a U.S. Navy SEAL in charge of Iraqi special operations training, went to Basrah Palace by vehicle convoy. Army Colonel James H. Coffman arrived at Basrah Palace to advise Interior Minister Jawad Bolani, and reported to Petraeus that the operation stood a 50-50 chance of success.[100]

Despite the bad turn of events on March 25, the next day Maliki publicly demanded that the militias lay down their arms and hand over their leaders within 72 hours. Fighting continued on March 26 and spread beyond Basrah to the southern Iraqi cities of Kut, Diwaniya, and Hillah, as well as to Zubayr, about 8 kilometers southwest of Basrah, where militiamen overran two police stations. The next day, the fighting spread to Nasiriyah, where the local Iraqi SWAT unit and its CJSOTF advisers fought off JAM militants in a 56-hour battle.[101] The Basrah confrontation was escalating into a war between the Sadrists and the government across the entire south.

On March 27, Austin and U.S. Embassy's political-military counselor Marcie Ries flew to Basrah and then to the Basrah Palace to meet with Maliki. Still upset with the British, Maliki embarrassed Brigadier Free by ejecting him from the meeting, after which the Iraqi leader criticized the United Kingdom for letting militias take control of Basrah and MNF-I for not doing enough to help in the present crisis, before demanding more coalition air support. Providing close air support was problematic, because the forward air controllers in the military transition teams were still en route and the Iraqi units in the city seemed neither to understand fully the rules of engagement nor to be able to provide MND-SE with accurate coordinates. Calming down Maliki, Austin convinced the Iraqi leader to allow coalition advisers, including the British, to integrate more closely with Iraqi units to help provide the air support he requested. Maliki also ordered additional Iraqi units to deploy to Basrah, including the 1st Iraqi Army Division's headquarters and the rest of its 1st Brigade, as well as alerting four other divisions to be prepared to offer support.[102]

Meanwhile, JAM groups launched a counterattack throughout Basrah, in what was to become the militia's high-water mark during the operation. Police chief Jalil's convoy was hit by an IED that killed 3 of his guards, after which Jalil reported that 28 police stations and army strong points had been simultaneously attacked at dawn. Hundreds of police officers were still defecting to the militias, and in the city's Maqil District, militiamen who had overrun a police station and checkpoint and blocked an ISF relief column trying to reach beleaguered troops at the Camp Apache ammunition depot. This time, the inexperienced 52d Brigade, 14th Iraqi Army Division, located in positions close to the JAM stronghold neighborhoods of Hayaniyah and Qibla, faced the worst of the fighting and simply disintegrated, with half of its 3,000 soldiers deserting.[103]

The Iraqi Army in Basrah, already demoralized by its defeats at the hands of the Sadrists, began to come apart as the weakness of the Iraqi logistics system derailed the Prime Minister's offensive operations. A CJSOTF adviser who observed Iraqi planning efforts in Basrah Palace noted in a March 28 report: "There is no logistical resupply or support plan. The majority, if not all Iraqi forces are critically short of food, fuel, water, and ammunition. In several cases, units have none of the previous supply items mentioned. The reported average ammunition stores in the IA [Iraqi Army] are 4 magazines per man, but it is likely less than that. All of the commanders appear to understand that they are being led to disaster."[104] Without their own combat service support units, Iraqi Army units had been relying on privately owned gas stations to refuel their vehicles and local markets to purchase food, but when these closed down due to fighting, the Iraqis had no alternatives.[105] Iraqi forces requested U.S. and British air support to stem the rout of their forces, but as before, the Iraqis' lack of situational awareness and disinclination to mitigate civilian casualties sometimes led the coalition representatives to refrain from conducting the strikes. On one occasion, Iraqi commanders handed American advisers a napkin with numbers on it and instructed them to "bomb here." When the advisers could not translate the numbers into grid coordinates, the Iraqis explained that the numbers were, in fact, a phone number, and that the man who answered the phone would know the location to bomb. When the Americans called the number, they were told to "bomb the white truck in the intersection . . . we know you can see the truck," with no other explanation.[106]

As these actions unfolded in Basrah, the fighting also intensified in Baghdad, where JAM fighters from Sadr City and other militia-dominated neighbors had begun coordinated attacks against the coalition and the Iraqi Government. What had begun as a short-term security operation in one city was becoming a full-blown Shi'a civil war, with the Maliki government's fate in the balance. Writing to Gates on March 30, Petraeus reported "at this point, my assessment is that Prime Minister Maliki has bit off more than he can chew in Basra."

Maliki "remains in his own world," Petraeus judged, and the Iraqi leader had "put the credibility of his government on the line in Basra."[107] The biggest problem, in Petraeus's view, was the mismatch between Maliki's "publicly stated objectives," essentially to eliminate the militias, and the actual capabilities of the Iraqi security forces to do it. Petraeus noted that the coalition was trying to provide Maliki with as much advice as possible "to improve planning and to help the Iraqis establish a battle rhythm" and provide essential enablers such as attack aviation, ISR coverage, and logistics. Such enablers, Petraeus said, could "put Maliki in an advantageous position for future negotiations" based on Ambassador Crocker's recommendation to Maliki to "think hard about a political agreement to enable this to come to as good a conclusion as possible."[108] However, the MNF-I commander appeared to have little faith that Maliki could actually win outright the civil war he had inadvertently entered.

Reinforcements Arrive

The situation in Basrah remained tense on March 28. Realizing that something needed to be done to repair Maliki's relationship with the British and to provide more coalition surveillance and air support to the Iraqis, Austin had dispatched his MNC-I deputy commander, U.S. Marine Major General George J. Flynn, and several hundred U.S. personnel to Basrah, including a 120-member Marine Corps tactical operations center to integrate into the MND-SE headquarters and the Basrah Operations Center. The arrival of so many Americans at the British headquarters was awkward. On one hand, many on the British staff realized that the truce with Fartusi, the British drawdown, and a lack of political will were some of the root causes for the violence in Basrah and they welcomed the U.S. assistance. Others saw it as an American takeover of MND-SE. For White-Spunner and Free, however, the open fighting in Basrah meant that the truce was no longer in effect, the gloves needed to come off, and U.S. involvement was needed to stave off disaster. In any case, the arrival of the MNC-I contingent and the Marine Corps' aviation assets suddenly gave MND-SE a capacity and combat power the British had not had in Basrah since 2003.

Flying immediately into Basrah, Flynn and Free met with Lieutenant General Freiji (who continued in his job thanks to his decades-long relationship with Defense Minister Abdel Qader) and the newly appointed 14th Iraqi Army Division commander, Major General Aziz Swaidy, to advise the Iraqis on how to salvage the situation. At the same time, U.S. F-16s, F/A-18s, Predators, and AH-64 Apaches began to hunt down the JAM rocket teams attacking Iraqi and MND-SE bases, while the first U.S. MiTT with the lead battalion of the 1st Brigade, 1st Iraqi Army Division, arrived and immediately called in air strikes to relieve 14th Division troops pinned down near Basrah University. "Once we had forward air controllers on the ground to verify targets, it really made a difference," Free reported later.[109] Help had finally arrived.

Between March 29 and 30, the rest of the Iraqi reinforcements trickled into the city. Troops from Colonel Charles A. Flynn's 1st Brigade, 82d Airborne Division, also arrived from Tallil to embed with the Iraqis and to help MND-SE coordinate fires. Meanwhile, on March 29, Iraqi special operations forces and their CJSOTF mentors commenced Operation LIGHTNING ANVIL, a series of nightly raids into the city with the support of the Scots Guards' Warrior Infantry Fighting Vehicles that would kill 75 militia fighters over the following month.[110] The British Task Force SPARTAN also would assist, conducting covert surveillance on targets for the strike teams.[111]

As White-Spunner returned to Basrah on March 30, the reinforced Iraqi units and their coalition enablers were finally massing to retake the city. White-Spunner and Free agreed to insert British MiTTs with the 14th Iraqi Division and then retroactively requested permission from London the next day, though given that the United Kingdom's reputation was on the line, there was little chance of the request being denied. Rhine Company, 1st Battalion, The Royal Regiment of Scotland, and D Squadron, Royal Dragoon Guards, were assigned to the 14th Iraqi Army Division's three brigades, as well as to Freiji's headquarters. The decision to embed British advisers marked a major shift in the British approach to Basrah. By April 1, 14 of the 38 Iraqi units in the city had coalition MiTTs attached to them.[112]

The Tide Turns

Despite the coalition and Iraqi reinforcements, the situation remained fragile, and to some Iraqi leaders in Baghdad seemed on the point of failure. With Maliki away from Baghdad and disheartening reports coming out of Basrah, some of Maliki's political opponents sought to take advantage of what they perceived to be the Prime Minister's misstep. Expectedly, the Sadrists, with help from former Prime Minister Ibrahim al-Ja'afari and Ahmad Chalabi, began an attempt to engineer a no-confidence vote against Maliki, while an Iraqi Parliamentary delegation flew to Tehran to consult with the Iranians about the crisis. Under Iranian pressure to negotiate, Moqtada Sadr issued a nine-point cease-fire letter on that day, instructing his followers to cooperate with the Iraqi Government and labeling those who publicly displayed their weapons as criminals, even though his steps fell short of the Iraqi Government demand that the Sadrists lay down their arms. In exchange for the Sadrists' disarmament, Maliki's government promised to leave the rest of the Sadrists alone and allow them to participate in the next elections.[113]

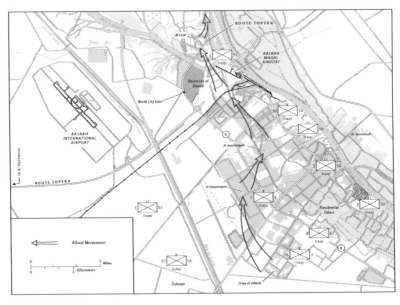

Map created by the official cartographer at the U.S. Army Center of Military History, Washington, DC.

Map 18. Basrah Battle, March–April 2008.

364

The political situation in Baghdad looked grim for the Prime Minister, whose allies found themselves on the defensive as the Sadrists attempted to organize a no-confidence vote in the Iraqi Parliament. Back in Basrah, however, events outpaced the political negotiations in Baghdad and continued to turn in the Prime Minister's favor. At noon on March 30, Royal Dragoon Guards' tanks crashed through blockades in Hayaniyah to allow the 1st Brigade, 1st Iraqi Army Division, to fight the militia for an hour before pulling back. Simultaneously, Interior Minister Bolani and a force of 300 men advanced to the port at Umm Qasr and found that militia groups had already abandoned it and had unwisely all gone to Basrah to take part in the battle there.[114] Having achieved a symbolic victory and survived a week of militia bombardment, Maliki flew back to Baghdad on April 1 to deal with the political crisis that had arisen in his absence.

As the Prime Minister departed Basrah, beleaguered Basrawis, ready for change after months of being terrorized by the militias and angry at JAM for turning its weapons on the Iraqi security forces, began reporting the names and locations of hundreds of militia members on anonymous tip lines set up by MND-SE. Basrah's Shi'a citizenry, fed up with the militias' criminal behavior and religious extremism, welcomed the arrival of the mostly Sunni Iraqi Army reinforcements, who had deployed from the 1st Iraqi Army Division in Anbar Province. The integration of the MiTTs with Iraqi units also had increased the effectiveness of coalition air strikes and restored confidence to the Iraqi troops. Coalition staff support at Iraqi headquarters improved coordination between the disparate Iraqi security forces. More importantly, it allowed Flynn, White-Spunner, and Free to help Lieutenant General Freiji develop a more coherent plan to clear Basrah's districts systematically, instead of Freiji's erratic headlong rushes into the city. While Freiji preferred to conduct yet another hasty attack on the JAM stronghold of Hayaniyah, Flynn and MND-SE convinced him to establish freedom of maneuver by first regaining control of the city's main arteries. On April 2, Iraqi troops successfully cleared militia roadblocks and seized key intersections, while coalition air support easily destroyed militia fighters defending in the open.[115]

Source: DoD photo by Corporal Daniel Angel (Released).

Marines and Iraqi Forces During Fighting in the Latif District of Basrah on May 3, 2008.[116]

The same evening, Maliki announced a 7-day cease-fire (eventually extended to 11 days), though militia elements continued heavy indirect-fire attacks against Iraqi and MND-SE bases. The next day, the Prime Minister also announced plans to create 25,000 jobs for Basrah and to spend $100 million for reconstruction.[117] The lull allowed Iraqi Government officials to implement a modestly successful weapons buy-back program, reestablish logistics, receive additional reinforcements (including the 7th Iraqi Army Division's 26th Brigade with its U.S. Army MiTTs), and organize for future clearing operations as MND-SE gathered vital targeting information.[118] With the arrival of the 26th Brigade, Maliki's forces in Basrah now included two Sunni-majority brigades from Anbar whose soldiers and officers had no qualms about fighting against Basrah's Shi'a militias, a dramatic change from the militia-influenced local Iraqi Army and police units.

Determined to press his advantage against the Sadrists, Prime Minister Maliki used the terms of the cease-fire to continue operations by relabeling Operation CHARGE OF THE KNIGHTS a law-enforcement operation focused on arresting criminals based on warrants, and not directed against any particular group.[119] Mainstream JAM members generally upheld the cease-fire, though some Special Groups ignored it and continued to fight. With these initiatives in motion, Maliki won a political victory when, at an April 5 meeting of Iraq's major political parties, the mainstream Shi'a, Kurdish, and Sunni parties unanimously sided with the Prime Minister rather than with the Sadrists. Reporting to Gates on April 6, a cautiously optimistic Petraeus noted that JAM had been "bruised during the last couple of weeks" and their "supplies fairly exhausted." "Overall, it appears that Prime Minister Maliki's government is emerging from this crisis on a fairly solid basis," the MNF-I commander assessed, an outcome he had not contemplated when Maliki began his ill-advised expedition 2 weeks earlier.[120]

SINBAD Redux

When Maliki's cease-fire ended on April 12, Iraqi security forces spent the next 2 days isolating the militia strongholds in the Qibla, Hayaniyah, Timinyah, and Five-Mile Districts, the same restive neighborhoods Operation SINBAD had failed to bring under control 15 months before. The Sunni-majority 26th Brigade also successfully cleared the Qibla area with little opposition, a fact that MND-SE leaders took as a sign of weakening militia resistance. As the Iraqi troops swept through Qibla, they found large stockpiles of abandoned arms collected on sidewalks, while local residents welcomed the Iraqi troops and pointed out militia hideouts.[121] Learning from the key mistake of Operation SINBAD, Iraqi engineers constructed strongpoints at strategic sites after clearing these areas so they could then be held. By chance, on April 14, soldiers from the 14th Iraqi Army Division's 51st Brigade engaged a JAM cell firing from a house in the Jubailah District and discovered the kidnapped CBS journalist Richard Butler inside.[122]

The same aspects of the Qibla clearing were repeated over the next 2 months as the Iraqi brigades and their coalition advisers cleared other areas of the city. Seeing the ominous signs, large numbers of JAM members began to flee, many of them to the town of Qurnah 70 kilometers to the northwest, or across the border to Iran. Most of their senior leaders had already left. After being released by the British in December 2007, Ahmed al-Fartusi had been recaptured in Baghdad on March 4—before CHARGE OF

THE KNIGHTS began—in a coalition operation to capture Special Groups leader Hajji Shibl, a member of Qais al-Khazali's Asa'ib Ahl al-Haqq (League of the Righteous). Fartusi was meeting with Shibl ostensibly on behalf of the United Kingdom to negotiate the release of the British hostages taken from the Finance Ministry in 2007, and was re-released by MNF-I shortly after his capture.[123] When CHARGE OF THE KNIGHTS began, Fartusi fled to Beirut, where he issued threats against the British forces for breaking the truce, an absurd accusation, considering the heavy JAM bombardment against British and Iraqi Government troops.[124] The notorious militia-linked Captain Jaffar of Basrah's Special Crimes Unit, who had been responsible for the 2005 abduction of two UK soldiers, escaped to Iran in the midst of the fighting, as did a number of other JAM leaders.[125] The departure of JAM's senior leaders after the first week of fighting significantly weakened the resolve of the remaining militiamen and resulted in an uncoordinated insurgent defense of their districts, leading White-Spunner and others in MND-SE to express surprise at "how quickly the Shi'a militias crumbled."[126]

From the early days of the operation, however, there had been signs that the Sadrist militiamen in Basrah were not used to the kind of hard fighting against coalition troops that the Shi'a militants of Baghdad had become accustomed to by 2008. As the Marine Corps' aviation assets arrived in Basrah during the weekend of March 28-29, for example, MND-SE and MNC-I officers had watched night-vision video feeds of militiamen milling about the streets seemingly unaware that coalition sensors could detect them in the dark. As a result, the clearing of JAM's main base in the Hayaniyah District on April 19 turned out to be anticlimactic. MND-SE's unmanned aerial vehicles (UAVs) identified militia fighting positions and IED emplacements for the Iraqis days before the assault. On the morning of the attack, British artillery fired a large number of flares and noise rounds to frighten the remaining militiamen before eight Iraqi Army battalions moved in against little resistance. Flynn advised General Freiji to attack the district north to south to ensure that units did not get too far ahead of their line of advance, while Freiji wanted to conduct multiple attacks at different entry points. Freiji agreed to Flynn's suggestion, but changed plans the morning of the attack by rushing into the heart of the district with only his personal security detail and four tanks, luckily finding no resistance. Iraqi forces discovered over the next 2 days an estimated 50 caches with approximately 150 IEDs, 200 rockets, and 300 mortars.[127]

The remaining clearing operations in Basrah city followed a similar pattern as in Qibla and Hayaniyah, and finally ended on May 6 in the Latif District. General Freiji left Basrah the next day, replaced by the able Major General Mohammed Jawad al-Hawadi, who had been present and performed well throughout the operation. Freiji returned to Baghdad to become an adviser to his old friend, Minister of Defense Abdel Qader, while Basrah's police chief, General Jalil, was reassigned to a staff position in Baghdad.

Hawadi's first test as Freiji's successor was to clear the town of Qurnah on May 13. Freiji, who had planned the operation before his departure, was insistent on clearing the town despite Flynn's warnings that coalition air support was in short supply, having since been reallocated to support operations in Baghdad and northern Iraq.[128] Even without extensive air support, however, the operation went smoothly, highlighting that Sadrist resistance had completely collapsed and marking the close of Operation CHARGE OF THE KNIGHTS.

For JAM, the battlefield defeat in Basrah had been severe. Interior Minister Bolani estimated that 210 Sadrist militiamen had been killed, 600 wounded, and 155 captured, numbers that represented about one-sixth of JAM's original fighting strength in Basrah.[129] The coalition had 4 killed and 15 wounded. The result of the 50-day operation was unchallenged Iraqi Government control of Basrah, which was now occupied by about 20,000 Iraqi soldiers loyal to the Maliki government to ensure that the city did not fall back into Sadrist hands.[130]

THE BATTLE FOR SADR CITY

By the time the battle in Basrah had shifted in favor of Maliki and the coalition, a new and even bigger battle had opened in Baghdad, where the Sadrists and their allies undertook a large-scale attack against the Green Zone, the site of the U.S. Embassy and MNF-I headquarters and the seat of government for the absent Prime Minister Maliki. The Sadrist offensive prompted, in turn, a fierce battle for Sadr City that had been years in the making.

The Quintessential Safe Haven

Sadr City had been a thorn in the side of the coalition for years and had only grown more dangerous for coalition units over time. Since the deadly April 2004 ambush that killed eight 1st Cavalry Division Soldiers at the outset of the April uprisings, the coalition had had only a limited presence in and around the Sadrist-dominated neighborhood. Within Sadr City, roughly three categories of insurgent fighters enjoyed a safe haven. JAM fighters loyal to Moqtada Sadr concentrated on defending the Shi'a population in Sadr City and other Shi'a enclaves under the authority of the Office of the Martyr Sadr. The Shi'a militant Special Groups, meanwhile, received specialized training in Iran and were employed throughout the capital in a more offensive role under the authority of Iranian-sponsored militias such as Qais al-Khazali's Asa'ib Ahl al-Haqq or Abu Mahdi al-Muhandis' Kata'ib Hizballah. The third element was a criminal component that exploited the lawlessness and violence in the city, operating much like a mafia organization but invoking the name of JAM to cover its activities. Together, these militants totaled an estimated 1,000-2,000 active fighters in Sadr City, but coalition officials believed Moqtada Sadr could mobilize as many as 20,000 for a larger uprising.[131]

Source: DoD photo by Staff Sergeant Jason Bailey, Joint Combat Camera Center, (Released).

A View of the Sadr City Area of Baghdad, March 29, 2008.[132]

The isolation of Sadr City from the rest of Baghdad had begun with the onset of the surge in early 2007. Colonel Billy Don Farris's 2d Brigade, 82d Airborne Division, the first surge brigade, was assigned much of east Baghdad, including the restive Adhamiyah and Sadr City, two districts with a combined population approaching 3 million people, approximately 40 percent of Baghdad's total. "We occupied a piece of terrain that had turned south and had one company living in it . . . and we didn't know who was who when we started. It was time to start over," Farris later recalled.[133] Before the surge and Farris's arrival, northeast Baghdad had been assigned to a U.S. battalion headquartered 40 kilometers away on the large U.S. forward-operating base near Taji, but once given responsibility for the area, Farris's brigade began to erect massive 4-meter-high concrete walls to control population flow across east Baghdad. At the same time, the paratroopers set about targeting and dismantling insurgent networks and installing joint security stations and combat outposts to keep a closer watch on the neighborhoods alongside local Iraqi units.

Unlike the rest of his area of operations, however, Farris was not able to move directly against militants inside Sadr City. The coalition's agreement with Maliki to restrict operations in the politically sensitive Shi'a neighborhood meant Farris was limited to isolating the enclave and conducting occasional targeted strikes against JAM and Special Groups leaders.[134] Moqtada Sadr had declared a 6-month cease-fire after the Karbala fiasco in August, but the cleric's subtle wording essentially authorized the Special Groups to continue attacking coalition forces. A number of militia leaders disregarded Sadr's orders in any case—a fact that enabled the coalition to better distinguish Special Groups leaders from the more loyal JAM commanders who observed Sadr's directive.[135]

One raid against JAM leaders in fall 2007 illustrated the difficulty of operating against the militants who used Sadr City as a base. A U.S. detachment making a nighttime raid on October 20 to capture a lieutenant of militia leader Abu Dura was surprised by dozens of militiamen and forced to call for close air support. According to MNF-I estimates, the ensuing air strikes killed more than 40 JAM fighters, but the Sadrists were quick to claim that the coalition had killed dozens of civilians, including worshippers at a Shi'a mosque.

The controversy over collateral damage immediately became a political crisis. Clearly under pressure from the Sadrists, Maliki demanded that MNF-I seek his approval for any future coalition activities in and around Sadr City.[136] Petraeus reported to Gates that "we thus find ourselves walking a fine line between conducting aggressive operations against Shi'a extremists (particularly targets in Sadr City) and keeping the GOI [Government of Iraq] on board to negotiate the UNSCR [United Nations Security Council Resolution] and Strategic Partnership Declaration."[137] Concerned that the incident could push Maliki and other Shi'a parties into opposing the renewal of the soon-to-expire UNSCR that authorized the coalition's presence in the country, Petraeus agreed that any further action in Sadr City would require joint approval from Maliki and MNF-I.

While Farris's freedom of action was further curtailed following the controversial October raid, he insisted that much more needed to be done in Sadr City, which had become an even more dangerous insurgent safe haven after the raid.[138] Farris had a point. The cohesion of the Sadrist movement had been strained for years, but the ability to retain the Sadr City sanctuary allowed JAM and the Iranian-backed Special Groups freedom of movement the ability to project power against the coalition and Maliki's Iraqi

Government forces throughout Baghdad.[139] By the time Farris handed over his area to Colonel Hort's 3d Brigade, 4th Infantry Division, on March 10, 2008, Farris's brigade had constricted Sadr City by encircling it with checkpoints and joint security stations.[140] Farris remained frustrated because he could not do more directly, as did Hammond, who told his staff at MND-B that "sooner or later we are going to have to deal with Sadr City. It just can't sit there. It just can't be a haven."[141]

Source: U.S. Army photo by Staff Sergeant Luis Orengo (Released).

Major General Jeffery Hammond, Commander of MND-B, Greets Baghdad's Governor Tah'an.[142]

Nevertheless, Hammond's clear priority for MND-B operations was AQI, which he believed remained the "greatest threat to sustainable security" in Baghdad. Upon taking command of MND-B in December 2007, Hammond had requested that the coalition's special operations forces reduce its focus on Shi'a militant targets in order to apply more resources to pursuing AQI.[143] The MND-B commander's judgment put him somewhat at odds with both Hort and Austin, who shared the view by spring 2008 that JAM and the Special Groups, by virtue of their Iranian-supported explosively formed penetrators (EFPs) network, posed the greatest danger to coalition troops in central Iraq.[144]

Fissures within the Sadr Movement

The political constraints on coalition actions against the Sadr City militants began to loosen in January 2008 when the Sadrists sharpened their opposition to the Maliki government in Parliament and JAM groups precipitated a clash with Maliki's closest advisers. On January 18, hundreds of JAM and Special Groups fighters surrounded a mosque in the Shu'la neighborhood of northwest Baghdad, where Iraqi national security adviser Mowaffaq Rubaie had gone to attend Ashura services. Demanding Rubaie's surrender, the Sadrist fighters had only been thwarted by the timely arrival of an armored convoy led by Interior Minister Jawad Bolani, which had enabled Rubaie's escape through a hail of stones and Molotov cocktails. The action did not lead to a wider clash but made the Maliki government look weak and vulnerable in its own capital.[145]

In these actions, the Sadrists had begun to remove the political buffer between the JAM/Special Groups sanctuary and a coalition intent on eliminating it.[146] Targeting the Sadr movement militants in the Baghdad region was complicated because it was unclear who comprised the Special Groups and who really controlled JAM in Baghdad. To begin with, opinions differed within the coalition and the Iraqi Government over which Shi'a militant groups to target. For almost 2 years, MNF-I and its commands had considered the Special Groups to be "Shi'a extremists" that were "irreconcilable" and under heavy Iranian influence, and would have to be targeted by coalition units and special operators. By contrast, coalition officials considered "mainstream JAM" groups—many of them loyal to Moqtada Sadr—to be more nationalist and "reconcilable," and better approached by pressuring or enticing them to seek political avenues rather than violence to advance their interests. Prime Minister Maliki and his advisers, however, took precisely the opposite view. They believed that Moqtada Sadr was the one who had become extremist and irreconcilable, while the Special Groups—especially those under Qais al-Khazali and Asa'ib Ahl al-Haqq—had more mature leaders who could be "reconciled" and persuaded to lay down their arms in favor of entering the political process. In political terms, Maliki also continued to view Khazali as a preferred alternative to the troublesome Sadr, one who could potentially split Sadr's grassroots base and deliver some of it to Maliki's Da'wa Party. To explore Maliki's idea, coalition officials held discussions with the captive Khazali in late 2007 and early 2008, during which Khazali spoke of wanting to transform his militant group into a political party and sever ties with the Iranian regime. It was unclear if he was sincere or if the Iran-based militant leaders running his organization, Akram Kabi and Mohammed Tabatabai, were interested in such ideas in any case.[147] Indeed, similar "heretical" ideas on Sadr's part had caused Khazali himself and others to split from mainstream JAM.

The situation was further complicated by other Shi'a parties that tended to use nominal JAM groups to mask their own militant activities. This was particularly true of what the Shi'a militants referred to as the "Khamenei groups," former JAM fighters who had been coopted by deputies of the Quds Force. Evidence also began to emerge in January 2008 that some Special Groups members were, in fact, Badr Corps members and that some violence previously attributed to JAM actually originated from ISCI and Badr operatives.[148]

Coalition officials were well aware of the troubled relationship between Moqtada Sadr's loyalists and the Special Groups. The attack on Rubaie in Shu'la had almost turned into a clash between JAM militants loyal to Sadr and Asa'ib Ahl al-Haqq fighters loyal to Khazali, who had quarreled outside Rubaie's mosque over which group had the right to take Rubaie prisoner. Sadr also had been harsh against "rogue JAM" commanders in 2007, sending "noble JAM" or "golden JAM" tribunals from Najaf and Karbala to enforce discipline by expelling or even executing JAM commanders deemed to be disobedient to Sadr's leadership. These fractures had been exacerbated by disagreements within the

Sadr movement over Sadr's August 2007 freeze on JAM operations—disputes that began to mount again as the expiration of the 6-month moratorium in late February approached.

As the freeze was set to expire, Sadr decided, with a dramatic flourish, to extend JAM's 6-month cease-fire by sending sealed envelopes to be opened by all of his clerics at Friday sermons, where his decision was publicly announced in mosques across Iraq. Because the movement was already fracturing, the renewed cease-fire did little to allay concerns over Sadr's ability to control whether it would be followed. Petraeus remained hopeful that the splintering offered opportunities to accommodate the reconcilable element in the Sadr movement, but he cautioned Gates by stating that "we fully anticipate that Iran will continue to pursue ways to exploit the Special Groups and other elements and parties for their purposes as the Sadr movement fractures."[149] Two weeks later, in early March, further signs of the disarray among JAM's top ranks came when Sadr suddenly declared that he was temporarily withdrawing from his leadership responsibilities to further his religious education.

The Sadrist Attack on the Green Zone

Coalition officials in Iraq at the time of the Basrah and Sadr City battles assumed that the Sadrist attack against the coalition and the Iraqi Government in Baghdad in late March was a response to Maliki's operation against Sadrist militias in Basrah. In retrospect, however, signs appeared that the Sadrist offensive in Baghdad was a preplanned operation whose start actually preceded the CHARGE OF THE KNIGHTS. For instance, Sadr's extension of the freeze on JAM operations in late February exempted the Special Groups, whom he authorized to resume attacks against the coalition. This was an important change in light of Sadr's crackdown on rogue violators of the freeze order in late 2007 and early 2008. One likely sign of the resumption of Special Groups operations was that EFP attacks and other violent incidents significantly increased in the week before Maliki went to Basrah. In the week after Farris and Hort's transfer of authority, violent incidents in the city almost tripled from the previous week.[150]

Furthermore, the Shi'a militants' indirect-fire attacks against the Green Zone, which marked the beginning of the Sadrist offensive, began 1 day before Maliki went to Basrah, not after. On March 23, the militias began raining rockets—most of them fired from Sadr City—at the Green Zone after a 6-month period in which indirect-fire attacks against the zone had been almost nonexistent.

As the barrage of rockets fell on the seat of the Iraqi Government, the scale of the Sadrist offensive was not immediately apparent. Rockets had fallen on the Green Zone often, but this latest wave emerged as something new. Indirect-fire attacks gradually escalated in the first 5 days of the Sadrist offensive (March 23-28), during which militants launched 91 separate barrages that dropped a total of 344 rockets and mortar rounds on the Green Zone, opening what became the most intense insurgent bombardment of the entire war.[151] These indirect-fire attacks coincided with a coordinated JAM assault against all 11 ISF checkpoints around Sadr City belonging to the 11th Iraqi Army Division and the 1st National Police Division. During the attacks, JAM gunmen abducted 14 Iraqi soldiers in Kadhimiyah District and kidnapped General Secretary of the Council of Ministers Tasheen al-Shaikhli from his home.

Initially, the Sadrists were aided in late March and early April by extensive seasonal sandstorms that hampered the coalition's ability to use sensors and air weapons teams to detect the militias' indirect-fire teams. A curfew imposed on Baghdad's neighborhoods usually kept the Sadrists from operating at night for fear of being spotted on Baghdad's deserted streets. Under cover of the sandstorms, Sadrist rocket and mortar teams were able to bombard the Green Zone and its environs during daylight hours when the militiamen could blend into the dense populations of Sadr City and other Shi'a neighborhoods.[152]

As the bombardment continued, the U.S. Embassy compound and military headquarters in the Green Zone frequently came under fire. In one incident, a rocket landing on the MNSTC-I gym killed several troops inside. By the second week of April, Petraeus and Crocker's headquarters began to resemble a refugee camp as more than 1,000 embassy and MNF-I personnel sought shelter in the hardened embassy building rather than remain in the poorly shielded trailers and sleeping huts outside.[153]

The coordinated assault demonstrated Sadr's operational reach to express his displeasure with the coalition's presence and Maliki's government. As Maliki's surprising Basrah offensive began on March 25, Sadr continued his own offensive in Baghdad with calls for a "civil disobedience protest" and declared an end to the 6-month cease-fire that he had recently extended in February. The day before, in a BBC (British Broadcasting Corporation) interview, Petraeus had publicly implicated the Iranian regime, stating "the rockets that were launched at the Green Zone yesterday, for example . . . were Iranian-provided, Iranian-made rockets."[154] Sadr City in effect had become not only a Shi'a militia safe haven but also an instrumental staging area for an Iranian proxy war against the coalition. Considering the dramatic change in events, Petraeus informed Gates "this week we have shifted our stance from nation-building back to warfighting."[155]

Route Gold

The intense indirect-fire attacks against the Green Zone—originating mainly from Sadr City and other areas east of the Tigris, though a few attacks originated from Jihad and Shu'ala/Hurriyah in west Baghdad—led coalition commanders to decide to seize the lower portion of Sadr City to deny its use as a militia firing point and to push JAM and the Special Groups northeast so they could not bombard the Green Zone with mortars and rockets. The coordinated rocket and checkpoint assault also encouraged Maliki to remove most of the restrictions that had stymied anti-militia efforts for years. With Maliki's permission on March 25, the same day Maliki's Basrah offensive began, Hort's brigade launched an operation to reclaim the checkpoints the militias had seized and establish a foothold in the southern sections of Sadr City, objectives that Hort's troops and their partnered Iraqi units accomplished quickly.

The next phase to gain control of Sadr City entirely, however, would take an additional 45 days and would also strain the Iraqi Army and National Police in Baghdad to the breaking point. Maliki had given permission for coalition and Iraqi forces to enter the Ishibiliya and Habbibiya neighborhoods south of Route Gold—the name coalition troops gave to Quds Street, which ran east-west across the lower quarter of Sadr City—but had ordered that only indirect strikes would be allowed into portions of Sadr City to the north of Route Gold. Typically, JAM and Special Groups rocket teams would cross to the south

Colonel John Hort (left). Source: DoD photo by Sergeant Zachary Mott (Released).

Colonel John Hort, Commander of the 3d BCT, 4th Infantry Division, With Admiral Michael Mullen, Chairman of the Joint Chiefs of Staff.[156]

of Route Gold, launch rockets west across the Tigris River, and then move back north to fade into the depths of Sadr City. To eliminate the rocket firing points in Ishibiliya and Habbibiya, Hort's brigade launched another operation to seize the one-third of Sadr City south of Route Gold.

The operation was the first major coalition move into Sadr City since the 1st Cavalry Division's operations there in 2004. It was also an existential threat to the Sadrists' power base in Baghdad. In addition to serving as the most effective launching point for JAM rocket attacks in the city, Ishibiliya and Habbibiya contained the Jamila market, the country's largest shopping district and, as Hammond referred to it, a "cash cow" for JAM's racketeering networks.[157] For both its indirect-fire utility and its sources of cash, Sadr City south of Route Gold was key terrain that the Sadrists would fight hard to keep, resulting in 40 days of the most intense urban fighting in Iraq since the Fallujah operations of 2004. Hort originally had allocated just a Stryker cavalry squadron—the 1st Squadron, 2d Cavalry Regiment—to seize the neighborhoods south of Route Gold, but after EFPs destroyed six Stryker vehicles in the first week, it became clear that more U.S. troops would be required. A combined arms battalion, the 1st Battalion, 68th Armored Regiment, soon joined the operation along with additional tank companies. The battalion's M1 Abrams tanks and M2 Bradleys proved to be of high value during the urban fighting because of their armor protection and firepower. Eventually, Hort would commit almost an entire brigade's worth of combat power to gain control of the rocket launch sites.

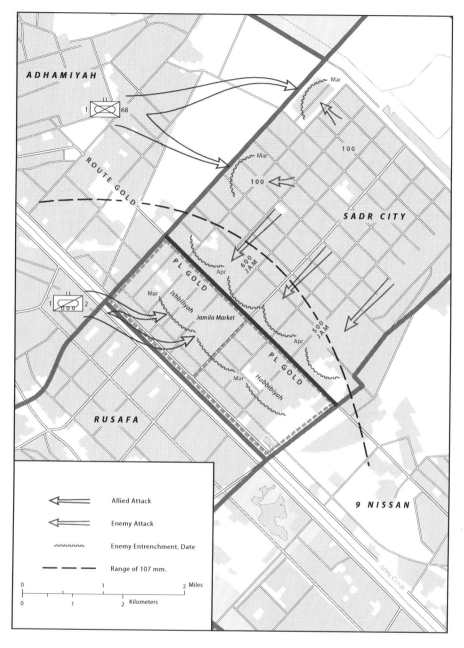

Map created by the official cartographer at the U.S. Army Center of Military History, Washington, DC.

Map 19. Sadr City, March–May 2008.

The plan also called for a significant role for the Iraqi Army in what coalition commanders hoped would be a validation of their capability. However, as both the 1st Battalion, 68th Armored Regiment, and the 1st Squadron, 2d Cavalry Regiment, pushed northeast, they found it difficult to keep their Iraqi counterparts in the fight for several reasons. Since the launch of the Baghdad Security Plan, the Iraqi Army in Baghdad had been mainly a checkpoint-oriented army—comfortable with static security positions, but reluctant and incapable of conducting coordinated maneuver and offensive operations.[158] The Iraqi Army division assigned to Sadr City was manned by many east Baghdad residents who were well aware of JAM and the Special Groups' ability to threaten their families.[159] As a result, up to 700 Iraqi soldiers, many of whom were thought to have families in Sadr City, deserted in the first 2 days of fighting. Those units that remained intact did so mainly because of the influence of their embedded American advisers.[160]

Observing the difficulty of keeping the Iraqi units committed to the tough fighting, a frustrated Hammond suggested in an update briefing to Petraeus that the coalition should allow the Iraqi units and leaders involved in the operation against Baghdad's militias to fail. Only by failing and taking losses, Hammond reasoned, would the Iraqi security forces learn their lesson the hard way and realize the need to improve. For Petraeus, Hammond's recommendation was detached from the gravity of the situation. The fighting in Baghdad was not a training exercise, but a pivotal battle of the war, the MNF-I commander replied, one that neither the coalition nor the Iraqi Government could afford to lose. Petraeus also judged that the battle had unexpectedly presented the coalition and the Iraqi security forces the chance, finally, to destroy the Shi'a militias, and that MND-B needed to seize that opportunity.[161]

Maliki already had come to a similar conclusion, and the political battle between the Prime Minister and the Sadrists in Baghdad continued to escalate in the first days of April. With operations against JAM now in full swing across Baghdad and the entire south, Maliki took steps to remove the JAM problem permanently, declaring that the Sadrists "would lose the right to participate in the political process" if JAM was not disbanded.[162] Moqtada Sadr responded by declaring that JAM would disband only if directly ordered to do so by Grand Ayatollah Sistani—a political intervention that Sistani was highly unlikely to make—and by calling for a "million-man march" in Baghdad on April 9, the 5-year anniversary of Saddam's fall. Sadr's call for an April 9 protest appeared to be a scheme to have tens of thousands of Sadrists march through Baghdad toward the Green Zone. With this in mind, MNF-I planners began to consider the danger that mobs of angry Sadr followers could penetrate the Green Zone perimeter—something similar to the overrunning of the U.S. Embassy in Tehran in 1979. This would create a no-win situation in which either the coalition's headquarters might be overrun or coalition troops might be forced to fire heavy weapons on Sadr's followers. With the situation in Basrah turning against him, however, Sadr abruptly canceled the march the day before it was to occur likely over fears of violence against JAM and a low turnout, either of which could further weaken his position.[163]

Two days later, on April 11, the Sadrists were dealt another blow when assassins killed senior Sadrist leader Riyad al-Nuri in Najaf. The murder hit close to home: Nuri was Sadr's brother-in-law and had been one of the Sadr lieutenants, along with Qais al-Khazali, suspected of murdering Abdul Majid al-Khoei in Najaf in April 2003.

The Battle of the "Gold Wall"

While the coalition and Iraqi attack into Ishibiliya and Habbibiya drew a fierce response from JAM and Special Groups, the next phase would draw an even greater one. The 11th Iraqi Army Division and the 3d Brigade Combat Team, 4th Infantry Division, had established themselves firmly in outposts south of Route Gold, but JAM and Special Groups still had freedom of movement throughout the warren of alleyways and streets that connected northern and southern Sadr City. With the area south of Route Gold tenuously secured, on April 15 Hort and the 3d Brigade Combat Team, 4th Infantry Division, began building a concrete wall the length of the sector to partition Sadr City and separate Ishibiliya and Habbibiya from the northern two-thirds of the Sadrist enclave.[164]

Source: DoD photo by Sergeant Joseph Rivera Rebolledo (Released).

Soldiers Emplace Concrete Barriers Across Route Gold in Sadr City.[165]

The appearance of Hort's units erecting enormous concrete barriers across Route Gold brought the Sadrist militiamen into the open as JAM and Special Groups commanders realized the wall would permanently separate them from their rocket-launch areas and the Jamila market. The militia commanders began to hurl their fighters at the wall builders to try to prevent this outcome. In Hammond's words, "JAM impaled itself on the wall," losing hundreds of fighters in an unequal fight against coalition units whose capabilities had evolved significantly since the grinding fight on the same streets 4 years earlier.

As the battle along the wall unfolded, the ground fight in Ishibiliya and Habbibiya and the air strikes in Sadr City looked old and new. The ground fight brought to bear the fundamentals of armored and dismounted combat in an urban environment. The precision air war, however, demonstrated an unprecedented level of technology that changed how the coalition could lethally engage a safe haven and support the ground war. Within days, Hort controlled or directly accessed national-, theater-, division-, and brigade-level ISR assets that included Global Hawk, Predator, and Shadow UAVs; close air support and air weapons teams of AH-64 Apaches; aerostat balloons; guided multiple-launch rocket systems (GMLRS); and large numbers of coalition snipers.[166] Although the 3d Brigade Combat Team, 4th Infantry Division, was still restricted from maneuvering north of Route Gold, these multiple layers of surveillance and strike capabilities had a devastating effect on the thousands of militiamen attacking the brigade combat team and its Iraqi partner units. Hundreds of JAM fighters died in fruitless assaults on the wall. The militiamen's indirect-fire attackers suffered as well: coalition air weapons teams launched 85 attacks (with a total of 200 Hellfire missiles) that destroyed many of the militias' Iranian-trained 107-mm rocket teams.[167]

In the week that began on May 7, the coalition dealt what amounted to knockout blows to JAM and its leaders in Baghdad. Hort received from the CJSOTF a 30-man Navy SEAL sniper platoon with experience in Fallujah and Ramadi and deployed them just beyond the leading edge of the wall construction. From there, with the added protection of Bradley fighting vehicles and Abrams tanks, their deadly fire could reach a mile into Sadr City's grid-like streets. The snipers quickly made an impact. Shortly after their arrival, a sandstorm grounded all coalition air assets, slackening the pressure the air weapons teams could place on the militia enemy. As JAM attempted to exploit the drop-off in coalition air support during the sandstorm, the Navy snipers were not affected, registering kills of 46 fighters in 1 day. By May 15, after 8 days on the wall, Navy snipers had killed 67 militiamen.[168] Meanwhile, the ISOF Brigade and their CJSOTF advisers launched nightly dismounted assaults into Sadr City and conducted heliborne-targeted raids against Sadrist leaders.[169] These missions, combined with targeted raids launched by the counter malign Iranian influence special operations task force, ground down JAM's fighting capabilities and gave them no respite during the hours of darkness.

Source: U.S. Air Force photo by Technical Sergeant Adrian Cadiz (Released).

A Massive Sandstorm Affected the Battle of Sadr City.[170]

The coalition also had been tracking JAM and Special Groups leaders who were meeting in trailers adjacent to Sadr City's Imam Ali Hospital, where the militia commanders believed their proximity to a protected site would shield them from attack. Hort and MND-B had other ideas. After MND-B made targeting calculations to limit collateral damage, MNF-I and U.S. Central Command (CENTCOM) gave permission for a GMLRS strike on the militia meeting place. On April 29, 2 days after the sandstorm subsided, the GMLRS struck the trailers precisely, killing several top militia leaders while causing no damage to the nearby hospital. With JAM and Special Groups leaders and fighters dying at an alarming rate, most of the remaining leaders fled to Iran to escape the coalition's increasingly lethal reach.[171]

The End of the Sadr City Battle

On May 10, Moqtada Sadr and the Government of Iraq agreed to a cease-fire. The 14-point agreement required JAM to end all armed activities, accede to government control of Sadr City, and agree not to carry weapons in public. In return, the Maliki government agreed to limit raids against JAM and to reopen the roads into Sadr City.[172]

As the Route Gold wall neared completion and with renewed confidence in the ISF's capability, Maliki urged General Aboud Qanbar and other ISF commanders to move Iraqi troops quickly into northern Sadr City to exploit the militias' tactical defeat. Hammond and Petraeus, less confident about ISF's abilities, cautioned General Aboud to act more deliberately than Maliki wished, but as had been the case in Basrah, the Prime Minister and his advisers were intent on attacking much more quickly than their coalition counterparts thought wise.[173]

The Route Gold wall was completed in a little over a week after the cease-fire agreement on May 18, and 2 days later two Iraqi brigades moved north across Route Gold and occupied Sadr City without a fight. After 4 years during which both the coalition and the ISF had avoided major operations in Sadr City out of dread of a large-scale confrontation with the Sadrists, the Iraqi Army and its coalition advisers had walked into the Sadrists' largest stronghold unopposed, just as they had done in Basrah. Rather than turning either Basrah or Sadr City into an Iraqi Stalingrad, as many analysts believed they could do, the militias had turned and fled, proving they were no military match for the ISF and coalition forces together.

The Shi'a militias' losses in Baghdad were severe and unsustainable. The coalition commands estimated that between March 23 and May 10, coalition troops killed 700 militia fighters in the battle for Sadr City, with an unknown number of additional militiamen wounded. The Sadrists publicly announced they had lost at least 1,000 killed.[174] Coalition casualties in April had been high as well, with 41 troops killed in that month. After the seizure of Sadr City, May 2008 was a different story: the 19 deaths during the month were the fewest for the coalition since the 2003 invasion.[175]

Nor had the fight gone against the Shi'a militias just in Sadr City. In other parts of the Iraqi capital that had been militia strongholds, U.S. units and their partnered ISF units had been able to seize territory from JAM and other Shi'a militant groups as well. In the Rashid neighborhood, for example, Colonel Theodore Martin's 1st Brigade, 4th Infantry Division, was in the midst of taking over control from Colonel Ricky D. Gibbs's

4th Brigade, 1st Infantry Division, when the militia uprising began. Though the local 5th National Police Brigade had withered under attacks from JAM, Martin's and Gibbs's brigades had been able to strengthen the two other National Police brigades and the 43d Iraqi Army Brigade in southwest Baghdad and to establish new joint security stations to control the former JAM-dominated territory.[176]

The end of the Sadr City militia safe haven brought with it a sharp decrease in the militias' ability to deploy EFPs in the Baghdad region. After May 2008, increased surveillance and coalition activity decreased the militias' freedom of movement and made it harder for insurgents to emplace larger arrays of EFPs. Instead, militia groups were forced to emplace single EFPs that were significantly less effective against coalition forces. Beyond Baghdad, Shi'a militants were still able to emplace larger arrays of EFPs and maintain their level of lethality, but overall, the Sadr City battle permanently reduced EFP effectiveness across Iraq, and showed how important a safe haven the slum had been.[177]

***

In Basrah and Sadr City, MNF-I was compelled to commit to a battle it had not anticipated and to draw its attention away from a final showdown with the Sunni insurgency in Mosul. Even so, Operation CHARGE OF THE KNIGHTS was a milestone in the Iraq War. After 5 years of campaigning, it was nearly unimaginable that such a large-scale operation would be necessary in what many coalition leaders had considered the sleepy backwater of the south, among a supposedly homogeneous Shi'a population. However, unchecked intra-Shi'a competition for influence, control, and resources proved to be just as destabilizing as the sectarian conflict roiling central Iraq. The operation in Basrah also dispelled the fallacy that a smaller British troop presence hunkered down at Basrah Air Station and the accommodation with a militia leader had reduced violence and had prompted the Iraqis to resolve their own problems. While MND-SE's withdrawal from Basrah city had temporarily lowered attacks against British forces, it had ceded the city to militias and left the population without protection. The repositioning to Basrah Air Station removed British combat power from the equation when neither the Iraqi police nor Army was ready to secure the city. When militia forces filled the security vacuum, they made Operation CHARGE OF THE KNIGHTS an inevitability, even if it was inconvenient for the coalition at the time. General Freiji's UK adviser, Colonel Richard Iron, later explained to the press:

> We have made some terrible mistakes in Iraq. . . . We released 120 of their prisoners and withdrew out of town, but when we moved out, lawlessness took over. As 90 percent of the attacks were against us, we thought that if we moved out we would remove the source of the problem. But actually Jaish al-Mahdi had been fighting us because we were the only obstacle to their total control.[178]

The Iraqi security forces' poor performance during the first 3 days of Operation CHARGE OF THE KNIGHTS exposed a critical flaw in the British approach to training, advising, and assisting the Iraqi security forces. Colonel Iron later noted that the United Kingdom decided early in the war not to embed MiTTs with the Iraqi Army. "The argument against MiTTs at the time was that we could not guarantee their protection; since we were so short of troops we could not provide them dedicated support at the same time as running our own operations. In retrospect, this was a poor decision: resourcing MiTTs should have been the first use of our troops, before our own operations."[179] Instead, the British had followed a concept of monitoring, mentoring, and training only at the training center at Shaibah, west of Basrah, but did not conduct partnered operations with the Iraqi units they had trained.

After the 10th and 14th Iraqi Army Division troops completed their training at Shaibah, Binns noted, "We didn't then mentor them when they deployed on operation, and that was the significant difference between the way that we approached support and the way that the Americans approached support in Basra."[180] The difference between the U.S. and British approach to mentoring was not lost on several British commanders, who recognized the missing critical component. Whenever raising the issue from the field, British officers faced resistance from the UK Permanent Joint Headquarters in London, England, where British leaders deemed embedding too dangerous as well as contrary to British plans for troop reductions.[181]

With JAM and Special Groups hold over Basrah and Sadr City and with Amarah broken, several conclusions emerged. The militia groups that had defied the Iraqi Government since fall 2003 had lost at least 2,000 fighters killed, half of them in Baghdad alone. Ultimately, after 4 years of recoiling from operations against the militants in Sadr City and Basrah, the coalition had seen JAM and Special Groups resistance crumble more quickly than anyone had predicted, indicating perhaps that the militia threat had been overstated for at least 3 years. JAM was rendered operationally ineffective for more than a year, and even then, it would likely not return in the same form. The coalition and Iraqi troops conducting the March-June 2008 operations had overmatched the militias and come close to destroying them. Conversely, the Iranian regime had nearly lost its proxy militias altogether. The various Iranian attempts to broker cease-fires between the militias and the government were not intended to stabilize Iraq, but to rescue the Iranians' most important militant proxies from extinction.

In political terms, the civil war between the Iranian-backed Shi'a militant groups and the Shi'a-led Maliki government had ended in a clear victory for the Prime Minister who, by summer 2008, was unquestionably Iraq's most powerful politician and bore little resemblance to the weak Maliki that Stephen J. Hadley had described to the National Security Council principals in November 2006. For the 5 years since the collapse of the Iraqi Ba'athist state in April 2003, nonstate factions and militant groups had appeared to be stronger than the new Iraqi state, but with the defeat of the Shi'a militant groups, the Maliki-led Iraqi state had retaken control of most of the country's territory. With the Prime Minister strengthened politically and his most troublesome Shi'a political rivals swept from the field, coalition leaders now anticipated Maliki would be free to sign the U.S.-Iraq Status of Forces Agreement without impediment—an expectation that Maliki soon frustrated.

ENDNOTES - CHAPTER 8

1. Multi-National Corps-Iraq (MNC-I), Operation PHANTOM PHOENIX, December 24, 2007, p. 5, Chief of Staff of the Army (CSA) Operation IRAQI FREEDOM (OIF) Study Group archives, Army Heritage and Education Center (AHEC), Carlisle, PA. All unpublished documents in this chapter, unless otherwise stated, are in the CSA OIF Study Group archives, AHEC, Carlisle, PA.

2. Ibid., p. 5.

3. Ibid., p. 20.

4. Manuscript (Ms), *On Point*, Vol. IV, Chapter 7, Fort Leavenworth, KS: Combat Studies Institute, September 25, 2014, p. 4.

5. Multi-National Force-Iraq (MNF-I), Secretary of Defense (SECDEF) Weekly Update, December 31, 2007-January 6, 2008.

6. Report (Rpt) for Congress, Catherine Dale, "Operation Iraqi Freedom: Strategies, Approaches, Results, and Issues for Congress," Rpt No. RL34387, Washington, DC: Congressional Research Service, April 2, 2009, p. 99, available from *https://www.fas.org/sgp/crs/natsec/RL34387.pdf.*

7. Ms, *On Point*, Vol. IV, Chapter 5, p. 30.

8. Stephen Farrell, "U.S. Attack in Iraq Is No Surprise to Many Insurgents," *The New York Times*, January 9, 2008, available from *http://www.nytimes.com/2008/01/09/world/middleeast/09diyala.html?ex=1357534800&en=99eca6d59d9d1192&ei=5090&partner=rssuserland&emc=rss&pagewanted=all&_r=0.*

9. MNF-I, SECDEF Weekly Update, January 7-13, 2008.

10. Ibid., January 14-20, 2008.

11. DoD photo by Private 1st Class Kirby Rider, "Tunnel Rat," February 17, 2008, Released to Public, available from *https://www.flickr.com/photos/mnfiraq/4315038658/in/faves-138659840%40N02/.*

12. Ms, *On Point*, Vol. IV, Chapter 5, p. 31; Bill Roggio, "Senior al Qaeda in Iraq leader killed in Miqdadiyah," *Long War Journal*, January 16, 2008, available from *http://www.longwarjournal.org/archives/2008/01/senior_al_qaeda_in_i_1.php.*

13. Ms, *On Point*, Vol. IV, Chapter 5, p. 31.

14. "Operation Marne Thunderbolt," Washington, DC: Institute for the Study of War, available from *http://www.understandingwar.org/operation/operation-marne-thunderbolt.*

15. Bill Roggio, "Coalition airstrikes pound al Qaeda in Iraq positions in southern Arab Jabour," *Long War Journal*, January 20, 2008, available from *http://www.longwarjournal.org/archives/2008/01/coalition_pounds_al.php.*

16. MNF-I, SECDEF Weekly Update, January 7-13, 2008.

17. Bill Roggio, "34 al Qaeda killed in day's fighting during Phantom Phoenix," *Long War Journal*, January 12, 2008, available from *http://www.longwarjournal.org/archives/2008/01/34_al_qaeda_killed_i.php.*

18. "Operation Marne Thunderbolt."

19. MNF-I, SECDEF Weekly Update, January 14-20, 2008.

20. Ibid.

21. U.S. Army photo by 1st Lieutenant Jonathan J. Springer, "Ear Protection," January 13, 2008, Released to Public, available from *https://www.flickr.com/photos/mnfiraq/4314073315/in/album-72157623309921276/*.

22. MNF-I, SECDEF Weekly Update, January 14-20, 2008, and January 21-27, 2008.

23. U.S. Army photo by Specialist Kieran Cuddihy, "Vehicle Cover," January 17, 2008, Released to Public, available from *https://www.flickr.com/photos/mnfiraq/4314073707/in/faves-138659840%40N02/*.

24. MNF-I, SECDEF Weekly Update, January 14-20, 2008, and January 21-27, 2008.

25. Ibid.; January 28-February 3, 2008; and February 4-10, 2008.

26. Major Sean Wilson, "Operation reconciles insurgents with coalition forces," Mountaineer Online, n.d., available from *http://www.drum.army.mil/mountaineer/Article.aspx?ID=2600*.

27. Sudarsan Raghavan and Amit R. Paley, "Sunni Forces Losing Patience With U.S.," *The Washington Post,* February 28, 2008, available from *https://www.pressreader.com/usa/the-washington-post/20080228/281496451982476*.

28. DoD photo by Staff Sergeant Russell Bassett, "Diyala's Breadbasket two months later: A success story [Image 8 of 8]," DVIDS Identifier 80653, March 8, 2008, Released to Public, available from *https://www.dvidshub.net/image/80653/diyalas-breadbasket-two-months-later-success-story*.

29. Raghavan and Paley, "Sunni Forces Losing Patience with U.S."

30. "Operation Iron Harvest," Washington, DC: Institute for the Study of War, available from *http://www.understandingwar.org/operation/operation-iron-harvest*.

31. "Operation Marne Thunderbolt."

32. Sudarsan Raghavan, "Woman Sets Off Suicide Bomb In Shiite Area Of Baghdad," *The Washington Post*, February 18, 2008, available from *http://www.washingtonpost.com/wp-dyn/content/article/2008/02/17/AR2008021702262.html*.

33. U.S. Army photo by Specialist Nicholas A. Hernandez, "Pointing Fingers," January 7, 2008, Released to Public, available from *https://www.flickr.com/photos/mnfiraq/4314073227/in/album-72157623309921276/*.

34. MNF-I, SECDEF Weekly Update, February 4-10, 2008.

35. Ibid., February 11-17, 2008.

36. Ibid.

37. Ms, *On Point*, Vol. IV, Chapter 5, p. 33.

38. MNF-I, SECDEF Weekly Update, December 31, 2007-January 6, 2008.

39. E-mail, General (Ret.) David H. Petraeus to Colonel Joel Rayburn, November 24, 2015.

40. MNF-I, SECDEF Weekly Update, February 18-24, 2008.

41. Ibid., February 25-March 2, 2008.

42. U.S. Army photo by Sergeant Laura M. Bigenho, "Austin Assumes Command of Multi-National Corps—Iraq [Image 1 of 3]," DVIDS Identifier 77347, February 14, 2008, Released to Public, available from *https://www.dvidshub.net/image/77347/austin-assumes-command-multi-national-corps-iraq*.

43. Interview, Vincent McLean, Combat Studies Institute (CSI) Contemporary Operations Study Team, with Lieutenant General Lloyd Austin, May 12, 2010.

44. Ms, *On Point*, Vol. IV, Chapter 7, p. 12.

45. Testimony of Graham Binns, Iraq Inquiry (UK Chilcot Inquiry), January 15, 2010, pp. 3-6, available from *http://www.iraqinquiry.org.uk/media/42505/100115am-binns.pdf*, accessed March 7, 2016. (Note: *http://www.iraqinquiry.org.uk/about.aspx*.)

46. Tim Ripley, *Operation Telic: The British Campaign in Iraq 2003-2009*, Lancaster, UK: Telic-Herrick Publications, 2014, Kindle Ed., location No. 8683 of 11586.

47. Testimony of Binns to UK Government's Iraq Inquiry, pp. 17-18; David H. Ucko and Robert Egnell, *Counterinsurgency in Crisis*, New York: Columbia University Press, 2013, p. 65; Ripley, *Operation Telic*, location No. 8702.

48. Testimony of Binns to UK Government's Iraq Inquiry, p. 18.

49. Memo, Lieutenant General Raymond T. Odierno for General George W. Casey, Jr., Commander, MNF-I, January 8, 2007, sub: January 2007 Provincial Security Transition Assessment.

50. Thomas Harding, "US 'delayed UK pull-out from Basra'," *The Telegraph*, September 10, 2010.

51. UK House of Commons Defence Committee, UK Operations in Iraq, Rpt No. 13, London, UK: House of Commons, July 19, 2006, p. 11; Ucko and Egnell, *Counterinsurgency in Crisis*, p. 67; Des Brown, "Government and Security in Iraq: The Evolving Challenge," *RUSI Journal*, Vol. 151, No. 3, June 2006, pp. 10-13.

52. Interview, Colonel Frank Sobchak, CSA OIF Study Group, with Colonel Christopher Conner, Combined Joint Special Operations Task Force (CJSOTF) Commander, December 10, 2015.

53. Ucko and Egnell, *Counterinsurgency in Crisis*, p. 67.

54. Mona Mahmoud, Maggie O'Kane, and Ian Black, "UK has Left Behind Murder and Chaos, says Basra Police Chief," *The Guardian*, December 17, 2007, available from *http://www.theguardian.com/world/2007/dec/17/iraq.military*.

55. U.S. Army photo by Sergeant Nicole Dykstra, "Security Handover [Image 3 of 3]," DVIDS Identifier 69352, December 16, 2007, Released to Public, available from *https://www.dvidshub.net/image/69352/security-handover*.

56. Prime Minister Maliki was loath to transfer both civil and security authority over to Governor Waeli, who was frequently in conflict with Baghdad's central government. It required U.S. State Department efforts to reconcile the two, paving the way for the elaborate arrangement whereby Waeli handled civil affairs and Mohan handled security matters.

57. UK House of Commons Defence Committee, UK Land Operations in Iraq 2007, Rpt No. 1, London, UK: House of Commons, December 3, 2007, pp. 30-32. See also Ucko and Egnell, *Counterinsurgency in Crisis*, p. 67; Ripley, *Operation Telic*, location No. 8753.

58. Testimony of Barney White-Spunner, *Iraq Inquiry* (UK Chilcot Inquiry), January 7, 2010, p. 4, available from *http://www.iraqinquiry.org.uk/media/53037/White-Spunner%202010-01-07%20S1.pdf*, accessed March 7, 2016.

59. Testimony of Binns to UK Government's Iraq Inquiry, pp. 32-33.

60. Ibid., p. 25.

61. Ucko and Egnell, *Counterinsurgency in Crisis*, p. 58.

62. Testimony of Binns to UK Government's Iraq Inquiry, p. 26.

63. Richard A. Oppel, Jr., "In Basra, Militia in Control after Infiltration of Police," *The New York Times*, October 9, 2005; Interview, Colonel Joel Rayburn, CSA OIF Study Group, with Lieutenant Colonel Jim Sindle, March 7, 2016.

64. Mahmoud, O'Kane, and Black, "UK has left behind murder and chaos, says Basra police chief."

65. Ucko and Egnell, *Counterinsurgency in Crisis*, p. 58.

66. "Iraqi soldiers free CBS journalist from captors," CNN, April 14, 2008, available from *http://www.cnn.com/2008/WORLD/meast/04/14/basra.journalist.freed/index.html?iref=nextin*.

67. "Iraqis Protest Poor Security in Basra," CBS News, March 8, 2008, available from *http://www.cbsnews.com/news/iraqis-protest-poor-security-in-basra*.

68. Yiffat Susskind, "Who Is Killing the Women of Basra?" CommonDreams.org, January 8, 2008, available from *http://www.commondreams.org/views/2008/01/10/who-killing-women-basra*.

69. "2008 Country Reports on Human Rights Practices: Iraq," Washington, DC: U.S. Department of State, February 25, 2009.

70. Testimony of Binns to UK Government's Iraq Inquiry, p. 11.

71. Ripley, *Operation Telic*, location No. 8664; Richard Iron, "Basra 2008: Operation Charge of the Knights," Jonathan Bailey, Richard Iron, and Hew Strachan, eds., *British Generals in Blair's Wars*, Surrey, UK: Ashgate Publishing, 2013, p. 188.

72. Ripley, *Operation Telic*, location No. 8666.

73. Testimony of White-Spunner to UK Government's Iraq Inquiry, pp. 6-7.

74. Personal notes from meeting, James Sindle, State Department Political Officer, Basrah Regional Embassy Office, April 2008.

75. DoD photo by Petty Officer 3d Class Jannine Hartmann, "Opening of new Department of Boarder Enforcement [Image 2 of 9]," DVIDS Identifier 107074, August 4, 2008, Released to Public, available from *https://www.dvidshub.net/image/107074/opening-new-department-boarder-enforcement*.

76. Iron, "Basra 2008," pp. 188-189; Ucko and Egnell, *Counterinsurgency in Crisis*, p. 68; Jack Fairweather, *A War of Choice: Honour, Hubris and Sacrifice: The British in Iraq*, London, UK: Jonathan Cape, 2011, pp. 328-332.

77. Iron, "Basra 2008," pp. 188-189; Ripley, *Operation Telic*, location No. 8824; Fairweather, *A War of Choice*, pp. 330-331.

78. Iron, "Basra 2008," p. 189; Fairweather, *A War of Choice*, p. 333.

79. MNF-I, SECDEF Weekly Update, March 3-9, 2008; Testimony of White-Spunner to UK Government's Iraq Inquiry, p. 10.

80. MNF-I, SECDEF Weekly Update, March 3-9, 2008; Iron, "Basra 2008," p. 189; Ripley, *Operation Telic*, locations No. 8824, 8830; Fairweather, *A War of Choice*, p. 334.

81. Ned Parker, "Radical Shiite cleric's bloc quits Iraqi ruling coalition," *Los Angeles Times*, September 16, 2007.

82. Ripley, *Operation Telic*, location No. 8863; MNF-I, SECDEF Weekly Update, March 10-16, 2008.

83. DoD photo by Staff Sergeant Lorie Jewell, "Mowaffaq Rubaie tells P4 of Prime Minister Maliki's plans to carry out operations in Basrah," March 21, 2008, Released to Public.

84. Ripley, *Operation Telic*, location No. 8874; MNF-I, SECDEF Weekly Update, March 17-23, 2008.

85. Testimony of White-Spunner to UK Government's Iraq Inquiry, p. 11.

86. Interview, CSA OIF Study Group with Major General Julian Free, January 28, 2014.

87. Ucko and Egnell, *Counterinsurgency in Crisis*, p. 68.

88. Iron, "Basra 2008," p. 194.

89. Michael R. Gordon, Eric Schmitt, and Stephen Farrell, "U.S. Cites Planning Gaps in Iraqi Assault on Basra," *The New York Times*, April 3, 2008.

90. Iron, "Basra 2008," p. 193; Ripley, *Operation Telic*, location No. 8891.

91. Ripley, *Operation Telic*, location No. 8897.

92. Ibid., location No. 8930.

93. Interview, CSA OIF Study Group with Sindle, March 7, 2016.

94. Ripley, *Operation Telic*, location No. 8947.

95. Ibid.

96. Ucko and Egnell, *Counterinsurgency in Crisis*, p. 68; UK House of Commons Defence Committee, *UK Operations in Iraq and the Gulf*, Rpt No. 15, London, UK: House of Commons, July 22, 2008, p. 7, available from *http://www.publications.Parliament.uk/pa/cm200708/cmselect/cmdfence/982/982.pdf*, accessed March 7, 2016.

97. Testimony of White-Spunner to UK Government's Iraq Inquiry, p. 17.

98. Duane L. Mosier, "The Road to Al Amarah: Operation Yarborough and U.S. Army Special Forces Soldiers in Southern Iraq (January-June 2008)," *Small Wars Journal*, November 4, 2010.

99. Ripley, *Operation Telic*, location No. 8960.

100. Ibid.

101. Mosier, "The Road to Al Amarah."

102. Fairweather, *A War of Choice*, p. 337; Ripley, *Operation Telic*, location No. 8986; MNF-I, SECDEF Weekly Update, March 17-23, 2008.

103. Iron, "Basra 2008," p. 190; Ripley, *Operation Telic*, location No. 9030 and location No. 9025; Ucko and Egnell, *Counterinsurgency in Crisis*, p. 68; UK House of Commons Defence Committee, *UK Operations in Iraq and the Gulf*, Rpt No. 15, London, UK: House of Commons, July 22, 2008, p. 7.

104. Sitrep, MNF-I Liaison Cell to MNF-I and CJSOTF, 1450 hours [2:50 pm], March 28, 2008.

105. Paper, *Operational Detachment Alphas 9515*, Commander's Sitrep comments, March 28-29, 2008.

106. E-mail, Lieutenant Colonel (Ret.) Mark Grdovic to Colonel Frank Sobchak, August 19, 2014, sub: Chief of Staff of the Army Operation IRAQI FREEDOM Study Group.

107. MNF-I, SECDEF Weekly Update, March 24-30, 2008.

108. Ibid.

109. Ripley, *Operation Telic*, location No. 9035; Interview, CSA OIF Study Group with Major General Free, January 28, 2014.

110. Mosier, "The Road to Al Amarah."

111. Ripley, *Operation Telic*, location No. 9252.

112. Ucko and Egnell, *Counterinsurgency in Crisis*, p. 69; Testimony of White-Spunner to UK Government's Iraq Inquiry, p. 32; Interview, CSA OIF Study Group with Free, January 28, 2014; Major T. G. S. Perkins, "Mitting in Basra during OP Telic 11—an OC's Perspective," Edinburgh Castle, Scotland, UK: *Royal Regiment of Scotland Journal*, March 2009, p. 36.

113. Sholnn Freeman and Sudarsan Raghavan, "Sadr Tells His Militia to Cease Hostilities," *The Washington Post*, March 31, 2008; Ripley, *Operation Telic*, location No. 9172.

114. Ripley, *Operation Telic*, location No. 9152.

115. Iron, "Basra 2008," p. 191.

116. DoD photo by Corporal Daniel Angel, "Captain Matthew Clinger and Sergeant Robert Lower, 1st ANGLICO, Fire Control Team 6 joint tactical air controller and team chief, provide security with 3rd Battalion, Quick Reaction Force 1, 1st Iraqi Army Quick Reaction Force soldiers while other Iraqi forces search the neighborhood for criminals and illegal weapons in the Latif district in Basra, Iraq, May 3," May 3, 2008, Released to Public, available from *http://www.marines.mil/Photos.aspx?igphoto=152265*.

117. Stephen Ferrell and James Glanz, "More Than 1,000 in Iraq's Forces Quit Basra Fight," *The New York Times*, April 4, 2008; Qassim Abdul-Zahra, "Al-Maliki vows crackdown in Baghdad," *USA Today*, April 3, 2008.

118. Iron, "Basra 2008," p. 191.

119. MNF-I, SECDEF Weekly Update, March 31-April 6, 2008.

120. Ibid.

121. Iron, "Basra 2008," p. 192.

122. "Iraqi soldiers free CBS journalist from captors."

123. MNF-I, SECDEF Weekly Update, March 3-9, 2008.

124. Hala Jaber, "We will spill British blood, warns Sheikh Ahmad Fartusi," *Sunday Times*, September 14, 2008.

125. Ripley, *Operation Telic*, location No. 9182.

126. Testimony of White-Spunner to UK Government's Iraq Inquiry, p. 19.

127. Iron, "Basra 2008," p. 192; Interview, CSA OIF Study Group with Sindle, March 7, 2016.

128. Iron, "Basra 2008," p. 193.

129. Ripley, *Operation Telic*, location No. 9286.

130. Ucko and Egnell, *Counterinsurgency in Crisis*, p. 69; Peter Mansoor, "The British Army and the Lessons of the Iraq War," *British Army Review*, No. 147, Summer 2009, p. 13.

131. Paper, Major Tom Sills and Commander Doreen Fussman, *Battle of Phase Line Gold, Sadr City, Iraq: Coalition Forces and Iraqi Security Forces Partnering for Iraq, Integrating Forces, Combat Operations*, March 23-May 20, 2008, CSA OIF Study Group archives at AHEC, Carlisle, PA, August 6, 2008, pp. 4-5.

132. DoD photo by Staff Sergeant Jason Bailey, Joint Combat Camera Center, "Sadr City," March 29, 2008, Released to Public, available from *https://www.flickr.com/photos/mnfiraq/4315761833/in/faves-138659840%40N02/*.

133. Interview, Donald Wright and Timothy Reese, CSI Contemporary Operations Study Team, with Colonel Billy Don Farris, May 6, 2008.

134. Command Rpt, January 2007-February 2008, 2d Brigade, 82d Airborne Division, pp. 4-6.

135. MNF-I, SECDEF Weekly Update, October 28-November 3, 2007.

136. Ibid., October 14-20, 2007.

137. Ibid.

138. Notes from meeting between Colonel Billy Don Farris and Lieutenant General Raymond T. Odierno, December 23, 2007.

139. Marisa Cochrane, "Special Groups Regenerate," Iraq Rpt No. 11, Washington, DC: Institute for the Study of War, available from *http://www.understandingwar.org/sites/default/files/reports/IraqReport11.pdf*, accessed May 18, 2016.

140. Interview, CSI Contemporary Operations Study Team with Colonel John Hort, December 10, 2009.

141. Interviews, CSI Contemporary Operations Study Team with Colonel Farris, May 6, 2008; CSI Contemporary Operations Study Team with Major General Jeffrey Hammond, Combat Studies Institute, Fort Leavenworth, KS, January 21, 2010.

142. U.S. Army photo by Staff Sergeant Luis Orengo, "MND-B leaders meet with Baghdad governor [Image 4 of 4]," DVIDS Identifier 76873, February 11, 2008, Released to Public, available from *https://www.dvidshub.net/image/76873/mnd-b-leaders-meet-with-baghdad-governor*.

143. Ms, *On Point*, Vol. IV, Chapter 7, p. 11.

144. Interview, CSI Contemporary Operations Study Team with Hammond, January 21, 2010.

145. Interview, CSA OIF Study Group with Mowaffaq Rubaie, October 4, 2014.

146. "International Crisis Group: Iraq's Civil War, the Sadrists and the Surge," Middle East Rpt No. 72, Washington, DC: Council on Foreign Relations, February 7, 2008, p. 14.

147. Interview, Colonel Joel Rayburn, CSA OIF Study Group, with Colonel (Ret.) Derek Harvey, May 18, 2016.

148. MNF-I, SECDEF Weekly Update, January 14-20, 2008.

149. Ibid., February 18-24, 2008.

150. MNF-I, SECDEF Weekly Update, March 17-23, 2008.

151. Paper, Sills and Fussman, *Battle of Phase Line Gold, Sadr City, Iraq*, p. 11.

152. Interview, Colonel Joel Rayburn, CSA OIF Study Group, with Oubai Shahbandar, May 18, 2016.

153. Ibid.

154. MNC-I Chronology, February 2007-May 2008; "Iran 'behind Green Zone attack,'" BBC News, March 24, 2008.

155. MNF-I, SECDEF Weekly Update, March 24-30, 2008.

156. DoD photo by Sergeant Zachary Mott, "Chairman visits Sadr City, tours revitalized Jamilla Market [Image 6 of 6]," DVIDS Identifier 101161, July 7, 2008, Released to Public, available from *https://www.dvidshub.net/image/101161/chairman-visits-sadr-city-tours-revitalized-jamilla-market*.

157. Interview, CSI Contemporary Operations Study Team with Hammond, January 21, 2010.

158. Ibid.

159. Paper, Sills and Fussman, *Battle of Phase Line Gold, Sadr City, Iraq*, p. 3.

160. 3d Brigade Combat Team, 4th Infantry Division, Operation STRIKER DENIAL backbrief, April 16, 2008. The interview with Hammond provides details of his encounters with the U.S. advisers to the 42d and 44th Brigades of the 11th Iraqi Army Division. He recounts the remarkable heroism of Major Mark Rosenberg, who held his Iraqi battalion in place and pushed it into the fight despite the leaders often wanting to withdraw and abandon the fight. Major Rosenberg was killed several days into the fight by an EFP strike to his vehicle; he was traveling to refit after 2 days of fighting without sleep.

161. E-mail, Petraeus to Rayburn, March 9, 2016.

162. MNF-I, SECDEF Weekly Update, April 7-13, 2008.

163. Interview, CSA OIF Study Group with Shahbandar, May 18, 2016.

164. 3d Brigade, 4th Infantry Division, Operation IRAQI FREEDOM, December 2007-March 2009, Presentation, n.d.; Paper, Sills and Fussman, *Battle of Phase Line Gold, Sadr City, Iraq*, p. 2; MNC-I Chronology.

165. DoD photo by Sergeant Joseph Rivera Rebolledo, "MND-B Soldiers help improve security in Sadr City neighborhood [Image 1 of 2]," DVIDS Identifier 86930, May 3, 2008, Released to Public, available from *https://www.dvidshub.net/image/86930/mnd-b-soldiers-help-improve-security-sadr-city-neighborhood*.

166. David E. Johnson, M. Wade Markel, and Brian Shannon, *The 2008 Battle of Sadr City: Reimagining Urban Combat*, Santa Monica, CA: RAND Corporation, 2013, p. 55, available from *http://www.rand.org/pubs/research_reports/RR160.html*, accessed March 7, 2016.

167. Ibid., p. 57.

168. Paper, Sills and Fussman, *Battle of Phase Line Gold, Sadr City, Iraq*, p. 15.

169. Interview, CSA OIF Study Group with Colonel Conner, December 10, 2015.

170. U.S. Air Force photo by Technical Sergeant Adrian Cadiz, "Limited Visibility," April 17, 2008, Released to Public, available from *https://www.flickr.com/photos/mnfiraq/4316448914/in/faves-1386598 40%40N02/*.

171. MNC-I Chronology; Interviews, CSI Contemporary Operations Study Team with Hammond, January 21, 2010; CSI Contemporary Operations Study Team with Hort, December 10, 2009.

172. Cochrane, "Special Groups Regenerate," p. 17.

173. Ibid.; Interview, CSI Contemporary Operations Study Team with Hammond, January 21, 2010. MNF-I weekly updates in the spring of 2008 portray optimism of Iraqi security forces' growing capabilities.

174. Paper, Sills and Fussman, *Battle of Phase Line Gold, Sadr City, Iraq*, p. 19.

175. MNF-I, SECDEF Weekly Update, April 28-May 4, 2008; MNC-I Chronology.

176. Ms, *On Point*, Vol. IV, Chapter 7, p. 15.

177. "Analysis of Explosively Formed Penetrator (EFP) Explosions Against Coalition Forces in Iraq," Alexandria, VA: Institute for Defense Analysis, October 24, 2008.

178. James Hanning, "Deal with Shia prisoner left Basra at mercy of gangs, colonel admits," *Independent*, August 3, 2008.

179. Iron, "Basra 2008," p. 190.

180. Testimony of Binns to UK Government's Iraq Inquiry, pp. 16-17.

181. Ripley, *Operation Telic*, location No. 8689.

CHAPTER 9

THE SURGE CULMINATES, SUMMER 2008

The coalition commanders faced a situation in spring 2008 they had not anticipated. Since formulating the surge campaign plan during spring 2007, General David Petraeus and other senior coalition leaders had expected to fight al-Qaeda in Iraq (AQI) to the finish before shifting their main effort to the Shi'a militant groups at some point in late 2008, by which time the surge brigades would have left Iraq. Instead, the coalition had defeated the Shi'a militants by May 2008, far sooner than anyone thought possible. The coalition commanders now had to shift back to defeating AQI in northern Iraq with fewer troops at their disposal.

Prime Minister Nuri al-Maliki had complicated Petraeus's "north first" strategy with Operation CHARGE OF THE KNIGHTS, but the Prime Minister's gambit had several strategic benefits. By the operation's end, the fighting had routed Jaysh al Mahdi (JAM), the Iraqi Government had defeated Iran's militant proxies, and the Sadrists had lost any hope of ousting Maliki from power. With JAM and other Shi'a militias at a much-diminished capacity, there were fewer explosively formed penetrator (EFP) attacks, U.S. casualty rates dropped and criticism of the campaign in the United States slackened. U.S. commanders hoped this would allow them to resume the fight against AQI with fewer distractions.[1]

Still, the situation posed a conundrum for Lieutenant General Lloyd Austin, the Multi-National Corps-Iraq (MNC-I) commander, who was fighting different enemies at opposite ends of the country during the summer of 2008. He had to consolidate the gains his troops and the Iraqi security forces had won against the Sadrists in Baghdad and the south while dealing a knockout blow to AQI in the far north. These objectives would require increased reliance on the Iraqi security forces (ISF). The operations of summer 2008 also unfolded against the backdrop of changing political dynamics in Iraq that would make it increasingly difficult for U.S. leaders who hoped to put the U.S.-Iraqi security relationship on a stable long-term footing.

THE END OF THE SURGE

By July 2008, the last of the five surge brigades that had helped secure Baghdad and its surrounding belts had redeployed, requiring MNC-I to reallocate forces to fill the gaps. All told, the loss of the surge brigades, when combined with the drawdown of support personnel, resulted in a reduction of 22,000 troops, roughly one-seventh of the U.S. military strength at the peak of the surge.[2] MNC-I also faced the drawdown of international forces throughout 2008. Multi-National Division-Center (MND-C) felt the losses most acutely. By December 2008, Major General Michael L. Oates's 10th Mountain Division would be responsible for every province south of Baghdad except Basrah, an area about the size of California.[3] After the June 2008 departure of the last 550 Australian combat troops from Dhi Qar Province, Oates moved Colonel Philip Battaglia's 4th Brigade Combat Team (BCT), 1st Cavalry Division, from the northern reaches of MND-C's area of operations to fill the gap.[4]

Similar moves took place in August after the nation of Georgia recalled its 2,000-man 1st Georgian Brigade from Kut when fighting broke out with Russia back at home. The rapid withdrawal of the brigade, which departed Iraq on U.S. Air Force C-17s only 72 hours after the Russian invasion, forced MNC-I to shift an artillery brigade quickly to their sector.[5] The Georgian withdrawal also had larger international implications. The United States considered Russia the aggressor in its invasion of Georgia, assisted in returning Georgian units home, and issued stern diplomatic condemnations, raising concerns about the future of any United Nations (UN)-approved security agreements in Iraq given Russia's veto on the UN Security Council. Approximately 900 Polish troops redeployed from Diwaniya in October 2008 as well.[6] In total, 16 coalition partners withdrew from Iraq during 2008.[7]

Because of the reduction in U.S. and coalition forces, the remaining 15 U.S. combat brigades would have to cover more ground with fewer resources, and often single brigades were responsible for entire provinces. This left few U.S. forces with which to reinforce Multi-National Division-North (MND-N), where the 2d Cavalry Regiment occupied all Diyala Province; the 1st BCT, 10th Mountain Division, covered Kirkuk Province; 1st BCT, 101st Airborne Division, oversaw Salahadin as well as some northwestern portions of Baghdad; and the 3d Armored Cavalry Regiment (ACR) had the largest territorial responsibility, covering Ninawa Province, including Mosul and a large portion of the Jazeera desert.[8]

The smaller U.S. force would encounter a much-improved security situation throughout much of the country. In Multi-National Force-West (MNF-W), where the Sunni Awakening had been underway for more than a year, the Marines maintained security despite losing 8 of 14 infantry battalions as part of the post-surge drawdown. Levels of violence continued to fall in Baghdad and Diyala as well. In June 2007, Iraq had experienced an average of 180 attacks of all kinds per day, but by mid-July 2008, attacks numbered fewer than 21 per day, a level not seen since January 2004.[9]

Only in Ninawa Province was there a marked deterioration in security. By late spring, one-third of all violent incidents in Iraq took place there, especially in the long-suffering provincial capital city of Mosul. This is where the coalition and the Iraqi Government turned their attention in mid-2008.

OPERATION DEFEAT AL-QAEDA IN THE NORTH

Prime Minister Maliki's decision to conduct a large-scale operation in Basrah had derailed Multi-National Force-Iraq's (MNF-I) plans to conduct a U.S.-Iraqi offensive in Mosul during March 2008. However, even as the coalition focused on battling the Shi'a militants in southern Iraq and Baghdad, MNC-I planned to return the coalition's main effort to Mosul at some point. In early February, following the disappointing results of Operation PHANTOM PHOENIX in Diyala, General Raymond Odierno and Petraeus already had pressed Major General Mark Hertling to shift Multi-National Division-North's (MND-N) manpower and intelligence, surveillance, and reconnaissance

(ISR) focus to Ninawa.[10] In late March 2008, Austin and MNC-I began Operation DEFEAT AL-QAEDA IN THE NORTH (OPDAN), a synchronization of the division-level operations in northern Iraq that would last for the entirety of XVIII Airborne Corps' rotation as MNC-I. OPDAN focused on Mosul and its surrounding regions. The city's importance to AQI's strength elsewhere in Iraq had become clearer as the group lost its grip in western and central Iraq. Forced out of Baghdad and denied access to Anbar, AQI had no choice but to regroup in the far north and fight to retain a foothold in the country. Petraeus told reporters in early March that, while Baghdad was crucial for al-Qaeda to win in Iraq, Mosul and its surrounding areas were vital for the terrorist group's survival. One senior MNC-I officer agreed, later commenting, "If AQI had a Pentagon, it would be in Mosul."[11]

During the months that the coalition and the Iraqi Army fought Shi'a militias in the south, Mosul's security situation continued to deteriorate. Between February and April 2008, AQI attacked nine coalition and ISF combat outposts in the city with large suicide car or truck bombs smuggled from Syria, destroying several of the compounds. The influence of Ba'athist insurgent organizations—the Awda ("Return") Party and the Naqshbandi Army—had grown as well.[12]

The departure of the surge brigades between February and July, however, meant that the coalition would have fewer resources for the operation than coalition commanders had hoped. In late March, when the coalition had planned for the Mosul operation to begin, Austin and MNC-I still had 19 U.S. brigades at their disposal, with Colonel Billy Don Ferris's 2d Brigade, 82d Airborne Division, the only one of the 5 surge brigades already redeployed. By the time the unplanned fighting against the Shi'a militias wound down in May 2008, MNC-I had redeployed a division's worth of combat power and stood weaker than it had been in March. MNC-I would have to conduct its northern operations with only 16 U.S. brigades. Austin had no spare brigades with which to reinforce Hertling's MND-N.

Austin took several steps to compensate for the loss of combat power for the north. He encouraged his Iraqi counterparts to shift ISF units from relatively quiet areas to reinforce Iraqi divisions engaged in intense fighting in hot spots in northern Iraq. He also began to expand some of his own units' areas of responsibility. On April 11, to relieve some of the pressure on Hertling's stretched force, Austin moved the boundary between MNF-W and MND-N some 80 kilometers north, giving the Marines in the somewhat pacified Anbar Province responsibility for portions of Ninawa and Salahadin Provinces that Hertling's units could not adequately cover. The additional territory, designated Temporary Area of Operations Mameluke, was an 80-mile wide strip of the Jazeera desert that ran from the Syrian border to just north of Lake Tharthar. In this area, the Marines of I Marine Expeditionary Force (I MEF) would interdict foreign fighters along the southern infiltration routes from Syria before they could reach Baghdad or other major population centers.[13] The shrinking of MND-N's area of operations enabled the 3d ACR to focus its combat power on Mosul and enabled 1st Brigade, 101st Airborne Division, to focus on Salahadin's populated areas.[14]

Source: DoD photo by Staff Sergeant Margaret Nelson (Released).

**Kirkuk Governor Abdul-Rahman Mostafa, Major General Mark Hertling,
and Colonel David Paschal.[15]**

In another measure to mitigate the dearth of maneuver brigades for OPDAN, MNC-I gave responsibility for the vast western Ninawa Province—the northern Jazeera area where AQI had previously stationed its "border emir" in Sinjar and where the 3d ACR had created a U.S.-Iraqi light reconnaissance troop to cover the border zone in 2005—to an ad hoc interdiction force comprised of the corps military intelligence brigade and special operations forces (SOF). Colonel Robert Ashley's 525th Battlefield Surveillance Brigade (BfSB), which MNC-I moved from the Iranian border in Diyala Province to Tal Afar in early April, would use its ISR assets to watch for foreign fighter crossings from Syria. The Combined Joint Special Operations Task Force (CJSOTF) provided a battalion tactical command post and advanced operational base to be the 525th BfSB's action arm, with the CJSOTF element and the 525th BfSB collocating their headquarters to ensure tight coordination.[16]

The battlefield surveillance brigade's umanned aerial vehicles (UAVs), joint surveillance target attack radar systems (JSTARs) downlinks, and long-range reconnaissance capabilities helped locate AQI elements for targeting by the CJSOTF and by some elements of the 3d ACR. For their part, the CJSOTF detachments used armed Toyota HiLux trucks and stripped their High Mobility Multi-Purpose Wheeled Vehicles (HMMWV) of improvised explosive device (IED) armor protection, doors, and even windows to be able to conduct long-range desert interdiction missions.[17] These patrols found that the border area again had become an insurgent sanctuary. The special operators engaged in running gun battles with AQI technical vehicles and discovered abandoned AQI training compounds as well as mammoth caches of arms and supplies. One such location in western Ninawa stretched across a 19-structure compound and had weapons and explosives hidden in the walls of buildings, where, among other items, the U.S. commandos found M–16 rifles that had been provided to Lebanon as part of the foreign military sales program.[18] The cache also contained so many IED-making materials that it exceeded the ability of the green berets to destroy it with their own explosives. A B–52 strike completed the job.[19] In another instance, a Special Forces team discovered a well-kept and expansive house in the middle of the desert, miles from the nearest settlement, where they captured a one-legged man whom they later determined to be AQI's third in command.[20]

Despite discoveries like these, the BfSB, CJSOTF, and 3d ACR lacked sufficient maneuver and aviation assets to cover the massive area they were assigned, which was larger than the state of Massachusetts. Despite its designation as a battlefield surveillance brigade, the 525th BfSB had deployed to Iraq in September 2007 without fully changing from a standard military intelligence brigade to a BfSB. Most significantly, it lacked its authorized cavalry squadron that would have given it a way to attack the targets generated by the brigade's ISR assets.[21] As a result, the BfSB often detected foreign fighter crossings but could not do anything about it. This frustrated both 3d ACR commander Colonel Michael A. Bills and 525th commander Ashley. "The sheer distance involved was very problematic," Ashley said later. "[T]here were occasions that we could see things coming over the border and we were not able to react to them."[22]

Closer to Mosul, Iraqi commanders repositioned their units to operate in zones that the coalition could not cover. The 3d Iraqi Division, normally responsible for western Ninawa Province, assumed responsibility for the AQI-dominated towns on Mosul's western outskirts, placing nine Iraqi battalions there to free the 2d Iraqi Division to focus on the city itself. On May 1, General Riyadh Jalal Tawfiq's Ninawa Operations Command became fully operational, ready to oversee both Iraqi divisions in the impending Mosul operation.[23] With clearing operations inside the city planned for mid-May, Tawfiq's Iraqi units created a cordon of checkpoints and combat outposts around the city and gathered intelligence indicating that AQI's ranks in Ninawa included a large number of foreign fighters who had traveled from Syria.[24] Many of these foreign fighters had come to Mosul via Abu Ghadiyah's Syria-based facilitation network, including AQI fighters who killed 13 Iraqi police officers on May 2, in an attack that Petraeus judged "could not have been carried out without the acquiescence of Syrian officials at some level."[25]

Mosul: Operation MOTHER OF TWO SPRINGS

On May 10, 2008, the day after the Iraqi Government and the Sadrists agreed to a cease-fire in Baghdad, Tawfiq launched the long-anticipated operation to clear AQI from Mosul's neighborhoods. As Bills's 3d ACR cut off insurgent supply routes into the city, including the major route from Tel Afar to Mosul, the Iraqi 2d Division and Iraqi special operations forces (ISOF) conducted 17 cordon and search operations inside the city along with targeted raids to round up high-value individuals from AQI and other Sunni militant groups.[26] As he had done in Basrah, Prime Minister Maliki arrived soon after the operation began with his interior minister and defense ministers in tow to take command and turn the security operation into a political initiative. Reaching Mosul on May 14, Maliki named the Iraqi-led Operation UMM AL-RABIYAIN (MOTHER OF TWO SPRINGS) and began to assert Baghdad's authority over the local government and security forces.

Unlike their counterparts in Basrah, the Iraqi units in Mosul did not suffer desertions in the early days of fighting, and AQI did not attempt to challenge the government forces in direct firefights. During the first week, Iraqi forces detained over 1,000 suspects, of which just under 200 had known connections to either AQI or its political front, the Islamic State of Iraq (ISI).[27] At the same time, coalition special operators stepped up operations against AQI in northern Iraq, carrying out 69 raids against the group between May 12 and 18 that yielded 117 AQI-linked detainees, including 2 senior AQI commanders. On May 14, U.S. special operators in western Ninawa managed to capture Abu Umar al-Tunisi, one of AQI's most senior Syria-based facilitators, generating additional targets by keeping news of the capture quiet and exploiting information obtained from his hideout.[28]

The Iraqi-led clearing of Mosul continued to the end of May, by which time General Tawfiq's troops had conducted 177 battalion-level operations. One Iraqi raid uncovered what was probably AQI's main distribution hub for IEDs and car bombs in Mosul: a building in east Mosul that contained more than 11 tons of homemade explosives and other bomb-making materials.[29] At the same time, the U.S. special operators in western Ninawa exacted a heavy toll, detaining 32 AQI members in intelligence-driven raids on foreign-fighter facilitation networks in the 4 weeks following the launch of Operation MOTHER OF TWO SPRINGS.[30] The intense operations had a noticeable effect on the group's ability to move freely and pay its operatives. "Some low-level AQI fighters are abandoning the organization due to lack of pay, and . . . the head of AQI, Abu Ayyub al-Masri, may have ordered a month-long halt of the flow of foreign fighters into Iraq," Petraeus reported to Secretary of Defense (SECDEF) Robert Gates on May 25.[31] With the security operations proceeding smoothly, coalition and Iraqi officials turned their attention to reconstruction projects. Maliki allocated $100 million for that purpose, just as he had for Basrah and Sadr City.[32]

It was not yet clear if AQI had been defeated in Ninawa. Near the end of May, Iraqi Minister of Defense Abdel Qader reported that he considered the clearing of Mosul only 40 percent complete, prompting Petraeus to conclude that the joint U.S.-Iraqi operation would not reach the "hold" phase of "clear, hold, and build" until the end of July.[33] Appearing to confirm this assessment, by early July MNF-I reported that 68 percent of all attacks in Iraq took place in the Multi-National Division-North (MND-N) area of operations.

Although AQI could not control territory, it mounted a counterattack of assassinations and intimidation against Iraqi officials and civilians. On June 6, insurgent gunmen nearly killed Ninawa Governor Duraid Kashmoula as he traveled through a formerly AQI-held neighborhood, and on June 27, the governor had another near miss when an AQI car-bomb attack on his office killed 18 people and wounded another 80.[34] On July 9, insurgents attacked a Kurdistan Democratic Party compound in Mosul during a visit by General Tawfiq, killing eight people in an unsuccessful assassination attempt against the Iraqi commander. The car bombing came the same week Petraeus reported that insurgents had assassinated 16 Mosul police officers in the space of 30 days, including a police brigadier responsible for issuing identification badges in the city.[35] The following week, MNF-I recorded a 20 percent increase in attacks in Ninawa, a disheartening trend that led Austin and MNC-I to deploy an additional Stryker battalion from Baghdad to Mosul to reinforce the 3d ACR.[36]

The persistence of the insurgent groups in the Mosul area was caused by several complex problems. Without a large and capable border force, northwestern Iraq remained a porous throughway for foreign fighters and for AQI members. Economic conditions made it difficult for the Iraqi Government to enlist local tribes to help cut down the foreign fighter flow. An ongoing drought in the Jazeera desert limited Ninawa's agricultural output and led some sheikhs to smuggle goods, arms, and foreign fighters.[37] The many small towns west and north of Mosul were difficult to secure and remained important safe havens for AQI and other militant groups. Some of the towns between Tel Afar and Mosul, such as Muhallabiyah and Sheikh Ibrahim, were under the near-complete control of the extremists—some captured by the 3d ACR in 2005 but later released—and would later function as important bases for the Islamic State of Iraq and Syria (ISIS). Hertling's subordinates identified no fewer than 22 different militant groups operating in the MND-N area of operations, many with facilitation networks extending into Syria.[38] Whenever the coalition and ISF pushed AQI away from Ninawa's populations, other groups, such as the Ba'athist Naqshbandi Army, filled the void and continued attacks against coalition troops and Iraqi officials.[39]

Finally, the ethnic fault lines running through Ninawa Province challenged the coalition as well as the Iraqi Government. Most of the Iraqi troops who conducted Operation MOTHER OF TWO SPRINGS were Kurdish. In discussions with American officials, the citizens of Mosul often referred to the Iraqi Army units in their city as peshmerga.[40] In addition, the Sh'ia-majority 6th Brigade, 2d National Police Division, which had deployed from Baghdad for the operation, often dealt with Mosul's population in a heavy-handed manner that Bills described as "pretty cruel." The police brigade's presence in the city grew so counterproductive that Bills persuaded General Tawfiq to redeploy it to Ninawa's desert areas to search for enemy fighters.[41] As Bills and the 3d ACR observed, the people of Mosul remained wary of the ISF and felt they were being policed by Sh'ia and Kurdish troops with an anti-Sunni agenda.

These ethnic fissures made Hertling and Bills skeptical about the idea of creating large Sons of Iraq groups in Ninawa Province—and, in Hertling's view, in Diyala as well. Both feared AQI would infiltrate any Awakening groups in Ninawa. Bills believed the diverse demographics of Ninawa meant that Sons of Iraq groups would make the province even more volatile.[42] Having been involved in the early days of the ineffective Iraqi Civil Defense Corps in 2003–2004, Hertling also saw limited utility in creating what he called a "highly paid neighborhood watch program" and was concerned about dissolving such groups once they had been created. He also believed they would drain human capital from more crucial areas. "Once you pay an Iraqi to stand around with a gun they are not going to want to do a whole lot of other things," he later said. "We had doctors, lawyers, and teachers all joining the Sons of Iraq, even [some of] the police, because they were assured payment from the Americans and usually the payment for the doctors and lawyers was higher than they were getting as a doctor or lawyer."[43]

Because of these concerns, Hertling and MND-N decided not to create an Awakening movement on the scale that had taken place in MNF-W, MND-C, and Multi-National Division-Baghdad (MND-B). Instead, U.S. commanders in the north pressed their Iraqi counterparts to recruit new ISF battalions from the local Ninawa population, including Yezidis and Sunnis from western Ninawa, but the ethnic and sectarian fissures in the province and its capital remained a persistent problem.[44]

CONSOLIDATING VICTORY AGAINST THE SHI'A MILITANT GROUPS

As Operation MOTHER OF TWO SPRINGS proceeded in Mosul, coalition and ISF units in southern Iraq and Baghdad attempted to consolidate the gains made against the Shi'a militant groups from March to May, especially against the Sadrists. The defeat of the Shi'a militants in Iraq's southern cities created an opportunity for the coalition to extend its presence to areas that had been dangerous territory for it since 2004. On May 24, just 4 days after Prime Minister Maliki sent Iraqi Army troops to occupy Sadr City, U.S. Ambassador Ryan Crocker visited Karbala and Najaf to mark the arrival of new provincial reconstruction teams (PRTs). This was a significant step since violence had kept the PRTs for most southern provinces on protected compounds in Hillah or Basrah for almost 2 years.[45] Having PRTs in the Shi'a shrine cities expanded the coalition's political and diplomatic role in the critically important religious hub of the south.

In Baghdad, coalition and Iraqi forces continued clearing operations in neighborhoods that had long been militia strongholds, confiscating large quantities of weapons and explosives. U.S. troops maintained their presence in Sadr City south of Route Gold, while the Iraqi Army and police with a few coalition advisers occupied Sadr City's northern neighborhoods. In the 3 weeks following the Iraqi Army's May 20 entry into Sadr City, Iraqi troops seized 118 weapons caches, including 90 EFPs and "enough rifles to equip nearly three battalions," Petraeus reported on June 8.[46]

Coalition troops also conducted targeted raids against some of the militia-affiliated Iraqi officials whose political top cover waned once the Prime Minister turned against the militias. In one high-profile case on May 24, coalition special operators and the Iraqi National Police Emergency Response Unit arrested the director general of the Iraqi corrections system, who had used his position to torture prisoners, extort money from families, and back death squad killings by Shi'a militants.[47]

Though most militia leaders had fled and their foot soldiers had dispersed, a few Shi'a militant cells in Baghdad continued attacks against American troops and other Iraqis. On June 4, as Shi'a militants prepared to fire improvised rocket-assisted munitions against a U.S. patrol base near Sadr City, a rocket detonated prematurely, killing the militants and some bystanders. The explosion left 18 Iraqis dead, 30 wounded, and destroyed 15 houses.[48] Two weeks later, a car bomb at a busy bus stop in the Shi'a-majority Hurriyah neighborhood killed at least 27 civilians and wounded 50. Responding to the attack, the local coalition unit, Colonel William B. Hickman's 2d Brigade, 101st Airborne Division, quickly discovered that the bombing against mostly Shi'a civilians had not been the work of AQI, but of a local Special Groups commander who wanted the Shi'a civilians of Hurriyah to believe there was still a Sunni terrorist threat in the neighborhood to justify his militia. As Petraeus put it, the attack was meant "to reduce perceptions of security in the neighborhood, justify Shi'a militia presence, and discourage the return of displaced Sunni families. We have presented evidence to the Iraqi Government in an effort to get them to publicly identify Special Groups (SG) as being responsible for the attack."[49]

The Transformation of JAM

The defeat of JAM did not end the threat of Shi'a insurgency. However, it did force the largest of the Shi'a militant groups to change. In the wake of his militia's operational downfall, on June 13, Moqtada Sadr announced that he intended to reorganize the Mahdi Army into two components: the Mumahidun, a civic and humanitarian organization, and a specialized militant wing that would operate secretly. According to the Mumahidun project guide, its members would be unarmed and strictly disciplined, and any violation of this policy would be dealt with harshly.[50] The Baghdad-based Hazem al-Araji and nine other Sadrist clerics would lead this reformed movement.[51]

In July, Sadr followed up his earlier announcement by proclaiming the formation of the Promised Day Brigade, an organization of Sadrist militants authorized to continue resistance against U.S. troops. In Petraeus's view, this was "not an entirely deft move," because by announcing the creation of a new militia, Sadr ran the risk of having the Maliki government exclude his candidates from the upcoming provincial elections since, by law, no illegal militia could participate. Petraeus also noted that because "Sadr and most senior SG leaders are now in Iran, this action may increase perceptions that the Sadr Trend's militia is beholden to and responds to direction from Iran. Sadr's statement also exposes Iran's role in facilitating violence in Iraq, thereby giving lie to Iran's repeated commitments to stop lethal aid and support the Iraqi government."[52]

Ultimately, however, these changes aided Sadr because Maliki, anticipating a political showdown with Abdul Aziz al-Hakim and the Islamic Supreme Council of Iraq (ISCI) in the upcoming provincial elections, had reached out to his defeated Sadrist foes to negotiate a Da'wa-Sadrist reconciliation prior to the elections, something that Petraeus and other coalition leaders did not anticipate.[53] Reconciliation with Maliki meant the new incarnations of the Mahdi Army could work largely unmolested by the Iraqi Government. The flight of the militia commanders to Iran had left a new political power vacuum in east Baghdad and the southern provinces, one that Maliki's Da'wa Party and Hakim's ISCI hastened to fill prior to the provincial elections scheduled for late 2008.

Ali Faisal al-Lami and the Sadr City Assassinations

As Sadr attempted to revamp his militia, many Special Groups members and JAM fighters opposed the truce Sadr had declared and were reluctant to stop fighting coalition forces. Some had left JAM to join Asa'ib Ahl al-Haqq (AAH) or Kata'ib Hizballah.[54] Evidence that other Special Groups were filling the void after JAM's defeat was evident in Baghdad in the summer of 2008. In June, MND-B moved troops and other support elements into Sadr City to follow up May's military victory with civic action against the militia-affiliated politicians who had controlled the district. Because the militia loyalists who held the formal district council leadership had fled when the Shi'a militant groups left, U.S. officials hoped to establish a provincial reconstruction team in Sadr City and empower a new, anti-Sadrist chairman of the district council. AAH, however, did not intend to let this happen. On June 24, 2008, a bomb detonated in a Sadr City District Advisory Council meeting, killing six Iraqis, two American Soldiers, and two State Department officials, including 57-year-old Deputy PRT Chief Stephen Farley. Another U.S. official, who stepped out of the room moments before the blast, survived. The sophisticated bomb plot involved explosives packed in the headrest of an office chair that the attackers knew the meeting attendees would use.[55]

U.S. troops quickly uncovered a trail of evidence that led back to Ali Faisal al-Lami, a longtime aide to Iraqi politician Ahmad Chalabi. A senior official on Chalabi's de-Ba'athification committee, Lami was closely allied with AAH and apparently had helped plan the assassination of Farley and other officials, intending to kill the new anti-Sadrist district council head. He also had long been suspected by other Iraqi officials of using the de-Ba'athification committee's security details as death squads against Sunnis and Ba'athists, especially in west Baghdad. After the Sadr City bombing, Lami traveled to Beirut for consultations with Lebanese Hizballah, likely in connection with his mission to "unify Shi'a extremists throughout the region," as Petraeus described it.[56] He also had probably intended to wait there until the investigation of the bombing had passed. On August 27, however, Lami unwisely flew back to Iraq, where U.S. troops arrested him as he arrived at the Baghdad International Airport and moved him to the U.S. detention center at Camp Cropper, where he would remain for a year. "We believe Ali Faisal was directly involved in the 24 June attack in Sadr City against the District Advisory Council that killed two State Department employees, two Coalition Soldiers, and members of the council," Petraeus reported to Gates on August 31.[57] Petraeus also revealed to Gates that Lami was a member of the militant group headed by Akram al-Ka'abi, a reference to AAH. At Camp Cropper, Lami admitted to knowledge of sectarian death squad killings against former Ba'athists. He also asserted that Chalabi had been involved in the killings of former regime members, Iraqi Members of Parliament, and journalists, and that Chalabi had shared information on 450 former Ba'athists with Shi'a death squads so the Ba'athists could be targeted.[58] Perhaps not coincidentally, unknown assailants tried but failed to assassinate Chalabi in Baghdad on September 5, just days after Lami's capture, killing two bodyguards but missing Chalabi himself.[59]

Attacks like those in Hurriyah and the Sadr City District Council tempered the sense that the coalition and the Maliki government had won a decisive victory against the Shi'a militants. The day after the Sadr City bombing, Iraqi police liaison to Sadr City, Ferat Attriyeh, claimed that although the Iraqi Government had forced JAM and the Special Groups to give up their overt control over the slum, the militant groups remained present in the shadows. "They are still working inside the city. There are killings, lootings, they come and go in unmarked cars. They threaten anyone who works with U.S. forces. Outside the wall, they are still in control."[60]

Amarah and Operation LOOK SOUTH

Farther south, the Shi'a militants suffered another significant defeat as the coalition and Maliki government turned to the longtime militia stronghold of Amarah, the capital of Maysan Province. While Basrah and Sadr City represented endpoints of a sophisticated and deadly Iranian smuggling network, Maysan and Amarah were the network's hub.[61]

Under Major General Jonathan Shaw, MND-SE left Maysan in April 2007 and transferred responsibility to the Iraqis.[62] With no coalition military presence, the province's importance as a transit and supply point from Iran increased throughout 2007 and early 2008 as some of the militia commanders and fighters who fled Baghdad in the early days of the surge moved into Amarah.[63]

As the Sadr City battle wound down in May 2008, Austin asked the CJSOTF, MND-C, and other special operations forces (SOF) to develop plans to address the Amarah problem. Austin selected the CJSOTF plan, Operation YARBOROUGH, because it offered operational effects with minimal forces, allowing MNC-I to focus on Mosul. After the success of Iraqi security forces and the coalition in Basrah and Sadr City, the CJSOTF plan played on the Sadrist fears that a large-scale coalition offensive was imminent. Rather than follow through with YARBOROUGH, the CJSOTF hit the militias with a series of deception operations and raids designed to convince them to abandon Maysan before sustaining what could be heavy losses.

To prepare for the action, the CJSOTF moved a company of the ISOF brigade, an additional operational detachment, and the majority of its special operations aviation contingent, which included helicopters, an MC-130 transport capable of leaflet drops, and an AC-130 gunship to Tallil Airfield in neighboring Dhi Qar Province. The operation began on May 9 when an armed Predator UAV killed JAM fighters on a major road to Amarah. Over the next several days, ISOF troops and their CJSOTF advisers launched raids into Amarah and established temporary checkpoints on roads surrounding the town, capturing militiamen and telling the local population that the coalition was preparing for a major offensive. At the same time, the MC-130 dropped leaflets announcing that civilians should consider evacuating the city ahead of the impending operation. Overflights by F-16s and Predator UAVs increased, some of which bombed uninhabited desert areas to create the perception that the coalition was conducting air strikes against remote militia hideouts. As early as May 15, the operations began having an effect, as reports emerged that local militants were stockpiling weapons and emplacing IEDs. The raids, checkpoints, overflights, and leaflet drops continued for several weeks, with the addition of a feigned ground assault and the airdrop of humanitarian aid supplies to "refugees" from an imaginary attack, all designed to further fray the militia leaders' nerves. When CJSOTF operators learned that militia leaders had ordered civilians to pick up and destroy the coalition leaflets, they printed new "wanted poster" leaflets with photographs of those responsible for the order, dropping 10,000 on Amarah the following night. As some JAM and Special Groups leaders fled to Iran, the CJSOTF dropped additional leaflets that listed those who had fled and warned those staying behind that they had been abandoned and left to die. By early June, the operation had achieved its desired effect: the majority of Maysan's militia leaders had panicked and escaped to Iran rather than stay and face what they expected would be a Fallujah-style coalition attack.[64]

Source: U.S. Navy photo by Petty Officer 2d Class Jack G. Georges (Released).

Air Force Loadmasters Prepare to Drop Pallets of Humanitarian Aid During Operation YARBOROUGH.[65]

The operation in Amarah was part of a broader MNC-I approach to defeat the Iranian-sponsored Shi'a militant networks in southern Iraq. Even before Operation YARBOROUGH, Austin had decided the time was right to accept risk in the southern Baghdad belts and push toward the Iranian border region.[66] Securing Baghdad and Basrah had not solved the problem of the rampant Iranian smuggling network through Maysan, Dhi Qar, and Muthanna Provinces. Ten days after the fighting ended in Sadr City, MNC-I issued the order for Operation LOOK SOUTH to snuff out the networks and directly counter malign Iranian influence. However, much of this area fell within the British Multi-National Division-Southeast (MND-SE) area of operations. Operation LOOK SOUTH creatively avoided the politically charged question of changing the British boundaries by establishing a temporary area of operations on May 30 that effectively carved out Maysan, Dhi Qar, and Muthanna Provinces from MND-SE for MND-C to control indefinitely.[67] Officially, the multinational division boundaries had not changed, but the reality on the ground told another story. The British readily accepted the unofficial and unconventional change in responsibility across much of MND-SE and would see their area gradually shrink throughout the summer.[68] The newly arrived U.S. 10th Mountain Division, which replaced Major General Rick Lynch's 3d Infantry Division as MND-C at the end of May 2008, had four brigades to cover this vast expanse of southern Iraq. Under the command of Oates, the 10th Mountain Division further expanded MND-C's area of responsibility following the scheduled departure of the Polish-led Multi-National Division-Central South (MND-CS) in October.[69]

Major General Michael Oates (left). Source: DoD photo by Staff Sergeant Michel Sauret (Released).

Major General Michael Oates, With Major General Othman Ali Farhood al-Ghanimi, 8th Iraqi Army Division Commander.[70]

The day after Oates took command of MND-C and Operation LOOK SOUTH kicked off, Prime Minister Maliki ordered Iraqi forces in Maysan Province to clear Amarah. The operation differed from those in Sadr City and Basrah since the 10th Iraqi Army Division planned it with American support. It was also to be Oates's first operation. After hearing his counterparts' overcomplicated plan that called for several uncoordinated axes of advance that would lead to violent engagements inside the city, Oates gently suggested changes that simplified the operation and spared Amarah's population. In the revised plan, the Iraqi Army would deploy a brigade to clear the capital from west to east toward the Iranian border, while Oates would position SOF east of the capital to interdict fighters attempting to flee toward the border.[71]

On June 19, troops from the 10th Iraqi Division and their U.S. advisers entered Amarah unopposed, an achievement born from the success of Operation YARBOROUGH. As the soldiers began to clear the city, they discovered large weapons and munitions caches that included almost 500 mortar rounds and 700 antitank mines.[72] Over the course of a week, the ISF detained 65 suspected insurgents and found 52 weapons caches, some containing EFPs.[73] Along with the dozens of militiamen, the Iraqi troops detained several senior local officials with Sadrist militant ties, including both the provincial governor and the provincial chief of police. Iraqi leaders in Baghdad also replaced the brigade responsible for the Iraq-Iran border in Maysan Province that had been ineffective for several years.[74]

On June 2, Prime Minister Maliki flew to Amarah, continuing his practice of being personally present for large-scale ISF operations. He arrived to find Iraqi Army units increasingly confident as they witnessed the defeat of the Shi'a militants in a third major militia stronghold city. "We saw a positive indicator of the growing confidence of the ISF in a bit of graffiti seen on the Yugoslav Bridge in the vicinity of Amarah last week," Petraeus reported to Gates. "Presumably a JAM/SG member had scrawled on the bridge, 'We'll be back.' Below it, someone from the ISF responded with, 'We'll be waiting for you'."[75]

As had happened in Basrah and Baghdad after extensive shaping operations, another Shi'a insurgent base had fallen with relative ease into ISF and coalition hands. For the first time since 2003, the Iraqi Government controlled the entire lower Tigris River Valley from Baghdad to the sea, unvexed.

THE UNFINISHED BUSINESS OF THE SURGE

Return to Normality in Baghdad

As the clearing operations in militia-dominated neighborhoods continued, the once-extreme violence in Iraq's capital dropped to levels experienced in other capitals of the developing world. In early July, MNF-I's spokesmen announced that the violence was at its lowest level since the war began. Economic activity had improved as well. On July 11, official Iraqi and U.S. economic reports calculated that the Iraqi economy was growing at an annual rate of between 8 and 9 percent. At the same time, the Gulf Region Division of the Army Corps of Engineers — Iraq's largest employer — reported that only 3 percent of its active projects faced security-related delays, down from more than 20 percent in fall 2007.[76]

By midsummer 2008, life in Baghdad had returned to normal, something that Petraeus and MNF-I looked to encourage. In one example, Petraeus had MNF-I assist farmers in the lower Diyala Valley near Baghdad with the crop dusting of 159,000 acres of date palms to increase the yield of one of Iraq's most important agricultural exports. Petraeus also worked to reopen Baghdad's public swimming pools (nicknamed "Operation SPEEDO"), calculating that this would give idle young men something to do and offer respite from the summer heat and sporadic electricity.[77]

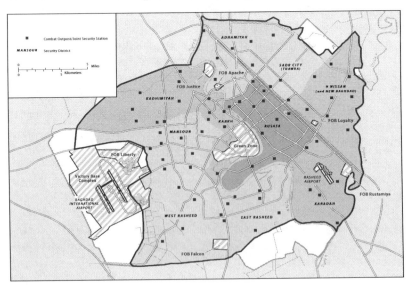

Map created by the official cartographer at the U.S. Army Center of Military History, Washington, DC.

Map 20. U.S. Forward Positions, Baghdad, 2007–2008.

Baghdadis who had shunned public places at night in 2006 and 2007 now filled restaurants and shops. Commercial areas such as the city's famous riverside Abu Nuwas Street reopened. In late August, a crowd of about 50,000 attended a soccer match in Baghdad, the largest sporting event since the 2003 invasion, with no security problems marring the occasion.[78] To capitalize on the growing sense of improvement among Iraqis, Petraeus ordered U.S. military vehicles to "adhere to Iraqi traffic patterns and assume a lower profile with less aggressive and provocative security procedures" of the sort that had long raised Iraqis' ire. Petraeus also directed U.S. units to begin removing what he called "detritus of war" from the streets of Baghdad and other cities, including the vast mass of concertina wire, sandbags, and construction material that had accumulated over 5½ years of violence.[79]

Source: DoD photo by Staff Sergeant Ian M. Terry (Released).

Iraqis Celebrate the Removal of Concrete Barriers From a Marketplace in Samarra.[80]

A more complicated problem arose in the resettlement of those Iraqis who had been forced to flee their homes during years of sectarian violence, especially in Baghdad and other parts of central Iraq. An estimated 5 million refugees and internally displaced persons, or roughly 17 percent of the Iraqi population, had not returned home following the sectarian cleansings of 2005–2007.[81] This had far-reaching political implications, especially with provincial elections scheduled to take place in late 2008. According to one U.S. Government report, of those displaced persons who attempted to return to Baghdad, "up to 70% . . . could not resettle in their own homes, either because someone else was living there or because the ethnic composition of the neighborhood made it unsafe."[82] The lack of a uniform procedure for adjudicating property disputes between squatters and displaced persons had destabilizing potential, possibly encouraging both sides to elicit support from local militias.[83]

Nevertheless, Petraeus considered the situation promising as the summer ended. Reporting to Gates in the first week of September, he noted that almost 50,000 displaced Iraqi families had returned to Baghdad since December 2007, a figure that represented about a quarter of a million people. The U.S. brigade in the Rashid District reported almost 1,500 families returned home in the last week of August alone.[84] To help matters, the government announced that Iraqi troops would evict squatters from illegal residences; and Iraqi ministries would disburse compensation payments to squatters forced to move.[85] It surprised U.S. commanders that "Sunni and Shi'a alike seem generally receptive to the resettlement process," though Iraqi media reports made it clear that the return of internally displaced persons (IDPs) was popular and a welcome sign that the civil war was ending.[86]

Still, the return of IDPs was not entirely peaceful. Two Members of Parliament who attempted to organize the return of hundreds of mostly Sunni families to west Baghdad had their homes blown up. One of the Parliamentarians, Mithal al-Alusi, accused Baghdad Operations Commander General Abud Qanbar of blocking the return of Sunni families, since bombers destroyed Alusi's empty home, even though an Iraqi military checkpoint was just a few meters away.[87] Nevertheless, by summer's end such attacks were rare with an average of only four violent incidents per week across all of Baghdad Province.[88]

Petraeus Promoted, Odierno Returns

Petraeus oversaw these changes in Baghdad with the knowledge that his tenure as MNF-I commander was almost over. Spring 2008 saw an unexpected shuffle among senior U.S. commanders in the Middle East. In early March, Admiral William "Fox" Fallon suddenly resigned his post as U.S. Central Command (CENTCOM) commander after allowing scholar-journalist Thomas Barnett to quote him in unguarded moments and cast him as a lone figure opposing the White House's supposed drive toward war with Iran.[89]

With Fallon gone, CENTCOM Deputy Commander Lieutenant General Martin Dempsey filled the position temporarily. This led to an immediate change in the rapport between CENTCOM and MNF-I, which had been troubled during Fallon's tenure. The relationship changed further in April 2008 when President George W. Bush nominated Petraeus as CENTCOM's next permanent commander beginning in the fall. At the same time, Bush nominated Odierno, who had only left Baghdad in February and had been preparing to become Vice Chief of Staff of the Army, to succeed Petraeus as MNF-I commander. The two generals underwent a Senate confirmation hearing together in late May and were confirmed a few days later. The Department of Defense (DoD) scheduled the MNF-I change of command for mid-September.

As a result of the impending promotion to command of CENTCOM, Petraeus began to look beyond the Iraq theater. With Fallon out of the picture, Petraeus took on some of the regional military diplomacy that normally would fall to the CENTCOM commander. Both with and without Crocker, Petraeus made visits in spring and summer 2008 to Saudi

Arabia, Bahrain, Lebanon, and Jordan, meeting with heads of state and senior security officials in each country to press them to improve their relations with the Iraqi Government and to crack down on foreign fighters and terrorist financiers. However, circumstances forced him to increasingly turn his attention to the deteriorating situation in Afghanistan and Pakistan. Odierno, meanwhile, faced the prospect of returning for a third command tour in Iraq, but this time with a break of only 7 months. He was slated to become the first U.S. officer since General Lucian Truscott to command at division, corps, and army levels in the same theater of war.

Questioning the Coalition Force Presence

The change in security conditions shifted attitudes toward the U.S. military presence in the country among both Iraqis and some coalition leaders. Even before the spring campaign against the Shi'a militants had played out, some senior U.S. leaders had begun to indicate that security conditions in Iraq warranted shifting military resources to Afghanistan where security had deteriorated. In early April, the new chairman of the Joint Chiefs of Staff, Admiral Michael Mullen, said that troop commitments in Iraq prevented the United States from meeting force requirements in Afghanistan and elsewhere.[90] The following week, Bush announced that he would suspend the drawdown of U.S. troops in Iraq after the departure of the last of the surge brigades in July, but on the same day, he instructed the U.S. military to begin planning for "conditions-based reductions" in Iraq to free up forces for Afghanistan. At the same time, the Army announced an end to 15-month deployments for units going to Iraq: after August 1, Army units would serve 12-month rotations.[91]

As the signs of a U.S. withdrawal mounted, the continued U.S. presence in Iraq became a major political issue among the Iraqi parties competing in the country's provincial elections. The UN Security Council resolution that provided the legal justification for U.S. military involvement expired at the end of 2008, so Washington pursued a bilateral status of forces agreement (SOFA) that would allow a continued American presence. In mid-March, Ambassador Robert Loftis, a State Department expert on status of forces agreements, arrived in Baghdad with a team of technical experts to negotiate a new agreement. White House staffer Brett McGurk accompanied Loftis to negotiate a parallel strategic framework agreement (SFA) covering the broader U.S.-Iraqi relationship in economic and diplomatic matters.

By mid-May, the talks bogged down. The Maliki government was not keen on separating the SOFA from the broader SFA, preferring one comprehensive document that defined all future U.S.-Iraq relations. Petraeus also reported that Maliki hesitated to use "his political capital to urge the Council of Representatives to support the SFA" because he feared it might hurt his Da'wa Party and fracture his political coalition.[92] The Prime Minister's concern reflected changing public attitudes. The improved security situation in central and southern Iraq had increased the Iraqi public's confidence in their government security forces and led them to question the need for a continued coalition military presence. National polls of Iraqis in spring 2008 found that about two-thirds of Iraqis disapproved of the presence of coalition troops in the country, while a similar portion of Iraqis expressed confidence in the Iraqi Army and National Police. In keeping with these polled attitudes, 144 of the 275 members of the Iraqi Parliament signed a letter on May 11 calling for a timetable for the withdrawal of coalition forces.[93]

A few high-profile incidents by U.S. troops did not help the situation. On May 9, a U.S. Soldier in MND-B used a Koran for target practice at a firing range near the Baghdad Airport. Local Iraqis quickly learned of the event, forcing MND-B Commander Major General Jeffery Hammond to issue a formal apology and meet with local Iraqi leaders to soothe their anger.[94] Nevertheless, the incident made national news in Iraq and helped fuel anti-coalition sentiment. Three weeks later, a committee of the Iraqi Parliamentary parties called for the Iraqi Government to reject the draft statement of principles for the U.S.-Iraqi relationship, increasing the pressure on Maliki to drive a hard bargain in the SOFA negotiations.[95]

At the same time, Moqtada Sadr organized a series of protests in Baghdad, the first of which drew 10,000 participants just a week after the Iraqi Army occupied Sadr City. "Although the demonstrations were fairly small compared to those in the past, basically representing the size of Friday congregations, they indicate the need for Iraqi leaders to begin to make the case for these accords," Petraeus noted.[96] In public statements, the Sadrists and their Iranian allies began drawing parallels between the draft U.S.-Iraq SOFA and the 1964 U.S.-Iran SOFA, a military agreement between the U.S. Government and the Shah that the Ayatollah Ruhollah Khomeini had used to build opposition to the Shah's rule. Other Iraqis also drew parallels with the Portsmouth Treaty of 1948 between the Iraqi monarchy and Great Britain, a highly unpopular agreement that had led to a near-revolt in Baghdad. At the time, the significance of these previous agreements was lost on the U.S. officials negotiating the SOFA and SFA, but for Iraqis and Iranians they were full of historical meaning. MNF-I noted that Iraqi political factions were particularly sensitive to questions about whether U.S. forces would continue to have the authority to detain Iraqis, conduct unilateral operations, and maintain bases in the country. The question of legal immunity for contractors and third-country nationals employed by the United States was also a sensitive one on which many Iraqi politicians were not inclined to give the United States a great deal of leeway.[97]

The Iranian regime also exerted significant behind-the-scenes influence. Though the Iranians had suffered a setback with the operational defeat of their Iraqi militia proxies, they retained enough influence with the Iraqi political parties to obstruct the U.S.-Iraqi negotiations. On June 7, Maliki traveled to Tehran to meet with Ayatollah Ali Khamenei and Qassem Soleimani, ostensibly to confront the Iranian leaders with evidence of their destabilizing activities in Iraq, but in reality, the discussions revolved around Iranian opposition to the U.S.-Iraq SOFA. The Iranian leaders denied that any high-level Iranian authorities had been involved in arming the Iraqi Shi'a militias and told Maliki that the SOFA and SFA were "unacceptable" and constituted a "new occupation of Iraq."[98] "Given the Supreme Leader's strident language about the United States during the visit, we can expect the Iranians to continue their strategic communications campaign against U.S.-Iraq SF/SOFA negotiations inside Iraq and in the regional media," Petraeus reported after Maliki's trip.[99]

With political conditions making the SOFA negotiations difficult, Crocker proposed to Maliki on June 26 that the two governments should sign a temporary "bridging agreement" that would allow U.S. forces to operate in Iraq until they could reach a longer-term

SOFA.[100] Two days later, however, a single incident by U.S. special operators almost derailed the entire SOFA process. On June 28, the special operations task force conducted a raid in a small town near Karbala that targeted the wrong house in a search for a Shi'a militant. Unfortunately, the targeted house belonged to Prime Minister Maliki's sister, and in the course of the raid, the special operators killed one of her bodyguards, a young man who was one of Maliki's relatives.[101]

The raid infuriated Prime Minister Maliki, who, like many Iraqi leaders, found it impossible to believe that the coalition had raided his family and killed one of his relatives by mistake. In addition, the raid had taken place in one of the nine provinces supposedly under full Iraqi control, but local Iraqi security officials asserted the coalition had conducted the operation without their knowledge. The incident was a clear setback for the United States, coming at the worst possible time in the stormy negotiations over unilateral U.S. military operations and immunity from Iraqi law for U.S. Government personnel and contractors.[102]

Allegations in the same week that the United States was using Iraq as a base to conduct operations inside Iran compounded the problem. In late June, *The New Yorker* magazine published an article by journalist Seymour Hersh that claimed U.S. SOF had been sending operatives into Iran to prepare the way for an American war against the Iranian regime. The story raised Iraqi ire and lent credence to the Iranian regime's claims that the United States wanted to retain bases in Iraq for the precise purpose that Hersh claimed. Partly to contain the damage from the Hersh story and from the raid in Karbala, Petraeus took Prime Minister Maliki and Iraqi National Security Adviser Mowaffaq Rubaie to visit the special operations headquarters in Iraq, the first time senior Iraqi officials were briefed there.[103] Maliki's past opposition toward special operations raids against Shi'a militant targets and the recent killing of his relative at the hands of U.S. commandos added tension to the visit. The trip was intended to provide the Iraqi leaders the most up-to-date operational picture as well as to make the special operations activities more transparent. At the headquarters, Maliki and Rubaie visited an operations center, inspected the elite commandos' high-tech equipment, and received assurances that U.S. special operators were neither slackening their efforts against AQI nor using Iraq as a platform to make raids into Iran. The special operations commanders "gave a terrific presentation that clearly impressed and moved the PM [Prime Minister]," Petraeus reported afterward, adding that Maliki "addressed our troops in the most complimentary terms and stressed again the importance of the U.S. to the fate of a free Iraq."[104] For his part, Petraeus hoped that the visit had watered down some of Maliki's opposition to a SOFA.[105]

Senator Barack Obama in Baghdad

The day after Maliki's visit to Balad, another factor injected itself into the U.S.-Iraq SOFA negotiations. In the ongoing U.S. Presidential election campaign, Democratic candidate Barack Obama called for the United States to set a fixed timetable for withdrawal from Iraq. On July 4, Obama expanded on his plans, indicating that, if elected, he would withdraw all U.S. troops from Iraq within 16 months. Just days later, on July 19, Prime Minister Maliki told German journalists that he too believed American forces could safely be withdrawn from Iraq over a 16-month period, apparently endorsing Obama's campaign platform with a statement that Petraeus described as "a politically incautious remark." The Iraqi Prime Minister mentioned the same 16-month withdrawal timetable in a videoconference with Bush, in which Maliki also said he saw no need for any non-American coalition forces beyond 2009.[106]

On July 21, 2 days after Maliki's public remarks, Senator Obama met with Petraeus and Crocker in Baghdad as part of a visiting congressional delegation that also included future SECDEF Charles Hagel and Senator Jack Reed of Rhode Island. In the course of a long briefing on the situation in Iraq, Obama laid out several arguments for withdrawing U.S. troops.

(Seated left to right) Senator Charles Hagel, General David Petraeus, Senator Barack Obama, Ambassador Ryan Crocker, and Senator Jack Reed. Source: DoD photo by Staff Sergeant Lorie Jewell (Released).

Tense Discussions on Iraq War Strategy During a Congressional Delegation Visit on July 21, 2008.[107]

The meeting was collegial, but tense. Petraeus and Crocker argued that sectarian violence had slowed, but political progress had not yet matched the security gains. It was thus premature to assume Iraq could remain stable without U.S. troops. Much of the discussion between Obama and Petraeus dealt with shifting responsibility to Iraqi security forces, with Obama arguing that the United States needed to force the Iraqi Government to assume the lead in providing security, an idea Obama's advisers labeled "conditional engagement." Petraeus, however, noted that that approach had failed in 2006 and warned against handing the ISF more than they could handle. Obama also argued that the Iraq campaign was a distraction from the fight against Osama bin Laden and al-Qaeda in Afghanistan and Pakistan. Petraeus replied that al-Qaeda itself had declared Iraq the central front in its war against the West. The general also noted that calls to shift troops from Iraq to use them against bin Laden would require the United States to invade Pakistan—bin Laden's likely location. Obama and Hagel argued that Petraeus's recommendations to maintain a large U.S. force in Iraq were infeasible, given the strain the Iraq War was placing on the U.S. Government, especially with an expanding financial crisis. Petraeus replied that he understood that, in setting Iraq policy, U.S. leaders had to consider the larger strategic picture, but as the MNF-I commander his duty was to give his best military advice on accomplishing the mission in his theater of operations. He indicated that it was up to his political superiors to accept his recommendations or change his mission. The visiting senators seemed to be pressing Petraeus to preclude that process by tailoring his military advice to a policy, Petraeus said.

After the contentious meeting, Petraeus and Obama met one-on-one, with the senator inquiring if there was anything additional that the general wanted to offer privately. Petraeus responded by asking Obama to maintain his flexibility on Iraq and suggested that withdrawal within 16 months of taking office would too rapid and might jeopardize the progress made during the surge. It would be a suggestion that eventually bore fruit, as the 16-month timetable stretched to almost 3 years, with the last U.S. forces withdrawing December 2011.[108] Other voices in Iraq amplified the arguments Petraeus and Crocker had made. Later in their visit, for example, the senators met Sunni Awakening leaders who warned that a hasty U.S. military withdrawal from Iraq would likely lead to a return to violence.[109] After the July 21 discussions, it seemed clear that if Senator Obama became President, then an expedited U.S. withdrawal from Iraq was likely.

MALIKI'S WARNING SIGNS: DIYALA, THE ISOF, AND THE SOFA

Diyala: Operation GLAD TIDINGS OF BENEVOLENCE, July–August 2008

As coalition leaders focused on completing the campaign against AQI in Mosul and institutionalizing the long-term U.S.-Iraq military relationship, the Prime Minister's attention was on a different agenda. In the wake of his victory over his Sadrist rivals in Operation CHARGE OF THE KNIGHTS, Maliki increasingly structured Iraqi security operations toward his personal objectives. U.S. troops had conducted three large-scale operations in Diyala since summer 2007; the most recent in January 2008 found little evidence of a large AQI presence in the province's populated areas. However, Maliki's priorities differed from those of the coalition, and the Prime Minister decided in late July to conduct another large operation in Diyala. This one, which the Prime Minister named Operation BASHIR AL-KHAIR (GLAD TIDINGS OF BENEVOLENCE), was ISF-led.

To oversee the Iraqi part of the operation, Maliki ordered Iraqi Ground Forces Commander Lieutenant General Ali Ghaidan to take charge of the newly created Diyala Operations Command, another regional command like those the Iraqis had in Baghdad, Basrah, and Ninawa.[110] Ghaidan brought most of the 1st Iraqi Division and a brigade of the 9th Iraqi Mechanized Division to reinforce the 5th Iraqi Division already stationed in Diyala. For Hertling and MND-N, the lead U.S. units in the operation would be Colonel John RisCassi's 2d Stryker Cavalry Regiment, which deployed to Diyala in July to replace Colonel Jon Lehr's 4th Brigade, 2d Infantry Division, and Colonel Patrick White's 2d Brigade, 1st Armored Division. RisCassi's troops would focus on Baqubah and on the seam between Diyala and Salahadin Provinces, while White would focus on the rural areas near Balad Ruz.

Petraeus reported to U.S. leaders that Maliki indicated that he intended to begin a Diyala operation in July.[111] Maliki's decision to shift the focus of the ISF from Mosul to Diyala surprised Hertling and other MND-N leaders. They believed their forces in Diyala had almost completed the necessary clearing operations in the province and were ready to enter the hold and build phase.[112] For his part, Petraeus was pleased to see the Iraqis taking the initiative, reporting to Gates that ISF planning and preparation "demonstrates that they have learned a great deal since the start of the Basrah operation in March."[113]

This optimism did not last long as Operation GLAD TIDINGS OF BENEVOLENCE quickly derailed. Petraeus cautioned that in Diyala the ISF would operate along sensitive ethnic and sectarian fault lines. "Unlike the situation in predominantly Shi'a Amarah and Basrah, this offensive [would] have to deal with a mixed population of Shi'a Arabs, Sunni Arabs and Kurds, plus the presence of peshmerga forces from the KRG [Kurdistan Regional Government]," he observed on July 20.[114] As 50,000 Iraqi and U.S. troops began new clearing operations during the last week of July, Iraqi commanders seemed more interested in establishing an ISF presence in the province's mixed-sect and mixed-ethnicity areas than in pursuing AQI. The Iraqi Army and police activities in the province seemed particularly focused on slowing Diyala's Sunni Awakening groups, which had grown rapidly since fall 2007. Sunni distrust grew quickly as ISF began setting up checkpoints to control the movement of Diyala's population.[115] In the first 2 weeks of the operation, the ISF arrested more than 1,100 Sunnis, many of whom were members of the Sons of Iraq. The arrests created the impression that Maliki was employing the ISF to combat the perceived political threat of the Awakening, which looked poised to dominate the upcoming provincial elections, rather than the security threat of AQI.[116] In response, on August 11, the Sunni-led Diyala provincial council voted to sack Major General Ghanem al-Qureishi, the Diyala provincial police chief who had pressured the Sons of Iraq for months. This led to a confrontation with Maliki, who had consistently backed Qureishi.

The following day, tensions worsened when Iraqi Army troops and Kurdish peshmerga came close to an armed clash in the upper Diyala Valley. The Iraqi Army units pushing north in Diyala arrived on the outskirts of Khanaqin, a Kurdish-majority town guarded by the 34th Peshmerga Brigade since 2003, and ordered the peshmerga to depart within 24 hours. This confrontation quickly escalated to a national political crisis as the peshmerga troops refused to leave. Khanaqin was on the de facto dividing line between territory controlled by the Iraqi Government in Baghdad and the Kurdistan Regional Government (KRG) in Erbil, and the demand for the peshmerga to withdraw equated to a demand by Baghdad for the KRG to cede territory that Kurdish leaders considered part of Kurdistan.

Source: DoD photo by Petty Officer 2d Class Paul Seeber (Released).

Diyala Provincial Police Chief Major General Ghanem al-Qureishi Converses With a Colleague.[117]

The Khanaqin confrontation came 2 months after the Iraqi and Kurdistan Governments had rejected a recommendation by UN Envoy Staffan DeMistura to designate several of the disputed territories along the Green Line—including upper Diyala—under the control of one government or the other.[118] The tense tactical standoff surprised the Kurdish political leaders, who began to question the reliability of their political alliance with the major Shi'a parties in Baghdad, an agreement that had dominated Iraqi politics since 2003.[119] The standoff also shocked coalition leaders, because it represented an unexpected Shi'a-Kurdish dispute rather than the Sunni-Shi'a sectarian conflict that had dominated the 2005–2007 period. To avoid the outbreak of a Shi'a-Kurdish war that would serve no one's interest but AQI's, Hertling and MNF-I J–3 Major General Michael Barbero began intense shuttle diplomacy between ISF and peshmerga commanders, making clear to each side that the other was prepared to fight. Meanwhile in Baghdad and Erbil, senior U.S. generals and diplomats encouraged Prime Minister Maliki and KRG leaders to reach a political solution. Nevertheless, as U.S. commanders in Diyala discovered, the Shi'a Arab ISF commanders along the Green Line were just as eager for a fight against the Kurds as the Sunni Arabs had been.

The ISOF Diyala Raid

With the standoff in Khanaqin still unresolved, Sunni-Shi'a sectarian tensions boiled over when Prime Minister Maliki employed Iraqi troops against the Diyala provincial government that had sacked police chief General Qureishi. One week after Qureishi's firing, the Prime Minister's office—through counterterrorism service chief, General Talib Kenani—ordered the ISOF to arrest Hussein al-Zubaidi, Diyala's Sunni governor. The ISOF raid, which the CJSOTF refused to support because of the lack of evidence linking any of the targets to insurgent activity, turned into a fiasco. On the night of August 18, ISOF elements raided the governor's office in Baqubah, arresting two prominent local Sunni politicians, killing the governor's secretary, and wounding four Iraqis in a clear attempt at political intimidation.[120] As the Iraqi commandos left, they became involved in a firefight with local police and fired on American forces assisting the police. It took the personal intervention of General Ali Ghaidan to untangle the mess. The incident infuriated Petraeus, who "condemned the operation in the strongest terms" and "emphasized to the [Iraqi Government] that Coalition support for the ISF is dependent upon their adherence to the rule of law." "PM [Prime Minister] Maliki has ordered an investigation, but this incident is lamentable (especially as the PM ordered it)," Petraeus wrote to Gates a few days after the raid.[121]

These politicized ISF activities and the battle for political control in the province overshadowed the fact that in remote parts of Diyala, U.S. units were still working to track down AQI's top leaders and prevent the group from retaining sanctuaries. White's troops focused on Balad Ruz, where coalition commanders believed AQI leader Abu Ayyub al-Masri might be.[122] Making contact with the enemy proved difficult, especially in the area that U.S. troops called the "Turki Bowl" south of Balad Ruz. In the first 2 weeks of operations in the Turki Bowl, White's brigade experienced no direct firefights, but lost more than 30 vehicles to IEDs. It was unclear whether the IEDs were part of an active enemy defense or merely part of an abandoned defensive belt network. Either way, in the dry, reed-choked irrigation canals that crisscrossed the area, White's troops found hundreds of ammunition caches before withdrawing in late August.[123] Meanwhile, in the Baqubah area, RisCassi's cavalry troopers found the security situation much-improved from the previous fall, but they still encountered occasional booby-trapped houses and a new type of threat—female suicide bombers. By the late summer of 2008, female bombers wearing suicide vests had become a persistent danger in Baqubah and Muqdadiyah, where they often passed through security checkpoints without being fully searched by male Iraqi troops used to avoiding public contact with women.[124]

Despite these activities, the ISOF raid in Baqubah and the ISF-peshmerga tensions in Khanaqin cast a pall over Operation GLAD TIDINGS OF BENEVOLENCE and diminished its tactical gains. The politically motivated clearing and checkpoint operations stoked ethno-sectarian tensions in the province but did little damage to AQI's residual capability. The operation "really spiked the sectarian violence in Diyala," Hertling later conceded, adding that the operation "almost had a complete falling apart of what we had established over 9 months." Rather than being a culminating victory against Sunni terrorists in Diyala, the operation had become, in Hertling's estimation, "one of the biggest downers of our time over there."[125]

The ISOF Under Maliki: The "Dirty Brigade"

The disturbing ISOF raid in Baqubah was the culmination of a year-and-a-half-long effort by Prime Minister Maliki to take full control of the ISOF, Iraq's premier counter-terrorism force, and use it against his rivals. From 2008 onward, Iraqis increasingly saw the ISOF as Maliki's political tool. That commando force, hailed as heroes for its role in the 2004 battles in Najaf and Fallujah, became known in popular parlance as the "dirty brigade" or, in a throwback to the days of Saddam Hussein, the "Fedayeen Maliki."

Source: DoD photo by Petty Officer 1st Class Daniel Mennuto (Released).

ISOF Commandos Conduct Night Missions Near Amarah With a CJSOTF Adviser.[126]

This was a significant shift from early 2007 when the ISOF brigade was considered the crown jewel of the ISF. Originally created in late 2003 as the 36th Commando Battalion and continuously mentored and advised by the CJSOTF, the unit had grown in size and capability to the point that it could conduct short-notice heliborne assaults and integrate information received by its human intelligence networks into operations. The ISOF were under the operational control of the coalition, but having seen the organization's performance against AQI and Sadrist militias, Maliki had long sought more authority over the unit. Unable to convince coalition leaders to permit substantive changes to the ISOF's command control arrangement, Maliki opted for a fait accompli in January 2007 by issuing an executive order removing the brigade and its parent headquarters, the Iraqi

Counterterrorism Command, from the Ministry of Defense and placing it under his own Office of the Commander in Chief.[127]

The CJSOTF, which had considerable influence over the brigade because of its authority to approve leadership changes and its control over the unit's pay and finances, resisted Maliki's politicization of the ISOF.[128] CJSOTF leaders argued to MNF-I that if the ISOF brigade was beholden solely to the Prime Minister, it would become his Praetorian Guard, and political or sectarian targeting would undoubtedly follow. Removing the brigade from the Ministry of Defense also would upend the basic institutional services needed to keep the ISOF brigade functioning, such as recruiting, pay, logistics, medical care, and intelligence.[129]

With the Counterterrorism Command an unstaffed shell incapable of operating as a higher headquarters and MNF-I siding with the CJSOTF, Maliki's executive order initially had little impact. However, the coalition's unified opposition to Maliki's moves changed in the summer of 2007 when Navy SEAL Rear Admiral Edward G. Winters III took command of the Iraqi National Counterterrorism Force Transition Team, a special operations organization created to help the ISOF brigade shift to full Iraqi control. Winters was convinced that the unit could not reach its full potential under the Ministry of Defense where bureaucratic infighting made funding, logistics, and maintenance a perennial headache.[130] Winters also believed sectarian officers in the Ministry of Defense subverted the ISOF brigade mission against insurgents and militias.[131] Over CJSOTF's objections, Winters and other senior special operations leaders in Iraq recommended that the Iraqis create an organization similar to United States Special Operations Command (SOCOM)—an independent entity to control the country's special operations budget and act as its own armed service, representing ISOF interests at the ministerial level. In Winters's view, the proposed SOCOM-like counterterrorism organization should report directly to the chief executive, thereby removing layers of bureaucracy that slowed responses to national-level terrorist incidents.[132] Because this idea mirrored Maliki's executive order and a transition to Iraqi control would have to happen at some point, Winters asked Petraeus to endorse Maliki's proposal. Petraeus was initially noncommittal in part due to the CJSOTF's opposition to the plan, but after Winters enlisted the support of a senior special operations commander in summer 2007, Petraeus relented and endorsed the proposal.[133]

The decision slowly changed the nature of the ISOF as Maliki loyalists moved into key leadership positions and the Counterterrorism Command grew from a shell to a functioning headquarters. Lieutenant General Taleb Dhia Kanani and Lieutenant General Abdul Ghani al-Asadi, two officers with a history of service in Saddam's Army but no special operations experience, received top positions in the Counterterrorism Command and Service, prompting concern among CJSOTF officers and senior ISOF leaders. Kanani, a Maliki loyalist, previously had angered ISOF members when he investigated unfounded allegations that the Iraqi commandos had executed civilians during a March 2006 raid of a JAM compound in Adhamiyah. Many ISOF commandos "were convinced that Kenani was the devil incarnate," recalled a CJSOTF commander.[134] Iraqi leaders also resisted the move. "[Maliki] just put two Iranians in charge of the ISOF brigade," Colonel Fadhil Jamil al Barwari, the brigade's Kurdish commander, told a CJSOTF adviser upon hearing of the appointments.[135] Under Kanani's oversight, Shi'a officers with ties to

Maliki but little or no special operations experience began to replace experienced ISOF officers. CJSOTF advisers noticed alarming trends, "witnessing punitive reassignments of officers [and] ethnically oriented organizational changes," and concluded that Maliki was cementing personal control of the brigade with these actions.[136] These changes, combined with other officer reassignments, amounted to placing "Shi'a sectarian commissars meant to watch over and make sure the ISOF does only the bidding of the Shi'a government," according to one CJSOTF commander.[137] When Winters confronted Kenani about the personnel changes, the Iraqi general claimed the increase in Shi'a ISOF officers was the result of Kurds and Sunnis not wanting to leave their homes and move to the ISOF headquarters in Baghdad.[138]

As the leadership of the brigade changed, the CJSOTF struggled to keep the unit nonsectarian, insisting on maintaining ethnic quotas among the ISOF's enlisted recruits to preserve the brigade's original balanced composition of 61 percent Shi'a, 24 percent Sunni, and 12 percent Kurdish.[139] Recruits submitted to polygraphs and counterintelligence interviews to confirm they were not members of militias. Strict entry requirements also helped maintain the brigade's makeup, with only 42 percent of applicants passing the unit's selection course during 2008.[140] On several occasions, these entry requirements blocked large groups of Shi'a soldiers that arrived without warning, alleging their assignment to the brigade as replacements.[141]

Nevertheless, the purge of the brigade's leadership and infiltration of its commanding headquarters had a sectarian impact. By early 2008, CJSOTF advisers noticed a higher failure rate when the brigade struck politically sensitive Shi'a targets and concluded that the new leadership was tipping off the targets or steering the raids toward token, low-level Shi'a militants.[142] Testing their theory, CJSOTF advisers helped loyal ISOF soldiers submit lengthy, "near perfect" target packages against Shi'a targets, but they were rejected without explanation every time, while similar packages for Sunni targets received easy approval.[143] At the same time, CJSOTF leaders concluded that Iraqi leaders had begun to give the ISOF sectarian missions or to dispatch them against Maliki's political opponents. When such missions occurred, the CJSOTF advisers refused to accompany the ISOF commandos and notified MNC-I, who in turn worked with MNF-I to lodge formal protests.[144] On some occasions, the ISOF brigade conducted operations at the behest of Prime Minister Maliki and only informed the CJSOTF after the missions were concluded.

The August 2008 ISOF raid against the Diyala governor's office was a turning point for CJSOTF leaders, who began to question their continued collaboration with the organization they had created. Concluding that the sectarian influence ran too deep to repair, CJSOTF advisers began to distance themselves from any ISOF operations that resembled sectarian intimidation and instead began to work more closely with the Ministry of the Interior's Emergency Response Units, six elite special weapons and tactics battalions patterned after the FBI's hostage rescue teams and national counterterrorism teams.[145] The CJSOTF's separation from the ISOF was jarring to the many U.S. and Iraqi special operators who had worked closely in combat for almost 5 years. Many of the rank-and-file ISOF members recognized the sectarian change to their unit, but were powerless to stop it. "You taught us about being Iraqis . . . You taught us that our ethnicity is not part of it, [that it should be] Iraq first," one saddened ISOF leader told a CJSOTF commander. "You taught us better than this."[146]

Maliki and the SOFA

During the summer of 2008, U.S. leaders began to realize that the biggest impediment to a status of forces agreement was Maliki himself. U.S. leaders had believed that what held the Prime Minister from reaching a long-term military relationship with the United States was opposition from Shi'a militant factions and the Iranian regime, so if those two groups were neutralized, Maliki could sign a binding agreement. The American leaders initially believed that the military victory over Iran's proxies in spring 2008 had removed the SOFA's biggest impediment, but they soon realized they were wrong. From his espousal of Senator Obama's 16-month withdrawal timeline to his misuse of the ISF in Diyala, Maliki demonstrated that he viewed the continued U.S. military presence as an obstacle to his personal objectives. He was also reluctant to be, as Petraeus put it, "the first Iraqi leader to legitimize a foreign military presence in Iraq."[147]

Nevertheless, Bush and other senior U.S. leaders pressed the Iraqi leader to finalize the U.S.-Iraqi agreement in August. Realizing the U.S. approach needed a reboot, Bush instructed White House official Brett McGurk, Ambassador David Satterfield, and Pentagon official Mark Kimmitt to take over the SOFA negotiations from Ambassador Loftis and his team. To give his new negotiators greater leeway, Bush authorized them to offer the Maliki government a specific timeline for U.S. troop withdrawal, something the President previously refused to consider. As the new talks got underway, Maliki and his advisers pressed the American team for a general withdrawal of U.S. combat forces by December 31, 2010, but conceded a need for a residual force beyond that date to train the Iraqi security forces.[148]

On August 4, the two sides agreed that the final U.S.-Iraq security accord would specify a departure date between 2010 and 2011, an understanding that led the U.S. negotiators to assume Maliki had accepted the terms of the SOFA. However, they were wrong.[149] As days passed, it became clear that Maliki had not agreed with his own negotiators and had developed "cold feet" about the agreement, perhaps out of concern that Ayatollah Ali Husayni Sistani would oppose it, as Petraeus reported on August 10.[150]

On August 21, the negotiators finally agreed that U.S. combat troops would leave Iraq by the end of 2011, a concession that U.S. officials hoped would finally secure Maliki's backing for the SOFA.[151] Even with the specified departure date, however, the negotiators on both sides understood that the agreement could be extended or rolled over later, meaning that a full U.S. military departure would not be set in stone. To close the deal, U.S. officials arranged a videoconference between Bush and Prime Minister Maliki on August 22, in which the American President made a personal entreaty to Maliki to sign the SOFA and settle the two countries' military relationship. To the dismay of Petraeus and senior U.S. leaders, the Iraqi Prime Minister appeared nervous and noncommittal, declining Bush's entreaty and claiming the matter needed more study and consideration.

The inconclusive meeting left U.S. leaders to question whether the events of 2008, in which Maliki had effectively overpowered his strongest political rivals, left the Prime Minister less inclined to strike an agreement with the United States rather than more. Commenting on the episode to Gates, Petraeus wrote that, in front of the President, Maliki had "delayed and dissembled, generally demonstrating considerable vacillation and lack of confidence."[152] Recounting the details of the videoconference to his senior general officers the following morning, a frustrated Petraeus concluded that Maliki had failed an important test of statesmanship. "There was just no leadership in that room," Petraeus said.[153]

In retrospect, what appeared to Petraeus and others as Maliki's lack of confidence may simply have been the Prime Minister's effort to stave off an agreement he saw as unnecessary. Maliki's opposition to the SOFA may have reflected his growing confidence, because of his successes in Basrah, Sadr City, Amarah, and his takeover of the ISOF brigade. In the days following the inconclusive videoconference, Maliki surprised his U.S. counterparts again by dismissing the Iraqi negotiating team led by a senior foreign ministry official and replacing it with the same group of Da'wa Party advisers who had negotiated the UNSCR rollover in late 2007. Led by Mowaffaq Rubaie, the new negotiating team emphasized that any U.S.-Iraqi agreement would have to stipulate that apart from advisory teams and PRTs, U.S. troops would withdraw from all Iraqi cities by June 30, 2009. To senior U.S. leaders, this withdrawal would happen over time anyway and thus be accepted with little cost.[154] Nevertheless, the unresolved negotiations meant that Petraeus would be leave command in Iraq without a settled legal justification for his forces to remain beyond the end of the year.

***

Summer 2008 found the situation in Iraq much changed in the space of a year. Violence in Baghdad almost had ceased, the Shi'a militants had been routed, and AQI had been forced into the far north of the country. As large numbers of U.S. troops redeployed outside Iraq, the coalition's morale was high. An impressive display of U.S. military commitment came at Camp Victory on July 4 when Petraeus presided over a reenlistment ceremony for 1,215 U.S. service members in the ornate rotunda of Faw Palace, an event that MNF-I considered the largest mass reenlistment ever held.[155] A week later, when Petraeus and Crocker presided over their last Campaign Assessment and Synchronization Board together, the coalition leaders concluded that the coalition already had achieved the near-term security objectives of the 2007 joint campaign plan. In their estimation, the time had come to shift "from directly protecting the population to jointly achieving a level of security that can be maintained by Iraqi security and civil institutions with reduced Coalition involvement."[156]

Petraeus himself spent his last weeks in Iraq shifting focus from Iraq to Afghanistan and other pressing problems he would soon be responsible for as CENTCOM commander. In early August, while U.S. and Iraqi troops conducted Operation GLAD TIDINGS OF BENEVOLENCE in Diyala, the MNF-I commander traveled to Afghanistan to assess what he anticipated would be a challenge rivaling that of Iraq and a major issue during the next Presidential administration.[157] On August 17, Petraeus reported to Gates that the situation in Afghanistan was deteriorating and would require "'thickening the force,' both by generating more Afghan forces and by creating 'Awakening' style security arrangements wherever possible—in addition to increasing the Coalition forces there."[158] Petraeus's solution for Afghanistan would thus be to take pages from the Iraq playbook that had worked for him.

In operational terms, the surge had indeed achieved most of its objectives by summer 2008. The populations of central, southern, and western Iraq in particular were returning to a normal way of life. But the events of the summer showed that political objectives would be more difficult. As the pressure of violence decreased, Iraqis had begun to assert their sovereignty both in seeking to take over the leadership role in security operations and in driving a hard bargain for a long-term U.S.-Iraqi security agreement. The uncertainty of the U.S. Presidential election campaign affected the situation as well, given Obama's well-publicized plans to withdraw from Iraq.

The continuing ethno-sectarian conflict in Diyala disappointed U.S. commanders in the north who had hoped to deal AQI a knockout blow and stabilize the restive province. Prime Minister Maliki's refusal to sign a U.S.-Iraq SOFA struck a major blow to senior U.S. leaders in Baghdad and Washington, casting doubt on whether the strategic gains of the Iraq War could be consolidated. The problematic role of the Iraqi security forces in ethno-sectarian political disputes and the emerging tendency of Prime Minister Maliki to consolidate power were ominous signs of future instability. The Prime Minister's actions made it unclear whether the coalition could accomplish its goals of good governance and national reconciliation—goals that coalition leaders believed necessary to ensure Iraq's long-term stability. Finally, the campaign in Mosul remained unfinished. Though U.S. and Iraqi troops had pursued AQI to remote corners of the country, the extremists still could conduct limited but complex attacks in the north. As Petraeus prepared to leave Baghdad, all of this unfinished business would fall to his successor, General Odierno.

ENDNOTES - CHAPTER 9

1. Interview, Contemporary Operations Study Team with Lieutenant General Lloyd Austin, Combat Studies Institute (CSI), Fort Leavenworth, KS, May 2010, p. 6. All unpublished documents in this chapter, unless otherwise stated, are in the Chief of Staff of the Army (CSA) Operation IRAQI FREEDOM (OIF) Study Group archives, Army Heritage and Education Center (AHEC), Carlisle, PA.

2. Michael O'Hanlon and Ian Livingston, "Iraq Index," Washington, DC: Brookings Institution, January 2011, available from *https://www.brookings.edu/wp-content/uploads/2016/07/index20120131.pdf.*

3. Manuscript (Ms), *On Point*, Vol. IV, Chapter 7, Fort Leavenworth, KS: Combat Studies Institute, September 25, 2014.

4. "Australians End Combat Role in Iraq," CBS News, June 1, 2008, available from *http://www.cbsnews.com/news/australians-end-combat-role-in-iraq/.*

5. Multi-National Force-Iraq (MNF-I), Secretary of Defense (SECDEF) Weekly Update, August 11-17, 2008.

6. "Poles' Departure to be Marked," *Stars and Stripes*, October 2, 2008, available from *http://www.stripes.com/news/poles-departure-to-be-marked-1.83710.*

7. Stephen A. Carney, *Allied Participation in Operation IRAQI FREEDOM*, Washington, DC: U.S. Army Center of Military History, 2011, Charts 32, 33.

8. Ms, *On Point*, Vol. IV, Chapter 7, p. 16.

9. MNF-I, SECDEF Weekly Update, August 18-24, 2008.

10. Ms, *On Point*, Vol. IV, Chapter 7, pp. 22, 25.

11. Interview, CSI Contemporary Operations Study Team with Colonel Jeffrey Bailey, Fort Leavenworth, KS, August 16, 2010, p. 5.

12. Ms, *On Point*, Vol. IV, Chapter 7, pp. 29-30.

13. Ibid., p. 25.

14. Ibid., p. 24.

15. DoD photo by Staff Sergeant Margaret Nelson, "Southern Kirkuk Civil Service Corps established to train and employ its citizens [Image 1 of 6]," DVIDS Identifier 108298, August 11, 2008, Released to Public, available from *https://www.dvidshub.net/image/108298/southern-kirkuk-civil-service-corps-established-train-and-employ-its-citizens*.

16. Interview, CSI Contemporary Operations Study Team with Bailey, August 16, 2010, p. 6.

17. Ms, *On Point*, Vol. IV, Chapter 7, p. 28; Interview, Colonel Frank Sobchak, CSA OIF Study Group, with Colonel Kevin Leahy, Combined Joint Special Operations Task Force (CJSOTF), J-3 Deputy, November 7, 2014.

18. Interview, CSA OIF Study Group with Leahy, November 7, 2014.

19. Interview, Colonel Frank Sobchak, CSA OIF Study Group, with Brigadier General (S) Scott E. Brower, Special Operations Task Force Commander (Cdr), June 2, 2014.

20. Interview, Colonel Frank Sobchak with Colonel Chris Connor, CJSOTF Cdr, December 10, 2015.

21. Ms, *On Point*, Vol. IV, Chapter 7, p. 26.

22. Ibid., p. 28.

23. XVIII Airborne Corps, MNC-I Chronology, 2008-2009, May 1, 2008, entry.

24. Interview, CSI Contemporary Operations Study Team with Lieutenant Colonel Jeffrey LaFace, Fort Leavenworth, KS, July 2010, p. 10; MNF-I, SECDEF Weekly Update, May 5-11, 2008.

25. MNF-I, SECDEF Weekly Update, May 12-18, 2008.

26. Ms, *On Point*, Vol. IV, Chapter 7, p. 34; Interview, CSI Contemporary Operations Study Team with LaFace, July 2010, p. 10.

27. Bill Roggio, "Operation Lion's Roar nets more than 1,000 suspects," *Long War Journal*, May 16, 2008, available from *http://www.longwarjournal.org/archives/2008/05/operation_lions_roar.php*.

28. MNF-I, SECDEF Weekly Update, May 12-18, 2008.

29. MNF-I, SECDEF Weekly Update, May 26-June 1, 2008.

30. Ibid.

31. MNF-I, SECDEF Weekly Update, May 19-25, 2008.

32. MNF-I, SECDEF Weekly Update, May 26-June 1, 2008.

33. MNF-I, SECDEF Weekly Update, May 19-25, 2008.

34. XVIII Airborne Corps, MNC-I Chronology, 2008-2009, entries for June 6, 2008 and June 27, 2008.

35. MNF-I, SECDEF Weekly Update, July 7-13, 2008.

36. MNF-I, SECDEF Weekly Update, July 14-20, 2008.

37. MNF-I, SECDEF Weekly Update, July 7-13, 2008.

38. Interview, CSI Contemporary Operations Study Team with Lieutenant General Mark Hertling, Fort Leavenworth, KS, February 2010, p. 4.

39. MNF-I, SECDEF Weekly Update, June 2-8, 2008.

40. Ms, *On Point*, Vol. IV, Chapter 7, p. 32.

41. Ibid., p. 37.

42. Ibid., p. 44.

43. Ibid., p. 43.

44. MNF-I, SECDEF Weekly Update, August 18-24, 2008.

45. XVIII Airborne Corps, MNC-I Chronology, 2008-2009, May 24, 2008, entry.

46. MNF-I, SECDEF Weekly Update, June 2-8, 2008.

47. MNF-I, SECDEF Weekly Update, May 19-25, 2008.

48. MNF-I, SECDEF Weekly Update, June 2-8, 2008.

49. MNF-I, SECDEF Weekly Update, June 16-22, 2008.

50. "Shiite Cleric Al-Sadr Suspends Mahdi Militia Operations-MP," *Aswat al-Iraq*, August 28, 2008, available from *http://www.thefreelibrary.com/Shiite+cleric+Al-Sadr+suspends+Mahdi+militia+operations+-MP.-a0184155667*, accessed May 18, 2016.

51. Ned Parker, "In Iraq, Muqtada Sadr's Followers Struggle for Relevance," *Los Angeles Times*, November 10, 2008; Sudarsan Raghavan, "Sadr Movement Seeks Its Way As Others Gain Power in Iraq," *The Washington Post*, December 5, 2008, p. A1; Asharq Al-Aswat, "Inside Al-Sadr's Al-Mumahhidun Project," *Asharq al-Awsat*, January 2, 2009, available from *https://eng-archive.aawsat.com/theaawsat/features/inside-al-sadrs-al-mumahhidun-project*.

52. MNF-I, SECDEF Weekly Update, June 9-15, 2008.

53. Joel Rayburn, *Iraq After America: Strongmen, Sectarians, Resistance*, Stanford, CA: Hoover Institution Press, 2014, p. 194.

54. Hamza Hendawi, "Warrior with AK-47 Becomes Cleric with Pseudonym," Associated Press, August 12, 2008.

55. MNF-I, SECDEF Weekly Update, August 15-31, 2008.

56. Ibid.

57. Ibid.

58. XVIII Airborne Corps, MNC-I Chronology, 2008-2009, September 3, 2008, entry.

59. Ibid., September 5, 2008, entry.

60. "Shiite Militia Reemerges in Baghdad After Weeks of Quiet," Fox News, June 25, 2008, available from *http://www.foxnews.com/story/2008/06/25/shiite-militia-reemerges-in-baghdad-after-weeks-quiet.html.*

61. Interview, CSI Contemporary Operations Study Team with Lieutenant Colonel Edward Bohnemann, 2d Squadron, 7th Cavalry, Cdr, Fort Leavenworth, KS, July 21, 2010.

62. UK House of Commons Defence Committee, UK Land Operations in Iraq 2007, Report (Rpt) No. 1, London, UK: House of Commons, December 3, 2007.

63. MNF-I, SECDEF Weekly Update, June 2-8, 2008.

64. Duane L. Mosier, "The Road to Al Amarah: Operation Yarborough and U.S. Army Special Forces Soldiers in Southern Iraq (January-June 2008)," *Small Wars Journal,* November 4, 2010; Interviews, CSA OIF Study Group with Leahy, November 7, 2014; with Conner, December 10, 2015.

65. U.S. Navy photo by Petty Officer 2d Class Jack G. Georges, "Special Ops Provide Humanitarian Supplies [Image 1 of 7]," DVIDS Identifier 91629, May 21, 2008, Released to Public, available from *https://www.dvidshub.net/image/91629/special-ops-provide-humanitarian-supplies.*

66. MND-C Backbrief to MNC-I Operation Order (OPORD) 08-02 (Operation BLUE RIDGE MOUNTAIN), August 10, 2008.

67. Interview, Colonel Joel Rayburn, CSA OIF Study Group, with Lieutenant Colonel Jim Sindle, March 2016.

68. MND-SE Backbrief to MNC-I OPORD 08-02, July 17, 2009; MND-C OPORD 08-02, August 10, 2008.

69. MND-C Backbrief to MNC-I OPORD 08-02, August 10, 2008.

70. DoD photo by Staff Sergeant Michel Sauret, "Leaders discuss stability, growth," DVIDS Identifier 102730, July 14, 2008, Released to Public, available from *https://www.dvidshub.net/image/102730/leaders-discuss-stability-growth.*

71. Interview, Colonel Joel Rayburn and Lieutenant Colonel Matthew Zais, CSA OIF Study Group, with Lieutenant General Michael Oates, December 3, 2014.

72. MNF-I, SECDEF Weekly Update, June 16-22, 2008.

73. Ibid.; Interview, CSI Contemporary Operations Study Team with Lieutenant Colonel Bohnemann, July 21, 2010; MNF-I Battlefield Update Assessment, June 25, 2008.

74. MNF-I, SECDEF Weekly Update, June 16-22, 2008.

75. Ibid.

76. XVIII Airborne Corps, MNC-I Chronology, 2008-2009, July 11, 2008, entry.

77. Emma Sky, *The Unraveling: High Hopes and Missed Opportunities in Iraq,* New York: Public Affairs, 2015.

78. MNF-I, SECDEF Weekly Update, August 15-31, 2008.

79. MNF-I, SECDEF Weekly Update, September 8-14, 2008.

80. DoD photo by Staff Sergeant Ian M. Terry, "Mayor of Samarra sends a message to the people: Tear down that wall [Image 3 of 4]," DVIDS Identifier 159574, March 23, 2009, Released to Public, available from *https://www.dvidshub.net/image/159574/mayor-samarra-sends-message-people-tear-down-wall*.

81. Brian Katulis, Mark Lynch, and Peter Juul, "Iraq's Political Transition after the Surge," Washington, DC: Center for American Progress, September 2008, p. 17.

82. Rpt for Congress, Rhoda Margesson, Andorra Bruno, and Jeremy Sharp, "Iraqi Refugees and Internally Displaced Persons: A Deepening Humanitarian Crisis?" Washington, DC: Congressional Research Service, Rpt No. RL33936, February 2013, available from *http://fas.org/sgp/crs/mideast/RL33936.pdf*.

83. Katulis, Lynch, and Juul, "Iraq's Political Transition after the Surge," p. 18.

84. MNF-I, SECDEF Weekly Update, September 1-7, 2008.

85. MNF-I, SECDEF Weekly Update, August 15-31, 2008.

86. MNF-I, SECDEF Weekly Update, September 29-October 5, 2008.

87. Interview, Colonel Joel Rayburn, CSA OIF Study Group, with Mithal al-Alusi, September 23, 2015.

88. MNF-I, SECDEF Weekly Update, August 15-31, 2008.

89. Thomas P. M. Barnett, "The Man between War and Peace," *Esquire*, April 2008, available from *http://www.esquire.com/news-politics/a4284/fox-fallon/*, accessed March 13, 2016.

90. XVIII Airborne Corps, MNC-I Chronology, 2008-2009, April 2, 2008, entry.

91. XVIII Airborne Corps, MNC-I Chronology, 2008-2009, April 10, 2008, entry.

92. MNF-I, SECDEF Weekly Update, June 30-July 6, 2008.

93. U.S. House, Committee on Foreign Affairs, Subcommittee on International Organizations, Human Rights, and Oversight, Testimony of Steven Kull: Iraqi Public Opinion on the Presence of US Troops, 110th Congress, 2d Session, July 23, 2008, available from *https://drum.lib.umd.edu/bitstream/handle/1903/10182/Iraqi%20Public%20Opinion%20on%20the%20Presence%20of%20US%20Troops.pdf?sequence=1&isAllowed=y*, accessed June 5, 2018.

94. XVIII Airborne Corps, MNC-I Chronology, 2008-2009, May 9, 2008, entry.

95. MNF-I, SECDEF Weekly Update, May 26-June 1, 2008.

96. Ibid.

97. Ibid.

98. MNF-I, SECDEF Weekly Update, July 14-20, 2008.

99. MNF-I, SECDEF Weekly Update, June 9-15, 2008.

100. XVIII Airborne Corps, MNC-I Chronology, 2008-2009, June 26, 2008, entry.

101. XVIII Airborne Corps, MNC-I Chronology, 2008-2009, June 28, 2008, entry.

102. Qassim Zein and Hannah Allam, "In Maliki's hometown, grief and questions after deadly U.S. raid," McClatchy DC, June 2008, available from *http://www.mcclatchydc.com/news/nation-world/world/article24490081.html*.

103. MNF-I, SECDEF Weekly Update, June 30-July 6, 2008.

104. Ibid.

105. MNF-I, SECDEF Weekly Update, July 7-13, 2008.

106. MNF-I, SECDEF Weekly Update, July 14-20, 2008.

107. DoD photo by Staff Sergeant Lorie Jewell, "Obama, Senators, Receive Briefing From Top U.S. Commander [Image 4 of 5]," DVIDS Identifier 104677, July 21, 2008, Released to Public, available from *https://www.dvidshub.net/image/104677/obama-senators-receive-briefing-top-us-commander*. From left to right, Senator Charles Hagel, General David Petraeus, Senator Barack Obama, Ambassador Ryan Crocker, and Senator Jack Reed.

108. MNF-I, SECDEF Weekly Update, July 21-27, 2008.

109. XVIII Airborne Corps, MNC-I Chronology, 2008-2009, July 25, 2008, entry.

110. Ms, *On Point*, Vol. IV, Chapter 7, p. 55.

111. MNF-I, SECDEF Weekly Update, June 30-July 6, 2008.

112. Ms, *On Point*, Vol. IV, Chapter 4, p. 55.

113. MNF-I, SECDEF Weekly Update, July 21-27, 2008.

114. MNF-I, SECDEF Weekly Update, July 14-20, 2008.

115. MNF-I, SECDEF Weekly Update, July 28-August 3, 2008.

116. Ms, *On Point*, Vol. IV, Chapter 7, p. 63.

117. DoD photo by Petty Officer 2d Class Paul Seeber, "Operation Glad Tidings of Benevolence Begins," DVIDS Identifier 106771, July 29, 2008, Released to Public, available from *https://www.dvidshub.net/image/106771/operation-glad-tidings-benevolence-begins*.

118. MNF-I, SECDEF Weekly Update, June 2-8, 2008.

119. XVIII Airborne Corps, MNC-I Chronology, 2008-2009, entries for August 13, 2008, and August 16, 2008.

120. Marisa Sullivan, "Maliki's Authoritarian Regime," Washington, DC: Institute for the Study of War, 2013, p. 12; David Witty, "The Iraqi Counter Terrorism Service," Washington, DC: Brookings Institution, 2015, p. 18; Shane Bauer, "Iraq's New Death Squad: America has built an elite and lethal counterterrorism force. But who's calling the shots?" *Nation*, June 3, 2009, available from *http://www.thenation.com/article/iraqs-new-death-squad/*, accessed May 18, 2016.

121. MNF-I, SECDEF Weekly Update, August 18-24, 2008.

122. Interview, CSI Contemporary Operations Study Team with Colonel Bailey, August 16, 2010, p. 10; Ms, *On Point*, Vol. IV, Chapter 7, p. 56.

123. Ms, *On Point*, Vol. IV, Chapter 7, pp. 57-58.

124. Ibid., p. 59.

125. Interview, CSI Contemporary Operations Study Team with Lieutenant General Hertling, February 2010, p. 14.

126. DoD photo by Petty Officer 1st Class Daniel Mennuto, "Iraqi special forces conduct night work," DVIDS Identifier 99267, May 10, 2008, Released to Public, available from *https://www.dvidshub.net/image/99267/iraqi-special-forces-conduct-night-work.*

127. Witty, "The Iraqi Counter Terrorism Service," p. 10.

128. Ibid., p. 9.

129. Interview, Colonel Frank Sobchak, CSA OIF Study Group, with Colonel Mark Mitchell, CJSOTF, J-3 Cdr, September 29, 2014.

130. Office of the Special Inspector General for Iraq Reconstruction, *Iraqi Security Forces: Special Operations Force Program is Achieving Goals, but Iraqi Support Remains Critical to Success,* Washington, DC, October 25, 2010, pp. 15-16; Interviews, Colonel Frank Sobchak, CSA OIF Study Group, with Lieutenant General Kenneth Tovo, CJSOTF Cdr, Special Operations Division-Iraq Commanding General (CG), August 19, 2014; Colonel Sobchak, CSA OIF Study Group, with Rear Admiral Edward Winters, Iraqi National Counterterrorism Force Transition Team Cdr, October 22, 2015.

131. Interview, CSA OIF Study Group with Winters, October 22, 2015.

132. Ibid.; Interviews, CSA OIF Study Group with Tovo, August 19, 2014; Colonel Frank Sobchak, CSA OIF Study Group, with Lieutenant General (Ret.) Francis Kearney, Special Operations Component CG, October 16, 2015.

133. Interview, CSA OIF Study Group with Winters, October 22, 2015.

134. Interview, CSA OIF Study Group with Tovo, August 19, 2014.

135. Interview, Colonel Frank Sobchak, CSA OIF Study Group, with Lieutenant Colonel (Ret.) Patrick Morrison, Iraqi Special Operations Forces, Brigade Senior Adviser, Iraqi National Counter Terrorism Force Transition Team, September 22, 2014.

136. Robert Tollast, "Maliki's Private Army," *National Interest,* December 31, 2012.

137. Interview, CSA OIF Study Group with Mitchell, March 10, 2014.

138. Interview, CSA OIF Study Group with Winters, October 22, 2015.

139. Witty, "The Iraqi Counter Terrorism Service," p. 16.

140. Ibid., p. 13.

141. Interview, CSA OIF Study Group with Morrison, September 22, 2014; Witty, "The Iraqi Counter Terrorism Service," p. 16.

142. Interview, CSA OIF Study Group with Morrison, September 22, 2014.

143. Ibid.

144. Interview, Vince McLean, CSI Contemporary Operations Study Team, with Colonel Scott Brower, March 13, 2014.

145. Interview, CSA OIF Study Group with Morrison, September 22, 2014; Sullivan, "Maliki's Authoritarian Regime," p. 12; Interview, CSA OIF Study Group with Brower, June 2, 2014; Major Dave Butler, "Lights Out: ARSOF Reflect on Eight Years in Iraq," *Special Warfare,* January-March 2012.

146. Interview, CSA OIF Study Group with Brower, June 2, 2014.

147. MNF-I, SECDEF Weekly Update, August 15-31, 2008.

148. MNF-I, SECDEF Weekly Update, August 4-10, 2008.

149. XVIII Airborne Corps, MNC-I Chronology, 2008-2009, August 4, 2008, entry.

150. MNF-I, SECDEF Weekly Update, August 4-10, 2008.

151. XVIII Airborne Corps, MNC-I Chronology, 2008-2009, August 21, 2008, entry.

152. MNF-I, SECDEF Weekly Update, August 18-24, 2008.

153. Interview, Colonel Joel Rayburn, CSA OIF Study Group, with Major Wilson Blythe, March 6, 2015.

154. MNF-I, SECDEF Weekly Update, August 25-31, 2008.

155. Corporal Frances Goch, "1,215 Servicemembers Re-Up in Iraq," www.army.mil, July 4, 2008, available from *http://www.army.mil/article/10642/1215-servicemembers-re-up-in-iraq/*; MNF-I, SECDEF Weekly Update, June 30-July 6, 2008.

156. MNF-I, SECDEF Weekly Update, July 7-13, 2008.

157. MNF-I, SECDEF Weekly Update, August 4-10, 2008.

158. MNF-I, SECDEF Weekly Update, August 11-17, 2008.

CHAPTER 10

CONCLUSION: THE SURGE, 2007-2008

The change in the operational situation in Iraq from the beginning of the surge to its end was sweeping. By mid-2008, most of the Sunni insurgents that had threatened the Iraqi state's very existence in 2006 had either switched sides or fled to remote areas where they posed little danger to Iraq's heartland. The Iraqi security forces that had struggled to function in 2006 had grown by more than 140,000 troops and operated throughout the country. The Iranian-backed Shi'a militias that had dominated large swaths of Baghdad and southern Iraq had been defeated. The Syria-based foreign fighter network that had funneled thousands of terrorists into Iraq was neutralized. Life in Baghdad had returned to normality just 2 years after the carnage of 2006. Anbar, Iraq's most restive province in 2006, was now at its most peaceful. For the first time since 2003, the Iraqi Government controlled the lower Tigris and Euphrates River valleys from Baghdad to the sea, and pacification of the upper Tigris and upper Diyala valleys seemed within reach.

All this seemed unlikely after Multi-National Force-Iraq's (MNF-I) failed transition campaign in late 2006 when its internal strategic review acknowledged both a deteriorating security situation and a joint campaign plan with misaligned ends, ways, and means. General George W. Casey, Jr., sought to correct this and check the descent into sectarian civil war by accelerating the transition to Iraqi control and prodding the Nuri al-Maliki government into confronting the Shi'a militias and reconciling with the Sunnis. Casey had believed that drawing down was the surest way of maintaining an extended—albeit reduced—U.S. presence in Iraq, thus achieving the nation's objectives. By the end of 2006, President George W. Bush no longer found this persuasive. The White House strategy review that had begun in the summer gathered steam in the fall and finally culminated in January 2007 with the announcement of the "new way forward" that included a surge of U.S. troops and a new commander. Replacing Casey as MNF-I commander 1 month later, General David Petraeus developed and implemented a strategy, distinct in many respects from its predecessor but most markedly so in its intentional realignment of ends, ways, and means.

The surge, of course, provided the coalition with additional means, chiefly the 5 U.S. brigade combat teams (BCTs) that arrived between January and May 2007 to raise the total number of U.S. combat brigades in Iraq to 20—the highest it had been since the invasion. Two more Marine rifle battalions and a regimental-sized expeditionary unit also deployed as part of the surge, joining with forces already on the ground to expand MNF-I's operational reach into enemy sanctuaries throughout central Iraq. The commitment of an additional division headquarters and its combat aviation brigade facilitated this geographical expansion by providing focused command and control—particularly across Baghdad's southern "belts." In 2007, the arrival of several additional provincial reconstruction teams extended the coalition's reach, capitalizing on security gains to improve local governance and economic development. A surge of enablers gave BCT commanders capabilities that dramatically increased intelligence collection and analysis, force protection, and population control. For example, full-motion video, document exploitation, and signals intelligence gave tactical leaders increased targeting proficiency and precision.

Time remained a finite resource, though. Frequently mentioning the tyranny of the "Washington and Baghdad clocks," Petraeus sought to buy time in the United States by emphasizing the need for patience and promising to report on the effects of the surge to Congress in September 2007. In Iraq, Petraeus and U.S. Ambassador Ryan Crocker pursued reconciliation and capacity building as U.S. forces refocused on the reduction of sectarian violence. Even so, political progress came haltingly as Iraqi factions resisted compromise in the complex communal struggle for power and the Iranian and Syrian regimes intervened in the process.

The "new way forward" ushered in no sweeping change of the Iraq War's desired end state, but Petraeus described his objectives differently, making protecting the civilian population preeminent and setting a goal of a "baseline of security" by mid-2008 and "sustainable stability" by the spring of 2009. Neither Petraeus nor Lieutenant General Raymond Odierno believed quickly shifting to Iraqi control made sense so long as the Iraqi Government and its security forces were complicit in sectarian violence. As MNF-I's emphasis on "Iraqi Army lead" and "provincial Iraqi control" receded, the reduction of violence emerged as the key measure of success, encouraging coalition units to concentrate on resolving the internecine struggle and allowing reconciliation at the local level. The coalition's new metrics reflected Petraeus and Odierno's judgment that transition could not precede reconciliation.

At the tactical level, Petraeus and Odierno pressed U.S. commanders to establish a persistent presence among the population. In Baghdad, this led to the creation or expansion of dozens of joint security stations and combat outposts. The decision to maximize forward presence allowed a tactical change that eventually had a remarkable operational impact. BCT commanders positioning their battalions forward reported a sharp rise in intelligence tips that often blossomed into targetable information. As units successfully prosecuted those targets, killing or arresting insurgents and sectarians, more Iraqis came forward with information, confident their tips would be heeded. As the cycle continued, its effects compounded and expanded, dealing both insurgents and militias punishing blows that shifted the initiative to the coalition for the first time since 2004.

This same virtuous cycle enabled the spread of the Awakening that had begun in Ramadi in 2006. The spread of combat outposts facilitated engagement opportunities with local leaders that, at times, led to accommodations or cease-fires with former insurgents. As U.S. forces expanded their presence throughout western and central Iraq, Sunni tribes and insurgent groups fighting a desperate multi-front war against al-Qaeda in Iraq (AQI), the coalition, and—especially in mixed-sect areas—Shi'a militias and the Iraqi security forces sought truces with their American foes. At the same time, U.S. commanders exploited this opportunity to persuade their erstwhile Sunni opponents to turn their guns against their common enemies, namely AQI and its extremist allies. Seizing such an opportunity often entailed tremendous risk for U.S. commanders, since Sunni fighters did not fall neatly and consistently into the categories of "reconcilable" and "irreconcilable." While the Awakening was unquestionably an organic movement borne of Sunni discontent and an acknowledgment of their perilous prospects, there is likewise little doubt that the actions taken by senior coalition leaders helped nurture and spread the budding movement.

Lines formed by tribal loyalties and insurgent affiliations with AQI blurred within the slightly broader context of a war within a war as clans and houses struggled for dominance in a local area. Odierno considered accepting the risk associated with this bottom-up reconciliation one of his most important decisions as Multi-National Corps-Iraq (MNC-I) commander. To ease the Maliki government's fears of a Ba'athist resurgence and to solidify the security gains of the Awakening as it spread from Anbar into Baghdad, the "belts," and beyond, the coalition created organizations and processes to link these bottom-up efforts with the central government. Sectarian biases and suspicions were difficult to overcome, and—though the ranks of the Sons of Iraq steadily grew well into 2008—the idea that a loose patchwork of local accommodations with U.S. units would eventually lead to a broad interconnected "quilt" knit together by national reconciliation proved difficult to fulfill. Nonetheless, in the near term, employing forward-positioned American forces as a means of brokering ceasefires and enlisting Sunni fighters in the struggle against AQI threatened Sunni extremists by denying AQI its long-term safe havens and restricting its freedom of action.

Additional U.S. forces did not obviate the need for operational art. Commanders had to employ combat units in relation to key terrain and adaptive enemies. Not unlike the Sunni and Shi'a militants battling for control of Baghdad, coalition commanders made Iraq's capital their main effort. As surge BCTs flowed into Iraq during the first half of 2007, Odierno placed them in the city, but he also distributed headquarters and battalions in the "belts" arcing north and south, where they began to push into sanctuaries that had long been without coalition presence. In June, with all of his forces in place, Odierno launched simultaneous operations across Baghdad and the "belts" even as MNC-I continued to exploit the Awakening in Anbar. Odierno's innovation was to use four U.S. division-sized units in and around Baghdad for synchronized operations to secure the population and interdict "accelerants" that infiltrated the city from safe havens—many in the "belts." With the arrival of "accelerants" halted, AQI and Shi'a militias were unable to stoke the sectarian fires through high-profile attacks.

By the fall of 2007, MNF-I had retaken the initiative, and AQI was reeling. Still, in spite of the surge, the coalition had to rely on economy-of-force efforts in Mosul and Basra. As the pressure increased in Baghdad and Anbar became more inhospitable to AQI fighters, the group's leadership in Iraq retreated up the Diyala and Tigris River Valleys, regrouping in Mosul. A battle for that city loomed in early 2008, but Prime Minister Maliki had other plans, launching an offensive against the Sadrists in Basra and Sadr City. Significant security gains in Baghdad and the impending drawdown of coalition forces did not eliminate the challenge Lieutenant General Lloyd Austin faced when he succeeded Odierno as MNC-I commander in early 2008. Thanks to an AQI stronghold in Mosul and Maliki's unexpected decision to fight the Sadrists, MNC-I had to expand its operational footprint even as its troop levels steadily fell. Furthermore, Iraq's factions continued to posture for advantage in the ongoing communal struggle for power, particularly as the various parties prepared for provincial elections.

The successes and disappointments of the surge had much to do with unity and disunity of effort. A close, cooperative relationship between Petraeus and Crocker enhanced the joint campaign and amplified the surge's military effects. In mid-2007, the Multi-National Security Transition Command-Iraq (MNSTC-I) modified its approach under a new commander, General James Dubik, and synchronized its support to the Iraqi security forces with MNC-I. By contrast, Multi-National Division-Southeast's (MND-SE) deviation from the MNF-I campaign plan in 2007 brought the British and American divergence to a head in 2008 and sowed the seeds for the crisis that precipitated Operation CHARGE OF THE KNIGHTS. Most notably, the Maliki government sought different end states than those of the United States—a point that became more prominent during the negotiations over a U.S.-Iraq status of forces agreement.

With the departure of the last surge BCT in the summer of 2008 and provincial elections set for early 2009, the surge had culminated. The coalition's military gains were indisputable, setting the stage for a steady yet unprecedented drop in attacks soon after Petraeus departed for U.S. Central Command and Odierno returned to Baghdad to take his place. What remained to be seen was whether the U.S.-led coalition could translate the surge's hard-fought operational gains into a stable and secure Iraq.

PART II:
FROM SURGE TO
WITHDRAWAL

CHAPTER 11

ZERO ATTACKS, SEPTEMBER-DECEMBER 2008

ODIERNO TAKES COMMAND

General Raymond T. Odierno assumed command from General David H. Petraeus on September 16 in Faw Palace at Camp Victory during a ceremony presided over by Secretary of Defense (SECDEF) Robert Gates. Odierno's respite from Iraq had lasted barely 7 months, but the character of the conflict had changed dramatically in his absence. The combined coalition-Iraqi offensive against Jaysh al-Mahdi (JAM) in Basrah and Baghdad in the spring, along with renewed operations against al-Qaeda in Iraq (AQI) in Diyala and Mosul in the late summer, had reduced the level of violence to near-record lows by the time Odierno took command. Territory that had been in enemy hands in 2006 and 2007 was largely under Iraqi Government control by the fall of 2008, and the Sunni and Shi'a militant groups that had appeared on the verge of overwhelming the Iraqi Government in 2006 were in retreat nearly everywhere. After a year and a half of intense combat operations under the surge, Odierno's first task as Multi-National Force-Iraq (MNF-I) commander would be to shift the coalition's focus onto the many noncombat activities and nontraditional missions needed to complete the operational victory the coalition troops, Iraqi security forces (ISF), and Sons of Iraq had won in 2007-2008.

Source: DoD photo by Jerry Morrison (Released).

General Raymond Odierno With Secretary of Defense Robert Gates During the MNF-I Change of Command Ceremony.[1]

Since giving up command of Multi-National Corps-Iraq (MNC-I) to Lieutenant General Lloyd J. Austin in February, Odierno had spent almost all of the intervening months preparing to return to Baghdad. In the weeks before he took charge of MNF-I, he and his close advisers pondered how they might need to adapt the campaign plan. In Odierno's view, by late summer 2008 the coalition needed to "shift from security primacy to political primacy" and focus on supporting Iraqi political actions rather than conducting major security operations. Odierno still believed that fully defeating AQI and Iranian-sponsored militant groups required intense military operations. But, if mainstream Iraqi political groups would use the constitutional process, the coalition could support the governance and economic reforms needed to make a lasting political reconciliation. Overall, Odierno expected that MNF-I's mission was to be stability and support operations, as well as peacekeeping.

Accordingly, Odierno planned to update the Joint Campaign Plan to reflect the new priorities and invited a team of external experts to Baghdad to assist with this update. He also reorganized MNF-I's intelligence resources and directed them toward political issues, social movements, and broader regional dynamics, leaving MNC-I's intelligence units to handle tactical and security-related matters. Odierno expected that support for the impending Iraqi provincial elections of January 2009 would be among the coalition's top priorities once he took command, and that the subsequent 1-year period between provincial and national elections would be decisive for achieving the end state of the campaign. Above all, Odierno anticipated that the not-yet-finalized U.S.-Iraq security agreement would significantly alter the conditions under which his forces operated, as the Iraqi Government continued to assert greater independence and more control over the coalition's activities. With the changed security environment and the likely expiration of the United Nations Security Council Resolution (UNSCR) under which the coalition had operated, Odierno believed the Iraqi Government would press for visible changes in the coalition's mode of operations. This would include a reduction in his forces' footprint in Baghdad and other cities and the return of the Republican Palace to Iraqi control.

Of course, MNF-I's troop strength had already diminished by the time Odierno took command. As the 15-month tours of the surge brigades ended, the U.S. force in Iraq had returned to its late-2006 size of 15 brigades. Odierno and his advisers believed that political pressures both in Iraq and in the United States eventually would dictate further force reductions with the brigades that remained gradually assuming a training, advisory, and overwatch role, leaving Iraqi forces responsible for security operations. As he left for Baghdad in early September, Odierno speculated that within 24 months MNF-I might evolve into an Office of Military Cooperation (OMC)—an "OMC-Egypt on steroids"—with five U.S. brigades, which he considered "the minimum amount in case it goes south."[2]

Zero Attacks

On September 19, 3 days after Odierno took command of MNF-I, there were no civilian casualties in the entire country for a 24-hour period. This was only the fourth occurrence since the 2003 invasion.[3] October saw only 983 security incidents of all kinds, the lowest total since January 2004. On October 31, there was another 24-hour period without any civilian casualties.[4] In the last week of November, there were 111 security incidents, the lowest weekly total since the end of 2003. In December, there were fewer than 600.[5] High-profile attacks such as car bombings fell to their lowest levels since 2004, though they still accounted for almost half of the casualties. The change was unmistakable: in 2007, an average of 124 coalition troops, Iraqi troops, and civilians were killed or wounded each day, but for 2008, the average was 47 per day.[6]

Source: DoD photo by Staff Sergeant J. B. Jaso (Released).

A U.S. Soldier Plays Foosball With Children in Husseniyah Nahia.[7]

Although the ISF continued to lose more than 100 soldiers or police each month, especially in areas such as Mosul, life for civilians in central and southern Iraq returned to what Iraqis considered normal. Baghdad residents encountered a new problem with the volume of traffic on its streets, similar to other Arab capitals, and Iraqi officials began exploring options for mass transit projects.[8] In a symbolic move, the famous Mutanabi book market reopened in December, 21 months after it had been destroyed by an AQI car bomb in March 2007.[9]

Source: DoD photo by Specialist Grant Okubo (Released).

Prime Minister Nuri al-Maliki at a Ceremony Reopening Baghdad's Historic Mutanabi Book Market.[10]

The Push for Improved Governance

With the improved security conditions, however, came heightened expectations among Iraqi civilians of a "peace dividend" with restored essential services and economic activity. As violence receded in central and southern Iraq, the long-standing shortage of electricity became the public's top concern, one that threatened to undermine the government's legitimacy. The Ba'athist regime provided unlimited free electricity, and the new Iraqi Government sought to follow that policy. Fall 2008 saw occasional angry protests by thousands of Baghdadis against the Minister of Electricity. Coalition leaders noted with worry that a large portion of Iraqi civilians believed public services had been better under Saddam Hussein, a perception that militants might exploit to inflame the security situation. In his third week in command, Odierno reported to Washington that electricity had become "the number one problem in Iraq."[11] However, the Iraqi ministries typically lacked the will or capacity to follow suit, leaving the Maliki government dogged by public dissatisfaction.

While the surge provided Maliki the breathing space needed to address the country's thorny political challenges, U.S. leaders in the Green Zone feared that he could not or would not do so, particularly in parts of Iraq that had been under militant control. Even though Iraqi security forces were mostly able to establish a presence in liberated areas, the restoration of other government functions and essential services often lagged far behind.

To better assess the Government of Iraq's performance and institutional capacity, MNF-I and the U.S. Embassy commissioned a Governance Assessment Team (GAT) under Colonel H. R. McMaster and Ambassador Larry C. Napper. Over several weeks in 2008, the team of civilian and military experts, many of whom had served on the Joint Strategic Assessment Team (JSAT) in 2007, investigated Iraq's ministerial capacity, provincial administration, economic development, and political progress to determine how to help the Iraqi Government to reestablish the level of governance demanded by its population. The GAT validated what many coalition units had seen at the local level: corrupt and often sectarian state institutions, a shortage of quality mid-level officials, and the legacy of an overly complex Ba'athist bureaucratic system diminished government capacity and impeded political progress.[12]

The GAT found that money was not the problem: the Iraqi Government was not poor. Oil revenues increased by almost 10 percent from 2007 to 2008, spurred by the improved security situation in the north and anti-corruption measures at the Bayji refinery. By mid-2008, the Iraqi Government was exporting about 1.8 million barrels per day at export prices of roughly $83 per barrel.[13] The Iraqi economy was growing at a rate of about 7 percent, and the government budget grew a whopping 22 percent from 2007 to 2008. The result was a government that had vast oil wealth at its disposal but little capacity to spend it effectively. The Maliki government "had more money than it knew what to do with," observed Colonel Rick L. Waddell, a senior economist on the GAT.[14]

The problem, the GAT found, was that Iraqi civil servants responsible for finances were incapable of executing the government budget. In many ministries, senior civil servants had been purged as Ba'athists in 2003-2004, leaving only inexperienced junior officials or incompetent political appointees. Meanwhile, those professional civil servants who remained went about their duties as though they were still in the sanctions-era bureaucracy of Saddam Hussein, when the goal had been to hoard resources rather than spend them and even minor decisions were made at the highest possible level.[15] Risk aversion was still prevalent in early 2008, when most decisions were made by ministers selected for political loyalty rather than for professional competence.

Because the central Iraqi Government lacked the capacity to spend its budget, the GAT recommended that local agencies be given more spending authority. Doing so would require political changes. Public finance management experts brought in by the coalition to analyze the convoluted process by which funds flowed from Baghdad to the provinces found that the central government did not distribute resources equitably to Sunni and Kurdish provinces.[16] When the ministries allocated money or resources to the provinces, it was usually in a halting, unpredictable manner under the close control of ministerial officials using an antiquated paper-and-courier-based distribution system.[17] Similarly, without a modern banking system that facilitated electronic funds transfers, cash payments were the norm, facilitating corruption.

To help overcome this lack of government capacity, the GAT recommended that the coalition increase its advisory effort to the Iraqi ministries. The GAT found that, despite spending tens of billions of dollars on reconstruction through the Iraqi Reconstruction Management Office and other agencies, the U.S. Embassy was ineffective in improving the ministries, partly because it lacked sufficient advisory personnel and access to the Iraqi ministries. The GAT recommended that MNF-I use military officers to augment the Embassy's advisers and military resources to ensure that coalition officials could travel to the ministries.[18]

The next major recommendation from the GAT involved connecting improvements in governance and economic development at the local or provincial level to the ministries in Baghdad. The provincial reconstruction teams (PRTs) and the embedded provincial reconstruction teams (EPRTs) worked together with the brigades at the local level striving to encourage this connection and good governance within their areas of operations. However, there was only so much they could accomplish on their own. In Diyala Province, for example, Colonel Jon S. Lehr's 4th Stryker Brigade Combat Team (BCT), 2d Infantry Division, discovered that the province's budget, consisting of billions of Iraqi dinars, was managed by "an elderly woman in the basement of the provincial center using a ledger pad, straight ruler, and a pencil."[19] In Mosul, officials were unable to establish a municipal garbage collection program. Under Iraq's centralized system of government, responsibility for trash collection fell under the Ministry of Public Works in Baghdad, which Michael Ensch of the Army Corps of Engineers described as "absolutely dysfunctional."[20] Local EPRTs spent significant time and resources attempting to resolve these types of problems, but any improvement was short-lived if not sustained with assistance from the ministries in Baghdad.

Connecting the Iraqi provinces to the central government was not a straightforward matter. During years of insurgency, large swaths of the country had fallen out of contact with Baghdad. At the same time, the ministries had been a literal battlefield during the violence of 2006-2007, and ministerial officials had often lived and worked under siege, hunkering down and unable to attend to the business of governance. U.S. units and diplomats in 2007-2008 often found themselves trying to reestablish a working relationship between the central government and its outlying territories. To forge connections across the levels of government, U.S. forces frequently used "helicopter diplomacy" in which U.S. helicopters ferried provincial and central government officials between the capital and provinces.[21] In many cases, the U.S. commanders and diplomats who transported senior ministerial officials to the provinces found that their Iraqi counterparts were visiting the provinces for the first time and had never met their branch staffs there. This improved communication in the short term, but systemic changes were needed to ensure cooperation endured after the coalition left.

THE NORTHERN IRAQ PROBLEM

The Arab-Kurd Conflict

Among the problems Odierno faced was the worsening territorial dispute between Arabs and Kurds over the fate of the oil-rich city of Kirkuk. As Odierno took command in mid-September, Arab-Kurd tensions threatened to fracture Iraq's governing coalition and reignite the civil war—albeit along a different axis. In August, Iraqi Army troops and Kurdish peshmerga had come close to blows in the town of Khanaqin. That town and other parts of northern Diyala had been under peshmerga control since the early days of the war, but as the Iraqi security forces (ISF) proceeded up the Diyala Valley to clear AQI support zones during Operation GLAD TIDINGS OF BENEVOLENCE, they had aggressively entered areas the Kurdish Government considered under its control. The 34th Peshmerga Brigade, which had occupied and worked to pacify Khanaqin since 2003, in turn defied orders from the Maliki government to withdraw and give way to Iraqi Army troops. Instead, the peshmerga had dug in, and both sides braced themselves for a possible civil war. U.S. military advisers in the area had worked to defuse the confrontation, but commanders on both sides, Arab and Kurdish, seemed eager to fight.[22]

The armed standoff had grown serious enough that Major General Mark P. Hertling and his Multi-National Division-North (MND-N) hastily deployed additional troops and advisers to the Khanaqin area to separate the Arab and Kurdish units and prevent a costly battle between Iraqi forces that were supposed to be on the same side. "It was one of my three worst days in Iraq," Hertling would later recall.[23] For his part, Hertling was determined not to become embroiled in this Iraqi-Kurdish brinksmanship, telling all involved that in the event of ISF-peshmerga fighting, U.S. forces would support neither side. "I would pull back all my advisors," Hertling told them. "I would tell all my other forces to return to their [bases]. I wasn't going to take sides on this, and [they] would be responsible for any bloodshed."[24] Defusing the situation ultimately required Prime Minister Maliki and President Jalal Talabani to order their respective ISF and peshmerga commanders to stand down, after which leaders in Baghdad and Erbil negotiated a deal under which Kurdish police patrolled the city and the peshmerga withdrew.[25]

In one of his first acts as MNF-I commander, Odierno instructed MNC-I Commander General Austin to increase the number of U.S. advisers with all Iraqi units in eastern

Diyala to prevent further Arab-Kurd confrontations.[26] The narrow escape in Khanaqin showed that a conflict that had largely pitted Sunnis and Arabs against one another before 2008 had the potential to develop into a full-scale Arab-Kurd fight as well. It also showed that the Shi'a-Kurdish political coalition, which dominated Iraqi politics since Maliki's rise to power in 2006, was beginning to falter under the weight of competing claims over disputed territories and the broader implementation of Article 140 of the 2005 Iraqi Constitution, which called for a referendum on Kirkuk's future status and a de-Arabization of the city. The war against AQI and other Sunni terrorist groups had united the Kurdistan Regional Government and the Shi'a-led government in Baghdad against a common enemy, but as the AQI threat receded, the unresolved question of the relationship between Kurdistan and the central government remained, with the potential to cause conflict. If the Kurdish and Arab parties that made up Iraq's national unity government began warring among themselves, the political implications would be "catastrophic," a visiting White House official warned Odierno in Baghdad. The fighting would be viewed externally as a sign that "the progress was not real."[27]

Operations to Finish AQI in Mosul: Operation MOTHER OF TWO SPRINGS II

The dispute in Khanaqin was particularly costly because it was a distraction from the ongoing operations in Mosul, where, since late spring 2008, the coalition and ISF had been attempting finally to destroy AQI in the city. In the early fall, Operation MOTHER OF TWO SPRINGS II was a three-phased effort to target important AQI figures, clear the remaining neighborhoods where AQI enjoyed support zones, and then restore Mosul's civilian governance capacity.[28] Throughout the early fall, coalition and Iraqi special operators carried out targeted raids against AQI leaders in Mosul in advance of large-scale operations by U.S. and Iraqi conventional forces planned for mid-October. Some of these shaping operations yielded significant results. On October 5, special operators in Mosul cornered and killed Abu Qaswarah, a Swedish militant who had been among AQI's most prominent field commanders and its northern emir before becoming overall deputy to AQI commander Abu Ayyub al-Masri.[29] The materials found with Abu Qaswarah were a treasure trove of records rivaling the Sinjar records in scale and detailing hundreds of AQI attacks over time.[30] The files also revealed the organization's financial networks, operational guidance, line and block charts, and even guidance on operational security.[31] These records yielded strategic insights about AQI's inner workings and led to further raids that netted dozens of other AQI members.

At the same time, a series of raids against AQI's "Finance Emirs" constricted the organization's cash flow. AQI fighters received little or no pay for several weeks, forcing them to rely on crime, extorting payments from businesses such as the Northern Oil Company, the AsiaCell phone company, and the state-owned Northern Cement Company.[32] AQI leaders also demanded money from government employees and small businesses such as neighborhood pharmacies, a practice that eroded the group's support.[33]

Source: DoD photo by Staff Sergeant JoAnn Makinano (Released).

A Soldier From 3d Armored Cavalry Regiment Conducts a Patrol in Mosul.[34]

In a desperate bid to polarize Ninawa Province and attract local Sunni Islamist support, AQI tried to incite sectarian war against Ninawa's Christian population. In early October, Abu Omar al-Baghdadi, leader of AQI's political front, the Islamic State of Iraq, declared war on Christians, directing assassinations, bombings, and threats that eventually caused 13,000 of the city's Christians to flee their homes—more than half of Mosul's Christian population.[35] Meeting on October 12, Maliki and the Iraqi National Security Council concluded that AQI and other insurgents had infiltrated Mosul's police force and were undermining the city's security from within.[36] The impending coalition-ISF operations would therefore include two additional National Police brigades to replace or reinforce Mosul's local policemen.[37] Maliki and other ministers also decided to remove Ninawa Operations Commander Lieutenant General Riyadh Jalal Tawfiq, a Sunni officer who had previously commanded the 9th Division in eastern Baghdad, and replace him with Major General Hassan Kareem Khudeir, a Shi'a officer who had also served in Baghdad and was believed to have close ties to Maliki's Da'wa Party. Maliki and other Iraqi leaders were concerned that the instability in Mosul could disrupt the provincial elections scheduled for January 2009 just as it had in January 2005. Odierno believed the coalition itself might have to stop the intimidation of Mosul voters.[38] Iraqi leaders believed that the outcome of Ninawa's provincial elections would have national significance and would shape the elections scheduled for 2010.[39] These political concerns heightened the stakes for the impending security operations in the province.

Source: DoD photo courtesy Joint Combat Camera Center Iraq (Released).

U.S. Soldiers Intercept a Vehicle Whose Occupants Had Been Observed Emplacing a Roadside Bomb in Mosul.[40]

On October 15, Iraqi Army and police forces working with MND-N units began clearing Mosul of suspected insurgent cells and recovering buildings that had fallen into insurgent hands.[41] MNF-I had expected the Mosul operations to last until mid-January, but AQI's operational tempo and leadership had been so disrupted that resistance faded quickly, especially as additional Iraqi National Police, Iraqi Army, and coalition troops flowed into the city.[42] By October 26, Odierno reported to Gates that the city was stabilized and insurgent attacks across Iraq were slackening.[43] Whether these security gains would last depended on political reform and improved governance.

The Abu Ghadiyah Raid and the Disruption of the Foreign Fighter Network

In addition to its losses in Mosul, AQI suffered another major setback on October 26 after a daytime raid struck the Syrian border town of Albu Kamal, opposite the Iraqi town of Al Qa'im on the Euphrates River. Abu Ghadiyah, the young Iraqi militant who was the long-time head of AQI's vast foreign fighter facilitation network in Syria, was killed during the operation. For at least 3 years, the majority of al-Qaeda's foreign fighters had been funneled into Iraq by Abu Ghadiyah and his network of facilitators, including most AQI suicide bombers. The Albu Kamal raid was a significant blow to the extremist organization, hindering foreign fighter flow for months while temporarily severing the connection between the jihadist organization and its regional supporters. MNF-I concluded that this reduced the number of non-Iraqi suicide bombers available to AQI commanders in Mosul and forced them to adjust and appoint new field emirs.[44] Syrian officials publicly denounced the raid and claimed to have no knowledge of Abu Ghadiyah's activities, but evidence of the Assad regime's direct support for AQI's foreign fighter network indicated that the regime's protests were disingenuous.

With their lead border facilitator dead and with clearing operations in Mosul gaining momentum, some remaining AQI leaders fled to western Ninawa and the Jazeera desert, the same area where Abu Ghadiyah's foreign fighters had long made their way toward Mosul and the Tigris Valley.[45] Since 2004, the western Ninawa city of Tel Afar had been a favored staging base for AQI and its foreign fighters, and in fall 2008, Odierno noted the need to deploy additional Iraqi and coalition troops there to prevent AQI from again reestablishing it as an insurgent stronghold.[46] Much of the responsibility for stepping up the coalition presence in the Tel Afar and Jazeera area would fall to Multi-National Force-West (MNF-W) because MNC-I had reassigned western Ninawa and the Syrian border zone in the Jazeera desert to MNF-W earlier in the year in order to free MND-N to focus on Mosul.[47] By early December, MNF-W's operations near the border made it difficult for AQI leaders and fighters to move along the Jazeera infiltration routes through which they had once traveled freely; and the Syrian-based network Abu Ghadiyah had headed struggled to send more than a trickle of foreign fighters into Iraq.[48]

Aftermath of the Mosul Operations

By early November, the ISF-led operations in Mosul had driven most AQI fighters from the city. Violence dropped to near zero, and the Christian families who had fled in October began returning.[49] AQI's previously powerful Mosul networks were in disarray, forced to forgo their usual distributions of cash to allies and clients in other provinces during October and November. Captured AQI members reported they had not been paid in many months.[50]

Resolving the longer-term causes of violence in Ninawa would take more than clearing operations and the sustained disruption of AQI's terrorist operations. Despite the heavy presence of Iraqi forces, MND-N believed that there was no rule of law in the city.[51] For years, it had been difficult to get terrorists and insurgents convicted in Mosul's courts, where AQI and other groups were able to intimidate or bribe Iraqi officials and even occasionally break prisoners out of jail. In addition, Mosul's unemployment rate was 70 percent, making the city's residents vulnerable to criminal and insurgent influence.[52] The fighting across Ninawa also created thousands of long-term displaced persons (2,500 in Tel Afar alone) who could be radicalized. The province was divided ethnically and politically, creating fissures that AQI and others exploited. MND-N believed Ninawa's Kurdish deputy governor and local Kurdish Democratic Party (KDP) chief, Kesro Goran, was locked in a power struggle with Arab parties ahead of the 2009 provincial elections that Arabs who had boycotted the January 2005 elections hoped to use to retake control of the provincial government.[53]

There were also questions of the reliability of ISF in the province. As AQI lost its grip on Mosul and western Ninawa, the group offered large cash rewards to Iraqi soldiers or police who assassinated American troops, a move that probably caused two incidents in November during which rogue Iraqi soldiers killed U.S. troops in Mosul and Biaj. In the Biaj killings, fellow Iraqi soldiers helped the assassin flee toward the Syrian border before loyal Iraqi border troops caught him.[54]

The task of tackling these issues would fall to new MND-N leadership. On December 9, General Mark Hertling and his 1st Armored Division handed responsibility for northern Iraq to Major General Robert L. Caslen, Jr., and the 25th Infantry Division, the same division that the 1st Armored had replaced as MND-N only a year before.

THE QUEST FOR STABILIZATION

The Joint Campaign Plan Assessment Team

Improvements in security came much faster than MNF-I leaders had anticipated, leading them to seek parallel economic and political progress.[55] To identify such opportunities, Odierno and Ambassador Ryan Crocker formed a Joint Campaign Plan Assessment Team (JCPAT), bringing in a wide range of experts to "review the ways in which we promote reform without undermining the GoI's [Government of Iraq's] exercise of sovereignty and how we must operationalize our procedures in response to the changing strategic environment."[56]

Led by retired Marine General Anthony Zinni, the JCPAT included Ambassador Ronald Neumann, Ambassador Robin Raphel, future Under Secretary of Defense for Policy Michelle Flournoy, historian Kimberly Kagan, future White House official Colin Kahl, and Brookings Institution scholar Kenneth Pollack.[57] After weeks of inquiry in Iraq, the team determined in late October that "the positive developments in Iraq were very real, but very fragile."[58] Making the gains of the surge last would take political reconciliation. The Iraqi Government would need to integrate the Sons of Iraq into the ISF, continue political engagement with the Sunni Awakening, and build government capacity.[59] However, the JCPAT noted that the necessary shift from security operations to stabilization would reduce coalition advantage.[60] The team warned that Prime Minister Maliki was becoming less interested in a sustained U.S. military presence in Iraq, especially if he concluded that withdrawal offered him an opportunity to consolidate power further.[61] The JCPAT cautioned against direct action against the Iranian regime and argued that a "strong, unified Iraqi polity" was the best way to minimize Tehran's influence.[62]

Like the earlier JSAT, the JCPAT gave MNF-I and the U.S. Embassy an analytical basis for a new campaign plan to reflect changing conditions.[63] Most of its conclusions and warnings would prove accurate, but in 2008 MNF-I found remedies increasingly difficult to implement, especially where Iraqi political reconciliation was concerned.

Transition of the Sons of Iraq

Operations between May and November 2008 brought Mosul firmly under government control and pushed AQI and other northern insurgent groups farther away from the population centers of the upper Tigris Valley. Like the JCPAT experts, coalition leaders believed the Sunni insurgency's future strength depended on nonmilitary variables. The most important was the future of the Sons of Iraq, the armed manifestation of the Sunni Awakening that had done so much damage to AQI in Anbar and the Baghdad region since late 2006. Having recruited and paid more than 100,000 Sons of Iraq, MNF-I agreed to transfer them to the government's payroll by the end of 2008, in exchange for Maliki's acceptance of the program. MNC-I began the transfer in early October 2008, starting with the 51,000 in the Baghdad region, the majority of whom received their monthly salary of $300 from a special government committee without incident.[64]

Source: DoD photo by Specialist Chuck Gill (Released).

Members of the Gazaliyah Guardians, a West Baghdad Awakening Group, Register for Payment From the Iraqi Government.[65]

Source: DoD photo by Staff Sergeant James Hunter (Released).

An Iraqi Army Officer Pays a Sons of Iraq Member in Ameriyah.[66]

Beyond Baghdad, however, the transition was less smooth. MNF-I and Maliki agreed to shift all Sons of Iraq to official government employment in 2009, with 20 percent of them to be absorbed into the ISF, but there were early signs that it would be difficult to hold the Maliki government to this pledge. As preparations began in November to transfer the 8,000 Sons of Iraq in Diyala to government control, coalition leaders became alarmed by continued sectarian tension between the Shi'a-led ISF and the largely Sunni Sons of Iraq that had emerged during security operations in Diyala in July and August. In the space of a few weeks, government forces detained several Sons of Iraq leaders, with one, Sheikh Bashir al-Judani, dying in the custody of the Interior Ministry's Major Crimes Unit. Confronting Maliki on the matter on October 23, Odierno warned that the ISF's behavior would undermine the government's legitimacy and create instability as the important January provincial elections approached. Maliki defended the raids against Sunni leaders that he considered to be "Ba'athists" and claimed that one Sunni detainee in Diyala was suspected of carrying out the 1999 assassination of Ayatollah Muhammad Sadiq Sadr, Moqtada Sadr's father.[67]

The dispute over the Diyala Sons of Iraq illustrated the problems in the broader relationship between the Sunni Awakening and the Maliki government. In Sunni-dominated Anbar, the Maliki government had been relatively quick to endorse the Awakening and accept a paid security role for thousands of local Sons of Iraq. However, in the mixed-sect Baghdad belts, Maliki and his Shi'a colleagues had been much more skeptical of the Sons of Iraq, demanding a long vetting process especially in the areas that had seen the most sectarian violence and displacement before 2008. In mixed-sect Diyala, where Sunnis were a demographic plurality but where the balance of power among the ethno-sectarian communities was still in question, government skepticism of the Awakening and the Sons of Iraq hardened into recalcitrance. The Sunni election boycott of January 2005 had allowed Shi'a and Kurdish minorities to control Diyala's police and provincial government, but the Sunni Sons of Iraq could potentially reverse that if mobilized for the January 2009 provincial elections. Maliki and other Shi'a government leaders also believed many of the Sons of Iraq were simply Sunni insurgents who had made a temporary pact with the coalition but would eventually return to warfare against the Shi'a-led government.[68] Their fears were not unfounded: coalition officials saw multiple signs of AQI and other Sunni insurgent groups attempting to recruit Sons of Iraq members back into the insurgent camp.[69]

There were other reasons for government officials to distance themselves from the Sons of Iraq as well. Senior Iraqis assigned by the Prime Minister to manage the Sons of Iraq portfolio faced frequent pressure from Shi'a parties and Iranian-sponsored militants, accusing them of empowering Sunni militants. Bassima Luay Hasun al-Jaidri, the Maliki loyalist who headed the Iraqi Government committee overseeing Sons of Iraq integration, became the subject of a criminal investigation along with her military deputy, while another committee member, Major General Mudher al-Mawla, was wounded in an early December assassination attempt.[70]

The success of transferring the Sons of Iraq to the government would determine whether the Sunni Awakening would endure and would act as a bellwether of the Maliki government's support of broader reconciliation efforts. The events of late 2008, however, demonstrated that the Maliki government did not share MNF-I's sense of urgency or the coalition's belief that the Awakening and the Sons of Iraq were the key to preventing a badly damaged AQI from regaining a foothold in Iraq's Sunni areas.

Diminishing American Casualties

American casualties dropped dramatically in summer 2008. U.S. units had suffered 961 fatalities in 2007, making it the costliest year of the war.[71] In 2008, U.S. fatalities dropped to 322, even with the large-scale offensives of the surge campaign, and weekly battle casualties dropped 57.8 percent between 2007 and 2008.[72] By the summer of 2008, U.S. casualties from non-battle incidents such as electrocution, fires, mine resistant ambush protected (MRAP) rollovers, and suicides began to approach the number of combat casualties. In both September and November 2008, U.S. non-battle deaths (15 in September and 10 in November) exceeded those killed in action (8 in September and 6 in November).[73]

To cut down on fatal accidents, MNF-I assigned Task Force SAFE, a group Petraeus had originally created to investigate deadly electrocutions in troop buildings, to assess vehicle rollovers and other accidents and then suggest preventive measures.[74] The investigation paid particular attention to MRAP accidents, with good reason. The MNF-I investigators discovered that 51 percent of MRAP accidents were due to vehicle rollovers, incidents that well-trained drivers knew how to avoid. MNF-I leaders endorsed the investigators' conclusion that "the MRAP must be treated in training as a combat vehicle, hence requiring crews to undergo the same level of comprehensive training we provide to crewmen for all other weapons systems."[75]

The U.S.-Iraq Security Agreement

Even though coalition commanders expected to have 15 brigades in 2009, they knew that the United States and its partners might be forced to withdraw all troops by the end of 2008. As the months passed, the yet-unsigned U.S.-Iraqi security agreement came to occupy a large portion of MNF-I's attention. Before taking command, Odierno had learned from counterparts in the White House that Maliki was "getting cold feet" about the draft U.S.-Iraq agreement allowing U.S. troops to remain in the country after 2008. With elections on the horizon in both 2009 and 2010, the Iraqi Prime Minister was reluctant to expend the political capital necessary to finalize the deal.[76] Meeting with White House official John Hannah in Baghdad the day before his change of command, Odierno learned that the negotiations were proving deeply divisive for the Iraqi political leadership. The religious parties in particular were publicly against the agreement, though behind closed doors most Iraqi political leaders acknowledged that the sudden departure of U.S. troops at year's end would be disastrous. Addressing rumors that the George W. Bush administration was thinking through a "Plan B" in case the negotiations collapsed—such as returning to the UN to ask for an extension of the UN Security Council Resolution (UNSCR) 1790—Hannah revealed to Odierno that "there is no Plan B." Either the two sides would finalize the agreement or U.S. and other coalition troops would leave by the end of December.[77]

For his part, Odierno believed the security agreement would require extensive MNF-I planning and would likely change the way that U.S. troops operated inside Iraq.[78] It was unclear, for example, whether and how the tens of thousands of contractors working for MNF-I would function and whether they would remain immune from Iraqi laws. Planning for the contractors' possible departure was complicated by a Defense Department order that prevented MNF-I from holding discussions with contractors about post-2008 arrangements.[79] The delay in signing the U.S.-Iraq agreement also put other coalition countries in limbo, because most governments were waiting for the United States to conclude its bilateral agreement with the Maliki government before pursuing their own.[80]

Inside Iraq, the security agreement quickly became the most polarizing domestic political issue as the provincial election season began. Sharp disagreements among the major Iraqi parties paralleled ethnic and sectarian rifts. Among the Shi'a parties, the Sadrists and their allies demanded the immediate expulsion of U.S. troops and organized numerous public protests against the agreement. They prevented Maliki from publicly embracing the agreement out of fear of losing ground to Iranian-backed parties in the January 2009 provincial elections—though both Maliki and Islamic Supreme Council of Iraq privately supported a continued strategic relationship with the United States. Among the Sunni parties, leaders such as Vice President Tariq Hashimi publicly argued against an indefinite American military presence, demanded restraints on U.S. operations against Sunni targets, and pressed for the release of Sunni detainees. Privately, however, most Sunni leaders expressed fears that a U.S. withdrawal would lead to a Shi'a campaign of violence against the Sunni population. Only the Iraqi Kurds publicly expressed full support for a continued U.S. presence, and some Kurdish leaders even suggested that U.S. troops could remain in Kurdistan if the government in Baghdad did not ultimately approve a status of forces agreement. Addressing the Council of Representatives, Speaker of Parliament Mahmud Mashadani wryly observed that where the U.S.-Iraq security agreement was concerned, Iraq's Sunni politicians opposed it in public but supported it in private, Shi'a politicians supported it in public but opposed it in private, and Kurdish politicians supported it in both public and private.

In addition to the Sadrists, some other parties saw opposing the security agreement as a way to weaken Maliki, whom they felt was concentrating too much power in Baghdad. Odierno observed that some Iraqi leaders considered constraining Maliki a higher priority than legalizing the U.S. military presence, which many Iraqis assumed would continue with or without an agreement. "Our assessment is that some Iraqi leaders have mistakenly concluded that the U.S. is not sincere about the necessity of a SOFA [status of forces agreement] and we will continue to operate in Iraq without an agreement when the UNSCR expires," Odierno observed in his first weekly report to Gates in September.[81]

Iranian pressure was a significant factor as well. Upon returning to Baghdad in mid-September, Odierno reported to Gates that he was surprised by "the constant negative drumbeat regarding the SOFA" coming from Iran and was concerned that "Iran has seized the messaging initiative" with "an effective and wide-ranging" propaganda campaign.[82] By late October, Odierno concluded that Maliki had been swayed by Iranian influence and was delaying the agreement to drive a harder bargain with the United States.[83] To counter the Iranian regime's influence, Odierno directed MNF-I leaders to brief their Iraqi counterparts on the numerous security activities that would immediately cease and the vast capabilities that would no longer be at the Iraqi Government's disposal if the coalition suddenly departed. He also advised MNF-I planners to quietly conduct "prudent planning should we be absent a legal framework" when the UNSCR expired.[84]

Nevertheless, on November 27, the Iraqi Parliament approved the security agreement, though Sunni support only came after making the pact subject to a nationwide referendum. Passage followed a series of heated Parliamentary sessions with walkouts by the

Sadrists and other anti-American parties and the sudden resignation of the notoriously erratic Speaker Mashadani. The raucous scenes on the floor of the Parliament did not bode well for future U.S.-Iraqi relations.

Among other stipulations, the final agreement required U.S. combat forces to redeploy outside of Iraq's cities, villages, and localities by June 30, 2009. Complete withdrawal of all U.S. forces from Iraq would follow by December 31, 2011. In the interval, the agreement would place further constraints on U.S. operations: searching households would require a warrant, and arrests or detention of Iraqis would require prior approval from an Iraqi court. Finally, as residual damage from the Nisour Square incident, most of the U.S. military's contractors would lose their immunity to Iraqi law.

Source: DoD photo by Sergeant 1st Class Derren Mazza (Released).

President George W. Bush and Iraqi Prime Minister Nuri al-Maliki Sign the U.S.-Iraq Security Agreement.[85]

The Departure of the Coalition and Redrawing of Battle Space

Dragging out the negotiations led several smaller coalition members to withdraw. In October, the Polish contingent that had long served as the Multi-National Division-Central South (MND-CS) headquarters left, handing Forward Operating Base Echo in Diwaniyah over to a U.S. battalion. The South Korean troops in Iraqi Kurdistan withdrew from Erbil in early December, ending the mission of Multi-National Division-North East (MND-NE). Ten other smaller coalition contingents also left by the end of the year, forcing significant tactical changes. "We cannot underestimate the effect of losing our coalition partners," Odierno wrote to Gates on October 5. "In many cases, they relieved U.S. forces from internal security requirements as well as occupying key battle space. This will cause us to expand U.S. responsibilities as we reduce our footprint."[86] It was essential that

MNF-I maintain a forward presence in each province, Odierno judged, and to cover the new gaps MNC-I would have to make boundary and battle space changes for the remaining units just 9 months after Austin had redrawn unit boundaries following the departure of the surge brigades.[87] In November, Multi-National Division-Baghdad (MND-B) took control of the southern portions of Baghdad province previously held by Multi-National Division-Center (MND-C). MND-C, meanwhile, extended its battle space south to encompass the provinces of Maysan, Dhi Qar, and Muthanna. It also prepared to assume oversight of Multi-National Division-Southeast (MND-SE) following the planned 2009 withdrawal of British troops from Basrah. MND-N expanded its battle space to Erbil to cover the territory previously overseen by the South Korean headquarters of MND-NE.[88]

Source: U.S. Army photo by Specialist Creighton Holub (Released).

U.S. and Romanian Army Soldiers Review Plans During an Observation Mission Near Nasiriyah.[89]

The departure of coalition partners affected the various headquarters in Baghdad as well. Since 2003, the United Kingdom and Australia had provided up to 20 flag officers to the staffs of the theater and operational commands; their impending absence would leave a gap that Odierno believed would require 12 additional U.S. generals to fill.[90] Even harder to replace would be Task Force KNIGHT, the British special operations contingent that had played an important role in the campaigns against AQI and other extremist groups and had an especially significant effect against AQI's car-bomb networks in Baghdad. But with the expiration of the UNSCR, the British were reluctant to leave their special operators open to charges of violating European Union human rights legislation, illustrating one of the complexities of coalition warfare in the 21st century.[91]

***

For the coalition, the situation on the ground in Iraq felt like a military victory by late 2008. With only a handful of violent incidents on most days, Iraq had begun to resemble other countries in the Middle East. AQI, which once had seemed capable of causing the collapse of the Iraqi state, was on the run in a shrinking corner of northwest Iraq, with its most important Syria-based kingpin dead and its foreign fighter networks in disarray. With the security situation improving to a degree that would have been unthinkable at the beginning of the year, MNF-I's intent to shift to a stabilization mission seemed timely and necessary to cement the security gains.

However, warning signs abounded. The incapacity of the government meant that Iraqi leadership in stabilization tasks such as governance and economic development would come slowly. The receding of AQI in northern Iraq gave way to a potential Arab-Kurd war in which the governments in Baghdad and Erbil would be on opposite sides. Finally, there was the turbulent way in which the U.S.-Iraqi SOFA had been reached. The Sadrists and the Iranian regime had been able to use the issue to regain some of the political advantage they had lost during the spring of 2008. At the same time, Prime Minister Maliki had proved to be a reluctant signer, leading some coalition leaders to question whether he intended to maintain a long-term security relationship with the United States.

As if to illustrate the difficulty of the situation for the United States, the December 14 ceremony in Baghdad to mark the passage of the security agreement ended in chaos when an Iraqi journalist threw his shoes at President Bush in protest during a joint press conference with Maliki. It was Bush's final public act related to the Iraq War. Barely a month later, the United States would have a new President and a dramatically different Iraq policy.

ENDNOTES - CHAPTER 11

1. DoD photo by Jerry Morrison, "Secretary of Defense [Image 11 of 13]," DVIDS Identifier 115860, August 16, 2008, Released to Public, available from *https://www.dvidshub.net/image/115860/secretary-defense.*

2. General Raymond T. Odierno Iraq Notebook No. 1, August to October 18, 2008, p. 13, not dated but probably was in July, before taking command. All unpublished documents in this chapter, unless otherwise stated, are in the Chief of Staff of the Army (CSA) Operation IRAQI FREEDOM (OIF) Study Group archives, Army Heritage and Education Center (AHEC), Carlisle, PA.

3. MNF-I, SECDEF Weekly Update, September 15-21, 2008.

4. MNF-I, SECDEF Weekly Update, October 27-November 2, 2008.

5. MNF-I, SECDEF Weekly Update, November 24-30, 2008; and December 29, 2008-January 4, 2009.

6. MNF-I, SECDEF Weekly Update, December 29, 2008-January 4, 2009.

7. DoD photo by Staff Sergeant J. B. Jaso, "Table Time," September 8, 2008, Released to Public, available from *https://www.flickr.com/photos/mnfiraq/4316536564/in/album-72157623189185653/.*

8. MNF-I, SECDEF Weekly Update, November 17-23, 2008.

9. Eric Owles, "Then and Now: A New Chapter for Baghdad Book Market," *The New York Times*, December 18, 2008.

10. DoD photo by Specialist Grant Okubo, "Prime Minister Maliki attends Mutanabi Book Market reopening [Image 4 of 4]," DVIDS Identifier 137986, December 18, 2008, Released to Public, available from *https://www.dvidshub.net/image/137986/prime-minister-maliki-attends-mutanabi-book-market-reopening*.

11. MNF-I, SECDEF Weekly Update, September 29-October 5, 2008.

12. Governance Assessment Team Rpt, Baghdad, Iraq, April 2008, p. 2; Interview, Combat Studies Institute (CSI) Contemporary Operations Study Team with Brigadier General H. R. McMaster, November 20, 2010; David Petraeus, "How We Won in Iraq," *Foreign Policy*, October 29, 2013, available from *http://www.foreignpolicy.com/articles/2013/10/29/david_petraeus_how_we_won_the_surge_in_iraq*.

13. Report to Congress, *Measuring Stability and Security in Iraq*, Washington, DC: Department of Defense, June 13, 2008, pp. v, 11.

14. Interview, CW2 Andrew Wickland with Major General Rick Waddell, November 13, 2014.

15. Governance Assessment Team Rpt, Baghdad, Iraq, April 2008, p. 5.

16. Ibid., p. 3; Manuscript (Ms), *On Point*, Vol. IV, Fort Leavenworth, KS: Combat Studies Institute, September 25, 2014, Chapter 9, p. 21.

17. Interview, Wickland with Waddell, November 13, 2014.

18. Ibid.

19. Ibid.

20. Ibid.

21. Ibid.

22. MNF-I, SECDEF Weekly Update, August 25-31, 2008.

23. MNF-I Quarterly Cmd Rpt, October 1-December 31, 2008.

24. Quil Lawrence, "A Precarious Peace in Northern Iraq," Middle East Research and Information Project, October 1, 2009, available from *http://www.merip.org/mero/mero100109*.

25. Ibid.

26. MNF-I, SECDEF Weekly Update, September 1-7, 2008; September 8-14, 2008; and September 15-21, 2008.

27. Odierno Iraq Notebook No. 1, September 15, 2008, entry.

28. Ms, *On Point*, Vol. IV, Chapter 7, p. 75; Interview, CSI Contemporary Operations Study Team with Lieutenant General Lloyd Austin, May 12, 2010.

29. Bill Roggio, "US Forces kill al Qaeda in Iraq's Deputy Commander," *Long War Journal*, October 15, 2008, available from *http://www.longwarjournal.org/archives/2008/10/us_forces_kill_al_qa_1.php*.

30. MNF-I, SECDEF Weekly Update, October 6-12, 2008.

31. Odierno Iraq Notebook No. 1, October 14, 2008, entry.

32. MNF-I, SECDEF Weekly Update, September 1-7, 2008.

33. MNF-I, SECDEF Weekly Update, September 15-21, 2008.

34. DoD photo by Staff Sergeant JoAnn Makinano, "Al Qirwan neighborhood [Image 6 of 38]," DVIDS Identifier 142402, December 24, 2008, Released to Public, available from *https://www.dvidshub.net/image/142402/al-qirwan-neighborhood*.

35. Odierno Iraq Notebook No. 1, October 10, 2008, entry; MNF-I, SECDEF Weekly Update, October 6-12, 2008; Aidan Jones, "Killings force 13,000 Christians to flee Mosul," *The Guardian*, October 24, 2008.

36. Odierno Iraq Notebook No. 1, October 12, 2008, entry.

37. MNF-I, SECDEF Weekly Update, October 6-12, 2008. Odierno also contemplated recruiting 700 Ninawa Province Christians for the National Police, though there is no indication this initiative was ultimately undertaken. See Odierno Iraq Notebook No. 1, October 13, 2008, entry.

38. Odierno Iraq Notebook No. 1, October 13, 2008, entry.

39. Odierno Iraq Notebook No. 1, October 12, 2008.

40. DoD photo courtesy Joint Combat Camera Center Iraq, "U.S. forces search car [Image 3 of 4]," DVIDS Identifier 124327, October 15, 2008, Released to Public, available from *https://www.dvidshub.net/image/124327/us-forces-search-car*.

41. MNF-I, SECDEF Weekly Update, October 6-12, 2008.

42. MNF-I, SECDEF Weekly Update, November 3-9, 2008.

43. MNF-I, SECDEF Weekly Update, October 20-26, 2008.

44. MNF-I, SECDEF Weekly Update, November 3-9, 2008.

45. Ibid.

46. Odierno Iraq Notebook No. 1, October 6-7, 2008, entry.

47. Quarterly Cmd Rpt, October 1-December 31, 2008, MNF-I, February 10, 2009.

48. Odierno Iraq Notebook No. 1, December 16, 2008, entry.

49. MNF-I, SECDEF Weekly Update, October 27-November 2, 2008.

50. MNF-I, SECDEF Weekly Update, December 22-28, 2008.

51. Odierno Iraq Notebook No. 1, December 10, 2008.

52. MNF-I, SECDEF Weekly Update, November 3-9, 2008.

53. Odierno Iraq Notebook No. 1, December 10, 2008, entry.

54. MNF-I, SECDEF Weekly Update, November 10-16, 2008; and November 24-30, 2008.

55. Interview, Lynne Chandler Garcia, CSI Contemporary Operations Study Team, with Vice Admiral David H. Buss, U.S. Navy, Fort Leavenworth, KS, April 26, 2012.

56. MNF-I, SECDEF Weekly Update, October 6-12, 2008, p. 4.

57. Interview, Lieutenant Colonel Robert Kirkland, U.S. Army Center of Military History (CMH), with Admiral David Buss, June 25, 2009.

58. Interview, Colonel Joel Rayburn, CSA OIF Study Group, with Kenneth Pollack, February 11, 2016.

59. Ibid.

60. Interview, Lieutenant Colonel William Shane Story, MNF-I Historian, with General (Ret.) Anthony C. Zinni, October 24, 2008.

61. Interview, CSA OIF Study Group with Pollack, February 11, 2016.

62. Ibid.

63. Interview, Kirkland with Buss, June 25, 2009.

64. MNF-I, SECDEF Weekly Update, September 29-October 5, 2008; and November 10-16, 2008.

65. DoD photo by Specialist Chuck Gill, "Iraqi Government Assumes Control of Sons of Iraq [Image 11 of 12]," DVIDS Identifier 117573, September 18, 2008, Released to Public, available from *https://www.dvidshub.net/image/117573/iraqi-government-assumes-control-sons-iraq*.

66. DoD photo by Staff Sergeant James Hunter, "Sons of Iraq in northwest Baghdad receive first payment [Image 3 of 3]," DVIDS Identifier 128885, November 9, 2008, Released to Public, available from *https://www.dvidshub.net/image/128885/sons-iraq-northwest-baghdad-receive-first-payment*.

67. Odierno Iraq Notebook No. 1, October 23, 2008, entry; MNF-I, SECDEF Weekly Update, December 1-7, 2008.

68. Interview, CSA OIF Study Group with Michael Pregent, June 12, 2014.

69. Odierno Iraq Notebook No. 1, entries for October 4, 2008, and October 23, 2008.

70. MNF-I, SECDEF Weekly Update, December 1-7, 2008.

71. Chart, Operation IRAQI FREEDOM, Iraq Coalition Casualties: Fatalities by Year and Month, available from *http://icasualties.org/iraq/ByMonth.aspx*, accessed May 13, 2015.

72. Ibid.; Rpt, Center for Army Analysis, Casualty Analysis-Trends for Operations IRAQI FREEDOM and ENDURING FREEDOM (2008-2009).

73. MNF-I, SECDEF Weekly Update, September 29-October 5, 2008; and November 24-30, 2008.

74. MNF-I, SECDEF Weekly Update, September 1-7, 2008; October 29-November 5, 2008; August 4-10, 2008; August 18-24, 2008; and September 8-14, 2008.

75. MNF-I, SECDEF Weekly Update, August 18-24, 2008.

76. Odierno Iraq Notebook No. 1, July 28, 2008, entry.

77. Odierno Iraq Notebook No. 1, September 15, 2008.

78. Odierno Iraq Notebook No. 1, August 12, 2008.

79. MNF-I, SECDEF Weekly Update, October 27-November 2, 2008.

80. Odierno Iraq Notebook No. 1, August 5, 2008, entry.

81. MNF-I, SECDEF Weekly Update, September 15-21, 2008.

82. Ibid.; and MNF-I, SECDEF Weekly Update, September 22-28, 2008.

83. MNF-I, SECDEF Weekly Update, October 20-26, 2008.

84. MNF-I, SECDEF Weekly Update, October 27-November 2, 2008.

85. DoD photo by Sergeant 1st Class Derren Mazza, "Bush visits Iraq, meets Maliki [Image 7 of 10]," DVIDS Identifier 136588, December 14, 2008, Released to Public, available from *https://www.dvidshub.net/image/136588/bush-visits-iraq-meets-maliki*.

86. MNF-I, SECDEF Weekly Update, September 29-October 5, 2008.

87. Ibid.

88. MNF-I, SECDEF Weekly Update, November 17-23, 2008.

89. U.S. Army photo by Specialist Creighton Holub, "Teamwork," November 4, 2008, Released to Public, available from *https://www.flickr.com/photos/mnfiraq/4316569490/in/album-72157623313790500/*.

90. MNF-I, SECDEF Weekly Update, November 3-9, 2008.

91. MNF-I, SECDEF Weekly Update, October 13-19, 2008.

CHAPTER 12

OUT OF THE CITIES, JANUARY-JUNE 2009

A NEW IRAQ POLICY FOR THE UNITED STATES

The arrival of the Barack Obama administration in January 2009 brought a dramatic change in the American policy and posture in Iraq. As a candidate, then-Senator Obama had advocated a withdrawal of U.S. forces from Iraq, and upon taking office, he moved quickly to implement this plan.

In late October 2008, before the Presidential election, General Raymond Odierno approved the early departure of one brigade based on Iraq's improving security conditions, but in early December he recommended to the Joint Chiefs of Staff that U.S. forces remain in Iraq for the full 3 years specified in the December 2008 Security Agreement, at levels based on local conditions.[1] Odierno envisioned a "flexible plan" that would include deliberate decision points at which commanders in Iraq would have the latitude to make "careful transitions" in U.S. troop levels.[2]

However, the new administration's policy guidance ran counter to Odierno's recommendation. On President Obama's first day in office, the National Security Council (NSC) tasked Odierno and Ambassador Ryan Crocker to develop three different options for the timed drawdown of U.S. troops in a fixed period of either 23 months, 19 months, or 16 months. The last of these reflected the time that Obama had pledged to withdraw American forces. The NSC specified that none of these options was to be conditions-based.

On January 28, 2009, Odierno and Crocker told Washington that the 23-month withdrawal timeline offered the least risk to security and political gains, but the President chose the 19-month timeline. The specifics of the drawdown were important: Obama directed that the U.S. "combat mission" should end within the 19-month period, after which no U.S. "combat troops" could remain in Iraq. However, an undetermined residual force could remain beyond the expiration of the "combat mission" to lend military assistance. The NSC left Odierno and Crocker to determine the exact purpose and size of the military assistance mission while also instructing Crocker to define the size of the U.S. diplomatic mission.[3]

As they highlighted the risks of rapid withdrawal, Odierno and Crocker ran into resistance. When the National Intelligence Council prepared a draft national intelligence estimate on Iraq in February 2009, Odierno and Crocker objected to what they believed was an overly optimistic assessment of the security situation both considered unsustainable without a major U.S. military presence. Odierno and Crocker were concerned that a too-rosy intelligence estimate would encourage policymakers to disengage without considering the negative consequences.[4] It was also the third year in a row that Multi-National Force-Iraq (MNF-I) had disagreed with a national intelligence estimate on Iraq.

At the same time, MNF-I hosted a RAND Corporation team conducting a congressionally mandated "withdrawal study" to assess whether U.S. troops should stay in the country through 2011 or withdraw sooner.[5] The options that the study team was asked to consider, which were potentially faster than those the President envisioned, illustrated the mounting political pressure to reduce the U.S. troop presence in Iraq.

POLITICAL CULMINATION OF THE SURGE: THE JANUARY 2009 PROVINCIAL ELECTIONS

By early 2009, Washington was more optimistic about Iraq than those struggling with the obstacles on the ground. Certainly, the January 2009 Iraqi provincial elections had gone well. Many Sunnis had boycotted the previous provincial elections in 2005, as had the Sadrists, and both groups had thus been frozen out of local government for the 4 years that followed. During that time, the Sadrists and Sunni rejectionist groups had conducted separate, multi-year insurgencies against the Iraqi Government and the coalition. The January 2009 elections provided an opportunity to redress local political imbalances that had been one of the most important drivers of conflict. The incumbents who had won power in the boycotted January 2005 election were reluctant to hold provincial elections in 2009, fearing they would lose some local power. However, pressure from the Awakening, the Sadrists, the Iraqi Shi'a clerical leaders in Najaf, and the United States forced the issue. The voting took place January 31 except in the three predominantly Kurdish provinces, which planned to vote later, and in Kirkuk, where the Arab-Kurd political deadlock made voting impossible.

The 2009 provincial vote was the most peaceful election Iraq had experienced since the 2003 invasion. During the 2005 elections, there were more than 400 attacks per week. To prevent similar events in 2009, Multi-National Forces-Iraq (MNF-I) and the Iraqi security forces (ISF) carried out a series of spoiling attacks, supported by a surge of intelligence, surveillance, and reconnaissance (ISR) resources from U.S. Central Command (CENTCOM).[6] With 750,000 Iraqi soldiers, police, and other government officials deployed, the 2009 elections saw less than a quarter of the attacks that had taken place in 2005, though five Sunni candidates in Mosul were assassinated before the voting.[7]

The January 2009 elections brought sweeping change to Iraq's local governments. The Iraqi electorate penalized the incumbent parties, whom Iraqis blamed for the sectarian warfare of 2006-2008, voting them out of power in each of the 14 provinces that held an election.[8] MNF-I found the results encouraging on several levels. The Sunni communities that had boycotted the election 4 years earlier turned out to vote in large numbers in Anbar, Ninawa, Salahadin, and Diyala. In many cases, they voted for candidates associated with the Awakening who had advocated national reconciliation, factors that Odierno and MNF-I believed would begin to reverse the broader Sunni community's perception of its own marginalization.[9] Parties that ran on secular nationalist platforms polled significantly better than Islamist parties, reversing the trend of the 2005 national elections. Parties associated with Iran polled most poorly of all—especially the Islamic Supreme Council of Iraq (ISCI), which lost control of seven southern governorships. Most significant in Odierno's view was that the Sunni "Hadba Gathering" bloc headed by Osama Nujaifi, Sheikh Abdullah al Yawar, and other Ninawa notables took control of the Ninawa provincial council from the Kurdish parties that had won it in 2005. MNF-I hoped the transfer of power in Mosul from Kurdish politicians to Sunni ones would rob al-Qaeda in Iraq (AQI) and other rejectionist groups of their remaining political support in the province that was AQI's sole remaining sanctuary.[10] These political trends seemed to bode well for the national elections scheduled for late 2009 or early 2010, and seemed to indicate that the surge campaign of 2007-2008 might have set the stage for a stable Iraq.

DRAWDOWN AND CHANGE OF OPERATING POSTURE FOR MNF-I

After the January elections, MNF-I turned its full attention to implementing Obama's new drawdown policy and implementing the security agreement that the George W. Bush administration had finalized in late 2008. Under Obama's directive, MNF-I would need to reduce U.S. troop levels from 142,000 in February 2009 to about 50,000 at the end of summer 2010, a reduction that would require a near-continual redeployment of troops, redrawing of unit boundaries and transfer of responsibilities across the country. The diminishing force also would have to change the way it operated. The U.S.-Iraq security agreement specified that U.S. troops would leave Iraq's cities by June 30, 2009, after which American units could no longer conduct unilateral operations or raids but would have to work through their ISF counterparts to obtain warrants from Iraqi courts ahead of any operation. They would also be required to coordinate their movements and operations with their ISF counterparts—with the Iraqis having the power to veto U.S. operations.

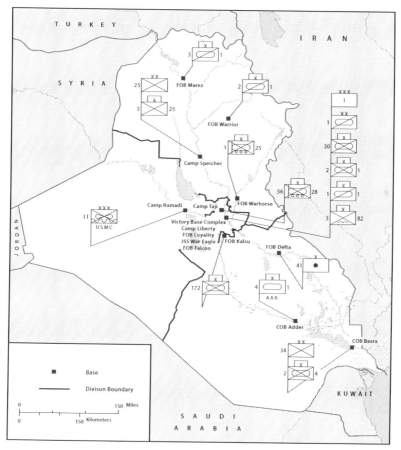

Map created by the official cartographer at the U.S. Army Center of Military History, Washington, DC.

Map 21. MNF-I Unit Disposition, June 2009.

459

Most of the units that would have to adopt this different way of operating were newly arrived. The annual turnover of coalition units that had taken place between February and April in each year since 2004 occurred again in 2009. The number of U.S. brigades in Iraq held steady at 15, but the overall troop strength had decreased. By February, MNF-I's total strength was down to 147,000, from a high of 182,000 at the height of the surge in October 2007.[11] It would continue to fall through the summer. In early March, Odierno announced that MNF-I would shrink by another 12,000 American and 4,000 international troops by September. As the drawdown progressed, MNF-I would lose most of its multi-national character, becoming almost a solely American force. Most of the foreign contingents already had departed Iraq with the expiration of the United Nations (UN) Security Council Resolution at the end of 2008.

On March 31, the British Multi-National Division-South East (MND-SE) departed Iraq as well, ending Great Britain's 6-year deployment in southern Iraq. During that time, British units had suffered 179 troops killed and more than 5,000 wounded. In a ceremony at the Basrah airfield, British Foreign Secretary David Miliband watched as MND-SE handed control of its area of operations to Major General Michael Oates's Multi-National Division-Center (MND-C), which had been gradually expanding its battle space southward from Baghdad since June 2008 and would be renamed MND-South after the British departure.

Source: DoD photo by Specialist Darryl Montgomery (Released).

**British Major General Andrew Salmon, Commander of MND-SE,
Hands Responsibility for Southern Iraq to U.S. Major General Michael Oates,
Commander of MND-C.[12]**

The withdrawal of MND-SE left Multi-National Corps-Iraq (MNC-I) with four U.S.-led division headquarters. In addition to Oates's MND-C headquarters in the south, Major General Robert Caslen's 25th Infantry Division remained in control of Multi-National Division-North (MND-N), with about 23,000 troops spread among its 4 brigade combat teams (BCTs). In March, II Marine Expeditionary Force (MEF) arrived to assume duties as Multi-National Force-West (MNF-W) in Anbar, replacing I MEF. In the same month, Major General Daniel Bolger's 1st Cavalry Division arrived to become Multi-National Division-Baghdad (MND-B), replacing Major General Jeffery Hammond's 4th Infantry Division in command of 35,000 U.S. troops and 6 BCTs in the Baghdad region. These four divisions would fall under a new corps command. A few days after the British departure, Lieutenant General Lloyd Austin and XVIII Airborne Corps departed as well, replaced by Lieutenant General Charles H. Jacoby, Jr.'s I Corps in early April. The XVIII Airborne Corps' year in Iraq had opened with the unexpected war against the Shi'a militant groups across central and southern Iraq but had ended with Iraq at its calmest since the 2003 invasion. Whereas Austin had assumed command of 20 U.S. brigades and more than 10,000 international troops in early 2008, Jacoby took command of a force that by September would consist of only 12 U.S. brigades covering the entire country. Jacoby also inherited a shrinking support structure. By the end of March, the coalition had 133,000 contractors supporting its operations, a decrease of 18,000 since the beginning of 2009.[13]

With this smaller operating force and fewer enablers, Odierno and his senior commanders had 5 months, February through June, to make as much progress as possible. During these last months of relatively unconstrained operations, MNF-I worked to accelerate the development of the ISF that would have to take full responsibility for their nation's security by midsummer. Odierno's units also intended to maintain pressure on AQI in northern Iraq with a final U.S.-Iraqi offensive against the extremist group in its remote sanctuaries. MNF-I and the U.S. Embassy hoped to continue reconciliation initiatives such as the Sons of Iraq and to fragment further the Sunni insurgency, bringing additional portions of it to the negotiating table. At the same time, MNF-I intended to neutralize the Iranian regime's Shi'a militant proxies and prevent their resurgence in Iraqi cities. Above all, MNF-I would have to vacate its many bases, outposts, and joint security stations in the Iraqi cities without allowing enemy forces to exploit them. This was a tall order.

IRAQI SECURITY FORCES DEVELOPMENT

The Iraqi Army and Iraqi National Police, which would have to fill the gap as the coalition's troops diminished, had come a long way since the civil war of 2006, when Sunni and Shi'a militants had outmatched an ISF riddled with sectarianism and corruption. The ISF's overall strength had grown rapidly, reaching 565,000 soldiers and police by the end of 2008, compared to 323,000 2 years earlier.[14] At the time of Obama's policy change in January 2009, the Iraqi Army had 175 combat battalions along with 5 special operations battalions and 5 infrastructure security battalions.[15] These units and the Iraqi police had taken the lead role in securing the January 31 provincial elections, splitting duties between them so that an inner ring of police guarded polling sites while the Iraqi Army secured an outer perimeter, with coalition troops in an overwatch role. The Interior Ministry had even deployed 500 female police officers to search and counter the threat of female suicide bombers as the voting took place.[16] With roughly 750,000 Iraqi soldiers, Iraqi police, and coalition troops on duty election day, the voting occurred without incident. After passing the test of election security, in February and March the ISF displayed a growing capability to conduct population security when it deployed more than 40,000 soldiers and police to secure the Arba'een pilgrimage route to Karbala in response to a wave of attacks against Shi'a pilgrims. The following month, the ISF secured more than a million pilgrims as they gathered for a Shi'a religious holiday in Samarra.[17]

However, beyond these relatively simple infantry- and police-based security activities, MNF-I found it difficult to develop the Iraqi military's more advanced capabilities. In early 2009, the Iraqi Ministry of Defense established a program to oversee the purchase and fielding of M1A1 tanks from the United States, an addition that would finally give Iraq's ground forces an offensive capability.[18] The new tanks would be a critical capability in an Iraqi military that the coalition and Minister of Defense Abdel Qader intended to grow to a strength of 352,000, with 14 army divisions. But in spring 2009, coalition and Iraqi military leaders learned that the rest of the Iraqi Government and Parliament was willing to fund only 253,000 Ministry of Defense forces, far fewer than Qader and MNF-I expected and believed the security situation required as U.S. forces withdrew. Finding ways to overcome the shortfalls in funding and manpower fell to Lieutenant General Frank Helmick's Multi-National Security Transition Command-Iraq (MNSTC-I).[19]

Meanwhile, the Iraqi Air Force, which once was one of the most capable in the Middle East, lagged far behind the army. Though the Iraqi Ministry of Defense was moving ahead with plans to expand its air force personnel to about 6,000 and to open a training center at Tikrit air base, the air force lacked a modern jet fighter. Plans for Iraq to buy F-16s and their accompanying training aircraft from the United States moved slowly because of the same budget shortfall that cut the Ministry of Defense's overall troop strength. The Iraqi Air Force had an air operations center capable of overseeing 350 sorties per week, but it lacked the broader air traffic control capability needed to control Iraq's airspace.[20]

Development of the small Iraqi Navy outpaced the air force. It operated 40 or more patrols each week in the Persian Gulf, where about 90 percent of Iraq's oil exports flowed through vulnerable terminals. The Iraqi Navy also was building a new pier and seawall at the country's only port of Umm Qasr, where the Navy would station a fleet of newly purchased Italian patrol boats.[21] Despite these positive developments, the coalition's program to train the Iraqi Navy fell victim to politics in 2009. Odierno and other U.S. leaders hoped to maintain as large a force of trainers and advisers from other countries as possible, particularly from Great Britain. The Nuri al-Maliki government, unfortunately, did not share MNF-I's sentiment. After the departure of MND-SE, MNF-I and its North Atlantic Treaty Organization (NATO) counterparts hoped to quickly negotiate an agreement with the Iraqi Government under which a British military assistance mission could remain in the country, including the naval contingent training the Iraqi Navy in Umm Qasr.

In late 2008, the United Kingdom (UK) and Iraq agreed that British troops could remain in the country until May 31, 2009, while the two countries negotiated a longer-term arrangement. However, as the deadline approached, Maliki seemed to view British training with ambivalence and sought only to limit the legal immunities for UK forces. At times, the Iraqi officials seemed driven by their long-standing resentment of their former British colonial masters. Iraqi politics played a role in the rocky negotiations as well. "[T]he PM [Prime Minister] sees a UK agreement as a political vulnerability exploitable by his political rivals," Odierno reported to Secretary of Defense (SECDEF) Robert Gates after the Anglo-Iraqi negotiations stalled in mid-May.[22] In the meantime, with no settled UK-Iraq agreement, other NATO countries were reluctant to deploy their own contingents of trainers and advisers, leaving NATO Training Mission-Iraq (NTM-I), the multinational training arm of MNSTC-I, at just two-thirds of its required strength.[23] In the last days of May, with no legal basis for staying in the country, the remaining British contingent, including the entire UK naval training mission, left for Kuwait to await news of whether the Iraqi Government would allow them to return. At the 11th hour, Maliki and the UK Government reached an agreement that would permit British forces to remain in Iraq for an additional year, but Maliki limited the British contingent to just five ships and 100 troops ashore, far fewer British troops than MNF-I had hoped to include in the NATO training mission.[24]

That Maliki was willing to allow a severe disruption in the training and advisory program for one of Iraq's military services surprised and dismayed coalition commanders, but it was a sign of things to come. Within days of the UK-Iraq agreement, Maliki and Qader began pressing U.S. leaders to change the name of MNF-I to U.S. Forces-Iraq to reflect the departure of the other national contingents.[25]

THE CONTINUING PURSUIT OF AQI

Back to Diyala and Mosul

As the coalition withdrawal from the Iraqi cities drew closer, MNF-I leaders and their Iraqi counterparts decided to conduct additional combined operations in northern Iraq where AQI still had sanctuaries and support. Despite a series of four large-scale security operations in Diyala in 2007-2008, the province remained unstable. Diyala was "a microcosm of the nation's political challenges, with its Shi'a population maintaining close ties across the Iranian border via the Old Silk Road, its Ba'athist enclave serving as a key Sunni buffer zone, AQI attempting to hang on, and Arabs and Kurds disputing the status of northeastern parts of the province," Odierno wrote to Gates in March.[26] Some AQI commanders and fighters fleeing the fall 2008 operations in Mosul had been able to make their way back to their old sanctuaries in the sparsely populated badlands east of the Diyala River and in the Hamrin Mountains to the west, where they were beyond the reach of coalition and Iraqi troops but close enough to populated areas to launch attacks, especially against the Sons of Iraq. The Diyala Operations Command was created in 2008 to partner with MND-N and coordinate ISF activities against this threat, but by early 2009, Prime Minister Maliki had grown frustrated with its performance and sacked its commander. The residual AQI presence in Diyala was both a security and political threat, because AQI attacks had the potential to cause Sunni-Shi'a or Arab-Kurd strife as the newly elected provincial council parties attempted to form a local government in which Sunnis were likely to have the leading role.[27]

Source: DoD photo courtesy U.S. Navy (Released).

**An Explosive Ordnance Technician Prepares to Destroy a Bunker
During Operations in Diyala Province.[28]**

MNC-I and Iraqi forces launched a series of operations in spring 2009 to push AQI out of its remote sanctuaries and prevent the group from launching attacks into the cities of the Diyala Valley as coalition troops prepared to leave. In early March, a large operation involving the 1st Brigade, 25th Infantry Division, and the 21st Iraqi Army Brigade took aim at AQI in the countryside near Balad Ruz, especially in the area coalition troops called the Turki Bowl, which had been difficult for U.S. units to clear in 2008. As U.S. and Iraqi soldiers pushed into parts of the Turki Bowl that were inaccessible except on foot or motorcycle, they uncovered extensive AQI bunker complexes, some of which had to be reduced by air strikes after firefights with the extremists.[29] A second phase of the operation in late March uncovered large remote weapons and ammunition caches that AQI had abandoned.[30]

Meanwhile, farther north, U.S. and Iraqi troops cleared the areas around Hamrin Lake between Muqdadiyah and Khanaqin, another hard-to-access area where AQI groups had a safe haven for several years.[31] AQI responded by showing it could attack larger nearby towns. A late March suicide bombing killed 26 civilians in Jalawla near the shores of Hamrin Lake, and 2 deadlier bombings the following month in Baqubah killed 80 people.[32]

The operations near Khanaqin risked rekindling the political crisis that had taken place when Iraqi Army troops and peshmerga faced off against each other the previous fall. Arab-Kurd tensions already had been stoked again in February when Prime Minister Maliki decided to deploy the 12th Iraqi Division to the vicinity of Kurdish-controlled Kirkuk, ostensibly to protect oil infrastructure in the area but in actuality to assert political advantage over Iraq's Kurdish parties.[33] When Iraqi troops began to push toward Khanaqin again in April, the Iraqi Army, the peshmerga, and MNC-I exchanged liaison officers and conducted a combined rehearsal of the operation in order to avoid another confrontation.[34] It was a cooperative model that Odierno would apply along the entire Green Line in 2010.

U.S. and Iraqi troops conducted further clearing operations in Mosul at the same time. As had been the case in Diyala, the late 2008 operations in Mosul had disrupted AQI but not fully dislodged the group from its long-term support zones in and around the city. Part of the problem was the ISF's inability to hold neighborhoods once they were cleared. "In the past, the ISF in Mosul have been reluctant to maintain a presence in cleared neighborhoods, favoring raids and checkpoints instead," Odierno explained to Gates in February 2009.[35] This assessment followed a difficult week during which four AQI suicide car bombs targeted Iraqi and coalition troops, with one of them killing 3d Battalion, 8th Cavalry Regiment, commander Lieutenant Colonel Gary Derby and his three-man personal security detail.[36]

Source: U.S. Air Force photo by Staff Sergeant JoAnn S. Makinano (Released).

U.S. Army Soldiers and Iraqi Police Search Houses in West Mosul During Operation NEW HOPE.[37]

On February 20, MNC-I and the ISF launched Operation NEW HOPE, which Odierno described as a "comprehensive COIN [counterinsurgency] operation" involving six additional U.S. battalions, as well as forces from both the 2d and 3d Iraqi Divisions in Ninawa.[38] By the beginning of March, the combined U.S.-Iraqi troops had established a presence in AQI's former neighborhoods and appeared to have disrupted the extremists' operations, especially its ability to collect funds through extortion.[39] Within days of entering the neighborhoods, Iraqi and coalition units began to report a significant increase in tips from the local population. The increased tips drove targeted operations against AQI leaders such as the Islamic State of Iraq's "Minister of Oil," who was captured in the first week of March.[40] A few weeks later, coalition special operators apprehended a series of senior terrorist leaders in the area, including Ahmad Mohammed Ali al-Tai, the AQI "Wali" (governor or guardian) of the entire Mosul region.[41]

Yet the sprawling metropolis of 2 million people was not wholly under coalition-ISF control, especially the city's old quarter, where a maze of narrow streets and passageways made clearing and holding operations difficult. In the medieval neighborhoods of Old Mosul, AQI maintained a presence that it used to launch an average of 35 attacks per week across Mosul in April and May, far higher than the weekly average in any other province.[42] On April 9, an AQI suicide bomber drove a dump truck packed with 10,000 pounds of explosives into an Iraqi police compound in south Mosul just as a U.S. patrol entered. The attack killed 5 U.S. Soldiers and 3 Iraqis while wounding more than 60 people. It was the largest U.S. death toll from a single attack in more than a year.

To combat the AQI threat in Old Mosul, a combined force of the 1st Iraqi National Police Brigade, a local police battalion, and U.S. forces systematically cleared the thousands of buildings. By late May, an Iraqi emergency response battalion had arrived to become the hold force.[43] The operations appeared to have significant results: MNF-I observed in late May that AQI's improvised explosive device (IED) and indirect fire attacks in Mosul had become largely ineffective.[44] MNF-I also learned that AQI financiers had lost the ability to extort funds from their richest targets in the north, including the AsiaCell phone company, Bayji oil refinery, and Badush cement factory, leading to an assessment of a 50 percent drop in income.[45]

Despite the progress, both coalition and Iraqi commanders felt that fully securing Mosul would require several more months beyond the June 30 deadline for withdrawing U.S. forces from the cities. After patrolling the city himself, Odierno believed MNF-I needed 4 to 6 additional months, in part, because AQI leaders were desperate to maintain a foothold in the city and were committing resources from across Iraq to the fight. In April, Ahmad Zayd, one of AQI's captured Mosul emirs, had told coalition officials that AQI considered Mosul "its last opportunity at retaining viability in the country of Iraq," indicating that the group would invest heavily in regenerating its presence in the city if coalition-ISF military pressure were relieved.[46]

Rampant corruption in Mosul's courts worried coalition leaders as well. Hundreds of AQI and other insurgent detainees captured during the springtime operations were freed by intimidating or bribing judges and other Iraqi officials.[47] Similarly, AQI and other insurgent groups infiltrated the Mosul police forces. To counteract the penetration, the coalition and the Interior Ministry opened a new police college with a vetted training cadre that could screen recruits to keep out AQI sympathizers, but this process of generating trusted police would take time.[48]

Source: DoD photo by Specialist Daniel Nelson (Released).

General Raymond Odierno Meets With MNC-I Commander Lieutenant General Charles Jacoby and MND-N Commander Major General Robert Caslen, Jr., in Mosul.[49]

In response to these concerns, Ninawah Operations Commander Major General Hassan Karim and MND-N commander Caslen provided a joint assessment to their chains of command in which they recommended that coalition troops remain inside the city until October 31. Even though Odierno doubted Maliki would accept the 4-month extension beyond the June 30 deadline, he was able to convince the Iraqi Ministry of Defense to dispatch two additional army brigades to the city later in the month.[50] Nevertheless, in mid-June, Odierno reported to Gates that "our commanders remain uneasy about our reduced presence in Mosul," just days before the withdrawal deadline.[51]

AQI's Resilience

AQI had staying power in Ninawa Province because its Syria-based foreign-fighter network had been rebuilt after the raid that killed Abu Ghadiyah in October 2008. Under the leadership of a new kingpin called Abu Khalaf, the former Ghadiyah network pushed North African AQI operatives from Syria into Mosul to carry out suicide attacks. Working through CENTCOM, MNF-I provided the Tunisian Government with information to interdict the jihadi network, but not before the Tunisian terrorists had carried out several major attacks in Mosul. On March 31, a Tunisian suicide truck bomber attacked a police headquarters next to Mosul's main train station, and on April 9, another Tunisian drove the explosive-laden truck that killed five U.S. Soldiers and three Iraqis.[52] As AQI's Mosul networks came under intense pressure during Operation NEW HOPE in March and April, AQI leaders apparently requested a surge of suicide bombers from the Syria-based facilitation network, which helped the terrorist group maintain its operations in Mosul even as its local networks were dismantled.[53]

The reemergence of the Syria facilitation network forced MNC-I to position additional ISR resources in western Ninawa where AQI's "Border Emir" had operated earlier, and to conduct additional spoiling raids on the infiltration routes across the Jazeera desert.[54] The problem was not just a Syria-based one, however. In early May, MNF-I reported the discovery of a Kurdish AQI "battalion" that pushed fighters and weapons into the Mosul area from the east. Meanwhile, far to the south, some AQI operatives rousted from Ninawa Province returned to the seam between the northern Baghdad belts and eastern Anbar. Those who migrated back to the Abu Ghraib and Karmah areas attempted to reconstitute support bases in areas from which the Sons of Iraq had driven them during 2007-2008.[55] Within Baghdad itself, AQI's car bomb network was being rebuilt after a long period of near-dormancy.[56]

As these AQI networks began to reactivate, they benefited from complacency in Baghdad. In early March 2009, AQI struck the Interior Ministry in east Baghdad and killed or wounded 71 job applicants who were queued there. On March 10, an AQI suicide bomber penetrated a government-sponsored reconciliation conference in Abu Ghraib, killing 33, including an Iraqi Army battalion commander.[57] In both cases, MNF-I found that the ISF had experienced a breakdown in discipline and situational awareness, a problem that later allowed AQI to conduct 7 coordinated car bombings against Shi'a neighborhoods that killed and wounded more than 100 civilians.[58] These vulnerabilities in the ISF defenses indicated to coalition commanders that AQI could exploit the impending departure of U.S. troops from the city. MNF-I also noted that AQI had stepped up attempts to regain freedom of movement in the western Baghdad belts and in Ramadi by striking agreements with other local insurgent groups, thereby positioning themselves to respond to coalition and ISF countermeasures as well as take advantage of the coalition departure on June 30.

To counter the increase in ISF checkpoints in central Iraq in 2008, AQI began using large numbers of female suicide bombers, whom Iraqi police and soldiers tended not to check closely. In 2008, there were 36 attacks by female suicide bombers, compared to just 7 for all of 2007.[59] In late November, a Sunni cleric in Dhuluiyah helped coalition and Iraqi troops uncover a ring of 21 AQI women.[60] Three months later, in February 2009, Iraqi forces arrested Samira Ahmed Jassim, a woman from Diyala known as the Mother of Believers, who had orchestrated 28 female suicide bombings in the previous 18 months and was suspected of recruiting more than 80 female suicide bombers on behalf of the AQI-allied group Ansar al Sunna. Once detained, the Mother of Believers revealed that she specifically targeted rape victims for recruitment, capitalizing on their sense of shame in Iraqi society, and that Ansar al Sunna sometimes organized the rapes in the first place in order to create recruitment opportunities.[61] AQI and Ansar al Sunna's female suicide bombers were particularly effective at penetrating security for large gatherings such as Awakening meetings or pilgrimages.

Having suffered from a loss of public support in 2007-2008 because of its brutal practices in Sunni areas, AQI adjusted its tactics in early 2009 to lessen collateral damage from its attacks against coalition targets. AQI fighters began using Russian-made RKG-3 armor-piercing grenades to attack coalition-armored vehicles, which did not cause the level of civilian casualties that large IEDs tended to do. In the 6-week period coinciding with Operation NEW HOPE during March-April 2009, there were 46 RKG-3 attacks against coalition targets, and the throwers detained were often youths paid to conduct the attacks, rather than hardened AQI members.[62]

Source: U.S. Marine Corps photo by Lance Corporal James F. Cline III (Released).

RKG-3 Grenades.[63]

As the late spring operations to clear Old Mosul began, premeditated "green on blue" attacks reappeared, something that was difficult to counter or predict. On May 2 at a combined U.S.-Iraqi outpost south of Mosul, two Iraqi soldiers opened fire on U.S. Soldiers, killing two Americans and wounding three. One shooter was killed, while the second was captured along with an Iraqi police captain who had facilitated the attack. The incident, the fourth of its kind since late 2008, illustrated AQI's continued ability to attack vulnerable U.S. troops in a partnership role.[64]

While seeking to limit civilian casualties in Sunni areas, AQI sought to cause more of them in Shi'a areas. The first half of 2009 saw an expansion in AQI's use of suicide vest (SVEST) attacks to infiltrate through checkpoints and carry out high-profile bombings in gatherings and crowded areas. In mid-April, SVEST attacks killed more than 400 civilians in 1 week, with significant attacks taking place in Diyala just as Iraqi and coalition troops were clearing AQI caches and hideouts there. In one attack in Muqdadiyah, a suicide bomber killed 57 Iranian pilgrims in a restaurant, while another SVEST attacker killed 53 Iraqis at the Kadhimiyah shrine in Baghdad. At the end of the bloody week, special operators traced the SVEST operation to a cell near Balad, and, as the operators closed in on the target, seven of the cell members detonated their SVESTs, killing themselves before capture.[65] The following week, police in Kirkuk caught a would-be SVEST attacker and made an important tactical discovery. The bomber was so heavily drugged that he almost died from the narcotic, suggesting that in some cases AQI might manipulate unwilling bombers.[66]

In another important aspect, however, AQI's early 2009 adaptations were less successful: the VBIED network struggling to reestablish itself in Baghdad proved far less effective than its 2006-2007 predecessors. On April 29, for example, of 12 coordinated AQI car bombs, only half detonated; coalition forces found that the other 6 had been packed with simplistic, low-yield munitions that lacked the sophistication and size of previous AQI VBIEDs.[67]

At the same time as AQI's botched car bombs, the group benefited from an Iraqi Government failure in information operations during a bizarre, high-profile incident spearheaded by Maliki's office. In late April, Maliki and his spokesmen announced that Iraqi troops had captured Abu Omar al-Baghdadi, the leader of the Islamic State of Iraq, AQI's political organization. Strangely, however, the Iraqi officials detaining the man did not grant MNF-I access to "Baghdadi" or immediately share information from his interrogations, and based on multiple sources, MNF-I confidently judged that the Iraqis had not in fact captured Baghdadi. Nevertheless, for almost a month, Maliki and Iraqi Government spokesmen continued to declare that "Baghdadi" had been captured and was making "confessions" that implicated a large number of prominent Sunni politicians and Sons of Iraq leaders in acts of terrorism. Despite MNF-I's warnings that the captured man was an impostor, the Maliki government used the information to issue arrest warrants for several Sunni leaders, including some associated with the Iraqi Islamic Party.[68] Not until June 2009 did the Maliki government admit its mistake, which had already done serious damage to its credibility on counterterrorism just days before the June 30 transition to Iraqi security lead in Iraqi cities. In retrospect, the incident represented another warning sign of Maliki's tendency to issue specious claims in order to centralize his power base further and to seek retribution against Sunni politicians and leaders.

THE CHALLENGE OF RECONCILIATION

Problems With the Sons of Iraq: The Adel Mashhadani Affair

By late April 2009, MNF-I reported that 18,000 Sons of Iraq had been absorbed into Iraqi Government jobs, but there were signs that the overall reconciliation initiative was in danger as U.S. troops prepared to leave some of the key urban areas where the Awakening had flourished during the surge.[69] The Baghdadi hoax and the political fallout from the Maliki government's actions against Sunni leaders came at a sensitive time for the Sons of Iraq program, which had been transferred to the Iraqi Government just weeks beforehand. Many Sons of Iraq leaders distrusted the Maliki government's intentions and considered slow salary payments and arrests of the group's members evidence of the Prime Minister's ill will toward the program. MNF-I and MNC-I acted as a buffer between government and Sons of Iraq, often protecting the group's leaders from arrest. However, on March 28, 2009, MNF-I sent special operators with Ministry of Interior forces to arrest a prominent Sons of Iraq leader in Baghdad.

Adel al-Mashhadani headed a large Sons of Iraq group in the east Baghdad neighborhood of Fadhil and was closely associated with senior political leaders such as Ayad Allawi. After having originally helped to quell the Sunni insurgency in east Baghdad, Mashhadani had become a local mafia boss. "We have known for months that Mashhadani was extorting store owners, setting up illegal checkpoints, and refusing to cooperate with ISF, and a warrant was issued for his arrest," Odierno explained to Gates the day after the arrest, while describing Mashhadani as "a charismatic leader whose brutality led to his arrest."[70] Mashhadani was taken into custody without incident, but in the hours after his capture, his Sons of Iraq followers fought Iraqi troops and U.S. Soldiers from 5th Squadron, 73d Cavalry Regiment, part of General Bolger's MND-B. About 15 of Mashhadani's men were killed, and the situation turned into an all-night standoff after Baghdad Operations Commander General Abud Qanbar deployed 3 Iraqi battalions to surround Fadhil. At dawn, more than 100 of the remaining Mashhadani followers surrendered, ending the crisis.[71]

Source: DoD photo by Staff Sergeant James Selesnick (Released).

Troops of 3d BCT, 82d Airborne Division, Rush to the Scene of Fighting Between Iraqi Security Forces and Adel al-Mashhadani's Sons of Iraq Group.[72]

The public outcry from Iraq's Sunni community led MNF-I to expect widespread Sons of Iraq desertions. However, few of the 92,000 Sons of Iraq left their positions in the aftermath of the Mashhadani arrest, though slow salary payments stemming from the early 2009 budget cuts fueled Sunni perceptions of government bias against them.[73] To alleviate these concerns, MNF-I and Iraqi Government officials convened a conference of Sons of Iraq leaders from around the country in Baghdad in mid-May and assured them continued U.S. and Iraqi Government support.[74] In the coming years, however, these assurances would mean little. An Iraqi court eventually sentenced Mashhadani to death, and the Maliki government executed him in January 2014.

Reconciliation With the Iraqi Ba'athists in Syria

The Baghdadi and Mashhadani affairs also came at a bad time for the coalition's effort to reconcile with former Iraqi military officers and Ba'athist officials living in Syria and Jordan who supported the insurgency. Maliki had used the fictional Baghdadi confessions to allege a vast Sunni terrorist conspiracy against his government involving AQI, the Ba'ath Party, and the Sunni parties in the Iraqi Parliament, all with the complicity of the Syrian regime of Bashar al-Assad. Maliki's claims came just weeks after MNF-I's Force Strategic Engagement Cell (FSEC) had opened negotiating channels with the Political Council for the Iraqi Resistance. This umbrella group included Jaysh al-Islami, and Syria-based New Ba'ath Party leader Mohammed Yunis al-Ahmad, who had long been associated with the Sunni insurgency in Ninawa and was a rival to Izzat Ibrahim al-Douri among the remnants of the Saddam Hussein regime. The FSEC's objective had been to get these insurgent groups to declare and enforce cease-fires inside Iraq. FSEC had opened these channels in December 2008 via former republican Guard General Raad Hamdani, who had connections with former military officers living outside Iraq. He and FSEC had encouraged those officers to apply for reinstatement of their jobs or pensions under the 2008 Iraqi Government law that had revised Coalition Provisional Authority (CPA) Order No. 2.[75]

In both the cease-fire discussions and the reintegration of former military officers, MNF-I stressed to interlocutors that Sunni insurgent and Ba'athist leaders would have to reconcile with the government. However, Maliki's anti-Ba'athist stance threatened the FSEC's outreach efforts. The same week that the FSEC made contact with Ahmad, the Maliki government angered Sunnis by demanding that Iraqi President Jalal Talabani approve the execution of General Sultan Hashem, Iraq's former Minister of Defense, who had been sentenced to death for his part in the anti-Kurdish Anfal campaign of the late 1980s.[76] Hashem was reviled by Iraqi Shi'a and Kurds but remained popular in his native Mosul, leading coalition officials to fear that his execution would destabilize the north. Ultimately, Talabani stood firm and denied Maliki's request, temporarily subduing the sectarian sparring.

The coalition differed in 2009 from Maliki and his allies on the prospect of reconciliation with former regime officers and officials based in Syria and Jordan. Maliki was skeptical, believing that the Ba'athists were behind most of the insurgent and terrorist violence and were determined to overthrow the democratic government. Maliki also disagreed with the United States as to whether Bashar al-Assad could be persuaded to crack down on the Syrian-based terrorist and insurgent networks. Engaging Assad on this was a centerpiece of the new Obama administration's Middle East policy, so U.S. delegations quickly began visiting Damascus, Syria. For his part, Odierno worked in spring 2009 to operationalize the Obama administration's new Syria policy by brokering security talks among Iraq, Syria, and the United States to secure the porous Syria-Iraq border. In initial bilateral talks with the Iraqis, however, Syrian representatives rebuffed Baghdad's concerns about Iraqi Ba'ath Party members in Damascus and instead protested the raid against Abu Ghadiyah the previous October.[77] Despite these inauspicious beginnings, U.S. leaders in Washington instructed MNF-I to conduct bilateral military-to-military talks with the Assad regime and share information on foreign fighter networks operating in Syria. Leading the U.S. delegation, the MNF-I chief of staff, Major General Guy Swan, proposed a trilateral assessment of Syria-Iraq border crossings to curtail terrorist and criminal activities there. The Assad regime responded by pressing for a broader discussion on economic and political issues, essentially seeking to end the U.S.-led isolation of Syria.[78] For their part, MNF-I leaders believed that the United States could pressure the Syrian regime to crack down on terrorist networks. MNF-I officers reported that Assad was worried that the future drawdown of U.S. troops could lead to the fragmentation of Iraq and a spillover of unrest to Syria.[79]

Back in Baghdad, however, Maliki and other Iraqi leaders were convinced of the Assad regime's bad faith and declined to participate in the trilateral initiative. In retrospect, the Iraqis had good reason for this view. Throughout the spring and summer, the Syrian regime's provocative actions on the border and tolerance of AQI undercut the idea of shared security interests with either Iraq or the United States.[80]

The Rise of Jaysh ar-Rejal at-Tariq al-Naqshbandi

Some of Maliki's concerns about a Ba'athist resurgence inside Iraq were justified. As AQI struggled to maintain its presence in the upper Tigris Valley and Mosul in the face of U.S.-Iraqi security operations, another insurgent organization began to take over the militant leadership role that AQI had held since 2005. The Jaysh ar-Rejal at-Tariq al-Naqshbandi (JRTN), or Naqshbandi Army, was a militant group associated with Douri's wing of the Ba'ath Party and ideologically founded on a curious mixture of Ba'athism and Sufi Islamism. JRTN had grown out of a Sufi order of Iraqi military officers led by Douri during Saddam's "Faith Campaign" of the 1990s, but after the fall of Saddam's regime, it had become a potent militant group enjoying a base of support in Hawijah, eastern Anbar, and Mosul.[81] While AQI sought headlines with its operations, JRTN preferred to work behind the scenes.[82] Though Douri and some other JRTN leaders were themselves Sufi, the group tended to be associated with Sunni nationalist interests, and its main political cause was to prevent the Kurdish takeover of Kirkuk and other disputed territories of the north. By late spring 2009, MNF-I noted JRTN's increasing militant activities in Mosul where AQI had once held sway and considered them a threat to long-term stability.[83] MNF-I observers also noted that JRTN seemed well funded but carefully masked its role in terrorism. JRTN leaders seemed willing to enter into tactical alliances with AQI and other terrorist groups hoping to claim credit for driving coalition troops out of northern cities after the June 30 withdrawal deadline.[84] Though the Ba'athists and Douri appeared in 2009 to be far from power and out of the Iraqi political mainstream, the local strength of JRTN indicated that Douri's loyalists would remain a force capable of influencing politics and potentially destabilizing areas of northern Iraq in the future.

THE IRAN PROBLEM

As MNF-I formulated its plans to withdraw from Iraqi cities and drawdown U.S. forces in the country, its commanders grappled with the difficult problem of ensuring that Iran's militant proxies did not regain their former strength in central and southern Iraq. The military defeat of Shi'a militants in 2008 led to more than half a year of subdued activity on their part, but, during the first weeks of 2009, they increased their attacks against U.S. units and the ISF with assistance from the Iranian regime. In mid-January, Shi'a militants in west Baghdad launched the first rocket attacks against Camp Victory in more than a month, and U.S. and Iraqi troops investigating the firing points found ammunition manufactured in Iran. The use of explosively formed penetrators (EFP) increased, killing three U.S. Soldiers in January. Late in the month, U.S. troops captured a five-man, Iranian-trained EFP cell.[85]

These and other attacks against coalition units elsewhere in southern Iraq were the work of the same three major Shi'a militant groups that had fought the coalition in 2008: Kata'ib Hizballah (KH), Asa'ib Ahl al-Haqq (AAH), and the remnants of Jaysh al-Mahdi, now renamed the Promised Day Brigade. MNF-I adopted different approaches toward each group. MNF-I sought to neutralize Moqtada Sadr's newly reorganized Promised Day Brigade before it reached maturity by disrupting its activities, fracturing its existing networks, and deterring it recruitment. Against KH, the militant group created by Quds Force proxy Abu Mahdi al-Muhandis, MNF-I destroyed its cells wherever they could be found. Throughout the first weeks of 2009, the coalition carried out intelligence-driven raids against both the Promised Day Brigade and KH, including operations that led to the capture of one of Abu Dura's senior lieutenants and that disrupted KH's indirect fire teams in Basrah.[86]

MNF-I's strategy for AAH, the group commanded by the imprisoned Qais al-Khazali, was similarly adjusted toward reconciliation rather than conflict. In late 2008, Odierno agreed to support the Maliki government's negotiations with Khazali and his followers, by which Maliki hoped to persuade the group to disarm and become a political party. The decision brought an end to the conflicting positions that the Maliki government and MNF-I had held since 2006, during which time the coalition had targeted AAH while Maliki had attempted sporadic political reconciliation talks with the group. In return for ceasing its targeting of AAH, MNF-I required that the group end all acts of violence, decommission its weapons, stop accepting support from the Iranian regime, and no longer take or hold hostages. When both Prime Minister Maliki and AAH representatives agreed that their negotiations would include a "roadmap" toward these points and that AAH members would observe a cease-fire with the coalition, MNF-I agreed in early January to stop targeting AAH and to release four imprisoned members.[87] MNF-I also demanded that AAH provide proof of life for U.S. Army Sergeant Ahmed al-Taie whom it kidnapped in November 2006, and for the five British citizens AAH had abducted from the Iraqi Ministry of Finance in 2007.[88]

Odierno and other senior U.S. commanders were not sanguine about the reconciliation with AAH, especially as they learned more about its commanders' deep connections to other irreconcilable Shi'a militants.[89] Unfortunately, however, the 2008 security agreement required the United States to turn over all its detainees to the Iraqi Government. Odierno believed MNF-I needed to get as much as possible for releasing Khazali and the hundreds of AAH members in U.S. detention centers rather than eventually setting them free with no quid pro quo.[90]

Through February, AAH members appeared to abide by the cease-fire, but there were signs the cease-fire would not last. The Islamic Revolutionary Guard Corps of Iran (IRGC) Quds Force continued to train and equip Iraqi militants at camps in Iran, and EFP strikes against U.S. troops began to rise in the latter half of the month, with eight EFP attacks taking place in a 6-day period. From his base in Iran, AAH deputy commander Mohammed Tabatabai began recruiting militants willing to conduct attacks that could not be traced back to AAH, probably to circumvent the cease-fire.[91]

Iran's military posture indicated that it considered it important to maintain proxies inside Iraq for use against the United States in the event of a larger regional conflict. Throughout March 2009, MNF-I observed the Iranian regime continuing to train, equip, and direct Iraqi Shi'a militant groups—including Sadr's Promised Day Brigade—to attack the coalition. MNF-I also saw indications that KH might ramp up attacks against U.S. troops as they withdrew from the Iraqi cities, and that KH continued to receive support from Lebanese Hizballah. Coalition analysts also tracked KH's attempts to construct "mega-IRAMs" carrying a 1,000-kilogram warhead that could be used in a mass-casualty attack against U.S. facilities, something KH had repeatedly tried to do since 2007.[92]

Against this backdrop, MNF-I's negotiations with AAH began to break down. Although the MNF-I FSEC met with 250 Baghdad-based Special Groups members in March hoping to reach an agreement, by April it was clear that AAH members no longer accepted the January cease-fire.[93] With the suspension of reconciliation talks, AAH stepped up its indirect-fire attacks against the Green Zone, targeting the U.S. Embassy, and MNF-I prepared to resume operations against the militant group.[94]

Ironically, as AAH walked away from the talks, Sadr reached out to MNF-I himself. After months of special operations raids against his Promised Day Brigade, Sadr sent an intermediary to Odierno to request the release of a Sadrist prisoner. Judging the prisoner to be relatively low threat, Odierno agreed, telling Gates on May 3 that he would "see if this leads to anything."[95]

With targeting restrictions against AAH lifted, the coalition and ISF resumed raids against the group with mixed results. On April 27, a coalition raid in Kut went awry and resulted in the death of an Iraqi woman with connections to local Shi'a politicians. The incident, which quickly made national news in Iraq, led an outraged Maliki to demand that coalition special operators cease all raids. To get the Prime Minister to back off this demand, Odierno agreed that all future counterterrorism raids would be cleared through the Iraqi Government. The following week, on May 5, Iraqi troops captured a large weapons cache at the Amarah home of Hayder Gharrawi, an AAH affiliate and longtime IRGC Quds Force associate. The cache included, among other munitions, 50 rocket rails and 151 EFP plates. Along with the weapons, the Iraqi troops also discovered letters dating from November 2007 written by Jason Creswell, one of the British citizens AAH abducted from the Ministry of Finance in 2007. The find indicated that Creswell had been alive months after the abduction and that he had been in the hands of an Iraqi militant with long-time connections to the Iranian regime.[96]

Less than 2 weeks after the Gharrawi raid, MNF-I reported that AAH and other Quds Force proxies had stepped up their indirect fire against the Green Zone by 125 percent since April, and that the 27 EFP attacks in the first half of May already exceeded the total of 25 for the month of April.[97] A few days later, MNF-I noted that senior AAH members had returned from Iran to the west Baghdad neighborhoods of Hurriyah and Sh'ula, apparently to prepare for a summer offensive against the coalition.[98]

Odierno and newly arrived U.S. Ambassador Chris Hill were incensed to learn in late May that IRGC Quds Force commander Qassem Soleimani planned to visit Erbil in the Kurdistan Region on June 6. Confronting Iraqi President Talabani, Odierno and Hill protested that "Soleimani's presence inside of Iraq would send the wrong message" at a time when his militant proxies were intensifying their war against the U.S. presence in the country.[99] The same week that Soleimani intended to be in Erbil, Iraqi troops captured a truckload of 59 improvised rockets being moved by a Shi'a militant group through Maysan Province near the Iranian border, along the same route from the Shalamcheh border crossing point that Soleimani's subordinates used to move weapons to central Iraq to attack U.S. troops and facilities.[100]

Despite the resumption of attacks by the Quds Force's Iraqi proxies, in early June MNF-I agreed to a proposal by the Maliki government to reopen reconciliation talks with AAH. At the Iraqi Government's request, Odierno agreed to release Laith al-Khazali, the younger of the Khazali brothers who had been captured with Qais al-Khazali and Ali Mussa Daqduq in Basrah in 2007. Under the deal worked out among the Khazalis, the Maliki government, and MNF-I, Laith al-Khazali would travel to Iran to persuade Akram al-Kabi and other AAH commanders to enforce the cease-fire agreed to by Qais al-Khazali. The Maliki government hoped these arrangements would convince AAH to disarm itself in time to participate in the 2010 Parliamentary elections as a political party. Odierno hoped that Laith al-Khazali's entreaties to AAH commanders would "further split AAH into reconcilables and non-reconcilables."[101] After 2 weeks of freedom, MNF-I officials noted that Laith al-Khazali was keeping his end of the bargain by pressing AAH members to agree to the cease-fire. In a grim show of good faith, on June 21 AAH turned over to the Iraqi Government the remains of two of the five British citizens taken from the Ministry of Finance. One of the dead was Jason Creswell, whose letters soldiers had found in Amarah just weeks before.[102]

As the June 30 deadline approached, MNF-I's work to neutralize the Iranian-sponsored Shi'a militants remained far from complete, and the withdrawal from the cities would make it difficult for U.S. units to maintain contact with the enemy. A further difficulty was that the U.S. units in southern Iraq in spring 2009 were operating in that region for the first time and had little local knowledge or understanding of the enemy there. For 6 years, the four southernmost provinces had been the responsibility of the British units of MND-SE, which had extensive local information, long-standing relationships, and human intelligence networks. However, much of the British knowledge did not transfer in the transition between MND-SE and the 10th Mountain Division in March. This loss of operational understanding was compounded when the 34th Infantry Division of the U.S. Army National Guard, deploying to Iraq for the first time, replaced the 10th Mountain Division just 7 weeks later. At that point, MNF-I's understanding of the operating environment in the far south was significantly degraded.

The Mujahedin e Khalq (MeK) Conundrum

MNF-I's problem with Iranian proxies was linked to the continuing challenge of the MeK, an Iranian opposition group that Tehran wanted to see expelled from Iraq. In the early days of the Iraq War, the Iranian regime had enlisted the help of the Badr Corps to pressure and occasionally attack the MeK at its base at Camp Ashraf in Diyala, and encouraged the Iraqi Government to take diplomatic actions against it.

The MeK problem was complicated. Its members were protected by UN authority, but many countries designated it a terrorist organization. As a result, few countries were willing to accept MeK members as refugees. In any case, its cult-like leadership prevented many of them from leaving. In private conversations in late 2008, Maliki had assured MNF-I leaders that his government would not forcibly deport MeK members to Iran. However, other Iraqi officials had told U.S. counterparts that the Iraqi Government would require Camp Ashraf residents to return to Iran or move to a third country and would deal with any MeK political activities through the Iraqi judicial system.[103] MNF-I and the U.S. Embassy were caught between their obligation to protect the MeK under international law and the requirement eventually to cede control of Camp Ashraf to the sovereign Iraqi Government. Turning the MeK camp over to Iraqi control appeared to U.S. officials to be certain to doom the residents to abuses or to forced repatriation to Iran, where death sentences awaited many of them.

As June 30, 2009, approached, it appeared that elements of the Iraqi Government intended to expel MeK from Camp Ashraf, which U.S. troops had turned over to Iraqi control. Fearing the MeK members would seek asylum in Europe and escape prosecution, the Iranian regime increased pressure on Maliki to extradite them.[104] In response, Iraqi leaders planned to conduct a census of the camp and issue arrest warrants for MeK leaders—a move with international implications.[105] On February 20, the Iraqi Government assumed full authority over Camp Ashraf, with U.S. forces providing overwatch from nearby Forward Operating Base Grizzly. Shortly after assuming control, Iraqi officials initiated their census of the Camp Ashraf population, though they refrained from executing arrest warrants.[106] During the following weeks, Iranian pressure became more evident. On February 25, an Iranian unmanned aerial vehicle (UAV) entered Iraqi airspace and overflew the Camp Ashraf area, nearly 129 kilometers from the Iranian border, for more than an hour before U.S. troops shot it down.[107] Days later, in a meeting with President Talabani, Iranian Supreme Leader Ali Khamenei demanded "the implementation of our agreement regarding the expulsion of the [MeK] hypocrites." Talabani reportedly replied that the Iraqi Government would expel the group.[108] During a trip to Iran during the same period, Iraqi National Security Adviser Mowaffaq Rubaie announced that the camp would close within 2 months.[109]

In a public relations move during mid-March, the MeK claimed Iraqi troops had beaten its members when entering the camp in an attempt to expel some of them.[110] Meanwhile, the Iranian regime continued to accuse the United States of training the MeK to conduct operations in Iran, an accusation perhaps meant to justify the Iranians' own surrogate activities in Iraq.[111] Tensions over MeK and Camp Ashraf would continue through the spring and summer, with no resolution in sight.

LEAVING THE CITIES

The Departure From Baghdad

By June 2009, U.S. troops already had left most Iraqi cities. Among the urban centers that still had U.S. garrisons, MNF-I leaders found Mosul to be the most worrisome, given the continuing presence of AQI. The most complicated and largest withdrawal, however, would take place in Baghdad, where, by the end of the surge, U.S. troops maintained more than 80 forward operating bases, combat outposts, and joint security stations. These would have to be reduced to one-sixth that number by June 30.

General Abud Qanbar Hashim al-Maliki (left). Source: DoD photo by
Sergeant Travis Zielinski (Released).

Major General Daniel Bolger, Commander of MND-B, Greets General Abud Qanbar Hashim al-Maliki, CG, Baghdad Operations Command (BOC).[112]

U.S. units required several months to prepare for the departure from the city. In February, when Bolger's 1st Cavalry Division succeeded Hammond's 4th Infantry Division as MND-B, the division controlled 6 BCTs and 35,000 troops across its area of operations. Several of the BCTs were still based within the city on large urban forward operating bases such as Loyalty, Rustamiyah, and Justice. To move out on schedule without disrupting Baghdad's security, Bolger decided to shift his units into "belt posture."[113] MND-B's brigades and battalions would move their command posts and support bases to the belts outside the city while shrinking their presence inside it. From their new bases in the belts, MND-B's units would remain close enough to respond to ISF requests for help if necessary. As Bolger put it, after June 30, the division would focus on securing the "doughnut" around Baghdad and would leave the ISF to secure "the hole in the doughnut"—the city itself.[114] The approach amounted to a return to the operating posture that MND-B had taken in 2005-2006, with U.S. units distancing themselves from populated areas and consolidating on large bases on the outskirts of the city.

Combined operations and planning continued despite the shift. After June 30, U.S. units still partnered with Iraqi brigades and divisions, and maintained an extensive advisory presence in Baghdad. However, there were no unilateral U.S. operations. In anticipation of the day when Iraqi units would plan and lead their own operations in the city, some U.S. units began merging their operations centers with those of their Iraqi partners.

Colonel Joseph Martin's 2d Brigade, 1st Infantry Division, for example, relocated its command post inside the west Baghdad headquarters of the Iraqi 6th Division, the brigade's partner unit.[115] Elsewhere in Baghdad, Bolger and MND-B agreed with their Iraqi counterparts to maintain a U.S. presence at key joint security stations (JSS) across the city. The process of selecting which stations would remain in operation proved difficult. Bolger urged General Qanbar and his BOC to keep 17 of Baghdad's 55 joint security stations open, but Qanbar and the BOC agreed only to 14. To Bolger's disappointment, the BOC insisted on closing three joint security stations in sensitive Shi'a-majority neighborhoods, including JSS Sadr City—the outpost that U.S. troops had fought hard to create during the campaign against Jaysh al-Mahdi in 2008. Nevertheless, the Iraqi Government agreed that after June 30, 1,000 U.S. troops would remain as advisors at the 14 remaining urban JSS.[116]

By mid-June, U.S. units were making their final moves out of Baghdad and other cities. The operations against AQI in Diyala and Ninawa had ended, and U.S. troops had turned over their final base in Mosul.[117] To reduce the visible presence of U.S. troops in the Baghdad area and reinforce Iraqis' perception that MND-B was leaving the city as the U.S.-Iraq security agreement required, Bolger ordered his units to move to reverse cycle operations, making routine movements such as logistical resupply convoys only during nighttime hours.[118]

Militant groups marked the approaching withdrawal deadline with significant attacks that were likely meant to assert that the U.S. withdrawal amounted to an insurgent victory. On June 24, a massive car bomb in Sadr City killed 69 Iraqis and wounded more than 100 in an all-too-familiar scene in the Shi'a slum neighborhood. On June 28, troops from the 2d Battalion, 5th Cavalry, were traveling near Sadr City when their convoy was hit by a series of EFPs, severing both legs of battalion commander Lieutenant Colonel Timothy Karcher. Immediately after evacuating their commander to the military hospital in the Green Zone, Karcher's men suffered another EFP attack that killed Sergeant Timothy David.[119] David was the last U.S. Soldier killed in Baghdad ahead of the withdrawal. On July 1, MND-B, which at its peak during the surge had controlled 9 U.S. brigades, now commanded 4 brigades and 20,000 U.S. Soldiers, and the Iraqi capital was without U.S. operating units for the first time since April 2003.

***

The days immediately following the withdrawal from the cities were calm, but there were some warning signs. Although the U.S.-Iraqi committees had worked out detailed coordination guidelines for how U.S. forces would function after June 30, Iraqi officials in Baghdad initially refused to allow American troops to provide security for U.S.-funded governance and economic development projects. This decision delayed some key projects for several weeks. Although the Iraqi Government eventually reversed this decision, there was a sharp drop-off in U.S.-ISF combined patrols in July. Senior U.S. commanders worried the decline in combined operational tempo would allow militant groups to become active again.[120] The new requirement for a warrant from an Iraqi judge for all counterterrorism raids also constrained U.S. military operations at first, although Bolger and MND-B later realized that, because Iraqi courts had very broad jurisdiction, a cooperative judge in Baghdad could authorize raids "practically unlimited in time or space."[121] Judicial warrants for military operations proved awkward for U.S. units. As Bolger later described, "War is not police work, and the entire idea of searching for terrorists with a warrant sure seemed to mix the two."[122]

In their first days of planning and executing operations on their own, ISF commanders impressed MNF-I leaders by completing complex security missions in Anbar and central Iraq. In one instance, the Interior Ministry was able to coordinate multiple ISF agencies during a targeted counterterrorism raid near Rutbah.[123] In another, the ISF managed to plan and provide security for 2 million pilgrims traveling to the Kadhimiyah shrine in northwest Baghdad.[124] In mid-July, Odierno reported that coordination among the Iraqi Army, Interior Ministry, and Sons of Iraq in Anbar had enabled the Iraqis to respond to car-bomb attacks and increase the frequency of patrols and searches.[125]

Yet, there were a few ominous signs of what some ISF leaders intended to do with their new autonomy. In late July, Iraqi Army and police forces carried out an operation at the MeK compound at Camp Ashraf that turned deadly. The Maliki government had deployed police to the MeK compound, but its residents blocked the camp entrance and initiated a standoff. On July 28, Iraqi police and army forces forced the issue, using bulldozers and tanks to break through the gates and enter the compound to establish a police station there.[126] To the Iraqi troops' surprise, MeK members blocked the Iraqi vehicles' advance with their bodies. The ensuing violence left 9 dead and more than 200 wounded before the Iraqi troops halted their attempt.[127] In Odierno's view, the Iraqi Government had overestimated its forces' capabilities, while the MeK had miscalculated that the Iraqis would refrain from using force.[128]

Meanwhile, a series of events in Mosul indicated that as Generals Karim and Caslen had feared, AQI was taking advantage of the U.S. forces' absence in the city to pressure the ISF leaders who were now responsible for Ninawa's security. In a 6-day period in early July alone, AQI carried out seven attacks against ISF leaders in the city, prompting Odierno to warn that the group was repeating the tactics that had "effectively broke[n] the IA and IP [Iraqi Army and Iraqi Police]" in Mosul in 2004 and 2006.[129] In the weeks to come, AQI would exploit the coalition's departure from the cities by launching an offensive not just in Mosul, but also in Baghdad, where AQI bombers would carry out some of the war's largest attacks at the very edge of the Green Zone.

ENDNOTES - CHAPTER 12

1. Multi-National Force-Iraq (MNF-I), Secretary of Defense (SECDEF) Weekly Update, October 27-November 2, 2008. The brigade in question was 2d Brigade, 101st Airborne Division.

2. MNF-I, SECDEF Weekly Update, December 1-7, 2008.

3. MNF-I, SECDEF Weekly Update, February 9-15, 2009.

4. Ibid.

5. Ibid.

6. MNF-I, SECDEF Weekly Update, January 12-18, 2009.

7. MNF-I, SECDEF Weekly Update, January 26-February 1, 2009.

8. Joel Rayburn, *Iraq After America: Strongmen, Sectarians, Resistance,* Stanford, CA: Hoover Institution Press, 2014, pp. 42-43.

9. MNF-I, SECDEF Weekly Update, February 9-15, 2009.

10. MNF-I, SECDEF Weekly Update, February 16-22, 2009.

11. Michael E. O'Hanlon and Jason H. Campbell, "Iraq Index," Washington, DC: Brookings Institution, January 30, 2009, p. 24.

12. DoD photo by Specialist Darryl Montgomery, "Multi-National Division - Center, Multi-National Divison [sic]- Southeast combine, creating Multi-National Divison [sic]- South [Image 2 of 2]," March 31, 2009, DVIDS Identifier 161631, Released to Public, available from *https://www.dvidshub.net/image/161631/ multi-national-division-center-multi-national-divison-southeast-combine-creating-multi-national-divison-south.*

13. MNF-I, SECDEF Weekly Update, April 13-19, 2009, pp. 4-5.

14. O'Hanlon and Campbell, "Iraq Index," p. 32.

15. Department of Defense (DoD) Report (Rpt) to Congress, *Measuring Stability and Security in Iraq,* March 2009, p. 34, available from *http://www.defense.gov/Portals/1/Documents/pubs/Measuring_Stability_and_ Security_in_Iraq_March_2009.pdf,* accessed January 19, 2016.

16. MNF-I, SECDEF Weekly Update, January 5-11, 2009; January 12-18, 2009; and January 26-February 1, 2009.

17. MNF-I, SECDEF Weekly Update, February 9-15, 2009, p. 1, and March 2-8, 2009, p. 2.

18. MNF-I, SECDEF Weekly Update, February 2-8, 2009, p. 2; February 9-15, 2009; March 2-8, 2009.

19. MNF-I, SECDEF Weekly Update, May 11-17, 2009, p. 2.

20. DoD Rpt to Congress, *Measuring Stability and Security in Iraq,* March 2009, p. 34.

21. Ibid.; MNF-I, SECDEF Weekly Update, February 9-15, 2009.

22. MNF-I, SECDEF Weekly Update, May 18-24, 2009, p. 4-5.

23. MNF-I, SECDEF Weekly Update, February 23-March 1, 2009, p. 5.

24. MNF-I, SECDEF Weekly Update, June 1-7, 2009, p. 5.

25. MNF-I, SECDEF Weekly Update, June 8-14, 2009, p. 5.

26. MNF-I, SECDEF Weekly Update, March 2-8, 2009.

27. Ibid.

28. DoD photo courtesy U.S. Navy, "Ready to blast a bunker," DVIDS Identifier 160252, March 22, 2009, Released to Public, available from *https://www.dvidshub.net/image/160252/ready-blast-bunker.*

29. MNF-I, SECDEF Weekly Update, March 9-15, 2009.

30. MNF-I, SECDEF Weekly Update, March 23-29, 2009.

31. MNF-I, SECDEF Weekly Update, March 9-15, 2009.

32. MNF-I, SECDEF Weekly Update, March 23-29, 2009.

33. MNF-I, SECDEF Weekly Update, February 23-March 1, 2009, p. 3.

34. MNF-I, SECDEF Weekly Update, April 27-May 3, 2009, p. 2.

35. MNF-I, SECDEF Weekly Update, February 16-22, 2009.

36. MNF-I, SECDEF Weekly Update, February 9–15, 2009.

37. U.S. Air Force photo by Staff Sergeant JoAnn S. Makinano, "Combined Effort," March 1, 2009, Released to Public, available from *https://www.flickr.com/photos/mnfiraq/4522120013/in/album-7215 7623734024453/*.

38. MNF-I, SECDEF Weekly Update, February 16-22, 2009.

39. MNF-I, SECDEF Weekly Update, February 23-March 1, 2009.

40. MNF-I, SECDEF Weekly Update, March 2-8, 2009.

41. MNF-I, SECDEF Weekly Update, April 6-12, 2009.

42. MNF-I, SECDEF Weekly Update, May 4-10, 2009.

43. MNF-I, SECDEF Weekly Update, May 18-24, 2009, p. 2.

44. MNF-I, SECDEF Weekly Update, May 11-17 2009; and May 25-31, 2009.

45. MNF-I, SECDEF Weekly Update, March 30-April 5, 2009; and June 8-14, 2009.

46. MNF-I, SECDEF Weekly Update, March 30-April 5, 2009.

47. MNF-I, SECDEF Weekly Update, April 13-19, 2009; and June 1-7, 2009.

48. MNF-I, SECDEF Weekly Update, March 2-8, 2009, p. 2.

49. DoD photo by Specialist Daniel Nelson, "Joint Briefing Conducted to Discuss the Future of Ninewa [Image 8 of 9]," DVIDS Identifier 169538, May 2, 2009, Released to Public, available from *https://www. dvidshub.net/image/169538/joint-briefing-conducted-discuss-future-ninewa*.

50. MNF-I, SECDEF Weekly Update, March 30-April 5, 2009; and May 4-10, 2009, p. 2.

51. MNF-I, SECDEF Weekly Update, June 1-7, 2009; and June 8-14, 2009.

52. MNF-I, SECDEF Weekly Update, April 13-19, 2009; and April 6-12, 2009.

53. MNF-I, SECDEF Weekly Update, April 20-26, 2009.

54. MNF-I, SECDEF Weekly Update, May 4-10, 2009.

55. MNF-I, SECDEF Weekly Update, February 23-March 1, 2009.

56. MNF-I, SECDEF Weekly Update, November 10-16, 2008.

57. MNF-I, SECDEF Weekly Update, March 9-15, 2009.

58. MNF-I, SECDEF Weekly Update, April 6-12, 2009.

59. Corey Siemaszko, "'Mother of Believers,' Suspected of Recruiting More than 80 female Suicide Bombers, Arrested in Iraq," *New York Daily News*, February 3, 2009.

60. MNF-I, SECDEF Weekly Update, November 24-30, 2008.

61. Siemaszko, "'Mother of Believers,' Suspected of Recruiting More than 80 female Suicide Bombers, Arrested in Iraq."

62. MNF-I, SECDEF Weekly Update, March 16-22, 2009; March 23-29, 2009; and April 6-12, 2009.

63. U.S. Marine Corps photo by Lance Corporal James F. Cline III, "Thermal grenades, rocket propelled grenade projectiles, and other munitions were found by U.S. military personnel attached to the 3rd Battalion, 1st Brigade, 1st Iraqi Army Division, Military Transition Team, at a weapons cache near Lake Tharthar, Iraq, Oct. 7, 2007, during Operation Sattar. The unit is deployed with Multi-National Forces-West in support of Operation IRAQI FREEDOM in the Anbar province of Iraq," DIMOC Identifier 071007-M-IS307-032, October 7, 2007, Released to Public, modified (cropped).

64. MNF-I, SECDEF Weekly Update, April 27-May 3, 2009.

65. MNF-I, SECDEF Weekly Update, April 20-26, 2009.

66. MNF-I, SECDEF Weekly Update, April 27-May 3, 2009.

67. Ibid.

68. MNF-I, SECDEF Weekly Update, April 20-26, 2009; and May 18-24, 2009.

69. MNF-I, SECDEF Weekly Update, April 27-May 3, 2009, p. 4.

70. MNF-I, SECDEF Weekly Update, March 23-29, 2009; and March 30-April 5, 2009.

71. MNF-I, SECDEF Weekly Update, March 23-29, 2009.

72. DoD photo by Staff Sergeant James Selesnick, "Patrol in Baghdad [Image 25 of 28]," DVIDS Identifier 169445, March 29, 2009, Released to Public, available from *https://www.dvidshub.net/image/169445/patrol-baghdad*.

73. MNF-I, SECDEF Weekly Update, March 30-April 5, 2009.

74. MNF-I, SECDEF Weekly Update, May 11-17, 2009.

75. MNF-I, SECDEF Weekly Update, December 1-7, 2008; and December 22-28, 2008.

76. MNF-I, SECDEF Weekly Update, March 16-22, 2009.

77. MNF-I, SECDEF Weekly Update, April 20-26, 2009.

78. MNF-I, SECDEF Weekly Update, June 8-14, 2009.

79. MNF-I, SECDEF Weekly Update, June 1-7, 2009.

80. MNF-I, SECDEF Weekly Update, March 23-29, 2009, and May 18-24, 2009.

81. Rayburn, *Iraq After America*, pp. 108-109.

82. Interview, Colonel (Ret.) Derek Harvey with Major Jeanne Hull, December 11, 2014.

83. MNF-I, SECDEF Weekly Update, February 23-March 1, 2009.

84. MNF-I, SECDEF Weekly Update, April 27-May 3, 2009; and May 4-10, 2009.

85. MNF-I, SECDEF Weekly Update, January 12-18, 2009; and January 26-February 1, 2009.

86. MNF-I, SECDEF Weekly Update, January 26-February 1, 2009, p. 2.

87. MNF-I, SECDEF Weekly Update, December 29, 2008-January 4, 2009, p. 2.

88. MNF-I, SECDEF Weekly Update, January 5-11, 2009; and January 26-February 1, 2009.

89. MNF-I, SECDEF Weekly Update, January 12-18, 2009, p. 1.

90. Interview, Chief of Staff of the Army (CSA) Operation IRAQI FREEDOM (OIF) Study Group with General Raymond T. Odierno, January 25, 2015.

91. MNF-I, SECDEF Weekly Update, February 9-15, 2009; and February 23-March 1, 2009.

92. MNF-I, SECDEF Weekly Update, February 23-March 1, 2009; and March 30-April 5, 2009.

93. MNF-I, SECDEF Weekly Update, March 16-22, 2009.

94. MNF-I, SECDEF Weekly Update, April 20-26, 2009; and April 27-May 3, 2009.

95. MNF-I, SECDEF Weekly Update, April 27-May 3, 2009, p. 3.

96. MNF-I, SECDEF Weekly Update, May 4-10, 2009, p. 2.

97. MNF-I, SECDEF Weekly Update, May 11-17, 2009, pp. 2-3.

98. MNF-I, SECDEF Weekly Update, May 18-24, 2009, p. 3.

99. MNF-I, SECDEF Weekly Update, May 25-31, 2009, p. 3.

100. MNF-I, SECDEF Weekly Update, June 1-7, 2009, pp. 2-3.

101. MNF-I, SECDEF Weekly Update, June 8-14, 2009, p. 2.

102. MNF-I, SECDEF Weekly Update, June 15-21, 2009, p. 2.

103. MNF-I, SECDEF Weekly Update, November 10-16, 2008, p. 3; MNF-I, Quarterly History, October 1-December 31, 2009, pp. 23-24; MNF-I, SECDEF Weekly Update, December 15-21, 2008.

104. MNF-I, SECDEF Weekly Update, February 9-15, 2009, p. 2; Gawdat Bahgat, "United States-Iranian Relations: The Terrorism Challenge," *Parameters*, 2009, p. 98, available from *http://strategicstudiesinstitute. army.mil/pubs/parameters/Articles/08winter/bahgat.pdf*, accessed December 1, 2015.

105. MNF-I, Quarterly History, January 1-March 31, 2009, pp. 29-30.

106. MNF-I, SECDEF Weekly Update, February 16-22, 2009; MNF-I, Quarterly History, January 1-March 31, 2009, pp. 29-30.

107. Rod Nordland and Alissa J. Rubin, "U.S. Says It Shot Down an Iranian Drone Over Iraq," *The New York Times*, March 16, 2009, available from *http://www.nytimes.com/2009/03/17/world/middleeast/17iraq. html?_r=0*, accessed December 2, 2015.

108. Rania Abouzeid, "At Tehran's Bidding? Iraq Cracks Down on a Controversial Camp," *Time*, July 29, 2009, available from *http://content.time.com/time/world/article/0,8599,1913399,00.html*, accessed December 2, 2015; Lincoln Bloomfield, Jr., "Mujahedin-e Khalg (MEK/PMOI) and the Search for Ground

Truth About its Activities and Nature: An Independent Assessment by Ambassador Lincoln Bloomfield, Jr.," August 16, 2011, available from *http://www.delistmek.com/MUJAHEDIN-E-KHALQ-AN-INDEPENDENT-ASSESSMENT.pdf*, accessed December 2, 2015.

109. MNF-I, Quarterly History, January 1-March 31, 2009, pp. 29-30; MNF-I, SECDEF Weekly Update, March 16-22, 2009, p. 5.

110. "Iranians at Iraq camp allege abuse," CNN, March 16, 2009, available from *http://www.cnn.com/2009/WORLD/meast/03/16/iran.iraq.us/*, accessed December 2, 2015.

111. MNF-I, SECDEF Weekly Update, March 30-April 5, 2009, p. 3.

112. DoD photo by Sergeant Travis Zielinski, "Air Cavalry hosts top Iraqi general [Image 1 of 2]," DVIDS Identifier 202953, September 11, 2009, Released to Public, available from *https://www.dvidshub.net/image/202953/air-cavalry-hosts-top-iraqi-general*.

113. Ms, *On Point*, Vol. V, Chapter 5, p. 93.

114. Ibid., Chapter 5, p. 96.

115. Ibid., p. 111.

116. Ibid., p. 94.

117. MNF-I, SECDEF Weekly Update, June 1-7, 2009, p. 1.

118. Ms, *On Point*, Vol. V, Chapter 5, p. 99.

119. Ibid., p. 130.

120. Ibid., p. 100.

121. Ibid., p. 95.

122. Ibid., p. 96.

123. MNF-I, SECDEF Weekly Update, June 29-July 5, 2009, p. 2.

124. MNF-I, SECDEF Weekly Update, July 13-19, 2009, p. 1.

125. MNF-I, SECDEF Weekly Update, July 20-26, 2009, p. 1.

126. MNF-I, Quarterly History, July 1-September 30, 2009, p. 22.

127. MNF-I, SECDEF Weekly Update, July 27-August 2, 2009, p. 1.

128. Ibid., p. 2.

129. MNF-I, SECDEF Weekly Update, July 6-12, 2009, p. 1.

CHAPTER 13

TOWARD THE DEFEAT OF AQI, AUGUST 2009-JULY 2010

Prime Minister Nuri al-Maliki and other leaders hailed Multi-National Force-Iraq's (MNF-I) June 30, 2009, withdrawal from Iraqi cities as a significant Iraqi achievement. However, with U.S. troops leaving the population centers, al-Qaeda in Iraq (AQI) and other insurgent groups tried to show that the government could not secure Iraq's cities on its own. Although it had lost the ability to operate openly and hold territory, AQI lashed out in late 2009 in a series of attacks in Baghdad that shook the Maliki government.

In the months that followed, MNF-I and the Iraqi Government fought back and regained ground lost to AQI. Together, they mounted operations that dealt the group a near-fatal blow in spring 2010. They did so against a difficult backdrop of changing U.S. strategic guidance, the Arab-Kurdish political conflict, a protracted Iraqi election crisis, and a creeping consolidation of power by Maliki. These factors combined to dim hopes for Iraq's future stability.

THE AUTUMN 2009 BOMBINGS

AQI Shifts its Strategy

As MNF-I planned its move away from Iraqi cities during 2009, its leaders expected that AQI would intensify its attacks to discredit the Iraqi security forces. Even ahead of the June 30 withdrawal deadline, MNF-I believed that AQI was shifting its strategy. Under constant pressure from both coalition brigade combat teams (BCTs) and special operations forces, and having lost much of its popular support, AQI refocused its attacks on MNF-I and Iraqi Government targets to avoid civilian casualties.

AQI's capacity had plummeted from its high during 2006-2007, when the organization had controlled large swaths of northern and central Iraq and seemed on its way to creating a bona fide "Islamic State of Iraq (ISI)." By mid-July 2009, MNF-I estimated that the combined strength of all Sunni Arab resistance groups in the country, including AQI, had fallen to between 1,450 and 3,550 fighters, too few to operate as an insurgent army.[1] Likewise, across the country, the number of security incidents hovered around 200 per week, a rate consistent with summer 2003 levels.[2]

Only in Ninawa Province could AQI carry out a high rate of attacks and infiltrate Iraqi Government ranks to strike from within those ranks. During the winter of 2008-2009, AQI operatives and their contacts within the Iraqi Army and National Police carried out several insider or "green on blue" attacks against U.S. military detachments in the Mosul area. The attackers usually were Iraqi security force (ISF) members recruited or coerced by AQI or other insurgents, and they principally targeted coalition advisers embedded in ISF units. One such attack in February 2009 killed members of a U.S. police transition team in Mosul and proved that AQI and other groups continued to be able to penetrate the Mosul police force.[3]

The Mosul police themselves were hit even harder as violent incidents nearly doubled after the coalition's departure from the city. In the first week after the withdrawal of U.S. combat units, AQI and its allies carried out seven assassination attempts against senior ISF leaders in Mosul. During the first 6 weeks after the withdrawal, they killed at least 68 policemen in the Mosul area.[4] General Raymond T. Odierno reported to Secretary of Defense (SECDEF) Robert Gates that the intensified pressure against Mosul's security forces resembled the insurgent campaigns that had led to the collapse of the city's police force in 2004.[5] A shortage of more than 5,000 policemen and 1,300 investigating officers in the undermanned Ninawa police force made the situation worse.[6]

Despite its continued activities against the ISF in Mosul, AQI suffered serious setbacks in far northern Iraq. It faced constant pressure from the extensive system created to target the group's foreign fighter networks. For almost 6 years, AQI and its allies had been reinforced by Salafi militants from throughout the Arab world, most entering via Syria. During 2009, that system broke down as the United States and other countries made a concerted effort to disrupt them.

While the group facilitating the flow of foreign fighters had regenerated somewhat in early 2009, it had never fully recovered from the 2008 raid that killed Abu Ghadiyah. On the heels of the loss of Abu Ghadiyah, the network suffered another blow when Lebanese authorities arrested a major Kuwaiti AQI facilitator with the nom de guerre "Al Hajj."[7] By mid-2009, Abu Khalaf, Abu Ghadiyah's successor, fled Syria under pressure from Bashar al-Assad's security forces, relocating into the Iraqi border area.[8] Within Iraq, MNF-I had begun shifting some coalition troops to the Syrian border zones as coalition units left the cities in late spring, a move that MNF-I judged had reduced the foreign fighter flow even further, to an estimated rate of only five per month.[9] The wider network of AQI's Salafi militant allies suffered another setback in July when coalition special operations forces (SOF) and Iraqi troops captured four top leaders of Ansar al Islam during a 24-hour period in Mosul, including Mullah Halgurd, a Kurdish militant who served as the group's deputy leader.[10]

Since late 2008, the coalition had sought to limit AQI's local financing in Ninawa. For several years before 2009, AQI had extorted large sums of money from the AsiaCell phone company, Iraq's second-largest mobile phone provider. However, when AsiaCell stopped payments in mid-2009, AQI blew up three of the company's cell towers and attacked the company's headquarters building in Baghdad.[11] Ninawa Governor Atheel Nujaifi also asked for coalition help to rein in corruption within his provincial government, which he believed was providing cash to AQI. Multi-National Division-North (MND-N) responded by forming a joint interagency task force in Mosul to address both government corruption and AQI financing.[12]

These and other initiatives against AQI made it nearly impossible for the group to operate openly. Reviewing AQI's mid-2009 operations, Odierno noted that the organization had reverted to its earlier terrorist tactics. Where it once had been able to control terrain and carry out a wide variety of attacks that included improvised explosive devices (IEDs) and complex ambushes, pressure now limited the group to high-profile bombings about once every 3 weeks—a 70 percent reduction since the dark days of 2007-2008. On July 6, Odierno fatefully predicted to his staff that AQI would increasingly have to rely on high-profile car bombings.[13]

"Bloody Wednesday," August 19, 2009

Odierno's prediction came true the following month as AQI began a string of bombings in Baghdad that were among the deadliest of the entire war. On the morning of August 19, two large truck bombs struck Iraq's Finance Ministry and Foreign Ministry just a few minutes apart. The bombs devastated the buildings as well as the lines of employee cars queued to enter the ministry compounds for the start of the workday. Two more blasts followed in commercial districts elsewhere in the city. The day's final death toll listed 75 killed with another 749 injured.[14]

The bombings stunned the Iraqi population and the government, which had seen Baghdad settle in a relatively safe pattern after the summer 2008 end of the Sadrist uprising. The attacks also undermined the Maliki government's assertion that the ISF could secure Iraq's cities after the departure of coalition troops. Under intense public scrutiny, Prime Minister Maliki immediately blamed the Syrian regime and Syrian-based "Saddam loyalists." The Prime Minister had visited Damascus only 1 day before the bombings expressly to reestablish Iraq-Syria relations after a long rupture, but in the wake of the bombings, he broke off relations once again. Within days, the Iraqi Interior Ministry began to arrest suspects associated with the Ba'ath Party. On August 23, the government broadcast a confession by one suspect who said that he acted under orders from Iraqi Ba'athists in Syria, after which Iraq expelled the Syrian ambassador in Baghdad, an act that the Syrian regime reciprocated in Damascus.[15] Maliki also declared that Iraq would not participate in the nascent trilateral talks on counterterrorism and border security by the United States, Iraq, and Syria.

Despite the Iraqi Government's insistence on Syrian involvement, MNF-I saw no evidence that anyone other than AQI had planned and executed the August 19 bombings. For Odierno and other coalition leaders, the main failing had been the lax security measures of a complacent ISF, a factor that MNF-I leaders had been concerned about since beginning the transition out of the cities in the spring. "[O]ur joint, interagency assessment is that AQI is responsible for the bombings. We have no evidence directly linking any foreign entities," Odierno reported in early September.[16] Nevertheless, Odierno signaled his support for the international pressure Maliki was putting on Syria, given the Assad regime's long-standing support for AQI facilitators.[17]

As conflict with the Assad regime intensified, the Iraqi Government took steps to address some of its security problems. Eleven ISF commanders were arrested for negligence in allowing the August attacks and Iraqi police and Army units were placed on alert, with all leave canceled. The operational pace of coalition special operations forces units returned to pre-June 30 levels, indicating that the Iraqi Government was willing to drop many of its reservations about coalition counterterrorism raids.[18] This showed quick results: by late September, AQI had compartmentalized its operations, tasking individuals rather than cells, a security measure that made complex operations more difficult.[19] Within MNF-I, coalition leaders hoped the bombings had been a "wakeup call" or an "Iraqi 9/11" for ISF leaders who underestimated the continuing terrorist threat.[20]

The October 25th Bombings

Within weeks, further attacks in Baghdad proved these speculations premature. On October 25, AQI operatives based in the western Baghdad belt struck the Ministry of Justice and the nearby Ministry of Public Works in two coordinated vehicle bombings. The attacks caused more than 800 casualties, a higher toll than the August 19 attacks, and showed that the increased security measures were insufficient.

AQI's political front, the ISI, immediately claimed responsibility in an online statement declaring that "suicide bombers targeted the dens of infidelity and pillars of the rejectionist Shi'ite state in the land of the caliphate."[21] Nevertheless, as he had done in August, Maliki again blamed the Syria-based Iraqi Ba'ath for the bombings. The continued difference of opinion between U.S. commanders and Maliki was significant. U.S. leaders insisted the Iraqi Government still faced an AQI problem and should not have relaxed internal security measures. Maliki claimed the security problem originated outside Iraq, and that the coalition forces drew violence to the Iraqi cities by their presence.

The October 25 attack showed that AQI had made inroads in the western belt between Baghdad and Anbar, including the former AQI safe havens near Lake Tharthar. "It is clear to me that AQI is trying to reestablish itself along the seam between Anbar and Baghdad provinces," Odierno had written in mid-September. A few weeks later MNF-I had noted that AQI high-profile bombings in eastern Anbar were damaging the credibility of the ISF and the provincial government.[22] A Mercedes bus used as a vehicle bomb on October 25 resembled a similar bomb found 2 weeks before in an AQI car-bomb factory in Abu Ghraib, just west of Baghdad. In response, MNF-I and Iraqi troops increased their patrols in the "seam" area to an average of 27 per day by the beginning of November.[23] MNF-I found that the October 25 suicide bombers had probably been detainees in either the U.S. or Iraqi systems, leading Odierno to halt all releases of AQI-affiliated prisoners and slow down transfers of MNF-I's remaining 7,000 detainees to Iraqi Government custody.[24]

In Baghdad itself, the October 25 bombing led to tighter ISF physical security measures, especially regarding traffic congestion which the attackers had used to move through the city undetected.[25] The bombings showed that the Iraqi security forces relied on fake bomb detection wands that soldiers and police uselessly waved around vehicles at checkpoints—phony equipment a British businessman had sold to Baghdad for tens of millions of dollars with the collusion of corrupt Iraqi officials.

Beyond the security shortfalls in Baghdad and eastern Anbar, broader dynamics made central Iraq less secure than it had been since late 2007. The initial transfer of the Sons of Iraq to Iraqi Government payrolls had gone relatively smoothly in late 2008 and early 2009. Within 6 months, however, the government had become chronically late paying the Sunni militias and had begun arresting their leaders, rounding up 25 from July to September 2009.[26] Much of the government's hostility stemmed directly from Prime Minister Maliki, who "considered some of these Sons of Iraq groups to be nothing more than terrorists who were now getting paid for operating checkpoints," according to Ambassador Christopher Hill.[27] By fall 2009, Odierno was deeply concerned that the Iraqi Government's failure to embrace the Awakening and the Sons of Iraq was creating an opening for AQI.[28] AQI's attempted resurgence took place in the cyber realm as well. Though it enjoyed less popular support than ever inside Iraq, the group continued to use its sophisticated media outlets to broadcast propaganda throughout the region, claiming to be regaining its former strength. The coalition's seeming inability to counter AQI and ISI propaganda—as well as that from Jaysh ar-Rejal at-Tariq al-Naqshbandi and Shi'a militant groups—frustrated MNF-I leaders, who had sought but not received authority to shut down AQI-affiliated media outlets.[29]

The December 8th Bombings

Despite the Iraqi Government's tighter security measures, the MNF-I J-2 predicted in mid-November that another major attack was likely to occur around December 15.[30] The estimate would prove to be prescient. On December 8, suicide car bombers targeted the Ministry of Finance, a major Iraqi courthouse, and a busy overpass near the Ministry of Labor. AQI immediately claimed responsibility for the attacks that killed 50 Iraqis and wounded more than 200.[31] The combined ISF-coalition response to the attacks was quicker and more thorough than in August and October, when the ISF had waited to ask for coalition help. Coalition technicians determined that the same bombing ring had carried out the October and December attacks.[32]

The attacks did less damage than the earlier ones mainly because of the ISF's improved operational procedures, but evidence that AQI could still penetrate into the heart of Baghdad shook public confidence in the Maliki government. The day after the bombings, the Iraqi Parliament summoned the Prime Minister to an unprecedented 6-hour, closed-door session to grill him on his handling of Iraq's security. Partly to deflect blame from himself and avoid a no-confidence vote, Maliki sacked General Abud Qanbar, the long-time head of the Baghdad Operations Command.[33]

According to Gates, the December 8 bombings showed that AQI was "down, but not out."[34] Two weeks after the attacks, MNF-I reported that some Iraqi civil servants had stopped going to work in the ministries out of fear.[35] With national elections just weeks away, Iraqi politicians responded by exchanging accusations of blame, including Maliki. In the days after the attacks, the Prime Minister asserted that the bombings had been the work of AQI sympathizers who had infiltrated the ISF, an allegation that MNF-I leaders warned Maliki would reinforce Iraqis' doubts about the ISF's ability to protect the population.[36]

THE "RESPONSIBLE DRAWDOWN"

Despite the AQI offensive, the March 2010 national elections had the potential to produce a national unity government that could help heal Iraq's ethno-sectarian divisions and further eclipse Iraq's Sunni and Shi'a militant groups. As a result, U.S. commanders believed that 2010 would see U.S. forces complete the transition to stability operations. It would also be a year of troop reductions. Given President Barack Obama's instructions to end the U.S. combat mission by September 2010, U.S. forces would have to conduct a "responsible drawdown," as the President termed it, from about 100,000 U.S. troops to 50,000 by the end of August.

With U.S. units withdrawing from Iraq's cities and shifting to stability operations, Odierno adjusted the joint campaign plan that had governed the coalition's military and civil activities. In fall 2009, he enlisted a team of experts led by General (Ret.) Leon LaPorte to examine the strategic situation in the country and recommend changes. The Joint Campaign Plan Assessment Team (JCPAT) viewed a renewed civil war as more likely than a return to large-scale insurgency, and recommended that the command concentrate on preventing civil war. LaPorte's team also suggested lowering the Iraqi expectation for continued U.S. military presence and assistance, noting, "Iraqis do not seem to accept that there will be a major decline in U.S. presence starting in summer 2010."[37] Finally, the JCPAT noted a disconnect between MNF-I's conditions-based approach to the impending troop drawdown and the time-based guidance Obama had given earlier in the year and urged the command to adapt to the political deadlines.[38]

The JCPAT's conclusions matched a September 2009 internal strategic risk survey that asked dozens of senior MNF-I, Multi-National Corps-Iraq (MNC-I), and U.S. Embassy leaders to identify the most significant risks to U.S. strategic goals in Iraq. Two emerged: the danger of an Arab-Kurd war, and the unwillingness or inability of the Iraqi Government to "balance" against "malign Iranian influence." The officials surveyed also identified sectarianism, a lack of economic development, and ineffective governance as obstacles to stability.

With these recommendations and risks in mind, Odierno decided that U.S. troops should shift from full-spectrum operations to stabilization operations. As U.S. troops withdrew, MNF-I and MNC-I would transfer their activities to the Iraqis and U.S. Embassy. To manage their much-reduced forces, MNF-I and its many subordinate commands would consolidate into one headquarters, U.S. Forces-Iraq (USF-I), at the beginning of 2010. The new USF-I would no longer be a coalition command since other nations had pulled their forces out of Iraq in 2009, with the exception of small contingents assigned to the North Atlantic Treaty Organization (NATO) Training Mission-Iraq.

The new campaign plan, published November 15, 2009, codified these changes, which were further detailed in a new operations order, OPORD 10-1, released January 1, 2010. The order laid out how the future USF-I would shift to stability operations while simultaneously drawing down to a "transition force" by August 30, 2010, the date set by Obama for the end of U.S. combat operations in Iraq. The order also directed USF-I's subordinate units to focus on three major tasks for 2010: the "responsible drawdown of forces" to fewer than 50,000 troops by the end of August; support for the conduct of the March 2010 Parliamentary elections; and the August 2010 transition from Operation IRAQI FREEDOM to Operation NEW DAWN, in which new Advise and Assist Brigades (AABs) would replace the combat brigades that had been deploying to Iraq since 2003.[39] After August 2010, the command would continue to perform counterterrorism operations, but the vast majority of its forces would focus on developing Iraqi Government and security force capacity while completing a full "responsible redeployment" no later than December 31, 2011, as stipulated in the 2008 Security Agreement. OPORD 10-1's "end state" envisioned "an increasingly competent and capable GoI [Government of Iraq], an ISF capable of maintaining internal security and . . . a foundation for a lasting U.S.-Iraq security partnership."[40]

To oversee the new mission, Odierno reorganized his headquarters for the remainder of the campaign, merging the three previously independent operational headquarters into a single command. MNC-I and MNF-I merged and the Multi-National Security Transition Command (MNSTC-I) became an Advise and Train directorate within the new amalgamated headquarters. In the new structure, Odierno would have three deputy commanders: one each for Advise and Train, Operations, and Support. These changes shrank the size of the operational headquarters elements to 2,200 personnel by spring 2010, very different from the 7,000-strong headquarters of the surge era.[41]

Beyond Odierno's headquarters, MNF-I's four multinational divisions shifted to three U.S. divisions—north, center, and south—each with two AABs augmented with dozens of senior officers and noncommissioned officers to embed with partner ISF units. OPORD 10-1 envisioned a "transition force" of just more than 53,000, divided between about 12,000 troops and enablers at the USF-I level; about 18,000 troops and enablers at the division and theater levels; and about 23,000 troops in the AABs.[42] Geographically, Major General Anthony Cucolo's 3d Infantry Division was responsible for northern Iraq, Major General Terry Wolff's 1st Armor Division focused on Baghdad and Anbar, and Major General Vincent Brooks's 1st Infantry Division covered all of southern Iraq. This transition force was in far fewer locations than in previous years. From a peak of 495 bases and installations at the height of the surge, MNF-I had reduced its presence to just 281 bases by the publication of the new campaign plan on November 15, and decreased to fewer than 100 by September 2010. The closure of almost 400 bases and installations in a space of about 2 years proved a vast logistical undertaking, requiring a significant share of MNF-I/USF-I's manpower and planning capacity. As the bases closed, USF-I reduced the large population of support contractors from a high of approximately 160,000 in 2008 to fewer than 60,000 by late 2010.[43]

Not all of the senior leaders in Baghdad were completely satisfied with the new campaign plan and OPORD 10-1. USF-I Deputy Commanding General for Operations Lieutenant General Charles Jacoby had misgivings about the timing of the headquarters consolidation given the 2010 election season, the drawdown of brigades, and ongoing security operations in areas such as Ninawa. Jacoby believed these activities still required a separate corps headquarters to manage. "We should have gotten to 50,000 and gotten steady before [reorganizing]," Jacoby said later. "Trying to [shift to stability operations] in the middle of the election . . . where we were trying to get Iraqi units positioned to replace U.S. units as we were moving chess pieces off the battlefield at a quicker and quicker pace, was an operationally flawed concept."[44]

For Odierno, the changes in the Joint Campaign Plan and OPORD 10-1 were part of the inevitable U.S. exit from Iraq. He believed the U.S. campaign had always been destined to end by handing off security responsibilities to the Iraqi Government and its forces, but he also understood that the earlier transition plan of 2005-2006 was attempted too soon. Surveying the situation in late 2009, Odierno believed that the conditions for a resumption of the transition plan were now present, with a greatly expanded ISF deployed across the country and the Iraqi political groups competing far less through violence than through elections and the government structures.[45] If the political progress could continue, then USF-I could accept the risk involved in drawing down by almost 50 percent to the transition force level of 53,000, Odierno judged.

Iraqi Security Forces Shortfalls and Competition With Afghanistan

There were risks to the new campaign plan. The continued development of the ISF was not a sure thing. For U.S. forces to depart without a return of violence and instability the ISF had to improve its operational capabilities and expand its geographic coverage while the Iraqi Government took over full responsibility for funding it. By late 2009, the government's budget was in crisis. The recession of 2008 and the accompanying drop in oil prices had created a significant funding shortfall. The Iraqi cabinet responded by cutting the ISF development budget to half of what was required to produce what USF-I considered the "minimum essential capability."[46]

The financial problems came at a particularly bad time. USF-I had assumed the oil-rich Iraqi Government would be able to pay for the many costly capabilities needed for the country to defend itself without U.S. troops. The slashing of the defense budget risked the building of an air defense capability and the creation of an Iraqi Air Force. Accordingly, Odierno asked the Pentagon for $3.5 billion in security assistance to make up the difference. The cash-strapped Pentagon resisted until Odierno warned the Joint Chiefs that the shortfall threatened the President's withdrawal timeline.[47]

The budget crunch was not the only problem. By this point, Afghanistan had become a higher priority than Iraq for the U.S. Government. When the President ordered the drawdown of U.S. combat brigades in Iraq, Odierno advised that the mission could be accomplished with fewer combat troops. However, the scarce "enablers" — combat support systems such as intelligence, surveillance, and reconnaissance (ISR) and special operations forces — would need to remain in larger numbers through 2011 so that the combat units would not lose situational awareness, mobility, and force protection. Odierno also believed the Commanders' Emergency Response Program (CERP) and the congressionally sponsored Iraqi Security Forces Fund would become more important as U.S. units left.[48] Throughout 2009, the U.S. commands in Iraq found themselves competing with Afghanistan for enablers and funds at every level.

Early in 2009, U.S. Central Command (CENTCOM) commander General David H. Petraeus had reapportioned 40 percent of the Iraq theater's ISR to Afghanistan, a decision that Odierno believed introduced unnecessary risk to the Iraq mission. Petraeus believed himself under pressure from senior U.S. leaders to shift assets to Afghanistan, which the President concluded had long been under-resourced. This pressure mounted after the President announced on December 1, 2009, that the United States would send an additional 30,000 troops to Afghanistan for an 18-month "surge." The decision pushed Petraeus to accelerate the movement of forces into Afghanistan through the U.S. logistics network in the Middle East, a change in priorities for ports, shipping, and air bases that restricted the flow of resources into Iraq.[49]

Source: DoD photo by Sergeant Alexander Snyder (Released).

Soldiers Load a C-130 Aircraft at Balad Air Base, Iraq, Bound for Bagram Air Base, Afghanistan.[50]

OPORD 10-1, USF-I's plan for a transition force of 53,000 after August 2010, did not reflect Obama's intent to leave a "residual force" of between 35,000 and 50,000 in Iraq. The troop level that MNF-I leaders considered a minimal "floor" exceeded the White House's "ceiling" by 18,000. Odierno did not resist making Afghanistan the main U.S. effort, but he bristled at the idea that additional resources for Afghanistan should come from Iraq rather than from other theaters.[51] Illustrating Odierno's point, the last Marine command left Anbar in January 2010, handing over responsibility for the province to the 1st Armored Division. After 6 years in western Iraq, where they had done some of their hardest fighting since World War II, the Marines shifted to Afghanistan's Helmand Province. Thereafter, U.S. ground operations in Iraq would fall solely to the U.S. Army.

Source: DoD photo by Sergeant Daniel Schneider (Released).

Marines Case the Colors of II Marine Expeditionary Force During a Ceremony Marking the End of the Marines' Presence in Anbar Province.[52]

The war in Afghanistan also put considerable pressure on the special operations elements in Iraq. While the Combined Joint Special Operations Task Force (CJSOTF) effort in Iraq remained unchanged, in 2009 the special operations task force shifted its main effort to Afghanistan. In July, the Ranger elements from the task force departed Iraq, handing other joint SOF elements responsibility for countering malign Iranian influence. The next month, the joint task force shifted its forward headquarters to Afghanistan, leaving a smaller command and control element in Iraq.

Tension in U.S. Civil-Military Relations in Baghdad

The ISF budget shortfall and downgrading of the Iraq theater's importance in U.S. strategy came as USF-I and other DoD elements worked to implement the President's instructions to hand "lead agency responsibility" to the State Department by September 2010. USF-I leaders identified more than 1,000 functions and missions the U.S. Embassy would need to take over in 2010 and 2011. But MNF-I representatives learned that their U.S. Embassy counterparts did not intend to continue some of what USF-I considered to be core U.S. military functions in the country. For example, the State Department and other civilian agencies were not equipped to train the Iraqi Army and police in the way the U.S. military had done since 2005. The very different capabilities of USF-I and the U.S. Embassy led many senior USF-I leaders to believe the State Department would discontinue—or fumble—many mission-essential tasks once U.S. troops left.

The departure of Ambassador Ryan Crocker in mid-2009 struck a blow to U.S. military and U.S. Embassy relations and made the handover of responsibility more difficult. The close rapport Odierno and his command enjoyed with Crocker ended when Ambassador Chris Hill arrived in 2009 with what he believed was a Presidential mandate to "civilianize" the U.S. presence in Iraq and to make the Baghdad Embassy a "normal" U.S. diplomatic mission in which the ambassador was the President's personal representative with final authority over all operations in the country.[53]

Source: DoD photo courtesy Joint Combat Camera Center Iraq (Released).

**U.S. Ambassador to Iraq Christopher R. Hill With Iraqi Policemen
in Qadisiyah Province.[54]**

Hill's desire to assert embassy control over military activities led to considerable tension. After his first embassy briefing, a joint meeting with MNF-I and Iraqi governors, Hill fumed at what he perceived to be the Embassy's subordination to its military counterparts. He asked his staff "whether this was how briefings had always been conducted, with the commanding general handling 95 percent of it while the ambassador sat like a bobble head doll, nodding his approval."[55] Afterward, he declared that he would lead future meetings, which would be attended by equal numbers of soldiers and diplomats. Hill also reduced the civil-military working groups and asserted embassy authority over security and administrative functions but later blamed his uniformed counterparts for any friction. "[T]he military really had some trouble letting go," he said, because "the military and its camp followers were used to running everything in Iraq."[56]

In addition to differing views on the civil-military relationship, Hill and the U.S. military commanders had differing conceptions of the Iraq conflict. Having just emerged from the intense operations of the surge, U.S. military leaders regarded the relative stability of 2009 as fragile and dependent on continued security operations and political progress. Hill, by contrast, appeared to believe that Iraq had stabilized, and it was time for the U.S. military to leave. He pushed back against Odierno's idea of "drivers of conflict" that needed to be addressed to consolidate security. Hill also believed the United States should extricate itself from what he saw as Iraqi business. Toward this end, he began withdrawing long-standing embassy participation in Iraqi Government security and economic functions, later commenting that he was "appalled by the idea that anyone but Iraqis should be in attendance at an Iraqi national security meeting."[57] Hill also sought to extricate the United States from a number of international issues in which MNF-I had played a leading role, such as the complex matter of the Mujahedin e Khalq (MeK). The ambassador and his embassy team considered the MeK issue to be a "constant irritant" that should be left to the Iraqis or an international body such as the United Nations (UN), and he prohibited U.S. negotiators from interacting with the group.[58]

These disagreements over strategy soon became clashes of personality. As top leaders disagreed, relations became tense at lower levels as well. After 5 years of being housed with MNF-I in the Republican Palace in Iraq's Green Zone, the U.S. Embassy moved to its immense new compound in early 2009. Once there, Hill's staff gradually limited MNF-I's presence in the building, severing many of the day-to-day, civil-military working relationships that had existed since the days of the Coalition Provincial Authority (CPA) and Combined Joint Task Force-7 (CJTF-7). After half a decade of increasingly close partnerships, the U.S. diplomats and military officials in Baghdad were returning to the fractious civil-military relations that had developed between Ambassador Paul Bremer and Lieutenant General Ricardo Sanchez. This deterioration would hamper the U.S. mission in Iraq after 2009, when the country would enter a protracted political crisis for which the U.S. military and diplomatic representatives in Baghdad would advocate sharply different responses.

THE COMBINED SECURITY MECHANISM

One major political challenge of early 2010 was the continued Arab-Kurd conflict in northern Iraq. Having ceded provincial power by their misguided boycott of the January 2005 provincial elections, the Sunnis of northern Iraq voted in large numbers in January

2009 and won majorities or pluralities in Ninawa, Salahadin, and Diyala. Though the Sunni vote represented an embrace of the political process and thus a political defeat for AQI, it also precipitated a political struggle that threatened to spill over into violence and destabilize the country through the last 3 years of the U.S. military presence in Iraq.

The August 2008 confrontation between Arab troops and Kurdish peshmerga in Khanaqin was just the first in a series of low-level standoffs. Upon assuming command of MND-N in late 2008, Major General Robert Caslen concluded that "the peace dividend of the surge was that the Iraqi Army now had the ability to focus on what had previously been their adversary, the Kurds," and that the central government in Baghdad was intent on rolling back the Kurdistan Regional Government's control of Kirkuk.[59] "We quickly found ourselves in the middle of an ethnic conflict," Caslen recalled. "There were 12 separate times that there was a standoff between Kurds and Arabs with guns pointed at each other . . . [and] American soldiers standing in between."[60]

Kirkuk and Khanaqin were not the only flashpoints. In Ninawa Province, the Sunni Hadba Gathering, a party running on an anti-Kurdish platform, won 19 of the provincial council's 37 seats in the January 2009 elections and promptly formed a provincial government under Atheel Nujaifi with greatly reduced Kurdish participation.[61] In response, Ninawa's Kurdish leaders withdrew from their posts and refused to recognize Nujaifi as governor.[62] The situation came to a head in May 2009 when peshmerga forces prevented Nujaifi from traveling to Bashiqa, an oil-rich, Kurdish-administered district east of Mosul.[63] The governor turned back to Mosul before the situation escalated, claiming Kurdish leaders had issued a "shoot to kill" order if he attempted to enter the town. These continuing jurisdictional disputes between the Kurdistan Regional Government and its Arab counterparts caused ethnic strains all along the Green Line. By summer 2009, Odierno concluded that tension between Kurds and Arabs was the "No. 1 driver of instability" in all of Iraq, creating a real threat of ethnic civil war.[64]

Source: DoD photo by Sergeant Christopher Kozloski (Released).

Ninawa Provincial Governor Atheel Nujaifi Addresses Iraqi Police Academy Graduates in Mosul.[65]

Combined Checkpoints and the Golden Lions

One problem was that the Green Line was not an internal boundary, but a demilitarized zone, with peshmerga checkpoints set up to the north, Iraqi Army checkpoints some distance to the south, and a seam of often populated territory between the two. AQI and other insurgents used this seam to move with relative ease from the Syrian border to Mosul, and as far east as Kirkuk.[66] All along the Green Line, Sunni insurgent groups exploited Arab-Kurd tensions and stoked ethnic conflict. In Taza, a majority Turkoman town of 20,000 just south of Kirkuk, an AQI car bomb in June 2009 killed 75 and wounded 254, leaving locals convinced that AQI had targeted the quiet town to "ignite the sectarian sedition in Iraq."[67] The attack was just one in a series of provocative bombings made possible by the absence of a security presence within the seam.

Doing away with this causeway of insurgent activity was not a simple matter of maneuvering troops to establish a security presence. The U.S. forces that traditionally acted as the neutral security presence for several years continued to drawdown throughout 2009, leaving MND-N without the troops or the time for peacekeeping. In an effort to establish an effective security presence within the disputed area and build confidence between Arabs and Kurds, Odierno formulated a tripartite peacekeeping arrangement known as the Combined Security Mechanism. Odierno and other U.S. commanders recognized that the problem was political. "The problem was not that a Kurdish policeman and an Iraqi soldier would necessarily go to guns on each other," one U.S. brigade commander recalled. "It was because their leadership would."[68] The aim of the Combined Security Mechanism was cooperation between militaries first, and then, in Odierno's words, "have the political stuff follow."[69] By October, the concept evolved into a series of Combined Security Areas with checkpoints reporting to regional Combined Coordination Centers, all jointly manned by peshmerga, ISF, and U.S. troops.[70] A committee comprised of Jacoby, Iraqi Lieutenant General Ali Ghaidan, and a senior Kurdish security official pored over maps to plot the precise locations and boundaries of the security areas and checkpoints. The meetings were complex, back-and-forth negotiations with U.S. officers mediating between the two Iraqi groups.[71] "There were differences in things that did not seem important to us but were important to them," said one senior U.S. officer, and U.S. officials found themselves "moving [checkpoints] sometimes only hundreds of yards to make people happy."[72]

Source: DoD photo by Petty Officer 1st Class Matthew Leistikow (Released).

An Iraqi Federal Policeman, a U.S. Army Soldier, and a Kurdish Peshmerga Fighter, Members of the Golden Lions Combined Security Force, on Patrol Near the Green Line.[73]

The most innovative security mechanism was a Combined Security Force made up of equal parts ISF, peshmerga, and U.S. troops who manned the combined checkpoints and patrolled the security areas together. To bring the three forces together, MND-N set up joint training schools for platoons of Iraqis, Kurds, and Americans.[74] Each squad in the combined platoons was ethnically mixed, with soldiers from all three armies eating, sleeping, and training as a cohesive unit. To enforce the single unit identity further, the mixed force was given the name "Golden Lions" and outfitted in distinctive uniforms worn by both Kurds and Arabs.[75] By summer 2010, the Golden Lions were performing their mission throughout northern Iraq's disputed territories, part of the first Arab-Kurd peacekeeping mechanism along the Green Line in the country's history.

Still, the combined checkpoints and Arab-Kurd units needed an accompanying political consensus to prevent ethnic conflict, as one incident in early 2010 illustrated. As the combined checkpoints were erected along the Green Line in January 2010, Odierno insisted that the peshmerga dismantle their unilateral checkpoints inside the disputed internal boundaries areas.[76] However, the new joint security architecture failed in its first major test. On February 1, 2010, the Sunni Arab governor of Ninawa, Atheel Nujaifi, set out from Mosul in a convoy of dozens of vehicles to visit the peshmerga-occupied eastern districts of the province, but Kurdish leaders in Erbil deployed peshmerga and zerevani (Kurdish police) to block Nujaifi's way into the Kurdish-held districts.[77] Kurds along the route assaulted the governor's convoy and briefly fired at Nujaifi's vehicles. Nujaifi's entourage responded by arresting nine Kurds on the scene and jailing them in Mosul on "terrorism" charges.[78] The situation worsened when Kurdistan Regional Government (KRG) officials, most likely acting on orders from KRG President Massoud Barzani, arrested eight Arabs, escalating the affair into a hostage exchange crisis.[79] The situation was finally resolved on February 22, when Deputy Prime Minister Rafe al-Issawi and U.S. officials arranged the simultaneous release of the hostages from both sides.

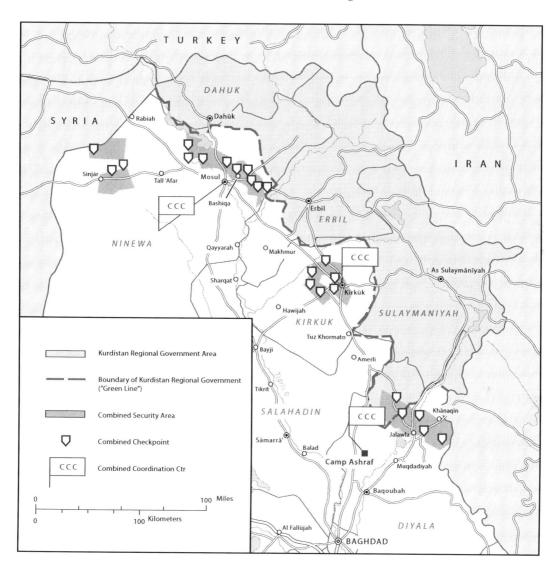

Map created by the official cartographer at the U.S. Army Center of Military History, Washington, DC.

Map 22. Combined Security Mechanism, 2010-2011.

The episode showed the fragility of the peace along the Green Line where U.S. officials had been surprised by what Odierno termed "a complete breakdown within the peshmerga forces in implementing the agreed-upon joint security architecture."[80] It also showed that preventing civil war would not be easy, and that the United States played an essential moderating role among the rival Iraqi political groups.[81]

THE EVISCERATION OF AL-QAEDA IN IRAQ, JANUARY–MAY 2010

The bombings of autumn 2009 had shown that AQI remained a potent threat despite having lost almost all its territory during 2008–2009. The group also had succeeded in sowing discord among the fractious political parties as they prepared for the Parliamentary elections of March 2010. However, within weeks of AQI's final high-profile attacks against the Iraqi ministries in Baghdad on December 8, 2009, USF-I, coalition SOF, and the Iraqi security forces began a series of operations that would bring AQI closer to defeat than at any point during the long Iraq War. The crushing of AQI in spring 2010 would change the organization in unanticipated ways, greatly reducing its capacity to harm the Iraqi population and interrupt the political process. The decimation of AQI would also lay the groundwork for the terrorist group's later evolution into the Islamic State of Iraq and the Levant (ISIS).

Breaking the Bombing String

The autumn 2009 bombings had a significant impact on Iraqis, even though the last of the three did far less damage than the rest. With Iraq's March 7, 2010, Parliamentary elections just weeks away, USF-I leaders were concerned that AQI could disrupt the political process or perhaps thwart voting in some areas as it had done in 2005. Accordingly, U.S. and Iraqi SOF focused on AQI in Mosul and other strongholds ahead of the voting. Investigations of the autumn bombings had yielded a great deal of intelligence about AQI's structure and operations, so that USF-I analysts believed by January that they had a clearer idea of AQI-ISI's inner workings than at any other point in the Iraq War.[82]

This new understanding of AQI's organization paid off on January 4, when U.S. and Iraqi troops simultaneously struck 16 targets in Mosul, resulting in several high-profile captures and the death of several more leaders, including AQI's "Border Wali" who was responsible for bringing foreign fighters into the north.[83] The following week brought another significant gain in Baghdad, where on January 12, U.S. and Iraqi SOF foiled a fourth set of coordinated car bombings, breaking the string of massive attacks against the Iraqi Government.[84] Just 10 days later, on January 22, U.S. SOF conducted a raid that killed Abu Khalaf, the senior AQI facilitator who had inherited Abu Ghadiyah's Syria-based foreign fighter network after the latter's death in October 2008. Though pressure from the Syrian regime already had marginalized Abu Khalaf, his death still hurt AQI's Syria-based network.[85]

AQI's setbacks in Mosul and on the border did not prevent the group from attacking the Arba'een pilgrimage in early February, when AQI suicide bombers and IEDs killed and wounded more than 500 of the several million pilgrims making their way to Karbala. The January U.S.-Iraqi operations did appear to break AQI's momentum in Baghdad after the carnage of the fall, and the biggest gains against the extremist group were still to come.

The Wali of Baghdad

The Maliki government's erroneous claim to have captured Abu Omar al-Baghdadi in April 2009 harmed its credibility. Ironically, it proved the first step toward the devastation of AQI's senior leaders the following year. Ahmad Khamis al-Majma'i, the AQI detainee that Maliki's forces mistakenly thought was Baghdadi was, in fact, one of the AQI leader's lieutenants who sometimes acted as Baghdadi's stand-in.[86] In the course of his interrogations, Majma'i explained how Baghdadi and his organization moved and operated to evade detection, information that allowed the Iraqi Government to begin infiltrating AQI's Baghdad networks.[87]

The first major payoff from Majma'i's information was the capture of AQI's so-called wali (governor or guardian) of Baghdad, a Moscow-born, 35-year-old former Ba'athist named Manaf al Rawi, whom the Iraqi Government believed had masterminded the autumn bombings. After Saddam Hussein's fall in 2003, Rawi had been recruited by Abu Musab al-Zarqawi and had fought in the first battle of Fallujah before being captured by coalition troops in June 2004. Task Force 134, the command responsible for coalition detention operations, had released him in November 2007, after which Zarqawi's successor Abu Ayyub al-Masri integrated him back into AQI's operational network, making him head of AQI's Baghdad operations by the end of 2008.[88] On March 11, 2010, Iraqi federal police arrested Rawi just 2 miles from Camp Victory, after which ISF interrogators held him for more than a week without informing USF-I.[89] For an additional 2 weeks, Iraqi officials did not allow USF-I access to Rawi, perhaps wary of sharing their detainee after the embarrassing public disagreement with MNF-I leaders over the falsely identified Abu Omar al Baghdadi the year before. Prime Minister Maliki did not allow USF-I officers to join Rawi's interrogation until April 4, the same day a string of AQI car bombs in Baghdad struck the Iranian, Egyptian, and German Embassies, with another bomb defused at the French Embassy.[90]

As USF-I joined the questioning, Rawi gave his captors detailed and extensive information about himself, the AQI leadership network, and the group's plans.[91] According to Rawi, AQI in Baghdad had been subdivided into three sectors, one encompassing the east side of the city and two more covering the north and south halves of the west side. The group's internal communications were governed by security measures so strict that Rawi and other AQI sub-leaders never personally met their superiors, but instead received instructions only by courier or from ISI "minister of war" Abu Ayyub al-Masri— an arrangement that left Rawi with wide latitude to plan and carry out operations in the city as he saw fit.[92]

Among other plots, Rawi explained that Masri had entrusted him with the early planning of a major external operation ordered by AQI senior leader Ayman al-Zawahiri—a high profile attack against the 2010 FIFA World Cup games in South Africa.[93] He also revealed that AQI had hatched a plot to hijack aircraft and fly them into Iraq's Shi'a shrines to incite a sectarian war, as their former leader Zarqawi had intended by the Samarra mosque bombing of 2006.[94] The threat to the shrines prompted a rapid response from the Iraqi Government, for which such an attack would have spelled disaster. Government ministries scrambled to account for Iraqi planes and examine the backgrounds of Iraqi pilots, while USF-I moved quickly to deploy an antiaircraft capability to Najaf and other threatened areas.[95] The plot against the shrines did not come to fruition, however, because AQI's top leaders were about to meet their end.

The Elimination of AQI's Senior Leadership

In addition to these plots, Rawi provided information that led directly to Masri and Baghdadi. Along with Rawi's lengthy confessions, which were later broadcast on Iraqi and regional television, information released by disgruntled AQI members via social media in 2013-2014 explained how Rawi's capture eventually led to the evisceration of almost the entire AQI/ISI leadership. Masri had instituted extreme operational security measures in fall 2009 after the death of AQI operations chief Brigadier General Mohammed Nada al-Juburi (also known as al-Ra'i). Both Baghdadi and Masri had remained in a static location, with the latter only communicating with Rawi by courier and then relying on Rawi to disseminate his orders to the other provincial walis. Also actively involved in the dissemination of Masri's orders was Ibrahim Awwad al-Samarra'i, (also known as Abu Bakr al-Baghdadi or Ibrahim al-Badri), the future ISIS caliph whose Baghdad home served as the primary distribution point for AQI senior leaders' correspondence.[96]

In an AQI organization whose leadership had been depleted by 6 years of rapid turnover, Masri had come to place great trust in Rawi due to the latter's long jihadi pedigree and experience, but this reliance would prove to be the AQI leader's undoing. Operating on Rawi's information, ISF troops captured the complete AQI records for Anbar Province, which included orders from Masri to the AQI walis for Anbar and Ninawa to supply Rawi with revenue, fighters, and suicide bombers. Taken at face value, the AQI records showed that as much as 80 percent of AQI's revenue in Ninawa was being sent to Rawi to finance operations in Baghdad.[97]

The captured documents provided an operational and administrative picture so complete that, according to Prime Minister Maliki, gaining corroboration though detainee interrogations was relatively easy. In effect, the same clandestine bureaucracy that had served AQI so well in the past, enabling it to remain resilient in the face of severe attrition, now proved lethal to the group. As part of a combined U.S.-ISF operation that the Iraqis called LION'S LEAP, the exploitation of the captured AQI documents led to the immediate capture of several senior AQI leaders. They were Abdallah Azzam Misfir al-Qahtani (also known as Sinan al Saudi), a former Saudi Army officer who was the architect of the planned World Cup attack; Tariq Hassan Abd al-Qadir (also known as Abu Yasin al-Jaza'iri), the AQI emir of west Baghdad; and Muzahim al-Janabi, who oversaw AQI's operations in southern Baghdad from his base in Lutufiyah.[98]

These three high profile captures yielded information exposing the hiding place of Masri and Baghdadi in the Tharthar region approximately 10 kilometers outside the city of Tikrit, on the edge of the former area of operation (AO) Bedrock and just a short distance west of Major General Anthony Cucolo and MND-N's headquarters at Camp Speicher.[99] In a manner eerily reminiscent of Saddam Hussein, or later, Osama bin Laden, the two AQI men had lived in a simple mud building since September 2009, communicating with AQI senior leaders in Pakistan and a handful of key subordinates through trusted couriers.[100] A measure of how removed Masri had become from the day-to-day administration of his own organization can be seen in one AQI member's claim that following al-Ra'i's death, Masri appointed a new operations chief—a former Ba'athist colonel named Samir Abd Mohammed al-Khlifawi (aka Hajji Bakr)—without having any prior contact with or knowledge of the man.[101] Apart from their wives, the only individuals present at the house were Baghdadi's son and Masri's aide de camp. Masri's own wife later claimed to the Arabic press that during her time living near Lake Tharthar she never saw any trace of the ISI that her husband purportedly led.[102]

On April 18, 2010, U.S. troops and their counterparts from the Iraqi 54th Brigade identified Masri's and Abu Omar al-Baghdadi's isolated safe house and set up a cordon around it to prevent the AQI leaders from escaping.[103] Once the American and Iraqi troops revealed themselves, the women living in the house came outside and, after some initial denials, admitted that Baghdadi was there. After a failed attempt to persuade Baghdadi to surrender, the troops raided the house, and after a firefight, Baghdadi, Masri, Baghdadi's son, and Masri's aide blew themselves up rather than be captured.[104]

The seizure of the AQI leaders' hideout yielded a trove of documents and more than six terabytes of data that enabled special operations forces to mount a series of assaults against other AQI leaders. In the days following the April 18 raid, U.S. and Iraqi forces captured and interrogated 16 AQI senior aides and their bodyguards.[105] On April 20, U.S. and ISF troops killed Ahmad Ali Abbas Dahir al-Ubayd, AQI's commander for northern Iraq, and 3 days later captured Mahmoud Suleiman, a leading AQI operations officer in Anbar.[106] On May 4 in west Baghdad, U.S. troops and ISF counterparts dealt AQI-ISI another major blow when they captured Abu Abdullah al-Shafi, the head of Ansar al Islam, who had been one of the few leaders of the jihad to survive 7 years into the war and had been considered a potential successor to Masri. Coinciding with other AQI losses and mass surrenders in the Hamrin Mountains of Diyala and Sharqat in Ninawa, these raids crippled the group.[107] By mid-May, Odierno reported that at least 32 of AQI's top 42 leaders had been killed or captured since the beginning of March, the most severe leadership losses the organization had suffered since beginning operations in Iraq in 2003.

Measuring the Impact on AQI

The thousands of handwritten letters, documents, CDs, computers, and audio recordings captured by coalition troops yielded tremendous insight into AQI's inner workings, including direct correspondence between Masri and al-Qaeda senior leaders in Pakistan.[108] Among the information recovered was Masri's last major operational plan to target a large number of Christian churches in Baghdad. The information also confirmed previous coalition assessments that AQI was suffering from both financial and manpower shortages, indicating the degree to which the group already had declined prior to the deaths of its leaders.[109]

Source: DoD photo by Private 1st Class Jared Eastman (Released).

Major General Anthony Cucolo, Commander of MND-N.[110]

While coalition and Iraqi SOF units carried out the raids that destroyed AQI's operational leadership, Cucolo and MND-N undertook an offensive against AQI's vast financial empire in northern Iraq. In early 2010, U.S. analysts came to understand the extent to which Iraq's northern petroleum industry had become a black market that fed insurgent groups of all kinds, especially through the trafficking of the gasoline produced at Iraq's largest refinery in Bayji.

Smugglers routinely stole gasoline from tankers once they left Bayji and resold the stolen gas to illegal roadside gas stations that dotted the highways in northern Iraq, many of them affiliated with AQI. The process involved not just AQI and other insurgent groups, but also a vast network of government officials, trucking outfits, and gas station owners.[111] Cucolo and Major General Nasser Ghanam, commander of the 2d Iraqi Army Division in Mosul, formulated a combined plan to disrupt this illicit network. The controversial Ghanam previously served as a brigade commander in Abu Ghraib, where he notoriously attempted to repress Abu Azzam's large Awakening group against MNF-I's wishes in 2007. In Mosul, however, Ghanam seemed more eager to assist his U.S. partners.[112] Under Ghanam and Cucolo's combined direction, 3 MND-N battalions intercepted gasoline smugglers at the Iraq-Syria border north and west of Mosul while Ghanam's troops and Iraqi border forces shut down all 117 of the identified illegal gas stations in the north and arrested the operators at each one.[113] The shutdown of the gas stations disrupted the black market cash flow at precisely the time AQI found itself desperate for money and new leaders.

The cumulative loss of leadership and finances crippled AQI. Even before the April 18 raid, USF-I had estimated that AQI's strength had been cut to fewer than 100 fighters in Mosul and Baghdad and no more than 1,000 in the entire country. The April and May raids slashed these numbers further.[114] In early May, Odierno reported to Gates that AQI "had never before lost so many key leaders or been tested as they were now." By June, both U.S. and Iraqi officials judged that AQI effectively had been cut off from secure communications with the broader al-Qaeda network.[115] The documents captured later from Osama bin Laden's compound in Abbottabad in 2011 supported this as bin Laden was still seeking detailed biographies for the new AQI leadership as late as June 2010.[116] Not until mid-July 2010 were al-Qaeda's senior leaders able to reestablish direct communications with AQI leaders inside Iraq.[117] Isolated from their counterparts outside Iraq, AQI's remnants inside Iraq fell into disarray during the late spring of 2010 with various mid-level leaders jockeying to fill the group's power vacuum. Subsequent AQI insider accounts painted a picture of the group's network in chaos.[118]

Even so, the remaining AQI leaders of Baghdad and Mosul moved quickly to demonstrate that their organization was not extinct. On May 10, 2010, AQI operatives carried out coordinated attacks against 24 targets in Mosul, Baghdad, Fallujah, Hillah, and Basrah, killing 119 and wounding more than 350.[119] In Tel Afar on May 14, they detonated a truck bomb on the field during a children's soccer match and followed with suicide vest bombers amidst the crowd of panicked parents, causing more than 130 casualties.[120]

Nevertheless, for USF-I leaders the AQI operations of May-June 2010 showed that the effectiveness and sophistication of the group's attacks had greatly diminished. To gather their resources to maintain a presence in Mosul and Baghdad, AQI's remnants had to cede many of their former operating areas to other insurgent groups such as the Naqshbandi Army.[121] There were still "decentralized cells . . . attempting to continue to execute the last orders given," Odierno noted, but these had no hope of disrupting the ongoing Iraqi election process or achieving AQI's ultimate goal of destabilizing the Iraqi Government.[122] It was an assessment the captured Wali of Baghdad shared. Interviewed in his captivity on May 18, Manaf al-Rawi told CNN, "It is 80 to 100 percent harder to operate for al Qaeda these days."[123]

THE IRAQI POLITICAL CRISIS

The Disputed 2010 Elections

The rapid U.S.-Iraqi operations that decimated AQI's leadership in early 2010 had taken place alongside a protracted political crisis that threatened to undermine the security gains. The Iraqi Parliamentary election of March 2010 was a high-stakes contest for control of the two traditional pillars of the Iraqi state: vast oil revenues that reached more than $100 billion in 2010 and a huge security sector of over 900,000 troops and police. The political battle of 2010-2011 would have profound consequences for the U.S. campaign in Iraq, casting a shadow over USF-I's plans and initiatives as U.S. forces began to drawdown.

Four major coalitions competed in the election. As in 2005, the major Kurdish parties formed a Kurdish Alliance to secure their share of the new Parliament. Iraq's Sunnis, meanwhile, followed the Kurdish example by forming a single electoral list headed by former Prime Minister Ayad Allawi, reversing the fragmentation that had hurt Sunni prospects in 2005. The country's Shi'a parties had fragmented into two large coalitions by 2010: Prime Minister Maliki's State of Law coalition, with the Da'wa Party at its center; and the Iraqi National Alliance comprised of ISCI, Badr, and the Sadrists.

The period prior to the election was volatile. As the parties published their candidate lists in December and January, the Iraqi Parliament's de-Ba'athification committee—formed under Ahmad Chalabi's leadership in the early years of the war—threw the election campaign into disarray. Led by Chalabi's deputy, Ali Faisal al-Lami—only recently released from a year of U.S. captivity after his role in the assassinations of U.S. officials in Sadr City in 2008—the committee used its dubious legal authority to nullify the candidacy of more than 500 allegedly Ba'athist-linked candidates, including some who previously had been elected to Parliament.[124] The move weakened Allawi's Sunni-majority Iraqiyah coalition that had a large number of former Ba'athists while helping the Shi'a-majority coalitions, leaving the Sunni community to conclude that their candidates were being specifically targeted.[125]

After months of security planning, Iraqi and American officials were pleased when the elections occurred on March 7 with little violence. From their base in the Green Zone, Maliki and his State of Law allies believed they would win about 120 seats in the new 325-seat Parliament, a total that would have given them a leading role in forming the next government.[126] However, the results of the vote were a surprise to all involved. As the tallies came in from Iraq's provinces in mid-March, Iraqiyah finished first in the voting, gaining 91 seats to Maliki and State of Law's 89.[127] The unexpected result was due at least in part to Allawi's success in attracting secular Shi'a voters, who elected a dozen Shi'a candidates from Baghdad and the south as part of the Sunni-majority Iraqiyah. Maliki and State of Law, conversely, did poorly in Sunni-majority areas and lost ground in Shi'a provinces to the Sadrists, who unexpectedly increased their seat count from 29 to 40.

According to the standard interpretation of the Iraqi constitution and the 2005 precedent, the electoral result meant that Allawi and Iraqiyah should be given the first chance to form a new government. Maliki and his allies, however, had other plans. As the official results were announced in late March, Maliki secured a ruling from Iraq's constitutional court that whatever parties could form the largest post-electoral bloc would win the right to form a government, regardless of the election results. The decision was legally questionable and, given Chief Justice Medhat Mahmood's previous connections to Maliki during the Site 4 and Jadriyah Bunker scandals, many Sunnis saw the ruling as overt sectarianism and illegitimate. With trust in Iraq's legal system undermined, the electoral process devolved. Maliki took the matter further by demanding recounts in areas where his coalition had done poorly and accusing the United States and the UN of undercounting his coalition's votes. He publicly denounced Iraq's electoral commission as complicit and signaled his intention not to recognize Iraqiyah's victory. Privately, Maliki sent threatening messages to several members of Iraq's Independent High Electoral Commission before attempting to obtain arrest warrants against them. The matter concerned Odierno enough for him to consider the possibility of USF-I providing security for the electoral commission's headquarters.[128] Further complicating the situation, Lami's de-Ba'athification committee disqualified an additional 52 candidates on April 26—an act applauded by Maliki as he fought to maintain his hold on power.[129]

Maliki's Consolidation of Control

Signs that Maliki intended to use government institutions to alter the election out-come in his favor worried USF-I leaders, who had already become alarmed by the Prime Minister's consolidation of control of Iraq's security forces and intelligence community in 2009-2010. Over the course of 2009, Maliki had asserted his power over operational Iraqi units via the Office of the Commander in Chief, headed by General Faruq al-Araji. Eventually he circumvented the Ministry of Defense to take control of command appointments and issue tactical orders without using the formal chain of command.

A similar process played out in the Iraqi intelligence community. The United States had expended great effort professionalizing Iraq's principal intelligence apparatus, the Iraqi National Intelligence Service (INIS), under the leadership of the former military officer Mohammed Shahwani, a Sunni Turkoman who opposed Iranian involvement in Iraq. For 6 years, Shahwani led the INIS in a clandestine war against Iranian-sponsored operatives inside Iraq, including some operatives from the Shi'a-led rival intelligence agency, the Ministry of State for National Security Affairs. When Shahwani suddenly resigned in the wake of the autumn 2009 bombings in Baghdad, Maliki seized control of the INIS and dismissed 376 intelligence officers, often using de-Ba'athification as a justification. In their place, Maliki appointed political loyalists, many from the Da'wa Party. The new Da'wa-affiliated intelligence officers had difficulty in penetrating Iraq's Sunni communities and often focused on regime preservation and the targeting of the Prime Minister's political opponents rather than on AQI. Some experts, especially those in CJSOTF, believed this purge of capable Sunni intelligence officers blinded the Maliki government from observing the resurgence of the ISI and its transformation into ISIS in later years.[130]

Maliki also obtained control of the Special Tactics Unit (STU), a small INIS paramilitary unit that had been constructed as part of Iraq's intelligence infrastructure, but had eventually entered into an advisory relationship with the CJSOTF. Under Maliki's authority, the STU was removed from the INIS and attached to the Counterterrorism Service, which was itself under the direct control of the Prime Minister's office. In the description by CJSOTF commander Colonel Mark Mitchell, the STU in its new incarnation became a "hit squad" used to "disappear" Sunni election candidates or to arrest them on vague corruption charges. The STU often held its detainees without acknowledgement in the unit's private detention facilities in Baghdad, where CJSOTF officials who attempted to inspect the facilities were denied access. In the face of the STU's behavior, the CJSOTF withdrew its advisers and severed ties with the unit in March 2010.[131]

The Election Crisis

As Maliki began a campaign of chicanery to overcome his election loss and hold onto the premiership, postelection events split the senior U.S. officials. Odierno warned Washington that Iran was trying to block Allawi and Iraqiyah from forming a government and aimed to assemble Iraq's Shi'a parties into a governing coalition under Tehran's domination. In a April 4 memo, Odierno cautioned that Iran's electoral manipulation could result in "the worst case scenario for security, stability, and our continued strategic partnership with Iraq as it excludes significant Sunni participation, potentially causes the Iraqi people to lose faith in the democratic process, as the leading candidates are excluded from the government formation." The result could be "a compromise Shi'a Prime Minister who is beholden to Iran."[132]

Hill and other senior U.S. Embassy officials disagreed, arguing that there were limits to Iranian influence that prevented Tehran from becoming as dangerous as Odierno and USF-I believed. Hill's political counselor, Gary Grappo, argued, "in many places in Iraq, the Iranians were doing a great job of wearing out their welcome," and that while Iran was trying to "buy off" Iraqi politicians to obtain greater influence, few Iraqis were cooperating.[133] In answer to Odierno's warnings, on April 20, Hill himself told President Obama and Secretary of State Hillary Clinton that "the risk of Iraq becoming an Iranian client state was 'negligible'."[134]

Despite Hill's assurances, days after the vote results were announced in Baghdad, Iraqi President Jalal Talabani flew to Tehran to broker discussions among the major Shi'a parties about a consensus Prime Ministerial candidate—and about returning Talabani himself to the President's office.[135] Though the Shi'a parties did not agree on a candidate—largely because of their collective resolve to deny Maliki's return to power—the conference in Tehran appeared to offer the Iranian regime the chance to steer the government formation process. Having expected a chance to form his own government, Allawi warned in May that the electoral machinations could potentially drive the country back into a civil war that would "not remain within the borders of Iraq. It will spill over and has the potential to reach the world at large, not just neighboring countries."[136]

As the month of May passed with no new government, and with the Iranian regime and Maliki blocking Allawi's path, Odierno expressed reservations about continuing the "Responsible Drawdown of Forces" to 50,000 Soldiers by the August 2010 deadline.[137] The USF-I commander remained concerned about Maliki's use of extraconstitutional powers to usurp the role of the security and intelligence ministries. Odierno and some other U.S. officials also believed Maliki's attempt to overturn the election constituted a dangerous power grab that might eventually destabilize the political situation and return Iraq to sectarian violence, unraveling the extensive security and political gains the United States had made. Odierno was so concerned with the direction Maliki seemed to be taking that he warned Washington that Maliki might stage "a rolling coup d'état of the Iraqi state."[138]

Hill agreed with the assessment of Maliki's intentions, but unlike Odierno, the ambassador believed Maliki's return to the premiership was the best outcome for U.S. interests. Iraq required a Shi'a leader, Hill told other U.S. officials in Baghdad, and Maliki, as the strongest of the Shi'a leaders, would be the most reliable U.S. partner. Allawi had, in Hill's view, disqualified himself by relying on a mostly Sunni coalition; a situation that Hill believed was the equivalent of a black South African politician leading a white Afrikaner political party.[139] Echoing this sentiment, political counselor Gary Grappo later commented, "[R]ealistically speaking there was no chance . . . that Allawi, himself a Shi'a, would win the election as the leader of a largely Sunni political coalition. . . . 60 to 65 percent of the country was Shi'a, [and] after what they had experienced not only under Saddam but all previous regimes, they were not about to trust this crowd that was basically the leftovers from the Saddam era."[140] Hill also believed it was not appropriate for the United States to meddle too deeply in internal Iraqi affairs. Iraq was a sovereign nation, Hill told Vice President Joseph Biden, and "picking and choosing winners (and losers) was way beyond anything we could do. . . . Perhaps back in 2004 or 2005, but in

2010 Iraq was its own country with its own political system, which we would interfere with at our peril."[141]

After discussions with Biden in Washington in the late spring, Odierno had understood that U.S. leaders intended to remain neutral in the government formation negotiations among the Iraqi parties. However, in talks with Iraqi leaders in Baghdad in July, Biden signaled that the United States would not support Allawi's candidacy as Prime Minister and implied that the United States had decided to help Maliki retain the premiership. This change of plan confounded Odierno, who warned Biden that if Maliki were allowed to prevail over the Iraqiyah coalition that had technically won the elections, the Prime Minister and his allies could be counted on to conduct reprisals against the Sunni-majority Iraqiyah in order to marginalize them politically, probably reigniting sectarian violence in the process. To answer these concerns, Biden told Odierno and other U.S. officials in Baghdad that Iraq's Shi'a, Sunnis, and Kurds would always detest one another, just as the Irish and the British had, and implied that trying to construct a national reconciliation pact among them was futile.[142]

***

The summer of 2010 found Iraq in a much-improved security condition but a precarious political situation. USF-I and the ISF had rebounded from AQI's massive autumn bombings and had pulverized the terrorist group, neutralizing its ability to conduct large-scale attacks. In northern Iraq, after fits and starts, USF-I's combined security initiative offered a means to keep the peace between Arabs and Kurds along Iraq's volatile Green Line. These developments seemed to offer hope that the reduced transition force could successfully conduct the stabilization operations needed to cement the gains of the surge.

These hopes began to founder, however, as the disputed Iraqi election results dragged into a political crisis. The Sunni-majority Iraqiyah electoral victory in March 2010 marked the political culmination of the Sunni Awakening, but the combined efforts of Prime Minister Maliki, the Shi'a political parties, and the Iranian regime threatened to nullify Iraqiyah's victory. The situation caused a split within the U.S. Government that found USF-I and the U.S. Embassy on opposite sides, exacerbating the divide that had opened between the two with the arrival of Hill in 2009. By late summer, with Iranian and American policymakers ironically aligning against the candidacy of Allawi, Maliki remained in his position as caretaker Prime Minister, standing athwart the constitutional government formation process so that it could not proceed without him. Instead of a functioning government, for the foreseeable future Iraq would have a bitter Sunni-Shi'a divide that threatened to rekindle the embers of sectarianism. This political crisis overshadowed USF-I's evisceration of AQI and cast doubt on the U.S. ability to cement the gains of 2007-2009.

ENDNOTES - CHAPTER 13

1. Multi-National Force-Iraq (MNF-I), Quarterly History, July 1-September 30, 2009. All unpublished documents in this chapter, unless otherwise stated, are in the Chief of Staff of the Army (CSA) Operation IRAQI FREEDOM (OIF) Study Group archives, Army Heritage and Education Center (AHEC), Carlisle, PA.

2. Quarterly Command (Cmd) Report (Rpt), July 1-September 30, 2009, MNF-I, October 2009, p. 34. Security incidents are based on coalition and host nation reports and are defined as attacks against infrastructure and government organizations; found and cleared bombs (IED and mines); detonated bombs; sniper, ambush, grenade, and other small arms attacks; and mortar, rocket, and surface to air attacks.

3. MNF-I, SECDEF Weekly Update, February 23-March 1, 2009.

4. MNF-I, SECDEF Weekly Update, July 6-12, 2009; and August 10-16, 2009.

5. MNF-I, SECDEF Weekly Update, July 6-12, 2009.

6. Ibid., August 10-16, 2009.

7. Ibid.

8. USF-I, Quarterly History, January 1-March 31, 2010.

9. MNF-I, Quarterly History, July 1-September 30, 2009.

10. MNF-I, SECDEF Weekly Update, July 20-26, 2009; Bill Roggio, "Iraqi troops detain deputy leader of Ansar al Islam," *Long War Journal,* August 4, 2009, available from *http://www.longwarjournal.org/archives/2009/08/iraqi_troops_detain.php*, accessed June 1, 2016.

11. MNF-I, SECDEF Weekly Update, August 3-9, 2009.

12. MNF-I, SECDEF Weekly Update, August 10-16, 2009.

13. MNF-I Battle Update Assessment (BUA), July 6, 2009; MNF-I, Quarterly History, July 1-September 30, 2009.

14. MNF-I, Quarterly History, July 1-September 30, 2009.

15. MNF-I BUA, August 25, 2009.

16. MNF-I, SECDEF Weekly Update, August 31-September 6, 2009.

17. Ibid.

18. MNF-I, SECDEF Weekly Update, August 24-30, 2009.

19. MNF-I, SECDEF Weekly Update, September 21-27, 2009.

20. MNF-I, Quarterly History, July 1-September 30, 2009.

21. "Al Qaida Linked Group Claims Baghdad Bombings," Radio Free Europe, October 27, 2009, available from *http://www.rferl.org/content/AlQaedaLinked_Group_Claims_Baghdad_Bombings/1861891.html*, accessed June 1, 2016.

22. MNF-I, SECDEF Weekly Update, September 7-13, 2009; and October 12-18, 2009.

23. MNF-I, SECDEF Weekly Update, October 26-November 1, 2009.

24. Ibid.

25. MNF-I, Quarterly History, July 1-September 30, 2009.

26. Quarterly Cmd Rpt, July 1-September 30, 2009, MNF-I, p. 11.

27. Interview, Dr. Lynne Garcia, Contemporary Operations Study Team, with Ambassador Christopher R. Hill, U.S. Ambassador to Iraq, May 14, 2012.

28. Interview, Chief of Staff of the Army (CSA) Operation IRAQI FREEDOM (OIF) Study Group with General Raymond T. Odierno, January 25, 2015.

29. MNF-I, SECDEF Weekly Update, November 2-8, 2009.

30. MNF-I, Quarterly History, October 1-December 31, 2009.

31. Ibid.

32. MNF-I, SECDEF Weekly Update, December 7-13, 2009.

33. MNF-I, Quarterly History, October 1-December 31, 2009.

34. MNF-I, SECDEF Weekly Update, December 7-13, 2009.

35. MNF-I, SECDEF Weekly Update, December 14-20, 2009.

36. MNF-I, Quarterly History, October 1-December 31, 2009.

37. Ibid.

38. Briefing, MNF-I, Joint Campaign Plan Assessment Team Outbrief, October 27, 2009; quote from MNF-I, Quarterly History, October 1-December 31, 2009.

39. Briefing, USF-I Commander's Conference Overview of OPORD 10.01.4: Stability Operations, August 21, 2010, Military History Institute (MHI), AHEC, Carlisle, PA.

40. MNF-I, Quarterly History, October 1-December 31, 2009.

41. Manuscript (Ms), *On Point*, Vol. V, Book IV, Chapter 3, Fort Leavenworth, KS: Combat Studies Institute, September 25, 2014, p. 49.

42. MNF-I, Quarterly History, October 1-December 31, 2009.

43. USF-I, Quarterly History, January 1-March 31, 2010.

44. Ms, *On Point*, Vol. V, Chapter 6, p. 8.

45. Informal discussion, Lieutenant Colonel Joel Rayburn with General Raymond T. Odierno, Chief of Staff of the Army, October 4, 2013, Washington, DC.

46. MNF-I, Quarterly History, October 1-December 31, 2009.

47. MNF-I, SECDEF Weekly Update, November 9-15, 2009; USF-I, Quarterly History, January 1-March 31, 2010.

48. MNF-I, Quarterly History, October 1-December 31, 2009.

49. Interview, Colonel Joel Rayburn, Chief of Staff of the Army (CSA) Operation IRAQI FREEDOM (OIF) Study Group, with Michael Bell, March 25, 2016.

50. DoD photo by Sergeant Alexander Snyder, "From Iraq to Afghanistan," March 28, 2009, Released to Public, available from *https://www.flickr.com/photos/mnfiraq/4522176789/in/album-72157623734045725/*.

51. Interview, CSA OIF Study Group with Odierno, January 25, 2015.

52. DoD photo by Sergeant Daniel Schneider, "1st Armored Division transfer of authority takes place at Camp Ramadi, Iraq [Image 4 of 4]," DVIDS Identifier 243130, January 23, 2010, Released to Public, available from *https://www.dvidshub.net/image/243130/1st-armored-division-transfer-authority-takes-place-camp-ramadi-iraq*.

53. Christopher R. Hill, *Outpost: Life on the Frontlines of American Diplomacy: A Memoir*, New York: Simon & Schuster, 2014, p. 351.

54. DoD photo courtesy of Joint Combat Camera Center Iraq, "Ribbon-cutting ceremony near Scania re-opens highway segment from Baghdad to Basra [Image 2 of 17]," DVIDS Identifier 177403, June 2, 2009, available from *https://www.dvidshub.net/image/177403ribbon-cutting-ceremony-near-scania-re-opens-highway-segment-baghdad-basra*.

55. Hill, *Outpost*, p. 350.

56. Interview, Garcia, CSI Contemporary Operations Study Team, with Hill, May 14, 2012; Christopher R. Hill, "How the Obama Administration Ignored Iraq: One ambassador's story of an exit strategy gone wrong," *Politico*, October 2, 2014.

57. Hill, "How the Obama Administration Ignored Iraq."

58. Interview, Garcia, CSI Contemporary Operations Study Team, with Ambassador Gary Grappo, Minister Counselor for Political Affairs, July 30, 2012, U.S. Embassy, Iraq.

59. Interview, Steven Clay, CSI Contemporary Operations Study Team, with Lieutenant General Robert Caslen, July 19, 2012.

60. Ibid.

61. Rania Abouzeid, "Arab Kurd Tensions Could Threaten Iraq's Peace," *Time*, March 24, 2009, available from *http://content.time.com/time/world/article/0,8599,1887189,00.html*.

62. Ramzy Mardini, "Factors Affecting Stability in Northern Iraq," West Point, NY: Combating Terrorism Center, August 15, 2009, available from *https://www.ctc.usma.edu/posts/factors-affecting-stability-in-northern-iraq*.

63. Ibid.

64. Interview, Steven Clay, CSI Contemporary Operations Study Team, with Odierno, May 10, 2012.

65. DoD photo by Sergeant Christopher Kozloski, "Ninewah Iraqi police fulfill Ministry of Interior's Iraqi police training requirement, setting the stage for Iraqi police primacy in region [Image 1 of 5]," DVIDS Identifier 172802, May 11, 2009, Released to Public, available from *https://www.dvidshub.net/image/172802/ninewah-iraqi-police-fulfill-ministry-interiors-iraqi-police-training-requirement-setting-stage-iraqi-police-primacy-region*.

66. Interview, Clay, CSI Contemporary Operations Study Team, with Odierno, May 10, 2012.

67. "Dogs to search for bomb victims in Iraq," Associated Press, June 21, 2009, available from *http:// www.nbcnews.com/id/31459332/ns/world_news-conflict_in_iraq/#.VCltmPldWFV*.

68. Interview, Steven Clay, Contemporary Operations Study Team, with Colonel George Larry Swift, Cdr, 1 BCT 1AD USD-N, January 10, 2012.

69. Interview, Dr. Donald Wright, Contemporary Operations Study Team, with Odierno, CG USF-I, May 10, 2012.

70. Interview, Steven Clay, Contemporary Operations Study Team, with Major General Anthony Cucolo, CG MND-N, USD-N 3 ID, December 7, 2011.

71. Interview, Dr. Lynne Garcia, Contemporary Operations Study Team, with General Charles Jacoby, CG I Corps MNC-I, June 4, 2011.

72. Interview, Dr. Lynne Garcia, Contemporary Operations Study Team, with Major General (Ret.) James Hunt, DCG MNC-I, March 1, 2012.

73. DoD photo by Petty Officer 1st Class Matthew Leistikow, "Town assessment [Image 16 of 28]," DVIDS Identifier 272254, April 13, 2010, Released to Public, available from *https://www.dvidshub.net/ image/272254/town-assessment*.

74. Interview, Clay, Contemporary Operations Study Team, with Cucolo, CG MND-N, USD-N 3 ID, December 7, 2011.

75. Interview, Garcia, Contemporary Operations Study Team, with Jacoby, CG I Corps MNC-I, June 4, 2011.

76. Chief of Staff Notes, General Raymond T. Odierno, January 20, 2010.

77. USF-I, Quarterly History, January 1-March 31, 2010.

78. MNF-I, SECDEF Weekly Update, February 1-7, 2010; Briefing, CENTCOM Commanders Update, February 9, 2010.

79. Briefing, disputed internal boundaries update to Brigadier General John G. Rossi (USF-I Effects Coordinator), March 3, 2010; MNF-I, SECDEF Weekly Update, February 8-14, 2010.

80. USF-I, Quarterly History, January 1-March 31, 2010.

81. MNF-I, SECDEF Weekly Update, February 22-28, 2010.

82. USF-I, Quarterly History, January 1-March 31, 2010.

83. Ibid.

84. MNF-I, SECDEF Weekly Update, January 11-17, 2010.

85. USF-I, Quarterly History, January 1-March 31, 2010.

86. Muhammad Al-Tamimi, "Former Leading Members in Al-Qa'ida Say Replacements for Al-Baghdadi and Al-Masri Are Ready; Expect Revenge Soon," *Al-Hayat*, April 30, 2010.

87. The Iraqi Government broadcast Majma'i's video confessions on Al-Iraqiyah, Iraq's state-run television news channel, on April 20, 22, and 26, 2010.

88. Ibid., on May 10, 2010, and May 14, 2010.

89. Scott Stewart, "Jihadists in Iraq: Down For the Count?" Stratfor Global Intelligence, April 29, 2010, available from *http://www.stratfor.com/weekly/20100428_jihadists_iraq_down_count*, accessed July 23, 2010; USF-I, SECDEF Weekly Update, March 22-28, 2010.

90. USF-I, Quarterly History, April 1-June 30, 2010.

91. Interviews, CSI Contemporary Operations Study Team with Lieutenant General Robert W. Cone, Fort Leavenworth, KS, February 27, 2012, and May 21, 2012, p. 5; Bill Roggio, "Al Qaeda in Iraq confirms deaths of al Masri, Baghdadi," *Long War Journal*, April 24, 2010, pp. 1-2, available from *http://www.longwarjournal.org/archives/2010/04/al_qaeda_in_iraq_con.php*, accessed May 1, 2012.

92. "Death Industry," *Al-Arabiyah*, May 14, 2010.

93. Ibid.

94. USF-I, Quarterly History, April 1-June 30, 2010.

95. MNF-I, SECDEF Weekly Update, April 5-11, 2010.

96. Abu Ahmad, "The Concealed Truths About al-Baghdadi's State," April 5, 2014, available from *http://fundforfallenallies.org/news/2014/09/25/here-finalized-osc-translation-aq-loyalist-abu-ahmads-account-isil-and-its-origins*, accessed June 1, 2016.

97. The Iraqi Government broadcast reports on the captured documents and the insights about AQI's organization they yielded during the newscasts of state-run Iraqiyah news channel on April 19, 20, and 26, 2010; May 17, 2010; and December 13, 2010.

98. Al-Iraqiyah Television, May 17, 2010; Al-Iraqiyah Television, April 26, 2010.

99. Al-Iraqiyah Television, April 19, 2010.

100. Al-Iraqiyah Television, April 20, 2010; Al-Iraqiyah Television, April 26, 2010.

101. Ahmad, "The Concealed Truths About al-Baghdadi's State."

102. As related by Abbas Fadil, Cdr of the 54th Iraqi Army Brigade. See also Sadiq Al-Iraqi, "Abu-Ayyub al-Masri's Wife: We Arrived in Baghdad after the Fall of Saddam Husayn's Regime; My Husband Was Vague and Extremist," *Al-Riyadh*, April 29, 2010.

103. "Death Industry," *Al-Arabiyah*, May 7, 2010.

104. USF-I, Quarterly History, April 1-June 30, 2010.

105. Interviews, CSI Contemporary Operations Study Team with Cone, February 27, 2012; and May 21, 2012, p. 5; Roggio, "Al Qaeda in Iraq confirms deaths of al Masri, Baghdadi."

106. Bill Roggio, "Al Qaeda in Iraq is 'broken', cut off from leaders in Pakistan, says top US general," *Long War Journal*, June 5, 2010, p. 3, available from *http://www.longwarjournal.org/archives/2010/06/al_qaeda_in_iraq_is.php*, accessed August 2, 2012.

107. Muhammad Al-Tamimi, "Al-Qa'ida Faces Real Danger in Himrin Mountains," *Al-Hayat*, April 28, 2010.

108. Newscasts, *Al-Iraqiyah*, April 19, 20, and 26, 2010. These were the regular newscasts on Iraqi state-run television.

109. Ibid., April 20, 2010.

110. DoD photo by Private 1st Class Jared Eastman, "A Dog Face Hero Remembered [Image 1 of 2]," DVIDS Identifier 266728, April 4, 2010, Released to Public, available from *https://www.dvidshub.net/image/266728/dog-face-hero-remembered*.

111. Manuscript (Ms), *On Point*, Vol. V, Book III, Chapter 6, Fort Leavenworth, KS: Combat Studies Institute, September 25, 2014, pp. 24-25.

112. Ibid.; USF-I, Quarterly History, April 1-June 30, 2010.

113. Ibid.

114. Quarterly Cmd Rpt, April 1-June 30, 2010, USF-I, p. 47.

115. Roggio, "Al Qaeda in Iraq is 'broken,' cut off from leaders in Pakistan, says top US general."

116. Letter, UBL to Atiyatullah Al-Libi, SOCOM-2012-0000019-HT, available from *https://www.ctc.usma.edu/posts/letter-from-ubl-to-atiyatullah-al-libi-4-original-language-2*.

117. "Testimony to End Bloodshed among Mujahideen in the Levant," Al-Fajr Media Center, May 2, 2014.

118. "Struggle Over Power Between Al-Sadr, Those Who Seceded From Him; Al-Qa'ida Tries To Attract Islamic Army," *Al-Hayat*, August 22, 2010.

119. Ms, *On Point*, Vol. V, Chapter 6, p. 16.

120. Quarterly Cmd Rpt, April 1-June 30, 2010, USF-I, p. 49.

121. Quarterly History, April 1-June 30, 2010, USF-I.

122. Jane Arraf, "General Odierno: Al Qaeda in Iraq Faces Serious Financial Crunch," *Christian Science Monitor*, July 2, 2010, available from *http://www.csmonitor.com/World/Middle-East/2010/0702/General-Odierno-Al-Qaeda-in-Iraq-faces-serious-financial-crunch*, accessed June 1, 2016; USF-I, Quarterly History, April 1-June 30, 2010.

123. Jomaneh Karadsheh, "Al Qaeda Commander: How I Planned Iraq Attacks," CNN, May 18, 2010, available from *http://www.cnn.com/2010/WORLD/meast/05/20/iraq.al.qaeda/*, accessed June 1, 2016.

124. Joel Rayburn, *Iraq after America: Strongmen, Sectarians, Resistance*, Stanford, CA: Hoover Institution Press, 2014, p. 211.

125. Rpt for Congress, Kenneth Katzman, "Iraq: Politics, Governance, and Human Rights," Washington, DC: Congressional Research Service (CRS), 2014, pp. 6-7.

126. Rayburn, *Iraq after America*, p. 212.

127. Leila Fadel and Karen DeYoung, "Ayad Allawi's Block wins most Seats in Iraqi Parliamentary Elections," *The Washington Post*, March 27, 2010, available from *http://www.washingtonpost.com/wp-dyn/content/article/2010/03/26/AR2010032602196.html*, accessed June 9, 2015.

128. Quarterly History, January 1-31, USF-I, March 2010, p. 8.

129. Ian Black, "Iraq Election Chaos as 52 Candidates are Disqualified," *The Guardian*, April 26, 2010.

130. Mariska Sullivan, "Maliki's Authoritarian Regime," Middle East Security Report No. 10, Washington, DC: Institute for the Study of War, April 2013, p. 16; E-mail, Colonel (Ret.) Mark Mitchell, former CJSOTF-AP Cdr, to Colonel Frank Sobchak, February 20, 2016, sub: Follow up questions.

131. Interviews, Colonel Frank Sobchak, CSA OIF Study Group, with Colonel Mark Mitchell, CJSOTF-AP Cdr, September 29, 2014; and February 8, 2016; E-mail, Mitchell to Sobchak, February 20, 2016, sub: Follow up questions.

132. USF-I, SECDEF Weekly Update, March 29-April 4, 2010.

133. Interview, CSI Contemporary Operations Study Team with Grappo, July 30, 2012.

134. Hill, *Outpost*, p. 376.

135. Quarterly Cmd Rpt, April 1-June 30, 2010, USF-I, p. 11.

136. Martin Chulov, "Iraq Risks Sectarian War, Warns Election Winner Iyad Allawi," *The Guardian*, May 10, 2010.

137. USF-I, SECDEF Weekly Update, March 19; April 4, 5-11, 19-25; April 26-May 2; and May 17-23, 2010; Colonel Thomas Goss notebook, entries for May 28, 2010, and March 10-11, 2014. Goss was Lieutenant General Cone's executive officer.

138. Hill, *Outpost*, p. 371.

139. Mark Moyar, *Strategic Failure: How President Obama's Drone Warfare, Defense Cuts, and Military Amateurism Have Imperiled America*, New York: Threshold Editions, 2015, p. 82.

140. Interview, CSI Contemporary Operations Study Team with Grappo, July 30, 2012.

141. Hill, *Outpost*, p. 384.

142. Emma Sky, *The Unraveling: High Hopes and Missed Opportunities in Iraq*, New York: Public Affairs, 2015, pp. 334-338.

CHAPTER 14

FROM NEW DAWN TO ZERO, AUGUST 2010-DECEMBER 2011

In June 2010, just weeks after Iraqi President Jalal Talabani led government formation talks among Iraq's Shi'a political parties in Tehran, the U.S. Senate confirmed General Lloyd Austin as the next commander of U.S. Forces-Iraq (USF-I) and General Raymond Odierno as the next Chief of Staff of the U.S. Army. The handover between the two was scheduled for the end of August, coinciding with President Barack Obama's directed change of mission for USF-I and the departure of the last U.S. combat brigades. After Austin's assumption of command, the U.S. operation in Iraq would be renamed from "IRAQI FREEDOM" to "NEW DAWN" to signal the shift to a noncombat mission.

Odierno used his final month in Iraq to begin determining what forces and resources the United States would need after December 2011 when the U.S.-Iraq security agreement expired. As his staff analyzed what might be accomplished with a residual force of various sizes and capabilities, Odierno concluded that it would take at least 25,000 troops to sustain a strategic partnership with Iraq.[1]

Back in the United States, Austin had begun work on the residual force question as well. Before taking command, he oversaw wargames based on the possible scenarios facing the United States as the U.S.-Iraq security agreement expired in late 2011, including the chance the United States would be forced to "go to zero." The wargames highlighted that without a residual U.S. force, USF-I would find it difficult to hand off hundreds of military activities to the U.S. Embassy, wind down support for provincial reconstruction teams, and deactivate the existing command and control structures. The United States would also be hard pressed to maintain stability along the Kurdish-Arab Green Line or help the Iraqis prevent the resurgence of the Islamic State.[2]

Vice President Biden (left) General Odierno (right) and Ambassador Jeffery (center).
Source: DoD photo by Sergeant 1st Class Roger Dey (Released).

Vice President Joseph R. Biden Meets General Raymond Odierno and Ambassador James Jeffery in Baghdad.[3]

On August 31, Obama announced an end to "the American combat mission in Iraq," a step he had first promised as a Presidential candidate more than 4 years earlier. Operation IRAQI FREEDOM had concluded, Obama declared, and Iraqis now had taken the lead for their own security, though USF-I would remain on hand until the end of 2011 to advise and assist them. The President added that the promise of American partnership was contingent on the Iraqis moving forward "with a sense of urgency to form an inclusive government that is just, representative, and accountable to the Iraqi people."[4] At the same time, Obama said that U.S. involvement in Iraq had to be balanced against other pressing issues such as Afghanistan and the need to restore America's economic strength at home.[5]

The day after the President's remarks, September 1, 2010, Austin took command from Odierno in a formal ceremony in Baghdad. Odierno's departure as USF-I commander coincided with the replacement of Ambassador Christopher Hill, whose relationship with Odierno and his command had grown more tense as the Iraqi election impasse deepened. Instead of Hill, Austin would partner with U.S. Ambassador James Jeffrey, a veteran Arabist who had served as an Army officer in Vietnam and, unlike Hill, arrived at the Embassy with extensive Iraq experience. Together, Austin and Jeffrey set out to repair the civilian-military relationship that had deteriorated during Hill's tenure, bringing their staffs together for combined planning and team building.[6]

Behind Austin are (left to right) Vice President Biden, Secretary of Defense Gates, Chairman of the Joint Chiefs of Staff Admiral Mullen, and U.S. Central Command Commander General Mattis. Source: DoD photo by Sergeant 1st Class Roger Dey (Released).

General Lloyd Austin During His Assumption of Command of USF-I from General Raymond Odierno.[7]

THE INTERREGNUM

Austin and Jeffrey took up their duties in a nation that had been trying to form a government for almost 6 months. In early 2006, the Iraqi political parties' inability to reach an agreement while the country slipped into civil war had hamstrung General George Casey, Jr., and Multi-National Force-Iraq (MNF-I). In 2010, with the country far less violent than in 2006, the Iraqis were even more deeply deadlocked, as Prime Minister Nuri al-Maliki worked to prevent Ayad Allawi from forming a new government in the hope of eventually forcing all of the parties to agree that only he could be Prime Minister.[8] To prevent Allawi's Sunni-majority Iraqiyah coalition, which had won a plurality of Parliamentary seats, from being shut out of power, Vice President Joseph Biden suggested in late summer that Maliki return as Prime Minister but share power with a new strategic policy council to be headed by Allawi. In Biden's concept, Allawi's council would determine policy and strategy for the Iraqi security forces (ISF), the Iraqi defense budget, and the particulars of the U.S.-Iraq strategic relationship. The idea, while politically creative, was flawed. Iraq's Maliki-friendly courts were sure to challenge the council's constitutionality. Without firm constitutional justification, the proposed compromise amounted to a gentlemen's agreement that would rest on the goodwill and good faith of the major parties—a risky venture, considering Maliki made it clear he did not intend to dilute his power as commander in chief.

The prolonged negotiations over the formation of the government came at the same time U.S. officials expected to coordinate with their ISF counterparts to transfer many military and diplomatic activities. The uncertainty of the political situation made Iraqi officials reluctant to make decisions. Reconciliation initiatives stalled as well, as USF-I had difficulty getting officials of Maliki's caretaker government to demonstrate continued support for the Sons of Iraq, which continued to face attacks and intimidation from Sunni insurgents.[9] As the months passed, U.S. commanders also found their ISF counterparts and caretaker government officials unwilling to act against militant groups as intensely as they had in 2008 and 2009, especially Shi'a militants.[10] After Shi'a militants rocketed the U.S. Embassy on September 23, U.S. officials noted the perpetrators had little fear that the ISF would pursue them. By mid–October, a full month had passed since USF-I or the ISF had attacked the top-tier militant networks in a meaningful way. Some U.S. officials suspected the Iraqi militants were testing the new commander, Austin, to gauge his reaction.[11]

Like the United States, the Iranian regime had become impatient with the pace of Iraq's government formation as the stalemate dragged on through the summer. By September, Iranian leaders had decided to support Maliki and had begun to pressure Iraq's Kurdish and Shi'a leaders to back Maliki as well. In Tehran, General Qassem Soleimani, head of the Islamic Revolutionary Guard Corps (IRGC) Quds Force, reportedly reminded Iraqi leaders that U.S. forces would soon leave Iraq, but Iran would always be their powerful neighbor. Soleimani's terms to the Iraqis were simple: Maliki would remain Prime Minister, Talibani would remain President, and the U.S. military would be forced to leave Iraq by the end of 2011 as the U.S.-Iraq security agreement required. Iraqi leaders who cooperated would benefit from Iranian political assistance and cash payments, while those who defied Iran would suffer "dire consequences."[12] With both the United States and Iran backing Maliki's return, all that remained was for Iraq's other major parties to negotiate for as much power as possible in a second Maliki government.

OPERATION NEW DAWN AND THE "RESPONSIBLE DRAWDOWN OF FORCES"

The Advise and Assist Mission

In Operation NEW DAWN, Austin and his command continued to work with ISF even as they withdrew. Austin saw three components to his mission.[13] First, U.S. forces would advise, train, assist, and equip the ISF "so that they are capable of COIN [counterinsurgency] operations, maintaining internal security, and have developed the foundation for external defense." Second, U.S. forces would conduct combined operations to neutralize al-Qaeda in Iraq (AQI) and other violent extremist networks. Third, U.S. forces would help increase the capacity of the Iraqi ministries and other institutions.[14] Additional key tasks included helping to reduce Kurd-Arab tensions and balancing Iranian influence.[15]

To accomplish these missions, Austin had an initial force of 50,000 troops, with 7 Advise and Assist Brigades (AABs) spread across the three remaining U.S. divisions. In his initial guidance, Austin warned that USF-I could not afford to be surprised since the diminished U.S. troop level in the country left the command little flexibility and depth. To maintain their situational awareness and force protection, the AABs needed closer relationships with the ISF.[16] Austin noted that USF-I would have to rely on Iraqi units to secure the American lines of communication during the final withdrawal if it came.[17]

The AABs were a departure from the Army's preference to train its combat units mainly for high intensity conflict while treating stability operations as a secondary focus. Instead, the AABs were designed expressly for the new post-combat mission in Iraq, with their organization and training modified to better assist Iraqi units—army, police, and border forces. Some AAB commanders saw this new role as analogous to that of the observer-controllers at the Army's combat training centers, mentoring and conducting operations simultaneously.[18] In addition, the AABs provided their Iraqi partners with intelligence and targeting assistance, air and logistics support, planning, and command and control. The AABs' mission also included helping improve Iraqi governance, especially by providing security for the provincial reconstruction teams (PRTs) still operating across Iraq. Some AAB commanders even saw supporting the PRTs as their primary mission.[19]

Each AAB contained a civil affairs company, psychological operations teams, combat camera teams, and additional contracting officers and lawyers. Each brigade also had a human terrain team comprised of civilian social scientists—anthropologists, sociologists, and political scientists—to analyze local Iraqi political and economic dynamics. The brigades also had five Stability Transition Teams (STTs), which were essentially the military transition teams (MiTTs), special police transition teams (SPTTs), and border transition teams (BTTs), renamed. Each STT had 14 senior officers and noncommissioned officers (NCOs) who worked with ISF counterparts until the expiration of the security agreement at the end of 2011.[20] Unlike their predecessors, the STTs were organic to the

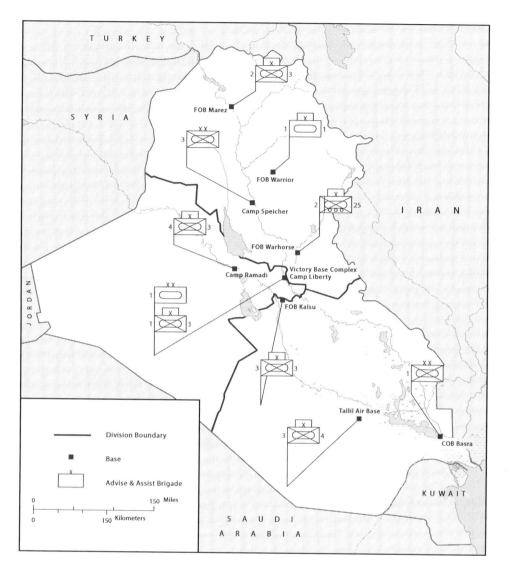

Map created by the official cartographer at the U.S. Army Center of Military History, Washington, DC.

Map 23. Disposition of U.S. Forces, USF-I Operation NEW DAWN, September 2010.

brigades, reflecting lessons learned from the 2005-era transition teams that suffered from unity of command challenges and lacked support when operating independently inside a brigade's battlespace.[21] Making the STTs part of the brigade's structure also made them more flexible. If certain Iraqi units needed more mentoring than others, an AAB commander could shift STT members from more capable units to advise less capable ones.[22]

The earlier transition teams had focused on the battalion level of the Iraqi Army, but the STTs paired with brigades and divisions instead. Partnering at the higher level freed transition teams to assist the Iraqi border forces, an element of the ISF that had a reputation for looking the other way as Iranian weapons and agents were smuggled into Iraq.[23] In one instance highlighting the border guards' ineffectiveness, during the 36th Infantry Division's 8-month deployment to Iraq's nine southern provinces in 2011, the Iraqi Border Police did not seize a single contraband weapon.[24]

Along with their nontraditional organization, the AABs underwent very different pre-deployment training than COIN-oriented brigade combat teams. NCOs and junior officers attended an abridged civil affairs course at Fort Bragg, NC, to develop governance and reconstruction skills and add capabilities and depth to the few PRTs assigned to each brigade. Almost every Soldier attended Arabic language classes, and key leaders received additional training, often at the State Department's Foreign Service Institute. Many units were trained in city management and civic administration. Some AABs sent leaders to train with the U.S. Border Patrol; others worked with the U.S. Department of Agriculture. Reflecting hard lessons from the early phases of the MiTT program, the STTs were assigned to their AABs early enough to attend pre-mission training with the rest of the brigade. Even the PRTs, usually including their assigned State Department personnel, attended pre-mission training.[25]

In contrast to USF-I's drawdown and changed missions, special operations forces (SOF) in Iraq prepared for a long-term presence, believing they would remain for counterterrorism and security force assistance missions long after conventional forces left. Envisioning an enduring mission similar to those in the 1990s in Kuwait and Colombia, special operations elements altered their command structure and rotational policies. To sustain the unity of effort, SOF leaders created a new headquarters, Joint Forces Special Operations Component Command-Iraq (JFSOCC-I), headed by a Special Forces general officer who would command Combined Joint Special Operations Task Force-Arabian Peninsula (CJSOTF-AP) and all other special operations elements in Iraq. To promote unity of effort further, SOF leaders ended the 7-year-old policy of rotating 5th and 10th Special Forces groups as the CJSOTF-AP headquarters every 7 months. The 5th Special Forces Group (Airborne) received permanent responsibility for the CJSOTF-AP headquarters, freeing the 10th Special Forces Group to refocus on Europe. This new arrangement, prompted by years of frustration due to the differing approaches between the two groups, matched a 2004 proposal that SOF leaders had rejected in favor of the rotational policy.

Below the SOF headquarters level, there would be no drawdown in forces, with the USF-I commander insisting that the CJSOTF maintain its full complement of three battalion-sized task forces that would be the last units to leave Iraq in the event of a full withdrawal. Those task forces increased the length of their deployments from 7 to 9 months to avoid rotating units and headquarters at the same time and to match more closely the conventional units' deployment schedule. Maintaining a large special operations footprint as U.S. conventional forces drew down was challenging. Much of the success of special operations forces in previous years came from their symbiotic relationship with conventional forces that provided base security, logistics support, medical evacuation, and quick reaction capabilities. As conventional forces receded across Iraq, many special operations elements had to be repositioned to maintain their support.[26]

Among the AABs, the declared end of combat operations and the constraints of the security agreement created an entirely new operational rhythm, making their experience fundamentally different from the COIN-oriented brigades that had come before them. As the number of brigades in USF-I shrank, the amount of territory each AAB covered grew, which paradoxically forced some AABs to increase the number of bases they occupied in order to maintain contact with the Iraqis they advised.[27] The larger areas of responsibility created logistical and medical evacuation challenges, with each AAB commander forced to weigh carefully where to position Soldiers safely so that any casualties could be evacuated to medical facilities within the "golden hour."

The pace of security operations slowed significantly as Iraqis assumed the lead, in part due to the security agreement's requirement for U.S. units to obtain evidence-based warrants from Iraqi judges before offensive operations. Local reconstruction projects slowed as well once the State Department and the U.S. Agency for International Development (USAID) took the lead in U.S. development efforts. Projects based on military necessity that were commonplace during earlier years, such as hiring unemployed Iraqis to pick up garbage to eliminate improvised explosive device (IED) hiding spots, no longer passed muster. Reflecting the transition to Iraqi civil authority, the PRTs and AABs coached Iraqi officials to nominate their own reconstruction projects, approving only those that could be sustained after the United States departed.[28]

To a certain degree, Operation NEW DAWN represented a return to Casey's transition plan from 2005 to 2006, but under more favorable circumstances. Many U.S. officers cited the same rationale for the diminished American role that MNF-I had used 4 years earlier, arguing that an American drawdown would push the Iraqis to improve their own capabilities and avoid the dependency trap. For example, Major Jason Bullock, a battery commander in 1st Battalion, 82d Field Artillery, echoed the same concerns that Casey and General John Abizad had had with Iraqi dependency and praised the security agreement as a way to overcome those concerns:

> The U.S. military is still full of [Soldiers] who would much rather do everything unilaterally, but good leaders know that's a road to nowhere, except more time in Iraq. The security agreement was a forcing function not only for U.S. troops to embrace partnership and try to develop the ISF, but also a wakeup call for the ISF that we are not going to be here forever and they are on the clock to get to the level they need to get to before we leave.[29]

The Battle of the Palm Grove

The first significant test of the idea that USF-I's units should coach from the sidelines as the ISF took responsibility for security within Iraq's borders came shortly after Austin took command. On September 11, 2010, in Diyala Province where politicized Iraqi Army leaders had kept USF-I advisors at arm's length, a large Iraqi force became bogged down in an engagement against a much smaller Sunni insurgent force in an agricultural area about 50 miles from Baghdad.[30] When locals reported to a nearby Iraqi Army unit that a group of AQI fighters had gathered in a palm grove to construct bombs, an initial ISF attack against the insurgents collapsed on contact. After the first assault failed, at least seven different Iraqi units responded to the scene, each unable to mount a coordinated attack against an AQI force that may have been as small as a squad. A number of senior

Iraqi officials descended on the area, including the commander of Iraqi Ground Forces Command, General Ali Ghaidan, and watched ISF units mount a series of unsuccessful assaults in column formation. The situation did not improve until U.S. Soldiers from 2d Brigade, 25th Infantry Division, the local AAB, arrived with rotary wing reconnaissance, close-air support from attack helicopters, and indirect fire. On September 12, U.S. F–16s dropped two 500-pound bombs on the AQI position—the first such airstrike since June 2009—after which Iraqi troops maneuvered into the palm grove to find the AQI fighters gone. The Iraqi troops had failed to establish a cordon around the area as U.S. firepower dislodged the insurgents, apparently allowing the AQI men to escape.[31]

Source: DoD photo by Sergeant Brandon Bolick (Released).

Iraqi and U.S. Soldiers Maneuver During the Battle of the Palm Grove.[32]

This incident provided several lessons for the USF-I command team. The Iraqis had made contact with the enemy before notifying the nearest U.S. unit that they might need assistance, so that the AABs and their subordinate formations had been forced to deal with the action as it unfolded.[33] As they had been trained to do, the local U.S. troops under Lieutenant Colonel Robert Molinari had refrained from taking over the battle from the Iraqis. In Molinari's words, he had taken "an appetite suppressant" when it had come to letting his more capable U.S. Soldiers take the lead and instead focused on providing as much assistance as the ISF leaders were willing to accept.[34] Similarly, Lieutenant General Robert Cone, USF-I's deputy commander for operations, had monitored the situation and instructed USF-I's subordinate commanders to wait for the Iraqis to ask for assistance rather than offer it unsolicited. In Cone's view, since the Iraqis would soon have to conduct such engagements without U.S. operational support, they had to stop relying on immediate U.S. assistance.[35]

The Battle of the Palm Grove showed that Iraqis' capacity for independent action was limited. In its aftermath, Cone concluded that USF-I's top priority for ISF development should be training the Iraqis in combined operations at the platoon and company level, where they had failed at the Palm Grove. Cone also reviewed the Iraqis' problems with command and control, another shortfall during the fighting. In his opinion, the Iraqi regional commands that had proliferated during 2007-2009—including the Diyala Operations Command, which technically had been responsible for the battle—had received a great deal of attention but did not serve the longer-term interests of the Iraqi Army. Cone believed the Iraqis needed an operational organization that looked beyond immediate tactical problems in specific locations, a function that the disparate operations commands could not fulfill. Accordingly, Cone avoided direct dealings with Iraqi division commanders and instead used General Ghaidan, commander of the Iraqi Ground Forces Command (IGFC), as his primary interlocutor, in hopes of developing the IGFC into a senior-level headquarters focused on the welfare of the Iraqi Army as an institution, capable of maintaining and training fielded forces and capable of thinking beyond the next crisis.[36]

Back in Diyala, the AAB's battalion-level after-action review revealed that the Iraqi troops not only had struggled with basic conventional tactics, but had also mistreated local citizens and detainees, a counterproductive factor in a COIN campaign.[37] In the aftermath of the September 11-12 fiasco, Molinari found the 5th Iraqi Army division far more willing to seek the AAB's help, which eventually resulted in collective training and battalion-level live fire exercises.[38] In the larger sense, the Battle of the Palm Grove left U.S. commanders with the unsettling sense that years of training and billions of dollars of expenditure might have accomplished little.

COIN Capabilities vs. Modernization

The debacle in Diyala illustrated how far the Iraqi forces were from the capability the U.S. military thought that they needed. In 2009, Prime Minister Maliki had believed his security forces capable of maintaining domestic order in Iraq, and U.S. leaders generally had agreed. The Iraqi Army that the U.S.-led coalition helped create was proficient at internal security tasks such as staffing checkpoints and conducting light patrols. However, Iraqi leaders had been overconfident in the ISF's broader abilities to operate without U.S. assistance. Although Iraqi leaders decided to purchase M1A1 tanks, M113 armored personnel carriers, attack helicopters, and M198 howitzers, Iraqi units in 2010 could neither execute combined-arms operations at any level nor defend and control their own airspace. In 2009, MNSTC-I estimated Iraq needed another 12 years to become self-sufficient in defense matters, a decade beyond the term of the U.S.-Iraq security agreement, but the same assessment also had optimistically assumed no serious threat from another regional state, a diminishing level of sectarian conflict, and a waning insurgency.[39]

In the aftermath of the Diyala incident, Austin and his command conducted a thorough assessment of the state of the Iraqi Army in October 2010, with sobering results. Many Iraqi commanders were absent, and in some cases driven by political allegiance rather than professional responsibilities. The Iraqi Army and Iraqi police did not cooperate. The Iraqi Army's logistics and unit staffing systems were abysmal. Across the army, ammunition remained in short supply. In some units, soldiers "hot bedded" in bunks due to a shortage of barracks space.[40]

Lieutenant General Cone (second from left). Source: DoD photo by Staff Sergeant Daniel Yarnall (Released).

Lieutenant General Robert Cone, USF-I Deputy CG for Operations, With General Ali Ghaidan, Commander of the Iraqi Ground Forces Command.[41]

Another major problem was that constant operations against AQI and other militant groups wore their combat units down. Iraqi leaders rarely pulled units from the front lines to refit and train, often leaving them in the fight until they became combat ineffective. But even if Iraqi units could have rotated through training, the army as a whole lacked a training management system, a fact that Austin labeled his "number one gap and concern for ISF" in November 2010. Without it, the United States could not be confident the Iraqi Army could maintain its proficiency following USF-I's departure.[42]

Fixing these problems was difficult. Iraq's inability to form a government hindered USF-I's efforts to help Bagdad plan and modernize its forces. Iraqi defense budget shortfalls further complicated matters.[43] As the Iraqis' newly purchased U.S.-built military hardware began to arrive, the government struggled to pay for and maintain it. By the end of 2010, the Iraqis had received 3 Bell helicopters and 51 of the projected 140 M1A1 tanks, but the government only budgeted a third of the estimated $1.5 billion needed to maintain the new equipment. The shortfall created the risk that the ISF's expensive new systems might quickly fall into disrepair.[44]

Source: DoD photo by Technical Sergeant Randy Redman (Released).

An M1A1 Abrams Tank From the Iraqi 9th Mechanized Division.[45]

The Interior Ministry was just as problematic as the Defense Ministry. Austin had hoped the Iraqi police could assume a larger security role, freeing Iraqi Army units to refit and train. However, as U.S. commanders took stock in late 2010, they concluded that the Iraqi police were not ready to take over the internal security role from the Iraqi Army, and that USF-I's efforts and resources supporting the police would be better directed to the army.[46] Terminating assistance to Iraq's police forces was a significant shift. Since 2005, the U.S. command in Baghdad had viewed "police primacy" in Iraq's security affairs as a critical component of the U.S. campaign based on an assumption that a successful counterinsurgency required effective civil policing. Though the security situation had improved greatly since the dark days of 2006 and 2007, there had been no commensurate growth in the capability of the Iraqi police—provincial or federal—that would enable them to relieve the army of its internal security role. The federal police also resisted cooperation with the Iraqi Army, and often avoided cooperation with local police.[47]

Elsewhere among the Interior Ministry's forces, Iraq's border forces remained undermanned and poorly equipped despite several years of effort to improve them. The forces at the ports of entry on the Iranian border near Basrah required special attention, in Austin's judgment. In the west, USF-I had no visibility on the operations at the three border crossing points in Anbar. North of Anbar there was concern that the Kurdistan Workers' Party (PKK) had infiltrated some of the police formations.[48] USF-I recognized a few encouraging signs, notably the CJSOTF-advised Emergency Response Brigade, which had a reputation for a willingness to "hit anyone," fuse intelligence, conduct network targeting and crime scene exploitation, and carry out professional development and leader training. Austin remarked that units like this would be important for force protection as USF-I departed.[49] Unfortunately, they were rare.

The End of U.S. Detention Operations

The 2008 U.S.-Iraq security agreement also required USF-I to transfer detention operations to the Iraqis. In summer 2010, USF-I completed a 19-month process of releasing or relinquishing custody of more than 22,000 detainees and closing the U.S. theater internment facilities, finally fulfilling former Secretary of Defense (SECDEF) Donald Rumsfeld's 2004 goal of getting the United States "out of the Iraqi prison business."

Under the terms of the security agreement, all detainees held by the coalition had either to be released or transferred to Iraqi correctional facilities with an arrest warrant or detention order approved by Iraqi officials. This task fell principally to Task Force 134 commander Major General David E. Quantock, a military police officer who had been previously assigned to fix the failed detention operations at Abu Ghraib in 2004. As USF-I's lead for detention operations from late 2008 to spring 2010, Quantock had to sort through the detainee population and determine those too dangerous to release. Working with the military police, criminal investigation division (CID) agents, intelligence personnel, and 56 lawyers, the task force ultimately released over 12,000 detainees and transferred another 8,000 to Iraqi custody.[50] A further 400 foreign fighters from 22 countries were repatriated through the International Committee of the Red Cross.[51]

The task force found sorting dangerous detainees from benign ones difficult, despite having continually segregated its detainee population based on threat level. To issue the arrest warrants or detention orders that USF-I needed to transfer internees to Iraqi authorities, Iraqi courts required either confessions or two eyewitness statements. Given the potential for retribution, eyewitness testimony was rare, and the original coalition arrest packets often could not be shared with the Iraqi courts because they contained classified information. The coalition's modern forensic techniques, such as identifying fingerprints on an IED, explosive residue detection, videotapes or photographs of a criminal act, or DNA evidence, appeared too many Iraqi judges almost like "witchcraft," Quantock observed.[52] After a series of education programs for judges and negotiations with Iraqi officials, local courts slowly accepted some of these techniques as evidence, but corruption among the Iraqi judges remained a problem. In the restive city of Mosul, for example, judges often released inmates within 24 to 48 hours of transfer from USF-I. Sectarianism also played its part, Quantock noted, with the Maliki government "almost exclusively asking for Shia releases," often in the face of substantial evidence against the detainees.[53]

Even physically transferring detainees to Iraqi control was not simple. U.S. officials and international human rights organizations worried that Iraqi prisoners would be subject to torture and abuse after being transferred from the well-regulated coalition detention facilities to the less-regulated Iraqi prisons. To guard against this, Task Force (TF) 134 transferred detainees only to facilities that met United Nations (UN) standards. The task force also initiated several programs to improve the Iraqi corrections system to those levels, including constructing a $28 million facility aimed at logisticians, mid-level supervisors, and wardens, and organizing several academies that could train 700 Iraqi prison guards at a time.[54] As Iraqi corrections officers completed their training, they part-nered with U.S. guards for additional mentorship, assuming responsibility compound by compound within each detention facility.[55] Corrections Assistance Transition Teams, the detention equivalent of MiTTs, comprised of military police, engineers, medical officers, and lawyers, crisscrossed Iraq weekly to inspect Iraqi prison facilities and certify them according to international standards.[56]

Source: U.S. Army photo by Private 1st Class Candace Mundt (Released).

Major General David Quantock With Iraqi Ministry of Justice Official Dara Nour al-Deen.[57]

As inmates were transferred to Iraqi control, TF 134's footprint shrank quickly. By the end of 2009, the task force oversaw one military police brigade in a mainly advisory role, down from two military police brigades in 2008. In September 2009, TF 134 shut down the sprawling Camp Bucca, with facilities capable of holding over 30,000 detainees, and shifted Bucca's remaining inmates to the Camp Taji theater internment facility, which itself reverted to Iraqi control in March 2010. When USF-I consolidated its operational subordinate commands in early 2010, TF 134 furled its colors, becoming a directorate within USF-I, with Quantock at its head as a deputy USF-I commander for detention operations.

In July 2010, Quantock's successor in that post, Major General Jerry Cannon, com-pleted the handover of the Camp Cropper Theater Internment Facility to the Iraqi Minis-try of Justice (MoJ), with the exception of 225 high-value detainees that the United States continued to hold until the end of 2011.[58] The handover of Camp Cropper to the Iraqi Gov-ernment was inauspicious. Within days, the camp ran out of potable water and sewage overflowed in the detainees' living areas, prompting the Iraqis to request the return of American assistance and advisors. To make matters worse, as these problems arose, the prison warden disappeared and four top Islamic State leaders escaped.[59]

Throughout 2011, USF-I's detention directorate helped the Iraqi Justice Ministry consolidate control of detention operations which were fragmented across several ministries. This effort suffered, however, from the fact that like other ministries, the Ministry of Justice was without a minister during the interregnum period, and few mid-level bureaucrats were willing to make important decisions on their own.[60]

At the same time, USF-I worked to resolve the future of the 60 remaining detainees, with the Lebanese Hizballah commander Musa Daqduq among them. U.S. officials aimed to establish a degree of confidence that the final detainees could be handed over to the Iraqi Government and held in a maximum security facility without risk that they could escape and return to the battlefield. Unfortunately, many released detainees had already returned to the fight. Scores released in the final months and days of the Iraq campaign eventually assumed leadership roles in the Islamic State of Iraq and Syria (ISIS), prompting a senior Special Forces officer to quip to Army historians in 2015, "I really hope we kept the biometric information from all the detainees we took."[61]

IRAQ'S POLITICAL DESTABILIZATION

The Erbil Agreement

By late November 2010, Iranian pressure on Maliki's behalf forced the Iraqi Shi'a parties to accept his return as Prime Minister. Even the Sadrists dropped their objections, though Maliki reportedly agreed to hand over some of his party's southern governorships to Sadrists as part of the deal. With the Shi'a bloc unified at last—however begrudgingly—the major Iraqi factions met in Erbil to hammer out the conditions of Maliki's return.[62] The specific terms of the Erbil Agreement of December 10, 2010, remained secret, but the public learned that Maliki agreed to a power-sharing arrangement including an expanded presidency council of Maliki, Talabani, Barzani, and Iraq's two Vice Presidents to decide major policy questions. In addition, Ayad Allawi's Iraqiyah would have the right to select a Defense Minister with the provision that the choice would not be a politician, nor would the new Interior Minister and Iraqi National Intelligence Service (INIS) director. To secure the Kurdish parties' backing, Maliki reportedly agreed to their demands for greater control over their region's oil reserves and revenues.[63] Maliki ultimately honored none of these pledges, but making them allowed him to hold onto the premiership. Iraq had been without an elected government for 278 days, the longest such period any modern parliamentary democracy had experienced at that point.

The Shi'a Militant Problem

U.S. and Western leaders hailed the Erbil Agreement and looked forward to a return to political stability in Iraq. For USF-I, however, the aftermath of the Erbil Agreement brought the return of old enemies. In the first days of January 2011, Kata'ib Hizballah (KH), the Iraqi Shi'a militant group most closely controlled by Iran's Quds Force and General Qassem Soleimani, attacked both the Camp Victory base complex and Forward

Operating Base (FOB) Kalsu, 50 miles south of Baghdad near the town of Iskandariyah. At Camp Victory, KH fired nine 107 mm rockets and one 240 mm rocket from fixed sites close to the camp's perimeter, indicating the group had sufficient time to prepare its firing positions and coordinate its attack. At FOB Kalsu, the main base of the 3d Armored Cavalry Regiment, KH attacked with six 240 mm rockets and nine large 333 mm improvised rocket-assisted munitions (IRAMs). The use of so many IRAMs, a signature Quds Force weapon, led Austin to conclude that both the Iraqi Shi'a militants and their Iranian sponsors had decided to pressure the United States to leave Iraq in 2011.[64]

Source: DoD photo by Airman 1st Class Brian Ferguson (Released).

Improvised Rocket-Assisted Munitions.[65]

Captured IRAM launchers

Amid these attacks, Moqtada Sadr made an unexpected return to Iraq on January 5, following 4 years in Iran. In his initial public appearances, Sadr told his followers to support the ISF and signaled his approval of the U.S. troop withdrawal timeline, but he once again called for resistance against U.S. troops. USF-I analysts concluded correctly that his return would create trouble for USF-I in the year to come.[66] By late March, Sadr's Promised Day Brigade restarted its operations against U.S. troops, hitting the Green Zone with 4 rockets in an attack that would have been more damaging had a U.S.-Iraqi quick-reaction force not raided the firing point and found 16 more rockets on improvised rails attached to timers.[67]

These attacks were part of a trend of increasing Shi'a militant activity across Iraq. On March 20, Shi'a militants conducted seven assassination attempts over a 5-hour period in Baghdad. USF-I concluded that Qais Khazali's Asa'ib Ahl al-Haqq (AAH) was responsible for the attacks, one of which severely wounded the commander of the 6th Iraqi Army Division.[68] Fifteen months after his release from U.S. detention as part of the Force

Strategic Engagement Cell's (FSEC) attempt to reconcile with the Shi'a militants, Khazali once again was waging war against the United States and its Iraqi partners.

The Day of Rage and the Return of Political Violence

The resurgence of Shi'a militant attacks accompanied an unexpected political challenge to Maliki's government. The wave of Arab Spring uprisings across North Africa and Syria in early 2011 swept into Iraq as well. As the Mubarak regime crumbled in Egypt during February 2011, large demonstrations against the Maliki government broke out in Baghdad and other major cities such as Basrah and Nasiriyah. The protesters initially demanded political reforms, a crackdown on government corruption, and the improvement of electricity and other public services. Unlike in Egypt, where protesters demanded both the ouster of the Mubarak regime and a change in the system of government, in Iraq, protesters were content with their democratic form of government but demanded a leadership change. By mid-February, an ad hoc grouping of disaffected youths, Sunni activists, Sadrists, Iraqi communists, and other small anti-Maliki factions brought tens of thousands of Iraqis into the streets to demand that Maliki step down. A smaller but similar movement arose in Kurdistan, where young activists demonstrated against corruption within the Kurdistan Regional Government (KRG).[69]

On February 25, 1 month after the massive Cairo, Egypt, protests, activists in Baghdad, Sulaimaniyah, and 10 other Iraqi cities organized a "Day of Rage" against Iraq's ruling parties. The results were ugly. Maliki attempted in advance to dissuade Iraqis from participating, warning that AQI or Ba'athist militants might use the gathering to incite violence.[70] The protests went forward anyway, and Iraqi and Kurdish security forces fired into the crowds in some cities, killing at least 29 protesters. In Baghdad, Iraqi troops quelled a large demonstration in Tahrir Square by firing at protesters. In Basrah, where Iraqi units refrained from such measures, the crowds forced the provincial governor, a Da'wa Party member, to resign.

The Day of Rage passed with 43-recorded protests across the country, though, to the surprise of many, no terrorists launched attacks against the large crowds. Responding to the popular pressure, Maliki announced he would limit himself to two terms as Prime Minister and reduce the salaries of senior officials. In the days following the Day of Rage, Iraqi Government officials reportedly offered cash, car loans, or land to Iraqi journalists to change the tone of their coverage.[71]

But Da'wa Party loyalists and security officers also began a wide-ranging crackdown, arresting hundreds of protest organizers. "The intelligence services are collecting information about activists and after the demonstrations they have been making arrests and detaining people," one organizer told reporters in early March.[72] The measures dampened popular enthusiasm for the anti-Maliki demonstrations, leading U.S. officials in Baghdad to report, "We anticipate PM [Prime Minister] Maliki will conclude that he has been strengthened by the relative[ly] small scale of the protests and the ISF's success in ensuring security."[73]

The protests' anti-Maliki energy dissipated partly because of other political dynamics that distracted from the demonstrators' original purpose. In northern Iraq, Kurdish leaders used the Day of Rage demonstrations as a pretext to deploy a division-sized peshmerga force to Kirkuk and to disputed areas of the Diyala valley, only withdrawing after a month of negotiations with the government. The peshmerga incursion heightened Arab-Kurdish tensions and gave Maliki an issue with which to appeal to Arab anti-Kurdish sentiment just when the protests against him were most intense. In Mosul, thousands of Sunni Arabs, including Ninewa governor Atheel Nujaifi, protested against KRG President Massoud Barzani and demanded that the U.S. military not remain in Iraq beyond December 2011.[74] Some U.S. observers interpreted Barzani's deployment of Kurdish troops to Kirkuk and Diyala as efforts to convince the United States that it was still needed as a guarantor of peace along the Green Line.[75] Whatever the case, U.S. Division-North (USD-N) commander Major General David Perkins, whose 1st Armored Division had succeeded Major General Anthony Cuccolo's 3d Infantry Division as USD-N, declined to have his troops drawn into the standoff between Kurdish and Iraqi Army units, insisting to both sides they would have to resolve the crisis on their own.[76]

In another distraction from the anti-Maliki movement, Iraq's Shi'a parties staged large protests in March and April against Bahrain's Sunni minority regime, which had cracked down on Bahraini Shi'a protestors and invited Saudi troops to help restore order in the country.[77] The Iraqi Parliament suspended its work in protest, and Maliki and other Iraqi leaders warned that the Bahrain crisis could expand into a regional sectarian war. Large rallies led by Moqtada Sadr in particular became not just a domestic Iraqi political issue, but also a serious concern for the United States. Highlighting the presence of the U.S. Fifth Fleet in Bahrain, Sadr and other Iraqi Shi'a leaders accused the United States of supporting the crackdown on Bahrain's Shi'a and used that accusation to denounce the U.S.-Iraqi status of forces agreement being negotiated by the Obama administration and the Maliki government.[78] This illustrated that gaining popular or Parliamentary support for keeping U.S. troops in the country beyond 2011 would be difficult for Maliki and his allies.

In contrast to the uprisings that eventually toppled dictators in Tunisia, Egypt, Libya, and Yemen and caused a civil war in Syria, the protest movement against Maliki fizzled out for reasons specific to Iraq. Other than Moqtada Sadr, none of Iraq's major political figures joined the protests. The protesters also found organizing via social media difficult because of Iraq's frequent electricity shortages—which, ironically, were one of the causes of the protests in the first place. The Iraqi protests also did not draw the same attention in the west that those in other countries had, though there was some criticism of the methods Maliki loyalists used against activists. In June 2011, Human Rights Watch reported that the ISF in Baghdad had stood by while Maliki supporters attacked protesters or had participated in the violence against protesters. At protests on June 10, "instead of protecting peaceful demonstrators, Iraqi soldiers appeared to be working hand in hand with the thugs attacking them," a Human Rights Watch report related, adding that the Ministry of Defense had deployed more than 150 plainclothes security officers to infiltrate the protests and intimidate or attack the demonstrators.[79] The intimidation of activists continued outside the protests, culminating in the September assassination of Hadi al-Mahdi, a popular radio talk show host who had been an important protest organizer. Four hours before being murdered at his Baghdad home, Mahdi posted on Facebook that Da'wa Party loyalists had issued death threats and were on their way to intercept him.[80] The assassination marked the seventh such killing of an Iraqi journalist in 2011.

These killings were just one sign that the political violence that had plagued Iraq from 2004 to 2006 was reappearing. The vacant Ministry of Defense and Interior positions remained problematic for the Iraqi and U.S. Governments as the status of forces agreement (SOFA) negotiations progressed, but when Maliki named nominees for the posts, Ali Faisal al Lami, the de-Ba'athification committee chairman who had disrupted the 2010 elections, blocked the appointments on grounds that the candidates had Ba'athist ties. Lami's maneuver had a violent outcome.[81] On May 26, 2011, professional-style gunmen shot him in his car near Sadr City.[82] It was just one of many attacks on Iraqi Government officials that spring. As Iraq scholar Michael Knights noted, a wave of killings of Iraqi officials meant that by June 2011, "senior Iraqi politicians and bureaucrats were attending multiple funerals per week."[83] Chalabi blamed Lami's murder on Ba'athists, but U.S. analysts concluded that Lami's former allies in AAH, which had grown increasingly friendly with Maliki in 2011, were behind the attack. When Austin brought up Lami's death with Maliki, the Prime Minister unsympathetically noted that Lami "had a lot of blood on his hands."[84]

The Return of AQI and End of the Sons of Iraq

As the Shi'a militant groups reemerged in early 2011, AQI demonstrated that it had begun to recover from the attacks of the previous year. The resurgence began with the scramble among AQI members to form a new leadership cadre in April-May 2010, a process that resulted in the takeover of the organization by figures connected to the former regime of Saddam Hussein.

In contrast to the orderly succession of Abu Ayyub al-Masri as AQI leader after Abu Musab al-Zarqawi's death in June 2006, there is no evidence that AQI anticipated or planned for the catastrophic leadership losses of spring 2010. According to internal documents from al-Qaeda in Pakistan, Atiyah Abd ar-Rahman contacted AQI on April 22 to authorize the group to appoint interim leaders on its own until al-Qaeda's central leaders could reestablish reliable communications.[85] AQI publicly acknowledged the deaths of its leaders on April 25, but waited until mid-May to announce its new leaders officially, who emerged after much infighting.[86] Despite its heavy losses, the group still had a small number of surviving leaders qualified to take over.

According to former AQI ally Mullah Nadhim al-Juburi, those familiar with AQI's internal structure expected a new emir of the Islamic State of Iraq (ISI) to come from AQI members with jihadi pedigrees and extremist religious credentials, such as Shaykh Yunis al-Mashhadani, engineer Abd al-Rahim al-Ani, or Abdallah al-Mufti.[87] Instead, the weeks following the deaths of Abu Ayyub al-Masri and Abu Umar al-Baghdadi witnessed a takeover of AQI by militants who tended to have Ba'athist as well as religious backgrounds.

According to AQI insider accounts, Samir Abd Muhammed al-Khlifawi, known more commonly as Hajji Bakr, a former Ba'athist colonel and AQI's newly appointed operations chief, moved quickly to seize control of the organization. Lacking the requisite religious credentials to serve as emir himself and hobbled by past ties to senior Ba'athists such as Izzat Ibrahim al-Douri, Hajji Bakr aimed to install as ISI's new emir his own protégé, Ibrahim Awwad al-Samarra'i (known to other jihadists as "Abu Du'a" or, later, as Abu Bakr al-Baghdadi or Caliph Ibrahim), a little-known cleric elevated to the AQI shura council less than 3 months before the deaths of Masri and Abu Umar al-Baghdadi.[88] Like many of ISI's senior leaders, Abu Bakr al-Baghdadi had been a detainee at Camp Bucca, released after 11 months in 2004 as a low-threat detainee. Some AQI members later claimed that amid the dispersal of AQI leaders during April–May 2010, Hajji Bakr used his control over the organization's courier network to create the appearance of consensus support for Abu Bakr al-Baghdadi and to rig a shura council vote in his favor.[89] One AQI member later claimed that a majority of AQI's imprisoned leaders opposed Baghdadi's appointment, but they were unable to influence the process.

Source: ISIS propaganda image.

Samir Abd Muhammad al-Khlifawi, Known More Commonly as Hajji Bakr.[90]

To appease al-Qaeda leaders in Pakistan, Hajji Bakr and Abu Bakr al-Baghdadi appointed Nu'man Salman Mansur al-Zaydi, a Moroccan trained in Afghanistan by bin Laden's lieutenants, to succeed Abu Ayyub al-Masri as war minister of the ISI. Zaydi had traveled to Iraq in 2006 and 2007 and displayed an anti-Shi'a sectarian ideology reminiscent of that of Zarqawi. Following his appointment as "war minister," he announced a new offensive to avenge Abu Ayyub al-Masri.[91] In contrast to Masri, however, Zaydi played little role in AQI's internal politics, content to let Hajji Bakr and Abu Bakr al-Baghdadi oversee matters so long as they did not interfere with his ability to wage jihad.

Once in control of the entirety of AQI, Hajji Bakr reorganized the movement in ways that resembled the Ba'ath, forming a new secret police (mukhabarat) cadre under a commander named Abu Safwan Rifai to prevent further leadership losses.[92] In short order, the AQI mukhabarat grew to 100 members who worked to purge internal dissent and had wide-ranging authority above that of the provincial walis. From the ranks of these mukhabarat, ISIS leaders later would draw the commanders of the paramilitary forces of the "Islamic Caliphate" across Syria and Iraq.[93] Hajji Bakr and Abu Bakr al-Baghdadi also formed a new shura council that included jihadists with Ba'athist ties.[94] In addition to Hajji Bakr and Abu Safwan Rifai, other key members of the new shura council included the former Iraqi Army colonel Fadel Ahmad Abdullah al-Hayali (aka Abu Muslim al-Turkmani or Hajji Mu'tazz), Abd al Rahman Mustafa al-Qaduli (aka Abu Ali al-Anbari or Abu Alaa al-Afiri), and former Iraqi Army captain Adnan Ismail Najm al-Bilawi (aka Abu Abd al-Rahman al-Bilawi).[95] Bilawi would later become the top intelligence official within ISIS, while Hayali and Qaduli, both Turkomans from Tel Afar, would become ISIS's key operational commanders.

These new ISI leaders concentrated in their early months on replenishing the organization's empty coffers rather than stepping up attacks against coalition forces or the Iraqi Government.[96] By the beginning of 2011, they had recovered enough to restart large-scale terrorist activities. In mid-January, they launched six suicide attacks over a span of 4 days that killed 8 Iraqi soldiers and 38 civilians, and wounded more than 250 more Iraqis. The worst attacks occurred on January 20, when a pair of suicide car bombers killed or wounded 147 Arba'een pilgrims in Karbala.[97] The ISF had planned ample security measures for the pilgrimage, but Austin observed after the attack that "with six million pilgrims on the road, it's hard to protect them all."[98] On January 27, a suicide car bomber killed or wounded more than 100 people in a funeral procession in central Baghdad, showing that AQI, now calling itself the ISI almost exclusively, had regained its ability to breach the capital and cause mayhem.[99]

Alongside these mass-casualty attacks, ISI focused on targeting Iraqi Government and ISF officials, and began to do damage on a scale that Iraq had not seen for more than a year.[100] On January 17-19, ISI suicide bombers carried out large attacks in Ramadi, Tikrit, and Baqubah, the first of which attempted—for the third time—to assassinate the Anbar provincial governor but managed to kill the deputy governor instead. The attacks continued in February, with a three-car-bomb assault near the KDP headquarters in Kirkuk and multiple attacks against ISF and Shi'a pilgrims in Samarra that caused hundreds of casualties.[101]

The rejuvenated ISI benefited from the Maliki government's rejection of the Sons of Iraq, the group that had had a decisive, crushing impact on AQI in 2007-2008. Throughout most of 2010 and 2011, the Maliki government stopped finding government jobs for Sons of Iraq members. As of July 2010, only 41,000 of an estimated 94,000 Awakening members had been hired and integrated into the government, with only 9,000 in security jobs.[102] At the same time, the Interior Ministry began stripping Awakening movement security forces of their rank and salary, effectively leaving many unemployed.[103] The Maliki government blamed the problems on budget shortages, but many Sunnis perceived the freeze as evidence of the government's reluctance to integrate them into the state. Former Awakening Council leader Nathem al-Jabouri opined in late 2010 that Sahwah members had only two options: "Stay with the government, which would be a threat to their lives, or help al-Qaeda by being a double agent."[104]

Events seemed to support Sunni frustration, such as the Interior Ministry's decision to bypass the Sons of Iraq when hiring large numbers of new police for Ninewa Province in early 2011. USF-I leaders pressed the Iraqi police commands to hire former Sons of Iraq temporarily as contractors until government jobs became available, but the Interior Ministry rebuffed the idea of a mixed force of contractors and government employees on legal grounds. USF-I reports identified "Shia dominance within the MoI," as the real reason.[105] In the meantime, USF-I looked for other ways to find the Sons of Iraq useful, paid work and prevent them from returning to their former lives as insurgents. USF-I tried assigning some of the Sons of Iraq to pursue human intelligence on the Syrian border and in Sunni provinces but this was unsuccessful. A program to offer $4,000 small-business grants in lieu of government jobs met with no more success. Another proposal involved retraining Sons of Iraq members to be farmers, tractor repairmen, or gas station attendants, but the Maliki government had little interest.[106]

The strongest evidence that ISI had begun to regain its strength came on March 29 when its militants carried out one of the deadliest strikes of the war against provincial leaders. A group of about 10 insurgents disguised as Iraqi police attacked the Salahadin provincial council building in Tikrit with a car bomb, small arms fire, and suicide vests. Once inside the government center, the militants took hostages and then systematically slaughtered them during a protracted gun battle with the ISF. The ISF assaulted the building twice, finally securing it 5 hours later. Five Iraqi soldiers died in the fighting while 53 Iraqi civilians were killed, including 3 provincial council members and 2 journalists. Nearly 100 others were wounded. U.S. troops did not participate in the assault but responded to Iraqi requests for ISR and close-air support.[107] The attack sent shockwaves through the Sunni communities of northern Iraq, which had presumed after spring 2010 that ISI had been neutralized. The provincial reconstruction team for Salahadin reported that the province's population was "stunned" by the violence and that the general sense of security that had grown in the previous months had all but vanished after the attack.[108]

The apparent resurgence of ISI, coupled with Iraq's growing political instability and questions about the ISF's effectiveness led Austin to request that 4th AAB, 1st Armored Division deploy to Iraq in May to replace 4th AAB, 1st Cavalry Division in USD-N. The Joint Staff and Defense Department had hoped that the brigade in Iraq could return home without a replacement, but Austin believed the removal of an AAB from northern Iraq would be too risky given the deterioration in security and political conditions. The deployment of the additional AAB was unpopular within the Pentagon, since it would slow the drawdown and complicate USF-I's withdrawal, but the additional brigade would give Austin a fresh reserve force for the remainder of the mission.[109]

Austin's decision proved prescient, as on August 15, ISI hit 17 cities nearly simultaneously with a series of bombings, killing 74 and injuring over 300. The attacks produced the most casualties Iraq had experienced in a single day for over a year.[110] Shi'a and Christian neighborhoods in Kut, Baghdad, Baqubah, Karbala, and Najaf bore the brunt. Less than 2 weeks later, ISI hit the massive Sunni Umm al Qura Mosque in West Baghdad with a suicide-bomber, wounding 30 and killing 28, including a Member of Parliament.[111] To many analysts, the strikes, launched during the month of Ramadan, appeared to be an attempt by ISI to reignite the sectarian civil war that had been nearly extinguished but was being given new life by Maliki's partisan moves. ISI's spokesman appeared to confirm as much, promising, "Do not worry, the days of Zarqawi are going to return soon," in the wake of the bombings.[112]

The ISI, which had been on life support for most of 2010, was back in force. Hajji Bakr had managed to transform what had been the largely symbolic leadership of the ISI into a supreme authority for the organization, with himself as the power behind Abu Bakr al-Baghdadi. His restructuring of the group's leadership cadre had recast former Ba'athist officers as leaders of the global jihad, and their military expertise soon would make the organization more effective than its earlier incarnations under Zarqawi and Abu Ayyub al-Masri. These developments set the group down the path that would lead to the Islamic State's conquest of large swaths of northern and western Iraq.

The Mujahedin e Khalq Problem, Continued

The quandary of what to do with the UN-protected but terror-listed MeK, which had bedeviled U.S. commanders and diplomats since 2003, came to the fore again when a debacle at the MeK camp in Diyala gave U.S. officials a preview of how the Iraqi Government intended to treat the group once the U.S. military left. The Iraqi Army had assumed control of external security at Camp Ashraf, the MeK's base, in June 2010, after which the MeK and Iraqi troops had confronted each other in clashes that U.S. forces could not sort out due to ambiguous rules of engagement and force protection guidelines. As Colonel Malcolm Frost and his 2d Brigade, 25th Infantry Division, the local AAB in Diyala, worked to advise and assist their ISF counterparts, Frost concluded that Camp Ashraf and the MeK would have to be handled carefully to prevent violence. If not restrained, Frost judged, the Shi'a-dominated Iraqi Government would settle old scores with the MeK and fulfill Iran's wish of forcing the organization to leave Iraq.[113]

Major General Perkins (center), Colonel Frost (right).
Source: DoD photo by Sergeant Brandon Bolick (Released).

Major General David G. Perkins, Commander of MND-N, With Colonel Malcolm Frost, Commander, 2d BCT, 25th Infantry Division, and Iraqi Officers.[114]

Frost's predictions came true in early April. After the drawdown of U.S. observers from the direct vicinity of Camp Ashraf, Frost discovered that the Iraqi Ground Forces Command had ordered the Diyala Operation Center to attack the MeK compound. Frost persuaded Diyala Operations Commander Lieutenant General Tariq Abd Al-Wahb Jasim Mahdi al-Assawi to refuse the order, but Assawi was quickly relieved of his command and replaced by his deputy, who followed the IGFC order. On April 8, while IGFC commander General Ali Ghaidan looked on, the 5th Iraqi Army division moved into Camp Ashraf and immediately clashed with the MeK there. As the Iraqi and MeK casualties mounted, Frost led his own headquarters and medics back to Camp Ashraf, ignoring ISF demands to remain outside the camp's perimeter, and set up an aid station for the hundreds wounded inside the compound.[115] UN officials on the scene reported 34 people killed and more than 300 wounded in the fighting, the vast majority of them MeK members.

The crisis at Camp Ashraf led to tense confrontations between U.S. officials and the Maliki government. Commenting on the situation to CENTCOM and the Pentagon, Austin reported that senior Iraqi officials had been "consistently deceitful" when questioned about what was happening.[116] Ambassador Jeffrey and the U.S. Embassy continued to work with the UN to try to resolve the fate of the MeK, but the Iraqi Government appeared determined to remove the group forcibly from Camp Ashraf even if it required violence.[117]

THE PATH TO ZERO

Operation NEW DAWN, which debuted in August 2010, was intended as a stability operation as U.S. troops left Iraq, but after 9 months, the country was less stable than when the operation began. Transferring security affairs to Iraqi control had ground to a near halt during the long political stalemate after the March 2010 elections. The Shi'a militant groups and AQI-ISI had both returned to the battlefield, reviving security threats that once seemed finished. Austin, Cone, and other USF-I leaders realized the ISF were not ready to handle Iraq's security on their own.

The ISF's violence against the protesters and the MeK in spring 2011 put U.S. commanders in an awkward position: USF-I's mission was to empower the ISF, but if ISF leaders reverted to Saddamist-type practices and functioned as a political tool for Prime Minister Maliki, they would call U.S. security assistance into question. In the 8 months remaining in USF-I's mission, whether the United States and Iraq reached an agreement on a residual force or not, U.S. troops would have further to go than anyone had anticipated to support the goal of leaving behind a stable, self-sufficient Iraqi state.

Planning for Post-2011: A Residual Force

On January 25, 2011, Austin met with Chairman of the Joint Chiefs of Staff Admiral Michael W. Mullen and General James N. Mattis, the CENTCOM commander, to discuss the requirement for a new status of forces agreement that would leave a residual force in Iraq. Mullen and Mattis proposed a 24,000-strong force built around three advise-and-assist brigades and some "boutique" items like special operations forces and aviation support that could be drawn down easily if necessary.[118] Mattis noted that keeping at least one brigade in northern Iraq would mitigate Arab-Kurd tensions along the Green Line and that any force could be drawn down as conditions improved.[119] Austin reported that both Prime Minister Maliki and Ayad Allawi supported the idea, at least privately. Mattis believed Maliki would agree to a force of up to 25,000 U.S. troops as long as they were only in a training role.

In February, Austin and his USF-I staff analyzed the pros and cons of residual forces ranging from 10,000 to 24,000 and concluded that the risk of mission failure grew as the force level dropped, and that the residual force should not be smaller than a full strength division.[120] The Iraqi security forces, though improving, would be hard-pressed to assume responsibility for Iraq's internal and external security by the end of the year. The Iraqis would have a continued need for security assistance and capacity-building after 2011, but Austin believed it would not be possible for U.S. forces to provide it from outside Iraq. Austin also worried about the potential for the Iranian regime to fill the void left by the departing U.S. military presence and the danger to U.S. troops if the withdrawal proceeded too quickly.[121] To hedge against future instability, USF-I hoped, in addition to the residual force, to preposition enough equipment at different locations in Iraq to enable the United States quickly to deploy a force of three BCTs to the country.[122]

In Austin's and Cone's view, strategic risk and security should shape U.S. decisions. A robust residual force would not only benefit Iraq but also provide security assurances for Turkey, Jordan, Kuwait, and Israel.[123] However, Austin also believed it would be difficult to steer deliberations in Washington away from troop numbers and costs.[124] Cone worried that discussions about residual force would focus solely on trainers and would shortchange force-protection requirements.[125]

These military recommendations for a residual force ran counter to the preferences of the Obama administration. In late 2010, administration officials suggested to reporters that the United States could get by with between 5,000 and 10,000 troops in Iraq. Reports were that the President himself was considering a force that small. By April, Obama confirmed these reports, making clear to senior U.S. officials that maintaining more than 10,000 troops was no longer an option, a constraint that frustrated SECDEF Robert Gates as well as the U.S. military leadership in Iraq.[126]

Inauspicious Start for SOFA Negotiations

Negotiations with the Maliki government about a new SOFA and a residual force intensified in spring 2011, with the expiration of the existing agreement only 8 months away. With time growing short, negotiators on both sides tacitly agreed U.S. troops could remain past the deadline without a finalized SOFA if the Iraqi Government formally requested them.[127] On April 16, Maliki told visiting Congressman John Boehner, speaker of the House of Representatives, that while he felt Iraqi forces could secure the country after 2011, he would welcome American training and equipment.[128] On May 8, Maliki had a similar meeting with Senators John McCain and Lindsey Graham, Austin, and Jeffrey, but when the visiting congressmen pressed him about the need for agreement on a residual force, the Iraqi leader countered that the U.S. Government had not yet told him what kind of force it wished to leave in Iraq after 2011. Without a specific proposal, the Prime Minister had had nothing to present to the Parliament, so the issue had languished.[129] The senators later wrote that Austin and Jeffrey told them after the meeting that U.S. leaders in Washington had not yet decided how many troops to propose.

Maliki's shaky political standing hampered the negotiations as well. Some polls indicated that less than 20 percent of Iraqis wanted U.S. troops to remain, but at the same time Iraqis were worried about the security vacuum following an American withdrawal.[130] Sadrist resistance to the negotiations put Maliki in a political bind, given his dependence on the Sadrist Parliamentary bloc for his position as Prime Minister.[131] In late May, Sadr led a large protest against the SOFA and threatened to reconstitute the Jaysh al Mahdi militia if the U.S. military remained.[132]

Maliki created additional unrest himself. During a Parliamentary recess in May, Maliki violated the Erbil Agreement by naming his allies Faleh al-Fayadh and former Minister of Defense Abdel Qader to ministerial-level national security posts, but maintained the Ministries of Defense and Interior portfolios himself.[133] These moves deepened the public battle between Maliki and Ayad Allawi, who remained in a position to threaten Maliki's shaky governing coalition. Maliki feared that if he committed publicly to a new SOFA and residual force, Allawi would attack his policy on nationalist grounds and rob him of his thin margin of support.[134] Maliki himself was at times ambivalent toward the SOFA, as a continued U.S. presence would likely be an obstacle to his consolidation of power. Meanwhile, Obama had set August 1 as an unpublicized deadline for the Iraqis formally to request a residual force. During a videoconference with Obama in June, Maliki asked for additional time to shore up political support for the agreement and cited Allawi's opposition as an obstacle.[135] In July, President Talabani convened a meeting of the major political blocs in hopes of reaching a unified position in favor of U.S. military support, but Allawi's bloc refused to agree to a residual force until the 2010 Erbil Agreement was implemented and the vacant security minister posts filled.[136]

Despite the political turmoil, many Iraqi military leaders considered some American military presence necessary. Abdel Qader, now Maliki's chief advisor on defense matters, had consistently acknowledged that the ISF would require continued training through 2018.[137] In July, Major General Fadhel Barwari, the ISOF commander, told *The New York Times*, "The Americans need to stay because we don't have control over our borders."[138] The next month, Iraqi chief of defense General Babakir Zebari told reporters, "Iraqi soldiers and officers would like the American forces to stay in Iraq until they're capable of doing the job 100 percent. . . . If I were asked about the withdrawal, I would say to politicians, 'The U.S. Army must stay until the Iraqi Army is fully ready in 2020. . . . If America withdraws its forces and one of the neighboring countries causes problems, then we're going to have a problem'."[139]

The Spike in Shi'a Militant Attacks

As the SOFA negotiations intensified, the Iranian regime's Shi'a proxies escalated attacks against U.S. troops. In southern Iraq, violence steadily rose from May onward, but since the Shi'a militants spared the ISF, most ISF units in the south were reluctant to defend U.S. troops and installations from the militias as the U.S.-Iraq security agreement required them to do. Austin warned his superiors that if the attacks continued, USF-I would be forced to conduct unilateral operations against the groups, likely with U.S. casualties.[140] The munitions used plus the increasing accuracy of the attacks pointed toward greater Iranian involvement particularly in the U.S. Division-South (USD-S) area of responsibility.[141] Austin wanted U.S. training teams to partner with Iraqi units to disrupt the smuggling routes for the Shi'a militants' lethal supplies from Iran, but local governments in southern Iraq resisted the kind of cooperation Austin desired.[142] In one case, the Sadrist Provincial Council in Basrah attempted to outlaw the movement of USF-I throughout the province. Local courts appeared to operate a "catch-and-release" program for any Shi'a militants detained.

On June 6, Kata'ib Hizballah fired an IRAM from the Iraqi-controlled portion of FOB Loyalty near Sadr City, killing 7 Americans and wounding 30.[143] Further south, by mid-June, the Iranian-backed militias continuously harassed USD-S with IRAM and EFP attacks. To fire the heavy, difficult-to-guide IRAMs, the Shi'a militants used launch points close to American bases and troop concentrations, sometimes building houses with a false roof, such as a plastic tarpaulin, near the base perimeter, and then removing the roof just before firing the IRAM.[144] In late June, a Kata'ib Hizballah IRAM at FOB Shocker, 5 miles from the Iran-Iraq border, killed three Soldiers and wounded seven more just days before the outpost was due for transfer to the ISF. The attack brought the number of U.S. Soldiers killed in June to 14, with more than 50 wounded, making it the deadliest month for U.S. forces in over 2 years. Over April, May, and June, 21 Soldiers were killed and 105 wounded—triple the previous 3 months' casualties.[145] Violence against the civilian population rose as well. Iraqis suffered 340 killed in June, the most recorded in a year.[146]

In response, Austin ordered CJSOTF to launch unilateral raids against Shi'a militant technicians and facilitators across the south.[147] Nevertheless, in July the number of attacks in the country escalated to 13 per day, a 30 percent increase over the average of the previous 6 months.[148] On July 10, AAH bombarded FOB Garry Owen with rockets, killing one American Soldier. On July 12, the group launched more than 40 rockets at the base, and on July 16, they followed with four IRAMs, though these attacks caused no casualties. The same month, Stuart Bowen, the special inspector general for Iraq reconstruction, declared in a report to Congress that Iraq was less safe than a year before.[149]

Following AAH's July 16 attack, Austin bluntly told Maliki that the ISF were not engaging Shi'a militant groups. The USF-I commander also asked the Iraqi leader to warn Iran not to confuse USF-I's restraint with weakness. Maliki replied that he had sent the same message to Tehran only days before and had dispatched his own national security advisor to emphasize the warning, but the Prime Minister also told Austin that USF-I's unilateral raids against Shi'a targets were a political problem for him and pressed Austin to return to combined U.S.-Iraqi operations. After almost 2 months of elevated attacks and ISF failure to counter them, however, Austin received Maliki's assurances with skepticism.[150]

Despite the Prime Minister's entreaties, USF-I continued unilateral operations and captured one of the suspects in the late June attack against FOB Shocker. Partnered U.S.-ISF operations, meanwhile, rounded up some of the Shi'a militants responsible for IRAM attacks in Basrah, while ISF-led operations in Maysan Province netted 70 low-level Shi'a militants in late July and early August. However, USF-I's efforts to get the Iraqi Government and ISF to pressure the Shi'a militias met little success. Despite the rising Shi'a militant threat, the ISF continued to generate mostly Sunni targets for partnered counterterrorism operations, and Iraqi judges often refused to issue warrants for individuals suspected of taking part in attacks.[151] U.S. units and advisors also noted that the Shi'a militant groups regularly infiltrated ISF units, creating a problem that would continue to plague USF-I's advisory mission.[152]

PREPARING FOR EXIT

The "Waterfall" and Withdrawal From the Green Line

As it became clearer to USF-I and U.S. Embassy negotiators that the residual U.S. force in Iraq would be much smaller than the 24,000 troops they initially recommended, Austin gradually began to decrease the U.S. military presence. First, he withdrew U.S. troops from the 22 combined security checkpoints along the Green Line in Major General

David Perkins's USD-N, placing them into an overwatch role. As USD-N receded from the checkpoints, U.S. commanders hoped they could convince Arab and Kurdish units to continue cooperation along the Green Line, but this proved difficult.[153] USD-N initially withdrew forces from the combined security checkpoints in Diyala and Ninawa, but had difficulty extricating themselves from the bilateral checkpoints manned by Iraqi police in Kirkuk. Eventually, USD-N and the Iraqis agreed the "Golden Lions," the Iraqi unit consisting of Iraqi Army, Iraqi police, and members of the peshmerga militia, would assume responsibility for the Kirkuk checkpoints as the last of the U.S. forces moved into overwatch positions on July 22.[154]

Next, Austin consolidated the three U.S. division headquarters. Since its arrival in January, attacks on the 36th Infantry Division USD-S by Shi'a militants had increased, with local ISF in the south doing little to stop them.[155] Concerned that the 36th Division headquarters devoted much of its effort to force protection, Austin redeployed the division headquarters early and merged the remaining units in U.S. Division-Center (USD-C) and USD-S into a single division under Major General Bernard Champoux's 25th Infantry Division headquarters. After the 36th Infantry Division's departure, Champoux and his command served as the main command-and-control element for USF-I's final maneuvers out of Iraq. This move allowed Austin to continue to staff the Arab-Kurd fault line in the north and Baghdad, but rendered southern Iraq an economy-of-force mission.[156]

The End of the Special Operations Mission

The realization that U.S. troop strength—including special operations forces—might drop to zero by the end of 2011 caught the CJSOTF off guard. Most special operations leaders had anticipated continued counterterrorism and advisory missions after conventional forces left, believing that a full withdrawal was a "throw-away course of action . . . that's never going to happen."[157] Yet the U.S. special operations mission already had undergone dramatic changes since 2008. By 2011 the ISOF, CJSOTF's principal Iraqi partner, had become a capable organization, described by several CJSOTF commanders as the best special operations unit in the Middle East. The unit had expanded from one to two brigades, one with two national-level counterterrorism battalions, and the second with regional commando battalions in Basrah, Mosul, Diyala, and Anbar.[158] These Iraqi units conducted nighttime helicopter assaults in Mi–17 helicopters flown by Iraqi pilots as a matter of routine. They had developed their own human intelligence networks, and even had their own ISR aircraft and joint terminal attack controllers for close air support.

But the sectarianism that seeped into the organization since its 2007 transfer to the control of Prime Minister Maliki's Office of the Commander in Chief degraded the CJSOTF's ability to conduct operations with ISOF elements. The Prime Minister had used the ISOF to intimidate Sunni politicians and other political opponents in addition to targeting terrorists, and the CJSOTF slowly had distanced itself from the ISOF as the Iraqi force became politicized. In December 2008, the ISOF had arrested 35 politicians only weeks before Iraq's provincial elections.[159] In May 2009, the brigade arrested four of the nine newly elected provincial council members in Diyala.[160] In May 2010, the brigade again arrested a politician in Diyala who had openly criticized the ISOF's politicized role.[161] When these raids occurred, the CJSOTF declined to participate and raised objections with their Iraqi counterparts in the Counter Terrorism Service headquarters.

While partnered operations with the ISOF against AQI continued, missions against Shi'a targets rarely were approved.[162] In one instance, Cone submitted 10 potential targets, all of them involving rocket attacks. Counterterrorism director General Talib Kenani approved two Sunni targets immediately, but disapproved the remaining eight Shi'a targets because they did not have "the right intelligence."[163] In a further display of sectarian tone deafness, Counter Terrorism Service leaders chose to have the ISOF brigade's elite Iraqi Counter-Terrorism Force change uniforms. The uniform of Iraq's national Army was replaced with jet black coveralls, which matched the all black clothing worn by the Mahdi Militia during the dark days of Iraq's civil war—a similarity immediately recognized by Sunni leaders across Iraq.

Because of these trends, the CJSOTF shifted its focus from the ISOF to a partnership with the Emergency Response Brigade (ERB), an Interior Ministry unit modeled upon the FBI hostage rescue and special weapons and tactics teams. The CJSOTF had formed the ERB as a police counterpart to the ISOF brigade, and some of the brigade's elements, such as the Hillah special weapons and tactics (SWAT) battalion, had been paired with Special Forces advisors since 2003.[164] The ERB commander, Brigadier General Noman Dakhil Jawad, was a Shi'a officer unafraid of arresting fellow Shi'a Iraqis who were accused of sectarian crimes or targeting American forces. This independence caused at least one CJSOTF commander to warn Jawad to lower his profile or risk drawing Prime Minister Maliki's attention.[165] It was a prescient warning. In March 2011, Maliki loyalists in the federal police tried to arrest Jawad on charges of corruption, but when the policemen arrived, his troops drove them off. Nevertheless, after Jawad's subsequent arrest, a Saddam-era officer whom USF-I linked to Kata'ib Hizballah took his place and abruptly ended the ERB's partnered operations against Shi'a targets.[166] The CJSOTF noted that the new commander exclusively targeted Sunnis, including Sunni political leaders, often without warrants. In July, after the ERB's Hillah SWAT battalion and CJSOTF advisors conducted a series of operations against Iranian-backed Shi'a militias, several of the Hillah battalion's leaders were arrested and jailed.[167] By August, the CJSOTF had collected enough evidence to persuade Austin to sever ties with the ERB. Breaking the news was difficult for the brigade's Special Forces advisors, with some of the Green Berets and the ERB constables they had fought alongside nearly brought to tears when they learned of the decision.[168]

The Race to Build ISF Capacity

Building capacity within the Iraqi security forces always had been a crucial component of the transition plan. As debate continued over the residual force question, Cone, who had once overseen the U.S. Army's National Training Center, pressed Iraqi Army leaders to develop basic combined-arms capabilities through collective training.[169] As he did so, the USF-I advisory brigades urged their Iraqi Army counterparts to pull units out of day-to-day operations to train, with mixed results. In April, the Iraqi military commenced Exercise Lion's Leap, in which Iraqi units simulated hostage rescues; cordon and search operations; air assaults; and reconnaissance operations with a combination of air, land, and naval forces.[170] In addition, the 8th, 9th, and 14th Iraqi Army divisions all conducted major training exercises in 2011, but the Iraqis' capacity to undertake more sophisticated training as the number of American military trainers diminished remained in question.[171]

Source: DoD photo by Captain Chad Ashe (Released).

Soldiers From the Iraqi Army's 12th Division Take Part in Exercise Lion's Leap.[172]

The effort to modernize the Iraqi Army created some additional challenges. As American-made equipment made its way to Iraqi units,[173] the Iraqis required two separate logistics systems, one for the newer American-made systems and the other for the Soviet bloc equipment the Iraqis had fielded from 2003 to 2009. Many units ended up with a mix of Soviet and American equipment and encountered shortages of nearly every category of supply. The communications systems in the American tanks were not compatible with those in the eastern bloc legacy vehicles, so that many units had to rely on hand and arm signals or cell phones for tactical communications.[174]

Meanwhile, the United States continued to work with the Iraqi Government to purchase F–16 fighter aircraft, which U.S. officials believed would tie the Iraqi military closer to the United States and serve as a counterbalance to Iran's rising influence in the region.[175] Iraq would pay for the F–16s from oil revenues, with an expected cost of $4.2 billion, including parts and related weapons.[176] However, the air force had a difficult time recruiting personnel, training its pilots, and maintaining its planes, leaving Austin concerned that the Iraqis might not be able to sustain an F-16 force over the long term without U.S. mentorship.[177]

USF-I found it difficult to work with Iraqi defense officials to solve these and many other similar problems. With Maliki serving as both Minister of Defense and Minister of Interior in addition to his responsibilities as Prime Minister, obtaining the necessary administrative approval for crucial ministerial functions was slow. USF-I officials noted that in the uncertain political environment, Iraqi bureaucrats feared making decisions that could have political implications, with the result that Iraq's national-level defense systems were incapable of planning more than 6 to 8 weeks in advance. As Cone described it, the national security ministries in 2011 were in "a general state of paralysis."[178]

The "paralysis" had come in part from an unprecedented consolidation of power within the ISF, as Prime Minister Maliki purged professional officers in key leadership positions across the ISF and replaced them with his supporters. In 2011, Maliki replaced 5 of the 14 division commanders, substituting Shi'a Da'wa party loyalists for proven Sunni and Kurdish commanders.[179] The Kurds, who felt the reassignments most acutely, made their frustrations public, with General Babakir Zebari, Iraq's Chief of Defense and commander of the Joint Headquarters, providing President Talibani a report that alleged General Mohan Freiji, who had become a senior advisor to the Minister of Defense after being removed as the Basra Operations Commander, had "spearheaded a campaign to rid all Kurdish influence and destroy Kurdish roles within the MoD."[180] Zebari's report alleged that Prime Minister Maliki had orchestrated a slow takeover of Iraq's security apparatus, a process that began with the creation of the Office of the Commander in Chief (OCINC), which Zebari described as "a shadow headquarters" that "diluted" and "stole" the power of the Joint Headquarters. Following the creation of the OCINC, Maliki quietly took control of Iraq's special operations forces and its intelligence services, along with their substantial and secret budgets. With the most effective elements of the Iraqi security forces under Maliki's control, OCINC and other Da'wa officers in key positions began a campaign "assigning officers with sectarian ties to various units and divisions in the Army." Zebari asserted that in 2009 Kurdish loyalists intercepted a secret letter from General Freiji to other Shi'a conspirators in the Ministry of Defense describing methods to accomplish these objectives. These included forcing Kurdish and Sunni officers to retire, flooding unqualified Shi'a militia members into the senior ranks of the Army, and "finding charges" that could be levied against senior officers unwilling to support Maliki's sectarian consolidation.[181]

By 2010, Maliki's labors had borne fruit, and in addition to the changes that left only two Kurds and two Sunnis in command of the 14 divisions in the Iraqi Army, Shi'a officers had taken control of all of the department and directorate level positions in the Ministry of Defense. Shi'a generals held three of the four service commands, with Sunnis completely excluded, and the Baghdad Operations Command was ordered to report directly to Maliki, bypassing the Joint Headquarters.[182] Zebari's report argued that as USF-I rushed to prepare the Iraqi security forces for the unanticipated complete withdrawal of American forces, a slow cancer was overtaking the organization from within.

THE RETROGRADE

The Collapse of SOFA Negotiations

The new U.S. defense secretary, Leon Panetta, arrived in Baghdad on July 11, 2011, for talks with President Talabani and Prime Minister Maliki on the long-term U.S. presence in Iraq. Panetta emphasized the need for U.S. force protection and for the Iraqi Government to appoint defense and interior ministers. Maliki expressed confidence that the Iraqis could take care of Iraq's internal security with limited U.S. assistance in intelligence, logistics, border control, air space control, and collective training. Panetta replied that if the Iraqis wanted U.S. assistance, they should formally request it sooner rather than later.[183] Speaking to U.S. troops after his meetings, a frustrated Panetta said, "I'd like things to move a lot faster here, frankly, in terms of the decision-making process. I'd like them to make a decision, you know: Do they want us to stay? Don't they want us to stay? . . . Damn it, make a decision."[184]

Source: DoD photo by Technical Sergeant Jacob N. Bailey (Released).

Secretary of Defense Leon Panetta Meets With U.S. Troops Following Negotiations With Iraqi Leaders About an Extension of the U.S.-Iraq Status of Forces Agreement.[185]

In late July, Jeffrey and Austin made their rounds of the Iraqi political leaders to stress the importance of arriving at a decision on the SOFA quickly, but when the political blocs met on August 2, ostensibly to decide Iraq's policy on the SOFA, they adjourned for the 30-day Ramadan holiday instead.[186] In the meantime, Maliki's acting Minister of Defense, Sadun al Dulaymi, agreed with Austin that there was an urgent need for a continued U.S. military mission, but declined to formalize arrangements without Parliamentary approval.[187]

On the eve of Obama's August 1 deadline for a formal Iraqi request for a residual U.S. force, Ambassador Jeffrey and Brett McGurk reported that Maliki could meet all the U.S. administration's requirements with two exceptions. He did not yet have Parliamentary approval for the extension of troops and, because of pressure from the Sadrist bloc, he could not guarantee U.S. troops immunity from prosecution in the Iraqi judicial system. Both points crossed redlines for the U.S. negotiators and leaders, although Panetta advocated continuing the negotiations to maintain a 10,000-man residual force in Iraq.

Meanwhile, Lieutenant General Robert Caslen, named director of the Office of Security Cooperation that would succeed USF-I at the end of 2011, met with senior U.S.

officials in Washington as he prepared to deploy to Baghdad in August. In one meeting, a senior White House official warned Caslen to be prepared not to have any troops under his command after 2011, because the President intended not to maintain a residual force in Iraq. Instead, the official said, the President would insist that the Iraqi Parliament approve the SOFA—a demand that would be a poison pill, since Maliki would not risk a no-confidence vote on his premiership. "We know it is not going to happen . . . and it will look like the Iraqis were the ones that made it happen," the official told Caslen.[188] Arriving in Baghdad shortly after the meeting, Caslen met with Austin and Jeffrey and relayed the warning, but the general and ambassador assured Caslen that U.S. leaders remained committed to leaving a residual force in the country.[189]

Back in Washington, the administration was reducing the size of the projected residual force. On August 13, Obama informed the National Security Council (NSC) principals that he had revised his earlier position and would now only authorize a maximum of 3,500 U.S. troops to remain in Iraq, supported by an additional 1,500 troops that would periodically rotate in and out of the country as contingencies arose. The smaller force and rotational posture were ideas that General James Cartwright, the Vice Chairman of the Joint Chiefs of Staff, had suggested to White House officials without the knowledge of Panetta or Mullen. In Iraq, the revised numbers caught McGurk and Jeffrey off guard and unable to explain the change, as hours before they had been negotiating with the Iraqis for a residual force of 10,000. The smaller force would still require Iraqi Parliamentary approval and immunity from Iraqi law but would provide much less capability to help defend Iraq.

Assessing the costs and benefits of the SOFA and unnerved by the change in the size of the residual force, many Iraqi politicians concluded that they would expend far too much political capital and incur too much risk in exchange for a small force with limited capabilities. Thus, when the Iraqi Parliament returned from its Ramadan holiday in early September, the negotiating teams made no progress resolving these issues. As September passed without an agreement, Austin declared October 15 as the deadline for a decision, since beyond that point "the laws of physics," as he put it, would make it impossible for USF-I to withdraw by the end of the year.[190]

As that deadline approached, Austin and USF-I began to realize that an agreement was unlikely. On October 1, Austin reported to Panetta that Maliki simply could not find a way to balance the need for a continued U.S. troop presence with the political fallout he anticipated if he pushed the Iraqi Parliament to a public vote on the matter.[191] For a brief time, Austin considered "freezing" 5,000 troops in place to force the Parliament to vote on the SOFA.[192] He also proposed signaling U.S. commitment to stay by accelerating the arrival of the 3d Infantry Division headquarters, which was scheduled to deploy to Iraq as a subordinate unit under OSC-I, and reflagging it as the United States Training Mission-Iraq by the beginning of December as USF-I redeployed.[193]

However, by October 7, Austin accepted that he would be unable to retain either the advise-and-assist brigades or aircraft within Iraq's borders after 2011. He ordered USF-I to begin planning to augment Caslen's OSC-I, which would have to assume responsibility for the entirety of the U.S. military mission by the end of the year.[194] The official word came on October 21, when Obama spoke with Prime Minister Maliki via video teleconference for the first time since June and informed the Iraqi leader that the United States would indeed reduce its forces in Iraq to zero by the end of 2011.

Maliki's Crackdown

Political turbulence followed in the weeks after the announcement that U.S. troops would withdraw. KRG President Massoud Barzani leveled the public charge that Maliki and his allies had submitted to pressure from Iran not to sign the SOFA. Acting Minister of Defense Sadun Dulaymi, considered a Maliki ally, charged that Maliki had violated the Iraqi constitution in an attempt to seize power.[195] Meanwhile, the Prime Minister took steps to solidify control of an Iraqi military that would no longer be partnered with U.S. military units. In the Iraqi general officer ranks, Maliki removed several senior military leaders who had been closely associated with the United States, including General Nasier Abadi, an experienced air force officer who had been Iraq's vice chief of defense. Maliki ordered Abadi's retirement just days after finalizing the agreement to buy American F–16s, even though Abadi had overseen Iraq's F–16 program for several years.[196]

With U.S. troops set to depart, U.S. officials saw signs that Maliki feared the prospects for a coup against him once his government no longer had the backing of American military units. Caslen observed that Libyan leader Muammar Gaddafi's brutal murder by rebels on October 20, 2011, the day before Obama's Iraq withdrawal announcement, panicked the Prime Minister. Recalling a meeting with Austin and Maliki shortly after Gaddafi's death, Caslen said, "All Maliki could talk about was 'that better not happen to me . . . there better not be a coup, or I will be dragged through the streets'."[197]

Maliki's fears probably drove what happened next. Three days after Obama announced the U.S. withdrawal, the Maliki government arrested 600 people across the country, mostly Sunnis, to quash what Maliki said was a Ba'athist coup plot revealed to him by the new Libyan Government. However, the government's list of supposed plotters made the allegations seem implausible, since it included people who had long since left the Ba'ath Party and others who were already dead.[198] USF-I reported that the arrests aroused "the ire of Sunni officials and tribal sheikhs."[199] In Salahadin, the Sunni-majority provincial council responded to the crackdown by voting on October 27 for a federal, semi-autonomous region modeled upon the KRG—an arrangement they believed might insulate the province from what they viewed as Maliki's authoritarian consolidation of power in Baghdad.[200] Within days, the Sunni-led provincial councils in Ninewa, Diyala, and Anbar followed suit, fully reversing their provinces' 2005 rejection of the federalism provisions in the Iraqi constitution.[201] Maliki declared these moves unconstitutional and dispatched troops to Salahadin to suppress Sunni protests and to Baqubah to arrest the Diyala provincial governor.[202]

Similar trouble appeared on the Arab-Kurd front as U.S. troops began to leave. Even before it was decided there would not be a residual force, peshmerga forces had moved into the combined security areas in northern Iraq as U.S. troops departed. In November, when USF-I transferred FOB Warrior in Kirkuk to Iraqi Army control, Kurdish police attempted to block Iraqi Army units from entering the base. With only weeks before the departure of U.S. forces, Austin found himself making a final attempt to prevent Kurd-Arab tensions from escalating into war. One senior Kurdish politician visiting Washington summed up the situation shortly after Maliki's crackdown and the Kirkuk confrontation. "Many Americans seem to think this [the U.S. military withdrawal] means the end of the power struggle in Iraq . . . it does not. Now that the Americans are going, we will see the real start of the struggle for power in Iraq, not the end."[203]

The Final Convoys

USF-I's final withdrawal from Iraq over a 7-week period in 2011 was an extraordinary logistical feat for a U.S. force that had maintained large bases in the country for more than 8 years and for U.S. commanders who, until the last moment, had not expected to have to leave completely. The scale of the final retrograde movement out of Iraq—the "waterfall" that USF-I had planned for—was a sizable and rare effort. Austin's decision to keep as many troops as possible working with the ISF until late 2011 meant that when it was announced on October 21 that U.S. forces would withdraw fully, USF-I had fewer than 60 days to redeploy 40,000 Soldiers and about 36,000 contractors. Those personnel would have to dispose of the vast amount of equipment that had accumulated since 2003, including 45,000 pieces of rolling stock and 13,000 shipping containers. Although a small portion of that equipment would be transferred to the ISF, most would have to be driven to ports in Kuwait or Jordan or flown from Baghdad. USF-I's personnel would exit by convoying to Kuwait or flying out of Baghdad.[204]

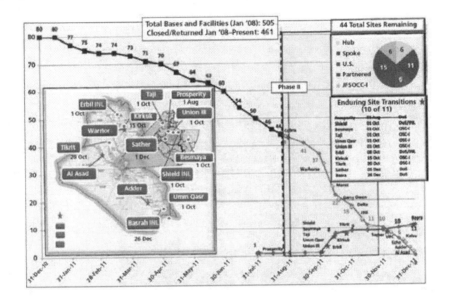

Source: USF-I briefing slide (Released).

Chart 1. U.S. Military Base Closures (December 2010-December 2011).[205]

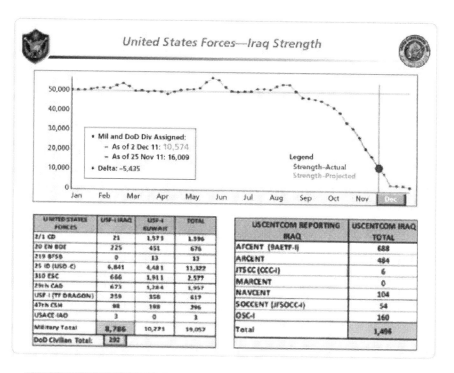

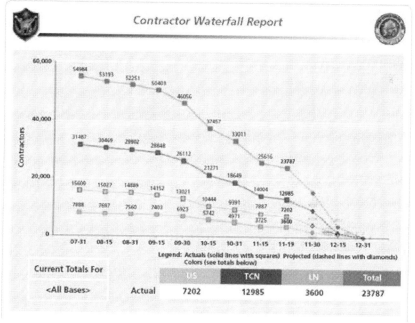

Chart 2. Troop Drawdown and Contractor Drawdown.[206]

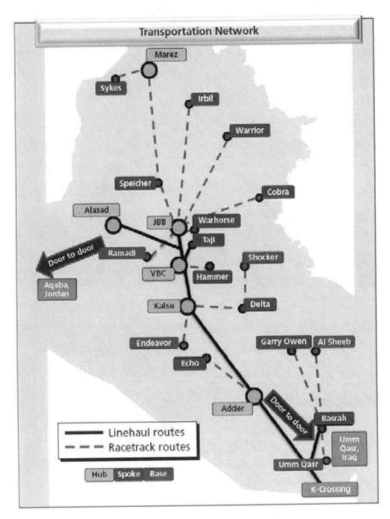

Source: USF-I briefing slide (Released).

Chart 3. Transportation Sustainment Spine in Iraq for Operation NEW DAWN.[207]

To manage the exit, Austin relocated USF-I's command nodes to Al Asad airbase and to Kuwait and prepared to hand the enormous Victory base complex over to the Iraqis.[208] A CENTCOM contracting fusion cell helped manage the contractor drawdown, since USF-I had no mechanism to verify the whereabouts of individual contractors.[209] A few U.S. military elements continued their operations in Iraq up to the last days of the USF-I presence. USF-I had asked the Iraqi Government to take custody of USF-I's remaining detainees before the end of the year, but Prime Minister Maliki declined the request, forcing American detention operations elements to continue their work until the end of December.[210]

Likewise, the remaining special operators of the CJSOTF continued daily operations up to the unit's final day in Iraq, with many of the operations meant to protect the large American convoys leaving Iraq. With three battalion-sized task forces still in Iraq, the CJSOTF would have to manage a rapid drawdown at the same time Austin expected them to serve as a covering force as U.S. troops withdrew. As Colonel Scott Brower, the CJSOTF commander at the time, described it, the CJSOTF would be "screening for USF-I, literally doctrinally screening, as the conventional forces were withdrawing down route Tampa heading for Kuwait."[211] To keep the Shi'a militias off-balance and deter their attacks, Austin authorized the CJSOTF to launch preemptive strikes.[212] At times, the CJSOTF operated unilaterally, but usually it conducted partnered operations—sometimes with its Soldiers wearing Iraqi uniforms and in vehicles painted to match the ISF as a way to lower their signature.[213]

Source: DoD photo by Master Sergeant Cecilio Ricardo (Released).

Airmen of the 407th Air Expeditionary Group Prepare to Depart Iraq in a C-17 Globemaster III Cargo Aircraft.[214]

By the beginning of December 2011, USF-I had only 5 bases in Iraq, and between 500 and 800 U.S. Soldiers were leaving the country each day.[215] Austin had long worried about the vulnerability of U.S. troops as they convoyed through southern Iraqi territory where the Iranian-sponsored Shi'a militant groups had a heavy presence. His concerns had deepened in September after reports that IRGC Quds Force affiliates were occasionally interfering with U.S. convoys, raising the prospect that attacks against USF-I's last convoys might yield propaganda images of burning U.S. vehicles on the Iraqi highways.[216] As the retrograde movement unfolded, however, the U.S. convoys and their ISF escorts made their way to Kuwait unharrassed, indicating that the Iranian regime and its proxies decided ultimately not to impede USF-I's exit.

Source: DoD photo by Staff Sergeant Caleb Barrieau (Released).

General Lloyd Austin Cases the USF-I Colors at Camp Victory on December 15, 2011.[217]

By early December, Camp Victory, where more than 50,000 Americans had once been based, resembled a ghost town. A small air operations center remained at the Baghdad Airport to support the U.S. Embassy and OSC-I, but on December 1, USF-I handed its Iraqi counterparts possession of the empty Faw Palace, the former seat of American military power. On December 15, Panetta and Austin presided over a final ceremony at Camp Victory to case USF-I's colors. It was an event attended by Iraq's senior military officers, but Prime Minister Maliki chose not to join them, and the front-row seat that USF-I reserved for him remained empty. "No words, no ceremony, can provide full tribute to the sacrifices that have brought this day to pass," Panetta told the crowd, adding that though the cost had been high for the United States and the Iraqi people, "Those lives were not lost in vain. They gave birth to an independent, free and sovereign Iraq."[218] Following the ceremony, Austin boarded an aircraft and departed Iraq, taking JFSOCC-I commander Brigadier General Darsie Rogers and the last USF-I elements in Baghdad with him.

***

Three days after the ceremony at Camp Victory, the final U.S. convoy assembled at Contingency Operating Base (COB) Adder near Nasiriyah in the early morning hours of December 18. To throw off any final symbolic enemy attack, the troops had spread disinformation to local officials the day before that they would be remaining in place for the time being. However, at 2:30 am, more than 500 Soldiers loaded into 110 vehicles and began their trek in the dark, arriving at the Kuwaiti border shortly before dawn.

Source: DoD photo by Master Sergeant Cecilio Ricardo (Released).

The Final USF-I Convoy Reaches the Kuwaiti Border as the Sun Rises on December 18, 2011.[219]

Among the troops in the last convoy was an American Soldier who had arrived in the United States as an Iraqi immigrant in 2009 and had enlisted in the U.S. Army the following year. As the convoy waited in the night to depart COB Adder, the Soldier spoke to a *New York Times* reporter, but declined to give his name out of fear for the safety of his family that remained in Iraq. Asked for his thoughts on the withdrawal, he observed, "The Iraqis are going to wake up in the morning, and nobody will be there."[220]

ENDNOTES - CHAPTER 14

1. Colonel Thomas Goss Notebook, entries for July 26, 2010, August 12, 2010, August 20, 2010, August 21, 2010, and August 22, 2010; Interview, Colonel Matthew D. Morton, Chief of Staff of the Army (CSA) Operation IRAQI FREEDOM (OIF) Study Group, with Colonel Matthew Q. Dawson, October 8, 2014. All unpublished documents in this chapter, unless otherwise stated, are in the CSA OIF Study Group archives, Army Heritage and Education Center (AHEC), Carlisle, PA.

2. Plans Notes, United States Forces-Iraq (USF-I), J-5, August 5, 2010, Military History Institute (MHI), AHEC, Carlisle, PA.

3. DoD photo by Sergeant 1st Class Roger Dey, "Vice President Joe Biden Arrives in Baghdad [Image 4 of 17]," DVIDS Identifier 313982, August 30, 2010, Released to Public, available from *https://www.dvidshub. net/image/313982/vice-President-joe-biden-arrives-baghdad.*

4. Barack Obama, "President's Address to the Nation," August 31, 2010, available from *https:// www.whitehouse.gov/the-press-office/2010/08/31/remarks-President-address-nation-end-combat-operations-iraq*, accessed September 23, 2014.

5. Ibid.

6. Rick R. Brennan, Jr., et al., *Ending the U.S. War in Iraq: The Final Transition, Operational Maneuver, and Disestablishment of United States Forces-Iraq,* Washington, DC: RAND Corporation, 2013, p. 78; USF-I, Secretary of Defense (SECDEF) Weekly Update, September 13-19, 2010.

7. DoD photo by Sergeant 1st Class Roger Dey, "Austin leads USF-I into New Dawn [Image 9 of 17]," DVIDS Identifier 315675, September 1, 2010, Released to Public, modified (cropped), available from *https:// www.dvidshub.net/image/315675/austin-leads-usf-into-new-dawn*.

8. Brennan et al., *Ending the U.S. War in Iraq,* p. 51.

9. USF-I, SECDEF Weekly Update, July 12-18, 2010; and September 20-26, 2010.

10. Plans Notes, USF-I, J-5, August 30, 2010.

11. Plans Notes, USF-I, J-5, September 23, 2010.

12. Ali Khedery, "Why we stuck with Maliki—and lost Iraq," *The Washington Post,* July 3, 2014.

13. Plans Notes, USF-I, J-5, September 4, 2010.

14. USF-I, Mission and Approach in Stability Operations, September 1-December 31, 2011, MHI.

15. Briefing, USF-I Commander's Conference, Overview of October 1, 2004: Stability Operations, August 21, 2010, MHI.

16. Goss Notebook, September 1, 2010, entry.

17. Plans Notes, USF-I, J-5, May 26, 2010, MHI.

18. Interviews, Vincent McLean, Contemporary Operations Study Team, with Colonel Peter Newell, Commander (Cdr), 4th Brigade Combat Team (BCT), 1st Armored Division, December 7, 2011; Steven E. Clay, Contemporary Operations Study Team, with Colonel Roger Cloutier, Cdr, 1st BCT, 3d Infantry Division, May 7, 2012.

19. Gary Sheftick, "Deploying brigade to test 'advise and assist' concept," *Army,* Vol. 59, No. 5, May 2009.

20. Michael E. O'Hanlon and Jason H. Campbell, "Iraq Index," Washington, DC: Brookings Institution, January 31, 2012, p. 13; Manuscript (Ms), *On Point,* Vol. VI, Fort Leavenworth, KS: Combat Studies Institute, September 25, 2014, Chapter 9, p. 18; President Barack Obama, "Responsibly Ending the War in Iraq" Speech, Camp Lejeune, NC, February 27, 2009, available from *https://obamawhitehouse.archives.gov/the-press-office/remarks-president-barack-obama-ndash-responsibly-ending-war-iraq*, accessed October 1, 2014.

21. Interviews, CSI Contemporary Operations Study Team with Newell, December 7, 2011; with Cloutier, May 7, 2012; Lynne Chandler Garcia, CSI Contemporary Operations Study Team, with Colonel Michael Eastman, Cdr, Task Force 2-29 FA, 4th BCT, 1st Armored Division, April 20, 2012; Sergeant Benjamin Kibbey, "Advise and Assist Brigade: A familiar unit with a new mission in Iraq," *Army,* Vol. 60, No. 8, August 2010.

22. Manuscript (Ms), *On Point,* Vol. V, Conclusion Chapter, "The Approach of a New Dawn," Fort Leavenworth, KS: Combat Studies Institute, September 25, 2014.

23. Ibid.

24. Ms, *On Point*, Vol. VI, Chapter 1, p. 39; Interview, CSI Contemporary Operations Study Team with Major General (Ret.) Eddy Spurgin, April 17, 2014, pp. 4-8.

25. Interviews, CSI Contemporary Operations Study Team with Newell, December 7, 2011; with Cloutier, May 7, 2012; with Eastman, April 20, 2012; Kibbey, "Advise and Assist Brigade."

26. Interviews, Colonel Frank Sobchak, Chief of Staff of the Army's Operation IRAQI FREEDOM Study Group, with Colonel Mark Mitchell, CJSOTF-AP Cdr, September 29, 2014, February 8, 2016; Interview, Vince McLean, Contemporary Operations Study Team, with Colonel Scott Brower, CJSOTF-AP Cdr, March 13, 2014; E-mail, Colonel (Ret.) Mark Mitchell, to Colonel Frank Sobchak, Sub: Follow up questions, February 20, 2016.

27. Interview, Vincent McLean, Contemporary Operations Study Team, with Colonel Peter Newell, Cdr 4th BCT, 1st Armored Division, December 7, 2011.

28. Interview, Steven Clay, Contemporary Operations Study Team, with Colonel (P) Roger Cloutier, Cdr 1st BCT, 3d Infantry Division, May 7, 2012; Interview, Dr. Lynne Garcia, Contemporary Operations Study Team, with Colonel Michael Eastman, Cdr TF 2-29 FA, 4th BCT 1st Armored Division, April 20, 2012.

29. Ms, *On Point*, Vol. V, Chapter 2, p. 45.

30. Interviews, Colonel Matthew D. Morton, CSA OIF Study Group, with Colonel David Funk, October 31, 2014; with Colonel Robert Molinari, October 31, 2014.

31. Michael R. Gordon, "In Iraq, Clearer Image of U.S. Support," *The New York Times*, September 13, 2010, available from *http://www.nytimes.com/2010/09/14/world/middleeast/14military.html?_r=1&scp=8&sq=diyala&st=cse*, accessed October 14, 2014; Transcript, Broadcast by Mary Louise Kelly and Robert Siegel over National Public Radio, October 4, 2014, sub: Battle Raises Questions On Iraq Security Readiness, available from *http://www.npr.org/templates/transcript/transcript.php?storyId=130323848*, accessed October 14, 2014.

32. DoD photo by Sergeant Brandon Bolick, "Operation New Dawn [Image 7 of 15]," DVIDS Identifier 321225, September 13, 2010, Released to Public, available from *https://www.dvidshub.net/image/321225/operation-new-dawn*.

33. Interviews, CSA OIF Study Group with Colonel Funk, October 31, 2014; with Colonel Molinari, October 31, 2014.

34. Transcript, Kelly and Siegel, September 13, 2010; Interview, CSA OIF Study Group with Molinari, October 31, 2014.

35. Interviews, Colonel Matthew D. Morton, CSA OIF Study Group, with Colonel Thomas J. Goss, October 9, 2014, West Point, NY; with Molinari, October 31, 2014.

36. Interview, CSA OIF Study Group with Goss, October 9, 2014; Goss Notebook, March 27, 2010, entry.

37. Interview, CSA OIF Study Group with Goss, October 9, 2014; Memorandum for the Record, HQ, Forward Operating Base Warhorse, 1st Battalion, 21st Infantry Division, and 2d Airborne Battalion, 25th Infantry Division, September 17, 2010, sub: Operation AL HADID PALMS After Action Review, September 11-13, 2010.

38. Interview, CSA OIF Study Group with Molinari, October 31, 2014.

39. Briefing, MNSTC-I, Shaping the Long-Term Security Partnership with Iraq, to General Raymond T. Odierno, Cdr, MNF-I, February 24, 2009; Brennan et al., eds., *Ending the U.S. War in Iraq*, Washington, DC: RAND Corporation, 2013, pp. 157-158.

40. Plans Notes, USF-I, J-5, October 23, 2010.

41. DoD photo by Staff Sergeant Daniel Yarnall, "Lt. Gen. Cone attends Senior Working Group meeting [Image 7 of 10]," DVIDS Identifier 330630, October 19, 2010, Released to Public, available from *https://www.dvidshub.net/image/330630/lt-gen-cone-attends-senior-working-group-meeting*.

42. Plans Notes, USF-I, J-5, November 11, 2010.

43. Ibid.

44. USF-I, SECDEF Weekly Update, December 13-19, 2010; July 12-18, 2010; and September 13-19, 2010.

45. DoD photo by Technical Sergeant Randy Redman, "Exercise Lion's Leap demonstrates full range of Iraqi military capabilities [Image 4 of 8]," DVIDS Identifier 392005, April 18, 2011, Released to Public, available from *https://www.dvidshub.net/image/392005/exercise-lions-leap-demonstrates-full-range-iraqi-military-capabilities*.

46. Interview, CSA OIF Study Group with Goss, October 9, 2014.

47. Plans Notes, USF-I, J-5, May 21, 2010; and May 25, 2010; White Paper, "New Approach to Police Primacy and Creation of an Iraqi Corps," June 4, 2010; White Paper, "J-5 (Plans) Police Primacy," n.d., MHI; Plans Notes, USF-I, J-5, August 9, 2010; and November 10, 2010.

48. Plans Notes, USF-I, J-5, November 20, 2010.

49. Ibid.

50. Interview, Vincent McLean, CSI Contemporary Operations Study Team, with Major General David E. Quantock, CG JTF-134, December 12, 2011.

51. Interview, Vincent McLean, CSI Contemporary Operations Study Team, with Colonel David Glaser and Lieutenant Colonel Zane Jones, Cdr and DCdr, 42 Military Police Brigade, December 12, 2011.

52. Interview, CSI Contemporary Operations Study Team with Quantock, December 12, 2011.

53. Interview, McLean, Contemporary Operations Study Team, with Quantock, CG JTF-134, December 12, 2011.

54. Interview, Dr. Robert Rush, U.S. Army Center of Military History (CMH) with Brigadier General David E. Quantock, CG JTF-134, May 29, 2009.

55. Interview, CSI Contemporary Operations Study Team with Colonel Glaser and Lieutenant Colonel Jones, December 12, 2011.

56. Interview, Lynne Garcia, CSI Contemporary Operations Study Team, with Colonel Mack Huey, Cdr 89th Military Police Brigade, February 24, 2012; Interview, CSI Contemporary Operations Study Team with Quantock, December 12, 2011.

57. U.S. Army photo by Private 1st Class Candace Mundt, "Transfer of Detainee Operations to Iraqi Government Underway," DVIDS Identifier 260536, March 15, 2010, Released to Public, available from *https://www.dvidshub.net/image/260536/transfer-detainee-operations-iraqi-Government-underway*.

58. USF-I, SECDEF Weekly Update, July 12-18, 2010.

59. Interview, Lieutenant Colonel Wes Melnick, MNF-I Historian, with Major General Nelson Cannon, DCG for Detainee Operations and Provost Marshall General for Iraq, December 14, 2010.

60. Interview, Melnick, MNF-I Historian, with Cannon, Deputy CG for Detainee Operations and Provost Marshall General for Iraq, December 14, 2010.

61. Interview, Colonel Frank Sobchak, CSA OIF Study Group, with Army Special Forces Officer who asked for anonymity, May 12, 2015.

62. Emma Sky, *The Unraveling: High Hopes and Missed Opportunities in Iraq*, New York: Public Affairs, 2015, p. 329.

63. Joel Rayburn, *Iraq after America: Strongmen, Sectarians, Resistance*, Stanford, CA: Hoover Institution Press, 2014, pp. 214-215.

64. USF-I Weekly Assessment, January 3-9, 2011.

65. DoD photo by Airman 1st Class Brian Ferguson, "Near the Al Rashid hotel in Baghdad, Iraq (IRQ), after a rocket attack launched from this blue trailer, which contains tubes used as launchers damaged the hotel," DIMOC Identifier 75M45QZ_9KXLEK6C3, October 26, 2003, Released to Public.

66. Ibid.

67. USF-I, Quarterly History, January 1-March 31, 2011, p. 43.

68. Ibid.

69. Liz Sly, "Egyptian Revolution Sparks Protest Movement In Democratic Iraq," *The Washington Post*, February 12, 2011.

70. USF-I Quarterly Cmd Rpt, January 1-March 31, 2011, p. 10.

71. Andrew Raine, "Iraq Authorities 'Using Violence and Bribes' to Curb Dissent," *National*, March 2, 2011, available from *http://www.thenational.ae/news/world/middle-east/iraq-authorities-using-violence-and-bribes-to-curb-dissent*, accessed June 3, 2016.

72. Ibid.

73. Quarterly Cmd Rpt, January 1-March 31, 2011, USF-I, p. 11.

74. USF-I Weekly Assessment, April 4-10, 2011.

75. Colonel Keith A. Casey, Interview by CSI, April 28, 2014, pp. 12-13; Colonel Paul Garcia, CSI, August 26, 2014, pp. 5-7; International Crisis Group, "Iraq and the Kurds: Confronting Withdrawal Fears," Middle East Report No. 103, March 28, 2011, pp. 25-27, available from *https://www.crisisgroup.org/middle-east-north-africa/gulf-and-arabian-peninsula/iraq/iraq-and-kurds-confronting-withdrawal-fears*, accessed June 15, 2018.

76. Lieutenant General David Perkins, Interview by CSI, May 4, 2012, pp. 14-15.

77. Associated Press, "Bahrain Troops Lay Siege to Protestors' Camp," CBS News, March 16, 2011, available from *http://www.cbsnews.com/news/bahrain-troops-lay-siege-to-protesters-camp/*; Associated Press, "Bahrain declares martial law; Saudis send troops," CBS News, March 15, 2011, available from *http://www.cbsnews.com/news/bahrain-declares-martial-law-saudis-send-troops/*.

78. Tim Arango, "Shiites in Iraq Support Bahrain's Protestors," *The New York Times*, April 1, 2011.

79. Human Rights Watch, "Iraq: Attacks by Government-Backed Thugs Chill Protests," June 30, 2011.

80. Annie Gowen and Aziz Alwan, "Hadi al-Mahdi, Slain Iraqi Journalist, Warned of Threats," *The Washington Post*, September 10, 2011.

81. Joel Wing, "Iraq Finally Moves Forward with Security and Planning Ministers," *Musings on Iraq*, April 4, 2011, available from *http://musingsoniraq.blogspot.com/2011/04/iraq-finally-moves-forward-with.html*, accessed June 3, 2016.

82. USF-I Weekly Rpt, May 22-28, 2011; Tim Craig, "In Iraq, Head of de- Baathification Panel is Killed," *The Washington Post*, May 26, 2011, available from *https://www.washingtonpost.com/world/thousands-of-sadr-supporters-rally-against-us-in-baghdad/2011/05/26/AGx1gqBH_story.html*, accessed June 3, 2016.

83. Michael Knights, "Iraq's Relentless Insurgency: The Fight for Power Ahead of U.S. Withdrawal," *Foreign Affairs*, August 2011, available from *https://www.foreignaffairs.com/articles/middle-east/2011-08-22/iraqs-relentless-insurgency*.

84. Ibid.

85. "Testimony To End Bloodshed Among Mujahideen in the Levant," Al-Fajr Media Center, May 2, 2014.

86. Abu Rumman, Muhammad, "Iraq's Al-Qa'ida After the Killing of its Two Leaders: Between Total Collapse and Regaining Initiative," *Al-Ghadd*, April 26, 2010.

87. Mullah Nadhim was assassinated by AQI in west Baghdad in 2011; "Defected Al-Qa'ida Leader Reveals that Al-Mashhadani, Al-Ani, and Al-Mufti Prominent Candidates To Succeed Abu-Umar al-Baghdadi," *Al-Sumariyah News*, May 13, 2006.

88. Ahmad, Abu, "The Concealed Truths About al-Baghdadi's State," April 5, 2014; William McCants, "The Believer: How an Introvert with a Passion for Religion and Soccer Became Abu Bakr al-Baghdadi, Leader of the Islamic State," *The Brookings Essay*, September 1, 2015, available from *http://csweb.brookings.edu/content/research/essays/2015/thebeliever.html*, accessed May 26, 2016.

89. Ahmad, Abu, "The Concealed Truths About al-Baghdadi's State," April 5, 2014.

90. Islamic State of Iraq and Syria (ISIS) propaganda image from their magazine *Rumiyah*, Iss. 1.

91. "Al-Nasir Lidin Allah Cruel, Intensely Extremist; Entered Iraqi Twice, Is Inclined To Abetting Sectarian War," *Al-Hayah*, May 16, 2010; "A Statement from the War Ministry of the Islamic State of Iraq," Al-Fajr Media Center, May 13, 2010.

92. Kyle Orton, *Governing the Caliphate: Profiles of Islamic State Leaders*, London, UK: Centre for the Response to Radicalisation and Terrorism at the Henry Jackson Center, 2016, pp. 12-13.

93. Walid, Ala, "'The Inghimasiyun' and the 'Dhabbihah' and the Terror of the 'Islamic State,'" *Al-Quds al-Arabi*, August 12, 2014.

94. Ahmad, Abu, "The Concealed Truths About al-Baghdadi's State," April 5, 2014.

95. The latter of these would later assume Nu'man's duties as *wazir al-harb* (war minister) following ISIS's February 2014 break with al-Qa'eda.

96. Various discussions with Kyle Orton, Henry Jackson Center, @wikibaghdady, December 15, 2013.

97. USF-I, Quarterly History, January 1-March 31, 2011, p. 40.

98. Ibid., p. 41.

99. Ibid.

100. Ibid., p. 40.

101. Ibid., p. 41.

102. Duraid Adnan and Timothy Williams, "Sunnis in Iraq Allied with U.S. Rejoin Rebels," *The New York Times*, October 26, 2010.

103. Leila Fadel, "Iraq's Awakening Stripped of Their Police Ranks," *The Washington Post*, September 26, 2010.

104. Adnan and Williams, "Sunnis in Iraq Allied with U.S. Rejoin Rebels," *The New York Times*, October 26, 2010.

105. Quote from Quarterly Cmd Rpt, April 1-June 30, 2011; USF-I, July 1, 2011, p. 133. See also Quarterly Cmd Rpt, January 1-March 31, 2011; USF-I, May 15, 2011.

106. Ibid., April 1-June 30, 2011, USF-I, July 1, 2011; and January 1-March 31, 2011, USF-I, May 15, 2011.

107. Ibid., January 1-March 31, 2011; USF-I, May 15, 2011, p. 44.

108. Ibid.

109. Ms., *On Point*, VI, Chapter 2, pp. 43-44.

110. AFP, "74 Killed as Bombs Tear through 17 Iraqi Cities," Emirates247.com, August 16, 2011, available from *https://www.emirates247.com/news/world/74-killed-as-bombs-tear-through-17-iraqi-cities-2011 -08-16-1.413505*.

111. British Broadcasting Company, "Baghdad Mosque Attack: Suicide Bomber Kills at least 28," BBC. com, August 28, 2011, accessed July 14, 2016.

112. Michael Schmidt, "Threat Resurges in Deadliest Day of Year for Iraq," *The New York Times*, August 11, 2011.

113. Brigadier General Malcolm Frost, Interview by CSI, November 21, 2013.

114. DoD photo by Sergeant Brandon Bolick, "Kirkush military base visit [Image 3 of 4]," DVIDS 366435, January 11, 2011, Released to Public, available from *https://www.dvidshub.net/image/366435/ kirkush-military-base-visit*.

115. Frost, Interview by CSI, November 21, 2013.

116. USF-I Weekly Assessment, April 4-10, 2011.

117. Ibid.; USF-I Weekly Assessment, October 30-November 5, 2011; and USF-I Weekly Assessment November 13-19, 2011.

118. Plans Notes, USF-I, J-5, January 25, 2011, and January 27, 2011.

119. Ibid., March 15-16, 2011; and March 18, 2011.

120. Ibid., February 7, 2011; and March 1, 2011; Interview, Colonel Joel Rayburn and Colonel Frank Sobchak, CSA OIF Study Group, with Gen (Ret.) Lloyd Austin, USF-I CG, October 4, 2016.

121. Ibid.

122. Interview, CSA OIF Study Group with General Lloyd Austin, February 6, 2015.

123. Plans Notes, USF-I, J-5, January 21, 2011.

124. Ibid., February 7, 2011; and March 1, 2011.

125. Michael R. Gordon, "Iran's Master of Iraq Chaos Still Vexes U.S.," *The New York Times*, October 3, 2012, available from *http://www.nytimes.com/2012/10/03/world/middleeast/qassim-suleimani-irans-master-of-iraq-chaos-still-vexes-the-us.html*, accessed October 1, 2015.

126. Robert M. Gates, *Duty: The Memoirs of a Secretary at War*, New York: Vintage Books, 2014, pp. 553-555; John D. Banusiewicz, "Gates Wraps Up Iraq Visit, Arrives in UAE," American Forces Press Service, April 8, 2011, available from *http://archive.defense.gov/news/news/newsarticle.aspx?ID=63493*, accessed June 3, 2016.

127. Ibid.

128. Ms, *On Point*, Vol. VI, Chapter 2, p. 14.

129. Dexter Filkins, "What We Left Behind," *New Yorker*, April 28, 2014.

130. James Franklin Jeffrey, "Behind the U.S. Withdrawal from Iraq," *The Wall Street Journal*, November 2, 2014.

131. Rebecca Santana, "Iraqi Cleric Muqtada al Sadr: Resist the US by All Means Necessary," Associated Press, January 8, 2011; Jomana Karadsheh and Joe Sterling, "In Iraq, a Popular Cleric Cranks up Anti-U.S. Rhetoric," CNN, January 8, 2011, available from *http://www.cnn.com/2011/WORLD/meast/01/08/iraq.sadr/*, accessed May 25, 2017.

132. USF-I Weekly Assessment, May 22-28, 2011.

133. USF-I Weekly Assessment, June 5-11, 2011.

134. USF-I Weekly Assessment, June 12-18, 2011; Brennan et al., *Ending the U.S. War in Iraq*, pp. 104, 107-108.

135. Michael S. Schmidt and Tim Arango, "Despite Difficult Talks, U.S. and Iraq Had Expected Some American Troops to Stay," *The New York Times*, October 21, 2011.

136. USF-I Weekly Assessment, July 3-9, 2011; and June 19-25, 2011.

137. Plans Notes, USF-I, J-5, June 18, 2011; Gregg Carlstrom, "Leaving Iraq: Debating Obama's Withdrawal Timeline," *World Politics Review*, May 4, 2010, available from *http://www.worldpoliticsreview.com/articles/5490/leaving-iraq-debating-obamas-withdrawal-timeline*, accessed May 26, 2016.

138. Tim Arango, "Taking Lead, Iraqis Hope U.S. Special Operations Commandos Stay," *The New York Times*, July 2, 2011.

139. This is a compilation of direct quotes from two sources: Liz Sly, "Iraq needs help defending its borders after U.S. troops leave in 2011," *Los Angeles Times*, August 12, 2010, available from *http://articles.latimes.com/2010/aug/12/world/la-fg-iraq-military-support-20100812*; and *Al Arabiya News*, "Iraq's Top Army Officer Says US Must Stay," August 11, 2010, available from *https://www.alarabiya.net/articles/2010/08/11/116344.html*, accessed May 25, 2017. Someone also indicated the quote together is actually Agence France Presse Wire Service, August 11, 2010.

140. USF-I Weekly Assessment, April 25-May 1, 2011.

141. USF-I Weekly Assessment, May 8-14, 2011.

142. Plans Notes, USF-I, J-5, March 29, 2011.

143. Muhanad Mohammed, "Five U.S. troops killed in Iraq attack," *Reuters*, June 6, 2011, available from *http://www.reuters.com/article/us-iraq-violence-us-idUSTRE7551QG20110606*; Interview, CSI Contemporary Operations Study Team with Colonel Andrew Gainey, March 19, 2014, pp. 7-12.

144. Ms, *On Point*, Vol. V, Chapter 5, p. 18.

145. Quarterly Cmd Rpt, April 1-June 30, 2010, USF-I, pp. 32-34; and July 1-September 30, 2011, USF-I, pp. 28-29; Mohammed Tawfeeq and Joe Sterling, "US official: Iraq 'less safe' than it was last year," CNN, July 30, 2011.

146. Quarterly Cmd Rpt, April 1-June 30, 2010, USF-I, pp. 32-34; and July 1-September 30, 2011, USF-I, pp. 28-29; Tawfeeq and Sterling, "US official: Iraq 'less safe' than it was last year."

147. USF-I Weekly Assessment, June 26-July 2, 2011.

148. Quarterly Cmd Rpt, July 1-September 30, 2011, USF-I, October 2011, pp. 28-29; Tawfeeq and Sterling, "U.S. official: Iraq 'less safe' than it was last year."

149. Tawfeeq and Sterling, "U.S. official: Iraq 'less safe' than it was last year."

150. USF-I Weekly Assessment, July 10-16, 2011; Interview, Colonel Joel Rayburn, CSA OIF Study Group, with SECDEF Robert Gates, July 21, 2014.

151. USF-I Weekly Assessment, June 12-18, 2011.

152. USF-I Weekly Assessment, July 10-16, 2011; July 31-August 6, 2011; and June 5-11, 2011.

153. Interview, CSI Contemporary Operations Study Team with Lieutenant General David Perkins, Fort Leavenworth, KS, May 4, 2012, pp. 5-6.

154. USF-I Weekly Assessment, July 10-16, 2011; and July 31-August 6, 2011.

155. Interview, CSI Contemporary Operations Study Team with Major General (Ret.) Spurgin, April 17, 2014, pp. 4-8.

156. Plans Notes, USF-I, J-5, January 18-19, 2011; Interviews, CSA OIF Study Group with Goss, October 9, 2014; with Major General Brian Owens, April 29, 2014, Stuttgart, Germany.

157. Interview, Colonel Frank Sobchak, CSA OIF Study Group, with Brigadier General (S) Scott Brower, CJSOTF-AP Cdr, June 2, 2014.

158. The two battalions of the national level brigade were originally known as the Iraqi Counterterrorism Force, 36th Commando Battalion.

159. Marisa Sullivan, "Maliki's Authoritarian Regime," Washington, DC: Institute for the Study of War, p. 12; Shane Bauer, "Iraq's New Death Squad: America has built an elite and lethal counterterrorism force. But who's calling the shots?" *Nation*, June 3, 2009.

160. David Witty, "The Iraqi Counter Terrorism Service," Washington, DC: Brookings Institution, 2015, p. 18; International Crisis Group, "Loose Ends: Iraq's Security Forces between U.S. Drawdown and Withdrawal," Middle East Report No. 99, Washington, DC, October 26, 2010, pp. 15-16, available from *https://www.crisisgroup.org/middle-east-north-africa/gulf-and-arabian-peninsula/iraq/loose-ends-iraq-s-security-forces-between-us-drawdown-and-withdrawal*, accessed May 20, 2018.

161. Witty, "The Iraqi Counter Terrorism Service."

162. Interviews, CSI Contemporary Operations Study Team with Brigadier General (S) Brower, March 13, 2014; CSA OIF Study Group with Brigadier General (S) Brower, June 2, 2014; E-mail, Colonel (Ret.)

Mark Mitchell, former Cdr, CJSOTF-AP, to Colonel Frank Sobchak, February 20, 2016, sub: Follow-up questions; Interview, Sobchak with Colonel Mark Mitchell, Cdr, (CJSOTF-AP), September 29, 2014.

163. Interview, Steven Clay, CSI Contemporary Operations Study Team, with Lieutenant General Robert W. Cone, Deputy CG, USF-I Operations, February 27, 2012.

164. Major Dave Butler, "Lights Out: ARSOF Reflects on Eight Years in Iraq," *Special Warfare*, January-March 2012.

165. Interview, CSA OIF Study Group, with Brigadier General (S) Brower, June 2, 2014; E-mail, Colonel (Ret.) Mark Mitchell, former CJSOTF-AP Cdr, to Colonel Frank Sobchak, subj: Follow up questions, February 20, 2016.

166. Plans Notes, USF-I, J-5, March 29, 2011.

167. Ms, *On Point*, Vol. VI, Chapter 4, p. 6.

168. Interviews, CSI Contemporary Operations Study Team with Brigadier General (S) Brower, March 13, 2014; CSA OIF Study Group with Brigadier General (S) Brower, June 2, 2014; E-mail, Mitchell to Sobchak, February 20, 2016, sub: Follow-up questions; Interview, CSA OIF Study Group with Mitchell, September 29, 2014.

169. USF-I Weekly Assessment, January 3-9, 2011.

170. USF-I Weekly Assessment, April 25-May 1, 2011; and September 25-October 1, 2011.

171. Interviews, CSI Contemporary Operations Study Team with Lieutenant Colonel John D. Cross, March 25, 2014, pp. 5-15; CSI Contemporary Operations Study Team with Lieutenant Colonel Timothy A. Brumfield, March 14, 2014, pp. 5, 14-15; Regimental History of HQ, 3d Armored Cavalry Regiment, Operation NEW DAWN, August 2010-August 2011, August 3, 2011, entry.

172. DoD photo by Captain Chad Ashe, "Live fire exercise preps IA soldiers for Lion's Leap [Image 4 of 4]," DVIDS Identifier 393444, April 19, 2011, Released to Public, available from *https://www.dvidshub.net/ image/393444/live-fire-exercise-preps-ia-soldiers-lions-leap*.

173. USF-I Weekly Assessment, January 31-February 6, 2011; and September 25-October 1, 2011.

174. Quarterly Cmd Rpt, April 1-June 30, 2011, USF-I, July 1, 2011. This source is for both paragraphs, and includes a note that Iraq had 123 M1A1 tanks by June 30, 2011. USF-I Weekly Assessment, May 22-28, 2011; and August 21-27, 2011.

175. Barbara Starr, "U.S.: Iraq looking to buy F-16 fighters," CNN, July 12, 2011, available from *http:// www.cnn.com/2011/US/07/12/iraq.fighter.jets/*, accessed June 10, 2015.

176. Adam Entous, Ben Lando, and Nathan Hodge, "U.S. Set to Sell Fighters to Iraq," *The Wall Street Journal*, July 12, 2011.

177. Brennan et al., *Ending the U.S. War in Iraq*, p. 186; USF-I Weekly Assessment, August 21-27, 2011; Plans Notes, USF-I, J-5, May 17, 2011.

178. Interview, CSI Contemporary Operations Study Team with Cone, March 21, 2012.

179. Marisa Sullivan, "Maliki's Authoritarian Regime," Middle East Security Report 10, Washington, DC: Institute for the Study of War, April 2013, pp. 16-19.

180. Letter, General Babakir Zebari to Iraqi President Jalal Talibani, Subj: Report, September 4, 2011.

181. Ibid. All quotes are from this letter, and the paragraph includes paraphrasing from the letter.

182. Ibid.

183. Jim Garamone, "Panetta Calls for Iraqi Decision on Future U.S. Presence," American Forces Press Service, July 11, 2011, accessed October 1, 2014, available from *http://archive.defense.gov/news/newsarticle.aspx?id=64631*, accessed June 3, 2016; Jim Garamone, "Austin Gives Insights into Drawdown, Possible Aid to Iraq," American Forces Press Service, July 11, 2011, accessed October 1, 2014, available from *http://archive.defense.gov/news/newsarticle.aspx?id=64629*, accessed June 3, 2016.

184. Garamone, "Panetta Calls for Iraqi Decision on Future U.S. Presence."

185. DoD photo by Technical Sergeant Jacob N. Bailey, "U.S. Secretary of Defense Leon E. Panetta speaks to troops at Camp Victory, Iraq," DIMOC Identifier 110711-F-RG147-606, July 11, 2011, Released to Public.

186. USF-I Weekly Assessment, July 24-30, 2011; and July 31-August 6, 2011.

187. USF-I Weekly Assessment, August 21-27, 2011.

188. Interview, CSA OIF Study Group with Lieutenant General Robert Caslen, December 18, 2014.

189. Ibid.

190. Ms, *On Point*, Vol. VI, Chapter 2, p. 21.

191. USF-I Weekly Assessment, September 25-October 1, 2011.

192. Plans Notes, USF-I, J-5, October 3-5, 2011.

193. USF-I Weekly Assessment, January 31-February 6, 2011; and September 4-10, 2011.

194. USF-I Weekly Assessment, October 16-22, 2011.

195. Ibid.

196. Ramzy Mardini, "Maliki Arrests Potential Opponents," Washington, DC: Institute for the Study of War, December 14, 2011, p. 1.

197. Interview, Colonel Joel Rayburn and Colonel Matthew Morton, CSA OIF Study Group, with Caslen, Chief, OSC-I, November 7, 2014.

198. USF-I Weekly Assessment, October 23-29, 2011; Mardini, "Maliki Arrests Potential Opponents," p. 3.

199. USF-I Weekly Assessment, October 23-29, 2011.

200. Ibid.

201. Rayburn, *Iraq after America*, p. 220.

202. Ibid., pp. 220-221.

203. Ibid., p. 253.

204. Assocation of the U.S. Army, Institute of Land Warfare, "Third Army: Empowering Theater Responsiveness by Synchronizing Operational Maneuver," *Army*, Vol. 62, No. 3, March 2012.

205. USF-I briefing slide, December 14, 2011, Released to Public.

206. Ibid.

207. Ibid.

208. Interview, Combat Studies Institute with Major General Arthur Bartell, December 23, 2013.

209. Molly Dunigan, "A Lesson from the Iraq War: How to Outsource War to Private Contractors," *Christian Science Monitor*, March 19, 2013, available from *http://www.csmonitor.com/Commentary/Opinion/2013/0319/A-lesson-from-Iraq-war-How-to-outsource-war-to-private-contractors*, accessed December 12, 2014; Interview, Combat Studies Institute with Brigadier General Kenneth D. Jones, February 4, 2014; Interview, Combat Studies Institute with Major General Camille Nichols, November 19, 2013.

210. USF-I Weekly Assessment, October 30-November 5, 2011; and November 6-12, 2011.

211. Interview, CSA OIF Study Group with Brigadier General (S) Brower, June 2, 2014.

212. Interviews, CSI Contemporary Operations Study Team with Brigadier General (S) Brower, March 13, 2014; CSA OIF Study Group with Brigadier General (S) Brower, June 2, 2014; E-mail, Mitchell to Sobchak, February 20, 2016, sub: Follow-up questions.

213. Ibid.

214. DoD photo by Master Sergeant Cecilio Ricardo, "Last airmen flying out of Iraq [Image 14 of 17]," DVIDS 501089, December 18, 2011, Released to Public, available from *https://www.dvidshub.net/image/501089/last-airmen-flying-out-iraq*.

215. Dennis Steele, "The Sun Sets on Operation New Dawn, but Shadows Remain," *Army Times*, January 2012, pp. 52-55, available from *http://www.ausa.org/publications/armymagazine/archive/2012/01/Documents/Steele_0112.pdf*, accessed December 2, 2014.

216. Plans Notes, USF-I, J-5, August 31, 2011; Plans Notes, USF-I, J-5, September 14, 2011.

217. DoD photo by Staff Sergeant Caleb Barrieau, "End of mission ceremony [Image 6 of 29]," DVIDS Identifier 500737, December 15, 2011, Released to Public, available from *https://www.dvidshub.net/image/500737/end-mission-ceremony*.

218. Jennifer Griffin, "Reporters Notebook: Panetta Formally Ends U.S. Military Mission in Iraq," FOX News, December 15, 2011, available from *http://www.foxnews.com/world/2011/12/15/panetta-formally-ends-us-military-mission-in-iraq.html*.

219. DoD photo by Master Sergeant Cecilio Ricardo, "Tactical road march [Image 16 of 16]," DVIDS Identifier 501377, December 18, 2011, Released to Public, available from *https://www.dvidshub.net/image/501377/tactical-road-march*.

220. Tim Arango and Michael S. Schmidt, "Last Convoy of American Troops Leaves Iraq," *The New York Times*, December 18, 2011.

CHAPTER 15

EPILOGUE: THE OFFICE OF SECURITY COOPERATION
AND THE RETURN OF THE IRAQ WAR, 2012-2014

In December 2011, the decision not to leave a residual U.S. force in Iraq left Lieutenant General Robert Caslen and the 150 personnel of the new Office of Security Cooperation-Iraq (OSC-I) unexpectedly in charge of the large-scale security assistance mission that a theater headquarters and more than 40,000 U.S. troops had been performing just weeks before. U.S. leaders made the change from a large U.S. military command to a small embassy-based cooperation office against the backdrop of what many U.S. observers believed was an increasingly stable Iraq, a strengthening Iraqi state and Iraqi security forces (ISF), and a manageable set of security threats. Over the ensuing 2½ years, the experiment of using a stripped-down OSC-I to consolidate the U.S. campaign gains fell fall short of the mark. From 2012 to 2014, Iraq slipped back into civil war, and the Islamic State of Iraq (ISI) regenerated fully into the new Islamic State of Iraq and the Levant (ISIL/ISIS), with the U.S. military powerless to stop either event.

AFTER U.S. FORCES-IRAQ (USF-I): CRACKDOWNS AND DISARRAY

Maliki's Purges

On December 12, 2011, as the few remaining U.S. troops in Iraq prepared to leave, President Barack Obama and Prime Minister Nuri al-Maliki met in Washington, DC, to mark the end of the U.S. military presence in Iraq. Early in the day, the two leaders visited Arlington National Cemetery to lay wreaths at the graves of troops killed in the Iraq War. Later, in a joint press conference at the White House, they emphasized that their two countries would have a different relationship moving forward. Welcoming Maliki as "the elected leader of a sovereign, self-reliant, and democratic Iraq," Obama noted that levels of violence in Iraq remained low despite the U.S. troop withdrawal and declared, "what we have now achieved is an Iraq that is self-governing, that is inclusive, and that has enormous potential." As the President saw it, Iraq could be "a model for others that are aspiring to create democracy in the region." Both Obama and Maliki acknowledged that their governments were at odds over the question of whether Syrian leader Bashar al-Assad should leave power, but in general, the two leaders hailed the future strategic partnership between their countries.[1]

Three days later, on the same day that General Lloyd Austin and Secretary of Defense (SECDEF) Leon Panetta cased U.S. Forces-Iraq's (USF-I) colors in a ceremony at Camp Victory, Iraqi politics began to descend into chaos. Prime Minister Maliki's seat would be empty during the December 15 ceremony ending the U.S. military mission in Iraq, as he had to tend to other matters. Maliki, back in Baghdad after his brief visit to Washington, instead used the day to call for the Iraqi Parliament to sack his own deputy Prime Minister, Sunni politician Saleh Mutlaq. Mutlaq had given television interviews denouncing Maliki as a dictator and criticizing the United States for leaving Iraq in an authoritarian state. "Maliki is worse than Saddam Hussein," Mutlaq told an Iraqi TV channel on

December 13, "because at least Saddam was a builder, but Maliki has done absolutely nothing." Mutlaq told CNN the same day that he had been "shocked" to hear Obama welcome Maliki as a "democratic" leader, considering that Maliki had arrested hundreds of people and deployed troops against some of Iraq's provincial governments in the preceding weeks. Mutlaq told CNN that:

America left Iraq with almost no infrastructure. The political process is going in a very wrong direction, going toward a dictatorship. . . . People are not going to accept that, and most likely they are going to ask for the division of the country. And this is going to be a disaster. Dividing the country isn't going to be smooth, because dividing the country is going to be a war before that and a war after that. . . . There will be a day whereby the Americans will realize that they were deceived by al-Maliki . . . and they will regret that.[2]

On the same day that Maliki announced his initiative to impeach Mutlaq, the Prime Minister's security forces deployed across the Green Zone, surrounding the homes of several senior Sunni politicians, rendering them virtually under house arrest. Over the following days, Maliki government officials revealed that they had arrested several of Vice President Tariq Hashimi's bodyguards and that the men had confessed that Hashimi had allegedly ordered them to bomb Maliki's convoy as it passed through the Green Zone on November 28. On December 18, Iraqi state television broadcast the bodyguards' videotaped confessions implicating the Vice President in terrorism, while elsewhere Iraqi judicial officials prepared to issue an arrest warrant for Hashimi. By that evening Hashimi, Iraq's most senior Sunni politician, was a fugitive, having fled Baghdad on an Iraqi airways flight to Erbil to be sheltered by Kurdistan Republican Guard (KRG) President Massoud Barzani. From Kurdistan, Hashimi and his representatives made statements declaring his innocence and claimed the bodyguards had confessed falsely under torture. Their claims would later be strengthened by the fact that one of the bodyguards who confessed on television died in the custody of Maliki's security forces, with evidence indicating he was beaten to death.[3]

Hashimi (left), Tawfiq (center). Source: DoD photo by Sergeant Patrick Lair (Released).

Iraqi Vice President Tariq al-Hashimi With Ninawa Operations Commander Lieutenant General Riyadh Jalal Tawfiq in 2008.[4]

On the same day that the Maliki government moved against Hashimi and Mutlaq, it also moved to consolidate power in the ethnic powder keg of Diyala Province. In response to the Diyala provincial council having passed a resolution that would begin the process to transform the province into an autonomous region similar to the Kurdish provinces, Maliki charged the Sunni governor with holding an illegal vote and ordered Iraqi security forces, aided by Jaysh al-Mahdi (JAM) and Badr militiamen, to take control of the provincial government center. The governor, who like Hashimi was a member of the Iraqi Islamic Party, fled to Kurdistan along with a majority of the provincial council.[5]

Back in the Green Zone, as these events were unfolding in the immediate aftermath of USF-I's departure, the Iraqiyah bloc to which Hashimi belonged suspended its participation in Maliki's cabinet and called for U.S. intervention to force Maliki to give up sole control of Iraq's security forces and to implement the December 2010 power-sharing agreement. Throughout 2011, the Prime Minister had failed to fulfill his pledge to appoint new security ministers selected by the other parties. Instead, he had named himself as acting head of the Ministry of Defense and Ministry of Interior and also retained control of the Iraqi intelligence community, signaling that he intended to consolidate personal control of the most potent arms of the Iraqi Government. Only with the pressure of the August bombings, did Maliki appoint one of his allies as acting Minister of Defense, itself a violation of the Erbil Agreement. After Hashimi's removal, the Prime Minister paused his pressure against Mutlaq and other senior Sunni leaders, but the December crackdown still left the Iraqi political class in a state of shock. Maliki had shown by his actions that he was willing to use his security apparatus against any rival, with even the country's most senior political leaders not protected. "Welcome to the post-occupation Iraq," one senior Iraqi official in the Green Zone told his American counterparts.[6]

OSC-I's Rocky Start

The jarring purge of Iraq's top Sunni leader occurred as the U.S. military in Baghdad was going through a jarring period of its own. The U.S. decision to withdraw USF-I fully from Iraq without a residual force meant that as of December 18, 2011, Lieutenant General Robert Caslen's OSC-I was the only U.S. military organization in the country. The U.S. Government had long planned to transition the military mission in Iraq from USF-I to OSC-I at the end of 2011, but Caslen and virtually all the planners involved in that process had assumed that as OSC-I director, Caslen would still be a de facto operational commander with thousands of troops at his disposal. Until very late in the decision-making process, U.S. military leaders had believed that Caslen would have a large OSC-I staff to inherit the functions of the USF-I headquarters and would have the 3d Infantry Division headquarters available to carry out a large training mission with thousands of military advisors and trainers. Instead, after the final ceremony marking the deactivation of USF-I in Baghdad on December 15, Caslen and the 157 personnel of OSC-I found themselves in charge of a military mission that had required the combined efforts of 40,000 U.S. troops just a few weeks before.

Caslen (right), Perkins (left). Source: DoD photo by Specialist Brandon Bednarek (Released).

Lieutenant General Robert Caslen With U.S. Division-North (USD-N) Commander Major General David G. Perkins.[7]

The OSC-I mission almost collapsed before it could begin. The rapid withdrawal of USF-I's 40,000 troops and more than 30,000 contractors in the space of 2 months in late 2011 was a marvel of logistical planning and execution, but in that intense drawdown period the U.S. Government failed to resolve significant problems that endangered OSC-I's ability to function. With USF-I's departure, OSC-I would be operating in the country as part of the U.S. diplomatic mission, covered by the Vienna Convention and given diplomatic immunities and privileges by the Iraqi Government. But as the end of December 2011 approached, Caslen and U.S. Embassy officials had difficulty getting the Maliki government to issue visas for the U.S. military personnel who would be arriving in Baghdad or staying behind from USF-I to make up the OSC-I staff. They had even more trouble getting the Iraqis to issue visas for the several thousand contractors who were meant to provide the bulk of OSC-I's transportation, logistical, and security support, but who lacked legal protections under the Vienna Convention. Within the Iraqi Government, Maliki required that his own office approve U.S. military and contractor visas, greatly slowing the process.[8] Most of OSC-I's contractors had entered Iraq on a U.S. Government identification card, not a passport or visa, and thus as the end of December approached, more than half of them had to leave while they could still do so. Caslen also discovered in December that the U.S. Government had not yet acquired land-use agreements from the Iraqi Government for the training sites that OSC-I was supposed to continue operating. With just 2 days left before the end of the year and many U.S. Government offices in Washington shut down for the holidays, a desperate Caslen finally managed to enlist the aid of Undersecretary of Defense Ashton Carter to strike a last-minute ministerial agreement with Iraqi Minister of Defense Sadoun Dulaimi that would allow OSC-I to continue to operate.[9]

Carter's timely intervention saved Caslen's mission, though many of OSC-I's missing contractors would still have to spend several months working through a friction-filled visa process before returning to work inside Iraq.[10] However, the North Atlantic Treaty Organization (NATO) aspect of the U.S. security assistance mission did not survive the transition from USF-I to OSC-I. U.S. officials had assumed that the NATO Training Mission-Iraq (NTM-I), which had been present in Iraq since the early days of the war and had come to play a central role in the Iraqi Army's officer education system, would continue beyond 2011 under a new agreement with the Iraqi Government. However, in the final weeks of 2011, NATO's continued participation became unlikely. NATO officials were reluctant to leave their training mission in place without the substantial U.S. military protection that disappeared when USF-I withdrew from the country. They were also unwilling to leave NATO personnel in Iraq without guarantees of immunity from Iraqi law that the Maliki government seemed unwilling to give, and in any case, Iraqi officials were just as slow to extend visas to NATO officials as to U.S. officials and contractors. Though Caslen traveled to Brussels ahead of the end of year deadline to lobby NATO officials to stay in Iraq, he and other U.S. officials were unable to convince NATO leaders to continue the training mission. As a result, NTM-I ceased work as the year ended.[11]

Despite the loss of a residual force and the departure of the NATO contingent, Caslen still considered OSC-I an operational component of U.S. Central Command (CENTCOM) with a mission to preserve the security gains already achieved in Iraq.[12] There were several tasks Caslen considered essential to this goal. Having served as the commander of Multi-National Division-North (MND-N) at the end of the surge and seen firsthand the damage that al-Qaeda in Iraq (AQI) and other extremist organizations could do, he believed it was OSC-I's responsibility to assist the ISF in ensuring that these groups did not regain a foothold in the country. He also had to manage intra-Iraqi tensions along the Green Line in 2008-2009 and believed OSC-I had a role to play in preventing conflict between Arabs and Kurds in the north. In central Iraq and the south, he believed OSC-I's security assistance effort should mitigate Iran's malign influence so that Iraqis could chart their own future without external manipulation. In a related area, he hoped OSC-I could help the Iraqi Government build security cooperation relationships with other Arab states in the region to counterbalance Iran's influence. Finally, he believed OSC-I had an important role to play in restraining Prime Minister Maliki's authoritarian tendencies, especially since he judged that security threats to the Iraqi Government tended to bring out the worst in the Prime Minister.[13]

These would prove to be ambitious tasks for a military organization with no combat power and few personnel, and they were made more complicated by a newly assertive Iraqi bureaucracy. As December 2011 waned, Caslen and his small staff were consumed in dealing with Iraqi Government requirements and processes not faced by previous U.S. military organizations in Baghdad. Senior Iraqi officials later admitted that the Maliki government purposely made things difficult for U.S. counterparts as USF-I departed as a way of signaling that there would be a new way of conducting business.[14] Without the authorities that had come with being a named operation such as Operation IRAQI FREEDOM (OIF) or Operation NEW DAWN, OSC-I's every move was subject to Iraqi law and oversight by the Iraqi Government bureaucracy. In one example, USF-I left behind 1,200 vehicles in Iraq for OSC-I's use, but because they had been brought into the country before 2012, Iraqi officials declared that they could not be registered with the Iraqi Government, leaving anyone driving them subject to arrest. Any new vehicles OSC-I brought into the country could be registered, Iraqi officials ruled, but that process might take as long as 9 months.[15] In other instances, Iraqi officials often delayed the movement of U.S. Embassy supply convoys until the proper paperwork could be produced, at one point forcing the Embassy to issue Meals Ready to Eat (MREs) to its personnel for a short period.[16]

There were also difficulties fitting OSC-I into the U.S. diplomatic mission. U.S. inter-agency planners in Washington had envisioned that the U.S. security assistance mission in Iraq could continue with little disruption by simply transferring USF-I's training, advisory, and foreign military sales (FMS) functions—and the personnel and equipment to execute them—to the U.S. Embassy's control. The budgets to fund those activities would be transferred from the Department of Defense (DoD) to the State Department. However, this plan went astray from the start. With a large-scale security assistance mission and OSC-I grafted onto it, the U.S. Embassy that Ambassador James Jeffrey oversaw at the beginning of 2012 was the largest in the world, with more than 16,000 diplomats and contractors, its own fleet of helicopters, mine resistant ambush protected (MRAP) vehicles, unmanned aerial vehicles (UAVs), three hospitals, and large quick reaction forces. Despite its size, the Embassy simply was not postured to continue the vast array of tasks that had fallen to USF-I as a warfighting organization. Jeffrey believed that U.S. officials in Washington never understood that his and Caslen's organizations were not simply "USF-I Lite" and had little capacity to conduct the security, governance, and rule of law activities that the U.S. military had carried out before 2012, or to continue to broker Sunni-Shi'a and Arab-Kurd outreach. Jeffrey remarked in early 2012, "I don't have the people to follow up. It's all gone."[17]

What military assets did remain behind did not necessarily mesh well with the Embassy. The expanded U.S. Embassy structure came with huge financial and administrative costs that forced Jeffrey and other senior diplomats to spend a great deal of their time trying to get the hybrid organization to operate effectively. USF-I and DoD planners had worked hard to bequeath the Embassy a range of military capabilities that the American diplomatic staff in Baghdad was unused to managing, and considered unnecessary for a diplomatic mission in any case. For example, the Embassy never used the MRAPs USF-I had left it and quickly abandoned the UAVs and helicopters as well.[18]

The presence of an unusually large military contingent inside the Embassy also created friction. OSC-I worked under the umbrella of the U.S. Mission in Iraq (USM-I), but was not like any other security cooperation office in the world. Unlike the other division heads working in the Embassy, Caslen had been nominated for his position by the President and confirmed by the Senate, which made him and OSC-I an awkward fit within the Embassy's hierarchy.[19] Asked by Army researchers to describe the relationship between the Embassy's other divisions and OSC-I after USF-I's departure, one embassy official observed that the two sides "are going in the same direction, but we are still in different boats."[20] In a few instances, embassy officials bristled at some of OSC-I's military trappings. Many OSC-I service members continued to wear their uniforms, a practice that the Embassy's regional security office (RSO) viewed as problematic for force protection.

In the RSO's view, the sight of uniformed Americans could lead Iraqis to think the U.S. military occupation had resumed and to respond violently.[21] When Caslen created a J-2 intelligence cell within his staff, senior embassy security officers opposed the move, arguing that OSC-I had no need of an independent intelligence capability. Caslen and his J-2 saw it differently, arguing that the increased level of militant attacks in Baghdad in 2012 created a risk that OSC-I needed to monitor. With U.S. military officials embedded in key Iraqi Government offices, OSC-I was in a better position to gather information about what Iraqi leaders were thinking and planning than were many other U.S. agencies.[22]

OSC-I's greatest bureaucratic difficulties lay in its authorities and funding. As an organization that was neither a military command nor a mere security cooperation cell within a standard embassy, OSC-I was caught between the models under which DoD and State Department organizations normally operated and received funding. Like other military organizations inside U.S. Embassies that oversaw security assistance, OSC-I was responsible for managing foreign military sales and foreign military financing to the Iraqi Government under Title XXII of the U.S. legal code—the section of U.S. law that governed State Department activities. The U.S. Foreign Assistance Act limited Title XXII military security cooperation cells to no more than six people—very different from OSC-I's 157. At the same time, U.S. officials in Washington appeared to expect OSC-I to continue some of USF-I's military activities, but without being a U.S. military command that had authorities under Title X of the U.S. code—the section of U.S. law that governed DoD. This awkward arrangement made it difficult for OSC-I to work with the DoD agencies that had previously worked with USF-I. Despite the fact that both Caslen and CENTCOM commander General James Mattis considered Caslen to be one of Mattis's subordinate commanders and behaved accordingly, the two men's respective organizations did not follow suit. Since OSC-I was not a Title X DoD organization, the CENTCOM bureaucracy was not technically OSC-I's higher headquarters and was not bound to use its Title X operational funds to support the military organization in Baghdad.

In case after case, CENTCOM and the DoD bureaucracy behaved as though the State Department were responsible for reimbursing CENTCOM for any military costs to support OSC-I, and the State Department reciprocated. One example dealt with the C-130 ring route that the U.S. Air Forces Central Command (AFCENT) flew in support of OSC-I personnel in Baghdad, Taji, and Tikrit. For years, AFCENT had funded the flights out of its Operation IRAQI FREEDOM and Operation NEW DAWN contingency budgets, but with the end of those named operations, the source for continued funding was unclear. Since OSC-I was technically a division of the U.S. Embassy, CENTCOM sought to shift the cost for the flights to the State Department, but for their part, State Department officials considered the flights Title X activities being carried out by uniformed military personnel. Since the ring route flights were a vital lifeline that OSC-I could not operate without, the planes continued to fly amid the bureaucratic dispute, leaving Caslen and his staff caught in the middle trying to figure out who would fund the operations. The result was one DoD organization billing another DoD organization for the cost of supporting its own mission.[23] An even thornier problem arose when ARCENT ruled that without a named military operation, it would not provide OSC-I with postal or finance service or even to deploy an Army veterinarian into Iraq to conduct the required inspections for MREs stored for emergencies. As far as U.S. Army Central (ARCENT) leaders were concerned, the Iraqi Theater of Operations had closed and was no longer their responsibility.[24] With ARCENT declining to support military activities inside Iraq, the U.S. Embassy passed their bills—such as the costs required to fly their fleet of military helicopters—directly to Caslen's OSC-I, which had no way of paying for them.[25]

Working out these and many other such bureaucratic problems dominated OSC-I's first several months of operation after USF-I's departure. Caslen and other U.S. military officials in Baghdad found themselves expending the bulk of their energy in simply figuring out how to secure the authorities and resources necessary to remain in Iraq, rather than in keeping up the momentum of USF-I's relationships with and assistance to the ISF. Within weeks after USF-I's departure, it was becoming painfully clear that OSC-I would not be able to perform all of the essential elements of the security assistance mission by itself without the personnel management, logistics, and signal support that would have come with a residual force.[26]

THE UNRAVELING OF IRAQI POLITICS

The wave of arrests in the Iraqi provinces carried out by Prime Minister Maliki's officials from October onward and the crackdown on Sunni political leaders in the Green Zone had a significant political effect in 2012. After the broad Sunni rejection of the U.S.-sponsored political process in 2004-2006, the Awakening and the surge campaign had helped turn the vast majority of Iraqi Sunnis back to participation in the political process. The elections of 2009 and 2010 had signified that Sunnis generally perceived their interests could be better secured through politics than through violence, and through mainstream Sunni political parties rather than through militant groups. The events of late 2011 and early 2012 showed that the Sunni community's mainstream political center, represented by the Awakening and the Iraqiyah coalition, was weakening. As had been the case since 2009, local Awakening leaders in central Iraq were under constant pressure from ISI and other militant groups and faced harassment and pressure from Maliki's government. Attacks against members of the Sons of Iraq were common, as were assassinations of Awakening leaders. In one high-profile instance in January 2012, Mullah Nathem Jabouri, the Sunni cleric from Dhuluiyah who had been a founding member of the Mujahedin Shura Council but had later become a vocal anti-AQI Awakening leader, was shot to death in west Baghdad by suspected ISI assassins shortly after criticizing the group in a television interview. Jabouri had arrived in Baghdad only a short time before to assist Maliki's office with outreach to Sunni groups who were willing to oppose ISI, but his killing sent a clear message that the government could not protect people like him from Sunni extremist groups.[27]

Vice President Hashimi's case had a similar impact on mainstream Sunni politics. Hashimi was an abrasive politician whom many U.S. officials did not particularly care for, but he had received almost a quarter of a million votes in the 2010 election and thus represented a large Sunni constituency, especially in Baghdad's Adhamiyah district. If mainstream Sunni politicians like him or Saleh Mutlaq were to be purged, then hundreds of thousands of Sunnis might drift toward more radical political options. As if on cue, just weeks after the purging of Hashimi, Saddam's former Ba'athist deputy Izzat ad-Douri broke almost 9 years of silence by releasing a videotaped speech on April 7, 2012, in which he called for Iraqis to unite with "the heroic Iraqi resistance" against "the Persian Safavid enemy," claiming they had come to dominate the Iraqi Government in Baghdad.[28] The appearance of Douri, who in addition to leading a wing of the Ba'ath Party in exile was also the de facto leader of the Naqshbandi Army, indicated that the Ba'athist leader recognized there might be an opportunity to reoccupy some of the political space that Iraqiyah and the Awakening had dominated since 2006.

A final element in the weakening of the Sunni political center came as Maliki took a page from Saddam's political playbook. Before 2003, Saddam had often kept Iraq's Kurdish and Shi'a communities under control by selecting politicians from those communities who were willing to work with his regime and then letting the largesse of the Ba'athist state flow through them to the Shi'a- and Kurdish-majority provinces. The politicians who volunteered to assist the Ba'athist dictator had no natural political following, but became powerful in their home communities because they were a gateway to the state's resources. In 2012, Maliki adopted a similar approach toward Iraq's Sunnis. Rejecting cooperation with the Iraqiyah politicians whom Iraqi Sunnis had elected to represent them, Maliki instead looked for Sunni political partners who had no grassroots following but could be counted upon to act as channels for state resources to the Sunni community that might buy some popular allegiance to Maliki's rule. One such partner that Maliki chose was the former insurgent financier Mishaan Jabouri, the former ally of Uday Hussein who had tried to take power in Mosul in 2003 and had had to flee the country to evade arrest on corruption charges in 2005. Once outside Iraq, he had become a militant ally of the Syrian regime and Muammar Gaddhafi and had also run a satellite TV station dedicated to broadcasting terrorist propaganda videos, including of attacks against U.S. troops. He had been charged in absentia with promoting terrorism, but in March 2012, Maliki and his allies invited Mishaan to return to Baghdad, cleared him of the terrorism charges, and encouraged him to form a political bloc to compete against Iraqiyah in Iraq's northern provinces.[29]

The Reemergence of Ahl al-Haqq (AAH)

Maliki was taking a similar divide-and-rule approach to Shi'a politics, where he was attempting to sponsor a competitor to Moqtada Sadr's political bloc in Baghdad and the south. Since late 2006, when Maliki and his allies had decided that Moqtada Sadr was too great a political threat to the Da'wa Party, the Prime Minister had been seeking a political pact with Qais al-Khazali's militant group Asa'ib Ahl al-Haqq (AAH). Maliki had long believed that Khazali, as a former disciple of Moqtada Sadr's father, could potentially draw grassroots support away from Sadr and shore up Maliki's political coalition. In the last week of December 2011, Maliki brought 5 years of negotiations with Khazali and AAH to fruition, reaching an agreement under which all criminal charges against AAH would be dropped and the group would be allowed to operate in the open as a political party. By December 26, Khazali was back in Najaf after more than a year of exile in Iran. On January 1, with Maliki's permission, Khazali held a large "victory" rally in west Baghdad's Tahrir Square to celebrate the departure of U.S. troops.[30] As the Prime Minister and his Da'wa allies had hoped, the rift between AAH and the Sadrists was immediate—and violent. Within hours of the AAH victory rally, Khazali's men were fighting gun battles against Sadr's followers in Sadr City and other parts of Baghdad, prompting Moqtada Sadr to accuse Khazali and AAH of being power-hungry "killers without a religion."[31]

Maliki's validation of AAH's activities offered the group a way to advance its long-term objective of developing an influential political-religious network in major Iraqi cities while maintaining a militant wing in a manner modeled upon Lebanese Hizballah. AAH was rebranding itself as a nationalist Islamic resistance organization that participated in local politics, but it also would continue to operate a large militia and take an active part in the regional "Axis of Resistance" led by the Iranian regime.[32] By the end of January, AAH had opened political offices in Baghdad and Basra and was laying the groundwork to begin political activities as affiliates of Maliki's State of Law coalition. They had also opened a think tank in Beirut affiliated with Lebanese Hizballah. As 2012 progressed, the group would open political offices in Hillah, Najaf, Khalis, and Tal Afar as well, expanding the presence of their militia along with their new political deployment.[33]

Meanwhile, as the turf war heated up between AAH and the Sadrists, a reign of terror descended upon neighborhoods where Shi'a resistance groups had a significant presence. In several cities, Shi'a militants regularly attacked Iraqis whose behavior they considered sinful, killing dozens of owners of liquor stores and other establishments the militiamen deemed to be un-Islamic. In the first few weeks of 2012, Shi'a militants who were most likely AAH or Promised Day Brigade members also murdered or abducted hundreds of Iraqi youths who participated in the Western-style "Emo" trend of clothing and hairstyles, a lifestyle the Shi'a militiamen believed involved homosexuality. The militiamen usually carried out the killings by stoning their victims to death. The wave of murders began after the Ministry of Interior itself pledged to stamp out what it considered the "Satanic" Emo subculture, showing that the ministry was on the side of the murderers rather than the victims.[34] The Maliki government apparently had normalized AAH as a political organization without requiring that the group stop its extremist activities.

In late February, as part of a prisoner exchange with the Maliki government, the newly normalized AAH handed over to Iraqi officials a wooden casket containing the remains of U.S. Army Staff Sergeant Ahmed al-Taie. The Iraqi-born Taie, the last American Soldier missing in Iraq, had been abducted by Shi'a militiamen as he made an ill-advised visit to family members in south Baghdad on October 23, 2006, and had quickly wound up in AAH's hands. AAH had sent Taie's family ransom demands and proof of life videos in 2006 and 2007, but he died in the militia's custody at some point after that, probably while in captivity in Iran. Under the exchange agreement with the Maliki government, AAH faced no criminal prosecution or legal measures for the American sergeant's kidnapping and murder.[35]

The Quest for a No-Confidence Vote

Meanwhile, in the weeks after the purging of Vice President Tariq Hashimi, Prime Minister Maliki continued his effort to consolidate power in Baghdad. For months, Maliki had gradually asserted control over the Iraqi Government's independent institutions that had been created in the 2005 constitution as a check on just such a consolidation of power. By early 2012, the Iraqi judiciary, government auditors, and inspectors general were largely under the Prime Minister's control. In mid-April 2012, Maliki arrested the head of

Iraq's election commission, the official whom Maliki had accused of conspiring with the United States and United Nations (UN) to deny the Prime Minister his fraudulent victory in the Parliamentary elections of 2010. When the election chief was released after a few days in jail, the man fled to Kurdistan, leaving Iraq's electoral body in disarray.[36]

Other Iraqi leaders watched these developments with growing concern. On April 28, just days after the purge of the election commission chief, KRG President Massoud Barzani, Iraqi President Jalal Talabani, Parliament Speaker Osama al-Nujayfi, Ayad Allawi, and Moqtada Sadr met in Erbil and produced a written demand that Maliki accept a two-term limit as Prime Minister and reverse his consolidation of control over agencies of the government.[37] Maliki responded by declaring in a televised interview that he had become the target of a foreign-inspired coup attempt.[38]

Maliki's opponents reached their breaking point by the summer of 2012. In June, Iraqiyya, the Sadrists, the Islamic Supreme Council of Iraq (ISCI), and Barzani joined forces to present to President Talabani a list of 173 Parliamentarians who had pledged to support a no-confidence vote that would end Maliki's premier-ship. Unfortunately for the Parliamentary factions, the list immediately found its way from Talabani to Maliki, who began pressuring individual Members of Parliament into recanting and quickly killed the initiative. The Iranian regime helped Maliki in this fracturing of the opposition bloc by making it clear to senior Iraqi politicians that the Iranians did not intend to allow Maliki to be unseated.[39] By mid-2012, the Iraqi Prime Minister's support for the embattled Bashar al-Assad in Syria had made Maliki indispensable in Iranian leaders' eyes, and the Iranian regime used its political advantage to help break up the opposition coalition. In the days following the opposition leaders' joint call for a no-confidence measure, Iranian regime officials succeeded in pressuring both Moqtada Sadr and Jalal Talabani to abandon their support for an immediate vote, and the danger to Maliki dissipated for the time being.[40]

Source: UN photo by Eskinder Debebe.

**Iraqi Prime Minister
Nuri al-Maliki.[41]**

THE SPILLOVER OF THE SYRIAN CIVIL WAR

Iraq's domestic political dysfunction in 2012 was related to the deepening Syrian civil war. The Iraqi factions that had faced each other in a civil war of their own from 2005 to 2008 now found themselves on opposite sides of the brutal conflict.[42] By the end of 2011, the Maliki government was in effect intervening in the Syrian war on the side of Bashar al-Assad and his Alawite regime. Although Maliki and other Iraqi Shi'a leaders had long considered Assad an enemy because of the Syrian dictator's support for AQI and other terrorist groups in Iraq and although Maliki had actually demanded a UN tribunal against Assad in late 2009, by mid-2011 Iraqi Government policy had reversed itself. As popular uprisings spread and regional pressure mounted on the Syrian regime, the Maliki government came to its defense, extending political, economic, and security support to its one-time enemy. The change in the Iraqi Government's stance was partly induced by Iran, but Iraqi Shi'a leaders also feared that the fall of Assad's Shi'a Alawite regime would lead to a Sunni Islamist regime in Damascus that would sponsor a renewed jihad against the Iraqi state.[43]

It was not an unfounded fear. Most of the Sunni opposition to Assad in 2011 and 2012 came from anti-regime activists and from the newly forming Free Syrian Army, but from the early stages of the Syrian war, ISI played a significant role as well, as did its network of Salafi allies inside Syria. Since 2003, AQI and other Salafi militant groups in Iraq had used Syria as their strategic depth, supported by a vast network of Syrian-based Salafi mosques, clerics, and militants that enabled AQI and others to conduct insurgent and terrorist operations inside Iraq. In 2011-2012, this arrangement began to reverse itself, as Iraqi militant networks became a logistical base that enabled militants to carry out operations inside Syria.

Source: Photo courtesy of Kremlin.ru.

Syrian President Bashar al-Assad.[44]

Al-Qaeda's senior leadership also recognized the potential of expanding their global jihad into Syria. Assad's regime had been weakened by months of internal strife, and the terrorist group already had a network of agents and support cells in place from the years of sanctuary that Assad had provided. As such, in August 2011, al-Qaeda's senior leadership and ISI agreed to send a cadre of experienced Syrian and Iraqi jihadists back into Syria with the objective of creating an Islamic state there that would become part of a larger regional caliphate. The new group, named Jabhat al-Nusra li Ahl al Sham (The Support Front for the People of the Levant) quickly became one of the most effective insurgent groups fighting against Assad's government due to its discipline and military training.[45]

Support for the Syrian insurgency went far beyond militant networks, however. Iraqi Sunnis tended to sympathize with Syrian Sunnis, whom they viewed as fighting a Shi'a minority government backed by the Iranian regime—a situation many Sunnis believed analogous to their own position inside Iraq.[46] After 8 years in which Iraq's Shi'a Islamist parties had been in the ascendency, Iraqi Sunnis began to envision the establishment of a Sunni state in Syria to reverse their own fortunes. If Syria were to become a Sunni power, Iraqi Sunnis reasoned, then Iraq's Sunnis might use the support of Syrian Sunnis to regain control of Baghdad or at least to renegotiate a greater share of power.[47] As a result, from an early stage in the Syrian conflict, Iraq's Sunni tribes provided material support for the Syrian opposition, particularly in eastern Syria, where large tribes such as the Shammar, Obeid, and Dulaim spanned the porous Iraq-Syria border. The tribes offered the same safe haven to Syrian insurgents that had once been offered to Iraqi insurgents, reversing the flow of weapons and militants that had in earlier years gone from Syria into Iraq.

In addition to the Iraqi Sunni tribes, ISI saw the Syrian civil war as a godsend, providing the organization with a much-need territorial refuge inside Syria where it could regroup, recruit new fighters, and then eventually resume operations in Iraq. Throughout 2012, Syrian border towns such as Deir ez-Zor and Albu Kamal were flooded with Iraqi fighters, many belonging to ISI. For ISI and its allies, the conflicts in Iraq and Syria had merged into a single theater of jihad, with militant operations aimed both west toward Damascus and Aleppo, and east toward the Tigris River Valley and Baghdad.

Just as Iraq's Sunni jihadis were becoming heavily involved in Syria, Iraq's Shi'a militant groups were likewise deciding that they had a role to play in supporting their fellow Shi'a confessionals in the Syrian civil war. By mid-2012, Iraqi Shi'a militants were flowing into Syria from groups such as AAH, Kata'ib Hezbollah, and the Badr Corps. The Iraqi Shi'a fighters' deployment into Syria was part of the Iranian regime's effort to reinforce Assad's Alawite forces that could not match the rebel manpower in a country where Sunnis outnumbered Alawites by 15 to 2. As the Assad regime faced escalating military pressure from the rebels in 2012, Iran channeled Iraqi Shi'a fighters to Damascus and other Syrian cities, often routing them via Iran to be trained and equipped before joining Iran's Revolutionary Guard Corps or Lebanese Hizballah. This flow of Shi'a militants increased once AAH leader Qais al-Khazali and KH leader Abu Mahdi al-Muhandis returned to Baghdad following the withdrawal of U.S. troops in late 2011.[48] At first, the Shi'a militant groups kept their role in the Syrian fighting quiet, but signs of AAH's involvement became unmistakable when funerals of AAH members killed in Syria began to take place with rising frequency.[49]

By fall 2012, the Shi'a militant groups' involvement was overt and escalating. Several Iraqi Shi'a militant groups and Lebanese Hizballah teamed up to contribute fighters to the newly formed Liwa Abu al-Fadl al-Abbas, an Iranian-sponsored militant conglomerate that operated as an auxiliary force for Assad.[50] Throughout 2012, these Iraqi Shi'a militias circulated internet videos of themselves fighting in the streets of Damascus to defend the Shi'a shrine of Sayyeda Zeinab, the daughter of Imam Ali. Located southeast of Damascus, the Zeinab shrine was not just a symbolic location, but was also key terrain that the Assad regime needed to keep the Damascus Airport open.[51] Back in Iraq, the Shi'a militant groups used the defense of the Zeinab Shrine as a recruiting tool and a pretext for providing auxiliaries to the Assad regime. The majority of the Iraqi Shi'a fighters in Syria traveled through the Baghdad International Airport, where they enjoyed tacit Iraqi Government support as they moved openly — and armed — through the facility. Iraqi officials also did little to stop Iranian overflights through Iraqi airspace to deliver military aid to Assad, despite entreaties by the Obama administration and other Western powers.[52]

The Syrian war had a profound effect on Iraqi Kurdistan as well. By late 2012, Syrian Kurdish militias were taking control of the Kurdish-majority areas of northern Syria where the regime's power had receded. There they began setting up a new autonomous region they called West Kurdistan, or Rojava, that bordered on some Kurdish-held territories of Iraq. In the autonomous zone, a Syrian branch of the PKK that called itself the Democratic Union Party (PYD) was dominant, and it fielded a militia called the People's Protection Units (YPG) to hold its newly gained territory. As an offshoot of the PKK that had posed a serious danger to Turkey, the PYD was a rival of the Turkish-allied KDP of Massoud Barzani and was also affiliated with Kurdish separatists who would likely view a new autonomous Syrian Kurdistan as a base from which to launch a renewed insurgency inside Turkey. The PYD would soon become a new force with significant implications for the stability of the KRG.

RETURN OF THE SUNNI INSURGENCY

The Issawi Crackdown and Sunni Protest Movement

Almost exactly a year after authorizing the December 2011 ISF raid against Iraq's most senior Sunni politician, Vice President Tariq Hashimi, Prime Minister Maliki repeated the act, this time against the most senior Sunni minister in his own cabinet, Finance Minister Rafe al-Issawi. Well-regarded by the international community and fellow Iraqis as a non-sectarian, pragmatic technocrat, Issawi had been a tangential target in the Hashimi raids. Both he and Deputy Prime Minister Saleh Mutlaq had seemed to escape the purge by making peace with Maliki in early 2012 despite their vehement criticism of the Prime Minister before that. By late 2012, relations between Maliki and Issawi had soured, and the Finance Minister had become Maliki's biggest political target. On December 19 and 20, Iraqi special operations forces surrounded Issawi's home and offices in the Green Zone as Iraqi Government spokesmen announced the Finance Minister was being sought on the charge of supporting terrorism through his alleged connections to the Sunni militant group Hamas al-Iraq. Issawi took refuge in the home of Parliament Speaker Osama al-Nujaifi, where he reported in a news conference that 150 of his guards, staff, and family members had been arrested.[53]

Source: U.S. Navy photo by Petty Officer 1st Class Mario A. Quiroga (Released).

Iraqi Sunni Leader Rafe al-Issawi.[54]

The accusation that Issawi was a material supporter of Hamas al-Iraq was a familiar one to U.S. officials, since Maliki had previously leveled it in 2010. At that time, then-USF-I commander Odierno had given the Prime Minister a report from USF-I analysts concluding that the charge was false, and Odierno's opposition to the charge had helped Issawi survive a potential purge. In December 2012, however, it seemed clear that Maliki intended to use the allegation to sideline yet another senior Sunni leader. U.S. officials had regarded Issawi as a moderate Sunni with whom Maliki could cooperate in 2011, but the push for his removal from the government in 2012 indicated that deeper purges would come.

One reason for Maliki's lack of restraint against top Sunni leaders was that Iraqi President Jalal Talabani, who had often played a mediating role between Iraq's Sunni and Shi'a parties and had helped defuse tensions between Maliki and Iraqiyah the year before, had suffered a debilitating stroke and had become incapacitated. With Vice President Hashimi already purged but no new Sunni Vice President nominated in his place, Talabani's absence meant that the Iraqi presidency council was not present to help restrain

Maliki's targeting of his political opponents. For his part, Issawi described the attack against him as a larger "pre-election blow" intended to weaken Iraqiyah prior to the spring 2013 provincial elections.[55] Within days of the raids, Issawi fled Baghdad to the relative safety of Ramadi, becoming a fugitive from his own government as Hashimi had been.

The Sunni community's reaction to the purging of Issawi was not as calm as its reaction to Hashimi's arrest a year before. Unlike Hashimi, Issawi was a senior leader of a major Iraqi tribe, the Albu Issa of eastern Anbar, and he was also a popular civic leader who had worked as a surgeon in the Fallujah hospital in 2004. His arrest sparked immediate outrage among both his tribe and the Sunni communities of Anbar and the north. Able to take refuge in his tribe's territory rather than flee the country, Issawi defied the Maliki government's arrest warrant and spoke publicly throughout Anbar condemning Maliki's treatment of Iraqi Sunnis and labeling the Prime Minister a dictator. The public demonstrations of support for Issawi quickly grew into anti-government protests throughout Iraq's Sunni territories, where youth unemployment reached 40 percent and accusations of unlawful detention of Sunnis by the Maliki government had provoked anger for months.[56] Within days of the arrests in the Green Zone, the country had a full-fledged Sunni protest movement on its hands, with crowds numbering in the tens of thousands in Sunni cities such as Mosul, Fallujah, Ramadi, Tikrit, and Hawijah, and even in Baghdad's Sunni-majority district of Adhamiyah. The protests were supported by powerful Sunni leaders inside and outside of Iraq, such as Khamis al Khanjar, a wealthy Sunni businessman with Ba'athist ties living in Jordan, who helped fund supportive media broadcasts and the construction of camps for Anbari protestors.[57] By mid-January, virtually every significant Sunni city had a large protest camp at its center, with near-continuous political rallies and televised speeches by Sunni leaders airing their angry grievances against the Maliki government, including many Sunnis who had been leaders of the Awakening and Sons of Iraq.

In response, Maliki deployed Iraqi security forces to surround the Sunni protest camps nearest to Baghdad, especially Fallujah and Ramadi. In those cities and a few others, the government's mostly Shi'a police and soldiers established a perimeter of checkpoints and outposts and kept a tense watch on the protest camps. Young Sunni protesters reciprocated, keeping watch on the government troops just dozens of yards away. With the armed soldiers and angry protestors in such close proximity, it was merely a matter of time before the situation became explosive. Maliki dispatched Sunni deputy Prime Minister Saleh Mutlaq to Anbar in hopes of calming the protesters, but the move backfired when thousands of Fallujah protesters attacked Mutlaq with stones. The Deputy Prime Minister and his entourage barely escaped with their lives.[58] Embarrassingly for Mutlaq, who had moved from being Maliki's chief Sunni opponent to his chief Sunni ally in the space of a year, the assault was caught on video and televised throughout Iraq.

The situation soon deteriorated further. On January 25, demonstrators headed to a rally in Fallujah clashed with Iraqi soldiers at a checkpoint. When the protesters pelted the soldiers with rocks, the troops fired into the crowd, killing 9 demonstrators and wounding about 60 more. Hours later, Sunni gunmen retaliated by attacking an army checkpoint in northern Fallujah and killing two soldiers. These incidents signaled that Anbar was slipping into open rebellion, with tribal leaders who had once partnered with

U.S. troops joining in the militant opposition to the Maliki government. Speaking on behalf of other tribal leaders, Awakening council chairman Sheikh Ahmed Abu Risha gave the government 1 week to deliver the soldiers responsible for the protesters' deaths, after which, he warned, "if the government has not heeded our demand, we will launch jihad against army units and posts in Anbar."[59]

The weeks following the Fallujah violence brought an escalation of violence across Iraq, including a return of the kind of bombings that had once been common in Shi'a neighborhoods in Baghdad. On January 27, for example, a bomb near a Shi'a funeral procession in Baghdad's Zafraniyah neighborhood killed 31 people, including 8 police officers.[60] Some of the violence took on overtones of the Syrian war. The large demonstrations in Sunni cities often included flags and banners of the Free Syrian Army, indicating that the Syrian civil war was continuing to spill over into internal Iraqi matters, with Iraqi Sunnis on the rebel side of the Syrian conflict and the Maliki government on the Assad regime's side. Eventually these dynamics came to a head in Iraq's western desert. When a force of dozens of Syrian soldiers came under rebel attack at a border crossing point near Ninewa Province, the Syrian troops fled into Iraq, where government forces gave them shelter. The Iraqi troops then attempted to transport the Syrians to a safer part of Syria by busing them through Anbar Province, but on March 4, 2013, in western Anbar, the entire Iraqi-Syrian force of about 50 troops was ambushed and massacred by Sunni gunmen. A week later, ISI claimed responsibility for the killings in a statement that declared—not inaccurately—that the incident was proof of collusion between the Maliki government and Bashar al-Assad.[61]

With the situation in Anbar and Ninewa provinces growing worse by the week, Maliki decided in March that the provincial elections scheduled for the following month would not be held in those two provinces.[62] Meanwhile, as sporadic clashes between Sunni protesters and the Iraqi security forces continued, observers noted in March that the black flags of the ISI had appeared for the first time at rallies in Ramadi, an omen of what was to come.[63]

The Hawijah Massacre

The confrontation between Maliki's government and the Sunni protest movement exploded into large-scale violence in April, just days after the country held its provincial elections. The flashpoint came in Hawijah, the restive Sunni town near Kirkuk that had long been a stronghold for Ba'athist insurgents loyal to Izzat ad-Douri and the Naqshbandi Army, and by April 2013 home to a large protest camp. The provincial elections on April 20 took place largely without incident across the country, but on the following day, gunmen attacked an ISF checkpoint in Hawijah and killed an Iraqi soldier. Suspecting that the killers had blended in with the protesters, ISF commanders issued a deadline for the protesters to turn over the perpetrators. It passed without result.[64] In response, during the early hours of April 23, 2013, Iraqi troops under the direction of Iraqi Ground Forces commander General Ali Ghaidan moved in to break up the camp and arrest suspects. The facts of what followed are in dispute, but what is clear is that gunfire quickly broke out between the two sides and left scores of casualties. According to an investigation by the Iraqi Parliament, when the shooting finally stopped, more than 40 civilians and 3 Iraqi soldiers were dead, and more than 100 civilians were wounded.[65] Other sources claimed more than 100 civilians had been killed; though the Ministry of Defense claimed only 3 soldiers and 23 "militants who were using the demonstration as a safe haven" had died.[66]

The massacre in Hawijjah touched off the most intense fighting Iraq had seen since 2008, most of it in sensitive areas along the Green Line. Hours after the Hawijah incident, Sunni militants who were likely affiliated with the Naqshbandi Army (JRTN) overran government troops in towns south of Kirkuk and cut the main Kirkuk-Baghdad highway, leading to several days of battles with government troops before the insurgents withdrew. On April 25, the clashes spread to Mosul, where large-scale gunfights left as many as 40 people dead. The violence expanded the following day to Baghdad, where several Sunni mosques were bombed. On April 27, Sunni gunmen in Fallujah pulled five plainclothes government security men out of a car and executed them, perhaps in an attempt to prevent the ISF men from reconnoitering for a Hawijah-like assault on the Fallujah protest camp. The Maliki government suspected that Ahmed Abu Risha's nephew was among those who executed the five government men, indicating the extent to which members of the Awakening in Anbar might have turned against the government. Four bombings in Shi'a towns south of Baghdad at the end of the weekend brought the death toll for April to more than 700, making it the deadliest month for Iraqis since 2008.[67]

The fighting led to a further breakdown in political dialogue and an intense escalation in sectarian tensions. When the violence reached the mixed-sect towns near Kirkuk, KRG President Massoud Barzani deployed peshmerga to the city to occupy positions beyond the normal Green Line. Parliament Speaker Osama Nujaifi blamed Maliki for the violence and called for the Prime Minister to resign and a new government to be formed.

Meanwhile, in a nationally televised speech amid the fighting, Maliki had warned that continued "sedition" against his government would lead to full-scale civil war. "What happened in Hawija . . . and other places, is a point in which we should stop and think because it might lead to sectarian strife," the Prime Minister said. "Everyone would lose. Whether he is in the north, the south, east or west of Iraq, if the fire of sectarianism starts, everyone's fingers will be burned by it."[68] The Prime Minister's prediction—or threat—would come true within months.

THE ISLAMIC STATE OF IRAQ AND SYRIA (ISIS)

The "Breaking the Walls" Campaign

The events of late 2012 and early 2013 were a godsend for Abu Bakr al-Baghdadi and his ISI, which since July 2012 had been engaged in a campaign aimed at reigniting Iraq's civil war and unifying the wars in Syria and Iraq. For the 9 months preceding the Hawijah massacre, Baghdadi and his organization had carried out attacks that both exacerbated and exploited Iraq's worsening political conflict. On July 21, 2012, Baghdadi announced the Islamic State's "Breaking the Walls" campaign, an initiative that took many pages from Abu Musab al-Zarqawi's 2004-2006 playbook for provoking a large-scale Sunni-Shi'a civil war. Central to the strategy was the reliance on car bombs: 24 separate waves of AQI's signature weapon aimed at fomenting sectarian strife through spectacular attacks that would garner disproportionate media attention. The waves were spread out over four phases and demonstrated ISI's technical capabilities, tactical skills, and ability to conduct an operational level campaign that adapted as the situation changed.

The first phase of "Breaking the Walls" from July through October 2012 consisted of 137 car bombs that hit cities ranging from Basrah to Mosul and varied widely in targets and density. Government, military, and civilian targets were hit in patterns that made it difficult to discern a broader objective, but ISI's ability to mass up to 30 car bombs on a single day indicated that they had fully regenerated AQI's car bombing capabilities. While ISI replicated one of AQI's most effective tactic by incorporating car bombings in its Breaking the Walls campaign, it added new elements such as attacking the Iraqi state's detention facilities in order to free hardened fighters and return them to battle. The first such attack in September 2012 only freed 100 prisoners, including 47 death row inmates, but the operations would quickly grow to be more frequent and effective, eventually hitting a total of eight prisons.[69]

Phase II, covering the next 4 months, saw a total of 112 car bombs that hit the Shi'a enclave of Sadr City, as well as the Green Line separating the Kurdish provinces and the remainder of Iraq. The Green Line attacks in particular indicated operational level flexibility and tried to exacerbate Kurdish/Shi'a tensions caused by Maliki's executive order creating the Tigris Operational Command that would inject non-Kurdish Iraqi Army units into Kurdish provinces. Phase III, with 137 car bombs, principally targeted Baghdad from February to May, with large waves of 20 or more hitting the capital about every 30 days. Analysts suspected that the surge and pause periods indicated ISI needed time to construct the complex weapons, and that the car bomb factories were again located in the Baghdad belts—the same location as AQI's brutal 2005-2007 campaigns. Also mirroring AQI's earlier campaigns, a majority of the bombers themselves appeared to foreign fighters who flowed into Iraq through Syria and down the same infiltration routes tracing the Tigris and Euphrates Rivers. A majority of the attacks targeted Baghdad's Shi'a community and were portrayed by ISI as reactions to the Maliki government's excesses against Sunni protesters in Fallujah, Hawijah, and other parts of Anbar Province.[70]

Abu Bakr al-Baghdadi's Split From Zawahiri and al-Qaeda

Amid its spring 2013 attacks on the Iraqi Shi'a and the Maliki government, ISI suddenly precipitated a rift within the wider Salafi jihad that had far-reaching consequences. On April 8, 2013, Abu Bakr al Baghdadi announced that ISI had merged with Jabhat al-Nusra and formed the Islamic State of Iraq and Syria (ISIS), attempting to highlight the unity of jihadist forces and that fighting in Syria and Iraq effectively erased the post-World War I interstate border. Baghdadi's announcement was imprudent and premature. The next day, Abu Mohammed al Jolani, the leader of Jabhat al-Nusra, rejected the claim, insisting that he had not been consulted prior to the media announcement. For a time, Zawahiri attempted to mediate between the two groups, publicly intervening and ordering each operational level commander to wage war only in their respective theaters: Iraq for Bagdadi and Syria for Jolani.[71] In the aftermath of this series of announcements, which also included promises from Jolani that his group would remain loyal to al-Qaeda, Jabhat al Nusra fractured, with a number of its followers leaving to join Baghdadi and ISIS. Less than a month later, open fighting broke out between the two groups.

Much of the break between ISI and Jabhat al-Nusra had been long brewing and echoed some of the same disputes that had existed between Abu Musab al-Zarqawi, the leader of AQI, and his senior leadership in Pakistan, namely Ayman al-Zawahiri. Jabhat al Nusrah and al-Qaeda's senior leaders had become uncomfortable with the brutal tactics of ISI and the implementation of Sharia law in areas where it lacked popular support first. The mass executions—particularly of Shi'a Muslims—beheadings, and horrific online videos designed to inspire fear and terror as a prelude to civil war were seen by al-Qaeda and Jabhat al Nusra as dangerous moves that could ultimately damage public support and turn the population against the group in a replay of the 2007-2008 Sahwah. Instead of such tactics, Jabhat al Nusrah followed policies that aimed, more or less, to win "hearts and minds" through economic assistance and social services while avoiding overt demonstrations of radicalism and extremism that would antagonize local communities.[72] With neither group willing to compromise on what they believed was the most effective strategy, splintering and conflict were inevitable.

To some degree, the rift between ISIS and al-Qaeda's senior leadership also represented an attempt by the Iraqi franchise of al-Qaeda to challenge the organization's leaders in Pakistan. In claiming to lead the jihad in both Iraq and Syria and to have authority over Jabhat al-Nusrah, Abu Bakr al-Baghdadi was actually asserting authority over the entire jihadist enterprise in the northern Arab world and mounting a direct challenge to Zawahiri's leadership. The relationship between Baghdadi and Zawahiri would deteriorate as the civil war in Iraq deepened and eventually fracture in February 2014 when Zawahiri formally disavowed any relationship with ISIS as an al-Qaeda affiliate.[73]

The Abu Ghraib Prison Break

The final 3 months, or Phase IV, of Breaking the Walls, from May to July 2013, were the temporal and operational culmination of the campaign for the newly renamed ISIS. The attacks were timed to magnify the effects of the Hawijah massacre and Maliki's brutal reaction to the Sunni protests. ISIS car bombs surged with nearly half of the attacks of the entire campaign occurring in the 3-month period after the Hawijah incident. Statistically the change was breathtaking: during all of 2010 and 2011, there were between 5 and 10 car bombs per month, but for the last 3 months of Breaking the Walls, this number shot up to 80 to 90 attacks per month.[74] These attacks would help make 2013 become Iraq's most deadly year since 2007, with a total of 7,818 civilian fatalities.[75]

The last phase of Breaking the Walls also saw the culmination of ISIS's attacks on Iraqi prisons. On July 21, 2013, exactly a year after Baghdadi had announced the campaign, ISIS breached Abu Ghraib, the most heavily defended prison within the Iraqi detention system, in a highly sophisticated attack that was synchronized with a simultaneous attempted prison break in Taji. While their suicide bombers hit key guard posts, ISIS struck the prison's security force with sustained mortar fire from multiple directions. Those attacks were followed closely by suicide car bombs that breached the prison gates to make way for a ground assault force that went cell to cell freeing somewhere between 500 and 1,000 prisoners, including ISIS "minister of war" Abdul Rahman al Bilawi and several other ISIS leaders who were awaiting execution on death row.[76]

ISIS's operations expanded the group's ranks with hardened fighters freed from the Iraqi prisons and prompted a return of the Shi'a militias in the Baghdad region. By May 2013, checkpoints manned by Shi'a militiamen sprouted across Baghdad as they had done in 2006. Likewise, incidents of unidentified assailants wearing Iraqi police uniforms seizing Sunnis out of their beds in the middle of the night crept back into news reports, as well as the accompanying occurrence of the mejhool, or unidentified bodies, discovered dumped in empty lots or floating in the Tigris.[77] The Iraqi Government's reaction to the renewed car bombing campaign—a policy of mass arrests of military age Sunni males—only served to worsen the situation and exacerbate tensions.[78] ISIS exploited the militia and government reactions in its media messaging, connecting them with the government's abuses in Fallujah, Hawijah, and other locations and creating an impression that Sunnis faced genocide and extinction. As in the dark days of the Iraqi civil war, many Iraqi Sunnis again had to choose between a government they considered a sectarian and authoritarian enemy or a brutal religious extremist group that at least offered them protection in exchange for submission. Typical of the Sunnis caught in this dilemma was one leader who told a former U.S. official in Baghdad, "I was never sectarian before . . . I love my country. I'm a nationalist. But I've become sectarian now because there's nowhere else for a moderate or secularist to be. We're losers. I've become as sectarian as the people I used to hate."[79]

THE DETERIORATION OF THE IRAQI SECURITY FORCES, 2012-2014

As ISIS and other Sunni militant groups grew stronger during 2013, the Iraqi security forces were not up to the challenge. ISIS's July 2013 Abu Ghraib attack was a tactical tour-de force that displayed exactly the kind of combined-arms capability that USF-I had struggled to build in the Iraqi Army, while the terrorist bombing offensives of 2013 showed that the ISF was struggling to protect Iraq's vulnerable cities and population from attacks by the resurrected Sunni insurgency. By virtually any measure, the ISF in 2013 were less capable than they had been in 2010 and were growing weaker in both capability and confidence, mostly because the worrisome trends that Austin and Cone observed in 2010-2011 had accelerated. As they had foreseen, the Iraqi Army's training program dissipated as U.S. troops left the country, so that many Iraq divisions stopped sending units to collective training and commanders often diverted their training budgets to other purposes or to corrupt practices. As Austin had predicted, the Iraqi Army's maintenance practices continued to deteriorate without U.S. assistance. Iraqi officers who bought into the U.S.-inspired model of training and skills development watched with dismay as the Ministry of Defense and major units abandoned it.

After USF-I's departure, the politicization of officer appointments that had begun the previous year accelerated, with appointments typically issued through Prime Minister Maliki's Office of the Commander in Chief. Changes first occurred at the regional headquarters outside of the traditional chain of command which had been effective at coordinated operations because they commanded all security forces in their area of responsibility—police, army, border security, infrastructure security, and others. During 2012, 4 of the 10 commanders in these headquarters were replaced, and 1 new Operational Command created, with Maliki appointing the new commander himself. The new command enflamed Arab-Kurd tensions as its area of responsibility included disputed areas in Kirkuk and parts of Salahadin province. Disagreements over the move's implementation boiled over into open Kurd-Arab conflict in December 2012 when peshmerga forces briefly exchanged fire with Iraqi Federal Police in Tuz Khurmato.[80]

Similar sectarian consolidation occurred at the division level, with Maliki replacing 6 of 14 commanders in 2012, capping the replacements of 5 other commanders in 2011. All together, these changes left a massive ethnic imbalance, with 11 divisions led by Shi'a officers, including the 1st Division in Sunni dominated Anbar and the 2d Division in Eastern Ninewa/Mosul. Only two Sunni commanders and one Kurdish commander remained, and one of the Sunni commanders was known as a long-term Maliki loyalist who had been implicated in sectarian violence against Sunnis. In making his appointments, Maliki had bypassed Iraq's constitution, refusing to submit his nominees for Parliamentary approval as required.[81] Many of the newly appointed officers had little military experience and few qualifications other than personal loyalty to the Prime Minister. Politicization also occurred in the junior officer ranks as candidates for entry into the Iraqi military academy tended to be connected to Iraq's political factions.[82] These were bad omens for future performance of the Iraqi Army as inexperienced officers replaced veteran commanders.

Within the Iraqi military's general staff, decision-making authority increasingly resided in the senior generals most closely associated with Maliki: OCINC director Faruq al-Araji, MOD chief of operations Abud Qanbar, counterterrorism director Talib Kenani, and IGFC commander Ali Ghaidan. These four, all Shi'a, effectively ran the ministry and its ground forces, even though the ministry was nominally under the direction of Defense Minister Sadoun Dulaimi and Chief of Defense Staff General Babakir Zebari. In reality, neither Dulaimi nor Zebari had any real authority.[83]

Under the direction of the four Maliki-loyalist generals, the Ministry of Defense made some consequential changes after 2011. Perhaps the most significant was the creation of a new command in spring 2012 to oversee operations in the Jazeera-Badiyah region, the vast desert area of western Iraq that spanned the country's long border with Syria. Concerned that ISI and other Sunni militant groups were once again establishing a cross-border sanctuary from which to attack Iraqi (and Syrian) cities, Maliki's OCINC directed the Ministry of Defense to establish the new command not by raising new combat units, but by reassigning each Iraqi division's existing commando battalion—generally the most experienced and best trained soldiers—to the control of the new headquarters. It was a disastrous move whose negative effects soon rippled across the Iraqi Army. By mid-2012, many of the Iraqi divisions had already lost the heightened manpower levels that Petraeus, Dubik, and Odierno had convinced the Iraqi Government to give them during the surge period. As a result, most of the Iraqi divisions and brigades of 2012 operated at an effective strength of about 70 percent, a steep drop from the 120 percent (or more) staffing levels of the surge period. When the order came to give up their commando battalions to the Jazeera-Badiyah command, many of the remaining divisions suddenly found themselves with an effective strength of less than 60 percent of what they were authorized.[84] The problem was made worse by the fact that the prevalence of "ghost soldiers" in the Iraqi Army's ranks—soldiers who received a salary from corrupt commanders but who were not actually present in the force--had increased sharply in 2012. One former Iraqi division commander estimated that some Iraqi divisions might have 60 to 70 percent of their authorized troops on the rolls, but that once ghost soldiers were factored out, their effective strength would be little more than 40 percent.[85]

These trends were clear to many of the U.S. military officials assigned to the U.S. Embassy, such as U.S. defense attaché Colonel Charles "Tony" Pfaff, an experienced U.S. Army foreign affairs officer who had served in assignments throughout the Middle East. In an after action report written in early 2014, Pfaff documented the impressions he had formed after arriving in Baghdad in fall 2012. The Iraqi security forces had "good leaders, brave soldiers and police, as well as effective weapons and equipment," he noted, but institutional issues such as "overlapping chains of command, poor administration, continued sectarian influences, and limited logistic, command and control, and intelligence capabilities" resulted in "poor performance in the field." On paper, the Iraqi security forces had expanded significantly from 2010 to 2013. The Ministry of Defense's forces had ostensibly grown from 245,000 in 2010 to 271,400 in 2013, and the Ground Forces Command by 2013 supposedly fielded more than 193,000 troops in 14 divisions and independent brigades. Across Iraq, these forces were augmented by the Interior Ministry's 531,000 police—up from 413,613 in 2010. In addition to its local police, facilities guards, border guards, and oil police, the Interior Ministry had more than 30 SWAT teams as well as 44,000 Federal Police deployed in 4 divisions. Despite their notional strength, the forces that numbered more than 800,000 soldiers and police suffered a string of battlefield defeats from 2013 onward. Pfaff concluded these factors were the culmination of "corrupt legacy practices that diverted resources away from the fight and created poor conditions for soldiers and police as funds for food, housing, fuel, and maintenance were siphoned off." Commanders who often purchased their positions of authority—sometimes reportedly paying as much as half a million dollars for division or brigade commands—recouped their investment by diverting equipment and supplies or by striking bargains with "ghost soldiers" to remain home in exchange for splitting their salaries with their commanders. The soldiers who remained at their posts had to shoulder heavier burdens of combat under austere conditions, and from late 2012 onward Iraqi units fighting against ISIS tended to experience mass desertions in combat.[86]

As the Iraqi security forces were hollowed out in this manner, ISF units entered into what Pfaff described as "a vicious circle where risk aversion stemming from poor conditions drove indiscriminate practices that alienated the population and empowered its adversaries. This, in turn, encouraged greater risk aversion, as not only was there little incentive to take risks on behalf of leaders responsible for these conditions, but also little reason to take risks on behalf of a population that resented them." Pfaff listed a few significant turning points in 2013 when the relationship between the Iraqi security forces and the country's Sunni community broke down. The April 2013 incident in Hawijah, when General Ali Ghaidan's troops had fired on a Sunni protest camp and had killed more than 40 people, had inflamed tensions and made "protesters elsewhere . . . afraid that the ISF would conduct similar attacks against them." The situation worsened after the Hawijjah killings when ISF troops "reportedly under orders from Maliki, attempted to arrest Dulaymi tribal shaykh Ali Hatem al Sulaiman, killing three bodyguards [and] again setting the ISF against the Sunnis in Anbar," Pfaff recounted. Finally, in late September 2013, hundreds of ISIS fighters entered the western Anbar towns of Rawa and Anah to attack government facilities and blow up bridges over the Euphrates River to prevent the Jazeera-Badiyah command from sending reinforcements to the area. The attack against the two towns had foreshadowed the fall of Fallujah to ISIS 3 months later, Pfaff believed.[87]

OSC-I director Lieutenant General Robert Caslen reached many of the same conclusions as Pfaff. Under Prime Minister Maliki's leadership, the upper ranks of the Iraqi military became riven by sectarianism, Caslen observed. "The Iraqis preserved ethnic and sectarian diversity in the military's upper ranks, as instructed by the Americans," Caslen said in 2013. "But the nation's divisions permeated even that arrangement. Officers routinely bypassed the chain of command to deal with soldiers from similar backgrounds," reflecting the deep distrust among military leaders of different sects.[88] Caslen believed much of Maliki's behavior, which appeared sectarian and authoritarian to outside observers, was the result of the Prime Minister's insecurity in his position. Shortly after assuming his position as OSC-I director at the end of 2011, the American general had been surprised to realize that Maliki had considered it part of USF-I's role inside Iraq to secure the Maliki government against major attacks or coup attempts. Meeting with Caslen to discuss OSC-I's role, Maliki had made it clear that he assumed Caslen and OSC-I would somehow continue to provide that kind of security after USF-I's departure and the expiration of the U.S.-Iraq security agreement. Caslen believed that when Maliki realized that OSC-I had no means to keep him in power and the U.S. Government no inclination to do so, the Iraqi leader decided to govern differently, greatly expanding his use of the ISF against political rivals to secure his own position.[89]

Like Pfaff, Caslen saw the Iraqi military deteriorate as it became more politicized. When tensions between the Maliki government and Massoud Barzani's KRG flared in early 2013, Caslen believed that in the event of a clash between the Iraqi Army and the Kurdish peshmerga along the Green Line, the Army would find itself at a serious disadvantage. Maliki had attempted to intimidate Barzani and the Kurdish forces by deploying Iraqi units to the Kirkuk region in 2012. However, the Prime Minister's troops could not match the peshmerga's capabilities and coordination, Caslen believed, meaning that Baghdad would be unlikely to win in a military confrontation with the Erbil government. As if to illustrate Caslen's point, in May 2013 the Kurdish commander of an Iraqi brigade in the 4th Division refused orders to leave a disputed territory on the Green Line and instead defected to the peshmerga along with all of his Kurdish soldiers and their equipment.[90]

As fighting between the ISF and ISIS intensified in 2013, Pfaff noted some serious tactical and operational shortcomings within the Iraqi units. They had a good communications infrastructure but during the country's frequent power outages, it was useless, and Iraqi commanders were often forced to rely upon unsecure cell phones or landlines to communicate. Meanwhile, in combat the ISF "often rely on large formations when engaging terrorist targets and facilities, which are easily spotted by ISIL . . . as a result, ISIL fighters often have sufficient time to depart the target area before the ISF troops arrive."[91] Iraqi logisticians were good at stockpiling supplies and ammunition on bases, Pfaff observed, but extremely poor at supplying units on the move, meaning that "when they do move, ISF often find themselves outgunned with limited ammunition when confronted by ISIL fighters." Overall, Pfaff noted, the ISF was a force that often lacked adequate situational awareness in combat and had commanders who were afraid to take decisive action in a deteriorating security situation.[92] Within months, the factors that Pfaff observed would spell disaster for the Iraqi security forces and the Iraqi Government they were meant to defend.

THE ASCENDANCY OF ISIS

The Fall of Fallujah

The weakness of the Iraqi security forces and the gathering strength of the Sunni militant groups that opposed them was on full display in Anbar in the last days of 2013 and first days of 2014. For the third December in a row, Prime Minister Maliki ordered government security forces to arrest one of Iraq's top Sunni leaders, this time targeting Ahmed Alwani, a Member of Parliament who was also a leader of the Albu Alwan tribe in eastern Anbar. On December 28, Iraqi troops raided Alwani's home near Ramadi, arresting the Parliamentarian and killing his brother in the melee. The raid was the culmination of months of tensions between the Maliki government and Anbaris. By late 2013, Maliki and his security advisors concluded that western Anbar had become a safe haven for ISIS from which the group was staging its attacks against the government and against Baghdad's population. They were particularly concerned with Wadi Horan, a remote but strategic area connecting Iraq to Jordan and Saudi Arabia that had long been studied by Iraqi staff colleges because of its frequent use by smugglers and insurgents. The staff college students were correct, and during 2012-2013, ISIS fighters established bases in Wadi Horan and used them to train recruits and mount attacks against Iraqi population centers. On December 21, ISIS fighters emerged from Wadi Horan to attack the 7th Iraqi Division in Rutbah, killing 17 senior officers including the division commander and wounding scores more. The boldness of the attack shocked the Iraqi Army defenders throughout the province and buckled their morale.[93]

By then, the protest camps in Fallujah and Ramadi had become the epicenter of Sunni opposition to Maliki, and the Prime Minister believed ISIS and other terrorist groups were using the protesters as cover while they set up "headquarters" in both cities. Maliki said as much in a national speech on December 25 in which he announced his intention to raze the protest sites, and 3 days later, the same day as the Alwani raid, Iraqi security forces began dismantling the camps.[94] The raid and the razing of the camps prompted 40 Sunni Members of Parliament to resign in protest, while a prominent Sunni cleric called for Sunni ISF members to defect and defend the protest camps against the government.

On January 2, just 2 days after the camps were leveled, Sunni rebels attacked. In Ramadi, the rebels made only modest headway, but in Fallujah, the government forces quickly collapsed. On January 3, ISIS fighters seized Fallujah's main mosque and declared the city an Islamic emirate. By January 4, most of Fallujah was in rebel hands, with various armed Sunni groups—some tribal, some associated with the Ba'ath Party, some ISIS—holding different parts of the city while the ISF retreated to areas outside it. Within days of the initial rebel attack, the insurgent cleric Abdullah Janabi, who had led Fallujah's rebels in 2004, had returned to the city and called for a general insurrection.[95]

The Maliki government had a larger problem than just ISIS. The rebels were a broad front that included ISIS, other longstanding insurgent groups, and some parts of the Sunni Awakening. One example was the rebel militia created by Dulaimi sheikh Ali Hatem

Suleiman, who formerly had been one of the leaders of the Ramadi Awakening council and had allied with Maliki in the 2009 and 2010 Iraqi elections.[96] Nevertheless, as its predecessor organization AQI had done in Fallujah in 2004, ISIS quickly seized leadership of the rebellion through its superior organization and resources, even though most rebels considered themselves to be fighting to topple Maliki rather than establish a caliphate. By mid-January, the Sunni rebels and the government forces had settled into a violent standoff throughout eastern Anbar, with each side launching near-daily local attacks and casualties mounting on both sides.

With a major city 30 miles from Baghdad in insurgent hands, Iraq held Parliamentary elections on April 30. The question of whether Nuri al-Maliki would return for another term as Prime Minister dominated the voting, despite the broad opposition to his premiership from the political parties outside his State of Law coalition. Unlike 2010, Iraq's Sunni and secular parties did not join in an electoral bloc as they had done under Ayad Allawi's Iraqiyah. As a result, Maliki's State of Law finished far ahead in the voting, taking 92 seats while the nearest second-place finisher, Muqtada Sadr, finished with just 34. Maliki himself garnered more than 720,000 popular votes, almost half a million more than the next most popular candidate, Ayad Allawi. The Prime Minister had paused the military operations around Fallujah while the voting took place, but on May 9, he directed a force led by the Iraqi special operations forces to resume an offensive against the city. Though it stalled after a few days, the election result and Maliki's control of the security forces made him seemed poised in late May to dominate the process of forming a government yet again.

The Fall of Mosul

Neither Maliki nor any other Iraqi leader knew it, but the country was about to be plunged into a deep crisis that would threaten the Iraqi state's very existence. As Maliki and the other political parties prepared to negotiate a new government in early June 2014, Iraq's second-largest city of Mosul fell into enemy hands. Though control of Mosul had always been tenuous, the Iraqi Government's grip on the city and its 2-million-strong population had weakened after the U.S. withdrawal, largely due to the worsening relationship between the population and government security forces. In 2013, Maliki had appointed Lieutenant General Mehdi Gharrawi of the Federal Police to command Mosul's security forces, despite Gharrawi's notorious history as a National Police commander in west Baghdad. In 2006, Gharrawi's troops had terrorized the Sunni population of west Baghdad, and Gharrawi himself had narrowly escaped prosecution on charges of murder and torture.[97] He had been relegated to unimportant positions for a few years but had been dispatched to Ninewa by the Prime Minister as the security situation deteriorated there after USF-I's withdrawal. Gharrawi's checkered history made him a poor choice to take over a force that already suffered from poor training, low staffing, and tense relations with Moslawis. The weakness of Gharrawi's troops led them to rely on checkpoints to screen for insurgent fighters, but the checkpoints also served to harass the local Sunni population.[98] Ambassador James Jeffrey later noted that the security forces in Mosul "had lost the support of the people because they had a sectarian policy, and I saw it with my own eyes."[99]

The war against ISIS and other insurgents in Anbar also made Mosul vulnerable. By June 2014, the local brigades of the Iraqi Army had been stripped of significant man-power, equipment, and heavy weapons to support operations in Anbar. The resulting shortfalls within the 2d and 3d Iraqi Army divisions in Ninewa were compounded by the rampant problem of ghost soldiers in their ranks, with thousands of soldiers splitting their salaries with their commanders in order to be excused from reporting for duty. The 6th Brigade of the 3d Iraqi Division, for example, had only about 500 troops on hand in early June, significantly fewer than the 2,500 being reported to higher headquarters.[100] Similar manning issues afflicted the rest of Ninewa's security forces. Local authorities later estimated that of the 25,000 soldiers and police who were supposed to be securing Mosul in June 2014, fewer than 10,000 were actually present.[101]

The thinness of the ISF ranks in Mosul was exposed in spectacular fashion in early June 2014. Before dawn on June 6, a force of perhaps 300 ISIS fighters assaulted the north-west portion of the city.[102] In Musherfa, a key entry point into Mosul, only about 40 Iraqi soldiers were on duty to oppose the ISIS attack.[103] In nearby Tamoz 17 district, an ISIS column of 15 pickup trucks and two captured HMMWVs easily routed an Iraqi police bat-talion owing to the ISIS fighters' superior firepower.[104] "In my entire battalion we ha[d] one machine gun," recalled Colonel Dhiyab Ahmed al-Assi al-Obeidi, the police battalion commander, while "In each pickup, [ISIS] had one."[105] Over the next several days, ISIS flooded the city with hundreds of trucks carrying heavy weapons and fighters.[106] By June 9, approximately 2,000 ISIS fighters had entered the city, and assaulted the main force of ISF defenders at the Mosul Hotel. Attacking the hotel with a military water tanker loaded with explosives, the ISIS men set off an explosion large enough to be felt throughout city, shaking the confidence of the remaining government troops west of the Tigris.[107]

Source: ISIS propaganda image.

A Convoy of ISIS Fighters Moves Through Mosul Shortly After Capturing the City.[108]

An ISF exodus from Mosul followed. ISF morale crumbled when the two senior Iraqi Army officers on the scene, General Abud Qanbar and General Ali Ghaidan, took their security details and left west Mosul on the evening of June 9. As word spread that the senior commanders had fled the battlefield, most of the remaining soldiers and police followed suit, abandoning thousands of vehicles and heavy weapons and leaving the city's main military bases and airport undefended, shortly to fall into ISIS's possession.[109] As the ISF fled, ISIS fighters also captured Mosul's branch of the Iraqi Central Bank and seized what may have been more than $400 million in currency, instantly making them the wealthiest terrorist group in the world.[110]

The people of Mosul were dumbstruck by the sudden disappearance of the government's troops seemingly without a fight. As one businessman who witnessed the battle put it, "The city fell like a plane without an engine . . . [ISIS] were firing their weapons into the air, but no one was shooting at them."[111]

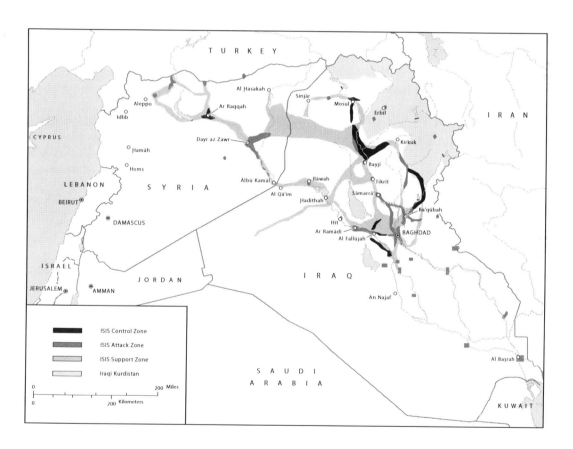

Map created by the official cartographer at the U.S. Army Center of Military History, Washington, DC.

Map 24. ISIS Sanctuary, June 2014.

The Camp Speicher Massacre

The collapse of the ISF in Mosul opened the road down the Tigris River Valley. Taking advantage of the ISF retreat, ISIS pressed its offensive south toward Baiji, Tikrit, and Samarra. By midday on June 11, ISIS fighters in 30 unarmored trucks rolled into Tikrit, taking control of the city center without firing a shot. The Tikriti police force had already melted away the previous day as word of the disaster in Mosul spread.[112] When ISIS seized downtown Tikrit on June 11, the thousands of Iraqi Army and Air Force troops based outside the city at Camp Speicher were thrown into confusion as they assumed that the ISIS juggernaut would soon swamp the base. Many troops at Camp Speicher were unarmed trainees at the base's air force school, and among these trainees panic spread, especially after some found the base's armory empty.[113] Many trainees, spurred by phone calls from their families in Baghdad and the south, took the ill-advised decision to flee the base. On June 12, thousands of them shed their uniforms and forced their way through the main gate of Camp Speicher unarmed and in civilian clothes. The exact details of the flight from the base are unclear owing to conflicting accounts and the subsequent killing of most of those who fled. Lieutenant General Ali Freiji, who in 2006-2008 had partnered with U.S. troops to pacify the Triangle of Death south of Baghdad, was now the commander of Camp Speicher, and though he raced to the gate with his security detail to stop the flood of deserters, more than 3,000 troops poured out of the camp.[114] Many of the deserters walked down the highway in an orderly file toward waiting trucks that local Tikritis had apparently promised would escort them south to safety. Instead, those who boarded the trucks found themselves captured by ISIS fighters. After sorting the captives by sect, the ISIS men executed about 1,700 Shi'a troops, dumping their bodies into mass graves or the Tigris River Valley and posting photos on the internet.[115]

The mass murder shocked the country and threw the Shi'a population of Baghdad and the south into a panic. Blame for the incident was unclear. Many of the surviving soldiers claimed they had received orders from officers to abandon Camp Speicher.[116] Some said their instructions had come from Ali Freiji himself, and initial accounts of the massacre repeated that rumor, but military and Parliamentary investigations later in 2014 cleared the general and assessed that he had done his best to stop the disaster.[117] It was a dark moment for Freiji, who had worked effectively with U.S. troops during the surge and who former Minister of Defense Abdel Qader rated as the top officer in the Iraqi Army.

The Popular Mobilization

By the end of June, as the holy month of Ramadan approached, ISIS was in control of three major Iraqi cities (Mosul, Fallujah, and Tikrit) and a large swath of the upper Tigris River Valley. ISIS fighters were pressing against Sinjar, Tel Afar, Kirkuk, and the Shi'a shrine city of Samarra, with the ISF and the Kurdish peshmerga seemingly powerless to stop them. Having won an equally stunning military victory against the ISF, ISIS followed up with a stunning political and religious coup. On June 29, the group declared that it had reinstituted the worldwide Caliphate and that its leader, Abu Bakr al-Baghdadi, would henceforth rule as Caliph Ibrahim. On July 4, Abu Bakr al-Baghdadi appeared publicly for the first time to give a sermon in the Nur al-Din Mosque in Mosul on the first Friday of Ramadan. He preached to a congregation of thousands of terrified Moslawis who had been searched by armed ISIS fighters at the entrances, directed where to sit, and told only that the day's sermon would be delivered by "the commander of the faithful."[118] In a 21-minute sermon, Baghdadi echoed the words of Islam's first caliph, his namesake Abu Bakr, demanding Muslims' obedience, asking for support for his caliphate, and emphasizing the theme of jihad.[119] ISIS media specialists produced a professional-grade video of Baghdadi's sermon and quickly broadcast it on the internet.

Source: Department of State photo (Released).

ISIS Leader Abu Bakr al-Baghdadi.[120]

Baghdadi's sermon was a masterstroke, demonstrating that he and his organization were more strongly positioned than the al-Qaeda leaders in hiding in Pakistan. By appearing in the open in a major city in the Arab heartland, Baghdadi had accomplished something Osama bin Laden and Ayman al-Zawahiri had never managed, a fact that vaulted him to a position of authority in the global jihadist movement. The Mosul appearance was useful as recruiting propaganda among jihadists across the globe, proving that ISIS's caliphate was a reality. Baghdadi's declaration of re-establishing the caliphate, an issue that Abu Musab al-Zarqawi and Ayman al-Zawahiri had hotly debated, had considerable religious significance. According to some religious figures, the reestablishment of the caliphate obligated Muslims to come to its defense, although such an interpretation was not uniform and many prominent scholars asserted Baghdadi had insufficient prominence to make such a declaration.

ISIS spokesmen declared that the group intended to attack Samarra, Baghdad, and Karbala. Baghdadi's sermon and takeover of much of northern Iraq convinced the population of the capital that the threat was real.[121] The fall of Mosul and Tikrit shattered Iraqi confidence in their Army and led many to conclude that ISIS was capable of defeating the roughly 60,000 Iraqi soldiers and police who defended the capital. On June 12, Grand Ayatollah Ali al-Sistani issued a fatwa calling for volunteers to defend Baghdad, secure the country's Shi'a shrines, and support Iraq's Sunnis and other minorities against ISIS attack.[122] Though Sistani may have intended his fatwa as a call to reinforce the Iraqi security forces, it spurred a vast expansion of the country's Shi'a militias. Within days, Moqtada Sadr, AAH, the Badr Corps, and Kata'ib Hizballah had all formed new groups to accept tens of thousands of volunteers who were coming forward to respond to Sistani's call.[123]

On June 15, the Iraqi Parliament codified Sistani's fatwa by declaring the volunteers official auxiliaries of the Iraqi military known as the Population Mobilization Forces (PMF). Overall command of the PMF fell to Iraqi national security advisor Falah Fayadh, with the Iranian-sponsored former Badr Corps operative Abu Mahdi al-Muhandis as the PMF's deputy commander.[124] Virtually every Shi'a political faction and leader formed their own popular mobilization units under the auspices of the PMF, while Prime Minister Maliki pledged a large government budget for their equipment and salaries, a move that incensed Sunnis as it laid bare the government's motives for abandoning the Sons of Iraq. Within weeks, more than 90,000 volunteers had swelled the PMF ranks and drifted toward the front lines, where the remnants of the Iraqi security forces had established positions to slow ISIS's advance.[125]

Iraq's Shi'a parties and most Baghdadis considered the PMF necessary to prevent Baghdad from falling, even though by mid-July ISIS, with its lines of communications overextended, showed little intention of trying to attack the city. Instead of continuing toward Baghdad in large numbers, ISIS had turned toward smaller objectives such as the dams near Haditha and Mosul, isolated ISF garrisons in Salahadin and Kirkuk Provinces, and areas north of Baqubah in the Diyala River Valley.[126] Nevertheless, the Iranian regime's Quds Force and its commander Qassem Soleimani launched a high-profile advisory effort, rushing IRGC Quds Force advisors to the PMF in areas contested by ISIS, such as the Diyala valley. It was an excellent opportunity for Iranian strategists. For decades, Soleimani and other IRGC commanders who had lived through the Iran-Iraq War as their formative experience had considered the Iraqi Army a potential threat to the Iranian regime. With the collapse of several Iraqi Army divisions and the appearance of the PMF, Soleimani and his peers had an unexpected chance to promote a parallel security structure to compete with the Iraqi Army for legitimacy, under the overwhelming influence of the Quds Force and its militia proxies.

The fall of Mosul ended Maliki's chance for a third term as Prime Minister. He had staked his reputation on his ability to provide security, but the swift collapse of the security structure he had overseen and failure of the senior military leaders he had appointed created a political backlash he could not survive. Even as Maliki attempted to regain political legitimacy by pledging government funding for the PMF, the other political parties began to organize against him in a way they had not done in 2010. On July 9, Grand Ayatollah Sistani tipped the balance against Maliki by writing privately to Da'wa Party leaders that Iraqi leaders needed "to speed up the selection of a new Prime Minister who has wide national acceptance" and a "new vision" in order to address the country's "critical circumstances."[127] With top cover from Sistani, the Da'wa leaders and other parties moved to form a new government without Maliki. On July 15, the Parliament elected Diyala native Salim Jabouri, a Sunni, as speaker, following on July 24 by electing senior PUK official Fuad Masum as Iraq's new President in place of Jalal Talabani. On August 11, Masum nominated Da'wa Party Parliamentarian Haider Abadi, a British-educated engineer, as Iraq's new Prime Minister.

Source: DoD photo by D. Myles Cullen (Released).

Prime Minister Haider Abadi.[128]

THE START OF OPERATION INHERENT RESOLVE

The United States restricted its military support to the Iraqis while Maliki still served as Prime Minister. A small task force from U.S. Army Central (ARCENT) under the command of Major General Dana Pittard had arrived in Baghdad on June 15 to assess the military situation and begin coordination with the Iraqi Army, but U.S. leaders had refrained from providing more direct support in the weeks after the fall of Mosul. U.S. officials believed Maliki needed to step aside in order for the campaign to halt ISIS to succeed, and they conditioned security assistance on his replacement by a new Iraqi premier. This policy stance created resentment among many Iraqis, especially Shi'a, who concluded that the United States had been willing to let ISIS threaten Baghdad in order to gain leverage to remove Maliki. The Iranian regime and its Iraqi allies highlighted the difference between the U.S. and Iranian responses to the crisis, and even some long-time U.S. partners voiced their frustration. Mowaffak Rubaie summed up this attitude when he told journalists, "Who arrived here to save us three days after Mosul fell? Not the Americans. They only sent abysmal airstrikes 3 months later when their citizens were beheaded. The speed of the Iranian response to Baghdad and Erbil was the next day."[129]

With Abadi in place, U.S. military involvement steadily increased and, in fact, direct U.S. activity against ISIS had already begun the week before Abadi's appointment. From August 1-4, ISIS attacked outposts in Sinjar and near the Mosul Dam, sending the peshmerga reeling and forcing tens of thousands of Kurds, Yezidis, Christians, and other minorities to flee. At Jebel Sinjar, ISIS fighters massacred hundreds of Yezidis and pursued Yezidi civilians who fled onto the bare mountain and became stranded there. At Mosul Dam, ISIS members came close enough to the dilapidated structure to worry Iraqi and U.S. officials that they could seize the dam's controls and flood the Tigris River Valley from Mosul to Samarra. On August 6, ISIS attacked east from the Tigris River Valley and overran the Christian towns of eastern Ninewa, killing non-Sunni men and enslaving women and children. Within hours, the ISIS fighters were less than 20 miles from Erbil, with peshmerga defenses appearing to collapse and open the road to the Kurdish capital. In response to the threat, on August 8, U.S. aircraft began bombing ISIS positions west of Erbil, while U.S. special operations forces provided advisors to peshmerga units. The airstrikes reversed the ISIS momentum immediately, halting the terrorist group's advance and enabling peshmerga units to stabilize a defensive line.

On the same day, CENTCOM named ARCENT commander Lieutenant General James Terry as commander of the counter-ISIS campaign, and Terry began to organize a task force headquarters at ARCENT's main base in Kuwait. Terry and a small staff—limited in size by a troop cap set by U.S. officials in Washington—joined Pittard's organization in Baghdad and set up a Combined Joint Operations Center with Iraqi Army counterparts at forward operating base (FOB) Union III, across the street from the U.S. Embassy in the Green Zone. Terry's task force also organized a small operations center in Erbil from which to coordinate with peshmerga counterparts. By August 18, under the cover of U.S. airstrikes, peshmerga troops had halted ISIS's advance along the Green Line and had begun to push the group's fighters slowly back toward the Tigris River.

Carter (center), Jones (left), Terry (right). Source: DoD photo by U.S. Army Sergeant
1st Class Clydell Kinchen (Released).

**SECDEF Ashton Carter With U.S. Ambassador to Iraq Stuart Jones and ARCENT
Commander Lieutenant General James Terry.**[130]

Significant changes in the military organization on both the Iraqi and American sides
soon followed. On September 23, Prime Minister Abadi dissolved the Office of the Commander in Chief, the organization Maliki and General Faruq al Araji had used to exert
control over the Ministry of Defense, and ordered the immediate retirement of General
Abud Qanbar and General Ali Ghaidan, the two senior officers whose flight from Mosul
had demoralized the city's defenders.[131] The following day, SECDEF Carter ordered the
Army's 1st Infantry Division headquarters to deploy 500 Soldiers to Baghdad, Erbil, and
Kuwait to take over for Pittard's task force as a new Combined Joint Forces Land Component Command-Iraq. The division would do so as part of the newly named Operation
INHERENT RESOLVE, the name given to the campaign against ISIS in both Syria and
Iraq under Terry's command. Though the number of troops deployed inside Iraq as part
of Operation INHERENT RESOLVE remained limited by the U.S. Government's self-imposed cap, the operation included a large NATO contingent to train Iraqi units.

By the end of October, Major General Paul Funk and his 1st Infantry Division headquarters reached Baghdad and Erbil to begin their mission as Combined Joint Forces
Land Component Command-Iraq, meant to repair the broken Iraqi Army and coordinate
close air support for the Iraqi and peshmerga troops in contact with ISIS. Just shy of 3
years after the last U.S. units had left Baghdad, the U.S. Army had returned.

ENDNOTES - CHAPTER 15

1. Office of the Press Secretary, "Remarks by President Obama and Prime Minister al-Maliki of Iraq in a Joint Press Conference," Washington, DC: The White House, December 12, 2011, available from *https://obamawhitehouse.archives.gov/the-press-office/2011/12/12/remarks-president-obama-and-prime-minister-al-maliki-iraq-joint-press-co.*

2. Arwa Damon and Mohammed Tawfeeq, "Iraq's leader becoming a new 'dictator,' deputy warns," CNN, December 13, 2011, available from *http://www.cnn.com/2011/12/13/world/meast/iraq-maliki/.*

3. Ghaith Abdul-Ahad, "Corruption in Iraq: 'Your son is being tortured. He will die if you don't pay'," *The Guardian*, January 15, 2012, available from *http://www.theguardian.com/world/2012/jan/16/corruption-iraq-son-tortured-pay*; Rami Ruhayem, "Hashemi trial: Murder plots detailed in Iraqi court," BBC News, June 3, 2012, available from *http://www.bbc.com/news/world-middle-east-18301600.*

4. DoD photo by Sergeant Patrick Lair, "Iraqi Vice President Visits Mosul [Image 2 of 4]," DVIDS Identifier 78254, February 24, 2008, Released to Public, available from *https://www.dvidshub.net/image/78254/iraqi-vice-President-visits-mosul.*

5. Joel Wing, "Iraq's PM Maliki Flexes his Muscles in Diyala Province Again," *Ekurd Daily*, January 26, 2012, available from *http://ekurd.net/mismas/articles/misc2012/1/kurdsiniraq149.htm*; Joel Wing, Musings on Iraq Blog, December 28, 2011, available from *http://musingsoniraq.blogspot.com/2011/12/push-to-make-iraqs-diyala-province.html*; "Iraqi Shi'ite rally against autonomy push in Diyala," Reuters, December 15, 2011, available from *https://www.reuters.com/article/us-iraq-autonomy-diyala/iraqi-shiite-rally-against-autonomy-push-in-diyala-idUSTRE7BE1F920111215*; Ramzy Mardini, "Iraq's Recurring Political Crisis," Washington, DC: Institute for the Study of War, February 16, 2016, available from *http://www.understandingwar.org/backgrounder/iraqs-recurring-political-crisis#_edn5.*

6. E-mail, Lieutenant Colonel Joel Rayburn to Karim Sadjadpour, December 15, 2011.

7. DoD photo by Specialist Brandon Bednarek, "Generally speaking [Image 4 of 8]," DVIDS Identifier 477278, October 20, 2011, Released to Public, available from *https://www.dvidshub.net/image/477278/generally-speaking.*

8. Tim Arango, "U.S. Planning to Slash Iraq Embassy Staff by as Much as Half," *The New York Times*, February 7, 2012, available from *http://www.nytimes.com/2012/02/08/world/middleeast/united-states-planning-to-slash-iraq-embassy-staff-by-half.html?pagewanted=all&_r=0*, accessed January 8, 2015.

9. Interview, Chief of Staff of the Army (CSA) Operation IRAQI FREEDOM (OIF) Study Group with Lieutenant General Robert Caslen, December 18, 2014, West Point, NY.

10. Interview, Center for Army Lessons Learned (CALL) with Lieutenant General Robert Caslen, November 24, 2012, OSC-I, Interviews, Vol. II, p. 8.

11. Plans Notes, United States Forces-Iraq (USF-I), J-5, October 14-18, 2011, November 6-12, 2011, November 13-19, 2011, and November 20-29, 2011, Military History Institute (MHI), AHEC, Carlisle, PA.

12. Interview, CALL with Lieutenant General Robert Caslen, March 23, 2012, OSC-I, Interviews, Vol. I, p. 16.

13. Caslen, interview by CALL, March 23, 2012, OSC-I, Interviews, Vol. I, p. 21; OSC-I, "Iraq and the Office of Security Cooperation-Iraq," command briefing n.d., submitted by Caslen, p. 2.

14. Interview, CALL with Caslen, March 23, 2012, Newsletter OSC-I, Interviews, Vol. I, No. 12-12, Leavenworth, KS: Center for Army Lessons Learned, August 2012, p. 24; interview with Mark Hunter,

November 26, 2012, OSC-I, Interviews, Vol. II, p. 56. Special Agent Mark Hunter served as the Senior Regional Security Officer at USM-I; CSA OIF SG with Caslen, December 18, 2014, West Point, NY.

15. Interview, CALL with Kenneth Harvey, J3 Director of Training and Operations Officer OSC-I, November 14, 2012, OSC-I, Interviews, Vol. II, p. 164; with Dean Raab, Legal Advisor for OSC-I, December 15, 2012, OSC-I, Interviews, Vol. II, p. 106.

16. Interview, CSA OIF Study Group with Caslen, December 18, 2014, West Point, NY.

17. Ambassador James Jeffery, interview by CALL, March 30, 2012, OSC-I, Interviews, Vol. I, p. 5.

18. Ibid., pp. 12-13; Interview, CALL with Mark Hunter, November 26, 2012, OSC-I, Interviews, Vol. II, p. 56.

19. Interview, CALL with John Hall, November 16, 2012, OSC-I, Interviews, Vol. II, p. 91. Colonel John Hall served in the OSC-I Initiatives Group.

20. Interview, CALL with Mark Libby, November 18, 2012, OSC-I, Interviews, Vol. II, p. 52.

21. Interview, CALL with Hunter, November 26, 2012, OSC-I, Interviews, Vol. II, p. 60.

22. Ibid., p. 62; Interview, CALL with Harold Reeves, September 24, 2012, OSC-I, Interviews, Vol. II, p. 155.

23. Interview, CALL with Karl Krause, J8 Director of Resource Management for OSC-I, January 14, 2013, OSC-I, Interviews, Vol. II, p. 214.; CALL with Kenneth Harvey, November 14, 2012, OSC-I, Interviews, Vol. II, p. 163.

24. Interview, CALL with Dean Raab, December 15, 2012, OSC-I, Interviews, Vol. II, pp. 103-104.

25. Interview, CALL with Kenneth Harvey, November 14, 2012, OSC-I, Interviews, Vol. II, p. 165; with Karl Kraus, January 14, 2013, OSC-I, Interviews, Vol. II, p. 213.

26. Interview, CSA OIF Study Group with Caslen, December 18, 2014, West Point, NY.

27. E-mail, Lieutenant Colonel Joel Rayburn to Mithal Al-Alusi, January 24, 2012.

28. "Leader of Saddam Hussein's Baath party 'criticises Iraq Government'," *The Telegraph*, April 8, 2012, available from *http://www.telegraph.co.uk/news/worldnews/middleeast/iraq/9193383/Leader-of-Saddam-Husseins-Baath-party-criticises-Iraq-Government.html*.

29. *London Al-Hayah Online* [in Arabic], March 24, 2012, Report from Baghdad by Mushriq Abbas: "Mish'an al-Jabburi Tells Al-Hayah: I Returned to Baghdad and Call for the Return of Izzat al-Duri and Harith al-Dari."

30. Joel Rayburn, *Iraq after America: Strongmen, Sectarians, Resistance*, Stanford, CA: Hoover Institution Press, Stanford University, 2014, p. 225; Wyer, p. 12.

31. Rayburn, *Iraq after America*, p. 225; Wyer, p. 12.

32. Wyer, pp. 6-10.

33. Ibid., p. 13.

34. Ahmed Rasheed and Mohammed Ameer, "Iraq militia stone youths to death for 'emo' style," Reuters, March 10, 2012, available from *http://www.reuters.com/article/2012/03/10/us-iraq-emo-killings-idUSBRE8290CY20120310*; Rayburn, *Iraq after America*, p. 206.

35. "Missing U.S. soldier killed by Shiite group," *USA Today*, February 27, 2012, available from *http:// usatoday30.usatoday.com/news/military/story/2012-02-27/iraq-us-soldier-shiite/53267618/1*.

36. Ben Van Heuvelen, "Iraqi Leaders Criticize Nouri al-Maliki after Arrest of top Elections Official," *The Washington Post*, April 17, 2012.

37. Joel Wing, "Why the Talk of a No Confidence Vote Against Iraq's Premier Maliki Remains Just Talk," *Musings on Iraq*, May 30, 2012, available from *http://musingsoniraq.blogspot.com/2012/05/why-talk-of-no-confidence-vote-against.html*.

38. "Deja Vu All Over Again? Iraq's Escalating Political Crisis," Middle East Report No. 126, New York: International Crisis Group, July 30, 2012, available from *https://www.crisisgroup.org/middle-east-north-africa/ gulf-and-arabian-peninsula/iraq/deja-vu-all-over-again-iraq-s-escalating-political-crisis*.

39. Rayburn, *Iraq after America*, p. 227.

40. Stephen Wicken, "Sadr's Balancing Act on Maliki," Washington, DC: Institute for the Study of War, June 18, 2012, available from *http://www.understandingwar.org/backgrounder/sadr's-balancing-act-maliki#_edn19*; Kenneth Pollack, "Iraqi Elections, Iranian Interests," Washington, DC: The Brookings Institution, April 4, 2014, available from *http://www.brookings.edu/blogs/markaz/ posts/2014/04/04-pollack-iraq-national-elections-2014-iranian-interests*.

41. UN photo by Eskinder Debebe, "Secretary General Meets Prime Minister of Iraq," Photo No. 404634, July 22, 2009, United Nations News and Media Photo, available from *https://www.unmultimedia.org/s/photo/ detail/404/0404634.html*.

42. William Young, David Stebbins, Bryan Frederick, and Omar al-Shahery, "Spillover From the Conflict in Syria: An Assessment of the Factors that Aid and Impede the Spread of Violence," Santa Monica, CA: RAND Corporation, 2014, p. 45.

43. Rayburn, *Iraq after America*, pp. 228-229.

44. Photo courtesy of Kremlin.ru, "President of Syria Bashar al-Assad [photo 6 of 11]," October 21, 2015, Released to Public, available from *http://en.kremlin.ru/events/President/news/50533/photos/42160*.

45. Daniel L. Byman and Kenneth M. Pollack, "The Syrian Spillover: Is anyone prepared for the unintended consequences of the war for Syria?" *Foreign Policy*, August 10, 2012, available from *http://foreignpolicy. com/2012/08/10/the-syrian-spillover/*.

46. Rayburn, *Iraq after America*, p. 231.

47. Phillip Smyth, "From Karbala to Sayyida Zaynab: Iraqi Fighters in Syria's Shi'a Militias," *CTC Sentinel*, Vol. 6, No. 8, August 2013, p. 28.

48. Will Fulton, Joseph Holliday, and Sam Wyer, "Iranian Strategy in Syria," Washington, DC: American Enterprise Institute, May 2013, pp. 23-24.

49. Michael Knights, "Iran's Foreign legion: The Role of Iraqi Shiite Militias in Syria," PolicyWatch 2096, Washington, DC: The Washington Institute for Near East Policy, June 27, 2013, available from *http:// www.washingtoninstitute.org/policy-analysis/view/irans-foreign-legion-the-role-of-iraqi-shiite-militias-in-syria*.

50. Fulton, p. 25.

51. Michael Gordon, "Iran Supplying Syrian Military via Iraqi Airspace," *The New York Times*, September 4, 2012, available from *http://www.nytimes.com/2012/09/05/world/middleeast/iran-supplying-syrian-military-via-iraq-airspace.html*.

52. Michael Gordon, "Tensions Rise in Baghdad with Raid on Official," *The New York Times*, December 20, 2012.

53. Gordon, "Tensions Rise in Baghdad with Raid on Official."

54. U.S. Navy photo by Petty Officer 1st Class Mario A. Quiroga, "Iraqi Deputy Prime Minister Dr. Rafi al-Issawi responds to inquires from Service Directorate-Generals and local media during the central services meeting at the Government Center in Baqubah, Iraq, Aug. 9, 2008. Ministry members, Diyala tribal sheiks, and Service Directorate-Generals discussed ongoing provincial reconstruction and funding for the Diyala province during the meeting," DIMOC Identifier 75M2OT5_5V7AZBEB0, August 9, 2008, Released to Public, modified (cropped).

55. PBS, "The Rise of ISIS," *Frontline*, season 33, episode 2, October 28, 2014, available from *https://www.pbs.org/wgbh/frontline/film/rise-of-isis/*.

56. Ibid.

57. Anthony Cordesman and Sam Khazi, *Iraq in Crisis: A Report of the CSIS Burke Chair in Strategy*, New York: Center for Strategic International Studies, May 2014, p. 98; "Protestors Attack Iraqi Deputy PM, Guards Open Fire," Voice of America, December 30, 2012, available from *http://blogs.voanews.com/breaking-news/2012/12/30/protesters-attack-iraqi-deputy-pm-guards-open-fire/*.

58. Ahmed Maher, "Iraq Sunnis Threaten Army Attacks After Protest Deaths," BBC News, January 26, 2013, available from *http://www.bbc.com/news/world-middle-east-21206163*.

59. Michael Schmidt, "434 People Killed in Iraq Since US Pulled Out," *The New York Times*, January 27, 2012, available from *http://www.nytimes.com/2012/01/28/world/middleeast/suicide-bomber-attacks-funeral-procession-in-iraq.html*.

60. Al-Salhy, Suadad, "Al Qaeda claims killing of Syrian soldiers in Iraq," Reuters, March 11, 2013, available from *http://www.reuters.com/article/2013/03/11/us-syria-crisis-iraq-qaeda- idUSBRE92A07B20130311*.

61. Alistair Lyon, ed., "Iraq Postpones Local Elections in two Provinces," Reuters, March 19, 2013, available from *http://www.reuters.com/article/2013/03/19/us-iraq-elections-idUSBRE92I0A020130319*, accessed June 1, 2015.

62. PBS, "The Rise of ISIS."

63. Interview, CSA OIF Study Group with John Hall, March 16, 2015, with quotations derived from notebook excerpts from April 21-22, 2013; and e-mail from John Hall, March 19, 2015.

64. Wladimir van Wilgenburg, "Implications of the Hawija 'massacre' and Kirkuk Protest Movement," *Today's Zaman*, May 12, 2013, available from *http://www.todayszaman.com/orsam_implications-of-the-hawija-massacre-and-kirkuk-protest-movement_315156.html*, accessed June 1, 2015; Rayburn, *Iraq after America*, p. 238.

65. Priyanka Boghani, "In Their Own Words: Sunnis on Their Treatment in Maliki's Iraq," PBS, October 28, 2014, available from *http://www.pbs.org/wgbh/frontline/article/in-their-own-words-sunnis-on-their-treatment-in-malikis-iraq/*.

66. Joel Rayburn, "Iraq is Back on the Brink of Civil War," *New Republic*, May 8, 2013, available from *http://www.newrepublic.com/article/113148/iraqs-civil-war-breaking-out-again*, accessed June 2, 2015.

67. Tim Arango, "Iraqi Premier Urges Talks but Vows to Battle Insurgents," *The New York Times*, April 25, 2013, available from *http://www.nytimes.com/2013/04/26/world/middleeast/iraqi-premier-urges-calm-but-vows-to-continue-military-strikes.html?_r=0*.

68. Aki Peritz, "The Great Iraqi Jail Break," *Foreign Policy*, June 26, 2014; Jessica D. Lewis, "Middle East Security Report 14: Al-Qaeda in Iraq Resurgent, The Breaking the Walls Campaign, Part I," Washington, DC: Institute for the Study of War, September 2013, p. 7.

69. Lewis, "Al-Qaeda in Iraq Resurgent, Part I."

70. Michael Weiss and Hassan Hassan, *ISIS: Inside the Army of Terror*, New York: Regan Arts, 2015, pp. 184-185.

71. Hassan Hassan, "A Jihadist Blueprint for Hearts and Minds is Gaining Traction in Syria," *The National*, March 4, 2014.

72. Liz Sly, "Al-Qaeda Disavows any Ties with Radical Islamist ISIS group in Syria, Iraq," *The Washington Post*, February 3, 2014.

73. Lewis, "Al-Qaeda in Iraq Resurgent, Part I"; Weiss and Hassan, *ISIS*, p. 93.

74. "Iraq's annual death toll highest in five years—UN," BBC News, January 1, 2014, available from *http://www.bbc.com/news/world-middle-east-25568687*.

75. Aki Peritz, "The Great Iraqi Jail Break," *Foreign Policy*, June 26, 2014; Mushreq Abbas, "Al-Qaeda Militants Raid Iraq's Abu Ghraib, Taji Prisons," *Al Monitor*, July 25, 2013.

76. Jessica Lewis, Ahmed Ali, and Kimberly Kagan, "Iraq's Sectarian Crisis Reignites as Shi'a Militias Execute Civilians and Remobilize," Washington, DC: Institute for the Study of War, June 1, 2013, available from *http://www.understandingwar.org/backgrounder/iraqs-sectarian-crisis-reignites-shia-militias- execute-civilians-and-remobilize*.

77. Lewis, "Al-Qaeda in Iraq Resurgent, Part I."

78. Weiss and Hassan, ISIS, p. 93.

79. Marisa Sullivan, "Maliki's Authoritarian Regime," Middle East Security Report 10, Washington, DC: Institute for the Study of War, April 2013, pp. 12-14.

80. Ibid., pp. 16-19.

81. Knights, "Iran's Foreign legion."

82. Babakir Report; Ibid.

83. Interview, Colonel Joel Rayburn, CSA OIF Study Group, with Major General (Ret.) Aziz Swaidy, May 11, 2016.

84. Ibid.

85. Paper, Colonel C. Anthony Pfaff, "Strength and Weaknesses of Iraqi Security Forces," June 2014.

86. Ibid, p. 10.

87. Ibid., pp. 1-3, 7.

88. Interview, CSA OIF Study Group with Caslen, December 18, 2014, West Point, NY.

89. Ibid.

90. Pfaff, p. 10.

91. Ibid., p. 12.

92. Ibid.

93. Interview, CSA OIF Study Group with Swaidy, May 11, 2016.

94. Kirk Sowell, "Maliki's Anbar Blunder," *Foreign Policy*, January 15, 2014.

95. Ibid.

96. Ibid.

97. Rowan Allport, "A Year after Mosul," June 2, 2015, available from *http://www.hscentre.org/security-and-defence/year-mosul/*, accessed April 12, 2016.

98. Yasir Abbas and Dan Trombly, "Inside the Collapse of the Iraqi Army's 2d Division," July 1, 2014, available from *http://warontherocks.com/2014/07/inside-the-collapse-of-the-iraqi-armys-2nd-division/*, accessed April 12, 2016.

99. Suadad Al-Salhy and Tim Arango, "Sunni Militants Drive Iraqi Army Out of Mosul," available from *http://www.nytimes.com/2014/06/11/world/middleeast/militants-in-mosul.html?_r=0*, accessed April 12, 2016.

100. Ned Parker, Isabel Coles, and Raheem Salman, "How Mosul Fell: A General's Story," p. 6, available from *http://graphics.thomsonreuters.com/14/10/MIDEAST-CRISIS:GHARAWI.pdf*, accessed April 12, 2012.

101. Ibid.

102. The five districts were Musherfa, Haramut, Tamoz 17, Hay al-Islah al-Ziraie, and Hay Tanak; Parker, Coles, and Salman, "How Mosul Fell," pp. 2, 4.

103. Parker, Coles, and Salman, "How Mosul Fell," p. 6.

104. Ned Parker, Isabel Coles, and Raheem Salman, "Special Report: How Mosul fell - An Iraqi general disputes Baghdad's story," p. 7, available from *http://uk.reuters.com/article/us-mideast-crisis-gharawi- special-report-idUSKCN0I30Z820141014*, accessed April 13, 2016.

105. Ibid., p. 6.

106. Ibid., p. 4.

107. Ibid., p. 6.

108. Islamic State of Iraq and Syria (ISIS) propaganda image, available from *https://www.longwarjournal.org/archives/2014/06/isis_holds_military_parade_in.php*.

109. Parker, Coles, and Salman, "Special Report: How Mosul fell."

110. Jack Moore, "Extremists In Iraq May Have Looted $430 Million From Mosul's Central Bank," June 11, 2014, available from *http://www.businessinsider.com/430m-looted-from-mosuls-central-bank-2014-6?IR=T*, accessed April 13, 2016. The cash was in the form of 500 billion Iraqi dinars as well as a separate stockpile of gold bullion.

111. Ibid.

112. Ibid.

113. Raheem Salman, "Survivors demand justice after Iraq massacre," September 5, 2014, available from *http://www.reuters.com/article/us-iraq-crisis-massacre-idUSKBN0H021L20140905*, accessed April 14, 2016.

114. Interview, CSA OIF Study Group with Lieutenant General Ali al-Freiji, September 2015.

115. Slater, "The Paper Tiger of the Tigris."

116. Salman, "Survivors demand justice after Iraq massacre."

117. "Iraqi probe delves into Speicher Camp massacre," *Al-Arabiya English,* November 28, 2014, available from *http://english.alarabiya.net/en/News/middle-east/2014/11/28/Iraqi-probe-delves-into-Speicher-Camp-massacre.html,* accessed April 14, 2016.

118. Alissa J. Rubin, "Militant Leader in Rare Appearance in Iraq," July 5, 2015, available from *http://www.nytimes.com/2014/07/06/world/asia/iraq-abu-bakr-al-baghdadi-sermon-video.html?_r=0,* accessed April 14, 2016; Martin Chulov, "Abu Bakr al-Baghdadi emerges from shadows to rally Islamist followers," July 6, 2014, available from *http://www.theguardian.com/world/2014/jul/06/abu-bakr-al-baghdadi-isis,* accessed April 14, 2016.

119. Chulov, "Abu Bakr al-Baghdadi emerges from shadows to rally Islamist followers"; "ISIS Abu Bakr al-Baghdadi first Friday sermon as so-called 'Caliph'," *al-Arabyia English,* available from *http://english.alarabiya.net/en/webtv/2014/07/05/ISIS-s-chief-Baghdadi-in-first-purported-video-as-caliph-.html,* accessed April 15, 2016.

120. Department of State photo, "Wanted: Information that brings to justice . . . Abu Bakr al-Baghdadi: Up to $25 Million Reward," n.d., Released to Public, available from *https://rewardsforjustice.net/english/abu_dua.html.*

121. "ISIS urges militants to march to Baghdad," *Al Arabiya English,* available from *http://english.alarabiya.net/en/News/2014/06/12/ISIS-militants-plan-to-march-on-Baghdad.html,* accessed April 19, 2016.

122. "The Iraqi People Voluntary Army of Al Hashd Al Shaabi Moralistic Democracy: The Popular Mobilization Forces," available from *https://www.nationstates.net/nation=al_hashd_al_shaabi/detail=factbook/id=main,* accessed April 19, 2016.

123. Ahmed Ali with Kimberly Kagan, "The Iraqi Shi'a Mobilization to Counter the ISIS Offensive," June 14, 2014, available from *http://www.understandingwar.org/backgrounder/iraqi-shi'-mobilization-counter-isis-offensive,* accessed April 15, 2016.

124. "The Iraqi People Voluntary Army of Al Hashd Al Shaabi Moralistic Democracy: The Popular Mobilization Forces," available from *https://www.nationstates.net/nation=al_hashd_al_shaabi/detail=factbook/id=main,* accessed April 19, 2016.

125. Joel Wing, "Iran And Its Shiite Militias Mobilize In Iraq Interview With Phillip Smyth," June 16, 2014, available from *http://musingsoniraq.blogspot.com/2014/06/iran-and-its-shiite-militias-mobilize.html,* accessed April 15, 2016; Ahmed Ali with Kagan, "The Iraqi Shi'a Mobilization to Counter the ISIS Offensive"; Bilgay Duman, "A New Controversial Actor in Post-ISIS Iraq: al-Hashd al-Shaabi (The Popular Mobilization Forces)," ORSAM Report No. 198, May 2015, pp. 10-12, available from *http://www.orsam.org.tr/en/enUploads/Article/Files/2015527_198raporengweb.pdf,* accessed April 15, 2016.

126. "Iraq: Security situation and internally displaced people in Diyala, April 2015," Oslo, Norway: The Norwegian Country of Origin Information Centre, April 24, 2015, pp. 7-8, available from *https://www.ecoi.net/en/file/local/1115404/1226_1441804342_topical-note-security-situation-and-internally-displaced-people-in-diyala.pdf,* accessed April 20, 2016.

127. Loveday Morris, "A Letter from Sistani Turned the Tide Against Iraq's Leader," *The Washington Post,* August 13, 2014, available from *https://www.washingtonpost.com/world/middle_east/a-letter-from-sistani-turned-the-tide-against-iraqs-leader/2014/08/13/3b3426cf-60ee-4856-ad26-d01a9c6cc9c3_story.html,* accessed June 13, 2016.

128. DoD photo by D. Myles Cullen, "CJCS visits Baghdad [Image 10 of 15]," DVIDS Identifier 1834314, March 9, 2015, available from *https://www.dvidshub.net/image/1834314/cjcs-visits-baghdad*.

129. Janine Di Giovanni, "The Militias of Baghdad," November 26, 2014, available from *http://www.newsweek.com/2014/12/05/militias-baghdad-287142.html*, accessed April 19, 2016. U.S. citizens refers to the journalists James Foley and later Steven Sotloff, and Peter "Abdul-Rahman" Kassig.

130. DoD photo by U.S. Army Sergeant 1st Class Clydell Kinchen, "Secretary of defense walks [Image 4 of 14]," DVIDS Identifier 2085574, July 23, 2015, Released to Public, available from *https://www.dvidshub.net/image/2085574/secretary-defense-walks*.

131. Ned Parker, "Iraq PM Abadi retires two top generals after Islamic State conquests," Reuters, September 23, 2014, available from *https://www.reuters.com/article/us-iraq-crisis-army/iraq-pm-abadi-retires-two-top-generals-after-islamic-state-conquests-idUSKCN0HI1K320140923*.

CHAPTER 16

CONCLUSION: FROM SURGE TO WITHDRAWAL

The post-surge period was marked by dramatic changes in the character of the Iraq conflict and in the U.S. approach to it. By the end of 2008, the security situation had improved to a degree that had seemed unthinkable in early 2007, when U.S. casualties and incidents of violence had risen to their highest levels of the war. Where insurgent attacks inside Iraq had once averaged over 140 per day, by the end of 2008 the coalition routinely experienced days with no attacks at all throughout the entire country. The provincial elections of January 2009, in which Iraqi voters in almost every Arab province elected parties running on a nationalist law and order platform boded well for political stability as well. General Raymond Odierno and Multi-National Forces–Iraq (MNF-I) recognized the profound change in the character of the conflict, and as a result MNF-I and its units began to shift their focus from counterinsurgency to stability operations—the activities necessary to sustain the military victory won during the surge.

At the same time, however, interest in the United States was waning. By early 2009, the "Washington clock" that General Peter Petraeus had spoken about in 2007-2008 had run out. After the financial crisis of 2008, U.S. Government officials and American foreign policy experts began to argue that counterinsurgency was too costly during a time of shrinking resources. As a result, the Iraq strategy and plans put in place in early 2009 reflected limits on U.S. military activity rather than the idea that the surge had created opportunities that could be exploited.

After its signing, the 2008 U.S.-Iraq security agreement and its provision that U.S. troops would withdraw fully from Iraq by the end of 2011 loomed over every aspect of the U.S. military campaign. The agreement forced MNF-I to adjust its operations and plans in significant ways, such as the stipulation that U.S. troops would withdraw from Iraqi cities in June 2009, as well as new requirements for almost all U.S. units to coordinate their operations through their Iraqi military and police counterparts. The movement of U.S. troops out of the cities created vulnerabilities that al-Qaeda in Iraq (AQI) exploited in the massive autumn bombings of August-December 2009, which discredited the Maliki government to such an extent that it nearly collapsed.

As the date for withdrawal from the cities approached, civil-military cooperation suffered and the relationship between MNF-I and the U.S. Embassy devolved into a level of dysfunctionality equal to that between Combined Joint Task Force-7 (CJTF-7) and the Coalition Provisional Authority. Still, MNF-I and its civilian counterparts were able to cooperate closely enough to implement Odierno's vision of a "combined security mechanism," a de facto peacekeeping mission along the Green Line under which U.S., Iraqi, and Kurdish security forces operated and coordinated together to prevent the very real threat of an Arab-Kurdish war in the north.

While the Combined Security Mechanism was helping to stabilize northern Iraq, several factors were undermining Iraq's stability elsewhere. In 2010, the Sons of Iraq movement that had helped turn the tables in 2007-2008 began to wilt under pressure from AQI on one hand and the Maliki government on the other. The Iranian regime's Quds Force intensified its campaign to try to force the United States out of Iraq using militant proxies such as Kata'ib Hizballah and other Shi'a militias, while the Syrian regime of Bashar al Assad continued its involvement with AQI and other Sunni insurgents despite U.S. outreach to the Assad regime. Nevertheless, the Syrian regime could not save AQI from the most successful series of security operations of the entire war, which came in early 2010 and nearly destroyed the terrorist organization. The Iraqi political deadlock that ensued after the country's parliamentary elections of March 2010 undermined these successes by once again polarizing Iraqi politics along sectarian lines and setting Prime Minister Maliki against the Sunni political bloc associated with the Awakening. When the Arab Spring movement swept across the Middle East in 2011, the unpopular Maliki government found itself the target of popular disaffection because of the government's failure to improve governance and public services.

Against this backdrop, U.S. commanders raced against the clock in 2010-2011 to prepare the Iraqi security forces (ISF) to defend the country by themselves after the departure of U.S. troops, and the U.S. Army's specially designed Advise and Assist Brigades began to rotate to Iraq for that purpose. After United States Forces-Iraq's (USF-I) August 2010 change of mission from combat operations to advise and assist operations, however, USF-I leaders had fewer and fewer means with which to counter the Shi'a militants and other adversaries. By late 2010, USF-I leaders had to work hard to prevent retrograde operations from becoming the U.S. command's main effort. At the same time, commanders had to develop new tactics, techniques, and procedures for the Advise and Assist Brigades that operated "by, with, and through" Iraqi forces. USF-I commander General Lloyd Austin and his headquarters also had to conduct continual planning to push the "waterfall" (of the ultimate U.S. troop withdrawal) as far to the right as possible, thereby leaving the greatest number of forces in place and preserving options to the last possible moment in 2011 as the United States formulated its policy on troop strength in Iraq.

As U.S. troops prepared to depart the country, clear signs emerged that USF-I's main enemies were reemerging. Under new leadership and reinvigorated by the onset of the Syrian civil war, AQI rebounded during 2011 and began forming itself into what would eventually become the Islamic State in Iraq and Syria (ISIS). Shi'a militant groups, meanwhile, stepped up their attacks against U.S. troops in mid-2011 in an attempt to position themselves to gain credit for driving USF-I out of Iraq, as Lebanese Hizballah had done before the Israeli withdrawal from Lebanon in 2000. The Iranian-backed militias also conducted these attacks partly to better position themselves for political power in the post-U.S. period.

Even before 2011, USF-I leaders were seeing early signs of the deep problems within the ISF that would later cause that force to unravel in the face of ISIS in 2014. Austin noted in particular the difficulty within the ISF of maintaining complex weapons systems and performing logistics functions. At the same time, signs of Prime Minister Maliki's politicization of ISF leadership and establishment of regime protection forces—such as the Iraqi special operations forces—were unmistakable, pointing to the difficulty of completing a security assistance mission within a "sovereignty trap" in which a host nation government's aims diverge increasingly from our own, but that host nation remains the means by which we intend to secure our interests. Falling oil prices also led the Iraqi Government to cut the ISF's budget, making it impossible for USF-I and the ISF to remain on track with ISF development plans such as the generation of the new Iraqi Air Force. The

Iraqi Government also cut payments to the Sons of Iraq, partly due to its budget deficits and partly for sectarian reasons aimed at preventing a Sunni resurgence.

Most importantly for the completion of the USF-I mission, however, the effort to leave a residual force in place after 2011 failed. U.S. military plans did not anticipate the fall 2011 decision to withdraw all troops. These plans were based on mistaken assumptions that the State Department would have the capacity and the will to sustain USF-I's many military missions upon assuming control of the security assistance mission. The shift in security assistance and ISF development from military units to contractors failed after 2010, and at the same time, "soft power" did not fill the vacuum as U.S. military planners had assumed and officials in Washington had asserted.

As a result, at the end of 2011 the Office of Security Cooperation-Iraq—the organization created to assume the security assistance mission after USF-I's closure—was left in a situation similar to that of CJTF-7 in 2003: under-resourced and lacking the authorities and tools necessary to preserve U.S. interests. This mismatch of ends and means was more serious than U.S. Government leaders understood in 2011-2012, partly because of the U.S. misinterpretation of low reported levels of violence and the difficulty of maintaining situational awareness as U.S. forces drew down.

The unfortunate aftermath of the U.S. military withdrawal is now well known: in 2013, after a series of political moves by Maliki that alienated much of Iraq's Sunni community, the country began to return to a state of civil war. By the first week of 2014, Fallujah was back in insurgent hands, soon to become an ISIS stronghold. Five months later, in June 2014, Mosul fell to ISIS and the four Iraqi Army divisions in Ninewa and Salahadin Provinces evaporated. In the ensuing chaos, ISIS fighters advanced all the way to the outskirts of Baghdad and to the hinterland of Erbil, prompting a massive expansion by Iraq's Shi'a militia organizations to defend the country's capital. By the end of summer 2014, U.S. forces had begun to return to Iraq to stiffen the ISF and to conduct a new campaign against ISIS, but without the benefit of the military infrastructure the United States had shut down in 2011. The war that had begun in 2003 was far from over.

PART III:
FINAL CONCLUSIONS

CHAPTER 17

CONCLUSION: LESSONS OF THE IRAQ WAR

In a way, it would be reassuring to believe that the mistakes the United States made in the Iraq War were the result of unintelligent leaders making poor decisions. If that were so, then the United States could be assured of avoiding similar mistakes in the future simply by selecting better, more intelligent leaders. However, this is not the case. The overwhelming majority of decisions in the Iraq War were made by highly intelligent, highly experienced leaders whose choices, often in consensus, seemed reasonable at the time they were made, but nonetheless added up over time to a failure to achieve our strategic objectives. Examining the reasoning behind these decisions and the systemic failures that produced them should be the first task in analyzing the Iraq War's lessons. What follow are examinations of some of those key decisions, and in some cases their unintended consequences, as well as their implications for future wars.

SELECTED STRATEGIC IMPLICATIONS FOR FUTURE WARS

State Collapse

The operation to change the Ba'athist regime of Saddam Hussein escalated into the unintentional collapse of the Iraqi state, an outcome that went beyond U.S. objectives and for which the U.S. military was not prepared. Part of the Iraqi state was bound to collapse because of the U.S.-led invasion, but coalition provisional authority (CPA) orders 1 and 2 led to a far more sweeping implosion than U.S. leaders intended. A large part of the instability that followed between 2003 and 2011 was the predictable consequence of this implosion, after which factions of all kinds, including extremist militants, rushed to fill the void.

The invasion of Iraq showed that even an operation designed as a limited regime decapitation can precipitate state collapse in centralized, authoritarian political systems, after which must follow either martial law imposed by a large military presence or civilian authority prepared to step in and immediately assume responsibility for governance—itself a massive undertaking. If this does not happen, the void will at least partly be filled by malignant actors. In Iraq, coalition leaders made a conscious decision not to impose martial law in Iraq in the aftermath of the fall of Saddam's regime, but they also had not prepared an interim authority ready to do more than manage a humanitarian crisis that did not materialize. The resulting power vacuum and governance gap have never been fully filled by the post-Saddam Iraqi state.

Technology Does Not Always Offset Numbers

The Iraq War demonstrated that technological advancements only go so far in enabling reduction of our military end strength and our forces on the ground. Stability and counterinsurgency (COIN) operations in Iraq, and in general, are troop-intensive activities. In addition, irregular warfare by its nature is a political-military endeavor in which every operation has political implications, which is why establishing relationships with local Iraqis and developing an understanding of local socio-cultural dynamics was so important. That task requires human interaction more than it requires the application of technology. Against this backdrop, the de facto cap on U.S. troop strength in Iraq and the reduction of ground troops in the Army's transformed brigade combat teams (BCTs) combined to create an absolute shortage of ground forces for the prosecution of stability and COIN operations in Iraq. In future wars, the United States must guard against its historical American predilection to assume technology or qualitative warfighting superiority can be a substitute for troop numbers.

The Iraq War also highlighted the mistaken assumptions that influenced the pre-2003 debate over whether the U.S. military would—or should—be capable in the future of fighting two major regional conflicts simultaneously. In the pre-2003 period, U.S. military leaders and planners accepted that the United States need only maintain the combat power and forces required to win in one theater of war while holding in another, after which U.S. forces would be able to pivot to the second theater of war and win there as well—a concept nicknamed "win-hold-win." In the simultaneous conflicts in Iraq and Afghanistan—neither of which reflected the nature of a major regional conflict in defense planning—the U.S. military was not able to "win-hold-win." Instead, long-term stability operations severely taxed ground forces optimized for decisive conflict such as Operation DESERT STORM and created a shortage of ground forces. Strategic defeat was almost assured by artificial constraints on combat power in either theater and by this overall shortage of ground forces. This fact holds implications for potential future contingencies around the world. It is not clear, after the Iraq War, that the U.S. military has retained sufficient ground forces to fight successfully in more than one major regional conflict at a time. Furthermore, the inability of ground forces to accomplish the objectives of the win-hold-win concept indicate that the basic strategic premise itself is inadequate.

Coalition Warfare

The multinational coalition's political and diplomatic value for the United States was not matched by its operational effectiveness inside the Iraq theater. Coalition warfare was largely unsuccessful for several reasons. Following the model established in the Balkans, the U.S. military allocated independent division battlespace to the coalition partners in Multi-National Division-Central South (MND-CS) and Multi-National Division-Southeast (MND-SE), but in doing so uncoupled most of southern Iraq from the broader U.S. military campaign. The Polish-led MND-CS operated under strict national caveats that restricted its units in restive, Shi'a-militant-influenced areas of the country. In the British case, MND-SE became increasingly disconnected from Multi-National Corps-Iraq's (MNC-I) planning and operations, with both the U.S. command in Baghdad and the British command in Basra operating as though events in central Iraq and far southern Iraq were unrelated. As Iranian malignant influence mounted in 2006 and after, U.S. commanders pressed the British contingent in southern Iraq to disrupt the Islamic Revolutionary Guard Corps (IRGC) and its Shi'a militant proxies, a step that Whitehall prevented. When the United States adopted the surge strategy in 2007, the differences between the new U.S. approach in central Iraq and the British transition strategy in southern Iraq could not be reconciled.

These differences illustrated problems that stemmed from assuming the coalition's contributing nations held a common understanding of and commitment to the strategic objective. They did not. The success of any coalition depends on the establishment and maintenance of such a common understanding and commitment. Without these elements, the predictable result is coalition partners who operate with caveats that can become self-defeating.

The United Kingdom's (UK) operations in Iraq are a case in point. By 2006, the British Government had decided to withdraw its forces gradually from Iraq in order to increase significantly its troop presence in Afghanistan. This decision made deployments in Iraq and Afghanistan a zero-sum matter, a fact whose implications British policymakers apparently never discussed with their U.S. counterparts. The need to pull forces from Iraq to send to Afghanistan became even more critical after the 2003 strategic restructuring and defense cuts that dramatically reduced the size of the British Army began to take effect.[1] As a result, MND-SE was forced to reduce forces on a strict timetable, giving the command almost no flexibility as conditions changed. Resolving this strategic dilemma, as U.S. commanders in Baghdad wished to do, would have required discussions and an agreement between U.S. and British national leaders that did not take place.

Despite the disconnect between the operational commands in Baghdad and MND-SE, the British contribution in Baghdad was significant. Until mid-2009, when the British national contingent departed Iraq, British special operators played a crucial role in the fight against al-Qaeda in Iraq (AQI). British and Australian officers played key roles in Combined Joint Task Force-7 (CJTF-7), Multi-National Force-Iraq (MNF-I), MNC-I, and Multi-National Security Transition Command-Iraq (MNSTC-I) as well as MNSTC-I's North Atlantic Treaty Organization (NATO) element, NATO Training Mission-Iraq (NTM-I). Senior British officers often led MNF-I's planning, reconciliation, and governance efforts, exerting outsized influence on the conduct of the coalition campaign. Over the course of this 6-year interaction, the working relationship between U.S. and British officers grew increasingly close and eventually shifted to Afghanistan. From 2002 onward, a generation of U.S. Soldiers learned to assume that in any major operation they would be serving alongside British counterparts, especially at the operational level. From the British perspective, however, it is not clear that the same is true. Given the British Government and public's deeply negative view of the Iraq War, participation of British forces in future U.S.-led campaigns cannot be taken for granted.

The Iraq War also showed that the under-resourcing of defense forces by almost all our allies, including the United Kingdom, would require a new approach to the integration of allies into future campaigns. Throughout the 1990s, the U.S. military assumed that any large-scale U.S. operation would include major allies. In the future, we can no longer assume our allies will be willing to participate, at least on the terms we require; nor can we assume they will retain the military capabilities to add value to operations when they do. If countries with limited capabilities and overly restrictive national caveats participate in future conflicts as allies, the challenge of integrating them can be mitigated somewhat by diffusing coalition contingents across U.S. headquarters rather than giving allied contingents their own independent battlespace as was done in MND-SE and MND-CS.

Security Force Assistance and Security Sector Reform

U.S. national interests probably will require the military to conduct large-scale security force assistance in the future, either in conflict or outside of conflict, so the Army must sustain institutional capabilities for missions of this kind. Building indigenous foreign forces on a scale of the Iraq War requires a specialized force structure and training base within the conventional Army, not just special operations forces. The U.S. military may be called upon to stand up MNSTC-I or Combined Security Transition Command-Afghanistan type organizations in the future, and thus the Army should have the doctrine and force structure capable of doing so quickly. In Iraq, the Army waited 6 years before creating the Advise and Assist Brigades. In future conflicts, this should be done more rapidly, or it would be even better if the capability were retained in the peacetime Army.

In the future, security assistance and security sector reform must go hand in hand. Both are necessary; neither is sufficient by itself. In Iraq, the United States had to build military forces, self-sufficient administrative systems within the military and the Ministry of Defense, and law enforcement organizations. Building combat power through the construction of tactical units alone, as was done in the first 3 years of the Iraq War, was a short-term solution that squandered precious time and created an illusion of progress. Institutional development of combat support, combat service support, and ministerial functions must occur in parallel with the creation of tactical units.

Holistic security assistance means that the United States must also build law enforcement institutions. This includes police, a confinement system, and an adjudication system, yet in Iraq, the United States did not have an integrated approach. U.S. leaders assigned responsibility for the police function to MNSTC-I and provided congressionally approved Iraqi security force (ISF) funds, but they assigned the other two functions to the U.S. Embassy's Rule of Law Task Force, which could not access ISF funds. The result was a massive operational police force but an inadequate confinement and adjudication capability.

The effort to build an effective ISF also faced unity of effort challenges, with responsibility for local police, paramilitary police, and military forces assigned at various times to different departments within the U.S. Government. After 3 years, this problem was finally resolved when authority, responsibility, and funding for all security forces, to include the police, were assigned to the Department of Defense (DoD). In the future, such an arrangement should be the model. If regulatory or statutory change is not possible to attain unity of effort, organizations responsible for building non-military security forces—such as the police—must be appropriately organized and funded. They currently are not.

Building capable and independent security forces requires years, potentially decades, of interagency efforts. The insistence of senior military leaders, nearly consistently across the span of the Iraq War, that Iraqi forces would be able to stand on their own after "just" another year or two was counterproductive. If the United States is to undertake such projects in the future, senior military officers should caution their political leaders from the onset that their path will be long, slow, and frustrating. While such a commitment is costly, it does pay dividends. Maintaining involvement and presence not only helps protect the investment in training host nation security forces, but it also provides some degree of influence with local political leaders.

Democratization and the Sovereignty Dilemma

Since the early 20th century, the United States has assumed that democratization brings greater stability. However, as the post-September 11, 2001 (9/11), wars have shown, elections are not always stabilizing events. U.S. commanders long believed the emergence of an elected Iraqi Government would have a calming effect, but the elections of 2005 exacerbated ethno-sectarian conflict and contributed to the civil war that followed. The haste with which the Coalition carried out that process—holding two parliamentary elections, drafting a constitution, and hosting a referendum on that constitution—heightened tensions by raising the stakes of each event and provided insufficient time for reconciliation. Iraq went from the removal of the Ba'ath regime to an approved constitution in roughly 30 months. By comparison, the fledgling United States—a nation with a tradition of democracy and a robust civil society—spent 12 years navigating a similar path. Iraq's 2010 parliamentary elections were similarly destabilizing, providing Prime Minister Maliki a pathway to consummate his authoritarian and sectarian tendencies.

The Iraqi political process demonstrated one of the enduring problems with the American approach to COIN. Once a partner government feels that its survival is assured, the U.S. ability to influence it declines. This often means that the partner government will arrest reform and reconciliation programs before they are complete—especially programs that would threaten the political or economic elite. As a result, often the root causes of insurgency will remain intact and ready to flare back up under the right conditions. U.S. leaders will continue to confront these dynamics in the future as the United States works through host nation governments to advance its national interests. Overcoming such a deep challenge will require a counterintuitive application of U.S. national power. As security improves, the United States will likely have to increase its commitment of key elements of national power—especially within the economic and diplomatic realms—in order to maintain sufficient influence so as to build a lasting peace.

U.S. misperceptions regarding democratization and sovereignty were linked directly to another key strategic error. The United States equated the end of fighting with the end of the war, but war involves more than fighting. By focusing heavily on metrics involving violent incidents, U.S. leaders assumed that Iraq was more stable than it actually was. As a result, they deluded themselves about the length of commitment required and gave away tactical and operational successes only to achieve strategic failure. Strategic success would have required an acceptably stable state that Iraqis considered legitimately representative of majority and minority groups, but U.S. leaders struggled to define how to accomplish that objective and focused on comfortable tactical and operational tasks that were necessary but not sufficient.

The Role of External Actors

COIN and counterterrorism are exponentially more difficult if enemy groups enjoy sanctuaries, especially in neighboring countries. The United States must develop a whole-of-government approach for neutralizing such sanctuaries, which have posed a problem for the United States since the end of World War II. From an early stage in the war, Syria and Iran played a highly destabilizing role in Iraq. Both sought to bog the

U.S.-led coalition down to gain advantage in the regional political struggle and deter the United States from seeking regime change in their countries. They also opposed the creation of a new U.S.-allied Iraqi Government. They gave sanctuary and strategic assistance to the Sunni and Shi'a insurgencies, respectively, and contributed materially to the killing and wounding of tens of thousands of Iraqis and hundreds, if not thousands, of coalition troops. U.S. military and civilian leaders recognized this problem early in the war but never formulated an effective strategy for ending or even neutralizing it. U.S. leaders refrained from direct measures against those regimes, and instead left the matter to MNF-I, a U.S. theater command that could only operate against Syrian and Iranian operatives and proxies inside Iraq itself—with very rare exceptions. As a result, the Syrian and Iranian regimes became more and more emboldened. In particular, the Iranian regime produced sophisticated and lethal technology for their Iraqi proxies to use against U.S. troops, and U.S. forces had difficulty keeping up with the evolution of Iranian weapons such as explosively formed penetrators and improvised rocket-assisted munitions (IRAMs). These weapons killed and wounded scores of U.S. troops, but the United States responded to them only at the tactical and operational levels, not the strategic. By imposing artificial geographic boundaries on the conflict, the United States limited the war in a way that made it difficult to reach its desired end states.

The United States also never formulated a successful strategy for addressing the destabilizing influence of other regional states, including some U.S. allies. Turkey, Jordan, and the Gulf states all played roles of varying significance in Iraq, not all of them positive. The United States had difficulty persuading the Gulf States to crack down on terrorist facilitators who supported AQI and other Sunni militant groups in Iraq. The Jordanian Government was reluctant to crack down on facilitators and sympathizers for the Sunni insurgency based in Jordan. The Turkish Government came close to war with the Kurdistan Regional Government (KRG) on several occasions. The Turkish air and ground operations against the Kurdistan Workers' Party (PKK) inside Iraqi Kurdistan in 2007-2008 nearly collapsed the Iraqi governing coalition in Baghdad at a time when the United States was trying to parlay the security gains of the surge into political reconciliation. The United States also failed to persuade the Gulf States to fully embrace the new Iraqi Government and encourage its reintegration into the Arab world in political, economic, and security terms.

In any conflict with major regional implications, the United States must expect all of the countries in a region to respond to U.S. actions. From the initiation of hostilities, the motives and potential actions of regional players must be taken into account and an interagency response developed. In the Iraq War, U.S. leaders seemed to believe that other regional nations would not react. When they did, U.S. leaders rejected strategic action and instead chose operational or tactical responses. Although the United States should always be wary of expanding a conflict to other nations, U.S. leaders should consider the option of escalation—including with military power—when neighboring states become de facto combatants. In Iraq, the U.S. inability to find an effective response to Syrian and Iranian proxies made accomplishing our political and military objectives almost impossible.

Military Leadership and Strategic Implementation

Innovative commanders emerged during the war and were empirically successful, but the process of encouraging and institutionalizing innovations was uneven. It is also not clear that the Army rewarded their performance through the promotions process or by supporting the replication of their successful innovations. With only a few exceptions, it does not appear that the Army examined how the tactical leaders who innovated in Iraq became innovators in the first place. Most often, it appears they learned what was required through peer-to-peer interaction on the battlefield, not in institutional venues back home. Indeed, it seems that the most successful innovators were actually inverting policy rather than operating within policy, most notably in the case of the brigade and battalion-level COIN approaches of 2005-2006, which took place during a time of the transition strategy. This is a fact the Army has not really confronted, and it seems possible that the Army in the Iraq War actually tended to penalize successful leaders who challenged their commanders.

Some of these issues clearly extended to strategic leadership as well. Theater and operational commanders were continually forced to deal with problems that could only truly be resolved at the policy level, by higher authorities in Washington or in allied capitals. The two most significant examples were that Iraq theater commanders often operated without the benefit of a coherent regional strategy, and that Iraq theater commanders were forced to mitigate the national caveats and policies of coalition partners. In addition to these examples, at several points of the war—the surge most prominently—military leaders found themselves in the awkward role of defending strategy in the political realm. As a result, the line between military and political roles at times became blurred.

A better concept for the role of military leaders in war might be that of shared responsibilities of senior political and military leaders.[2] The belief in a hard line between the civil and military spheres is a mistaken one, and the experience of the post-9/11 wars has shown that, while civil leaders unequivocally retain final decision authority, military leaders should share the responsibility for ensuring the quality of important decisions. Specifically, military and civil leaders who embark upon war have a shared responsibility to ensure that war aims are achievable and that strategies, policies, and campaigns are tied to those aims and have a reasonable probability of success. It is also incumbent upon them to ensure, together, the integrity of the decision-making process and the fidelity of the information used in that process; the organizational capacity to execute in a sufficiently coherent way, then adapt quickly enough as change happens; and the sustained legitimacy of the war.

There is an organizational dimension to the implementation of these strategic factors. Future conflicts will require the integration of different elements of national power, but the U.S. interagency often lacks the capability of managing this integration. The current methodology of making policy via the National Security Council is sufficient for setting policy parameters, but it is insufficient for implementing and adapting. As Robert Komer noted in "Bureaucracy Does Its Thing," the U.S. system was too slow to adapt to the changing character and demands of the Vietnam war, and more than 3 decades later in Iraq, it remained too slow.

OPERATIONAL LESSONS

The Operational Impact of Key Policy Decisions

The Short-war Assumption. U.S. leaders and planners operated under the constant assumption that the war would be short. At no point in the war, even during the surge, did U.S. leaders believe the campaign was more than 18 or 24 months from the point when U.S. troops could be withdrawn and responsibility for security handed over to the Iraqis.

The short-war assumption drove DoD's planning, and the "patch chart" of units scheduled to deploy often drove operational planning in the theater. The same assumption, at times, drove procurement and modernization decisions, with the Army and Marine Corps often deciding to fund future capabilities ahead of the operational needs of the Iraq theater. Such a decision was wholly logical, given the assessment from the theater headquarters that the war would wind down within the next year or so. Some leaders, such as Secretary of Defense (SECDEF) Robert Gates, were able to overcome institutional inertia temporarily and champion procurement projects that met the immediate operational needs of the conflict, but in general, the bureaucracy still "did its thing."

The fact that U.S. leaders retained the short-war assumption for as long as they did created some long-term negative consequences within the U.S. military. One such consequence was the creation of a de facto "away team" and "home team" within the U.S. officer corps, wherein a population of officers in certain career fields, services, and units deployed much more frequently than the rest. This phenomenon, in turn, created a division in worldview among military leaders.

Constant Constraint on Force Levels. Throughout the war, the commands in Iraq had too few troops to accomplish their military missions. As a matter of policy, DoD leaders and strategic-level commanders enforced a de facto cap on U.S. troop strength in the Iraq theater and effectively discouraged lower-level commanders from requesting more troops. DoD and military leaders did this for a variety of reasons, including the belief that the U.S. ground services were too large, outdated and unwieldy, and therefore sending more troops to Iraq would hinder building more agile forces against future threats. Another reason for the force cap was the assessment that additional forces could be counterproductive by creating "antibodies" among the Iraqi public as well as a "dependency cycle" that could prevent the Iraqi Government and its security forces from taking full responsibility for their nation's security. Institutional concerns also loomed large, with Washington worrying that extended and back-to-back deployments would burn out and even cripple the all-volunteer force. Requirements from other theaters, namely Afghanistan, competed for limited resources in what became a zero-sum game. At other points in the war, the cap was driven by domestic political considerations.

The consequence of the troop cap was that at no point during the war, even during the surge period, did the in-country commanders meet their troop-to-task ratios or have enough troops to defeat both the Sunni insurgency (including AQI) and the Iranian regime-backed Shi'a militants simultaneously. The campaign to stabilize Iraq most likely required far more time than it would otherwise have needed as a result, time that ultimately would not politically be available. The dearth of U.S. troops in late 2003 and early 2004 gave room to the Sunni and Shi'a insurgencies to gather strength. As U.S. troops withdrew later in the war, it meant that their departure left the United States with little influence over the behavior, effectiveness, and development of the ISF, which were rendered far less capable and far more politicized as U.S. combat support waned.

The question of force levels was not just an operational one. Senior civilian and military leaders did not always make accurate assessments of the force levels required to perform the missions they assigned, nor put in place personnel policies that would make those force levels available. The problem was further exacerbated by a reluctance to increase the size of the Army and Marine Corps because of concerns that such an expansion would come at the cost of procurement and research and development.

Several steps should be taken to avoid these sorts of problems in future conflicts. First, strategy should be driven by the traditional method of balancing of ends, ways, and means rather than by force levels. This should be done in conjunction with civilian leadership as a part of the national security decision-making process. That process should include discussions on what is actually feasible at different force constraints, and should incorporate a continuous discussion about risk that matches the changing operational situation. Second, the assumption that U.S. Soldiers, by their mere presence, create ill effects must be banished from our strategic thought. While Iraqis chafed at the continued presence of U.S. Soldiers, many Iraqis also considered it essential for Americans to stay until their country was truly stabilized and self-sufficient. American military personnel consistently served as the most effective brake to sectarian conflict, with U.S. forces often acting as the only honest broker trusted by a majority of Iraqis.

Another important step to address potential future force constraint challenges would be for senior military leaders to consider increasing the size of the force, especially the Army and Marine Corps, as soon as the United States is committed to a major conflict. Repeatedly, the military has downsized after a major conflict to the degree that it does not have enough forces to fight the next war. This historical reality, when paired with the time required to obtain funding and authority for expansion, as well as the interval needed to recruit and train those new forces, makes early action essential. If the decision is not made early enough to increase the size of the force sufficiently, it is possible or even likely that, by the time that additional forces become available, they will arrive too late to have an operational effect. Senior military leaders should be extremely skeptical of assessments that a conflict will be over too quickly to benefit from such a growth. It is far easier to cancel such growth than to deal with the operational and strategic consequences of having insufficient forces.

Ad Hoc Organizations. After the invasion of April-May 2003, which was executed at the operational level by standing headquarters (U.S. Central Command [CENTCOM], Third Army, and V Corps), the war was fought by ad hoc organizations. Rather than use standing headquarters and commands, the Army and DoD chose instead to create new organizations to perform the functions of the theater command and its subordinate headquarters that handled the development of the ISF and detention operations. Almost all of the most important operational commands in Iraq, such as CJTF-7, MNF-I, MNSTC-I, and Task Force 134, were established mainly by joint manning documents and staffed by individual augmentees provided by the services. Only MNC-I did not fall into this category, since it was based upon the standing U.S. Army corps headquarters that rotated into theater on a yearly basis. The ad hoc commands all suffered greatly from low staffing at the outset, though MNF-I eventually grew far larger than its original design.

DoD leaders chose to use ad hoc organizations partly because they believed the Iraq War would be short and therefore large standing headquarters would be costly and unnecessary, and partly because they wished to keep the standing commands—such as CENTCOM and other army-level commands—available for other operations. The large, capable Coalition Forces Land Component Command (CFLCC), for example, sat under-utilized in Kuwait for the duration of the war, waiting to be used in a contingency that never came. The consequence of using an ad hoc manning process was that the U.S. operational commands in Iraq were mainly headquarters that did not train together, lacked cohesion, and suffered from high personnel turnover, all of which hampered their effectiveness. While the tactical units that fought the war avoided the pitfalls of the Vietnam war's year-long individual replacement program, the headquarters that planned and managed the conflict were saddled with exactly that burden.

Since the withdrawal of U.S. forces from Iraq in 2011, the trend toward ad hoc headquarters has accelerated as a number of standing headquarters have been eliminated or reduced as cost savings measures. V Corps, the headquarters that planned the invasion of Iraq, is no more; and the Army Service Component Commands (ASCCs), which could form the basis for a future CFLCC, have had their personnel authorizations cut nearly in half. In 2014, U.S. Army Central (ARCENT) had sufficient manpower to assume the mission immediately as a CJTF for operations in Iraq in addition to its ASCC duties. Today such a shift would not be possible. Given the concrete value that standing headquarters demonstrated repeatedly during the Iraq War, it would be wise to arrest, if not reverse, the near free fall reduction in their strength.

Army Transformation and the War. The Army's 2003-2004 decision to continue with transformation while fighting in Iraq and Afghanistan had severe operational implications. Army leaders decided that the transformation process would eventually produce a larger number of more capable BCTs for the Iraq theater and other contingencies, but by continuing with transformation in a time of conflict, they rendered some brigades unavailable for deployment as they were reorganized and refitted. The most serious consequence of this decision was the Army's need in 2005 to operationalize the strategic reserve, the Army National Guard, and deploy large portions of it to Iraq.

As a result, about half of the brigades deployed to Iraq during the 2005 rotation were National Guard units taking part in the first large-scale operational deployment of the National Guard since the Korean war. Though most of these units and individuals performed admirably, their deployment meant that for the make-or-break year of Iraqi elections, which President George W. Bush considered the critical period for his Iraq strategy, half of the Army brigades in theater were reserve units rather than more experienced and trained active component units.

The deployment of transformed brigades had other unintended consequences. The tactical improvements gained through transformation generally were offset by losses in troop strength in each brigade, a factor of critical importance in COIN operations. The Reconnaissance, Surveillance, and Target Acquisition (RSTA) squadrons, in particular, often proved unequal to their assigned tasks; and it would be hard to imagine a RSTA

624

squadron conducting a movement to contact as 3-7 Cavalry did while it fought its way to Baghdad in 2003. Breaking up division resources and decentralizing them into the transformed brigades also had other consequences. The demise of the Division Support Command and Division Artillery undoubtedly would make made it more challenging for a division commander to weight the main effort, and repeating the tactical success of the invasion could be more difficult. At times during the invasion, for example, all of the 3d Infantry Division's assigned and attached artillery battalions were firing in support of one brigade—a seemingly unrealistic scenario now that each brigade commander owns his own artillery battalion. While some of these division resources are making a fragile comeback, it is difficult to see how the partial reversals will have a decisive impact. When evaluated in the context of the Iraq War, transformation at best produced few concrete gains; at worst, it produced a net negative result.

Overly Optimistic Planning. Throughout the war, planners in DoD and in the theater assumed that the security situation in Iraq would improve over time, and that the theater would require fewer U.S. troops in the future. At no point other than in late 2006 and early 2007 did strategic thinking reflect the idea that the security situation could worsen and require more U.S. troops. U.S. military plans generally were aligned with General John P. Abizaid and General George W. Casey, Jr.'s assumption that the new Iraqi Government would be seen as legitimate and dampen militant resistance. The opposite proved to be true. U.S. military leaders stuck with the campaign plan of 2004-2005 even though several studies done in 2005—including the ones completed by MNF-I and U.S. Embassy Red Team in Baghdad—concluded that it was not succeeding. The planning of large operations such as IRAQI FREEDOM is a shared civil-military responsibility, and both military and civil leaders failed to reassess the appropriateness of the 2004-2005 campaign plan despite evidence that it needed to change. Senior military leaders and their staffs must be able to better identify strategic inflection points and alter their plans when such transitions occur.

The Understanding of the Environment Across the Force

Throughout the war, U.S. units suffered from a limited understanding of the operating environment in Iraq. In the prewar planning and the execution of the invasion, U.S. units did not understand the inner workings of the Ba'athist regime or the Iraqi security sector, and assigned too much importance to the formal structures of the government. Intelligence reports underestimated the impact of decades of international sanctions and their effects on Iraq's infrastructure and Iraqi society. The United States also did not understand the relationships and rivalries among the various Iraqi factions, political parties, communities, and tribes. As a result, U.S. units found it difficult to discern the enemy's strategic and operational intent throughout the war—and to discern the motivations of the factions and individuals that comprised the post-Saddam Iraqi Government and security forces. As a result, U.S. units' actions sometimes exacerbated preexisting conflicts among Iraqis, especially in cases in which Coalition forces inadvertently sided with one party against another in a long-standing local struggle. These struggles often appeared to be a matter of the Iraqi Government versus the insurgency (in which the Coalition naturally aligned with the representatives of the government) when in fact the disputes often long predated the 2003 invasion. Too often U.S. units were manipulated into taking part in local conflicts that were not necessarily germane to the broader fight against our enemies.

U.S. units also had difficulty understanding the relationships among the various enemy groups, so that early in the war they failed to detect, among an array of insurgent groups that appeared loose and disparate, the existence of an insurgency that could coordinate and synchronize its activities at the operational level across the country. In the mid-years of the war, U.S. forces also failed to detect deep fissures among insurgent groups—on both the Sunni and Shi'a sides—that might have been exploited to fracture the insurgency well before the Sunni Awakening. U.S. units also did not appreciate the degree to which the former regime elements in the Sunni insurgency were linked to AQI and other Islamist extremist groups, so that the Ba'athist role inside AQI was opaque to the United States when it evolved into an Iraqi-led organization in 2009-2010.

Because U.S. forces often did not understand the dynamics that drove local political conflict, they did not grasp the linkages between local conflicts and national politics. The dictum that "all politics is local" was truer in Iraq than we generally understood: virtually every powerful faction in the central Iraqi state owed its national-level strength to a local constituency. As a result, Iraqi political figures often became directly involved in local matters to preserve or advance their national-level power, to either the benefit or detriment of the coalition. Though the coalition often had limited leverage over Iraqi factions at the national level, our units had virtually unlimited power at the local level, where they could issue contracts to whomever they pleased, arrest whomever it was necessary to arrest, or partner with whomever it suited them to partner. Because U.S. leaders often did not understand the relationship between local politics and national politics, they rarely turned their ability to make or break any local Iraqi faction into advantage over national-level Iraqi factions or leaders.

Operational Art Considerations

The Army has not yet captured the operational art lessons of the Iraq War and incorporated them into doctrine or military education. At the time of this writing, Lieutenant General (Ret.) James M. Dubik's monograph, *Operational Art in Counterinsurgency*, remains one of just a few works on this topic. What follow are a series of lessons that the Army should incorporate into its doctrine on operational art.[3]

The Absence of an Operational Reserve. The constraint on U.S. force levels throughout the war meant that, aside from brief periods, the United States fought the Iraq War without an operational reserve inside the theater. At almost every stage of the war, U.S. forces inside Iraq were fully committed, meaning that U.S. commanders accepted more risk than U.S. doctrine would normally dictate. In several cases, U.S. commanders found it difficult to respond to operational-level surprises, such as the fall of Mosul in November 2004, the Samarra Mosque bombing in 2006, and the Basra and Sadr City battles of spring 2008.

In future conflicts, senior Army leaders should do everything possible to ensure that they have sufficient troops in theater to be able to maintain a capable reserve. In the case of Iraq, the reserve should have been at least two battalions in size and should have been a mechanized or Stryker force. If strategic constraints prevent leaders from having enough aggregate forces to task unassigned units to the mission, it is better to maintain a reserve and accept risk in some locations rather than go without. Assigning a unit that already has battlespace to be an "on call" reserve, as was the case in 2004, is not a viable option and has the potential to create catastrophic results for both the location requiring a reserve force and the location from which the "on call" reserve is inevitably pulled.

Economies of Force. The dearth of U.S. troops also meant that operational command-ers were forced to employ risky economies of force throughout the war, often under-re-sourcing areas that were important to Iraqi stability or to the enemy. The need to employ economies of force meant that U.S. commanders faced a constant tradeoff between the need to disrupt the Sunni insurgency's use of the Syrian border zone as a strategic base (and the Shi'a insurgency's similar use of the Iranian border zone) and the need to employ enough troops in central Iraq to secure and stabilize the Baghdad region. In the most costly instance of this tradeoff, MNF-I shifted significant combat power from central Iraq to the Syrian border zone in 2005, dealing the Sunni insurgency tactical defeats in its border sanctuaries but leaving the Baghdad region open to sectarian violence that almost tore the country apart. At no point in the war, even during the surge, did U.S. command-ers have enough forces at their disposal—either U.S. or Iraqi—to operate at an adequate level in both central Iraq and the border zones.

While nearly every military commander throughout history probably has wished for more forces, in Iraq, some of the causes of the malady of insufficient forces were self-induced. Particularly during the 2005-2006 timeframe, senior commanders sought to "starve" U.S. forces of manpower in order to force them to turn over more responsibility to Iraqis. This was thought to be a method that would empower and prepare the Iraqis more quickly to take responsibility for their own security, thereby attaining the theater end state more quickly. In reality, it had the opposite effect, creating considerable gaps in the coalition's situational awareness and propelling the country more quickly toward civil war. Future operational leaders should recognize the ill effect of purposely creating risky economies of force and determine better methods of transitioning responsibility to host nation forces quickly.

Boundaries. Too often, coalition unit boundaries did not take local political, social, or tribal dynamics into account, thereby hampering a unit's effectiveness and creating seams that our enemies could exploit. The U.S. units that occupied Iraq in 2003 made boundary choices that reflected U.S. military doctrine but sometimes made little sense in the Iraqi context. The most significant early example was the inclusion of Diyala in MND-North Central's (MND-NC) area of operations. Diyala was separated from much of the rest of the MND-NC area of operations by the Hamrin Mountains and was more linked to Baghdad than to the Tigris River Valley. This decision also artificially cut the upper Tigris River Valley, an insurgent hotbed, into two separate division areas of operation. Not until late 2005 were Mosul and Tikrit finally included in the same division area of operations, and even then, the Diyala Valley remained part of MND-North's (MND-N) battlespace.

Similarly, the unfortunate arrangement of MND-CS's battlespace made first Karbala and Najaf, and later Diwaniyah, artificially separate from the other major cities of central southern Iraq, creating many seams that the Sadrist insurgency and the IRGC Quds Force could exploit. Finally, at various times the vast Jazeera area north of the Euphrates—the

Ba'athist regime's main smuggling area during the 1991-2003 sanctions period—was a seam between MNF-West (MNF-W) and MND-N which the Sunni insurgency heavily exploited.

To address these issues, boundaries must be constantly reevaluated, perhaps to the point of creating a doctrinal mandate to review unit boundaries quarterly or at least semi-annually during sustained conflicts. In Iraq, with a few notable exceptions, shifting unit boundaries usually only occurred because of the surge or withdrawal of coalition forces. Even in those cases, often little thought was given as to how to restructure boundaries. In the future, boundaries must be reviewed on a recurrent basis to assess whether they adequately reflect the changing human terrain and enemy situation.

Key Terrain. The coalition's arrangement of battlespace also failed in some cases to emphasize properly Iraq's key terrain. The most significant example of this was that from 2003 through 2006, the coalition's operational commands did not recognize the importance of the "belts" around Baghdad and their critical role in securing the city. Only in late 2006 did MNC-I realize what most Iraqis knew: that Iraqi Governments had for decades used the belts to secure the approaches to Baghdad and that the belts had been the basis of Saddam's plans to defend the capital in 2003. From an early stage, AQI considered the belts vital to control Baghdad. Later the IRGC Quds Force and Badr Corps intended to use them to cleanse the Baghdad region of Sunnis. Nevertheless, not until the arrival of III Corps in late 2006 did the coalition formulate a comprehensive plan to control the belts.

It has become almost a cliché for operational level planners to assess a nebulous "will of the people" or "public support" as the center of gravity in a conflict against insurgents. While these issues are critical, they are more appropriately strategic centers of gravity and reflect tasks that do not fall wholly within the military's purview. At the operational level—even in fights against insurgents and other irregulars—key terrain is still important and ignoring this fact is perilous. The U.S. military should reemphasize the doctrinal importance of terrain in insurgencies, noting that guerrillas need logistics bases, training areas, sanctuaries, and areas from which to launch large-scale attacks. Human terrain matters, but so does geographic terrain.

Decentralized Assets for a Decentralized Fight. The U.S. force that invaded Iraq in 2003 was trained to maneuver and fight in divisions, meaning that scarce assets such as intelligence, surveillance, and reconnaissance (ISR) and fire support were managed at division or corps level. As the war proceeded, U.S. operations became increasingly decentralized to the brigade and battalion level, and over time enabler resources such as ISR were pushed to lower and lower levels. By 2009, some battalion commanders controlled more unmanned aerial vehicles (UAVs) and intelligence assets than the V Corps commander had in the 2003 invasion.

In institutional terms, the Army needs to further integrate operational decentralization in its organizational structures (tables of organization and equipment [TOEs]), rather than having units returning from a combat zone turn in the equipment and assets useful to them in war and recreate their prewar TOEs.

Transitions

The decision to rotate units into the theater on an annual basis had significant implications for operations, as many units that rotated into the theater tended to only formulate plans that extended to the end of their 1-year rotation. Those plans often sought to conduct a successful 1-year campaign based on new approaches rather than sustaining whatever the units that preceded them had been doing. As a result, U.S. units tended to emphasize quick but sometimes short-lived effects rather than longer-term stability. In one example early in the war, U.S. leaders rejected as too slow Brigadier General David Perkins's suggestion to build a new electrical infrastructure that would meet Baghdad's full demand within 3 years. Perkins then returned to the theater 3 years later to find that no major upgrades to the Iraqi electrical grid had taken place, and Baghdad's demand still far outpaced supply.

The turbulent unit transitions that took place at least once a year also hampered relationships between coalition units and local Iraqis. U.S. units came and went so frequently that productive relationships were forgotten. Often the extensive knowledge about the local operating environment that units developed was not fully transmitted to incoming units. This was made worse by the frequent changes that accompanied the drawdown of U.S. troops.

A potential solution could have been to align brigades and divisions permanently to one theater and one specific area of operations until the cessation of hostilities or the withdrawal of forces. Under such a model, if a brigade operated in west Baghdad on its first deployment, it would expect to be deployed to that same area—even to the same forward operating bases (FOBs) and joint security stations (JSSs) if possible—for the remainder of the conflict. When that brigade redeployed to its home station, it would remain in virtual contact with the unit that replaced it, even reading its classified daily reports and conversing with the deployed unit's leadership. Such a pattern, used by special operations units for the majority of the war, could have created long-term buy in and commitment for coalition forces and Iraqis alike as the unit would know that their actions had long-term relevance. It might not be possible to assign units always back to their same area of operations given the turbulence associated with Army transformation and the ebb and flow of overall force structure. However, it would have been better than the haphazard assignment of forces that often saw brigades switched not only across different provinces in Iraq, but also between the Iraqi and Afghan theaters.

A second potential solution would be to deviate from the normal command rotational schedule, keeping commanders in key positions such as brigades, divisions, and corps headquarters deployed for multiple years or even the duration of the conflict. While such a solution would undoubtedly be an incredible personal and family burden, it would almost certainly have alleviated the dilemma of repeated annual transitions. Nor would such a solution be without historical precedent. In the Civil War and World War II, senior leaders knew that they were committed for the duration of the conflict, itself a considerable motivating factor to achieve success. Similarly, during the post-9/11 conflicts, some senior special operations commanders remained deployed for years at a time, and Casey commanded MNF-I for 2½ years.

Metrics

Throughout the Iraq War, U.S. operational commands found it difficult to determine whether their plans were succeeding or failing, especially as conditions in the theater changed. U.S. commanders and their staffs never came to a consensus on what they ought to be measuring to know whether their units were effective. For most of the war, units and civilian agencies tended to measure their activities or inputs rather than the outcome of those activities: money spent, Iraqis trained, insurgents killed or captured, or other such measures. Until 2006, the coalition essentially measured success by the holding of Iraq's three elections, the generation of ISF, and the drawdown of coalition troops. During the surge, the United States emphasized the completion of "benchmarks" to gauge strategic progress. But for both the pre-2007 measures of success and the 2007 benchmarks, it would have been possible to show progress in every specified metric but still fail in the overall mission—exactly the situation in which the coalition found itself in late 2006. For future operations, the Army must reexamine its measures of effectiveness, and U.S. units must have better ways of determining whether they are succeeding in their missions.

At a different level, the Army should consider reassessing trends that emphasize the use of metrics at the expense of difficult to measure professional judgment. In some ways, Army leaders have become too enamored with the "fetishization" of statistics and metrics.[4] At times in Iraq, metrics and statistics were seen as hard truths or facts, when they often only provided a snapshot in time of a portion of the situation. Examples of this phenomenon include the transition readiness assessment, the size of the Iraqi security forces, and the calculation of whether U.S. brigades could be withdrawn in 2006. While our Army relishes quoting Carl von Clausewitz, in practice we have come to rely excessively on the Jominian theory of war and its emphasis on scientific method, an imbalance that requires adjustment. As a force, we should re-emphasize the traditional German military concept of "Fingerspitzengefuhl," which loosely can be considered a commander's sense and intuition of the battlefield in making decisions.

Iraqi Security Force Development

The years-long effort to create a self-reliant and effective ISF failed for a variety of reasons, highlighting the extreme difficulty and complexity inherent in building another nation's institutions. Though the development of the ISF was often named as the U.S. operational commands' main effort, it was never the top priority in terms of resources or manpower. The main vehicles for developing the ISF (MNSTC-I and the transition teams) were under-resourced for most of the war. The 2005 decision to have specialized units and transition teams rather than regular brigades and divisions lead ISF development meant that the mission never received the full attention of DoD or the theater command. For better or worse, the development of the ISF was effectively a secondary mission for most U.S. units until the arrival of the Advise and Assist Brigades in 2010.

The development of the ISF also suffered from disunity of effort for the first 2½ years of the war when the theater command did not have unified responsibility for the security ministries and their forces. Even after MNF-I gathered all ISF development functions under MNSTC-I at the end of 2005, MNC-I and MNSTC-I did not unify their campaign plans until mid-2007 when Dubik and Lieutenant General Raymond T. Odierno synchronized the generation of Iraqi forces with MNC-I's campaign plan so that the ISF's force generation and replenishment directly supported MNC-I's counteroffensive.

Dubik and Odierno modeled their relationships with the ISF on the one within the U.S. Army between the Training and Doctrine Command (TRADOC) and U.S. Army Forces Command (FORSCOM). Dubik and MNSTC-I, as the ISF's de facto TRADOC, took responsibility for the ISF's initial training, retraining, and brigade-level combat training center. Odierno and MNC-I, as the ISF's de facto FORSCOM, used embedded transition teams and unit partnership to continue training in the field. When the operational commands adopted this approach in 2007, it helped achieve a greater unity of effort for ISF development.

The most significant problem in building the ISF was failing to account for the political pressure upon and corruption within the Iraqi forces. Too often, the coalition generated Iraqi military or police units or assisted offices of the Ministry of Defense or Ministry of Interior without fully understanding the ways in which political networks extended into the security forces and security ministries. Rarely did the coalition's intelligence-gathering apparatus invest as much effort in understanding the ISF and the Iraqi Government as it did analyzing the enemy. Iraqi commanders often operated under political pressures their coalition counterparts could not discern or answered to familial or political connections that were opaque, all of which made their behavior and decision making seem at times inexplicable and made full partnership between coalition and Iraqi units difficult to achieve.

Addressing this problem, likely one of the most vexing of the entire war, is not easy. Its roots return to the U.S. decision to transfer sovereignty to the Iraqis in June 2004—an action that was originally intended to occur years later. Once sovereignty is returned to a defeated or collapsed power, a large degree of control over the construction of that state's institutions is lost. As difficult as it would be, given the host nation's political push to return sovereignty as soon as possible, every effort must be made to delay the transfer of power to allow institutions to incubate under the umbrella of international protection from corruption. The longer institutions are able to grow without the threat of corruption and political pressure, the more likely those institutions will be able to resist them on their own. Furthermore, in Iraq, U.S. leaders usually acted as if the issue of sovereignty was black and white—once sovereignty had been granted, the United States should completely acquiesce to the will of the newly sovereign nation. While respecting sovereignty has usually been a bedrock of U.S. values and foreign policy, it does not mean that the United States should not apply the appropriate levers in order to convince host nation leaders to make the best decisions. As one U.S. general remarked to Army historians, the United States had the money and guns to try to influence Iraqi policy—including the selection of security force leaders—but often gave both away without caveat or condition.[5]

The Iraq War was the scene of a long debate between using standing units to develop host nation security forces through partnership and using specialized, ad hoc transition teams. Transition teams often faced challenges that inhibited their performance, including poor cohesion, insufficient size, lack of unity of command, and haphazard staffing. As a result, their efforts to prepare ISF were inconsistent. By contrast, standing units partnered with Iraqi forces experienced few of the problems that beset transition teams. While such a solution still had considerable challenges inherent to the monumental task of rebuilding a nation's security forces and infrastructure, it appears that using standing units is the best approach to developing foreign indigenous forces. Constructing the ISF was also hindered by a series of decisions that inhibited their effectiveness from the tactical to the institutional level. Formal partnership between U.S. advisors and Iraqi units often focused on staff functions and rarely occurred below the battalion level, preventing growth at the squad, platoon, and company level: the basic building blocks of tactical formations. Logistics functions were not built in parallel with tactical units, crippling the long-term ability of the Iraqis to sustain themselves and creating additional opportunities for corruption. Similarly, armor and artillery formations, as well as engineers, were neglected initially, delaying the possibility of developing true combined arms capabilities. Combined together, these decisions enfeebled ISF development and delayed transition of security responsibilities to Iraqi forces.

Detainees

Throughout the war, U.S. forces struggled with the question of what to do with the enemy captured on the battlefield. Having decided at the outset not to treat them as prisoners of war who may be detained legally until the cessation of hostilities, the United States never found a workable solution to the problem of handling "security detainees" or "enemy combatants" within a sovereign nation. The improvised systems for reviewing whether detainees were a security risk were so imperfect as to allow large numbers of Sunni insurgents in particular to return to the battlefield. So pervasive was this phenomenon that most of the senior Iraqi leaders of AQI and later ISIS were at one time in U.S. custody but let go, including ISIS leader Abu Bakr al Baghdadi. The political dynamics that dominated the Iraqi Government, meanwhile, created a similar result among captured Shi'a insurgents, a large number of whom were released back onto the battlefield because of pressure from Baghdad or by the terms of the 2008 U.S.-Iraq security agreement.

The phenomenon of insurgents reappearing on the battlefield repeatedly after U.S. troops captured them created a deep level of distrust between the tactical units who fought and captured the militants and the higher echelon commands that designed policies that released them. The perception that the operational commands were following a "catch and release" policy became widespread among U.S. units, so much so that the detainee policies created perverse incentives among U.S. troops, especially on operations against militants who had been previously captured and released. The repeated reappearance of militants on the battlefield also undermined the Iraqi population's confidence in the coalition and gave life to conspiracy theories that the United States was releasing dangerous fighters back into the war in order to perpetuate sectarian conflict.

The likelihood that U.S. forces will continue to operate against militias or insurgents in the future means that the detention conundrum that began in Afghanistan and Iraq will recur. The Army must relook its doctrine, training, and organization for detention operations and ensure that it is as appropriate for the handling of security detainees as it is for the handling of enemy prisoners of war. At the national level, the United States should lead an effort to revisit and potentially update portions of the Geneva Conventions and international law to reflect the current environment of nonstate actors and multinational terrorist organizations who exploit loopholes within current detention protocols.

At the same time, military leaders should press for a revision of U.S. policies that led to detainee problems in Iraq. If, in future conflicts, the United States again chooses to regard its captured enemies as something other than enemy prisoners of war, then U.S. leaders can expect once again to see the enemy released back onto the battlefield repeatedly through imperfect security review procedures, to see detainee abuse cases emerge, and to see our troops forced into debilitating moral dilemmas.

Multinational and Interagency Campaign Planning

Iraq showed that the United States needs better doctrine for strategic campaign planning. The United States and its coalition allies invaded Iraq without the detailed civil-military plans necessary to stabilize the country after regime change. Over time, the theater command and the U.S. Embassy developed sophisticated plans for meeting coalition objectives in Iraq, but they did so in an ad hoc fashion, by trial and error. General David H. Petraeus and Ambassador Ryan C. Crocker refined multinational and interagency planning in the Joint Strategic Assessment Team and Joint Campaign Plan of 2007, which Odierno and Austin later carried forward, but these processes have not been captured in U.S. doctrine.

At no point during the war was the joint campaign planning that took place in Baghdad matched by similar interagency planning or synchronization in Washington. Future conflicts will require the integration of many different elements of national power, but the Iraq War showed that the United States currently lacks the capability of managing this integration. The United States should actively support regulatory or statutory changes such as a "Goldwater-Nichols" for interagency reform. At a minimum, such reform should include interagency assignments as a requirement for General Officer or Senior Executive Service level promotions; increased funding for civilians to attend military schooling at all levels (basic course, advanced course, command and general staff college, as well as senior staff college); mandatory civilian participation at combat training centers (CTCs), battle command training programs (BCTPs), and other training; and creation of a civilian quick reaction corps with short notice deployments included in their recruitment contracts.

Conventional-SOF Integration

At the outset of the Iraq War, U.S. conventional and special operations forces were unaccustomed to operating together in the same area. U.S. military doctrine at that time encouraged a segregation of conventional forces and special operations forces (SOF) into different areas of operation, and this was the way U.S. forces conducted the invasion of 2003. As the coalition settled into largely static geographic areas of operation after the invasion, conventional and SOF units found it necessary to share battlespace. For at least the first 2 years of the war, this arrangement was often awkward, as conventional commanders often found SOF raids disruptive and uncoordinated, while SOF commanders sometimes found conventional units constraining to the SOF mission. As early as fall 2003, however, conventional and SOF commanders found ways to integrate their operations, and by 2005 Casey and MNF-I sought to institutionalize these methods at the theater level. By the time of the surge, most SOF and conventional units in Iraq had become highly adept at synchronizing their operations, able to generate intelligence, coordinate targeting, and execute operations together with astonishing speed—a factor that created heavy pressure on AQI in particular and nearly resulted in that organization's defeat in 2010. A generation of tactical commanders in both conventional and SOF units learned how to operate together between 2003 and 2011, to devastating effect. As with the war's other innovations, the integration of special and conventional operations is a perishable skill that will atrophy over time if it is not captured in U.S. military doctrine, training, and organization. As one U.S. general officer observed after 2011, "everyone will be inclined to return to their own corners now."[6]

Some Army leaders have also noted the role reversal between SOF and conventional units: before the 9/11 attacks, foreign internal defense (FID) had been nearly exclusively the role of special operations forces, specifically the Army Special Forces regiment. Special Forces groups were oriented regionally and considerable effort and expenditure was put into training their personnel to speak foreign languages and understand different cultures. The doctrinal mission of direct action, while still one of the regiment's core tasks, was not of equal importance to FID. During the wars in Iraq and Afghanistan, Army Special Forces groups increasingly focused on direct action, leaving large-scale FID missions to conventional forces—as is the case, at the time of this writing, in much of Operation INHERENT RESOLVE. It appears, for example, that the doctrinal guideline that a Special Forces Operational Detachment Alpha (ODA) should train a host nation battalion was ignored during certain periods of both conflicts. While this report recognizes U.S. special operations forces will never be of sufficient size to rebuild an entire country's security forces, its leaders should revisit the current imbalance between FID and direct action, and shift the focus of Special Forces groups back toward their more traditional role in FID.

The Role of the Reserve Component

At an individual level, reserve component troops made significant contributions to the war. The operational commands could not have been staffed without them, especially as changes in the operating environment required the creation of new organizations to deal with specific problems, such as Task Force 134.

At the unit level, the Army's 2004 decision to operationalize the nation's strategic reserve, the Army National Guard, had important implications inside the Iraq theater. This was especially true during the pivotal election year of 2005, when the National Guard provided 8 of the 16 Army brigades in the theater. The majority of National Guard units and commanders performed well, especially at the platoon and company level. But the difficult experiences of the 48th BCT in the Triangle of Death, 1-184 Infantry Regiment in Baghdad, 2-28 BCT in Ramadi, and 278th Regimental Combat Team (RCT) in Kirkuk—all in 2004-2006—left senior U.S. commanders with the impression that assigning battlespace to National Guard brigades carried significantly more risk than assigning battlespace to active brigades. As a result, MNF-I did not assign brigade or division battlespace to National Guard units again until 2009. The increased title 10 burden the National Guard will have in a shrinking Army requires significant reforms. Additional

funding is required to ensure Guard units are equipped on par with active forces, personnel rules should ensure deployable units are fully staffed, and policies should increase
the number of mandatory annual training days.[7]

The Role of Contractors

The U.S. military's reliance on contractors to provide services and other support in
theaters of war, a development that followed the drawdown of uniformed U.S. troops in
the 1990s, gave them a critical role throughout the Iraq War. This trend accelerated when
senior military and civilian leaders substituted force management levels or troop limitations for traditional strategic reviews. As a result, contractors performed military support
tasks that the units in Iraq could not do themselves, such as some logistics functions, part
of the training of the ISF, and even the securing of large coalition bases. At some points
in the war, the coalition had more contractors inside the theater than uniformed troops.

Contractors came with their own challenges, however. Before the surge period, the
operational commands did not have reliable systems for tracking the activities and
locations of contractors, meaning that they occasionally disrupted military operations
or strayed into dangerous situations without the awareness of battlespace owners. In
addition, the Iraqi population mostly did not distinguish between the actions of coalition military units and Western contractors and often held the coalition responsible for
contractors' negative activities. The most significant case was the Blackwater contractors'
killing of 17 Iraqis in Nisour Square in Baghdad in September 2007, an incident that had
strategic implications for the remainder of the war because it made the Iraqi Government
deeply reluctant to accept the presence of U.S. and coalition contractors without legal
restrictions on their activities.

MNSTC-I faced two contractor-related issues. First, the requirements in theater
changed faster than the contracting system could accommodate. The late summer 2007
decision by coalition commanders that the police development contract should be
changed to the advising of provincial chiefs of police took 8 months to implement, far too
long for the operational needs of the campaign. Second, contracts in which contractors
phase themselves out of work—a necessary part of "phasing in" host nation security
forces to do the job themselves—are hard to write and provide incentives for contractors
to underperform. In one case, coalition commanders realized in 2007 that the MNSTC-I
contract to train the Iraqi National Police had failed—in 3 years—to produce a single
policeman capable of training his fellow Iraqis. When the contract was passed to the
Italian Carabinieri, the paramilitary force produced an Iraqi training cadre capable of
instructing students in just 6 months.

The Importance of Headquarters

U.S. senior commanders learned over the course of the war to value tactical and operational headquarters. Stabilization and COIN operations generated a myriad of nonstandard tasks that often required the hands-on involvement of leaders, such as engagements
with political, ISF, or tribal leaders. Many of these tasks endured even as U.S. units gave
up responsibility for tactical security so division, brigade, and battalion headquarters
continued to play central roles in the campaign even as their companies and battalions

drew down. In some cases, missions required a full headquarters structure but few troops, such as the Combined Security Mechanism, the peacekeeping-style mission created by Odierno to prevent Arab-Kurd conflict along the disputed boundaries in northern Iraq.

U.S. commanders also learned the consequences of using ad hoc, joint manning document headquarters rather than standing headquarters. Time after time, when creating new organizations in Iraq, DoD and CENTCOM relied on ad hoc headquarters rather than standing army, corps, or division headquarters, only to see the new organizations suffer from a lack of cohesion, inadequate training and proficiency, and low staffing. Senior leaders such as Petraeus concluded from their experience in Iraq that a standing headquarters of any kind will always outperform an ad hoc, individual augmentee-filled organization. Yet DoD favored ad hoc joint headquarters for a variety of reasons: to ensure all the services contributed to the headquarters; to leave standing commands intact for other contingencies and war plans; and because U.S. leaders assumed the missions for which the ad hoc organizations had been created would be short and need not disrupt future plans and operations. Iraq showed the pitfalls of such an approach.

The Role of the Division

The 2003 invasion was fought by divisions maneuvering through battlespace and synchronizing the operations of their brigades and other assets. Once the coalition divisions took up largely static areas of operation after the invasion, the proper role of the division in the broader campaign was not entirely clear. Over time, the management of the Iraq campaign was decentralized to the brigade level. As the modular brigades became severed from their organic division headquarters, frequently operating under the control of divisions with whom they had little familiarity, divisions sometimes had difficulty finding an appropriate role in synchronizing tactical activities. In some extreme cases, divisions acted as the equivalent of area support groups for diverse and sometimes only loosely coordinated brigade operations, especially divisions with vast battlespace and diverse operating environments. In other cases, divisions found a productive role in maintaining an operational-level enemy picture and coordinating brigade and battalion operations to overcome seams that insurgents might exploit.

In either case, the Iraq War did not yield a clear picture of the future operational role of the division. Some divisions took on a level of responsibility, management of assets, and control of territory equivalent to that of a traditional corps headquarters. At the height of the surge, for example, Multi-National Division-Baghdad (MND-B) controlled five U.S. brigades, but also exercised de facto control, or at least controlling influence, over four Iraqi divisions, tens of thousands of Iraqi police, and more than 50,000 Sons of Iraq. Similarly, in some cases U.S. brigades took on a level of responsibility equivalent to or even exceeding that of a traditional U.S. division. In 2007, Colonel Ricky Gibbs's 4th Brigade, 1st Infantry Division controlled no fewer than nine U.S. battalions and exercised de facto control of thousands more Iraqi troops. In the same year, Colonel Michael Kershaw's 2d Brigade, 10th Mountain Division, had slightly over 5,000 U.S. troops in the "Triangle of Death" south of Baghdad, but also exercised de facto control over more than 20,000 Iraqi troops and Sons of Iraq, giving 2d Brigade, 10th Mountain Division, more manpower and a span of control greater than that of a standard U.S. division.

Stability Operations

Stability operations are a crucial part of fighting and winning the nation's wars. However, large-scale stability operations require specialized skills and troop-to-task ratios. A stability operation on the scale of Iraq is likely to require more specialized expertise and combat support than the Army currently retains in its inventory. If—or when—tasked again to undertake a large-scale stability operation, the Army must be better prepared to deploy quickly combat support capabilities and specialized personnel. To do so, the Army should both maintain the civil affairs growth that occurred over the last decade and continue to balance stability training with combined arms maneuver training. At the same time, certain capabilities could be effectively "warehoused" within TRADOC to be able to be reactivated on short notice. Such capabilities would include military governance, economic reconstruction, agricultural development, human assessment teams, and military assistance and advisory teams, at a minimum.

Strategic Communications

The coalition was never able to keep pace with the enemy's strategic communications. Its process was reactive, bureaucratically slow and centralized, and not considered a critical mission. Commanders often remarked that strategic communications required approval at corps and force level—or often higher. One commander in south Baghdad noted that he could not obtain corps approval to display a billboard or distribute leaflets featuring a wanted insurgent, but that he incongruously had the authority to drop joint direct attack munitions (JDAMs) on insurgent positions or buildings. The coalition's inability to influence the informational battlespace in a timely manner or to provide the necessary authorities to commanders who were engaged in a decentralized and local conflict was a symptom of the U.S. military culture that did not place a high priority on strategic communications or information operations and a U.S. Government averse to the risks associated with fighting a war of ideas. As the world becomes more reliant on digital information, this challenge will become more acute, as most Army tactical capabilities are still primarily flyer, leaflet, and loudspeaker platforms. Engaging in the digital conflict of ideas in real time or near real time, as our adversaries already do, will require structural, doctrinal, and legislative change across the joint and interagency spectrum.

TACTICAL AND OPERATIONAL INNOVATIONS

The tone of this study of the Iraq War often has been critical, highlighting the significant errors from which the United States and the Army must learn, but this is not meant to overshadow the Army's significant tactical and operational adaptations and innovations. The units deployed to Iraq made strides in COIN warfare, stabilization operations, counterterrorism, security assistance, and many other areas that would have been unthinkable in 2003. This flexibility and adaptability will be important for generations of future leaders who may face similar tactical and operational problems. What follows is a selection of some of the more significant innovations and adaptations.

The initial adaptation to COIN from 2003 to 2006. Well before the publication of a COIN manual in December 2006, U.S. units had made great progress in applying such an approach in their areas of operation. Many units demonstrated surprising flexibility in rediscovering and applying COIN tactics—albeit unevenly—often without any support from their institutional and educational systems. The campaign histories of 2003-2006 are replete with such examples of units and commanders who taught themselves to fight in a way they had not been instructed to do.

Agility from 2006 onward in reconciliation at the local level. Agile, flexible, and open-minded commanders and units made the Awakening possible. Later, U.S. units displayed great creativity in synchronizing bottom-up and top-down political accommodation, so that by the time of the surge, battalion and brigade commanders had invented the concept of "maneuvering to reconciliation"—i.e., planning security operations with a view to opening up new reconciliation initiatives. In 2007, the operational commands created an entire infrastructure to manage and enable the Sons of Iraq, while creating the Force Strategic Engagement Cell (FSEC) to parlay local cease fires into political progress wherever possible. These innovations had little to guide them in existing doctrine.

The use of Commanders' Emergency Response Program (CERP) funds. Army commanders and units developed the capacity and knowledge to use money as a COIN and stabilization tool, so much so that by 2007 most leaders acknowledged that money for projects had become as important as ammunition on the battlefield. By then, the pre-2003 practice of centralized control of small funds by contracting officers and field ordering officers had given way to spending billions of dollars by U.S. units across a spectrum ranging from microeconomic projects to much larger-scale initiatives such as paying of the Sons of Iraq. While considerable debate exists on the long-term efficacy of such efforts, there is little question that Army commanders' adroit use of the funds helped tamp down many of the underlying causes of instability for the short term, thereby buying time to re-establish security and rebuild the ISF. A more detailed review of this topic is warranted, given the uneven long-term effects and the concern that such "expeditionary economics" caused more harm than good.

The operational synchronization of military and civil activities. The U.S. units who fought after 2005 had learned to integrate their operations with civil activities and non-military organizations in ways the Army of 2003 could not have envisioned. The creation of provincial reconstruction teams (PRTs) to pursue stabilization objectives; the integration of MNF-I (and USF-I) with U.S. Embassy-Baghdad, both organizationally and in planning; and the specific revision of MNF-I campaign plans by the civil-military Joint Strategic Assessment Team in 2007 (and by its successors in later years) are the most significant cases in point. In many instances, U.S. military leaders and units learned to connect their military operations explicitly to the achievement of a sustainable political outcome in their areas of operation, though this was not accomplished, ultimately, at the strategic level.

A series of intelligence innovations. During the war, a combination of organizational changes and technological improvements gave tactical level units, sometimes down to the brigade and even battalion level, access to national level intelligence from all of the three major intelligence collection disciplines. These made it possible for U.S. forces to identify enemy networks and target them for either disruption or political reconciliation. They also enabled an unprecedented increase in counterterrorism operations tempo (OPTEMPO). These changes coincided with an extraordinary forward deployment of the defense intelligence community that made defense intelligence more responsive to operational demands and equipped commanders with better knowledge and capabilities than could have been dreamt of in 2003. These deployments, coupled with the ability to reach back to national capabilities, enabled commanders to understand better the various threats the coalition faced and at times to get within the decision cycle of those adversaries.

Establishing an effective medical evacuation system. During the span of the war, the U.S. Army's medical community constructed the most effective medical evacuation system in the history of warfare. At the point of injury, individual Soldiers were issued medical kits with tourniquets and advanced bandages with coagulant material. Frontline medics were provided additional training and new trauma equipment that greatly increased a casualty's chance of survival. In order to preserve the "golden hour," casualties were swiftly evacuated to forward-based surgical teams and then sent on to a regionally located combat support hospital where they received further treatment and stabilization. Those facilities pioneered many new trauma techniques, such as whole blood transfusions and massive blood loss protocols, which were later passed on to civilian trauma specialists. If necessary, casualties were sent to the Landstuhl Regional Medical Center in Germany where they were further stabilized before being sent on to the national military hospitals in the Washington, DC, area. Hundreds, if not thousands, of grievously wounded casualties lived because of these innovations, leading to unprecedented survival rates.

The creation of the Combined Security Mechanism. This initiative to prevent conflict along the disputed internal boundary (the "Green Line") helped avert an Arab-Kurd war that had seemed inevitable in 2007-2008. For a critical period of 2 years, it kept the peace between the Iraqi Government in Baghdad and the KRG in Erbil until it was dismantled during the U.S. military withdrawal of 2011. It should serve as a model for peacekeeping and peace enforcement within the U.S. military.

***

The Iraq War has the potential to be one of the most consequential conflicts in American history. It shattered a long-standing political tradition against preemptive wars. John Quincy Adams's presumption that America should not go "abroad searching for monsters to destroy" was erased, at least temporarily.[8] In the conflict's immediate aftermath, the pendulum of American politics swung to the opposite pole with deep skepticism about foreign interventions.

In terms of geostrategic consequences, the war produced profound consequences. At the time of this project's completion in 2018, an emboldened and expansionist Iran appears to be the only victor. Iraq, the traditional regional counterbalance for Iran, is at best emasculated, and at worst has key elements of its government acting as proxies for Iranian interests. With Iraq no longer a threat, Iran's destabilizing influence has quickly spread to Yemen, Bahrain, and Syria, as well as other locations. As the conflict expanded beyond its original boundaries, the colonial creation that was the Iraqi-Syrian border was effectively erased. Bashar al-Assad, having misjudged his ability to control the Salafist foreign fighters that he gave safe haven for the better part of a decade, found himself

639

threatened by the very forces that he had exploited to avert an American invasion—an invasion that in actuality was never forthcoming. Syria was plunged into a vicious civil war that devolved into a brutality only seen in the worst conflicts of the 20th century, resulting in a death toll that has topped half of a million, repeated use of chemical weapons, and the worst refugee crisis since World War II. Kurdistan evolved from a proto-state into a de-facto nation, a development that has created deep tensions with Turkey. The danger of a Sunni-Shi'a regional conflict, with potentially globally destabilizing effects, is now greater than at any time since the original schism. Zarqawi's goal appears to be on the cusp of becoming reality.

The human and material cost of the conflict was staggering. Nearly 4,500 American military personnel lost their lives in the fighting, and another 32,000 were wounded—many of them grievously. More than 300 soldiers from other coalition nations also perished. Estimates on Iraqi casualties vary wildly, ranging from roughly 200,000 killed to more than a million. Monetary costs, for the United States only, are similarly hard to approximate due to the challenge in estimating future costs for veterans' care and the interest on loans taken out to finance the war. There is no question that the war has been expensive, ranging even among the lower estimates from a cost of over 800 billion to nearly 2 trillion dollars.

At the same time, there are those who argue that the Iraq War, as well as the conflict in Afghanistan, represent historical aberrations with few germane lessons. Supporters of this position posit that conflicts involving COIN and nation-building sit far from the World War II style of "traditional war" for which the Army typically has been held responsible. Such potentially existential conflicts are so much harder to prepare for, they argue, that investing time on COIN related tasks would be counterproductive, if not irresponsible. Adherents of the position that the Army should return to its "traditional" warfighting role also suggest that it is relatively easy to train "down" from high intensity conflict against other armies.

The authors of this study conclude that such positions are intellectually specious. Ironically, many of the same arguments were made before the invasion of Iraq and during the first few years of the war. As a result, precious lives and time were lost before the Army adapted to the character of the conflict and was able to regain the initiative. It is one of this study's core premises that there are additional complexities in COIN that often do not exist in more conventional conflicts. Translating national political guidance into battles and campaigns that blend both traditional maneuver and deft political efforts that target the drivers of conflict is a complicated art. Leaders at all levels in COIN have to be able to integrate the fields of political science, culture, and regional history simultaneously with military strategy to achieve success. Long-term security force assistance, a staple of COIN, is difficult, dangerous, and frustrating. Peacebuilding, the process of nurturing reconciliation, building durable and tolerant institutions, and carrying out political and economic transformation are intensely challenging tasks. U.S. efforts toward this end in Iraq were inefficient, disjointed, and ultimately unsuccessful.

Given the consequences and the cost of the Iraq War, it is essential that the Army studies what went wrong and why. The Army must also capture the innovations and adaptations that produced tactical and operational successes. Above all, the United States must not repeat the errors of previous wars in assuming that the conflict was an anomaly with few useful lessons. This project was commissioned by the Army's senior leadership in part because they believed the Army had spent the first few years of the Iraq War relearning the lessons of the Vietnam conflict. Hopefully, *The U.S. Army in the Iraq War* will help prevent that error from being repeated.

While the next war that the United States fights may be different from the conflicts in Iraq and Afghanistan, it would be risky to assume that it will be so different as to render the lessons of those conflicts moot. The character of warfare is changing, but even if we face peer or near-peer competitors in future conflicts, they are likely to employ a blend of conventional and irregular warfare—what is often called "hybrid warfare" or "operations in the gray zone." The United States may not have the luxury of choosing the next war it fights. Our enemies are aware of the challenges we faced in Iraq and Afghanistan and will incorporate lessons that they have derived from these conflicts against us.

The failure of the United States to attain its strategic objectives in Iraq was not inevitable. It came as a byproduct of a long series of decisions—acts of commission and omission—made by well-trained and intelligent leaders making what seemed to be reasonable decisions. At one point, in the waning days of the Surge, the change of strategy and the sacrifices of many thousands of Americans and Iraqis had finally tipped the scales enough to put the military campaign on a path towards a measure of success. However, it was not to be, as the compounding effect of earlier mistakes, combined with a series of decisions focused on war termination, ultimately doomed the fragile venture.

It is for the efforts and immeasurable sacrifices of our Soldiers that this work is dedicated. Above all, this history is meant to be a permanent record of their accomplishments and their willingness to give the last full measure of devotion for their own country and for the people of Iraq.

ENDNOTES - CHAPTER 17

1. Officially titled "Delivering Security in a Changing World," the cuts restructured infantry regiments, eliminated tank squadrons and artillery batteries, and reducing the Army by more than 1,000 Soldiers.

2. See Lieutenant General (Ret.) James Dubik, *Just War Reconsidered*, Lexington, KY: University Press of Kentucky, 2016.

3. Lieutenant General (Ret.) James M. Dubik, *Operational Art in Counterinsurgency: A View from the Inside*, Washington, DC: Institute for the Study of War, July 2012.

4. Boris Zelkin, *Nate Silver and the Fetish of Data Driven Journalism*, available from *https://amgreatness.com/2017/02/07/nate-silver-fetish-data-driven-journalism/*.

5. Interview, Colonel Joel Rayburn and Major Jeanne Godfroy with Lieutenant General H. R. McMaster, August 14, 2015.

6. Interview, Major Jeanne Godfroy, Chief of Staff of the Army (CSA) Operation IRAQI FREEDOM (OIF) Study Group, with Major General Patrick Higgins, April 29, 2014, Reston, VA.

7. Increasing the number of mandatory annual training days has been shown to have a negative impact on retention of reserve component personnel. Yet, at the same time, it would be difficult, if not impossible, to increase the combat capabilities of battalion size and larger National Guard units without similarly increasing mandatory training days. If this quandary is not resolvable at the macro scale, then at a minimum, an increase in training days should be applied on a smaller scale to specific units—with reserve component personnel informed during recruitment that they will be joining a unit with a higher OPTEMPO.

8. John Quincy Adams, speech to U.S. House of Representatives on Independence Day, July 4, 1821, available from *http://teachingamericanhistory.org/library/document/speech-on-independence-day/*.

AFTERWORD

The U.S. Army War College (USAWC) was honored to support the effort for this study and to publish these volumes. Since our vision is to develop strategic leaders and ideas invaluable to the Army, the Joint Force, and the Nation, the publication of these volumes is emblematic of this study's purpose. In fact, this study represents what Secretary of War Elihu Root envisioned when he established the USAWC in 1901. He directed its students to consider three important strategic issues: national defense, military science, and responsible command—aspects which are relevant to this study.

It is our hope these volumes will prompt and enable further studies on other levels and aspects of the wars in Iraq and Afghanistan. In addition to hundreds of hours of interviews, as a byproduct of this work, over 30,000 pages of documents were declassified, and will be made available online. Over time, all of these primary sources will be reviewed and reassessed by others, including the Staff College and USAWC students, as a way to continue to improve as a profession. To further assist with studying these volumes, we are publishing them in a searchable digital format, negating the need for a lengthy index. Additionally, while this is an extensive study, it is by no means complete. Many areas fell outside the scope of this study and will require further in-depth research, areas such as logistics, humanitarian assistance, special operations, and conventional mutual efforts, along with U.S. Central Command's (CENTCOM's) decisions and wider U.S. and international partner decisions, which impacted the strategic and operational direction and resources in Iraq itself.

This study reinforces the importance of what we do at the USAWC as part of professional military education and the need to continue to innovate and improve our efforts. The central problems in Iraq and Afghanistan typically started at the strategic level. We rightfully need to address the many operational and tactical issues highlighted throughout this study. However, that is not sufficient to solve the overall challenges we will face in the foreseeable future. We have to get the strategy right and be prepared for the inevitable natural tendency toward strategic drift and strategic depreciation. The U.S. Army has traditionally had an almost overwhelming faith in technology and doctrine, on the changing character of war, which is often reflected in this study. We can and will analyze and learn from it. At the same time, we cannot overcommit to the lessons from this war. As Dr. Mike Neiberg, our USAWC Chair of War Studies, recently reinforced to me, "The next war we fight will be quite different and will render many of the operational and tactical suggestions here overcome by events." The question is which ones? At the USAWC, we are committed and will further reinforce the importance of the study of strategy, the nature of war, and the essence of leadership and decision-making at the strategic level, and at the sometimes "Gordian Knot" nexus of strategy and operations.

On this the 100th anniversary of the end of World War I, I am mindful that this study is part of a longstanding tradition within our Army to critically assess past strategies, operations, and decisions to inform decisions and actions in the future. This commitment to self-evaluation, study, and adaptation serves not only to ensure the future readiness of our Army, but honors those who likewise committed themselves to the security and defense of our Nation during this conflict.

MAJOR GENERAL JOHN S. KEM
Commandant
U.S. Army War College

SELECT BIBLIOGRAPHY

INTERVIEWS

Interviews Conducted by the CSA's OIF Study Group

Alex Alderson
Mithal al-Alusi
Lieutenant Colonel Charles Armstrong
General Lloyd Austin
Colonel Jeffrey Bannister
Colonel (Ret.) Michael Bell
Brigadier General Scott E. Brower
Colonel J. B. Burton
President George W. Bush
Major General Nelson Cannon
General (Ret.) George W. Casey, Jr.
Lieutenant General Robert Caslen
Ross Coffey
Colonel Chris Connor
Colonel Matthew Q. Dawson
Lieutenant General (Ret.) James Dubik
Brigadier General Billy Don Farris
Major General (UK) Julian Free
Lieutenant General Ali al-Freiji
Colonel David Funk
Lieutenant General (Ret.) Jack Gardner
Major General Walter E. Gaskin
Secretary Robert M. Gates
Colonel Thomas J. Goss
Colonel John Hall
Colonel Jeff Hannon
Colonel (Ret.) Derek Harvey
Major General (Ret.) Najim Jabouri
General (Ret.) John M. Keane
Lieutenant General (Ret.) Francis Kearney
Lieutenant Colonel Scott Kimmell
Colonel Dale Kuehl
Lieutenant General (United Kingdom)
  Graeme Lamb

Colonel Kevin Leahy
General (Ret.) James N. Mattis
Colonel (Ret.) Kevin McDonnell
Brigadier General Herbert Raymond
  "H. R." McMaster
Brigadier General (Ret.) Michael Meese
Colonel (Ret.) Mark Mitchell
Major General Benjamin R. Mixon
Colonel Robert Molinari
Lieutenant Colonel (Ret.) Patrick Morrison
Lieutenant General Michael Oates
General Raymond T. Odierno
Major General Brian R. Owens
General (Ret.) Peter Pace
Secretary Leon Panetta
General (Ret.) David H. Petraeus
Lieutenant Colonel Kurt J. Pinkerton
Kenneth Pollack
Michael Pregent
Secretary Condoleezza Rice
Colonel Bryan Roberts
Mowaffaq Rubaie
General (Ret.) Peter J. Schoomaker
Oubai Shahbandar
Major General (UK) Jonathan Shaw
Lieutenant Colonel Kent Strader
Major General (Ret.) Aziz Swaidy
Brigadier General Robin Swan
Brigadier General Sean Swindell
General (Ret.) James D. Thurman
Lieutenant General Kenneth Tovo
Major General Rick L. Waddell
Rear Admiral (Ret.) Edward Winters
General (Ret.) Anthony C. Zinni

Institute for Defense Analyses

Colonel Julian "Dale" Alford
Sheikh Aifan Sadoun al-Issawi
Sterling Jensen
Major General (Ret.) Thomas Jones

Brigadier General Robert B. Neller
Colonel (Ret.) Richard Welch
Major General Richad C. Zilmer

Washington, DC: Institute for the Study of War

Colonel J. B. Burton

Colonel David W. Sutherland

Combat Studies Institute

Lieutenant General Lloyd Austin
Colonel Jeffrey Bailey
Lieutenant Colonel Edward Bohnemann
Brigadier General (S) Scott E. Brower
Lieutenant Colonel Timothy A. Brumfield
Vice Adm. David H. Buss
Lieutenant General Robert Caslen
Colonel John W. Charlton
Colonel Roger Cloutier
Lieutenant General Robert W. Cone
Colonel Christopher Conner
Lieutenant Colonel Douglas C. Crissman
Lieutenant General John D. Cross
Major General Anthony Cucolo
Lieutenant General Martin Dempsey
Lieutenant General (Ret.) James Dubik
Colonel Michael Eastman
Colonel Billy Don Farris
Colonel Paul E. Funk II
Colonel Andrew Gainey
Brigadier General Michael X. Garrett
Colonel Ricky D. Gibbs
Colonel Christopher P. Gibson
Ambassador Gary Grappo
Major General Jeffrey Hammond
Lieutenant General Mark Hertling

Colonel James Hickey
Ambassador Christopher R. Hill
Colonel John Hort
Major General (Ret.) James Hunt
General Charles Jacoby
Colonel Michael M. Kershaw
Lieutenant Colonel Jeffrey LaFace
Colonel Jon S. Lehr
Major General Rick Lynch
Lieutenant General Herbert Raymond "H. R." McMaster
Lieutenant Colonel Patrick R. Michaelis
Lieutenant General Benjamin R. Mixon
Colonel Peter Newell
Lieutenant General David Perkins
Colonel Walter Piatt
Brigadier General David Quantock
Colonel Bryan T. Roberts
Lieutenant Colonel Jim Sindle
Avanulus Smiley
Major General (Ret.) Eddy Spurgin
Lieutenant Colonel Mark W. Suich
Colonel Steven J. Townsend
Colonel Stephen Twitty
Colonel John C. Valledor
Command Sergeant Major Tommy William

646

Marine Corps History and Museums Division

Major Kurt Ebaugh
Colonel Craig S. Kozenjesky
Colonel Lawrence D. Nicholson

Colonel Richard L. Simcock
Colonel (Ret.) Richard Welch

Center for Army Lessons Learned

Lieutenant General Robert Caslen
Colonel John Hall
Colonel Kenneth Harvey
Mark Hunter
Ambassador James Jeffrey

Colonel Karl Kraus
Mark Libby
Colonel Dean Raab
Harold Reeves

U.S. Army Center of Military History

Brigadier General John R. Allen
Vice Admiral David H. Buss
Major General Peter Devlin
Major General Joseph Fil
Colonel Christopher P. Gibson

Colonel Michael M. Kershaw
General Raymond T. Odierno
Brigadier General David Quantock
Major General Douglas M. Stone

BOOKS

Andrade, Dale, *Surging South of Baghdad: The 3d Infantry Division and Task Force Marne in Iraq, 2007-2008*. Washington, DC: U.S. Army Center of Military History, 2010.

Bailey, Jonathan, Richard Iron, and Hew Strachan, *British Generals in Blair's Wars*. Surrey, UK: Ashgate Publishing, 2013.

Baker III, James A. and Lee H. Hamilton, *The Iraq Study Group Report*. New York: Vintage Books, 2006.

Bush, George W., *Decision Points*. New York: Crown Publishers, 2010.

Carney, Stephen A., *Allied Participation in Operation IRAQI FREEDOM*. Washington, DC: U.S. Army Center of Military History, 2011.

Casey, Jr., George W., *Strategic Reflections: Operation Iraqi Freedom, July 2004-February 2007*. Washington, DC: National Defense University Press, 2012.

Cordesman, Anthony and Sam Khazi, *Iraq in Crisis: A Report of the CSIS Burke Chair in Strategy*. New York: Center for Strategic International Studies, May 2014.

Cucullu, Gordon and Chris Fontana, *Warrior Police: Rolling with America's Military Police in the World's Trouble Spots*. New York: St. Martin's Press, 2011.

Fairweather, Jack, *A War of Choice: Honour, Hubris and Sacrifice: The British in Iraq*. London, UK: Jonathan Cape, 2011.

Gates, Robert M., *Duty: Memoirs of a Secretary at War*. New York: Knopf, 2014.

Hill, Christopher R., *Outpost: Life on the Frontlines of American Diplomacy: A Memoir*. New York: Simon & Schuster, 2014.

Isenberg, David, *Shadow Force*. London, UK: Praeger Security International, 2009.

Kagan, Kimberly, *The Surge: A Military History*. New York: Encounter Books, 2009.

Mansoor, Peter R., *Surge: My Journey with General David Petraeus and the Remaking of the Iraq War*. New Haven, CT: Yale University Press, 2013.

Matlak, Regis W., *The Nightmare Years to Come?* Washington, DC: National Defense University Press, 2014.

McChrystal, Stanley, *My Share of the Task: A Memoir*. New York: Penguin Group, 2013.

McWilliams, Timothy S. and Kurtis P. Wheeler, eds., *Al-Anbar Awakening, American Perspectives*, Vol. I. Quantico, VA: Marine Corps University Press, 2009.

Metz, Steven, *Decisionmaking in Operation Iraqi Freedom: The Strategic Shift of 2007*. Carlisle, PA: Strategic Studies Institute, U.S. Army War College, 2010.

Montgomery, Gary W. and Timothy S. McWilliams, eds., *From Insurgency to Counterinsurgency in Iraq, 2004-2009: Al-Anbar Awakening*, Vol. II, Iraqi Perspectives. Quantico, VA: Marine Corps University Press, 2009.

O'Hern, Steven, *The Intelligence Wars: Lessons from Baghdad*. New York: Prometheus Books, 2008.

Rayburn, Joel, *Iraq After America: Strongmen, Sectarians, Resistance*. Stanford, CA: Hoover Institution Press, 2014.

Ricks, Thomas E., *The Gamble: General David Petraeus and the American Military Adventure in Iraq, 2006-2008*. New York: Penguin Press, 2009.

Ripley, Tim, *Operation Telic: The British Campaign in Iraq 2003-2009*. Lancaster, UK: Telic-Herrick Publications, November 2014.

Robinson, Linda, *Tell Me How This Ends: General David Petraeus and the Search for a Way Out of Iraq*. New York: Public Affairs, 2008.

Rosen, Nir, *Aftermath: Following the Bloodshed of America's Wars in the Muslim World*. New York: Nation Books, 2010.

Sky, Emma, *The Unraveling: High Hopes and Missed Opportunities in Iraq*. New York: Public Affairs, 2015.

Ucko, David H. and Robert Egnell, *Counterinsurgency in Crisis*. New York: Columbia University Press, 2013.

Weiss, Michael and Hassan Hassan, *ISIS: Inside the Army of Terror*. New York: Regan Arts, 2015.

West, Bing, *The Strongest Tribe: War, Politics, and the Endgame in Iraq*. New York: Random House, 2009.

Woodward, Bob, *The War Within: A Secret White House History, 2006-2008*. New York: Simon Schuster, 2008.

Wright, Robin, *Dreams and Shadows: The Future of the Middle East*. New York: Penguin Press, 2008.

ARTICLES

Abbas, Yasir and Dan Trombly. "Inside the Collapse of the Iraqi Army's 2d Division." July 1, 2014. Available from *http://warontherocks.com/2014/07/inside-the-collapse-of-the-iraqi-armys-2nd-division/*.

Abouzeid, Rania. "At Tehran's Bidding? Iraq Cracks Down on a Controversial Camp." *Time*, July 29, 2009. Available from *http://content.time.com/time/world/article/0,8599,1913399,00.html*.

Ahmed, Farook. "Offensive Operations in MND-C, June 2007-January 2008." Washington, DC: Institute for the Study of War, January 2008.

Ali, Ahmed with Kimberly Kagan. "The Iraqi Shi'a Mobilization to Counter the ISIS Offensive." Washington, DC: Institute for the Study of War, June 14, 2014. Available from *understandingwar.org/backgrounder/iraqi-shi'-mobilization-counter-isis-offensive*.

Allport, Rowan. "A Year After Mosul." London, UK: Human Security Centre, June 2, 2015. Available from *http://www.hscentre.org/security-and-defence/year-mosul/*.

Association of the U.S. Army, Institute of Land Warfare. "Third Army: Empowering Theater Responsiveness by Synchronizing Operational Maneuver." *Army*, Vol. 62, No. 3, March 2012.

Bahgat, Gawdat. "United States-Iranian Relations: The Terrorism Challenge." *Parameters*, 2009. Available from *http://strategicstudiesinstitute.army.mil/pubs/parameters/Articles/08winter/bahgat.pdf*.

Bill, Brian J. "Detention Operations in Iraq: A View from the Ground." *International Law Studies*, Vol. 86, 2010.

Brown, Colonel James, Lieutenant Colonel Erik Goepher, and Captain James Clark. "Detention Operations, Behavior Modification, and Counterinsurgency." *Military Review*, Vol. 43, May-June 2009.

Browne, Des. "Government and Security in Iraq: The Evolving Challenge." *RUSI Journal*, Vol. 151, No. 3, June 2006.

Butler, Major Dave. "Lights Out: ARSOF Reflect on Eight Years in Iraq." *Special Warfare*, January-March 2012.

Chiarelli, Major General Peter W., and Major Patrick R. Michaelis. "Winning the Peace: The Requirement for Full-Spectrum Operations." *Military Review*, Vol. 85, July-August 2005.

Coll, Steve. "The General's Dilemma." *New Yorker*, September 8, 2008. Available from *http://www.newyorker.com/magazine/2008/09/08/the-generals-dilemma*.

Crider, Jim. "Inside the Surge: One Commander's Lessons in Counterinsurgency." Working Paper, Washington, DC: Center for a New American Security, June 2009.

Detwiler, Elizabeth. "Iraq: Positive Change in the Detention System." Washington, DC: U.S. Institute of Peace, July 1, 2008. Available from *http://www.usip.org/publications/iraq-positive-change-in-the-detention-system*.

Donnelly, Thomas and Vance Serchuk. "U.S. Counterinsurgency in Iraq: Lessons from the Philippine War." AEI Online, November 1, 2003. Available from *http://www.aei.org/publication/u-s-counterinsurgency-in-iraq/*.

Dowdy, John. "Stabilizing Iraq's economy: An interview with the DOD's Paul Brinkley." *McKinsey Quarterly*, March 2010. Available from *http://www.mckinsey.com/insights/public_sector/stabilizing_iraqs_economy_an_interview_with_the_dods_paul_brinkley#*.

Feaver, Peter D. "The Right to Be Right: Civil-Military Relations and the Iraq Surge Decision." *International Security*, Vol. 35, No. 4, Spring 2011.

Filkins, Dexter. "What We Left Behind." *The New Yorker*, April 28, 2014.

Fulton, Will, Joseph Holliday, and Sam Wyer. "Iranian Strategy in Syria." Washington, DC: American Enterprise Institute, May 2013.

Gaughen, Patrick. "Fight for Diwaniyah: The Sadrist Trend and ISCI Struggle for Supremacy." *Backgrounder*, Vol. 17, Washington, DC: Institute for the Study of War, January 6, 2008. Available from *http://www.understandingwar.org/backgrounder/fight-diwaniyah*.

Grossman, Elaine M. "Rehabilitating Iraqi Insurgents." *National Journal*, Vol. 39, No. 33, 2007.

Hamilton, Eric. "Iraq Report: The Fight for Mosul, March 2003-March 2008." Washington, DC: Institute for the Study of War, March 2008.

Institute for the Study of War, Washington, DC. "Operation Iron Harvest." Available from *http://www.understandingwar.org/operation/operation-iron-harvest*.

Institute for the Study of War, Washington, DC. "Operation Marne Thunderbolt." Available from *http://www.understandingwar.org/operation/operation-marne-thunderbolt*.

Institute for the Study of War, Washington, DC. "Operation Phantom Thunder." Available from *http://www.understandingwar.org/operation/operation-phantom-thunder*.

Kagan, Kimberly. "Iraq Report: From 'New Way Forward' to New Commander, January 10, 2007-February 10, 2007." Washington, DC: Institute for the Study of War.

Katulis, Brian, Mark Lynch and Peter Juul. "Iraq's Political Transition after the Surge." Washington, DC: Center for American Progress, September 2008.

Kibbey, Sergeant Benjamin. "Advise and Assist Brigade: A Familiar Unit with a New Mission in Iraq." *Army*, Vol. 60, No. 8, August 2010.

Knarr, William et al. *Al Sahawa—The Awakening*, Vol. II, Al Anbar Province, Multi-National Force-West, Area of Operations Atlanta. Alexandria, VA: Institute for Defense Analyses, 2013.

_____. *Al Sahawa—The Anbar Awakening*, Vol. IIA, Anbar Province Area of Operations Atlanta—The Insurgency. Alexandria, VA: Institute for Defense Analyses, 2013.

_____. *Al Sahawa—The Awakening*, Vol. IIIB, Al Anbar Province, Area of Operations Denver, Haditha-Hit Corridor. Alexandria, VA: Institute for Defense Analyses, 2013.

_____. *Al Sahawa—The Awakening*, Vol. IV, Al Anbar Awakening: Area of Operations Topeka, Ramadi Area. Alexandria, VA: Institute for Defense Analyses, 2013.

_____. *Al Sahawa—The Awakening*, Vol. IV-A, Area of Operations Topeka, East Ramadi, and the Shark Fins. Alexandria, VA: Institute for Defense Analyses, 2013.

Knights, Michael. "Iran's Foreign legion: The Role of Iraqi Shiite Militias in Syria." *PolicyWatch 2096*, Washington, DC: The Washington Institute for Near East Policy, June 27, 2013. Available from *http://www.washingtoninstitute.org/policy-analysis/view/irans-foreign-legion-the-role-of-iraqi-shiite-militias-in-syria*.

_____. "The Evolution of Iran's Special Groups in Iraq." West Point, NY: Combating Terrorism Center, November 1, 2010.

Kuehl, Dale. "Testing Galula in Ameriyah: The People Are the Key." *Military Review*, March-April 2009.

Lawrence, Quil. "A Precarious Peace in Northern Iraq." Middle East Research and Information Project, October 2009. Available from *http://www.merip.org/mero/mero100109*.

Lewis, Jessica, Ahmed Ali, and Kimberly Kagan. "Iraq's Sectarian Crisis Reignites as Shi'a Militias Execute Civilians and Remobilize." Washington, DC: Institute for the Study of War, June 1, 2013. Available from *http://www.understandingwar.org/backgrounder/iraqs-sectarian-crisis-reignites-shia-militias-execute-civilians-and-remobilize*.

Mansoor, Peter. "The British Army and the Lessons of the Iraq War." *British Army Review*, No. 147, Summer 2009.

Mardini, Ramzy. "Factors Affecting Stability in Northern Iraq." West Point, NY: Combating Terrorism Center, West Point, August 15, 2009. Available from *https://www.ctc.usma.edu/posts/factors-affecting-stability-in-northern-iraq*.

_____. "Maliki Arrests Potential Opponents." Washington, DC: Institute for the Study of War, December 14, 2011.

Mosier, Duane L. "The Road to Al Amarah: Operation Yarborough and U.S. Army Special Forces Soldiers in Southern Iraq (January-June 2008)." *Small Wars Journal*, November 4, 2010.

Perkins, Major T. G. S. "Mitting in Basra during OP Telic 11—an OC's Perspective." *Royal Regiment of Scotland Journal*, March 2009.

Petraeus, General David H. "Ambassador Ryan Crocker: Diplomat Extraordinaire." *Army*, Vol. 61, No. 4, April 2011.

_____. "Learning Counterinsurgency: Observations from Soldiering in Iraq." *Military Review*, January-February 2006.

Pollack, Kenneth. "Iraqi Elections, Iranian Interests." Washington, DC: The Brookings Institution, April 4, 2014. Available from *http://www.brookings.edu/blogs/markaz/posts/2014/04/04-pollack-iraq-national-elections-2014-iranian-interests*.

Roggio, Bill. *Long War Journal*. Available from *http://www.longwarjournal.org*.

Schippert, Steve and Nick Grace. "The Fiction of Abu OMarch al-Baghdadi." *Threats Watch*, December 5, 2007.

Sheftick, Gary. "Deploying brigade to test 'advise and assist' concept," *Army*, Vol. 59, No. 5, May 2009.

Smyth, Phillip. "From Karbala to Sayyida Zaynab: Iraqi Fighters in Syria's Shi'a Militias." *CTC Sentinel*, Vol. 6, No. 8, August 2013.

Stewart, Scott. "Jihadists in Iraq: Down For The Count?" Stratfor Global Intelligence, April 29, 2010. Available from *http://www.stratfor.com/weekly/20100428_jihadists_iraq_down_count*.

The Norwegian Country of Origin Information Centre, Oslo, Norway. "Iraq: Security situation and internally displaced people in Diyala, April 2015." April 24, 2015. Available from *https://www.ecoi.net/en/file/local/1115404/1226_1441804342_topical-note-security-situation-and-internally-displaced-people-in-diyala.pdf*.

Ucko, David H. "Lessons from Basrah: The Future of British Counter-Insurgency." *Survival*, Vol. 52, No. 4, August-September 2010.

Wicken, Stephen. "Sadr's Balancing Act on Maliki." Washington, DC: Institute for the Study of War, June 18, 2012. Available from *http://www.understandingwar.org/backgrounder/sadr's-balancing-act-maliki#_edn19*.

Wing, Joel. Musings on Iraq. Available from *http://musingsoniraq.blogspot.com*.

Witty, David. "The Iraqi Counter Terrorism Service." Brookings Institution, 2015.

MONOGRAPHS AND REPORTS

Bernard, Cheryl et al. *The Battle Behind the Wire: U.S. Prisoner and Detainee Operations from World War II to Iraq*. Santa Monica, CA: RAND Corporation, 2011.

Bloomfield, Jr., Lincoln. "Mujahedin-e Khalg (MEK/PMOI) and the Search for Ground Truth About its Activities and Nature: An Independent Assessment by Ambassador Lincoln Bloomfield, Jr." August 16, 2011.

Bowen, Jr., Stuart W. *Learning from Iraq: A Final Report from the Special Inspector General for Iraq Reconstruction*. Washington, DC: U.S. Government Printing Office, 2013.

Brennan, Jr., Rick R. et al. *Ending the U.S. War in Iraq: The Final Transition, Operational Maneuver, and Disestablishment of United States Forces-Iraq*. Washington, DC: RAND Corporation, 2013.

CALL Handbook 09-27. Commander's Guide to Money as a Weapons System: Tactics, Techniques, and Procedures. Fort Leavenworth, KS: Center for Army Lessons Learned, 2009.

Center for Strategic and International Studies. Final Report on Lessons Learned: Department of Defense Task Force for Business and Stability Operations, June 2010.

Center for Strategic and International Studies. Independent Commission on the Security Forces of Iraq. Report, September 6, 2007. Available from *https://usiraq.procon.org/sourcefiles/iraqsec.9-6-07.pdf*.

Cochrane, Marisa. "Special Groups Regenerate." Iraq Report No. 11, Washington, DC: Institute for the Study of War, August 29, 2008. Available from *http://www.understandingwar.org/sites/default/files/reports/IraqReport11.pdf*.

Cochrane, Marisa. "Iraq Report 12: The Fragmentation of the Sadrist Movement." Washington, DC: Institute for the Study of War, January 2009.

Combating Terrorism Center at West Point. "Al-Qa'ida's Foreign Fighters in Iraq: a first look at the Sinjar Records." December 19, 2007. Available from *http://tarpley.net/docs/CTCForeignFighter.19.Dec07.pdf*.

Cordesman, Anthony and Sam Khazi. *Iraq in Crisis: A Report of the CSIS Burke Chair in Strategy*. New York: Center for Strategic International Studies, May 2014.

Council on Foreign Relations. "International Crisis Group: Iraq's Civil War, the Sadrists and the Surge." Middle East Report No. 72, February 7, 2008.

Dale, Catherine. "Operation Iraqi Freedom: Strategies, Approaches, Results, and Issues for Congress." Report for Congress, Congressional Research Service, Report No. RL34387, April 2, 2009. Available from *https://www.fas.org/sgp/crs/natsec/RL34387.pdf*.

Department of Defense. *Measuring Stability and Security in Iraq*. Report to Congress, March 2009. Available from *http://www.defense.gov/Portals/1/Documents/pubs/Measuring_Stability_and_Security_in_Iraq_March_2009.pdf*.

Duman, Bilgay. "A New Controversial Actor in Post-ISIS Iraq: al-Hashd al-Shaabi (The Popular Mobilization Forces)." ORSAM Report No. 198, May 2015. Available from *http://www.orsam.org.tr/files/Raporlar/rapor198/198eng.pdf*.

Institute for Defense Analysis. "Analysis of Explosively Formed Penetrator (EFP) Explosions against Coalition Forces in Iraq." October 24, 2008.

International Crisis Group. "Deja Vu All Over Again? Iraq's Escalating Political Crisis." Middle East Report No. 126, July 30, 2012. Available from *https://www.crisisgroup.org/middle-east-north-africa/gulf-and-arabian-peninsula/iraq/deja-vu-all-over-again-iraq-s-escalating-political-crisis*.

International Crisis Group. "Loose Ends: Iraq's Security Forces between U.S. Drawdown and Withdrawal." Middle East Report No. 99, Washington, DC: International Crisis Group, October 26, 2010. Available from *https://www.crisisgroup.org/middle-east-north-africa/gulf-and-arabian-peninsula/iraq/loose-ends-iraq-s-security-forces-between-us-drawdown-and-withdrawal*.

Johnson, David E., M. Wade Markel, and Brian Shannon. *The 2008 Battle of Sadr City: Reimagining Urban Combat.* Santa Monica, CA: RAND Corporation, 2013.

Kagan, Frederick W. *Choosing Victory: A Plan for Success in Iraq.* Phase I Report, Washington, DC: American Enterprise Institute, January 2007.

Katzman, Kenneth. "Iraq: Politics, Governance, and Human Rights." Report for Congress, Washington, DC: Congressional Research Service (CRS), 2014.

_____. "Iraq: Post-Saddam Governance and Security." Report for Congress, Washington, DC: CRS, July 2008.

Lamb, Christopher J., Matthew J. Schmidt, and Berit G. Fitzsimmons. "MRAPs, Irregular Warfare, and Pentagon Reform." Institute for National Strategic Studies Occasional Paper 6, Washington, DC: National Defense University, June 2009.

Lewis, Jessica D. "Al-Qaeda in Iraq Resurgent, The Breaking the Walls Campaign, Part I." *Middle East Security Report 14*, Washington, DC: Institute for the Study of War, September 2013.

Margesson, Rhoda, Andorra Bruno, and Jeremy Sharp. "Iraqi Refugees and Internally Displaced Persons: A Deepening Humanitarian Crisis?" Report for Congress, No. RL33936, Washington, DC: CRS, February 2013. Available from *http://fas.org/sgp/crs/mideast/RL33936.pdf*.

Manuscript (Ms), Combat Studies Institute (CSI). *On Point.* Vol. II, September 25, 2014.

_____. *On Point.* Vol. IV, September 25, 2014.

_____. *On Point.* Vol. V, September 25, 2014.

_____. *On Point*. Vol. VI, September 25, 2014.

Naland, John K. "Lessons from Embedded Provincial Reconstruction Teams in Iraq." Special Report No. 290, Washington, DC: U.S. Institute of Peace (USIP), October 2011. Available from *https://www.usip.org/sites/default/files/SR290.pdf*.

Office of the Special Inspector General for Iraq Reconstruction. *Full Impact of Department of Defense Program to Restart State-Owned Enterprises Difficult to Estimate*. Washington, DC, 2009.

_____. *Iraqi Security Forces: Special Operations Force Program is Achieving Goals, but Iraqi Support Remains Critical to Success*. Washington, DC, October 25, 2010.

O'Hanlon, Michael E. and Jason H. Campbell. "Iraq Index." Washington, DC: Brookings Institution, January 31, 2012.

Perito, Robert M. *The Iraq Federal Police: U.S. Police Building under Fire*. Special Report, Washington, DC: USIP, October 2011.

Petraeus, General David H. *Situation in Iraq, 8-9*. Report to Congress, April 2008. Available from *http://iraq.usembassy.gov/uploads/3m/Gl/3mGlIE3hK_bMMKoly4AKAQ/petraeus-testimony-8-april-2008.pdf*.

Polin, R. B. "The Counter-IED Fight in Iraq." P-4949, Alexandria, VA: Institute for Defense Analyses, February 2013.

Schwartz, Moshe. "The Department of Defense's Use of Private Security Contractors in Afghanistan and Iraq: Background, Analysis, and Options for Congress." Report for Congress No. R40835, Washington, DC: CRS, May 13, 2011.

Singer, P. W. "Can't Win With 'Em, Can't Go to War Without 'Em: Private Military Contractors and Counterinsurgency." *Policy Paper No. 4*, Washington, DC: Brookings Institution, September 2007.

Sullivan, Marisa. "Maliki's Authoritarian Regime." *Middle East Security Report 10*. Washington, DC: Institute for the Study of War, April 2013.

UK House of Commons Defence Committee. *UK Land Operations in Iraq 2007*. Report No. 1, London, UK: House of Commons, December 3, 2007.

_____. *UK Operations in Iraq*. Report No. 13, London, UK: House of Commons, July 19, 2006.

_____. *UK Operations in Iraq and the Gulf.* Report No. 15, London, UK: House of Commons, July 22, 2008. Available from *http://www.publications.parliament.uk/pa/cm200708/cmselect/cmdfence/982/982.pdf.*

U.S. Congress, Congressional Budget Office. *Contractor's Support of U.S. Operations in Iraq.* Washington, DC, August 2008.

_____. Government Accountability Office. *Military Operations: Actions Needed to Better Guide Project Selection for Commander's Emergency Response Program and Improve Oversight in Iraq.* Washington, DC, 2008.

_____. Government Accountability Office. *Rebuilding Iraq: Integrated Strategic Plan Needed to Help Restore Iraq's Oil and Electricity Sectors.* Washington, DC, May 2007.

U.S. Department of State. *2008 Country Reports on Human Rights Practices: Iraq.* February 25, 2009.

Young, William, David Stebbins, Bryan Frederick, and Omar al-Shahery. "Spillover From the Conflict in Syria: An Assessment of the Factors that Aid and Impede the Spread of Violence." Santa Monica, CA: RAND Corporation, 2014.

UNPUBLISHED PAPERS

Cochran, Sandy and Captain Kelly Howard. Paper, *MNF-I Chronology Reference.* November 12, 2008.

Condrey, Major Jason. *The Commander's Emergency Response Program: A Model for Future Implementation.* Fort Leavenworth, KS: School of Advanced Military Studies, July 4, 2010.

Harvey, Derek. "Intelligence During the Surge." May 11, 2015, unpublished manuscript.

Joint Chiefs of Staff Working Paper (draft, version 8). November 22, 2006.

Sky, Emma. *The Unraveling: High Hopes and Missed Opportunities in Iraq.* New York: Public Affairs, 2015, Kindle edition, Surge memoir (draft).

Taylor, Master Sergeant Keith. *CERP Misappropriation.* Paper, Fort Bliss, TX: U.S. Army Sergeant Majors Academy, April 28, 2011.

NEWS OUTLETS AND NEWSPAPERS

ABC News

Al Monitor

al-Fajr Media Center

al-Ghadd

al-Hayat

al-Quds al-Arabi

al-Sumariyah News

Alarabiya

American Forces Press Service

American Spectator

Asharq al-Aswat

Associated Press

Aswat al-Iraq

Baltimore Magazine

BBC News

Business Insider

CBS News

CNN

DoD News

Eurasia Insight

Foreign Policy

Fox News

Huffington Post

Independent

Inter Service Press News Agency

Iraq News Monitor

Islamic Republic News Agency

Jerusalem Post

Los Angeles Times

Nation

Nation States

National Interest

New Republic

New York Daily News

New York Sun

Newsmine

Newsweek

PBS

Politico

Radio Free Europe

Reuters

Stars and Stripes

Sunday Times

The Daily Beast

The Guardian

The National

The New York Times

The Telegraph

The Wall Street Journal

The Washington Post

USA Today

Voice of America

ABBREVIATIONS

AAB	Advise and Assist Brigade
AAH	Asa'ib Ahl al-Haqq
ACR	Armored Cavalry Regiment
AEI	American Enterprise Institute
AFCENT	Air Forces Central Command
AHEC	Army Heritage and Education Center
AIF	anti-Iraqi forces
AO	area of operation
AOB	Advanced Operational Base
AQI	al-Qaeda in Iraq
ARCENT	U.S. Army Central (U.S. Army component of CENTCOM)
ASCC	Army Service Component Commands
BCT	Brigade Combat Team
BfSB	Battlefield Surveillance Brigade
BOC	Baghdad Operations Command
BRAC	Base Realignment and Closure
BTT	border transition team
BUA	Battle Update Assessment
CACE	Corps Analysis and Control Element
CALL	Center for Army Lessons Learned
CENTCOM	U.S. Central Command
CERP	Commanders' Emergency Response Program
CEXC	Combined Explosives Exploitation Cell
CF	Coalition Forces
CFLCC	Coalition Forces Land Component Command
CG	Commanding General
CIA	Central Intelligence Agency
CID	Criminal Investigation Division
CJCS	Chairman of the Joint Chiefs of Staff
CJSOTF	Combined Joint Special Operations Task Force
CJSOTF-AP	Combined Joint Special Operations Task Force–Arabian Peninsula
CJTF	Combined Joint Task Force
CJTF-7	Combined Joint Task Force-7
CLC	Concerned Local Citizens
CMH	U.S. Army Center of Military History
COB	Contingency Operating Base
COIC	Counter-IED Operations and Integration Center

COIN	counterinsurgency
COL	colonel
CPA	Coalition Provisional Authority
CRS	Congressional Research Service
CSA	Chief of Staff of the Army
CSI	Combat Studies Institute
CSIS	Center for Strategic and International Studies
DCSINT	Deputy Chief of Staff for Intelligence
DIA	Defense Intelligence Agency
DoD	Department of Defense
EFP	explosively formed penetrator
EOD	explosive ordinance disposal
EPRT	embedded provincial reconstruction teams
ERB	Emergency Response Brigade
ERU	Emergency Response Unit
FBI	Federal Bureau of Investigation
FID	foreign internal defense
FIFA	Federation Internationale de Football Association
FMS	foreign military sales
FMV	full-motion video
FOB	forward operating base
FORSCOM	U.S. Army Forces Command
FPS	Facilities Protection Service
FRAGO	fragmentary order
FSEC	Force Strategic Engagement Cell
GAT	Governance Assessment Team
GMLRS	guided multiple-launch rocket systems
GOI	Government of Iraq
HMMWV	High Mobility Multi-Purpose Wheeled Vehicle (aka "Humvee")
I MEF	I Marine Expeditionary Force
IA	Iraqi Army
IED	improvised explosive device
IFCNR	Implementation and Follow-Up Committee for National Reconciliation
IGFC	Iraqi Ground Forces Command
IIP	Iraqi Islamic Party
INIS	Iraqi National Intelligence Service
IO	Information Operations
IP	Iraqi Police

IRAM	improvised rocket-assisted munition
IRGC	Islamic Revolutionary Guard Corps of Iran
ISCI	Islamic Supreme Council of Iraq
ISF	Iraqi security forces
ISG	Iraq Study Group
ISI	Islamic State of Iraq
ISIL	Islamic State of Iraq and the Levant
ISIS	Islamic State of Iraq and Syria
ISOF	Iraqi special operations forces
ISR	intelligence, surveillance, and reconnaissance
ITFC	Iraq Threat Finance Cell
JAM	Jaysh al-Mahdi (aka Mahdi Army)
JCPAT	Joint Campaign Plan Assessment Team
JCS	Joint Chiefs of Staff
JDAM	Joint Direct Attack Munition
JFSOCC-I	Joint Forces Special Operations Component Command-Iraq
JIEDDO	Joint Improvised Explosive Device Defeat Organization
JRTN	Jaysh ar-Rejal at-Tariq al-Naqshbandi
JSAT	Joint Strategic Assessment Team
JSS	joint security stations
KDP	Kurdistan Democratic Party
KH	Kata'ib Hizballah
KRG	Kurdistan Regional Government
LNO	liaison officer
LTC	lieutenant colonel
MEF	Marine Expeditionary Force
MeK	Mujahedin e Khalq
MEU	Marine Expeditionary Unit
MHI	Military History Institute
MiTT	Military Transition Team
MNC-I	Multi-National Corps–Iraq
MND	Multinational Division
MND-B	Multi-National Division–Baghdad
MND-C	Multi-National Division-Center
MND-CS	Multi-National Division–Central South
MND-N	Multi-National Division–North
MND-NC	Multi-National Division–North Central
MND-NE	Multi-National Division–Northeast

MND-SE	Multi-National Division–Southeast
MNF-I	Multi-National Force–Iraq
MNF-W	Multi-National Force–West
MNSTC-I	Multi-National Security Transition Command–Iraq
MOD	Ministry of Defense
MRAP	mine resistant ambush protected
NATO	North Atlantic Treaty Organization
NCO	noncommissioned officer
NDU	National Defense University
NDU-CISA	National Defense University-College of International Security Affairs
NPR	National Public Radio
NSA	National Security Agency
NSC	National Security Council
NTM-I	NATO Training Mission–Iraq
OCINC	Office of the Commander in Chief
ODA	Operational Detachment Alpha
ODIN	Observe, Detect, Identify, and Neutralize
OIF	Operation IRAQI FREEDOM
OMC	Office of Military Cooperation
OPDAN	Operation DEFEAT AL-QAEDA IN THE NORTH
OPORD	operation order
OPTEMPO	operations tempo
OSC-I	Office of Security Cooperation-Iraq
OSD	Office of the Secretary of Defense
PIC	Provincial Iraqi Control
PJCC	Provincial Joint Coordination Center
PKK	Kurdistan Workers Party
PM	Prime Minister
PMF	Population Mobilization Forces
POTUS	President of the United States
PRT	provincial reconstruction team
PSC	private security contractor
PUK	Patriotic Union of Kurdistan
PYD	Democratic Union Party
RCT	regimental combat team
ROE	rules of engagement
RPG	rocket-propelled grenade
RSO	regional security office

RSTA	reconnaissance, surveillance, and target acquisition
SCIRI	Supreme Council for the Islamic Revolution in Iraq
SDE TIR	Strategic Debriefing Element Tactical Interrogation Report
SEAL	Sea, Air, and Land Teams
SECDEF	Secretary of Defense
SFA	strategic framework agreement
SG	Special Groups
SGS	secretary to the general staff
SIGACT	significant activity
SOCCENT	Special Operations Command Central
SOCOM	Special Operations Command
SOF	special operations forces
SOFA	status of forces agreement
SPTT	Special Police Transition Team
SSI	Strategic Studies Institute
STT	Stability Transition Team
STU	Special Tactics Unit
SVEST	suicide vest
SWAT	Special Weapons and Tactics
TF	Task Force
TFBSO	Task Force for Business and Stability Operations
TOE	table of organization and equipment
TRADOC	U.S. Army Training and Doctrine Command
UAV	unmanned aerial vehicle
UK	United Kingdom
UN	United Nations
UNSCR	United Nations Security Council Resolution
USAHEC	USAWC's Army Heritage and Education Center
USAID	United States Agency for International Development
USAWC	U.S. Army War College
USD-C	U.S. Division-Center
USD-N	U.S. Division-North
USD-S	U.S. Division-South
USF-I	United States Forces-Iraq
USIP	U.S. Institute of Peace
USMC	U.S. Marine Corps
VBIED	vehicle-borne improvised explosive device
VP	Vice-President

VTC	Video Teleconference
WMD	weapons of mass destruction
YPG	People's Protection Units

MAP SYMBOLS

Armor	
Cavalry	
Cavalry (Armored)	
Field Artillery (Self-Propelled)	
Infantry	
Infantry (Airborne)	
Infantry (Air Assault)	
Infantry (Mechanized)	
Infantry (Stryker)	

Battery, Company, or Cavalry Troop	I
Battalion or Cavalry Squadron	I I
Regiment or Group	I I I
Brigade	X
Division	X X
Corps	X X X

I Corps	
II Marine Expeditionary Force	
Multi-National Division–Baghdad	MND-B
1st Armored Cavalry Division	
82d Airborne Division	
2d Brigade Combat Team, 101st Airborne Division (Air Assault)	
6th Brigade, 2d National Police Division (Iraqi)	
11th Armored Cavalry Regiment	
1st Brigade, 25th Infantry Division (Stryker)	
2d Battalion, 114th Field Artillery	

ABOUT THE CONTRIBUTORS

JOEL D. RAYBURN is a U.S. Army colonel (COL) with 25 years of experience in intelligence and political-military affairs. A 1992 graduate of the U.S. Military Academy, he served in a series of assignments as an artillery officer in Germany, Bosnia, and Kuwait before transferring to the military intelligence corps in 1996. From 2002 to 2005, COL Rayburn taught British and Middle Eastern history at West Point, NY. From 2005 to the present, he has focused on political-military affairs in the greater Middle East, including several combat deployments in Iraq and Afghanistan and multiple assignments at U.S. Central Command. From 2013 to 2016, he directed the Army's Operation IRAQI FREEDOM Study Group, which was tasked with writing the Army's history of the Iraq War. COL Rayburn is the author of *Iraq After America: Strongmen, Sectarians, Resistance* (Hoover Press, 2014). He holds master's degrees from Texas A&M University and the National War College.

FRANK K. SOBCHAK began his career as a military intelligence officer and deployed to Kuwait in 1993. After completing special forces training, he was assigned to 5th Special Forces Group (Airborne) where he commanded Operational Detachment Alphas (ODAs) through various missions, including a deployment to Kosovo. Following detachment command, he taught classes in world history and peacekeeping at the U.S. Military Academy. Colonel (COL) Sobchak then returned to 5th Group, commanding a company in Iraq during 2005. He was next assigned as a Congressional liaison for U.S. Special Operations Command. From 2011 to 2013, COL Sobchak commanded the U.S. Army Garrison in Natick, Massachusetts. After serving as a senior fellow for the Chief of Staff of the Army's Operation IRAQI FREEDOM Study Group, he became the organization's director in 2017. Colonel Sobchak has published articles in various journals and magazines, including *Military Review, Military Intelligence Professional Bulletin, Infantry*, and *Armor*. He holds a bachelor's degree in military history from the U.S. Military Academy and a master's degree in Arab studies from Georgetown University.

JEANNE F. GODFROY served in the Military Intelligence Corps, deploying to Bosnia in October of 2001 and then to Iraq as part of the 101st Airborne Division (Air Assault) in August of 2002. Lieutenant Colonel (LTC) Godfroy went back to Iraq in 2004 to work directly for the commander of the Multi-National Security Transition Command-Iraq (MNSTC-I). She returned to Iraq for a third tour from 2008 to 2009, and served as an advisor to the Iraqi Directorate General of Intelligence and Security and in the Force Strategic Engagement Cell (FSEC) where she helped orchestrate national reconciliation initiatives. From 2009 to 2011, LTC Godfroy taught courses on international relations and civil war in the Department of Social Sciences at West Point. She subsequently served as the 2nd Infantry Division's secretary to the general staff (SGS) in the Republic of Korea. LTC Godfroy left active service in the Army in the fall of 2012, and spent a year studying street gangs and narcotics at the Council on Foreign Relations as an international affairs fellow. She returned to active duty to become one of four lead researchers on the Chief of Staff of the Army's Operation IRAQI FREEDOM Study Group. LTC Godfroy presently works as a strategy and management consultant for IT Cadre in Ashburn, Virginia, and she performs her U.S. Army Reserve duties in the department of social sciences at West Point. She holds a bachelor's in history from the U.S. Military Academy and a master's and doctorate in public and international affairs from the Woodrow Wilson School at Princeton University.

MATTHEW D. MORTON served as a cavalryman in Germany and the Balkans as a company grade officer before instructing in the Department of History at West Point. As a field grade officer, he served on general staffs in Germany, Iraq, Afghanistan, the Pentagon, and as a regional fellow at the Marshall Center. Colonel (COL) Morton is the author of *Men on Iron Ponies, The Death and Rebirth of the Modern U.S. Cavalry*. He is the assistant chief of staff for future plans and policy, U.S. Army Central/Third Army. COL Morton received his commission from the U.S. Military Academy and received his doctorate in history from Florida State University.

JAMES S. POWELL is a U.S. Army colonel (COL) and strategic plans and policy officer. After graduating from the U.S. Military Academy at West Point, New York, in 1992, he served with field artillery units at Fort Campbell, Kentucky, and Baumholder, Germany. Following these operational assignments, he returned to West Point and taught military history from 2002 to 2004. After a tour in Iraq as the campaign planner for III Corps from December 2006 to February 2008, COL Powell was assigned to the Pentagon, serving first as speechwriter for the Chief of Staff of the Army and later as military advisor to the Director of Net Assessment in the Office of the Secretary of Defense. He deployed to Afghanistan in June 2017, working in the plans directorate of the Resolute Support headquarters. COL Powell holds a doctorate in history from Texas A&M University and is a graduate of the School of Advanced Military Studies at Fort Leavenworth, Kansas, where he also served as a seminar leader following completion of the Advanced Strategic Leadership Studies Program. His book, *Learning under Fire: The 112th Cavalry Regiment in World War II*, was published in 2010.

MATTHEW M. ZAIS served the first half of his career as an infantry officer in the 82nd Airborne Division, 101st Airborne Division, and as Mountain Phase Ranger Instructor. Lieutenant Colonel (LTC) Zais later taught American foreign policy and international relations in the department of social sciences at the U.S. Military Academy. After transitioning as an Army Strategist, he served in the Defense Threat Reduction Agency, as the executive officer of the Chief of Staff of the Army's Operation IRAQI FREEDOM Study Group, and as deputy director of the Strategic Initiatives Group at U.S. Army Cyber Command. He currently serves as the director for Iraq on the National Security Council and as an adjunct professor in the Security Studies Program at Georgetown University. His deployments include Haiti and Iraq. LTC Zais graduated from the U.S. Military Academy with a bachelor's in economics and holds a master's of public administration and a doctorate from Princeton University.

Made in the USA
Middletown, DE
24 September 2024

61310091R00393